THE CONDESCENSION OF GOD

"And at midnight there was a cry made..."

Matthew 25:6

Sean Michael Morris

ISBN-13: 978-1492967446

TABLE OF CONTENTS

PREFACE

John Knox was derided in his day for being too much of an Old Testament prophet. The caricature drawn may have been correct had it not been for the overwhelming idolatry and superstition that then pervaded the professing church of the 16th century. But so it was that darkness covered with its veil the eyes of the ignorant, that their eyes should be holden from steadfastly looking upon Jesus Christ the *Righteous*. Thus these poor souls beheld only the forms and traditions of the ecclesiastical body in which Satan then reigned as usurper; and, in consequence, they were shut up to the gospel promises by this works-righteousness offered them. It was into this scene which the character Knox appeared - *with all his thundering judgments*. Knox, filled with the Spirit, came convinced of the evil disease that had taken fast hold upon his nation of Scotland *and* of the prescription needed to see an end of the darkness. Thus he was not *too much* an Old Testament prophet. He came amourning because there was something to be lamented in the church of the day. Carnal men, who are at all times at home and happy in this world, will never understand the likes of Knox.

My question to the reader is: how shall the church today arise from the ashes in which she lies? We who have drunk the moral anesthetic called, in our day, *the gospel* – how shall we awake? Declension has brought us back to another dark age, where the prophet and priest are just as profane as they were in Knox's day and the people are as ignorant as they were then too; thus we need another reformation. Not a return to the doctrine of Calvin *or* Arminius, but to the apostles' doctrine!

When immersed in the darkness of sleep, it never feels pleasant to at once be aroused by the blazing shock of harsh white lights. And so, it is rarely pleasing to be so awakened from such sinful slumber by the call of fiery preaching. We have, *ad infinitum*, sermons, books, classes, and whole conferences devoted to the fear of God – and yet we have not employed the knowledge we've acquired. The very thing we need most is the very thing we cannot acquire! How shall we attain unto the fear of God, that we may "serve him acceptably" (Heb. 12:28)? It's time we stop giving assignments to our keynote speakers, and wait upon God! Surely if *God* assigned a man to the task, we would learn our lesson aright! We need a man who has been taken down to the third hell – a man who has ascended up the burning mount! How could the Ninevites resist such irresistible preaching from a man who came fresh from hell (*see*, Jon. 2:2)?

I believe God's found a man.

Reader, *will you hear?*

- *Jake Gardner*

TO THE READER

To the Reader

> "For I determined not to know any thing among you, save Jesus Christ, and Him crucified" – 1 Corinthians 2:2

My reader, I am not determined after this determination of Paul in 1 Corinthians 2:2, for there is more to be known! Paul

RELATED SERMONS

"Leaving the Foundation" - Jake Gardner

called it "wisdom" (1 Cor. 2:6) - wisdom which is, in our day, lying undiscovered beyond the "first principles" of the faith (Heb. 5:12, 6:1). God be praised for all the efforts of God's people! Indeed we have, in this generation, set forth to prove the narrow entrance of "the strait Gate" (Matt. 7:13-14) with considerable success, but my burden is to prove and make clear the light of God's wisdom for *the pathway beyond*. Verily, "strait is the gate", but Christ also said, "narrow is the **way**" (Matt. 7:14). There is much left unsaid concerning this holy "Way" (John 14:6), and we, in regenerate circles, are too often coveting the high chair of spiritual infancy! Can life be sustained on nothing more than milk? Many push away the plate of maturity with unfounded confidence, saying, "I don't want to know anything else." Is this admirable? We live in a generation of spiritual babies who have lost their appetite for meat! There are more nightmares to be told of all those who choked on the bones…and most remain overwhelmed. Shall we fear the meat because many have choked on it? Shall we never eat it because others have not had the grace to consume it? Dear reader, bone-chokers have gone "whereunto also they were appointed" (1 Pet. 2:8), but whither is your appointment? The 66 books of the Bible have become like a 66-mile high Mountain, and when men cower at its height long enough, they become satisfied at its foundation.

David exclaimed, "Who will bring me into the strong city" (Ps. 61:9)? We would do well to answer with him in his reverential song – "Wilt not Thou, O God, which hadst cast us off?" (Ps. 61:10) – and wilt not Thou, O God, Who has left us without guidance, without courage, blubbering at the foot of Thy holy Mountain?

> *If we would mount up on wisdom's-wings*
> *We would soar to heights the Spirit brings*
> *Being compelled thereto, to sing - to sing – Great is our God!*

The chapters henceforth written, though vast and exhausting, are meant to guide and direct the regenerate man into the pathway of life, which is, without variableness, up this 66-mile high Mountain of glory. This is not a message to the unconverted public. This is written to God's true people, to the end that truth might be established, unity might be perfected, faith might be purified, and the Bride might be beautified.

"Leaving the first principles" does not mean we are, God forbid, going on to "other truths" which have viable significance outside of Jesus Christ and Him crucified (Heb. 6:1). We are not leaving Christ, for then we would be as a cell without a *Nucleus* or a master builder without a *Foundation*. We are not leaving these first principles so as to study other things which are irrelevant to them, but rather we are *building upon them*. Let my reader understand: every truth finds its relevance in the Person and work of Christ, and every step along "the narrow way" is done in the Person who is "The Way" (John 14:6).

In this writing I do repeat myself many times, but mind you, I do not think it to be redundant. Given the unfamiliarity of the content of which I have set forth to prove with the general difficulty of understanding it, that it is complex when standing alone, and how that it is of greater complexity when in connection with spiritual parallels all throughout the scripture, I find that, without repetition, these doctrines are impossible to understand. Repetition is a methodology used in the inspired scripture of the Bible, thus one should never despise the use of repetition, for then one would have to despise the Bible. Consider the four gospels – Matthew, Mark, Luke, and John – they are repetitions one of another in many ways, but each are approaching Christ from different spiritual angles, with different majoring themes, ending in different spiritual truths as the final communication to the spiritually capable reader, and though this book is incomparable to inspired writings which are God-breathed, I do hope that it is led by the Spirit enough that such technique and methodology to communicate spiritual truth can be used for your spiritual edification.

Also, it is absolutely necessary that you read the chapters in order to understand what I am saying and meaning with the words or phraseology that I am using, lest you misunderstand, misinterpret, misbalance, or misapply what I am teaching through the scripture. When I have once established a biblical principle or a biblical phrase in its exact meaning, then I will continue to use that phrase without reference to its exact meaning in later chapters. The chapters, principles, doctrines, and ideas build upon one another. Some chapters can be read outside of the context of the former chapters, and behold, much truth can still be gleaned, but I assure you that you will not understand what I am saying or meaning *in full*. Beware lest you wrest my words to your own destruction, lest you are found a slanderous criminal in the sight of God. I say this, especially, to those who refuse to study the whole context of each chapter, who do not take the time to study the entire book. May the Lord have mercy, in Jesus' Name.

The inspired scripture does present the heart of God in its entirety, in perfect balance. This is a Divine wonder! Furthermore, this Book, the very letters of inerrancy, is committed to preachers to steward. Woe to the most of us, I say to "the preachers", for we are called to represent God, and who is able to preach and expound such mysterious and holy Words? Through preaching, can we make visible

2

The Invisible? From our tongues, can we utter an oration fit for the Only Wise? Left speechless before the brightness of His Image, can we speak for Him? "Who is sufficient for these things" (2 Cor. 2:16)? To the humiliation of every God-called preacher, or every God-ordained ready writer, we are put to this task which conquers our pride. Whatever we are ingratiated to say or pen, there is some ugly smudge of self and sin which lurks about the uninspired text. We cannot tell where it is, otherwise, by God's grace, we would remove it with all speed. It is therefore impossible, except by God's own exhale of grace, that a writing could be so clear a depiction of God's entire heart on a certain matter. When one would endeavor to make sinners heavy in godly sorrow, how often do they go away too *light hearted*? When one would endeavor to make known the mysteries of God's grace by promise, expecting that, at last, their tongue will surely let loose the age old "AMEN" of the saints, and then say, "Bold I approach the eternal Throne, to claim the crown through Christ my own", and yet, alas, in whatever we preached or wrote – "they saw Him, they worshiped Him: but *some doubted*" (Matt. 28:17). May God have mercy upon our foul breath, our finite fingers; for we endeavor to write letters and words which shall never pass away. We are of all men most needy for grace! The commandment of God does lay heavy upon us: "If any man speak, let him speak as the oracles of God" (1 Peter 4:11). May God have mercy upon us!

Take the book of Hebrews as an example: By approximation, the 1st chapter, ¾ of the 2nd chapter, ¼ of the 4th chapter, ¼ of the 5th chapter, a 3rd of the 6th chapter, the 7th, 8th, and 9th chapters, ½ of the 10th chapter, the 11th chapter, and ¼ of the 12th chapter all focus on the glory of *God's grace*. When a man is reading these portions of Hebrews under the illumination of the Spirit, it is as if God is bidding you to open your eyes, like Abraham, and "look now toward heaven, and tell the stars" (Gen. 15:5). Praise God! As the stars of heaven bend you back and widen your eyes in wonder, you would be overwhelmed at the sight of God's love if He gave you eyes to see. There are so many promises, elaborated and made alive like a colorful galaxy burns in otherworldly flames, promises which are eternal in saving power like the undying stars stand fast and abide. Then, according to God's Fatherly wisdom, the reader is intermittently led to look upon a different scenery – namely, the terrifying warnings written in the other portions of Hebrews (¼ of chapter 2, chapter 3, ¾ of chapter 4, ¾ of chapter 5, 2/3 of chapter 6, ½ of chapter 10, and ¾ of chapter 12) - but you see, the reader has been made able to endure them in their proper application. The wrathful warnings of God, understood and applied alone, without love, or the love of God standing alone, without God's wrathful warnings, is as the elements of table salt. Standing alone, sodium and chlorine are poisonous, but when they are compounded together they created the life-preserving, life-giving substance called salt. We too must be balanced, like this compound, for we "are the salt of the earth" (Matt. 5:13). He that eateth a little honey falling from the trees (1 Sam. 14:25-29) will have energy enough to survive the war. A man caught up in heaven (Eph. 2:6), looking down, would not fear the flames of hell in any unrighteous regard (1 John 4:17-18).

My reader, I do state all of this because most chapters in this book ("The Condescension of God") were not meant to guide you "to the top of Pisgah" that you might see the Promised Land (Deut. 34:1). These chapters do not have the balance and perfect application of inspired scripture, that you might be intermittently solaced with God's gracious love. Nay, this book was to prove what is left unproven, to a generation who has unfounded confidence while in a spiritual position of woe and wrath. This book, according to my burden, is a guide to lead you to Mount Sinai, that you might learn to fear. If need be, my reader, resort to the last chapter for the comforts of Pisgah. The balm of Gilead does yet remain in Zion (Jer. 8:22), and even in this book (see the last chapter); though for the most part I am seeking to wound you with an injury, given by a true friend (Prov. 27:6).

THE CONDESCENSION OF GOD
CHAPTER 1

A Poetical Introduction: *Look at the Cross*

"No man taketh it from Me, but I lay it down of Myself.
I have power to lay it down, and I have power to take it again."
- *Jesus Christ*

The ABC's of God's unfathomable condescension begins, firstly, with a look at the cross. Without contest, the deepest thinker of humanity staggers to grasp the concept of God's momentary Humanity – by incarnation – and furthermore, His death at the hand of wicked men! Oh, my reader! Consider that *woeful* and *wonderful* scene again! God Incarnate self-surrendered His Body to die – and in what circumstance? He was man-stolen by treacherous men, who were motivated by their hatred of God within, and they beat Him and bound Him, they crowded around Him and challenged Him, and the weakened Omnipotent cried aloud: "My God, my God, why hast Thou forsaken Me" (Psalm 22:1, Matt. 27:46, Mk. 15:34)?! Look HERE – "Look at the Cross" – at God's wrath and love, sovereignty and weakness, pleasure and pain; an unfathomable condescension! The most vivid revelation of God to man was in the Person of Jesus Christ. The most comprehensive demonstration of the personal qualities of God, namely His hallowed wrath and love, was climactic and cumulative when the Man Jesus Christ was publically displayed crucified, afterward resurrected, then ascended, and finally enthroned. The Lamb was slain in innocence before the apocalypse of wrath, forerunning the Great Tribulation; Lo, He made manifest the Day of salvation. The lovingkindness of God was revealed in the Person, life, and actions of Christ, but foremost of all when He willingly laid down His life. Jesus is The Good Shepherd, and in Him is *no greater love*.

> John 10:14-18
> [14] I am the Good Shepherd, and know My sheep, and am known of Mine. [15] As the Father knoweth Me, even so know I the Father: and I lay down My life for the sheep. [16] And other sheep I have, which are not of this fold: them also I must bring, and they shall hear My voice; and there shall be one fold, and one Shepherd. [17] Therefore doth My Father love Me, because I lay down My life, that I might take it again. [18] No man taketh it from Me, but I lay it down of Myself. I have power to lay it down, and I have power to take it again. This commandment have I received of My Father.

"No man taketh it from Me," the humiliated Sovereign declared! Jesus Christ has "POWER to lay it down" and "POWER to take it again," and He became powerless before the hatred of humanity by the power of His Divinity!

Immeasurable, just love and severe, holy wrath were simultaneously revealed to be in the gruesome crucifixion of so valuable a Person, to pacify a wrath so unalterable by any less of a cost. When Christ became sin, God's anger consumed and forsook so perfect a Divine Man, and yet the Father sent Jesus to *this end*. The Father & The Son – they both confess an equal responsibility! Jesus Christ *CHOSE* to lay down His life, and simultaneously as a second witness, the Father *GAVE* His Son for propitiation. Of the Father it was written, "God so loved the world, that **HE GAVE** His only begotten Son," and "**HE** hath **MADE** Him TO BE SIN for us, Who knew no sin" (John 3:16, 2 Corinthians 5:21). God's just anger burns to kill sin, and so also, it burns to destroy sinful men, and when Christ BECAME SIN God killed Him, but it was through the hands and feet of human men! The Sovereign killed His own Person in the form of an Incarnated Human, in and through the hands of a sinning, God-hating humanity. Oh! That Christ would disrobe Himself from Divinity, that He would come to earth and walk amongst sinful humanity, and, lo, that He would robe Himself with the garments of our disgusting and wretched sin, lawfully becoming what God hated about men! So God led Christ to the hill, to hang Him on display, to show the world This Object of God's wrath in dismay. Christ did there suffer – in perfect proportion – as a representation of God's hatred for sin! The Absolute and most perfect Dignity – The Second Person of the Trinity – was SHAMED and made NAKED for an evil, undeserving, and unthankful humanity! Jesus Christ foreknew it, He did, of His own will, eternally and within time choose it! From thence we can understand a love that tasted death for every man. "I have loved you," Jesus said (John 15:12), and "greater love hath no man than this, that a man lay down his life for his friends" (John 15:13).

> *This is goodness from the Good Shepherd*
> *Dual benevolence for the world to reverence*
> *And should we ever cease from wondering at such a time in history*
> *That this unthinkable death was a victory!?*

> *"Alas and did my Savior bleed and did my Sovereign die.*
> *Would He devote that sacred head for such a worm as I?"*

> *It was a priceless Life – Jesus, the Christ –*
> *well able to envelop innumerable transgressions;*
> *Innumerable days of ceaseless praise will never overstate the glory of God's atoning*
> *substitution!*

> *That He, even He,*
> *Came forth from His throne,*
> *Descended to the earth, and to His own,*
> *Incarnated as a man, with a purpose to die,*
> *Initiating a plan, that, in Him, all death would die*
> *That He, for men, became a wrath-enveloping substitution,*
> *That He was mangled and blood-red, hated on earth until He was dead!*

> *Heaven's Potentate was encircled and overpowered, and by sinful men!?*

6

They were raging in hatred of Him with every emotion within!
Apparently succeeding to rid themselves of His presence among men
Until finally, at last, they thought they were free to go on in sin…

But then God reciprocates the deed,
He crucifies men in Christ that they might rise again after His lead,
And Christ, risen and alive, sends salvation into the world that hated Him,
that they might then be freed!
For their needs He did bleed! They nailed Him unto His death,
that He might overcome it for the rest,
His death brought forth life, overcoming hatred with love,
and night with light, that of a truth it was said,
He was the dying seed which gave life to those in need.

Just wrath was pacified! God is righteous to justify the ungodly, hell-deserving sinners of the world! God is just, therefore, to justify us; because Christ became our sin, we are made alive in Him, and this is a sound declaration: "To declare, I say, at this time His righteousness: that He might be just, and the justifier of him which believeth in Jesus" (Romans 3:26). "One drop of Christ's blood is worth more than heaven and earth." – Martin Luther

The Man, Christ, was so valuable a Life
that salvation was borne from Emanuel's veins!
He washed a world of sin!
In Him an innumerable company is resurrected to endless days!

And what is absolutely necessary for so magnificent a victory,
Is that God was not carelessly outwitted to lose
His Son at the hands of free-will sinners undone!
*The **free will** of man held no priestly knife in this sovereign,*
eternal, salvific plan!
The Father was the transcending Great High Priest,
and He is the author of every chapter of the plan;
In His hand He held the knife to condemn all sin in One Man.
Every finger may have been the finger of man,
But they gripped the knife of salvation
to slay the world's sin in One Sacrificial Propitiation.
The knife in hand, the final blow, was God's judgment against sin
– let all the world know!
His work, His way, He sacrificed His Son for all in one day!

God so loved the world, He gave His Son as a gift,
Sinners did not steal God incarnate because they were swift.
*The future is not determined by the **freewill** actions of men,*
Even if they misbehave, do wickedly, or sin.

God determined the salvation of the Adamic race in Jesus Christ,
By His free will He chose, and He snuffed out the fires of eternal woes.
The Lord a symphony did compose!
The sound of a mystery played throughout history!

[30] There is no wisdom nor understanding nor counsel against the LORD.

Even while a man may prepare his heart for an evil act of sin, the Lord uses it all for His **good** and glorious purpose. He uses the evil sins of men for His mighty, sovereign, eternal plan. He used the sinful hearts and hands of Joseph's brethren to send Joseph to Egypt. They did evilly prepare their hearts but it was from the Lord. Read how they did indeed think evil, but God meant good by it, thus He had governance over the evil in their hearts. Joseph explained this in Genesis 50:20.

> Genesis 50:20
> [20] But as for you, **ye thought evil against me; but God meant it unto good**, to bring to pass, as it is this day, to save much people alive.

It was the sin of Joseph's brethren that they betrayed and sold Joseph to Egypt, even so, but God takes *OWNERSHIP* of it because it was God's plan. What sin was in the heart of Joseph's brethren? How did this come to pass? His brethren began to hate Joseph in their heart, and from this horrid and bitter hatred they conspired to sell him to Egypt. They indeed made a plan in their own wicked heart, nevertheless, read how it was the plan of Joseph's brothers, **while simultaneously**, it was the Lord's plan. Beginning with Genesis 37:4…

> Genesis 37:4
> [4] And when **his brethren saw that their father loved him more than all his brethren**, they hated him, and could not speak peaceably unto him.

Thus they planned and **conspired**…

> Genesis 37:18-20
> [18] And when they saw him afar off, even before he came near unto them, **they conspired** against him to slay him. [19] And they said one to another, Behold, this dreamer cometh. [20] Come now therefore, and let us slay him, and cast him into some pit, and we will say, Some evil beast hath devoured him: and we shall see what will become of his dreams.

By what was written and afore proven by scripture, we ought to expect that God was in control of their hearts, thus Joseph freely confesses this in Genesis 45. Read how it was God's plan as well, yet He is innocent of any unrighteousness, altogether lovely, and pure!

> Genesis 45:5-8
> [5] Now therefore be not grieved, nor angry with yourselves, that ye sold me hither: **for God did send me** before you to preserve life.

> [6] For these two years *hath* the famine *been* in the land: and yet *there are* five years, in the which *there shall* neither *be* earing nor harvest. [7] And **God sent me before you** to preserve you a posterity in the earth, and to save your lives by a great deliverance. [8] **So now** *it was* **not you** *that* **sent me hither, but God**: and He hath made me a father to Pharaoh, and lord of all his house, and a ruler throughout all the land of Egypt.

Joseph was able to confess this, but can you? Please do not harden your heart against the scriptures simply because they cannot be logically digested. Likewise to Joseph's confession, the Holy Spirit inspired the psalmist of Psalm 105 to give credit to God in the same way. Again God was in complete, sovereign control!

> Psalm 105:16-22
> [16] Moreover He called for a famine upon the land: He brake the whole staff of bread. [17] **He sent** a man before them, *even* Joseph, *who* was sold for a servant: [18] Whose feet they hurt with fetters: he was laid in iron: [19] Until the time that his word came: the word of the LORD tried him. [20] The king sent and loosed him; *even* the ruler of the people, and let him go free. [21] **He made** him lord of his house, and ruler of all his substance: [22] To bind his princes at his pleasure; and teach his senators wisdom.

By the hands of Joseph's brethren *God sent Joseph*; even in their sinful thoughts *God was Lord*, and He was working a mighty plan of salvation! As God did with the hands of Joseph's brethren, He did the same thing with Judas, the Jews, and the Romans when they betrayed Jesus Christ, that it might rightly be said that *God sacrificed His own Son*. The Lord takes **OWNERSHIP** of this sinful plan of the Jews in a multitude of places throughout scripture. If the Lord did not send Joseph by the hands of his brethren, then He did not crucify His own Son, both would have been the happening of *the free will of man*. If it was the happening of the free will of man and God merely orchestrated and allowed the circumstances and scenarios to transpire, then it would have been the **foreknowledge** of God alone that was active in the crucifixion of Jesus Christ, and that was God's full part in the matter. It was not singly the **foreknowledge** of God only but it was the **determinate counsel** of God as well!

> Acts 2:23
> [23] Him, being delivered **by the determinate counsel and foreknowledge of God, ye have taken, and by wicked hands** have crucified and slain:

God appointed the men to their disobedient, wicked conspiracy so that God was able to take sure *ownership* of Christ's death. In 1 Peter 2:8 it is written that the disobedient were **appointed** instead of freely choosing, and mind you, we could have known this already by the previous scripture that revealed God's relationship to the heart of all men (Prov. 16:1, 9, 21:1, 30).

> 1 Peter 2:8
> [8] And a stone of stumbling, and a rock of offence, *even to them* which stumble at the word, being disobedient: **whereunto also they were appointed.**

In Isaiah 53 God takes *pleasure* in His plan to kill His own Son as an offering for sin, and, He is innocent, again, of all unrighteousness! In Isaiah 53:10, God claims complete ownership and authorship of the plan and its execution; while in Acts 3:13-15 God holds the Jews responsible for this sin, telling them it was their desire of evil, and they will be punished for it if they fail to repent and believe. It is a paradox. Please read carefully – first, Isaiah 53:10, and then Acts 3:13-15:

> Isaiah 53:10
> [10] **Yet it pleased the LORD to bruise Him**; He [God] hath put Him to grief: **when Thou [God] shalt make His soul an offering for sin**, He shall see His seed, He shall prolong His days, and the pleasure of the LORD shall prosper in His hand.

> Acts 3:13-15
> [13] The God of Abraham, and of Isaac, and of Jacob, the God of our fathers, hath glorified His Son Jesus; **Whom ye delivered up**, and denied Him in the presence of Pilate, when he was determined to let Him go. [14] But **ye denied the Holy One and the Just**, and desired a murderer to be granted unto you; [15] And killed the Prince of life, Whom God hath raised from the dead; whereof we are witnesses.

Indeed, "whatsoever the LORD **pleased**, that did He in heaven, and in earth" and "it **pleased** the LORD to bruise" and crucify His Son (Ps. 135:6, Isaiah 53:10)! God took *ownership* of the most momentous event in all time! God has provided "gates of righteousness," and Christ is "this Gate of the LORD, into which the righteous shall enter" (Ps. 118:19-20) – praise God! "Every house is builded by some man; but **He that built all things is God,**" and "strait is the Gate, and narrow is the Way which leadeth unto life" (Heb. 3:4, Matt. 7:14)! Let everyone praise the LORD as the psalmist says, "I will praise Thee, for Thou hast heard me, and art become my salvation" (Psalm 118:21)! Christ has become our salvation by "**the LORD's doing,**" when, namely, "the stone which the builders refused is become the head stone of the corner. **This is the LORD'S doing**; it is marvellous in our eyes" (Psalm 118:22-23)! "This is the day which the LORD hath made!" And will you rejoice and be glad in it (Psalm 118:24)? The disciples were offended that Christ was smitten by men, but will you be offended *that God smote Christ*? God said, "**I will smite the Shepherd**, and the sheep of the flock shall be scattered abroad" (Matt. 26:31). The Son of Man has gone to the crucifix "as it was **determined**" of Him, nevertheless God holds men in a simultaneous responsibility, and "woe unto that man by whom He is betrayed" (Lk. 22:22)!

I say again, God took *ownership* of the most momentous event in all time! This event was **the greatest sin of man against God**, for they crucified the Lord of glory, but since it was a sovereign work of God it was **the greatest display of God's love** to give and kill His Son, likewise the Son willingly laid down Himself under the Father's death sentence, and more so, this was **the greatest display of God's wrath** to require the value of His Own Life as the only capable means to pacify the magnitude of His just anger against sin and sinners. The sovereignty of God behind the crucifixion of Christ is carefully detailed in the book of Romans with much more explanation than Psalm 105, which gave only a snapshot of God's sovereignty in Joseph's betrayal, slavery, and rise to power. In Romans, God declares His mysterious purpose behind why He killed His own Son, and how that He did it by blinding His own people. *Through* the "fall," "diminishing," and "casting away" of God's chosen people Israel (Romans 11:15), the Gentiles are grafted into the Tree of Salvation! God determined that it would be through the "fall" of Israel that the Gentiles would be saved (Rom. 11:11). How can their fall be the casting away of God? Did God cast them away in response to their sin only, or was God the author of this unsearchable plan!? Their fall into sin was that they rejected and crucified Christ, and God was the author and executor of these events through ordination, specifically in that He made them "slumber" in blindness and deafness (Romans 11:8). It was because they were blinded and made deaf that they did reject Christ, thus God's Sovereign control is the cause and determining factor of sin and righteousness. So when a man is blind or deaf it was God's **election** that determined it. Please read carefully:

> Romans 11:7-10
> [7] What then? Israel hath not obtained that which he seeketh for; but **the election** hath obtained it, and **the rest were blinded** [8] (According as it is written, **God hath given** them **the spirit of slumber**, eyes that they should **not see**, and ears that they should **not hear**;) unto this day. [9] And David saith, Let their table be made a snare, and a trap, and a stumblingblock, and a recompence unto them: [10] Let their eyes be darkened, that they may not see, and bow down their back alway.

Election is manifest by blindness and sight. Blindness or sight determines the actions of a person. The state of the heart is blindness or sight; God is in control of the heart, and the heart is the fountain the "issues of life" (Prov. 4:23). Dear reader, be astonished and wonder that God, He, Himself, caused the "casting away" of Israel through the most horrendous, vile, and immeasurably wicked sin, satisfying a wrath which was ready to eternally burn trillions of men. Yet He, Himself, caused the sin! And by it provided innumerable benefits and **worldwide reconciliation**, mercy to triumph over judgment in every nation through heaven's High Priest making the

13

Offering – The Sacrifice – of an impossible Person to bring an impossible peace, an eternally valuable propitiation upon an altar on earth, and lo! The Holy Man arose to herald the victory in heaven's High courts! Ascending to the heights men and angels behold His rites! And lo, and behold, men and angels, the world and animals of the stable, they do all wonder at the meekness of this Man Who had footsteps of thunder – His birth, His might, His weakness is power in the most royal right! For only the King, the Judge, could save the convicts from eternal death, through LOVE. And now, worldwide reconciliation! That is, namely, salvation to the Gentiles.

> Romans 11:11-15
> [11] I say then, Have they stumbled that they should fall? God forbid: but *rather* **through their fall** salvation *is come* unto the Gentiles, for to provoke them to jealousy. [12] Now if the **fall** of them *be* the riches of the world, and the **diminishing** of them the riches of the Gentiles; how much more their fulness? [13] For I speak to you Gentiles, inasmuch as I am the apostle of the Gentiles, I magnify mine office: [14] If by any means I may provoke to emulation *them which are* my flesh, and might save some of them. [15] For if **the casting away of them** *be* **the reconciling of the world**, what *shall* the receiving *of them be*, but life from the dead?

It is a glorious plan, nevertheless, it was the "casting away" of Israel and the "salvation" of the Gentiles. Yes, God caused, ordained, and made the Gentiles find Him. He manifested Himself to them, was found of them, for they were given *eyes to see*, *ears to hear*, and *hearts to savingly believe*. Please read carefully: God's election to salvation is evident in that the Gentiles were saved; God's election to damnation is evident in that Israel was a disobedient and gainsaying people.

> Romans 10:19-21
> [19] But I say, Did not Israel know? First Moses saith, I will provoke you to jealousy by *them that are* no people, *and* by a foolish nation I will anger you. [20] But Esaias is very bold, and saith, **I was found of them that sought Me not; I was made manifest unto them that asked not after Me.** [21] But to Israel He saith, All day long I have stretched forth My hands unto **a disobedient and gainsaying people.**

Election is God's choice. When He has chosen, He brings that choice to pass by His own sovereign might to give or take away sight, to soften or harden hearts. God hardens in a plan or purpose of *wrath*, God softens in a plan or purpose of *mercy*. It is in reference to those who are elect that it was written, "For they are not all Israel, which are of Israel" (Rom. 9:6). This is to say that God did not grant that all of Israel could come to Christ, but a remnant did come by the sovereign distribution of saving faith. If you are not of this faith, you cannot become a spiritual child of Israel. Jesus Christ did in all of Israel preach! But He knew just who were the very ones that He would reach! With this idea in reference, consider John chapter 6. This chapter contains, arguably, the most antagonistic sermon He could have given to the flesh of men, and to justify His words, Jesus Christ said: "No man can come to Me, except the Father which hath sent Me draw him," and, "it is the spirit that quickeneth; the flesh profiteth nothing: the words that I speak unto you, they are spirit, and they are life. But there are some of you that believe not" (John 6:44, 63-64). Jesus preached with the understanding that only those who were granted ears to hear would hear, and that is a gift from God. He called all to come, but only those of whom God called by His sovereign power could come. He preached to all, but only those who had the quickening of the Spirit brooding upon their dead souls could hear, believe, and live by Him. "The preaching of the cross is foolishness to them which are perishing" (1 Cor. 1:18). God must give and take away saving faith and repentance, and this is **sober thinking**, "for I say, through **the grace given** unto me, to every man that is among you, not to think of himself more highly than he ought to think; but to **think soberly**, according as **God hath dealt** to every man **the measure of faith**" (Romans 12:3).

Our faith is a calling, a calling irresistible and effectual, ordained before the world began. It is all of HIM, the Lord God, "Who hath saved us, and **called us** with an holy calling, not according to our works, but according to His own purpose and grace, which was given us in Christ Jesus before the world began" (2 Timothy 1:9). This calling is ever under the Presidency of God in Christ so that we may humbly confess that all faith or repentance is a gift from God. This ought to make us increasingly meek to longsuffer sinners until God, if He wills, may grant them repentance, till then and for all there is therefore hope. Thus it was written, "In meekness instructing those that oppose themselves; **if God peradventure will give them repentance** to the acknowledging of the truth; and that they may recover themselves out of the snare of the devil, who are taken captive by him at his will" (2 Timothy 2:25-26). Therefore all boasting is excluded – on what basis? That all things, whether works or faith, are not of ourselves but a gift from God. It is therefore highminded pride to claim that, of yourself, you have saving faith, or of your freedom of will you chose God. On the contrary, "there is none seeketh after God" and "we love Him, because He first loved us" (Romans 3:11, 11:18-25, 1 John 4:19). ALL GLORY TO GOD! "For Who maketh thee to differ from another? And what hast thou that thou didst not receive? Now if thou didst receive it, why dost thou glory, as if thou hadst not received it" (1 Cor. 4:7)? The determinate working of God that is active within time and eternally pre-ordained is termed in Romans 9:16 & 18.

> Romans 9:16
> [16] So then *it is* not of him that willeth, nor of him that runneth, but of God that sheweth mercy.

> Romans 9:18
> [18] Therefore hath He mercy on whom He will *have mercy*, and whom He will He hardeneth.

Truly, man may seek after repentance and faith. They can will for it, they can run after it, but unless God shows mercy they cannot find it. Even as Esau desired to be saved, but lo, "when he would have inherited the blessing, he was rejected: for **he found no place of repentance, though he sought it carefully with tears**" (Heb. 12:17). Esau madly pursued salvation! In agonizing tears, "he cried with a great and exceeding bitter cry," and "said unto his father, Hast thou but one blessing, my father? Bless me, even me also, O my father. And Esau lifted up his voice, and wept" (Gen. 27:34, 38)! How could it be that a man could so greatly desire and run after salvation, and yet he finds no repentance and faith? There is only one answer – **the hatred of God**. God says, "I **hated** Esau, and laid his mountains and his heritage waste for the dragons of the wilderness" (Mal. 1:3). This was the purpose of God for Esau which was purposed through election, as God had said: "Jacob have I loved, but Esau have I hated" (Rom. 9:13). For those unlike Esau, the few and precious elect of God, when they find repentance and faith they are humbled to hate themselves, hallowed by a first and forceful grace, struck alive into an amazement that God's love was first, saving, faith-giving, and finishing. GRACE! "Even so at this present time also there is a remnant according to the election of grace. And if by grace, then is it no more of works: otherwise grace is no more grace. But if it be of works, then is it no more grace: otherwise work is no more work" (Rom. 11:5-6). If there is a remnant saved, "the election hath obtained it, and the rest were blinded" (Rom. 11:7).

If you have been made into a faithful and godly saint, it is because you have "obtained mercy of the Lord" (1 Cor. 7:25) as "His workmanship" (Eph. 2). If you have become fearless and double-hearted toward repentance, bent on backsliding, and floundering in fearlessness before a Holy God Who demands FEAR, this is the end of your unhappy predestination *if you are never changed*! God is evidently hardening your heart, for, "who He will He hardeneth!" On the contrary, "Happy is the man that feareth alway," and back again, "but he that hardeneth his heart shall fall into mischief" (Prov. 28:14). You are responsible in heaven's court for your crimes, and yet, God "hath blinded [your] eyes, and hardened [your] heart; that [you] should not see with [your] eyes, nor understand with [your] heart, and be converted," that Christ should heal you (John 12:40). With God is the power of the clay, to make one vessel to see and the other blind! Blessed are you, oh man, if Jesus Christ comes to you in your lifetime and has compassion on your blind, pitiful estate. He is the potter, and with a little clay He can turn all your darkness into day. "How were thine eyes opened? He answered and said, A man that is called Jesus made clay, and anointed mine eyes, and said unto me, Go to the pool of Siloam, and wash: and I went and washed, and I received sight" (John 9:6-11). "But now, O LORD, Thou art our Father; we are the clay, and Thou our Potter; and we all are the work of Thy hand" (Isaiah 64:8)! Praise God!

The love and hatred of God moves a softening and hardening, OMNIPOTENT HAND, well able to mold the billions of clay hearts from every race, tribe, and tongue, even class, category, and status – the rich and the poor – every creature and more throughout all their goings, and since they were born they are

16

mastered by the mold of His mysterious art. Blessed is the man that can say, "By Thee have I been holden up from the womb: Thou art He that took me out of my mother's bowels: my praise shall be continually of Thee" (Psalm 71:6).

> *From eternity past love moved Him to choose the cast, the Potter molded the clay making **performers** for the Glory Day, that in theater of time God might display a salvation through God making temples of clay His redeeming habitation, to magnify Himself in a culmination and manifestation that will cause the world to wonder at an incorruptible glorification. A glorification that is the beginning at the end, an eternal life in a recreated, new earth, a new world and better birth than the beginning of Eden in its goodness and worth. We love Him because He first loved us, we are the cast set for this task, and before physical creation we were ever in the mind of God as His loving meditation, that He would ordain us for His momentous and universal occasion.*

This purpose of God's election is what determines their faith and salvation, as we have been carefully noting so far. However, given the difficulty of grasping this subject, the responsibility of man in tension with the justice of God, it is needful to carefully note each crystallized fixture set in geometric perfectness to behold the doctrinal jewel of the Lord as a whole. It is apparent that election determines all things… but what determines election? It cannot be the *foreknowledge* God has of what man will do, because God is sovereign over what man will do. He would not elect based upon what man will do – for He determines it! Election determines what man will do, but what determines election? The *free will* of God motivates election! Free will does exist, but *only* in God. We are to know that election is simply according to *the purpose of God*, and that is all. God does not allow man to know all the facets of His eternal judgment and purposes. It pleases the Lord that His judgments and ways are, "past finding out," even as the Holy Ghost did rightly extol: "O the depth of the riches both of the wisdom and knowledge of God! How unsearchable are His judgments, and His ways past finding out" (Romans 11:33)! Will you agree?

The impossibility of election being determined by foreknowledge of works is a very important doctrine one MUST understand, seeing that those of the persuasion of the free will doctrine are convinced that this is the case and point of Romans 9:11. The mastermind of the Holy Spirit used the apostle Paul to formulate the treatise of unconditional, eternal election through the ensamples of the Old Testament historical men, Jacob (Israel) and Esau, and the historical people as a whole, the Israelites in the days of Moses and the Egyptians, but the Egyptians were represented by their king who was called Pharaoh. These four peoples in view are of specific representation, Paul argued, that *Jacob* and the *Israelites* were instruments of mercy that God "afore prepared unto glory," and that *Esau* and the *Egyptians* were "vessels of wrath fitted to destruction." God's eternal purpose was a willing, or a

17

desire, to make His power known to the world by a public display of His wrath on the Egyptians (Pharaoh) for their refusal to release Israel. The use of the wording, "fitted to destruction" and "afore prepared," shows the purpose of God before these men or peoples were created or born, and thus, not in reference to what they were going to do in works. To show the determination and foreknowledge of God through eternal election, Jacob and Esau are first used as persons of election to prove this point. Thus the subject of investigation at hand in a question is - did election happen according to God's foreknowledge of works or simply by election alone? Please read Romans 9:6-24 before we continue.

In Romans 9:12-13, the purpose of God was distinct in His will for the two individuals. God's plan for the two is that "the elder shall serve the younger," and this was to prove that, "Jacob have I loved, but Esau have I hated." He loved Jacob in ordaining him to be the inheritor of the covenants and promises which were the blessings of salvation. The line of the seed is through generations of saved men – Abraham, Isaac, and then Jacob. Romans 9:12-13 was God's elective plan and purpose governed by His will of love or hatred, which is, mercy or wrath. This election was before their creation and birth, meaning that it was before they DID ANYTHING at all. Pointedly then, election must not be of works. As it is written:

> Romans 9:11-13
> [11] (For *the children* being not yet born, neither having done any good or evil, that the purpose of God according to election might stand, not of works, but of Him that calleth;) [12] It was said unto her, The elder shall serve the younger. [13] As it is written, Jacob have I loved, but Esau have I hated.

The entire point of these passages is to show that God's election was not according to works but according to election, and election is entirely separate from any reference or motivation stimulated by a knowledge of works; thus making impossible the claim that election is based upon a foreknowledge of works. The very passage demands the same interpretation of election as is written in Romans 11:7, and elsewhere.

> Romans 11:7
>
> [7] What then? Israel hath not obtained that which he seeketh for; but the election hath obtained it, and the rest were blinded.

Furthermore, seeing that it was before Jacob and Esau were created or born that the election was made, their creation was a fitting, an afore preparation to one of two destinies – wrath or mercy – the glory of His hatred through punishing plagues or the glory of His love through a shackle-breaking salvation! Therefore they are no more significant or involved in their purpose, destiny, deeds, and fate as much as clay is molded under the unavoidable will of the forming Potter. God has power over each vessel to make one of *honour* (unto a merciful salvation) and the other of *dishonour* (unto a wrathful damnation). As God made Jacob and Esau for His purposes, they were *fitted* and *prepared* for that purpose, and this is the reason "fitted to destruction" and "afore prepared unto glory" are used in Romans 9:22-23. As God did with the individuals, Jacob and Esau, so it is with the nations of people called Israel and Egypt. And now, lo, you may be confused. You may be questioning many things regarding the character and innocence of God. Yes, my reader, this view of sovereignty provokes the questions, "Is there unrighteousness with God?" and again, "Why doth he yet find fault? For who hath resisted His will" (Romans 9:14, 19)? If all this work is God's, even all the sin, how can He yet punish and find fault with men? If you feel provoked to answer God with a question, "how is this righteous?" know that there is no unrighteousness with God even though it appears that there is. If you feel compelled to ask, "Why doth He yet find fault" or "why does He yet hold men accountable and responsible for their sins that He ordains under His mighty sovereign power," the scriptures answer this question directly. The answer to this question is a humbling one where you must come to know your place before an unsearchable, mysterious, infinitely Holy God: "Nay but, O man, **who art thou** that repliest against God? Shall the thing formed say to Him that formed it, **Why hast Thou made me thus**" (Romans 9:20).

"who art thou that repliest against God?" – Rom. 9:20	'shall the work say of Him that made it" – Isa. 29:16
"shall I answer Him" – Job 9:14	'shall the thing framed say of Him that framed it" – Isa. 29:16
"who can say" – Job 36:23	
"who may say unto Him" – Eccl. 8:4	'shall the thing formed say to Him that formed it" – Rom. 9:20

"If thou hast done foolishly in lifting up thyself, or if thou hast thought evil, lay thine hand upon thy mouth" (Prov. 30:32).	"What doest Thou?" – Eccl. 8:4 "What doest Thou?" – Job 9:12 "What doest Thou?" – Daniel 4:35 "What makest Thou?" – Isa. 45:9 "Why hast Thou made me thus?" – Rom. 9:20

Do you not know? Have you not heard that you are but a "potsherd" fashioned by God? What insanity would it be for clay to think, argue, or speak!? And yet, this arena of earth-dwellers does not know the silent humility that a clay pot has before its Pottery Maker! We need to learn from the silence of clay pots! And how infinitely more insane it is for human beings to question God! The curve of respect clay has to its dignified potter on earth is infinitely out-steeped by the curve of humanity to the Almighty. God says you are proud! You are proud if you think you should understand, you need to understand, or you must understand, and so you argue to comprehend, or you have the audacity to question! Does your heart argue with God? Answer God then! Listen to the Potter's preaching – **"Woe unto him that striveth with his Maker!** *Let* the potsherd *strive* with the potsherds of the earth. **Shall the clay say to Him that fashioneth it, What makest Thou?** or thy work, He hath no hands" (Isa. 45:9)? If He makes you to damn you for the glory of His wrath, will you now add to your reprobate insanity by saying to God – "What makest

Thou?" This is the clear interpretation and meaning of Romans 9 on the doctrine of election, and, those who are humble enough to leave the limitations of human logic when seeking a comprehension of an incomprehensible God will be forced to confess like Nebuchadnezzar, Daniel 4:35:

> "And all the inhabitants of the earth *are* reputed as nothing: and He doeth according to His will in the army of heaven, and *among* the inhabitants of the earth: and none can stay His hand, or say unto Him, **What doest Thou**?" (Dan. 4:35)

Don't say it. You don't know His eternal mind, you are blind to His glorious, harmless, righteousness that is omniscient and outside of time. Will you make yourself the teacher, questioner, creator, or speaker, and tell God that you see, and that He is blind on this point that He has revealed to you within time? "Surely your turning of things upside down shall be esteemed as the Potter's clay: for shall the work say of Him that made it, He made me not? Or shall the thing framed say of Him that framed it, He had no understanding" (Isa. 29:16)? Oh house of Israel and all the hellish heathen, hear God! "Cannot I do with you as this potter? Saith the LORD. Behold, as the clay is in the Potter's hand, so are ye in Mine hand" (Jer. 18:6). If the heathen rage and rise to blaspheme, if they frame mischief with lies, oh Lord Jesus! "Thou shalt break them with a rod of iron; Thou shalt dash them in pieces like a Potter's vessel" (Psalm 2:9)! Lord Jesus, You "shall rule them with a rod of iron; as the vessels of a Potter shall they be broken to shivers" (Rev. 2:27)! "Be wise now therefore" all ye men of the earth, "be instructed ye judges of the earth" (Psalm 2:10)! "O the depths of the riches both of the wisdom and knowledge of God" (Rom. 11:33)! "A brutish man knoweth not; neither doth a fool understand this. When the wicked spring as the grass, and when all the workers of iniquity do flourish; it is that they shall be destroyed for ever" (Psalm 92:4-7). Deep, wise, and great are His works, and the righteous shall be glad at the end. What are you, my reader? What are we? WHAT IS MAN!?

> "If he will contend with Him [God], he cannot answer Him one of a thousand. He is wise in heart, and mighty in strength: who hath hardened himself against Him [God], and hath prospered? Which removeth the mountains, and they know not: which overturneth them in His anger. Which shaketh the earth out of her place, and the pillars thereof tremble. Which commandeth the sun, and it riseth not; and sealeth up the stars. Which alone spreadeth out the heavens, and treadeth upon the waves of the sea. Which maketh Arcturus, Orion, and Pleiades, and the chambers of the south. Which doeth great things **past finding out**; yea, and **wonders without number**. Lo, **He goeth by me, and I see Him**

20

not: He passeth on also, but I perceive Him not. Behold, He taketh away, who can hinder Him? who will say unto Him, **What doest Thou?** If God will not withdraw His anger, the proud helpers do stoop under Him. **How much less shall I answer Him, and choose out my words to reason with Him?**" (Job 9:3-14)

The end of a true study of God, namely theology, is a wonder at His infinite loft, an elevation that surpasses our humble knowledge and understanding! God's achievements dwarf every man's skyscraper; the Lord of glory is a galaxy maker! Architect and Engineer with pen in hand, calculating on paper they carefully planned, but the Lord spoke without moving His hand! Lo, and BEHOLD! Void to creation, darkness to illumination, chaos to innumerable creatures applauding God in standing ovation, all this, even, a type of Christian recreation! The same works and words were shadows to personal salvation. To be carnally minded, you will be vile and interrogating, you will be arrogantly investigating, but when will you stop? When will you finally agree with Paul, and exclaim: "O the depth of the riches both of the wisdom and knowledge of God! How unsearchable are His judgments, and His ways past finding out" (Romans 11:33)?!

Can you believe it? That salvation is like the first creation; our beginning is like the earth's formation? "And the earth was without form, and void; and darkness was upon the face of the deep. And the Spirit of God moved upon the face of the waters. And God said, Let there be light: and there was light. And God saw the light, that it was good: and God divided the light from darkness" (Gen. 1:2-4). The world now is in darkness blinded, Satan is enthroned in the carnally minded. "But if our gospel be hid, it is hid to them that are lost: In whom the god of this world hath blinded the minds of them which believe not, lest the light of the glorious gospel of Christ, Who is the image of God, should shine unto them" (2 Cor. 4:3-4). My darkness was illuminated by a **COMMAND**, and there was separation. "For God, Who **COMMANDED** the light to shine out of darkness, hath shined in our hearts, to give the light of the knowledge of the glory of God in the face of Jesus Christ" (2 Cor. 4:6). Let not man reason like the reprobates! Let no man think up some accusing question for God, some reprimand! "Lie not against the truth" that salvation is God given by God's sovereign **COMMAND** (James 3:14)!

Spiritual light to shine out of humanities depraved darkness is a **treasure** that comes from the command of God in election. As it is written, "But we have this **treasure** in earthen vessels, that the excellency of the power may be **of God**, and **not of us**" (2 Cor. 4:7). Formless wickedness is recreated into righteousness when the Spirit moves upon sinners. At the command of Light comes a revelation of Christ, and Christ's likeness is the formation and mighty transformation. "Now the Lord is that Spirit: and where the Spirit of the Lord is, there is liberty. But we all, with open face beholding as in a glass the glory of the Lord, are **changed into the same image** from glory to glory, even as by the Spirit of the Lord" (2 Cor. 3:17-18). Our confession is that, it was not when I was pleased, that then I chose God, that then I savingly called upon Him, that it was then that I did genuinely will and run after Him, "but when it pleased God, Who separated me from my mother's womb, and called me by His grace, **to reveal His Son in me**," it was then that I was saved (Gal. 1:15-16)!

These truths of God's sovereignty are **biblically** true but not always **apparently** true. It is not always apparent by the plain reading of scripture that God is Sovereign over all things. What is most righteously and needfully inculcated is *the responsibility of man*, their vileness and crimes motivating a Holy God to an enormity of just recompenses and punishments. But when the scriptures which we have concisely overviewed thus far are properly believed, the conclusion is clear: God's justice in the punishment of sinners is irreconcilable to the full spectrum of revelation concerning all the features of God's active will, works, responsibility, and sovereignty. The incomprehensible paradigm proven in Romans 9 is not the primary context scripture was written in. By saying this I mean to point out that the most exhaustive form scripture is written in is the context where God's justice is vindicated, understandable, and justified, when addressing the gross crimes of the wicked. If one built theology solely based upon the scripture which is apparently paradoxical to other inspired scripture, we would have a great problem. This needs to be exemplified, and please, pause and pray for wisdom as we proceed.

We have accounted how God was in control of the betrayal of Joseph, and the crucifixion of Jesus, and how God takes ownership of them both as His work and doing. We have seen that men are simultaneously held responsible for their sin. So who was responsible for the sin of taking God's people as slaves in Egypt? What does a simple reading of Exodus chapter 1 conclude? *Lesson: things are not always what they appear to be, what is **apparent** is not always what is **actual**.*

> Exodus 1:6-14
> [6] And Joseph died, and all his brethren, and all that generation. [7] And the children of Israel were fruitful, and increased abundantly, and multiplied, and waxed exceeding mighty; and the land was filled with them. [8] Now there arose up a new king over Egypt, which knew not Joseph. [9] And he said unto his people, Behold, the people of the children of Israel *are* more and mightier than we: [10] Come on, let us deal wisely with them; lest they multiply, and it come to pass, that, when there falleth out any war, they join also unto our enemies, and fight against us, and *so* get them up out of the land. [11] Therefore they did set over them taskmasters to afflict them with their burdens. And they built for Pharaoh treasure cities, Pithom and Raamses. [12] But the more they afflicted them, the more they multiplied and grew. And they were grieved because of the children of Israel. [13] And the Egyptians made the children of Israel to serve with rigour: [14] And

they made their lives bitter with hard bondage, in morter, and in brick, and in all manner of service in the field: all their service, wherein they made them serve, *was* with rigour.

A simple reading of the text shows how the events came to pass. It seems *apparent* that they have a free will and are understandably responsible for their actions and sin. Their thought process is accounted of, they have prepared their heart and devised their way, but one thing is to be remembered! God holds their hearts in His hand and directs them after His determinate counsel and will! Read as the Psalmist of Psalm 105 gives an explanation of the events of Exodus 1 which were not recorded there. It is the hidden, higher, and lofty work which only God can author.

> Psalm 105:24-25
> [24] And He increased His people greatly; and made them stronger than their enemies. [25] **He turned their heart** to hate His people, to deal subtilly with His servants.

It is inaccurate to build theology on just what is written in Exodus 1. We must take into account the whole of scripture. Does not the Spirit expressly teach us that the way of God is revealed in comparing spiritual with spiritual, and that is meant to say, scripture with scripture? This is the way of the Holy Ghost, "which things also we speak, not in the words which man's wisdom teacheth, but which the Holy Ghost teacheth; comparing spiritual things with spiritual" (1 Corinthians 2:13). It is easy to oversimplify biblical history by only one perspective of understanding when there are two perspectives to take into account. What two perspectives? **First, God does not want the Egyptians to sin by taking captive His people Israel. Second, God does want the Egyptians to take His people captive. It cannot be said that God wanted men to sin, most would agree to this, but in the same manner that God does not want any man to sin, likewise He genuinely does not want anyone to perish.** He holds men responsible for their sins even though He is in control, but this does not mean they have a free will, thus their condemnation is His ordination and it is comprehensibly unjustified in our eyes (**or ways**), but it is justified in His. Indeed, "it is God that justifieth" (Romans 8:33). If you have any questions for Him about that, it is just your stinking, filthy pride; these things are too wonderful for us to understand – we must hear, learn, trust, and obey!

We must put a difference here. All things God does are just, and He is justified in His doings, but not necessarily in our comprehension. We cannot understand His justice in all His works, because His sovereign works are hidden from us. In all of our reasoning, we cannot get a logical peek into the righteousness of His majesty when He rules in His eternal sovereignty. Contrasting this *hidden justice*, there is a *comprehensible justice* where God pointedly justifies His doings according to our understanding. The context of God's doings where the Lord is comprehensibly justified in our eyes, this is God in the ways of man. When men try to understand the righteousness of God while His sovereign election and predestination is in view, God's answer is that: *we are forbidden to understand why we have become what He formed us to be, or how our creative purpose and eternal destiny is just.* God does not need to vindicate the righteousness of sovereign predestination, nor does He desire to. It is sin for us to question it! Therefore these things are hidden from us, **secret to God**, and all else is that which is **revealed** and belonging to us. "The **secret things** belong unto the LORD our God: but **those things which are revealed** belong unto us and to our children for ever, that we may do all the words of this law" (Deuteronomy 29:29). NOTE: the sovereignty of God makes justice incomprehensible, but there remains a justice which condescends to your comprehension...more will be spoken on this later as these two themes build and develop in this chapter.

In Exodus 10 we can see the same hidden, sovereign works of God, but **this time we don't have to go to another book to read about it.** In Exodus 10 God says to Pharaoh, "how long wilt thou refuse to humble thyself before Me? Let My people go, that they may serve Me" (v. 3). It is clear that God **wants** His people to be released, and Pharaoh **is sinning** against God in his obstinate pride. God's clear commanded desire is to let His people go. This is **the genuine will** of God concerning Pharaoh but this is not His determinate will... did you know there are *two wills* in God? God desires Pharaoh not to sin and His people to be released, and simultaneously, He desires that Pharaoh would refuse to let the people go. Why? So that God can show great and mighty signs of wrath and judgment against the sin of Pharaoh, on behalf of His love for Israel, to the end that Israel might know that God is the LORD! You may ask where I am getting all of this. Well, in verses 1-2 of Exodus chapter 10, all these things can be clearly seen, and likewise, in Romans 9:17-18, & verse 22.

> Exodus 10:1-4
> [1] And the LORD said unto Moses, Go in unto Pharaoh: for **I have hardened his heart**, and the heart of his servants, **that I might shew these My signs before him**: [2] And that thou mayest tell in the ears of thy son, and of thy son's son, what things I have wrought in Egypt, and My signs which I have done among them; **that ye may know how that I *am* the LORD**. [3] And Moses and Aaron came in unto Pharaoh, and said unto him, Thus saith the LORD God of the Hebrews, **How long wilt thou refuse to humble thyself before Me?** let My people go, that they may serve Me. [4] Else, if thou refuse to let My people go, behold, to morrow will I bring the locusts into thy coast:

> Romans 9:17-18 & 22
> [17] For the scripture saith unto **Pharaoh**, Even for this same purpose have I raised thee up, that I might shew My power in thee, and that My name might be declared throughout all the earth. [18] Therefore hath He mercy on whom He will *have mercy*, and whom He will He hardeneth......[22] *What if God, willing to*

24

shew *His* wrath, and to make His power known, endured with
much longsuffering the vessels of wrath fitted to destruction:

It cannot be said that God does not want His people to be set free, because
God never commands something He does not want (or will). He certainly was not
acting or lying when He commanded Pharaoh to let His people go. He was not acting
or lying when He was grieved over the unwillingness of Pharaoh to humble himself
before the Lord's command. This grief is illustrated in the words "**How long** wilt
thou refuse" written in verse 3. This is a real and genuine will of God which was
working in a tension against the determinate will of God that motivated the Lord to
harden Pharaoh's heart. How can these two wills, desires, and deeds of the Lord be
completely contradictory and genuine at the same time? How can they both be
presently active at the same instance of history, and yet both be completely real,
emotional wills in God? There is no way we can know the answer to these questions,
but one thing is for sure – *God is not a man* – consequentially man ought to be
comfortable with the idea that we cannot fully understand Him.

There is a will of God that is determinate and another that is responsive to
the responses of men. The determinate will of God turns men's hearts and determines
their response; the other will of God is changeable, resistible, and interactive to the
responses of men. God's resistible will was His desire that Pharaoh would let the
people go, that Pharaoh would not sin, and that Pharaoh would not be hardened
through pride. God was using Pharaoh as an instrument of His wrath and hatred, and
He hardened him through an eternal, predestinated plan and purpose which was for
His own glory – this was His eternal, irresistible, unchanging will. God hated
Pharaoh from eternity past, and at present that eternal hatred hardened his heart;
simultaneously, God loved Pharaoh and did not want him to sin, so much so that He
was grieved over his continuance to sin.

> Isaiah 55:8-9
> [8] For My **thoughts** *are* not your **thoughts**, neither *are* your **ways**
> My **ways**, saith the LORD. [9] For *as* the heavens are higher than
> the earth, so are My **ways** higher than your **ways**, and My
> **thoughts** than your **thoughts**.

We must humble ourselves to Who God reveals Himself to be. We must
not arrogantly expect or demand some kind of comprehensive summary of the justice
of His judgments, as if we have some kind of seat of reason or authority in the
courtroom of heaven. God has not invited you as a jury in His courtroom! Indeed, a
true study of all that is given to us in the holy scripture will cause us to exclaim in
unspeakable wonder, "O the depth of the riches both of the wisdom and knowledge
of God! how unsearchable are His judgments, and His ways past finding out"
(Romans 11:33)!

I define all the attributes of God which are employed for determination,
which are accomplished by His irresistible will, as **God in the ways of God**. They

are holy ways, separate ways, and they are not even comprehensible to **the ways of man**. In Isaiah 55:8-9 the Lord seeks to make this point. We cannot even comprehend God's thoughts, because He is outside the dimension of our thinking capacity. An ant cannot understand the moral conscience of a human being, nor can we understand the conscience or consciousness of God; what it is like for Him to think or do anything in His will or ways. An ant to a human is a six-foot height difference; a human to God is higher still, even as the earth to the immeasurable expanse of the heavens in outer space. Expanding on and on, no man can measure its distance and no telescope can see its end. STOP & BE STILL, & CONSIDER the WONDER: God condescends to us as men. He seeks a relationship with us. Undoubtedly, this motivated the purpose of God to relate to us *in the ways of man*. God in the ways of God – He is omnipotent, omnipresent, and omniscient, eternal, determinate, and irresistible. He is everywhere, always, uncreated, and evermore. He is mightily other than us, HOLY, that we could have no relationship with Him unless He condescends to our low estate of mean, dustic faculties. Men are dustic, made of dust and dirt, thus all our splendor is in the meekness of dustic dynamics. We are not omnipresent; we have one location. We are not omnipotent; we must be spoken to in a manner which does not destroy our feeble frames. We are not omniscient, and therefore we need to learn lessons from the Judge. We are temporarily in flesh and subject to the governance of time and deterioration. Our will is not determining but relative, responsive, emotional, changing, and interactive to events we have no foreknowledge of. The two contexts, spectrums, paradigms, and relationships are in two separate ways consistently logical to the features attributed to God and man, but God takes on both *simultaneously*. Please let me accumulate the scriptural case for this.

God in the Ways of God

"God is not a man" – Num. 23:19

"He is not a man" – 1 Sam. 15:29

"For I am God and not a man" – Hos. 11:9

"For I am the LORD" – Mal. 3:6

"He is not a man" – Job 9:32

God is omniscient and man is not. God is not a man, thus He would never need to change His mind; what He wills, He does. Not only does God know all things but He can do all things; He is omnipotent. God is not even limited to time or space, nor any single place; He is omnipresent. THESE are the ways of God. Since He is this way in His person, when He is in THESE ways at any certain time, what God wills or thinks, what He speaks or does – it is irresistible, determinate, eternal, invariable (Jas. 1:17), changeless (Mal. 3:6), and immutable (Heb. 6:17-18). There is something the inspired word of God is seeking to make known to humanity when it states that, "God is not a man" (Num. 23:19), and again, "He is not a man" (1 Sam. 15:29). Furthermore, concerning the deeds of God in response to sin or righteousness, resulting in damning wrath or salvation for those in Covenant promise with God, He says, "I am God and not a man" (Hos. 11:9), and again, "I am the LORD, I change not" (Mal. 3:6)…but if ever God does act inconsistent with His higher ways, it is then

26

we must remember, even again, "He is not a man" (Job 9:32). The subject matter which is contained within the scope of the former two sentences is so vast and shockingly relevant to you and me, that to discover and explain its significance with decent success, the body of text will stretch across this entire book, but as for the beginnings of our study, let the readers be introduced to these words and phrases, and understand first, "**God in the ways of God**":

> Malachi 3:6
> "For I am **the LORD, I change not**; therefore ye sons of Jacob are not consumed." (Ex. 32:10, Neh. 9:31)

> James 1:17
> "Every good gift and every perfect gift is from above, and cometh down from the Father of lights, **with Whom is no variableness, neither shadow of turning.**"

> Ecclesiastes 3:14
> I know that, whatsoever God doeth, it shall be **for ever**: nothing can be put to it, nor any thing taken from it: and God doeth it, that men should fear before Him.

What He is in Person He is in His ways, which are His thoughts, words, and deeds:

> Numbers 23:19
> [19] God *is* **not a man**, that He should **lie**; neither the son of man, that He should **repent**: hath He said, and shall He not do *it*? or hath He spoken, and shall He not make it good?

> 1 Samuel 15:29
> "And also the Strength of Israel will not **lie** nor **repent**: for He **is not a man**, that He should **repent**."

> Hebrews 6:17-18
> [17] Wherein God, willing more abundantly to shew unto the heirs of promise the **immutability of His counsel**, confirmed *it* by an oath: [18] That by two immutable things, in which *it was* **impossible for God to lie,** we might have a strong consolation, who have fled for refuge to lay hold upon the hope set before us:

> Titus 1:2
> "In hope of eternal life, which God, **that cannot lie**, promised before the world began;"

> Romans 11:29
> "For the gifts and calling of God are without **repentance**."

God always fulfills His will and therefore controls the **heart** and **spirit** of man:

> Revelation 17:16-17
> [16] And the ten horns which thou sawest upon the beast, these shall hate the whore, and shall make her desolate and naked, and shall eat her flesh, and burn her with fire. [17] For **God hath put in their hearts to fulfil His will**, and to agree, and give their kingdom unto the beast, **until the words of God shall be fulfilled**.

> Deuteronomy 2:30
> [30] But Sihon king of Heshbon would not let us pass by him: for the LORD thy **God hardened his spirit, and made his heart obstinate**, that He might deliver him into thy hand, as *appeareth* this day.

> > NOTE: God passively and ordinately hardens men's hearts. We cannot say that He thinks the evil thoughts Himself... Does He harden their hearts passively through circumstances, or through His own work in the heart? Whatever it is, God takes ownership of it. We would transgress our comprehension boundaries to presume we could fully understand how God does what He says He does.

His purposes and thoughts are mightily Godlike and therefore irresistible:

> Isaiah 14:24-27
> [24] The LORD of hosts hath sworn, saying, Surely **as I have thought**, so shall it come to pass; and **as I have purposed**, *so* shall it stand: [25] That I will break the Assyrian in My land, and upon My mountains tread him under foot: then shall his yoke depart from off them, and his burden depart from off their shoulders. [26] This *is* the purpose that is purposed upon the whole earth: and this *is* the hand that is stretched out upon all the nations. [27] For **the LORD of hosts hath purposed**, and who shall disannul *it*? and His hand *is* stretched out, and who shall turn it back?

His purposes, thoughts, and will are His counsel and pleasure:

> Isaiah 46:10-11
> [10] Declaring the end from the beginning, and from ancient times *the things* that are not *yet* done, saying, **My counsel** shall stand, and **I will do all My pleasure:** Calling a ravenous bird from the east, the man that executeth **My counsel** from a far country: yea, **I have spoken it**, I will also bring it to pass; **I have purposed it**,

28

I will also do it.

Job 23:13

[13] But He *is* in one *mind*, and who can turn Him? and **what His soul desireth, even *that* He doeth.**

In all things whether past, present, or future we can be assured that what is done on earth is done "for to do whatsoever Thy hand and Thy **counsel determined** before to be done" (Acts 4:28). Be it a sin against mankind, small or great, or be it the greatest sin against God, namely the crucifixion of Jesus Christ, it is done according to "whatsoever Thy hand and Thy **counsel determined** before to be done" (Acts 4:28).

Acts 4:23-31

[23] And being let go, they went to their own company, and reported all that the chief priests and elders had said unto them. [24] And when they heard that, they lifted up their voice to God with one accord, and said, Lord, Thou *art* God, which hast made heaven, and earth, and the sea, and all that in them is: [25] Who by the mouth of Thy servant David hast said, Why did the heathen rage, and the people imagine vain things? [26] The kings of the earth stood up, and the rulers were gathered together against the Lord, and against His Christ. [27] For of a truth against Thy Holy Child Jesus, Whom Thou hast anointed, both Herod, and Pontius Pilate, with the Gentiles, and the people of Israel, were gathered together, [28] **For to do whatsoever Thy hand and Thy counsel determined before to be done.** [29] And now, Lord, behold their threatenings: and grant unto Thy servants, that with all boldness they may speak Thy word, [30] By stretching forth thine hand to heal; and that signs and wonders may be done by the name of Thy Holy Child Jesus. [31] And when they had prayed, the place was shaken where they were assembled together; and they were all filled with the Holy Ghost, and they spake the word of God with boldness.

And this has been the teaching and recognition through all the centuries, but will you recognize it? Regarding the common thought of the Jews toward the "movement" which arose with Jesus Christ, it was spoken in the light of the irresistible sovereignty of God:

Acts 5:38-39

[38] And now I say unto you, Refrain from these men, and let them alone: for if this **counsel** or this work be of men, it will come to nought: [39] **But if it be of God, ye cannot overthrow it; lest haply ye be found even to fight against God.**

According to His **counsel**, things are predestinated to **salvation**:

> Ephesians 1:11
> [11] In Whom also we **have** obtained an inheritance, **being predestinated according to the purpose of Him Who worketh all things after the counsel of His own will**:

According to His **ordination**, men are predestinated to **condemnation**:

> Jude 4
> [4] For there are certain men crept in unawares, **who were before of old ordained to this condemnation**, ungodly men, turning the grace of our God into lasciviousness, and denying the only Lord God, and our Lord Jesus Christ.

God sets the course for all damned men to be just as Eli's sons who, "hearkened not...because the LORD would slay them" (1 Sam. 2:25). Like as it was said of the Canaanites, even so it will be said to all that it is ordained upon, "it was of the LORD to **harden their hearts**...that He might destroy them utterly" (Josh. 12:20). A panoramic view of God's sovereignty reveals that God is in control of the full expanse of things in the universe of His creation; He rules the systems made by man – like kingdoms, classes, authority, and prosperity (or man's inventions and works) – all of this! In every kingdom on earth, and more, all is under God's control, but look closer! A zoomed-in picture of God's sovereignty at work is that He "declareth unto man what is his thought"! Amos 4:13 reveals this panoramic and zoomed in detail of God's sovereign glory with descriptive language that is God-breathed. Wonder as you read it:

> "For, lo, He that formeth the mountains, and createth the wind, and **declareth unto man what is his thought**, that maketh the morning darkness, and treadeth upon the high places of the earth, The LORD, The God of hosts, is His Name" (Amos 4:13).

God "declareth unto man what is his thought," so that, a "man's goings are of the LORD; how can a man then understand his own way" (Proverbs 20:24)? God calls nations of men, with kings, armies, and orders of authority and rule, they all obey His orders and serve His purposes, but like brute animals they don't even know it! He calls them like as a human makes a "hiss" (Isa. 5:26), as a master to a trained pet, like to a ravenous bird (Isa. 46:11), and they all like bees and flies come swarming forth for war (Isa. 7:18, Zech. 10:8) – an ordered chaos! God's commands from heaven are declared in the hearts of man! He elaborates on His sovereign powers in the humiliation of one of the world's greatest human sovereigns, Nebuchadnezzar by name. God self-declares that He does all great things, and He rules all great men. "He increaseth the nations, and destroyeth them: He enlargeth the nations, and straiteneth them again. He taketh away the heart of the chief of the people of the earth, and causeth them to wander in a wilderness where there is no way. They grope in the dark without light, and He maketh them to stagger like a drunken man" (Job 12:23-25). "Shall a trumpet be blown in the city, and the people not be afraid? Shall there be evil in a city, and the LORD hath not done it" (Amos 3:6)? Behold, God is sovereign!

Put your mind at rest from trying to understand perfectly, dear saint; you cannot understand how this is just. In the greatest treatise we have in the whole of scripture arguing the defence of God's absolute sovereignty, all the evidence and truth leads the readers to one question – "if all this is true, how can God be just in condemning us?" This very question is asked and answered in Romans chapter 9; read carefully and find the answer:

> Romans 9:18-23
> [18] Therefore hath He mercy on whom He will *have mercy*, and **whom He will** He hardeneth. [19] Thou wilt say then unto me, **Why doth He yet find fault? For who hath resisted His will?** [20] Nay but, O man, **who art thou that repliest against God?** Shall the thing formed say to Him that formed *it*, **Why hast Thou made me thus?** [21] Hath not the potter power over the clay, of the same lump to make one vessel unto honour, and another unto dishonour? [22] What if God, willing to shew His wrath, and to make His power known, endured with much longsuffering the vessels of wrath fitted to destruction: [23] And that He might make known the riches of His glory on the vessels of mercy, which He had afore prepared unto glory,

My dear brethren, my fellow vessels of clay, if we cannot understand the footstool of God, how can we understand His heavenly Throne of Judgment? If we cannot understand things on earth, which is His footstool, how can we understand His Throne Judgments made in heaven? If we cannot reach our hand to grasp the circumference of His pinky finger, how can our comprehension grasp the incomprehensible mind of our Maker!? Our every supplication should be preceded with an awareness of our state before this Awesome Deity! Many men murmur against God, but Abraham saw it a weighty thing to even speak to God. In righteousness he had faith, in humility he did premeditate, before speaking to God he did inculcate: "Behold now, **I have taken upon me** to speak unto the Lord, **which am but dust and ashes**" (Genesis 19:27).

Mankind may desire to supplicate, but no prayer can he worthily generate.
But dust and ashes I am, just an earthly creature.
Under the Sun I burn, in the night a sleeper.
As for God, I cannot grasp His pinky finger!

God sows together the threads of time, He is arrayed in it like a kingly gown,
Until finally, BEHOLD, He is descending, and His coming is Heaven-bringing,
Because God transforms everything, all around, by Heavenly Jerusalem coming down!

His Kingdom blooms after apocalyptic dooms,
the beauty of a heavenly flower falling to earth like a rain shower.
Mountains melting, the earth under God's smelting.
The heavens rolled back, and nothing is left intact.
In pools of blood, He returns wicked men to the mud.
But the saints, they will not break,
Even while the earth staggers and shakes.
From dust and ashes they will arise, alive, like lightning to the sky they will be
translated, having glorified eyes to see God–face to face–the same One Who they
once carnally hated. They will wonder, still, at His right hand majesty, even though
they are now glorified-sinless, everlastingly

Gathered around with gaping eyes – wondering how – IT IS THE END OF DAYS!
Heavenly saints, GASP! It is the end, AT LAST!
For, lo, The Rod of Iron He's grasping!
The Universe Bows...Hallelujah!
The Nations in recreation, He subdues all scholastically.
God becomes all in all, and the Father takes supremacy!

Guard your mind from pride, for we sit at the foothills of His condescension! In all your learning, saint, learn to silently trust, giving glory to the God of wonders! If we cannot understand even how He is, that He is three and one, how can we think to understand the galaxies of His Judgment and the intricacies of His ways? If you saw Him rightly, dear one, you would remember that God is greater and more fearful than the Leviathan. If you understood "Him of Whom we have to do," you would not answer Him again.

So fearful is the sight of the Almighty that He says, "there shall no man see Me, and live" (Ex. 33:20)! God dwelt in the midst of and walked with Judah and Israel. It was written, "Judah was His sanctuary, and Israel His dominion" (Psalm 114:2). Oh Israel! Did you know that when sitting on the Banks of the Red Sea, there the sea caught a glimpse of the Almighty! Oh Israel, it is because God was in the midst of thee! Therefore was it said that thou art His sanctuary. "The sea saw it, and fled: Jordan was driven back. The mountains skipped like rams, and the little hills like lambs. What ailed thee, O thou sea, that thou fleddest? Thou Jordan, that thou wast driven back? Ye Mountains, that ye skipped like rams; and ye little hills, like lambs? Tremble, thou earth, at the presence of the Lord, at the presence of the God of Jacob; which turned the rock into a standing water, the flint into a fountain of waters" (Psalm 114:3-8). What ailed the sea ought to ail you and me. What struck the sea to flee? It was because of WHOM it did see, and the God of Israel has made a Covenant with you and me! He turns mountains into rams, rivers to shining walls. He can make Mount Everest into a skipping ram, the Rocky Mountains into lambs. The wicked were born to be damned, the righteous in a merciful, mysterious walk, preplanned. Now saints, He is your Shepherd, and by His written word He calls. Do you hear His voice? His commands do not necessitate man's free will to choose, but, "of His own will begat He us with the word of Truth, that we should be a kind of firstfruits of His creatures" (James 1:18).

In His mercy He has condescended to our humble finite state. So great is the Leviathan that he does not "make many supplications unto thee? Will he speak soft words unto thee? Will he make a covenant with thee?" Indeed he does none of these things (Job 41:3-4). How much more fearful is it that the Almighty creator of the Leviathan has condescended to speak soft words to us and make a Covenant with man? Even at the sight of the Leviathan you would be cast down to the ground! Do you think you will fight with the Leviathan? "Lay thine hand upon him, remember the battle, do no more. Behold, the hope of him is in vain: shall not one be cast down even at the sight of him? None is so fierce that dare stir him up: who then is able to stand before Me? Who hath prevented Me, that I should repay him? Whatsoever is under the whole heaven is Mine" (Job 41:8-11). God has condescended to our humble stature and spoken soft works to us. These words are in the softness of a page contained in a holy Book. Should we then wrangle with God? Are we forgetting the gravity of this great God, "Who only hath immortality, dwelling in the light which no man can approach unto; Whom no man hath seen, nor can see: to whom be honour and power everlasting" (1 Tim. 6:16)!? Should we receive His written word with less fearful trembling than if we were in His very presence as it was spoken? Before His brilliant face that shines like the edges of the sun, no man would even be able to stand before Him, let alone question His Almighty Judgments. It would be a serpent's pride to even question what was spoken; how then can you question what is written?

"A King that sitteth in the throne of judgment scattereth away all evil with His eyes."
(Proverbs 20:8)

Will you lay your hand upon the majesty of His Judgment and intermeddle with wisdom before His throne? Are you so arrogant as to suppose you could judge the price of His justice or the value of His sayings? You strike war with God if you fight against His word, but if you were there would you not be cast down even at the sight of Him? If none can stand before the Leviathan, who can stand before God? No, we will fall as dead men in His Holy presence. He has spoken to us in soft words, even through the words of an inspired, holy Book. He has made a covenant with us! Let us therefore not stumble at what is written. It is pride to seek an understanding of forbidden knowledge. The **highminded** do fret in anxiety until they vent their ungodly wrath and wrangle against the higher things of God. God hides things from us for our good, and these things we cannot understand. Job grievously sinned against the Lord by transgressing the limitations of his understanding; he ventured to judge God and contended with the justice of His doings. My reader, you who unceasingly strain because you heart cries out, "how can this be righteous?!" You need the humility of Job, but I hope it comes at a lesser cost than how he did obtain it. God said to Job fearful sayings so that you would learn to copy his humility. Now listen up! Will you lay your hand upon your mouth? The Leviathan is a whimper next to the Almighty's temper. Before this beast you may die but your soul to the Almighty will fly with an eternal destiny by and by.

Job 40:1-14

¹ Moreover the LORD answered Job, and said, ² Shall he that contendeth with the Almighty instruct *Him*? he that reproveth God, let him answer it. ³ Then Job answered the LORD, and said, **⁴ Behold, I am vile; what shall I answer Thee? I will lay mine hand upon my mouth.** ⁵ Once have I spoken; but I will not answer: yea, twice; but I will proceed no further. ⁶ Then answered the LORD unto Job out of the whirlwind, and said, ⁷ Gird up thy loins now like a man: I will demand of thee, and declare thou unto Me. ⁸ Wilt thou also disannul My judgment? wilt thou condemn Me, that thou mayest be righteous? ⁹ Hast thou an arm like God? or canst thou thunder with a voice like Him? ¹⁰ Deck thyself now *with* majesty and excellency; and array thyself with glory and beauty. ¹¹ Cast abroad the rage of thy wrath: and behold every one *that is* proud, and abase him. ¹² Look on every one *that is* proud, *and* bring him low; and tread down the wicked in their place. ¹³ Hide them in the dust together; *and* bind their faces in secret. ¹⁴ Then will I also confess unto thee that thine own right hand can save thee.

There are many things written and taught by the Lord. Except we have faith, they will serve as a stumbling block to our harm. If we don't have the humble faith wherein we receive the Word of God as "seeing Him Who is invisible," we will not fear His Word as we ought, and we will be offended like the rest. If we believe not, we forget the glory of His majesty. If we believe not, we forget the limitations of our earthly tabernacle and proudly err. In the earthly days of Christ Jesus, He preached a message causing most people to offend. After the message was preached, "many therefore of His disciples, when they had heard this, said, This is an hard saying; who can hear it? When Jesus knew in Himself that His disciples murmured at it, He said unto them, Doth this offend you? **What and if ye shall see the Son of Man ascend up where He was before** (John 6:60-62)?" "Thou, even Thou, art to be feared: and who may stand in Thy sight when once Thou art angry" (Psalm 76:7)?

Jesus knew that their pride had caused them to overlook the Lordship and brilliant glory of the One Who was speaking to them. If the same message was given from the ascended glory of His Throne, the place that He was before the humiliation of His incarnation, these men would not have been offended. It was their unbelief that caused this prideful offense at what was spoken. What they heard by the hearing of the ear was not received because they remembered not Who it was that spoke with them. **Because they could not understand,** they were offended. What arrogance! Job learned this same lesson and we must learn it too. Have you begun to abhor yourself, you who wrangle with God in offense? Take heed to Job's example of repentance and humble yourself, as it is written:

Job 42:1-6

[1] Then Job answered the LORD, and said, [2] I know that Thou canst do every *thing*, and *that* no thought can be withholden from Thee. [3] Who *is* he that hideth counsel without knowledge? therefore have I uttered that I understood not; things too wonderful for me, which I knew not. [4] Hear, I beseech Thee, and I will speak: I will demand of Thee, and declare Thou unto me. [5] I have heard of Thee by the hearing of the ear: **but now mine eye seeth Thee.** [6] **Wherefore I abhor** *myself*, **and repent in dust and ashes.**

My reader, whether sinner or saint, read of the Son of Man ascended in glory:

Daniel 7:13-14
[13] I saw in the night visions, and, behold, One like **the Son of Man** came with the clouds of heaven, and came to the Ancient of days, and they brought Him near before Him. [14] And there was given Him dominion, and glory, and a kingdom, that all people, nations, and languages, should serve Him: His dominion is an everlasting dominion, which shall not pass away, and His kingdom that which shall not be destroyed.

Can **the Son of Man** be "betrayed" by him who is but a "grass blade" (Luke 22:22, 1 Pet. 1:24, Isa. 40:7-8)? Can He Who "was given dominion, and glory, and a kingdom, that all people, nations, and languages, should serve Him," be shaken, mistaken, or asleep in a tempestuous sea so that He and those given Him are by waves overtaken? Though the waves wax bold and things appear undetermined of old, by the declarative word of God are things rightly told that the end from the beginning did the Potter mold. "His dominion is an everlasting dominion, which shall not pass away," and though "the heathen rage" and devise a tempestuous snare, it is of God that "many sons" might His glory share (Ps. 2:1, Acts 4:25, Heb. 2:10). In one moment He could command "twelve legions" (Matt. 26:53), and He is not intimidated by the "enchained dark demons" (Jude 1:6); their "time is short" (Rev. 12:12) for the cause in which they are employed to rend "the veil that is His flesh" (Heb. 10:20), to redeem "every race" of men (Rev. 5:9), to have all the world by Christ possessed. As "foaming waves" (Jude 1:13) they sought to oppress, all His glory they sought to suppress, but He with an innumerable company will this world possess, and "His Kingdom" is "that which shall not be destroyed" (Dan. 7:13-14).

This work of humility is the grace of God! In the same sermon Jesus preached, "No man can come to Me, except the Father which hath sent Me draw him: and I will raise him up at the last day" (John 6:44). And again, "It is the spirit that quickeneth; the flesh profiteth nothing: the words that I speak unto you, they are spirit, and they are life. But there are some of you that believe not.....Therefore said I unto you, that no man can come unto Me, except it were given him of My Father" (John 6:63-65). If the Spirit of God will quicken you to receive the biblical instruction of the sovereignty of God and the justice of man's responsibility, you will be like Job and wonder that *these things* are too wonderful for you. **Faith sees Him** (Heb. 11:27, 2 Cor. 3:18)! Let us therefore repent in dust and ashes.

God in the ways of God: it is the higher thoughts and ways of God which man cannot comprehend – it is the secret contents of the scripture which we are only able to blindly trust. Of these ways we are instructed, yet only God can understand them. However, there are **ways** in which we are instructed that we are able to understand – God relates to us in **the ways of man**.

God in the Ways of Man

Isaiah 57:15
"For thus saith the **high** and **lofty One** that **inhabiteth
eternity**, Whose name is **Holy**; I dwell in the **high**
and **holy place**, <u>with him also</u> that is of a **contrite** and
humble spirit, to revive the spirit of the **humble**, and
to revive the heart of the **contrite ones**."

We must put a difference between what is revealed to our understanding (what is in our ways) and those things which are hidden from our understanding, secret, and solely understood by God (in His ways). "The **secret** things belong to the LORD our God: but those things which are **revealed** belong unto us and to our children for ever, that we may do all the words of this law" (Deut. 29:29). We are sinful creatures created by an exalted and hidden Creator Who dwells in an unapproachable and lofty arena called heaven: The "high and holy place." If God will speak, then His words bear this title, "Thus saith the High and Lofty One that inhabiteth eternity, Whose name is Holy; I dwell in the high and holy place" (Isa. 57:15). With such a title and Person we should be sharply aware of our low, vile, and unholy person and passions; therefore when He speaks we would be "of a contrite and humble spirit" (Isa. 57:15). There should be a *keeping* of ourselves before this God, a *slowness* to speak or think, and a *readiness* to hear. Why? "For God is in **heaven**" and we are "upon **earth**" (Eccl. 5:1-2). As it is written, "Keep thy foot when thou goest to the house of God, and be more ready to hear, than to give the sacrifice of fools: for they consider not that they do evil. Be not rash with thy mouth, and let not thine heart be hasty to utter any thing before God: **for God is in heaven, and thou upon earth**: therefore let thy words be few" (Ecclesiastes 5:1-2).

"Our Father which art in heaven…come…in earth…as it is in heaven"
– Matthew 6:9-10

If He would speak and relate to us, then it would be by an infinite condescension! In Isaiah 57:15 God reveals this condescension. God is in heaven, a place of infinite height, holiness, and loft. We are on earth, a place infinitely beneath, below, and unholy. God does inhabit eternity, timelessly and terribly filling all things with Himself, and yet we are a single vessel of perishable clay in a single space of matter and time. Even under the degeneration and deterioration of time we cannot stay standing. As the earth rotates and time passes, we cannot but wither, wrinkle, and waste away. And lo! It is an infinite condescension for God to come and dwell upon this revolving earth with men. It is condescension because of the place from which He comes – namely heaven! Heaven bestows upon Him endless honors and adorations as it and all its inhabitants therein are exercised by the impossible powers that pour forth from the Being of this Person. Billows of endless and sweeping glory rouse heaven's creatures to gasping explosions of ecstatic wonder. What an unimaginable humbling and dishonor it is for Him to dwell upon the devil's earth (2 Cor. 4:4). If this God finds you worthy, if He chooses you as an earthen vessel to dwell in, then your soul will be likewise exercised by heaven's King! You too will be overwhelmed into an ejaculatory joining with heaven's choir. By understanding where He is from and who you are, you may become *this humble one*. As He saith, "I dwell in the high and holy place, **with him also** that is of a *contrite* and *humble* spirit, to revive the spirit of the *humble*, and to revive the heart of the *contrite ones*" (Isa. 57:15). God is high, so high, but let the world wonder that He would come here below, so low, that He would dwell with you and me. "Though the LORD *be* high, yet hath He respect unto the lowly: but the proud He **knoweth** afar off" (Ps. 138:6). Now if He comes to you and is still yet hidden from this world, if they pay no attention to Him still, this coming down to the earth is a great humbling of God and condescension to man.

Hallowed is the place of His dwelling in heaven. When God shows man how High and hallowed He is, when He shows us the place of His dwelling in heaven, it ought to bring our minds to the low place of blind obedience. He dwells in heaven! Well then, what can be said of His works on earth? Up there is a language, life, learning, and location we know nothing of. It is HOLY. His works below are therefore mind-shattering in greatness! He does gather "the winds in His fists," bind "the waters in a garment," and establish "all the ends of the earth" (Prov. 30:3-6). These works declare an incomparable wisdom and knowledge in God. Therefore men, mere earth-inhabiters, should have a boundless awe of the wisdom and knowledge of a God Who doth infinitely stride in secret wonders. Ascending to heaven and descending to earth, it is God that worketh all things for His glory and Name which are unknowable, unbearable, and eternally significant. If we cannot tell or teach ourselves these things, nor find out the ways in God, then we ought to be teachable, believing, and obeying! When He speaks and teaches therefore, "add thou not unto His words, lest He reprove thee, and thou be found a liar" (Prov. 30:3-6). This is the humble confession we need to believe: "I neither learned **wisdom**, nor have the **knowledge of the holy. Who hath ascended up into heaven, or descended?** Who hath gathered the wind in His fists? Who hath bound the waters in a garment? Who hath established all the ends of the earth? What is His name, and what is His Son's name, if thou canst tell? Every word of God is pure: He is a shield unto them that put their trust in Him. Add thou not unto His words, lest He reprove thee, and thou be found a liar" (Proverbs 30:3-6).

"Great is the LORD, and greatly to be praised;
and His greatness is unsearchable" – Ps. 145:3

What does God want us to understand? "God is greater than man" (Job 33:12-13) and therefore He "giveth NOT account of any of His matters" to man (Job. 33:12-13). If you think that you have found something to strive with God about, "Behold, IN THIS THOU ART NOT JUST: I will answer thee, that **God is greater than man**. Why dost thou strive against Him? **For He giveth not account of any of His matters**" (Job 33:12-13). "Woe unto him that striveth with his Maker! Let the potsherd strive with the potsherds of the earth" but let not the potsherd strive with the Potter (Isa. 45:9). God is an incomprehensible Person dwelling in an incomprehensible place; likewise are all His matters. There is a realm of things which God says is "secret" (Deut. 29:29). *I will forewarn you of a danger, of error you may commit*: The wonder of the Trinity and that God is an uncreated mystery; most are not offended with these two things. They say, "Amen," even though they don't understand it. Men are humbled that He is three and one, content that we cannot understand how there was never a time when He had a beginning. Why? HE IS GOD. Now listen! As soon as an Armenian sees God making a judgment they can't understand, they contend with Him about it. As soon as a Calvinist sees God in a way that is inconsistent with His sovereignty, they have a problem with it. Oh that you would silence your biases and break before HIS HAMMER (Jer. 23:29).

God is incomparable to the greatest nobility or majesty on earth and therefore is worthy of the highest degree of respect that HE is "right" and "most just." We are earth-dwelling creatures of His creation, even "the work of His hands." He gave you a mouth to praise Him and a mind to be overwhelmed with a holy perplexity and awful wonder. Now consider this! "Shall even he that hateth right govern? And wilt thou condemn Him that is most just? Is it fit to say to a king, Thou art wicked? And to princes, Ye are ungodly? How much less to Him that accepteth not the persons of princes, nor regardeth the rich more than the poor? **For they all are the work of His hands**" (Job 34:17-19). "Behold, God exalteth by His power: who teacheth like Him? **Who hath enjoined Him His way? Or who can say, Thou hast wrought iniquity? Remember that thou magnify His work, which men behold. Every man may see it; man may behold it afar off. Behold, God is great, and we know Him not, neither can the number of His years be searched out**" (Job 36:22-26). He uses flying angels to declare the day of His judgment! He is the Creator that "made heaven, and earth, and the sea, and the fountains of waters" (Rev. 14:6-7); therefore when you read what He writes, even the journals, biology, physiology, and psychology of God – "FEAR GOD and GIVE GLORY to HIM" (Rev. 14:6-7). "And I saw another angel fly in the midst of heaven, having the everlasting gospel to preach unto them that dwell on the earth, and to every nation, and kindred, and tongue, and people, Saying with a loud voice, Fear God, and **give glory to Him**; for the hour of His judgment is come: and **worship Him that made**

heaven, and earth, and the sea, and the fountains of waters" (Rev. 14:6-7).

No man "hath enjoined Him His way," and "we know Him not" (Job 33:22-26). "His ways are everlasting" (Hab. 3:6) and "we cannot find Him out" (Job 37:23). "There is no searching of His understanding" (Isa. 40:28). He is Almighty God; "Who hath **measured** the waters in the hollow of His hand, and **meted out** heaven with the span, and **comprehended** the dust of the earth in a measure, and **weighed** the mountains in scales, and the hills in a balance? **Who hath directed the Spirit of the LORD, or being His counsellor hath taught Him? With whom took He counsel, and who instructed Him, and taught Him in the path of judgment, and taught Him knowledge, and shewed to Him the way of understanding?** Behold, the nations are as a drop of a bucket, and are counted as the small **dust** of the balance: behold, He taketh up the isles as a **very little thing**. And Lebanon is not sufficient to burn, nor the beasts thereof sufficient for a burnt offering. All nations before Him are as **nothing**; and they are counted to Him less than **nothing**, and **vanity**. To whom then will ye liken God? or what likeness will ye compare unto Him" (Isa. 40:12-18)? He has "measured" the humanly immeasurable, "comprehended" the numbers of the earth that are humanly innumerable, His balances and scales are precisely perfect expanding in universal length and accuracy, and all this immeasurable immensity is caught up in the hollow of His hand.

"who art thou that repliest against God?" – Rom. 9:20
"shall I answer Him" – Job 9:14

"What doest Thou?" – Eccl. 8:4
"What doest Thou?" – Job 9:12
"What doest Thou?" – Daniel 4:35
"What makest Thou?" – Isa. 45:9

"Shall not the Judge of all the earth do right?" – Gen. 18:25
"Is there unrighteousness with God?" – Rom. 9:14
"Who hath enjoined Him His way?
Or who can say, Thou hast wrought iniquity?" – Job 36:23

My dear reader, God is omnipresent, omnipotent, and omniscient. These three characteristics are solely His. But Oh! God does lay aside all three of these glories to relate to men in **the ways of men**. There is a way that is God's – omnipresence, omnipotence, and omniscience – and yet there is another way in which God does relate to men - **God in the ways of man**. If it were not so, we could not survive His presence and power. We would not understand His will, word, or work. Oh my reader, oh that you would understand this great condescension! You would be as I am now, powerless, perplexed, and full of praise! Bless His Holy Name! Consider Abraham.

Abraham discoursed with God about the justice of His judgments under an infinite condescension. When doing so, he did wisely and fearfully understand himself to be unworthy for such a conversation, and more so, unworthy to even speak a word if ever he was given a glimmering secret of what God was about to do. His inquiries and answers back to God were not without trembling of soul, not without deep and loathsome reflections of his own demeaning presence and clay-tongued speech as such a matter of discussion did light upon him from God. Can dust and ashes understand the justice and judgment of an eternal, uncreated, timeless, omnipresent, omnipotent, omniscient, and almighty God? Loathing himself as Isaiah did while in the presence of God's enthroned presence (Isa. 6), he did present the humble inquiry, "Shall not the Judge of all the earth do right" (Gen. 18:25)? There is a righteousness at work active in the Person of God that is comprehensible to man, and yet if our ash-like comprehension does climb the angelic ladder of His higher revelations, it will be sin to think that we could even understand God's righteousness, justice, and judgment. We must learn the wonder of this question that Abraham was able to righteously ask, a question that would have been forbidden to speak in heaven (Rom. 9:20).

Isaiah 55:9
*"For as the **heavens** are higher than the **earth**,*
*so are **My ways** higher than **your ways**, and **My thoughts** than*
***your thoughts**."*

To be humble, one must look up, see, and find out – how high are the heavens above the earth? "Look unto the **heavens**, and see; and behold the clouds which are **higher than thou**" (Job 35:5). Until we see this, we cannot understand the mystery of God's condescension. God *came down* to Abraham! Consider all the matters of God's condescension. God came down and did eat and drink man's food and water! Solomon wondered at the prospect of God coming down to men, saying, "But will God in very deed dwell with men on the earth? Behold, heaven and the heaven of heavens cannot contain Thee; how much less this house which I have built" (2 Chron. 6:18)! God is infinite in space, unlimited in all characteristics, and yet, though the heaven of heavens cannot contain Him, He that hath no limit, will God indeed limit Himself to a single location and dwell there? Yet even more so, would God eat man's food? He allowed Abraham a little service with "a little water," to run and bow before Him, and then Abraham "hastened into the tent unto Sarah" to "make ready quickly three measures of fine meal." Abraham "ran into the herd" and fetched a calf for a young man to hastily dress (Gen. 18:2-7). Abraham had this supreme privilege, and "he stood by them under the tree, and they did eat" (Gen. 18:8). Is this not the context of an infinite condescension? Is God in any need of water for His feet, rest for His body, and meat for His hunger? God, "Who only hath immortality, dwelling in the light which no man can approach unto; Whom no man hath seen, nor can see: to Whom be honour and power everlasting," EVEN HE did say: "I will take no bullock out of thy house, nor he goats out of thy folds. For every beast of the forest is Mine, and the cattle upon a thousand hills. I know all the fowls of the mountains: and the wild beasts of the field are Mine. If I were hungry, I would not tell thee, for the world is Mine, and the fulness thereof. Will I eat the flesh of bulls, or drink the blood of goats" (Psalm 50:9-13)?

Can Abraham wash the feet of God? "Can a man take fire in his bosom, and his clothes not be burned? Can one go upon hot coals, and his feet not be burned" (Prov. 6:27-28)? Then how could one reach forth and touch the feet of God which are "like unto fine brass as if they burned in a furnace" (Rev. 1:15)? A man cannot even touch the ark of God and live…how more the feet of God!? While the apostle John was in heaven in the presence of God, did he ever dare approach God and think to do Him some kindness by washing His feet, which from everlasting are clean? How did Abraham put forth his hand to touch the feet of God as "Uzzah put forth his hand to the ark of God" (2 Sam. 6:6)? As the oxen shook the cart and Uzzah saw a need, the feet of God were dirty and Abraham did reach forth and wash them. How? Is this not an infinite condescension? To be in the presence of God's ark was a dangerous thing; nevertheless men were able to keep standing. Howbeit when men enter into the presence of God, a place where they may behold His burning feet of bronze, there they will fall down as dead. On the plane of earth, a lower ground, the few and privileged did know the hallowed feeling as they drew near to a condescended Creator. God does hide His glory, for our safety, that He might tenderly draw near in a diminished form and visage compatible to our weak and feeble frames. This Preferred King condescends to make servants of men, stepping down in an earthly gown He allows Abraham to wash His feet. Even God, "Whose shoe's latchet I am not worthy to unloose" (John 1:27).

God is Omnipresent

Can God indeed be limited to a single place, so humbling Himself as to lay aside His **omnipresence**? God "dwelleth on high!" God "humbleth Himself to behold the things that are in heaven, and the earth," but will He come and visit the earth in a limited space of time to walk in a certain place? This is an awesome wonder, for no one "is like unto the LORD our God, Who **dwelleth on high**" (Psalm 113:5-6). "What is man, that Thou art mindful of him? and the son of man, that Thou visitest him" (Psalm 8:4)? Will God limit Himself not only to a single place, but a certain frame of limited energy that man might rightly say to Him as He stands with a company of angels, "rest yourselves under the tree" (Gen. 18:4)? Does God need rest? "Thus saith the LORD, The heaven is My throne, and the earth is My footstool: where is the house that ye build unto Me? and **where is the place of My rest**" (Isaiah 66:1)? It is written, "Behold, He that keepeth Israel shall neither slumber nor sleep" (Psalm 121:4)! "Hast thou not known? hast thou not heard, that the everlasting God, the LORD, the Creator of the ends of the earth, fainteth not, neither is weary? **there is no searching of His understanding**" (Isaiah 40:28). What is time to God? Men are so weak, finite, and insignificant; we cannot even sit under the Sun and live. We will dehydrate, burn, blister, break into a fever, and die. "What is man?" And again, what is time? Time is merely the rotation of the earth. Men are so insignificant that we will wither, sag, waste, bruise, break down, and age while simply undergoing the rotations of the earth. Old men are so wasted under the effect of time – sagged, hunched, hurting, and disproportioned – they have become an unrecognizable creature from the man they once were just some thousands of rotations ago. And God! God wants to meet with you before your skin melts like wax under time and gravity. Surely it is right for us to understand that this is an infinite condescension.

> "And he said, I beseech Thee, **shew me thy glory**. And
> He said, I will make all **My goodness** pass before thee,
> and I will proclaim the name of the LORD before thee;
> and will be gracious to whom I will be gracious, and
> will shew mercy on whom I will shew mercy. And He
> said, **Thou canst not see My face: for there shall no
> man see Me, and live.** And the LORD said, Behold,
> there is a place by Me, and thou shalt stand upon a
> rock: And it shall come to pass, while My glory passeth
> by, that I will put thee in a clift of the rock, and will
> cover thee with My hand while I pass by: And I will
> take away Mine hand, and thou shalt see My back
> parts: but My face shall not be seen." (Exodus 33:18-
> 23)

When heaven invades earth and God fulfills the prayer, "Thy Kingdom Come," the proudest men of the earth will flee. Having nowhere to go, they will cry out, "Hide us from the face of Him that sitteth on the Throne, and from the wrath of the Lamb" (Rev. 6:16). This is the fulfillment of what is written, "And I saw a GREAT WHITE THRONE, and Him that sat on it, **from Whose face the earth and the heaven fled away**; and there was found no place for them" (Rev. 20:11). Yet can it be?! Can it be that Abraham did look upon the face of God without burning up? Consider the shining sun that makes the day. No man is so bold, so unflinching and straight-faced, to look upon the sun. The stoutest men will hide their eyes from its shining strength. If ever there is a man so proud to lock eyes upon this earthly light, then those around him of the meeker sort will find a helpless blind man left to their care. This arrogant man now humbled, he would never leave the proud ground from which he stood when he opposed the burning, earthly sun except by the care of those meek men who "led him by the hand" (Acts 9:8). Is this light of any earthly significance? Even it can humble the sons of pride, but lo, how much more the face of Almighty God? Can you believe it? "If I have told you **earthly things**, and ye believe not, how shall ye believe if I tell you of **heavenly things**" (John 3:12)?

How much more the face of God, even His countenance which is "as the sun shineth in his strength" (Rev. 1:16)? The face of God is the chief glory of God; not even Moses could see His face and live! God said, "Thou canst not see My face: for there shall no man see Me, and live" (Ex. 33:18-23). God *passed by* Moses and Moses could scarcely survive it. Even to *pass by* the poor man Moses he had to hide in the "clift of the rock!" Not even the rock was enough to withhold the dangerous presence of God's glory *passing by*. Do you think it was like a gentle breeze and soft whispers? "And, behold, **the LORD passed by**, and a great and strong wind rent the mountains, and brake in pieces the rocks before the LORD; but the LORD was not in the wind: and after the wind an earthquake; but the LORD was not in the earthquake:

42

and after the earthquake a fire; but the LORD was not in the fire: and after the fire a still small voice" (1 Kings 19:11-12). Not even the rock of unmovable mountains can stay still or intact. They will fracture and quake at the impact of God's holy presence. They cannot hold together when God passes by, nor could they, save God strengthens the rock with the shield of His hand. God covered the opening behind Moses as he hid in the clift because only the hand of God can safely shield and reflect the majesty of God's passing glory. Only after He was passed by, it was then that God said, "I will take away Mine hand, and thou shalt see My back parts: but My face shall not be seen" (Ex. 33:18-23). This was the time when His "glory passeth by!" Moses had to run away and take cover from God as He passed by, but Abraham ran to God and requested that He passed him not by. How can this be? "He ran to meet them from the tent door" and said, "pass not away I pray Thee from Thy servant" (Gen. 18:2-3). It is an infinite condescension. Even the mountains run away from God. Even they are "ailed" at His approaching! Mindless, sightless, and senseless, inanimate mountains are more humble than earthly princes: They stand up, skip, and flee for safety from their Maker Who dwells in a whirlwind of impossibility (Psalm 114:3-7).

God is Omnipotent

God must lay aside His **omnipotence** to speak and relate to creatures of insignificance. Nothing living can bear the power of the GREAT I AM. He always was and is; "and the LORD God formed man of the dust of the ground, and breathed into his nostrils the breath of life; and man became a living soul" (Gen. 2:7). By His breath we breathe – He is THE LIFE – but when He arises like the sun over this cursed earth and the brightness of His burning glory approaches, all creatures will obey the command given of old; "Enter into the rock, and hide thee in the dust, for fear of the LORD, and for the glory of His majesty. The lofty looks of man shall be humbled, and the haughtiness of men shall be bowed down, and the LORD alone shall be exalted in that day. For the day of the LORD of hosts shall be upon every one that is proud and lofty, and upon every one that is lifted up; and he shall be brought low" (Isa. 2:10-12). As Moses fled for cover, even so, this great company of sinners – "the kings of the earth and the great men, and the rich men, and the chief captains, and the mighty men, and every bondman, and every free man" – they shall "go into the clefts of the rocks, and into the tops of the ragged rocks, for fear of the LORD, and for the glory of His majesty, when He ariseth to shake terribly the earth." Therefore God says, "Cease ye from man, whose breath is in his nostrils: for wherein is he to be accounted of" (Isa. 2:21-22)? If the Lord comes down to earth without any condescension, every exalted earthly power or majesty will scramble like roaches for cover. As worms flee to their holes and moles into the dust, even so the men of high degree will scramble and flee, crawling on their hands and knees, diving into the place of their accounted glory: the company of worms and the coverings of dust. "Wherein is he to be accounted of?" Behold, the mighty men of the world will finally see! They will happily agree with God that they are worms, and they will earnestly hope the LORD would leave them in their holes. Nevertheless, "they shall move out of their holes." "The nations shall see and be confounded at all their might: they shall lay their hand upon their mouth, their ears shall be deaf. They shall lick the dust like a serpent, they shall move out of their holes like worms of the earth: they shall be afraid of the LORD our God, and shall fear because of Thee" (Micah 7:16-17).

He that "sitteth upon the circle of the earth" sat down before Abraham (Isa. 40:21-23). The earth was His footstool and yet His feet are now grasped by the tiny hands of Abraham (Isa. 66:1). "He stood, and measured the earth: He beheld, and drove asunder the nations; and the everlasting mountains were scattered, the perpetual hills did bow" – this is the strength and glory of God! In this way everlasting He is, Godlike in every way, unchanging and limitless, eternal and strong, omnipotent, omniscient, holy, and never wrong; "His ways are everlasting" (Habakkuk 3:6). Yet now, lo, God sits before Abraham, stands in his company, beholds the humble dwelling of an earthly tent, and walks among His creature being comforted by Abraham's manufactured structures which are grasshopper-like and meager. Abraham stretches out animal skins or woven hairs spun by needle working men; in them he is housing God and comforting Him within, but God, behold, He "stretcheth out the heavens as a curtain, and spreadeth them out as a tent to dwell in!" "Have ye not known? Have ye not heard? Hath it not been told you from the beginning? Have ye not understood from the foundations of the earth? It is He that sitteth upon the circle of the earth, and the inhabitants thereof are as grasshoppers; that stretcheth out the heavens as a curtain, and spreadeth them out as a tent to dwell in: That bringeth the princes to **nothing**; He maketh the judges of the earth as **vanity**" (Isaiah 40:21-23). Can vanity verily serve God? All things are possible with God. Do you see that God must lay aside omnipotence and omnipresence to employ earthly servitude?

Isaiah 55:9
*"For as the **heavens** are higher than the **earth**,*
*so are My **ways** higher than **your ways**, and My **thoughts** than*
***your thoughts**."*

We have seen something of the **ways** of God, but what about the **thoughts** of God? God is **omnipresent**; however, He reveals Himself most often in a relational way to man from one localized place. In this localized place, He does what man is limited to do. God is everywhere and in every place, thus for Him to walk from one place to the other is not possible, for He is in all places. In Genesis 3:8-9, God is walking in the Garden of Eden after Adam and Eve sinned. They heard the noise of Him and hid themselves, and God said, "Where art thou?" "And they heard the voice of the LORD God walking in the garden in the cool of the day: and Adam and his wife hid themselves from the presence of the LORD God amongst the trees of the garden. And the LORD God called unto Adam, and said unto him, Where art thou" (Gen. 3:8-9)? God was confined to one place walking in Eden. This is not very startling, but what is more notable is that God not only was in one localized position, but the knowledge that He related to Adam with was as if He did not know where they were. This knowledge was as if God was subject to His location and His knowledge was limited to His observation from that single position. This is as if He was limited to the five sensory observations which are in man as He walked in the garden. In the ways of man, He related to the man Adam. He knew where Adam was already, but He wanted to have a relationship in the ways of man.

Likewise to the Edenic scene God said, "Where is Abel thy brother?" But He knew already, seeing his "blood crieth unto" Him "from the ground." He asked the question in a spectrum of relationship necessary to condescend to man. "And the LORD said unto Cain, Where is Abel thy brother? And he said, I know not: Am I my brother's keeper? And He said, What hast thou done? the voice of thy brother's blood crieth unto Me from the ground" (Gen. 4:9-10). This condescension can be clearly seen simply by a localized voice, for the Lord could speak with an innumerable number of voices from His innumerable Presences that are everywhere! Then His voice would be like the rolling thunder in strength, "as many waters," and men would not be able to endure such a terror, let alone converse with Him in such a glory (Revelation 1:15). A simple reading of scripture is edifying and illuminating without considering all these things. It does not have to be understood in each passage how the Lord condescends from His ways to our ways. However, given the passage and subject of study, it will become increasingly relevant to understand this condescension and two spectrums of relationship.

Judge then who is speaking in this verse: man or God? "I will go down now, and see whether they have done altogether according to the cry of it, which is come unto Me; and if not, I will know." In Genesis 18:20-21, God spoke to Abraham **as if He did not know** the sins that have been committed in Sodom and Gomorrah and **He had to go down into the city and see it for Himself to know** for sure, like He said, if "the cry" is accurate to what is actually there. All of this is as if He is not already in the city! "And the LORD said, Because the cry of Sodom and Gomorrah is great, and because their sin is very grievous; I will go down now, and see whether they have done altogether according to the cry of it, which is come unto Me; and if not, I will know" (Gen. 18:20-21). Abraham is aware that God already knows about the sin in Sodom and Gomorrah, but the emphasis left to us is the gravity of when God **visits**. He is establishing a relationship with us based upon our limitations, and He desires that we remember the magnitude of what is happening when He visits or does draw near!

God is Omniscient

God is omniscient. Would God ever need to scan a city with His eyes, walk the length of it to observe the sin, or search the Garden of Eden by walking the whole terrain as to find His hiding humans, Adam and Eve? The sin of Sodom and Gomorrah, Adam and Eve, or any other sin committed throughout all time…was it hidden from His observance? Would God ever need to be restricted to one radius of sight so that all other things cannot be seen by Him, and, if He were searching for something, would He need to look *here* and *there*, *to* and *fro*, as a man would do when he turns his head and moves his eyes? A man existing in one place surely would, but God is in all places and sees all things. Nevertheless, it is written in 2 Chronicles 16:9, "For **the eyes of the LORD run to and fro** throughout the whole earth, to shew Himself strong in the behalf of them whose heart is perfect toward Him." Here, it is as if the eyes of the Lord are confined in one place at one single time. And again in Psalm 33:13-14, "The LORD looketh from heaven; He beholdeth all the sons of men. From the place of His habitation He looketh upon all the inhabitants of the earth."

Even though the scriptures speak this way, we still do know that His eyes are not restricted to one place, that they are in every place, as it is written in Proverbs 15:3: "The eyes of the LORD are in **every place**, beholding the evil and the good." Nothing is hidden from His sight, as it is written in Hebrews 4:13: "Neither is there any creature that is not manifest in His sight: but all things are naked and opened unto the eyes of Him with Whom we have to do." He sees not as man sees, but He can look into the heart, as it is written in Psalm 44:21: "Shall not God search this out? for He knoweth the secrets of the heart." And again in Proverbs 15:11: "Hell and destruction are before the LORD: how much more then the hearts of the children of men?" God's omnipresence is a way of His Highness, and it should humiliate humans in the lower world, for in it we can see a great amplification of the Lord's omnipotence and omniscience. David scribed this wonder well when he wrote Psalm 139:1-10:

> "To the chief Musician, A Psalm of David. O LORD, Thou
> hast searched me, and known me. Thou knowest my
> downsitting and mine uprising, Thou understandest my
> thought afar off. Thou compassest my path and my lying
> down, and art acquainted with all my ways. For there is not
> a word in my tongue, but, lo, O LORD, Thou knowest it
> altogether. Thou hast beset me behind and before, and laid
> Thine hand upon me. **Such knowledge is too wonderful**
> **for me; it is high, I cannot attain unto it.** Whither shall I
> go from Thy spirit? or whither shall I flee from Thy
> presence? If I ascend up into heaven, Thou art there: if I
> make my bed in hell, behold, Thou art there. If I take the
> wings of the morning, and dwell in the uttermost parts of
> the sea; Even there shall Thy hand lead me, and Thy right
> hand shall hold me."

Can you see how David describes God as a Being infinitely and wonderfully beyond human comprehension? Even so, dear reader, an unknowable God makes Himself knowable by a condescension in *the ways of man.* Thus, we understand what it means for God to look "to and fro" for a man who has a perfect heart, and why? Well, when we read this text, then the emotion that we have experienced when we looked for someone or something of value is aroused in our

46

minds, and we understand that this is the heart of God on this matter. Our ways in those cases when we look for something precious, this is used by God to communicate His heart and mind toward us even though He does not have to look for anything. So also, when God's eyes are upon you, it is to communicate a special sense that He is with you, though His eyes and presence and everywhere. Do you see how this language of God in the ways of man does communicate a very special message, a message which we could not otherwise understand? You see, we know the safety, comfort, and strength of faithful companions like a friend, wife, or fellow soldier. Their eyes are upon you for friendship, intimacy, and protection, but how much more is communicated to us when God speaks of His relational connection with us in such understandable terms as this – that His eyes are upon you. This communicates well, by language of a condescension in the ways of man, that God cares – even a care and devotion that "will guard your hearts in Christ Jesus" (Php. 4), that is, when you believe the "too wonderful" (Ps. 139) realities of God never leaving you nor forsaking you, ever-hearing you, even "from His holy heaven with the saving strength of His right hand" (Ps. 20:6)!

Peradventure, while Abraham and God communed one with another on that green hill overlooking the plains, and then, a crumb of secret judgment fell from the table of heaven so that Abraham caught a glimmer of what was about to happen to Sodom and Gomorrah, and what awful amazement is this that God did allow Abraham to reply to God a little – even to ask that fearful, otherwise forbidden question – "Shall not the Judge of all the earth do right" (Gen. 18:25)? If God did not come down but rather Abraham went up to the lofty, holy, clean, and eternal abode of heaven, "the high and holy place" (Isa. 57:15), the place where the higher ways of God orchestrate all the happenings of men (Job 1:6-12), then it would have been sin for Abraham to speak to God like he did when God was on earth.

From heaven God does look to earth, and do you see the amazement?! God comes to the earth and visits men behind the veil of condescension! Hear ye His own declaration: "Thus saith the LORD, The heaven is My throne, and the earth is My footstool: where is the House that ye build unto Me? And where is the place of My rest? For all those things hath Mine hand made, and all those things have been, saith the LORD: but to this man will I look, even to him that is poor and of a contrite spirit, and trembleth at My word" (Isa. 66:1-2). However, if a man was brought up to God to catch a glimpse of all those high wonders "before the LORD" (Job 1:6-12) in His eternal abode, of which, if a man was translated to see and hear – those things which he would see, who can bear to hear!? Like "such an one caught up into the third heaven," "caught up into paradise," there in this place, what would be heard is "unspeakable words which it is not lawful for a man to utter" (2 Cor. 12:2, 4). In this place, "the high and holy place," the apostle John fell down as a dead man before God. Without strength, without words, without fleshly life or boldness to converse with the Almighty, it is there he was as a dead man. The closest he ever came to the I AM, "The Life" (John 14:6), the Wellspring of Life Eternal, it is then that he was shocked "at His feet as dead" (Rev. 1:17). The Life of God is a deadly energy of lightning, strikingly awful for everything living, prostrating all in a paralysis of praise "as dead."

When confronted by the potent and Brilliant Life of God, then the dust settles down, is without strength, and is dead. In our clayish creations, we may surmise a proud ascent to the heavens. We may be so infatuated with ourselves that we would build upon or trust our own logical and self-defined justice, and so, repeat that ancient apostate cry, "Let us build us a city and a tower whose top may reach unto **heaven**, and let us make us a name" (Gen. 11:4). I denounce this cry! Nay! There is no Name but His which reacheth to the heavens, and when His justice drops down, we will all be confounded, humbled, and broken under His heavenly language of justice and truth. My reader, do you want to be "as gods," at the height of the heavens, knowing justice and judgment, "good and evil" with the same sophisticated stature as God (Gen. 3:5)? If you listen to the voice of the devil you will share his fate, "for thou hast said in thine heart, I will ascend into heaven, I will exalt my throne above the stars of God: I will sit also upon the mount of the congregation, in the sides of the north: I will ascend above **the heights of the clouds**; I will be like **the most High**. Yet thou shalt be brought down to hell, to the sides of the pit" (Isa. 14:13-14).

"Look unto the heavens, and see;
And behold the clouds which are higher than thou." – Job 35:5

If ever you are "caught up" there where Elijah could not take himself, if ever you appear before this great God wherein is the place of His Kingdom, you will not understand the riding of His heavenly cavalry which gallops in flames of fire, nor their mysterious whirlwind-like speed (2 Kings 2:10-12). Up there the wisest become witless. Senseless and unable to stand, holy men scarce know what to worship because the image of God's Majesty shines upon all God's holy angels (Rev. 19:10, 22:9). Likewise there is a similar difficulty when the Image of God shines upon earthen vessels. At this time the foolish of the earth are confounded to conclude, "the gods are come down to us in the likeness of men" (Acts 14:11). "Which when the apostles, Barnabus and Paul, heard of, they rent their clothes, and ran in among the people, crying out" (Acts 14:14). "Sirs, why do ye do these things? We also are men of like passions with you" (Acts 14:15), they said, even as the angels told the wisest and holiest of men humbled on the higher ground of heaven, "See thou do it not: I am thy fellowservant, and of thy brethren that have the testimony of Jesus: **worship God**" (Rev. 19:10, 22:8-9)! The wisest on earth are fools in heaven as the fools on earth grossly err to worship clay pilgrims endued with heavenly power. We are used to worshipping the reflection of God during our sojourning on earth, because, if we were confronted by His face we could not endure it. "No flesh should glory in His presence" (1 Cor. 1:29). Christ Jesus had to lay His right hand upon John's melted soul as a gentle touch of mercy to endure (Rev. 1:17, Psalm 18:35). At former times it was angels that strengthened men when they were exercised by the most debilitating, heavenly visions. Most often throughout history it was angels that

48

conversed with men in the stead of God on matters of human significance, for what man can endure the "great voice as of a trumpet" and "many waters" (Rev. 1:10, 15)? Understand God, my reader, that if He spoke to you in His greatness without a condescension then you too would cry out, "Let not God speak with us, lest we die" (Exodus 20:19)! And God will say to you as He said to them – "[you] have well spoken that which [you] have spoken" (Deut. 18:17).

Until God says, "Understand O son of man," how can we understand (Dan. 8:17)? This was the voice of an angel and yet Daniel said, "as he was speaking with me I was in a deep sleep on my face toward the ground: but he touched me, and set me upright" (Dan. 8:17-18). Again at another time, when apocalyptic visions did burst upon Daniel's sides, he "fainted and was sick certain days" (Daniel 8:27). Of what he saw, "none understood it" (Dan. 8:27). Visits from heaven are violent to the flesh; scarcely can the earth endure its holy purity and power. At another time, Daniel saw a "great vision" and said, "there remained no strength in me: for my comeliness was turned in me into corruption, and I retained no strength," until "behold, an hand touched me, which set me upon my knees and upon my palms of my hands" (Dan. 10:5-12). We are clouded creatures dwelling on a cursed earth, but when heaven (by a measure) comes down or ever we go up, we will be like Daniel and become "dumb" (Dan. 10:15). We will be unable to speak without His empowering touch. We cannot stand stable under the weight of heaven's glory. Rightly did Daniel exclaim, "O my lord, by the vision my sorrows are turned upon me, and I have retained no strength. For how can the servant of this my lord talk with this my lord? For as for me, straightway there remained no strength in me, neither is there breath left in me. Then there came again and touched me one like the appearance of a man, and he strengthened me, and said, O man greatly beloved, fear not: peace be unto thee, be strong, yea, be strong. And when he had spoken unto me, I was strengthened, and said, Let my lord speak; for thou hast strengthened me" (Dan. 10:15-19). Nay, ye men of the earth, God is not interested in your swelling muscles, nor will you be able to flex them in His Almighty Presence. As it is for your carnal muscles, likewise it is for your intellectual might and muscular wits – you would not be able to pick up the dumbest dumbbell in heaven, and below this, you could not lift up your own self! **"The foolishness of God is wiser than men; and the weakness of God is stronger than men"** (1 Cor. 1:25). Thou wilt not speak unless you are spoken to, but will you answer Him rudely now when He does speak to you softly in the writing of a Book? Will you murmur against God's secret (Deut. 29:29) higher things? Live out now, on earth, what you will say then in heaven, even though here you only see darkly (2 Cor. 3:18) and are clothed in fleshly sin: "I know that Thou canst do every thing, and that no thought can be witholden from Thee. Who is He that hideth counsel without knowledge? Therefore have I uttered that I understood not; things too wonderful for me, which I knew not. I have heard of Thee by the hearing of the ear: but now mine eye seeth Thee. Wherefore I abhor myself, and repent in dust and ashes" (Job 42:2-6).

Job 37:19-24

"Teach us what we shall say unto Him; for we cannot order our speech by reason of darkness. Shall it be told Him that I speak? if a man speak, surely he shall be swallowed up. And now men see not the bright light which is in the clouds: but the wind passeth, and cleanseth them. Fair weather cometh out of the north: with God is terrible majesty. **Touching the Almighty, we cannot find Him out**: He is excellent in power, and in judgment, and in plenty of justice: He will not afflict. **Men do therefore fear Him: He respecteth not any that are wise of heart**."

Shall a cricket declare the beauty and exactitude of a famous, castle-like city on earth? Even so, an orator for heaven who can find save when He the Holy Ghost comes down from heaven? I am less than a wretched cricket squeaking in the blindness of the night; at all times I am thus except when the Holy Spirit is lighting upon me. My wretched insufficiency is like the monotonous racket of a thousand shouting crickets. I am a nuisance, an annoyance to all peaceful prospects. Those singers of the daylight are covered in fair feathers of artistic color. They sing with a sweet sound and vibrant melodies. Yet the blackness of night is welcomed by the chattering laughter of hyenas, the creeping of scaly creatures, and those shrieking crickets. I am not sophisticated enough for heaven, I deserve to sweat under the curses of the earth, and had there never been a dispensation of mercy which recreates malefactors into new creatures (2 Cor. 5:17), none would enter the heaven's new creation. Concerning the things of earth, I fare well on their expertise. It is no hardship for me to compete with bloody rags and putrid messes. Like boils on the human body, I am a swelling infection upon this earth. Yet to mingle myself with those holy subjects which do lie in the depths of God (1 Cor. 2:10), those matters written in the Holy Book, "who is sufficient for these things" (2 Cor. 2:16)? Shall a cricket correct the conscience of God and offer a sharper or more definite execution of justice? It would be a thorn in the way of God or as a barrier of briers before His charging stride. "Who would set the briers and thorns against Me in battle? I would go through them, I would burn them together," says God (Isa. 27:4)! If you argue with His word you argue with fire; be sure of this, you will be broken and burned (Jer. 23:29).

I am not as sophisticated as a crippled gnat stuck on its back, flying circles upon a tabletop. I have no more wisdom than an insect mindlessly burned out, endlessly drawn to fly into a light bulb's burning heat. This is its slow suicide, pound by pound the flying creature's body is melted away. I am not as civilized as these creeping things: next to me they are complex creatures! I am as a boneless worm, and lower – I am faceless, graceless, and helpless. "**As for God His way is perfect**:" "Dominion and fear are with Him, He maketh peace in His high places. Is there any number of His armies? And upon whom doth not His light arise? How then can man be justified with God? Or how can he be clean that is born of a woman? Behold even

50

to the moon, and it shineth not; yea, the stars are not pure in His sight. How much less man, that is a **worm**? And the son of man, which is a **worm**" (Job 25:2-6, Isa. 41:14)?

The sun is an emblem of the love of God shining upon all of His creatures; night is an scenery representative of evil, a time and hour when the wicked awake to do evil (1 Thess. 5). Night is the hour in which God has ordained for evil, because it is then that "the beasts of the forest do creep forth" (Ps. 104:20). There are "rulers of the darkness of this world" which reign in secret evils. If I do confide in them or ever arise to take their counsel on righteousness, likewise if ever I do trust in my fleshly wisdom supposing I have a self-sufficient mind, it is then that I am trusting in "the vanity of [my] mind" (Eph. 4:17). Humans: we are fallen creatures of no hope, who by creation are unfit, unwise, and without light, "having the understanding darkened, being alienated from the life of God through the ignorance that is in them, because of the blindness of their heart: Who being past feeling have given themselves over unto lasciviousness, to work all uncleanness with greediness" (Eph. 4:18-19). If we take counsel and learn the judgments of this lower earth, we are having "fellowship with the unfruitful works of darkness" (Eph. 5:11). To attain the mind of God and find His judgments, which alone are right, wise, and saving, then we need the

God removes His Divinity like as a King would remove His robes of royalty, that henceforth, they become approachable and relatable in other ways which were formerly impossible in the scenery of court and crown. In the case of God, He relates in ways which are not His own ways: He wills and speaks words which are inconsistent and irreconcilable to omniscience, but it is so that He may have a relationship to clay creatures. He disrobes Himself from His ways and clothes Himself with ours, but even when the humble raiment of humanity's ways do clothe Him – HE IS STILL GOD – thus He does simultaneously and everlastingly coexist on the higher ground of His higher ways at the same time.

gift from His hand which was said to be "the spirit of wisdom and revelation in the knowledge of Him: The eyes of your understanding being enlightened", and illuminated, as with "the light of the knowledge of the glory of God" (Eph. 1:17-18, 2 Cor. 4:6). You see, there is night and there is light. An orator of the night is pale in comparison to the orators of light, so it is infinitely more contrasting to compare an orator of earth to the speakers of heaven. A conscience of clay cannot be compared to the conscience of God. There is no room for flesh upon Christ's throne, and if you will share a coheir's seat there, it will be because God killed your flesh and hid you in Jesus, "in Whom is no darkness at all" (1 john 1), "in Whom are hid all the treasures of wisdom and knowledge" (Col. 2:3, 3:3).

If Abraham got to the top of Jacob's ladder, there would be no more conversation, but blazing through the fullness of Abraham's being, will, emotions,

51

and sensations would be the saying, "O man, who art thou that repliest against God? Shall the thing formed say to Him that formed it, Why hast Thou made me thus" (Rom. 9:20)? A snapshot of sovereignty would not excite sinful murmurings in this holy habitation. If you were there, you would be what you are: dead, dusty ashes. You would be forbidden to do what God has forbidden. You would sit in a holy, silent adoration if ever sovereign ordinances were being spoken in that place. Nothing in you could rise up and wonder, "Is there any unrighteousness with God" (Rom. 9:14) or "Shall not the judge of all the earth do right" (Gen. 18)? When God collects all of His clay on His Judgment Day, they will not speak but be spoken to! They will not stand up but bow down on demand. Devilish and dark angelic majesties alongside intellectual humans from all earthly masteries, they all will be clay features before the Potter-like Preacher as He pronounces from the Books their eternal abode. Thrice it is written for the Three Persons of the Trinity, "Unto Me every knee shall bow, every tongue shall swear" and "confess." Every knee, God says, "of things in heaven, and things in earth, and things under the earth" (Isa. 45:23, Romans 14:11, Php. 2:10)! In the arena of earth there is a humbling of the Person of God, and there, shockingly, He does not disallow men to converse with Him on matters "revealed" (Deut. 29:29), to the end that men might come to know God. Look with me further into the condescended omniscience of God, that the thoughts of God might become more manlike and earthly, within reach to be understood by the infinitely unworthy – God in the ways of man.

Disrobed from omniscience and by way of condescension, God **wills** and speaks **words**. There is a counsel and will that cannot be changed as afore mentioned, "God **is not a man**, that He should lie; neither the son of man, that He should repent: He hath said, and shall He not do it? Or hath He spoken, and shall He not make it good" (Numbers 23:19)? Again, this is sensible for the qualities and characteristics inherent in God. How could He ever need to repent or change His mind, seeing that He knows everything and transcends time? How could He ever need to change His mind from one will to another as if He would be regretful of a decision made or an outcome and event undetermined? Why would He ever go back on His Word, or lie, seeing that what He says determines everything else? These sovereign ways are certainly not our ways. We can say that they are higher than our ways, as it is written they are the ways of God. However, are you seeing that there are other ways that God uses, even our ways, and this great condescension affects even His purposed will and spoken word? Did you know that there are two ways God uses, simultaneously, and there are therefore two wills in God? My reader, look closely now at the scriptural description of *God in the ways of man.*

God is not a man that He should lie, and He is not a man that He should repent, but did you know He repents and goes back on His word all throughout biblical history? God has a will that is determinate and a will that is like the will and ways of man. Therefore, I have categorized the second spectrum of relationship God uses by means of condescension as **God in the ways of man**. It is the way of man to repent. Our words do not determine everything. Even so we can therefore go back on them, and likewise, when we speak words, they can fail to come to pass. This is not confusing to us because this is common humanity, but for God to will and speak in these capacities is an amazing condescension!

Jeremiah 18:7-11

[7] At what instant I shall speak concerning a nation, and concerning a kingdom, to pluck up, and to pull down, and to destroy it; [8] If that nation, against whom I have **pronounced**, turn from their evil, **I will repent of the evil that I thought to do unto them**. [9] And at what instant I shall speak concerning a nation, and concerning a kingdom, to build and to plant it; [10] If it do evil in My sight, that it obey not My voice, then **I will repent of the good, wherewith I said I would benefit them**. [11] Now therefore go to, speak to the men of Judah, and to the inhabitants of Jerusalem, saying, Thus saith the LORD; Behold, I frame evil against you, and devise a device against you: return ye now every one from his evil way, and make your ways and your doings good.

In a matter of judgment and wrath God can and does speak "to pluck up, and to pull down, and to destroy." God can and does whole-heartedly "pronounce" these judgments with the full intention of doing it. Therefore He *genuinely* thinks to do this wrathful judgment. But if they turn from their sin, God says He will *repent,* or change His mind, of "the evil **I thought** to do unto them." God was not playing a fake role. He was *genuinely* thinking to do this evil to them.

God can speak for blessing and salvation "to build and to plant" with the full intention to do it, but if they do afterwards turn to sin then God will "repent of the good, wherewith **I said I would** benefit them." I repeat, God can pronounce a salvific blessing and *fully intend* to do it, and if they do afterwards turn to wickedness He can **go back on what He said He would do**. I am not sure if you are thinking this…but how can God *genuinely think* to do good to a people at a certain instance in time, only to change His mind at a later time because of the evil He sees them doing, unless, somehow, God did not know that the people were going to do the evil that they did. Somehow God's former thoughts and intents were *genuine* as if He was *limited* from a *foreknowledge* of what was going to happen later, and also, as if He was limited from a *determinate power* whereby He is able to make all things happen according to His will. If He knew beforehand of the evil that was later done, then how could He have genuinely thought or spoken a blessing to them? If you say He was not genuine, then He didn't genuinely repent (or change His mind), and this, according to the verse, is not possible because it clearly states that God will repent (change His mind). If He did not genuinely think to do it, then He would not have to repent of it. The will of God that is able to repent is therefore responsive to the actions and deeds done within time; therefore as God observed the deeds done, then His will changed. What is the source of all the questions of how this can be possible with God? It is that this repentance of God is an operation inconsistent with *omniscience* and *absolute sovereignty*. It is as if God is in the ways of a man… right?

It is as if the actions and deeds were not foreknown so that the will, heart, salvation, and emotion in God which preceded the actual commission of the deeds observed were entirely unaffected and separate from <u>Godlike</u> qualities – omniscience to name one. This localizes the will of God into the limitations of time so that He does genuinely respond to the will of man as if He was not outside of time and in complete determination of the will of man at the same time. It is as if God's will is in the limitations of <u>manlike</u> capacities and ways. How can He genuinely intend to bless a person that He has already determined from eternity past to hate and destroy, only then to change His mind from intending to bless someone when the manifestation of their wicked rebellion takes place, and surely, even this rebellion God did ordain to happen by an eternal intent and unchanging purpose?

Please let me be repetitive and inculcate these truths… the scriptures certainly do. There is a counsel of God that cannot be changed, right?

> "The LORD of hosts hath sworn, saying, Surely as I have
> **thought**, so shall it come to pass; and as I have **purposed**, so
> shall it stand: That I will break the Assyrian in My land, and upon
> My mountains tread him under foot: then shall his yoke depart
> from off them, and his burden depart from off their shoulders.
> This is the **purpose** that is **purposed** upon the whole earth: and
> this is the **hand that is stretched out** upon all the nations. For
> the LORD of hosts hath **purposed**, and who shall disannul it?
> And his **hand is stretched out**, and who shall turn it back?" (Isa.
> 14:24-27)

This is easy enough to understand. Who can stand against God? Therefore whatever He decides to do, He will do. The counsel of God is His purpose, intention, plan, will, and pleasure - all of these things cannot be resisted. All of this can be summed up into God's will. There is a will in God that cannot be changed, resisted, stood against, or hindered, and it will always be accomplished. This is easy for us to understand since this is inherent in the characteristics that God would own in the powers of Himself. Such powers are *omniscience*, *omnipotence*, and *omnipresence*. As God laid aside His omnipotence and omnipresence, likewise He lays aside His omniscience (in a sense)! Consider Genesis 6:5-7.

> "And **GOD saw** that the wickedness of man was great in the
> earth, and that every imagination of the thoughts of his heart was
> only evil continually. And it **repented** the LORD that He had
> made man on the earth, and it grieved Him at His heart. And the
> LORD said, I will destroy man whom I have created from the
> face of the earth; both man, and beast, and the creeping thing, and
> the fowls of the air; for it **repenteth** Me that I have made them"

(Genesis 6:5-7).

Can God repent? It says, AFTER "**GOD SAW**" the wickedness of man, it was then that He "**repented**". After seeing that this is what humanity was incessantly doing, as if He did not have omniscience as to already know what they would do before He made them, He was *now* sorry He made man, and He changed His mind, deciding to no longer keep them alive, by destroying all men except Noah and his family. God has a changeless mind and will, and yet here is a genuine repentance *in the ways of man*. It is as if God related to men in a genuine will to keep them alive, for the good of them, but because of their sin, He was minded to destroy them <u>now</u>, therefore He was repenting. He was once minded toward them in a good, loving, favorable will, as if He could say that this love was uninterrupted by a consciousness of their future rebellion and His future repentance, as if He could say that He loved them so much so that He would affectionately express to them how He wanted them to stay alive, how He wanted to never have to judge them for doing this deed, which is to say in other words, "neither came it into My heart" (Jer. 7:31), when speaking of what that the people did evilly commit.

Yet, if God had a will to save them and a mind to keep them alive and prosper them, why did He not determine their salvation by His irresistible grace and sovereign counsels? God is relating to them *in the ways of man,* that's why. When God is **in the ways of God**, if He desired for men to be saved, He would turn their heart into faith and repentance. This is God's irresistible will, word, and counsel that works through the sovereign influences of His omnipotence which govern *the interior capacities of men*. The will that is contrary, genuine and simultaneous to this will is **God in the ways of man**. This is God's resistible will, word, and counsel that works through limited and humanlike influences which are *exterior from the interior capacities of men*. The omniscience of God can never be nonexistent, but somehow God relates to men *in the ways of men* wherein He has a genuine will active and completely irrelevant from omniscience and all the ways of God.

God in the Ways of God	God in the Ways of Man
Irresistible will, word, and counsel.	Resistible will, word, and counsel.
❖ Influential through interior capacities to save.	❖ Influential through exterior capacities to save.
Incomprehensible justice of condemnation.	Comprehensible justice of condemnation.
Incomprehensible justice of salvation.	Comprehensible justice of salvation.
Changeless and eternal counsel, will, mind, emotion, and word.	Changing and temporary counsel, will, mind, emotion, and word.
Isaiah 14:27	Romans 10:21, Isaiah 65:2
"His hand is stretched out, and who	*"All day long I have stretched forth*

Can God be undecided over what He will do, or in other words, can He be unsure?

> "…therefore now put off thy ornaments from thee, **that I may know what to do with thee**" (Exodus 33:5).

> "How shall I…how shall I…how shall I…how shall I…**Mine heart is turned within Me, My repentings are kindled together**" (Hos. 11:8).

In striving to save the house of Judah, God published the horror of His curses which He purposed to do in hopes that they would hear of the coming doom and repent. Can God hope or say, "it may be" in this circumstance?

> **"It may be** that the house of Judah will hear all the evil which I purpose to do unto them; that they may return every man from his evil way; that I may forgive their iniquity and their sin."
> (Jeremiah 36:3)

You can see the genuine hope God has mentioned again just a few verses later:

> **"It may be they will** present their supplication before the LORD, and will return every one from his evil way: for great is the anger and the fury that the LORD hath pronounced against this people."
> (Jeremiah 36:7)

Notice that God is using exterior influences to try to bring man to repentance, *as a man* would seek to change another man's mind. Men cannot change another man's mind or will except by exterior means. They cannot reach into another man's heart and change it. Now God can, but in these instances He relates to men in a genuine will through *the ways of man*, even to the laying aside of the inevitable emotions consistent with and operable in omniscience and sovereignty. Again, like publishing the judgments and curses in Jeremiah 36:3 & 36:7, the Lord has His prophet Ezekiel display future banishments with the same good, loving, willing hope.

> "Therefore, thou son of man, prepare thee stuff for removing, and remove by day in their sight; and thou shalt remove from thy place to another place in their sight: **it may be they will consider**, though they be a rebellious house." (Ezekiel 12:3)

One could conjecture that God is not sincerely bound in these manlike limitations, that He is acting it out or something of this sort, meaning that He would not be able to say within Himself, "it may be they will consider", in sincerity. THIS IS WRONG.

Consider the following passage:

> "The just LORD is in the midst thereof; He will not do iniquity:
> every morning doth He bring His judgment to light, He faileth
> not; but the unjust knoweth no shame. I have cut off the nations:
> their towers are desolate; I made their streets waste, that none
> passeth by: their cities are destroyed, so that there is no man, that
> there is none inhabitant. **I said, Surely thou wilt fear me, thou
> wilt receive instruction; so their dwelling should not be cut
> off, howsoever I punished them: but they rose early, and
> corrupted all their doings."** (Zephaniah 3:5-7)

His attempts for their salvation by a genuine, willing love are in a context as if God is limited to the influential and relational capacities *of a man*, and is therefore subject to the free will of men, therefore the justice of their condemnation is vindicated because of the righteousness of God that He did all that *He could have done* to save them. This is a comprehensible justice that God is reasoning with His people in, which is logical recompense based upon our deeds and His deeds, as if we were free to choose as a self-governing creature, and as if God is subject to our free will so that His ability to influence our free will is solely by exterior actions, as if God could not change our will without our conscious understanding that it is being changed by God instead of our free decisions ("Howbeit he meaneth not so, neither doth his heart think so" (Isa. 10:7)). God vindicates salvation and condemnation based upon these terms of comprehension, as if God is altogether relating to us in the limitations, capacities, and conversations of *the ways of men*.

> "Now will I sing to my wellbeloved a song of my beloved
> touching His vineyard. My wellbeloved hath a vineyard in a very
> fruitful hill: And He fenced it, and gathered out the stones
> thereof, and planted it with the choicest vine, and built a tower in
> the midst of it, and also made a winepress therein: and He looked
> that it should bring forth grapes, and it brought forth wild grapes.
> And now, O inhabitants of Jerusalem, and men of Judah, judge, I
> pray you, betwixt Me and My vineyard. **What could have been
> done more to My vineyard, that I have not done in it?**
> wherefore, when I looked that it should bring forth grapes,
> brought it forth wild grapes? And now go to; I will tell you what I
> will do to My vineyard: I will take away the hedge thereof, and it
> shall be eaten up; and break down the wall thereof, and it shall be
> trodden down:" (Isaiah 5:1-5)

In the Person of God by condescension: successfully or unsuccessfully yet sincerely and hopefully, God does strive to save His people through the means of outward, exterior works or attempts of a saving communication (as if He does not know what they will do, as if He is unable to savingly influence His people, and is subject to attempts and hopes to turn or change their free will). The terror of warnings (Jer. 36:3, 7), the demonstrations and teachings of prophets' words and deeds (Ezek. 12:3), chastisements and just punishments for past sins as to gain what God hopes for, which is a present repentance wrought in the people of God (Zeph. 3:5-7), and more than what is listed here…all of these instances are examples of what God means when He says in Isaiah 5:1-5: "What could have been done more to My vineyard, that I have not done in it?" God was sincerely stretching out His hands hoping for their repentance (Rom. 10:20-21), and He demonstrates this sincerity by saying to Himself (as if He is assuring Himself of future hopes), "**Surely thou wilt fear Me, thou wilt receive instruction; so their dwelling should not be cut off**" (Zeph. 3:7) – and yet they refused the hopeful, loving, saving, good will of a merciful God Who self-declares that He has a universal love when He saith:

> "I have no pleasure in the death of him that dieth, saith the Lord GOD: wherefore turn yourselves, and live ye" (Ezek. 18:32).

> "Have I any pleasure at all that the wicked should die? Saith the Lord GOD: and not that he should return from his ways, and live" (Ezek. 18:23)?

> "For He doth not **afflict willingly** nor grieve the children of men" (Lamentations 3:33).

> "To subvert a man in his cause, the Lord approveth not" (Lamentations 3:36).

How can this be logically reconciled or justly understood by our meager conceptions of justice? If God did not declare Himself to be sovereign, a hidden governor of our hearts, then this is very understandable, but those doctrines of His sovereignty, election, predestination, salvation and condemnation in the higher ways of God (**God in the ways of God**) are forbidden to be understood by men: henceforth we should be well content to relate to God in a context which we can understand, in a condescending relationship **in the ways of man**, and leave those higher things to be acknowledged and appropriated in their rightful places.

> "But Esaias is very bold, and saith, I was found of them that sought Me not; I was made manifest unto them that asked not after Me. But to Israel He saith, **All day long I have stretched forth My hands unto a disobedient and gainsaying people.**" (Romans 10:20-21)

> "I am sought of them that asked not for Me; I am found of them that sought Me not: I said, Behold Me, behold Me, unto a nation that was not called by My name. **I have spread out My hands all the day unto a rebellious people,** which walketh in a way that was not good, after their own thoughts;" (Isaiah 65:1-2)

58

"**His hand is stretched out**, and who shall turn it back" (Isa. 14:27)?

God explains that He is just in condemning His people because, "All day long I have stretched forth My hands unto a disobedient and gainsaying people" (Rom. 10:20-21). What He has done to save them, He states, is, "All day long I have stretched forth My hands," and this makes them without excuse or answer when He does destroy them. This sense of justice has a logical answer, and it is contradicting the sense of God's work in the higher sense (God in the ways of God) which men are forbidden to understand, question, or answer God in any wise. Bending over, as it were, from the arena of heaven unto humanity, by this great condescension, God converses with man, yet when His steeped Person is lifted back up into the realm of His Godlike loft, those things which appeared to be a free will of our own, are revealed to be what they are in truth: formations and ordinations of His hand, as if He intimately molded a piece of clay for His own purpose, pleasure, and glory! As it is written, "His hand is stretched out, and who shall turn it back" (Isa. 14:27)? When God is no longer bent over in condescension, as it were, and He doth stand up straight, He is as He is in heaven, where there is no condescension. Up there, it is then that God is God, in His ways, as He is in His infinite powers The Sovereign, and what He does in heaven, no man can comprehend or even question! "Nay but, O man, who art thou that repliest against God? Shall the things formed say to Him that formed it, Why hast Thou made me thus? Hath not the Potter power over the clay, of the same lump to make one vessel unto honour, and another unto dishonour" (Rom. 9:20-21)?

Look at the hopeful love of God behind the sending of Jesus Christ. God hoped to save the Jews by the sending of so royal a Messenger:

> "**Then said** the Lord of the vineyard, What shall I do? I will send My Beloved Son: **it may be** they will reverence Him when they see Him" (Luke 20:13).

Do you see the exact parallel here that it is as the former passages? And what is the emphasis we can take away from this? It was the good mind of God to send so valuable a Person for so merciful a salvation, and yet they killed Him! God relates to them as if He had no omniscience of this deed, but in pure love, He minded their condemnation after their free will justly determined this cursed, wrathful fate. When the Lord of the vineyard saw what they did, afterwards, "He shall come and destroy these husbandmen, and shall give the vineyard to others" (Lk. 20:16). The focal point of their salvation or condemnation hinges upon their deeds, and so by their deeds the favor and love of God is stedfast or changed into wrath and condemnation. This is a comprehensible justice by way of condescension.

Calvinists relate to God in the spectrum of His sovereignty, His eternality, and His changeless mind and will of love or hatred. They believe that God loves or hates all men with an eternal, unchanging, determining love or hatred, and this is true.

However, simultaneously, there is another counsel, will, mind, emotion, love, and hatred of God genuinely coexisting, and yet it is logically contradicting. It is another jewel of God's impossible wonders for men to praise Him for. A Calvinist would never believe that God would love or desire to save a man who He does not save, because He would save those He desires to save with His irresistible grace. They would never believe that God loves someone within time – the same one that He hates outside of time – but this is possible because there is a temporary, condescending will coexisting with an eternal, unchanging will. Therefore Calvinists conclude that God loves a select and limited amount of people which are determined to be covered by the blood; a limited atonement. ***Limited Atonement* = *Limited Love*.**

Now consider again the generation of Jesus Christ. God gave most of Israel "the spirit of slumber, eyes that they should not see, and ears that they should not hear," so that only "the election hath obtained" salvation "and the rest were blinded" (Rom. 11:7-8). Those that were blinded were not the elect, therefore they were hated by God with a changeless and eternal wrath. NOW, will you know that there is another will in God besides this hatred: a will that is genuine, within time, and perfect in love, only it is not active in sovereign operations to save, which means therefore that it is limited to manlike limitations, powers, and ways to save, but it is nevertheless all the while willing, hopeful, and striving (in thought, word, and deed) till all deeds of love are expended and nothing else can be done? Jesus Christ eternally hated the damned generation that crucified Him, and simultaneously, He desired to save them, He sought to save them, and He had weeping lamentations over the fact that they refused to be saved. My reader, THIS IS LOVE! Can you read the following passages and honestly conclude that Jesus Christ did not love them?

> "And **when He was come near, He beheld the city, and wept over it**, Saying, If thou hadst known, even thou, at least in this thy day, the things which belong unto thy peace! but now they are **hid from thine eyes**. For the days shall come upon thee, that thine enemies shall cast a trench about thee, and compass thee round, and keep thee in on every side, And shall lay thee even with the ground, and thy children within thee; and they shall not leave in thee one stone upon another; because **thou knewest not the time of thy visitation**." (Luke 19:41-44)

> "O Jerusalem, Jerusalem, which killest the prophets, and stonest them that are sent unto thee; **how often would I have gathered thy children together, as a hen doth gather her brood under her wings, and ye would not!** Behold, your house is left unto you desolate: and verily I say unto you, Ye shall not see Me, until the time come when ye shall say, Blessed is He that cometh in the name of the Lord." (Luke 13:34-35)

This weeping, lamenting Savior is brokenhearted that Israel and Jerusalem "would not" repent even though He is as a willing Hen "often" reaching to "gather

her brood." God could have saved Jerusalem, even as He could have saved Sodom and Gomorrah, but He is restrained by a simultaneous, contradicting will (Matt: 11:20-24). Could you hate a people with an eternal hatred, have no desire to save them or any pity to regard them, and so you blind them to damn them into everlasting perdition, and then, in a separate location another person of yourself does look upon and behold all of this happening and you weep through desperate brokenness wishing it were not so?! You cannot do this because YOU ARE NOT God...but God can. Could it be that Christ loved those that are hopelessly damned by God, by and through the Spirit of the Father which hated and damned them according to His own pleasure, and now this Spirit of love reigns in love through us toward eternally hated men, that we as Christ live in love toward the elect and non-elect? How do you love all men if God loves only some men? Away with logical consistency and Calvinistic simplicity!

As further proof of the genuine love of God to save the 1st century Jews, consider Luke 13:6-9 and Mark 11:12-21 in comparison to their Old Testament parallel, Isaiah 5:1-5:

> "He spake also this parable; A certain man had a fig tree planted in his vineyard; and **he came and sought fruit thereon**, and **found none**. Then said he unto the dresser of his vineyard, Behold, these three **years I come seeking fruit** on this fig tree, and find none: cut it down; why cumbereth it the ground? And he answering said unto him, **Lord, let it alone this year also, till I shall dig about it, and dung it**: And if it bear fruit, well: and if not, then after that thou shalt cut it down" (Luke 13:6-9).

> "And on the morrow, when they were come from Bethany, He was **hungry**: And seeing a fig tree afar off having leaves, **He came, if haply He might find any thing thereon**: and when He came to it, **He found nothing** but leaves; for the time of figs was not yet. And Jesus answered and said unto it, No man eat fruit of thee hereafter for ever. And His disciples heard it. And they come to Jerusalem: and Jesus went into the temple, and began to cast out them that sold and bought in the temple, and overthrew the tables of the moneychangers, and the seats of them that sold doves; And would not suffer that any man should carry any vessel through the temple. And He taught, saying unto them, Is it not written, My house shall be called of all nations the house of prayer? but ye have made it a den of thieves. And the scribes and chief priests heard it, and sought how they might destroy Him: for they feared Him, because all the people was astonished at His doctrine. And when even was come, He went out of the city. And in the morning, as they passed by, they saw the fig tree dried up from the roots. And Peter calling to remembrance saith unto Him,

Master, behold, **the fig tree** which thou cursedst is **withered away**" (Mark 11:12-21).

In the first passage of scripture, Luke 13:6-9, we can see a metaphor which clearly communicates God's mind and heart toward His Israelite people. They are His planted vineyard and to them He comes seeking fruit. After finding none for three years, it is then that the good will to save Israel is held fast again, and the servant says, "let it alone this year also, till I shall dig about it, and dung it", so that it is understood by us that if this vineyard is cut down, it is after that God had done everything that could have been done to it. Therefore the Lord could have said, "What could have been done more to My vineyard, that I have not done in it? Wherefore, when I looked that it should bring forth grapes, brought it forth wild grapes" (Isa. 5:4)? In the second passage we can see this metaphor directly connected with the very deeds of Christ to Israel, emblematic in His deeds towards the Temple. As God sought fruit on His vineyard in the OT, and as the lord sought fruit on the vineyard of Luke 13:6-9, so also Christ is "hungry" for fruit from Israel, and He has come to seek it out, "if haply He might find any thing thereon", but like the fig tree "He found nothing". So also, we can see that time has run out for Israel! That now the Temple is forsaken by God! "The fig tree" which was cursed just "withered away" when it bore no fruits for Christ's hunger, and so also, God did cast away Israel with a deluding curse and turned to the Gentiles to save them! Do you disbelieve it? Is this not what is meant in the fullness of the parable afore mentioned? Read it carefully:

> "Hear another parable: There was a certain householder, which planted a vineyard, and hedged it round about, and digged a winepress in it, and built a tower, and let it out to husbandmen, and went into a far country: And when the time of the fruit drew near, he sent **his servants** to the husbandmen, **that they might receive the fruits of it**. And the husbandmen took his servants, and beat one, and killed another, and stoned another. Again, he sent other servants more than the first: and they did unto them likewise. **But last of all he sent unto them his son, saying, They will reverence my son.** But when the husbandmen saw the son, they said among themselves, This is the heir; come, let us kill him, and let us seize on his inheritance. And they caught him, and cast him out of the vineyard, and slew him. When the lord therefore of the vineyard cometh, what will he do unto those husbandmen? They say unto him, he will miserably destroy those wicked men, and will let out his vineyard unto other husbandmen, which shall render him the fruits in their seasons. Jesus saith unto them, Did ye never read in the scriptures, **The stone which the builders rejected, the same is become the head of the corner: this is the Lord's doing, and it is marvellous in our eyes?** Therefore say I unto you, **The**

62

kingdom of God shall be taken from you, and given to a nation bringing forth the fruits thereof. And whosoever shall fall on this stone shall be broken: but on whomsoever it shall fall, it will grind him to powder. And when the chief priests and Pharisees had heard His parables, they perceived that He spake of them. But when they sought to lay hands on him, they feared the multitude, because they took him for a prophet" (Matthew 21:33-46).

This very moment was foretold thousands of years ago, all the way back to Deuteronomy 32 (the song of Moses). God had just mightily saved Israel through the instrumentality of Moses, and thus He is called their "Father" (Deut. 32:6); they are His purchased possession (Deut. 32:6, 9), "the apple of His eye" (Deut. 32:10), and an eagle's young under her wings (Deut. 32:11). "So the LORD alone did lead him, and there was no strange god with him" (Deut. 32:12). Nevertheless, Israel rebelled and turned to idolatry (Deut. 32:15-17) insomuch that the Lord "abhorred them because of the provoking of His sons, and of His daughters. And He said, I will hide My face from them, I will see what their end shall be" (Deut. 32:19-20), and so God did. Then God said this: "They have moved Me to jealousy with that which is not God; they have provoked Me to anger with their vanities: **and I will move them to jealousy with those which are not a people; I will provoke them to anger with a foolish nation**" (Deut. 32:21). Israel moved God to jealousy, so God prophesies that He will move them to jealousy, and how? This is a prophecy of the casting away of Israel, and their jealousy, when God does turn to the Gentiles for salvation. Paul quotes this very verse to mean this very thing in Romans 10:19. So Paul further comments, "I say then, Have they stumbled that they should fall? God forbid: but rather through their fall salvation is come unto the Gentiles, for **to provoke them to jealousy**" (Rom. 11:11). Thus God accounts of His works long before they were to come to pass, and explains, Israel will rebel (Deut. 32:15-17), God will forsake them and hide His face (Deut. 32:18-20), He will then choose the Gentiles in their stead to make them jealous (Deut. 32:21), He will nearly annihilate Israel in His wrath (Deut. 32:26-27), and He will repent of His wrath when He sees that Israel is humbled (Deut. 32:36). Now God knew that Israel would rebel just as He states in Deuteronomy 32, and in another place He said, "I knew that thou wouldest deal very treacherously, and wast called a transgressor from the womb", and again, "I knew that thou art obstinate, and thy neck is an iron sinew, and thy brow brass; I have even from the beginning declared it to thee; before it came to pass I shewed it thee: lest thou shouldest say, mine idol hath done them, and my graven image, and my molten image, hath commanded them" (Isa. 48:8, 4-5). This is the foreknowledge of God, for He is omniscient, but there are other verses which show the condescended relationship of God to Israel during this prophesied, predestinated course of Israel's rebellion, rejection, and near annihilation.

Just as God said to Israel, as it were in the parable, sincerely:

"But last of all He sent unto them His Son, **saying, They will reverence My son**" (Matt. 21:37).

"Then said the Lord of the vineyard, What shall I do? I will send My Beloved Son: **it may be** they will reverence Him when they see Him" (Luke 20:13).

So also the Lord said of Israel before they finally rebelled unto near annihilation:

"For He **said, Surely they are My people, children that will not lie: so He was their Savior**" (Isa. 63:8).

You see? There is a will, desire, and spoken word which is as if God is minded this way toward Israel because He does not have a foreknowledge that they will eventually rebel. This is His will and word in the condescension (God in the ways of man). And again in Psalm 81:10-16 the Lord explains His good will to save, that, if they would have just obeyed Him, He was completely willing, desirous, earnest, and fervent to save them forever:

"I am the LORD thy God, which brought thee out of the land of Egypt: open thy mouth wide, and I will fill it. But My people would not hearken to My voice; and Israel would none of Me. So I gave them up unto their own hearts' lust: and they walked in their own counsels. **Oh that My people had hearkened unto Me, and Israel had walked in My ways! I should soon have** subdued their enemies, and **turned My hand** against their adversaries. The haters of the LORD **should have** submitted themselves unto Him: **but their time should have endured for ever.** He should have fed them also with the finest of the wheat: and with honey out of the rock should I have satisfied thee" (Psalm 81:10-16).

Can you see it so clearly? As Jesus wept, mourned, and lamented over the damnation of the 1st century Jews, so also here, in generations beforehand which were types of the 1st century Jews, God is lamenting over Israel's rebellion saying, Oh! "Oh that My people had hearkened unto Me, and Israel had walked in My ways!" It is clear that He wanted them to be saved, He wanted them to be obedient, so that, even then, God would have done what we wanted to do, which was what? God would have, as He said – "soon have subdued their enemies", and not just for a little while. Do you see how that God said, "I **should** have soon subdued their enemies"? Again He says, "the haters of the LORD **should** have submitted themselves unto Him", and not just for a little while. God had in His mind that this should have happened FOREVER, and that Israel never would have been destroyed, thus He said – "their time **should** have endured for ever". God says that He chose the Gentiles as an afterthought because Israel provoked His wrath in Deuteronomy 32, and so also thereafter, Israel should not have rebelled but continued forever without

64

falling according to the good will, hope, and love of God that they "will not lie", and He would then, unto forever, be "their Savior" (Isa. 63:8). Could the Lord be any clearer about His will to save them when He says things like this?

> **"I said, Surely thou wilt fear Me, thou wilt receive instruction; so their dwelling should not be cut off, howsoever I punished them: but they rose early, and corrupted all their doings"** (Zephaniah 3:7).

Even so, it is true that there is a condescension by which God has a resistible, changeable, will, with resistible and changeable words, and this relationship of God by way of condescension (God in the ways of man) is mysteriously paradoxical and contradictory to the sovereign, eternal, determinate, irresistible, changeless, and predestinating will and words of God (God in the ways of God).

God in the ways of man is logically irreconcilable to **God in the ways of God**. God seeking fear, seeking to know by trial, seeking to know their repentance and doing all the means by which He would justly expect them to repent (as if He, by His own ordination, is not hardening and softening their hearts in every present moment of time while they live); this is God in the ways of man exhausting all the means to save sinners and wayward saints, and after those means are lovingly and hopefully executed by the Omnibenevolent will of God (**God in the ways of man**), if they still don't repent and believe, it is then that God vindicates their damnation and justifies Himself in it because of what He has done to save them, and what they have done in response to His wooing ("All day long I have stretched out My hand"). This is a sense of justice which is comprehensible to men, a justice that is responsive to our own actions and responses to God's actions and responses. This is a justice which is an antithesis and contradiction from sovereign justice in the invisible, higher ways of God. The justice of God's damnation of sinners based upon their responses to His pursuit of their salvation is understandable by men because we feel as though we have a free will, or are justly guilty of those sins we are committing because we do not sense the invisible hand of God hardening our hearts. It is not confusing to us but we feel guilty, and we are. However, in the light of the higher workings of God, His sovereign hardenings or softenings, how can we be held accountable for our actions if they are all ordained by His determining will? Therefore, in the light of the full spectrum of God's relationship to man, namely in the light of His higher ways (God in the ways of God), it is then that the justice of God to punish men based upon their deeds is not a comprehensible justice because we do not have a free will. Yet if we do not, then the justice of God judging us based upon our deeds is a relational experience made possible through a great condescension God has undergone to have a relationship with us, and though He has given us a snapshot of His higher workings by the written revelation of inspired scripture, we must understand that this work of God is incomprehensible, humanly illogical, and inconsistent with God's condescension, which is, **God in the ways of man** saving, judging, and condemning on the basis of our works (rooted in the presence or absence of faith) in a logical vindication of His own works based upon the guilt they have for their unlawful deeds.

Oh Calvinist, will you not collapse as you read the following ways of God by condescension? They do break the boundaries of your theological system, and why? Your theology is built under the unbiblical premise that theology must be logically consistent instead of biblically consistent. In truth, we must take off our shoes from off our feet, as it were, and take off our human comfort in everything that makes logical sense. The scriptures argue that God is humanly incomprehensible, and how much more all of His ways? Nevertheless, it is sensible and logical, in truth, to understand that God cannot be understood. God relates to men outside of the realm of sovereignty, and, the significance of this you will see. According to all of these passages, did not God choose Israel so that their fruits "should" remain (Ps. 81:10-16), which is to say that they should have persevered? Could this be at all relevant in the New Covenant so that God could say to us who are in Christ, that we are chosen so that our fruit "should remain" forever (John 15:16)? But if it is like as they were chosen, and our "should" (John 15:16) is like as their "should" (Ps. 81:10-16), what does that mean for us? Calvinist, you may be leaning upon a broken reed. God's condescension affects God's will, word, counsel, and therefore, His promises, which then do affect the doctrine of *eternal security*.

THE SIMULTANEOUS
GENUINE WILLS OF GOD
CHAPTER 2

"He putteth his mouth in the dust; if so be there may be hope." – Lamentations 3:29

Lesser Matters

When the LORD commanded Moses to go to Egypt and deliver the Israelites, Moses resisted his commission by God. The Lord did not intend to send anyone with Moses; He chose Moses alone. Then Moses gave three objections to the commission of God (Ex. 4:1, 10, 13), until finally, "the anger of the LORD was kindled" (Ex. 4:14). Moses would have been sufficient to speak, though he said "I am not eloquent," for the Lord said, "Now therefore go, and I will be with thy mouth, and teach thee what thou shalt say" (Ex. 4:10, 12). When Moses persisted to resist the will/counsel of God (God in the ways of man), God repented of this genuine intention. God's righteous anger against Moses' resistance shows the sincerity of God's will/counsel to send Moses alone. A will/counsel/intent that can be *resisted* is a desire that is after *the ways of man*, but since this is the Lord's will being resisted, it is therefore called **God in the ways of man**. After the Lord's repentance, He said to Moses: "Is not Aaron the Levite thy brother? I know that he can speak well. And also, behold he cometh forth to meet thee: and when he seeth thee, he will be glad in his heart. And thou shalt speak unto him, and put words in his mouth: and I will be with thy mouth, and with his mouth, and will teach you what ye shall do" (Ex. 4:14-15). This entire scenario was chronicled without the will/intent/counsel of **God in the ways of God** accounted of. Nevertheless, **God in the ways of God** (His will/counsel/intent/command) cannot be resisted, changed, refused, or repented of.

The final blow which liberated the Israelites from Egyptian bondage was "by strength of hand" from the Lord (Ex. 13:16). "The LORD slew all the firstborn in the land of Egypt, both the firstborn of man, and the firstborn of beast," thus the Israelites were commanded to "sacrifice to the LORD all that openeth the matrix, being males" (Ex. 13:15). The Lord said, "Sanctify unto Me all the firstborn, whatsoever openeth the womb among the children of Israel, both man and of beast: it is Mine" (Ex. 13:2). Long after this was commanded and the Israelites made their way to Sinai, sin arose, wrath was kindled, and rebellion was punished, but in the process of events the Lord repented of His former decision about the firstborn of Israel. He changed His mind on what He was claiming for Himself! He said, "And I, behold, I have taken the Levites from among the children of Israel **instead of all the firstborn** that openeth the matrix among the children of Israel: therefore the Levites shall be Mine" (Num. 3:12). Question: If God can change His mind on a purpose like this, could He then change His mind on a purpose of salvation? **God in the ways of God** counseled, willed, and desired to have the Levites as His possession, thus the genuine will (God in the ways of man) to take the firstborn of the matrix was changed. God's will (God in the ways of God) was made manifest through circumstances that were predestined to change until God's final decision remained.

In these two examples, it is clear that certain circumstances arose that changed God's will. The Sovereign will of God was determining the opposite of what was originally the will of God, thus both wills were the antithesis of the other. Logically, in the capabilities and limitations possible within the willing/thinking faculties of a man, both of these wills could not genuinely exist at the same time, therefore (logically) we would think one of the wills is not a genuine desire that God had – kind of an act, maybe. This is not the case with God even though, logically, He cannot be understood (nor can this twofold will be experienced within man's capacity), we can understand that He has revealed Himself through a **condescension** – in terms that the lens of our limited capacity & understanding can see – **God in the ways of man**. Overall, we must understand that we can't understand! We must be at peace with the incomprehensible greatness of God which makes Him unknowable, and then we can be thankful for the condescension of God which reveals Him in ways which are like ours so that we might understand Him. We must reconcile ourselves with a **biblical premise** (contrary to mainstream, modern scholarship) – that all theological systems must be biblically, ***not logically*** consistent.

Weightier Matters

Some may think that God is able to change His mind on ***lesser matters*** (as the scenarios presented above), but what of matters wherein the lives of men are at stake? A close study will prove that the dualistic, paradoxical wills in God is unlike faculties operable in men. After Moses obeyed God's sending, he set out to travel to Egypt. While Moses was "by the way in the inn," God was wroth with him because he failed to circumcise his son (born of Zipporah). Now pay close attention, please! We know that Moses was a "vessel of mercy" (Rom. 9:23), which means that he was loved with "an everlasting love" (Jer. 31:3), or an uninterrupted love, therefore God had an eternal and unchanging will/desire/intention/purpose/counsel that Moses would live on, deliver Egypt, and be "faithful in all His house" (Heb. 3:5), and yet, "it came to pass by the way in the inn, that the LORD met him, and **sought to kill him**" (Ex. 4:24). Could the LORD intend/desire/will/purpose to kill Moses and actively seek to accomplish this by smiting him with a sickness!? God was seeking/working according to His just and angry counsel/will "to kill him," yet simultaneously, God had a contrary will/intent/desire/purpose to keep Moses alive! The sovereign will of God to keep Moses alive was actively working/seeking to fulfill this desire by ***mercifully softening his heart*** (Rom. 9:16, 18), thus Moses was granted faith to repent and obey God. Moses obeyed just in time, saving his life, but he had to force Zipporah to circumcise his son. As for this scenario, it is clear: One will in God is *resistible* and the other is **irresistible** (Rom. 9:19), but both are genuine and simultaneous! One is the will of God that is according to *the ways of man*, the other is the will of God according to *the ways of God*. Let it therefore be known unto us that the ways of God are **unthinkable** (Isa. 55:9), **unknowable** (Rom. 11:33), and **incomprehensible** (Job 38:2-4, 39:1-2, 42:3).

> *Modern and historical scholarship has built theological systems of biblically incorrect tenets that are logically consistent! It is the unbiblical premise that they hold to which misguides them – the premise that every tenet must be logically consistent. Before telling others about the Holy Scriptures, might I say, let us hear them first! And what do they say? They instruct us that we cannot understand GOD! And those things which we can understand, God's condescension in the ways of man, are biblically distinct from those things that we cannot understand, God in the ways of God. Men presume that the scriptures are to be consistent with their logical understanding, and therefore men confine their interpretations to what they understand – what they deem as possible, logical, consistent, and right for God to think, say, and do, and they shun anything that they cannot understand.*

My reader, thus saith God – "Declare, if thou hast understanding" (Job 38:4)! Will you answer God? Do you have understanding? Let every man say nothing! If we speak, we have "words without knowledge" (Job 38:2). If we cannot understand how the foundations of the earth were laid (Job 38:4), the time schedule for every individual animal to give birth (Job 39:1-2), and all other facets of the creation of God, how then shall we understand the Creator Who has infinitely condescended to "make a covenant" with us (Job 41:4)? Men speak against the sovereign ways of God as they are revealed in the Covenant, but they should rather say, as Job, "I will lay mine hand upon my mouth" (Job 40:4). Yea, God says to us, "Who art thou that repliest against God? Shall the thing formed say to Him that formed it, Why hast Thou made me thus" (Rom. 9:20)? If we question God, we follow in the arrogant error of Job. A face-to-face meeting with God would rearrange your mindset, and as Job, you would say, "I abhor myself, and repent in dust and ashes" (Job 42:6). Men seek to keep the righteousness of God on the same logical level as their ways, the ways of men, but God infinitely exceeds the comprehension of men in all His ways! Therefore men unknowingly (in a zeal without knowledge) condemn God and disannul His judgments.

Oh man, "hast thou an arm like God? Or canst thou thunder with a voice like Him? Deck thyself now with majesty and excellency; and array thyself with glory and beauty. Cast abroad the rage of thy wrath: and behold every one that is proud, and abase him. Look on every one that is proud, and bring him low; and tread down the wicked in their place. Hide them in the dust together; and bind their faces in secret" (Job 40:9-13). If we are not like God in arm or strength, majesty or excellency, beauty and glory, wrath and countenance, power and secrecy, how then could we have a mind like God's to understand His wisdom /will/ ways/ works/ justice/ judgments/ counsels? Will we condemn His ways because He has forbidden us to understand them? Will we seek to make God like men and bind Him to the logical righteousness which men seem to have in their own will or ways? Then we are disannulling His judgments – condemning Him – and this is gross pride against the wonderful things of God. When the humble wonder at the workings of God, the proud stumble and do rage with accusation, yet every written word in the Book of God should be attended to with a trembling of soul as if it was spoken out of a consuming fire with earth-rending thunder (Ex. 20). "Is not My word like as fire? Saith the LORD; and like a hammer that breaketh the rock in pieces" (Jer. 23:29)?

"Lean not on thine own understanding" (Prov. 3:5), "fear the LORD" (Prov. 8:13), and recognize that God is wisdom that we don't have or understand. He says of Himself, "Counsel is Mine, and sound wisdom: I AM UNDERSTANDING; I have strength" (Prov. 8:14). "I lead in the way of righteousness, in the midst of the paths of judgment" (Prov. 8:20). It is wise for us to fear God that we might "hear instruction, and be wise, and refuse it not" (Prov. 8:33), but many a man does contend against the Sovereignty of God and seek to instruct men that God's ways are only and always like men, or men contend that God cannot be anything but sovereign and they discount the condescension. God says, "Shall he that contendeth with the Almighty instruct Him" (Job 40:2)!? Cease, man, cease! Be not as the wicked whose crime was, God says, "thou thoughtest that I was altogether such an one as thyself: but I will reprove thee, and set them in order before thine eyes" (Psalm 50:21).

With holy severity God sought to kill Moses, and likewise God sought to kill another disobedient prophet named Jonah. When Jonah "rose up to flee" "from the presence of the LORD," he fled by a boat to Tarshish (Jonah 1:3). The sea was "raging," even as the anger of God raged against Moses! God sought to kill Jonah and Jonah knew it. Jonah said, "I know that for my sake this great tempest is upon you" (Jonah 1:12). The boat could not bring safety to Jonah. God's wrath was so relentless that if Jonah had stayed in the boat, all the other men would have perished with him. The anger of God was as the waves of the sea, whose raging was in a perpetual unrest until Jonah was apprehended from the boat. God's anger is pacified by the sacrifice of the sinner, and thus, the waves were at peace after Jonah was cast forth. Jonah was pursued by the curses of the Almighty. He was taught of God as Moses was, as it is written, "Thy wrath lieth hard upon me, and Thou hast afflicted me **with all Thy waves**. Thy fierce wrath goeth over me; Thy terrors have cut me off. They came **round about me daily like water; they compassed me about together**" (Psalm 88:7, 16-17). Jonah could have finished the psalm with a perfectly parallel lamentation, for Jonah did say in Jonah 2:3: "For Thou hadst **cast me into the deep, in the midst of the seas; and the floods compassed me about: all Thy billows and Thy waves passed over me.**"

God's fierce anger was burning bright,

70

To finish a purpose with no mercy in sight,
But who can tell if the Lord will not repent and turn darkness into light,
Saving men from a wrathful, just plight?
When men do turn from sin,
God may turn from the intent or spoken promise to kill men,
But men must know the danger and working of a will,
That burns and pursues sorrow-less sinners to kill,
Even if there is a paradoxical, contradicting, perpetual, loving will, that is
determining election, predestination, and causing salvation without exception.

All this, is so that, when regenerate men are unrepentant still,
They will not think solely of God's sovereign, loving will,
So as to keep them from seeking repentance by a solace of salvific promises still.

Nevertheless Jonah "cried" in repentance (Jonah 2:2), made vows of obedience (Jonah 2:9), thus he did experience the saving power of God! "Salvation is of the LORD" (Jonah 2:9)! It happened to Jonah as it did happen to Nineveh, "**God saw their works, that they turned from their evil way**; and **God repented of the evil**... and He did it not" (Jonah 3:10). Jonah knew that God was "a gracious God, and merciful, slow to anger, and of great kindness, and **repentest**" (Jonah 4:2) of wrath and impending destructions. Jonah experienced it himself! What is amazing is that God ensured the destruction of Jonah with deeds (angry consuming waves), and greater than that, God ensured the destruction of Nineveh with a prophetic promise of WOE. He said, "Yet forty days, and Nineveh shall be overthrown" (Jonah 3:4), without any condition or appeal for possible mercy. The people did not know God would have mercy. They said, "**Who can tell** if God will turn and **repent**, and turn away from His fierce anger, and we perish not" (Jonah 3:9)? When God did repent, He changed His mind "of the evil that He **had said** that He would do unto them" (Jonah 3:10). Therefore, as God was to individual persons (Moses and Jonah), He is to whole cities containing multitudes of persons.

God said to righteous Hezekiah when he was sick, "set thine house in order: for thou shalt die, and not live" (Isaiah 38:1). Could or would God go back on this word/will/counsel/desire/intention/purpose/work? "Then Hezekiah turned his face toward the wall, and prayed unto the LORD, and said, Remember now, O LORD, I beseech Thee, how I have walked before Thee in truth and with a perfect heart, and have done that which is good in Thy sight. And Hezekiah wept sore. Then came the word of the LORD to Isaiah, saying, Go, and say to Hezekiah, Thus saith the LORD, the God of David thy father, I have heard thy prayer, I have seen thy tears: behold, I will add unto thy days fifteen years. And I will deliver thee and this city out of the hand of the King of Assyria: and I will defend this city" (Isaiah 38:2-6). The Lord changed His mind and word because of the faith Hezekiah evidenced by "prayers and supplications with strong crying and tears unto Him that was able to save him from death, and was heard in that he feared" (Heb. 5:7)! The Lord said to Hezekiah, "**I have seen thy tears**" (Isaiah 38:5)! And so He changed His mind/will/counsel and spoken word. Do you ever pray like this? Or, is your heart like an "adamant stone" against the wrathful warnings of God, so that they do never terrify you as they ought, so that you can never tell when they are nigh to fall upon you, for, you cannot even remember them, nor apply them, because you are inoculated from them? You have memorized all the promises of God! But you trample them underfoot by your disobedience! Do you have "the same spirit of faith, according as it is written," "my flesh trembleth for fear of Thee; and I am afraid of Thy judgments" (2 Cor. 4:13, Psalm 119:120)!? Don't you want to be like Jesus Christ, Who…

> **"Who in the days of His flesh, when He had offered up prayers and supplications with strong crying and tears unto Him that was able to save him from death, and was heard in that He feared"** (Hebrews 5:7).

Sophisticated and "at ease" (Amos 6:1), the worldly-wise seminary professors teach without callused knees.
In proud intellectualism they profess to be masters of grace, not knowing they are provoking God to His face.
The wrath of God they do daily tease while the flesh of men they do please, by worldly morality and counterfeit spirituality the genuine guilt of a troubled conscience is put to rest and appeased.

They teach that tearful prayers are extreme emotionalism, and hours of prayer are a misunderstanding of grace,
But they do, with Jesus, create a schism; their passionless persona has made heresies of disgrace.

Nay rather, I will come to the Garden and find my Lord, weeping tears of dreadful blood!
In this school I will stay, the foolish, narrow path is the "babes'" (Matt. 11:25) biblical way.
While others seek heady knowledge let us rather say, Lord teach us, Lord teach us, "Lord, teach us to pray" (Luke 11:1).

Contend against these "doctors" of theology whose counterfeit grace is a satanic doxology.
They forsake humble revelation and have created their own carnal amalgamation,
Because devilish wisdom (James 3:15) darkens their own imagination (Jer. 7:24).
Tearless and on a Titanic of deception, they make ready themselves for hell's reception,
Because the foolish ways of God are their rejection.

Oversimplifying scripture to be seen solely in the spectrum of
sovereignty teaches men not to fear.
This solidifies confidence to the regenerate man even when his
conscience is seared (Prov. 14:16).

God does set His mind to destroy, wrath to this end He does deploy, but before the terror of this anger does accomplish the cause for which it was sent forth, men have a window of time to repent. The wrath of God was deployed and purposed against the wicked King Ahab, and God said, "Behold, I will bring evil upon thee, and will take away thy posterity, and will cut off from Ahab him that pisseth against the wall, and him that is shut up and left in Israel" (1 Kings 21:21). More than this, a specific word declared the fate of Ahab himself, saying, "Thus saith the LORD, in the place where dogs licked the blood of Naboth shall dogs lick thy blood, even thine" (1 Kings 21:19). This did come to pass (1 Kings 22:38), however, Ahab obtained a little mercy after he first heard this word from God. **God is watchful at the response of men**, and depending on His sovereign will, men *may* receive a little mercy. "And it came to pass, when Ahab heard those words, that he rent his clothes, and put sackcloth upon his flesh, and fasted, and lay in sackcloth, and went softly. And the word of the LORD came to Elijah the Tishbite, saying, **Seest thou how Ahab humbleth himself before Me?** Because he humbleth himself before Me, I will not bring the evil in his days: but in his son's days will I bring the evil upon his house" (1 Kings 21:27-29). The Lord did intend to cut off the house of Ahab while Ahab was yet alive so that he would be tormented with the experience of familial death. Yet in the mercy of God, because Ahab humbled himself, God did change His will/intent/desire/purpose with a drop of mercy for a "vessel of wrath" (Rom. 9:22). Such a "*cool drop*" of mercy may now be granted within the hours of every man's allotted life span, but when the sands of time no longer sink, when time and flesh are swallowed up into a timeless eternity, a single will in God of endless, perfect hatred will disallow even *one drop of cool water* to interrupt the everlasting, conscious, tormenting affliction of flaming fire (Luke 16:24). A *little* fear now may afford a little pity from God; this is surprising love! But to be surprised by everlasting hatred who can bear!? "The sinners in Zion are afraid; fearfulness hath surprised the hypocrites. Who among us shall dwell with the devouring fire? Who among us shall dwell with everlasting burning" (Isaiah 33:14)?

1) The noteworthy things that do affect and change the mind of God.
2) The inner-wrestlings of a timelessly eternal, dually relational, condescending God.

The pursuing wrath of God (in the ways of man) would have killed Moses, Jonah, Nineveh, and Ahab. This will was pacified and repented of when God did observe repentance by men. As in bullet point number one: God's will and purposeful emotion was changed as He experienced the regret and humiliation of men in their change of mind. The crisis of God's judgment did affect them, thus God did reconsider His decision to reject them. Aside from what can be drawn from the events themselves, look at bullet point number two just above: God's will to kill (God in the ways of man) was changed by the unchanging will of God to keep them alive (God in the ways of God), yet their sovereign election to live was manifest by God giving faith to their hearts (causing repentance) – *repentance wrought **when** they beheld the genuine will of God to destroy them.* These men repented while unconscious of the secret, sovereign workings of God. How did they repent? They repented by beholding, believing, and responding to the will of God in wrath (in the ways of man), but modern teachings of sovereignty exclude this will from being possible or experiential to a saved man. Thus, they strengthen the unrepentant hearts of men by "promising them life" (Ezek. 13:22), and yet repentance may come if such men saw a promise of death pursuing after them. Life could come *through* repentance – repentance wrought within a man by the sober instruments of death hanging over or impending upon them. "I will praise Thee with uprightness of heart, when I shall have learned **Thy righteous judgments**. I will keep Thy statutes: **O forsake me not utterly**" (Psalm 119:7-8)! A sense of duty may motivate at diverse times, a sense of right may motivate in diverse manners, but when the "fleshly lusts" that "war against the soul" (1 Pet. 2:11) do overwhelm us, when they do gain an advantage over the will of righteous men, how can they resist, overcome, and obey? At such an hour, the secret of repentance can be found in the fervent emotion that motivated this cry – "O forsake me not utterly!" The ability to obey will come by a healthy fear, knowing this: if you don't obey God, then He will utterly forsake you. For many it will be an *uncertain* fight for eternal life, a fight we may lose if there is no understanding of this kind of fear (1 Cor. 9:26). Many run for "an incorruptible" crown (1 Cor. 9:25-26) and yet fail to obtain it because the race is hard: "But I," Paul says, "I keep under my body, and bring it into subjection: lest that by any means, when I have preached to others, I myself should be a **castaway**" (1 Cor. 9:27). Paul understood the castaway capabilities of God's wrath and took heed, saying, "I therefore so run, not as uncertainly; so fight I, not as one that beateth the air" (1 Cor. 9:26).

My reader, FACE IT! There are times when the saints are sleeping. They are as Lot when he was dwelling in a place or position that endangered his eternal life, and from here he heard the angel say – "we will destroy this place!" Then Lot "seemed as one that mocked" because of his careless ease. Unable to repent, his soul slept on… can you relate? Christians today are fast asleep in damnable conditions – in sin – plugging their ears into silence from the alarms of God's holy Writ, alarms which declare sure destruction for their situation. The mercy of God deployed another warning to lingering Lot the next morning. "Then the angels hastened Lot, saying, Arise, take thy wife, and thy two daughters, which are here; **lest thou be consumed** in the iniquity of the city" (Gen. 19:15). Lot was first warned, and now again, but he lingers…and still the mercy of God more fervently followed him, even with forceful and final warnings – "And **while he lingered**, the men **laid hold** upon his hand, and upon the hand of his wife, and upon the hand of his two daughters; **the LORD being merciful unto him**: and they brought him forth, and set him without the city" (Genesis 19:16). Mercy forced him out to the edge of the city, and lo, Lot stands on the edge of salvation. Here he is revived to reach forth for a final and stedfast resolve – saving repentance! "**Lest thou be consumed**" was the message of God's mercy to this beloved saint! And again the angel strives with righteous Lot using terror as his persuasion: "And it came to pass, when they had brought them forth abroad, that he said, Escape for thy life; look not behind thee, neither stay thou in all the plain; escape to the mountain, **LEST THOU BE CONSUMED!**" (Gen. 19:17). Again the angel pleads, "**LEST THOU BE CONSUMED**," therefore the mocking, lingering, at ease mentality was shaken out of Lot like one that awaketh out of sleep (Eph. 5:8, 14, Matt. 25:5)! Lot awakens to an acceptable repentance and keeps it from this point onward – FEARING – hasting to follow God's warnings exactly. This haste, focus, and exact obedience in Lot saved his eternal soul! But sadly, his wife, who was exercised by the same mercies, looked back. "**Lest thou be consumed**" gripped Lot with the saving mind of racing faith, one that wins the prize (1 Cor. 9:24-27)! This consuming fire chased away this righteous man! And he knew that if it caught him, it would have burned him, now and forever, for it was "the vengeance of eternal fire" (Jude 7) that never burned out, that is still burning today, begun on earth and now burning in hell! How do you minister to the elect of God, preacher? This is God's wisdom, His stinging "goads," "given from one Shepherd" (Eccl. 12:11), and "the Lord knoweth how to deliver the godly out of temptations" better than us (2 Peter 2:9)! So narrow was the way of God, so scarce are they who hold to it, so terrifying are God's merciful messengers, that God, in infinite wisdom, left for Lot's generation a memorial statue of horror – Lot's wife. Those who passed by this "pillar of salt" (Gen. 19:26) were compelled to stop, to steadfastly look, and they all did learn something of what Lot learned. Oh the "terror" (2 Cor. 5:11)! The terror which is necessary for saving repentance! Lot's wife is left there for all to look upon! The woeful woman's face is fixed in the expression of hellfire FEAR! We should "look diligently," not back, but at them who looked back so as to learn from their error. We should look at the terror within Lot who fled from the consuming chaos of God's destroying wrath. We should "look diligently," brethren, even at the salt-fixed face of Lot's wife frozen in terror, lest we, like her, "fail of the grace of God" (Heb. 12:15). These are two witnesses in the cloud (Heb. 12:1) which still speak today – crying out – in the force of trumpet-loud terror, because God is seeking to keep us from looking around. Look straight on to Jesus (Heb. 12:2); let us look diligently! "Looking diligently lest any man fail the grace of God" (Heb. 12:15)!

God repented when He saw a circumcised son (Moses' son), Jonah crying and vowing, Nineveh sitting in ashes, Hezekiah in tearful entreaties, and Ahab in sackcloth and fasting – these were the means by which the sovereign will of God was manifest and accomplished. Therefore men ought to judge their election by blameless obedience, looking carefully at their walk with God through the lens of God's judgments and warnings. If Moses and Jonah had believed it was impossible that the arrows of God's wrath were ever aimed at them, then they would not have been saved! What about you, Calvinist - are you sure God can never be angry at you now that you have been born again or purchased by the blood? If so, PLEASE, let me reason further with you, peradventure God would grant this poor man wisdom that "scaleth the city" of Calvinism, that "casteth down the strength of the confidence thereof" (Prov. 21:22).

My reader, you may understand the applications that have been made thus far from these passages but still deny the applicability of these principles in the New Covenant, because the New Covenant, you think, is vastly different. I understand this thinking and intend to address it thoroughly. Please, keep studying with me as we make our way into the New Covenant. Indeed, we cannot take OT scenarios and apply them as NT experiences **unless** the NT applies them as NT experiences. To make our way there, let us overview some preliminary Covenants which will exercise our understanding in the language of the New Covenant – "*A Priestly Covenant,*" "*A Kingly Covenant,*" and "*The Abrahamic Covenant.*"

A Priestly Covenant

> ❖ *There are no conditions side by side the promises.*
> ❖ *A man must live worthy of the promises and gifts.*

In the previous instances reviewed, God was intent (God in the ways of man) on killing men, but repented, after He saw their repentance. In the following two scenarios, "A Priestly Covenant" and "A Kingly Covenant," God was intent on (by spoken promises) good salvific purposes. Firstly, in the priestly covenant, God was intent on perpetuating the priestly line of Ithamar which is *a type* of perpetuating life and salvation. Nevertheless when God saw the wickedness of the High priest, Eli, He repented of or changed His *will and word*! God did go back on "**a perpetual statute**" and "**an everlasting priesthood!**" A good promise/will/intent/purpose of salvific life (God in the ways of man) was changed because God beheld sinful, unrepentant rebellion in Eli. Eli's fate was sealed by this judgment of wrath which came through a repentance in God, nevertheless, the sovereign will of God to destroy him was always unrepentant, even though it became manifest in this way. God in the ways of God, in unchanging hatred from eternity past, did predestinate Eli to be one of the many "vessels of wrath."

Eli was the High Priest after the line of Ithamar. The lineage of priests wherein Eli was ordained was a product of a promise God made to Aaron. Ithamar and Eleazar were the only remaining sons of Aaron, and thus, they were the only remaining priestly lines. God promised them and said, "And thou shalt gird them with girdles, Aaron and his sons, and put the bonnets on them: and the priest's office shall be theirs for a **perpetual statute**: and thou shalt consecrate Aaron and his sons" (Exodus 29:9). God said that they were part of an "**everlasting priesthood**." God said, "And thou shalt anoint them, as thou didst anoint their father, that they may minister unto Me in the priest's office: for their anointing shall surely be an **everlasting priesthood** throughout their generations" (Exodus 40:15).

With the good words **perpetual** and **everlasting** binding them into holy covenant, do you think that the sons of Aaron did entertain the possibility of damnation? Is it impossible for binding conditions to exist when a promise is said to be *perpetual* and *everlasting*? If Eli relied on the promise deceitfully, excusing fear while in disobedience, it is because he thinks that he would never lose his priesthood or salvation. This would embolden a continuance of compromise. What was Eli's sin?

Eli sinned greatly against the Lord by not restraining his two sons from their wickedness. Eli preferred to honor his sons above the Lord. Of this God said, "Wherefore kick ye at My sacrifice and at Mine offering, which I have commanded in My habitation; and honourest thy sons above Me, to make yourselves fat with the chiefest of all the offerings of Israel My people?" (1 Samuel 2:29) Then the Lord says a staggering statement! The Lord is not hiding, worried, or afraid to make known, "**I said indeed** that thy house, and the house of thy father, should walk before Me **for ever**," but the Lord changes His mind and goes back on what He said because of the *unworthiness* and guilt He observed from Eli! Why? How? God can change His mind (God in the ways of man)! Henceforth be warned, He will not honor the wicked! The Lord finishes saying to Eli…

> "**but now the LORD saith**, Be it far from Me; for them that honour Me I will honour, and they that despise Me shall be lightly esteemed. Behold, the days come, that I will cut off thine arm, and the arm of thy father's house, that there shall not be an old man in thine house. And thou shalt see an enemy in My habitation, in all the wealth which God shall give Israel: and there shall not be an old man in thine house for ever. And the man of thine, whom I shall not cut off from Mine altar, shall be to consume thine eyes, and to grieve thine heart: and all the increase of thine house shall die in the flower of their age. [34] And this shall be a sign unto thee, that shall come upon thy two sons, on Hophni and Phinehas; in one day they shall die both of them. [35] And **I will raise Me up a faithful priest**, that shall do according to that which is in Mine heart and in My mind: and **I will build him a sure house; and he shall walk before Mine anointed for ever**. [36] And it shall come to pass, that every one that is left in thine house shall come and crouch to him for a piece of silver and a morsel of bread, and shall say, Put me, I pray thee, into one of the priests' offices, that I may eat a piece of bread" (1 Samuel 2:30-36).

This prophecy was fulfilled in the days of Solomon when Abiathar was ejected from the priesthood in 1 Kings 2:27. This rejection ended the line of Ithamar, as it is written: "So Solomon thrust out Abiathar from being priest unto the LORD; that he might fulfill the word of the LORD, which He spake concerning the house of

Eli in Shiloh." Abiathar was a son of Eli, Eli was in the line of Ithamar, and Zadok replaced Abiathar. From this point the line of Ithamar ceased to exist. If God can go back on "*a perpetual statute*" and "*an everlasting priesthood,*" can God go back on a promise for **perpetual** perseverance in the **everlasting** ordination of the New Testament priesthood of all believers (1 Pet. 2:9)? Not the priesthood of Ithamar but that of the New Covenant saints!? Regenerate Christians are called by Peter, "A Royal Priesthood" (1 Pet. 2:9)! Men argue that such words of everlasting mean, unequivocally and without condition, everlasting, but is this an oversimplification of the Covenant promise and an unbiblical, unhistorical, unscriptural interpretation? What about the word "*for ever*" (1 Sam. 2:35)? Is a Covenant made with **the seed of Aaron** different than a Covenant made with **the spiritual seed of Abraham**, or is it different from the Covenant made with **the seed of Christ**?

A Kingly Covenant

In biblical history, when God endeavors to save His people, He saves and anoints a man for the duty. Jesus Christ is Jesus, "the anointed One;" this is the meaning of the title "Christ." A faithful and faith-filled man does works of faith which save others. Even so, thus it was with King Saul. God said, "To morrow about this time I will send thee a man out of the land of Benjamin, and thou shalt **anoint him** to be captain over My people Israel, that he may **save My people** out of the hand of the Philistines: for I have looked upon My people, because their cry is come unto Me" (1 Samuel 9:16). "Then Samuel took a vial of oil, and poured it upon his head, and kissed him, and said, Is it not because the LORD hath anointed thee to be captain over His inheritance" (1 Samuel 10:1)? "**God gave him another heart**" (1 Sam. 10:9), and he, as the prophet prophesied, was "**turned into another man**" (1 Sam. 10:6). All the "signs" of a saved man were his experience (1 Sam. 10:9), as the prophet said to him, "**God is with thee**" (1 Sam. 10:7). "The Spirit of God came upon him, and he prophesied among them" (1 Sam. 10:10). Saul was made an under-king in the Kingdom of God by a prophet's blessing, the oil of God, the Spirit of power, and newness of heart and life. "The Spirit of God came upon Saul" (1 Sam. 11:6), and he led them to such a great deliverance that the Kingdom was established, "and all Israel rejoiced greatly" (1 Sam. 11:15)! Saul's valiant deeds are of the sort named by "The Hall of Faith" in Hebrews chapter 11. The Hebrews 11 elders and Saul "out of weakness were made strong, waxed valiant in fight, turned to flight the armies of the aliens" (Heb. 11:34)! Saul, "through faith subdued kingdoms, wrought righteousness," and "obtained promises" (Heb. 11:33)!

Israel and Saul were given clear conditions with the establishment of the kingdom (1 Sam. 12:14-15, 20-25). For an entire year, Saul reigned, faithful to God in these covenantal conditions. He did not "turn aside from following the LORD" with "all" his "heart" (1 Sam. 12:20), he did "only fear the LORD and did serve Him in truth" (1 Sam. 12:24) *for a whole year*! However, "when he had reigned *two years* over Israel" (1 Sam. 13:1), then he rebelled from God. Some may think that God did not intend to establish the Kingdom of Saul **forever**, but this is incorrect. After Saul's first rebellion, it was confirmed by Samuel - when Samuel was speaking to Saul, he said - "Thou hast done foolishly: thou hast not kept the commandment of the LORD thy God, which He commanded thee: **for now would the LORD have established thy kingdom upon Israel <u>for ever</u>**" (1 Sam. 13:13). God willed for Saul's kingdom to be established *forever* (God in the ways of man), but now God was discontinuing those thoughts!

At this Divine rejection God said, "**But now** thy kingdom shall not **continue**: the LORD hath sought Him a man after His own heart, and the LORD hath commanded him to be captain over His people, **because thou hast not kept that which the LORD commanded thee**" (1 Samuel 13:14). Even though this was said then (at Saul's first rebellion), I suspect that Saul repented of his sins which he committed here in the first rebellion, and, in response to the prophet Samuel's prayers, God repented of what He had purposed and said to Saul, how that He was going to take the Kingdom away from him. After this Saul went on to do great works of faith. It was written, "So Saul took the kingdom over Israel, and fought against all his enemies on every side, against Moab, and against the children of Ammon, and against Edom, and against the kings of Zobah, and against the Philistines: and whithersoever he turned himself, he vexed them. And he gathered an host, and smote the Amalekites, and **delivered Israel out of the hands of them that spoiled them**" (1 Samuel 14:47-48).

The Lord, at this point, had not forsaken Saul because Samuel was still continuing with him. This means that God was still on friendly terms with him, commissioning him (1 Sam. 15:1), and Israel was being delivered and secured under him (1 Sam. 14:47-48). David was not sought out and anointed yet, the Holy Spirit was not taken away from Saul yet, the evil spirit was not sent to Saul yet, and when the eventual reprobation of Saul transpired the LORD did repent again (1 Sam. 15:1), which means that He did decide to reject Saul *again* (1 Sam. 15:23), which must reveal that God had repented of the previous decision to reject him, otherwise God would not have repented again to reject him again. God must have heard the intercessions of Samuel who, doubtlessly, as this second rejection too, was "grieved" and "cried unto the LORD all night" (1 Sam. 15:11). The intercession must have availed last time when Samuel cried out like this, but this time, as Samuel attempts to intercede again even after the final rejection of Saul, it is to no avail. After the LORD finally "**repented** that He had made Saul King over Israel" (1 Sam. 15:35), then God reproved Samuel and says, "How long wilt thou mourn for Saul, seeing I have rejected him from reigning over Israel? Fill thine horn with oil, and go, I will send thee to Jesse the Bethlehemite: for I have provided Me a king among his sons" (1 Samuel 16:1). At this final repentance, there was an inability for intercession, an immediate fulfillment of the former word that God, "sought Him a man after His own heart and the LORD hath commanded him to be captain over His people" (1 Sam. 13:14), thus the anointing transpired (1 Sam. 16:13), the Holy Spirit came upon David and left Saul (1 Sam. 16:13-14), "an evil spirit from the LORD troubled" Saul (1 Sam. 16:14), God no longer answered nor commission Saul, and likewise, Samuel never saw Saul again unto death.

At the final repentance of God it was said, "The LORD hath rent the Kingdom of Israel from thee this day, and hath given it to a neighbor of thine, that is better than thou. And also **the Strength of Israel will not lie nor repent: for He is not a man, that He should repent**" (1 Sam. 15:28-29). God said He would not repent of this word that was just given, and He repented of the intention that was formerly at work (1 Sam. 15:35), but it is as if Samuel sought any means, as Nineveh, to obtain a repentance in the mind of God *if it was possible*. As Nineveh said, "*Who can tell* if God will turn and repent," also David said after the pronouncement of the death of Bathsheba's firstborn, "*Who can tell* whether God will be gracious to me, that the child may live" (Jonah 3:9, 2 Sam. 12:22). God did not repent at David's prayers, nor did He repent at Samuel's prayers, and as many other instances throughout history, there is a time when He will not repent (when He chooses not to/when His determinate counsel ordains it).

In the Sovereign purposes of God that are stated as predestinated purposes and counsels (God in the ways of God), the Godlike qualities of 1 Sam. 15:29 are exalted! Samuel said, "the Strength of Israel **will not lie nor repent: for He is not a man, that He should repent**" (1 Sam. 15:29). So in the Covenants, words, purposes, and counsels done in the context of "**God in the ways of God**," the establishment of the spoken word is given in like manners: Concerning the priesthood of Christ (Melchizedek) it was said, "The LORD hath sworn, and **will not repent**, Thou art a Priest for ever after the order of Melchizedek" (Psalm 110:4, Heb. 7:21). The predestinated counsel of God (God in the ways of God) can never change, can never fail, will never be repented of nor gone back on. Therefore, in those promises, Covenants, spoken words, and revelations which announce those things which are the staircase and platform for the manifestation of Christ, all things formerly done become significant in the light of Christ, that all things after are accomplished in the work and Person of Christ, that in Christ all the glory of God in a singular lens is manifest! Thus, God will not repent of the ordination of Christ after the priesthood of Melchizedek. Through the fall of Saul, David arose, yet through the same means God does manifest His eternal purposes. Through resisting God's revealed will men do fall, and through their fall the sovereign, hidden will of God does rise into your attention. The eternal purposes of God are woven throughout the rise and fall of past generations and Covenants!

We shall study each of these Covenants and generations in exhaustive detail, but by way of summary and introduction, let me begin by saying: *Through the fall* of the Exodus generation, the Abrahamic Covenant is pending until the work of Christ consummates and entirely fulfills it. *Through the fall* of Solomon, the Davidic Covenant is pending until the work of Christ consummates and entirely fulfills it. *Through the fall* of the Judaistic nation and people of God in the first century (at the first coming of Christ), the consummated promises of God for the full salvation of Israel is pending until the work of Christ consummates and entirely fulfills it, and temporarily ***through this fall*** the predestinated purpose to reconcile the whole (Gentile) world to Himself is manifest until the fulfillment of the Abrahamic and Davidic Covenants are accomplished wherein, conclusively, all of physical Israel will be saved, but it is at the end of time, after the fullness of the Gentiles comes in. Of what nature is this END? It is the resurrection, the condescension withdrawn, inaugurating the full reign of the Messianic King Jesus, Who will fully recreate the laws of all creation, remove the curses of sin, and fully reconcile, resurrect, redeem, and save His partially regenerated Christians who waited for Him on earth.

The Abrahamic Covenant was said to be spoken and determined in the word, intent, counsel, and ***ways of God***, therefore, the word was called an "**immutable counsel**" (Heb. 6:17-18). An immutable counsel is the will/word/promise/intent/Covenant which cannot be breached, which God will not repent of nor go back on, contrary to the will/word/promise/intent/counsel/covenant which he can repent of or go back on. Nevertheless, during the time of Abraham's sojourning, God revealed His will to be ***conditional*** instead of ***unchanging*** or ***immutable***. Of the Davidic Covenant, it was said to be in the ***unfailing faithfulness of God*** (Ps. 89:33), a spoken word that cannot be ***broken*** or ***altered*** (Ps. 89:34), a thing spoken and sworn to that ***He will not go back on*** or ***lie*** about (Ps. 89:35), yet for centuries the men of God were wondering, as with the Abrahamic Covenant, "where are Thy former lovingkindnesses, which Thou swarest unto David in Thy truth" (Ps. 89:49)? Why? Because the Lord did "cast off" (Ps. 89:38), make "void the Covenant" (Ps. 89:39), and did "cast his throne down to the ground" (Ps. 89:44). The Davidic Covenant did not come to pass as it was intended for the present generation, as did the Abrahamic Covenant, but it was so that, ***through the fall*** and failure of men, Christ would illuminate the world by a single work to the glory of God, wherein all the promises, shadows, Covenants, and prophecies are fulfilled in Him! As the fall of Saul manifested the rise of David, the breach of the Abrahamic and Davidic Covenants did manifest the need and make room for Christ, Who arose, and He will fulfill them in the end of days. As we reviewed the Kingly Covenant made with Saul, let's turn to the Abrahamic and Davidic Covenants.

THE ABRAHAMIC COVENANT
CHAPTER 3

It must be understood by the reader that there are promises, Covenants, and oaths that can be gone back on, changed, and repented of – yet in those things which are in the

----
RELATED SERMONS

"The Prophet Like Unto Moses"

– Sean Morris
----

predestinated purpose to manifest Christ in the earth (the determinate counsel of God/God in the ways of God), those promises, Covenants, and oaths cannot be gone back on, changed, or repented of. Heretofore in these next two addresses, the Abrahamic and Davidic Covenants, note how the fulfillment of these promises is pending because it is a genuine promise, Covenant, and oath *gone back on, changed,* and *repented of,* yet, a final fulfillment in an unchanging purpose that cannot be repented of will come - *the fulfillment of these Covenants in Christ.*

Tracing the Abrahamic Covenant

NOTE: *The people of the Covenant were a specific generation.*

> "And He said unto Abram, Know of a surety that **thy seed** shall be a stranger in a land that is not theirs, and shall serve them; and they shall afflict them **four hundred years**; And also that nation, whom they shall serve, will I judge: and afterward shall they come out with great substance. And thou shalt go to thy fathers in peace; thou shalt be buried in a good old age. But in **the fourth generation** they shall **come hither again**: for the iniquity of the Amorites is not yet full." (Genesis 15:13-16)

> "In the same day the LORD made a **covenant with Abram**, saying, Unto **thy seed** have I given this land, from the river of Egypt unto the great river, the river Euphrates: The Kenites, and the Kenizzites, and the Kadmonites, And the Hittites, and the Perizzites, and the Rephaims, And the Amorites, and the Canaanites, and the Girgashites, and the Jebusites." (Genesis 15:18-21)

At the establishment of the Abrahamic Covenant, God told him saying, "unto thy seed have I given this land," and the Lord named the boundaries of the Promised Land (Gen. 15:18-21). The Lord answered the question Abraham asked, saying, "whereby shall I know that I shall inherit it" (Gen. 15:8). God told Abraham that he would inherit the land in the generation of his seed that will inherit the land. Abraham will inherit the land through his seed, and specifically, his seed that will be in *the generation* that comes out of **four hundred years** in bondage. In the **fourth generation,** God says, "They shall come hither again" (Gen. 15:8, 13, 16). God promises Abraham that the **fourth generation** of people that come out of the bondage of Egypt will inherit the Promised Land in Abraham's stead - This is the Abrahamic Covenant.

The promise was to Abraham concerning *this* fourth *generation,* whose the number will be as the stars of heaven (Ex. 32:15). Thus was the genuine will/intent/word/promise/Covenant of God by oath to Abraham. Can this oath fail or be altered, changed, or broken? God named this generation as the inheritors, and so, as He promised, He came to them to deliver them from Egypt. Closely trace with me the special characteristics of this generation who became the primary type of NT salvation in reference by NT inspired writers. Below, tracing the book of Exodus, there is an account of all the salvific promises and oaths that God gave to this specific generation, wherein, God in the ways of man sought to save them.

Motivation and Intent for Salvation	"God remembered **His Covenant with Abraham**, with Isaac, and with Jacob" – Exodus 2:24
Salvation as a work of God based upon the faithfulness of God	"I am come down to deliver," "to bring them up out of that land," "unto the place" (the Promised Land) – Exodus 3:8
The spoken word of God	"And **I have said**, I will bring you up out of the affliction of Egypt unto the land of the Canaanites, and the Hittites, and the Amorites, and the Perizzites, and the Hivites, and the Jebusites, unto a land flowing with milk and honey." (Exodus 3:17)
The Promise of God	"And it shall come to pass, when ye be come to the land which the LORD will give you, according **as He hath promised**, that ye shall keep this service." (Exodus 12:25)
The Oath to their fathers	"And it shall be when the LORD shall bring thee into the land of the Canaanites, and the Hittites, and the Amorites, and the Hivites, and the Jebusites, **which He sware unto thy fathers** to give thee, a land flowing with milk and honey, that thou shalt keep this service in this month." (Exodus 13:5)

The Oath to the present Exodus generation	"And it shall be when the LORD shall bring thee into the land of the Canaanites, **as He sware unto thee** and **to thy fathers**, and shall give it thee," (Exodus 13:11)

The clear and genuine will/counsel/intent/word/promise/oath/Covenant of God to this generation is understood by the people themselves just as God communicated it to them. Serving as a confirmation of the words, God DID come down, and He DID deliver *them*. In this purpose, God did *win* the heart and faith of His people, and how? The good tidings of their deliverance (these promises) were confirmed by mighty deeds in the saving power of God, beyond their hopes or imaginations. These promises made up their gospel – and they responded with saving faith.

The Exodus Generation Saved by Faith

The Israelites responded in faith at the first presentation of the gospel. Upon the hearing of faith it is written that they worshipped God – "And Moses and Aaron went and gathered together all the elders of the children of Israel: And Aaron spake all the words which the LORD had spoken unto Moses, and did the signs in the sight of the people. And **the people believed**: and when they heard that the LORD had **visited** the children of Israel, and that He had looked upon their affliction, then they **bowed their heads and worshipped**" (Exodus 4:29-31).

The Israelites began well, in faith (as accounted Exodus 4:29-31), but their faith was soon lost because of the increased burden of labor and anguish of spirit. Under the power of Pharaoh's oppression the people were made faithless and deaf to the gospel of God, but God did not let go. God turned their heart back to Himself by a demonstration of His gospel power! Israel watched as Satan's Egypt contested with the power of God, and behold, the serpent did bruise, but God did crush. How? Seven miraculous plagues of wrath afflicted Egypt...but Israel, she dwelt in the midst of these stormy swarms of wrath as under an invisible shield! Israel wondered how they went on unharmed, and their faith was renewed to glorify God. God won their heart! Egypt came to recognize, confess, and believe that they were under the wrath of the God of Israel, even so, Israel came to recognize, confess, and believe that they were set apart and saved because they were loved by God!

7 Plagues

The swarm of flies – "to the end thou mayest know that I am the LORD in the midst of the earth. And I will put a division between My people and thy people: to morrow shall this sign be" (Exodus 8:22-23).

An unnamed Plague – "all the cattle of Egypt died: but of the cattle of the children of Israel died not one. And this is the "sever between the cattle of Israel and the cattle of Egypt" which He spoke of (Exodus 9:6, 4).

In the miracle of the boils – "the magicians could not stand before Moses because of the boils; for the boil was upon the magicians, and upon all the Egyptians," but there is no mention of it being upon the Israelites (Exodus 9:11).

The plague of hail mixed with fire – "the hail smote throughout all the land of Egypt all that was in the field, both man and beast; and the hail smote every herb of the field, and brake every tree of the field. Only the land of Goshen, where the children of Israel were, was there no hail" (Exodus 9:25-26).

The plague of locusts – Ex. 10:13-18 – the plague appeared to be only in the land of Egypt, for the locusts destroyed only what "the hail had left" "through all the land of Egypt" (Ex. 10:15). The plague of locusts was so grievous that the land was dark by the thick multitude of locusts that came over the land; it is suspected, as with the others (and the hail plague), that the Israelites were excluded.

The plague of darkness – The LORD then brought a "darkness over the land of Egypt, even darkness which may be felt" (Exodus 10:21). It is written of the Egyptians that "they saw not one another, neither rose any from his place for three days: but all the children of Israel had light in their dwellings" (Exodus 10:23).

The smiting of the firstborn - By all this time, the LORD won the hearts of the people by His mighty deeds; now they certainly believed. By the time the LORD pronounced His wrathful judgment to smite all the firstborn of the Egyptians, not one Israelite died (Exodus 11:6-7).

In the last plague, the firstborn of Israel could have died, but Israel demonstrated saving faith in that they believed and obeyed the gospel of their Passover, and so, they were **passed over by the wrath of God**. This is a famed *type* of Christ for New Testament believers, and to them it was their gospel. In it, the inspired writers declare, they received Christ "in a figure" (as Abraham, see Heb. 11:19), just like Abraham received Christ in a figure in his own lifetime. The Exodus generation took a lamb without blemish, roasted it in the fire, broke no bones of it, and ate unleavened bread with bitter herbs with their apparel girded. They ate it in haste and were gloriously saved from the destroyer when the LORD saw the covering of the Passover's blood. Not one Israelite went out of his house, defied the ceremony, and was slain by the destroyer. All of Israel stayed and observed the ordinance according to the word and commandment of the LORD through Moses. Firstly, look at their hearts of saving faith at the hearing of the Passover ceremony:

> Exodus 12:23-28: "For the LORD will pass through to smite the Egyptians; and when He seeth the blood upon the lintel, and on the two side posts, the LORD will pass over the door, and will not suffer the destroyer to come in unto your houses to smite you.

And ye shall observe this thing for an ordinance to thee and to thy sons for ever. And it shall come to pass, when ye be come to the land which the LORD will give you, according as He hath promised, that ye shall keep this service. And it shall come to pass, when your children shall say unto you, What mean ye by this service? That ye shall say, It is the sacrifice of the LORD'S passover, Who passed over the houses of the children of Israel in Egypt, when He smote the Egyptians, and delivered our houses. **And the people bowed the head and worshipped.** And the children of Israel went away, and **did as the LORD had commanded Moses and Aaron, so did they.**"

This ceremony was the first of several experiences which was soon to come upon the Israelites, all of which, according to the New Testament inspired writers, serve as examples of saving experiences by saving faith, administering a carnal and spiritual salvation, even to the degree that they received the pre-incarnate Person of Christ. This means that their freedom from Egyptian bondage was not a mere freedom from physical slavery, but a freedom from the slavery of sin. In the subsequent events after the Passover ceremony, we will see the gospel of an atoning sacrifice, the gospel of the Spirit's baptism, the gospel of the imperishable life of Christ, and the gospel of the unfailing Living Waters of Christ. Furthermore, the Israelites were called a "Church" that was "saved."

The Passover → (The Gospel of Sacrifice)	"Purge out therefore the old leaven, that ye may be a new lump, as ye are unleavened. For even **Christ our passover is sacrificed for us**" (1 Corinthians 5:7).	"**Through faith** He kept the **Passover**, and the sprinkling of blood, lest he that destroyed the firstborn should touch them" (Heb. 11:28).
The Red Sea Crossing → (The Gospel of the Spirit's Baptism)	"Moreover, brethren, I would not that ye should be ignorant, how that all our fathers were under the cloud, and all passed through the sea; And were all **baptized unto Moses** in the cloud and in the sea" (1 Corinthians 10:1-2).	"**By faith** they passed through the Red Sea as by dry land: which the Egyptians assaying to do were drowned" (Heb. 11:29). "Nevertheless He **saved** them for His name's sake, that He might make His mighty power to be known. He rebuked the Red sea also, and it was dried up: so He led them through the depths, as through the wilderness. And He **saved** them from the hand of him that hated them, and redeemed them from the

		hand of the enemy. And the waters covered their enemies: there was not one of them left. **Then believed they His words; they sang His praise**" (Psalm 106:8-12).
The Manna → (The Gospel of the Imperishable Life of Christ)	"And did all eat the same **spiritual meat**;" (1 Corinthians 10:3).	"As it is written, He gave them bread from heaven to eat. Then Jesus said unto them, Verily, verily, I say unto you, Moses gave you not that bread from heaven; but My Father giveth you **the true bread from heaven**. For the bread of God is He which cometh down from heaven, and giveth life unto the world" (John 6:32-33)…"And Jesus said unto them, **I am the bread of life**" (John 6:35). "Thou gavest also **Thy good Spirit** to instruct them, and witheldest not **Thy manna** from their mouth, and gavest them water for their thirst" (Neh. 9:20).
Water From the Rock → (The Gospel of the unfailing, Living Waters of Christ)	"And did all drink the same **Spiritual drink**: for they drank of that **Spiritual Rock** that followed them: and **that Rock was Christ**" (1 Corinthians 10:4). "**Living Water**" – John 4:10 "Jesus answered and said unto her, Whosoever drinketh of this water shall thirst again: But whosoever drinketh of the water that I shall give him shall **never thirst**; but the water that I shall give him shall be **in him a well of water**	"And gavest them bread from heaven for their hunger, and broughtest forth **water for them out of the rock** for their thirst, and promisedst them that they should go in to possess the land which Thou hadst sworn to give them" (Nehemiah 9:15). "And **they thirsted not** when he led them through the deserts: he caused the waters to flow out of the rock for them: he clave the rock also, and the waters gushed out" (Isaiah 48:21). "For My people have

		springing up into **everlasting life**" (John 4:13-14) "I will open rivers in high places, and fountains in the midst of the valleys: **I will make the wilderness a pool of water, and the dry land springs of water**" (Isaiah 41:18). "He that believeth on Me, as the scripture hath said, out of his belly shall flow **rivers of living water**" (John 7:38).	committed two evils; they have forsaken Me **the fountain of living waters,** and hewed them out cisterns, broken cisterns, that can hold no water" (Jeremiah 2:13). "And He said unto me, It is done. I am Alpha and Omega, the beginning and the end. I will give unto him that is **athirst** of the **fountain of the water of life freely**" (Revelation 21:6). Psalms 78:15-16, 105:41, 107:35, Exodus 17:6, Deut. 8:15
They Were A Church →		"This is he, that was in **the Church in the wilderness** with the angel which spake to him in the mount Sina, and with our fathers: who received **the lively oracles** to give unto us" (Acts 7:38). "Moses brought forth the people out of the camp **to meet with God**; and they stood at the nether part of the Mount" (Exodus 19:17). "And I will take you to Me **for a people, and I will be to you a God**: and ye shall know that I am the LORD your God, which bringeth you out from under the burdens of the Egyptians. And I will bring you in unto the land, concerning the which I did swear to give it to Abraham, to Isaac, and to Jacob; and I will give it you for an heritage: I am the LORD" (Exodus 6:7-8).	"Ye have seen what I did unto the Egyptians, and how I bare you on eagles' wings, and brought you unto Myself. Now therefore, if ye will obey My voice indeed, and keep My covenant, then ye shall be a **peculiar treasure** unto Me above all people: for all the earth is Mine…" (Exodus 19:4-5). "But ye are a chosen generation, a royal priesthood, an holy nation, a **peculiar people**; that ye should shew forth the praises of Him Who hath called you out of darkness into His marvellous light:" (1 Peter 2:9). "That at that time ye were without Christ, being aliens from the commonwealth of Israel, and strangers from the covenants of promise, having no hope, and without God in the world: But now in Christ Jesus ye who sometimes were far off are made nigh by the blood of Christ"

		(Ephesians 2:12-13).
They Were SAVED! →	"I will therefore put you in remembrance, though ye once knew this, how that the Lord, having **saved** the people out of the land of Egypt, afterward destroyed them that believed not" (Jude 1:5).	"He **SAVED** them" – Ps. 106:8 "He **SAVED** them" – Ps. 106:10 "Then **believed** they His words" – Ps. 106:12
They Had the SPIRIT! → **They Had CHRIST!** →	"the same **Spiritual meat**" – 1 Cor. 10:3 "**I am the Bread of Life**" – John 6:35 "the same **Spiritual drink**" – 1 Cor. 10:4 "that **Spiritual Rock**" – 1 Cor. 10:4 "**that Rock was Christ**" – 1 Cor. 10:4 "Neither let us **tempt Christ as some of them tempted**" – 1 Cor. 10:9 "**the Spirit of Christ which was in them**" – 1 Pet. 1:11 "**received Him in a figure**" – Heb. 11:19	"Searching what, or what manner of time **the Spirit of Christ which was in them** did signify, when it testified beforehand the sufferings of Christ, and the glory that should follow" (1 Peter 1:11). "And **I will walk among you, and will be your God, and ye shall be My people**" (Leviticus 26:12). "For the LORD thy God **walketh in the midst…**" (Deut. 23:14). "And what agreement hath the temple of God with idols? for ye are the temple of the living God; as God hath said, **I will dwell in them, and walk in them; and I will be their God, and they shall be My people**" (2 Corinthians 6:16).

Jesus Christ is called "our Passover" that is "sacrificed for us," thus herein the Israelites "received Him in a figure" (1 Cor. 5:7, Heb. 11:19). Without faith they could not have kept this Passover! As it is written, "**Through faith** He **kept the Passover**, and the sprinkling of blood, lest He that destroyed the firstborn should touch them" (Heb. 11:28). After receiving the sacrifice of Christ, in a figure, they were baptized by water when they were, "under the cloud, and all passed through the Sea" (1 Cor. 10:1), but this was NOT water ONLY! 1 Corinthians 10 affirms this as a **Spiritual** experience, otherwise it would not have been called a **baptism** – "**baptized** unto Moses" (1 Cor. 10:2). Baptism is a word which describes *a spiritual experience* *of salvation*, like as it is written in Romans 6:3-4 – "Know ye not, that so many of us as were **baptized** into Jesus Christ were **baptized** into His death? Therefore we are buried with Him by **baptism into death**: that like as Christ was raised up from the dead by the glory of the Father, even so we also should walk in newness of life" (Romans 6:3-4). This baptism is Spiritual and not only carnal, exactly as the Manna, or "meat," is called "Spiritual meat" (1 Cor. 10:3), just as the "drink" is called a "Spiritual drink" (1 Cor. 10:4), just as the "rock" was called a "Spiritual Rock," which "was Christ" (1 Cor. 10:4). In the crossing of the Red Sea it is, without contest, an act which required *saving faith*, an act which was made possible by *saving faith*, faith that was worthy enough to make it into the Hall of Faith – "**By faith** they passed through the Red Sea as by dry land: which the Egyptians assaying to do were drowned." The *faithless* Egyptians were drowned, but the *faith-filled* Israelites "were all **baptized** unto Moses in the cloud and in the Sea" (1 Cor. 10:2)! Praise God! After the Passover and Red Sea experience, Israel was promise laden and promise confirmed, passed over, blood covered, baptized, sanctified, and gospel freed!

By sin-remitting, sacrificial blood they were atoned, then they were baptized, thus Israel was now a "saved" (Jude 5, Ps. 106:8-12) people who were now called "the Church in the wilderness" (Acts 7:38). Did you know the scripture identifies these men as "**the Church**"? At Sinai they received "the lively oracles" of God (Acts 7:38), and this was a possession obtained only by God's holy people (Eph. 2:12-13). They were called out of Egypt by the power of God, and God says, see "what I did unto the Egyptians," "how I bare you on eagles' wings, and brought you unto Myself," therefore it is evident that this gathering was indeed a holy convocation (Ex. 19:4-5)! Gathering together before God as saved men and women, Israel became *the people of God* brought *nigh* to God. All others were, therefore, "far off" as "aliens from the commonwealth of Israel, and strangers from the Covenants of promise, having no hope, and without God in the world" (Eph. 2:12-13). Israel became God's "**peculiar** treasure" (Ex. 19:5), even as we understand NT, spiritual Israelites to be, as the Holy Ghost signifies, "a **peculiar** people" (1 Pet. 2:9, Tit. 2:14).

The Israelites were delivered and "did according to the word of Moses," "and the children of Israel journeyed from Rameses to Succoth, about six hundred thousand on foot that were men, beside the children" (Exodus 12:35, 37). This is the promised generation who were delivered from slavery that they might inhabit the Promised Land, thus God declares His express intention in saving them – UNDER BINDING OATH – "And I will take you to Me for **a people**, and I will be to you **a God**: and ye shall know that I am the LORD your God, which bringeth you out from under the burdens of the Egyptians. **And I will bring you in unto the land, concerning the which I did <u>swear</u> to give it to Abraham, to Isaac, and to Jacob; and I will give it you for an heritage: I am the LORD**" (Exodus 6:7-8). Can a people so mightily saved, who were blood-covered and baptized by so great a power of God, can they fall from their gospel of grace?

90

NT writers interpreted this generation as comparable, relatable, exemplary, and parallel to God's relationship to saved individuals in the New Covenant. They command us to look at them and learn from their salvation, but lo, we are directed to take warning by beholding, not just their beginning, but the final fate that they suffered! These applications are carefully detailed in 1 Corinthians 10:1-12. Please read the entire passage before we continue:

> "Moreover, brethren, I would not that ye should be ignorant, how that all our fathers were under the cloud, and all passed through the sea; and were all baptized unto Moses in the cloud and in the sea; and did all eat the same spiritual meat; and did all drink the same spiritual drink: for they drank of that spiritual Rock that followed them: and that Rock was Christ. But with many of them God was not well pleased: for they were overthrown in the wilderness. Now these things were our examples, to the intent we should not lust after evil things, as they also lusted. Neither be ye idolaters, as were some of them; as it is written, The people sat down to eat and drink, and rose up to play. Neither let us commit fornication, as some of them committed, and fell in one day three and twenty thousand. Neither let us tempt Christ, as some of them also tempted, and were destroyed of serpents. Neither murmur ye, as some of them also murmured, and were destroyed of the destroyer. Now all these things happened unto them for ensamples: and they are written for our admonition, upon whom the ends of the world are come. Wherefore let him that thinketh he standeth take heed lest he fall. There hath no temptation taken you but such as is common to man: but God is faithful, Who will not suffer you to be tempted above that ye are able; but will with the temptation also make a way to escape, that ye may be able to bear it" (1 Corinthians 10:1-13).

One must acknowledge, like Paul, that Israel was saved by the Passover and Red Sea Baptism, but look closer still. Israel was presently and progressively being saved by the Manna and the Water from the Rock, as Paul cites, and these things were not only CARNAL experiences. These were not merely carnal experiences of salvation, as noted before! It was said of the food they did eat in the wilderness (speaking of manna), that they "did all eat the same **spiritual meat**" (1 Cor. 10:3). Notice the words "spiritual meat" – this means that it was not just meat. Christ interprets the Manna to be a type of **spiritually** living by God; thus, He calls Himself the NT Manna that was sent by the Father from heaven to give life to the world – "As it is written, He gave them bread from heaven to eat. Then Jesus said unto them, Verily, verily, I say unto you, Moses gave you not that bread from heaven; but My Father giveth you **the true bread from heaven**. For the bread of God is He which cometh down from heaven, and giveth life unto the world" (John 6:32-33)…"And Jesus said unto them, **I am the bread of life**" (John 6:35). Seeing that Jesus is the bread from heaven, by interpretation this means that He is the source of spiritual life that is sent from heaven, and this also signifies that what He spoke on earth was life-giving to those who heard Him through faith. His words – take note – "they are Spirit, and they are Life" (John 6:63). Therefore, in like manner it was said of the Manna in the wilderness. It was *spiritually life-giving*, and when they received it by faith, God gave to them the Spirit of God in gospel virtue. As it is written again, "Thou gavest also **Thy good Spirit** to instruct them, and withheldest not **Thy manna** from their mouth, and gavest them water for their thirst" (Neh. 9:20). The disobedience of the Israelites in the OT inclines men to fancy that their experience of saving grace was merely carnal shadows which were absent of spiritual powers, spiritual life, and nearness to God – but this is not so. It was not a carnal salvation!

In like manner as the Manna, Christ was being revealed and received when God "turned the Rock into a standing water, the flint into a fountain of waters" (Psalm 114:8). The Israelites were *presently* and *progressively* persevering in salvation when they "did all drink the same **spiritual drink**: for they drank of that **spiritual Rock** that followed them: and **that Rock was Christ**" (1 Cor. 10:4). The Rock was smitten and poured forth, and the water is called a "spiritual drink." This means that it is a Spiritual type of Christ! This is why Jesus calls Himself, "Living Waters" (John 4:10). He is the waters that never fail, that are "springing up into everlasting life" (John 4:13-14, Jer. 2:13). If saving waters of a Spiritual salvation are waters that never fail, then God's people that are saved do *never thirst* (John 4:13, Neh. 9:15, Isa. 48:21), hence the appeal – "I will give unto him that is **athirst** of **the Fountain of the Water of Life freely**" (Rev. 21:6). This was prophesied before as a type of Christ in the major prophets (Isa. 48:18), and it came to pass when Jesus Christ came in the 1st century, and also, when He abideth on earth within Christian men, as Christ said – "He that believeth on Me, <u>as the scripture hath said</u>, out of his belly shall flow **rivers of living water**" (John 7:38). In this way Jesus Christ was the opening of rivers, the fountain in the valleys, the pool of water in the wilderness, and the springs of water in dry land, as it is written – "I will open rivers in high places, and fountains in the midst of the valleys: **I will make the wilderness a pool of water, and the dry land springs of water**" (Isaiah 41:18). Not only is the water from the rock a "spiritual drink," but the rock itself is "Christ!" Without contest, these men were spiritual men; hence they were savingly connected to Jesus Christ!

My dear reader, all of these things teach us that these individuals were regenerated, that they had the Spirit of God within them - in type, by law, spiritually speaking, and in reality, as it is written – it was "the Spirit of Christ which was in them" (1 Peter 1:11)! This is why 2 Corinthians 6:16 quotes the NT reality of God's indwelling presence as an OT reality – "…**as God hath said**, I will dwell in them, and walk in them; and I will be their God, and they shall be My people" (2 Cor. 6:16, Lev. 26:12, Deut. 23:14).

Israel believed the gospel at the Passover and the Red Sea crossing, and then they continued to believe the gospel at the Manna and the smitten Rock of life giving waters. However, in following Paul's burden in 1 Corinthians 10:1-4, we can see that he argues that Israel was SAVED, and yet, this is not the only thing Paul wants us to see. Read onward and take note of 1 Corinthians 10:5-12. This generation which did abound in spiritual salvation, whose faith was built upon 7 gospel messages giving an assurance to inherit the promised land, whose faith was wrought through the manifold mercy of seven sanctifying miracles in the land of Egypt – most of them did not ***continue in faith***. They, as Paul stated, "were overthrown in the wilderness" (1 Cor. 10:5), even though many continued for a long while in the steadfastness of faith. Paul is saying that they have become "our examples", of what? An example for "**our**" admonition, he says, meaning they are examples for us who are SAVED, and why (1 Cor. 10:11)? This is because these Israelites were saved, like us, but then they provoked God by wicked behavior…so much so that they were smitten down in wrath and "overthrown in the wilderness" (1 Cor. 10:5), and Paul specifically cites four ways in which the wrath of God overthrew them as examples for us, so that NT Christians do not fall into the same fate (1 Cor. 10:7, 8, 9, 10). Jude had the very same burden when he wrote to the saints. Does this sound familiar? "I will therefore put you in remembrance, though ye once knew this, how that the Lord, having **saved** the people out of the land of Egypt, afterward **destroyed them that believed not**" (Jude 1:5). Because this generation fell from gospel-grace unto their final reprobation, which we shall soon detail, they have become an example that we, as saved men and women like them, "should not lust after evil things, as they also lusted" (1 Cor. 10:6). 1 Corinthians 10 is a clear explanation of how these OT experiences are repeatable, that they were saved and then damned, and Paul thrusts the final fate of Israel's damnation right before the eyes of the NT Israelites so that they might take heed to themselves, lest they, in the same manner as Israel, do also "fall" (1 Cor. 10:12). "Wherefore let him that thinketh he standeth **take heed lest he fall**" (1 Cor. 10:12).

The New Testament writers do seek to put us in remembrance of the sure damnation we will undergo if we begin to be unbelieving, **though we do now, at present, savingly believe**. Look closely and you can see how this is what Jude is warning of, when he said – "I will therefore put you in remembrance, though ye once knew this, how that the Lord, having **saved** the people out of the land of Egypt, afterward **destroyed them that believed not**" (Jude 5). As Jude says, "I will therefore put you in remembrance, though ye once knew this" (Jude 5), Paul first said, "brethren, I would not that ye should be ignorant" (1 Cor. 10:1). Can you see how they are writing the very same burden? Read both chapters and you will see – it is the same message! Therefore we should "take heed" to ourselves as "brethren" (Heb. 3:12), as "holy brethren" who are "partakers of the heavenly calling", who have become the "house" of Christ on earth (Heb. 3:12, 1, 6)! Take heed for what? "Take heed, brethren, lest there be in any of you **an evil heart of unbelief**, in **departing from the living God**. But exhort one another daily, while it is called To day; lest any of you be hardened through the deceitfulness of sin. For we are made partakers of Christ, **if we hold the beginning of our confidence stedfast unto the end**" (Heb. 3:12-14). Again in Hebrews, the writer is writing about the same exodus generation who finally suffered the loss of their salvation.

Thus far the same burden and interpretation has been written in 1 Corinthians 10, Jude 5, and now Hebrews 3-4. See, this generation (namely approx. 600,000 men of war) lost their salvation, all except two men, though they partook of all the promises and oaths of the Covenant (Ex. 2:24, 3:8, 17, 12:25, 13:5, 11), wherein Christ was *spiritually* ministered unto them. They did not continue to believe, did not continue to receive Christ in figures, and consequentially, sinful works were wrought by the unbelief in their hearts. These spouts of rebellion did provoke God many times, until eventually, the Israelites provoked God to the point of no return – reprobation. They heard the gospel at the Passover, at the Red Sea, when the Manna fell, at Sinai, at the Rock of Waters, and finally, they heard the gospel the last time – but this time they denied it! What am I talking about? It was written that "**the gospel**" was "preached" "unto them: but the word preached did not profit them, not being mixed with faith in them that heard it" (Heb. 4:2). Do you wonder when this is? What gospel? We know that they received the gospel of the Passover, the Red Sea, the Manna, and the Rock, which were all types of Christ, but this "gospel" is found cited in Hebrews 4:2, and it was the last figure of Christ presented to them before their reprobation. Tragically, instead of spiritual life, their end was spiritual death, for, this time they denied the gospel instead of believing it.

This day is called "the day of temptation" or "the provocation" (Heb. 3:8). This is taught and applied to be **a possibility for a NT saint** in Hebrews chapters 3-4. Psalm 95 is quoted in verses 7-11 of Hebrews chapter 3:7-11. Hebrews 4 explains how they (the Exodus generation) came short of the promise (the gospel), and the NT Christians are warned likewise – "Let us therefore fear, lest, **a promise** being left us of entering into His **rest**, any of you should seem to **come short of it**" (Heb. 4:1). The warning is that, in like manner as Israel, we can come short of the promise of our salvation – "departing from the Living God" (Heb. 3:12, 4:1). NOTE: you cannot depart from what you have never been brought into, or, you cannot woefully leave what you have never savingly received, or, you cannot fall from what you have never arisen into, namely the salvation in God. The **rest** in Hebrews 4:1 is Israel's *typical* heaven (typically speaking), however the immediate, physical context of their rest was the literal inheritance of the Promised Land. Even so, our Promised Land (or rest) is Heaven, and according to Hebrews 4 we need to strive for it, lest we fall from it, like they did! As the OT Church was presently and progressively partaking of a Christ-empowering gospel, we too must be tried and found steadfast in our present progressive participation in Christ. Christ was then and is now! We too must persevere and not come short of a rest, promise, Covenant, and gospel that will consummate in our inheriting of the Kingdom of God – thus the rest is something to "labour" for, not rest for, nor should we rest in it as if we possess heaven now! "Let us labor therefore to enter into that rest, lest any man fall after the same example of unbelief" (Heb. 4:11). This rest is something we receive in the future, even though now, in another sense, we have spiritual rest in Christ from our own works. Nevertheless, we must labour because we must walk in His works (Heb. 4:1, 9, 11) –

RESTING IS WORKING. For NT Christians, the rest in Hebrews 4 is something we do not presently possess, a rest we do not rest in now, but rather, a rest we must labor for now so as to obtain it later, or, rest in it later. We, like the Israelites, are looking forward to a rest, an inheritance, and the consummating gospel in the future, but they fell short of theirs.

"For the upright shall dwell in the land, and the **perfect** shall remain in it" – Prov. 2:21

The frightening reality is that Israel was a partaker of the gospel and promises of God, the spiritual manifestations of Christ, the Covenant of Abraham, a salvation based upon the faithfulness of God, the spoken word of God, the promise of God, and the oaths of God, yet Hebrews 4:1 warns of *coming short of the promises* by unbelief! Numbers 14 gives an account of this day when they came short of and lost their salvation. God does not deny that He did promise them salvation. He says to them, "ye shall know My **breach of promise**" (Num. 14:34)! The word breach means break, and reader, we will see this more as we continue to study. God does this in many ways, many times – "breach for breach" (Lev. 24:20) and "break" for "break" (Ezek. 16:59, 17:18-19). Justly, unashamedly, and righteously, God says, "Doubtless ye shall not come into the land, concerning which **I sware to make you dwell therein**, save Caleb the son of Jephunneh, and Joshua the son of Nun" (Num. 14:30). My reader, Hebrews 4:1 should utterly stagger you! It is the New Testament application of what God called in the Old Testament – "**My BREACH OF PROMISE**" (Num. 14:34)! Do you remember all the promises and oaths of God that were upon this generation, confirming it, that they were supposed to inherit and take the Promised Land!? But God rose up their children in their stead, and this, my reader, is breaking what was promised before! Do you remember it? →

Motivation and Intent for Salvation	"God remembered **His Covenant with Abraham**, with Isaac, and with Jacob" – Exodus 2:24.
Salvation as a work of God based upon the faithfulness of God	"I am come down to deliver," "to bring them up out of that land," "unto the place" (the Promised Land) – Exodus 3:8
The spoken word of God	"And **I have said**, I will bring you up out of the affliction of Egypt unto the land of the Canaanites, and the Hittites, and the Amorites, and the Perizzites, and the Hivites, and the Jebusites, unto a land flowing with milk and honey." (Exodus 3:17)
The Promise of God	"And it shall come to pass, when ye be come to the land which the LORD will give you, according **as He hath**

	promised, that ye shall keep this service." (Exodus 12:25)
The Oath to their fathers	"And it shall be when the LORD shall bring thee into the land of the Canaanites, and the Hittites, and the Amorites, and the Hivites, and the Jebusites, **which He sware unto thy fathers** to give thee, a land flowing with milk and honey, that thou shalt keep this service in this month." (Exodus 13:5)
The Oath to the present Exodus generation	"And it shall be when the LORD shall bring thee into the land of the Canaanites, **as he sware unto thee** and **to thy fathers**, and shall give it thee," (Exodus 13:11)

The whole generation was killed off in the wilderness, even 600,000 men of war who refused to believe for the salvation that had already been given to them (Deut. 1:20-21). This was a generation whose number was supposed to be as the stars in number when they inherited the Promised Land, but this generation was reduced to two men of war! Even so, God decides to raise up their children in their stead. They refused to take the Promised Land as a gift of grace, and God condemned them to hell. He reprobated them without any possibility of repentance even though they sought after it with tears (Deut. 1:41-46 like as Heb. 12:17). My reader, I repeat, we know that they lost their salvation because they did once partake of Christ and the gospel (1 Cor. 10:1-4, etc.), and then they forsook the gospel which was preached to them while they stood on the edge of Heaven (Heb. 3:16-4:1)! On the edge of final perseverance their faith failed! HOW TERRFIYING! Verily, even the writer of Hebrews was AFRAID, therefore feelingly, he said – "LET US THEREFORE FEAR" (Heb. 4:1)! What about you?

For the Promised Land to be inherited by Israel, each man had to "cease from his own works" and walk in the faith and works of God, wherein He, as He said to them, would fight for them – even as He did fight for them in Egypt when He secured for them their exodus. With gospel-power, again, God said – "The LORD your God which goeth before you, He shall fight for you, according to all that He did for you in Egypt before your eyes" (Deut. 1:30). The people needed "**diligence** to the full assurance of hope **unto the end**: that ye be not **slothful**, but followers of them who through faith and patience **inherit the promises**" (Heb. 6:11-12), but they didn't have it! We must live by "faith and patience" also, which is active in "diligence" and "labour" (Heb. 4:11), and we must avoid slothfulness and lukewarmness (Heb. 6:11-12, Rev. 3:16). These deeds of faith do mandate an inheritance of the promises of God if we keep them **unto the end**, otherwise, like the Israelites, we will come short of them (Heb. 4:1). "Let us therefore fear, lest a promise being left us of entering into His rest, any of you should seem to come short of it" (Heb. 4:1).

We are warned of an "evil heart of unbelief" that would cause us to depart "from the living God," and we cannot depart from God if we were never with Him (Heb. 3:12). This is an example and charge to NT, regenerate Christians who are presently "partakers of Christ," that they do not undergo their own day of provocation until they are, like the Israelites, "cast away" (1 Cor. 9:27) or made "reprobates" (2 Cor. 13:5). When a saved man is "cast away" (1 Cor. 9:27), or in other words reprobated, he does fall away and lose his salvation – thus at this point repentance becomes an impossibility. This impossibility for repentance is a theme repeatedly pressed upon the recipients of the letter to the Hebrews, and it was a reality that this reprobated generation experienced in Deuteronomy 1:41-45. God commanded Israel to take the Promised Land – their gospel – but they refused, and right when the word of their reprobation was spoken they tried to repent…but it was too late.

> "Then ye answered and said unto me, We have sinned against the LORD, we will go up and fight, according to all that the LORD our God commanded us. And when ye had girded on every man his weapons of war, ye were ready to go up into the hill. And the LORD said unto me, Say unto them, Go not up, neither fight; for I am not among you; lest ye be smitten before your enemies. So I spake unto you; and ye would not hear, but rebelled against the commandment of the LORD, and went presumptuously up into the hill. And the Amorites, which dwelt in that mountain, came out against you, and chased you, as bees do, and destroyed you in Seir, even unto Hormah. And ye returned and wept before the LORD; but the LORD would not hearken to your voice, nor give ear unto you" (Deuteronomy 1:41-45).

They sought repentance "carefully with tears" (Heb. 12:17), and weeping (Deut. 1:45), "but the LORD would not hearken." An impossibility to repent is warned to NT Christians in Hebrews 6:6, 10:26-29, 12:15-17. In like manner, there is a repeated warning to the NT saints, a warning of sure damnation, if, like Israel, they do continue to disobey the voice of God. This would mean that they are willfully sinning (Heb. 2:1-4, 3:7-11, 4:7, 10:26, 12:25). Surrounding these passages is a glorious description of the Covenant of Christ elevated above the Covenant of Moses (Heb. 1, 2:5-18, 5:1-10, 7:1-10:18) – but NOTE – the superiority of the New Covenant is NOT the impossibility of wrath for the Church, but on the contrary, a MORE SURE and SEVERE wrath to backslidden saints. Hebrews is an argument that shows the Covenant of Christ to be a greater salvation, and if neglected by those who are presently saved, it is a greater, more severe, and surer condemnation (greater than it was for those who were disobedient to the Covenant made through Moses). To trace and prove this argument (inspired and applied by the Holy Ghost in Hebrews), I now turn.

Tracing Hebrews

❖ *Are the warnings in the book of Hebrews directed toward professed
believers who are actually unregenerate unbelievers that are
mingled in the midst of the Church congregation? Or, are the
warnings written toward true, regenerate believers?*

The book of Hebrews opens up by addressing the audience to be those
whom, by profession and in reality (the author including himself), have had the
purging work of salvation (2 Peter 1:9) through the blood of Christ, Who, "by
Himself purged our sins" (Heb. 1:3). The OT was delivered, "by the disposition of
angels" (Acts 7:53, Gal. 3:19), therefore the first chapter compares the excellence and
majesty of angels with that of Jesus Christ. The Law was given by "the angel which
spake" (Acts 7:38), but God "hath in these last days spoken unto us by His Son,
Whom He hath appointed heir of all things, by Whom also He made the worlds"
(Heb. 1:2). At the outset of the 2nd chapter of Hebrews, the author introduces the first
of many warnings of damnation which appear throughout the book of Hebrews.

> "Therefore we ought to give the more earnest heed to the things
> which we have heard, lest at any time we should let them slip.
> For if the word spoken by angels was stedfast, and every
> transgression and disobedience received a just recompence of
> reward; **How shall we escape**, if we neglect so great salvation;
> which at the first began to be spoken by the Lord, and was
> confirmed unto us by them that heard Him; God also bearing
> them witness, both with signs and wonders, and with divers
> miracles, and gifts of the Holy Ghost, according to His own
> will?" (Hebrews 2:1-4)

Seeing that Christ is so much greater than angels (Heb. 1), and "the word
spoken by angels was stedfast, and every transgression and disobedience received a
just recompence of reward" (Heb. 2:2), how much more steadfast is the word of One
greater than angels – the Son of God Himself? The superiority of Christ over the
angels is not revealed to mean that His grace disallows the consequence of wrath for
the fallen, but rather, a greater wrath for the fallen. How much greater and surer is the
"just recompence" of those who are in "disobedience" to the voice of the Son of God,
Whose voice, not the angels, did usher in the New Covenant? Christ, from "the
bosom of the Father" (Jn. 1:18), Who alone is sufficient to declare, express, and show
forth the image, declaration, and Person of the Father – He hath spoken the New
Covenant as One that "speaketh from heaven" (Heb. 12:25). The author argues that
we must be sure of Christ's greatness, specifically more so than the greatness of
angels, to what end? Christ's word is more severe in its recompense of just wrath
when it is disobeyed, beyond what the angel's word was. How much more promising

98

is wrath to those who hear the word of Christ, and then neglect it (though they were saved), so as to "hear His voice" "today" and yet they "harden" their "hearts" (Heb. 4:7, 3:15)?! The author desires to show the surety of damnation, the inability to "escape" (Heb. 2:3, 12:25) damnation, if indeed, those who are "purged" and saved do "neglect" (Heb. 2:3) or "refuse" (Heb. 12:25) to continue in the Covenant of grace, or in other words, "draw back" from faith (Heb. 10:38). As it was with the OT, even so, much more now, "Happy is the man that feareth alway: but he that hardeneth his heart shall fall into mischief" (Prov. 28:14). This is the first warning of the book of Hebrews (Heb. 2:1-4), and, it is parallel to the last (Heb. 12:25-29). From chapter 2 through 12, the book of Hebrews writes an argument to prove the utter inability to escape eternal damnation if, when you are presently saved, you do lose faith. This is to no wonder, for, we are "kept by the power of God through faith unto **salvation** ready to be revealed in the last time" (1 Peter 1:5).

The next warning is in chapters 3-4. The audience of this severe warning are those who are called, "**holy brethren**, partakers of the heavenly calling" (Heb. 3:1), who are also called the house of Christ on earth (Heb. 3:6); "made partakers of Christ" (Heb. 3:14). It cannot be argued that this warning is for counterfeit, professors of the faith (or false believers), for then they would be men who claim to believe but are not really **holy**. The text says that it is written to a people who are called "holy brethren" (Heb. 3:1). I repeat, this is not a crowd or congregation of mingled unbelievers and believers that the author is writing to; THEY ARE CALLED "holy brethren." Hebrews 3-4, as formerly addressed in detail, preaches the fear of losing salvation by referencing the OT breach of promise (Num. 14:34) as a NT reality (Heb. 4:1), applying it to NT Christians in the verse – "Let us therefore fear, lest, a **promise** being left us of entering into His rest, **any of you should seem to come short of it**." Unbelief is manifest through a hardened heart (Heb. 3:13, 15, 4:7). Hardness is manifest in disobedience of the heavenly voice that a Christian does hear, therefore – "To day, after so long a time; as it is said, To day **if ye will hear His voice, harden not your hearts**" (Heb. 4:7, 3:15). If one fears coming short of the promise (through unbelief, Heb. 4:1), he is then exhorted to hold fast and maintain his faith by seeing the great grace of Jesus (Heb. 4:14-16). This grace is help to the hardened. It is ever-accessible at the "throne of grace", so that, if a man has faith, then he can draw near to it without the fear of rejection (or boldly, see Heb. 4:16). Therefore if a man fears losing his salvation, let him fearlessly, or "boldly" (Heb. 4:16), come to the throne of grace to receive power to obey, softness of heart, and the ability to fulfill the mandate – "let us labour therefore" (Heb. 4:11). There is sufficient "help" to all our "needs" (Heb. 4:15-16) of heart change, right there, at the throne of grace, but there is no hope for a man who departs from grace, becomes fearless in disobedience, in continuance, until the day of his own provocation. Indeed, we have a need to obey His voice! Therefore regenerate reader, look to the throne of GRACE! The throne – the place of power, authority, rule, victory, and righteousness in God – has become for us a place where we can fearlessly and confidently draw near for helping power to obey, because, it has become a Throne of GRACE by the blood of Jesus. It is a Throne of unmerited favor and undeserved acceptance – God's pity for personal power! We are undeservedly accepted in unmerited favor, that we might serve and obey the active voice of God – herein is the end of saving faith!

The biblical life of saving faith does "labour" (Heb. 4:11) with "diligence" (Heb. 6:11, 11:6, 12:2, 15, 2 Peter 1:5, 10), therefore it is not "slothful" but steadfast (or patient, see Heb. 6:12). Faith fears a laborless life! The unction teaches us that faith without works would accuse the grace of God to be vain (1 Cor. 15:10, Matt. 25:26, 1 John 2:27). The terrifying fear of God did drive Paul to "labour" that he might "be accepted" of Christ at His "Judgment Seat" (2 Cor. 5:9-11). His faith gave him a confident awareness that he will, one day, appear before the Judgment Seat of Christ. This is what he meant in 2 Cor. 5:8 when he said that he is "confident" he will be "present with the Lord." Because Paul will be present with the Lord **at the "Judgment Seat"** (2 Cor. 5:10), he is driven to "labour," that whether on earth or in heaven, or as he phrased it, "that whether present or absent **we may be accepted of Him.** For we must all appear before the Judgment Seat of Christ; that every one may receive the things done in his body according to that he hath done, whether it be good or bad" (2 Cor. 5:9-10). Paul and the apostles knew this "terror of the Lord" personally. They taught this terror of the Lord corporately, like as Peter said - "If ye call on the Father, Who without respect of persons judgeth according to every man's work, pass the time of your sojourning here in fear" (1 Peter 1:17). Fatherhood and adoption does not mean we are to behave in fearlessness before God, as many incorrectly argue; this is a misinterpretation of Romans 8:15 (Furthermore, for an answer to the passage, "perfect love casts out fear", see the section entitled, "GOD IS LOVE"). "Let us therefore fear," Hebrews 4:1 commands, that we may fearlessly stay near God *in obedience*! Herein is the goal of all fear taught in Hebrews 4:1-16 – Faith fights to "lay hold on eternal life," not rewards, to "work out salvation," not rewards, therefore there is a "fear and trembling" (1 Tim. 6:12, Php. 2:12) in this work! The "acceptable" (Heb. 12:28-29) fear due unto His holiness is that He "is able" (Matt. 10:28) to cast us into hell, therefore let us "labor" (Heb. 4:11, 2 Cor. 5:9-10) and "work" (Php. 2:12, Jas. 2:21-24) by reigning grace "through righteousness" (Rom. 5:21), so that He Who "is able to destroy both soul and body in hell" does not destroy us (Matt. 10:28). Moving into the next warning, read Hebrews 5:11-6:1…

> "Of Whom we have many things to say, and hard to be uttered, seeing ye are dull of hearing. For when for the time ye ought to be teachers, ye have need that one teach you again which be the first principles of the oracles of God; and are become such as have need of milk, and not of strong meat. For every one that useth milk is unskilful in the word of righteousness: for he is a babe. But strong meat belongeth to them that are of full age, even those who by reason of use have their senses exercised to discern both good and evil. Therefore leaving the principles of the doctrine of Christ, let us go on unto perfection; not laying again the foundation of repentance from dead works, and of faith toward God" (Hebrews 5:11-6:1)

The next warning begins in Hebrews 5:11-12, and here we can see a clear address of the intended audience. Again, it is not counterfeit believers, but rather, "a babe," "milk"-drinking, "dull of hearing" (Heb. 5:11-12), "carnal" Christian who is called a "babe **in Christ**," yet most argue that such persons written to are outside of Christ (1 Cor. 3:1-3). These individuals are babes because they have fallen from the state of "perfection." This is referenced in Hebrews 6:1 and in 1 Corinthians 2:6. A babe is one who needs to establish, teach, or receive again "the first principles of the oracles of God", or otherwise called, "doctrine of Christ" (Heb. 5:12, 6:1). The first principles are those doctrines which are inherent in the gospel message. In other words, it is those things a man must receive, understand, retain, and believe **to be saved** – for it is "**repentance** from dead works" and "**faith** toward God" (Heb. 6:1). This is milk, thus Paul only preaches "Jesus Christ, and Him crucified" among them that are <u>not perfect</u>, because the gospel is the first principles. He preaches "wisdom" or "meat" "among them that are **perfect**" (1 Cor. 2:6, 3:1-2). This fallen state of the regenerate believer is a state that, in practice and conversation, he does walk after the flesh and not the spirit, therefore they are called "carnal" men who "walk as men" (1 Cor. 3:3-4), instead of "as Christ" (Php. 1:21, Col. 2:6) or "in the Spirit" (Gal. 5:16). Remember how it was said, "be not deceived" (1 Cor. 6:9, Eph. 5:6, Gal. 6:7), "there is therefore now no condemnation to them which are in Christ Jesus, **who walk not after the flesh, but after the Spirit**" (Rom. 8:1), "for **if ye live after the flesh, ye shall die**" (Rom. 8:13)? Many people quote the promise of Romans 8:1 without the condition (the latter half of the verse), which is, "**who walk not after the flesh, but after the Spirit**" (King James Version), but this half of the verse is taken out of most bibles because of the differing underlying manuscripts. "Nevertheless the foundation of God standeth sure, having this seal, The Lord knoweth them that are His. And, let every one that nameth the name of the Christ depart from iniquity" (2 Tim. 2:19), and those that depart from Him shall die (Heb. 3:12).

> "Therefore leaving the principles of the doctrine of Christ, let us go on unto perfection; not laying again the foundation of repentance from dead works, and of faith toward God, of the doctrine of baptisms, and of laying on of hands, and of resurrection of the dead, and of eternal judgment. And this will we do, if God permit. For it is impossible for those who were once enlightened, and have tasted of the heavenly gift, and were made partakers of the Holy Ghost, and have tasted the good word of God, and the powers of the world to come, if they shall fall away, to renew them again unto repentance; seeing they crucify to themselves the Son of God afresh, and put Him to an open shame" (Hebrews 6:1-6)

In Hebrews 6, the unperfected Christian has an urgent need to renew "faith" and "repentance" (Heb. 6:1) lest his "end is to be burned" (Heb. 6:8). This is a loss of the "assurance of hope unto the end" (Heb. 6:11). Most Calvinists seek to pervert these passages by arguing that the men in description were never saved. They argue that those who were – "once enlightened, and have tasted of the heavenly gift, and were made partakers of the Holy Ghost, and have tasted the good word of God, and the powers of the world to come" – are unbelievers, therefore these experiences are said to be pre-conversion experiences. This cannot be! It is said of these individuals that, after they do "fall away," they are reprobated from God, which means that they are unable to find *the repentance that they once had* – thus it says that it is "impossible...to **renew them again unto repentance**" (Heb. 6:4-6). They did "fall away," it says, meaning they fell away from a previous "repentance" that they did have, therefore in this "fall away" they cannot be renewed **again** to the former repentance which was acceptable to God, that they once had, and only a saved man can have an acceptable repentance in the sight of God. Therefore the experiences written Hebrews 6:4-5 cannot be the pre-conversion grace of God striving with a lost man. The man who was – "once enlightened, and have tasted of the heavenly gift, and were made partakers of the Holy Ghost, and have tasted the good word of God, and the powers of the world to come"– is a saved man, for this is an experience which works within a man an acceptable repentance.

> "For the earth which drinketh in the rain that cometh oft upon it, and bringeth forth herbs meet for them by whom it is dressed, receiveth blessing from God: But that which beareth thorns and briers is rejected, and is nigh unto cursing; whose end is to be burned" (Hebrews 6:7-8)

Furthermore, the experience described in Heb. 6:4-5 is metaphorically described as spiritual rain. Have you ever read of the "former rain" and the "latter rain" (Joel 2:23)? The same rain that Peter says is being poured out upon NT converts? Read Acts 2:16-21. With such an experience as Hebrews 6:4-5, the Christian is in the blessed wealth of life-giving power – UNDER THE RAIN – the very same rain that Joel prophesied would come, that Peter reaffirmed in Acts 2:16-21, and finally, it is spoken of again in Hebrews 6:7 in the same language – "the rain that cometh oft" (Heb. 6:7)! "The rain that cometh oft," IT IS UPON US! Therefore, if there are no "herbs meet" for so great a rain, but rather, there are "thorns and briers," this unrepentant Christian is "rejected" of God and "nigh unto cursing whose end is to be burned" (Heb. 6:8). The author's desire is that they would not be like the cursed field, that they would rather bear fruit by keeping repentance. He pleads with them to be renewed again in repentance, "**if God permit,**" for only He can grant repentance to them (Heb. 6:3, 2 Tim. 2:25). A renewed faith and repentance is the same thing as being renewed again "unto **perfection**" (Heb. 6:1). This renewal would make the Hebrew saints no longer "slothful" (Heb. 6:12) but rather "diligent" (Heb. 6:11), and therefore fruitful (see 2 Peter 1:5-17, Heb. 6:7-8) and obedient, having a justifiable (James 2:21) "full assurance of hope unto the end" (Heb. 6:11), because they are walking in the working of "faith and patience" which does "inherit the promises" (Heb. 6:12). What is the burden of the author? That they would "inherit the promises," like Abraham, who did perfect his faith (James 2:21-22) by obedient works, and thus he was found worthy to obtain the promises (Heb. 6:15). As the Lord hath said, "he that overcometh, and **keepeth My works** <u>unto the end</u>," he it is that will go to heaven. But what can be said of the man who Christ judges, and says, "I have not found **thy works perfect** before God" (Rev. 3:2)? This is sure death (Rev. 3:1), unworthiness (Rev. 3:4), and damnation, because the Lord will "blot out his name out of the book of life" (Rev. 3:5). Moving on to the next warning, read Hebrews 10:19-31...

> "Having therefore, **brethren**, boldness to enter into the holiest by **the blood of Jesus**, By a new and living way, which he hath consecrated for us, through the veil, that is to say, his flesh; And having an high priest over the house of God; Let us draw near with a true heart in full assurance of faith, **having our hearts sprinkled from an evil conscience**, and **our bodies washed with pure water**. Let us hold fast the profession of our faith without wavering; (for He is faithful that promised;) And let us consider one another to provoke unto love and to good works: Not forsaking the assembling of <u>**ourselves**</u> together, as the manner of some is; but exhorting one another: and so much the more, as ye see the day approaching. For if we sin wilfully after that we have received the knowledge of the truth, there remaineth no more sacrifice for sins, But a certain fearful looking for of judgment and fiery indignation, which shall devour the adversaries. He that despised Moses' law died without mercy under two or three witnesses: Of how much sorer punishment, suppose ye, shall he be thought worthy, who hath trodden under foot the Son of God, and **hath counted the blood of the covenant, wherewith he was sanctified**, an unholy thing, and hath done despite unto the Spirit of grace? For we know Him that hath said, Vengeance belongeth unto Me, I will recompense, saith the Lord. And again, The Lord shall judge His people. It is a fearful thing to fall into the hands of the living God" (Hebrews 10:19-31).

The next warning is in Hebrews 10:19-39. The audience in address is the "**brethren**" (Heb. 10:19), for only they would have "boldness to enter into the holiest by **the blood of Jesus**, by a new and living way" (Heb. 10:20). Only by the blood of Jesus Christ are men enabled to "draw near" to God by "faith" – a faith which makes their "hearts **sprinkled** from an evil conscience," a faith which makes their "bodies **washed** with **pure water**" (Heb. 10:22). Can an unbeliever be thus admonished? Do they have a sprinkled heart? Nay! The blood of the New Covenant (Heb. 9:20) that sprinkles (Heb. 9:19), purges (Heb. 9:22), sanctifies (Heb. 10:29), and justifies, is the blood of the Testator Himself (Heb. 10:19): Jesus Christ (Heb. 9:16). The brethren are appealed to on the basis of the Covenant of God's forgiveness (Heb. 10:16-17), wherein God does "remember no more" (Heb. 10:17) the brethren's sin – thus a Christian ought to "hold fast the profession of faith without wavering (for He is

103

faithful that **promised**)" (Heb. 10:23), and he ought to forget about the sins which God has forgotten about!

If these saints <u>do not</u> *judge God to be faithful* (Heb. 11:11), but rather think He is a liar (1 John 5:10), then they will think of themselves to be un-purged, un-sanctified, and un-washed. These same individuals know that they were formerly under the blood, but they have not held fast their first profession of faith. They are wavering...to them the blood of Jesus Christ has become unholy. Therefore it is said of such a man who continues in this, that he has "counted the **blood of the Covenant**, wherewith **he was sanctified, an unholy thing**" (Heb. 10:29). These individuals have been "sanctified" by "the blood of the Covenant" (Heb. 10:29), which is "the blood of Jesus" (Heb. 10:19), THEY ARE NOT UNBELIEVERS! They are regenerate believers who have not held fast the faith which would embolden them to draw near to God, the faith that the blood is holy and able to cleanse from sin!

On "the Day approaching," – Judgment Day – they will undergo the fearful judgment of Hebrews 10:26-27. These individuals were "sprinkled" and "washed" (Heb. 10:22) at salvation, but they failed to continue in this holy way by presently and progressively appropriating the gospel purchase of cleansing. A man must presently and progressively hold confidence in the purging power of the blood to persevere in Christ, so it is said in other terms which refer to gospel purchased power - at regeneration we are crucified and dead (Rom. 6:3-4), yet we must continue to mortify, crucify, and die (Rom. 8:13, Col. 3:5, Gal. 5:24). The Christians were charged, at present, to have their "bodies washed with pure water," and this is a salvific washing by present-tense appropriation, for, "we are kept by the power of God <u>THROUGH FAITH</u>." The beginning must endure to the end, "not by works of righteousness which we have done, but according to His mercy He saved us, by **the washing** of regeneration, and the renewing of the Holy Ghost" (Titus 3:5). The present-tense command to mortify, crucify, and die (Rom. 8:13, Col. 3:5, Gal. 5:24) is just alike to the present-tense command to be washed. It is a work of the Spirit of God, the substance that the OT shadow of washing did declare, as it is written, "And such were some of you: but ye are **washed**, but ye are sanctified, but ye are justified in the name of the Lord Jesus, and by the Spirit of our God" (1 Cor. 6:11).

The audience is those who are of "the house of God" (Heb. 10:21), fit to come into the holy place (Heb. 10:19), thus they must continue to assemble together (including the author), "not forsaking the assembling of **ourselves** together" (Heb. 10:25). Daily exhortation is a secret key for grace so that a man does not "draw back" in faith (Heb. 3:13). Knowing this, the conduct of their assembly is for the grave purpose of <u>maintaining salvation</u> by "**exhorting** one another: and so much the more, **as ye see the day approaching**," when the Judgment of God will be irreversibly given. A true Christian that discontinues his belief that he is "purged" by the blood of Christ (2 Peter 1:9), according to 2 Peter 1:4-11, is unable to walk in the obedience of abounding fruits (2 Peter 1:8), and therefore he is in danger of being "cast forth" from "The Vine" of Christ (John 15:1-7) – consequentially then, he will no longer be a partaker of the "heavenly calling" (Heb. 3:1, 2 Peter 1:10) which came by "election" (2 Peter 1:10) in Christ. Such men are compelled into the bondage of willful sin because they cannot draw near to God! Therefore they will be judged as Hebrews 10:26-27 warns. To "sin willfully after" receiving "the knowledge of the truth," is to "fall" from "repentance" without "renewal again" (Heb. 6:6). The comparative citation of the author is to "Moses' law" (Heb. 10:28). THIS IS VERY IMPORTANT. In this chapter, merciless, eternal death is warned for the NT Christian, just like merciless death is executed upon the OT Jew. What was the crime in Moses' law that would deserve a merciless death?

Hebrews 10:25-29 (NT Law)

Without MERCY → "…exhorting one another: and so much the more, as ye see the Day approaching. For if we sin willfully after that we have received the knowledge of the truth, there remaineth no more sacrifice for sins, but a certain fearful looking for of judgment and fiery indignation, which shall devour the adversaries. He that despised Moses' law **died without mercy** under two or three witnesses: Of how much sorer punishment, suppose ye, shall he be thought worthy who hath trodden under foot the Son of God, and hath counted the blood of the Covenant, wherewith he was sanctified, an unholy thing, and hath done despite unto the Spirit of grace?"

Numbers 15:28, 30-31 (Moses' Law)

With MERCY → "And the priest shall make an atonement for the soul that sinneth ignorantly, when he sinneth by ignorance before the LORD, to make an atonement for him; and it shall be forgiven him"

Without MERCY→ "But the soul that doeth ought presumptuously, whether he be born in the land, or a stranger, the same reproacheth the LORD; and that soul shall be cut off from among his people, because he hath despised the word of the LORD, and hath broken His commandment, that soul shall utterly be cut off; his iniquity shall be upon him"

Hebrews 10:28 references the teaching of the law found in Numbers 15. The 15th chapter of Numbers teaches that a man is worthy to obtain *forgiveness* by *an atoning sacrifice* **if** the sin which was committed was **not** done **willfully** (or presumptuously), but rather it was committed in *ignorance*. Willful or presumptuous sins are said to be (as in Hebrews 10:28) despising the word of God. This man, God said, "hath **despised** the word of the LORD, and hath broken His commandment," and so it is referenced in Hebrews 10:28 that they, "**despised** Moses' law," and finally in Hebrews 10:29, that they have done "**despite** unto the spirit of grace." Do you see how "**despised**," "**despised**," and "**despite**" are in direct parallel? He that "sinneth by ignorance" can have "atonement" and be "forgiven" (Numbers 15:28), but he that continues sinning "willfully after that we have received the knowledge of the truth, there remaineth no more sacrifice for sins," in the New Covenant or Old Covenant! This is a condition given for atoning mercies with OT sacrifices, and by NT inspiration this is carried over to the NT sacrifice of Christ. **Willful sin is unatonable sin**. If this was the severity of the Judgment of God in the Mosaic Covenant, *how much more severe* is the justice of God toward the rejection of a greater and more wonderful Covenant in Christ – thus it is said, "Of **how much sorer punishment**, suppose ye, shall he be thought worthy, who hath trodden under foot the Son of God, and hath counted the blood of the Covenant, **wherewith he was sanctified**, an unholy thing, and hath done **despite** unto the Spirit of grace" (Heb. 10:29). If one wishes to argue that Hebrews 10 is a warning to an unregenerate unbeliever, then one must conclude that an unbeliever can be sanctified by the blood of the Covenant (the blood of Jesus, Heb. 10:20)! If one wishes to argue that Hebrews 6 is a warning to an unregenerate unbeliever, then one must conclude that an unbeliever can repent acceptably and savingly before God (Heb. 6:6, note "renew again").

Nay, this is to regenerate believers who have become "**adversaries**" (Heb. 10:27), to whom will undergo the "vengeance" of God, and why? They are "**enemies of God**" through the crime of adultery (James 4:4), as it is written, "Ye **adulterers** and **adulteresses**, know ye not that the friendship of the world is **enmity with God**? Whosoever therefore will be a friend of the world is the enemy of God" (James 4:4). You cannot commit adultery as an unregenerate unbeliever; they were never betrothed to God in a Covenant like unto marriage in the first place. God's people (Heb. 10:30) can become "enemies," or "adversaries" (James 4:4, Heb. 10:27), who will have "judgment and fiery indignation" (Heb. 10:27) devouring them! Oh, but the burden of the author is that this would not happen! He does not leave them without encouragement (Heb. 10:32-34, 6:9-10)... rather, he would have them revive their former faith to obtain a steadfast patience, to the end that they "might receive the promise" (Heb. 10:35-36). He says, "Cast not away therefore your confidence, which hath great recompence of reward. For ye have need of **patience**, that, after ye have done the will of God, ye might **receive the promise**" (Heb. 10:35-36). Receiving the promise of eternal life, rather than coming short of it (Heb. 4:1), is and has been the burden of the author from the beginning.

Urging them to patience is urging them to perseverance. He did urge them in Hebrews 6:11-12, that they would be patient to "inherit the promises" *as Abraham* was perseverant to inherit his promises (Heb. 6:13-15, Jas. 2:21-25). In Hebrews 10:37-39, the author urges the readers in the same manner - that they would keep the faith with patience (perseverance) to "receive the promise" (Heb. 10:36), even as "the elders" of Hebrews 11 did persevere and obtain their promises. The author says that "we are not of them who draw back unto perdition," for, saints have an "unction" (1 John 2), a "Divine nature" (2 Peter 1:4), and the indwelling Spirit (Rom. 8:14), and it is these which we are "of." Thus God would lead us to follow those who "through faith" "obtained promises" (Heb. 11:33). "These all" "obtained a good report through faith" (as Abraham did), for their faith did "evidence" itself in the "substance" of persevering works, deeds, and labors of patient faith (Heb. 11). We are of the same Spirit, and therefore we are "of them [*the elders*] that believe to the saving of the soul," therefore let us follow their faith and not draw back from our nature "unto perdition" (Heb. 10:39-11:2). Let us, as they did, "lay aside very weight, and sin which doth so easily beset us, and let us run with **patience** the race that is set before us, looking unto Jesus" "diligently, lest any man fail the grace of God" (Heb. 12:1-2, 15) – becoming "cast away" (1 Cor. 9:27). Oh to escape the fate of one who is called, **"a root that beareth gall and wormwood,"** "whose heart turneth away this day from the LORD our God" (see Deut. 29:18)! The author of Hebrews references this passage to describe the damnable deed at hand, and warns the people of God to look unto Jesus as those elders of the faith did in the Hall of Faith – "looking diligently lest any man fail of the grace of God; lest any **root of bitterness** springing up trouble you, and thereby many be defiled" (Heb. 12:15).

"A **root that beareth gall** and **wormwood"** - Deut. 29:19	"the LORD shall blot out his name from under heaven" – Deut. 29:20
"**Root of bitterness** springing up" - Heb. 12:15	"blot out his name out of the book of life" – Rev. 3:5

Many a man, though they are beset by sin, though they are not diligent in the business of looking unto Jesus, though they hear all the words of these NT curses, even still, "when he heareth the words of this curse, that he blesseth himself in his heart, saying, I shall have peace, though I walk in the imagination of mine heart, to add drunkenness to thirst: The LORD will not spare him, but then the anger of the LORD and His jealousy shall smoke against that man, and all the curses that are written in this book shall lie upon him, and the LORD shall blot out his name from under heaven" (Deut. 29:19-20). Why? These men have become "**a root that beareth gall and wormwood**" (Deut. 29:18). Therefore the NT Covenant warns us of the same curses, how we might become this "**root of bitterness** springing up" (Heb. 12:15), that is (being interpreted), a man whose "heart turneth away this day from the LORD our God" (Deut. 29:18), failing to "look diligently," and failing "the grace of God" (Heb. 12:15). Oh, the horrifying reality! "Eternal security" teaches men to be as he that "blesseth himself in his heart, saying, I shall have peace," even though God warns of a curse upon men who are in unrepentant sin (Deut. 19:19). Preacher of peace to carnal Christians, preacher of eternal security, you are "making the word of God of none effect through your tradition" (Mar. 7:13)! You are blinding the eyes of the saints of God so that, even while they are beset by sin, they cannot apply the New Covenant "words of this curse," because they believe they are eternally secure. They do bless themselves in their heart, but lo, the vengeance of God hovers overhead. To such a man in the NT, God warns that He will "blot out his name out of the book of life" (Rev. 3:5), but this is just like the warning in the OT which was given to the Jews that God will "blot out his name from under heaven"

(Deut. 29:20). It is a false prophet's "flattery" (Prov. 6:24, Ezek. 12:24) to preach that a true Christian cannot "fall" (1 Cor. 10:12, 2 Peter 1:10, 3:17, Heb. 4:11, 6:6, 1 Tim. 3:6, 6:9), and when he does fall into Covenant-breaking adultery, will you say that God's "jealousy" does not "smoke against that man" (Deut. 29:20)?!?

The Exodus Generation →	"And ye returned and wept before the LORD; But the LORD would not hearken to your voice, nor give ear unto you" – Deut. 1:45
NT saints →	"For it is impossible…if they shall fall away, to renew them again unto repentance" – Heb. 6:4-6
Esau →	"For he found no place of repentance, though he sought it carefully with tears" – Heb. 12:17

Who is the "adversary" of Hebrews 10:26-27? Who is the "enemy" of James 4:4? It is those who have entered into the saving Covenant of God and have broken it; as adulterers. Such a man is no better than an adulterer against God (James 4:4), even a "fornicator, or a profane person, as Esau, who for one morsel of meat sold his birthright" (Heb. 12:16). So we, who by birthright (being born again) are bound by promises to an inheritance of our Father's Kingdom, glory, and salvation, yet if we do turn back from the faith we too will be reprobated without possibility to repent again (Heb. 6:4-6, 10:38). Then we will be as the Israelites (Deut. 1:40-45) and Esau, who, after their reprobation, sought to be as one who "inherited the blessing," and yet, both of them were "rejected"…they "found no place of repentance, though [they] sought it carefully with tears" (Heb. 12:17). Though the Israelites regretted their rebellion against God, though they sought repentance and "wept before the LORD," they could not find repentance (Deut. 1:40-45)! "If God permits" (Heb. 6:3), "peradventure," one will find repentance again (2 Tim. 2:25), but after the "tenth temptation" there will be a total annihilation (Num. 14:22) by reprobation.

"For the LORD thy God is **a Consuming Fire**, even a jealous God" – Deut. 4:24
"For our God is **a Consuming Fire**" – Heb. 12:29

The final warning is given in Hebrews 12:25-29, but to understand it we must understand what is meant by the author when he says, "our God is a consuming fire" (Heb. 12:29). The Consuming Fire which is in reference is from the scene of the former Church of God (Acts 7:37) which was gathered at Mount Sinai, also described in Hebrews 12:18-21. We must understand what it was like for the Old Covenant Church of God to come to Mount Sinai, that we who are of the New Covenant Church will know what is the significance of coming to *a holier Mountain*, called "Mount Sion," or Zion (Heb. 12:22).

The Calling of Moses was out of Egypt, through the Red Sea, and to Mount Sinai, whereat the Covenant was established by God, "a Consuming Fire". This scene was of immense significance! Henceforth we must closely note: 1) How holy was the

Mountain of Sinai, 2) of what significance and necessity is the fear of God at the inauguration of the Covenant, and 3) *was this fear maintained*? Things to be understood in the comparatively greater New Covenant are: 1) How much more holy is Mount Zion, 2) how much more fearful ought we to be in the Covenant of the Last Days, 3) and what fear are we commanded to (by grace) maintain, and likewise, what are the consequences if it is not maintained?

Holy Mount Sinai

Before God would draw near to and meet with Israel they had to be sanctified. "And the LORD said unto Moses, Go unto the people, and sanctify them to day and to morrow, and let them wash their clothes, and be ready against the third day: for the third day the LORD will come down in the sight of the people upon Mount Sinai" (Exodus 19:10-11). Oh the gravity that "Moses brought forth the people out of the camp **to meet with God**; and they stood at the nether part of the Mount" (Amos 4:12)! My reader, wonder in awe at the events wherein Moses, Aaron, the priests, and the people (in Exodus 19:20-24), were all prepared and warned of the deathly danger of this holy meeting.

Three days were set aside for sanctification and cleansing so that the people were "ready" (Ex. 19:11, 15). Thrice did God warn with the death penalty, if haply, unholy men did break through the boundaries to gaze upon the holy, and then God, "a Consuming Fire," would "break forth upon them" with devouring wrath like as He did descend upon Sinai – "in fire: and the smoke thereof ascended as the smoke of a furnace, and the whole Mount quaked greatly" (Ex. 19:18). "The whole Mount quaked greatly" at the Lord's terrifying descent, and all the people, and Moses, could do nothing else but quake and shake with the earth. "Tremble, thou earth, at the presence of the Lord, at the presence of the God of Jacob" (Psalm 114:7)!

> "And the LORD said unto Moses, go down, charge the people, lest they break through unto the LORD to gaze, and **many of them perish**. And let the priests also, which come near to the LORD, sanctify themselves, **lest the LORD break forth upon them**. And Moses said unto the LORD, the people cannot come up to the Mount Sinai: for Thou chargedst us, saying, set bounds about the Mount, and sanctify it. And the LORD said unto him, Away, get thee down, and thou shalt come up, thou, and Aaron with thee: but let not the priests and the people break through to come up unto the LORD, **lest He break forth upon them**" (Ex. 19:20-24).

The Lord came down in "a consuming fire" (Heb. 12)! The Lord will consume "the earth also and the works therein" (2 Pet. 3), and our God is such that it

109

is a "terrifying thing" to be in His hands. To be anywhere near to Him while there be some trespass or sin, He did and would, and thrice warned, He would "break forth upon them" (Ex. 19:24). Carnal men fear fire, others fear great waters, many feared the Leviathan, but who will not fear the Lord? "For, behold, the LORD cometh forth out of His place, and will come down, and tread upon the high places of the earth. And the mountains shall be molten under Him, and the valleys shall be cleft, as wax before the fire, and as the waters that are poured down a steep place. For the transgression of Jacob is all this, and for the sins of the house of Israel" (Mic. 1:3-5).

There were less and more holy places, also less and more holy things, and these were learned with carefulness. When God came down at the giving of the Covenant at Sinai, He said to Moses – "And thou shalt set bounds unto the people round about, saying, Take heed to yourselves, that ye **go not up into the Mount, or touch the border of it:** whosoever toucheth the Mount shall be surely put to death: There shall not an hand touch it, but he shall surely be stoned, or shot through; whether it be beast or man, it shall not live: when the trumpet soundeth long, they shall come up to the Mount" (Ex. 19:12-13).

The establishment of the Old Covenant was at this meeting with God – "And it came to pass on the third day in the morning, that there were thunders and lightnings, and a thick cloud upon the Mount, and the voice of the trumpet exceeding loud; so that all the people that was in the camp trembled. And Moses brought for the people out of the camp **to meet with God**…Mount Sinai was altogether on a smoke, because the LORD descended upon it in fire: and the smoke thereof ascended as the smoke of a furnace, and the whole mount quaked greatly. And when the voice of the trumpet sounded long, and waxed louder and louder, Moses spake, and God answered him by a voice" (Ex. 19:16-19). Then God spoke the Covenant of the Ten Commandments from the midst of **the Consuming Fire** – "And all the people saw the thunderings, and the lightnings, and the noise of the trumpet, and the mountain smoking: and when the people saw it, they removed, and stood afar off. And they said unto Moses, Speak thou with us, and we will hear: but **let not God speak with us, lest we die.** And Moses said unto the people, Fear not: for God is come to prove you, and **that His fear may be before your faces, that ye sin not**. And the people stood afar off, and Moses **drew near** unto the thick darkness where God was" (Exodus 20:18-21).

The Lord sought for His people to fear, even that "His fear may be before" their faces perpetually and forever, to the end "that" they "sin not" (Exodus 20:20). The scene was reemphasized so as to remind the Israelites, that they might continue to fear God, that their children might "learn to fear" Him too, that every generation would be sure to obey the voice of a God Who is "A Consuming Fire, even a jealous God" (Deut. 4:10, 24). Read carefully and consider the significance of the fact that God intended for His people to remember this fear – the fear of a Consuming Fire. He says…

"Only take heed to thyself, and keep thy soul diligently, lest thou forget the things which thine eyes have seen, and lest they depart from thy heart all the days of thy life: but teach them thy sons, and thy sons' sons; Specially the day that thou stoodest before the LORD thy God in Horeb, when the LORD said unto me, Gather Me the people together, and I will make them hear My words, **that they may learn to fear Me all the days that they shall live upon the earth**, and that they may teach their children. And ye came near and stood under the mountain; and the mountain burned with fire unto the midst of heaven, with darkness, clouds, and thick darkness. And the LORD spake unto you out of the midst of the fire: ye heard the voice of the words, but saw no similitude; only ye heard a voice. And He declared unto you His covenant, which He commanded you to perform, even ten commandments; and He wrote them upon two tables of stone" (Deuteronomy 4:9-13).

"Take heed unto yourselves, lest ye forget the covenant of the LORD your God, which He made with you, and make you a graven image, or the likeness of any thing, which the LORD thy God hath forbidden thee. **For the LORD thy God is a consuming fire, even a jealous God**" (Deuteronomy 4:23-24).

We have studied how the generation of the Exodus did not keep this fear. Over this fact, God Himself laments…Let these words of love reverberate through your soul!

"O that there were **such an heart** in them, **that they would fear Me**, and keep all My commandments always, that it might be well with them, and with their children for ever" (Deuteronomy 5:29)!

This is the lovingkindness of God wherein He related to the people after the counsel/intent/purpose/will/desire to save them (God in the ways of man), and they refused and were thus reprobated. In Deuteronomy 5, Moses retells the scene wherein God gave the Covenant to the Exodus generation because their children have risen up in their fathers' place as inheritors of the Promised Land. Do you remember that, when God damned their fathers, He spoke of taking their children in their stead? →

"But your little ones, which ye said should be a prey, them will I bring in, and they shall know the land which ye have despised. But as for you, your carcases, they shall fall in this wilderness. And your children shall wander in the wilderness forty years, and bear your whoredoms, until your carcases be wasted in the wilderness. After the number of the days in which ye searched the land, even forty days, each day for a year, shall ye bear your iniquities, even forty years, and ye shall know My breach of promise" (Numbers 14:31-34).

Read carefully how the prophet Moses did remind, reemphasize, and retell the day at Sinai again to them, when they were but children, and consider in your mind the significance, because 1) Hebrews 12:18-29 does this very thing in the New Testament, 2) as Moses was a prophet to the Israelites, in a like manner, Jesus is a prophet to Christians (Deut. 18:15), and 3) if the Israelites would have feared God by properly understanding and remembering the significance of this event, then they would have inherited the Promised Land, and in like manner, we are commanded to understand this scene for us, and therefore fear (Heb. 12:28-29), that it is sure we will inherit the Promised Land of heaven (or our rest, see Heb. 4:11), our New heavenly Jerusalem (Heb. 12:22). Even so, as much as they needed to understand this, so do we! But let's understand how *they* were taught, that we might learn what they learned.

Deuteronomy Chapter 5 *(Noted in broken sections)*

❖ Verse 5 – The Prophetic, Mediating, Intercessory Ministry of Moses

"¹ And Moses called all Israel, and said unto them, Hear, O Israel, the statutes and judgments which I speak in your ears this day, that ye may learn them, and keep, and do them. ² The LORD our God made a covenant with us in Horeb. ³ The LORD made not this covenant with our fathers, but with us, *even* us, who *are* all of us here alive this day. ⁴ The LORD talked with you face to face in the mount out of the midst of the fire, ⁵ **(I stood between the LORD and you at that time, to shew you the word of the LORD: for ye were afraid by reason of the fire, and went not up into the mount;) saying,**"

❖ Verses 6-21 – The Ten Commandments Restated

"⁶ I *am* the LORD thy God, which brought thee out of the land of Egypt, from the house of bondage. ⁷ Thou shalt have none other gods before Me. ⁸ Thou shalt not make thee *any* graven image, *or* any likeness *of any thing* that *is* in heaven above, or that *is* in the earth beneath, or that *is* in the waters beneath the earth: ⁹ Thou shalt not bow down thyself unto them, nor serve them: for I the LORD thy God *am* a jealous God, visiting the iniquity of the fathers upon the children unto the third and fourth *generation* of them that hate Me, ¹⁰ And shewing mercy unto thousands of them that love Me and keep My commandments. ¹¹ Thou shalt not take the name of the LORD thy God in vain: for the LORD will not hold *him* guiltless that taketh His name in vain. ¹² Keep the sabbath day to sanctify it, as the LORD thy God hath commanded thee. ¹³ Six days thou shalt labour, and do all thy work: ¹⁴ But the seventh day *is* the sabbath of the LORD thy God: *in it* thou shalt not do any work, thou, nor thy son, nor thy daughter, nor thy manservant, nor thy maidservant, nor thine ox, nor thine ass, nor any of thy cattle, nor thy stranger that *is* within thy gates; that thy manservant and thy maidservant may rest as well as thou. ¹⁵ And remember that thou wast a servant in the land of Egypt, and *that* the LORD thy God brought thee out thence through a mighty hand and by a stretched out arm: therefore the LORD thy God commanded thee to keep the sabbath day. ¹⁶ Honour thy father and thy mother, as the LORD thy God hath commanded thee; that thy days may be prolonged, and that it may go well with thee, in the land which the LORD thy God giveth thee. [17] Thou shalt not kill. [18] Neither shalt thou commit adultery. [19] Neither shalt thou steal. [20] Neither shalt thou bear false witness against thy neighbour. [21] Neither shalt thou desire thy neighbour's wife, neither shalt thou covet thy neighbour's house, his field, or his manservant, or his maidservant, his ox, or his ass, or any *thing* that *is* thy neighbour's."

❖ *Verses 22-23 – The Fearful Scene*

❖ *Verses 24-27 – The People's Response*

"[22] These words the LORD spake unto all your assembly in the mount out of the midst of the fire, of the cloud, and of the thick darkness, with a great voice: and He added no more. And He wrote them in two tables of stone, and delivered them unto me. [23] And it came to pass, when ye heard the voice out of the midst of the darkness, (for the mountain did burn with fire,) that ye came near unto me, *even* all the heads of your tribes, and your elders; [24] And ye said, Behold, the LORD our God hath shewed us His glory and His greatness, and we have heard His voice out of the midst of the fire: we have seen this day that God doth talk with man, and he liveth. [25] **Now therefore why should we die? for this great fire will consume us: if we hear the voice of the LORD our God any more, then we shall die.** [26] For who *is there of* all flesh, that hath heard the voice of the living God speaking out of the midst of the fire, as we *have*, and lived? [27] **Go thou near, and hear all that the LORD our God shall say: and speak thou unto us all that the LORD our God shall speak unto thee; and we will hear *it*, and do *it*.**"

❖ *Verses 28-29 – The Lord's Response and Lamentation*

❖ *Verses 30-33 – The Prophetic, Mediating, Intercessory Ministry of Moses and the Severity of Disobedience*

"[28] And the LORD heard the voice of your words, when ye spake unto me; and the LORD said unto me, I have heard the voice of the words of this people, which they have spoken unto thee: **they have well said all that they have spoken.** [29] **O that there were such an heart in them, that they would fear Me, and keep all My commandments always, that it might be well with them, and with their children for ever!** [30] Go say to them, Get you into your tents again. [31] But as for thee, **stand thou here by Me, and I will speak unto thee all the commandments, and the statutes, and the judgments, which thou shalt teach them, that they may do *them* in the land which I give them to possess it.** [32] Ye shall observe to do therefore as the LORD your God hath commanded you: ye shall not turn aside to the right hand or to the left. [33] Ye shall walk in all the ways which the LORD your God hath commanded you, **that ye may live**, and *that it may be* well with you, and *that* ye may prolong *your* days in the land which ye shall possess."

113

❖ God said that Israel "well said" that they could not hear God's voice, and live – therefore they needed a prophetic, mediating, intercessor - Moses.

❖ If they obeyed the voice of God through Moses (whose intercession was between the people and "a Consuming Fire"), then it was sure they would be saved, live, inherit the Promised Land (a type of our heaven).

❖ If they remembered the scene of Sinai so that God's "fear may be before" their faces, if they fulfilled the earnest desire/will/purpose/counsel/intent/Covenant of God "that there were such an heart in them," God says, "that they would fear Me, and keep all My commandments always, that it might be well with them," then they would have inherited the Promised Land. The saving manifestation of their faith would have been this FEAR.

The words that validated the need for the prophetic, mediating, intercessory ministry of Moses – these same words call for the ministry of Jesus Christ to the NT Church! This foretelling prophecy of Jesus Christ is in Deuteronomy 18:15-19 –

> "[15] The LORD thy God will raise up unto thee a Prophet from the midst of thee, of thy brethren, **like unto me**; unto him ye shall hearken; [16] **According to all that thou desiredst of the LORD thy God in Horeb in the day of the assembly, saying, Let me not hear again the voice of the LORD my God, neither let me see this great fire any more, that I die not.** [17] And the LORD said unto me, **They have well** *spoken that* **which they have spoken.** [18] I will raise them up a Prophet from among their brethren, **like unto thee**, and will put My words in his mouth; and he shall speak unto them all that I shall command him. [19] And it shall come to pass, *that* **whosoever will not hearken unto My words which he shall speak in My name, I will require** *it* **of him.**

Those who did not obey Moses were killed in extraordinary ways! If there is another Prophet, "like unto Moses," then we have the same need of intercession before God – "a Consuming Fire" – and we have the same need to fear lest we disobey. If we keep this fear/obedience to the words spoken by the prophet who stands in our stead before a Consuming Fire, then we will inherit eternal life! Has this not been the repeated burden and message throughout the book of Hebrews? Has not Hebrews already proven to us the validity and reality that God will fulfill the words spoken in Deuteronomy 18:19, speaking of Christ – "And it shall come to pass, that **whosoever will not hearken unto My words which he shall speak in My name, I will require it of him.**"

Indeed, Christ is our Prophet and Intercessor, yet He is also our God (a Consuming Fire). The Lord warns that when saved men do disobey the voice of

Jesus, it will be as when saved men disobeyed the voice of Moses! This is the burden of Paul's writing in 1 Corinthians 9:24-10:12. Paul warns that Christ can be tempted to wrath (1 Cor. 10:9) unto our eternal destruction, just as He was tempted to wrath unto the Israelites' eternal destruction. Hebrews 11 is the Hall of Faith, wherein the deeds of faith are exalted, in exemplification and reward, but on the contrary, 1 Corinthians 10:5-12 is the Hall of Death, wherein deeds of unbelief are warned to be punishable in the same manner, that we are, in like manner, eternally perishable, though we are saved now. How is the context speaking of salvation?

Paul establishes the context to be concerning salvation in 1 Corinthians 9:24-27. He states that the race is for an "incorruptible crown." He is teaching the people that they should run "not as uncertainly," but as one that will surely obtain the crown of eternal life (1 Cor. 9:26). How does a man run "uncertainly" (1 Cor. 9:26)? It is in the same way a man would walk out his Christian walk, being "ignorant" (1 Cor. 10:1). Let me explain. Paul wants them to be certain to obtain the incorruptible crown in the same way he makes sure his own winning finish of his own race, and he says, "I keep under my body, and bring it into subjection: lest that by any means, when I have preached to others, I myself should be a castaway" (1 Cor. 9:27). He says, "lest that by any means," showing that he is aware of the "means" by which he can become a castaway – namely, by not bringing his body into subjection. With this burden clearly applied to himself, Paul ends chapter 9 and goes into chapter 10, but he is still burdened over all the possibilities of castaway wrath. In this chapter, Paul is seeking to take away the ignorance of the Corinthians, as he says – "brethren, I would not that ye should be ignorant" (1 Cor. 10:1) – ignorant of what? Ignorant that saved men can perish by many "means!" Paul wants them to see multiple examples of how saved men did perish. We can see, then, how Paul is not just burdened for himself, but how he is aware of the "any means" by which the Corinthians can become "castaway" (1 Cor. 9:27). If the Corinthians continue in ignorance of the means by which they could become a castaway, then they are missing the entire burden of Paul – "Wherefore let him that thinketh he standeth take heed lest he fall" (1 Cor. 10:12). Rather, Paul says, "brethren, I would not that ye should be ignorant," in summary – that their fathers were saved, and yet, they fell as castaways (1 Cor. 10:1).

Firstly, don't be "ignorant" (1 Cor. 10:1) that they were saved – see 1 Cor. 10:1-4 (formerly reviewed).
Secondarily, note the "any means" (1 Cor. 9:27) they can fall – see 1 Cor. 10:5-10.
Finally, note the application of the author – see 1 Cor. 9:24-27, 10:5-6, 11-12.

The logic, argument, and interpretations are clear and consistent throughout the rest of the Bible. Christ is the Prophet like unto Moses, and our God, the Consuming Fire, can be tempted to wrath! 1 Corinthians 10:9 says, "neither let us **tempt Christ**, as some of them also tempted," for we, in like manner, will surely be destroyed! According to what God did to the Exodus generation, there is an unavoidable wrath in God when a saved man discontinues believing.

Christ, as our intercessor, mediator, and Covenant Testator, did deliver to us an infinitely greater and more glorious Covenant. 1) The call was "like unto Moses," 2) the Mount of the Covenant was like unto Sinai, 3) the need to fear is like unto the OT with Moses, but, 1) the call was greater than Moses and is therefore more severe if neglected, 2) the Mount of Zion is holier and more fearful than Sinai (of which they could not so much as touch it, and yet, we have fully ascended Zion and are upon it), thus 3) the need to fear is greater than it was with Moses!

The Call, Mount, and Fear of the Prophet Like Unto Moses – Jesus Christ

Hebrews 12:18-21 →The Covenant mediated by Moses, its establishment at Sinai, and the reason to FEAR and obey emphasized.

Hebrews 12:22-24 →The Covenant mediated by Christ, its establishment at Zion, and the greater reason to FEAR and obey emphasized.

> **"For ye are not come unto The Mount** that might be touched, and that burned with fire, nor unto blackness, and darkness, and tempest, and the sound of a trumpet, and the voice of words; which voice they that heard intreated that the word should not be spoken to them any more: (For they could not endure that which was commanded, And if so much as a beast touch the mountain, it shall be stoned, or thrust through with a dart: And so terrible was the sight, that Moses said, I exceedingly fear and quake:)" (Hebrews 12:18-21)

"For ye are not come unto the Mount" of Sinai (Hebrews 12:18) where that holy and "terrible sight" was seen (Heb. 12:21) when "Moses said, I exceedingly fear and quake." Rather, as the "Church of the firstborn" (Heb. 12:23), the writer speaks of a holier Mount of the New Covenant unto which we have already come.

> "**But ye are come unto Mount Sion**, and unto the city of the living God, the heavenly Jerusalem, and to an innumerable company of angels, to the general assembly and Church of the firstborn, which are written in heaven, and to God the Judge of all, and to the spirits of just men made perfect, and to Jesus the mediator of the New Covenant, and to the blood of sprinkling, that speaketh better things than that of Abel" (Heb. 12:22-24).

That which was seen in its holy terribleness at Sinai cannot be compared with the Mountain of Zion. The voice of God on earth, at Sinai, shook as all the people gathered before it. But the voice of our Covenant "speaketh from heaven," and will not shake Sinai only but the whole earth, not the earth only but also the heavens – such a shaking that all things will crumble and fail until only the Kingdom of God remains! Not Sinai only but the whole "earth also and the works therein" will be inflamed in fire "at His appearing and His Kingdom" (2 Tim. 4:1). Think of the heavenly sight that the apostle John saw – "And I looked, and, lo, a Lamb stood on the Mount Sion, and with Him an hundred forty and four thousand, having His Father's name written in their foreheads" (Rev. 14:1)!

> "**See that ye refuse not Him** that speaketh. For **if they escaped not** who refused Him that spake <u>on earth</u>, **much more shall not we escape**, if we turn away from Him that speaketh <u>from heaven</u>: Whose voice then shook the earth: but now He hath promised, saying, Yet once more I shake not the earth only, but also heaven. And this word, Yet once more, signifieth the removing of those things that are shaken, as of things that are made, that those things which cannot be shaken may remain. Wherefore we receiving a kingdom which cannot be moved, let us have **grace**, whereby we may serve God **acceptably** with **reverence** and **godly fear**: For our God is **A Consuming Fire**" (Hebrews 12:25-29).

Zion is the Mountain of our Covenant: both now and in the time to come.

Hebrews 2:5-18 exalts the means by which Christ did save in that He, **1)** being made into a human being (Heb. 2:9, 16), defeated the power of death that held man in bondage (Heb. 2:14-15), **2)** that He might afterward pass into the heavens (Heb. 4:14) as a "forerunner," that through His life He may bring "many sons to glory" (Heb. 6:20, 2:10). As Christ passed into the heavens by a death-defeating resurrection, we too partake of this "**heavenly** calling" (Heb. 3:1), "taste" and partake of "the **heavenly** gift" (Heb. 6:4), being made a partaker of Christ (Heb. 3:14), and thus, we have a basis of lawful and spiritual justification after the substance of "**heavenly** things" which the shadows of the OT declared (Heb. 8:5), being saved by a better sacrifice and blood that purifies the "**heavenly** things" with an incorruptible blood (Heb. 9:23-24, 1 Peter 1:18-19), and as partakers of this lawful and spiritual glorification, we are made to desire and seek what is prepared for us, namely a *country* and *city* that is "**heavenly**" (Heb. 11:16, 13:14), by a Covenant of One that came from heaven, ascended back into heaven, and "speaketh from **heaven**" (Heb. 12:25)! We therefore are "come unto **Zion**, and unto **a city** of the Living God, the **heavenly** Jerusalem, and to an innumerable company of angels, to the general assembly and Church of the firstborn, which are written in **heaven**, and to God the Judge of all, and to the spirits of just men made perfect, and to Jesus the mediator of the New Covenant, and to the blood of sprinkling, that speaketh better things than that of Abel" (Heb. 12:22-24).

Herein is the climactic scene of the Greater Mediator, Prophet, and Testator than Moses, who ascended a greater and holier mountain than Sinai, Who has passed from here to there for us (as He stands, even so, we stand in Him, spiritually and lawfully), and thus we ought to hold fast and keep with patience the Covenant delivered by Him (Heb. 2:1, 4:16, 6:11-12, 10:35-36) that we might follow the "Finisher" (Heb. 12:2), that it might be said of us that we are with Him where He is (John 17:24, 14:3). This will happen through a persevering faith which actualizes a translation (Heb. 11:5), that is, "when Christ, Who is our life, shall appear, then shall ye also appear with Him in glory" (Col. 3:4), because we lived and abode in the *heavenly things* (Col. 3:1-2, Php. 3:20, 4:8, Eph. 1:3, 2:6, 4:22-24, 1 Peter 2:11, Jas. 3:17), which is, a mortifying and death of the *earthly things* (Col. 3:5, Rom. 8:13, Gal. 5:24, Php. 3:19, Jas. 3:15). This Kingdom we have been born into (John 1:11-12), or translated into (Col. 1:13), is spiritually within us (Lk. 17:21). By its dominion, we have come to possess all things as one that inherits all that Christ owns (1 Cor. 3:22-23), because we relate to the Father in His life (Rom. 6:8-10); even now, we sit with/in Him (Eph. 2:6) on the Davidic Throne (Acts 2:29-36), thus we are presently in Zion and have ascended ***the holy hill*** in Christ (partially/spiritually/lawfully), and yet we await the consummating descent of the Kingdom of God to be upon the earth. We have been *resurrected* (Rom. 6:4), *regenerated* (Tit. 3:5), overcome *death* (Eph. 2:5), and *inherited* the Kingdom (Lk. 17:21), but we await a final consummating *resurrection* (1 Cor. 15:42-50), *regeneration* (Rom. 8:18-21, Php. 3:12-14), defeat of *death* (1 Cor. 15:54-57), and *inheritance* of the Kingdom of God (1 Cor. 15:50). "For now we see through a glass, darkly; but then face to face: now I know in part; but then shall I know even as also I am known" (1 Cor. 13:12). "Beloved, now are we the sons of God, and it doth not yet appear what we shall be: but we know that, when He shall appear, we shall be like Him; for we shall see Him as He is" (1 John 3:2).

Therefore verily, we are presently saved, and we are in a present progressive salvation where we are being saved continually. Those who are saved have met with God at Zion, for we are those who have received the Covenant of God, and yet it is not consummated, and we have an entire Promised Land to inherit which we only partially access now. We are as the Israelites at Sinai who had a need to follow God into the Promised Land. We too must "go forth therefore unto Him without the camp, bearing His reproach. For here have we no continuing city, but we seek one to come" (Heb. 13:13-14). The Prophet of this Kingdom (Who we are forewarned about by God in Deut. 18:19, "that whosoever will not hearken unto My words which He shall speak in My Name, I will require it of Him"), is He that the apostles (Peter, James, and John) saw glorified on the holy mount, as it was written – they "were eyewitnesses of His Majesty. For He received from God the Father honour and glory, when there came **such a voice to Him from the EXCELLENT GLORY**, This is My beloved Son, in Whom I am well pleased. And **this voice which came <u>from heaven</u>** we heard, when we were with Him in the holy mount. We have also a more sure word of prophecy; whereunto ye do well that ye take heed, as unto a light that shineth in a dark place, until the day dawn, and the day star arise in your hearts" (2 Pet. 1:16-19). "Whereunto ye do well that ye take heed," God says, for those who hear not God's "beloved Son" will undergo the warning of Deut. 18:19! Herein the Father did exalt Christ above the prophecy of old, and Christ was sanctified by a more sure word of prophecy, even above the renowned and famed prophets Moses and Elijah, for Moses and Elijah appeared with Jesus and spoke with Him! Above Moses! Above Elijah! While they stood beside the Lord Jesus in glory, it was then that – "Behold, a bright cloud overshadowed them: and BEHOLD **a voice out of the cloud**, which said, This is My beloved Son, in Whom I am well pleased; **HEAR YE HIM**" (Matt. 17:1-7)! HEAR HIM, Jesus Christ, above Moses and above Elijah! "He that cometh from above is ABOVE ALL: he that is of the earth is earthly, and speaketh of the earth: He that cometh from heaven is ABOVE ALL" (John 3:31).

With this voice from heaven, God did announce Christ as the Prophet like unto Moses (Deut. 18:15), the Testator (Heb. 9:16-17) of the New Covenant. Not only there on the Mountain, but again another time. The Father, The Son, and The Holy Ghost did show forth Their glory, simultaneously, when – "lo, the heavens were opened unto Him, and He saw the Spirit of God descending like a Dove, and lighting upon Him: and lo **a voice from heaven**, saying, This is My beloved Son, in Whom I am well pleased" (Matt. 3:16-17)! Never before was the Three Persons of God anointing, extolling, and glorifying such a Man! – for He was the Lord Who was given to us, "and the government shall be upon His shoulder: and His name shall be called Wonderful, Counsellor, The Mighty God, The Everlasting Father, The Prince of Peace. Of the increase of His government and peace there shall be no end, upon the throne of David, and upon His Kingdom, to order it, and to establish it with judgment and with justice from henceforth even for ever!" – but will we recognize this incomparable inauguration and tremble now at the words "**HEAR YE HIM**" (Matt 17:5)?!

God inaugurated Moses' ministry as prophet, intercessor, and mediator by a voice from a Consuming Fire which spake on earth. Greater than this is the burden of Hebrews 12:25-29: "See that ye refuse not Him that speaketh. For if they escaped not who refused Him that spake on earth, much more shall not we escape, if we turn away from **Him that speaketh from heaven**." His Kingdom is an everlasting Kingdom that cannot be shaken or moved. All of Christ's enemies will be placed under His feet, even death itself! A greater Kingdom, Covenant, Prophet, voice, Mountain, and inauguration – A greater shaking and fear to come wherein the earth and the heavens cannot bear the power, "Wherefore receiving a Kingdom which cannot be moved, let us have **grace**, whereby we may serve God **acceptably** with **reverence** and **godly fear**: For our God is **a Consuming Fire**" (Heb. 12:26-29)! A greater fear should be bound with a greater and holier Mount, Covenant, and Testator, if He is now refused or disobeyed, but will we come to understand that nothing else is acceptable, but "reverence and godly fear," wrought in the heart by grace, making us to attend to the words of the Covenant with a greater fear than what God sought to be maintained in the Israelite's heart – "For our God is a Consuming Fire" TODAY and NOW (Heb. 12:29)?!

119

When God was angry in the Old Covenant, "the earth shook and trembled; the foundations also of the hills moved and were shaken." Likewise in the end of days, the word will be fulfilled when – "men's hearts failing them for fear, and for looking after those things which are coming on the earth: for the <u>powers of heaven</u> shall be shaken" (Lk. 21:26). But will we, at present, fear God in such a manner, knowing that our God is a Consuming Fire with One Mediator, and every word on the pages of our New Testament should be trembled at as if it were presented by the voice of God's awesome and terrible FIRE which raged upon Mount Sinai? When will we attend to the New Testament with this remembrance, receiving it in this awful recollection, and realize evermore…it is not a man, nor was it Moses that spake in the old time, but it was the words of God – the Consuming Fire – Who will surely consume us if we disobey?! If hearts fail men at the end of time, should not our hearts fail us for fear <u>if we disobey</u> the words of this Book, for we have "tasted the powers of the world to come" and have beheld the glory of God in the face of Christ (2 Cor. 4:6) already! We must fear that we may ever be kept in faith, having a continual recognition to the severity of unbelief, and able to repeat the solemn words – "**I had fainted**, unless I had believed to see the goodness of the LORD in the land of the living" (Psalm 27:13). Remember, God is with us now! There is a greater presence in our midst than the apostle Paul. "Wherefore my beloved, as ye have always obeyed, <u>not as in my presence only</u>, [PAUL SAID] but **now much more** in my absence, work out your own salvation with **fear and trembling**. For **IT IS GOD** which worketh **IN YOU** both to will and to do of His good pleasure" (Php. 2:12-13).

The Lord said to Moses that His descent upon Sinai was for the purpose that: "Lo, I come unto thee in a thick cloud, that the people may hear when I speak with thee, and believe thee for ever" (Ex. 19:9). At the fearful sight wherein Israel beheld God, the Consuming Fire, Moses said, "I stood between the LORD and you at that time, to shew you the word of the LORD: for ye were afraid by reason of the fire, and went not up into the Mount" (Deut. 5:5). The people heard the voice and saw the fire, and said, "Let me not hear again the voice of the LORD my God, neither let me see this great fire any more, that I die not" (Deut. 18:16)! At these words the Lord said – "THEY HAVE WELL SPOKEN THAT WHICH THEY HAVE SPOKEN" (Deut. 18:17)!

Indeed they would have died; they could not bear to hear the voice of God, and they needed an intercessor and prophet. At the saying of these words from the people, God points to a parallel intercession at hand for Christ. Christ was sent BECAUSE what the people said was true, and well spoken, thus Moses prophesied – "The LORD thy God will raise up unto thee a Prophet from the midst of thee, of thy brethren, <u>like unto me</u>; unto him ye shall hearken; **According to all that thou desiredst of the LORD thy God in Horeb in the day of the assembly, saying, Let me not hear again the voice of the LORD my God, neither let me see this great fire any more, that I die not**" (Deut. 18:16)! The voice that spoke at Sinai did shake the earth; it came with such power that those who heard it could not endure it – the people knew THEY WOULD DIE. The voice of our Covenant at our Mountain,

Mount Zion, is spoken from heaven, and we who are "the Church of the firstborn" do behold the glory of God in heaven by a revelation in the Spirit of God, sent from heaven. We do partake of the realities of this Kingdom, have ascended Mount Zion, and experienced the powers that will shake the heavens! For this reason it was written that we have "tasted...the powers of the world to come" (Heb. 6:4-5). When the powers of the world to come were first revealed to us, behold, we were saved! We trembled in fear, turned from sin, and were saved! But do we have this deathly fear to obey, today? Do you have such a perception of the voice of God now, by faith through spiritual illumination?

"The earth shook, the heavens also dropped at the presence of God: even Sinai itself was moved at the presence of God, the God of Israel" (Psalm 68:8). "The hills melted like wax at the presence of the LORD, at the presence of the Lord of the whole earth" (Psalm 97:5) – what about YOU? Has God made known His Name to your inner man, has He revealed His glory to your mind, even as He will make it known to His "adversaries, that the nations may tremble at" His "presence?" As it is written, "Oh that Thou wouldest rend the heavens, that Thou wouldest come down, that the mountains might flow down at Thy presence, as when the melting fire burneth, the fire causeth the waters to boil, to make Thy name known to thine adversaries, that the nations may **tremble at Thy Presence**" (Isaiah 64:1-2)! Many serve and rejoice before the LORD – **UNACCEPTABLY**! – Because they do not "serve the LORD with **FEAR**, and rejoice with **TREMBLING**. Kiss the Son, lest He be angry, and ye perish from the way, when His wrath is kindled but a little. Blessed are all they that put their trust in Him" (Psalm 2:11-12). Everyone talks about serving God, and rejoicing, but are we rejoicing with *trembling*? Are you serving with *fear*? Do we understand the holiness of the presence of God, the severity of the words of our Covenant, the chronicles of deadly executions upon saved men who thought lightly of the Name of God? "God is **greatly to be feared** in the assembly of the saints, and to be had in **reverence** of all them that are about Him" (Psalm 89:7). Men must learn to be like the mountains round about God, and all those who have "so learned Christ" – they are saved (Eph. 4:20)!

> "The mountains quake at Him, and the hills melt, and the earth is
> burned at His presence, yea, the world, and all that dwell therein"
> (Nahum 1:5).

> "Before Him went the pestilence, and burning coals went forth at
> His feet. He stood, and measured the earth: He beheld, and drove
> asunder the nations; and the everlasting mountains were
> scattered, the perpetual hills did bow: His ways are everlasting"
> (Habakkuk 3:5-6).

> "The mountains saw Thee, and they trembled: the overflowing of
> the water passed by: the deep uttered his voice, and lifted up his
> hands on high. The sun and moon stood still in their habitation: at
> the light of Thine arrows they went, and at the shining of Thy

glittering spear" (Habakkuk 3:10-11).

"And the stars of heaven fell unto the earth, even as a fig tree
casteth her untimely figs, when she is shaken of a mighty wind.
And the heaven departed as a scroll when it is rolled together;
and every mountain and island were moved out of their places"
(Revelation 6:13-14).

"And I saw a great white throne, and Him that sat on it, from
Whose face the earth and the heaven fled away; and there was
found no place for them" (Revelation 20:11).

"Enter into the rock, and hide thee in the dust, for fear of the
LORD, and for the glory of His majesty. The lofty looks of man
shall be humbled, and the haughtiness of men shall be bowed
down, and the LORD alone shall be exalted in that day. For the
day of the LORD of hosts shall be upon every one that is proud
and lofty, and upon every one that is lifted up; and he shall be
brought low: And upon all the cedars of Lebanon, that are high
and lifted up, and upon all the oaks of Bashan, and upon all the
high mountains, and upon all the hills that are lifted up, and upon
every high tower, and upon every fenced wall, And upon all the
ships of Tarshish, and upon all pleasant pictures. And the
loftiness of man shall be bowed down, and the haughtiness of
men shall be made low: and the LORD alone shall be exalted in
that day. And the idols He shall utterly abolish. And they shall go
into the holes of the rocks, and into the caves of the earth, for fear
of the LORD, and for the glory of His majesty, when He ariseth
to shake terribly the earth. In that day a man shall cast his idols of
silver, and his idols of gold, which they made each one for
himself to worship, to the moles and to the bats; To go into the
clefts of the rocks, and into the tops of the ragged rocks, for fear
of the LORD, and for the glory of His majesty, when He ariseth
to **shake terribly the earth**"
(Isaiah 2:10-21).

Surely God hath set apart Christ! The Three Persons of the Trinity did extol
and inaugurate Him! And gave Him miracles to undo and turn upside down the
Kingdom of Satan on earth! Christ hath perfectly declared the invisible God (Col.
1:15). Therefore, if this is our Covenant's beginning, and we have such an extolled
Covenant Testator, and He does mediate between the Consuming Fire of heaven
preceding a worldwide shaking and regeneration, forerunning the final descent of the
everlasting Kingdom and glory of God, can we go on walking and talking with Him,
without FEAR? Could anything but fear be acceptable while we are standing upon
the holier Mount of Zion, even while the spiritual visions of His glory, fear, and
power burst upon our sides? Or, do you no longer have eyes to see and ears to hear?

After these witnesses, can we be so ill that we will not believe in Christ forever? God speaketh unto and through Christ, as with Moses. God did establish Moses' prophetic office, saying that Israel will "hear when I speak with thee, and believe thee for ever" (Ex. 19:9). How much more should we believe Christ forever, and hear what God hath spoken to Him, through Him, unto us by the Spirit of the "heavenly Dove"?!?

If God is with you, it is because He has broken you, and it was HIS VOICE that has broken you! As it is written, "For thus saith the High and Lofty One that inhabiteth eternity, Whose name is Holy, I dwell in the high and holy place, with him also that is of a **contrite** and **humble spirit**, to revive the spirit of the **humble**, and to revive the heart of the **contrite ones**" (Isaiah 57:15). Are you still broken? It is written, "He looketh on the earth, and **it trembleth**: He toucheth the hills, and they smoke" (Psalm 104:32), but is God looking upon you!? He says, "to this man will I look, even to him that is **poor** and of a **contrite spirit**, and **TREMBLETH AT MY WORD**" (Isaiah 66:2)! Have you ever trembled at His awesome, terrifying, majestic Presence? Do you still tremble today in an acceptable FEAR? Can you humbly confess to God, "**My flesh trembleth for fear of Thee; and I am afraid of Thy Judgments**" (Psalm 119:120). The writer of Hebrews commands you in Hebrews 12:28-29, that you must tremble *more than Moses and Israel*, for now, behold, all regenerate Christians do experience, see, and taste the thunderous and terrifying words, warnings, curses, and irrevocable Judgments of God, for to them they are spiritually revealed! Rightly did the psalmist write, "I will praise Thee with uprightness of heart, *when* I shall have learned Thy righteous judgments. I will keep Thy statutes: **O forsake me not utterly**" (Psalm 119:7-8)! Will you learn His "righteous judgments," and so, will you be able to praise Him acceptably, love Him rightly, kiss Him wholly, and therefore – "Serve the LORD with fear, and rejoice with trembling" (Psalm 2:11)? Partake of the revelations "in His Temple" (Psalm 29), and be thou instructed, all ye His saints…

Psalm 29
*" A Psalm of David. Give unto the LORD, O ye mighty, give unto the LORD glory and strength. Give unto the LORD the glory due unto His name; worship the LORD in the beauty of holiness. The voice of the LORD **is upon the waters**: the God of glory **thundereth**: the LORD is upon many waters. The voice of the LORD **is powerful**; the voice of the LORD **is full of majesty**. The voice of the LORD **breaketh the cedars**; yea, the LORD **breaketh the cedars of Lebanon**. He maketh them also to **skip like a calf**; Lebanon and Sirion like a young unicorn. The voice of the LORD **divideth the flames of fire**. The voice of the LORD **shaketh the wilderness**; the LORD **shaketh the wilderness of Kadesh**. The voice of the LORD **maketh the hinds to calve, and discovereth the forests: and in His temple doth every one speak of His glory.** The LORD sitteth upon the flood; yea, the LORD sitteth King for ever. The LORD will give strength unto His people; the LORD*

will bless His people with peace."

Calvinists and Armenians, have you heard Him speak because you are seeing "Him Who is invisible" (Heb. 11:27)? Look upon your God and abhor yourself, or perhaps you are a stranger to Zion. May God meet you now that you might say – "Now mine eye seeth Thee. Wherefore I abhor myself, and repent in dust and ashes" (Job 42:5-6)! Even so, Amen.

THE EXODUS GENERATION -
THE CONTRAST OF SUMULTANEOUS, GENUINE, PARADOXICAL WILLS IN GOD
CHAPTER 4

God in the ways of God	God in the ways of Man
God hated Pharaoh: The ordained hardening of Pharaoh's heart so that he would refuse to let the people go.	**God loved Pharaoh:** The commandment to let Israel go, and the lamentation of God over Pharaoh's sin when he refused to humble himself, this was the good will of love for Pharaoh because God desired that he would not sin.
God hated the Exodus Generation: The ordained hardening of the Exodus generation after their salvation, so that they would discontinue faith and fear.	**God loved the Exodus Generation:** The promises, Covenant, commandments, signs, salvation, chastening, strivings, and lamentations of God to save Israel.
The will is irresistible, determinate, incomprehensible, and logically unjustifiable to the mind of man. ~ Just Trust God ~	The will is resistible, dependent upon the response of man, comprehensible as if man has a free will, and logical in justice as if man's will was free, and therefore, fully responsible.

***The Lord's will (God in the ways of God) to Pharaoh
as an individual was like unto His will (God in the
ways of God) to the Exodus generation as a
congregation.***

In Exodus 10, as previously discussed, God commanded Pharaoh to let His people go, but Pharaoh refused. God hardened Pharaoh's heart to refuse His command because of the eternal purpose to use Pharaoh as an instrument of wrath (Rom. 9). Simultaneously, God did not want Pharaoh to sin against Him, commanded him to let His people go, and was grieved that he refused to humble himself (Ex. 10:3). ***God in the ways of God*** eternally hated Pharaoh while ***God in the ways of man*** loved Pharaoh. ***God in the ways of God*** did not want Pharaoh to let Israel go, while ***God in the ways of man*** did want Pharaoh to let Israel go, and furthermore He was grieved that he didn't let them go. Pharaoh, as a "vessel of wrath fitted to destruction," chosen to this end by election (Rom. 9:22), was used for the glory of

God to "shew His wrath and to make His power known" by plaguing Egypt, to the end that all the world would know the strength of God which is as a unicorn!

> "God brought them out of Egypt; He hath as it were the strength of an unicorn" (Numbers 23:22).

> "God brought him forth out of Egypt; He hath as it were the strength of an unicorn: He shall eat up the nations His enemies, and shall break their bones, and pierce them through with His arrows" (Numbers 24:8).

God loved and saved Israel – He became "God their Saviour, which had done great things in Egypt; wondrous works in the land of Ham, and terrible things by the Red Sea" (Psalm 106:21-22). These two instances (The Passover Night & The Red Sea Parting), along with the Covenant experience at Sinai – these three works of God are the complete salvation of Israel in its initiation – and their salvation is finished, or consummated (in type), when the gospel promises are fulfilled through their final inheritance of the Promised Land. Therefore, from the time of Sinai to the Jordan River they were already saved, they were being saved, and (by promise) they would be saved. The promises of the Abrahamic Covenant would be fulfilled in their inheritance of the Promised Land, just as our promises of our New Covenant will be fulfilled in our final resurrection and inheritance of the Promised Land (New Jerusalem).

God brought glory for Himself when "He made a way to His anger" (Ps. 78:49). "He cast upon them (*the Egyptians*) the fierceness of His anger, wrath, and indignation, and trouble" to the end that He "smote all the firstborn in Egypt; the chief of their strength in the tabernacles of Ham" (Ps. 78:51). By subduing the chief strength of Egypt, there sounded out a worldwide proclamation of God's power! GOD WAS FAMOUS! Inevitably, for those who are saved, at present, or those who will be saved in the future, God uses this exaltation of His glory as a testimony for their good (Rom. 8:28). The glory God obtains by destroying "vessels of wrath" is used to save and have mercy upon "vessels of mercy." Therefore in the death of Egypt's firstborn, the Israelites were saved from bondage, and through this display of strength the Israelites experience the powerful gospel of God. If the Israelites keep in memory this experiential faith, steadfastly, then they will endure to the end. A remembrance of these events that God did accomplish in the past does empower the Israelites at present to believe for, and thus experience, the same power of God. Therefore the condition for persevering in an empowering salvation is to persevere in faith's remembrances, as Moses said in Deut. 7:17-19 – "If thou shalt say in thine heart, These nations are more than I; how can I dispossess them? Thou shalt not be afraid of them: but shalt well **REMEMBER what the LORD thy God did unto Pharaoh, and unto all Egypt; The great temptations which thine eyes saw, and the signs, and the wonders, and the mighty hand, and the stretched out arm, whereby the LORD thy God brought thee out: so shall the LORD thy God do unto all the people of whom thou art afraid.**" The Israelites were saved from Egypt by faith, and they had to keep that faith unto the end to persevere their salvation, thus it might be said of them, as it is said to us, that they are "kept by the power of God through faith unto salvation ready to be revealed in the last time" (1 Peter 1:5).

After Israel's salvation, **God did continue to love Israel**, and this can be observed in how God **sought the perseverance** of their salvation. The perseverance of their salvation would be wrought by a keeping of faith, faith that is evidenced through a remembrance of Egyptian-Giant slaying power, and a Consuming, Fiery God of fear, because this would make Israel obey the voice of God. The Israelites did provoke God many times before Mount Sinai, but after the Covenant was established, and when they provoked Him still, God did smite them in His wrath, and many died. Before Sinai not one Israelite died, but after Sinai God was "willing to shew His wrath, and to make His power known," and as their unbelief continued, they eventually lost their salvation. They too, like Pharaoh, through the sovereign Counsel of God (in the ways of God), were "vessels of wrath fitted to destruction," but *their destruction was after their salvation*. The eternal purpose of God to bring glory to Himself was to show His wrath toward the saints who *lose their faith*. God is willing to show His wrath by damning the saved who lose their faith! Though this was the eternal purpose of God (God in the ways of God), the will of God (God in the ways of Man) was to persevere their salvation and fulfill His promises to them.

God in the ways of Man loved the Exodus generation and sought to persevere their salvation, yet simultaneously, *God in the ways of God* hated the Exodus generation and sought that they would lose their salvation by a discontinuance of saving faith. *God in the ways of man* loved and sought a persevering salvation by the "marvellous things" which He did in their sight.

> "**Marvellous things** did He in the sight of their fathers, in the land of Egypt, in the field of Zoan. He divided the sea, and caused them to pass through; and He made the waters to stand as an heap. In the daytime also He led them with a cloud, and all the night with a light of fire. He clave the rocks in the wilderness, and gave them drink as out of the great depths. He brought streams also out of the rock, and caused waters to run down like rivers. And they **sinned yet more** against Him by provoking the most High in the wilderness. And they **tempted God** in their heart by asking meat for their lust. Yea, they spake against God; they said, Can God furnish a table in the wilderness? Behold, He smote the rock, that the waters gushed out, and the streams overflowed; can He give bread also? can He provide flesh for His people? Therefore the LORD heard this, and was wroth: so a fire was kindled against Jacob, and anger also came up against Israel; **Because they believed not in God, and trusted not in His salvation:** Though He had commanded the clouds from above, and opened the doors of heaven, And had rained down manna

upon them to eat, and had given them of the corn of heaven. Man did eat angels' food: He sent them meat to the full. He caused an east wind to blow in the heaven: and by His power He brought in the south wind. He rained flesh also upon them as dust, and feathered fowls like as the sand of the sea: And He let it fall in the midst of their camp, round about their habitations. So they did eat, and were well filled: for He gave them their own desire; They were not estranged from their lust. But while their meat was yet in their mouths, The wrath of God came upon them, and slew the fattest of them, and smote down the chosen men of Israel. **For all this they sinned still, and believed not for His wondrous works.** Therefore their days did He consume in vanity, and their years in trouble. **When He slew them, then they sought Him: and they returned and enquired early after God. And they remembered that God was their rock, and the high God their redeemer. Nevertheless they did flatter Him with their mouth, and they lied unto Him with their tongues. For their heart was not right with Him, neither were they stedfast in His covenant. But He, being full of compassion, forgave their iniquity, and destroyed them not: yea, many a time turned He His anger away, and did not stir up all His wrath. For He remembered that they were but flesh; a wind that passeth away, and cometh not again.** How **oft did they provoke Him in the wilderness, and grieve Him in the desert! Yea, they turned back and tempted God, and limited the Holy One of Israel. They remembered not His hand,** nor the day when He delivered them from the enemy. How He had wrought His signs in Egypt, and His wonders in the field of Zoan: And had turned their rivers into blood; and their floods, that they could not drink. He sent divers sorts of flies among them, which devoured them; and frogs, which destroyed them. He gave also their increase unto the caterpiller, and their labour unto the locust. He destroyed their vines with hail, and their sycomore trees with frost. He gave up their cattle also to the hail, and their flocks to hot thunderbolts. He cast upon them the fierceness of His anger, wrath, and indignation, and trouble, by sending evil angels among them. He made a way to His anger; He spared not their soul from death, but gave their life over to the pestilence; And smote all the firstborn in Egypt; the chief of their strength in the tabernacles of Ham: But made His own people to go forth like sheep, and guided them in the wilderness like a flock. And He led them on safely, so that they feared not: but the sea overwhelmed their enemies. And He brought them to the border of His sanctuary, even to this mountain, which His right hand had purchased" (Psalm 78:12-54).

Therefore, this generation became the example of those who are damned (1 Cor. 10:4-5), as Paul said: "all these things happened unto them for ensamples" (1 Cor. 10:11). God does here command, through the apostle Paul, that the manner in which they were **saved,** *then* **damned**, would be remembered and taught to subsequent generations, that they "might not be as their fathers, a stubborn and rebellious generation." →

> "I will open my mouth in a parable: I will utter dark sayings of old: Which we have heard and known, and our fathers have told us. We will not hide them from their children, shewing to the generation to come the praises of the LORD, and His strength, and His wonderful works that He hath done. For He established a testimony in Jacob, and appointed a law in Israel, which He commanded our fathers, that they should make them known to their children: That the generation to come might know them, even the children which should be born; who should arise and declare them to their children: That they might set their hope in God, and not forget the works of God, but keep His commandments: **And might not be as their fathers, a stubborn and rebellious generation; a generation that set not their heart aright, and whose spirit was not stedfast with God.** The children of Ephraim, being armed, and carrying bows, turned back in the day of battle. They kept not the covenant of God, and refused to walk in His law; And forgat His works, and His wonders that He had shewed them" (Psalm 78:2-11).

Anyone who will be like these men, "like their fathers" (Ps. 78:57), they too will be damned. All those who are departing from the faith or have departed from the faith...now they know the signs of God's wrath that will come, or the signs that are upon them now – to the end they would repent and be not like them. The psalmist in 106 confesses the sins of his generation, that they were sinning even as the Exodus generation did sin, and was damned, yet he seeks mercy through **confession and repentance** –

> "Remember me, O LORD, with the favour that Thou bearest unto Thy people: O visit me with Thy salvation; That I may see the good of Thy chosen, that I may rejoice in the gladness of Thy nation, that I may glory with Thine inheritance. **We have sinned with our fathers, we have committed iniquity, we have done wickedly. Our fathers understood not Thy wonders in Egypt; they remembered not the multitude of Thy mercies; but provoked Him at the sea, even at the Red Sea.** Nevertheless He saved them for His name's sake, that He might make His mighty power to be known. He rebuked the Red Sea also, and it was dried up: so He led them through the depths, as through the

wilderness. And He saved them from the hand of him that hated them, and redeemed them from the hand of the enemy. And the waters covered their enemies: there was not one of them left. **Then believed they His words; they sang His praise. They soon forgat His works; they waited not for His counsel: But lusted exceedingly in the wilderness, and tempted God in the desert. And He gave them their request; but sent leanness into their soul.** They envied Moses also in the camp, and Aaron the saint of the LORD. The earth opened and swallowed up Dathan, and covered the company of Abiram. And a fire was kindled in their company; the flame burned up the wicked. They made a calf in Horeb, and worshipped the molten image. Thus they changed their glory into the similitude of an ox that eateth grass. **They forgat God their saviour, which had done great things in Egypt; Wondrous works in the land of Ham, and terrible things by the Red sea.** Therefore He said that He would destroy them, had not Moses His chosen stood before Him in the breach, to turn away His wrath, lest He should destroy them. **Yea, they despised the pleasant land, they believed not his word: But murmured in their tents, and hearkened not unto the voice of the LORD. Therefore He lifted up His hand against them, to overthrow them in the wilderness...**" (Psalm 106:4-26)

God sought for Israel to fear Him. He intended that they would, and gave them ten commandments with such fearful displays of power that Israel was afraid of dying (Ex. 20:19). The intent of God was, "that His fear may be before your faces, that ye sin not" (Ex. 20:20). This good will and love toward Israel was not determinate but *God in the ways of man*, therefore this good will was *resistible*. Israel went on to sin more - *ten times* they did tempt God - and eventually, nearly all the men in this generation were condemned to hell. G*od in the ways of God* directs and controls the hearts of men, but *God in the ways of man* laments in a genuine will that appears to be subjected to the free will of man, even though we know that there is no such thing. I say "subject to an appearance of free will," because God's emotions are not kindled or manifest until the deeds are committed, as if He didn't know they were going to sin, as if He didn't desire and ordain that they would sin (God in the ways of God), and as if He was unaware of what He was eventually going to do with them through their sin.

God's lamentation to this generation was, "O that there were such an heart in them, that they would **fear** Me, and keep all My commandments always, that it might be well with them, and with their children for ever" (Deut. 5:29)! Is this "O" not an exclamation of love and care toward Israel!? God loved them, but 600,000 men of war fell short of His promise and love by a fearless heart. God loved them and wanted them to fear, and simultaneously He was hardening their hearts in an eternal hatred which determined their hearts to be fearless and sinful. Do you see how there are simultaneous wills in God working from two separate planes of relational capacities in God (His ways and man's ways, in Sovereignty and in Condescension). These are not the ways of human beings, because we cannot genuinely will two things at once, that are opposites, but God can and does. **His ways are not our ways** (Isaiah 55:9). Shudder at His holiness and hear the cry of the godly go up: "O LORD, why hast Thou made us to err from Thy ways, and hardened our heart from Thy fear? Return for Thy servants' sake, the tribes of Thine inheritance" (Isaiah 63:17)!

In Conclusion – The Exodus generation, as a "vessel of wrath fitted to destruction," chosen to this end by election (Rom. 9:22), was used as an example of God's wrath to "shew His wrath and to make His power known" upon those individuals who do not keep a steadfast saving faith. The Lord was willing to show the world the severity of disobeying His voice! He was willing to show the world Psalm 90! Finally, He was willing to fulfill the Abrahamic Covenant by the manifestation and completion of all things in Christ, and so, He overpassed this generation for His own glory, changed the generation of choice, and prepared the promises for other men.

The wrath of God is able to be provoked, and if we understood the holiness of God aright, we would understand that the righteous are scarcely saved from the wrath of God. This was written by Peter, when he said, "And if the righteous scarcely be saved, where shall the ungodly and the sinner appear" (1 Peter 4:18)? Also note the life of Moses, who was a saved man (Heb. 3, 11), and he died in the wilderness with those who provoked God in rejecting the gospel (Heb. 4). However, Moses died for a different sin which was of the non-damnable kind. His sin was not a rejection of the gospel like as that wicked congregation in Numbers 14. Moses, along with Caleb and Joshua – they all believed the gospel of God and pled with the others to repent. No man, other than Moses, is more able to account of the dreamlike experiences of the exodus generation, how that they were a story of God's wrath! Moses' prayer in Psalm 90 does illustrate the willingness of God to show His wrath upon those who lose their salvation. With this generation, God wanted to make men know the **power** of His anger (Ps. 90:11), what manners God did and would **turn men to destruction** (Ps. 90:3), and the practical deeds of faith that unbelieving men do neglect, so that those who are still persevering may learn from and avoid their mistakes (Ps. 90:12). God was willing to cause Israel to pass away in His wrath, to make them a tale to be told, that men might number their days and apply their hearts to wisdom (Ps. 90:9), TODAY. Through Psalm 90, it is as if God is saying to the rest of the saved remnant in every generation – "O that there were such an heart in them, that they would fear ME" (Deut. 5:24). Read the fearful psalm and be ye taught of God, and imagine it! Imagine what terrible astonishment was in the heart of Moses when he did write this psalm…

Psalm 90
"A Prayer of Moses the man of God. Lord, Thou hast been our

131

dwelling place in all generations. Before the mountains were brought forth, or ever Thou hadst formed the earth and the world, even from everlasting to everlasting, Thou art God. **Thou turnest man to destruction; and sayest, Return, ye children of men.** For a thousand years in Thy sight are but as yesterday when it is past, and as a watch in the night. Thou carriest them away as with a flood; they are as a sleep: in the morning they are like grass which groweth up. In the morning it flourisheth, and groweth up; in the evening it is cut down, and withereth. For we are consumed by Thine anger, and by Thy wrath are we troubled. Thou hast set our iniquities before Thee, our secret sins in the light of Thy countenance. **For all our days are passed away in Thy wrath: we spend our years as a tale that is told.** The days of our years are threescore years and ten; and if by reason of strength they be fourscore years, yet is their strength labour and sorrow; for it is soon cut off, and we fly away. **Who knoweth the power of Thine anger? even according to Thy fear, so is Thy wrath. So teach us to number our days, that we may apply our hearts unto <u>wisdom</u>.** Return, O LORD, how long? and let it repent Thee concerning Thy servants. O satisfy us early with Thy mercy; that we may rejoice and be glad all our days. Make us glad according to the days wherein Thou hast afflicted us, and the years wherein we have seen evil. Let Thy work appear unto Thy servants, and Thy glory unto their children. And let the beauty of the LORD our God be upon us: and establish Thou the work of our hands upon us; yea, the work of our hands establish Thou it."

The Glory of God in the POWER of WRATH → "What if God, willing to shew His **wrath**, and to make His **power** known, endured with much longsuffering the vessels of wrath fitted to destruction" (Rom. 9:22).

The scarcity of salvation for those who do endure to the end cannot be properly understood until we are conscientious of the dual, simultaneous, and genuine wills of God that are actively working all the time, in tension/contradiction with one another. Noting one snapshot in time wherein the dual wills are easily seen will help us comprehend how there is a constant tension with the continuous wills of God every time God **experiences the observance of sin**, or as Psalm 90:8 put it, when sin is set in the light of His countenance. Some will still be inclined to doubt the genuine nature of this dual will that God has. This faculty in God, which is able to have simultaneous, contradictory wills, is not functional or possible in men. If we tried to mimic the experience of God we would have to fake one of the wills, therefore only one would be sincere and the other unreal. God can say to Adam, "Where art thou" (Gen. 3:9), while knowing where he is, and so can men. God can say to Cain, "Where is Abel thy brother" (Gen. 4:9), while knowing where he is, and so can men. These can be done to teach or relate with men, but can men lament over Israel's fearless heart, not wanting them to sin, while at the same time (by ordination and interior heart-hardening) cause it (because of an unchanging, unwavering, eternal hatred)? A vivid example of this dual work of God is in Exodus 32.

In Exodus 32, God **intended** to consume the whole congregation to death after their golden calf idolatry. God was not acting when He told Moses, "let Me alone, that My wrath may wax hot against them, and that I may consume them: and I will make of thee a great nation" (Ex. 32:10). This was **a genuine intention,** therefore God had to **repent** of this thinking, for it was genuine thinking – "And the LORD **repented of the evil which He thought to do** unto His people" (Ex. 32:14). Why did the Lord **repent**? Well, only *God in the ways of man* can repent, for the eternal, Sovereign will of God cannot repent, for He is not like a man (1 Sam. 15:29). There was an unchanging eternal purpose at work to use Israel as an example of salvation, and they were not to be destroyed here, but go on; thus God caused the Spirit in Moses to intercede with God that the Lord would repent. The eternal counsel never repented or changed, but the counsel in the context of *God in the ways of man* did, but both were simultaneously at work in the same, single, Triune God! God wanted to kill all of Israel, and simultaneously, the will of God which is existent in an unchanging eternity did not want to destroy them, therefore *God in the ways of man* repented. *God in the ways of God* determined the whole scene to the end that we would marvel and learn! The dumbest human is smarter than the smartest ant. Breaking the boundaries of species to compare differing creatures can help us understand how "other than" and "different" God is from man. God is not a man. God is not a greater species. The chasm that separates the creature from the Creator is beyond our comprehension, therefore there is condescension.

New Covenant Applications

The Israelites of the Exodus generation were given promises/ oaths/ Covenants of salvation without any mention of a condition. It seems impossible for a condition to interrupt the promises from being performed because the promises are said to be dependent upon the faithfulness and work of God alone, in the sufficiency of His spoken word. This manner in which God gives His promises is consistent throughout the Bible, leading all the way into the NT. I call it, "The Pattern of the Promises." However, there are conditions to the promises given. The first condition given to the Exodus generation was in Exodus 15. The promises given to the Israelites were without conditions directly beside them, but the conditions were given at other times, and because they are not given directly beside the promises, it is easy to misinterpret the scripture and presume that this implies the impossibility of conditions.

After Salvation: Lesson #1

133

Immediately after the Israelites were saved by faith in the Passover Lamb and were baptized by the Spirit of God, immediately AFTER salvation, then God gave the first verbal condition for the perseverance of their salvation (Ex. 15). This condition is emphasized for its importance, because it was the first thing that God spoke to them when He fully and finally delivered them from Egypt, and it was at the first instance of sin and rebellion after their salvation. The condition is given in Exodus 15:26, and it is emphasized as a means of present progressive salvation (through faith) in Jeremiah 7:21-23, 11:3-5. That is to say, our persevering faith is evident by obedience. This event in Exodus 15:26 was so emphatic that it was echoed by other prophets, like as the references of Jeremiah. Here is what happened...

The first emphasis, burden, and work of God with Israel was a "**trial** of their faith," but the Lord speaks of it in the terms, "there He **proved** them" (Ex. 15:25). This happened right out of the Red Sea baptism. God seeks to know the heart of His people by trial, by their deeds, as if He did not already know their hearts, know their future, and/or determine it. This is *God in the ways of man*. A man is limited to knowing a person by fruit because only God can see the heart. Man does not know the future, nor can he determine it. The genuine nature of this trial can be seen in chapter 16 when the Lord institutes further means of trial. "Then said the LORD unto Moses, Behold, I will rain bread from heaven for you; and the people shall go out and gather a certain rate every day, that I may **prove** them, whether they will walk in My law, or no" (Exodus 16:4). **As God did relate to the them in the context of "proving" and observing, "whether they will walk" in His law or not, here God gave conditions to their salvation, because salvation is kept, or lost, as much as their trying proves them to be faithful or unfaithful. The result of their testing will decide if their salvation will be verified or persevered.**

The trial was a three-day period of wilderness travel without finding water (Ex. 15:22), and when they found water it was bitter (Ex. 15:23). There they complained in distrust of the provisional hand of God, saying, "What shall we drink" (Ex. 15:24)? God showed them His provision by turning the bitter waters into sweet waters (Ex. 15:25). This is a type of their salvation – bitter bondage to sweet fellowship with God – and the Lord ensures a perseverance of provision, fellowship, and salvation, on one condition: "There He made for them a statute and an ordinance, and there He **proved** them, and said, **If thou wilt diligently hearken to the voice of the LORD thy God, and wilt do that which is right in His sight, and wilt give ear to His commandments, and keep all His statutes**, I will put none of these diseases upon thee, which I have brought upon the Egyptians: for I am the LORD that healeth thee" (Ex. 15:26).

Why is this a condition for salvation? Because God did show forth to the world His wrath upon the Egyptians (as "vessels of wrath fitted" to hell) by casting upon them the plagues of **disease**, the Lord is saying to Israel, generally speaking, if you do not meet this condition you will be damned to hell by the wrath of God, like as the Egyptians were damned, and so, the diseases of Egypt would come upon Israel.

In other words, as Egypt was damned in wrath, so will you be. God tries them with hard experiences to know their faith. Diligent obedience to **the voice of God** (commandments, statutes, laws) is the life of their faith, and it ensures the persevering of salvation and healing. It is when people turn away from obedience to God's voice that they are under the threats of damnation. A turning away from obedience is a turning away of faith. God testifies of this condition as damnation. This is the first condition given vocally, and it is the first instruction after their final deliverance from Egypt. This shows the supremacy of obeying God's voice as the chief expression of saving faith! False prophets are skilled at bewitching men with misapplied true promises, distracting them from the condition by which those promises are applicable, namely– OBEDIENCE.

In Jeremiah 7, God is making the argument that this generation (that of the Babylonian Captivity) is forsaken and damned, just like those who were punished when God forsook His own Tabernacle, when He allowed His throne to be stolen, etc. (Jer. 7:11-16). God is testifying to former works of damnation by referencing what He did at Shiloh, to put them in a fearful assurance that the same thing is happening to them. Men do not want to believe they will be damned under the wrath of God, especially if they have tasted of the lovingkindness and goodness of God, or the riches of His mercy. So the Lord reminds them of the condition given in Exodus 15 to show how He is justified in condemning them to hell. NOTE: it is easy for those who are saved to focus on the sacrificial atonement provided by God, rather than the condition by which that atonement is made possible in continuance; namely – OBEDIENCE.

> "Thus saith the LORD of hosts, the God of Israel; Put your burnt offerings unto your sacrifices, and eat flesh. **For I spake not unto your fathers, nor commanded them in the day that I brought them out of the land of Egypt**, concerning burnt offerings or sacrifices: **But this thing commanded I them, saying, Obey My voice, and I will be your God, and ye shall be My people: and walk ye in all the ways that I have commanded you, that it may be well unto you**" (Jeremiah 7:21-23).

They clave to imputed righteousness and atoning mercy, but did not exercise faith in the atonement through a diligence to obey, thus they were damned. A false balance that inoculates the people to this end is the craft of the false prophets in every generation. Take heed, Church! God said to them, "Behold, even I have seen it," and what does He see today (Jer. 7:11)? God said of these damned men, "This is a nation that **obeyeth not the voice of the LORD their God**, nor receiveth correction: truth is perished, and is cut off from their mouth" (Jer. 7:28). Will you fancy yourself to be fixed on the rock-solid foundation of salvation, even while you see the storm of judgment and death on the horizon for every living soul, even when you do not do what Jesus says? Read Matthew 7:24-27 and see otherwise! See that you are in sinking sand! Oh, how the false prophets do subtly deceive the people of

God to disobey under the guise of atoning mercy in Jesus! "The pastors are become brutish, and have not sought the LORD," and "who is the wise man, that may understand this? And who is he to whom the mouth of the LORD hath spoken" (Jer. 10:21, 9:12)? Again, God reemphasizes this day in Exodus 15:26 wherein God gave the condition for their salvation in Jeremiah 11:3-5, justifying their condemnation again:

> "And say thou unto them, Thus saith the LORD God of Israel; Cursed be the man that **obeyeth not the words of this covenant**, Which I commanded your fathers **in the day that I brought them forth out of the land of Egypt**, from the iron furnace, saying, **Obey My voice**, and do them, according to all which I command you: so shall ye be My people, and I will be your God: *That I may perform the oath* which I have sworn unto your fathers, to give them a land flowing with milk and honey, as it is this day. Then answered I, and said, So be it, O LORD" (Jeremiah 11:3-5).

By this condition the promises, Covenant, and oaths are bound. God says, "Obey My voice... so shall ye be My people, and I will be your God: **That I may perform the oath** which I have **sworn** unto your fathers, to give them a land flowing with milk and honey." This is not confusing. They were damned, yet God loved them, sought to save them, strove to do all that was possible for them (God in the ways of man), and still they refused to <u>OBEY</u>! Will you still deny this? Let God make His case for you in that He did exhaust the possibilities of His love (God in the ways of man) in trying to save Israel before they were in a damnable state.

> "Now will I sing to my wellbeloved a song of my beloved touching His vineyard. My wellbeloved hath a vineyard in a very fruitful hill: And He fenced it, and gathered out the stones thereof, and planted it with the choicest vine, and built a tower in the midst of it, and also made a winepress therein: and He **looked that it should bring forth grapes,** and it brought forth wild grapes. And now, O inhabitants of Jerusalem, and men of Judah, judge, I pray you, betwixt Me and My vineyard. **What could have been done more to My vineyard, that I have not done in it?** wherefore, when I looked that it should bring forth grapes, brought it forth wild grapes? And now go to; I will tell you what I will do to My vineyard: I will take away the hedge thereof, and it shall be eaten up; and break down the wall thereof, and it shall be trodden down: And I will lay it waste: it shall not be pruned, nor digged; but there shall come up briers and thorns: I will also command the clouds that they rain no rain upon it. For the vineyard of the LORD of hosts is the house of Israel, and the men of Judah His pleasant plant: and He looked for judgment, but

136

behold oppression; for righteousness, but behold a cry" (Isaiah 5:1-7).

As God said it metaphorically, now hear Him personally plead His love – "For He doth not afflict willingly nor grieve the children of men" (Lam. 3:33)…

> **"Have I any pleasure at all that the wicked should die? saith the Lord GOD: *and* not that he should return from his ways, and live?** But when the righteous turneth away from his righteousness, and committeth iniquity, *and* doeth according to all the abominations that the wicked *man* doeth, shall he live? All his righteousness that he hath done shall not be mentioned: in his trespass that he hath trespassed, and in his sin that he hath sinned, in them shall he die. Yet ye say, The way of the Lord is not equal. Hear now, O house of Israel; Is not My way equal? are not your ways unequal? When a righteous *man* turneth away from his righteousness, and committeth iniquity, and dieth in them; for his iniquity that he hath done shall he die. Again, when the wicked *man* turneth away from his wickedness that he hath committed, and doeth that which is lawful and right, he shall save his soul alive. Because he considereth, and turneth away from all his transgressions that he hath committed, he shall surely live, he shall not die. Yet saith the house of Israel, The way of the Lord is not equal. O house of Israel, are not My ways equal? are not your ways unequal? Therefore I will judge you, O house of Israel, every one according to his ways, saith the Lord GOD. Repent, and turn *yourselves* from all your transgressions; so iniquity shall not be your ruin. Cast away from you all your transgressions, whereby ye have transgressed; and make you a new heart and a new spirit: **for why will ye die, O house of Israel? For I have no pleasure in the death of him that dieth, saith the Lord GOD: wherefore turn *yourselves*, and live ye**" (Ezek. 18:23-32).

Many believe that God cannot damn a New Testament Christian because He promises He will not, but has God given any conditions to those promises? God promised that Israel would be saved as well. It is true that, according to the NT promises, we cannot lose our salvation, and by them we are assured an inheritance in the Promised Land of Heaven. This is all based upon the faithful word of God – but have you hardened your heart against the conditions of God? As sure as the promises are, so are the conditions to those promises! God "abideth faithful" to all His "faithful sayings" which He hath said, even – "If we suffer, we shall reign with Him: if we deny Him, **He also will deny us**" – and if we do not believe that He will deny us because we have been regenerated, even "if we believe not, yet He abideth faithful:" He cannot deny His own promise to deny us, i.e. His own faithful saying -"He cannot

137

deny Himself" (2 Tim. 2:11-13).

- ❖ The Israelites were given promises of eternal security – **So are we.**
- ❖ The promises were delivered in such a way that it was seemingly impossible that they could be bound with a condition by the nature of Who God is – **So are ours.**
- ❖ The promises were delivered in such a way that it was seemingly impossible that they could be bound with a condition by the content of the promises – **So are ours.**
- ❖ The Israelites' faith was tried and proven to see if they would obey – **So is ours.**
- ❖ They were tried in a Covenant of salvation that was not yet consummated, thus there is still an inheritance of the promises yet to obtain – **So are we.**
- ❖ The Israelites (the Exodus generation) failed the "Trial of Faith," and so they did not persevere to end – **So can we.**
- ❖ God is justified by the emphasis of the conditions that He gave to those promises – **the same with us.**

There is no question that the NT promises eternal security, but for many years I hardened my heart against the conditions and blinded myself from the actual teaching of scripture, thinking that the nature of the promise itself made impossible any condition, or, because there were no conditions side by side the plain promises, I thought there were no conditions at all. I did not know I was hardening my heart. Unconscious disobedience is the nature of my deception. Are you deceived? I was completely unaware of the two contexts by which God relates to men, and I only viewed God in the spectrum of His sovereign ways (God in the ways of God). Thus, I became a prey to the false doctrines of false prophets who allure the people with a confidence of salvation, even while they are breaking the commandments of God. May God reverse it, and restore what the locusts have eaten!

It is easy for men to trust a promise, but are we laying hold of the substances which those promises do proclaim? Many believe that they believe the promises, that God will confirm them unto the end that they may be blameless in the day of Christ (1 Cor. 1:8-9), but how many look at their life, conversation, and deeds to see if they are blameless, concluding that this is the evidence of their faith in that promise? Look not to a sentence on a page; look to Jesus, the Speaker and Writer of that promise – and cleave to Him, His works, His ways, and His present, continuous confirmation, and so, judge yourself rightly by the fruit in your heart instead of the creed on your lips. The devil can be in your heart while you kiss Christ with your mouth, as it is written, "Satan entered into him" (Jn. 13:27), so what about you? "Betrayest thou the Son of Man with a kiss?" (Lk. 22:48)

ABRAHAMIC EXEMPLIFICATION
CHAPTER 5

"...foundest his heart faithful before Thee..." – Neh. 9:8

The Covenant Promises Subject to Conditions

We have thoroughly reviewed the relevance and history of the Exodus generation and their reception of the Abrahamic Covenant. This generation was an example for those who lose their salvation, and contrasting them, Abraham is an example of persevering salvation. The Covenant to Abraham contained promises and ordinances which were given to the Exodus generation. When they did not continue in faith (evidenced by obedient works), God did not perform the promises. Likewise for Abraham, though he did not fall away and rather persevered in faith, if he would not have continued in faith God would not have performed the promises given to him. As God did to Abraham's seed, it was in like pattern to His dealings with Abraham himself, only Abraham **proved** faithful – "So then they which be of faith are blessed with faithful Abraham" (Gal. 3:9).

❖ God said to the Covenanted seed, OBEY, "**That I may** perform the oath which I have sworn" – Jer. 11:5

❖ God said to Abraham, OBEY, "**That the LORD may** bring upon Abraham that which He hath spoken of him." – Gen. 18:19

God said of Abraham, "**I will perform the oath** which I sware unto Abraham...**because** that Abraham **obeyed My voice**, and kept My charge, My commandments, My statutes, and My laws" (Gen. 26:3-5). Abraham's faith was maintained in obedience to the voice of his God. The faith he had at first was kept "**that he might become** the father of many nations; **according to that which was spoken**, So shall thy seed be" (Rom. 4:18), but do you realize that even the Abrahamic Covenant which was committed to Abraham was established through the hurdles of trial and conditions, that he was the example of persevering salvation and faith as he was proven in these trials, that his life is a thematic skeleton for the entire New Testament's depiction of salvation, and that those who are saved will be saved because they "walk in **the steps of that faith** of our father Abraham" (Rom. 4:12) from their beginning to their perseverant end (Heb. 6:11-20, James 2:14-26) all throughout like-trials?

❖ Genesis 12:1-3, the gospel **call**→ Hebrews 11:8-10.

❖ Genesis 17:1-2, **"perfect"**→
Matt. 5:48, 19:21, Lk. 6:40, 8:14, 1 Cor. 2:6, 2 Cor. 7:1, 13:9, 11, Gal. 3:3, Eph. 4:12-13, Php. 3:15, Col. 1:28, 4:12, 1 Thess. 3:10, 2 Tim. 3:17, Heb. 6:1, 13:21, Jas. 1:4, 2:22, 3:2, 1 Pet. 5:10, 1 Jn. 2:5, 4:12-18, Rev. 3:2.

❖ Genesis 17:15-19, imputed righteousness (*justification by faith*)→Romans 4:17-22, Hebrews 11:11-12.

❖ Genesis 22:12, "because thou hast obeyed My voice" (*justification by works*)→Hebrews 6:11-20 & James 2:14-26, Hebrews 11: 17-19.

Tracing Abraham's Life: The Trial of Faith

Biblical TRIAL → God seeking fear, and then, God finding fear, when it is observed by deeds…then salvation is assured.

The Lord sought the perseverance of Israel's (the Exodus generation) salvation, and in the same context, God seeks to know a saved man's faith. After a man is justified (by faith apart from works), God seeks to verify, vindicate, affirm, confirm, and justify this work by "justifying" men according to their works. Abraham is the first individual where *the Trial of Faith* is explicitly chronicled; likewise, he is the chief figure of "justification by faith" (Rom. 4), the chief figure of "justification by works" (James 2:14-26), and therefore he is the example of perseverance through a performance of oaths/covenants/promises (Heb. 6:11-20, 11).

God in the Ways of God	God in the Ways of Man
Elective/Predestinated & Exclusive Love	Universal, all-inclusive Love
Elective/Predestinated and irresistible will/counsel of salvation ❖ Determines the gift of faith for initial justification by faith ❖ Determines the perseverance of faith continuing in the heart ❖ In this way He determines a vessel to be blameless at the Coming Judgment.	Universal and Resistible will/counsel of salvation ❖ Makes the gospel call that is resistible. ❖ In **the Trial of Faith**, He seeks to know a man's heart as if He cannot see it. ❖ In **Visitation**, or **Final Judgment**, He judges based upon the success or failure of their trial (the deeds of faith found therein), as if election is irrelevant and deeds are the logical responsibility of man's free will.

Abraham's Election:

Abraham was elect according to the counsel of God in the ways of God, thus his salvation (justification by faith) and perseverance (justification by works) were all determined by God's predestination. In Genesis 18:19 God says, "I know him" – and this "know" is evidence that he is elect of God (God in the ways of God).

Abraham was elect according to the counsel of God that determined him to

140

be saved, persevere, and become the chief example of justification by faith (see Romans 4) and justification by works (see James 2:14-26). God in the ways of God did love Abraham with an everlasting love, and therefore he did persevere in faith to God (was justified by works), and consequentially God did perform the Covenant/promises in salvation.

If Abraham had not persevered in faith, he would have failed "**the Trial of his Faith**" wherein God sought to **know his faith by his works**. If Abraham had failed the trial of his faith, he would have failed to obtain the performance of the promises and Covenant, and therein was his salvation. Remember how God related to Israel after their salvation?

Israel

The Israelites received the gospel of the Passover, the Red Sea, the Manna, and the Rock; however, they were eventually reprobated when they denied "the gospel" (Heb. 3-4) at the Promised Land. All these instances were a type of salvation for them, an example of the difficulty of perseverance, and also, they were a picture of present progressive salvation. This idea is not well understood today. Most think the gospel and salvation are begun and completed at justification by faith. After this, all else is considered to be eternally inconsequential circumstances which always involve a "mere" sanctification. This is a great misunderstanding. The Bible does not say work out your sanctification with fear and trembling. It does not say work out your rewards with fear and trembling. God warns, "work out your own salvation with fear and trembling" (Php. 2:12).

The first emphasis, burden, and work of God with Israel is a "**trial** of their faith" – but the Lord speaks of it in the terms, "There He **proved** them" (Ex. 15:25). God seeks to know the heart of His people by trial – looking after their deeds – as if He did not already know their hearts, know their future, or determine it. This is God in the ways of man. A man is limited to knowing a person by fruit, because only God can see the heart. Man does not know the future, nor can he determine it. The genuine nature of this trial can be seen in Exodus chapter 16 when the Lord institutes further means of trial. Exodus 16:4 – "Then said the LORD unto Moses, Behold, I will rain bread from heaven for you; and the people shall go out and gather a certain rate every day, that I may **prove** them, whether they will walk in My law, or no." **As God did relate to the them in the context of "proving" and observing "whether they will walk" in His law or not, so God does give conditions to their salvation through the means by which their faith will be tested/tried and their salvation will be verified/persevered!**

Abraham

❖ Genesis 12:1-3, the gospel **call** → Hebrews 11:8-10.

God saved Abraham by the gospel calling in Genesis 12:1-3. He obeyed the

141

call, "Get thee out of thy country, and from thy kindred, and from thy father's house, unto a land that I will shew thee: And I will…I will…thou shalt…I will…and in thee shall all families of the earth be blessed" (Gen. 12:1-3). This obedience (obeying the gospel, 2 Thess. 1:8) was illustrative of our gospel experience, and, it was famed in the Hall of Faith: "By faith Abraham, when he was called to go out into a place which he should after receive for an inheritance, obeyed; and he went out, not knowing whither he went. By faith he sojourned in the land of promise, as in a strange country, dwelling in tabernacles with Isaac and Jacob, the heirs with him of the same promise: For he looked for a city which hath foundations, whose builder and maker is God" (Heb. 11:8-10). Abraham's faith in the gospel call that was bound with promises eventually became the primary illustration for salvation by faith apart from works, because Abraham was justified by faith alone before the law or circumcision. Therefore, Abraham is the father of faith, seeing he exemplifies this pure justification before the law. Many years, trials, and further revelations of this call and gospel were given to Abraham till, in Genesis 15:6, the Lord gives the most elaborate and explanatory revelation of the Covenant yet. When believing this promise it was written, "And he believed in the LORD; and he counted it to him for righteousness" (Gen. 15:6). This faith was exemplary for the Covenant of God with the Gentiles in Christ Who needed no circumcision, for Abraham "received the sign of circumcision, a seal of the righteousness of the faith which he had yet being uncircumcised: that he might be the father of all them that believe, though they be not circumcised; that righteousness might be imputed unto them also: And the father of circumcision to them who are not of circumcision only, but who also walk in the steps of the faith of our father Abraham, which he had being yet uncircumcised" (Rom. 4:11-12). Before circumcision he was justified; nevertheless he continued to believe and therefore passed the trials of his faith. Thus it is written of him, that through all the trials, he, in "hope believed in hope, **that he might become** the father of many nations; **according to that which was spoken**, So shall thy seed be" (Rom. 4:18).

❖ Genesis 17:15-19, imputed righteousness (justification by faith) → Romans 4:17-22, Hebrews 11:11-12.

This faith that was maintained was "**that he might become** the father of many nations" according to the promise of Genesis 12:1-3. He was 75 years old when the gospel call first came. The persevering faith that obtains Covenant promises is exemplified in the following reference after Romans 4:18, verses 19-22. "And being not weak in faith, he considered not his own body now dead, when he was about an hundred years old, neither yet the deadness of Sara's womb: He staggered not at the promise of God through unbelief; but was strong in faith, giving glory to God; And being fully persuaded that, what he had promised, he was able also to perform. And **therefore it was imputed to him for righteousness**" (Rom. 4:19-22). At this instance, Abraham continues with the understanding that faith must continue for the oath of God to continue. He knows that the oaths of God are subject to interruption, because God teaches him this. When Abraham was 99 years old (Gen. 17:1), He was warned of the necessity of perfection, and on this day he did exemplify perfect faith by believing that life could come from the dead (the deadness of Sarah's womb), and thus he received the gospel again (Christ bringing life from the dead, Gen. 17:15-19, Heb. 11:11-12). Do you not believe that Romans 4:18 is applying the consequence of possible interruption from fulfilling the Covenant promise that Abraham would be made "the father of many nations?" It is what the verse says plainly, but there is more proof. In Genesis 17:1-2, God gives the clear condition that the Covenant's performance hinges upon. When Abraham was 99 years old, God "appeared to Abram, and said unto him, I am the Almighty God; walk before Me, and **be thou perfect**. And **I will make My Covenant between Me and thee**, and will multiply thee exceedingly." Therefore, if Abraham didn't walk before God and be "perfect," then God would not perform or "make" the Covenant "according to that which was spoken" (Rom. 4:18). Now you may wonder, what is perfection?

❖ Genesis 17:1-2,   Matt. 5:48, 19:21, Lk. 6:40, 8:14, 1 Cor.
    "**perfect**"→   2:6, 2 Cor. 7:1, 13:9, 11, Gal. 3:3, Eph.
                         4:12-13, Php. 3:15, Col. 1:28, 4:12, 1
                         Thess. 3:10, 2 Tim. 3:17, Heb. 6:1, 13:21,
                         Jas. 1:4, 2:22, 3:2, 1 Pet. 5:10, 1 Jn. 2:5,

As stated before, Abraham exemplifies the workings of God as a skeleton for the NT. The burden of God to find His people perfect throughout the trial of their faith was first introduced in the trial of Abraham's faith, and the trial is of the such that, if Abraham failed it he would have come short of the promises/Covenant/salvation that God did speak to him; and to come short is erring from perfection. Falling from perfection, or being perfect, is the burden of the ministers in the New Covenant. The end goal of all the work of NT ministers is that they would present the saints perfect before God (Eph. 4:12), and in so doing none would fall short of the promised salvation in Christ. Jesus Christ, and all saving obedience necessary when walking in Him, was what they did "preach, warning every man, and teaching every man in all wisdom; **that we may present every man perfect in Christ Jesus**" (Col. 1:28). If you die having fallen from a state of "perfection" (Heb. 6:1, 1 Cor. 2:6) you will be damned. That is falling from perfection as a Christian (Col. 1:28-29, Eph. 4:12), which is, falling from **perfecting works** in Christ (Rev. 3:2), **perfected holiness** (2 Cor. 7:1), **perfected faith** (James 2:21-22, 1 Thess. 3:10), and as John addresses it, a **perfected love** (1 John 2:5, 4:12, 17).

We, in the New Covenant, are as Abraham because we have received a parallel gospel call that severs us from our house, land, and kindred (Gal. 5:24, Mk. 8:34-35, Lk. 14:26, Matt. 10:34-39, 12:49-50). We do maintain a strangeness and alienation to the world because God is an alien to the world, and we are the friends of God (Col. 1:21-22, Rom. 8:7-8, Eph. 2:1-3). "He was called the friend of God" (Jas. 2:23). We are strange because we, by Spirit and law, are not of the world (1 John 4:5-6, John 15:19, Gal. 6:14). We have been partakers of Christ's death; however, the consummating victory over death will not be actualized until after the fullness of the gospel of His Kingdom is consummated. We have been *resurrected* (Rom. 6:4), *regenerated* (Tit. 3:5), we have overcome *death* (Eph. 2:5), *inherited* the Kingdom (Lk. 17:21), but we await a final consummating *resurrection* (1 Cor. 15:42-50), *regeneration* (Rom. 8:18-21, Php. 3:12-14), defeat of *death* (1 Cor. 15:54-57), and *inheritance* of the Kingdom of God (1 Cor. 15:50). In this manner we await a "salvation to be revealed" (1 Pet. 1:5), which is not full yet, and we strive for the calling of this final freedom (Php. 3:14) as it daily draws "nearer than when we believed" (Rom. 13:11). This is the doctrinal logic behind present progressive salvation. Now, should it be any wonder that if a man discontinues to walk in the newness of life of the *resurrection* by an unrepentant indulgence of the *old man*, refuses the power of *regeneration* to then abide in the *death* which was once experientially overcome, despising the free *inheritance* of holiness which *the Kingdom of God* offers, that this man is doomed to the abyss of the anti-gospel hellfire? Those things are the gospel and Christ, and to deny them is to deny Him. Those who choose earth over heaven and the devil's kingdom over God's – they love hell and hate heaven. God will give them what their works justify for them.

Therefore we have to continue in saving faith through appropriating the gospel power and truths, which will maintain a strangeness and enmity with the world and a familiarity and walk according to heaven. We are chosen from darkness, death, the world & earth, the flesh, and dishonor. We are brought into the light, heavenliness, the Spirit, and holy honor. Maintaining a walk in the Spirit is maintaining the faith of the gospel call, which is, maintaining a walk in a perfect way – therefore God will perform the Covenant of our salvation to its completion. The *gospel by promise* (spiritually and lawfully) performs these things within us Christ's indwelling nature; the *gospel by command* is the present-tense command to walk in these things which we have already received at salvation (thus we will be presently/continuously saved), and if we maintain this perfect walk or God returns and finds us perfect then, we will be finally saved (at death or His return). The gospel by promise is – "I have given you the Land to possess it" (Num. 33:53), and, "The LORD your God which goeth before you, He shall fight for you, according to all that HE did for you in Egypt before your eyes" (Deut. 1:30). The gospel by command is the charge to "go up and fight" with "weapons of war" and the sword (Deut. 1:41) at the command of God – "Behold, I have set the land before you: go in and possess the land," (Deut. 1:8) and, "go up and possess it" (Deut. 1:21). God could have fought for them, but they must fight with Him, but they "set not their heart aright" so as to fight (Ps. 78:8). "The children of Ephraim, being armed, and carrying bows, turned back in the day of battle" (Ps. 78:9). So it is with us – all the things formerly addressed are given to us, put within us, promised for us, but we must presently take them, fight for them, and lay hold on them. Eternal life is a present possession in Christ (1 John 5:11-12), and yet we must daily "fight the good fight of faith" and "lay hold on eternal life" by standing against and prevailing over evil angels with the weaponry of God's war instruments (Eph. 6:10-18).

The Burden of Perfection: *the NT trial of faith in present progressive salvation.*

We have been made "strangers and pilgrims," but we must presently "abstain from fleshly lusts which war against the soul" (1 Pet. 2:11). We have been made now "light in the Lord" (Eph. 5:8) because Christ "delivered us from the power of darkness" (Col. 1:13), but now we must "walk as children of light" (Eph. 5:8). We were "foolish" (Titus 3:3), but now Christ has become to us "the wisdom of God" (1 Cor. 1:24), thus we must be "a wise man" (James 3:13) – "walk circumspectly, not as fools, but as wise" (Eph. 5:15). Notice how the "walk" is consistent with the Spiritual and lawful salvation that has already been accomplished. We are completed in this present progressive work by maintaining saving faith - this is perfection. "Walk before Me" in *these manners*, God commands in the NT, and in our Covenant, God says "be thou perfect" (Gen. 17:1).

❖ Genesis 22:12, "because thou hast obeyed My voice" (justification by works) → Hebrews 6:11-20 & James 2:14-26, Hebrews 11: 17-19.

When we stay away from the flesh, darkness, death, and the world, we are strangers and pilgrims who desire to continue to be strangers and pilgrims. Unregretful, unrepentant of the decision we have made to forsake all to follow Him against the potential lusts which can come from a house, properties of land, family, and kindred. This was Abraham's gospel and ours, but look at Abraham's perfect walk in perseverance.

> "These all died in faith, not having received the promises, but having seen them afar off, and were persuaded of them, and embraced them, and confessed that they were strangers and pilgrims on the earth. For they that say such things declare plainly that they seek a country. And truly, **if they had been mindful of that country from whence they came out, they might have had opportunity to have returned.** But now they desire a better country, that is, an heavenly: wherefore God is not ashamed to be called their God: for He hath prepared for them a city" (Heb. 11:13-16).

Abraham became a stranger, walked as a stranger, and continued to be a stranger; so must we continue to be, in life, light, righteousness, wisdom, and holiness, which is our alien strangeness in Christ; otherwise Christ will say, "I know you not whence ye are; depart from Me, all ye workers of iniquity" (Lk. 13:27). But if Abraham was "mindful of that country from whence" he "came out," then he would have "had opportunity to" return. But since he was steadfast in faith and repentance, according to the gospel call, he did steadfastly "desire a better country, that is, an heavenly!" So Abraham is the example of perseverance for us to follow in. The capstone of His perseverance is referenced directly after these verses in the Hall of Faith:

"By faith Abraham, **when he was tried**, offered up Isaac: and he that had received the promises offered up his only begotten son, Of whom it was said, That in Isaac shall thy seed be called: Accounting that God was able to raise him up, even from the dead; from whence also he received **Him** [Jesus] **in a figure**" (Heb. 11:17-19).

This is the capstone of the trial of his faith, as it says, "when he was **tried**." This mark of Abraham is used as the mark of his persevering faith. This is applied and taught to the NT Church in two other places, Hebrews 6:11-20 and James 2:14-26. Salvation begun was justification by faith (Rom. 4), salvation continued is the trial of faith wherein we continue to receive Jesus (like as Abraham "in a figure"), and maintaining this walk of perfection is when our works do demonstrate what is worthy of the virtue already given in the lawful/spiritual salvation (justification by works). "Was not Abraham our father **justified by works**, when he had offered Isaac his son upon the altar? Seest thou how faith wrought with his works, and by works was faith made **perfect**? And the scripture was fulfilled which saith, Abraham believed God, and it was imputed unto him for righteousness: and he was called the Friend of God. Ye see then how that by works a man is justified, and not by faith only. Likewise also was not Rahab the harlot justified by works, when she had received the messengers, and had sent them out another way? For as the body without the spirit is dead, so faith without works is dead also" (James 2:21-26).

Understanding the Trial of Faith

"Every way of man is right in his own eyes: but the LORD pondereth the hearts"
– Prov. 21:2

You see, God already knew Abraham by sovereign, eternal election. He said of him, "For **I know him**, that he will command his children and his household after him, and they <u>shall</u> <u>keep the way</u> of the LORD, to do justice and judgment; **that the LORD may bring upon Abraham that which he hath spoken of him**" (Genesis 18:19). The Lord already knew he would persevere, already elected him to persevere, but within time, God related to him in a manner which is not according to God in the ways of God. God sought to know him in another manner, as a man would seek to know something: through works, experiences, and trials. So the question is: Does God know you by trial? Though the Lord already knew Abraham (God in the ways of God), though he was the elect of God (God in the ways of God), God sought to know him through trial (temptation), thus it is written, "God did tempt Abraham" (Gen. 22:1). This is when He commanded Abraham to offer up Isaac, who was the promised child, and the Lord was *going to see* if Abraham still believed that by God's word He would bring life from the dead. This time it was not *the deadness of Sarah's womb* which tried him; rather it was the death of Isaac. Abraham believed that he was going to kill Isaac, but because he believed that Isaac would be killed, he was assured that Isaac would be raised from the dead according to the promise – "Accounting that God *was* able to **raise** *him* **up, even from the dead**" (Heb. 11:19). In this manner

Abraham continued to believe the gospel, passed the trial of faith, and *as if* God didn't already know Abraham, God said: "Lay not thine hand upon the lad, neither do thou any thing unto him: for **now I know** *that thou* **FEAREST** *God,* **seeing** thou hast not withheld thy son, thine only son from Me" (Gen. 22:12). God said "now I know" (God in the ways of man) because He was seeking to know Abraham **according to his works,** to prove (test or try) him as if He didn't already know his heart. God was operating as a man would when a man would seek to know another man, which means that God would seek to know another man by *works* and *experiential relationships.* This is the trial of faith in the condescension of God. Remember the thoughts of God toward Israel and all the ways that He sought to know them? "And thou shalt remember all the way which the LORD thy God led thee these forty years in the wilderness, to humble thee, and to **prove** thee, **to know what was in thine heart**, whether thou wouldest keep His commandments, or no" (Deut. 8:2).

 ⚌ Proving: Deuteronomy 7:22, 8:2, 13:3, 2 Chronicles 32:31, Job 23:10, Psalm 66:10, Malachi 3:2-3, Proverbs 17:3

  This knowing of God through trial, proving, and fire is a consistent theme throughout the scripture, for this is the hinge of the Covenant, promises, and salvation. The end of passing the trial is salvation because salvation is rewarded to every man who has saving faith. The question is: How will God find your faith to be when He tries you? Will He find it saving or staggering, enduring or fainting? The furnace of fiery trials is the course predestined for all God's twice-born children. It is written, "That the trial of your faith, being much more precious than of gold that perisheth, though it be tried with fire, **might be found** unto praise and honour and glory at the appearing of Jesus Christ: Whom having not seen, ye love; in Whom, though now ye see Him not, yet believing, ye rejoice with joy unspeakable and full of glory: Receiving the end of your faith, even the salvation of your souls" (1 Peter 1:7-9). God must find your faith out by works, then such a one will have the "praise and honour and glory," as Peter declares, or the "glory and honour and immortality, eternal life," as Paul declares (Rom. 2:7), both are indicative of Divine acceptance before the Judgment Seat of Christ. After Abraham was tried, and he passed, he did receive the assurance of his salvation through God's swearing in of the Covenant promises (Gen. 22:16-18). The writer of Hebrews applies this to the NT experience, pressing Christians to obtain a real assurance of their faith in the same way Abraham did. God said, "By Myself have I sworn, saith the LORD, for **because thou hast done this thing**, and hast not withheld thy son, thine only son...I will bless...I will multiply...in thy seed shall all the nations of the earth be blessed; **BECAUSE THOU HAST OBEYED MY VOICE**" (Gen. 22:16-18). What did saving faith look like? **OBEDIENCE to the VOICE OF GOD!** This is the repeated reasoning of God for why He performed the Covenant with Abraham, see Gen. 17:1-2, 18:19, 22:18, 26:5, and Romans 4:18. Therefore now, to us the burden of God is, as Genesis 17:1-2 states:

   "And we desire that every one of you do shew the <u>same diligence</u> to the full **assurance of hope unto the end**: That ye be not

147

slothful, but followers of them who through <u>faith</u> and <u>patience</u> **inherit the promises**. For when God made promise to Abraham, because He could swear by no greater, He sware by Himself, Saying, Surely blessing I will bless thee, and multiplying I will multiply thee. And so, **after he had patiently endured, he obtained the promise**" (Hebrews 6:11-15).

My reader, God will find you out. He must find you out, and though He *knows* your heart right now, though He *knows* your destiny by election, in condescension after the ways of man He seeks to *try you* and *know you* as if He has never known you for sure. Now consider your works, His voice of command, the hardness of your heart, and thus ask yourself the question, will He say to you, "now I know that thou FEAREST Me"? If you are regenerate, Christian, though God knows you eternally, and though He knows your heart right now, even though nothing is hidden from His sight so that He would never have to test anything or anyone to find anything out, God will do to you as He has tried Abraham's faith. He will, in this way, find you out. Will God find you faithful as "faithful Abraham" (Gal. 3:9)? God **"foundest** his heart **faithful"** through the trial of his faith, and therefore, He "madest a Covenant with him" (Neh. 9:8). "Be diligent that ye may be **found of Him** in peace, without spot, and blameless" (2 Peter 3:14).

Many would make the accusation that the doctrine of losing salvation is based upon a misunderstanding of grace, a reliance upon works, and a negating of faith. Ye hypocrites! If we believe we have received salvation, not apart from but through saving faith, how then is the loss of saving faith a salvation based upon works? The sovereignty of God is evidenced by a man's inability to come to Christ, because the man has an inability to believe, and because faith "is the gift of God" (Eph. 2) "according as God hath dealt to every man" (Rom. 12:3). But what if God, in His sovereignty, does show forth those who are elect as "vessels of wrath fitted to destruction" by their eventual discontinuance of faith and repentance, while formerly they were able to obtain salvation through faith and repentance, and conclusively, God glorifies His own eternal integrity before, during, and after their fall though it is an exultation of judgment outside the realm of our logical comprehension and understanding! Thus, it is a glorification of God's sovereignty. Of this glory, it is written, "no flesh can glory in His presence"; therefore these attributes of judgment are to be wondered at from below, a looking up at the loft of infinite purity in God's sovereign and just pleasure.

THE DAVIDIC COVENANT:
SEEKING A PERFORMANCE
OF THE PROMISES
CHAPTER 6

The Davidic Covenant was given in 2 Samuel 7 and 1 Chronicles 17. There are specific promises given in this Covenant. These promises were spoken and given to David and his seed just as the promises were given to Abraham and his seed. God said to David, "the LORD telleth thee that He will make thee an house" (2 Samuel 7:11). The Lord says of this house:

> "I will set up thy seed after thee, which shall proceed out of thy bowels, and **I will establish his kingdom. He shall build an house for My name**, and **I will stablish the throne of his kingdom for ever**. I will be his Father, and he shall be My son. If he commit iniquity, I will chasten him with the rod of men, and with the stripes of the children of men: But My mercy shall not depart away from him, as I took it from Saul, whom I put away before thee. **And thine house and thy kingdom shall be established for ever before thee: thy throne shall be established for ever**" (2 Sam. 7:12-16).

In Chronicles the Covenant states:

> "Furthermore I tell thee that the LORD will build thee an house. And it shall come to pass, when thy days be expired that thou must go to be with thy fathers, that I will raise up thy seed after thee, which shall be of thy sons; and **I will establish his kingdom. He shall build Me an house**, and **I will stablish his throne for ever**. I will be his Father, and he shall be My son: and I will not take My mercy away from him, as I took it from him that was before thee: **But I will settle him in Mine house and in My kingdom for ever: and his throne shall be established for evermore**" (1 Chronicles 17:10-14).

Three promises can be accounted of in this Covenant. Concerning David's seed, God says, 1) "I will establish his Kingdom," 2) "He shall build an house for My Name," and 3) "I will stablish the throne of his kingdom for ever." These three promises are emboldened above. Take note of what God says following these three promises in the text that is a lighter shade. Steadfast mercy, unfailing faithfulness, and persevering grace were promised to the seed of David – a covenanted relationship unlike what happened to Saul. When Saul sinned, God took away mercy from him and so went the kingdom, but with Solomon, God says, this would not be so even if he sins. If Solomon sinned, God said that He would "be his Father, and he shall be My son. If he commit iniquity, I will chasten him with the rod of men, and with the stripes of the children of men: But My mercy shall not depart away from him, as I took it from Saul, whom I put away before thee." On the basis of this fatherly relationship, it was therefore reasonable to believe the following PROMISE to be inevitable, irreversible, and without question, unalterable: "And thine house and thy kingdom shall be established for ever before thee: thy throne shall be established for ever." My reader, do you think this promise could be breached even though the content of the promise itself appears to be unconditional and unalterable?

❖ These promises were intended (God in the ways of man) for Solomon.

❖ These promises were intended (God in the ways of God) for Jesus Christ, *however, at the first it was understood that these promises were to Solomon and his immediate, subsequent generations.*

First, I desire to prove to you that these promises were intended for Solomon. I want to go through the accounts where David, the Lord, Solomon, and all the people acknowledge that this Covenant was to Solomon. Also, since it was not fulfilled in Solomon, seeing that he fell short of fulfilling the last promise, I want to draw out the reason he succeeded as far as he did, and why he failed in the end. Two of the three promises in the Covenant were performed and one promise was *breached.*

David understood the Covenant to be <u>for Solomon</u> and instructed Solomon to lay hold of it.

> 1 Chronicles 28:6-11
> [6] And He said unto Me, **Solomon thy son**, he shall build My house and My courts: for I have chosen him to be My son, and I will be his Father. [7] Moreover I will establish his kingdom for ever, **if he be constant to do My commandments and My judgments, as at this day.** [8] Now therefore in the sight of all Israel the congregation of the LORD, and in the audience of our God, keep and seek for all the commandments of the LORD your God: **that ye may** possess this good land, and leave it for an inheritance for your children after you for ever. [9] And thou, Solomon my son, know thou the God of thy father, and serve Him with a **perfect heart** and with a willing mind: for the LORD searcheth all hearts, and understandeth all the imaginations of the thoughts: **if thou seek Him, He will be found of thee; but if thou forsake Him, he will cast thee off for ever.** [10] Take heed now; for the LORD hath chosen thee to build an house for the sanctuary: be strong, and do it. [11] Then David gave to Solomon his son the pattern of the porch, and of the houses thereof, and of the treasuries thereof, and of the upper chambers thereof, and of

the inner parlours thereof, and of the place of the mercy seat"

In this passage we can clearly see the promises, the fatherly relationship of unconditional mercy, and the clear intent to "establish his [Solomon's] kingdom for ever." This is parallel to the account of the Covenant given to David in 1 Chronicles 17 & 2 Samuel 7, but in these two accounts there were no **IFs**, which would give the appearance that it is impossible to be cast off forever by God. There was not any conditional language at all. Emboldened in the text directly after the promise which was given in 2 Sam. 7 and 1 Chron. 17 is a condition that was not present when the scripture accounts the establishment of the Covenant. Have you ever studied all the "**IF**" warnings in the New Testament? Here in the Davidic Covenant, though the condition was not given in the accounts which detailed the reception of the Davidic Covenant, though the condition is written in another place in scripture, and though the Covenant seems to be unconditional by its very content, this condition binds still: "**if he be constant to do My commandments and My judgments, as at this day.**" In verse 8, notice the commonly used clause, "**that ye may,**" which frames the former address to remind us of the conditions. Keeping these conditions is maintaining saving faith, and like Abraham (Gen. 17:1-2), keeping these conditions is what it is to be found "**perfect**" in walk or heart before God. Thus David says in verse 9, "And thou, Solomon my son, know thou the God of thy father, and serve Him with a **perfect heart** and with a willing mind: for the LORD searcheth all hearts, and understandeth all the imaginations of the thoughts: **if thou seek Him, He will be found of thee;** but **if thou forsake Him, He will cast thee off for ever.**" Solomon does keep a perfect heart as to be given the throne of David (promise #1) and build the house of God (promise #2), but he fell from perfection after the house was built and therefore came short of the everlasting throne and Kingdom (as it was meant and intended for his immediate, physical seed). David is greatly burdened for Solomon to maintain a perfect heart. Read his prayer for Solomon, and consider, have you prayed these things for yourself? Solomon needed a perfect heart to build the Temple:

> 1 Chronicles 29:17-19
> [17] I know also, my God, that Thou triest the heart, and hast pleasure in uprightness. As for me, in the uprightness of mine heart I have willingly offered all these things: and now have I seen with joy Thy people, which are present here, to offer willingly unto Thee. [18] O LORD God of Abraham, Isaac, and of Israel, our fathers, **keep this for ever in the imagination of the thoughts of the heart of Thy people, and prepare their heart unto Thee**: [19] And give unto Solomon my son **a perfect heart,** to keep Thy commandments, Thy testimonies, and Thy statutes, and to do all these things, and to **build the palace**, for the which I have made provision.

Perfection in Solomon was a life of loving obedience to God, "and Solomon loved the LORD, walking in the statutes of David his father" (1 Kings 3:3).

A perfect heart strives and presses to obtain (Php. 3:14), fulfill (Rom. 8:4, Gal. 5:14, James 2:23), and lay hold (1 Tim. 6:12, 19) on the promises of God. Do you have this mind toward the promises of God in the NT? Saving faith is objectively defined by a carefulness to fulfill the Covenantal conditions, that it could not be said that a person savingly believes while their present behavior is to be blamed by one of the conditions of God. Most trust they are savingly believing God, and His promises, but are they keeping the conditions of those promises? Reader, are you burdened for "**perfection**?" Look how Solomon sets his face to build the Temple as we must set our face to "lay hold on eternal life" (1 Tim. 6:12).

> 1 Kings 5:5
> [5] And, behold, **I purpose** to build **an house** unto the name of the LORD my God, as the LORD spake unto David my father, saying, Thy son, whom I will set upon thy throne in thy room, he shall build an house unto My name.

David said to Solomon:

> 1 Chronicles 28:20
> [20] And David said to Solomon his son, Be strong and of good courage, and do it: fear not, nor be dismayed: for the LORD God, even my God, will be with thee; He **will not fail thee, nor forsake thee, until thou hast finished all the work for the service of the house of the LORD**.

He was not purposing or striving according to his own power to fulfill the promises. He was seeking God, that through the deeds of faith he would behave himself in a perfect way as David his father did. David said: "I will behave myself wisely in a **perfect** way. O when wilt Thou come unto me? I will walk within my house with a **perfect** heart" (Psalm 101:2). David can say, "I will behave" and "I will walk," nevertheless he knows that he can do nothing by himself. He confesses that "it is God that girdeth me with strength, and maketh my way **perfect**" (Psalm 18:32), and again, "The LORD will perfect that which concerneth me" (Ps. 138:8). Amen! So David said to Solomon in 1 Chron. 28:20 (written above), "Be strong and of a good courage, and do it... for the LORD God, even my God, will be with thee!"

When the Temple began to be built and the building was in process, the Lord spoke to Solomon yet another reminder of the conditions. If Solomon kept these conditions, he would have the performance of the promise he seeks, which is to *finish building the Temple*. If a man sets his face aright, he ought to be mindful of the conditions that he may be careful to fulfill them, even while those promises are partially fulfilled, or at present are being fulfilled. Grace at present does not ensure grace in the future; nay, only unless faith in perfection is kept, for we "are kept by the power of God through faith" (1 Pet. 1:5).

> 1 Kings 6:11-13

11 And the word of the LORD came to Solomon, saying, 12
Concerning this house which thou art in building, **if thou wilt
walk in My statutes, and execute My judgments, and keep all
My commandments to walk in them; then will I perform My
word with thee**, which I spake unto David thy father: 13 And I
will dwell among the children of Israel, and will not forsake My
people Israel.

David warned Solomon of conditions… then God did likewise through a
personal appearance before this choice man. It is doubly sure that Solomon was to
keep this ever in his mind, that God said, "**IF…THEN** will I perform My word with
thee, which I spake unto David thy father" (verse 12). God stated the conditions by
which He will perform genuine promises. David's clear understanding of the
principle of conditions is evident in how he warned Solomon of God's ability to
discontinue a promise because the covenanted people did discontinue their faith →

1 Kings 2:2-4
2 I go the way of all the earth: be thou strong therefore, and shew
thyself a man; 3 And keep the charge of the LORD thy God, to
walk in His ways, to keep His statutes, and His commandments,
and His judgments, and His testimonies, as it is written in the law
of Moses, that thou mayest prosper in all that thou doest, and
whithersoever thou turnest thyself: 4 **That the LORD may
continue His word which He spake concerning me, saying, If
thy children take heed to their way, to walk before Me in
truth with all their heart and with all their soul, there shall
not fail thee (said He) a man on the throne of Israel**.

Solomon kept the faith, was granted power through grace to finish the
Temple, and at the dedication prayer of the completed Temple he gave all the glory to
God. This prayer is after the cloud of glory had filled the Temple (1 Kings 8:10-11),
signifying God's acceptance of the Temple and the fulfillment of the promise. It was
all accomplished by God, through God, by grace through faith and not of works.
Solomon said, God "spake with His mouth unto David," "hath with His hand fulfilled
it," and "performed His word that He spake," "as the LORD promised." In this,
Solomon acknowledged two of the promises of the Covenant being fulfilled: 1) "I am
risen up in the room of David my father," and, 2) "have built an house for the name
of the LORD God of Israel" (verse 20).

1 Kings 8:15-20
15 And he said, Blessed be the LORD God of Israel, which **spake
with His mouth unto David** my father, and **hath with His hand
fulfilled it**, saying, 16 Since the day that I brought forth My
people Israel out of Egypt, I chose no city out of all the tribes of
Israel to build an house, that My name might be therein; but I
chose David to be over My people Israel. 17 And it was in the

153

heart of David my father to build an house for the name of the LORD God of Israel. [18] And the LORD said unto David my father, Whereas it was in thine heart to build an house unto My name, thou didst well that it was in thine heart. [19] Nevertheless thou shalt not build the house; but thy son that shall come forth out of thy loins, he shall build the house unto My name. [20] And the LORD hath **performed His word** that He spake, and **I am risen up in the room of David my father**, and sit on the throne of Israel, **as the LORD promised**, and have **built an house** for the name of the LORD God of Israel.

Solomon did "lay hold" of two promises by faith, but there was one left. Setting his face to the third promise of the Covenant was his next endeavor.

2 Chronicles 6:14-16

[14] And said, O LORD God of Israel, there is no God like Thee in the heaven, nor in the earth; which **keepest covenant**, and shewest mercy unto Thy servants, that **walk** before Thee with **all their hearts**: [15] Thou which hast kept with Thy servant David my father that which Thou hast **promised him**; and spakest with Thy mouth, and hast **fulfilled it with Thine hand**, as it is this day. [16] Now therefore, O LORD God of Israel, **keep with Thy servant David my father that which Thou hast promised him, saying, There shall not fail thee a man in My sight to sit upon the throne of Israel; yet so that thy children take heed to their way to walk in My law, as thou hast walked before Me.**

1 Kings 8:22-26

[22] And Solomon stood before the altar of the LORD in the presence of all the congregation of Israel, and spread forth his hands toward heaven: [23] And he said, LORD God of Israel, there is no God like Thee, in heaven above, or on earth beneath, who keepest covenant and mercy with Thy servants that walk before Thee with all their heart: [24] Who hast kept with Thy servant David my father that Thou promisedst him: Thou spakest also with Thy mouth, and hast fulfilled it with Thine hand, as it is this day. [25] Therefore now, LORD God of Israel, **keep with Thy servant David my father that Thou promisedst him**, saying, **There shall not fail thee a man in My sight to sit on the throne of Israel**; so that thy children take heed to their way, that they walk before Me as thou hast walked before Me. [26] And now, O God of Israel, **let Thy word, I pray Thee, be verified**, which Thou spakest unto Thy servant David my father.

Solomon was in "terror" (2 Cor. 5:11) over the conditions, and this is why he prayed for the performance, keeping, fulfillment, and verification of the promises.

154

When I was a Calvinist, I prayed for the fulfillment of the promises of God only because I saw that men did this in the scripture, but I didn't understand why. When I was a Calvinist, I warned about being a castaway only because I saw this in scripture, but I never had such a mindset that was evidently and personally in the apostle Paul. I could not understand how to have such a mind in the theological boundaries of Calvinism. Now here, Solomon was earnestly praying for the performance of the last and third promise given to him BECAUSE he is aware of the conditions, of perfection, and was desperately in need of God to prepare his heart in this way. God is a God that "keepest Covenant" (1 Chron. 6:14), and in Solomon's life God had "kept... that which" he "promised," and thus Solomon prayed for God to, "NOW THEREFORE," "keep with Thy servant David my father which Thou hast promised him, saying, There shall not fail thee a man in My sight to sit upon the throne of Israel" (2 Chron. 16). It was a promise to David, intended for Solomon, and Solomon prayerfully sought it, saying, "And now, O God of Israel, let Thy word, I pray Thee, be **verified**, which Thou spakest unto Thy servant David my father" (1 Kings 8:26). Solomon knew the promises that had been fulfilled, or would be fulfilled, were and would be fulfilled because God keeps His Covenant and mercy with His servants that are His servants indeed: "that walk before Thee with all their hearts" (2 Chron. 6:14), that "take heed to their way to walk in My law" (2 Chron. 6:16), and that is *perfection.* Solomon knew this. He knew that God could forsake him, his people, and the promises, if they didn't have perfect hearts. After the prayer, Solomon blessed the people in 1 Kings 8:54-66, and in verse 56-61, he clearly portrayed this burden of perfection: that God, to Solomon and Israel, would "incline our hearts unto Him, to walk in His ways, and to keep His commandments, and His statutes, and His judgments, which He commanded our fathers," would make "your heart therefore **perfect** with the LORD our God, to walk in His statutes, and to keep His commandments, as at this day." When Solomon prayed for the word of God to be fulfilled, verified, performed, and kept, he was praying for this **perfection** of heart, and therewith the obedient deeds that are necessary for a Covenant's performance.

Solomon's blessing after the Prayer:

> 1 Kings 8:54-66 (KJV)
> [54] And it was so, that when Solomon had made an end of praying all this prayer and supplication unto the LORD, he arose from before the altar of the LORD, from kneeling on his knees with his hands spread up to heaven. [55] And he stood, and blessed all the congregation of Israel with a loud voice, saying, [56] Blessed be the LORD, that hath given rest unto His people Israel, **according to all that He promised: there hath not failed one word of all His good promise, which He promised by the hand of Moses His servant.** [57] The LORD our God be with us, as He was with our fathers: let Him not leave us, nor forsake us: [58] **That He may incline our hearts unto Him, to walk in all His ways, and to keep His commandments, and His statutes, and His**

judgments, which He commanded our fathers. [59] And let these my words, wherewith I have made supplication before the LORD, be nigh unto the LORD our God day and night, that He maintain the cause of His servant, and the cause of His people Israel at all times, as the matter shall require: [60] That all the people of the earth may know that the LORD is God, and that there is none else. [61] **Let your heart therefore be perfect with the LORD our God, to walk in His statutes, and to keep His commandments, as at this day.** [62] And the king, and all Israel with him, offered sacrifice before the LORD. [63] And Solomon offered a sacrifice of peace offerings, which he offered unto the LORD, two and twenty thousand oxen, and an hundred and twenty thousand sheep. So the king and all the children of Israel dedicated the house of the LORD. [64] The same day did the king hallow the middle of the court that was before the house of the LORD: for there he offered burnt offerings, and meat offerings, and the fat of the peace offerings: because the brasen altar that was before the LORD was too little to receive the burnt offerings, and meat offerings, and the fat of the peace offerings. [65] And at that time Solomon held a feast, and all Israel with him, a great congregation, from the entering in of Hamath unto the river of Egypt, before the LORD our God, seven days and seven days, even fourteen days. [66] On the eighth day he sent the people away: and they blessed the king, and went unto their tents joyful and glad of heart for all the goodness that the LORD had done for David His servant, and for Israel His people.

In response to Solomon's prayer, the Lord appeared to him a second time with the same warning of conditions. Are you burdened and focused on the NT conditions? If God were to speak anything to the NT Churches today like as He did to the NT Churches in the province of Asia in Revelation chapters 2-3, His burden would be those things which we must do, those deeds which are the extension of a perfect heart, so that we can go to heaven and obtain the NT Covenant promises (Rev. 2:2-5, 9, 13-14, 19-20, 23, 26, 3:1-2, 8, 15). Are you burdened with the Lord's burdens? The second appearance of the Lord to Solomon:

2 Chronicles 7:17-22
[17] And as for thee, **if** thou wilt **walk** before Me, as David thy father **walked**, and do according to all that I have commanded thee, and shalt observe My statutes and My judgments; [18] **Then** will I stablish the throne of thy kingdom, **according as I have covenanted with David thy father,** saying, **There shall not fail thee a man to be ruler in Israel.** [19] But **if** ye turn away, and forsake My statutes and My commandments, which I have set before you, and shall go and serve other gods, and worship them;

156

^{20} Then will I pluck them up by the roots out of My land which I have given them; and this house, which I have sanctified for My name, will I cast out of My sight, and will make it to be a proverb and a byword among all nations. ^{21} And this house, which is high, shall be an astonishment to every one that passeth by it; so that he shall say, Why hath the LORD done thus unto this land, and unto this house? ^{22} And it shall be answered, Because they forsook the LORD God of their fathers, which brought them forth out of the land of Egypt, and laid hold on other gods, and worshipped them, and served them: therefore hath He brought all this evil upon them.

1 Kings 9:2-9
^{2} That the LORD appeared to Solomon the second time, as He had appeared unto him at Gibeon. ^{3} And the LORD said unto him, I have heard thy prayer and thy supplication, that thou hast made before Me: I have hallowed this house, which thou hast built, to put My name there for ever; and Mine eyes and Mine heart shall be there perpetually. ^{4} And **if** thou wilt walk before Me, as David thy father walked, in integrity of heart, and in uprightness, to do according to all that I have commanded thee, and wilt keep My statutes and My judgments: ^{5} **Then** I will establish the throne of **thy kingdom** upon Israel for ever, **as I promised to David thy father**, saying, **There shall not fail thee a man upon the throne of Israel**. ^{6} But if ye shall at all turn from following Me, ye or your children, and will not keep My commandments and My statutes which I have set before you, but go and serve other gods, and worship them: ^{7} Then will I cut off Israel out of the land which I have given them; and this house, which I have hallowed for My name, will I cast out of My sight; and Israel shall be a proverb and a byword among all people: ^{8} And at this house, which is high, every one that passeth by it shall be astonished, and shall hiss; and they shall say, Why hath the LORD done thus unto this land, and to this house? ^{9} And they shall answer, Because they forsook the LORD their God, Who brought forth their fathers out of the land of Egypt, and have taken hold upon other gods, and have worshipped them, and served them: therefore hath the LORD brought upon them all this evil.

Solomon did not keep a **perfect heart** (1 Kings 11:4) and therefore failed to obtain this third promise that was intended for him:

1 Kings 11:3-6
^{3} And he had seven hundred wives, princesses, and three hundred

concubines: and his wives turned away his heart. ^{4} For it came to pass, **when Solomon was old**, that his wives **turned away his heart** after other gods: and **his heart was not <u>perfect</u> with the LORD his God, as was the heart of David his father.** ^{5} For Solomon went after Ashtoreth the goddess of the Zidonians, and after Milcom the abomination of the Ammonites. ^{6} And Solomon did evil in the sight of the LORD, and went not fully after the LORD, as did David his father.

The Lord appeared to Solomon twice: he saw the glory of God in a cloud and fire consume the sacrifice, and he was as one of the faithful elders in Joshua's day, "who had seen all the great works of the LORD that He did for Israel" (Judges 2:7). Because these men saw all the great works of God, they stood faithful to God throughout the test of time and trial. As long as they were alive, the people of Israel followed their example. Those that "knew not the LORD, nor yet the works which He had done for Israel" (Judges 2:10) did rebel against God. What deceived the heart of so seasoned a saint, so choice a man as Solomon? What snare of pride or deceit of the devil was able to destroy the wisest man on the earth?

A commandment to the Kings of Israel was written by Moses in Deuteronomy 17:17 – "neither shall he multiply wives to himself, **that his heart turn not away.**" Solomon's heart did not turn away in a single day. He did not suddenly apostatize the day he had *too many wives*. The effect of many wives OVER TIME did slowly and steadily infect his heart to finally and eventually turn away from God. It was "when Solomon was old" that the effect of his many wives did turn his heart from **perfection**. Think of all the times that David and God warned Solomon to focus, take heed to, and be careful to remember the condition of a perfect heart. Solomon could have thought that, since he had a perfect heart then, at present in his today, then he would have a perfect heart 2 years from that day. He could have thought that he would never turn away from God after he saw all the great exploits of the Lord's faithfulness alongside two personal appearances. Nevertheless, God said that a perfect heart obeys His statutes and that Solomon should be careful and focused on obedience. One of God's statutes, if transgressed, warned of an inevitable and promised damnation to any caliber of saint, even the seasoned, elderly, wise, and virtuous King Solomon. It was a promise of God to damnation that, if Solomon multiplied wives, he would eventually turn from God. When God warns of the promise of spreading wickedness like leaven, spreading uncleanness like as it was by touch, or the certainty of corruption in some forbidden circumstance of company, God expects men to cast aside their self-confidence and arrogant reasoning. Solomon could have forgotten the commandment; he could have reasoned within himself, 'how many wives are too many?' He could have forgotten the commandment because he did not believe his heart could easily turn away from God. Since Solomon was sure he had a perfect heart at present and could discern no foolish thought or appealing temptation to turn away from God, seeing that he was so "perfect" in heart at present, he could have trusted he would not be turned away in the future.

Nevertheless, he put himself in a situation that promised damnation, and that situation did not damn him immediately but **over time**. NT Christian, do you know where the promises of damnation are in the NT? Do you know what the situations of damnation are in the NT?

Do you know what situations you can put yourself in that will damn you through seeds of infection and rebellion that are dormant at present, like Solomon's wives, yet with these seeds there is a promise of a growing, eventual, and effectual apostasy? Solomon was not conscientious of rebellion against God, nor was Eve, but the word of Almighty God did warn that Solomon's wives were a daily influence that is subtle, slow, yet sure, that he and those in situations like it will be led astray without knowing it. Do you know situations like this are in the NT? Perhaps you have never become aware of them because you never believed that the promises of your eternal life do hinge upon your obedience to these conditional commands and warnings. Though you are right with God now, though you love Him at present, and though you cannot perceive a future of eventual backsliding from Him, do you have the humility to believe God when He warns you that, just as Solomon was turned away, you can be "leavened" (1 Cor. 5:6-13) and made unclean (2 Cor. 6:17), and thus God judicially refuses to recognize you as His son or daughter (2 Cor. 6:17-18) just as He forsook King Saul and refused him as king henceforth. Like as Solomon's warning, both of these NT warnings are addressing your "company" (1 Cor. 5:9-11), "fellowship" (2 Cor. 6:14), and "yoking" (2 Cor. 6:14) with those who do not bear the fruits of a true confession in Christianity, and that they, if you choose to be in Christian company, practice, yoking, and fellowship with them, will infect you, turn your heart, "leaven" you, and cause you to be unclean in God's sight by their uncleanness. We are therefore commanded, as Solomon was, to remove ourselves from these persons because they create a harmful and dangerous spiritual environment which will eventually turn us away from God. This act of removing is the call of "purging" (1 Cor. 5:7) or "putting away" from the Church "that wicked person" (1 Cor. 5:9-13) until you are "perfected" in a "holiness" (2 Cor. 7:1), a "separateness," "wherefore come out from among them" (2 Cor. 6:17), God says!

Unwillingly and unconsciously, while maintaining a perfect and whole heart, we can commit this sin in its NT form, and as Solomon, our inevitable fate through time will be our corruption from a perfect and whole heart, even if we do not know what sin is causing our slow departure from God. A high-mindedness that you will be "ok", irrelevant of the promised woe of curse and corruption declared by God, is a high-mindedness which comes from a "trust" in the eternal security of salvation without any condition at hand to change the blessing, love, and salvific mind of God into a woeful, angry, damning, and cursing mind as a recompense to your own works – God is not mocked.

Nehemiah learned a severe lesson from Solomon's backsliding, and so should we. What deceived the wisest man on earth could certainly deceive you and I. Nehemiah warned of the deceptive allurement of disobedience, using Solomon as the example, saying, "Did not Solomon King of Israel sin by these things? Yet among many nations was there no king like him, who was beloved of his God, and God made him king over all Israel: nevertheless even him did outlandish women cause to sin" (Neh. 13:26). As "outlandish women" did cause Solomon to sin, so for us, unfruitful, un-perfected, backslidden, professing Christians will cause us to sin. Have you kept your church pure? Or do you win the world by yoking with the world? Friend, the world will win you if you do that. Thus said the Lord: **"Be not deceived: evil communications corrupt good manners"** (1 Cor. 15:33). Since Solomon did not, God says, "keep My Covenant," which was contained in, God says, "My statutes" (1 kings 11:11), therefore God says, "I will surely rend the Kingdom from thee" (1 Kings 11:11). The everlasting throne and secure Kingdom is breached for Solomon, likewise your eternal life will be (your throne – Eph. 2:6, Rev. 2:26-27, Lk. 19:11-27) if you do not keep the Covenant which is agreed upon conditions.

> 1 Kings 11:9-14
> [9] And **the LORD was angry with Solomon**, because his **heart was turned** from the LORD God of Israel, which had appeared unto him twice, [10] And had commanded him concerning this thing, that he should not go after other gods: but he kept not that which the LORD commanded. [11] Wherefore the LORD said unto Solomon, Forasmuch as this is done of thee, and **thou hast not kept My covenant** and **My statutes**, which I have **commanded** thee, **I will surely rend the kingdom from thee**, and will give it to thy servant. [12] Notwithstanding in thy days I will not do it for David thy father's sake: but I will rend it out of the hand of thy son. [13] Howbeit I will not rend away all the kingdom; but will give one tribe to thy son for David My servant's sake, and for Jerusalem's sake which I have chosen. [14] And the LORD stirred up an adversary unto Solomon, Hadad the Edomite: he was of the king's seed in Edom.

Bewilderment & Blindness by a Covenant Breached

The Davidic Covenant and the third promise therein was intended for Solomon, but God, through holy repentance, did change His mind because of the sinful offenses of Solomon & his seed. Consequentially, the eternal counsel that was hidden at first (the predestinated purpose for Christ to fulfill the Davidic Covenant and become the everlasting, enthroned King) is now manifest, but it was through the fall of Solomon & his seed, through repentance of the former counsel of God, and through the disannulment of the Covenant wherein Solomon would have had an everlasting throne from generation to generation in his immediate seed. In terms of the third promise of the Davidic Covenant, God did "cast his [David & Solomon's] throne down to the ground" (Psalm 89:44). Through a divine struggle with the sinfulness of man, through a repentance of a genuine good will/counsel/Covenant of God, through the fall of men, that which was predestinated arose.

Through Solomon's fall, the promise was breached, and the counsel of God given in the Davidic Covenant is mysteriously fulfilled through the manifestation of Jesus Christ. The sovereign counsel of God (God in the ways of God) is manifest through the change of the first intention (God in the ways of man), and this was a change undergone because of the sinfulness of man, but man did not change God, because the sinfulness of man is a manifestation of the sovereign will of God (God in the ways of God) working through a predestinated course of their individual lives. That is to say, because God ordained it, the hearts of men were **hardened** against the good will, counsel, and promise of God (God in the ways of man), so they resisted God and provoked Him to the disannulment of the Covenant. All these things still rest safely under the sovereignty of God's glorious purpose.

"Therefore hath He mercy on whom He will have mercy, and whom He will He **hardeneth**" – Rom. 9:18

"Who hath resisted His will?" – Rom. 9:19

Solomon sought God that He would give him and Israel a **perfect heart** to seek and serve God. A perfect heart is God-given and God-sustained; Solomon and Israel therefore sought for this "good and perfect gift" from the Father of Lights (Jas. 1:17). It was an earnest pursuit of God so that from God, as a gift from Him (Eph. 2:8-9), He would mercifully grant them a soft heart (Rom. 9:18) of saving faith wherein men can walk perfect before Him. I am reminded of the cry from Isaiah the prophet saying, "O LORD, why hast Thou made us to err from Thy ways, and **hardened our heart** from Thy fear? Return for Thy servants' sake, the tribes of Thine inheritance." (Isaiah 63:17). Through the centuries, along the timeline of man's existence, this cry has continually gone up to God. It is an expression depicting the great struggle between a salvific God and a sinful people with an acknowledgement of the sovereignty of God controlling all.

God did, through holy repentance, breach the Covenant of David as a retribution for their rebellion. Psalm 89 is devoted entirely to the lamentations, confoundedness, and bewilderment that the people of God underwent when the Lord departed from the relational grounds of His Covenant promises. The faithfulness of God is the central attribute of hope, exaltation, and prayer, but their great lamentation is that God HAS NOT accomplished what His faithful word had declared.

PSALM 89

❖ *Verses 2-4 The Covenant and Faithful Word*

[1] Maschil of Ethan the Ezrahite. I will sing of the mercies of the LORD for ever: with my mouth will I make known Thy faithfulness to all generations. [2] For I have said, **Mercy shall be built up for ever: Thy faithfulness shalt Thou establish in the**

very heavens. ³ I have made a covenant with My chosen, I have sworn unto David My servant, ⁴ Thy seed will I establish for ever, and build up thy throne to all generations. Selah.

❖ *Verses 5-18 The Name, Works, and Blessedness of God with His people*

⁵ And the heavens shall praise Thy wonders, O LORD: Thy faithfulness also in the congregation of the saints. ⁶ For who in the heaven can be compared unto the LORD? *who* among the sons of the mighty can be likened unto the LORD? ⁷ God is greatly to be feared in the assembly of the saints, and to be had in reverence of all *them that are* about Him. ⁸ O LORD God of hosts, who *is* a strong LORD like unto Thee? or to Thy faithfulness round about Thee? ⁹ Thou rulest the raging of the sea: when the waves thereof arise, Thou stillest them. ¹⁰ Thou hast broken Rahab in pieces, as one that is slain; Thou hast scattered Thine enemies with Thy strong arm. ¹¹ The heavens *are* Thine, the earth also *is* Thine: *as for* the world and the fulness thereof, Thou hast founded them. ¹² The north and the south Thou hast created them: Tabor and Hermon shall rejoice in Thy name. ¹³ Thou hast a mighty arm: strong is Thy hand, *and* high is Thy right hand. ¹⁴ Justice and judgment *are* the habitation of Thy throne: mercy and truth shall go before Thy face. ¹⁵ Blessed *is* the people that know the joyful sound: they shall walk, O LORD, in the light of Thy countenance. ¹⁶ In Thy name shall they rejoice all the day: and in Thy righteousness shall they be exalted. ¹⁷ For Thou *art* the glory of their strength: and in Thy favour our horn shall be exalted. ¹⁸ For the LORD *is* our defence; and the Holy One of Israel *is* our king.

❖ *Verses 19-37 The Choosing, Covenant, and Word of God spoken to David*

¹⁹ Then Thou spakest in vision to Thy holy one, and saidst, I have laid help upon *one that is* mighty; I have exalted *one* chosen out of the people. ²⁰ I have found David My servant; with My holy oil have I anointed him: ²¹ With whom My hand shall be established: Mine arm also shall strengthen him. ²² The enemy shall not exact upon him; nor the son of wickedness afflict him. ²³ And I will beat down his foes before his face, and plague them that hate him. ²⁴ But My faithfulness and My mercy *shall be* with him: and in My name shall his horn be exalted. ²⁵ I will set his hand also in the sea, and his right hand in the rivers. ²⁶ He shall cry unto Me, Thou *art* my Father, my God, and the rock of my salvation. ²⁷ Also I will make him *My* firstborn, higher than the kings of the earth. ²⁸ **My mercy will I keep** for him for evermore, and **My covenant shall stand fast with him.** ²⁹ **His seed also will I make *to endure* for ever, and** his throne as the days of heaven. ³⁰ If his children forsake My law, and walk not in My judgments; ³¹ If they break My statutes, and keep not My commandments; ³² Then will I visit their transgression with the rod, and their iniquity with stripes. ³³ Nevertheless My lovingkindness will I not utterly take from him, **nor suffer My faithfulness to fail.** ³⁴ **My covenant will I not break, nor alter the thing that is gone out of My lips.** ³⁵ Once have I sworn by My holiness that I will not <u>lie</u> unto David. ³⁶ **His seed shall endure for ever, and** his throne as the sun before Me. ³⁷ **It**

shall be established for ever as the moon, and *as* **a faithful witness in heaven**. Selah.

❖ *Verses 38-52 The Lamentation & Bewilderment over a Covenant Breached*

[8] But Thou hast cast off and abhorred, Thou hast been wroth with Thine anointed. [39] Thou hast **made void the covenant** of Thy servant: Thou hast profaned his crown by casting it to the ground. [40] Thou hast broken down all his hedges; Thou hast brought his strong holds to ruin. [41] All that pass by the way spoil him: he is a reproach to his neighbours. [42] Thou hast set up the right hand of his adversaries; Thou hast made all his enemies to rejoice. [43] Thou hast also turned the edge of his sword, and hast not made him to stand in the battle. [44] Thou hast made his glory to cease, and cast his throne down to the ground. [45] The days of his youth hast Thou shortened: Thou hast covered him with shame. Selah. [46] How long, LORD? wilt Thou hide Thyself for ever? **shall Thy wrath burn like fire?** [47] Remember how short my time is: wherefore hast Thou made all men in vain? [48] What man *is he that* liveth, and shall not see death? shall he deliver his soul from the hand of the grave? Selah. [49] Lord, where *are* Thy **former lovingkindnesses,** *which* **Thou swarest unto David in Thy truth?** [50] Remember, Lord, the reproach of Thy servants; *how* I do bear in my bosom *the reproach of* all the mighty people; [51] Wherewith Thine enemies have reproached, O LORD; wherewith they have reproached the footsteps of Thine anointed. [52] Blessed *be* the LORD for evermore. Amen, and Amen.

Notice the color coding that parallel the psalmist's lamentations:

What God Covenanted by Faithful Promise	What God Did By Holy Repentance
Verse 28 - **My mercy will I keep** for him for evermore	Verse 38 - Thou hast been wroth with Thine anointed Verse 46 - How long, LORD? wilt Thou hide Thyself for ever? **shall Thy wrath burn like fire?**
Verse 28 - My covenant shall stand fast with him. Verse 34 - **My covenant will I not break, nor alter the thing that is gone out of My lips.**	Verse 39 - Thou hast **made void the covenant** of Thy servant:
Verse 29 - his throne as the days of heaven. Verse 36 - his throne as the sun before Me.	Verse 39 - Thou hast profaned his crown *by casting it* to the ground. Verse 44 - cast his throne down to the ground.
Verse 33 - My lovingkindness will I not utterly take from him, **nor suffer My faithfulness to fail**.	Verse 38 - But Thou hast cast off and abhorred, Verse 49 - Lord, where *are* Thy former lovingkindnesses
Verse 35 - Once have I sworn by My holiness that I will not lie unto David.	Verse 49 - *which* Thou swarest unto David in Thy truth?

The psalmist is seeking the faithfulness of God (33), but the promised lovingkindness has been taken away (49). He is seeking for the keeping mercies of God (28), but God's wrath is burning like fire as to make void the Covenant, or in other words, "alter the thing that" was spoken, and though it is impossible for God to lie, the man of God searches for that "which Thou swarest unto David in Thy truth," because the oaths of His holiness have failed for *the time*. The man of God, like others, desires to declare the faithfulness of God. Yet, as he looks for the salvific promise, former lovingkindness, and wonderful mercy, instead he is forced to confess, "Thy wrath lieth hard upon me, and Thou hast afflicted me with all Thy waves" (Psalm 88:7). Without remedy, but God, the cries and desperate intercessions go up as His people helplessly draw nigh to the pit of death. "Mine eye mourneth by reason of affliction: LORD, I have called daily upon Thee, I have stretched out my hands unto Thee. Wilt Thou shew wonders to the dead? Shall the dead arise and praise Thee? Selah. Shall Thy lovingkindness be declared in the grave? Or Thy faithfulness in destruction? Shall Thy wonders be known in the dark? And Thy righteousness in the land of forgetfulness? But unto Thee have I cried, O LORD; and in the morning shall my prayer prevent Thee. LORD, why castest Thou off my soul? Why hidest Thou Thy face from me? I am afflicted and ready to die from my youth up: while I suffer Thy terrors I am distracted. Thy fierce wrath goeth over me; Thy terrors have cut me off" (Psalm 88:9-16).

> "In that day will I raise up the Tabernacle of David that is **fallen**, and close up **the breaches** thereof; and I will **raise up his ruins**, and I will **build it** as in **the days of old**: That they may possess the remnant of Edom, and of all the heathen, which are called by My Name, saith the LORD that doeth this" (Amos 9:11-12).

The verse above does prophesy of a day when God does "**build**" and "**raise up**" the Davidic Covenant, because for now, as you can see in Psalm 89, the Davidic Covenant is "**fallen**", utterly broken with "**breaches**" (breaks), so as to crumble into "**ruins**" (Amos 9:11-12). The Davidic Covenant is the second major and eternal Covenant that God did **breach**, and upon the breach of the Abrahamic Covenant the people of God suffered the same bewilderment as those in the Davidic. Psalm 77 reflects on the salvific works in the Abrahamic Covenant, when at that time, all such "favour" (77:7), "mercy" (77:8), "promise" (77:8), and "grace" (77:9) are no more. The psalmist who wrote Psalm 77 exudes the painful experience of when the God of the Bible is overwhelmingly absent. Hurled upon his soul is the overwhelming reality that God has hidden Himself. **Do you ever wonder where the God of the New Testament is?** It is a damnable sin for pastors and preachers to fail to say – "Where is the LORD?" (Jer. 2:8). The Spirit-filled psalmist said, "**I remembered God, and was troubled,**" but most people don't remember the God of the Bible as He has testified of Himself in the plain accounts of scripture – by doctrine, deed, and historical example. Most people worship an imaginary, self-invented, self-conforming god, a god they made up in their own mind. Children have imaginary friends, and adults have an imaginary god. In Jeremiah 2:8 men failed to say, "Where is the LORD," because they didn't remember the God of the Bible! In backslidden generations which span for years of time, if all this time is spent in the absence of God's great glory and promise, it is then that the righteous are troubled and the wicked are at ease. Where is the biblical God of the 1ˢᵗ century today? This is a troubling question… now look carefully at the prayers of this psalmist, and you will see that remembering God is remembering the deeds of His *mercy, favor, promise, grace,* and *tender mercies,* thus he recognizes that the absence of God's famous glory in these *wonderful works* is the *angry casting off* of the people of God. Psalm 77:3-9, "**I remembered God**, and was **troubled**: I complained, and my spirit was overwhelmed. Selah. Thou holdest mine eyes waking: I am so **troubled** I cannot speak. I have considered **the days of old**, the years of ancient times. I call to remembrance my song in the night: I commune with mine own heart: and my spirit made diligent search. Will the Lord **cast off** for ever? And will He be **favourable** no more? Is His **mercy** clean gone for ever? Doth His **promise** fail for evermore? Hath God forgotten to be **gracious**? Hath He in **anger** shut up His tender mercies? Selah" (Psalm 77:3-9).

God was confronting the psalmist of Psalm 77, and therefore he was troubled, and when this biblical, hidden, and holy God confronts you, you too will experience the same "enlargement of heart" (Ps. 119:32) with a divinely set hope in the written word (Psalm 119:49). There will be no hope put in men to change the hardness of your heart, but God alone. Under the intense conviction of a Covenant made void, you will cry to the Sovereign for help and hope, "incline not my heart to any evil thing" (Psalm 141:4), "And now, Lord, what wait I for? My hope is in Thee. Deliver me from all my transgressions" (Psalm 39:7-9). "Turn Thou me, and I shall be turned; for Thou art the LORD my God" (Jer. 31:18). "Heal me, O LORD, and I shall be healed; save me, and I shall be saved: for Thou art my praise" (Jer. 17:14). "Turn us again, O God, and cause Thy face to shine; and we shall be saved. O LORD God of hosts, how long wilt Thou be angry against the prayer of Thy people? Thou feedest them with bread of tears; and givest them tears to drink in great measure" (Psalm 80:3-5). "Return, we beseech Thee, O God of hosts: look down from heaven, and behold, and visit this vine; And **the vineyard which Thy right hand hath planted, and the branch *that* Thou madest strong for Thyself.** *It is* burned with fire, *it is* cut down: **they perish at the rebuke of Thy countenance.** Let Thy hand be upon the man of Thy right hand, upon the son of man *whom* Thou madest strong for Thyself. **So will not we go back from Thee: quicken us, and we will call upon Thy name. ¹⁹ Turn us again, O LORD God of hosts, cause Thy face to shine; and we shall be saved**" (Psalm 80:14-19).

"LORD, Thou wilt ordain peace for us: for Thou also hast wrought all our works in us" (Isa. 26:12).

The Covenant is there in word, but the performance thereof is absent. The very means of salvation, the instrumentality of His ways and works, these things are gone. It is impossible to replicate the workings of God. There is subservience in the people under the sovereignty of God. They do recognize that God is the Potter and they are but clay. When a Covenant is breached, the people are rejected of God, and therefore the two are only reconcilable by the free will of God.

When the Abrahamic & Davidic Covenants were breached, this left the people bewildered, blind, and in darkness. They became people and generations marked by blindness and rebellion. There are ways to be reconciled, called "the means of intercession," but these means cannot avail but by the free decision of the LORD to accept them. When the Lord arose in the zeal of His wrath, when He bent and aimed the bow of destruction to His people who were worthy of death, at this time Abraham interceded for Lot with success. This prayer of intercession arose while the prophet beheld the kindled wrath of God going forth on a purposeful pursuit. The will of God was in motion, active, and mounting to its execution, and thus the prophets do behold the vision of it bursting upon their sides, and thus we see them gasping for salvation. The Spirit-filled prophets did always cry for mercy! Like this, God makes manifest the manifold motives and bright attributes of His Person – justice against mercy wrestling in Divine tension. Prophetic intercessors were the sole human audience of these heavenly scenes. In similar ways throughout time, the prophets Moses, Samuel, David, Elijah, and Daniel did cast themselves at the feet of God to grasp the edge of His garment for healing, hope, and mercy. God was not always stopped from the pursuit of justice. The prophets could not always stay the heat of His anger against sin. Moses, Samuel, David, and Jeremiah could not avail. The Spirit of love in God was in hurtful mourning, but it was willing and yielding to a greater cause of justice upon criminal creatures.

How many religious men claim to be prayer warriors or intercessors? Intercession is to intercede between the wrath of a holy God impending upon a sinful people: God's people. An intercessor prays against the genuine, willing, and destroying wrath of God! Many men claim to be intercessors, but they know neither what it is nor what it is for! Intercession is for the promises of God to be performed, the love of God to be sustained, and the salvation of God's people to be persevered or restored! Amazingly, the doctrines from Calvinism and eternal security make impossible this work of intercession. Such men deny that God could be angry with His people, thus how would they intercede for them? For what purpose would they plead the promises to God if there was ONLY an everlasting, unchanging love at work in God? Without a condescended reality in God, then there would be no reason to intercede for the Covenanted, saved people of Israel, for, there could be no change of mind possible in God, and whatever anger had begun to be manifest within the realm of time would always be appearing now, because it was galloping from eternity past in a relentless hatred to destroy predestinated vessels of wrath, and thus, if a man stood against it so as to fill a gap, or turn it away, not only would this be vain, but such a one may be burned up and run over in the attempted intercession. It is an unthinkable endeavor to stand against an eternal, unchanging, irresistible, and destroying wrath of God! But it is not so; God can repent by the means of a condescended relationship with man, and therefore intercession is not a foolish, unsound, unthinkable, vain, and suicidal endeavor! Men do take hope in the fact that

God repented in time past from His anger over His people, so that, even though they are in such a generation of a Covenant breach, they cry out and pray – "Save us, O LORD our God". See Psalm 106:44-48:

> "Nevertheless He regarded their affliction, when He heard their cry: And **He remembered for them His covenant, and repented** according to **the multitude of His mercies**. He made them also to be pitied of all those that carried them captives. **Save us, O LORD our God, and gather us from among the heathen, to give thanks unto Thy holy name, and to triumph in Thy praise.** Blessed be the LORD God of Israel from everlasting to everlasting: and let all the people say, Amen. Praise ye the LORD" (Ps. 106:44-48).

Shockingly, it was revealed to David that the Covenant of God would be breached and then mysteriously fulfilled at latter times! David speaks of this in 2 Samuel 23:1-7, written below. David describes how the Davidic Covenant is breached as a result from some "**sons of Belial**", and in the following account, David says, that God will not fulfill that which He has begun in David's lifetime, which means that the Davidic house and throne will not continue to grow, and rather, it will decline and fall. David's very last words foretold the secret hope that David had, that eventually, but not immediately, God will fulfill the Covenant which was given to him. David obviously perceives a troublesome future ahead where his house will cease to hold the Throne of Israel *for a time*.

> "Now these be the last words of David. David the son of Jesse said, and the man who was raised up on high, the anointed of the God of Jacob, and the sweet psalmist of Israel, said, The Spirit of the LORD spake by me, and His word was in my tongue. The God of Israel said, the Rock of Israel spake to me, He that ruleth over men must be just, ruling in the fear of God. And He shall be as the light of the morning, when the sun riseth, even a morning without clouds; as the tender grass springing out of the earth by clear shining after rain. **Although my house be not so with God**; yet He hath made with me an everlasting covenant, ordered in all things, and sure: for this is all my salvation, and all my desire, **although He make it not to grow**. But the **sons of Belial** shall be all of them as thorns thrust away, because they cannot be taken with hands: But the man that shall touch them must be fenced with iron and the staff of a spear; and they shall be utterly burned with fire in the same place" (2 Sam. 23:1-7).

David said that it was "an everlasting covenant, ordered in all things, and sure" (2 Sam. 23:5); even so it is true, and God echoes this sure hope by expounding just how He will fulfill the word He spoke to David in a mysterious way, so

167

mysterious that the wisest prophets know it not. The fulfillment of this Covenant will be "great and mighty things which thou knowest not" (Jer. 33:3), God says, and He assures that some way, somehow, Christ will be the fulfillment of the Davidic Covenant so that, as is of necessity to be fulfilled: "David shall never want a man to sit upon the throne of the house of Israel" (Jer. 33:17). In this way, though God has altered the thing gone out of His mouth so as to cause the throne of David to cease, God still affirms to later generations – "The LORD hath sworn in truth unto David; **He will not turn from it**; Of the fruit of Thy body will I set upon Thy throne. If Thy children will keep My Covenant and My testimony that I shall teach them, their children shall also sit upon Thy throne for evermore" (Psalm 132:11-12) – meaning that this is one of God's eternal, everlasting purposes which He will not repent of or turn from. At the time of the psalm which contains this promise (Psalm 132), the Davidic Covenant was presently in desolation, and that is why the prophetic emphasis is that God "**will not turn from**" the Covenant's fulfillment! These words affirm that God will not turn from it so as to forget it, and He will eventually fulfill it! The Lord affirms again:

> "Behold, the days come, saith the LORD, that I will perform that good thing which I have promised unto the house of Israel and to the house of Judah. In those days, and at that time, will I cause the Branch of righteousness to grow up unto David; and He shall execute judgment and righteousness in the land. In those days shall Judah be saved, and Jerusalem shall dwell safely: and this is the name wherewith she shall be called, The LORD our righteousness. For thus saith the LORD; **David shall never want a man to sit upon the throne of the house of Israel**… " (Jer. 33:14-17).

> "Thus saith the LORD; **If ye can break My covenant** of the day, and My covenant of the night, and that there should not be day and night in their season; Then may also **My covenant be broken with David** My servant, that he should not have a son to reign upon his throne; and with the Levites the priests, My ministers. As the host of heaven cannot be numbered, neither the sand of the sea measured: so will I multiply the seed of David my servant, and the Levites that minister unto Me" (Jer. 33:20-22).

The latter verses from Jeremiah are a telling response to Psalm 89, possibly even to the cries of that very psalmist who prayed for answers. The proof which displays the Davidic Covenant's surety is said to be as God's covenant that He has made with the sun and moon – fixed unmovable in their places – and this is as it was said in Psalm 89:36-37: "His seed shall endure <u>for ever</u>, and his throne **as the sun before Me**. It shall be established <u>for ever</u> **as the moon**, and as a faithful witness in heaven. Selah" (Ps. 89:36-37). So God says in Jeremiah 33:20-21 the very same address: "If ye can break My Covenant of **the day**, and My Covenant of **the night**, and **that there should not be day and night in their season**; Then may also My Covenant be broken with David My servant, that he should not have a son to reign upon his throne". The eventual and mysterious fulfillment of this presently breached Davidic Covenant is an eternal, unchanging purpose of God, which He has determined in the powers of His own changeless ways (God in the ways of God).

Finally, what is profoundly notable with this Covenant's mysterious fulfillment is shown to us through what I call "the psalm of psalms," namely Psalm 110, because it is a one of a kind, metropolis depiction of Christ's future ministries, with astounding accuracy! In Psalm 110, we see Christ as the eternal Davidic King taking His seat at an everlasting throne, and furthermore, Christ as the eternal High Priest after an everlasting order which was before the Aaronic order! Doubtless, David knew very little of what all of these words meant comparatively to the unfolding of all the events that were yet to transpire for their fulfillment, but he knew something. Thus David knew that his throne would be eternally established, and in this way it was and is "ordered" and "sure" just as his dying words foretold. David does recognize in this psalm that, even though subsequent generations of his immediate house and throne are not ready for the Davidic Covenant's great fulfillment, nevertheless, God's "people shall be willing in the day of [His] power" in some latter generation wherein all these things shall be fulfilled. In this day, the King will be God Himself, David acknowledges, and some way, somehow, all earthly events shall be framed into this quintessential END where the LORD will be seated on His throne forever! Thus it is at the first of the psalm, David confesses – "**The LORD said unto my Lord, sit Thou at My right hand, until I make Thine enemies Thy footstool**" (Ps. 110:1).

> "A Psalm of David. **The LORD said unto my Lord, Sit Thou at My right hand, until I make Thine enemies Thy footstool**. The LORD shall send the rod of Thy strength out of Zion: rule Thou in the midst of Thine enemies. Thy people shall be willing in the day of Thy power, in the beauties of holiness from the womb of the morning: Thou hast the dew of Thy youth. **The LORD hath sworn, and will not repent, Thou art a priest for ever after the order of Melchizedek.** The Lord at Thy right hand shall strike through kings in the day of His wrath. He shall judge among the heathen, He shall fill the places with the dead bodies; He shall wound the heads over many countries. He shall drink of the brook in the way: therefore shall He lift up the head" (Psalm 110:1-7).

The Lord had two simultaneous, genuine wills. Firstly, Solomon and David's immediate seed through Solomon would be established into an everlasting house and Throne, un-fallen and fixed forever through the centuries, but since this was breached, therefore we can understand that this is manifest because of a forceful, time-changing, all-Covenant conforming purpose of God in Christ, as it were, galloping from eternity past – His brilliant incarnation into humanity, His penal, substitutionary, and atoning death, His victorious resurrection, and finally, His ascension unto the Davidic throne at the right hand of the Father.

INTERCEDING AGAINST WRATH
CHAPTER 7

1 Peter 4:17-18

[17] For the time is come that **judgment** must begin at the house of God: and if it first begin at us, what shall the end be of them that obey not the gospel of God? [18] **And if the righteous scarcely be saved, where shall the ungodly and the sinner appear?**

Wrath Pursuing Sinners

Simultaneous wills in God do animate a shocking Person for men to know, and tracing His terrible workings through the centuries will show the wisdom in the psalmist saying: "How terrible art Thou in Thy works! Through the greatness of Thy power Thine enemies submit themselves unto Thee... Come and see the works of God: He is terrible in His doing toward the children of men" (Ps. 66:3, 5). As for the mischievous and all wicked men, "God shall shoot at them with an arrow; suddenly shall they be wounded... and all men shall fear, and shall declare the work of God; for they shall wisely consider of His doing" (Ps. 64:7, 9). There has, and always will be, until the consummation of these Covenants, a present and continuous Divine struggle between the saving goodness of God and all men's wrath-inciting waywardness. Consider first the workings of God toward sinners; they who are without Covenant and promise, ever dwelling in the vanity of their mind.

"Behold, all souls are Mine; as the soul of the father,
so also the soul of the son is Mine:
the soul that sinneth, it shall die." (Ezekiel 18:4)

The godly Rolfe Barnard well understood this principle of God. He preached a sermon called The God of the Bible Kills People. This sermon, alongside another called Watching Men Die, well represents this fierce attribute of God's just and wrathful will to kill sinners. To be hunted by the arrows of God's justice, to know that the bow of His wrath is bent, that He hath made ready and aimed His arrows to be drunken with your blood – this is a biblical trauma many don't know! If sinners do not turn from their sin, what will God do?

"...God is **angry** with the wicked **every day**. If he [the sinner] turn not, He will whet His sword; **He hath bent His bow, and made it ready. He hath prepared for him the instruments of death; He ordaineth His arrows against the persecutors**" (Psalm 7:11-13).

What will God do? God has already bent His bow! He has already prepared the instruments of death! Oh, this generation is nearly mindless that this world is a world of Sinners in the Hands of an Angry God. Would to God this sermon, by

171

Jonathan Edwards, would cause the consciences of America to quake again. Within time, there is a humbling tension within the heart of an Omniscient, Omni-benevolent God, a tension between the love (Ezek. 33:11, John 3:16) and hatred of God (Psalm 5:5) that is beyond the spectrum of our comprehension. What would it mean for a sinner when, at present, "**the wrath of God abideth on him**" (John 3:36)? That is what is written: "He that believeth on the Son hath everlasting life: and he that believeth not the Son shall not see life; but **the wrath of God abideth on him**" (John 3:36). That is to say, the wrath of God dwells upon, continues upon, or rests upon the sinner…an active will of God, in just anger, held from its final satisfaction by the Sovereign mercy of God at tension. The potential of death is near, hovering overhead, ready to fall, and easily released. The wrath of God abiding upon a sinner is as a bow bent and ready, pointed at you [a sinner], and any moment the love of God could lose grip against it and release the justice of God that is aiming for your death. Life, righteousness, well-being, and the universe, for the glory of God, will be sustained and satisfied by the death of sinners. Yet until they all die, God's will to kill men is illustrative through Hosea 11:7-9: "**My repentings are kindled together.**"

> "And My people are bent to backsliding from Me: though they called them to the most High, none at all would exalt Him. How shall I give thee up, Ephraim? how shall I deliver thee, Israel? how shall I make thee as Admah? how shall I set thee as Zeboim? Mine heart is turned within Me, **My repentings are kindled together**. I will not execute the fierceness of Mine anger, I will not return to destroy Ephraim: for I am God, and not man; the Holy One in the midst of thee: and I will not enter into the city." (Hosea 11:7-9)

Admah and Zeboim are neighboring cities to Sodom and Gomorrah, which were destroyed in their destruction of fiery brimstone. God can, at present, be overtaken with the wrestling of "repentings." This is a wrestling of contradicting desires to save or to kill within the heart of God. God warns of the possibility of **sudden destruction** surprising the wicked. "He, that being often reproved hardeneth his neck, **shall suddenly be destroyed,** and that without remedy." (Proverbs 29:1) Oh sinner, above you are the eyes of God's glory beholding your thoughts, words, and deeds, and I plead with you to understand the weight of His watchings.

> "And He said unto them, Take heed, and beware of **covetousness**: for a man's life consisteth not in the abundance of the things which he possesseth. And He spake a parable unto them, saying, The ground of a certain rich man brought forth plentifully: And he thought within himself, saying, What shall I do, because I have no room where to bestow my fruits? And he said, This will I do: I will pull down my barns, and build greater; and there will I bestow all my fruits and my goods. And I will say to my soul, Soul, thou hast much goods laid up for many years; **take thine ease**, eat, drink, and be merry. But God said unto him, **Thou fool, this night thy soul shall be required of thee**: then

whose shall those things be, which thou hast provided? So is he that layeth up treasure for himself, and is not rich toward God." (Luke 12:15-21)

A sinner would never say within himself, "**take thine ease**," if he knew that the wrath of God was hovering over his head like a bent and strung bow, that death is so nigh and every decision is vitally careful, lest you decide against your eternal good and release the everlasting wrath of God upon your helpless and wretched soul. These are the words of the hell-bound man, "take thine ease!" He didn't know that he had less than 24 hours left in his life before God would require his soul. God said, "Thou fool, **this night** thy soul shall be required of thee."

Think of this nation in the celebration on New Year's Eve. In it, the people celebrate a false sense of liberty, new-year promises, and hopes of a prosperous next year. For this to be the time that their death sentence is executed is certainly a message from God. It reminds me of the rebellious partying: "let us eat and drink; for tomorrow we die" (1 Cor. 15:32). God is interrupting the very time of their futuristic hoping, boasting, and partying, and this is just what God did to the hopeful man in Luke 12:16-21. Are not these words the epitome of New Year's celebrations? "**And I will say to my soul, Soul, thou hast much goods laid up for many years; take thine ease, eat, drink, and be merry. But God said unto him, Thou fool, this night thy soul shall be required of thee: then whose shall those things be, which thou hast provided?" (Verses 19-20)**

> "Therefore **hell hath enlarged herself**, and **opened her mouth without measure**: and their glory, and their multitude, and their pomp, and he that rejoiceth, shall descend into it." (Isaiah 5:14)

Are you hunted by hell? Are you hunted by the very mouth of hell, to be swallowed up into the hole of God's justice? If you are swallowed up, you will remain there until you are cast into the Lake of Fire as an object of God's fierce hatred, eternally living that you might everlastingly die? "The sinners in Zion are afraid," scripture declares, and "fearfulness hath surprised the hypocrites. Who among us shall dwell with the devouring fire? Who among us shall dwell with everlasting burnings" (Isa. 33:14)? Will you be vomited out by the good will of God (Rev. 3:15-16), spewed out from the promising love of your Creator (Lev. 18:26-30), only to reside under the emotional distress and torturing experience of what you are in God's sight? The wicked are in hell because God is there, for He alone is the sustainer, creator, and maintainer of justice. The jubilee of everlasting life redounds to the glory of God, truly, but for what cause and triumph? It is an eternity without wickedness; an eternity beginning with the exclamation that wickedness has ceased to taint God's good creation and habitable palaces. That God, throughout all His good creation, or wherever the sole of His foot would walk, there is only righteousness, purity, peace, and God-centered charity. Finally, the wicked "shall drink of the wine of the wrath of God, which is poured out without mixture into the cup of His indignation; and he shall be tormented with fire and brimstone in the presence of the holy angels, and **in the presence of the Lamb**:" (Revelation 14:10)

Don't be carried away in the dream of sinners. Remember God, remember judgment, and remember righteousness! Don't let the illusion of happiness, the monotony of daily obligations, or pleasures steal your attention away from the cries of your conscience pointing you to your Creator! Before your soul is required and "your spirit shall return unto God Who gave it," remember HIM! Before suffering and evil come upon you, while it is yet day and there is still time to repent, remember your God. "**Remember now thy Creator** in the days of thy youth, **while the evil days come not**, nor the years draw nigh, when thou shalt say, I have no pleasure in them; While the sun, or the light, or the moon, or the stars, be not darkened, nor the clouds return after the rain: In the day when the keepers of the house shall tremble, and the strong men shall bow themselves, and the grinders cease because they are few, and those that look out of the windows be darkened, And the doors shall be shut in the streets, when the sound of the grinding is low, and he shall rise up at the voice of the bird, and all the daughters of music shall be brought low; Also when they shall be afraid of that which is high, and fears shall be in the way, and the almond tree shall flourish, and the grasshopper shall be a burden, and desire shall fail: because man goeth to his long home, and the mourners go about the streets: Or ever the silver cord be loosed, or the golden bowl be broken, or the pitcher be broken at the fountain, or the wheel broken at the cistern. Then shall the dust return to the earth as it was: and **the spirit shall return unto God Who gave it**." (Ecclesiastes 12:1-7)

Wrath Pursuing Saints

Without question this is God's mind toward sinners, but could or would God ever pursue a saint to kill him?

The scripture warns, "For **he that will love life, and see good days,** let him refrain his tongue from evil, and his lips that they speak no guile: let him eschew evil, and do good; let him seek peace, and ensue it. For the eyes of the Lord are over the righteous, and His ears are open unto their prayers: but **the face of the Lord is against them that do evil**" (1 Peter 3:10-12, Ps. 34:12-16). "**The face of the Lord is against them that do evil**", the scripture declares, but what happens when "the righteous" man turns to "do evil?" It is written again, "but when the righteous turneth away from his righteousness, and committeth iniquity, and doeth according to all the abominations that the wicked man doeth, **shall he live**? All his righteousness that he hath done **shall not be mentioned**: in his trespass that he hath trespassed, and in his sin that he hath sinned, **in them shall he die**" (Ezek. 18:24). God says that the righteous man's righteousness "shall not be mentioned," and in another place it is said, "his righteousness which he hath done **shall not be remembered**" (Ezek. 3:20). I had said that, till all sinners die, God's will to kill men is illustrative through Hosea 11:7-9: "**My repentings are kindled together.**" Do you remember the passage? Read it again below:

174

"And My people are bent to backsliding from Me: though they called them to the most High, none at all would exalt Him. How shall I give thee up, Ephraim? how shall I deliver thee, Israel? how shall I make thee as Admah? how shall I set thee as Zeboim? Mine heart is turned within Me, **My repentings are kindled together**. I will not execute the fierceness of Mine anger, I will not return to destroy Ephraim: for I am God, and not man; the Holy One in the midst of thee: and I will not enter into the city." (Hosea 11:7-9)

This wrestling within the heart of God was over "My people," God said, "bent to backsliding from Me." Backsliding is departing from God, a going backward, depicting the crime of those who were with God. This is unlike the heathen sinners who have never been near to God. They cannot backslide from Him because they were never with Him. The scarcity of salvation for those who endure to the end cannot be properly understood until we are conscientious of the dual, simultaneous, and genuine wills of God that are actively working all the time in tension and contradiction one with another – and they are minded for and against the perseverance of the Covenanted, righteous, and holy men of God when they commit sin. It was said of the righteous in their salvation comparatively to the dealings of God with sinners, "if **the righteous scarcely be saved**, where shall the ungodly and sinner appear" (1 Peter 4:18). The souls of the righteous that persevere to the end, they are **scarcely saved** from a shocking and near annihilation under a real, genuine anger of God. Trace with me the near annihilation of God's people. Study with me the stirrings of God's wrath when He "destroyed them not," but "yea, many a time turned He His anger away, and **did not stir up all His wrath**. (Ps. 78:37-42). Study with me the present progressive salvation of the righteous that perseveres by a rigorous and terrifying intercession against the very burning wrath of God.

> "Therefore He said that He would destroy them, **had not Moses**
> **His chosen stood before Him in the breach**, to turn away His
> wrath, **lest He should destroy them**."
> (Psalm 106:23)

> "stand in **the gap** before Me for the land, **that I should not**
> **destroy it**: but I found none." (Ezek. 22:30-31)

Before we walk the chronicles of this crisis, we must understand the tension of His simultaneous wills and understand them in view of God's will by vow, oath, promise, Covenant, salvation, calling, election, and choosing.

The Exodus Generation Partakers of
Salvation: Saved, Called, Elect, & Chosen ➔ *In these terms God willed their salvation.*

Deuteronomy 7:7-11
[7] The LORD did not **set His love upon you**, nor **choose** you,
because ye were more in number than any people; for ye were the

175

fewest of all people: [8] But because **the LORD loved you**, and because He would keep the oath which He had sworn unto your fathers, hath the LORD brought you out with a mighty hand, and **redeemed you** out of the house of bondmen, from the hand of Pharaoh king of Egypt.

God did "choose" Israel in redemptive love; therefore they are the elect and chosen. He "saved" them (Jude 5). When God elects and saves, He chooses them "**for a people**," that He might be their God. God spake in Exodus 6:6-7, "I am the LORD, and I will bring you out from under the burdens of the Egyptians, and I will rid you out of their **bondage**, and I will **redeem** you with a stretched out arm, and with great judgments: And I will take you to Me **for a people**, and **I will be to you a God**: and ye shall know that I am the LORD **your God**, which bringeth you out from under the burdens of the Egyptians" (Ex. 6:6-7). Scripture says, "Blessed is <u>the nation whose God is the LORD</u>; and the people whom **He hath chosen** for His own inheritance" (Psalm 33:12). With personable, tender affection, special only to God's elect vessels, people, and generation, thus God is to Israel: "When Israel was a child, then **I loved him**, and **called** My son out of Egypt" (Hos. 11:1). Israel was the **called** of God, and he was **called** into the wilderness for a Covenant like unto marriage.

> Ezekiel 16:8-9
> [8] Now when I passed by thee, and looked upon thee, behold, **thy time *was* the time of love**; and I spread My skirt over thee, and covered thy nakedness: yea, **I sware unto thee**, and entered into **a covenant** with thee, saith the Lord GOD, and **thou becamest Mine**. [9] Then **washed** I thee with water; yea, I throughly washed away thy blood from thee, and **I anointed thee with oil**.

> Jeremiah 2:2-3
> [2] Go and cry in the ears of Jerusalem, saying, Thus saith the LORD; I remember thee, the kindness of thy youth, **the love of thine espousals**, when thou wentest after Me in the wilderness, in a land *that was* not sown. [3] **Israel *was* holiness unto the LORD**, *and* the firstfruits of His increase: all that devour him shall offend; evil shall come upon them, saith the LORD.

Further attributes of their salvation are, "When Israel went out of Egypt, the house of Jacob from a people of strange language; Judah was His **sanctuary**, and Israel His **dominion**" (Psalm 114:1-2). This people became the hallowed sanctuary for the soles of His feet, a kingdom for dominion and rule by His immediate, actual presence. Thus far Israel is called "saved" (Jude 5), redeemed (Deut. 7:7-11, Ex. 6:6-7), "chosen" (Psalm 33:12, Deut. 7:7-11), His people (Ex. 6:6-7), loved (Deut. 7:7-11, Hos. 11:1, Ezek. 16:8, Jer. 2:2-3), "holiness" (Jer. 2:2-3), anointed with oil (Ezek. 16:9), in Covenant of marriage (Ezek. 16:8, Jer. 2:2), a son (Hos. 11:1), and "called" (Hos. 11:1). Read again the calling of Israel, the elect: "Thus saith the LORD, Israel is **My son**, even My **firstborn**: And I say unto thee, Let My son go, that he may serve Me: and if thou refuse to let him go, behold, I will slay thy son, even thy firstborn" (Ex. 4:22-23). These are the accolades of the elect, and God hath spoken to Israel, "**Live**; yea, I said unto thee when thou wast in thy blood, **Live**" (Ezek. 16:6). The word of God at Israel's election was "LIVE," and with this word they were scripted into Book of Life. All the elect written in the Book of Life are under certain requirements they must fulfill, lest of certain names it might be said, "it repented the LORD that He had" recorded their name there, "and it grieved Him at His heart" (Gen. 6:6). Blessed is the man whom God "will not blot out his name out of the book of life" (Rev. 3:5). What God spoke and established by name, spirit, law, justification, and work, He is able to remember no more (Ezek. 3:20), as a many effortlessly erases penciled names and letters, even so it is with God's timeless and judiciary liberties, and whosoever is blotted out is unrecoverable and lawfully nonexistent, never to be mentioned again (Ezek. 18:24).

Many times Israel was, as a whole inheritance, in danger of complete annihilation, and disinheritance (Ex. 32:10, 34:9, Deut. 9:25-29, Num. 14:12). Finally, God disinherited most of Israel, namely, no longer calling them His people (Hos. 1:9), divorcing them as His wife (Hos. 2:1), and delivering them to pitiless consumption (Hos. 1:6).However, before this great measure of wrath was irrevocably stirred up, "many a time turned He His anger away and did not stir up all His wrath" (Psalm 78:38). Many times He did speak and act to destroy them: "He said that He would destroy them, had not Moses His chosen stood before Him in the breach, to turn away His wrath, lest He should destroy them" (Psalm 106:23). During their salvation, before reprobation, God was pacified many times from executing their full destruction, and with *scarcity* Moses made intercession for their perseverance. This Divine struggle within God, for and against the salvation of the saved, reveals a frightening depiction of terror we are warned to remember (Heb. 12:28-29, 1 Cor. 10:12, 1 Peter 1:17, 2 Cor. 5:10-11). It is holiness in its purity, separate from man, not easily borne by our compromising comprehension, and when we (through grace) come to understand it, these ways are quickly acknowledged to be holy, higher, and "not of blood, nor of the will of the flesh, nor of the will of man, but of God" (John 1:13). "Exalt ye the LORD our God, and worship at His footstool; for He is holy" (Psalm 99:5).

THE NEAR ANNIHILATION
OF GOD'S PEOPLE
CHAPTER 8

"The earth also is defiled under the inhabitants thereof; because
they have transgressed the laws, changed the ordinance, broken
the everlasting covenant. Therefore hath the curse devoured the
earth, and they that dwell therein are desolate: **therefore the
inhabitants of the earth are burned, and <u>few</u> men left**." –
Isaiah 24:5-6

The Covenant of "the Called" in its Initiation: <u>THE GREAT PAUSE</u>

In Exodus 20, Moses drew near to God on behalf of the people and
delivered to them the Ten Commandments. Along with the Ten Commandments,
God gave the people many "judgments" that are recorded in Exodus 21through
Exodus 24. These four chapters entail various commandments of God, until finally,
by Exodus 24, Moses ascends the Mount of God. Why did Moses ascend up the
Mountain of God? God was teaching Moses about His Covenant agreement which He
desires to make with the people. This ascension up the Mountain marks the beginning
of when God began to initiate the Covenant. This exclusive meeting with God and
Moses lasted forty days and nights! With awe and wonder, Moses beheld visions of
heavenly realities, and he took note of instructions of how to replicate an earthly
simulation. On the day preceding Moses' ascent, the Israelite people gave a verbal
vow of commitment to the words of the Covenant which were thus far declared, and
also to those things which will be added to it (Ex. 24:3). The people verbally vowed,
the proper sacrifices were made (Ex. 24:4-6), the people were sprinkled by "the blood
of the Covenant" (Ex. 24:8), the "seventy elders of Israel" "saw the God of Israel" by
a partial ascension up the Mount, and finally, directly after the seventy elders did eat
and drink in the presence of God, the Lord specifically called Moses up into the
Mount alone to receive "tables of stone, and a law, and commandments," which God
wrote for Moses to "teach" Israel with (Ex. 24:9-12). Moses' last words were, "Tarry
ye here for us, until we come again unto you: and, behold, Aaron and Hur are with
you: if any man have any matters to do, let him come unto them" (Exodus 14:14).

> "And Moses went up into the Mount, and a cloud covered the
> Mount. And the glory of the LORD abode upon Mount Sinai, and
> the cloud covered it six days: and the seventh day He called unto
> Moses out of the midst of the cloud. And the sight of the glory of
> the LORD was like a devouring fire on the top of the Mount in
> the eyes of the children of Israel. And Moses went in the midst of

the cloud, and gat him up into the Mount: and Moses was in the Mount forty days and forty nights" (Ex. 24:14-18).

In the next forty days and forty nights, Moses was receiving all the holy and precautionary measures that must be taken, for what? That it might be possible to build a dwelling place for God! This had never been attempted or commanded before this point. To say the least, necessary preparations must be taken if the LORD, Who is terrifyingly holy, was going to dwell in the midst of a sinful people without devouring them in wrath. The Lord said, "Let them make Me a sanctuary; that I may dwell among them" (Ex. 25:8). Moses was taught of what measurements and materials the Tabernacle was to be made of, everything that was to be within it, and when all of this was completed, Moses would not have to go up the Mountain to commune in God's special and immediate presence. From then onward, "there," in the holy of holies, above the mercy seat, God says, "I will meet with thee, and I will commune with thee from above the mercy seat, from between the two cherubims which are upon the ark of the testimony, of all things which I will give thee in commandment unto the children of Israel" (Ex. 25:22). This was the great Covenant purpose!

It is God that sanctifies, it is His presence which makes all things holy, and He saved a people so that He might "dwell among the children of Israel" to "be their God!" Forty days and nights at the peaks of Sinai – only Moses & The Almighty – and then God "made an end of communing with" Moses, but while Moses tarried these forty days to come down, the people fell into idolatry. It is then that "**The Great Pause**" of the Covenant occurred! Shockingly, the very Covenant which Moses was receiving on the Mountain for forty days and nights was probated and then, after a great pause of indecision, it was scarcely established as it was originally initiated. After the idolatry, at first, God refused to make a Covenant with the people and ***nearly annihilated*** every one of them! Had not Moses interceded against God's ***just intention*** for ***total destruction***, then all the people would have been killed. God ***thought*** and ***moved*** to kill all of them! ALL, except Moses, were in the direct line of Divine wrath! Not a portion of them, nor half of them, but all of them! God was even wroth with those Israelites who did not sin in the uprising of idolatry, who did not participate in the reveling masses of idolaters. In all of it, God's forbearance against the iniquitous was tried. These people, who were precious in God's eyes, did learn that "it is a fearful thing to fall into the hands of the Living God" (Heb. 10:31), and that God does exercise vengeance, especially towards His people. Israel learns this now, right and early, that before God ever takes vengeance upon the rest of the world, firstly, His eye of judgment is upon Israel. "Vengeance belongeth unto Me, I will recompense, saith the Lord. And again, The Lord shall judge **His people**" (Heb. 10:30). Therefore it is written, "Thou shalt not tempt the Lord thy God" (Matt. 4:7).

"And the LORD said unto Moses, Go, get thee down; for thy people, which thou broughtest out of the land of Egypt, have corrupted themselves: They have turned aside quickly out of the

179

way which I commanded them: they have made them a molten calf, and have worshipped it, and have sacrificed thereunto, and said, These be thy gods, O Israel, which have brought thee up out of the land of Egypt. And the LORD said unto Moses, I have seen this people, and, behold, it is a stiffnecked people: **Now therefore let Me alone, that My wrath may wax hot against them, and that I may consume them: and I will make of thee a great nation**." (Exodus 32:7-10)

I have written on this passage more than once in this book. Nevertheless, consider it again, and after it, consider the whole trail of God's "repentings" until the devastating word was given by God - *"I am weary with repenting" (Jer. 15:9).* Beginning with Exodus 32, let's trace every repeat of this historical example. As we do this, let us consider the question, just how **scarce** is salvation? Peter concluded from biblical history that, "judgment must begin at the House of God", and in the judgments of God he saw that "the righteous are scarcely saved" (1 Peter 4:17-18). Do you know what Peter is talking about? After this chapter you may, if God permits. The wrath of God that was kindled in Exodus 32:10 was not easily pacified, and the Covenant underwent a "Great Pause." You must see the significance of this "**The Great Pause**," and how it is the first of many repentances of God which are to come!

The recently saved Israelites who are now precious and promise-bound, who now stand in the shadow of Sinai before a Covenant-determined God, and suddenly, God INTENDED to totally annihilate them and nullify the whole Covenant, deciding to begin again with Moses' seed. The people who were the objects of His love, the people that He saved by an outstretched arm of irresistible power, until Egyptian sovereignty bowed to the people whom they put into slavery – it was these very people that God was suddenly ready to destroy! While Moses was still upon the Mountain, God *saw the idolatry*…then He suddenly changed His mind and decided to destroy them rather than save them, and thereby He was refusing to dwell among them. When Moses heard this command of God, "GO, get thee down… let Me alone, that My wrath may wax hot against them, and that I may consume them" (Ex. 32:10), he did intercede for Israel (under the inspiration of the Holy Ghost). The spirits of intercessors do see and hear the secret judgments of God, and through great travail of soul therewith, through the full comprehension and spiritual sensation of sudden and impending dooms, behold, they cry out life-saving prayers. To many people, prayer is but an obligation. Or maybe it is an achievement of dedication. To spiritual men, it is an experience of ceaseless communion with the friendly face of God, at least until that friendship is interrupted by wrath, and immediately, prayer becomes a cause of interceding against the dangers at hand. Prayer is thus intermittent with intercessions for the dangers that threaten present progressive salvation. "The natural man receiveth not the things of the Spirit," which means, also, that he cannot comprehend the dimensions of Christian prayer. The most brutish sinner would call for help to any passerby, if, behold, some cause of carnal emergency and life-threatening alarm is upon him. If any man is frightened enough,

180

he will lift up his voice and call aloud! But what a sinner is blind to, even that does the Christian freely see (1 Cor. 2:10), and it is the "fearful looking" of those fiery judgments that are deep in the heart of God (Heb. 10:27)! A Christian does pray because he sees spiritual realities. Therefore he does call aloud for what he and others need! Christians are life-guarding men standing watch. They are the only messengers for the spiritually blind, they are to pray for and fight over what is completely out of humanity's natural mind. They are the only able men for spiritual emergencies, and the world does not understand their urgency.

> "Now therefore let Me alone, that My wrath may wax hot against them, and that I may consume them: and I will make of thee a great nation. And Moses besought the LORD his God, and said, LORD, why doth Thy wrath wax hot against Thy people, which Thou hast brought forth out of the land of Egypt with great power, and with a mighty hand? Wherefore should the Egyptians speak, and say, For mischief did He bring them out, to slay them in the mountains, and to consume them from the face of the earth? Turn from Thy fierce wrath, and repent of this evil against Thy people. Remember Abraham, Isaac, and Israel, Thy servants, to whom Thou swarest by Thine own self, and saidst unto them, I will multiply your seed as the stars of heaven, and all this land that I have spoken of will I give unto your seed, and they shall inherit it for ever. And the LORD repented of the evil which He thought to do unto His people" (Exodus 32:10-14).

"THE GREAT PAUSE" →   Exodus 32:15-34:10

& GOD's UNCERTAINTY →

(God in the Ways of Man)

"For the LORD had said unto Moses, Say unto the children of Israel, Ye are a stiffnecked people: I will come up into the midst of thee in a moment, and consume thee: therefore now put off thy ornaments from thee, **that I may know what to do unto thee**" (Exodus 33:5).

With two main reasons, Moses pleads a case to God, if haply, God's just wrath would be quenched and forgiveness would be won. Upon hearing Moses' intercession, then "the LORD **repented** of the evil which **He thought to do** unto His people" (Ex. 32:14). From this point (Exodus 32:15), all the way to Exodus 34:10 – this is "The Great Pause"! After yielding to Moses' intercession which he prayed in Exodus 32:10-14, all we know is that, for a time, God was undecided about what He was going to do with Israel. Moses' first intercession succeeded, and the life of the whole nation of Israel was spared, even all of those who repented of their idolatry were spared, but God had not decided whether He would dwell among the people as He had formerly explained to Moses that He would. In the meantime, Moses was desperate to try every possible means of intercession to regain the grace and favor of

God again, if haply, God might reinstate the Covenant that was told to him on the Mount - that the Lord, and no other, would dwell among them.

REMINDING GOD →

(God in the Ways of Man)

"I have set watchmen upon thy walls, O Jerusalem, which shall never hold their peace day nor night: ye that **make mention of the LORD**, keep not silence, And **give Him no rest**, till He establish, and till He make Jerusalem a praise in the earth" (Isaiah 62:6-7).

There are *three means of intercession* that the prophets do engage in, and in these means they do "wrestle" against God, but more specifically, they wrestle against the just, holy, and angry will of God, which is set to destroy – *Firstly*: intercession is done by the execution of justice and judgment upon guilty, unpardonable sinners. *Secondarily*: intercession is done by prayer which reminds God of the consequential effects of destroying wrath, namely, the glory of His Name that hinges upon what He will decide to do in the present circumstance, and the word, promises, and Covenants He has made with men in time past and present. *Thirdly*: intercession is done by a sacrifice or offering of some kind, which, when death is accomplished, it bears the penalty of the guilty sinner. With these three kinds of intercession in mind, let us study this Great Pause very carefully. Let us see the Divine struggle at hand, and how the holy intercessions of the prophet Moses did strive for mercy, amazingly, by standing against the fierce countenance of God which was pointed to destroy! As we acquaint ourselves with this, please remember, this is *the beginning* of the Covenant, and if Moses succeeds and the Covenant is established, then this marks the beginning of many centuries wherein God's prophets do wrestle in intercession concerning the same purpose of the Covenant – That this saying would be fulfilled: "I will dwell in them, and walk in them; and I will be their God, and they shall be My people…I will receive you, and will be a Father unto you, and ye shall be My sons and daughters, saith the Lord Almighty" (2 Cor. 6:16-18).

Moses does *five* works of intercession: in *two* acts of judgment and *three* prayerful entreaties. The two acts of judgment and the first prayer are all in Exodus 32:15-35, written below:

"And Moses turned, and went down from the mount, and the two tables of the testimony were in his hand: the tables were written on both their sides; on the one side and on the other were they written. And the tables were the work of God, and the writing was the writing of God, graven upon the tables. And when Joshua heard the noise of the people as they shouted, he said unto Moses, There is a noise of war in the camp. And he said, It is not the voice of them that shout for mastery, neither is it the voice of them that cry for being overcome: but the noise of them that sing do I hear.

And it came to pass, as soon as he came nigh unto the camp, that

182

he saw the calf, and the dancing: and **Moses' anger waxed hot, and he cast the tables out of his hands, and brake them beneath the mount. And he took the calf which they had made, and burnt it in the fire, and ground it to powder, and strawed it upon the water, and made the children of Israel drink of it.** And Moses said unto Aaron, What did this people unto thee, that thou hast brought so great a sin upon them? And Aaron said, Let not the anger of my lord wax hot: thou knowest the people, that they are set on mischief. For they said unto me, Make us gods, which shall go before us: for as for this Moses, the man that brought us up out of the land of Egypt, we wot not what is become of him. And I said unto them, Whosoever hath any gold, let them break it off. So they gave it me: then I cast it into the fire, and there came out this calf. And when Moses saw that the people were naked; (for Aaron had made them naked unto their shame among their enemies:)

Then Moses stood in the gate of the camp, and said, Who is on the LORD'S side? let him come unto me. And all the sons of Levi gathered themselves together unto him. And he said unto them, **Thus saith the LORD God of Israel, Put every man his sword by his side, and go in and out from gate to gate throughout the camp, and slay every man his brother, and every man his companion, and every man his neighbour. And the children of Levi did according to the word of Moses: and there fell of the people that day about three thousand men.** For Moses had said, Consecrate yourselves to day to the LORD, even every man upon his son, and upon his brother; that He may bestow upon you a blessing this day.

And it came to pass on the morrow, that Moses said unto the people, Ye have sinned a great sin: and **now I will go up unto the LORD; peradventure I shall make an atonement for your sin. And Moses returned unto the LORD, and said, Oh, this people have sinned a great sin, and have made them gods of gold. Yet now, if Thou wilt forgive their sin--; and if not, blot me, I pray Thee, out of Thy book which Thou hast written. And the LORD said unto Moses, Whosoever hath sinned against Me, him will I blot out of My book. Therefore now go,** lead the people unto the place of which I have spoken unto thee: behold, **Mine <u>angel</u> shall go before thee**: nevertheless in the day when I visit I will visit their sin upon them. And the LORD plagued the people, because they made the calf, which Aaron made." (Exodus 32:15-35)

183

The *first* act of intercession by judgment does reflect the mind & message of God. God was wroth, and so, "Moses' anger waxed hot." God decided against the Covenant, and so, Moses broke the tablets of the Covenant which contained the Ten Commandments. The message of God was clear – the Covenant is broken. Then Moses grinded the golden calf and had the people drink it. He knew that this was the object of God's jealousy and "curse" (Deut. 7:25-26).

The **second** act of intercession by judgment is when Moses killed the unrepentant. The call of Moses went forth, "Who is on the LORD'S side?" Those who answered from the idolatrous multitude, or those who were standing in their surrounding tents, these were the repentant people from the tribe of Levi. They came forward to be sent out, and for what? To kill their family members who engaged in the idolatry, who still, even now, remained unrepentant, and so...the Levites went forth to "slay every man his brother, every man his companion, and every man his neighbor!" With much anguish of soul, the Levites did mercilessly slay their friends and family!

Though severe judgment had been executed, Moses knew the Covenant was not yet reinstated. The sin of Israel was "great!" Moses contemplated a second ascent up the Mountain God, to appeal, if haply, God might forgive Israel for their sins, but Moses dared not ascend the Mount of God to make his request without executing due justice against the calf and its worshippers. What about you, preacher? God observed the death of those unrepentant men and women with fierce anger burning in His eyes. After all that could be done was done, and a part of Israel was executed-dead, the rest still stood in jeopardy...Moses said, "now I will go up unto the LORD; peradventure I shall make an atonement for your sin" (Ex. 32:30). Moses pleads for their forgiveness, to no avail. He offers himself as a sacrifice, and is denied. Furthermore, God still refuses to dwell among the people! God said, "therefore now go, lead the people unto the place of which I have spoken unto thee: behold, **Mine angel shall go before thee**: nevertheless in the day when I visit I will visit their sin upon them. And **the LORD plagued the people, because they made the calf, which Aaron made**" (Ex. 32:34-35). God lifted up His hand of wrath and sent forth a smiting plague upon the people, and behold, each man was in their plague of pain. Israel was full of the sounds of howling agony, and everyone knew – GOD IS STILL ANGRY. Yet, nobody knew the greatest loss which Moses was desperate to recover, that God would no longer dwell among the people. I repeat, God decided that an angel would dwell among them instead of Himself.

> "And the LORD said unto Moses, Depart, and GO...and I will send **an angel** before thee..." (Exodus 33:1-6).

The command was given to "GO." This showed that God meant to proceed with the Abrahamic Covenant, that He was intent on giving the Promised Land to Israel, but the forty days of instruction wherein God revealed His purpose to dwell among the people by a Tabernacle and all the incorporating laws (The Mosaic Covenant) was denied. Moses, "a man subject to like passions" as Jacob, did wrestle against the unwillingness of God to bless with the fulfillment of the Covenant. Moses sought "power with God" to "prevail," to reinitiate the Covenant, hoping that God's anger would only endure for "but a moment" (Gen. 32:28, Psa. 30:5), and that mercy might come in the morning. If so, then God's anger would be but a pause, a temporary refusal to commence this holy agreement with the people, and that His wrath was but a momentary probation of the Covenant. You see, God already repented of His wrath to totally annihilate the people of Israel (Ex. 32:14), and for God to reinstate the Covenant after the Great Pause, this requires further repentance in God – away from wrath and unto the former mercies in the Covenant. Note: God is not a man that we might wrestle with Him, yet if we are moved and inspired by the Holy Ghost, if we stand – not alone, but in One of the Persons of the Trinity – then through Him we can wrestle against Him (God in the ways of man). The soul exhaustion of spiritual wrestling is a sensory experience for interceding saints. It is a personal participation in the wrestlings of God's simultaneous and contradicting wills, in a clash – shifting and turning, they are rolling and burning, One against the Other – and, lo, they are wrestling all throughout the duration of time when God is **_undecided_**. This is just as God says in another place – "**My heart is turned within Me, My repentings are kindled together**" (Hos. 11:8)! This happens within time, and the holy prophet is included in the holy press – Will against Will – until at last, the ordination of His purpose chosen before is manifest as the final decision. For those of us who have been included in this Divine Mystery of wrestling repentances, by personal experience, it is as if we were lost betwixt the Persons of the Trinity for a while, straining against God yet compelled by God, in Him as one who is empowered to stand against Him. We may be weeping against God's wrath, but there is a transcending peace that we are safely in God. It is a resting, yet a working, nevertheless I wrestle, yet not I, but Christ wrestleth in me. Such experiences are inexpressible…like "unspeakable words, which it is not lawful for a man to utter" (2 Cor. 12:4). Nevertheless, at Moses' first attempt of prayerful intercession, he was not able to prevail with God. God's present judgment was to replace Himself with the Angel which He spoke of. God's judgment was further explained in the rest of Exodus 33:1-6.

> "And the LORD said unto Moses, Depart, and go up hence, thou
> and the people which thou hast brought up out of the land of
> Egypt, unto the land which I sware unto Abraham, to Isaac, and
> to Jacob, saying, Unto thy seed will I give it: And I will send **an
> angel** before thee; and I will drive out the Canaanite, the
> Amorite, and the Hittite, and the Perizzite, the Hivite, and the
> Jebusite: Unto a land flowing with milk and honey: **for I will not
> go up in the midst of thee; for thou art a stiffnecked people:
> lest I consume thee in the way.** And when the people heard
> these evil tidings, they mourned: and no man did put on him his
> ornaments. For the LORD had said unto Moses, Say unto the
> children of Israel, **Ye are a stiffnecked people: I will come up
> into the midst of thee in a moment, and consume thee:**

**therefore now put off thy ornaments from thee, that I may
know what to do unto thee.** And the children of Israel stripped
themselves of their ornaments by the mount Horeb." (Exodus
33:1-6)

The Lord is so holy and the people so sinful…He knows He cannot even
enter into the midst of them without becoming inflamed with holy anger, and when
God is so near there is a suddenness to justice. God said – "I will come up into the
midst of thee in a moment, and consume thee." Do you understand the difficulty?
One less holy than God could walk in the midst of Israel as they traveled to the
Promised Land. One less holy than God can be the instrument of God's deliverance
to conquer the Promised Land for Israel, but for God, Himself, to be so nigh – this
was a dangerously difficult happening! An Angel, one that is infinitely less holy than
God, one so much less in dignity and purity, can continue in the midst of Israel
without burning them up! An Angel in the Name of God is, by presence, person, and
expression, a mere shadow of God – a great condescension. An angel, though
exceedingly dignified, is infinitely less holy than God. This would be a lighter
presence for humanity's frame to bear. Comparatively to God, an angel may not be so
aggravated with human depravity. An Angel may be a presence Israel could draw
near to and survive with. We are able to look upon the shadow of God, and live, and
even so, we are able endure an Angelic visitation face to face. Not so with the
Almighty! Behold even the Holy Beasts of heaven, which do excel in
incomprehensible strength and dignity! Even they cannot do anything but cry, Holy!
Holy! Holy! before the Presence of God. No! They CANNOT look upon Him either!
They shield their faces from the Most Holy and dare not to look upon God (Isaiah
6:1-3). In choosing an Angel to replace the Lord, this is an infinite step down. God
was antagonized and appalled at sin, and having decided already that He will not
dwell among them, He thus contemplates what He should do with them further…God
says, "put off thy ornaments from thee, **that I may know what to do unto thee.**"

When God says that He does not know what to do…NOW is the time to
cast yourself down to the ground! At such a time, LET ALL FLESH BE SILENT
BEFORE GOD! "No flesh should glory in His presence" (1 Cor. 1:29)! By
interpretation, "the children of Israel stripped themselves of their ornaments by the
Mount Horeb" (Exodus 33:6). My reader, you will not find one decked-out,
ornament-sparkling, silver-wrist-watching, make-up precise, hair-perfect, picture-
conscience INTERCESSOR, no, not in all the world! What does your preacher look
like? Oh! Look how firmly composed he is while he prays! And his gentle
tones…away with them! They are so soothing to the ears – but he's just playing the
part – he is sounding for you a relaxing song! His tones are slow in pace, with
syllables L-O-N-G, but this is nothing but a spiritual baby's lullaby to keep you
asleep! My reader, what ever happened to biblical Christianity!? People are crying in
hell, and weeping – they are shouting and screaming! But we have painless preachers
as "church" leaders, and we have sleeping spectators on pews for bleachers! And you
tell the world that you believe in HELL!? What ever happened to, "**<u>Evening</u>**, and

morning, and at **noon**, will I pray, **and CRY ALOUD**: and He shall hear my voice" (Ps. 55:17)!? But these men pray in front of men that they might be heard of men! Are you surprised that your congregation never wakes up?! Your preacher is always well composed, but the man is deceiving you by a vain show. "Church people" substitute the shining countenance of God, and for what? A dim-lighted congregation before a brightly lit stage – they all watch their preacher glow as he puts on the act. Be astonished at this! For God says, "My people love to have it so" (Jer. 5:31)! Not so with Moses, he "was very meek, above all the men which were upon the face of the earth" (Num. 12:3). Rightly said! This preacher had his face upon the earth "before all the assembly" (Num. 14:5)! What about you, thou man of "church?" If you don't ever get on your face, then you are a preacher of pride, a peddler of God's holy word for a paycheck! Moses "fell upon his face" down to the earth (Num. 16:4)! He, with Aaron – they "fell on their faces" (Num. 14:5), "fell upon their faces" (Num. 20:6), "fell upon their faces" (Num. 16:22), and "fell upon their faces" (Num. 16:45)! What about you? "David and the elders of Israel…fell upon their faces" (1 Chron. 21:16), "Abram fell on his face: and God talked with him" (Gen. 17:3), "Joshua fell on his face to the earth" (Josh. 5:14), and "all the people," "they shouted and fell on their faces" (Lev. 9:24)!

When God does not know what to do, it is because the wrestling conflict of His simultaneous wills is unfinished! Amazing! At this time spiritual men behold the holy tension in God's mind! "For who hath known the mind of the Lord, that he may instruct Him? But we have the mind of Christ" (1 Cor. 2:16). Spiritual men are, alas, caught up in a mystery, caught up in a river whose motions is God! It is as if they are hidden behind a thick veil, caught up in a holy place, and there the servants of all men *travail in the Spirit*. These men plead for the promises because they are obsessed with how God saves sinners, and how He makes His name famous among men. Why do they *travail*? Imagine it! It is as the agony of a woman's birth! Imagine a woman crying aloud, and groaning, moan to moan, the delivering aid shouting, BREATHE! BREATHE! PANG to PANG, even so, intercession is comparatively the same. Intercessors **TRAVAIL**! Under bloody, flesh ripping, birth pangs, they are pained, and it is for those bound in God's angry chains. Unseen and unthanked, for lo, "He that is greatest among you shall be your servant" (Matt. 23:11).

In the flesh, what is more painful and gruesome than a woman giving birth? This honorable but flesh-tearing experience is the inevitable appointment for a woman to bring God's unborn humanity into life. Rightly said, so it is with spiritual intercessors! Only they are unheard, unseen, and in secret. That is, except for prayer meetings, but who goes to those anyway!? Therefore intercessors are without honor, thanks, and praise. Like a woman, but worse, they go through a like torment of spiritual birth all throughout their days. They do "travail in birth" for the souls of spiritual children "until Christ be formed" in them (Gal. 4:19). Paul described this when speaking to the Galatians, when he said, "My little children, of whom **I travail in birth** again until Christ be formed in you" (Gal. 4:19). This labor is wrought by the least of all men – the secret servants – praying for all humanity. Christians, they

187

are the clothing of the Chief Intercessor, Jesus Christ, Who is the Hero over hell and the secret Servant of all men. His secret salvation outwitted the world! They, thinking to exterminate Him, committed the greatest possible evil by killing the Person of God! But through this supposed extermination, God was working their greatest and only salvation. As it was with Christ, so it is with intercessors, it is their pain that works another's eternal pleasure – "so then death worketh in us, but life in you" (2 Cor. 4:12). They are the spiritual birth canal for an everlasting, newly-created life. Their strength is depleted in this most holy endeavor, and thereby they do become the weakest of men. "Who is weak, and I am not weak? Who is offended, and I burn not" (2 Cor. 11:29)? Weak, broken, and touched by God, they do not walk strong like other men. They have a lowly limp of deep humility, but they possess the treasure of unspeakable glory. They "wist not that the skin of" their face shines because they do talk with God (Exodus 34:29). As it was then, even so it is now, "And when He saw that He prevailed not against him, He touched the hollow of his thigh; and the hollow of Jacob's thigh was out of joint, as he wrestled with Him" (Gen. 32:25). Intercessors are not high-headed or barrel-chested, and when they walk they do limp.

Moses, having been denied once, having watched the people as they were plagued for their sin, and having received a direct command from God to proceed to the Promised Land without the reestablishment of the Mosaic Covenant, engages to wrestle God again! When most would give up and hang their head, until finally the Mountain vision of God's glorious promises do fade from memory... at this time Moses ROUSES himself! Even so my reader, BESTIR THYSELF for the vision of God! Moses considered what he might do, hoping that there was still time left to plead with God that He might change His mind. Moses dared not ascend the Mountain again, not after the commandment – "GO" – was solemnly given to him, but other than ascending the Mountain, how could Moses find audience with God? There was no Tabernacle made that Moses might go before the Presence of God to plead, and the Lord had already said that He will not come into the midst of the people. Moses, willing to risk his life, made a Tabernacle for the first time without the command of God. He attempted to make it like the one that was shown to him on the Mount. He had no other idea of how God might be willing to come and give him audience except by this Tent which was revealed to him beforehand. Given the haste that Moses was in and the short amount of time that he had, he made a Tabernacle...but it was not in hopes that God would come within the camp of Israel like the Covenant had stated, for the Lord had already said that He would kill the people if this happened. Moses made a Tabernacle and then went *outside of the camp* of Israel, if haply out there, God might visit the Tabernacle and give audience to Moses' earnest prayers! Only a man full of the Spirit of God knows the brevity of speaking again to God, after that He hath spoken once (Genesis 18:27, 30-32)! "Oh let not the Lord be angry, and I will speak!" This is the language of intercession from Abraham to the Almighty. Even so, under this heavy weight of godly fear, Moses endeavored, as Abraham said, "Behold now, I have taken upon me to speak unto the Lord."

"And Moses took **the tabernacle**, and pitched it **without the camp, afar off from the camp**, and called it the Tabernacle of the congregation. And it came to pass, that every one which sought the LORD went out unto the tabernacle of the congregation, which was **without the camp**. And it came to pass, when Moses went out unto the tabernacle, that all the people rose up, and stood every man at his tent door, and looked after Moses, until he was gone into the tabernacle. And it came to pass, as Moses entered into the tabernacle, the cloudy pillar descended, and stood at the door of the tabernacle, and the LORD talked with Moses. And all the people saw the cloudy pillar stand at the tabernacle door: and all the people rose up and worshipped, every man in his tent door." (Exodus 33:7-10)

God received Moses' mode of intercession and met with him face to face! The subject of wrestling and intercession is clear – "If Thy Presence go not with me, carry us not up hence... for wherein shall it be known here that I and Thy people have found grace in Thy sight? Is it not in that Thou goest with us? So shall we be separated, I and Thy people, from all the people that are upon the face of the earth" (Ex. 33:14-16). God received the intercession of Moses and granted that He would be with him and the people, and therefore, that which was taught and shown to Moses on the Mountain was now reinstated! The intercession dialogue is from verses 12-17, and the Lord says in verse 17, "I will do this thing." Before this meeting with God in the Tabernacle is over, Moses prays to God – "shew me Thy glory" (Exodus 33:18). The Lord says in response, "I will make all My goodness pass before thee..." (Exodus 33:19). The Lord tells Moses to prepare for another meeting the next morning, only this time Moses is to ascend Sinai again. Moses is also instructed to make "two tables of stone like unto the first" which he broke, that he might bring those with him up the Mountain (Ex. 34:1). This signifies that God may fulfill what He said to Moses, and reinstate the Covenant, but Moses is still in unrest. He senses that there is still fierce wrath burning in the heart of God. He considers the possibility that God will go back on His decision to reinstate the Covenant. Moses prepares everything, rises early, and ascends the Mount. There he sees the glory of God pass by him, and lo, the wrestle for the Covenant begins again! Moses is compelled to pray again:

"If now I have found grace in Thy sight, O Lord, let my Lord, I pray Thee, **go among us**; for it is a stiffnecked people; and pardon our iniquity and our sin, and **take us for Thine inheritance**" (Ex. 34:9).

Moses spends the next "forty days and forty nights" on top of Sinai – WRESTLING – and "he did neither eat bread, nor drink water" (Ex. 34:28). How do I know Moses was still wrestling against the wrath of God, and that God was still undecided to reinstate the Covenant? Moses explained exactly what he was doing at a later time, and said –

> "And I fell down before the LORD, as at the first, forty days and forty nights: I did neither eat bread, nor drink water, because of all your sins which ye sinned, in doing wickedly in the sight of the LORD, to provoke Him to anger. For I was afraid of the anger and hot displeasure, wherewith the LORD was wroth against you to destroy you. But the LORD hearkened unto me at that time also. And the LORD was very angry with Aaron to have destroyed him: and I prayed for Aaron also the same time…Thus I fell down before the LORD forty days and forty nights, as I fell down at the first; because the LORD had said He would destroy you. I prayed therefore unto the LORD, and said, O Lord GOD, destroy not Thy people and Thine inheritance…" (Deuteronomy 9:18-20, 25-26).

Only by the infinite power of God could Moses endure forty days and nights of wrestling against God's holy wrath. Jacob could scarce endure one night, and he wrestled for the lives of far fewer people. Vividly now, can you see the scarcity of their salvation, and that God "said that He would destroy them, **had not Moses His chosen stood before Him in the breach, to turn away His wrath,** lest He should destroy them" (Ps. 106:23)?! The scarcity of salvation for those who do endure to the end cannot be properly understood until we are conscientious of the dual, simultaneous, and genuine wills of God that are actively working, all the time, in tension and contradiction with one another, and that, within the single mind of the Godhead there can be multiple intentions, purposes, and considerable actions that His emotions are moving Him towards. In Hosea 11:8-9, the Lord speaks of it as His "repentings," or, the turnings, changes, and wrestlings within His mind and heart, each one pressing Him to a contradicting action at each moment. God, wrestling over what He would do, wrestling His own will, and prophets standing in His will for the wrestle, He says – **"How shall I** give thee up, Ephraim? **How shall I** deliver thee, Israel? **How shall I** make thee as Admah? **How shall I** set thee as Zeboim? **Mine heart is turned within Me, My repentings are kindled together**. I will not execute the fierceness of Mine anger, I will not return to destroy Ephraim: for I am God, and not man; the Holy One in the midst of thee: and I will not enter into the city" (Hosea 11:8-9). Perhaps now we can understand what the thoughts of God's heart were wrestling over when He said, "Ye are a stiffnecked people: I will come up into the midst of thee in a moment, and consume thee: therefore now put off thy ornaments from thee, **that I may know what to do unto thee**" (Ex. 33:5).

This was the *fourth* prayerful intercession of Moses since God's wrath
waxed hot.

Here, the Lord seals His acceptance of Israel and concludes the Great Pause. God clearly states, "Behold, I make a Covenant," AFTER FORTY DAYS AND NIGHTS! Moses hears the way and works that are of consequence to this

190

Covenant, praise God (Exodus 34:10-27)! Remember now, at the first forty days of Moses' communion with God on Sinai, the Lord was instructing Moses of merciful purposes and careful preparations. After this was denied, Moses spent another "forty days and forty nights" (Ex. 34:28) in PRAYER! I repeat, this second forty days and night, though equal in time to the other, was not for re-instruction or a further explanation of the Covenant…the entire time – ALL FORTY DAYS –was spent in intercession before the wrath of God! It took forty days until God was convinced to remake the former Covenant. Is this not amazing?! Now the message was clear that God was reinstating the Covenant. The word of instruction was given to rewrite the Ten Commandments, the way of salvation was made known, and Moses descended the Mountain with his face shining!

My reader, consider how valiantly and courageously Moses behaved, and how he risked his life in intercessions! Moses' first intercession availed to save Israel as a whole from total annihilation. The next two intercessions (by the execution of judgment) availed to pacify some wrath in God, and consequentially, Moses was emboldened to go before the Lord again on top of Sinai. Here, Moses sought further forgiveness by the intercession of prayer, and he was denied. Then the people were plagued, but nevertheless, Moses was adamant in the Holy Ghost! Absent of any command of God to continue in intercession, and contrary to the command already given – to "GO" – Moses found a way to get the attention of God – the Tabernacle pitched outside of the camp! "And Moses took the tabernacle, and pitched it without the camp, afar off from the camp, and called it the Tabernacle of the congregation. And it came to pass, that every one which sought the LORD went out unto the tabernacle of the congregation, which was without the camp. And it came to pass, when Moses went out unto the tabernacle, that all the people rose up, and stood every man at his tent door, and looked after Moses, until he was gone into the tabernacle. And it came to pass, as Moses entered into the tabernacle, the cloudy pillar descended, and stood at the door of the tabernacle, and the LORD talked with Moses" (Exodus 33:7-9). This is amazing! By the persistent intercessions of Moses, filled with the Holy Ghost, the people were spared. Finally, God knew what to do with them… but alas! It took FORTY MORE DAYS of intercessory wrestling against the burning heat of God's billowing wrath in order for the Covenant to be reinstated. With what difficulty was the Covenant of salvation established, *and this is just its beginning*! Do you think that Moses knew that salvation was scarce, if at all? He persevered in prayer, again and again, until finally, our ears tingle with astonishment to hear – God decided to "dwell among them." Indeed, "If the righteous scarcely be saved, where shall the ungodly and sinner appear" (1 Peter 4:18)?

The Divine Struggle Continues

Finally it was done, and the Covenant was established. Scarcely were the righteous saved from the wrath of God. Thus began the same Divine struggle for centuries…

Think about the contemplation of the Lord during The Great Pause. The

Lord wanted to go with them, dwell in their midst, and with His own Person, overthrow the armies of the Promised Land. He wanted to go with them "**in the way**" to the Promised Land (Ex. 33:3), but He hesitated. He knew of what scarcity they would survive His holy wrath, if and when He, and not an Angel, did dwell in their midst so as to immediately behold and experience (in a special way) the grotesque manifestation of their sin. He wanted to go with them "**in the way**" as a gentle Shepherd, but He decided, "I will not go up in the midst of thee; for thou art a stiffnecked people: lest I consume thee **in the way**" (Ex. 33:3). The Lord did leave them so that He did not consume, for a time, and for a short while He was wrestling in thought of what to do in this dangerous decision of great good, and, potentially, of great annihilation (Ex. 33:5).

The Covenant was reinstated – so what should we expect!? No more annihilation? No, my reader…a near annihilation of God's people. I am astonished at it. I sigh to write about it. But we need to face it! In the days to come, many will not escape the wrath of God. Alongside God "**in the way**," Moses summarized his (and Israel's) experience in a psalm. Please read it carefully and consider whether or not you know <u>this God</u>. These things were written because God decided *to dwell among them*. Thus, at the opening of the psalm, Moses said, "Lord, **Thou hast been our dwelling** place in all generations." It is one thing to dwell in some carnally special place that you like, or that is envied by men, but it is another thing for God to be your dwelling place.

> "A Prayer of Moses the man of God. Lord, **Thou hast been our dwelling place** in all generations. Before the mountains were brought forth, or ever Thou hadst formed the earth and the world, even from everlasting to everlasting, Thou art God. **Thou turnest man to destruction; and sayest, Return, ye children of men. For a thousand years in Thy sight are but as yesterday when it is past, and as a watch in the night. Thou carriest them away as with a flood; they are as a sleep: in the morning they are like grass which groweth up. In the morning it flourisheth, and groweth up; in the evening it is cut down, and withereth. For we are consumed by Thine anger, and by Thy wrath are we troubled. Thou hast set our iniquities before Thee, our secret sins in the light of Thy countenance. For all our days are passed away in Thy wrath: we spend our years as a tale that is told. The days of our years are threescore years and ten; and if by reason of strength they be fourscore years, yet is their strength labour and sorrow; for it is soon cut off, and we fly away. Who knoweth the power of Thine anger? even according to Thy fear, so is Thy wrath.** So teach us to number our days, that we may apply our hearts unto wisdom. Return, O LORD, how long? and let it repent Thee concerning Thy servants. O satisfy us early with Thy mercy; that

we may rejoice and be glad all our days. Make us glad according to the days wherein Thou hast afflicted us, and the years wherein we have seen evil. Let Thy work appear unto Thy servants, and Thy glory unto their children. And let the beauty of the LORD our God be upon us: and establish Thou the work of our hands upon us; yea, the work of our hands establish Thou it." (Psalm 90)

The Lord abode with them and chose them, that He might abide with them forever by the Covenant at Sinai. My reader, I want you to remember something. Before reaching Sinai but after the Red Sea crossing, while Israel traveled through the desert on the way there, Israel sinned and provoked God's wrath three times, yet no one died (Ex. 15, 16, 17). I conjecture that it was because, at Sinai, God meant to teach His people the fear of Him, that He might be respected when dwelling among them. Do you remember what happened at Sinai?

"And all the people saw the thunderings, and the lightnings, and the noise of the trumpet, and the mountain smoking: and when the people saw it, they removed, and stood afar off. And they said unto Moses, Speak thou with us, and we will hear: but let not God speak with us, lest we die. And Moses said unto the people, Fear not: for God is come to prove you, and that His fear may be before your faces, that ye sin not. And the people stood afar off, and Moses drew near unto the thick darkness where God was." (Exodus 20:18-21)

Before the Covenant at Sinai, Israel provoked God three times and no one died. Now let us study what happened after the Covenant at Sinai and after the Great Pause. Israel provoked God again, three times, and lo, the wrath of God did break forth upon the people. Their *near annihilation* at "The Great Pause" should have been a deep lesson. They should have known better, but they reverted to their former ways as if God had not instructed them.

"And when the people complained, it displeased the LORD: and the LORD heard it; and His anger was kindled; and the fire of the LORD burnt among them, and consumed them that were in the uttermost parts of the camp. And the people cried unto Moses; and when Moses prayed unto the LORD, the fire was quenched. And he called the name of the place Taberah: because the fire of the LORD burnt among them" (Numbers 11:1-3).

At the first temptation in Num. 11:1-3, Moses had no time to intercede before God's "anger was kindled," before "the fire of the LORD burnt among them, and consumed them that were in the uttermost parts of the camp." It was not until "the people cried" in repentance, and then Moses interceded and "prayed," that finally "the fire was quenched!" The place in which this happened is named in

193

memory of this great burning fire…it was called **Taberah**, which being interpreted, means *burning*.

In the second provocation, "the wrath of the LORD was kindled against the people, and the LORD smote the people with a very great plague," and "there they buried the people that lusted" (Num. 11:33-35). The name of the place was called "**Kibroth-hattaavah**," which means *graves of lust.* The third provocation was by Miriam and Aaron in Numbers 12, and in consequence, Miriam was struck with leprosy. The final provocation was called *the day of provocation*, and at this day, God reprobated all who are involved in the provocation. This was when spies were sent to spy out the Promised Land, and they returned to give an evil, unbelieving report (except for Caleb and Joshua). In turn, 600,000 men of war who were chosen to invade the Promised Land refused to obey God, and in consequence, the Lord said:

> "And the LORD said unto Moses, How long will this people
> provoke Me? and how long will it be ere they believe Me, for all
> the signs which I have shewed among them? **I will smite them
> with the pestilence, and disinherit them, and will make of thee
> a greater nation and mightier than they.**" (Numbers 14:11-12)

Again, like in Exodus 32:10, God sought to kill all of Israel! 600,000 men of war antagonized the justice of God to kill *all* of Israel, to altogether start again in another line. God said that He would "**disinherit them.**" Remember the cries of Moses at the fourth intercession that reinitiated the Covenant after "The Great Pause?" Moses pled, "Go among us; for it is a stiffnecked people; and pardon our iniquity and our sin, and **take us for Thine inheritance**" (Ex. 34:9). God took them for His **inheritance**, or possession, and did dwell among them, but here He sought annihilation of them, or to "**disinherit them.**" At the Great Pause, Moses cried this cry for forty days: "O Lord GOD, destroy not Thy people and **Thine inheritance**" (Deut. 9:26), and yet God, because of repetitive provocations, could *scarcely* bear their existence any longer!

Moses interceded, and availed, but not for the 600,000 men of war! The Lord repented of a *total annihilation*, and instead He only reprobated the 600,000 men of war. He chose to kill them over the next forty years, until their "carcasses be wasted in the wilderness" (Num. 14:33), and so, for forty years, He used them as an example for their sons and daughters to behold – watching men die – because God chose them for the Covenant in their fathers' stead. In grief, the Lord said, "How long shall I bear with this evil congregation, which murmur against Me? I have heard the murmurings of the children of Israel, which they murmur against Me" (Num. 14:27). It is finished for them, and there is no more mercy; God says, "in this wilderness they shall be consumed, and there they shall die" (Num. 14:35).

The merciful, loving, and saving Lord, Who delivered them from Egypt, could not continue along the way with the people to persevere them into the Promised Land, because their repeated sinfulness provoked God too far…into a will of wrath and destruction without any possibility of repentance or intercession. Israel didn't know that this would be the last temptation they had left, that after this there would be no more mercy. All the former provocations were able to be pacified, unto the preservation of most of Israel, but now, 600,000 men of war, representing the male adults and family heads of all the Israelite family lines, which are the male adults of a whole generation (minus the Levites), and all of them are ordained to destruction without repentance. This generation, in their wanderings through the wilderness for the next forty years, experienced what Moses wrote about in Psalm 90, in which he said – "For we are consumed by Thine anger, and by Thy wrath are we troubled. Thou hast set our iniquities before Thee, our secret sins in the light of Thy countenance. For all our days are passed away in Thy wrath: we spend our years as a tale that is told." Whether it was murmurings or some other rebellion of some sort, the wrath of God became increasingly more fatal upon the people as time continued. The lives preserved by intercession were less and less. After many provocations…then the temptation within the heart of God to destroy them surmounted the forbearance to preserve them. They did "tempt Me," God says, "now these ten times and have not hearkened to My voice" (Num. 14:22).

Threat of TOTAL ANNIHILATION #1 → Exodus 32:10, "…that I may consume them: and *I will make of thee a great nation.*"

Then the Sinai Covenant is Established, and…

BREAKING FORTH OF WRATH → 1ˢᵗ **Temptation**) Numbers 11:1-3, the Taberah-***burning.***

2ⁿᵈ **Temptation**) Numbers 11:33-35, the Kibroth-hattaavah-***graves of lust.***

3ʳᵈ **Temptation**) Numbers 12, Miriam struck with leprosy.

Threat of TOTAL ANNIHILATION #2→ 4ᵗʰ **Temptation**) Numbers 14:11-12, "I will smite them…disinherit them…*will make of thee a greater nation and mightier than they.*"

In the three temptations after the Covenant's establishment, Moses did intercede successfully, at least to preserve the generation from reprobation. God was still bringing most of them to heaven! In these three intercessions after Sinai, many people did die, but we don't see all that God was wrestling over in His heart, or all that Moses prayed to God in those hours and days. In "The Great Pause," we hear some of what God said, and some of what Moses interceded, and what God repented from…but in the subsequent three outbreaks of wrath, we can only imagine that the wrestle against wrath was like the former ones, or like wrestlings later chronicled in other centuries, such as Amos, for example, when he interceded before God in Amos 7:1-9.

A Revelation of Destroying Wrath → 1ˢᵗ) "then I said, O Lord God, forgive, I beseech Thee,

GIVEN TO AMOS

by whom shall Jacob rise? For he is small. **The LORD repented for this: It shall not be**, saith the LORD" – Amos 7:1-3

2**nd**) "Then said I, O Lord GOD, cease, I beseech Thee: by whom shall Jacob arise? For he is mall. **The LORD repented for this: This also shall not be**, saith the Lord God" – Amos 7:4-6

3**rd**) "Thus he shewed me: and, behold, the Lord stood upon a wall made by a plumbline, with a plumbline in His hand. And the LORD said unto me, Amos, what seest thou? And I said, A plumbline. Then said the Lord, Behold, I will set a plumbline in the midst of My people Israel: I will not again pass by them any more: And the high places of Isaac shall be desolate, and the sanctuaries of Israel shall be laid waste; and I will rise against the house of Jeroboam with the sword" – Amos 7:7-9

You see, there were three revelations of God's wrath to Amos, and behold how Amos wrestled them, until, two were repented of so that the mind of God changed, but the third one was established. This is the same scenario of how it was for Moses after the Covenant was established in Israel. There were four temptations – Burning, graves of lust, and leprosy were the results – but had not Moses interceded, like Amos, one can only imagine how the people would have been *totally annihilated*! Instead, my reader, by the grace of God, they were only *nearly annihilated*, but *this does not mean that God did not desire to totally annihilate them*! Back in Exodus 32:10 at Sinai, at the overflow of wrath which began "The Great Pause," do you remember how God wanted to totally destroy all of Israel and begin again with Moses? Well, in the wrestlings of the Almighty, one can only imagine this desire still rising in His heart – hotter and hotter in each subsequent temptation – until finally, at the fourth temptation in Numbers 14:11-13 – AGAIN – God speaks forth the commanded desire to totally annihilate Israel and start over with Moses! Both times God said to Moses, "I will make of thee a great nation," or, "I will make of thee a greater nation" (Exodus 32:10, Num. 14:12). Before Sinai, but after the Red Sea crossing, Israel tempted God and went on without any physical manifestation of wrath; yet again, even then, one can only imagine what is happening in the unseen realm, in the heavenlies, how the Divine struggle wrestled and the fires raged! Their salvation from these first temptations was with scarcity, no doubt. As the wrath of God was continually resisted by the will of God which pressed for mercy, even so, their salvation continued. This means that they continued on in perseverance, but with each temptation which continued, the wrath of God began to break forth into increasingly hard causalities. What the people could not learn by faith, they were taught by stroke and lash. They did not learn to fear the wrath of God which Moses secretly wrestled against and afterward reported to them; yet now this unseen wrath was breaking forth upon them! "Blessed are they that have not seen, and yet have believed" (John 20:29).

196

God will strike Israel to instruct Israel, if that's what it takes. He will do this until He says, "Why should ye be stricken any more? Ye will revolt more and more: the whole head is sick, and the whole heart faint" (Isaiah 1:5). "The blueness of a wound cleanseth away evil: so do stripes the inward parts of the belly" (Proverbs 20:30), but if after many stripes the heart is not made better…If after many stripes the heart is not healed and made right, with faith-filled fear, then they have wandered out from underneath their only safe haven – the love of God. "Keep yourselves in the love of God" (Jude 21); God says. KEEP YOURSELVES! The Godhead undergoes emotional trauma and lamentation as the will of God to destroy surmounts the love of God to forbear. Thus it was written: "O that there were such an heart in them, **that they would fear Me**, and keep all My commandments always, that it might be well with them, and with their children for ever" (Deut. 5:29)!

Now consider this, true Christian, you could have survived all of your provocations to God up to this point in your regenerated life – but unknowingly, will tomorrow be your *tenth temptation* that breaches the barrier of His lion-like, angry fire unto your quick annihilation!? The Israelites did not know they were walking into their *tenth temptation*. These things were accounted of in the heavenlies, as a secret. Israel was given clear commands, but they never laid them to heart in the fear of God. Oh, don't make the same mistake my beloved brethren! This generation of saved men and women, God's beloved Israel – they were "forgiven" – "from Egypt even until now" – Moses says, but behold how the day of their provocation came (Num. 14:19), how the longstanding forgiveness did run out! Israel was an adulterous woman, "she received not correction" (Zeph. 3:2); even so, the people were *nearly annihilated*. Then God repented, but lo, not of His wrath over the generation of male heads numbering 600,000 strong.

> "Surely it is meet to be said unto God, I have
> borne chastisement, I will not offend any
> more: That which I see not teach Thou me: if
> I have done iniquity, I will do no more." (Job
> 34:31-32)

This ought to have been the repentance of Israel after the first stripes of wrath. Yet now, this congregation goes into the wilderness to undergo, still more, further revelations of terror, and why? Because they will not keep the FEAR OF GOD in the midst of their heart (2 Cor. 5:9-11, Heb. 12:25-29, 12:15, 1 Peter 1:17, Luke 12:4-5).With difficulty and many casualties, the people came to understand – GOD IS HOLY.

Think of it! God warned of His intent to destroy all of Israel. Then Moses warned of it, and explained how difficult and scarce their salvation was, that God was moving after them, and that He had nearly executed an entire annihilation of them, had not Moses stood in the breach to turn away His wrath. When Moses stood before God upon Sinai, he cried – MERCY, PARDON, SALVATION! When Moses came down from the Sinai and stood before sinning saints, he commanded – REPENT,

Moses wanted them to understand the scarcity of salvation, and with what difficulty was it secured! Then God exercises the people, but not with the report of Moses alone. Moses was angry when he came down from the Mount; that is one thing...but Moses' weak face, trembling body, and honest reports didn't make the people fear. Even so, God did increasingly show them what Moses was reporting to them - God's burning WRATH. God is no longer licking up the sacrifices with the fire of His anger. The cry they should have heard from Moses, they now experience themselves, and they lift aloud the verity of it! God said – they will perish! Moses said – you nearly all perished! And now the people say – "WE ALL PERISH" (Num. 17:12)! Let these cries sink down into your ears, my reader: "**Behold, we die, we perish, we all perish.** Whosoever cometh any thing near unto the Tabernacle of the LORD shall die: shall **we be consumed with dying**" (Num. 17:12-13). This is the result of their next temptation after the day of provocation. In Numbers 16, 250 princes of Israel murmured against Moses. They proudly made diverse accusations against him, and did infect Israel with an evil suspicion. They did gather "**all the congregation** against them unto the door of the Tabernacle of the congregation" (Num. 16:19). Though these 250 princes did sin, God was not only intent on killing these 250 men! God was intent on destroying **all the congregation** of Israel, instantly! This is THE THIRD TIME where God threatens **TOTAL ANNIHILATION**! The Lord said...

Threat of TOTAL ANNIHILATION #3 →   "Separate yourselves from among this congregation, that I may consume them in a moment. And they fell upon their faces, and said, O God, the God of the spirits of all flesh, **shall one man sin, and wilt Thou be wroth with all the congregation**?" (Numbers 16:21-22)

As God called Lot out of Sodom and did forbear His wrath until Lot came out, so God commanded Moses and Aaron to flee from this congregation that they might escape an impending wrath which was intent on Israel's entire annihilation – sudden genocide – as in a **moment**! The Lord changed His mind at the intercession of Moses, and He had mercy. Now again, He repented and did not destroy the entire congregation. I repeat: this is the *third* time God was provoked to an entire annihilation. Those who desired to escape the sins of these men (Korah & the 250 princes) were given the opportunity, and Moses said:

> "Depart, I pray you, from the tents of thse wicked men, and touch nothing of theirs, lest ye be consumed in all their sins. So they gat up from the tabernacle of Korah, Dathan, and Abiram, on every side: and Dathan and Abiram came out, and stood in the

door of their tents, and their wives, and their sons, and their little children" (Num. 16:26-27, 2 Cor. 6:17-7:1).

Moses, by earnest entreaties under the inspiration of the Holy Ghost, resisted the command and will of God to annihilate all of Israel. God said to Moses and Aaron – "Separate yourselves" – then God repented, but lo, then Moses sounded forth the message of salvation – "Depart, I pray you." God said – "SEPARATE!" And then Moses said – "DEPART!" The same fearful calls are given to us in the New Testament, even to all that desire to escape the wrath of God – "Come out from among them, and be ye separate, saith the Lord, and touch not the unclean thing and I will receive you" (2 Cor. 6:17). Those that came out from the rebellious, unclean company, they survived (at least for now), and the earth "opened her mouth, and swallowed them up, and their houses, and all the men that appertained unto Korah, and all their goods. They, and all that appertained to them, went down alive into the pit, and the earth closed upon them: and they perished from among the congregation" (Num. 16:31-33). Those that are fearless and think all is well…they will suddenly fall into hell. When this happened, "all Israel that were round about them fled at the cry of them: for they said, Lest the earth swallow us up also. And there came out a fire from the LORD, and consumed the two hundred and fifty men that offered incense" (Num. 16:34-35).

Threat of TOTAL ANNIHILATION #4 →   "Get you up from among **this congregation**, that I may consume them as in a moment" (Num. 16:45).

The next day (without 24 hours passing by), Israel murmured against the Lord, and said, "ye have killed the people of the LORD" (Num. 16:41). They were dissatisfied, dishonoring, and disagreeing with the holy justice of God. When this happened, the Lord endeavored to kill all of Israel **again**. God commanded Moses the same thing – "Get you up from among **this congregation**, that I may consume them as in a moment" (Num. 16:45). This is the *fourth* time God righteously and genuinely intended to annihilate all of Israel, but this time the wrath of God had already "gone out from the LORD!" This means that the plague of total annihilation had already begun (Num. 16:46)! Again, the prophets wrestle for intercession, and yet there was none! Prayer did not avail and Moses knew they needed to do something else, something more…

"And Aaron took as Moses commanded, and ran into the midst of the congregation; and, behold, the plague was begun among the people: and he put on incense, and made an atonement for the people. **And he stood between the dead and the living; and the plague was stayed.** Now they that died in the plague were fourteen thousand and seven hundred, beside them that died about the matter of Korah" (Num. 16:47-49).

The scarcity of salvation was here exemplified, even the sovereign choice of God, though it is cloaked with the appearance of chance. Men are dying by the thousands, and the prophets rush to be a conflict to the plague. Only the timely intercession of a chosen prophet could intercede, until, he was the separation between the dead and the living. Without this, justice having its full swing, all of Israel would have been consumed – "in a moment" (Num. 16:45).

Do you think God is trying to give us a message? He is determinate to teach us something of His severity, the difficulty of salvation, and it is in no uncertain terms. Also He would teach us the need for separateness, holiness, and obedience. He desires to leave us in a terrifying, holy, admiration of this purpose in God – "I will dwell in them, and walk in them; and I will be their God, and they shall be My people" (2 Cor. 6:16). And, "If any man defile the Temple of God, him shall God destroy; for the Temple of God is holy, which Temple ye are" (1 Cor. 3:17). It was after this frightening scene took place, when all the people could see the very means of their perseverance before their eyes - an interceding body of a prophet – and how he scarcely kept back the killing, destroying, and annihilating justice of God! Who would stand in front of a stampede of thunder, but lo, prophets stand before God! What happened in the heavenlies before – now it lieth hard upon the people, and that which was a wrestle in secret, between God & prophet, now is displayed openly! Keep His holiness in the midst of your heart, and you will not need breathtaking stripes and awful emergencies to humble you into the dust. Stay in the dust, and God will lift you up with His love; otherwise He will strike you down with His wrath.

How could an Israelite forget this fear, now that it was learned by wrath-fires burning, Israelite men in the graves, leprosy, earth openings with human-swallowing power, and breaking forth clouds of fire? "Except ye see signs and wonders, ye will not believe" – but now the remnant that was alive did see the signs and wonders of His wrath. Now, finally…they believed what was formerly reported. Years went by, and tragically, they let it slip. God wants us to see the inescapable annihilation of all those who learn these lessons of saving faith and fear, and yet "let them slip" (Heb. 2:1). That is what the writer of Hebrews describes as their great demise. It was not that they never learned the way, but rather, what they did learn, they let slip. It was not that they never held the saving treasures of faith in their possession, that they never gripped the saving line of salvation fast, but that which they formerly held and gripped, they let slip. Mercy ran out because they sinned away their days of grace. "Therefore we ought to give the more earnest heed to the things which we have heard, lest at any time we should let them slip. For if the word spoken by angels was stedfast, and every transgression and disobedience received a just recompense of reward; How shall escape, if we neglect so great salvation; which at the first began to be spoken by the Lord, and was confirmed unto us by them that heard him" (Heb. 2:1-3). It would be a safeguard for us to understand, just this – what the writer of Hebrews is thinking about in this very warning! Look at the staggering truth! Hell is but a "slip" away!

How did Israel slip? Great lengths of time, coupled with the ever-consistent, faithful love from God (by Manna, provision, protection, and guidance), could contribute to the subtlety in which an Israelite would unknowingly become highminded and fearless. The fear of what was formerly experienced, though it was for a long time fervently remembered, yet now forgotten – and God will not remind Israel anymore through messages of reproof, but surprising and annihilating consummations arriving suddenly upon them. That which should have been unforgettable, we can forget, and if the reminders of God will not break your heart, you will be, from salvation, broken off. "Because of unbelief they were broken off, and thou standest by faith. Be not highminded, but fear: For if God spared not the natural branches, take heed lest He also spare not thee. Behold therefore the goodness and severity of God: on them which fell, severity; but toward thee, goodness, if thou continue in His goodness: otherwise thou also shalt be cut off" (Rom. 11:19-22). "Wherefore let him that thinketh he standeth take heed lest he fall" (1 Cor. 10:12).

In Numbers 21, Israel was stricken with another plague of wrath, and another in Numbers 25. In Numbers 25, the children of Israel sinned again, this time in the matter of Baalpeor. The wrath of God broke forth upon the people! Then the Lord commanded Moses to "take the heads of the people" which had sinned, and "hang them up before the LORD against the sun, that the fierce anger of the LORD may be turned away from Israel," but after this, the anger of God was still not turned away! Why? The intercession was still incomplete, because some mark of justice was compromised. Those which had sinned were hung up in execution, but while sin still progressed, the plague of wrath could not rest. Consider this graphic scene:

"And Israel abode in Shittim, and the people began to commit whoredom with the daughters of Moab. And they called the people unto the sacrifices of their gods: and the people did eat, and bowed down to their gods. And Israel joined himself unto Baalpeor: and **the anger of the LORD was kindled against Israel**. And the LORD said unto Moses, **Take all the heads of the people, and hang them up before the LORD against the sun, that the fierce anger of the LORD may be turned away from Israel**. And Moses said unto the judges of Israel, **Slay ye every one his men that were joined unto Baalpeor**."

[Why wasn't the plague of wrath stayed after all of this?]

"And, <u>behold</u>, **one of the children of Israel came and brought unto his brethren a Midianitish woman in the sight of Moses, and in the sight of all the congregation of the children of Israel, who were weeping before the door of the tabernacle of the congregation**. And when Phinehas, the son of Eleazar, the son of Aaron the priest, **saw it, he rose up** from among the congregation, and **took a javelin in his hand**; And **he went after the man of Israel into the tent, and thrust both of them**

through, the man of Israel, and the woman through her belly. So the plague was stayed from the children of Israel. And those that died in the plague were twenty and four thousand. And the LORD spake unto Moses, saying, Phinehas, the son of Eleazar, the son of Aaron the priest, **hath turned My wrath away from the children of Israel**, while he was zealous for My sake among them, that I consumed not the children of Israel in My jealousy. Wherefore say, Behold, I give unto him My covenant of peace: And he shall have it, and his seed after him, even the covenant of an everlasting priesthood; because **he was zealous for his God**, and made an atonement for the children of Israel." (Numbers 25:1-13)

Tearful intercession by prayer could not avail when intercessions of judgment were not perfectly complete. The plague was so fierce, the casualties so great, the congregation was "weeping before the door of the Tabernacle," and hoping, that their groaning might win God's pitiful eye. Nevertheless, Phinehas – the man of God – he saw the cause of the unbroken plague! God's command was to slay every one that were joined unto Baalpeor, and behold, there was one man yet in the very deed! On account of *this man's sin*, Israelite after Israelite was steadily slain by the anger of God. Because the sinner is still alive, alas, the burning justice does slaughter all! God is the determiner of justice, and on account of *this one man*, He is steadily and fiercely annihilating His people. If justice goes a hair unaccomplished, wrath may surmount its restraints. If you see wrath break forth, then look to God's judgments – look carefully so as to see them completed. In them dwelleth hope, life, and favor – "For His anger endureth but a moment; in His favour is life: weeping may endure for a night, but joy cometh in the morning" (Psalm 30:5). "Will the LORD be pleased with thousands of rams, or ten thousands of rivers of oil?" Just do exactly what He says. Will He be pleased with those men hanging up as a sacrifice to God, while at present, even now, the very sin that required their death is being committed!? "He hath shewed thee, O man, what is good; and what doth the LORD require of thee, but to do justly, and to love mercy, and to walk humbly with thy God" (Micah 6:7-8). We must love mercy, and yet, we must be merciless in the causes of justice. The wicked do wander from the word of the Lord being drawn about by inordinate loves, even "as a bird hasteth to the snare and knoweth not that it is for his life" (Prov. 7:23). Behold, the sinner went off in his mischief in the sight of all Israel, and Phinehas – HE "SAW IT!" "He rose up from among the congregation!" That is God's call: rise and obey! He rose up from the congregation because the rest of them were mistaken and amiss. Moses and "all the congregation of the children of Israel" that were "weeping before the door of the Tabernacle of the congregation," they were weeping instead of working – now- in the hour when God calleth for obedience! Do the difficult and keep judgment; don't neglect the javelin of God's holy justice. Be zealous for God. Phinehas rose up to kill; even so, it was that God might cease to kill. Had not Phinehas stood up and acted, the jealous wrath of God would have made a full end of Israel as the former times, even though all of

Israel did not sin.

This generation of Israelites became like a "tale that is told" (Ps. 90). Their offspring, chosen to enter the Promised Land, underwent the training yoke of hard things, waiting and watching till God made an end of every one of their fathers...until they buried the last one...only then God took up the journey back to the good land. God sought to burn within them a persevering fear by actual events of fire and blood. Otherwise, He promised that such an annihilation would come upon Israel that "all nations shall say, Wherefore hath the LORD done thus unto this land? What meaneth the heat of this great anger" (Deut. 29:24)? What happened in the sight of the Israelites, God would rehearse again in the sight of "all nations," that they all would come to know "the heat of this great anger!" Amazing! The Lord said He would smite the land with "plagues" and "sicknesses" (Deut. 29:22), "and that the whole land thereof is brimstone, and salt, and burning, that it is not sown, nor beareth, nor any grass growth therein, like the overthrow of **Sodom**, and **Gomorrah**, **Admah**, and **Zeboim**, which the LORD overthrew in His anger, and in His wrath" (Deut. 29:23). This did eventually happen, as it is written, "Except the LORD of hosts had left unto us a very small remnant, we should have been as **Sodom**, and we should have been like unto **Gomorrah**" (Isaiah 1:9). Preceding this climactic annihilation, there was centuries of wrestling, intercession, and Divine struggle. There was much repenting in the conversation of the prophets with God, that is, until every curse pursued and overtook Israel in the end (Deut. 28:15).

The remnant that survived the experience of this cursed annihilation, comparable to Sodom and Gomorrah, said, "Yet **many years didst Thou forbear them**, and testifiedst against them by Thy spirit in Thy prophets: yet would they not give ear: therefore gavest Thou them into the hand of the people of the lands. Nevertheless **for Thy great mercies' sake Thou didst not utterly consume them**, nor forsake them; for Thou art a gracious and merciful God" (Neh. 9:31). The greatness of God's mercy was understood through the lens of holy justice, that it is the mercy of God that they did *survive at all*. It was mercy that *some lived* and *not all died*. Can you say this? Do you understand this to be the mercy of God to save you, to persevere you "in the way" to your Promised Land? It is written, "**if the righteous scarcely be saved**, where shall the ungodly and the sinner appear" (1 Peter 4:18)!? Is this your understanding of God's relationship with the righteous, chosen, covenanted, saved individuals?

Before I press you on the matter of election, namely, on the vital application these passages have on those who strive, as the scripture demandeth, "to make your calling and election sure" (2 Pet. 2:10), I want you to see this peculiar mark of righteous men – how they had a deep understanding of the scarcity of salvation. They were marked with a peculiar understanding of fear toward God, the one and only God, Who has a dangerous and overtly sensitive holiness, and a wrath that was scarcely escapable and severe. "The fear of the LORD is the beginning of wisdom: and the knowledge of the holy is understanding" (Prov. 9:10).

There is a difficulty and scarcity for the righteous to be saved because they are so near in proximity to so holy a Lord of glory, and yet, they are so prone to deserve damnation by repeated, rebellious wanderings. The generation after the Exodus generation that Joshua led into the Promised Land, was faithful. Nevertheless they too had to learn the severity of God's wrath. LESSON #1 for this generation was at CITY CONQUEST #1 – Jericho. Have you ever heard of Achan? At the conquest of the first city in the Promised Land, Achan sinned. On account of his sin – *his sin alone*! – all of Israel was troubled and rendered powerless before their enemies. *One man's sin* did this! When they went to war 36 men died, and then God warned Joshua, saying, Israel was "accursed!" Let that stagger you! God said to His beloved servant Joshua, "Neither will I be **with you** any more, except ye destroy the accursed from among you" (Josh. 7:12). God said, destroy him or I will destroy you. Joshua's walk with God, the state of Israel as a nation, their ability to defeat their enemies, and with thirty six men already dead, Joshua knew the judgment of God was severe.

> "And Joshua, and all Israel with him, **took Achan** the son of Zerah, and the silver, and the garment, and the wedge of gold, and **his sons**, and **his daughters**, and his oxen, and his asses, and his sheep, and his tent, and **all that he had**: and they brought them unto the valley of Achor. And Joshua said, **Why hast thou troubled us? the LORD shall trouble thee this day.** And all Israel stoned him with stones, and burned them with fire, after they had stoned them with stones. And they raised over him a great heap of stones unto this day. So the LORD turned from the fierceness of His anger. Wherefore the name of that place was called, The valley of Achor, unto this day" (Joshua 7:24-26).

On account of *one man's sin*, all of Israel suffered under the wrath of God. *Think of the emotional pain as a consequence of this public execution!* Many soldiers who have seen the gore of war are haunted by its scenes of battle, whether awake or asleep. The cries of their fallen comrades do restlessly echo in the annals of their mind. For the Israelite, there was a very different cause, but a similar memory with a gruesome end. The common Israelite remembered the cries of Achan, his wife, and children, as they lifted their voices for mercy when they were stoned to death. Think of the gripping emotion in their cries as if they were pleading with you – looking right at you – begging mercy with their eyes. Think of the after-effect of this on the whole Israelite nation. Some men are driven to mad fury by jealousy over their wives. Some parents have murderous rage against kidnappers and sexual assaulters. With how much hatred, then, would the Israelite be angered with idols? To what extent would he go to see them all destroyed!? With what satisfaction would Israel make sure the destruction of all idols!

This understanding of the holiness of God is deeply in the mind of this generation heretofore. They learned to FEAR! This generation was not gripping the truth of salvation loosely, as one ready to slip. In a later time, in Joshua 22, when an altar was made as a witness and not for idolatry, ten tribes of Israel thought it was made for idolatry. Idolatry being committed within Israel was a serious crime, and knowing the God of Israel, all of Israel would be in grave danger because of it. It would be understood that either the idolaters would die or they would all die. Because of this, these ten tribes rallied together to "go up to war against" these two tribes which were suspected of idolatry. The ten tribes were willing to kill off the entire tribe if they did not repent. If Israel let judgment slip, they would slip into hell – THEY KNEW IT! Prepared for war and an immediate strike, the whole congregation pleads with these two tribes concerning their suspected rebellion. Take note: the knowledge of the Holy is pouring forth from the abundance of their heart.

> "Thus saith the whole congregation of the LORD, What trespass is this that ye have committed against the God of Israel, to turn away this day from following the LORD, in that ye have builded you an altar, that ye might rebel this day against the LORD? Is the iniquity of Peor too little for us, **from which we are not cleansed until this day, although there was a plague in the congregation of the LORD**, But that ye must turn away this day from following the LORD? **and it will be, seeing ye rebel to day against the LORD, that to morrow He will be wroth with the whole congregation of Israel.** Notwithstanding, if the land of your possession be unclean, then pass ye over unto the land of the possession of the LORD, wherein the LORD'S tabernacle dwelleth, and take possession among us: but rebel not against the LORD, nor rebel against us, in building you an altar beside the altar of the LORD our God. Did not Achan the son of Zerah commit a trespass in the accursed thing, and **wrath fell on all the congregation of Israel? and that man perished not alone in his iniquity.**" (Joshua 22:16-20)

These ten tribes spoke of two instances where the wrath of God broke out into *the whole congregation* – at the matter of Peor and Achan. Though a plague broke forth upon Israel because of the matter of Peor, the people were still not completely cleansed, even by this time. After the matter of Achan, they saw that "wrath fell *on all the congregation of Israel*… and that man perished **not alone** in his iniquity." These men were terrified for their own lives! They were moved and standing forth to the duty of intercession by judgment, in a moment! My reader, hear them speak! "It will be, seeing ye rebel to day against the LORD, **that to morrow He will be wroth with the whole congregation of Israel**"! Even David walked with God with this fearful manner of God's holiness in mind. When he sinned in numbering the people (1 Chronicles 21), look what he says:

> "And God sent an angel unto Jerusalem to destroy it: and as he was destroying, the LORD beheld, and He **repented Him of the evil**, and said to the angel that destroyed, **It is enough, stay now thine hand.** And the angel of the LORD stood by the threshingfloor of Ornan the Jebusite. And David lifted up his

eyes, and saw the angel of the LORD stand between the earth and the heaven, having a drawn sword in his hand stretched out over Jerusalem. Then David and the elders of Israel, who were clothed in sackcloth, fell upon their faces. And David said unto God, **Is it not I that commanded the people to be numbered? Even I it is that have sinned and done evil indeed; but as for these sheep, what have they done? Let Thine hand, I pray Thee, O LORD my God, be on me, and on my father's house; but not on Thy people, that they should be plagued**" (1 Chron. 21:15-17). God was intent on "three days" of destruction instead of a complete annihilation (1 Chron. 21:12), but the principle of God's repentance still stands. "Seventy thousand men" died, and lo, the angel was ready to destroy Jerusalem, but then…"the LORD repented Him of the evil, and said to the angel that destroyed the people, It is enough: stay now thine hand" (2 Sam. 24:15-16). How is it that God's people will perish, if they do perish, under a total annihilation? It is when God *does not repent* of the just will of entire annihilation in certain instances of His kindled anger. If Israel is saved, it will be because God "**repented** Him of the evil" that He thought to do, or on another occasion, was doing in Israel. Salvation comes by the lovingkindness of God wrestling against the just anger of God, until every stirring of annihilation is stayed, in some measure, as to preserve and persevere salvation. In this manner, the righteous are scarcely saved. However, my dear reader, what will happen if God is minded toward annihilation, and yet He says, "I am **weary** with **repenting**" (Jer. 15:9)?! What if God intends to execute His just wrath upon His people, and, though He repented *nine times* before and persevered Israel's salvation – what if He is weary of repenting from total annihilation? What if His weariness can only be comforted by annihilation?

LEARN TO FEAR GOD

Because of David – *this one man's sins* – God was wroth with the whole congregation! This is why David says, "as for these sheep, what have they done?" Does this amaze you?

Moses & Aaron → "shall **one man sin**, and wilt Thou be wroth with all the congregation?" – Numbers 16:22

The Surviving Israelites → "Behold, we die, we perish, **we all perish**…shall we be consumed with dying" – Numbers 17:13

2 ½ Tribes → "and it will be, seeing ye rebel to day against the LORD, that to morrow **He will be wroth with the whole congregation of Israel**." – Josh. 22:16-20

One Man → "behold, one of the children of Israel came and brought unto his brethren a Midianitish woman…And…Phinehas…went after **the man** of Israel into the tent, and thrust both of them through…" – Num. 25:1-13

One Man → Achan… "And Joshua said, **Why hast thou troubled us?** The LORD shall trouble thee this day. And all Israel stoned him with stones, and burned them with fire, after they had stoned them with stones" – Joshua 7:25

One Man → David… "**Is it not I** that commanded the people to be numbered? **Even I** it is that have sinned and done evil indeed; **but as for these sheep, what have they done?** Let Thine hand, I pray Thee, O LORD my God, be on me, and on my father's house; but not on Thy people, that they should be plagued" (1 Chron. 21:15-17).

Do you know the fear of God like as Moses warned, "if ye turn away from after Him, He will **yet again** leave them in the wilderness; and ye **shall destroy <u>all this people</u>**" (Num. 32:14-15)… "**be sure your sin will find you out**" (Num. 32:23)?

207

"I AM WEARY WITH REPENTING"
-JEREMIAH 15:6
CHAPTER 9

"Thou hast forsaken Me, saith the LORD,
thou art gone backward: therefore will I stretch out My hand
against thee, and destroy thee;
I am weary with repenting.*" – Jeremiah 15:6*
*"****I am weary with holding in****" – Jeremiah 6:11*

By *Covenant, vow, oath, promise, salvation*, and therefore, by God's *choosing* and *election* of Israel, it is clearly understood that God willed for their salvation (its beginning, present progression, and perseverance to finality). Along the sojourning and perseverance of their present progressive salvation, they provoked God to awful stirrings of His divine anger, and many a time He willed, purposed, intended, began to, and sought (God in the ways of man) to annihilate His people. If this will was **God in the ways of God**, it could not have changed, but God is not relating to Israel on the basis of His unchanging, higher, eternal, ways (God in the ways of God). "But being full of compassion," God "forgave their iniquity, and destroyed them not: Yea, many a time turned He His anger away, and did not stir up all His wrath. For He remembered that they were but flesh; a wind that passeth away, and cometh not again" (Ps. 78:38-39). "Therefore He said that He would destroy them, had not Moses His chosen stood before Him in the breach, to turn away His wrath, lest He should destroy them" (Ps. 106:23). Oh, the great necessity of intercessors! God, in the Holy Ghost and through His servant Moses, did stand against the will of God to destroy, being emboldened by the will of God to save, because this will of God was "willing and working" (Php. 2) within him to intercede. The surmounting of wrath did increasingly break forth upon the people, until finally, the entirety of the covenanted generation (aside from Caleb, Joshua, and the Levites) were cast away in reprobation without any means of intercession, divine repentance, or reversal of decision on the part of God. How do we know what is the will of God, or, which will is "**God in the ways of God**" while in the midst of the divine storm of God's own wills wrestling against each other? The will of God that comes to fruition as the final end was ***the eternal and unchanging*** will of God.

Sadly, the generations of Israel that lived on did follow in the works of *the exodus generation*, "Thus were they defiled with their own works, and went whoring with their own inventions. Therefore was the wrath of the LORD kindled against His people, insomuch that He **abhorred His own inheritance**" (Ps. 106:39-40). This is a fulfillment of the responsive, reactive will of God when He sees rebellious works, as He said in Leviticus 26:27-31, "Then I will walk contrary unto you also in fury...and cast your carcases upon the carcases of your idols, and My soul shall abhor you. And I will make your cities waste, and bring your sanctuaries unto desolation, and I will not smell the savour of your sweet odours." The salvation of the exodus generation was persevered through the intercession of the prophet Moses, as well as others (from the beginning until their reprobation). After Moses, God rose up like prophets as intercessors for His wayward people, and this continued throughout the centuries, but depending on the magnitude of sin being committed, intercession will succeed or fail. As the rebellion repeats itself, the love of God becomes exceedingly wearied to restrain the angry will of God to justly destroy. The angry will of God did intend to, and even begun to annihilate His people many times, and yet, still, through many means of intercession it was successfully and continually pacified so that the purpose to annihilate *was repented of*. So, through the repentance of God's will to destroy, God's mind to save is *scarcely secured*; yet what happens when God is "**weary with repenting**?" These are the words of the Lord in Jeremiah 15:6: "**I am weary with repenting**" – weary with changing His mind back into the former purpose which was to keep His people alive, which would be to persevere them as an object of His love. When God is weary of repentance, it is then that He thinks and purposes to destroy… it means that He is weary of changing His mind from destruction. At this time, the sovereign will of His eternal Godhead rises to its execution (God in the ways of God) in a will that cannot be repented of (1 Sam. 15:29). As it is written, "I thought to punish you, when your fathers provoked Me to wrath, saith the LORD of hosts, **and I repented not**" (Zech. 8:14).

Many times the Lord thought to annihilate, but now it is so, that, "like as the LORD of hosts **thought to do unto us**, according to our ways, and according to our doings, **so hath He dealt with us**" (Zech. 1:6). All the times of successful intercession which changed what God "thought to do unto" Israel, all the way up to this point, were choice and elect mercies given to men whose deeds necessitated such thoughts of annihilation rising in the mind of God, but now those former thoughts which were repented of have their execution upon Israel because they provoked Him long enough. To say, "I am weary with repenting," is to say, "I have changed My mind so many times as I sought after, spoke about, and was intent on destroying you, that now I am weary with changing My mind from annihilating you. I am weary of hearing the prayers of intercessors which formerly won My heart to repent and have mercy." Therefore God sets His heart, mind, and intent upon their destruction, declaring that, this time, "I have purposed it, and will not repent, neither will I turn back from it" (Jer. 4:28). Read the whole verse and see how destruction is in God's heart – "For this shall the earth mourn, and the heavens above be black: because I have spoken it, I have purposed it, and **will not repent, neither will I turn back from it**" (Jer. 4:28). This purpose and word is declared to be without repentance, or a turning back, for He is weary of mercy which did formerly and undeservedly preserve sinning saints.

Attempted Intercession
"Then said the LORD unto me, **though**

209

Moses and Samuel stood before Me, yet
My mind could not be toward this people:
cast them out of My sight, and let them go
forth" (Jer. 15:1).

Jeremiah the prophet attempts intercession for this generation of Israel that was under this terrifying, eternal indictment. He pleads on their behalf to God, "Hast Thou utterly rejected Judah? Hath Thy soul loathed Zion? Why hast Thou smitten us, and there is no healing for us? We looked for peace, and there is no good; and for the time of healing, and behold trouble! We acknowledge, O LORD, our wickedness, and the iniquity of our fathers: for we have sinned against Thee. Do not abhor us, for Thy name's sake, do not disgrace the throne of Thy glory: remember, **break not Thy covenant** with us" (Jer. 14:19-21). What is God's response to the intercessor, the prophet that stands in the breach to turn away His wrath? "Then said the LORD unto me, **though Moses and Samuel stood before Me**, yet My mind could not be toward this people: cast them out of My sight, and let them go forth" (Jer. 15:1). Even a prophet of the stature and reputation of Moses and Samuel, prophets that turned away God's wrath many times from His wayward, hell-deserving people, even for them He would not repent! At Moses' and Samuel's intercessions God arose to salvation, He dispensed the riches of His mercy again and again, and yet, for this people, God pronounces the woeful condition – "Thus saith the LORD unto this people, Thus have they loved to wander, they have not refrained their feet, therefore the LORD doth not accept them; He will now remember their iniquity, and visit their sins. Then said the LORD unto me [Jeremiah], **Pray not for this people for their good.** When they fast, I will not hear their cry; and when they offer burnt offering and an oblation, I will not accept them: but I will consume them by the sword, and by the famine, and by the pestilence" (Jer. 14:10-12).

What sweet and gladsome experience did Moses have for 40 days in uninterrupted glory on Mount Sinai, when God taught him all the intricacies of a Covenant which enabled the awesome nearness of His holy Presence? For forty days, Moses was mesmerized in worshipful anticipation of receiving God in their midst, seated upon His earthly throne (the ark), inside the holy Tent of His earthly abode. Yet, there is a bittersweet reality in this, for God is a *Great* and *Terrible* God. I will remind you that the fortieth day came, and lo, the sweet communion Moses was turned into bitter weeping and prayerful intercession, and following this, severe executions and blood-red streets, and then still more – God's angry, Covenant-breaking rebukes upon a wayward people until the man of God Moses was astonished in horror (Exodus 32-33)! The word that came to Moses on day 40 was, "Now therefore let Me alone, that My wrath may wax hot against them, and that I may consume them: and I will make of thee a great nation" (Ex. 32:10). As you may recall, this is the beginning of "The Great Pause," and this was not the last time Moses would stand in the gap against the will of God to totally annihilate…but look at and remember the mercy of God's eventual pardon even though it was scarcely attained. God did have mercy! Here, and onward through later intercessions, it was

210

His mercy that they were not **entirely consumed**, that only hundreds of thousands instead of millions perished, but when Ezekiel (a contemporary prophet with Jeremiah) echoed the same intercessions for his generation, even the same cries formerly pled by Moses, though he cried, "Ah Lord God! Wilt Thou destroy **all the residue of Israel** in Thy pouring out of Thy fury upon Jerusalem" (Ezek. 9:8), **God did not repent**! "Behold therefore the goodness and severity of God" (Rom. 11:22). At the hour of Israel and Judah's captivities, comparatively to the mercy dispensed in Moses' generation, it was a time when "God spared not" (Rom. 11:21).

Can we say that *God in the ways of man* did not will for this generation to be saved? Nay, Israel in this generation, as others, was representative of the "saved" (Jude 5), redeemed (Deut. 7:7-11, Ex. 6:6-7), "chosen" (Psalm 33:12, Deut. 7:7-11), people (Ex. 6:6-7), who were loved (Deut. 7:7-11, Hos. 11:1, Ezek. 16:8, Jer. 2:2-3), in "holiness" (Jer. 2:2-3), anointed with oil (Ezek. 16:9), in a Covenant of marriage (Ezek. 16:8, Jer. 2:2), called a son (Hos. 11:1), and the "called" (Hos. 11:1).This generation may not have experienced personal salvation; however, nigh to and on the eve of this judgment, there were numerous revivals in their righteous seasons, under certain kings like Asa, Jehoshaphat, Hezekiah, and Josiah. In Jeremiah 9:1-3, God shows the tender love He has for His people in that He is condemning them against His will (God in the ways of man).

> "Oh that my head were waters, and mine eyes a fountain of tears, that I might weep day and night for the slain of the daughter of my people! Oh that I had in the wilderness a lodging place of wayfaring men; that I might leave my people, and go from them! for they be all adulterers, an assembly of treacherous men. And they bend their tongues like their bow for lies: but they are not valiant for the truth upon the earth; for they proceed from evil to evil, and they know not Me, saith the LORD" (Jeremiah 9:1-3).

God's saving love to Israel laments (God in the ways of man), and simultaneously, God's eternal hatred of them is finally satisfied (God in the ways of God), but the way in which this eternal election of damnation was manifested within time was by their rejection, resistance, and spurning of His saving lovingkindness within time (God in the ways of man).

Alongside this lamentation, God accounts of the covenantal implications this surmounting of wrath had, in relation to His saved, redeemed, chosen, holy, anointed, people who are called His sons and wife – in Covenant. What does it mean for God *to repent not* and to destroy? Each prophet accounts of this work, rightly so, just as a judge ought to justify the Just. The prophets justify and make clear exactly what God has *repented of*, and what He has done, that, heretofore, His people might understand. Our merciful God knows our wretched forgetfulness, and so He employs prophets to record Divine happenings. *Before God repented*, Israel was loved (Deut. 7:7-11, Hos. 11:1, Ezek. 16:8, Jer. 2:2-3),but now God says, "I will love them no more" (Hos. 1:15). God's saving love toward Israel did save (Jude 5), redeem (Deut.

211

7:7-11, Ex. 6:6-7), and anoint them (Ezek. 16:9), even because they were His "chosen" "people" (Ps. 33:12, Deut. 7:7-11), His sons, and His wife. Yet now after God has *repented*, now there is no more love. God says, "My soul shall abhor you" (Lev. 26:30)! And consequentially He is refusing to dwell among Israel (Lev. 26:12, 31-32). Just as there is no more love, God renounces Israel as His people and wife (Hos. 1:9-10, 2:1), and His hatred is merciless unto reprobation like never before, with a very small remnant exempt (Isaiah 1:9, Hos. 1:6, 9:15-17).

For God to love Israel, He shows it by drawing near to dwell among them as their God. Therefore they, in this manner, become His people. Where His presence is, there His people are (Ex. 33:16). As it is written, "**And I will set My Tabernacle among you: My soul shall not abhor you. And I will walk among you, and will be your God, and ye shall be My people**" (Lev. 26:11-12). This is the establishment of the Covenant (Lev. 26:9). If God hates them, then behold, He will destroy His Tabernacle, or the House of His dwelling, and He will choose rather to leave His people. In this case we can understand that, now, God is choosing, saving, redeeming, and anointing another people to be His sons and daughters, His bride, and His people. Look at the deeds and consequences of God's love, opposed to the deeds and consequences of God's hatred. Contrastingly, God's love is seen in **Lev. 26:11-12**. When and if God says, "My soul shall abhor you," then He does to Israel the opposite of what His Covenant of love did formerly accomplish: "And I will make your cities waste, and **bring your sanctuaries unto desolation, and I will not smell the savour of the sweet odours**. And I will bring the land unto desolation: and your enemies which dwell therein shall be astonished at it" (Lev. 26:30-32). God did dwell among them, but now He says – "Woe also to them **when I depart** from them" (Hos. 9:12)! Again He says, "for the wickedness of their doings I will **drive them out of Mine House, I will love them no more**," and again, "there **I hated them**" (Hos. 9:15). The prophet Hosea proclaims, "My God will **cast them away**, because they did not hearken unto Him: and they shall be wanderers among the nations" (Hos. 9:17). God's message of hatred is clear, with all the implications therewith…

"The harvest is past, the summer is ended, and we are not saved" – Jeremiah 8:20

Therefore this people are hated and unloved because they have expended their "times" of mercy, or as another man of God has phrased it, they "sinned away their day of grace" (Jake Gardner). God said, using the impending birth of the prophet Hosea's unborn child – "Call her name Loruhamah: for **I will no more have mercy** upon the house of Israel; but I will utterly take them away" (Hosea 1:6). A people without mercy are a people without Covenant, Presence, promise, and salvation. Thus with the next child – "Then said God, Call his name Loammi: **for ye are not My people, and I will not be your God**" (Hosea 1:9). Where there was formerly a Covenant-bound relationship of love and near relation, God was now saying of Israel, "**She is not My wife, neither am I her husband:** let her therefore put away her whoredoms out of her sight, and her adulteries from between her breasts; lest I strip her naked, and set her as in the day that she was born, and make

212

her as a wilderness, and set her like a dry land, and slay her with thirst" (Hosea 2:1-3). As you know, this generation had no chance for Divine repentance in God, but the people did not know this until God revealed it to the prophets. The prophet Jeremiah, as previously noted, sought and wrestled against the Lord for repentance, but God forbade him to even pray for the people, for He said, "I am weary with repenting" (Jer. 15:6). This kind of relationship with God is not commonly understood, preached, or practiced, and though few have a knowledge of this manner of God's workings – the truth still stands. If we will be saved, it is by the unwearied repentings of God's mindedness to annihilate us, by the three means of intercession in continuing success along the sojourning of our salvation through time, that even while we are the elect of God (eternally and immutably), and though we be "the righteous," we are, in this way, "scarcely saved" (1 Peter 4:18)! Observing those of the exodus generation, and others, we cannot say that they were elect according to God's unchanging will, mind, purpose, counsel, calling, and election that Romans chapter 9 teaches (God in the ways of God). Those that are elect according to the counsel of *God in the ways of God*, they cannot fall away and will always persevere. Yet…will you understand that this perseverance is by a scarce escape from the lion-like justice of a holy, forbearing, omnipotent God? Truly, many claim to be intercessors by prayer and fervent wrestlings, but what are we interceding against? The only biblical intercession that exists is a standing against the anger of God, but since so many are unaware of this reality – the reality of God's anger over His people – there is a treacherous lightheartedness toward mercy, perseverance, and salvation! Everyone will make it, right!? It is time that these self-proclaimed intercessors are silenced into trembling over so holy an engagement! Away with them! "Her prophets are light and treacherous persons: her priests have polluted the sanctuary, they have done violence to the law" (Zeph. 3:4)! Follow them not, and walk not in their ways! "Be not rash with thy mouth, and let not thine heart be hasty to utter any thing before God" (Ecc. 5:2). "Keep thy foot when thou goest into the House of God, and be more ready to hear, than to give the sacrifice of fools: for they consider not that they do evil" (Ecc. 5:1).

"MERCY ON WHOM
I WILL HAVE MERCY"
-ROMANS 9:15
CHAPTER 10

"Now will I... have mercy... and will be jealous for My holy Name" – Ezekiel 39:25

RELATED SERMONS

"Sovereign Mercy" – Sean Morris

At the first part of chapter 1, we traced the absolute sovereignty of God as is taught in Romans chapter 9 (as the Calvinists would correctly understand it). In the logical flow of the chapter's argument, four persons or groups of persons are cited in the Old Covenant as examples of sovereign election, and by election I mean: elected unto salvation through an *eternal love*, or unto damnation through an *eternal hatred*. Referencing Jacob and Esau (Rom. 9:9-13) firstly, and the Israelites (Rom. 9:15) and Pharaoh (representative of the Egyptians, Rom. 9:17) secondarily, are two pairs which serve as examples for each predestination, unto heaven or hell. In a close study of these four persons/groups, we observed the sovereign and mysterious hatred of God upon Pharaoh in that it hardened Pharaoh's heart, and this made it evident to us that God was ordaining him to destruction. Do you remember how this was a *justice-shattering* hatred?! That is to say, it shatters *our comprehension* of justice, but it is, somehow, altogether just and righteous in God; however, any person reading the chronicles of Pharaoh's God-ordained hardening while still abiding in their limited and inferior ways of logic, would immediately feel emotionally harmed, even betrayed, thinking, "Is there unrighteousness with God" (Rom. 9:14)? Now hear me...As the predestinating HATRED of God provokes the question, "is there unrighteousness with God" (Rom. 9:14), the predestinating MERCY of God does likewise. It is *justice-shattering* mercy!

****
"I will...be **gracious** to whom I will be **gracious**, and will shew **mercy** on whom I will shew **mercy**" – Exodus 33:19

"I will have **mercy** on whom I will have **mercy**, and I will have **compassion** on whom I will have **compassion**" – Romans 9:15
****

This phrase in Romans 9:15, "I will have **mercy** on whom I will have **mercy**," was declared by God during "The Great Pause" of the Covenant, in Exodus 33:19. If you recall, this momentous word was given during Moses' second attempt

214

for intercession by prayer for the fallen Israelites. The Israelite covenant was presently broken (Ex. 32:19), God was pausing to decide what to do (Ex. 33:5), and Moses fled outside of the camp to attempt an intercessory meeting with God, because God would not come into their midst lest He consume them (Ex. 33:3, 7-11). Because Moses went outside of the camp, God came down and met with him. Moses wrestled Him, God turned at Moses' Spirit-empowered supplications, and then announced, "I...will be gracious to whom I will be gracious, and will shew mercy on whom I will shew mercy" (Ex. 33:19, Rom. 9:15)! Why is this an example of sovereign, mysterious, incomprehensible, *justice-shattering* mercy?

In response to the Israelite rebellion, the justice within God had decided upon the recompense of *total annihilation*. Clearly, God's intent, purpose, pursuit, and word was such (see Ex. 32:10). Even though this was almost immediately repented of after Moses' intercessory prayer, it was first desired by God, because this is unrestrained, pure, uncompromised *justice*. This was not an unjust thought in the heart of God, nor could God ever think or desire anything that was not perfectly and soundly just. Shockingly, the Lord pardoned Israel at this instance, but reader, we must understand that He does not always, consistently, nor continuously, pardon idolaters. Remember the justice of God upon Achan? Men alongside their women and children were mercilessly killed by God. Achan and his family personally underwent the justice of capital punishment, but at Israel's gathering at Sinai when they fell into idolatry, at once, they all deserved the same annihilation as Achan! However, as you can see, somehow there was still mercy for Israel but not for Achan. What is the difference between the one that was pardoned and rewarded heaven, compared to the other that was punished and rewarded hell? My reader, behold – it is the sovereign right of God! As He saith, "I will have mercy **ON WHOM** I will have mercy" (Rom. 9:15). When God mercifully pardoned Israel at the Sinai idolatry, it was not according to their works, for their works merited for them the death penalty. Therefore, do you see how this is *unexplainable* mercy! It is mercy which provokes the question, "Is there unrighteousness with God" (Rom. 9:14), and therefore this mercy was cited in Romans 9 as an example of *elective mercies*, which are and always have been irrelevant to "any good or evil" that a man does (Rom. 9:11) – it is outside of the realm of *comprehensible justice*, or, justice which is according to a man's deeds. God's covenanted law established at Sinai was thereafter implemented with faithfulness according to the letter, which means that God continued to demand death for all idolaters, as it is written. According to the written law there was absolutely, without partiality, no way to escape the death penalty! I repeat: there was no option for mercy, forgiveness, or pardon! God specifically commanded against pity or mercy in times of justice. God wrote justice in its impartial, universally equal letter, and throughout history the Lord wrought the letter of the law's execution upon so many that the fame of His justice was reckoned to be - "Shall not He render to every man **according to his works**" (Prov. 24:12). Thus was His justice universally, and thus He declares of Himself by the prophets: "Thou shewest lovingkindness unto thousands, and recompensest the iniquity of the fathers into the bosom of their children after them: the Great, the Mighty God, the LORD of hosts, is His name, great in counsel, and mighty in work: **for Thine eyes are open upon all the ways of the sons of men: to give every one according to his ways, and according to the fruit of his doings**" (Jer. 32:18-19).

Turning the page to the doctrine of eternal election, God's higher things, we have stepped out of the arena of the humanly comprehensible. What is famous about God in heaven? God's audience of holy angels, which circle about His sovereign throne, admire the eternal and mysterious purposes of election which unfold a circumstantial stage of God's eternal glory through humanity's final redemption. They rest, knowing that God is sovereign over human events, even though they appear to be an undeterminable chaos of freewill creatures. Elective mercy is mysteriously incomprehensible to man, but it is the glory and praise of God in heaven! Therefore to us it is *justice-shattering* MERCY, even the justice so consistently wrought severally upon millions of men and their nations – justice according to deeds. In this mercy, God pardoned Israel at "The Great Pause," unjustified by their works and therefore irrelevant of how they willed for idolatry and ran after revellings. "So then it is not of him that **willeth**, nor of him that **runneth**, but of **God that sheweth mercy**" (Rom. 9:16). Reader, be amazed! God can and does save people even against their **willing** and **running**, and again in another place He saith: "I was found of them that **sought Me not**; I was made manifest unto them that **asked not after Me**" (Rom. 11:20)! Are you unfamiliar with "THE GREAT PAUSE?" Carefully review the details of this Great Pause in the chapter titled, "The Near Annihilation of God's People." During "The Great Pause" there were several degrees of wrath which were repented of, until God decided to reestablish the Covenant as it was at the first. At the time of God's decision to reestablish the Covenant - even with IDOLATERS – God said that Israel is "WHOM" He has shown mercy and grace. From henceforth, Israel will continue to be a people before God, "WHOM," over and over, God shows elective mercy, peculiarly irrelevant of their works, partial to their advantage, to the shattering of comprehensible justice which was implemented in comparative experiences for other people or individuals within and outside of Israelite blood. For the Israelites, "as touching election, they are beloved for the fathers' sakes. For the gifts and calling of God are without repentance." This means that Israel will continue to be a people before God, now and forever, and their eventual and entire salvation before THE END of the world is a purpose of God that He will never repent of. How did Paul make the observation that Israel is elect by God's sovereign mercy? Paul cites the passage at "The Great Pause" – "I will have mercy **ON WHOM** I will have mercy" (Rom. 9:15). How does Paul make the observation that Israel is called with a calling that is "*without repentance*" in God? My reader, God confirms this elective purpose over and over again!

Under the section, "The Near Annihilation of God's People," there were four separate instances where God *actually spoke* a command, in paraphrase, to get out of the way so that He might totally annihilate Israel (Ex. 32:10, Num. 14:11-12, 16:21-22, 16:45). When God broke forth to judgment by sudden and annihilating plagues, we can see that God was minded to destroy Israel in the same heart of these four times where God was minded to total annihilation – which means, until the wrath-provoking sin was removed from before His holy eyes, GOD would NOT stop annihilating. This was for sure, and all Israel learned to acknowledge it! By spoken word, intention, and active annihilation, God desired to, and began to, totally annihilate His people to make a full end of them.

At a later time, the Assyrian and Babylonian Captivities, God's wrath did break forth into a paramount, unprecedented degree, and it was as God "thought to do" all those times before when He was moved to total annihilation, times which He did repent of, which were, Israel confesses, "according to our ways, and according to our doings" (Zech. 1:6). Read the entire verse: "But My words and My statutes, which I commanded My servants the prophets, did they not take hold of your fathers? and they returned and said, Like as the LORD of hosts <u>thought to do unto us,</u> **according to our ways, and according to our doings**, so hath He dealt with us" (Zech. 1:6). When Israel confesses, "so hath He dealt with us", God was doing what He thought to do all those times when He intended to, verbally declared, or began to annihilate His people – only those times God was stayed from His just wrath because of intercessory prophets. So now, at the time period of the book of Zechariah, Israel confesses, what God "thought to do unto us…so hath He dealt with us" (Zech. 1:6), and how? What did God do? God brought upon them the Assyrian and Babylonian Captivities - *a near annihilation*. The justice in God that burned for the letter's perfection lashed out from under the rule of Sovereign mercy unto its execution. That is to say, this justice was burning in the heart of God even while sovereign mercy barricaded its breaking forth. I REPEAT, even though it did not break forth in former times and seasons, it was still burning in God's heart. Even though mercy was administered and salvation maintained, it was still burning as a real, genuine, and living desire in the holy heart of God! When justice finally broke forth, it was because sovereign mercy let it loose, and those who died were rightly and justly judged **according to their works**, but God did not kill or make a **full end** even in the captivities, as accounted in the former section: "I Am Weary With Repenting." This, even this – *<u>the preservation of a few</u>* – this is how Israel came to understand MERCY! Do you understand it? "It is of the LORD'S <u>mercies</u> **that we are not consumed**" (Lam. 3:22)! Can you feel the thankfulness and wonder in their hearts when they said – "WE ARE NOT CONSUMED!" – thus they stand amazed in worshipful wonder! Near-annihilating wrath taught them the purest revelation of mercy! They did not understand mercy except by the justice of God's anger which **desired their *total annihilation***. Again they said, "Nevertheless for Thy great <u>mercies'</u> sake Thou **didst not utterly consume them, nor forsake them**; for Thou art a <u>gracious</u> and <u>merciful</u> God" (Neh. 9:31). Do you understand this biblical mercy? An utter and total annihilation was, and is, justice, and all of those persons who are not judged *according to their works* do escape the totally annihilating wrath of God, because, they are privileged objects of sovereign, *justice-shattering* mercy – "Mercy On <u>Whom</u> I Will Have Mercy."

"We should have been as Sodom, and we should have been like unto Gomorrah"

(Isaiah 1:9).

The prophet Ezekiel, more than any other of his contemporaries, undertook the burden to make plain the justice of God's continual desire for the total annihilation of Israel. In Ezekiel chapter 16, under God-breathed inspiration, Ezekiel makes the case that Israel has sinned against God to a greater degree than Sodom and Gomorrah, **whom** God did **NOT SPARE** from *total annihilation*. Thus Isaiah said of Israel, "We **should have** been as Sodom, and we **should have** been like unto Gomorrah" (Isa. 1:9). Israel should have been as Sodom and Gomorrah in *total annihilation*, because their wicked deeds demanded a worse punishment than Sodom and Gomorrah (Ezekiel 16). God's anger was burning hot like the Sodomite fires of annihilation (Deut. 29:23), but God's mercy lamented against it, and He said – "How shall I give thee up, Ephraim? How shall I deliver thee, Israel? How shall I make thee as Admah? How shall I set thee as Zeboim? *Mine heart is turned within Me, My repentings are kindled together*. I will not execute the fierceness of Mine anger, I will not return to destroy Ephraim: **for I am God, and not man**; the Holy One in the midst of thee: and I will not enter into the city" (Hos. 11:8-9). God was SO MOVED to total annihilation that, behold, He was staggering to restrain Himself! His changes of mind were tossing and turning! He had chosen – by sovereign mercy – that He would not totally annihilate Israel so as to, God says, "execute the fierceness of Mine anger," like as what He did to Zeboim and Admah (neighboring cities to Sodom and Gomorrah which were likewise burned) – and this is MERCY! To understand mercy is to feel you are an inhabitant of Zoar, and apart from any merit, in contradiction to the legal of justice, "The sun was risen upon the earth when Lot entered into Zoar" (Gen. 19:19:23), and you are spared! Praise God!

God called Jerusalem a *spiritual* Sodom and Gomorrah (Isa. 1:9-10), because they were followers of, and advancing in, Sodom's nature and deeds, like a child copies his father – kin to kin. To show the strength of this ungodly bond, Ezekiel said they were as *familial kindred* with Sodom, even *sisters*, and with Samaria too (Ezek. 16)! God says of Sodom and Gomorrah, "They were haughty, and committed abomination before Me: **therefore I took them away** as I saw good" (Ezek. 16:50). The iniquity of Jerusalem exceeded Samaria, who was also taken away in wrath, and comparing Jerusalem with her two sisters (Sodom + Gomorrah & Samaria), God declares –

> "Neither hath Samaria committed **half of thy sins**; but thou hast **multiplied thine abominations more than they**, and hast justified thy sisters in all thine abominations which thou hast done. Thou also, which hast judged thy sisters, bear thine own shame for thy sins that thou hast committed **more abominable than they**: they are **more righteous than thou**: yea, be thou confounded also, and bear thy shame, in that thou hast justified thy sisters…thou art a comfort unto them" (Ezek. 16:51-54).

Jerusalem's works demanded a greater, more fierce, annihilation from God,

218

BUT THEY DID NOT UNDERGO IT! A remnant was spared! Mercy is that a remnant was spared, that they were not as Sodom and Gomorrah's end – total annihilation. Thus God says, "I have overthrown some of you, *as God overthrew Sodom and Gomorrah*, and ye were as a firebrand plucked out of the burning" (Amos 4:11) – so a remnant was plucked out from the fire, alive, but not unmarked by the fires. They were heated, burned, and smelted. They were purified, for it was ordained of God that they did exist to praise God's sovereign mercy in holy, healthy, trembling fear. If Israel deserved the same as, or "should have been" as, Sodom and Gomorrah, which is TOTAL ANNIHILATION, but they were not, even while they were more wicked and hell-deserving of it, and instead God decided to save a remnant – this is elective, justice-shattering mercy, which is not according to their works.

How hot and how high were the fires of God's wrath? Look to the secret visions and gasping cries of the prophets, who alone do wrestle against these unseen, erupting potentials. Hear the contemporary prophet of this generation say, "I fell upon my face, and cried, and said, Ah Lord GOD! **Wilt Thou destroy all the residue of Israel** in Thy pouring out of Thy fury upon Jerusalem" (Ezek. 9:8)? And again, "Then fell I down upon my face, and cried with a loud voice, and said, Ah Lord GOD! Wilt **Thou make a full end of the remnant of Israel**" (Ezek. 11:13)? Even so, behold the visions of Amos as he pled against the mind of God to destroy:

> "Thus hath the Lord GOD shewed unto me; and, behold, He formed grasshoppers in the beginning of the shooting up of the latter growth; and, lo, it was the latter growth after the king's mowings. And it came to pass, that when they had made an end of eating the grass of the land, then I said, O Lord GOD, forgive, I beseech Thee: by whom shall Jacob arise? for he is small. **The LORD repented for this**: It shall not be, saith the LORD. Thus hath the Lord GOD shewed unto me: and, behold, the Lord GOD called to contend by fire, and it devoured the great deep, and did eat up a part. Then said I, O Lord GOD, cease, I beseech Thee: by whom shall Jacob arise? for he is small. **The LORD repented for this**: This also shall not be, saith the Lord GOD."
> (Amos 7:1-6)

Well did David Brainerd say, "let us always remember that we must through much tribulation enter in God's eternal Kingdom of rest and peace, **the righteous are scarcely saved, it is an infinite wonder that we have well rounded hopes of being saved at all**. For my part, I feel the most vile of all creatures living and I am sure sometimes that there is not such another existing on this side hell... Let us run, wrestle, and fight that we may win the prize and obtain that complete happiness to be 'holy as God is holy.'" He knew something about the thrice-holy countenance of God, and consequentially, he knew something of his own hell-deserving wretchedness, though he was one of "the righteous" (1 Peter 4:18), as Peter said. Brainerd wondered that God would *presently* and *progressively* save a man like himself, though he had already undergone regeneration. This concept of mercy was crystallized in his heart through the pressures of God's holy terror - hotter than the earth's mantle. Terror and humiliation was the "eyesalve" by which he washed his eyes, that he might behold **MERCY** as a beautiful <u>wonder</u> of God (Rev. 3); hushing the soul into silent admiration, piercing pride and awe-striking, leaving the stoutest champion humiliated, prostrated, and face-grounded in wonder. Such men as this learn to worship with ALL THEIR MIGHT! This same wonder of mercy is the renowned praise of God's righteous people throughout the centuries, and by the righteous I mean they that were humbled, convicted, redeemed, and persevered.

Men wondered at the mercy of God, that **because of it** they were not consumed, for they had holy revelations of their own just condemnation, they had a holy hatred of sin committed, and they had terrible visions of its aftermath after it was experienced, in a moment, when the reactive, perfectly holy will of God responded to sin. They learned the costliness and causes of sin, and it was bitter. They had a heavy mind and grave sensations of their present corruptions, that to be saved from underneath the inward pollutions of self was an infinite, incomprehensible, and unthinkable work of grace! Is this how you understand the mercy of God?

Those who know Brainerd do well understand that he had a deep and acute sense of his sinfulness, but I contend that it was because he had a lifetime of close encounters with The Sinless One – his Holy Judge and Savior. So, for us to understand the wondrous mercy of God, we must see that our sins provoke God to justly pursue our destruction and damnation, but through a holy, alien-righteous mercy, HE SAVES US! When we see that our sins caused God to flame hot enough for our annihilation, sending the prophets into the agonizing experiences heretofore accounted – it is

Who in this entire world of men does experience the soul-crushing, body-depleting, and near-death pressures of wrestling against God's wrath for personal and corporate salvation, as seen in the life of the beloved of God, King David? The famed missionary to the Native Americans, David Brainerd by name, was one man of such experience, but tragically, he is written off to be a man of melancholy, of mental and clinical sickness, but his rapturous experiences of nearness to God's presence, the length and depth of his prayer life, and the revival powers that followed, all of these things are the envy of the children of God. It is with brokenness and astonishment that I have come to conclude, that Brainerd was in a right-standing relationship with God, and thereby, he was sensitive to, and responsive to, his own sinfulness, being aware of God's reactive and changing wrath; all the while he was in pursuit of the promises of God to be performed, but how terrible it is that his life of lowly repentance and mourning is the hiss of God's people, as they just brush it off?! They are of a stronger constitution, you see...but Brainerd's power is their praise and they go on powerless all their days! Why!? Apparently they have sin that they don't know about! But Brainerd knew it – oh, how he knew his wrath-aggravating sin! The secret of Brainerd's success in the Spirit of God was this very breaking experience which "Americanized Christianity" spurns as a psychological instability, when, in truth, these experiences were death to the flesh so that Brainerd might live to God. This was not merely Brainerd's melancholy, but godly sorrow. It was his deep wrestling against then that OUR SIN becomes exceedingly sinful. Sin becomes the more abominable as anger and agony circle overhead, and then, suddenly, mercy is scarcely secured. Sins are *the more* abominable to men when they know that their eternal damnation was so worthy of applause amidst the Three Persons of the Trinity. Even so, God says to Ezekiel – "Cause them TO KNOW the abominations of their fathers" (Ezek. 20:4)! In this entire chapter, Ezekiel recounts three

wrath, followed by rising successes of mercies won! Thus power endued and rested upon this humble man! Brainerd was an example, like King David, whose experiences of personal soul-travail against God's wrath men do likewise spurn, so that men are nearly unaware of God's wrath altogether, and it is because they refuse to suffer it. Leonard Ravenhill rightly said, "I get calls from all over the world, everyone wants my anointing and mantle...but nobody wants my sackcloth and ashes".

instances where God intended, purposed, and sought after Israel's *total annihilation*, so that men might know the nearness of it, their *scarce* escape from it, and the threefold justice in it. Men do take for granted clouds of rain, but they never have or will after they are long exercised under the cloudless heat of the Sun.

It is the mercy of God that any at all, ever, did persevere and were finally saved, that of the many called, the multitudes, *few were still plucked out and hand-chosen* from the furnace of destroying fires, and, lo, a remnant was saved! Thus Ezekiel argues, but what is the heavenly jewel which crowns God's scepter of justice, that it, unto us, might be bowed for a kiss? Behold...

> "And ye shall know that I am the LORD, when I have wrought with you for **MY NAME'S SAKE, not according to your wicked ways, nor according to your corrupt doings**, O ye house of Israel, saith the Lord GOD" (Ezek. 20:44).

God would have men bow and kiss **His Name**, for under it we find a refuge for mercy. God's Name is most precious in the eyes of God, and it is able to stay the wrath of annihilation. When God would not spare men for His love that He has for them, then He spared them for His love that He has for His own Name. God would save His Name before He would save you, and seeing you are called by His Name, you are privileged to be under the covering of the greatest and highest pursuit of God – HIS GLORY! If you are identified with His Name, then "rejoice with trembling" (Ps. 2:11)! Everything that does now exist, everything that was created, it is all for God – "For Whom are all things, and by Whom are all things" (Heb. 2:10) – "For of HIM, and through HIM, and to HIM, are all things: to Whom be glory for ever" (Rom. 11:36). God loves His glory, He loves Himself, and He does things for Himself – chiefly! His own pleasure is satisfied in the exultation of His Name. Therefore – listen closely – God saves men whom He justly hates and pities men who deserve no pity, and why? It is not for the pity of their person, nay! It is the pity that God has toward HIS NAME! This is the greatest desire in God. For God so loved HIMSELF → He saved His people. God loveth The Most Lovely, adoreth The Most

Adorable, esteemeth The Most Right, and rejoiceth in The Most Good – and it is HIMSELF. God loves God, and when all of creation is in its creative order, it will praise, hallow, bless, and love Him right along with Him! His eye spared Israel from the wrath that was upon them before their conversion, and after their conversion, even though they sinned and rebelled against a magnificent degree of light, even though they left the safe haven of gospel-faith, still they were *selectively* and *progressively* saved from a burning justice in God which burned hot throughout their Christian pilgrimage – so hot, mind you, it is soul-gasping, wondrous MERCY that He did not make a ***full annihilation*** of them! And why did God forbear from total annihilation? Because He loved **The Name of God**! Of the Exodus generation, He said, "Nevertheless Mine eye spared them from destroying them, neither did I **make an end** of them in the wilderness" (Ezek. 20:17). And why? My reader, let the inspired prophet Ezekiel "proclaim" (Ex. 33:19) to you the "glory" (Ex. 33:18) of "the Name of the LORD" (Ex. 33:19), the same name spoken to Moses – the Name which is the refuge of elective and sovereign mercy, which prevents and triumphs over a total annihilating wrath in God!

Ezekiel 20:4-24

❖ **Near Annihilation #1**

"Wilt thou judge them, son of man, wilt thou judge them? ***cause them to know the abominations of their fathers****: And say unto them, Thus saith the Lord GOD; In the day when I chose Israel, and lifted up Mine hand unto the seed of the house of Jacob, and made Myself known unto them in the land of Egypt, when I lifted up Mine hand unto them, saying, I am the LORD your God; In the day that I lifted up Mine hand unto them, to bring them forth of the land of Egypt into a land that I had espied for them, flowing with milk and honey, which is the glory of all lands: Then said I unto them, Cast ye away every man the abominations of his eyes, and defile not yourselves with the idols of Egypt: I am the LORD your God. But they rebelled against Me, and would not hearken unto Me: they did not every man cast away the abominations of their eyes, neither did they forsake the idols of Egypt:* ***then I said****, I will pour out My fury upon them, to accomplish My anger against them in the midst of the land of Egypt.* ***But I wrought for My name's sake, that it should not be polluted before the heathen****, among whom they were, in whose sight I made Myself known unto them, in bringing them forth out of the land of Egypt. Wherefore I caused them to go forth out of the land of Egypt, and brought them into the wilderness. And I gave them My statutes, and shewed them My judgments, which if a man do, he shall even live in them. Moreover also I gave them My sabbaths, to be a sign between Me and them, that they might*

know that I am the LORD that sanctify them."

❖   Near Annihilation #2

"But the house of Israel rebelled against Me in the wilderness: they walked not in My statutes, and they despised My judgments, which if a man do, he shall even live in them; and My sabbaths they greatly polluted: **then I said,** *I would pour out My fury upon them in the wilderness, to consume them.* **But I wrought for My name's sake, that it should not be polluted before the heathen,** *in whose sight I brought them out. Yet also I lifted up My hand unto them in the wilderness, that I would not bring them into the land which I had given them, flowing with milk and honey, which is the glory of all lands; Because they despised My judgments, and walked not in My statutes, but polluted My sabbaths: for their heart went after their idols. Nevertheless Mine eye spared them from destroying them, neither did I make an end of them in the wilderness."*

❖   Near Annihilation #3

"But I said unto their children in the wilderness, Walk ye not in the statutes of your fathers, neither observe their judgments, nor defile yourselves with their idols: I am the LORD your God; walk in My statutes, and keep My judgments, and do them; And hallow My sabbaths; and they shall be a sign between Me and you, that ye may know that I am the LORD your God. Notwithstanding the children rebelled against Me: they walked not in My statutes, neither kept My judgments to do them, which if a man do, he shall even live in them; they polluted My sabbaths: **then I said,** *I would pour out My fury upon them, to accomplish My anger against them in the wilderness.* **Nevertheless I withdrew Mine hand, and wrought for My name's sake, that it should not be polluted in the sight of the heathen,** *in whose sight I brought them forth. I lifted up Mine hand unto them also in the wilderness, that I would scatter them among the heathen, and disperse them through the countries; Because they had not executed My judgments, but had despised My statutes, and had polluted My sabbaths, and their eyes were after their fathers' idols."*

Near Annihilation **#1** – MERCY – "But I wrought for My Name's Sake"
Near Annihilation **#2** – MERCY – "But I wrought for My Name's Sake"
Near Annihilation **#3** – MERCY – "Nevertheless I...wrought for My Name's Sake"

Concluding Parameters of MERCY – "I have wrought with you for My Name's Sake,

**not according to your wicked ways, nor
according to your corrupt doings**" (Ezek. 20:44).

Now do you believe that God's messages of mercy to saved men contain the phrase, "Lest thou be consumed" (Genesis 19), and that you are as brother Lot, even now, if you are regenerate? Yes, friend, your body of flesh is a "body of death" that is full of the venom of Sodom and Gomorrah. Now do you believe that, within the Person of God, there does burn a fire like that which broke forth upon Sodom and Gomorrah? Mercy! Mercy! It is mercy, because "WE SHOULD HAVE BEEN as Sodom" and "like unto Gomorrah" (Isa. 1:9); this is *justice-shattering* mercy! God poured forth His wrath upon Sodom and Gomorrah in apocalyptic fire, but for Israel and Judah, God wielded heathen nations as His hammer and axe to hew and dash His people into pieces (Isa. 10, Jer. 13). God announced this means of Israel's destruction since the days of Moses, saying:

> "**I said**, I would scatter them into corners, I would make the remembrance of them to cease from among men: **were it not that I feared the wrath of the enemy, lest their adversaries should behave themselves strangely, and lest they should say, 'Our hand is high, and the LORD hath not done all this.** For they are a nation void of counsel, neither is there any understanding in them. O that they were wise, that they understood this, that they would consider their latter end! How should one chase a thousand, and two put ten thousand to flight, except their Rock had sold them, and the LORD had shut them up" (Deut. 32:26-30)?

The Lord said – "I said" – meaning that He was intent on totally annihilating them, "were it not" that He would profane His own name and glory in the process. Israel was called by God's name, and if He destroyed them, then the heathen would rage in blasphemous glories over God's Name. It is written again by Ezekiel and Isaiah:

> Ezekiel 36:19-23
> "And I scattered them among the heathen, and they were dispersed through the countries: according to their way and according to their doings I judged them. And when they entered unto the heathen, whither they went, they profaned My holy name, when they said to them, These are the people of the LORD, and are gone forth out of His land. **But I had pity for Mine holy name,** which the house of Israel had profaned among the heathen, whither they went. Therefore say unto the house of Israel, Thus saith the Lord GOD; **I do not this for your sakes, O house of Israel, but for Mine holy name's sake**, which ye have profaned among the heathen, whither ye went. And **I will sanctify My great name**, which was profaned among the

224

heathen, which ye have profaned in the midst of them; and the heathen shall know that I am the LORD, saith the Lord GOD, when I shall be sanctified in you before their eyes."

Isaiah 48:9-11
"For My name's sake will I defer Mine anger, and **for My praise** will I refrain for thee, that I cut thee not off. Behold, I have refined thee, but not with silver; I have chosen thee in the furnace of affliction. **For Mine own sake, even for Mine own sake, will I do it: for how should My name be polluted? and I will not give My glory unto another**."

Psalm 106:8
"Nevertheless He saved them **for His Name's sake**, that He might make His mighty power to be known."

The Lord said, "I do not this for your sakes," but rather, He says in Isaiah, "for Mine own sake." (Isaiah 43:25) "I, even I, am He that blotteth out thy transgressions **FOR MINE OWN SAKE**, and will not remember thy sins." All the eyes of God's ransomed Church do fall upon God – The Glory of His Name – and all those who learn to savingly hope for mercy do solemnly hallow His Name! His Name, alone, became the most precious thing to man, because, it makes them precious to God! **"Hallowed be Thy Name**, Thy kingdom come…"

Those which came out of the captivities drank deep from the cup of God's wrath, but deeper yet from the mercy of God. Those who are saved are saved through God retaining not His anger forever – does that shock you!? Nevertheless He was angry! How many people who do believe in the sovereignty of God also believe that God *cannot* be angry with them? How many times did David find himself caught under the bent bow of God's anger (Ps. 32:1-5)? How many times did the godly pray like prayers as David, like Psalm 77:8 – "Is His mercy clean gone for ever? Doth His promise fail for evermore?" In God's eternality and sovereignty, and in unrepentant ordinations, He has chosen to save Israel before the end of time. For this purpose God spared a remnant of Israel, but take heed, it was by pacifying an able anger which

"Mine heart is turned within Me, My repentings are kindled together" – Hosea 11:8
****
Stand still for a moment and think of the will of God to save you wrestling with the will of God to destroy you, and a prophet there in the secret place, watching on, lifts up cries of intercessory prayers, and then, hardly and through much agony, by much scarcity, you are saved – yet all the while you never knew about or saw this great wrestling and the scarce Victor of MERCY Who triumphed over Wrath.

was rearing to annihilate, and, lo, it was engaged by an opposing will in God, and they wrestled, then wrath was scarcely surmounted…then subdued, and the stronger will in God which dispensed mercy was moved, strengthened, and made unconquerable, because it stands as the highest priority in God, that in preserving His people He preserves His Name. In the light of this justice-shattering mercy which no man can explain, in the light of a situation of justice which kindles an eternal, forever-burning, unrelenting wrath unto our total annihilation, the saints recognize and wonder – God saves – and they praise Him that His anger does not continue FOREVER! It is the mercy of God! →

> "Who is a God like unto Thee, that pardoneth iniquity, and passeth by the transgression of the remnant of His heritage? **He retaineth not His anger for ever, because He delighteth in mercy. He will turn again,** He will have compassion upon us; He will subdue our iniquities; and Thou wilt cast all their sins into the depths of the sea" (Micah 7:18-19).

If the election of God determines the predestination of salvation to arise in a perseverant end, its rise is through a thorny path and raging sea of *near annihilation*. The survival of the saints through this course unto a salvific end is the exclamation of great, *surpassing*, unthinkable, inexpressible mercy. The final, finishing, and entire salvation of Israel is the capstone event at the end of time. This is His eternal purpose and sovereign counsel (*God in the ways of God*), and though His mind, works, and will change many times, the sovereignty and eternality of His judgments made from everlasting are always exalted right beside the contrasting events, circumstances, and manifestations of God's condescension *in the ways of man*. Therefore God says, "For I am the LORD, **I change not**; therefore ye sons of Jacob **are not consumed**" (Malachi 3:6)! We must learn to relate to God in His condescension, but yet we must glorify God, knowing that every outcome is underneath His higher, secret, and full rule, because He is an unchanging, all-determining, predestinating King.

> "Hath not the potter power over the clay, of the same lump to make one vessel unto honour, and another unto dishonour? What if God, willing to shew His wrath, and to make His power known, endured with much longsuffering the vessels of wrath fitted to destruction: And that He might make known the riches of His glory on the vessels of mercy, which He had afore prepared unto glory" (Rom 9:21-23).

All of this mercy toward Israel was *the glory* of God's mercy toward "vessels of mercy," chosen beforehand that they would be saved. The mercy originated, and is sustained, by the supreme and highest lifeline – "My Name's sake," says the Lord – a higher plane above the reaching and cries of comprehensible justice, granting forgiveness even though their deeds required destruction. Thus the Lord says, "Ye shall know that I am the LORD, when I have wrought with you for My Name's sake, **not according to your wicked ways, nor according to your corrupt doings**" (Ezek. 20:44). God, Who was jealous for His Name, won for Himself the adoration of the remnant BY SAVING THEM. The GREAT mystery of how God does this work of salvation, and yet, still silences Satan from his accusatory demands for justice, is a mystery in which the holy angels look on with praises and

226

everlasting applause. Those fallen angels, now called devils, along with their once-or twice-dead kinsmen are amazed at the dispensation of mercy upon sinful men. In this way, God obtained the glory that He seeks to show in all the earth – "the exceeding riches of His grace in His kindness" (Eph. 2:7) toward the elect throughout all the ages of time, "that He might make known the riches of His glory on the vessels of mercy which He had afore prepared unto glory" (Rom. 9:23). The mercy of God which motivates election, as you can see, is a *justice-shattering* election, and when justice would demand destruction, God acts to defend His Name, yea, and for this chief cause He shows mercy. Are you understanding what the scriptures are saying? Consider God's own rendered reasons on matters of *justice-shattering* mercy and election:

> "**Speak not** thou in thine heart, after that the LORD thy God hath cast them out from before thee, saying, For **my righteousness** the LORD hath brought me in to possess this land: but for the wickedness of these nations the LORD doth drive them out from before thee. Not for **thy righteousness**, or for **the uprightness of thine heart**, dost thou go to possess their land: but for the wickedness of these nations the LORD thy God doth drive them out from before thee, and that He may **perform the word** which the LORD sware unto thy fathers, Abraham, Isaac, and Jacob. **Understand therefore**, that the LORD thy God giveth thee not this good land to possess it for **thy righteousness**; for **thou art a stiffnecked people**. **Remember**, and **forget not**, how thou **provokedst** the LORD thy God to wrath in the wilderness: from the day that thou didst depart out of the land of Egypt, until ye came unto this place, ye have been rebellious against the LORD. Also in Horeb ye provoked the LORD to wrath, so that **the LORD was angry with you to have destroyed you**" (Deut. 9:4-8).

God says in this passage – "**speak not**" – "**understand therefore**" – "**remember, and forget not**" – which means that this is a VERY IMPORTANT BURDEN the Lord was trying to communicate to the saved remnant of Israel! But oh! Men don't understand this today! You see, God wants men to understand the mercy of God in the light of the fact that they are worthy of *total annihilation*. Soul-humbling, mouth-stopping, terrifying, and awe-striking MERCY, is a MERCY which is undeserved! This is a MERCY that did reposition and suddenly move you just a hair out of the way of God's swinging wrath which was intent to bring your soul down to hell! God had mercy, even when His people were "**stiffnecked**" (Deut. 9:6), "**rebellious**" (Deut. 9:7), and even when God was "angry with [them] **to have destroyed [them]**" (Deut. 9:8) – He still had mercy! Therefore, as they were being saved they were commanded to confess that their salvation was not "**for [their] righteousness**" (Deut. 9:4), nor was it "**for the uprightness of [their] heart**" (Deut. 9:5), but God saved them because they were the remaining offspring of Israel which carried the banner of His name over their lives, and therefore, they were most precious to God. You could say that it was for their fathers' sake, and for the sake that God's word would have preeminent glory in the earth (Deut. 9:5), which, even still, is directly connected to the preservation and exultation of God's Name. This is what is meant when it was written: "as touching election, they are beloved for the Father's sake" (Rom. 11:28). Do you see how men need to understand the *totally annihilating* wrath of God, that they might understand mercy? When God is famous for fierce, angry, and destroying blows of perfect, sinless justice, and thus "repayeth them that hate Him to their face, to destroy them", and that, "He will not be slack to him that hateth Him, He will repay him to his face" (Deut. 7:10) – self-declaring that, in this way God is GOOD – for mercy to contradict, overpass, and triumph over this justice of judgment with heaven-high, incomprehensible, righteous, and eternal mercy, this is shocking! It is utterly amazing, and to mercy's recipients, it is knee-bowing, head-grounding, heart-melting, and finally, men and angels are irresistibly compelled unto perfect worship and ejaculatory praise! "Let all the earth keep silence before Him" (Hab. 2:20). Can you see it!? Wrath attempted the total annihilation of YOU, yes YOU, and if you are saved today, it is because sovereign mercy removed you from the reach of God's just and angry swing when He did intend to take you down to hell where you belong! Oh! For any criminal who feels how narrowly he escaped wrath throughout a lifetime of sojourning on a wicked world, then prostrated worship with silent admiration of God, even forever, seems like an unworthy privilege – that I, even I would have the honor to bow down in His presence and worship Him!? And for this we are insatiably satisfied to do! You can never satisfy this burning satisfaction to worship of God! Hallelujah! After one round of shouts and praises, heaven's bells still ring the same sounding ring – heaven praise Him, praise God – The Father, The Son, & The Holy Ghost!

History proclaims just how hallowed God's Name is to God, every time *justice-shattering* mercy is dispensed. Samson committed adultery, and had he lived in Moses' day, he would have died without mercy (Deut. 22:22). David committed adultery and murder, even the murder of one of the mighty men of God's army (Uriah the Hittite), and holy scripture justly declares, "whoso sheddeth man's blood, by man shall his blood be shed: for in the image of God made He man" (Gen. 9:6). Even still, God spared David's life! The prophet Hosea was commanded by God TO MARRY a harlot, and how extraordinary is this! Usually prophets are commanded to denounce them, prophesy woes upon them, or charge Kings, judges, or armies to ride forth and slaughter them! God's holy word demanded death by stoning for all harlots (Deut. 22:21). Could the letter of justice be any clearer when it says, "there shall be no whore of the daughters of Israel, nor a sodomite of the sons of Israel" (Deut. 23:17)? Even still, it is staggering that Rahab, the harlot, was the only individual saved from Jericho, and what was her deed of faith? She lied, even though the letter commands – "Thou shalt not bear false witness against thy neighbour" (Exo. 20:16). She lied to keep the Israelite spies hidden from the pursuing authorities of Jericho, and this lie was famed to be the deed of her salvation (James 2:25)! Rahab the harlot, of the condemned race of people that dwelt in the city of Jericho, of the condemned nation of Canaanites, with whom God forbade any agreement with, saying – "take heed to thyself, **lest thou make a covenant with the inhabitants** of the land whither thou goest, lest it be for a snare in the midst of thee" (Ex. 34:12), and again, "And **ye shall make no league with the inhabitants of this land**; ye shall throw down their altars" (Judges 2:2) – with her Israel made a covenant with. They had mercy upon her and let her live when God said, "thou shalt **smite them**, and utterly destroy them; thou shalt make no covenant with them, **nor shew mercy unto them**" (Deuteronomy 7:2). She came to dwell in the land of Israel, where God said, "they shall not dwell in thy land" (Ex. 23:33), and let it stagger you further! The woman who was a harlot, an occupation which God is utterly disgusted with – Rahab, who was of a nation which was so perverse that God said "the land is defiled" underneath them, "and the land itself vomiteth out her inhabitants" (Lev. 18:25), and how much more does God vomit out the inhabitants thereof – Rahab, even she was accepted, forgiven, shown pardon, and mercy, allowed to live on, and she was famed throughout the centuries as a saved woman (Heb. 11:13, Jas. 2:25). She was even one of the select few who were specifically mentioned in the genealogy of Jesus Christ – the sovereignly selected birth line of the Holy Messiah Himself (Matt. 1:5)!

Israel fell into idolatry under the leadership of Aaron, and yet Aaron, as well as a large majority of Israel, was pardoned and spared (Exodus 32-34), but Achan – only one generation later – he and all of his family died for lesser sins than full-blown calf worship (Josh. 7), which Aaron and Israel had committed. The wife of God, Israel, was an adulteress and a whore against God, her Husband, and in every respect He was deserving of a divorcement from her, and still more, the letter of the law demands the death of an adulterer, but God did not keep the *justice* as it was written in the law for the express purpose that He might make known the magnitude of His mercies. In all of these scenarios, we are forced to conclude that God HAD *justice-shattering* MERCY, and why? Because these people are those "on whom [He] will have mercy" (Rom. 9:15), and nothing more can be said of it! Let the clay look up, high above the spectrum of human observation, acknowledgment, understanding, and wisdom, and let it worship God, The Potter.

Great Is Thy Faithfulness

"And ye shall know that I am the LORD, when I have wrought with you for My Name's sake, **not according to your wicked ways, nor according to your corrupt doings**, O ye house of Israel, saith the LORD GOD" (Ezek. 20:44).

"He hath **not dealt with us after our sins; nor rewarded us according to our iniquities**" (Psalm 103:10).

When you exclaim, "the LORD is merciful and gracious!" (Ps. 103:8), exactly what are you thinking about? By what biblical and historical examples do you recognize that the Lord is "SLOW to anger and PLENTEOUS in mercy" (Ps. 103:8)? Just how slow is anger, and just how plenteous is mercy – can you explain it?

When you sing songs of praise, saying, "*Great Is Thy Faithfulness*" (Lam. 3:23), or, "*So Great Is His Mercy*" (Ps. 103:11), exactly what is the **GREATNESS** of God's faithfulness and mercy which is being magnified to you at that very moment? What are you thinking about? Are you making up your own unbiblical definitions of these things?

When you begin to fall in love with the Father-heart of God, and when you begin to see just how, amazingly, He is full of pity toward His saints –"**as a father pitieth his children**, so the LORD **pitieth** them that fear Him" (Ps. 103:13) – exactly what is so pitiful about God's pity toward His saints? What is so praise worthy about God's tender Fatherhood to you, His child?

"**The LORD is merciful and gracious, slow to anger, and plenteous in mercy**. He will not always chide: neither will He keep His anger for ever. **He hath not dealt with us after our sins; nor rewarded us according to our iniquities**. For as the heaven is high above the earth, **so great is His mercy** toward them that fear Him. As far as the east is from the west, so far hath He removed our transgressions from us. Like **as a father pitieth his children**, so the LORD **pitieth** them that fear Him. For He knoweth our frame; He remembereth that we are dust. As for man, his days are as grass: as a flower of the field, so he flourisheth. For the wind passeth over it, and it is gone; and the place thereof shall know it no more" (Ps. 103:8-16).

The inspired psalmist of Psalm 103 is praising God, that though God's wrath is so long a-kindled and burning, and so near the destruction of humanity's saints, because "our sins" and "our iniquities" merit this (Ps. 103:10), His anger is, nevertheless, NOT KEPT "for ever" and "always" (Ps. 103:9), for if it was kept always, then none of humanity's saints would be preserved – resulting in a total annihilation. Is this not what God is saying? And again, "For I will not contend for ever, neither will I be always

"*For the LORD shall judge His people, and repent Himself for His servants, when He seeth that their power is gone, and there is none shut up, or left*" (Deut. 32:36).
****
The Father pitieth His children when He seeth that their strength is gone, but not before!

This is the context of God's judgment of His children! This is biblical pity, when God is pacified from wrath when He sees that their strength is utterly gone, that most are annihilated, and how, look, the few that are left are on the verge of death – it is then that God pities them because He knoweth their frame, that they will all perish, if indeed His wrath continues. This is why the choicest of God's elect saints went through the agony of wrestling

230

wroth: for the spirit should fail before Me, and the souls which I have made" (Isa. 57:16). Again in this passage, God recognizes this chief explanation of mercy, namely, that the weakness of our frame would not survive a head-on collision with an angry God charging in the force of justice, and so God intends to preserve humanity's saints by remembering "our frame" and

against God's destroying anger, until, lo, they recognized that they were being brought to the point of death, and look, then they did plead for mercy because of this near-death experience, verifying it and glorifying God, that their strength is gone and now He has all the glory. This is a true experience of mercy on whom He has mercy! Think of all the saints pleading this very plea as they were pressed under the wrath of God, as it drove them to the precipice of destruction.

"that we are dust" (Ps. 103:14), and how shortly we are "gone" and "no more" existing, even as the as the flourishing life of a grass flower straightway withering under the hot sun – thus God must restrain and shade His wrath like He shades sunrays with clouds – IT IS FOR OUR SURVIVAL. All of these titles – "GREAT IS THY FAITHFULNESS" – "SO GREAT is His MERCY" – as a Father pitieth His children – what is the plenteousness of mercy – the slowness of anger – and what manner of grace God bestows – all of these titles are the exclaimed praises of saints when they behold this truth, that they were near to, under the scope of, and about to suffer total annihilation under God's wrath, but to God's great glory, the seemingly **forever** and **always-enduring** wrath that was pursuing them was suddenly overpassed and outrun by mercy, and mercy, like eagles' wings, did fly them to safety. For this, God is deemed slow to anger, in that He did not kill ALL of His people, and that He was not angry FOREVER! In remembering to preserve a small remnant, remembering to preserve His Name, is the same pointed meaning when God remembers *what we are* (our frame as dust & grass), and how that He might be mindful not to destroy us all.

Saints Who Recovered From Near Annihilating Wrath –
On What Appeal?

"Don't let me die, because then Your Name will die with me!"

When have you ever wrestled against the wrath of God for personal salvation like the choicest and most beloved saints of God did in their relationship with God? One who really understands biblical mercy, faithfulness, pity, and love, will also understand what to plead before God so as to obtain mercy for present continuous pardon and salvation.

I find that, as saints do wrestle against the destroying and annihilating wrath of God for present progressive salvation in their own lives, hoping to be saved from it even though it be by scarcity, they do use one chief appeal to arouse the emotions of mercy in God, which is that they, who are vessels of earth called by God's everlasting and worthy name, are now almost dead. God is attentive to this, because their death would cause God's praise to descend into silence with the dead man.

231

These men cried out that they were *nearing annihilation*, thus they were remembering that this is **the hour** and **moment** in which mercy is famed to save a saint from *total annihilation*! Therefore the saints did pray for mercy because they were being pressed toward death and destruction, so they cried – "be not silent to me" (Ps. 28:1), "put not Thy servant away in anger" (Ps. 27:9), "leave me not, neither forsake me" (Ps. 27:9), "lest, if Thou be silent to me, I become like them that go down into the pit" (Ps. 28:1), "let Thou bring me to nothing" (Jer. 10:24), "take me not away in the midst of my days" (Ps. 102:24). They knew this about God – "when He seeth that their power is gone, and there is none shut up, or left" – then His wrath is pacified and repented of, into saving mercies (Deut. 32:36). These saints do remind God of it, exactly when *their power is gone*, so that then they might obtain mercy which God says He gives, when He seeth that their power is gone (Deut. 32:36). They understood that if the wrath of God continues onward in its fiery pursuit, then it will drive them into the grave of death. Do you remember these scriptures?

> "But He, being full of compassion, forgave their iniquity, and destroyed them not: yea, many a time turned He His anger away, and did not stir up all His wrath. **For He remembered that they were but flesh; a wind that passeth away, and cometh not again**" (Ps. 78:38-39).

> "**For He knoweth our frame; He remembereth that we are dust.** As for man, his days are as grass: as a flower of the field, so he flourisheth. For the wind passeth over it, and it is gone; and the place thereof shall know it no more" (Ps. 103:14-15).

The saints understood biblical mercy, compassion, and faithfulness to be exclaimed by a scarce salvation from wrath – not that there is never any wrath, or that there are never any that perish under wrath, but, it is exclamatory that a small remnant, even a few, are spared from the entire regenerate multitude, scarcely though, and this is God's great faithfulness! And thus, they do ever remind God so that He will *remember* that they will perish unless God repents from His wrath. They remind Him what they are, namely flesh, a wind that passeth away, and dust. They remind Him of what their frame is so that God will not go too far and consume them to death. This is what is meant when the men cried this prayer into the ears and memory of God – "**How many** are the days of Thy servant" (Ps. 119:84). God makes men feel His wrath in shocking ways so that they come to understand that they are "appointed to death" (Ps. 102), that "the sorrows of death compassed [them]" and "the snares of death prevent [them]" (Ps. 18:4-6), and that "the terrors of death are fallen upon [them]" (Ps. 55:4-5); therefore they pray thus – "**LORD, make me to know mine end, and the measure of my days, what it is; that I may know how frail I am. Behold, Thou hast made my days as an handbreadth; and mine age is as nothing before Thee: verily every man at his best state is altogether vanity. Selah**" (Ps. 39:4-5). Do you know that God "turnest man to destruction; and sayest, Return, ye children of men" (Ps. 90:3)? As wrath is poured out, the godly men are "sighing" and full of "roarings," insomuch that they are distracted from eating (Job 3:24)! They become "feeble and sore broken" (PS. 38:8), their "bones" are "waxed old through [their] roaring all the day long" (Ps. 32:3), "[their] heart is sore pained within [them]...fearfulness and trembling are come upon [them], and horror hath overwhelmed [them] (Ps. 55:4-5), "the sorrows of hell compassed [them] about," so that, they are in "distress" unto an uplifted "cry" (Ps. 18:4-6), and "the pains of hell gat hold upon [them]" unto "trouble and sorrow" (Ps. 116:3)! As this is happening, it feels like it is **forever**, and they know that God, when He has mercy, it does – IN TRUTH – last **forever**, thus they pray and remind Him of this GREAT MERCY, saying…

"How long, LORD? wilt Thou hide Thyself **for ever**? shall Thy wrath burn like fire**? Remember how short my time is: wherefore hast Thou made all men in vain? What man is he that liveth, and shall not see death? shall he deliver his soul from the hand of the grave**? Selah" (Ps. 89:46-48).

"How long, LORD? wilt Thou be angry **for ever**? shall Thy jealousy burn like fire?" (Ps. 79:5)

"Wilt Thou be angry with us **for ever**? wilt Thou draw out Thine anger to all generations?" (Ps. 85:5)

"How long, LORD? wilt Thou hide Thyself **for ever**? shall Thy wrath burn like fire?" (Ps. 89:46)

"O LORD God of hosts, **how long** wilt Thou be angry against the prayer of Thy people?" (Ps. 80:4)

"O God, why hast Thou cast us off **for ever**? why doth Thine anger smoke against the sheep of Thy pasture? We see not our signs: there is no more any prophet: neither is there among us any that knoweth **how long**. O God, how long shall the adversary reproach? shall the enemy blaspheme Thy name **for ever**?" (Ps. 74:1, 9-10)

"To the chief Musician, A Psalm of David. How long wilt Thou forget me, O LORD? **for ever**? how long wilt Thou hide Thy face from me? How long shall I take counsel in my soul, having sorrow in my heart daily? how long shall mine enemy be exalted over me?" (Ps. 13:1-2)

"Be not wroth very sore, O LORD, neither remember iniquity **for ever**: behold, see, we beseech Thee, we are all Thy people." (Isa 64:9)

Today, men have no concept of two saving truths...Ravenhill correctly points to them as the Church's GREATEST NEED of REDISCOVERY – "One, **the majesty and the holiness of God**, and the other, **the sinfulness of sin**" (Leonard Ravenhill, Weep Between The Porch And The Altar). My reader, listen! Men believe that the wrath of God is upon them if they commit idolatry, adultery, or murder, but what about for a sinner in the Church congregation or an Achan in the holy camp? What about a failure to trust in the Lord to show the difference between true and false converts? Will God burn in castaway wrath for such things like this? Yes, reader, as He did to His beloved servant Joshua, as He did to David with various other sins which you would never consider to be "so sinful", so also God will do...and furthermore, God says in the New Covenant that sinners in the Church is as the crime of idolatry – and that includes saints who turn to sin and thus become unclean sinners! Do you know and watch after your congregation so closely, preachers? Or do you not know them so well? If you only knew that your success or failure on this matter holds the potential threat of the wrath of God, then perhaps you would make your ministry more than a Sunday job!

Read of all the times that God was angry with David, and how He did cast him off, and NOTE: David was not committing adultery and murder at any of these times, except one (Ps. 51), and yet God was still wroth with His beloved servant, enough so that God was casting him off in wrath. What are all these sins that David was committing? All of these other sins which David was committing were forgiven him, so much so they are not even mentioned again. David had an impeccable reputation – that he "did that which was right in the eyes of the LORD and turned not aside from any thing that He commanded him all the days of his life, save only in the matter of Uriah the Hittite" (1 Kings 15:5). If this is the case, then what sins was David committing in all of these psalms in which he was nearly drowning under the waves of God's raging wrath!? Pressed sore and near death, for nearly a "**forever**," wrath was kindled over his anointed head – thus did David cry – and he was delivered! It remains for us, therefore, to understand something of *the sinfulness of our sins* and *the holiness of God's majesty*.

"Great Is Thy Faithfulness" – Lamentations 3:23

> "**Great is Thy faithfulness**, O God my Father,
> There is no shadow of turning with Thee;
> **Thou changest not, Thy compassions, they fail not**
> As Thou hast been Thou forever wilt be."
> (Thomas Chisholm, "Great is Thy Faithfulness")

How many people sing the hymn, "Great is Thy Faithfulness," and yet they do not understand the context in which these exact words were written to describe, so that they would know exactly what is faithful about God's faithfulness!? Consider the whole passage of Lamentations again...

"It is of the LORD'S mercies that we are not consumed, because His **compassions fail not**. They are new every morning: **Great is Thy Faithfulness**" (Lamentations 3:22-23). God's *faithfulness* and *unfailing compassions* are magnified in that the people of God are not *totally annihilated*, but they were only brought *near to entire annihilation*, and the fact that they were ONLY brought to this point – a **near annihilation** instead of a **total annihilation** – this is God's great faithfulness and unfailing compassion! The greatness of our sin, colliding with the exceeding holiness of God, results to reveal to humanity that when a man is saved, it was because the force of God's faithfulness is greater than the greatness of sin which aggravated the force of holy justice. My reader, is this what you are meditating upon when you sing the hymn, "Great is Thy Faithfulness?" I am convinced that this nation is full of professing Christians that have never understood the meaning of this hymn, and so, they are not worshipping God according to the biblical truth of God's attributes, but rather according to their own interpretive imagination.

Also, see how the hymn says of God – "Thou changest not." Just in other words, it is written again of God, "there is no shadow of turning with Thee." Exactly what is being magnified here about the glory of God's *changelessness* which is so worthy of praise?

"For I am the LORD, **I change not**; therefore ye sons of Jacob **are not consumed**" – Malachi 3:6

Do you see it? What is being magnified about God's changelessness is that the people of God are not *entirely annihilated* as they deserve to be. God will not change on the matter of His decision that Israel shall be preserved and finally saved, and therefore He will not entirely destroy them as He does other nations of people. "I will not return to destroy Ephraim: **for I am God, and not a man**" (Hos. 11:9), which means, this decision was made in the glory of His sovereign purpose, which is *changeless*, predestinating, and determinate, and therefore the purpose is "**without repentance**" (Rom. 11:29). If this decision was spoken after the manner of God's condescension *in the ways of man*, then He could and would repent of it if He desired to. Is it not astonishing? Here again, the *near annihilating* wrath of God is still the glory of God's faithfulness, because He changes not on this point of decision. The famed hymn is saying – "Thou changest not" – which is to mean, "Therefore we are not entirely consumed!"

People quote the promises of God's faithfulness repeatedly. How often have you heard it said, "God is faithful." This is for a good reason! The scriptures focus on this attribute of God as the chief reason why men are enabled to persevere, but has it ever occurred to you that **God's faithfulness** has been the praise of God's people before the NT dispensation, and, we ought to look back to see what *is faithful about God's faithfulness*? Nehemiah 9 is a correct explanation of the mercy, forgiveness, and faithfulness of God as it was displayed throughout the centuries to His promise-bound people. As an introduction to Nehemiah 9, look now at verse 31, and don't forget what was written in Lamentations 3:22-23.

"Nevertheless for **Thy great mercies' sake** Thou didst not **utterly consume them**, nor forsake them; for Thou art a **gracious** and **merciful** God." – Nehemiah 9:31

From verses 1-30 of Nehemiah 9, the praying men recounted the troubled yet enduring relationship God had with His saved people. They were greatly mindful of how it played out through the centuries, unto that very day, as all those men were praying. They recognized the preciousness of the fact that, lo, they were yet alive, and this was an awesome mercy of God, because they deserved to be *totally annihilated*. When God allowed that a remnant would be saved, that of the many called still a few were chosen, and that God's wrath did not burn **forever**, but rather it was turned again into mercy, they recognized a breach of comprehensible justice, and that this was an achievement by sovereign mercy. God did send prophets to "judge them," to "cause them to know the abominations of their fathers" (Ezek. 20:4), and so they did now freely confess the praiseworthy truths – "He hath not dealt with us after our sins" (Ps. 103:10) – and if He did, then His anger would have burned *forever* unto *entire annihilation*.

"…but Thou art a God **ready to pardon, gracious** and **merciful, slow to anger**, and of **great kindness**, and forsookest them not" – Neh. 9:17

"Yet Thou in Thy **manifold mercies**" – Neh. 9:19

"…according to Thy **manifold mercies**" – Neh. 9:27

"…for Thou art a **gracious** and **merciful God**" – Neh. 9:31

"The LORD is **merciful** and gracious, **slow to anger**, and **plenteous in mercy**" – Psalm 103:8

"…that He might make known **the riches of His glory on vessels of mercy**…" – Rom. 9:23

Read Nehemiah 9, and then, think about it…what is so "**ready**" about God's *readiness to pardon*? See Nehemiah 9:17, how it says that God is "ready to pardon"? What is so ready, quick, and speedy about it? Also, what is so "**slow**" about the "**anger**" of God (Neh. 9:17)? What is so "**great**" about the "**kindness**" of God (Neh. 9:17)? What is so "**manifold**" about the "**mercies**" of God (Neh. 9:19)? And do you remember what Psalm 103 said about the **slowness** of God's **anger** and the **plenteousness** of His **mercy**, and also, do you remember Romans 9:23, how that it is God's eternal purpose to show the "**riches** of His glory on vessels of **mercy**?" Or in other words, God shows mercy to elect persons, but not *just* mercy… sinners don't get saved from just a little mercy. God showers upon them **the riches of His mercy** so as to save them, and it requires no less an amount! Therefore, here again, along with all the other questions, what is so **plenteous, manifold**, and "**RICH**" about the **mercy** of God? Can you answer these questions? Look at the context of the verses which are cited!

Now let's look at this situation from another angle. Because mercy is plenteous, manifold, and rich, therefore God's anger was slowed down, and for this reason the people praise God that He was "slow to anger." God's anger was burning

236

hotter, pursuing harder, and minded to a fast and quick annihilation, more than was ever manifested by a plague or a destroying power. He repented of it many times, until finally, He was weary of repenting (Jer. 15:6) – He refused to repent anymore of His angry thoughts toward His people. It was then that His people realized, "Like as the LORD of hosts **thought to do unto us**, according to our ways, and according to our doings, **so hath He dealt with us**" (Zech. 1:6). As the Lord thought to do but repented of it, again and again, now the Lord has thought and repented not, and what was it? It was *the near annihilation* of His people in the Assyrian and Babylonian Captivities, and the people of Nehemiah's day came out of it "as a firebrand plucked out of the burning" furnace of God's wrath, still alive, scarcely though, and now that they have returned back into the land of Israel they do solemnly confess to God – "Thou art just in all that is brought upon us; for Thou hast done right, but we have done wickedly" (Neh. 9:33). God thought to totally annihilate Israel, and then, in an unrepentant purpose, did set His face to Israel according to how He had "thought" before, and God dealt with them "according to [their] ways, and according to [their] doings" (Zech. 1:6), but the very fact that not all were totally annihilated is an unjustifiable mercy. It is a mercy that caused them to escape from the justice of God's judgment "according to [their] ways, and according to [their] doings" (Zech. 1:6), a mercy which was said to be ""**not according to your wicked ways, nor according to your corrupt doings**" (Ezek. 20:44), and again Israel says, "He hath **not dealt with us after our sins; nor rewarded us according to our iniquities**" (Psalm 103:10). Even so, when Israel praised God for His *faithfulness*, His *slowness to anger*, the *plenteous, manifold, richness* of His *mercy*, it was not that none could fall away and perish who were formerly saved, but it was that a few of the many which were of the saved multitude were preserved, and that there was not a *total annihilation* according to what they deserved!

"The whole land shall be desolate; **yet will I not make a full end**" – Jer. 4:27

"…destroy; but **make not a full end**" – Jer. 5:10

"I was but **a little** displeased" – Zech. 1:15

"…**I will not make a full end with you**" – Jer. 5:18

"In **a little** wrath" – Isaiah 54:8

"For I am with thee, saith the LORD, to save thee: **though I make a full end of all nations whither I have scattered thee**, yet will **I not make a full end of thee**: but I will correct thee in measure, and will not leave thee altogether unpunished" (Jer. 30:11).

"Fear thou not, O Jacob My servant, saith the LORD: for I am with thee; **for I will make a full end of all the nations whither I have driven thee: but I will not make a full end of thee**, but correct thee in measure; yet will I not leave thee wholly

237

unpunished" (Jer. 46:27-28).

> "For **a small moment** have I forsaken thee; but with great
> mercies will I gather thee. **In a little wrath** I hid My face from
> thee **for a moment**; but with everlasting kindness will I have
> mercy on thee, saith the LORD thy Redeemer" (Isaiah 54:7-8).

Shockingly, the wrath of God which nearly annihilated all of God's people is said to be when God was "but a little displeased," and it was but "a little wrath" (Zech. 1:15, Isa. 54:8)! What is so slow about God's slowness to anger? What is so little about God's wrath? What is so little about God's little displeasure? If we understood the sinfulness – the abominableness of our sin – like as God seeks to persuade us of (Ezek. 20:4), then we will understand how we DESERVED entire annihilation, how we do not deserve a small remnant to be spared alive, for, lo, a totally annihilating wrath is burning in the heart of God – THE JUST. The fact that a near-annihilating wrath came upon us, rather than a total annihilation, is slowness to anger, little wrath, and a little displeasure, comparatively to what God thought, intended, wanted, said, or could have done in the cause of pure, undefiled, unrestrained justice. If a remnant is spared, then, lo, we have much to be thankful for! This is RICH, PLENTEOUS, and MANIFOLD mercy which overcame the whelming storm of wrath which was alive in God's heart of justice, against us, the criminals, who have sinned in exceedingly sinful sins. This mercy wins for Israel a near annihilation instead of a total annihilation, and this is "not according to [our] wicked ways, nor according to [our] corrupt doings", and again, "He hath not dealt with us after our sins; nor rewarded us according to our iniquities" (Ezek. 20:44, Ps. 103:10)! This is how the biblical, inspired writers understood the mercy of God – the riches of it! The plenteousness of mercy is shown forth in that it was more manifold and numerous than our sins! Perhaps now we are prepared to understand what true worship is, and why God's people repeatedly praised God with the exact praise: "His mercy endureth for ever"!

His Mercy Endureth Forever

What is so magnificent about the ever-enduring mercy of God? Sin is so sinful, and God's wrath is so aggravated under the compulsion of His steep holiness, that regenerate men are brought low, scarcely saved from, and nearly consumed by wrath. See their great complaint in the former verses? They were suffering greatly under wrath so much that it seemed like it was FOREVER! But what is so magnified by saints who are saved from the nearly FOREVER-wrath which consumes most of the called? The few that are spared do exclaim, feelingly, that they do deserve to perish like all the others, nevertheless they do remain alive today to obtain Covenant promises, and why? God's MERCY ENDURETH FOREVER! It is MERCY that He did not retain anger forever, for this is what justice would have demanded! Nearly a forever-wrath does create, again, near-total annihilation.

238

"Who is a God like unto Thee, that pardoneth iniquity, and passeth by the transgression of the remnant of His heritage? He retaineth not His anger for ever, because He delighteth in **mercy**" (Mic. 7:18).

God's mercy endureth forever, of a truth, beyond the "forever" of wrath! Even though the saints are so exercised by wrath that they woefully exclaim – "will it burn forever?" – the mercy of God will overpass the mark at which wrath extends to, and so, the forever endurance of mercy is magnified in that it lasts **beyond** the persevering, annihilating wrath of God!

The book of Judges (recorded during the times of "the judges") contains many centuries of general apostasy. Century to century and judge to judge, there were intermittent periods of slight relief, but God exercised them all with great afflictions and bondages, and with an angry rod. When they began to call upon the name of the Lord – THEN – God would raise up some degree of relief by the hand of an abnormal leader, comparatively incapable to what was established in the glory of former generations. After the judges, then Samuel arose, and God gave Israel a King, of which He said – "I gave thee a king in Mine anger, and took him away in My wrath" (Hos. 13:11). With Saul's ascension to the throne, Israel was led into many more years of apostasy. In these times, many did "sit in darkness and in the shadow of death", "being bound" (Ps. 107:10), "afflicted" (Ps. 107:17), brought to "their wits' end" (Ps. 107:27), and yet, when the people of God returned and sought after Him, especially through the leadership of David and the prophets, then God "brought them out of the darkness and the shadow of death, and brake their bands in sunder" (Ps. 107:14), "He sent His word, and healed them, and delivered them from their destructions" (Ps. 107:20), "He bringeth them out of their distresses" (Ps. 107:28), and for what Divine reason? Upon the lips of God's people was, "O give thanks unto the LORD, for He is good: for His mercy endureth for ever" (Ps. 107:1), and four more times, again, "praise the LORD for His goodness" (Ps. 107:8, 15, 21, 31)! The "goodness" of God which is thank worthy and the ever-enduring mercy of God that is praise worthy – these attributes in God do not negate the possibility of God's people falling into reprobation and eternal demise – but after such perilous times have long transpired upon men, and, lo, a few are arising from the dungeons of affliction and sin, they do have hope to call upon the name of the Lord for salvation BECAUSE of God's goodness and mercy which endureth forever! God is still willing to save them, to raise them up, to hallow a small remnant! In the days of David's tribulation they came, all who were "in distress", "in debt", and "discontented" by false Christianity's ungodly rule of darkness and carnality; they "gathered themselves unto" David and "he became a captain over them" (1 Sam. 22:2). By God's enduring mercy, even though the priests were brutally slain by the demonic cruelty of King Saul, David and those with him arose out of obscurity to establish a season of salvation, as men that have spiritual sight, for a wasted, groping, and blind Israelite nation. David gathered the sheep, defended the helpless, and "fed them according to the integrity of his heart; and guided them by the skillfulness of his hands" (Ps. 78:72). From the pit of castaway wrath, salvation did ascend! Into the desert of overwhelming annihilation, behold what rivers of salvation God did send! And what praiseworthy attribute of God was on the lips of David and his comrades, after they were graciously brought on high!?

> "O give thanks unto the LORD; for **He is good; for His mercy endureth for ever**." – 1 Chronicles 16:34

God's mercy endureth forever beyond the endurance of wrath, and now, by God's good graces, David is able to ascend into the courts of God and praise Him before the newly established ark (1 Chron. 15)! So now, in 1 Chronicles 16, David writes the psalm that they sang to God in this day! After the establishment of the Davidic reign, and then, after the establishment of God's reign – the ark of the Covenant in its place – it was then that David *appointed singers* to ever stand before the ark of God – "to give thanks to the LORD, because His mercy endureth for ever" (1Chron. 16:41)! Amazing! Furthermore, David charged all of Israel to pray and praise God this exact way, saying – "O give thanks unto the LORD; for He is good; for His mercy endureth for ever." David commanded Israel seek after a further and more excellent salvation to be wrought in Israel beyond what is presently obtained, and that Israel should pray before God – "And say ye, **Save us, O God of our salvation, and gather us together, and deliver us from the heathen**, that we may give thanks to Thy holy Name, and glory in Thy praise" (1 Chron. 16:34-35). The scattering of Israel amidst the heathen powers evidenced that the Divine wrath of God was kindled, and that sin was frustrating God's promises. "The LORD's hand is not shortened, that it cannot save; neither His ear heavy, that it cannot hear: But your iniquities have separated between you and your God, and your sins have hid His face from you, that He will not hear" (Isa. 59:1-2).

Reader, please review Leviticus 26 & Deuteronomy 28 to understand the Old Covenant promises of God, so that when the psalmist or prophets did write about circumstances wherein one of the promises was not being fulfilled, then you will recognize it and understand that this is because the wrath of God was reacting to the presence of sin in an individual, or in the corporate body of Israelites. Take for example the promise in Deuteronomy 28:7: "The LORD shall cause thine enemies that rise up against thee to be smitten before thy face: they shall come out against thee one way, and flee before thee seven ways." By this we can understand that if Israel was defeated in battle, it was because of the wrath of God responding to the sin of Israel, like it was written again – "The LORD shall cause thee to be smitten before thine enemies: thou shalt go out one way against them, and flee seven ways before them: and shalt be removed into all the kingdoms of the earth" (Deut. 28:25).

When saints like David are in need of salvation from the heathen, they know that it is a sure reward to those who are worthy to receive the fulfillment of the promises of God. David instructed the people to pray, "save us, O God of our salvation, and gather us together, and deliver us from the heathen, **that we may give**

thanks to Thy Holy Name, and glory in Thy praise" (1 Chron. 16:35). His appeal to God for salvific mercy was not for His own sake, or that God would pity them, no, not this! But he prayed that God would love His name and save them for this reason – that "[they] may give thanks to [His] Holy Name, and glory in [His] praise"! Do you pray this way? David had in mind sovereign mercy; do you see it? This is the primary way the psalmists did appeal to God for pity and salvation.

"I have declared **Thy faithfulness** and Thy salvation"
– Psalm 40:10

David was in great straits! He felt as though he was suffocating underneath his own iniquities, and furthermore, heathen men were encroaching upon him (40:12-15). David knew that an alien victory against Israelite armies resulted from God's wrath in response to personal or corporate sin. This psalm recounts how David found deliverance from this "horrible pit" that he was in, and he says – "I waited patiently" and the Lord "heard my cry" (40:1)! What was David's cry? Not that he could never fall, nor was it that mercy and love from God could never discontinue or be withheld. On the contrary, David cried – "withhold not Thou Thy tender mercies from me, O LORD: let Thy lovingkindness and Thy truth continually preserve me" (40:11). Again David cried, "make no tarrying, O my God" (40:17). David understood the faithfulness of God and declared it to the great congregation (40:10); therefore in this psalm, he demonstrated a correct interpretation of God's faithfulness. How is it that Christianity has a completely different understanding of God's faithfulness? Death-like circumstances are described in 40:1-2, 12, so much so that David said – "therefore my heart faileth me." David was pursuing God's faithfulness for the performance of unfulfilled promises, by the appeasement of Divine wrath from its breaching powers, which means, David was seeking safety while yet in real danger.

"**Thy faithfulness**" – Psalm 88:11

God's faithfulness is in view for the psalmist of Psalm 88, but for what cause? At this moment, the psalmist confessed to God, "Thy wrath lieth hard upon me, and Thou hast afflicted me with all Thy waves…Mine eye mourneth by reason of affliction: LORD, I have called daily upon Thee, I have stretched out My hands unto Thee. Wilt Thou shew wonders to the dead? Shall the dead arise and praise Thee? Selah. Shall Thy lovingkindness be declared in the grave? **Or Thy faithfulness in destruction**? Shall Thy wonders be known in the dark? And Thy righteousness in the land of forgetfulness? But unto Thee have I cried, O LORD; and in the morning shall my prayer prevent Thee. LORD, why castest Thou off my soul? Why hidest Thou Thy face from me? I am afflicted and ready to die from my youth up: while I suffer Thy terrors I am distracted. Thy fierce wrath goeth over me; Thy terrors have cut me off" (Ps. 88:7-16). This man of God was drowning in an outpouring of wrath and Divine displeasure, and it was taking him to the point where he was "ready to die!" Thus his appeal was, "shall Thy lovingkindness be declared in the grave? Or **Thy faithfulness** in destruction" (Ps. 88:11)!? His main appeal for perseverance was, "Don't let me die, for Your Name will die with me!" At this point he was not experiencing the faithfulness of God which performs the Covenant promises, but rather, the wrath of God performing its curses, and thus he sought the promises of God through soul-travailing intercessions.

> "Hear my prayer, O LORD, give ear to my supplications: in **Thy faithfulness** answer me, and in **Thy righteousness**" – Psalm 143:1

> "Quicken me, O LORD, for **Thy Name's sake**: for **Thy righteousness' sake**" – Psalm 143:11

David had the faithfulness and righteousness of God in correct interpretation. During the time that he wrote this psalm, he was surrounded by "enemies" which did "afflict [his] soul" (Ps. 143:12), to the point where David was recognizing that God was hiding His face from him in wrath (Ps. 143:7), and therefore "the enemy" had, David says, "smitten my life down to the ground; he hath made me to dwell in darkness, as those that have been long dead" (Ps. 143:3). David knew that if he abode here in this spiritual avalanche of wrath, he would be soon swallowed up by death, and thus he said – "Hear me speedily, O LORD: my spirit faileth: hide not Thy face from me, lest I be like unto them that go down into the pit" (Ps. 143:7). David recognized that God was entering into judgment with him according to his sins, or the sins of Israel, and David understood that if God did not have sovereign mercy, if wrath took its course according to the judgment of holy justice, then, like all the others, David would come to a **full end** in *total annihilation*. Even so, David prayed – "in **Thy faithfulness** answer me, and in **Thy righteousness**. And **enter not into judgment** with Thy servant: for in Thy sight shall no man living be justified" (Ps. 143:1-2). David knew that God's faithfulness and righteousness would be declared forever, but this did not mean that none had ever perished who were formerly saved, but that of the many who were saved and then fell away, not all were judged and destroyed, and these saints, with a chosen multitude in the future, will be the object of God's final and forever righteousness and faithfulness, to perform all of the promises in the END of days. David just wanted to be a part of this holy and elect number who makes it to the END.

> "All Thy commandments are **faithful**: they persecute me wrongfully; help Thou me" – Ps. 119:86

Again in Psalm 119:86, the psalmist reached forth for the promises of God, hoping that he, by them, would be saved. When he wrote the psalm, lo, he was being brought to a *near annihilation* under God's wrath, as David was, and thus he said – "My soul fainteth for Thy salvation: but I hope in Thy word. Mine eyes fail for Thy word, saying, When wilt Thou comfort me? For I am become like a bottle in the smoke; yet do I not forget Thy statutes. How many are the days of Thy servant? when wilt Thou execute judgment on them that persecute me" (Ps. 119:81-84)? Again, the faithfulness of God does not mean that none can perish, or that some cannot be brought under God's wrath presently, and so the psalmist sought the performance of

242

God's promises with heart-rending intercessions.

When most people reckon the faithfulness of God in their life, they do it with mental assent, according to the text that they see written on a page, as if to just quote it, but they do not walk out in the very substance of grace, virtue, and power that the promise of God does provide. They are aloof to this like a drunken man, like a man "beholding his natural face in a glass: for he beholdeth himself, and goeth his way, and straightway forgetteth what manner of man he was" (James 1:23-24). This is a deception! "But whoso looketh into the perfect law of liberty, and continueth therein, he being not a forgetful hearer, but a doer of the work, this man shall be blessed in his deed" (James 1:25). Consequentially, men and women love the promises of God – they sing about them, memorize them, recite them – and lo, they are as powerless as a man without a promise. When I read of biblical men of sound and right conviction, I see that they were on an earnest and fervent pursuit to obtain the performance of Covenant promises, and therefore, with undying energy, they watched to see if any promise was under a present-tense breach, which meant that assaults of outbreaking wrath did exercise individual persons or the corporate nation. Also, I find that they were exercised by God's wrath until it made them say, "My flesh trembleth for fear of Thee; and I am afraid of Thy judgments" (Psalm 119:120).

> *If mercy is the central theme of the Bible, then let us understand also that the near annihilation of God's people is the central theme of the Bible which unlocks the mysteries of mercy – for this is the very point of praise in: "His mercy endureth forever!"*

When these men spoke of, declared, preached on, praised, and prayed for the faithfulness of God, they were not reckoning that they were spiritually safe, always saved, and continually "ok" just where they resided! People reckon the promises of God in a way which they feel means that they have no need to seek after their performance. They do not fear that the wrath of God is a threat to saving promises, and so, they have no fear of the present condition they are in, even if it is damnable. They are lulled to sleep by their heresies of grace, or should I say their heresies of God's faithfulness, so that they don't even know what a damnable condition is, or how to recognize it according to the NT promises. If you do arise into a persevering salvation in the course of your faith, it is by the sovereign grace of God, but it is NOT because God was never angry with you in all the days of your salvific pilgrimage. It is because God's mercy endureth forever, but this does not mean that wrath did not ever burn and pursue after your death and destruction! When you understand the near-annihilating wrath of God, then there will be nothing left that is better to say, but, "His mercy endureth forever," when indeed, finally, you are carried into a salvific position of grace.

When the Temple was built and finished in the days of Solomon, then they brought up the ark of God and put it in the most holy place, and after the priests left the holy place, they and the Levites did sound with the instruments of music "as one" man – "to make one sound to be heard in praising and thanking the LORD; and when they lifted up their voice with the trumpets and cymbals and instruments of musick, and praised the LORD, saying, **For He is good; for His mercy endureth for ever**: THAT THEN the House was **filled with a cloud**, even the House of the LORD; so that the priests could not stand to minister by reason of the cloud: for the glory of the LORD had filled the House of God" (2 Chron. 5:13-14). It is so compelling and soul-humbling for me to see how the Lord loves, foremost of all, this very phrase – "His mercy endureth for ever." There is no other statement of praise that is so repeated in all of scripture! If mercy is the central theme of the Bible, then let us understand also that the near annihilation of God's people is the central theme of the Bible which unlocks the mysteries of mercy – for this is the very point of praise in God's ever enduring mercy!

The Levites praised God with these divinely chosen words, and after Solomon's sermon and the prayer of dedication – "Fire came down from heaven and consumed the burnt offering and the sacrifices; and the glory of the LORD filled the House…And when all the children of Israel saw how the fire came down, and the glory of the LORD upon the House, they bowed themselves with their faces to the ground upon the pavement, and worshipped, and praised the LORD, saying, **For He is good; for His mercy endureth for ever**" (2 Chron. 7:1-3)! Forevermore it is praised, generation to generation, for – "the priests waited on their offices: the Levites also with instruments of musick of the LORD, which David the King had made to praise the LORD, **because His mercy endureth for ever**" (2 Chron. 7:6).

David and now Solomon, with their generations, did praise the Lord for His ever-enduring mercies, and David praised the Lord in the psalm written in 1 Chronicles 16:8-36. In this psalm, David looked upon the promises of the Abrahamic Covenant and praised God for their verity, and for them he also prayed, but this, and the fact that He is praising God that "His mercy endureth for ever" (1 Chron. 16:34), did not mean that none had ever failed the grace of God or come short of the Abrahamic Covenant promises! So also Jehoshaphat, a pursuer of the Covenant given to David, even he praised God as he sought the establishment of the Davidic promises with the very same glory of praise – "**Praise the LORD; for His mercy endureth for ever**" (2 Chron. 20:21) – but this was as he was trying to climb out of the distress of apostasy that he and his generation were born into. He was in the midst the battle when he lifted up this cry! "And when they began to sing and to praise, the LORD set ambushments against the children of Ammon, Moab, and mount Seir, which were come against Judah; and they were smitten" (2 Chron. 20:22). Another time of biblical revival like unto Jehoshaphat was in the days of Ezra, and they all, at the laying of the Temple foundation did shout and praise with the same words of perfect praise!

"And when the builders laid the foundation of the temple of the LORD, they set the priests in their apparel with trumpets, and the Levites the sons of Asaph with cymbals, to praise the LORD, after the ordinance of David king of Israel. And they sang together by course in praising and **giving thanks unto the LORD; because He is good, for His mercy endureth for ever** toward Israel. And all the people shouted with a great shout, when they praised the LORD, because the foundation of the house of the LORD was laid" (Ezra 3:10-11).

Are all of these events historically significant to you? It should enthrall you that such a seal of Divine pleasure and approval is given to this single praise of God. Oh! How much do we owe to the mercy of God!? Now, do you long to tell your Master His praise – "His mercy endureth for ever!" Do you want to learn to sing it in meter to God? Oh, to join the happy throngs of faithful men who sang in generations past, to sing this happy song of God's everlasting mercy which does, all things, outlast! Lo, and behold, at the beginning of FOREVER, look at the consummating praise which shall be sung at the fulfillment of the Davidic Covenant, when it finally has its mysterious establishment at the second coming of Christ:

"The voice of joy, and the voice of gladness, the voice of the Bridegroom, and the voice of the Bride, the voice of them that shall say, Praise the LORD of hosts: **for the LORD is good; for His mercy endureth for ever**: and of them that shall bring the sacrifice of praise into the house of the LORD. **For I will cause to return the captivity of the land, as at the first, saith the LORD**" (Jer. 33:11).

The Lord's mercy endures forever to establish His Covenant of salvation in its final consummation, and therefore men praise God that His mercy and faithfulness endure forever EVEN if, at present, mercy is not presently establishing the Covenant of salvation for regenerate individuals who are born into a backslidden generation. Do you believe that? Ezekiel 20 is like no other chapter in the whole of scripture, but by theme and purpose, there are many other chapters which are devoted to communicate the exact same theme at hand! Such chapters are Nehemiah 9, Deuteronomy 7, Psalm 89, and Psalm 106. By now you know the content of these chapters, but look with me at the very shocking attributes of God in view which I have yet to highlight!

Remember that Deuteronomy 7 addresses the Abrahamic Covenant promises, Psalm 89 the Davidic Covenant promises, and Nehemiah 9 and Psalm 106 address both the Abrahamic and Davidic promises. Each chapter is devoted to communicate how the promises have been breached in the former generation or generations (Deut. 7, Neh. 9, Psalm 106), and/or the promises have been and are being breached at the present generation (Psalm 89, Psalm 106). Furthermore, Psalm 89 and Psalm 106 are entirely devoted to the acknowledgment of the promises of God in the Covenants, which means that the psalmists rehearse what God said comparatively to what God did, but most importantly, these psalms are an intercessory lamentation for the Covenants that were presently breached, broken, cast off, and destroyed in their day; thus they cried out for salvation, but what is so amazing about the psalms is that they still praised the Lord for His faithfulness and mercy in that it is FOREVER ENDURING while they were in the midst of a breach of promise, while wrath was breaking forth, and they are bewildered in perplexity!

PSALM 89 - THE DAVIDIC COVENANT –

"I will sing of the mercies of the LORD for ever: with my mouth will I make known Thy faithfulness to all generations. Fro I have said, Mercy shall be built up for ever: Thy faithfulness shalt Thou establish in the heavens" (Psalm 89:1-2).

"And the heavens shall praise Thy wonders, O LORD: Thy faithfulness also in the congregation of the saints" (Psalm 89:5).

"O LORD God of hosts, who is a strong LORD like unto Thee? Or to Thy faithfulness round about Thee" (Psalm 89:8)?

"But My faithfulness and My mercy shall be with him: and in My Name shall his horn be exalted" (Psalm 89:24).

Amazing! Is it not? They were singing of the mercy and faithfulness of God, but they had no idea where it was, and they were in the utter agony and oblivion over how it was gone, how it failed, and the Covenant Throne was fallen. The praise does acknowledge a faith though, beyond the NOW, faith in a FOREVER which shall inevitably arise. Would it rise again in their lifetime? They didn't know…just like the praises of God which Habakkuk uttered in chapter 3, they pled – "in wrath remember mercy." They desired mercy in that hour for themselves, that God would not pass them by, that they might be hid in the day of wrath, but even though they lived on in a doomed generation, they still sang and praised the Lord for the incorruptible, everlasting, and sure salvation!

Habakkuk 3:16-19

"When I heard, my belly trembled; my lips quivered at the voice: rottenness entered into my bones, and I trembled in myself, that I might rest in the day of trouble: when he cometh up unto the people, he will invade them with his troops. Although the fig tree shall not blossom, neither shall fruit be in the vines; the labour of the olive shall fail, and the fields shall yield no meat; the flock shall be cut off from the fold, and there shall be no herd in the stalls: Yet I will rejoice in the LORD, I will joy in the God of my salvation. The LORD God is my strength, and He will make my feet like hinds' feet, and He will make me to walk upon mine high places. To the chief singer on my stringed instruments."

This is amazing to me! "Seek ye the LORD, all ye meek of the earth, which have wrought His judgment; seek righteousness, seek meekness: **it may be** ye shall be hid in the day of the LORD'S anger" (Zeph. 2:3). When you enter your church assembly and "sing of the mercies of the LORD for ever," what is so forever and faithful about the mercy of God that you are singing about? To the psalmists, it is not that those of the regenerate multitude can never fall away from or fail to obtain the promises of salvation, but it is that God will eventually and finally, in a great consummation, fulfill all the promises in the final resurrection, and thence changelessly, in this, forevermore.

PSALM 106 - THE ABRAHAMNIC & DAVIDIC COVENANT-

"Praise ye the LORD. O give thanks unto the LORD; for He is good: for His mercy endureth for ever" (Ps. 106:1).

This psalm is like as Psalm 89. Please read Psalm 106:4-5, 47-48. The psalmist expressed his fervent appeal for salvation, because he was presently under the wrath of God. He prayed for salvation, hoping that God may repent and remember the Covenant for him. The last verses of the psalm are prayers for saving grace, but unlike other psalms, this one does not end with a confident reckoning or a triumphant proclamation that God has heard, or will hear his prayer unto salvation. The psalm ends without any evidence that the man is confident that he is, or will be, saved. Therefore, even while he was presently under the wrath of God, to my amazement, the psalmist's opening line was – "His mercy endureth for ever!" This is the exact same opening used in Psalm 89. The psalmist desired for God to remember His Covenant (Lev. 26:42), which also is meant to include the man's personal salvation therein. The psalmist rehearsed how God's mercies had been magnified in past circumstances where God's people were wayward and backsliding (like as the law commands that a man should do, see Psalm 78:5-7)…but specifically, the psalmist rehearsed the **multitude of mercies** which are in God, how the psalmist said, "we have sinned with our fathers, we have committed iniquity, we have done wickedly" (Ps. 106:6) from the beginning of the Abrahamic Covenant, and after salvation in the Abrahamic Covenant, they "tempted God" to their great destruction, so much so that God "should destroy them" and did destroy many (Ps. 106:23), and yet, by the riches of His glorious mercy, God "saved" (Ps. 106:8) at the first, passed over great judgments presently and progressively, and continued to save a remnant, but lo, it was because Moses "stood before Him in the breach to turn away His wrath" (Ps. 106:23). After Moses' death (Ps. 106:33), it appears that the psalmist traced the future generations through Joshua, through the Judges, and up into and through the Davidic Covenant, until the final dispersion (I conjecture), and the psalmist recognized how many times Israel rebelled and deserved total annihilation (Ps. 106:34-43)…but God did not totally annihilate, and He did rather hear and save

247

His people when they were laden with "affliction,", and from there lifted up the intercessory "cry" for salvation (Ps. 106:44). The psalmist recognizes that this cry and answer of God for salvation was the praise of God's glory, that He "remembered for them His Covenant, and repented according to **the multitude of His mercies**" (Ps. 106:45). For this reason, being instructed by the near annihilation and scarce salvation of God's people throughout the centuries, the psalmist praised God's mercy, that it is a great "multitude" of mercies that "endureth for ever" (Ps. 106:45, 1)! Therefore the psalmist had hope that, though he was not presently saved, God may repent from destroying wrath and save him as he called upon Him. Therefore the psalmist ended the psalm with this uplifted cry – "Save us, O LORD our God, and gather us from among the heathen, to give thanks unto Thy Holy Name, and triumph in Thy praise. Blessed be the LORD God of Israel **from everlasting to everlasting**: and let all the people say, Amen. Praise ye the LORD" (Ps. 106:47-48). What is so good about God, what is thankworthy and praiseworthy, insomuch that it can be said – "His mercy endureth for ever" (Ps. 106:1)? NOT ALL of the regenerate people God are castaways! Nay, shockingly, a small remnant is spared for present and/or consummating salvation! "They shall inherit the land for ever…" (Isa. 60:21)! Is that what is amazing about the grace of God to you?

Deuteronomy 7 - THE ABRAHAMIC COVENANT-

"because the LORD loved you…" – Deut. 7:8
"because He would keep the oath which He had sworn unto your fathers…" – Deut. 7:8
 "He is God, the faithful God" – Deut. 7:9
"which keepeth Covenant and mercy" – Deut. 7:9

This **faithfulness** of God is mentioned in reference to the following: the parents of the audience that God was herein speaking to did fall away from their salvation and were lost, and God's mercy in its promised oath and covenant-keeping faithfulness were magnified in this very specific way – that the generation in Covenant with God was raised up for salvation in the stead of their parents! Israel did rather deserve total annihilation! God desired, and spoke to accomplish, a total annihilation of them (Numbers 14:11-12), but He did not do this, because He is an oath and Covenant-keeping God of mercy and faithfulness! Now, what is so loving, merciful, faithful, and oath-keeping about God? It is that some, even that anyone, even a small remnant of the whole multitude of regenerate persons were saved, in your generation, and/or in the end of time, and it is not that none can be lost, or fall away, who were of the number that were formerly saved! Furthermore, God forewarned this generation that if they did not obey His commandments which secured holiness from the Canaanite nations (see Deut. 7:11-12, 1-5, 25-26), even these people who are the remaining and preserved remnant, He would destroy "suddenly" (Deut. 7:4).

You see, God had made a name for Himself in the castaway-wrath He had

248

shown to the former generation, and He intended to keep the fame of this Name, that He – "repayeth them that hate Him to their face, to destroy them: He will not be slack to him that hateth Him, He will repay him to his face" (Deut. 7:10). This is why Moses titled the offspring of this reprobated generation with such downgrading terms, saying – "Behold, ye are risen up in your fathers' stead, an increase of sinful men, to augment yet the fierce anger of the LORD toward Israel" (Num. 32:14). Moses warned them, "if ye turn away from after Him [God], He will yet again leave them [Israel] in the wilderness; and ye shall destroy all this people" (Num. 32:15). Moses affirmed the surety of God's reprobating wrath as a dangerous potential, if indeed they sin in this way. Moses said – be sure of your eternal security? – NO! – He said, "be sure your sin will find you out" (Num. 32:23)! Turning back to Deuteronomy 7, see how the language here spoke very specifically that God would keep His Covenant and oath to the magnification of His mercy and faithfulness by keeping the next generation alive, and even they are warned of reprobation. Later generations came to understand the mercy and faithfulness of God by this very example in Deuteronomy 7. You can see this in their prayers, praises, and prophetic books, uttering the exact same meaning that is taught in Deuteronomy 7. Through the centuries of experience with God's Covenants, the people of God come to confess all the attributes of God as titles to His Name – NOT JUST MERCY! They said, the Lord is "The Great, The Mighty, and The Terrible God, Who keepest Covenant and mercy" (Neh. 9:32)! Nehemiah 9 is a comprehensive summary of centuries of Church history, and, as a foreground that sets the stage for the glory of God's everlasting, Covenant keeping mercy, Nehemiah rehearses centuries of near annihilation. Oh! It is the multitude of God's Covenant-keeping mercies that salvific mercy is even available at all for latter generations, even after God did reprobate former generations…thus God is "terrible" and merciful, and lo, behold, He has "goodness and severity" (Rom. 11:22)!

Amazingly, to the staggering of my soul into astonishment and worship, the ever enduring mercy of God is praised in backslidden generations even while there is no manifestation of mercy and no sign of relenting wrath, and lo, the promises remain breached! Why is this? How happy I am to declare to my reader their secret! These brethren of old did know that, *one day*, though it is not *their day*, the promises will be fulfilled, or in other words, though wrath is burning now it will not burn forever. Wrath seems like it burns forever, but Oh! God's mercy endures forever! Yea, there is a greater and longer lasting energy than wrath, at least for God's chosen people, and that is, "His mercy endureth for ever!"

God's Love in Creation:	God's Salvific Love in the Abrahamic Covenant:	The Past, Present, & Final Possession of the Land:
Verses 5-9	Verses 10-20	Verses 21-24

Psalm 136:1-26

(1) O give thanks unto the LORD; for He is good: **for His mercy endureth for ever.**

(2) O give thanks unto the God of gods: **for His mercy endureth for ever.**

(3) O give thanks to the Lord of lords: **for His mercy endureth for ever.**

(4) To Him Who alone doeth great wonders: **for His mercy endureth for ever.**

(5) To Him that by wisdom made the heavens: **for His mercy endureth for ever.**

(6) To Him that stretched out the earth above the waters: **for His mercy endureth for ever.**

(7) To Him that made great lights: **for His mercy endureth for ever:**

(8) The sun to rule by day: **for His mercy endureth for ever:**

(9) The moon and stars to rule by night: **for His mercy endureth for ever.**

(10) To Him that smote Egypt in their firstborn: **for His mercy endureth for ever:**

(11) And brought out Israel from among them: **for His mercy endureth for ever:**

(12) With a strong hand, and with a stretched out arm: **for His mercy endureth for ever.**

(13) To Him which divided the Red sea into parts: **for His mercy endureth for ever:**

(14) And made Israel to pass through the midst of it: **for His mercy endureth for ever:**

(15) But overthrew Pharaoh and his host in the Red sea: **for His mercy endureth for ever.**

(16) To Him which led his people through the wilderness: **for His mercy endureth for ever.**

(17) To Him which smote great kings: **for His mercy endureth for ever:**

(18) And slew famous kings: **for His mercy endureth for ever:**

(19) Sihon king of the Amorites: **for His mercy endureth for ever:**

(20) And Og the king of Bashan: **for His mercy endureth for ever:**

(21) And gave their land for an heritage: **for His mercy endureth for ever:**

(22) Even an heritage unto Israel his servant: **for His mercy endureth for ever.**

(23) Who remembered us in our low estate: **for His mercy endureth for ever:**

(24) And hath redeemed us from our enemies: **for His mercy endureth for ever.**

(25) Who giveth food to all flesh: **for His mercy endureth for ever.**

(26) O give thanks unto the God of heaven: **for His mercy endureth for ever.**

In every verse, the psalmist exalts this single phrase of praise, for, behold, it is to most perfectly describe the gracious powers in God which motivate a continued salvation! He speaks of the goodness of God in creation – mankind in their created beginning – the goodness of God in the salvation of Israel from Egypt unto the possession of the land, past, present, and final, and he praises the situation of need which God attended to with saving mercy – "Who remembered us in our low estate: for His mercy endureth for ever: And hath redeemed us from our enemies: for His mercy endureth for ever" (136:23-24) – all the way to newly created mankind in their end. Therefore, adjure thee, ye saints! As you wrestle for *perfection* in our holy pursuit for present progressive salvation in God, let us learn to pray as David prayed, wrestle as David wrestled, and win Covenant graces as David won them, and let us so conclude the chapter of our present troubles like him, and, lo, also the end of our lives – "[7] Though I walk in the midst of trouble, Thou wilt revive me: Thou shalt stretch forth Thine hand against the wrath of mine enemies, and Thy right hand shall save me. [8] The LORD will **perfect** that which concerneth me: **Thy mercy, O LORD, endureth for ever:** forsake not the works of Thine own hands" (Psalm 138:7-8).

THE RIGHTEOUS
JUDGMENT OF GOD
CHAPTER 11

"Children that will not lie" – Isaiah 63:8

God speaks of His people that they are "children that will not lie: <u>SO</u> He was their Savior" (Isa. 63:8), but He was not always their Savior...as the latter half of the text in Isaiah 63 describes, before long, God turned to be their "enemy" (Isa. 63:10) - and for what? This was "The Righteous Judgment of God." *If God's people turn against Him, He will turn against them.* If they become His enemy, then He will become their enemy. "The LORD is with you, <u>WHILE</u> ye be with Him; and if ye seek Him, He will be found of you; but if ye forsake Him, He will forsake you" (2 Chron. 15:2). What is the righteousness of this judgment? Let Paul declare it to us:

> "Or despisest thou the riches of His goodness and forbearance
> and longsuffering; not knowing that the goodness of God leadeth
> thee to repentance? But after thy hardness and impenitent heart
> treasurest up unto thyself wrath against the day of wrath and
> revelation of <u>the righteous judgment of God</u>; **Who will render to**
> **every man according to his deeds**: To them who by patient
> continuance in well doing seek for glory and honour and
> immortality, eternal life: But unto them that are contentious, and
> do not obey the truth, but obey unrighteousness, indignation and
> wrath, Tribulation and anguish, upon every soul of man that
> doeth evil, of the Jew first, and also of the Gentile; But glory,
> honour, and peace, to every man that worketh good, to the Jew
> first, and also to the Gentile: **For there is no respect of persons**
> **with God**." (Rom 2:4-11)

The righteous judgment of God is that He will "render to every man **according to his deeds**," without **respecting** a man's person and race. Compare "The Righteous Judgment of God" with what was said concerning eternal, elective mercies, which is, "Mercy On Whom I Will Have Mercy": It is written, "Ye shall know that I am the LORD, when I have wrought with you for My Name's sake, **not according to your wicked ways, nor according to your corrupt doings**" (Ezek. 20:44). In the one place (Rom. 2:4-11), God is magnifying the comprehensible *righteousness* and *justice* of His judgment in the salvation (Rom. 2:7 & 10) and condemnation (Rom. 2:8-9) of individuals, which He declares to be a judgment according to a man's deeds, but the other place (Ezek. 20:44) is magnifying elective mercy, the choice of God for salvation in an incomprehensible way which *shatters* our comprehension of justice in salvation and condemnation – a judgment which is, God says, "**not** according to your wicked ways, **nor** according to your corrupt doings" (Ezek. 20:44). "The Righteous Judgment of God" in the scriptures refers to the humanly comprehensible form of God's judgments for salvation & condemnation, and because it is comprehensible, it is therefore *God in the ways of man*. See the following table so as to refresh your mind of the consistent deeds wrought by God from two separate and contradicting ways.

God in the Ways of God	God in the Ways of Man
Irresistible will, word, and counsel.	Resistible will, word, and counsel.
❖ Influential through interior capacities to save.	❖ Influential through exterior capacities to save.
Incomprehensible justice of condemnation.	Comprehensible justice of condemnation.
Incomprehensible justice of salvation.	Comprehensible justice of salvation.
Changeless and eternal counsel, will, mind, emotion, and word.	Changing and temporary counsel, will, mind, emotion, and word.

Do you remember the different aspects of God portrayed in the separate portions of scripture, each one devoted to a different snapshot of the work of God in different *ways*? For example, Exodus 1:7-10 appears to be the full and complete account of when and how the Israelites came to be enslaved by the Egyptians; however, Psalm 105:23-25 shows the sovereign hand of God working behind the scenes in the events chronicled in Exodus 1:7-10, thus revealing that God was working in a secret and incomprehensible way to establish His counsel by influencing the hearts of men, which is, the influence of *interior capacities* within man to save or condemn. On the one hand, in Exodus 1:7-10, we can see the guilt and righteous condemnation of the Egyptians in that they hated and enslaved Israel, thus we would understand why God would condemn them in "The Righteous Judgment of God." However, in Psalm 105:23-25 we can see the sovereignty of God over their heart, will, and deeds, and that God's irresistible will and counsel controlled the will and counsel of men, but of course, when we see that none can nor did resist God's sovereign will, then it seems that the righteousness in justice was disannulled. Therefore men are compelled to ask, "Why doth He yet find fault? For who hath resisted His will" (Rom. 9:19)?

This instance with the Exodus generation is doubly emphasized from two dimensions, but so are most weighty matters of significance, matters like those dealing with the condemnation and salvation of generations and dispensations. As

Exodus 1:7-10 is an expression of the works of men in the ways of men without the secret of God's higher ways chronicled beside it, so it is in Isaiah 63:7-19. Likewise, Psalm 105:23-25 is an expression of the work of God (God in the ways of God) determining the works of the men that were chronicled in Exodus 1:7-10; in similar ways, so it is with Deuteronomy 32 in comparison to Isaiah 63, but Deuteronomy 32 highlights some other aspects of sovereignty besides *determination*. Both chapters (Deuteronomy 32 and Isaiah 63) are addressing the future captivity which will come upon God's people, but each one presents an entirely different aspect of God's ways and works in the matter (God in the ways of God & God in the ways of man).

Both chapters reveal the rebellion of Israel as the source of God's anger and righteous judgment against them (thus both present this aspect of judgment in the ways of man). However, in both of the chapters God said two different things:

> "**I said,** I would scatter them into corners, I would make the remembrance of them to cease from among men: Were it not that I feared the wrath of the enemy, lest their adversaries should behave themselves strangely, and lest they should say, Our hand is high, and the LORD hath not done all this" (Deut. 32:26-27).

> "For **He said,** Surely they are My people, children that will not lie: so He was their Savior" (Isaiah 63:8).

In Isaiah 63:8, God is relating to them in a genuine love and devotion, as if He does not know that they will eventually lie, as if He is limited in His abilities from the foreknowledge and determination of the future – and all of this magnifies the genuineness of God's desire to save His people, that He, at the first, *only* desired to save them and *never desired* to destroy them. God was relating to them as if He did not "know" the "imagination" of their heart, that they were liars, and that they would depart from Him for idolatry and rebellion, but God speaks in Deuteronomy 32 from another *glory* of consciousness wherein He exercises Himself in *omniscience*. God, in Deuteronomy 32, *declared the end from the beginning*, demonstrating His complete foreknowledge of their eventual apostasy, thus He says: "**I know their imagination which they go about, <u>even now</u>, before I have brought them into the land which I sware**" (Deut. 31:21). In fact, the entire song of Deuteronomy 32 is sung to put the children of Israel in remembrance of how God knew these things beforehand and how He testified to them it would happen, and this makes it all the more appalling that Israel will go on to do the wickedness described in the song. Those who were alive at the time when the song was first sung, and those in generations to come, all are extraordinarily without excuse because of this, and when they commit this eventual rebellion, they will do it by ignoring the witness of this song. Being doubly warned, they are doubly conscious; thus they are doubly condemned. God explicitly told Moses of their eventual treachery, saying:

> "And the LORD said unto Moses, Behold, thou shalt sleep with thy fathers; and **this people will rise up, and go a whoring after the gods of**

the strangers of the land, whither they go to be among them, and will forsake Me, and break My covenant which I have made with them. Then My anger shall be kindled against them in that day, and **I will forsake them**, and **I will hide My face** from them, and they shall be devoured, and many evils and troubles shall befall them; so that they will say in that day, Are not these evils come upon us, because our God is not among us? And I will surely hide My face in that day for all the evils which they shall have wrought, in that they are turned unto other gods. Now therefore write ye this song for you, and teach it the children of Israel: put it in their mouths, **that this song may be a witness for Me against the children of Israel**. For when I shall have brought them into the land which I sware unto their fathers, that floweth with milk and honey; and they shall have eaten and filled themselves, and waxen fat; then will they turn unto other gods, and serve them, and provoke Me, and break My covenant. And it shall come to pass, when many evils and troubles are befallen them, that **this song shall testify against them as a witness**; for it shall not be forgotten out of the mouths of their seed: **for I know their imagination which they go about, <u>even now</u>, before I have brought them into the land which I sware**" (Deut. 31:16-21).

My reader, please carefully note the song of Moses in Deuteronomy 32, and read it. This approach of God toward the rebellion of Israel contrasts Isaiah 63, each representing contrary perspectives in God's mind. It magnifies the treachery of God's people, God's foreknowledge (God in the ways of God) and holy hatred of their sin which is to come, and then at this time, before the crimes are committed, there is justice alive in God, because He sees and experiences this coming apostasy that is in the future, even now, because God is outside of time. Therefore, before the crimes are committed, God speaks of *His desire to fully annihilate them*, and the fact that He experiences the future events of apostasy now, even before they actually happen, we can see that *the just wrath in God is in magnification*. Thus He said: "**I said**, I would scatter them into corners, I would make the remembrance of them to cease from among men" (Deut. 32:26). God did "repent Himself for His servants" – but it was for *the glory of His own Name* – thus the exultant aim of this passage is the sovereign relations of God toward Israel in the light of their rebellion, His foreknowledge and therefore longsuffering of it, and how it required the justice of total annihilation. That is why He "**said**" what He "**said**"! Like as the "I said" of Deuteronomy 32, so also in Isaiah 48 God reaffirms His approach to Israel's eventual apostasy with the same high powers of foreknowledge in use, thus making plain His **ever-present desire to totally destroy them**, which in turn magnifies the remaining reason why He would even save them in the beginning and also thereafter their apostasy. Read the three verses in Deuteronomy, 31:21 & 32:26-27 and compare them with Isaiah 48:4, 8, & 9-11, and then read the entire passage of Isaiah 48:3-12 as a whole, and you will see the purpose of the song of Moses enlarged before you.

"I know their imagination which they go about, <u>even now,</u> before I have brought them into the land which I sware" (Deut. 31:21).

"I knew that thou art obstinate, and thy neck is as an iron sinew.... for I knew that thou wouldest deal very treacherously, and wast called a transgressor from the womb" (Isa. 48:4, 8).

"I said, I would scatter them into corners, I would make the remembrance of them to cease from among men: Were it not that I feared the wrath of the enemy, lest their adversaries should behave themselves strangely, and lest they should say, Our hand is high, and the LORD hath not done all this" (Deut. 32:26-27).

"For My name's sake will I defer Mine anger, and for My praise will I refrain for thee, that I cut thee not off. Behold, I have refined thee, but not with silver; I have chosen thee in the furnace of affliction. For Mine own sake, even for Mine own sake, will I do it: for how should My Name be polluted? And I will not give My glory unto another" (Isa. 48:9-11).

"I have declared the former things from the beginning; and they went forth out of My mouth, and I shewed them; I did them suddenly, and they came to pass. **Because I knew that thou art obstinate, and thy neck is an iron sinew, and thy brow brass; I have even from the beginning declared it to thee; before it came to pass I shewed it thee**: lest thou shouldest say, Mine idol hath done them, and my graven image, and my molten image, hath commanded them... **for I knew that thou wouldest deal very treacherously, and wast called a transgressor from the womb. For my name's sake will I defer Mine anger, and for my praise will I refrain for thee, that I cut thee not off.** Behold, I have refined thee, but not with silver; I have chosen thee in the furnace of affliction. **For Mine own sake**, even **for Mine own sake**, will I do it: for how should My Name be polluted? And I will not give my glory unto another. Hearken unto Me, O Jacob and Israel, **my called**; I am He; I am the first, I also am the last" (Isaiah 48:3-12).

God speaks of telling them this foreknowledge-empowered prophecy for the express purpose that they would give Him the glory for keeping them alive, being enabled to recognize that these things are of Him because they were exactly declared from the beginning by Him, before it all came to pass. When mercy is sinking down into the mouth of justice and hell, nearly swallowed and gone, there is only one foundation Rock which is able to keep a remnant above ground! God lifts up the banner, the crux of the matter, the hallowed title which is continually raised up through the centuries – HIS NAME – and it is the only reason God's people were not fully annihilated. Let everything that hath breath praise the Lord. To this let all men give thanks. God saved and saves because ***God was jealous for the reputation of His own Name*** amongst the heathen, who, God says, would surely glory over God if He used their instrumentality to *fully* destroy *all* of His people. God declares He will prevent this, and not only this, but He will heroically end man's earthly history, He declares, by drawing His sword of wrath to *fully annihilate the heathen*, and so, snuffing out their glory over God when He, by them, did almost entirely annihilate His people. What He would not do to His people, He will do to them.

The "**I said**" of Deuteronomy 32:26 speaks of the desire in God to fully annihilate His people, but the "**He said**" in Isaiah 63:8 reveals how God did not want to destroy them at all, and on the contrary, He tenderly, fervently, and in trustful hope desired to save them – being fully minded and devoted to this cause without any guile that the foreknowledge of their eventual treachery would incite in a human being. This is a clash of desires and wills from two separate ways in God, and thus, God did ***ever*** desire to fully annihilate them because of the foreknowledge of their apostasy, and at the same time He desired to save and ***never*** annihilate any of them. Deuteronomy 32:26 speaks of ***God's expectation*** of their rebellion, and therefore, His desire to fully annihilate them, and Isaiah 63:8 speaks of ***God's expectation*** that they will not rebel, His desire to fully save them and never annihilate them, and thus the crime of their rebellion against God is magnified, vilified all the more, for it grossly crosses God's good covenant and faithful love. God said that they "will not lie", and He meant it, was intent upon it in sincerity and truth, and this is a coexisting will ***simultaneously*** at work within God, even though it is in contradiction with the other will in God. Though this is impossible within man, it is not impossible within God, and shame on us if we simplify the Godhead to be limited to a man's capacities of willing, and thus, we would say that both of these wills are not genuine because it does not make sense to us, because it is not capable in us, because it is impossible for us to have contradicting, genuine wills, even if we were humanly enabled to exercise foreknowledge and sovereign determination. We would do well to avoid the woeful indictment, "Thou thoughtest that I was altogether such an one as thyself" (Ps. 50).

Though different aspects of the Lord's will are magnified in each passage, the account traces the same event of the eventual apostasy unto the captivities. Deuteronomy 32:5 speaks of the dispossessing of His children like as Isaiah 63 gives the account of His disowning of them. "Is He not thy Father that bought thee," Deut. 32:6 declares, but He dispossesses them. Like as this, in the account of Isaiah 63, the people cry to God with the same paternal acknowledgment and appeal - "Look down from heaven, and behold from the habitation of Thy holiness and of Thy glory: where is Thy zeal and Thy strength, the sounding of Thy bowels and of Thy tender mercies toward me? Are they restrained? Doubtless **Thou art our Father**, though Abraham be ignorant of us, and Israel acknowledge us not: **Thou, O LORD, art our Father**, our Redeemer; Thy name is from everlasting. O LORD, why hast Thou made us to err from Thy ways and hardened our heart from Thy fear? Return for Thy servants' sake, the tribes of Thine inheritance" (Isaiah 63:15-17). This is a frightening experience of reprobation.

Seeing that sovereign mercy (God in the ways of God) soars above the realm of man's comprehensible justice (that God does not save according to man's deeds), therefore God's contradicting and simultaneous will/work (God in the ways of man) would make clear the deeds of God toward men in the realm of comprehensible justice (which is a justice according to man's deeds), and when God relates to men in this realm, it is to teach and magnify this aspect of God – the understandable "**Righteous Judgment of God**." Therefore in Isaiah 63, since it is in the realm of God's will, counsel, and word, *in the ways of man*, which is limited from omniscience (at work through foreknowledge) and omnipotence (at work through determination to bring His saying to pass so as to make Israel faithful), God is seeking that men would understand exactly which sins would demand reprobation – which must be exceedingly sinful sins – but what is more exceedingly sinful than a child transgressing and defying the Paternal love of God to His children? The righteousness and justice of God to cast away His own children, which is a disowning of them, is a breach of the affections He formerly had in the Paternity of His Fatherhood (Isa. 63:15-16), because they breached their childlike trust, which is love toward God, and now, God turns upon them as His "enemy" (Isa. 63:10) and ignores their cries (Isa. 63:15) as He hides His face (Deut. 32:20) and hardens their hearts (Isa. 63:17). Can you see what deeds of Israel requited this response of God back to them? I hinted at it at the beginning:

"Children that will not lie" – Isaiah 63:8

According to the counsel of God in the ways of man, God covenanted with Israel with the conditional boundaries that they would be saved as long as they remained faithful to Him, and as much as they did not forsake Him, He would not forsake them. His Paternal love and familial security would remain as much as their childlike love, trust, and devotion remained. God covenanted with them on the basis that they would not lie to Him – but they DID. What would God require as justice for His child who, in this way, has become a liar? How exactly would it be phrased? First, let's trace the logic of the righteousness in God's justice from its scriptural beginning, and then we will be prepared to understand the edicts of retribution for backsliding and lying Christians.

The Righteous Judgment of God – By Principle: Horizontally & Vertically

Breach for Breach

"And if a man cause a blemish in his neighbour; **as he hath done, so shall it be done to him**; Breach for breach, eye for eye, tooth for tooth: as he hath caused a blemish in a man, so shall it be done to him again" (Lev. 24:19-20).

The righteous judgment of God in principle is, as formerly stated, "as he

258

hath done, so shall it be done to him," which is, whatsoever he did, to the degree he did it, let it be returned upon him. By principle, this was put in *practice* all across the scriptures and into the New Testament (Ex. 21:23-25, Deut. 19:21). This is the biblical presentation of "the righteous judgment of God". The scripture cited above, and the others mentioned in the parentheses, refer to the recompense of the law for a situation of two men, as a man "hath done" to another man, and likewise, other **horizontal** circumstances and crimes "man to man", but what is the principle of justice when a man sins against God **vertically**? By vertically I mean, "man to God"? What is the righteousness of justice from "man to God"?

It is said of God, "Surely He **scorneth** the **scorners**: but He giveth grace unto the lowly" (Prov. 3:34). "He," meaning God, scorns those that scorn Him, but in what way? Some of you may be hearing Elijah's mocking voice ringing in your memory when He mocked the prophets of Baal at their momentous face-off against each other before all the eyes of Israel, who all watched on under the grip of anticipation. This principle, written in Proverbs 3:34, is *not* **horizontal** *but* **vertical**, meaning not "man to man" justice but "God to man" justice. It is how God responds to the deeds of men when they are sinful towards Him. As righteous justice was horizontally, "breach for breach, eye for eye, tooth for tooth" (Lev. 24:19-20), so it is vertically; thus if a man scorns God, then God scorns him – *scorn for scorn*! Paralleling the context of Proverbs 3:34, Proverbs 1:20-33 is a real and lively example wherein God scorns the scorners, and He does it in the very words of inspired scripture. With strong and yet lamentable pleading, God calls out to scorners, "How long, ye simple ones, will ye love simplicity? And **the scorners delight in their scorning**, and fools hate knowledge" (Prov. 1:22) – but they refused and rejected His call, and so, they rejected repentance and salvation. Therefore they are scorners, thus God, according to justice, declares their woeful recompense for their behavior towards Him, and says:

> "**Because I have called, and ye refused;** I have stretched out My
> hand, and no man regarded; But ye have set at nought all My
> counsel, and would none of My reproof: **I ALSO will laugh at
> your calamity; I will mock when your fear cometh**; when your
> fear cometh as desolation, and your destruction cometh as a
> whirlwind; when distress and anguish cometh upon you. **Then
> shall they call upon Me, but I will not answer**; they shall seek
> Me early, but they shall not find Me: For that they hated
> knowledge, and did not choose the fear of the LORD" (Prov.
> 1:24-29).

These persons are scorners who *delight in scorning* (Prov. 1:22), and what does scorning look like <u>exactly</u>? They are *laughing* and *mocking* even though God is **calling out for them**. God's vertical recompense to them is a reflection of what they did to Him. He says, "I ALSO will **laugh**… I will **mock**," which is to say, He also will scorn like as they scorned. In this passage we can see that vertical justice is –

scorn for scorn, laugh for laugh, mock for mock, and refusal of call for refusal of call. God called to them and they refused His call, as it was said, "Because I have called, and ye refused," thus God did to them just "as [they] hath done" - "Then shall they call upon Me, but I will not answer" (Prov. 1:28). This saying, *refusal of call for refusal of call*, could be rephrased to, *silence for silence, rejection for rejection,* and *forsaking for forsaking.* Thus it is written, "The LORD is with you, while ye be with Him; and if ye seek Him, He will be found of you; but if ye forsake Him, He will forsake you" (2 Ch. 15:2). It is a fearful thing for the Lord to laugh and scorn! It is nearly inconceivable to the human mind that God would execute the justice of destruction upon sinners with the face of holy laughter, mockery, and scorning, even while they whimper for mercy and plead for pity. This expression of God is a high secret in God's awful justice against sin! Until sinners everlastingly cry in teeth-gnashing agony so as to never die, God will not be satisfied! While sinners have rest, God is in unrest; therefore the fires of that eternal Lake shall never diminish. Do you understand why? God is, "Holy, Holy, Holy, [and He is the] Lord God Almighty" (Rev. 4:8)! He will be happy, and heaven will shout Hallelujah when the Lake of Fire is finally filled with those predestinated souls of unrepentant sinners. "The Lord shall laugh at him [the sinner]: for He seeth that his day is coming" (Ps. 37:13).

This vertical justice of God fuels a responding and repaying of sin upon men for how they paid Him. This was a feared and well-known expectation in biblical saints, observable throughout the centuries of biblical history. David declared of the Lord:

> "With the **merciful** Thou wilt shew Thyself **merciful**; with an
> **upright** man Thou wilt shew Thyself **upright**; With the **pure**
> Thou wilt shew Thyself **pure**; and with the **froward** Thou wilt
> shew Thyself **froward**" (Ps. 18:25-26).

This is to say, furthermore, mercy for mercy, uprightness for uprightness, pureness for pureness, and frowardness for frowardness – in its vertical context of **man to God**, and mirrored back by God – **God to man**. God returns and visits those things, which are done to Him, back to man. Mercy, uprightness, and pureness are all vertical responses of God to men: men who live mercifully, upright, and pure toward God and man. Are you seeing the principle? God reflects the same character and deeds which man is doing toward Him ("as he hath done, so shall it be done to him", Lev. 24:19-20). We looked at how God would *scorn* a man, but are there any other ways in which we could examine how God would be *froward to a froward* man, as is said in Psalm 18:26? God scorning a man is breathtaking to imagine, but what about God being froward to a man? To be *froward* is to be: "perverse, ungovernable, and not willing to yield or comply with what is required" (Webster's 1828 Dictionary). The deeds of God's frowardness I intend to exhaustively address, but the verse below shows for a good introduction:

> "**Do good, O LORD, unto** *those that be* **good,** and *to them that*
> *are* upright in their hearts. As for such as turn aside unto their

crooked ways, <u>the LORD shall lead them forth</u> with the **workers of iniquity**: *but* peace *shall be* upon Israel" (Psalm 125:4-5).

God is *good for good*, and for the wicked, "the LORD shall <u>lead them forth</u> with the workers of iniquity," but who are these wicked men? They are such men that do "turn aside" – a turning which is a turn from *uprightness, purity, mercy,* and *goodness*; thus it is a turn from God, and therefore God turns from them, *turn for turn*, and leaves them to **the deception** of their sins, which is to say, "the LORD **shall lead them forth** with workers of iniquity." Did you know that God can lead people in the deception of their own sins? DECEPTION, and unrecoverable demise therein! Notice: This is a turn for turn in God's righteous justice toward them who turned from uprightness, namely, the regenerate turned back.

According to the glory of God's higher ways, a man cannot *continue* to be deceived by the sin-soaked counsel from his own heart, unless God first "gave them up unto their own hearts' lust" (Psa. 81:12). God can enjoin men to deception and sin, and then, "let [them] alone" to stay in their sins (Hos. 4:17), even though before they were rejected they were savingly with God (1 Sam. 16:1). If a man is led into deception, he is led, as it were, into a barren wilderness without one tree of saving wisdom, knowledge, and understanding – and so he is left there to die. Wisdom is not found by the will of man, but as a gift from God (James 1), and "a scorner seeketh wisdom, and findeth it not; but knowledge is easy unto him that understandeth" (Prov. 14:6). God is the governor of every pilgrim's progress. Pilgrims digress, and their steps take hold on hell, because of God's responsive reactions to evil, and "evil men understand not judgment" (Prov. 28:5).

When a Christian does not deal rightly with God, God will not deal rightly with him – *right for right* and *wrong for wrong*. A Christian, bound by the promises of God, attained his favorable estate in Christ when he did heartily promise/commit himself to God as a sacrifice (Rom. 12:1-2, Gal. 2:20, Rom. 6:1-3). If haply this Christian does not keep this oath and promise to God "unto the end", he has broken the Covenant of God made up of promises and oaths – *man to God* and *God to man*. God will justly respond, *break for break*, "for we are made partakers of Christ, if we hold the beginning of our confidence stedfast unto the end" (Heb. 3:14). *Break of promise and oath* for *break of promise and oath* – do you believe it?

> "For thus saith the Lord God; **I will even deal with thee as thou hast done**, which hast **despised the oath in breaking the Covenant**" (Ezekiel 16:59).

Therefore God saith again in another place, "Seeing <u>he despised the oath by breaking the covenant</u>, when, lo, he had given his hand, and hath done all these things, he shall not escape. Therefore thus saith the Lord GOD; As I live, surely <u>Mine oath</u> that he hath <u>despised</u>, and <u>My Covenant</u> that he hath <u>broken</u>, **even it will I recompense upon his own head**" (Ezek. 17:18-19). To be *froward* is to be "perverse, ungovernable, and not willing to yield or comply with what is required"

(Webster's 1828), and "the way of man is froward and strange" (Prov. 21:8). Therefore in this case, men dealt with God frowardly and strangely by *wronging* His righteous behavior. They ought to have been pure rather than froward. "As for the pure, his work is right," and they should have had the blessedness of *right for right* with God, but now it is *wrong for wrong, froward for froward*, and *strange for strange* (Prov. 21:8). Note: God did not break His Covenant so as to "cast them away" in the sense that He would cast all of them away forever – "destroy them utterly" and entirely (Lev. 26:44), but He will follow through with another sense of "casting away" (Rom. 11:15)

> **Breaking the Covenant**
>
> "And I took My staff, even Beauty, and cut it asunder, **that I might break My covenant** which I had made with all the people. And it was **broken** in that day: and so the poor of the flock that waited upon me knew that it was the word of the LORD" (Zechariah 11:10-11). (See Zech. 11:7-14 & Matt. 26:15)

which is different from the sense which is *entire annihilation* (Rom. 11:1-2). He will cast them away (Rom. 11:15) so as to cause their "fall" from salvation (Rom. 11:11-12), His own sovereign hand darkening their eyes of understanding into "blindness" (Rom. 11:7) and giving them a "spirit of slumber" (Rom. 11:8), so it is written: "eyes that they should not see, and ears that they should not hear" (Rom. 11:8). They provoked Him to jealousy (Deut. 32:16), therefore God shall deal with them likewise, and He shall provoke them to jealousy by choosing the Gentiles for salvation instead of them (Deut. 32:21) – *jealousy for jealousy*! This is the woeful happening prophetically foretold in ancient days: "And when the LORD saw it, He abhorred them, because of the provoking of His sons, and of His daughters. And He said, **I will hide my face from them**, I will see what their end shall be: for they are a very **froward** generation, children in whom is no faith" (Deut. 32:19-20).

They wronged His righteous faithfulness which was toward them, as is represented in Isaiah 63:8, and God did plead with them according to their wrong that they did toward His righteous goodness, saying – "I said, I will never break My Covenant with you" (Judges 2:1) – and this promise of God they despised by disobeying His commanding voice (Judges 2:2). On this the promises hinged and God dealt with them – *break for break* – thus He said: "Wherefore I also said, I will not drive them out from before you; but they shall be as thorns in your sides, and their gods shall be a snare unto you" (Judges 2:3). Hovering high above and transcending over the events of time as they unfolded through history, there is an unbreakable eternality in God's promise, though throughout time there were so many who perished in the justice of *break for break*. This is the mystery of damnation which God executed upon His backsliding children through the centuries. It was not that men understood it entirely so as to understand all the ways it was entirely just, but rather, they were *bewildered* and *confounded* about it. Thus they were led to pray to God – "Thou hast made void the Covenant of Thy servant" (Ps. 89:39). Their complaint was that it was VOID. They knew the promise and oath of God: "My Covenant will I not **break**, nor **alter** the thing that is gone out of My lips. Once have

262

I sworn by My holiness that I will not **lie** unto David" (Ps. 89:34-35). God's justice was termed *break for break* in Ezekiel 16 & 17, as formerly addressed, thus in Psalm 89, the bewildered prophet feels as though God is being *froward* and *deceptive*. The prophet feels as though he is beholding a froward face upon God, and in the stead of all the Israelites the prophet cries: "How long, LORD? Wilt Thou **hide** Thyself for ever? Shall Thy **wrath** burn like fire?...Lord, where are Thy former **lovingkindnesses**, which Thou **swarest** unto David in Thy **truth**" (Ps. 89:46, 49)? This prophet feels lied to even when God said, "I will not lie unto David" (Ps. 89:35).

Jeremiah knew the feeling of shame and adverse darkness under the shadow of the froward face of God. He cried, "O LORD, Thou hast **deceived** me, and I was **deceived**: Thou art stronger than I, and hast prevailed" (Jer. 20:7). And again, "Why is my pain perpetual, and my wound incurable, which refuseth to be healed? Wilt Thou be altogether unto me as a **liar**, and as waters that fail" (Jer. 15:18) – and Jeremiah knew that God had said of Himself that He would not -"suffer My faithfulness to fail" (Ps. 89:33). These cries of Jeremiah were all in the dilemma in which his personal, prophetic covenant that he had with God (Jeremiah 1) was breached, thus deception did mark some of his experiences throughout his personal ministry with God (Jer. 15 & 20), the details of which I will write later. Jeremiah was the intercessor for the generation of the captivities who also, like unto Jeremiah's personal experience, underwent the woeful darkness of the froward face of God when He turned their light into darkness, but unlike Jeremiah's quick restoration back into the favor of his covenant with God, this generation was never able to recover themselves. For them, just retributions of deception fell upon them alway. My reader, let these words of inspired scripture cry aloud in your conscience as if you were beholding Jeremiah himself: gasping, confounded, and crying loud and long – AHHHH! "Then said I, Ah, Lord GOD! Surely Thou hast **greatly deceived** this people and Jerusalem, saying, Ye shall have peace; whereas the sword reacheth unto the soul" (Jer. 4:10). The form of this deception is *break for break*, thus Jeremiah cries on behalf of the generation: "Do not abhor us, for Thy name's sake, do not disgrace the throne of Thy glory: remember, **break not Thy Covenant** with us" (Jer. 14:21) – but for them there was no hope (exempting a small remnant). Intercession was impossible: "Then the LORD said unto me, Though Moses and Samuel stood before Me, yet My mind could not be toward this people: cast them out of My sight, and let them go forth" (Jer. 15:1). Though it is impossible that God would eternally and everlastingly break His Covenant (Jer. 33:20), God is able to reprobate generations and persons from the company of those bound in this saving Covenant, for the glory of His wrath against lying children. To the "children that will not lie" (Isa. 63:8), God will not *show Himself* as a liar, and so He will save them by the keeping performance of His promises and oaths. It is impossible for God to be evil, impure, and froward; likewise it is "impossible for God to lie" (Heb. 6:8), but in retributive *deceptions,* God brings upon men the just penalty of their actions which are done vertically against Him, and thus He can *show Himself* to be *froward* to them. By show Himself, I mean that He appears to be this way in the deception of their own mind – *froward for froward, impure for impure, break for break,* and *lie for lie* –

263

nevertheless, in God's higher righteousness it cannot be so. "Wilt Thou be altogether unto me **as a liar**" (Jer. 15:18), Jeremiah said to God, though he knew that it was written of God that He "will not lie" (Ps. 89:35).

"Children that will not lie" – Isaiah 63:8

Children that will not lie believe that God does not lie; therefore they are nourished by persevering graces issuing from the root of God's promises. All men are liars, save those inhabited by and walking in the Spirit of truth, and as much as men abide in Him, they will keep the Covenant of their first confession firm until the end. They do believe in the faithfulness of God and so, by Him, are made faithful to the end. His faithfulness is the fountain of persevering graces, and those who disbelieve in His faithfulness believe that God is a liar. Therefore those who lie to God believe God is a liar! They believe that He is unfaithful, evil, and therefore a liar, so they are unfaithful and disobedient to Him. Under God's retributive powers of justice, God saith, "He that believeth not God **hath made Him a liar**; because He believeth not the record that God gave of His Son" (1 John 5:9-10). As it were, *froward for froward* and *lie for lie*. Judgment according to works vindicates the logical justice for God to cast away souls into deception, and in this way, at least, He shows Himself *froward, perverse, scornful,* and as a *liar*. According to what they have done, in response to and according to the light that they have had in the good promises of God, God shall do unto them (Num. 14:24).

Many men only meditate on the mercy of God and they spend a lifetime in the noble task of trying to discover the unfathomable riches in grace, but these riches of mercy, as wondrous as they are, are only half of the whole in two outstanding glories in God. One is: "the riches of His glory on the vessels of mercy" (Rom. 9:23), and the second, "His wrath, and to make His power known" upon "the vessels of wrath fitted to destruction" (Rom. 9:22). In other words, God wants men to know the faithfulness of His promises in their immeasurable expanse because of elective mercy, but not this alone – nay – but also its opposing force in God. If elective mercy was North then God would take men South, even to the lowest hell. Nay, God would not have men know His mercy alone, but He would take men to the gaping chasm of hell's mouth moving to swallow sinners with jaws of plaguing power – in all its gnashing terror and agony. He would have men know God's holy breach of promises and overruling wrath: "and ye shall know My breach of promise" (Num. 14:34). God says that He "will by no means clear the guilty" (Ex. 34:7). Men who spend their whole lives feasting on sin will, as it were, spend an eternity wishing they could vomit it out, but they will forever spasm and gag in the relentless sickness of regret and depression as souls locked up under the power of the second death.

What is the justice of God toward the generation where Numbers 14:34 is found, justice which merited the breach of promise? They believed God to be a liar, an unfaithful God, and so they feared He desired to destroy them. This they did say of God, and cried out, "Wherefore hath the LORD brought us unto this land, to fall by the sword, that our wives and our children should be a prey? Were it not better for us to return into Egypt" (Num. 14:3)? As they believed of God, as if He were a liar, even calling him a liar in accusation when their evil unbelief dictated their complaint, so He showed Himself, as it were, a liar, and reflecting their frowardness, He recompensed their fears upon them. "Say unto them, *As truly as* I live, saith the LORD, **as ye have spoken in Mine ears, so will I do to you**: Your carcases shall fall in this wilderness; and all that were numbered of you, according to your whole number, from twenty years old and upward, which have murmured against Me" (Num. 14:28-29). This is "The Righteous Judgment of God." As they believed of God, or, as they made God out to be, this they did to God: they scorned Him, beat Him, reproached Him, and were froward to Him, and so justice responded to the frowardness of their unbelief by *the fulfillment of that wicked belief*. Therefore it is said of God to men, He "will bring their fears upon them." God called Israel to go forth and inherit the Promises of everlasting life, but when He called, they did not answer. Thus God behaved as it is written, "I also will choose their **delusions**, and will **bring their fears upon them**; because when I called, none did answer, when I spake, they did not hear: but they did evil before Mine eyes, and chose that in which I delighted not" (Isa. 66:4). They believed God was evil, as if He were bent to destroy them, as a liar against His promises, laying in wait for their blood, and as an austere man. Thus God says, "Out of thine own mouth will I judge thee" (Lk. 19:21-22). "The fear of the wicked, it shall come upon him: but the desire of the righteous shall be granted" (Prov. 10:24), and again, "the fearful and unbelieving…and all liars, shall have their part in the Lake which burneth with fire and brimstone: which is the second death" (Rev. 21:8). "He that believeth not God hath made Him a liar" (1 John 5:9-10), even though it is "impossible for God to lie" (Heb. 6:18) just as it is impossible for God to be froward (which means perverse, evil, and unfaithful), but it is not impossible for God, to the wicked, to show Himself froward and as a liar, and so, the wicked will go to the grave with the bitter murmur, "wilt Thou be altogether unto me as a **liar**" (Jer. 15:18)?

This is the righteous judgment of God recompensed to lying children – "children of disobedience" (Eph. 5:6). They trusted in their own hearts, which told them that God is a liar, and thus they trusted in vanity. Wherefore it is written, "Let not him that is deceived trust in vanity: for vanity shall be his recompense" (Job 15:31). They sowed "vain words" (Eph. 5:6) and became "vain" men (James 2:20), thus they reaped vanity when they sought out their own deliverances after rejecting God's. How they judged God, they were judged, "for with what judgment ye judge, ye shall be judged: and with what measure ye mete, it shall be measured to you again" (Matt. 7:2). "Therefore shall they eat of the fruit of their own way, and be filled with their own devices" (Prov. 1:31). "They that plow iniquity, and sow wickedness, reap the same" (Job 4:8).

The prophets under the inspiration of God wrote extensively to reveal this realm of justice surrounding all the events that Israel underwent throughout the centuries. With the aid of metaphors, the prophets made this reality come alive, that by pictures of real events which men could identify with, they would, thereto, be equally gripped. These metaphorical events aided the preaching of spiritual truth, because they depicted the urgency and emotional distress that is parallel to the spiritual situation at hand between them and God, and so the people would understand more clearly what manner of emotional distress they ought to have in heart, if, by faith, they would receive the prophets' word of warning. Therefore, there are various pictures used to show the urgency at hand when, as it was many times, the protection of the promises were being breached, or were in danger of being breached.

The OT promises of God ensured the *corporate* (citywide & nationwide) and *individual lives* of the people to be in health and prosperity, so that when Israel was exalted in these ways, the image of God's reigning glory would be revealed to the surrounding nations. Israel was the only nation, people, and Kingdom God called His own. Thus, the name of the people became the Name of God, or they became, as it were, a belt around His loins (Jer. 13:1-8). Like a belt bound to the waist of the very Person of God, Israel was bound to the promises of health, life, and prosperity, but it was as long as they did obey, and in the event that a promise was breached because of sin, inciting wrath, then they would become sick, wounded, defeated, and destroyed (in varying degrees, in all types and areas). The promises given to individuals, comparatively to the promises given to the corporate nation of Israel as a whole, are of no major difference. A **break** is a *fracture*; like it is in a *bone*, so it is in a *stonewall*. It is a **gap** in a *stonewall*, or in the case of a person's *body of flesh*, it is a **wound**, and these expressions, alongside others, do figuratively represent a **broken promise**, or as it was said, a "**breach** of **promise**." I do therefore desire that the reader would understand the various prophetic pictures and expressions which are used to show the reality of *breach for breach*. Breach for breach = break for break, gap for gap, and wound for wound. As it is with the *individual* **bodies** of persons bound with promises, so it is with the *corporate* **city** and **nation** of persons together, that when they are in rebellion, they are invaded by aliens and destroyed – in other words, the citywide or nationwide person of Israel was *wounded*.

Life – Tribe & Company

Israel's continuance of life - in its health, success, and prosperity - is personal and bodily (Deut. 28:4), and furthermore, extending to the land (Deut. 28:3), family (Deut. 28:4), tribe, city, and nation. The promise of God ensured that all tribes would be intact and settled into their allotted inheritance within the Promised Land. When God destroyed an entire tribe, or a good majority, the people called it: "the LORD had made a **breach** in the tribes of Israel" (Judges 21:15). At another time, on a more individual basis, while David sought to bring the ark of God to himself, one of the carrying men, Uzzah by name, was struck dead for his transgression, and it was said of his death: "the LORD had made a **breach** upon Uzzah" (2 Sam. 6:8, 1 Chron. 13:11, 15:13). When men of Israel undertake the tasks to fulfill the objectives laid out by the promises of God, and they fail with broken efforts, broken works, while exploits of wrath through harmful plagues and death do trouble them, then they can be sure that something is disqualifying them from their promised right. Some may assume that these breaches are breaks, with no further spiritual parallels, but that it is where God broke forth upon one or some of them, when, had they done right before Him, He would not have breached them. This is a shallow understanding of the word breach. Consider the circumstance of *citywide* and *nationwide* matters when the word breach is used.

Life – City & Nation

"Also I set watchmen over you, saying, Hearken to the sound of the trumpet. But they said, We will not hearken" (Jer. 6:17).

When God speaks of His people as a city, or sometimes as a vineyard, God assures them that His promises do sustain Israelite protection and defense against all enemies that would, or do seek to, invade, so that, in the

> Psalm 33:16-17
> Psalm 35:1-3
> Psalm 68:1-2

case of an invasion there is an inevitable victory against them. It is said in Deuteronomy 28:7, "The LORD shall cause thine enemies that rise up against thee to be smitten before thy face: they shall come out against thee one way, and flee before thee seven ways." Again it is said, "And I will give peace in the land, and ye shall lie down, and none shall make you afraid: and I will rid evil beasts out of the land, neither shall the sword go through your land. And ye shall chase your enemies, and they shall fall before you by the sword. And five of you shall chase an hundred, and an hundred of you shall put ten thousand to flight: and your enemies shall fall before you by the sword" (Lev. 26:6-8). These promises proved to be real surety in the face of impossible circumstances; in real wars, shockwaves of Israelite victories gripped the nations with fear. The ripple effect went worldwide, and the nations esteemed the Israelite God as a God of war, but who knew it more – those smitten by the Presence of God or those empowered to smite standing in the Presence of God? Nay, none knew it more than the darling ransom of God, Israel by name. An Israelite learned to herald and hope in the good confession: **"The LORD is a man of war: the LORD is His Name"** (Ex. 15:3). Though the Israelites do cleave their hands to swords and spears and so make ready for the battle charge, they do never shout the courageous hoorah until the sacrifice is made! Nay, though the army is arrayed and at attention, every man's valiance is stayed until the ark of God enters the camp! The military acclamation of the Israelite army was: "The LORD saveth not with sword and spear: for the battle is the LORD'S" (1 Sam. 17:47)! Hands may cleave to the sword, but hearts only to the Lord.

As it is with the weaponry of "hand to hand" combat, so it is in the case of Israel's walls and fortified cities: built for protection and the vantage point of invaders at war. If Israel builds fortified cities of high walls and high towers, they may look down from the height of the walls and towers – but their hearts look up to the LORD. They are not out of reach of the enemy, except by the hiding place of His Presence. "My soul, wait thou only upon God; for my expectation is from Him" (Ps.

62:5), they pray. "Thou art my hiding place and my shield: I hope in Thy word" (Ps. 119:114), "for Thou hast been a shelter for me, and a strong tower from the enemy" (Ps. 61:3); "my fortress...my buckler...and my high tower" (Ps. 18:1). Fortresses of war may be the pride of the nations, emboldening them to boast and devour, but an Israelite painfully disdains this pride and reattributes all the successful instrumentality of any object of war to the glory of God. "Thou shalt hide them in the secret of Thy presence from the pride of man" (Ps. 31:20), the psalmist declares, and so "the Name of the LORD is a strong tower: the righteous runneth into it, and is safe," (Prov. 18:10) HALLELUJAH! Watchmen stand awake until daybreak and the alarm of war sounds ready the soldiers for war, but the prophets' preaching keeps men from vain hopes deceiving – "Thus saith the LORD; Cursed be the man that trusteth in man, and maketh flesh his arm, whose heart departeth from the LORD" (Jer. 17:5). They alarm men to the watchful eye of their Maker, and declare that this is the supreme matter. If men can wake up to God, then He will awake for them at a time of war. Thus it is written, "Except the LORD keep the city, the watchman waketh but in vain" (Psalm 127:1).

It is not the wall that protects Israel, just as it is not the sword that saves; it is God, through the agreement of His promises. The wall of protection circling a fortified city is like a barrier of the promises of God, and as a host of Israel is unbeatable while they are blessed by the power of God, so the wall of Israel is impregnable, unbreakable, and un-*breach*-able while it is sustained by His hand. The wall is protected and sustained by the promises of God, and if the promises of God are breached and invading aliens do attack, they will breach the wall of fortification and conquer. The aliens' victory through the breached wall is only a physical manifestation of the wrath of God which already breached the Israelite promises of salvation. Now, if in the time that the wrath of God is kindled against the people when God is intent on breaching the promises of their protection, being intent to destroy them by an invading host, if, before the invading host arrives, a prophet hears and sees the spiritual state of Israel as it is then, even beholding the wrath of God, as it were, breaking forth through a breach of promise, if that prophet stands in the breach to turn away God's wrath and avails, then the city is saved and the physical manifestation of their destruction never arrives. In this very context it is said of Moses:

> "Therefore He said that He would destroy them, had not Moses
> His chosen stood before him in the **breach**, to turn away His
> wrath, lest He should destroy them" (Psalm 106:23).

If enemy nations do conspire against Israel or Judah to say, "let us go up against Judah, and vex it, and let us make a **breach** therein for us, and set a king in the midst of it," "it shall not stand, neither shall it come to pass" unless God has inspired them to bring it to pass (Isa. 7:6). Prophets do hear the alarm of war (Jer. 4:21) from the trumpet of the watchman, as if then, at that very moment, he was sounding out the arrival of an invading host, and this is long before the day when it actually happens. They hear it as a spiritual utterance; they see it as a vision; they are overcome and outwitted by it as a revelation in the Spirit of God. It is as if they are "caught up" (2 Cor. 12:4), and they could say, "so the Spirit lifted me up, and took me away, and I went in bitterness, in the heat of my spirit; but the hand of the LORD was strong upon me" (Ezek. 3:14) – "whether in the body, or out of the body, I cannot tell: God knoweth" (2 Cor. 12:3). They feel it, experience it, are in the utter grip of it, as if they are in the death-grip of a Giant Man – thus at a time of judgment they are gripped by the wrath of God, by the noises of war, and by the travails of those weeping in pain under the suffering to come. It is then that these prophets do take upon themselves the holy and exhausting endeavor to wrestle the wrath of God, if haply, they could have grace to rise and stand against it, which is to intercede, and so shield it back. Just as the promises of God protected Israel, if then Israel was defeated, then it was the wrath of God, on the part and favor of the aliens, using them as His instruments of wrath to afflict Israel their recompense. Before the physical manifestation of the wrath of God, it is spiritually living as the real threat, and it must be taken with more urgency than physical enemies approaching on the horizon.

At times like these, the prophets were the only hope. The prophets who stood in the breach "stood between the dead and the living," pressed, as it were, in conflicts for eternity, even as Aaron did when he "stood between the dead and the living" as the plague of wrath broke forth upon Israel at the events surrounding the gainsaying of Korah (Numbers 16:46-48). Can you imagine it? Moses and Aaron frantically casting their holy bodies upon the ground! Having fallen upon their faces they dare not look up, and they plead and cry petitions of mercy! Moses and Aaron interceded against God's wrath set, at present, to fully annihilate Israel (Num. 16:45). Crying and pleading, the face of Moses lifts up from the ground and gives the brisk command to Aaron – "Take a censer, and put fire therein from off the altar, and put on incense, and go quickly unto the congregation, and make an atonement for them: for there is wrath gone out from the LORD; the plague is begun" (Num. 16:46)! Aaron, leaping from his knees to his feet with his priestly gown covered in dust, sprints with all his might across the camp of Israel toward the Tabernacle. Like running through the chaos of modern warfare, Aaron strides across the camp, and the plague is breaking forth upon the people like airborne artillery falling from the sky. His chest heaving for air, he prepares the censer of incense. Making it ready, he then "ran into the midst of the congregation; and, behold, the plague is begun among the people… and he stood between the dead and the living; and the plague was stayed" (Num. 16:47-48).

My reader, we should wonder at the time that Aaron took to run to and fro to prepare the intercession – how many thousands dead stacked upon thousands – until he stood right before the dead like a wall of protection from the plague, and thus, at the moment of his able intercession the plague of wrath was shielded. That sober stand of Aaron – how fearful it is! As it is in physical war, so it is in breaking and breaching wrath – every second counts! Is this how seriously you take intercession? Aaron, hasting for the intercessory stand, took a good while, and how

269

precious were those passing seconds for the living and the dead on that day! During the plague, though it was eventually stayed, in the elapse of time thereto "fourteen thousand and seven hundred" Israelites died (Num. 16:49). Real intercession stands to reflect and turn back real forces of wrath – even so, all intercessors stand for the noble cause of mercy and life. Yet onward in generations to come, not as Aaron, they wrestle against spiritual forces yet to manifest plagues or armies, but as Aaron they are raptured in the time-press of urgency as souls hang in the balance, and even, as they are slain before their eyes, YEA, before them is the same gripping scenery of Israelite slaughter as thousands fell and tens of thousands lifted their weeping cries to heaven; thus the visions seize the prophets in heart-wrenching agony. The prophets do not only hear the sound of the trumpet and the alarm of war, but voices of men and women weeping like an aerial view of a nationwide cry (Jer. 3:21, 4:15)!

> "For I have heard a voice as of a woman in travail, and the anguish as of her that bringeth forth her first child, the voice of the daughter of Zion, that bewaileth herself, that spreadeth her hands, saying, Woe is me now! For my soul is wearied because of murderers" (Jer. 4:31).

The howling agony to come they do see in their now, they hear it beforehand so that the prophesying of its coming electrifies their prophetic cries to the nation, and they do behold a man in agony! Can a man such as this be altogether ignored? Can the waters of emotion be altogether unstirred when they behold a man in the agony of the message and murder to come!? Howling and crying holy men should pierce the hearts of the unholy! Channels only, can you imagine the prophets living out the animation of such prophetic words - "Howl ye; for the day of the LORD is at hand; it shall come as a destruction from the Almighty. Therefore shall all hands be faint, and every man's heart shall melt: And they shall be afraid: pangs and sorrows shall take hold of them; they shall be in pain as a woman that travaileth: they shall be amazed one at another; their faces shall be as flames" (Isa. 13:6-8). Before the nationwide face of Israel is as flames, they do behold a prophet enflamed, amazed, speechless, weeping, and rent asunder – arising time and time again from gate to gate, preaching and pleading: "Thus saith the LORD!" It is a breaking burden, and thus it was declared:

> "The burden of the desert of the sea. As whirlwinds in the south pass through; so it cometh from the desert, from a terrible land. A grievous vision is declared unto me; the treacherous dealer dealeth treacherously, and the spoiler spoileth. Go up, O Elam: besiege, O Media; all the sighing thereof have I made to cease. Therefore are my loins filled with pain: pangs have taken hold upon me, as the pangs of a woman that travaileth: I was bowed down at the hearing of it; I was dismayed at the seeing of it. My heart panted, fearfulness affrighted me: the night of my pleasure hath He turned into fear unto me" (Isa. 21:1-4).

Can you imagine it? Imagine if you were a prophet dwelling in Israel, going about your daily business, or perhaps you were in the middle of the engagement of a sweet hour of prayer, and suddenly, you heard the horn of the watchman's trumpet sounding its citywide alarm in your heart? Then, after the trumpet's long sound, after the fear of annihilation and death grips your soul, then, in this state of emotional grip under the sensation of God, the very words of the Lord forcefully pound into your heart with spiritual power and authority! Thus is the reason why prophets *tremble*. According to the message they do sigh and cry. It is because they are dwelling in the spiritual reality of what will soon arise upon a condemned people, who, at its sudden arise will also tremble, but had they trembled with the prophet, they might have escaped the hour of wrath. Nevertheless, they will be seized with like agony the very moment they hear the actual trumpet of the watchman sound from their city wall. The prophets do see and hear things like this to amplify the message. Their bodily image makes real the words so that the people can see what danger they are in at that very moment, if haply they might understand that personal and national security are in danger and potential breach because the promises are, at present, being breached! This is the experience of a true prophet under the alarm of wrath, but false prophets preach the seductions of peace to a people in need of repentance. False prophets candy-coat poison by preaching the sweetness of the promises of God to a people disqualified from them. Their ministry is like a silent bite from a serpent while walking through the pricks of a thorny and swampy region. Like life-threatening venom moving through the veins of the body, so are false prophets through the city streets. "The prophets prophesy falsely, and the priests bear rule by their means; and My people love to have it so: and what will ye do in the end thereof" (Jer. 5:31)?

False prophets do see and hear false messages of peace. They are deaf to the alarms of God. Their theology forbids wrath and breaches, and if there was a breach in the wall of God's promised protection for Israel, they would neither have the courage or selfless care to stand in the gap and build it up again so that the wrath of God does not enter into the city. "Ye have not gone up into the gaps," God said, "neither made up the hedge for the house of Israel to stand in the battle in the day of the LORD" (Ezek. 13:5). Intercession is city-saving, and at the hour of wrath, the mercy of God looks for a man to stand in the breach! It is written, "And **I sought for a man** among them, that should **make up the hedge** (*wall*), and **stand in the gap** before Me for the land, that I should not destroy it: but I found none. Therefore have I poured out Mine indignation upon them; I have consumed them with the fire of My wrath: their own way have I recompensed upon their heads, saith the Lord GOD" (Ezek. 22:30-31). False prophets wear the clothes of an intercessor, but it is a lying vanity; they are neither rent, dusty, ashy, nor worn. God says of them that they do NOT stand in the breach or build up the wall: "And My hand shall be upon the prophets that see vanity, and that divine lies… because, even because they have seduced My people, saying, Peace; and there was no peace; and **one built up a wall, and, lo, others daubed it with untempered morter**" (Ezek. 13:9-10). Again the Lord says, "And her prophets have **daubed them with untempered morter**, seeing

271

vanity, and divining lies unto them, saying, Thus saith the Lord GOD, when the LORD hath not spoken" (Ezek. 22:28). The false prophets do build up the wall and fill the breach, but it is a counterfeit trust. Do you see it?! The true prophets give true promises in their rightful place, and they give true warnings in their rightful place, but if you fill a breach of promise by standing against the breaking forth of wrath at the gap in the wall with an unbiblical, misappropriated promise which the people are disqualified from, you are building the wall and filling the breach with a false promise – a false confidence like as untempered morter. False promises of peace give the perception that the wall of God's protection is standing firm, but they do fail to turn away the wrath of God in the midst of a spiritual dilemma like the crumbling of an untempered wall. Therefore the wrath of God comes and the actual walls of the defenced cities are breached, the cities are taken, and the people are ravaged with destruction. God warns:

> "Say unto them which **daub it with untempered morter, that it shall fall**: there shall be an overflowing shower; and ye, O great hailstones, shall fall; and a stormy wind shall **rend it**. Lo, when the wall is fallen, shall it not be said unto you, **Where is the daubing wherewith ye have daubed it?** Therefore thus saith the Lord GOD; I will even **rend it** with a stormy wind in my fury; and there shall be an overflowing shower in Mine anger, and great hailstones in my fury to consume it. So will I **break down the wall** that ye have **daubed with untempered morter**, and bring it down to the ground, so that the foundation thereof shall be discovered, and it shall fall, and ye shall be consumed in the midst thereof: and ye shall know that I am the LORD. Thus will I accomplish my wrath upon the wall, and **upon them that have daubed it with untempered morter**, and will say unto you, The wall is no more, neither they that daubed it; To wit, the prophets of Israel which prophesy concerning Jerusalem, and **which see visions of peace for her, and there is no peace**, saith the Lord GOD" (Ezek. 13:11-16).

> "Therefore this iniquity shall be to you **as a breach ready to fall**, swelling out in a high wall, whose breaking cometh suddenly at an instant" (Isa 30:13).

A breach in an actual city wall is sure destruction for a city, and so, the breaches of God's promises, which are the true defenders of Israel against alien foes, also are sure to end in the destruction of the city. If the promise is broken (breached), so is the wall. The false prophets speak peace – they promise the promises of security and salvation to a rebellious, disqualified, and unrepentant people. In principle, they see and believe there are no conditions to the promises of salvation. In this metaphor, the message is emblematic of the city and nationwide state of Israel, and we see that in this sense, like as other senses, it is *breach for breach, break for break*, and *gap for*

272

gap. When the people breach the Covenant, God breaches His promise, and when the promise is breached, then the wall is breached. Therefore true prophets build up the gaps, breaches, and breaks in the promises of God, and so also, metaphorically, the walls of Israel's protection. Again, in another metaphorical term God speaks on this wise - tearing down His oath-bound protection and blessing – "And now go to; I will tell you what I will do to my vineyard: I will take away **the hedge** thereof, and it shall be eaten up; and **break down the wall** thereof, and it shall be trodden down" (Isaiah 5:5). A generation given over to such breaches of promise and salvation do cry the lamentations, "Why hast Thou then **broken down her hedges**, so that all they which pass by the way do pluck her" (Psalm 80:12)? "Thou hast **broken down all his hedges**; Thou hast **brought his strong holds to ruin**" (Psalm 89:40).

Life – The Temple of God *(Tabernacle/House)*

"repair the breaches of the House" – 2 Kings 22:5

At the hour of wrath upon Israel, the walls are breached and the city is taken, and if the wrath of God is provoked far enough, then the house of God is defiled and destroyed. God says, "I will make your cities waste, and **bring your sanctuaries unto desolation**, and I will not smell the savour of your sweet odours" (Lev. 26:31). Read the heart-wrenching words of the prophet as he is rent by the emotional trauma of God Himself, and that the living prophetic word might rend you and me:

> "My bowels, my bowels! I am pained at My very heart; My heart maketh a noise in Me; I cannot hold My peace, because thou hast heard, O my soul, **the sound of the trumpet, the alarm of war**. Destruction upon destruction is cried; for the whole land is spoiled: **suddenly are My tents spoiled, and My curtains in a moment.** How long shall I see the standard, and **hear the sound of the trumpet**? For My people is foolish, they have not known Me; they are sottish children, and they have none understanding: they are wise to do evil, but to do good they have no knowledge" (Jeremiah 4:19-22).

Can you hear it?! Shame on you, reader, if you cannot gasp at such words! God says, "My bowels!" He is pained at His heart! He says that He hears the sound of the trumpet, **NOW**, long before it has sounded from the city wall, and behold – the whole land is destroyed. This is a matter much more grave than that of the land – the very Temple of God is laid waste in destruction. Speaking in reference to this, God said, "**suddenly are My tents spoiled, and My curtains in a moment**." Men who have experienced the trauma of war can understand the sudden fear that grips a city when the trumpet alarm sounds to warn of the approaching enemy hosts for war, but will you understand that the prophets are pained at their heart, **NOW**, in the fellowship of God's broken agony, and that they do ever hear the alarm of war and the declaration of destruction long before it arrives? If you knew a prophet and saw him tremble, dear reader, you'd better understand that *you should tremble too*. Oh Lord, have mercy. My reader, the Temple is like the fortified walls of the city; it is representative of the promises and salvation of God, and if it is destroyed and spoiled, then damnation has been executed in the fullest measure! Prophets do preach what they hear and see, and as they hear the alarm of war, they do also see the city as it will be at the war's aftermath. Read carefully of the visions that followed *the trumpet alarm of war* which was declared in the former passage above in Jeremiah 4:19-22. Think of it. At the prophetic sound of the trumpet horn was heart-rending pains, and then the first-Person utterances of God's anguish came out from a prophetic vessel of clay - an earthly vessel animated by heaven's anguish in God! "Be astonished, O ye heavens, at this, and be horribly afraid" (Jer. 2:12)! The trumpet sounds, and pouncing upon the prophet are the seizing emotions of God, and then the overflowing words of our Highness, the King, which He spoke in heaven, do come forth from this human figure which is comparable to dust and ashes – thus, God's voice is echoed throughout the lower world, the earth is instructed by the mouth of a prophet, and immediately after this, *visions*. God, knowing the end from the beginning, and dwelling outside the confinements of time, doth open to His prophet *the visions* of the future which He does lament over now, and lo, they burst upon the prophetic vessel with overwhelming power. Prophets do live in and walk out experiences yet to come, and behold, the lattice of the future opens before his eyes that he may gaze upon it, and declare it, hearken therefore and behold his visions:

> "**I beheld** the earth, and, lo, it was without form, and void; and the heavens, and they had no light. **I beheld** the mountains, and, lo, they trembled, and all the hills moved lightly. **I beheld**, and, lo, there was no man, and all the birds of the heavens were fled. **I beheld**, and, lo, the fruitful place was a wilderness, and all the cities thereof were broken down at the presence of the LORD, and by His fierce anger. For thus hath the LORD said, The whole land shall be desolate; yet will I not make a full end. For this shall the earth mourn, and the heavens above be black: because I have spoken it, I have purposed it, and I will not repent, neither will I turn back from it" (Jeremiah 4:23-28).

Can a man go up to heaven and return to the earth, yet still be the same as he was before? Can a man go down to hell and then back up to the earth, and then behave like other men? So it is with a prophet and the exploding visions which prostrate them; behold, when they arise they are ne'er the same. What they see they do experience as if it was <u>now</u>, thus they live out future realities as living messages at hand. When God speaks to His prophets, He doth also lift and move them, making them a living theater of prophetic revelations. They would stay prostrate as dead men, but God has plans and employments otherwise. As said to Ezekiel, "Sigh therefore, thou son of man, with the breaking of thy loins; and with bitterness sigh before their eyes. And it shall be, when they say unto thee, Wherefore sighest thou? That thou shalt answer, For the tidings; because it cometh: and every heart shall melt, and all hands shall be feeble, and every spirit shall faint, and all knees shall be weak as water: behold, it cometh, and shall be brought to pass, saith the Lord GOD" (Ezek. 21:6-7). When God reveals His command for future damnation unto His prophets, He commands them, He constrains them, and they are hurled into theatric movings of God's emotions; as it were, they are an alabaster box hurled to the ground and broken before the eyes of the people, filling the world with the scented savour of the knowledge of God.

When God reveals the command of judgment to a prophet, like as, "Thus saith the LORD; Say, A sword, a sword is sharpened, and also furbished: It is sharpened to make a sore slaughter" (Ezek. 21:9-10), He simultaneously enflames and animates the prophet with the rush of these imminent realities, saying to him: "**Cry and howl**, son of man: for it shall be upon My people, it shall be upon all princes of Israel: terrors by reason of the sword shall be upon My people: **smite therefore upon thy thigh**…thou therefore, son of man, prophesy, and **smite thine hands together**…", for God saith, "**I will also smite Mine hands together**, and I will cause my fury to rest: I the LORD have said it" (Ezek. 21:12-17). The prophets do prophesy a living, breaking, and burning word, and they, engulfed in the flames of it, burning alive, that the consuming flames do mesmerize the people to watch on – thus the people hear, see, and smell the knowledge of God. *God sets them on fire and the people come to watch them burn!* Ezekiel did **cry**, he did **howl**, and he **smote upon his thigh**, being overwhelmed by the prophetic Word, thus he was in clay-crumbling and holy seizures. He **smote his hands together** to portray the invisible God behind the veil of heaven Who will, God saith, "**smite Mine hands together**." "Is not My word like a fire? Saith the LORD; and like a hammer that breaketh the rock in pieces" (Jer. 23:29)? Understanding the mystery of prophecy is to behold, lo, not the spoken word only, but the demonstration of the Spirit and power which is influencing the prophetic men in holy animation, and you are filled with a holy assurance that these men are a wide open window into heaven, and gazing at them, you do gaze upon God! A prophet's *madness* is heaven's brightness, praise be to God! "Wherefore came this *mad fellow* to thee? …ye know the man, and his communication" (2 Kings 9:11).

As for prophetic revelations surrounding judgments toward the Temple, do you see how when the Temple is destroyed the whole land is destroyed? Read again, and see how the walls of the Temple are mentioned together along with the assemblies and ministrations which bring peace and salvation before the just anger of God.

> "And He hath violently taken away **His Tabernacle**, as if it were of a garden: He hath destroyed **His places of the assembly**: the LORD hath caused the <u>solemn feasts</u> and <u>sabbaths</u> to be forgotten

in Zion, and hath despised in the indignation of His anger the king and the priest. The Lord hath cast off **His altar**, He hath abhorred **His sanctuary**, He hath given up into the hand of the enemy **the walls of her palaces**; they have made a noise in **the House of the LORD**, as in the day of a solemn feast. The LORD hath purposed to destroy **the wall of the daughter of Zion**: He hath stretched out a line, He hath not withdrawn His hand from destroying: therefore He made the rampart and the wall to lament; they languished together. Her gates are sunk into the ground; He hath destroyed and broken her bars: her king and her princes are among the Gentiles: the law is no more; her prophets also find no vision from the LORD" (Lam 2:6-9).

The Temple was an emblem of *the Covenant*; which is all the promises of God in salvation. According to the words of Solomon, read how the Temple is the focal point of salvation, that we might understand, if the Temple is breached and broken, so also are the promises of salvation and the Covenant. At the time of the Temple's dedication and sanctification, Solomon preached a sermon, made a prayer, and gave a blessing. During the prayer he prays for *six* different circumstances where each one is a different experience of Divine wrath with differing individuals and companies, but in all *six* circumstances Solomon prays and points to one and only salvific hope to stand sure heretofore – God honoring His Name at His Temple. Men turn toward the Temple and so turn toward God, because the House is called after God's Name. It became the focal point of salvation, thus if it was destroyed then salvation is lost.

> "But will God indeed dwell on the earth? Behold, the heaven and heaven of heavens cannot contain Thee; how much less this house that I have builded? Yet have Thou respect unto the prayer of Thy servant, and to his supplication, O LORD my God, to hearken unto the cry and to the prayer, which Thy servant prayeth before Thee to day: That Thine eyes may be open **toward this house** night and day, even **toward the place of which Thou hast said, My name shall be there**: that Thou mayest hearken unto the prayer which Thy servant shall make **toward this place**. And hearken Thou to the supplication of Thy servant, and of Thy people Israel, when they shall pray **toward this place**: and hear Thou in heaven Thy dwelling place: and when Thou hearest, forgive" (1Ki 8:27-30).

"Toward this place" is now salvation, so that, circling and centering around the place called by God's Name, men recognize and understand that it is the LORD's salvation and work – "that all the people of the earth may know Thy Name, to fear Thee, as do Thy people Israel; and that they may know that this House, which I have builded, is called by Thy Name" (1 Kings 8:43). This House, therefore, is emblematic of God's Name and presence, and if it is destroyed then God's name and people are being destroyed, for even the people are called after God's name. When God's people are saved, they, alongside God's name, are exalted: "And all the people of the earth shall see that Thou art called by the Name of the LORD; and they shall be afraid of thee" (Deut. 28:10). Thus when the people are in salvific blessing and grace, they become "high above all nations which He hath made, in praise, and in name, and in honour," because Israel hath become a "holy people unto the LORD" (Deut. 26:19). These are the relational parallels attributed to those who are *connected to the Name of God*. So all the earth, and especially God's people, must learn to "fear this glorious and fearful Name, THE LORD THY GOD" (Deut. 28:58), and therefore fear the dwelling place of His presence which is called by His Name. God will maintain their fear of this place by plagues of wrath when necessary, that Israel will continue to cry, "Behold, we die, we perish, we all perish. Whosoever cometh any thing near unto the Tabernacle of the LORD shall die: shall we be consumed with dying" (Numbers 17:13)? The House, Presence, and Name of God ought to be a blessing, but it can become the support and exactor of every legislative curse upon Israel, if so be Israel hath merited such for themselves.

There are *means* to prevent wrath and maintain obedience with reverence to the Name of God, but if these means are neglected then the process of chastening and destruction begins. The fires and severity of chastening and destruction will change in degree and determination by the heart of the people: looming into hardness and disobedience or running into repentance and returning. Ordinances were given to the people which forced their travel from their states and countries to appear before and minister AT THE TEMPLE, and so they were brought nigh to God's Holy Name. At this place the ordinance rituals were practiced, some of which included a reckoning and re-invoking of their oaths with God (Deut. 26). Thus this Place, the Temple, is the place to come, Moses says, **"that thou mayest learn to fear the LORD thy God always"** (Deut. 14:23). These ordinances were to maintain and nourish the fear of God in the people. The Temple was the only place for atoning sacrifices which absorbed the wrath of God, as it was said: "Thou shalt therefore sacrifice the Passover unto the LORD thy God, of the flock and the herd, in **the place which the LORD shall choose to place His Name there**" (Deut. 16:2). This was the place where judgment went forth in its finality, being laced with the very Name of God, and here the judges did continually reside so that the people must, God says, "arise, and get thee up into **the place which the LORD thy God shall choose**" (Deut. 17:8), the Temple. "And it shall come to pass, that whosoever will not hearken unto My words which he shall speak in **My Name**, I will require it of him" (Deut. 18:19). This is the place of the firstfruits offerings where the people gave glory to God, before God, standing right before His Presence: "That thou shalt take of the first of all the fruit of the earth, which thou shalt bring of thy land that the LORD thy God giveth thee, and shalt put it in a basket, and shalt go unto **the place which the LORD thy God shall choose to place His Name there**" (Deut. 26:2). All rival places, altars, or any such thing which was used for worship, praise, judgment, blessing, and relational ministrations representative by the Name of God were thus destroyed. The Temple was the only place for these works, and certainly, the only *direction* to seek after God. Deuteronomy 12:1-7 summarizes the emphasis of all these things:

> "Ye shall utterly destroy all the places, wherein the nations which ye shall possess served their gods, upon the high mountains, and upon the hills, and under every green tree: And ye shall overthrow their altars, and break their pillars, and burn their groves with fire; and ye shall hew down the graven images of their gods, and destroy the names of them out of that place. Ye shall not do so unto the LORD your God. **But unto the place which the LORD your God shall choose out of all your tribes to put His name there, even unto His habitation shall ye seek, and thither thou shalt come:** And thither ye shall bring your burnt offerings, and your sacrifices, and your tithes, and heave offerings of your hand, and your vows, and your freewill offerings, and the firstlings of your herds and of your flocks: And there ye shall eat before the LORD your God, and ye shall rejoice in all that ye put your hand unto, ye and your households, wherein the LORD thy God hath blessed thee" (Deut. 12:2-7).

When a man understands the centrality of the Temple and its vital connections to all the promises and persevering graces in salvation, he sees that when or if the Temple is destroyed, so also are salvific promises. When the Temple is breached, the people are destroyed. When the Temple is breached, the heart of God is breached, even broken in agonizing hurt, even wounded with grievous wounds – emblematic and parallel to the breaches of promise, there is a breach (wound) in the very heart of God! Thus God said: "Woe is Me for **My hurt! My wound** is **grievous**: but I said, Truly this is a grief, and I must bear it. **My Tabernacle is spoiled, and all My cords are broken**: My children are gone forth of Me, and they are not: **there is none to stretch forth My tent any more, and to set up My curtains**" (Jer. 10:19-20). In such a case when the love of God is turned again toward His people, then the breaching wounds are healed within the heart of God, and therefore, God returns and repents of wrath, pities His people, and arises in jealousy for His Name (Joel 2:12-19). At such a time there is a Revival! That is, namely, a restoration of the breaches in salvation along with all its emblematic, physical manifestations (whether fortifying walls or hedges, the Temple, or all foundations thereof), and thus such ones which restore the Covenant do restore

> "O LORD, why hast Thou made us to err from thy ways, and hardened our heart from thy fear? Return for thy servants' sake, the tribes of thine inheritance. The people of thy holiness have possessed it but a little while: our adversaries have trodden down thy sanctuary" (Isaiah 63:17-18).
>
> "Our holy and our beautiful house, where our fathers praised Thee, is burned up with fire: and all our pleasant things are laid waste" (Isaiah 64:11).

these emblems: "And they that shall be of thee shall **build the old waste places**: thou shalt **raise up the foundations** of many generations; and thou shalt be called, **The repairer of the breach, The restorer of the paths to dwell in**" (Isa. 58:12).

Contrary to these prophecies of damnation and desolations, which are prophecies of breaches (first spiritually and then physically), so the prophecies of salvation and restoration are specified as, for example: "In that day will I raise up the Tabernacle of David that is fallen, and **close up the breaches thereof**; and I will **raise up his ruins**, and I will **build it as the days of old**: That they may possess the remnant of Edom, and of all the heathen, which are called by My Name, saith the LORD that doeth this" (Amos 9:11-12). At such a time like unto this prophecy, such men like Jehoash (guided under the counsel of the good man, Jehoiada the priest), Hezekiah, Josiah, Nehemiah, and Zerubbabel arose. Of the salvific work of revival through Jehoash, he did say, "Let them repair the **breaches** of the House, wheresoever any **breach** shall be found" (2 Kings 12:5). Of Hezekiah's salvific works, they are well-summarized under his preaching when he said:

> "Hear me, ye Levites, sanctify now yourselves, and **sanctify the House of the LORD** God of your fathers, and carry forth the filthiness out of the holy place. For our fathers have trespassed, and done that which was evil in the eyes of the LORD our God, **and have forsaken Him, and have turned away their faces from the Habitation of the LORD, and turned their backs.** Also they **have shut up the doors** of the porch, and **put out the lamps**, and **have not burned incense nor offered burnt offerings** in the holy place unto the God of Israel. Wherefore the wrath of the LORD was upon Judah and Jerusalem, and He hath delivered them to trouble, to astonishment, and to hissing, as ye see with your eyes. For, lo, our fathers have fallen by the sword, and our sons and our daughters and our wives are in captivity for this. Now it is in mine heart to **make a Covenant** with the LORD God of Israel, that His fierce wrath may turn away from us" (2 Chron. 29:5-10).

Josiah, like the good prophets, did intercede with breach-**amending** intercession (spiritually), thus he arose in the physical intercession "to repair the House of the LORD his God," that is, "to repair and **amend** the House" (2 Chron. 34:8, 10). During the heated days of Nehemiah, with danger crouching on every side, Israel prevailed through the reviving prophecies of Zachariah and Haggai, instruction in the law through Ezra, and godly and courageous leadership through Nehemiah: and "the people had a mind to work" and "**the walls of Jerusalem were made up, and the breaches began to be stopped**" (Neh. 4:6-7). Nehemiah's call was, "Let us rise up and build. So they strengthened their hands for this good work" (Neh. 2:18). They did, like the good prophets Zachariah, Haggai, Jeremiah, Daniel, and Ezekiel did do: they built with **tempered mortar** that would hold *a firm trust in time of need,* and so, the wrath of God was deflected spiritually and physically. Daniel's cries of intercession that he made did foreshadow and tell of this future restoration in the days of Nehemiah, when he said:

> "O Lord, according to all Thy righteousness, I beseech Thee, let Thine anger and Thy fury be turned away from Thy city Jerusalem, Thy holy mountain: because for our sins, and for the iniquities of our fathers, Jerusalem and Thy people are become a reproach to all that are about us. Now therefore, O our God, hear the prayer of Thy servant, and his supplications, and **cause Thy face to shine upon Thy sanctuary that is desolate**, for the Lord's sake. O my God, incline Thine ear, and hear; open Thine eyes, and **behold our desolations, and the city which is called by Thy name**: for we do not present our supplications before Thee for our righteousnesses, but for Thy great mercies. O Lord, hear; O Lord, forgive; O Lord, hearken and do; defer not, for Thine own sake, O my God: for Thy city and Thy people are called by Thy Name" (Dan 9:16-19).

As Daniel's intercessions, so were Nehemiah's labors for **the wall**, and thus was the face of Zerubbabel's works for the Temple. These men were energized by the mercy of God, as God did say: "I am returned to Jerusalem **with mercies**: **My house shall be built in it**, saith the LORD of hosts, and a line shall be stretched forth upon Jerusalem" (Zech. 1:16). And again, "The hands of Zerubbabel have laid the foundation of this House; **his hands shall also finish it**" (Zech. 4:9). Like unto the prophetic summary of Israel's fall written in Isaiah 63, the book of Lamentations depicts a historical snapshot from another angle; notwithstanding, both declare God to become "an enemy" (Lam. 2:5) against Israel, nearly annihilating all the lying children He did formerly love. Oh, what a shocking picture is painted with words! Pictures of wrath, ready wrath! The pointed, aimed, and intelligent focus of God's destroying wrath toward Israel was thus: "He hath bent His bow like an enemy: He stood with His right hand as an adversary, and slew all that were pleasant to the eye in the Tabernacle of the daughter of Zion: He poured out His fury like fire" (Lam. 2:4). Here, in greater detail, stringing together the themes at hand, read the following passages again:

> "And He hath violently taken away **His Tabernacle**, as if it were of a garden: He hath destroyed His places of the assembly: the LORD hath caused the solemn feasts and sabbaths to be forgotten in Zion, and hath despised in the indignation of His anger the king and the priest. The Lord hath cast off His altar, He hath abhorred His sanctuary, he hath given up into the hand of the enemy the walls of her palaces; they have made a noise in the house of the LORD, as in the day of a solemn feast. The LORD hath purposed to destroy the wall of the daughter of Zion: He

280

hath stretched out a line, He hath not withdrawn His hand from destroying: therefore He made the rampart and the wall to lament; they languished together. Her gates are sunk into the ground; He hath destroyed and broken her bars: her king and her princes are among the Gentiles: the law is no more; her prophets also find no vision from the LORD" (Lam 2:6-9).

False prophets, causes of wrath, deceptions, and emblematic barriers of salvation are breached; thus Jeremiah laments:

What thing shall I take to witness for thee? What thing shall I liken to thee, O daughter of Jerusalem? What shall I equal to thee, that I may comfort thee, O virgin daughter of Zion? **For thy breach is great like the sea: who can heal thee?** Thy prophets have seen vain and foolish things for thee: and they have not discovered thine iniquity, to turn away thy captivity; but have seen for thee false burdens and causes of banishment" (Lam 2:13-14).

In the most humiliating attempts for mercy, face down to the lowest press on the ground, so Jeremiah fought to intercede: "He putteth his mouth in the dust; if so be there may be hope" (Lam. 3:29), and gasping with intermittent cries, He said, "Hide not Thine ear at my breathing, at my cry" (Lam. 3:56). His chest heaving and his heart horrified-amaze, thus was his face in flames of emotion. The destruction of the Temple is the end of the last hope, and with its fall any wise man or prophet goes pale in terror. This is a spiritual hurt beyond language, and so, forgetting about bread and life, for this they would say, "our heart is faint; for these things our eyes are dim" (Lam. 5:17). This is like Nehemiah's intercessions which availed and awarded his God-sent mission to lead Israel to repair the wall, but look how he, at the first, was in secret weeping over the breaches therein! The messenger came to Nehemiah and said to him, "The remnant that are left of the captivity there in the province are in great affliction and reproach: **the wall** of Jerusalem also is broken down, and **the gates** thereof are burned with fire. And it came to pass, **when I heard these words, that I sat down and wept, and mourned certain days, and fasted, and prayed before the God of heaven**" (Neh. 1:3-4). Like as Nehemiah for the wall, so Jeremiah travails for the Temple: "How is the gold become dim! How is the most fine gold changed! The stones of the sanctuary are poured out in the top of every street. The precious sons of Zion, comparable to fine gold, how are they esteemed as earthen pitchers, the work of the hands of the potter" (Lam. 4:1-2). Those men who give God no rest, they have no rest! They are in "great heaviness and continual sorrow" (Rom. 9:2) because they are the forerunners for salvation. They are a nation's secret servants who bring it to exaltation. In restless pursuit they are God-empowered to the holy call: "I have set watchmen upon thy walls, O Jerusalem, which shall never hold their peace day nor night: ye that make mention of the LORD, keep not silence, And give Him no rest, till He establish, and till He make Jerusalem a praise in the earth" (Isa.

62:6-7).

Wound for Wound

An unrepentant purpose in God to destroy is as an unrepentant breach of a promise, which is as, speaking in typology, an unrepairable breach in a fortifying city wall or in the Temple of Israel, which likewise is as when there is no intercessor to stand in the gap to repair it – but have you noticed the connection between *breaches* and *wounds*? Briefly I have referenced the passage where the breaches are, in the very heart of God Himself, called wounds (Jer. 10:19-20), and these wounds are also imparted to the prophet's heart. They, the prophets, are His companions, thus they commune with and dwell in His pain. Seeing that God is able to be wounded, we can see another relational plane of "human to human" justice called "*breach for breach*" (Lev. 24:19-20), only now it is from "man to God" - *wound for wound*. God is hurt with a wound, and He says, "My wound is grievous" (Jer. 10:19); thus He returns to Israel their own deeds and inflicts wounds upon His people. He does this in "The Righteous Judgment of God" through retributive justice. God is moved to jealousy when the people forsake Him, therefore He does likewise move the people to jealousy as recompense: *jealousy for jealousy* (Deut. 32:16, 20-21). God's people breach their promise, as it were, wounding God, so God breaches His promise, and as it were, wounds them back.

Wounds are inflicted upon the body, affecting life, health, and strength. The promises of God for *personal* and *corporate* life, health, and strength can be summarized in two passages cited in the parentheses (Exodus 15:26, Psalm 103:2-5). These scriptures detail the promise of physical prosperity stemming from the Divine blessing; God says, "I am the LORD that healeth thee" (Exodus 15:26, Psalm 103:2-5), but we need to understand the other side of the token: "**I kill**, and…**I wound**" (Deut. 32:39). As a people would seek to repair a city wall's breaches for the sustenance of corporate life, one would suspect the address of such restoration to always be described in terms like building and mortar. Nevertheless, in another place, in the context to describe a city, nation, and people, God uses the word "**heal**" – "For thy **breach** is great like the sea: who can **heal** thee?" (Lam. 2:13-14), and this is no mistake. We must see the synonymous use of these prophetic words: *breaches* and *wounds*.

There are two purposes for God's glory and work in the earth which He is careful to perform: "See now that I, even I, am He, and there is no god with Me: **I kill**, and **I make alive**; **I wound**, and **I heal**: neither is there any that can deliver out of My hand" (Deut. 32:39). This twofold purpose is further revealed in the NT as, firstly, wrath through plaguing power upon individuals called "vessels of wrath fitted to destruction", and secondarily, the riches of glory on individuals called "vessels of mercy afore prepared unto glory" (Rom. 9:22-23). He is the God of eternal life through salvation, and eternal death through wrath; in these two veins is all His glory told. The praises of His people declare these twofold powers in God when they did

282

adoringly confess: "He that is our God is the God of **salvation**; and unto GOD the Lord belong the **issues from death**" (Psalm 68:20). Knowing such, we should pay good attention to the OT term "**I kill... I wound**," so that we might understand what is being said (physically and spiritually). Dear reader, this is the question to focus upon: what manner of glorious wrath is being revealed by this woeful *wounding* of God to man?

When God, having no mind to repent, breaches a promise unto a man's reprobation, prophetic language reveals that God is minded to wound with a mortal blow that cannot be bound up, called *an incurable wound*. This body that God wounds is another emblematic image that is a physical representation for salvation. The body and life of the whole person that receives the wounds now represents Israel as a whole, and in this metaphorical language, the prophets relate to God like as, and exactly parallel to, the emblems of the fortifying walls and the Temple of Israel, only now the *breaches* are called *wounds*. Attempting to prevent the dispersion, Jeremiah prays in intercession, but is denied (Jer. 15:1), and the reprobation transpires, as you know, but look at the prophetic terms for intercession, damnation, and salvation used below: *cures, sown or bound up wounds, and healing medicines.*

> "For I am with thee, saith the LORD, to save thee: though I make a full end of all nations whither I have scattered thee, yet will I not make a full end of thee: but I will correct thee in measure, and will not leave thee altogether unpunished. For thus saith the LORD, **Thy bruise is incurable, and thy wound is grievous. There is none to plead thy cause, that thou mayest be bound up: thou hast no healing medicines.**" (Jer. 30:12-13).

And again:

> "Therefore I will wail and howl, I will go stripped and naked: I will make a wailing like the dragons, and mourning as the owls. **For her wound is incurable; for it is come unto Judah; he is come unto the gate of my people, even to Jerusalem.**" (Mic. 1:8-9).

At another time Jeremiah himself was personally caught under the condemning wrath of God, but he did avail against it through personal intercession and repentance, unlike Israel. At this time he described the terror of his estate by this complaint and supplication unto God: "Why is my **pain perpetual**, and my **wound incurable**, which **refuseth to be healed**? Wilt Thou be altogether unto me as a liar, and as waters that fail" (Jer. 15:18)? In these same terms which reveal the threat of damnation, so the hope for salvation is likewise said: "Come, and let us return unto the LORD: for He hath **torn**, and He will **heal** us; He hath **smitten**, and He will **bind us up**" (Hos. 6:1). When God prophesied a coming salvation, therefore, He prophesied the healing of the wounds which He inflicted upon Israel, "for He doth not **afflict** willingly nor grieve the children of men" (Lam. 3:33). One prophecy in these terms was thus said: "Moreover the light of the moon shall be as the light of the sun, and the light of the sun shall be sevenfold, as the light of seven days, in the day that the LORD **bindeth up the breach** of His people, and **healeth the stroke of their wound**" (Isa 30:26).

Iniquity procures condemnation, and condemnation leaves the people stripped of hope and faith for salvation. This is, prophetically speaking, the wall of promises being breached – "ready to fall, swelling out in a high wall, whose breaking cometh suddenly at an instant" (Isa. 30:13). This staggering wall, weakened and swelling because of the wrath of God, is as the prophetic language that likens Israel to a failing body full of wounds and deadly blows because they cannot be bound up, meaning that they are sure to drain the lifeblood of the body. To declare the death of a nation, He preaches it by the metaphor of a *failing body*, thus signifying the actual nation's utter desolation and destruction. See below how this direct signification is made – where the body is the country/nation/people.

> "From the sole of the foot even unto the head there is no soundness in it; but **wounds**, and **bruises**, and **putrifying sores**: they **have not been closed**, neither **bound up**, neither **mollified with ointment**. Your country is desolate, your cities are burned with fire: your land, strangers devour it in your presence, and it is desolate, as overthrown by strangers" (Isaiah 1:6-7).

Do you see the synonymous connection to the prophetic language "body to nation"? One may wonder why God has used an additional metaphor to describe the same things. What benefit would come from the metaphor of the body and personal health (representative of Israel as a whole) that the city wall and Temple could not produce? With many common folk there is a naivety to war, and as for the Temple structure, it also is known by a select portion of Israel because not all are Levites, and depending on a man's age, wealth, education, and sex, in balance with personal, spiritual maturity, there could be a general ignorance of the Temple amongst the common people. A common person who cannot be aroused by the language of war may feel dull and unaffected because he or she has never experienced war, so it is difficult to identify with or imagine it. Such a man has never experienced the rush of battle or the looming potential of sudden death that can occur at any moment, with any slip. The troubling experience of war is undergone by a select portion of society, but troubles of body are experienced by all of humanity! Such men that cannot hear the language of alarms in war would otherwise remain emotionally dull if God did not take up another metaphor, a metaphor more widely experienced; hence the category of *personal, bodily health*.

Every man is taught to know the fear, sorrow, and emotional distress of wounds, sores, and feverish sicknesses. "Lo, all these things worketh God *oftentimes* with man" (Job 33:29), the scripture says. God writes of His practice of humiliating the common man, saying - "He is chastened also with pain upon his bed, and the multitude of his bones with strong pain: So that his life abhorreth bread, and his soul dainty meat. His flesh is consumed away, that it cannot be seen; and his bones that were not seen stick out. Yea, his soul draweth near unto the grave, and his life to the destroyers… then He [God] is gracious unto him, and saith, Deliver him from going down to the pit" (Job 33:19-24). "He looketh upon men, and if any say, I have sinned, and perverted that which was right, and it profited me not; He will deliver his soul from going into the pit, and his life shall see the light" (Job 33:27-28). Thus God, through sicknesses, wounds, pain, and near death experiences, exercises man, "that He may withdraw man from his purpose, and hide pride from man" (Job 33:17). Those who **cannot** relate to war **can** relate to bodily ailments. Think of it. Those that will not shake with the tremors of the earth as a host of invaders gallop their charge, perhaps they will tremble at the tremors of their own failing body. "Out of sight - out of mind", says the modern proverb… and sadly, sinners cozy up to a hibernating bear and sleep on the judgments of God, which, as in a moment, will awake to slay them. What a woeful condition is this? God's "judgments are far above out of [the sinner's] sight: as for all his enemies, he puffeth at them. He hath said in his heart, I shall not be moved: for I shall never be in adversity" (Ps. 10:5-6).

> "His troops come together, and raise up their way against me, and encamp round
> about my tabernacle" – Job 19:12

For many, war is out of sight and therefore, because of the sedating effect of iniquity, it is out of mind, but God would not have it so. Those roaring terrors of war beyond the city walls are "out of sight and out of mind" for many; thus God takes up another terror which comes straight at all men, even within them, and that is the invasion of plagues, sicknesses, wounds, and bodily ailments. When invading armies bruise the city wall and it is well-nigh breached, it is then that the soldiers lunge into their most valiant efforts to recover it, but when a hoard of alien organisms infect and assail the personal space of your own fleshly body – destroying it – it is then that the lazy heart awakes! A thief in the city or roaming the streets, this is one thing, but a thief in your house will unfold the hands at once! When the house around the heart caves in, then a sleepy soul arises and prays! The history of a person's health is a storehouse of personal alarms. The language of this metaphor has a rich library of memories to draw from to bring alive the message, memories which contain emotions and experiences to make alive spiritual urgency and agony.

Oh! How many prophetic languages the mercy of God doth undertake! Unctionized metaphors move once-born men, awaking them from the oblivion of sin. At sundry times in the course of life, men are and have been near to death by a sickness, and others nearer to death by a wound, but one thing is a sure commonality – when life is near its passing, men do seek God *at last*. At this time, no other desire can be compared to the value of the soul, and men become exceedingly aware of their END. Here, they are long exercised with the uncertainty of their end and the bitterness of a life wasted and spent. Here in this place is the horror of darkness which comes upon men because of a neglected and empty soul…and feelingly, it is as if life is out of his hands like as a freefall, and he is falling to his death with nothing to grasp on to. He has neither profit in what he has done with his hands, nor all that he has enjoyed under the sun. He thought death would slowly come upon him like the evening tide of the sea, or perhaps a soothing sunset arising to illuminate the heavens so that they become colorfully arrayed, and thus, the man thought he would have a long season of preparation for his death as it slowly seizes him through old age, but with the surprise of death's untimely touch standing at your door, it seems unreasonable and impossible that he would find God in time. He tries to "feel after Him and find Him" but He seems so far away while death and justice are so near (Acts 17:27). The oblivion of pleasure without God is gone, and the man is left wandering around his own empty and lonely soul, as if he has never known himself before. An empty soul to a dying man is as the shame of nakedness, and while he would flee for cover and privacy he has nowhere to go. In his heart is the relentless agony to flee, and alas, he cannot! He would look up for love, but behold, it is wrath, and while he would lie to himself and cover with a covering, "all things are naked and opened unto the eyes of Him with Whom we have to do" (Heb. 4:13), and at last he can feel it! "Dead man walking"! The executioner heralds as another man walks those short yards of death row, and so, sick and dying men feel as though death is knocking at their door...they are dying, and oh! Laden with sickness, they cannot walk toward death, but they sit still and watch as eternity steps toward them!

"As he came forth of his mother's womb, naked shall he return to go as he came, and shall take nothing of his labour, which he may carry away in his hand. And this also is a sore evil, that in all points as he came, so shall he go: and what profit hath he that hath labored for the wind? All his days also he eateth in darkness, and he hath much sorrow and wrath with his sickness" (Eccl. 5:15-17). Thus, the man has empty hands. He has nothing to carry with him into eternity, and furthermore, no Intercessor to guide his soul through the Judgment. A lifetime of memories makes a sinner ashamed to meet his Maker. His memory is like a burning furnace at its hottest heat, kindled by the precipice of eternity that is now in view. Eternally conscious, yet he is in "the now", and it has become a prison of suffocation like the pressure of a million pounds of ocean water over his head – he is, as it were, digesting in the belly of a whale – and now, alas, the devil's world is vomiting him into eternity. Unable to arrive and land upon the clean shores of God's holy heaven, he is hurled into hell as an unclean thing. On your death bed, alas, your life appears to be but a wind, a breeze, and now it is well-past and ready to cease. The fun is over. Your life was like a wild night of drunkenness, and the night is ready to pass, the dawn is ready to break, and on Judgment morning you will awake into hell's hangover. All you have is "now", and how suddenly death will arrive, with but seconds, minutes, moments, or days to wait – and you feel no power to turn your wretched will to God! Oh the terror of it! That your eternal soul could suddenly fly to its eternal destination and no man can hinder it! Now the songs of those Christian hymns do witness against you. "Once earthly joys I craved, sought peace and rest, now Thee alone I seek, give what is best" ("More Love To Thee, Oh Christ", Elizabeth Prentiss). The sinner cries, and cries, and cries, but with every vow he makes, he lies. Oh this wretched will! Oh this alienated mind! Had the torrents of death laid hold upon the sinner before now, just enough that he might peek into the realm of eternity which he sees so clearly, he may well have repented. Had he been alarmed over his own spiritual death early in life, he would have sought eternal life. These deathbed emotional compulsions are spiritual awakenings! Men become eternally conscious, and under its compulsion men prepare to meet their God Who dwells outside the canopy of time.

God knows how to wake men up! He shows men a monster mightier than the Leviathan – the face of death with teeth arrayed – and what can men think but that the devil's smile is upon their soul. The Old Serpent is ready to rejoice at every soul brought under the sting of sin. Consider the time press upon men who are struck with *a deadly wound*. Men who have a deadly wound are frantic, for now, with their own eyes they do behold a gaping hole in their body – their skin torn like a cloth, lacerated and mangled loose, with the fats of their body, like jelly, sprinkling and coating their raw flesh that surrounds the gaping, deep wound, whose valley exposes inches of red muscle right down to the bright, white bone – Haply, it is only a matter of time before blood gushes out of the wound, and you, by your own hand, must seek to plug the bleeding **IF YOU CAN**. What arteries, veins, and nerves are at hand, God knoweth, and now, perhaps for the first time, you must look death in the face and recognize – it could be only a matter of time. Wide wounds make for wide eyes, and at such a sight as this, there comes a certain grip of adrenaline, shock, and trauma that cannot be compared to much. Prophetic language touches pressure points to bring the soul into subjection. These are experiences in life that hang the soul in an uncertain balance, as from a thread before the chasm of eternity, and there is an unforgettable agony in the darkness of uncertainty, and like a sky high freefall you land where you land at your everlasting abode. It is as if the soul is in a freefall while the body lies still, and you are left with a paralyzing and uncontrollable fear! It is as if there is a chilling presence of evil and death near to you, and a kind of filthiness and uncleanness, like as the hot breath of the devil upon the back of your neck. You did not bid him welcome and you cannot bid him to leave – that old murderer. Thus men are haunted as they wait, AND SUDDENLY, that which was felt and feared is immediately seen, THE DEVIL, and he seizes the soul and drags a man to hell. To arouse these states of mind now, God knows best; thus He speaks prophetic woes in terms of incurable wounds, sicknesses, and sores. This is attention-grabbing language which should arouse the faculties of faith, fusing real experiences men have experienced in their personal life with the reality of their present spiritual dilemma, and so men remember the preciousness of time and the value of NOW. This is that men would be seekers of God! Jeremiah's intercession below does effectually link together the language of breaches, wounds, and the smiting of God upon the body – all used in reference to intercessions denied for Jeremiah's generation, God declaring **incurable wounds** to be the state of *castaways*.

"Let mine eyes run down with tears night and day, and let them not cease: for the virgin daughter of My people is **broken with a great breach, with a very grievous blow.** If I go forth into the field, then behold the slain with the sword! And if I enter into the city, then behold them that are sick with famine! Yea, both the prophet and the priest go about into a land that they know not. Hast Thou utterly rejected Judah? Hath Thy soul lothed Zion? **Why hast Thou smitten us, and there is no healing for us?** We looked for peace, and there is no good; **for a time of healing**, and behold trouble! We acknowledge, O LORD, our wickedness, and the iniquity of our fathers: for we have sinned against Thee. Do not abhor us, for Thy Name's sake, do not disgrace the throne of Thy glory: remember, break not Thy Covenant with us. Are there any among the vanities of the Gentiles that can cause rain? Or can the heavens give showers? Art not Thou He, O LORD our God? Therefore we will wait upon Thee: for Thou hast made all these things. Then said the LORD unto me, Thou Moses and Samuel **stood before Me**, yet my mind could not be toward this people: **cast them out of My sight**, and let them go forth" (Jer. 14:17-15:1).

Therefore let the reader understand…

When you are spiritually wounded, God is expecting you to see it and be alarmed about it, as we have discussed that the language is meant to alarm you, and He will warn you in the light of it that there is a certain amount of time left for you to find healing, binding up, medicines, and bandages, so that this does not become an incurable, mortal wound to the individual person or corporate body of Israel.

"before Me continually is grief and wounds. Be thou instructed, O Jerusalem, lest My soul depart from thee; lest I make thee desolate, a land not inhabited" (Jer. 6:7-8).

As false prophets filled the breach of the city wall with **"untempered morter"** (Ezek. 13:10-11, 14-15, 22:28), here they are **healing the hurt**, **wounds**, and **bodily injuries** of Israel falsely, with an appearance that it is healed, insomuch that it can be said that it was healed "slightly", but it is altogether a vain confidence. These false prophets deceive them so that the people do "look for peace, but no good came; and for a time of health, and behold trouble" (Jer. 8:15).

"They have **healed** also the **hurt** of the daughter of My people **slightly**, saying, Peace, peace; when there is no peace" (Jer. 6:14).
"For they have **healed** the **hurt** of the daughter of My people **slightly**, saying, Peace, peace; when there is no peace" (Jer. 8:11).
These false prophets deceive them so that the people do "look for peace, but no good came; and for a time of **health**, and behold trouble" (Jer. 8:15).

"When Ephraim saw his **sickness**, and Judah saw his **wound**, then went Ephraim to the Assyrian, and sent to   King Jareb: yet could he not **heal** you, nor **cure** you of your **wound**" (Hos. 5:13).

False prophets will also preach the liberty to turn to worldly wisdom, which in turn forsakes God's "foolish" ways, to the end that the people are rejected by God.

If the false prophets succeed to win the people by false confidences, then reprobation will come for the many called Israelites, till there be few left instead of none left, for God will not totally annihilate Israel. Thus God clearly states, in the language of wounds, hurt, and healing, a message which is continually repeated ever since it was first prophesied in Deuteronomy 32:26-43. It is the strange speech which defames God's holy Name, by which Israel is called, that motivates God to save a remnant which deserved, like the others, to be annihilated. Through this near annihilation, shockingly, God will make Israel righteous, and He will gather them again, but all of this is because the heathen have spoken the strange words – "outcast", and, "this is Zion, whom no man seeketh after" (Jer. 30:17)

"For I am with thee, saith the LORD, to save thee: **though I make a full end of all nations whither I have scattered thee, yet will I not make a full end of thee**: but I will correct thee in measure, and will not leave thee altogether unpunished. For thus saith the LORD, Thy **bruise** is **incurable**, and thy **wound** is **grievous**. There is none to plead thy cause, that thou mayest be **bound up**: thou hast no **healing medicines**. All thy lovers have forgotten thee; they seek thee not; for I have **wounded** thee with the **wound** of an enemy, with the chastisement of a cruel one, for the multitude of thine iniquity; because thy sins were increased. Why criest thou for thine **affliction**? thy sorrow is **incurable** for the multitude of thine iniquity: because thy sins were increased, I have done these things unto thee. Therefore all they that devour thee shall be devoured; and all thine adversaries, every one of them, shall go into captivity; and they that spoil thee shall be a spoil, and all that prey upon thee will I give for a prey. For I will **restore health** unto thee, and I will **heal** thee of thy **wounds**, saith the LORD; because they called thee an Outcast, saying, This is Zion, whom no man seeketh after. Thus saith the LORD; Behold, I will bring again the captivity of Jacob's tents, and have mercy on his dwellingplaces; and the city shall be builded upon her own heap, and the palace shall remain after the manner thereof" (Jeremiah 30:11-18).

"Behold, I will bring it **health** and **cure**, and I will **cure** them, and will reveal unto them the abundance of peace and truth. And I will cause the captivity of Judah and the captivity of Israel to return, and will build them, as at the first." (Jeremiah 33:6-7)

The experience described in scripture, which is as fatal, deathbed, incurable wounds, is indicative of the spiritual experience of darkness, God breaking His Covenant, and all that is understood to be the cursed trauma of "The Deception of God." God does not necessarily open up the earth to swallow men down straight into hell, but *the earth*, that is, their *flesh*, called "earthly members" (Col. 3:5), does open up and men are swallowed into the passions of hell which do incessantly and furiously rage in the flesh. It is not that God necessarily floods the earth, cities, or nations anymore, like as Noah's day, but He floods individual persons with spiritual floods and overwhelming billows of wrath – the soul frantically treading water for his very eternal life (Lam. 3:54). These are drowning billows which are declared by saints under the darkness, chastisement, and curse of God's wrath, and they do cry for a saving revelation of God's hidden face. Their soul is decaying, thus, their flesh follows after into a similar decay, and such descriptions they speak of are telling parallels to what has been said heretofore in other brilliant languages of life-gripping power.

The exhaustive perpetuity of the word "breach", which was be used ever since Numbers 14:34, is astounding, at least when its synonyms and parallels are identified and compared. Then we are able to see, like every other doctrine in the Bible, that there has been a progressive revelation and explanation of the doctrine of "breach of promise" (Num. 14:34) since the beginning.

As that first promise was breached, even so, when one studies through the centuries the rest of the promises which are given, and then, what God says in response to when they are not fulfilled, it becomes clear as day why certain descriptive vocabulary is used. The amplification which is given to the doctrine and word "breach" is utterly amazing to me. To name two of many in which we have studied in this chapter, we have studied how the Temple and the protective walls around Israel, which are emblems of the Covenant promise, are both breached in times of wrath. We have studied how other metaphors and synonyms are used to describe a breach, like the word "wound". So also, the fall of the Davidic Covenant is described in the very same term – breach. The house of David was promised to last for eternity, as you know, but that promise was breached in his son's lifetime, as you know, and therefore was the promise of the Covenant's final fulfillment spoken of in light of the former breach upon it, when God said: "In that day will I **raise up** the tabernacle of David that is **fallen**, and **close up the breaches thereof**; and I will **raise up his ruins**, and I will **build** it **as in the days of old**:"(Amos 9:11).

Equally relevant to us is the need to understand the beginning use and continual perpetuity of the doctrine of perfection, which, as you know, is directly connected to a breach of promise. Beside the perpetuity of the use of the word perfect in the NT alone, a correct view of biblical history would prove to us of what utter necessity the doctrine of perfection is for us today. Biblical history describes the lives, generations, and centuries of God's work of salvation in terms of personal and corporate *perfection*. Depending on if whether or not they obtained biblical "perfection," this determined their destiny of heaven or hell! The scripture **explicitly states** that Job (Job 1:1, 8, 2:3, 8:20), Noah (Gen. 6:9), Abraham (Gen. 17:1-2), Joshua (Deut. 18:13), David (Psalm 101), Solomon (1 Kings 11:4, with his repentance, which is in Ecclesiastes), and Hezekiah (1 Kings 20:3) went to heaven because they were *perfect*. As for all other heaven-bound men, even though it was not explicitly mentioned that they were "*perfect*," they, nevertheless followed the ways of them who were called "*perfect*." The scripture, likewise, does **explicitly state** that Abijam (1 Kings 15:3), Asa (1 Kings 15:14), and Amaziah (2 Chron. 25:2) went to hell because of a single indictment – that they were NOT *perfect*. Furthermore, every major vocation is taught the saving expression of their office and duties by the term *perfection*. Kings (Psalm 101), Priests (Lev. 22:21), Judges (2 Chron. 19:9), Warriors (Ps. 18:32), and all, were taught what it is to be *perfect* in the execution of their office, and depending on whether or not they were perfect, they went to heaven or hell. All other men and women of every generation were taught perfection in the principle of its meaning, even though the very word is not explicitly used. Let it therefore alarm us, if, haply, we don't understand what biblical perfection is! To firstly inherit, dwell in, and remain in salvation one must be PERFECT. "For the upright shall dwell in the land, and the **perfect** shall remain in it" (Prov. 2:21). "Behold, God will not *cast away* a *perfect man*, neither will He help the evil doers" (Job 8:20).

THE GLORY OF GOD IN WRATH
PERSONIFICATION, ANTHROPOMORPHISM, & ZOOMORPHISM
CHAPTER 12

Personification & Anthropomorphism

At such a time when wrath is without repentance so that the breaches of promise go on unfilled, lo, and behold, the prophets declare that the armies of God's wrath are rising upon the distant horizon! It is an amazing thing for God to fulfill the promises of God, that He would be so near a Warrior and King in Israel that He would fight for them, even through them, unto uncompromising victory, but how terrible is the warning in which God saith: "Woe also to them **when I depart** from them" (Hos. 9:12)! Woe that God, the only Good, would leave them, but let the reader understand that when God leaves Israel, He then joins the army of the invading enemy host to empower them by His infinite might!

"I the LORD have drawn forth My sword out of his sheath: it shall not return any more"
(Ezek. 21:5).

If an opposing alien host rearing up for the charge unsheathed all their swords – even with the loudest unanimous roar – they would be but grasshoppers of intimidation next to a Living God arrayed for the battle. Imagine, Almighty God, set forth in determination as a Warrior of Steel, saying, "I the LORD have drawn forth My sword." Enemy armies stand opposed, premeditating the utmost brutality to obtain the victory, and yea, they make themselves ready, even with valiant energy, solemn and stern countenances, every one of them set to kill the enemy they meet on the field, and thus –they unsheathe their sword – but how feeble is this house of cards when one army does not have a mere man in their cavalry charge?! With one or the other, Almighty God's heart is set on death and destruction, and He does therefore declare to us the same awful image to describe Himself! Yea, with an unwavering mind, He saith, arrayed as one with an unsheathed sword – "it shall not return any more" (Ezek. 21:5). A sword unsheathed in the arm of God, and He saith, "it shall not return"…this is to mean that it is propelled by *unrepentant wrath*, and therefore intercession is impossible. Had intercession been successfully attained, then the physical manifestation of an opposing army would not have come upon Israel. If God's sword had returned into His sheath, then the alien armies would have returned theirs. They are a hornet hive of servants under the Lord's command to send. Think of it! An army of swords in a million hands – but one Lord – directing every blade of the enemy raid! It was for this reason King David did earnestly pray: "Arise, O LORD, disappoint him, cast him down: deliver my soul from the wicked, **which is Thy sword: from men which are Thy hand**, O LORD, **from men of the world**" (Ps. 17:13-14)!

What terror it is that the wrath of God is personified in such a manner that God has unsheathed a sword of judgment and death! Again I say, and let it be clear – for God to say, "It shall not return any more" (Ezek. 21:5), is to say the same thing as, "I am weary with repenting" (Jer. 15), and for this purpose, the sword is reared back for the strike! This personification of wrath ought to cause the greatest warrior to cower. God, though depicted as a warrior, is an unapproachable force, and like wax before the fire, the mighty men will melt away. His footsteps are earthquakes, with His charging stride the earth does shake, and He will hew them down until their bones do break. "As wax melteth before the fire, so let the wicked perish at the presence of God" (Ps. 68:1-2). This sword drawn image is one of the many ways in which God takes up an illustration for His wrath through anthropomorphism. An unsheathed sword shows ready wrath, even reared back wrath, but other anthropomorphic images declare other attributes & messages.

The prophets declared wrath which was to come, and is not yet – how it would come as in a sudden moment when a man would awake, though it tarries long in hibernation. There are times when God does "rise up" (Num. 10:35) as a man would do who goes forth to war, and also, God does "awake" for "the judgment" as if He were lying down or fast asleep (Isa. 51:9, Ps. 7:6-7), and this shows that He did ignore the cause at hand until a sudden moment of time. And again, another more compelling message: "The LORD shall go forth **as a Mighty Man**, He shall stir up jealousy like **a Man of War**: He shall **CRY**, yea, **ROAR**; He shall prevail against His enemies. I have long time holden My peace; I have been still, and refrained Myself: **now will I CRY** like a travailing woman; **I will destroy and devour at once**" (Isa 42:13-14). The message is frightfully clear – GOD IS ANGRY – and in this way of descriptive speech, God uses anthropomorphism to rattle the cages of the animal-like, iniquitous sinners that He is angry with – so they feel hunted by God – even by God in the form of unrelenting vengeance and rage, even that He is *crying* and *roaring* after them in a devouring jealousy! Thus is the animation of God's mind in wrath!

"He breaketh me with breach upon breach, He runneth upon me like a Giant"
(Job 16:14).

Oh reader! What cry can be compared to a travailing woman? What roar can be compared to a jealous man of war who is valiant and strong – AND READY TO FIGHT, & TO DIE! For God to "go forth" with a cry and roar! How awful the image!! What would you do if you saw and heard God waking up and roaring exactly 1 mile away from you, and then with cries and roars, lo, He broke out into a sprinting stride in an angry pursuit to kill you!? Oh! This hotwires man's feeble understanding and leaves them speechless in a holy astonishment – and yet, there is more to tell! Few things are more intimidating than a charging mighty man of war, but even more than this, imagine the exact same raging man set to kill you, and he is also drunken or drugged. Numb to pain and mindless in rage, such a man can scarcely be restrained by force, for where sense of physical hurt or sure defeat would dissuade a man, or where reason and conscience would make a man aware of shame and guilt - his senses are stupid and his reasonability is madness. This is the experience of humanity, but what if it was likened to a charging, Mighty Deity? It is written, "Then the Lord **awaked as one out of sleep**, and **like a mighty man that shouteth by reason of wine**. And He smote His enemies in the hinder parts: He put them to a perpetual reproach" (Psa. 78:65-66). Earthly images of unstoppable forces are used to give men a small sense of the indescribably terrifying force that God is, so that the mind of men might understand – God is unstoppable – The Only Fierce. Like a mighty man, full of wine, or an intoxicated man in a fit of rage, when men are uncontrollably set to destroy another, this also is like as the uncontrollable human force behind a betrayed husband in the rage of jealousy, or again, a family member seeking revenge after their kin's blood was shed (called a pursuer of blood). At such a time as this, the anger in man is described as a restless anger, making men as mighty as they could be according to their earthen frames, but what if God is in such a restless anger, as if He was frantically out of control and boiling to pursue the adulterer who robbed Him of His wife, or the murderer of His child…He also being the Almighty?

Zoomorphism

God is infinitely beyond humanity, so as to be indescribable, but, in the effort of condescension to us, God describes Himself in the characteristics of men. This is called *anthropomorphism*, thus God takes upon Himself the attributes of humanity, but what if God takes upon Himself the attributes of animals? Considering the mightiest of men in the most terrifying fits of rage, however they are made uncontrollable or unstoppable by whatever circumstance, how much more are animals in strength and violence, which are not restrained by any reason or conscience? Thus God doth animate His wrath and power through *zoomorphism*. Zoomorphism is "the attributing of animal characteristics" to God, instead of human characteristics (Wiktionary). For example, Christ is called "**The Lion** of the tribe of Juda" (Rev. 5:5), and again, "I will be unto Ephraim **as A Lion**" (Hos. 5:14). Lions are called the King of the Animal Kingdom for a reason. The impregnable ranks of their pride do rule the countryside, and by their roar they do mark and guard their territories from other male lions or prides. In the wild, it is an unthinkable fear for a lion to steadfastly look upon you - for you know he is lusting after your blood. It is one thing to be threatened by a mighty man, or even a drunken man, as God warns, "I will tear and go away, I will take away and none shall rescue him" (Hos. 5:14), but what if God – The Lion – does make such a threat? "For I will be unto Ephraim **as a Lion**, and as a young Lion to the house of Judah: **I, even I, will tear and go away; I will take away, and none shall rescue him**" (Hos. 5:14). One of the ways that God shows the fierceness of His anger – which is not turned back – holding the promise of sure destruction, is that God is as terribly unconquerable as a Lion. In the face of a roaring Lion you will not render a reason, or vainly hope in a change of mind – it is an animal! Thus God doth show the unrelenting jeopardy of His mind toward sinners whose sin has reached the verdict of merciless annihilation. "Therefore I will be unto them **as a lion**: **as a leopard** by the way will I observe them: I will meet them **as a bear** that is bereaved of her whelps, and will rend the caul of their heart, and there will **I devour them like a lion**: **the wild beast** shall tear them. O Israel, thou hast destroyed thyself; but in Me is thine help" (Hos. 13:7-9). "The lion hath roared, who will not fear? the Lord GOD hath spoken, who can but prophesy" (Amos 3:8)? Those on the safari plains of Africa do know the terror of the saying, "The Lion hath roared, who will not fear" (Amos 3:8)?

Americans suppose they understand nature, but they are robbed from its experience! Sure, they can watch it from an illuminated box while seated in the comfort and safety of their living room couch, but a real-life experience of "The Wild" is fearful! There is a striking humiliation like no other when you, a mere biped, are standing before giant beasts which tower over you! Quadrupeds are of greater weight, speed, and power, and if you are caught in the open plains with them, then you will see the element for which they were created. Rhinos weigh upwards to 4000 pounds and they can run around 30 mph…in such a case when this animal turns to violence, safety could not be found even if you were in a safari jeep! Have you ever seen an elephant walk through a thick forest? They don't walk around trees very often, they just push them over and trample them down! Even an elephant's horns would make your heart rush if you found yourself outside of the safari jeep, but how much more a lion's roar? One swing of a lion's paw would filet your flesh like a tender child. If you are caught in its grip but a moment, you will not escape, but for a few seconds you may try to run, while your flesh is shredded under his retractable, three inch, razor sharp claws, and, lo, his mouth is just behind you to break your bones and rend your neck like you would a chicken. Nature channels and cinema experiences are one thing, and fantasy another, but when you have been near a pack of lions feasting on their prey, your heart will not slow down to rest until you are far from that place. They glance at you every once and a while as they feast in the bloodbath of their kill, and with red beards and full bellies they pass you by, for now.

"Thou huntest me **as a fierce Lion**: and again Thou shewest Thyself marvellous upon me" (Job 10:16).

The devouring power of a Lion leaves its prey unsalvageable - "Thus saith the LORD; As the shepherd taketh out of **the mouth of the lion** two legs, or a piece of an ear; so shall the children of Israel be taken out that dwell in Samaria in the corner of a bed, and in Damascus in a couch. Hear ye, and testify in the house of Jacob, saith the Lord GOD, the God of hosts, That in the day that I shall visit the transgressions of Israel upon him I will also visit the altars of Bethel: and the horns of the altar shall be cut off, and fall to the ground. And I will smite the winter house with the summer house; and the houses of ivory shall perish, and the great houses shall have an end, saith the LORD" (Amos 3:12-20). Even so, this generation is taught, by experience, the awful truth of these threats, and they say by confession: "He was unto me **as a bear lying in wait**, and **as a lion in secret places**. He hath turned aside my ways, and **pulled me in pieces**: He hath made me desolate" (Lam. 3:10-11)!

A lion is an animal that is raised up to learn the violence of hunting and killing, whose life is sustained by sharpened skills to do it well. It is an animal that lives by every kill – that kills to live – likewise with God are "the instruments of death", and as long as He lives, sin and sinners must die! If He were to die, then sin could remain alive to live forever, but with Him remaining yet alive it is impossible for this to be so. He exists to destroy sin, death, and evil! "God judgeth the righteous, and God is angry with the wicked every day. If he turn not, He will whet **His sword**; He hath bent **His bow**, and made it ready. He hath also prepared for him **the instruments of death**; He ordaineth **His arrows** against the persecutors" (Psa. 7:11-13). Instruments of death are His sword, His bow, and His arrows. God takes hold of these to reveal the emergency of wrath at hand, but like as the metaphorical image of the Lion's crouch, pounce, and roar, God is describing the urgent feeling of His powers but not necessarily the medium in which they are directed. God spoke of Himself as the Lion, but at other points He speaks of the actual destroyer to be "the Gentiles" (Jer. 4:5-10). "For a nation is come up upon my land, strong, and without number, whose teeth are the teeth of a lion, and he hath the cheek teeth of a great lion" (Joel 1:6). Why? God has left Israel and is now with the enemy nation, and He fights with and through them to destroy Israel!

When God takes hold on judgment, He takes hold on His "glittering sword" to make it warm and wet with blood. He takes hold on "Mine arrows," God says, that He may make them "drunk with blood." He takes hold on "My sword", He says, and this "shall devour flesh" (Deut. 32:39-43). Nevertheless, in the case of God turning upon Israel as His enemy to fight against them, His instruments of death are the entire population of Gentile humanity. Babylon, chosen to destroy Israel, was called "the hammer of the whole earth" (Jer. 50:23), and that is to say that they are God's HAMMER, God's weapon, which does not move without Him. At a time of triumph for Israel, it is said that Judah and Ephraim are His bent bow, and the sons of Zion the arrows, and as the sword of a mighty man – "the LORD shall be seen over them, and His arrows shall go forth as lightning: and the Lord GOD shall blow the trumpet, and shall go with the whirlwinds of the south" (Zech. 9:13-14). If the Lord is so seen over Israelite armies at war, in this soul-gasping, life-taking power, it should be equally as shocking to hear of the Gentiles that – "They come from a far country, from the end of heaven, **even the LORD, and the weapons of His indignation, to destroy the whole land**" (Isa 13:5). God takes the glory for it, and for this purpose He raises them up; God says, "Now have I brought it to pass, **that thou shouldest be to lay waste defenced cities into ruinous heaps**" (Isa 37:26).

These Gentiles nations are called "men which are Thy hand, O LORD" (Ps. 17:14). Assyria was called "The rod of Mine anger, and the staff in their hand is Mine indignation;" thus God calls them His "axe" wherewith He did hew down His people (Isa. 10:5-6, 15). God, literally, stands at the right hand of Israelite adversaries to bend their bow, and slay (Lam. 2:4). Thus God says, "I will spend Mine arrows upon them" (Deut. 32:23). At such a time as is said to be here, when God is spending His arrows, *and sparing not*, it was then that His anger was burning with the vehemence equivalent to "hell" (Deut. 32:22), which meaneth, it was flaming to devour the proud and swelling future of society - the *young man* and *virgin* – and so also the ancient past which remained alive in that day for venerable memories and respect - the *old man* – and even all those who would appear to deserve the pitiful face of pardon - the *suckling child* (Deut. 32:25).

Like the determined, fearless, relentless, and devouring look of a Lion, God commands "the sword" of men to slay, and says, "I will set Mine eyes upon them for evil, and not for good" (Amos 9:4). What kind of fear is God seeking to make manifest? Behold again, the prophet Ezekiel:

> "That all flesh may know that I the LORD have drawn forth my sword
> out of his sheath: it shall not return any more. Sigh therefore, thou son of
> man, with the breaking of thy loins; and with bitterness sigh before their
> eyes. And it shall be, when they say unto thee, Wherefore sighest thou?
> that thou shalt answer, For the tidings; because it cometh: and every heart
> shall melt, and all hands shall be feeble, and every spirit shall faint, and
> all knees shall be weak as water: behold, it cometh, and shall be brought
> to pass, saith the Lord GOD. (Ezek. 21:5-7)

The Glory of God in WRATH

"as natural brute beasts, made to be taken and destroyed" – 2 Peter 2:12
"My counsel shall stand, and I will do all My pleasure" – Isaiah 46:10

Professing Christians all over this world, of all denominations and creeds, and men of all other religions outside of that which is claimed under the name "Christianity", do make much of the love and mercy of God. It seems that there is a universal and natural conviction deep within the heart and conscience of every man, with few excluded, that God is GOOD. Yea, this is true, but they, "being evil," cannot understand what God's goodness is! As it is written, "O generation of vipers, how can ye, being evil, speak good things" (Matt. 12:34)?

"But these speak evil of those things which they know not:
but what they know naturally, as brute beasts, in those things they corrupt
themselves" – Jude 1:10

Men, blind to righteousness, "lovers of pleasures more than lovers of God" (2 Tim. 3:4), do have no sight of the GOODNESS of God's justice, so that they falsely justify themselves, and finally, they presume that the pleasures of sin will not lead to an eternity where God has pleasure in their displeasure, even in their pain and teeth-gnashing torments. In one sense, God has "no pleasure" in the death of the wicked (Ezek. 33:11), but in another sense we can understand that, from creation, men were "formed" (Rom. 9:20), "fitted" (Rom. 9:22), and created as "vessels of wrath" (Rom. 9:22), which means that they were created for the purpose of God's glory in WRATH – glory I say, to display breathtaking wrath and destruction for His own praise and honor, so that, the sovereign "pleasure" (Isa. 46:10) of this counsel is that they are "as natural brute beasts, **made to be taken and destroyed**" (2 Peter 2:12).

This is the glory of God! If saints shout eternal Hallelujahs in heaven, then the devil's family roars eternal horrors in hell. Not only the love of God, but the torments of hell, are "greater far than any tongue or pen can ever tell" (The Love of God)! God has predestined glory for Himself in the mercy of salvation, in reconciliation, but likewise in castaway destruction; not only love and redemption but also hatred and damnation. Hope and hopelessness, peace and anxiousness, ecstasy and agony, mercy and wrath, love and hate - eternity will never tell the end of the story of God's glory in these two veins! And which elect vessel are you? So many men want to and do sing of their various pleasures, and nearly all religious men sing of mercy, but the inspired writers and psalmists ALSO sang of God's wrath, even that it was the glory of God that fear seizes men unto unspeakable pains. Oh! How the world needs to be forewarned of *God's glorious wrath,* lest they meet with it in eternity because they never worshipped Him for it, on earth. Will you stop for a while and consider an honest question? Will you, my reader, join with those trillions of souls who are burning in hell underneath your feet? For just a moment of your time here on earth, I plead with you, please, will you think about what the souls in hell are forced to think about? Will you seek God for a deep understanding of the glory of God in hell, in eternal wrath, and not just in heaven and grace?

"PREPARE TO MEET THY GOD" – Amos 4:12

Holy angels underwent a difficult war with devils on earth, and at times they were restrained or hindered from accomplishing God's good purposes (Daniel). This is the scenery on earth below, but there is a different sight above – the scenery of God's unveiled glories! What think ye, thou devilish dominions and principalities, in the hour when God does look upon you? The darkest and most fierce host of the devil arrayed before the Almighty will then live out their lamentations which they did speak on earth: "What have we to do with Thee, Jesus, Thou Son of God? Art Thou come hither to torment us before the time" (Matt. 8:29)? Arrayed in earthly and angelic might, they all, with the renowned antichrist, shall be delivered over to the exhale of God. "The breath of the LORD like a stream of brimstone" (Isa. 30:33) "shall consume with the spirit of His mouth" (2 Thess. 2:8). The eyes of God, which are "a flame of fire" – even they shall look upon the "sons of pride" and bring them low. The eternal hatred of God contained within the Almighty shall be let loose by a fiery, Leviathan-like exhale, and that fire that shall begin will become an eternal lake which God will keep lit by His sustaining Presence. God shall encircle and compass them for a timeless eternity, taking upon Himself the task to be their Terror and Tormentor. They wish they could but die; yet at His feet their spirits shall live to forever die, eternally cast down as flaming, wailing carcasses, catching glimpses of His burning feet of brilliant, glowing brass as He walks about their midst. Locked under the eternality of His hatred to be condemned under the infinite power of God, His limitless intellect has created an eternal dungeon of death which is the anti-art of the Garden of Eden – for, here, every creation is the instrumentality of an excruciating execution.

The Garden of Eden did prosper as a life-abounding paradise, because God kept it. As "the LORD God planted a garden eastward in Eden; and there He put the man whom He had formed," likewise God planted a Lake of Fire in which to put wicked men whom He has "fitted for destruction" (Rom. 9). The Garden of Eden was called "the garden of the LORD" (Gen. 13:10) and "the garden of God" (Ezek. 31:9), a place of "joy and gladness," "thanksgiving and the voice of melody" (Isa. 51:3); likewise there is a place of "weeping and gnashing of teeth" (Matt. 8:12). Eden was the place where the Presence of God was "walking in the garden in the cool of the day" (Gen. 3:8), yet when devilish men and angels are "in the presence of the Lamb," there shall be a very different picture. The wicked "shall drink of the wine of the wrath of God, which is poured out without mixture into the cup of His indignation; and he shall be tormented with fire and brimstone in the presence of the holy angels, and **in the presence of the Lamb**" (Rev. 14:10). The presence of the Lamb was executing a very different purpose than that of Eden. The harmless Lamb has become a Lion upon His prey, seeking hurt, pain, and destruction upon everything that did hurt and taint God's good creation. Eden was a place of blessing, as was told in the sayings of God, "I the LORD do keep it; I will water it every moment: lest any hurt it, I will keep it night and day" (Isa 27:3). "A land which the LORD thy God careth for: the eyes of the LORD thy God are always upon it, from the beginning of the year even unto the end" (Deut. 11:12). Likewise, God will keep the Lake of Fire lit with His eyes so that nothing will ever interrupt His enemies' hurt, and "the smoke of their torment ascendeth up for ever and ever: and they have no rest day nor night" (Rev. 14:11).

"He crouched, He lay down as a Lion, and as a Great Lion: who shall stir Him up" (Num. 24:9)?

"The fear of a king is as the roaring of a lion: whoso provoketh him to anger sinneth against his own soul." (Proverbs 20:2)

It is the end, an eternal end, and now these pitiless criminals who are so vile in existence – these men and women who are the horror of heaven – now and forever they will suffer under the merciless rage of God:

When God emerges from silence, it will be with incomparable violence,
Like a Lion upon its prey, He will be the victor on Judgment Day.
It is a crime to have compassion when the Most Just massacres men.
Families will be seized with teeth-gnashing cries; mothers, brothers, and
sisters will look on with no earthly ties,
This Lion-like God will ignore all their cries, and every heavenly dignity
will shout Alleluia as every malefactor dies.
The passion of Christ the world thought was nice; they neglected it for
pleasure, and now they pay the price.

Eden was Eden because God walked in the midst of it in the cool of the day, but the Lake of Fire is the Lake of Fire because God walks in the midst of it in the heat of His fiery wrath. Behold the goodness and the severity of God – to them in Eden there was goodness, while they continued in His goodness – but who can endure the severity of the Lake of Fire? Behold God's goodness and severity, Eden and the Lake of Fire, and under the tent of time in this low earth, every generation did learn of His twofold purposes for all men – "the riches of His glory on vessels of mercy" and the power of His wrath assailing upon "vessels of wrath fitted to destruction" (Rom. 9:22-23), that through all ages and throughout time, these purposes alone would make up the two-piece garment of His glory.

"The heavens declare the glory of God and the firmament sheweth His handywork" (Ps. 19:1), so the atmospheric art of erupting clouds of smoke do surround the servants of the devil. These thick clouds are God's glorious curse upon sinners, suppressing any hope of light, or so much as a single breath of relief, while under the endless glory of God's wrath in fire. The collision of God and sinners results in the black clouds of punishing misery and lifeless suffocation. Nay, the faithful and sweet welcome of the morning sunshine of God's warm love to all creatures – the ever-faithful rays that pierced through the night and arose upon all darkness bringing life, hope, and a future – all these days on earth have been sinned away. They spent away all their days on earth discounting the firmament of brilliant colors and marvelous, artistic mixtures in their earthly sky, until the mist of their life evaporated into the volcanic atmosphere of God's handiwork in horror, maximized under smoking suffocation and clouds of torment.

The love of God evaporates! Eternity arrives and all sinners exasperate!
Creatures arrive before the judgment seat with nowhere to flee,
Angels and men, those who were wicked in sin, all are forced now to bow the knee.
Their heart yearns in some hopeful plea, their heart writhes the cry, "Pity me!"
Approaching the Sovereign He hears their heart cry,
But they left off to be urgent until it was time to die.
They tried to repent while upon their death bed,
They tried to find mercy as they had planned and always said.
But they died without grace because they lived a life that provoked God to the face!

They rejected Him all their days.
Even though He spoke, they followed their own ways.
A life with pleasure and full of sin, this was their choice time and time again,
And on their death bed they presumed they would have the grace to choose God
instead of all their sin.

Can sinners outwit God? Can they get all of their pleasure and be saved by a death
bed nod before the God they have defied, even though He cried, wept, and died?
Now they feel death's untimely touch, even the hand of God's justice which grips
their sinful soul,
And now they desire to come to God Who ever pled to make them whole.
But it's too late because sin has taken a toll,
Most men and women can't repent because they are lost and out of control.

"How long, ye simple ones, will ye love simplicity? and the scorners delight in their scorning, and fools hate knowledge? Turn you at my reproof: behold, I will pour out my spirit unto you, I will make known my words unto you. Because I have called, and ye refused; I have stretched out my hand, and no man regarded; But ye have set at nought all my counsel, and would none of my reproof: I also will laugh at your calamity; I will mock when your fear cometh; When your fear cometh as desolation, and your destruction cometh as a whirlwind; when distress and anguish cometh upon you. Then shall they call upon Me, but I will not answer; they shall seek Me early, but they shall not find Me: For that they hated knowledge, and did not choose the fear of the LORD: They would none of My counsel: they despised all My reproof. Therefore shall they eat of the fruit of their own way, and be filled with their own devices. For the turning away of the simple shall slay them, and the prosperity of fools shall destroy them. But whoso hearkeneth unto Me shall dwell safely, and shall be quiet from fear of evil." (Proverbs 1:22-33)

A wrath-bearing Body did bear the weight of <u>*wrath*</u>,
This is the Gateway for the righteous & narrow path,
But if His suffering you do shamefully neglect,
If His mercy you do not cherish and accept,
The wrath that fell on Him will fall upon you.

God made the Savior cry on a tree!
Sinner, will He do anything different to you and me?
If we neglect His caring calls, choose to love the Adamic lusts borne from the fall,
Make a mock at mercy, and for sin-soaked years of pleasure expect eternity to stall,
Will you think God is not meditating on your crying and tortured agony in hell?
Will you go on thinking, as you always have, that you are ok and all is well?

If God made the Savior cry on a tree, will He do anything different to me?

If Jesus bled for me there, under God's wrath,
what will wrath do to me if I choose the wicked path?
What happened in time, 2000 years ago,
will happen outside of time for an eternity of years, even so...
God will make men bleed like the hanging Savior was left in need,
God forsook Him and He will forsake you,
God bruised Him and He will break you,
He that made you will overtake you,
You will wish He never did create you,
With wrath He will overwhelm and hate you,
He slaughtered the sin-bearing Innocent, and will turn upon the guilty in vengeance,
And as He did ignore His cries, He will ignore your cries as you everlastingly die.

That forsaken Man on a tree,
You wonder now at His agony,
What it felt like when He cried, "Why hast Thou forsaken Me?"
But such a vision you will soon see, because from His wrath you did never flee!

"I know that, whatsoever God doeth, it shall be for ever:
nothing can be put to it, nor any thing taken from it:
and God doeth it, that men should fear before Him" (Eccl. 3:14).

THE DOCTRINE
OF REPROBATION:
CASTAWAY FOR CASAWAY,
FORSAKE FOR FORSAKE
CHAPTER 13

The personified, anthropomorphic, and zoomorphic expressions of the wrath of God are revelations of the glory of God's wrath which can all mean, essentially, that God forsook men. Why? God says that they have forsaken Him, and therefore He did forsake them – *forsake for forsake*:

> "And the LORD said unto Moses, Behold, thou shalt sleep with thy fathers; and this people will rise up, and go a whoring after the gods of the strangers of the land, whither they go to be among them, and will **forsake Me**, and **break My covenant which I have made with them**. Then my anger shall be kindled against them in that day, and **I will forsake them**, and **I will hide My face from them**, and they shall be devoured, and many evils and troubles shall befall them; so that they will say in that day, Are not these evils come upon us, because our God is not among us?" (Deut. 31:17)

Israel broke their agreement, so God broke His agreement. They broke their debts which were due to God, so God, being compelled by righteous justice, was innocent to revoke His. When God's people forsake Him (Jer. 2:13, 17), then God is constrained by the edicts of justice to do likewise. If the people behave foolishly and do what they ought not to do...and so they "give the sacrifice of fools" in the House of God because "they consider not that they do evil" (Ecc. 5:1), then God will surprise them in their foolishness by an awakening word – bold rebellion deserves a bold word – and thus, when they enquire of God to know His burden for them, He will say: "What burden? **I will even forsake you**, saith the LORD" (Jer. 23:33).

Though the primary burden of this book is to unveil to the reader "the scarcity of salvation," we must also recognize how difficult it is to lose one's salvation. The Lord did not forsake or "cast away" (1 Cor. 9:27) the Exodus generation until, as He said, the people "tempted Me now these ten times, and have not hearkened to My voice" (Numbers 14:22). These men were those who, God says, "have seen My glory, and my miracles, which I did in Egypt and in the wilderness," but after all of these "ten times" of repeated provocation, and after the many mighty signs and wonders which they did see, even still they would not obey the gospel call to conquer and take the Promised Land (Numbers 14:22, Ps. 78:9). God does give unrepentant men a "space to repent" before they become reprobated, irreconcilable, and hopelessly lost (Rev. 2:21). During the lifetime of such a one who is eventually reprobated, we must expect and understand that, though they were eventually reprobated, before this, God did exhaust His wooing powers in striving after them. God was seeking to make them faithful and obedient, but it was no avail. This *God-given* space and time to repent will be accompanied with the chastening of God, which is an effort to subdue the will of rebellion into repentance so as to bring men into "subjection unto the Father of spirits and live" (Heb. 12:9). The OT descriptions of chastening are described in four stages of severity in the circumstance of ongoing, unrepentant sin, and each stage is done before reprobation (Leviticus 26:16-17 [stage #1], 18-20 [stage #2], 21-22 [stage #3], and 23-26 [stage #4]). During this process of chastening, reprobation is the final straw – and then the privileges, advantages, and salvation inherent unto a son are taken away, like as if the child has become "lost" and "dead", and thus his inherited salvation is spent away, lost, and dead – thus God would say, "My son was dead" (Luke 15:23-24). According to biblical typology, this was done in various times, places, and generations, one of them being the captivities of dispersion (see Lev. 26:27-39). This chastening is for "profit," to work within us a yielding of fruit unto "His holiness" (Heb. 12:10); yet we must "endure" (Heb. 12:7) and be "exercised thereby" (Heb. 12:11), to the end that we obtain holiness, lest we faint under the chastening as Esau fainted, and think it reasonable to forfeit salvation for temporal lusts, pleasures, and carnal comforts like a satisfied belly full of food (Heb. 12:12-15, 16-17).

The Lord alone knows how long He will be merciful to a backslidden, un-perfected Christian, but we know that He does give a "space to repent" (Rev. 2:21). That space of time lasted nearly a year (at least) for God's choice and beloved servant, King David. David was standing to be blamed with damnable sin when he committed adultery and murder in the scenario with Bathsheba. The length of time that David existed in a blamable state before God, which is, in a state of rebellion without repentance, demonstrates how long this space of time can be…but we cannot limit it to this length either (for the decision belongeth unto God's sovereignty in every individual person's life). David was backslidden at least since the time he sinned with Bathsheba, and there was no repentance until after the child was born. Before the sin of Bathsheba, he should have been out at war with his army, and this also was a sin, and since this was before the sin of Bathsheba, then we cannot know exactly when his rebellion began. Nevertheless, nearly a year is a sufficient estimation, and this is a long time! Praise be to God for His great mercy!

> *"Lord, Thou hast won, at length I yield,*
> *My heart, by mighty grace compelled,*
> *Surrenders all to Thee;*
> *Against Thy terrors long I strove,*
> *But who can stand against Thy love?*
> *Love conquers even me"*
> (John Newton, "The Rebel's Surrender to Grace")

The time in which a man is in rebellion and yet unrepentant, and mercy is still available to him for the inward formation of repentance – this is the "space" given by God. In this time when a righteous man *falls*, he is still enabled to repent, for as long as God ordains that it is, namely, before he *falls away*. In such a time, it can be said that a man is *cast off* by the wrath of God, but there is still mercy if he repents; but if he does not, he will be a *castaway*. To *fall* is not the same thing as *falling away*, and likewise, when a man is *cast off*, he is not yet *cast away*. "For a just man **falleth** seven times, and riseth up again: but the wicked shall fall into mischief" (Prov. 24:16). "Though he **fall**, he shall not be **utterly cast down**: for the LORD upholdeth him with His hand" (Psalm 37:24). Like unto the word **fall**, the word **cast off** is used in reference to the experience of godly, regenerate saints in the OT who have fallen, and at present, the anger of God is kindled against them, but they are not reprobated…this means that they have the means available to pacify the wrath of God through repentance and intercession. Cited below are some references where "**cast off**" is used in regard to the experiences of godly, regenerate men. To be cast off is a manifestation of the wrath of God, and this can be demonstrated, for example, in a time of Israel's rebellion when God would not go out with the armies of Israel so as to empower a victory at war (Psalm 44:9). Also, to be "cast off" is an experience synonymous with what happens when God hides His face (Psalm 44:24). Both can be temporary, but they can turn into an everlasting experience (Psalms 44:23, 74:1, 77:7); yet to be forever cast off would also be referred to by the word *castaway*.

God is said to have breached the Mosaic and Davidic Covenants, and in this language it is said that God had **cast off** these promises and Covenants (Psalms 77:7, 89:38). At such a time, the prophets interceded with the cries, "**cast us not off forever**" (Ps. 44:23), which also meant, "**cast me not away from Thy Presence**, and take not Thy Holy Spirit from me" (Psalm 51:11). If the prophets were to succeed in intercession, then salvation, hope, and forgiveness would be on the horizon. After successful intercessions were obtained, the saint who was fallen was filled with a God-given assurance so that a prophetic vision of salvation is imparted to the heart, which in turn resulted in nothing else but bold praises to the Most High!

> "O God, Thou hast **cast us off**, Thou hast scattered us, Thou hast been displeased; O turn Thyself to us again…Wilt not Thou, O God, which hadst **cast us off**? And Thou, O God, which didst not go out with our armies? Gives us help from trouble…Through God we shall do valiantly: for He it is that shall tread down our enemies." (Psalms 60:1, 10-12, 108:11)

> "Rejoice not against me, O mine enemy: when I **fall**, I shall arise; when I sit in darkness, the LORD shall be a light unto me. I will bear the indignation of the LORD, because I have sinned against Him, until He plead my cause, and execute judgment for me: He will bring me forth to the light, and I shall behold His

righteousness. Then she that is mine enemy shall see it, and shame shall cover her which said unto me, Where is the LORD thy God? mine eyes shall behold her: now shall she be trodden down as the mire of the streets."
(Micah 7:8-10)

To be cast out of God's presence, like as it was phrased by David in Psalm 51:11 when he pled that he would not be reprobated, is applicably indicative of nationwide reprobation as well (Jer. 23:39, 52:3). If the wrath of God never gets to "this point" – the point of reprobation – God can redeem them as though He was never angry with them, as if He did not ever desire to destroy them (Zech. 10:6). A biblical synonym to **casting off** or **away** is the usage of the word **forsake**. 2 Chronicles 15:2, as formerly addressed, is the biblical principle of justice: *forsake for forsake,* which is like as *cast away for cast away.* It states, "The LORD is with you, while ye be with him; and if ye seek him, He will be found of you; but if ye **forsake** him, He will **forsake** you" (2 Ch. 15:2). God will forsake, does forsake, and has forsaken His people in His wrath, just as He **casts off** and **away** (Deut. 31:17), but to be **forsaken** *temporarily* is different than being **forsaken** *utterly* or *forever,* which is the meaning of the words *cast away* and *fall away.* Therefore the prophets did offer up their intercessions and prayers to prevent an ***utter*** and ***forever* forsaking** of themselves and God's people. A godly psalmist prayed, "O **forsake** me not **utterly**" (Ps. 119:8). This prayer well represents the fears deep in the heart of a well-saved man, for, such a man prays against the spiritual experiences he fears. King David cried this prayer over and over while he was under temporary manifestations of God's wrath, and one should be astonished with great perplexity if these prayers are altogether not on your tongue, for then, one may find out that what was temporary for David will be eternal for you.

"Hide not Thy face far from me; put not Thy servant away in anger: Thou hast been my help; leave me not, neither **forsake** me, O God of My salvation." (Psalm 27:9)

"O LORD, rebuke me not in Thy wrath: neither chasten me in Thy hot displeasure. For Thine arrows stick fast in me, and Thy hand presseth me sore. There is no soundness in my flesh because of Thine anger; neither is there any rest in my bones because of my sin. For mine iniquities are gone over mine head: as an heavy burden they are too heavy for me. My wounds stink and are corrupt because of my foolishness. I am troubled; I am bowed down greatly; I go mourning all the day long...**Forsake** me not, O LORD: O my God, be not far from me. Make haste to help me, O Lord my salvation." (Ps. 38:1-6, 21-22)

During a space of time wherein God has forsaken one or some, the prophets pray against *the length of time it endures* (Lam. 5:20), hoping to be redeemed from it. Yet, there is nothing as fearful as the Word of God which declares an **unrepentant**

306

forsaking in the heart of God. God said to reprobate generations, "And when this people, or the prophet, or the priest shall ask thee, saying, What is the burden of the LORD? Thou shalt then say unto them, What burden? **I will even forsake you, saith the LORD**...Therefore behold, I, even I, will **utterly forget** you, and I will **forsake you**, and the city that I gave you and your fathers, and **cast you out of My Presence**" (Jer. 23:33, 39). Though these realities are real, experiential, warned of, feared by the godly, interceded against by the prophets, and forever the doom of the reprobate – there are promises which declare that the **casting off**, **away**, and **forsaking** of God's wrath are *impossibilities* for God's people ((Jer. 31:37, 33:24, Psalm 94:14) → [casting off] (Psalm 94:14, 1 Sam. 12:22, 1 Kings 6:13, Neh. 9:31) → [forsaking]), but these scriptures refer to the *final* and *entire* annihilation of Israel, not the annihilation of *nearly all* except a *remnant,* and they in no way negate the validity or history when the many promise-bound saints rebelled throughout the centuries and thus lost their salvation. Parallel to this are the instances of God's *repentances*, but God promises with an unrepentant purpose that He will never *fully* and *entirely* annihilate His people (Rom. 11:29).

When God reprobates men, as seen throughout history, they are called **castaways** or **reprobates**. In Jeremiah, God spoke of them as "reprobate silver" (Jer. 6:30), which is cast away, useless, and without value, therefore it is unredeemable by the purifying fires of a smelting furnace. God's chastening is the fire of this smelting furnace, and as was formerly stated, when chastening ceases, then Paternal love ceases – thus the Father's son is dead. When God casts men away, as the prophet says in Hosea 9:17, "My God will **cast them away**," they are cast away from the Presence of God; thus God says, "Woe also to them when I **depart** from them" (Hos. 9:12), "I will **drive them out** of Mine House, I will love them no more" (Hos. 9:15). Experientially, God's presence is as the virtue of health and nourishment, like that which comes from a vine to make healthy and feed the branches grafted into it, but when a man is cast away from God, they are, as it were, cast away from "The Vine." The prophets declared this about people: "He hath laid my vine waste, and barked my fig tree: He hath made it clean bare, and **cast it away**; the branches thereof are made white" (Joel 1:7).

Do you remember the prophetic language of God when He did turn upon Israel as a man of war with the instruments of death, and as a devouring Lion? Could it ever be that these instruments of destruction could be turned toward a saint whom God loves, like as they were turned toward the city and nation of Israel? Could it be that they are turned toward a saint during this temporary period of time when God casts a man off, and, if they repent before He casts them away, then, lo, the sword of His wrath is returned to its sheath? David, the beloved of God, often confessed himself to be *cast off* by the Lord! At such a time, the instruments of death were taken up by the hand of God, as it were, and the sword of wrath was "drawn forth out of his sheath", yet, unlike those who were cast away, David interceded, repented, sought the face of his God, and thus, the sword returned to its sheath. The sword did slay him, but not *utterly*. The arrows were therefore taken up in the hand of God because of, David says, "Thine anger" (Ps. 38:3), but would you, my reader, ever believe that there has been a time in your walk with God that you could look up and perceive the bent bow of God aimed toward you? David did! God did not merely aim the bow at David, but He stuck him through with arrows! David said, "**Thine arrows** stick fast in me, and Thy hand presseth me sore" (Ps. 38:2). And again David said, "My **wounds** stink and are corrupt because of my foolishness" (Ps. 38:5). Aren't the arrows of God His instruments of death, which are meant for God's enemies? Indeed they are, and so is God's wrath, but will you know this biblical God which *nearly kills you to save you*, that *forbears wrath chiefly for Himself*? The wrath of God is temporarily kindled against His holy saints who do persevere, for if it would go on forever and always, then all would be ***utterly forsaken*** and ***cast away*** – but instead they are ***cast off*** and then recovered. "For I will not contend for ever, neither will I be always wroth: for the spirit should fail before Me, the souls which I have made" (Isa. 57:16).

The question I posed was thus, in other words: as Psalm 7:11-13 states that God bends His *bow* and *shoots* at sinners, and it also says that God judgeth the righteous, *is it possible for **saints** to become **sinners*** (at least temporarily) so that they are *pursued by God's wrathful and just instruments of death*? Though they may not be **cast away** like Jeremiah's generation, when it was said: "He hath bent His bow, and set me as a mark for the arrow. He hath caused the arrows to His quiver to enter into my reins" (Lam. 3:12-13), is it possible to be temporarily seized by the instruments of God's wrath and death, but then delivered from them, by the grace of God? Remember, the book of Lamentations is written as a lament over the reprobation of a generation which is a type of those who lose their salvation, and also remember the previous references which affirm this as an experience of the regenerate prophet – King David. Seeing these references, the reader must conclude to the affirmative. Yet again the question could be posed: is it possible for God, Who was a Lion of destruction toward those who are reprobated, turn upon the saved so as to devour them - like as the instruments of war were turned upon men? Of the generation which was dispersed (which was a type of losing salvation), it was said: "He was unto me as a **bear** lying in wait, and as a **lion** in secret places. He hath turned aside my ways, and **pulled me in pieces**: He hath made me desolate" (Lam. 3:10-11). There is no explanation for this, except that, during the time that His people are **cast off** but not **cast away**, they are considered *sinners* and *enemies* in the mind of God; otherwise He would not treat them as such. As with the arrows of wrath, so David confesses of the wounds of His wrath – "My **wounds** stink and are corrupt because of my foolishness. I am troubled; I am bowed down greatly; I go mourning all the day long" (Ps. 38:5-6).

As it is with the instruments of war and death, and the Lion-like devouring wrath, so it was with *the waves* of God's wrath as in the time of Jonah's destruction. He said, "All **Thy billows** and **Thy waves** passed over me... I am **cast out** of Thy sight" (Jonah 2:3-4); thus are the godly when they are "**cast off**" (Ps. 88:14). They do lament their complaint to God, "Thy **wrath** lieth hard upon me, and Thou hast afflicted me with all **Thy waves**" (Ps. 88:7, 42:7). So again it is written of the generation of Jeremiah, "**Waters** flowed over mine head; then I said, I am cut off" (Lam. 3:54). Thus all of these wrathful expressions of God are obviously linked together to reveal the same thing: "I am the man that hath seen affliction by the rod of His wrath…Surely against me is He turned; He turned His hand against me all the day" (Lam. 3:1, 3), and we know that God only turns in anger, as an enemy, toward sinners – therefore *saints* must be able to become *sinners* (during the time they are temporarily snared in unrepentant sin, a condition otherwise known as "cast off" or "fallen"). Now remember, they can recover their saintly standing, and if they don't, they will eventually be reprobated.

> "All the **sinners** of my people shall die by the sword, which say,
> The evil shall not overtake nor prevent us."
> (Amos 9:10)

> "**Brethren**, if **any of you** do err from the truth, and one convert him; Let him know, that he which converteth **the sinner** from the error of his way shall save a soul from death, and shall hide a multitude of sins."
> (Jas. 5:19-20)

Saints who are under the wrath of God have become His enemies (James 4:4), or adversaries (Heb. 10:27), as formerly addressed in detail. Such a state is a rebukable state (1 Tim. 6:14), which God seeks to prevent so as to make us "sons of God without rebuke" (Php. 2:15). If God's sons will be "without rebuke in the midst of a crooked and perverse nation", it will be because they are uncorrupted by the crookedness and perversion around them, but if they are corrupted, God saith: "They have corrupted themselves, their spot is not the spot of His children: they are a perverse and crooked generation" (Deut. 32:5). The rebuke of God is the mark of damnation (Hos. 5:9, Isa. 51:20), and of curse and destruction (Deut. 28:20); thus it is feared by the righteous who are cast off and backslidden (Psalms 38:1, 6:1). To be without rebuke is also to be "blameless and harmless" (Php. 2:15).

To be blameless is to be perseverant in grace (1 Cor. 1:8), and the NT letters attempt to recover and establish the saints so that they would be "unblameable in holiness before God, even our Father, at the coming of our Lord Jesus Christ with all His saints" (1 Thess. 3:13). To this end, the NT pastors wrote, preached, and labored (1 Thess. 5:23) – even for the Churches' "perfection" (1 Thess. 3:10, Col. 1:28-29) – and anyone who was sleeping to this burden had to awake to clear themselves from the dangerous threat of BLAME before Christ: "Wherefore, beloved, seeing that ye look for such things, be diligent that ye may be found of Him in peace, without spot, and blameless" (2 Peter 3:14).

To be blamable and rebukable, you are under an offence; thus Paul prays fervently for Christians to escape the terror of Judgment Day which can turn into and become a revelation of wrath for a man, if indeed the Christian is not "sincere and

309

without offence till the Day of Christ" (Php. 1:10). "Offence" is repeatedly spoken of as an expression for damnable sin (Rom. 9:33, 5:15, 18, 20, Matt. 18:7, Acts 24:16); even so it is defined in the OT as well (Hos. 5:15, Isa. 8:14). A man blamed as an offender is a "transgressor" (Gal. 2:18), and at this time a Christian becomes a "sinner" (Gal. 2:17) "fallen from grace" (Gal. 5:4).

To be blamable, rebukable, and under offence, is also to be at fault (1 Cor. 6:7, Rom. 9:19) – thus, as a Christian can become a sinner as in the verses referenced above (James 5:19-20), so also a Christian can become overtaken in a fault and in need of restoration: "Brethren, if a man be overtaken in a fault, ye which are spiritual, restore such an one in the spirit of meekness; considering thyself, lest thou also be tempted" (Gal. 6:1). All the redeemed will be those who "are without fault before the Throne of God" (Rev. 14:5). To fall is to fall into fault, to be kept by grace is to be kept from fault, and thus it is written – "Now unto Him that is able to keep you from falling, and to present you faultless before the presence of His glory with exceeding joy, to the only Wise God our Saviour, be glory and majesty, dominion and power, both now and ever. Amen" (Jude 24-25). God would have men know about, and avoid, the damnable condition of being found "faulty" before Him (Hos. 10:2). All this is to say, *saints can become sinners*; thus let us make no more excuses, no more great swelling word-acrobatics to somehow make the scripture mean something other than what the plain meaning is, and therefore let us hear the clear warning and charge: "work out your own salvation with **fear** and **trembling**" (Php. 2:12). Let us hear about and understand the race in which we run (1 Cor. 9:26), the striving which we strive in (1 Cor. 9:24-25), "lest...I myself should be a castaway" (1 Cor. 9:27), and so, let us not "be ignorant" (1 Cor. 10:1) that we can "fall" (1 Cor. 10:12), but in acknowledging this awful reality, let us therefore, by grace, avoid it! "Wherefore the rather, brethren, give diligence to make your calling and election sure: for if ye do these things, ye shall never fall: For so an entrance shall be ministered unto you abundantly into the everlasting kingdom of our Lord and Saviour Jesus Christ" (2 Peter 1:10-11).

"Behold, God will not *cast away* a *perfect man*, neither will He help the evil doers."
(Job 8:20)

"God will not cast away the perfect man", it is true, but not all of God's dear children do maintain Christian perfection. Do you? I am compelled to close this chapter with the poem of William Cowper titled "The Castaway". Anthropomorphism, personification, and zoomorphism of God's wrath are to teach us to fear, and this man wrote this poem with *similar* rhetorical powers as the scripture often wields. This poem remains as a death note for all to beware of! Cowper was a man who believed that he was cast away and without hope, and to read of such telling words of agony, one can only be silently amazed with horror...what a horror it must be to depart from the friendly Presence of God – FOREVER – to know it no more. Then, my reader, you are a castaway.

310

"THE CASTAWAY" – by William Cowper

"Obscurest night involv'd the sky, Th' Atlantic billows roar'd,
When such a destin'd wretch as I, Wash'd headlong from on board,
Of friends, of hope, of all bereft, His floating home for ever left.

No braver chief could Albion boast, Than he with whom he went,
Nor ever ship left Albion's coast, With warmer wishes sent.
He lov'd them both, but both in vain, Nor him beheld, nor her again.

Not long beneath the whelming brine, Expert to swim, he lay;
Nor soon he felt his strength decline, Or courage die away;
But wag'd with death a lasting strife, Supported by despair of life.

He shouted: nor his friends had fail'd, To check the vessel's course,
But so the furious blast prevail'd, That, pitiless perforce,
They left their outcast mate behind, And scudded still before the wind.

Some succour yet they could afford; And, such as storms allow,
The cask, the coop, the floated cord, Delay'd not to bestow.
But he (they knew) nor ship, nor shore, Whate'er they gave, should visit more.

Nor, cruel as it seem'd, could he, Their haste himself condemn,
Aware that flight, in such a sea, Alone could rescue them;
Yet bitter felt it still to die, Deserted, and his friends so nigh.

He long survives, who lives an hour, In ocean, self-upheld;
And so long he, with unspent pow'r, His destiny repell'd;
And ever, as the minutes flew, Entreated help, or cried—Adieu!

At length, his transient respite past, His comrades, who before
Had heard his voice in ev'ry blast, Could catch the sound no more.
For then, by toil subdued, he drank, The stifling wave, and then he sank.

No poet wept him: but the page, Of narrative sincere;
That tells his name, his worth, his age, Is wet with Anson's tear.
And tears by bards or heroes shed, Alike immortalize the dead.

I therefore purpose not, or dream, Descanting on his fate,

To give the melancholy theme, A more enduring date:
But misery still delights to trace, Its semblance in another's case.

No voice divine the storm allay'd, No light propitious shone;
When, snatch'd from all effectual aid, We perish'd, each alone:
But I beneath a rougher sea, And whelm'd in deeper gulfs than he."

THE DAMNABLE ABUSE &
MISAPPLICATION OF SOVEREIGN
ELECTION
CHAPTER 14

"Thou holdest mine eyes waking: I am so **troubled** that **I cannot speak**"– Psalm 77:4
"They that sow in **tears** shall reap in joy" – Psalm 126:5
"…the LORD hath heard the voice of my **weeping**" – Psalm 6:8

Woe to us! We have patterned-sleepers for saints! At ease, never-**troubled**, quick-**speaking**, **tearless**, no-**weeping** Calvinistic saints, fast asleep and comfortable in their beds of iniquity! Sleeping soundly, they can't wake up…because they have been taught to believe they can't ever die! Wake up! Wake up! And lo, the whole company cries for the "Christian" SNOOZE… The Holy Ghost saith, "Arise from the dead", "arise from the dead", "awake thou that sleepest, and arise from the dead" (Eph. 5:14), but they are caught up in their dreams already, and in them, lo, they are everlastingly alive!

In "An Alarm to the Unconverted", by Joseph Alleine, he wrote in disdain of misappropriated doctrines of election that hindered the initial salvation of unconverted sinners; however, there are like misrepresentations that hinder the present progressive and final salvation of converted saints. He said to the unconverted sinners, "You begin at the wrong end if you first dispute about your *election*. Prove your conversion, and then never doubt your election. If you cannot yet prove it, set upon a present and thorough turning. Whatever God's purposes be, which are secret, I am sure His promises are plain… Do not stand still disputing about your election, but set to repenting and believing. Cry to God for converting grace. Revealed things belong to you; in these busy yourself. It is just, as one well said, that they who will not feed on the plain food of the Word should be chocked with the bones." -Joseph Alleine, "An Alarm to the Unconverted"

In Calvinistic circles, the common and practical relationship with God is directly affected by misappropriations of sovereign election. The common individual does deduce: "Because I am saved, therefore I am elect. Because I am elect, God cannot be, and will never be, angry with me again…even when I am struggling with turning from this sinful affection or that. Therefore what I need to hear at this time of struggle (because I am God's regenerate son and a true Christian), is a greater revelation of His love – this is the answer to all my spiritual inadequacies. I am always loved by God, and it is not possible that God could ever have any other emotion or mind toward me, because I am always viewed in the finished work of Christ. God is eternal and therefore, so is His love toward me…therefore God never reveals sin to me as a message or means to condemn me, or having a mind or will to condemn me, but He reveals sin in my life to convict me – that is all. I must not mistake the revelation of my sin as a message of my condemnation in sin."

What saith the scripture? The common Calvinist is completely unconscious of "*God in the ways of man*" and outright denies Armenian aspects of God's circumstantial, reactive anger, which can include the potential of damnation. For the common Calvinist, "*God in the ways of God*" is all of God's relational ways in which He uses to think about, speak to, and perform works with mankind. As they understand God to be, that is all they believe exists – namely, His eternal, unchanging attributes (*God in the ways of God*). They do not relate to God by His condescension, and they are therefore snared in a misappropriation of the doctrine of election, which is a misappropriation of the higher, secret, and hidden things of God. Jeremiah, Joshua, Jacob, and Josiah did believe in the absolute sovereignty of God in salvation, predestination, and election, as a Calvinist would believe it, but they did not misappropriate God's higher ways to subvert and nullify His condescended ways.

JEREMIAH

We know that Jeremiah was the **elect** of God after the Lord's eternal counsel (*God in the ways of God*). Why? God said of him the famed and beloved scripture, "The LORD hath appeared of old unto me, saying, Yea, **I have loved thee with an *everlasting love*: therefore with lovingkindness have I drawn thee**"

> *If Jeremiah did relate to God only based upon His "everlasting love" and higher ways (**God in the ways of God**), then he would be in hell right now!*

(Jeremiah 31:3). Blessed be God that Jesus said, "no man can come to Me, except the Father which hath sent Me **draw him**" (John 6:44). If God loved Jeremiah with "an everlasting love," then this means everlasting…therefore there could never be an interruption of His everlasting, eternal, unchanging love; it is everlastingly the same and unchanging. God also, in His sovereignty and ways, is an everlasting, unchanging Being in will, counsel, decree, mind, emotion, and heart. True; however, there is a simultaneous, condescending will and relationship of God which can contradict and be wholly separate from the everlasting will of God. It is not that there could ever be an interruption of God's everlasting will, but that there is a separate will of God that is just as *genuine*, yet it can change, and it is confined to the reactive limitations of *the ways of man* – and also, this will of God is frightfully relevant to the daily, practical walk of a believer in Christ. Reader, let me get straight to the point of how relevant it is that we understand the simultaneous and contradictory wills in God – *If Jeremiah did relate to God only based upon His "everlasting love" and higher ways (**God in the ways of God**), then he would be in hell right now!* Why?

314

Did you know that even though God loved Jeremiah with "an everlasting love", the Lord intended to damn, and declaratively damned, Jeremiah during a specific time period of his sojourning as a prophet? This means that God was angry enough with Jeremiah that He desired to send him to hell. Jeremiah was disqualified from his prophetic office, promises, and covenant for a time, and he scarcely escaped damnation but by the surmounting mercies of an everlasting love. Jeremiah was loved with an everlasting love, and therefore was of "the elect" according to Romans chapter 9. An account of his election, ordination, and prophetic covenant is in Jeremiah, Ch. 1. Of Jeremiah's ordination, covenant, and promises, God said to him:

> "Be not afraid of their faces: **for I am with thee to deliver thee, saith the LORD.**" -Jer. 1:8 "Thou therefore gird up thy loins, and arise, and speak unto them all that I command thee: be not dismayed at their faces, lest I confound thee before them. For, behold, I have made thee this day a **defenced city**, and an **iron pillar**, and **brasen walls** against the whole land, against the kings of Judah, against the princes thereof, against the priests thereof, and against the people of the land. **And they shall fight against thee; but they shall not prevail against thee; for I am with thee, saith the LORD, to deliver thee.**" (Jeremiah 1:17-19)

Jeremiah was given one condition: "be not dismayed at their faces, lest I confound thee before them." While fulfilling this condition, Jeremiah was confirmed with the oaths and promises emboldened above. Along Jeremiah's pilgrimage, he fell into sin. Though he was in sin, he did not realize he was condemned in the sight of God – that is, until God confronted and verbally condemned him. Jeremiah was used to hearing the word of the Lord just drop upon him, suddenly, as it would happen to God's prophets, and yet in Jeremiah chapter 15, God delivered to Jeremiah the word of the Lord that condemned Israel, and this time, Jeremiah was included in the company that was condemned. God told Jeremiah that he too was under the burning fire of His wrath.

Jeremiah did not immediately fall after his prophetic ordination, which was at the beginning. It was a good while into his ministry, and after he had suffered much for the cause of God, for by this point in time he could call himself "a man of strife and a man of contention to the whole earth" (Jer. 15:10). This was after the people of Israel did "curse" Jeremiah (Jer. 15:10). Jeremiah's situation was heated, and persecution had already mounted upon him, so that without the preventative hand of God he would have been martyred. There were men that covenanted to kill Jeremiah, saying, "Let us destroy the tree with the fruit thereof, and let us cut [Jeremiah] off from the land of the living, that his name may be no more remembered" (Jer. 11:19). This plot was unknown by Jeremiah, therefore he said, "I was like a lamb or an ox that is brought to the slaughter and I knew not that they had devised devices against me" (Jer. 11:19). Yet the Lord protected him and revealed to Jeremiah this plot with the definitive judgment of God upon these scheming murderers…

> "Therefore thus saith the LORD of the men of Anathoth, that
> seek they life, saying, Prophesy not in the name of the LORD,
> that thou die not by our hand: Therefore thus saith the LORD of
> hosts, Behold, I will punish them: the young men shall die by the
> sword; their sons and their daughters shall die by famine: and
> there shall be no remnant of them: for I will bring evil upon the
> men of Anathoth, even the year of their visitation." (Jer. 11:21-
> 23)

Up to the time of Jeremiah 15, Jeremiah had experienced the faithful promises of God whereby he was securely protected. He was imperishable like a **"defenced city," "an iron pillar,"** and **"brasen walls!"** He experienced the blessed promise, **"they shall fight against thee but they shall not prevail against thee; for I am with thee, saith the LORD, to deliver thee"** (Jer. 1:17-19). Nevertheless, God departed from Jeremiah in this instance of his ministry. Read carefully to see Jeremiah's inclusion in the prophetic woe of condemnation to Israel:

> "Woe is me, my mother, that thou hast borne me a man of strife
> and a man of contention to the whole earth! I have neither lent on
> usury, nor men have lent to me on usury; yet every one of them
> doth curse me. The LORD said, Verily it shall be well with thy
> remnant; verily I will cause the enemy to entreat thee well in the
> time of evil and in the time of affliction. Shall iron break the
> northern iron and the steel? Thy substance and thy treasures will I
> give to the spoil without price, and that for all thy sins, even in all
> thy borders. **And I will make thee to pass with thine enemies**
> **into a land which thou knowest not: for a fire is kindled in**
> **Mine anger, which shall burn upon <u>you</u>.**" (Jeremiah 15:10-14)

The emboldened verse above is directed toward Jeremiah. Jeremiah is the "<u>**you**</u>" in the passage. Recognizing this word of condemnation and God's burning wrath, Jeremiah pled his case before God in hopes that He would repent of this word in Jeremiah 15:15-18. God responded to Jeremiah's prayers in Jeremiah 15:19-21. First, look at Jeremiah's prayers for mercy:

> "O LORD, Thou knowest: remember me, and visit me, and
> revenge me of my persecutors; **take me not away in Thy**
> **longsuffering:** know that for Thy sake I have suffered rebuke.
> Thy words were found, and I did eat them; and Thy word was
> unto me the joy and rejoicing of mine heart: for I am called by
> Thy name, O LORD God of hosts. I sat not in the assembly of the
> mockers, nor rejoiced; I sat alone because of Thy hand: for Thou
> hast filled me with indignation. **Why is my pain perpetual, and**
> **my wound incurable, which refuseth to be healed? wilt Thou**

be altogether unto me as a liar, and as waters that fail?"
(Jeremiah 15:15-18)

Jeremiah understood this word given in Jeremiah 15:10-14 as a message of condemnation to himself. He pled in verse 15, "take me not away in Thy longsuffering", because the word of the Lord was that he would be *taken away* from the land of Israel in the burning anger of God. Jeremiah pled for mercy from God by reminding Him of the suffering he had undergone in the Lord's service as a prophet ("for Thy sake I have suffered rebuke," "I sat not with the assembly of the mockers, nor rejoiced; I sat alone because of Thy hand: for Thou hast filled me with indignation"), and the joy and gladness he received upon his ordination and experience as a prophet ("Thy words were found, and I did eat them; and Thy word was unto me the joy and rejoicing of mine heart: for I am called by Thy name"). Jeremiah felt deceived by God. He felt as though he had done right, and therefore deserved to be protected by the promises which were formerly given, and since God's word was to take him away by wrath, he felt as though God had lied to him...Jeremiah's heart was deceiving him (Jer. 17:9). God set Jeremiah straight on how He had justly spoken this word of condemnation to him, when the Lord said: →

> "Therefore thus saith the LORD, **If thou return**, then will I bring thee again, and thou shalt stand before Me: and **if thou take forth the precious from the vile**, thou shalt be as my mouth: **let them return unto thee; but return not thou unto them**. And I will make thee unto this people a **fenced brasen wall**: and **they shall fight against thee, but they shall not prevail against thee: for I am with thee to save thee and to deliver thee**, saith the LORD. And **I will deliver thee out of the hand of the wicked, and I will redeem thee out of the hand of the terrible.**" (Jeremiah 15:19-21)

Do you see how Jeremiah was disqualified from his prophetic office because of the unrepentant sin detailed above? God gave three explanations of Jeremiah's rebellion that had caused this disqualification and condemnation, and God assured him that if he were to repent of his sins, God would grant the mercy he was seeking after, namely, that it would be restored, and He did this by reiterating the promises first given to Jeremiah at his prophetic ordination: the promises of God's delivering, protecting, and empowering hand, that he would not be taken away in the Babylonian Captivity, nor overcome by the people of Israel. Jeremiah's command by God to repent was, "if thou return," "if thou take forth the precious from the vile," and "let them return unto thee but return not thou unto them." The re-initiation of the prophetic office based upon his repentance was spoken in the word, "then will I bring thee again and thou shalt stand before Me," and "thou shalt be as My mouth." Standing before God and being His mouth are terms of a prophetic office (Jer. 15:1, 1 Kings 17:1, Ex. 4:12-16). With the prophetic covenant reestablished and unbreached, then God's delivering, protecting promises were re-initiated so that Jeremiah would again be "a fenced brasen wall," because God would be with him to deliver him like in former times.

Now consider this! Jeremiah was loved with "an everlasting love" (Jer. 31:3), and yet God was burning with anger in the intent of his damnation. Jeremiah was the foreknown elect of God (Jer. 1:5), and yet God had a simultaneous, contradicting will which was reactive to the disobedience of the chosen saint. God's eternal, irresistible, immutable, unchanging will and counsel is unaffected by the obedience or disobedience of the chosen saint; on the contrary, it is the determiner of obedience and disobedience. This is the hidden counsel of God in the higher ways of His secret workings, that it is "not of him that willeth nor of him that runneth, but of God that sheweth mercy" (Rom. 9:16). Yet there is a relational will of God which has

> *The scarcity of salvation for those who do endure to the end cannot be properly understood until we are conscientious of the dual, simultaneous, and genuine wills of God that are actively working all the time in tension/contradiction one with another, that God could have an everlasting and immutable will to save, and yet, a conflicting, condemning, wrathful will at present.*

infinitely condescended to man by operating in the ways of man, and therefore it is reactive and responsive to the obedience and disobedience of men. *If the higher, hidden, and sovereign ways of God had been Jeremiah's sole meditation, had he believed that there could be no danger, damnation, or anger in God because of an everlasting love, it is then that he would have perished in his own self-justifying and unrepentant deceit.* Nevertheless, Jeremiah did repent and was reinstated as God's prophet, *but had he been indoctrinated with the system of theology called Calvinism, he would have perished!* This misappropriation of the doctrine of election has become a complex snare of the devil that seduces God's people into an unbiblical confidence of salvation, a supposing that God accepts them while in a state of unrepentance. It is the age-old voice of the false prophets, saying, "Peace, peace; when there is no peace" (Jer. 6:14). "They say still unto them that despise Me, The LORD hath said, Ye shall have peace; and they say unto every one that walketh after the imagination of his own heart, No evil shall come upon you" (Jer. 23:17). Since the ancient times God has warned of these deceptive and twisted teachings that give the people an unalterable assurance in the promises and blessings of God, irrelevant of their behavior and performance. As it is written since the days of Moses:

> "Lest there should be among you man, or woman, or family, or tribe, whose heart turneth away this day from the LORD our God, to go and serve the gods of these nations; lest there should

be among you **a root that beareth gall and wormwood**; And it come to pass, when he heareth the words of this curse, **that he bless himself in his heart**, saying, **I shall have peace, though I walk in the imagination of mine heart**, to add drunkenness to thirst: <u>The LORD will not spare him, but then the anger of the LORD and His jealousy shall smoke against that man,</u> and all the curses that are written in this book shall lie upon him, and the LORD shall blot out his name from under heaven. And the LORD shall separate him unto evil out of all the tribes of Israel, according to all the curses of the covenant that are written in this book of the law..." (Deuteronomy 29:18-21)

Just as "**a root that beareth gall and wormwood**" sprung up in the Old Covenant (Deut. 29:18), the same "**root of bitterness springing up**" is warned of in the New Covenant (Heb. 12:15). The waters of salvation will not "*fail*" (Jer. 15:18), nor will God make His promises mutable as long as you diligently obey His voice: "looking diligently lest any man *fail* of the grace of God" (Heb. 12:15). Is this not enough for you? Then we will look at the lives of Joshua, Jacob, and Josiah. God wants us to understand that "the righteous are scarcely saved" (1 Peter 4:18). The scarcity of salvation for those who do endure to the end cannot be properly understood until we are conscientious of the dual, simultaneous, and genuine wills of God that are actively working all the time in tension/contradiction one with another, that God could have an everlasting and immutable will to save, and yet, a conflicting, condemning, wrathful will at present. What does this cause us to understand? We must consider our deeds and understand that they can provoke Christ (1 Cor. 10:9), and we must appropriate our everlasting election in a manner which does not disconnect us from our present progressive faith and repentance toward God, which then will connect us to a mindful care of our fruitfulness (2 Peter 1:8), to the end we would make our "calling and election sure" by what deeds of faith we, with perseverance, are ingratiated to "do" (2 Peter 1:10). "Do these things," Peter says, and this is a good trust in the finished work of Christ; thereby we are confirmed that He is finishing His work in us. "Wherefore the rather, brethren, give diligence to make your calling and **election sure**: for if ye do these things, ye shall never fall:" (2 Peter 1:10). Have you an appropriation, a doctrine, or an understanding of election? Let it be consistent with that holy charge and concern of the apostle Peter, a charge based upon what a saint does DO. It is an assurance based upon the sureness of election ("election sure") which is not dislocated from a man's performance, but vitally hinging upon one's own works done in and through Christ. So many are assured of their election but their election is not sure – therefore reader, make it sure!

JOSHUA

Joshua had a parallel confrontation by his Savior and God. He was exercised by the warning of eternal wrath so that he would never compromise strict, straightforward obedience. The promises and salvific covenant given to Joshua were clear:

> "And Moses called unto Joshua, and said unto him in the sight of all Israel, Be strong and of a good courage: for thou must go with this people unto the land which the LORD hath sworn unto their fathers to give them; and thou shalt cause them to inherit it. And the LORD, He it is that doth go before thee; He **will be with thee, He will not fail thee, neither forsake thee**: fear not, neither be dismayed." (Deuteronomy 31:7-8)

> "There shall not any man be able to stand before thee all the days of thy life: as I was with Moses, so **I will be with thee: I will not fail thee, nor forsake thee**." (Joshua 1:5)

Yet again there is a clear condition given – "Only be thou strong and very courageous, **that thou mayest observe to do according to all the law**, which Moses my servant commanded thee: turn not from it to the right hand or to the left, **that thou mayest prosper whithersoever thou goest**. This book of the law shall not depart out of thy mouth; but **thou shalt meditate therein day and night, that thou mayest observe to do according to all that is written therein: for then thou shalt make thy way prosperous, and then thou shalt have good success**" (Joshua 1:7-8). Joshua was the elect of God. He did not fail to fulfill these conditions, but God warned him again of the sure consequences if ever he did neglect the obedience of holy and just judgments. After Achan had caused 36 men of Israel to die under the wrath of God by his own, singlehanded rebellion, the Lord included Joshua in the same demise of wrath and condemnation unless he acted in obedience:

> "Therefore the children of Israel could not stand before their enemies, but turned their backs before their enemies, because they were accursed: **neither will I be with you any more, except ye destroy the accursed from among you**" (Josh. 7:12).

God said to Joshua that He would not leave him, but rather that He would "be with" him (Deut. 31:8), that He would not "fail" him or "forsake" him (Deut. 31:8, Josh. 1:5), and yet now God says that He will not be with him anymore!

Achan took of the forbidden spoil of Jericho, which God commanded not to be taken. Jericho's spoils were ordained by God to waste away into destruction, as hateful riches, wages won by wickedness and treachery. God said, "Thou shalt not seek their peace nor their prosperity" (Deut. 23:6)! Certain spoils of infamous sinners, by association, come to obtain the abominable identities of its owners, and so, the spoils – themselves – are doomed to suffer the same fate of destruction. Deuteronomy 13:16-18 speaks of such a scenario, a scenario which is telling of God's awe-striking severity with Joshua, even God's oath-breaking powers: →

> "And thou shalt **gather all the spoil** of it into the midst of the

street thereof, and shalt burn with fire the city, and **all the spoil thereof every whit**, for the LORD thy God: and it shall be an heap for ever; it shall not be built again. And **there shall cleave nought of the cursed thing to thine hand: that the LORD may turn from the fierceness of His anger, and shew thee mercy, and have compassion upon thee, and multiply thee, <u>as He hath sworn unto thy fathers</u>**; When thou shalt hearken to the voice of the LORD thy God, to keep all His commandments which I command thee this day, to do that which is right in the eyes of the LORD thy God" (Deuteronomy 13:16-18).

Joshua, knowing this passage well, was not paralyzed by confusion, as you may be, when God did thus warn Joshua of imminent damnation in the matter of Achan. His faith was not foiled; he was not in a craze over what seemed to be biblical contradictions. Branded upon Joshua's mind was now a holy resolve to make sure his election based upon what he did! Have you ever done that!? It is so easy to quote a promise with *ungodly simplicity,* removing care and consequence from personal morality and obedient deeds, couching yourself in imaginary assurances abounding forthwith to your relaxation, and why? Men have an unwavering confidence that a promise *cannot fail* – because of, they say, an everlasting and unconditional love in God – therefore election is sure with or without holiness. Myriads of men are "looking diligently" at the promises of God, and so, have come to understand that there are no sinful words, thoughts, or deeds that could interrupt saving grace…and lo, the conscience breaks loose from its "*beginning" "wisdom*" (Prov. 9:10), the man is rendered fearless – a fearless fool – set in opposition to and abhorrent of doing something, or anything at all, "lest any man fail of the grace of God" (Heb. 12:15). Spiritual eyes are gouged out, spiritual ears are deafened into silence, and Jesus speaks, "repent…or else I will come unto thee quickly and remove thy candlestick out of his place" (Rev. 2:5), and lo, they think the voice of impression which is coming upon them is the discouragement of false prophets or the condemnation of the devil.

Outside of a heretic's eyesight, in truth, a regenerate Christian has a new nature which affectionately and adamantly shouts – "God is faithful and His promises are sure!" – Rightly so! It is shouted loud to out-sound every lie. Yea, God's promises are true, trustworthy, lifesaving, worldwide regenerating, resurrection without end, and no one has ever gone to heaven while believing that God is a liar! Any one that "hath made him a liar" is damned for sure (1 John 5:10)! It is not that His promises fail, but that men come short of them (Heb. 4:1) – and this, how? By a failing faith, wrath-provoking disobedience, and impenitent rebellion, thus God executes the curses and conditions which those promises hinged upon. The promises of God do fill God's good mind as He thinks upon you, but simultaneously, His faithfulness is also to justice, to conditions and curses when necessary, therefore let all men understand: you will survive the pilgrimage journey of your salvation as long as the saving faith that you have is not turned into evil unbelief, evidenced by sinful

321

thoughts, words, and deeds. Heresies may excuse it, but if certain rebellion does exist with continuance, it will aggravate and arouse the hatred of God to break loose from its wrestling Opponent – God's love – and thereby wrath will arise unrestrained and God will judge you as a guilty sinner.

Come now! What is your understanding of the words of Jesus Christ, "Lo, I am with you always, even unto the end of the world" (Matt. 28:20)? Had Joshua believed that such a promise, commitment, and confirmation substantiates the impossibility that the contrary could ever be possible, he would have been damned. Oh how the words of God are wrested because Calvinism was not prayerfully, biblically, and successfully tested, thus on the basis of the words of Hebrews 13:5, "I will never leave thee, nor forsake thee," saints conclude that they cannot be left nor forsaken. They mistakenly blind themselves to the conditions of the New Covenant promises, concluding that the subject matter of the promises themselves make impossible the binding effect of any condition. This logic is an abominable snare. Had Joshua not heard the words, "neither will I be with you any more," would he have persevered to the end? Even David was terrorized by the reprobation of King Saul. As the next king in line to rule Israel, David carried with him the awful apprehension of reprobation – which is healthy – and it drove him to repentance when he had, at sundry times, left the God he loved. The terrifying possibility that the Holy Ghost could be taken from him just as it was taken from Saul, made David cry out the heart-rending words – "Cast me not away from Thy presence; and take not Thy Holy Spirit from me" (Ps. 51:11). Had not Saul's reprobation been his meditation, he would not have cried these words. Jeremiah would be in hell today if he was so indoctrinated by false hopes that he believed the wrath of God could never be kindled over his precious and loved soul. He would be in hell, had not he been convinced that he was going to hell, and by that fearful exercise he was "moved with fear" and found place of repentance (Heb. 11:7).

JACOB

❖ "Yea, he had **power over the Angel**, and <u>prevailed</u>: **he wept, and made supplication unto Him."** (Hos. 12:3-6)

❖ "As a prince hast thou **power with God** and with men, and hast <u>prevailed."</u> (Gen. 32:28)

❖ **"He <u>prevailed</u> not against Him"** (Gen. 32:25) → **"I will not let Thee go, except Thou bless me"** (Gen. 32:26)!

❖ "The Kingdom of heaven **suffereth violence, and the violent take it by force."** (Matt. 11:12)

The predestination of Jacob and Jeremiah have noteworthy parallels. The Lord foreknew Jeremiah in parallel terms which substantiate unconditional election in Romans chapter 9. God chose Jacob by election before he was born (Rom. 9:11) and therefore irrelevant to what he has done; likewise God said to Jeremiah, "**Before I formed thee in the belly I knew thee**; and before thou camest forth out of the womb I sanctified thee, and I **ordained** thee a prophet unto the nations" (Jer. 1:5). This foreknowledge is a foreknowing of a person before their birth, and that foreknowing is a foreordaining, a foreloving, and therefore fore-electing. This foreknowing substantiates a determining election as taught in Romans chapter 9, and is the same teaching referenced in Romans 8:28-30. "And we know that all things work together for good to them that love God, to them who are the called according to His purpose. For whom He did **foreknow**, He also did **predestinate** to be conformed to the image of His Son, that He might be the firstborn among many brethren. Moreover whom He did **predestinate**, them He also **called**: and whom He **called**, them He also **justified**: and whom He **justified**, them He also **glorified**" (Romans 8:28-30). The certain meaning of the word "foreknow" must be clarified.

"The foreknowledge of God here does not intend His prescience of all things future; by which He foreknows and foretells things to come, and which distinguishes him from all other gods; and is so called, not with respect to himself, with whom all things are present, but with respect to us, and which is eternal, universal, certain, and infallible; for in this sense He foreknows all men, and if this was the meaning here, then all men would be predestinated, conformed to the image of Christ, called by grace, justified and glorified; whereas they are a special people, whom God has foreknown: nor is this foreknowledge to be understood of any provision or foresight of the good works, holiness, faith, and perseverance of men therein, upon which God predestinates them to happiness; since this would make something out of God, and not His good pleasure, the cause of predestination; which was done before, and without any consideration of good or evil, and is entirely owing to the free grace of God, and is the ground and foundation of good works, faith, holiness, and perseverance in them: but this regards the everlasting love of God to His own people, His delight in them, and approbation of them; in this sense He knew them, He foreknew them from everlasting, affectionately loved them, and took infinite delight and pleasure in them; and this is the foundation of their predestination and election, of their conformity to Christ, of their calling, justification, and glorification: for these **He also did predestinate to be conformed to the image of His Son.**" – John Gill Commentary on Romans 8:29

Though God foreknew Jeremiah by election – even still – his election was not made sure within time except by persevering faith and repentance. Likewise it is for us: "Wherefore the rather, brethren, give diligence to make your **calling** and **election** sure: for if ye do these things, ye shall never fall" (2 Peter 1:10). We must understand what we must do (through faith) so that we do not fall. These two different senses and appropriations of "election" are among those "things" that Paul wrote of that are "hard to be understood, which they that are unlearned and unstable wrest, as they do also the other scriptures, unto their own destruction" (2 Pet. 3:16). Under the inspiration of God, Paul was the chiefest defender and explainer of the sovereignty of God. With the sovereignty of God in view alongside those workings and relationships of God that are contradictory and inconsistent with the higher plane of God's existence (**God in the ways of God**), things can become confusing. Consequentially, the system of theology known as Calvinism has wrested the doctrines of sovereignty and election so as to make void the salvation, will, election, and relationship of God's condescension (**God in the ways of man**). These different senses are confusing indeed, but if we remember the two distinct ways in which God has revealed and related to us throughout biblical history (**God in the ways of God** & **God in the ways of man**), and remember that these ways are consistently present throughout scripture, then these interpretations are not strange but soundly amazing. God's word is not simple, but hard and complex, yet when it is not wrested, and rather explained, we can escape the terrifying judgment written of old: "I have written to him the great things of My law, but they were counted as a strange thing" (Hos. 8:12). Let me attempt to steward these mysteries to you that we might also cry, when need be, the words and fears of David which were deeply in the heart of the beloved and elect saint, the apostle Paul: "Cast me not away from Thy presence" (Ps. 51:10). It is good to know what I must do as a regenerated saint, "lest I be a castaway" (1 Cor. 9:27)!

Remember Abraham? God foreknew him and had a foreknowledge of what he would do: "For **I know him**, that **he will** command his children and his household after him, and they shall keep the way of the LORD, to do justice and judgment; that the LORD may bring upon Abraham that which He hath spoken of him" (Genesis 18:19). This foreknowing was a sign of his eternal election (Rom. 9:11), and yet God tried him as if He did not already know him by eternal election. After Abraham was tried by deed, God was satisfied to continue his salvation, because his deeds were evidences of his faith. God said, "**Now I know** that thou fearest God, seeing thou hast not withheld thy son, thine only son from Me" (Gen. 22:12). Abraham was known by trial as if he was not already known by omniscient, eternal election (Known by trial – 2 Chron. 32:21, Hos. 8:1-5, Jer. 12:3). Abraham was sought out, tried, that God might know him in a different sense – by DEED – so that Abraham's salvation was made sure and immutable (Gen. 22:16-18, Heb. 6:11-18). A salvation made sure and immutable is a confirmation that their election is of the eternal, everlasting, and immutable counsel of **God in the ways of God** (as taught in Romans chapter 9). In the same manner, we are taught of a foreknowing which is an unconditional election (Rom. 9:11), and yet we are commanded to make our "calling and election sure" by our deeds (2 Peter 1:10). We are taught of a final judgment where our eternity will be unalterably determined and fixed, and this judgment is according to our DEEDS (2 Cor. 5:10-11). We are taught of a condescending will and relationship of God where the focal point of our present progressive favor, present progressive love, and present progressive salvation is according to our DEEDS. Remember why God saved Moses, Jonah, Nineveh (temporarily), Hezekiah, and Ahab (temporarily) according to **God in the ways of man**?

The focal point of their salvation with God was based upon the manifestation of their faith, evidenced by deeds. God saved Moses because He saw the bloody circumcision, and God saved Jonah because of his repentant crying and vowing (Jon. 2:9). In Nineveh, "God saw their works, that they turned from their evil way", and God turned from His word and intent to damn them. God saved Hezekiah, saying, "I have seen thy tears" (Isa. 38:5). God saved Ahab (temporarily) saying, "Seest thou how Ahab humbleth himself before Me? Because he humbleth himself before Me," God said, therefore He gave him mercy. Likewise in God's condescension (*God in the ways of man*), the Lord saved Jeremiah when He saw his repentance (Jeremiah 15). God saved Joshua when he sanctified Israel by the death of Achan and his family (Joshua 7).

God can know your election, foreknow your soul from everlasting, determine your predestination, and yet, simultaneously, He can relate to you as if He knew you not (responding to your disobedience with a mind of wrathful condemnation), trying you so as to know you by your deeds (as if He does not know them already by foreknowledge, as if He does not already know the depths of your heart, and as if He does not already know you by regeneration), and hang your eternal salvation upon your obedient success in faith which is evidenced through works, so that His eternal election is vindicated by a final judgment that is according to your works (as if election did not determine works) as the sense of God's comprehensible justice that the wicked (by deed) are damned and the righteous (by deed) are saved. Because God reacts to DEEDS in a relationship, will, and word of salvation which is *in the ways of man*, that salvific purpose and will to save you can be *changed* into a will to damn you.

Jacob, above all, is the chief example of an elect individual, but had he misappropriated the doctrine of election as Calvinism does, he would be in hell. Needless to say, he was loved by an everlasting love, for God said of him: "Jacob have I loved, but Esau have I hated" (Rom. 9:13, Mal. 1:2-3). Jacob had received the blessing of his father Isaac's inheritance and "the blessing of Abraham" (Gen. 28:4). Jacob went out at the command of his father Isaac to take a wife of Laban's house; unlike Esau, he obeyed his father. God promised to Jacob while asleep, robbed, humbled, broken, stripped of pride and hope, and alone in the wilderness, "Behold, **I am with thee**, and **will keep thee** in all places whither thou goest, and **will bring thee again** into this land; for **I will not leave thee**, until I have done that which I have spoken to thee of" (Gen. 28:15). At this time Jacob made the LORD his God according to what was spoken to him. He was resting himself on the words of God that He would **keep** him and **bring him again**, promising to be **with him**. These words Jacob believed and accepted by a vow of devotion, that he would follow God if the Lord kept him and brought him again (see Gen. 28:15, 20-21). Jacob built the House of God (Gen. 28:22), and from this point onward he became a worshiper of God. He walked with God as in a secret friendship, in a life which demonstrated righteousness, purity, lowliness, suffering, hope, and faith.

Throughout the 20 years of mock slavery to Laban, Jacob was faithful, honest, and patient. Jacob said that "with all my power I have served" (Gen. 31:6).

God blessed Laban for Jacob's sake (Gen. 30:27), and He was ever with Jacob (Gen. 31:5). Since Jacob was righteous, God rewarded him according to his righteousness (Gen. 30:33), "thus God hath taken away the cattle of your father [Laban], and given them to me," he confessed (Gen. 31:9). Jacob was greatly humbled and tried in the service of Laban, and yet he remained faithful (Gen. 31:38-42). Jacob knew that God was with him (Gen. 31:42), and he swore by God alone (Gen. 31:53); he had utterly forsaken the idolatrous gods of the house of Laban. All of this clearly represents the mind of God toward Jacob, His servant, that Jacob was obedient and in mutual cooperation with his LORD. In a life-threatening situation for Jacob, God defended him from Laban, yet as this trial came to an end, the purity of Jacob's camp was left defiled without his knowledge – there were idols in the camp!

Jacob was intent to meet with God, the same God that met with him at Bethel (Gen. 31:13). Returning to the land of his kindred meant a revisiting of Esau, and he had been left to boil in his bloodthirsty rage throughout the years of their separation. As never before, Jacob needed the blessing and protection of his God, but since the days of his friendship with God he had never had a defiled camp with secret idolatry dwelling in the midst. Now, the secrecy of friendship between Jacob and God was severely interrupted, and it was by a secret fellowship with idolatry. Jacob knew that a meeting with his LORD ought to be free from foolishness, disobedience, and idolatry, like as the command he gave to his people when returning to Bethel later in his life – "Put away the strange gods that are among you, and be clean, and change your garments: and let us arise, and go up to Beth-el; and I will make there an altar unto God, Who answered me in the day of my distress, and was with me in the way which I went. And they gave unto Jacob all the strange gods which were in their hand, and all their earrings which were in their ears; and Jacob hid them under the oak which was by Shechem" (Gen. 35:2-4). Jacob hated idolatry and thievery, and he declared it punishable by death, yet he didn't know that Rachel had stolen Laban's idols (Gen. 31:32).

After the encounter with Laban was past and "Jacob went on his way," then "the angels of God met him" (Gen. 32:1-2). An encounter with God's angels is of no small significance! God's angels encamp around the righteous for delivering protection and salvation (Ps. 34:17, 2 Kings 6:17), they do visit and commune with the righteous at pivotal times of salvation (Gen. 18:2-5, 19:2-3), and their presence can also denote some act of judgment of God's wrath, or, some discovery of sin so as to reckon its measure and report it back to God (Gen. 19:20-22). They could be vessels of God to administer a plague (1 Chron. 21:15-16, Gen. 19:22), or they could be the judges of the city, people, or nation at hand, whether it is worthy of a plague by the measure of iniquity. They would visit a city (as if God is not omniscient) so as to find out what the measure of their sin was that they might proportionately recompense it. Surely Jacob's encounter in Genesis 32:1-2 was not without significance. God's friendly face and willingness to bless, save, confirm, and be with Jacob had never changed...until there were idols in his camp! I do believe that Jacob was disconnected from God's host of salvation when they beheld the idolatry that he knew nothing of, and on account of this, God refused to, was intent against, and unwilling to bless Jacob, and thereby, God meant to leave him in the hands of his brother Esau to undergo a violent annihilation.

Some may consider this interpretation to be farfetched or unbiblical, but I would remind you of God's dealings toward His choice servant Joshua, that, when there were cursed objects in the midst of the camp of Israel in his day, God was ready to forsake him and all of Israel. Do you remember the words of the men of Israel who drank deeply of the knowledge of the Holy? They unforgettably and frightfully understood that "wrath fell on all the congregation of Israel…and that man perished not alone in his iniquity" (Josh. 22:20). Some would refuse to consider that God would be so offended and incited because of Rachel's idolatry that He would refuse to save Jacob, but you are underestimating the holiness of God, and you are judging based upon your own considerations. It does not matter that Rachel – alone – did sin. God is the same yesterday, today, and forever! He has consistently demonstrated a willingness to condemn others, and at times, all people, on account of just one, a few, or many men's sins. As for Jacob, what did he do? What did Jacob do to deserve this? That was a similar cry of David when God killed 70,000 Israelites on account of David's own sin (1 Chron. 21:14). He cried, "Is it not I that commanded the people to be numbered? Even I it is that have sinned and done evil indeed; but as for these sheep, what have they done" (1 Chron. 21:17)?

Jacob's encounter with the anger of God was as the secret wrestling of Moses against the mind of God to annihilate. Four different times God said He would destroy Israel completely (Ex. 32:10, Num. 14:11-12, 16:21-22, 41) and more times than this He did begin to destroy them, had not some intercessor prevailed by Holy Spirit-inspired wrestling. The wrestling of Moses against God during "The Great Pause" was not over until 4 separate intercessions by prayer and 2 intercessions by judgment had been completed, and then Moses, finally, wrestled God in intercession for forty days and nights, then the Covenant of God which had already been spoken of, which God had been intent on doing with Israel after their salvation from Egyptian bondage, the Passover Lamb, and the Red Sea crossing, was reestablished. This instance with Jacob is very similar…Jacob wrestled with God after his salvation from the wilderness of humiliation and horizontal abandonment, after the long and rigorous slavery of Laban's household, and then, after God had taken him thus far, bringing him all the way to this point that He might establish Jacob in the Covenant which was before spoken to him, which promised that the Lord would be with him to take him back to his own land safely (Gen. 28:12-22).

God came to dwell in the midst of Jacob and his camp, but He beheld an idol there! He was minded to leave them to their destruction, because He disdained being in their midst because of their idolatry, similar to God's mind in "The Great Pause" in Exodus 33:5. Jacob wrestled against the wrath of God all night long, even to the breaking of day (Gen. 32:24). Why did God refuse to bless Jacob in the Covenant and promise which He had been faithful to perform up to that day? So fierce was this wrestling that God sought to prevail against Jacob, and yet could not. "And when He saw that He prevailed not against [Jacob], He touched the hollow of his thigh; and the hollow of Jacob's thigh was out of joint, as he wrestled with Him" (Gen. 32:25). God's command to Jacob was, "let Me go, for the day breaketh," that He might leave Jacob to the sword of his bloodthirsty brother. Jacob, under the inspiration of the Holy Spirit, would not relent, but said, "I will not let Thee go, except Thou bless me" (Gen. 32:26). Jacob prevailed against the wrathful, unwilling mind of God (Gen. 32:28), and the Covenant was securely established with him henceforth. As God said to Jacob, "let Me go," so God said to Moses, "let Me alone" (Ex. 32:10), "separate yourselves from among this congregation" (Num. 16:21-22), and "get you up from among this congregation" (Num. 16:41), but by the grace of God, through the uprising, emboldening, interceding Holy Spirit, Moses and Jacob refused and stood against these commands given by their angry God! Salvation prevailed by scarcity because God found a man! Had not God found a man, an intercessor, it would have been as the time later spoken of: "And I sought for a man among them, that should make up the hedge, and stand in the gap before Me for the land, that I should not destroy it: but I found none. Therefore have I poured out Mine indignation upon them; I have consumed them with the fire of My wrath: their own way have I recompensed upon their heads, saith the Lord GOD" (Ezek. 22:30-31).

JOSIAH

Now consider the man Josiah for an example. This man was beloved of his God! He was one of the few men in history of whom the prophets, through God, prophesied his existence through calling him by his name, centuries and generations before his birth. Josiah was one of the last kings to rule in Judah. So late was his rule, he lived on the eve of judgment, in the very generation in which God was beckoning Babylon to come and make an end of His people's nation. God spoke of the name Josiah centuries before his birth, at the very nativity of apostasy under the twisted rebellion of Jeroboam; this was no mistake. At the arising of apostasy, God declared the END of it, and it was going to be by the man Josiah. God proclaimed to Jeroboam – to his face – that He, through Josiah, would avail to accomplish vengeance! God spoke of "Josiah by name," that he would be used to defile, destroy, and demolish this apostasy according to the mind of our Jealous God (1 Kings 13:2). When rebellion is born, God does, at times, longsuffer it to go on, and if He lets it rage on, it means immense Personal suffering, that God will be put in great weariness over the long continuance of sin. God longs for the death day of rebellion and sin! "Josiah by name" was born to bring penalty upon iniquity to God's satisfaction and rest – Hallelujah! What more than this could verify God's **everlasting love**, **foreknowledge**, and **election** of Josiah? Consider the scene of Josiah's prophecy...a no-named prophet, opposing king and nation, bold and unflinching in the face of this newborn rebellion against God, spoke what can be read in the following account:

> "And, behold, there came a man of God out of Judah by the word
> of the LORD unto Bethel: and Jeroboam stood by the altar to

burn incense. And he cried against the altar in the word of the LORD, and said, O altar, altar, thus saith the LORD; Behold, a child shall be born unto the house of David, **Josiah by name**; and upon thee shall he offer the priests of the high places that burn incense upon thee, and men's bones shall be burnt upon thee. And he gave a sign the same day, saying, This is the sign which the LORD hath spoken; Behold, the altar shall be rent, and the ashes that are upon it shall be poured out. And it came to pass, when king Jeroboam heard the saying of the man of God, which had cried against the altar in Bethel, that he put forth his hand from the altar, saying, Lay hold on him. And his hand, which he put forth against him, dried up, so that he could not pull it in again to him. The altar also was rent, and the ashes poured out from the altar, according to the sign which the man of God had given by the word of the LORD. And the king answered and said unto the man of God, Intreat now the face of the LORD thy God, and pray for me, that my hand may be restored me again. And the man of God besought the LORD, and the king's hand was restored him again, and became as it was before. And the king said unto the man of God, Come home with me, and refresh thyself, and I will give thee a reward. And the man of God said unto the king, If thou wilt give me half thine house, I will not go in with thee, neither will I eat bread nor drink water in this place: For so was it charged me by the word of the LORD, saying, Eat no bread, nor drink water, nor turn again by the same way that thou camest. So he went another way, and returned not by the way that he came to Bethel." (1 Kings 13:1-10)

Jeroboam introduced a system of religion peculiarly similar to Judaism, but acutely defiant of all God's righteousness. He made a falsified system of worship, supposedly to the one true LORD, and so he deceived the people that they would not go to the Temple anymore for worship. The people were led to believe that worship elsewhere, other than the Temple, was acceptable and directed to the same God of Israel which the people of Israel had historically worshipped up to that day. He set up two golden calves and called them the God of Israel (1 Kings 12:25-33), and Israel went a whoring after them. The inventor of this rebellion in the disguise of true religion, Jeroboam the son of Nebat, is mentioned by name more than any other criminal in the chronology of the kings. He, at this point, introduces such damaging and contagious doctrines that the people can scarce escape it, and continually, king after king, generation after generation, the people followed in his sins which he introduced in his generation. Therefore Jeroboam's name, and specifically – "the way of Jeroboam, and in his sin wherewith he made Israel to sin" – is referenced approximately thirty times throughout the generations (1 Kings 15:34). Josiah therefore, by the sovereign election of God, was a man set apart, unaffected and defiant against pressure and popular rebellion which did snare the masses! My reader, "know that the LORD hath set apart him that is godly for himself" (Psalm 4:3)! What does this mean? Glory and credit must be given to the sovereign grace of God! What an amazing accolade which strongly implied the everlasting love of God, that Josiah was prophesied by name as an instrument of God's pleasure, and that he would be an accomplisher of *perfect* obedience – "Josiah by name!"

Amazingly, as with David and others, Josiah's youth was spent in peculiar fervency for the righteous, good causes of God. He was "eight years old when he began to reign" in Judah. He was born in what God had intended to be the generation of wrath and judgment, the generation where He removed all the rest of His people into captivity and dispersion through the Babylonian invasion (2 Chron. 34:1). This is a shocking mystery, I mean, that God intended Josiah's generation to be the generation of wrath, which included the destruction of Josiah. Josiah would be the king upon whom the woeful curses of old were finally executed, he and his people, but because of his availing righteousness, Josiah did change the mind of God which at first was set against him; thus it was by intercession he did win peace for himself and Israel! Eternally, or in sovereignty (***God in the ways of God***), the Lord had always willed and determined for Josiah to be the second to last king in Judah, not the last. But in time, the simultaneous will of God (***God in the ways of man***) was minded to destroy him and Israel, and bring the whole people into the furnace of fire. Please follow carefully with me as I trace Josiah's life to show you the point of turning, wherein Josiah turned the mind of God through the intercessions of judgment and heartbreaking, terror-driven prayers for help and hope – and behold, the man beloved of God and famed of old, "Josiah by name."

As stated before, Josiah began to reign at eight years old (2 Chron. 34:1). Centuries had passed since the days of Jeroboam, and since then, the depravity of man had taken greater advantages to invent greater evils which were accepted because of the declining, degenerating conviction amongst the common people, who were, through the experience of sin, emboldened to further corruption unimaginable to previous generations. One generation of evil is unsatisfactory to the lusts of the next, until further mischief is wrought. "Hell and destruction are never full; so the eyes of man are never satisfied" (Prov. 27:20). Because apostasy springboards further apostasy, by the time Josiah was born, lo, the Bible was nowhere to be found...THERE WAS NO BIBLE! All that Josiah had to follow was the verbal traditions of the former kings which remained faithful to God in their lifetimes, kings who were very few in number. As much as Josiah knew of righteousness and truth – that he did! He "did that which was right in the sight of the LORD, and walked in the ways of David his father, and declined neither to the right hand, nor to the left" (2 Chron. 34:2). He probably learned of David's ways from the priesthood, elders, counselors, and ancients of his day. Therefore Josiah was a seeker of "the old paths", not a follower of the majority and all the kings of church history. He did as Jeremiah said: "Thus saith the LORD, Stand ye in the ways, and see, and ask for the old paths, where is the good way, and walk therein, and ye shall find rest for your souls" (Jer. 6:16).

When Josiah was 16 years old, and in "the eighth year of his reign, while he was yet young, he began to **seek** after the God of David his father" (2 Chron. 34:3). Josiah was seeking, listening, studying, meditating, and learning…and four years passed by. At 20 years old, "the twelfth year" of his reign, "he began to **purge** Judah and Jerusalem from the high places, and the groves, and the carved images, and the molten images. And they brake down the altars of Baalim in his presence; and the images, that were on high above them, he cut down; and the groves, and the carved images, and the molten images, he brake in pieces, and made dust of them, and strowed it upon the graves of them that had sacrificed unto them. And he burnt the bones of the priests upon their altars, and cleansed Judah and Jerusalem. And so did he in the cities of Manasseh, and Ephraim, and Simeon, even unto Naphtali, with their mattocks round about. And when he had broken down the altars and the groves, and had beaten the graven images into powder, and cut down all the idols **throughout all the land of Israel, he returned to Jerusalem**" (2 Chronicles 34:3-7).

Intercession by judgment began, and Josiah went forth all abroad to purge the land! AFTER he was finished doing all these things **"throughout all the land of Israel,"** NOTICE my reader, **"he returned to Jerusalem"** (2 Chron. 34:7). "The eyes of the LORD run to and fro throughout the whole earth, to shew Himself strong in the behalf of them whose heart is perfect toward Him," and surely, God was finding a man (2 Chron. 16:9)! After righteous judgment was wrought, Josiah returned. "Let judgment run down as waters, and righteousness as a mighty stream," then let the people of God offer sacrifices, offerings, prayers, and worshipful celebrations – and they will be accepted (Amos 5:24, Psalm 51:19). But if we persist to do evil and yet trust in God's promises, "and come and stand before Me in this House," God says, "which is called by My name, and say, We are delivered to do all these abominations" (Jer. 7:10), then we will suffer a like damnation according to the saying, "Is this House, which is called by My Name, become a den of robbers in your eyes? Behold, even I have seen it, saith the LORD," it is full of "the sacrifice of fools: for they consider not that they do evil" (Jer. 7:11, Eccl. 5:1).

Six years transpired as the man of God, Josiah, considered all the evil that Judah and Israel had done, and after 6 years of perpetual purging, he returned to Jerusalem "in the eighteenth year of his reign" (2 Chron. 34:8). He was 26 years old at this point, and he turned his face to purge "The House" of God (2 Chron. 34:8). "He set Shaphan the son of Azaliah, and Maaseiah the governor of recorder, to repair the house of the LORD his God" (2 Chron. 34:8). As all the men began "to repair and amend the House" and "the men did the work faithfully," God, in His great mercy toward Josiah, did provide for him a way of escape from wrath! You may think that Josiah had already escaped the wrath of God by this point in his life. You may think he was already fulfilling the course which was prophetically determined for him; but it was not so reader, not yet! **God is still angry enough with Josiah that he would perish** (2 Chron. 34:10, 12). Reader, we need to seek after and obey God with all the heart and conscience within us, and still yet understand that this does not mean that we have escaped wrath (in one sense), but we must do intercessory righteousness "until the fierce wrath of our God for this matter be turned from us" (Ezra 10:14).

While repairing the House of God, "and when they brought out the money that was brought into the House of the LORD, Hilkiah the priest found a book of the law of the LORD given by Moses" (2 Chron. 34:14). They found the BIBLE! This is great evidence that God is providing an opportunity for mercy, and we will see, by deeds, if Josiah will truly go through with God. Josiah was born in a day like the prophetic WOE:

> "Behold, the days come, saith the Lord GOD, that I will send a **famine** in the land, not a famine of bread, nor a thirst for water, but **of hearing the words of the LORD**: And they shall wander from sea to sea, and from the north even to the east, they shall run to and fro to seek the word of the LORD, and **shall not find it**. In that day shall the fair virgins and young men faint for thirst" (Amos 8:11-13).

Yet now, behold, Josiah has a chance to hear TRUTH, unadulterated by history, untainted by church degeneracy, unfollowed by most, and revealed to very few. Josiah found THE BIBLE! But can you believe it? At this point in Josiah's life, at 26 years old, after following the traditions of David which were verbally passed down to him with all of his heart, after 10 years of seeking and serving God – and now – even at this very moment, the wrath of God is burning upon him to destroy him! Do you believe it? Follow with me in the subsequent events after Josiah receives and hears the written word of God:

> "Then Shaphan the scribe told the king, saying, Hilkiah the priest hath given me a book. And Shaphan read it before the king. And it came to pass, **when the king had heard** the words of the law, that he **rent his clothes**. And the king commanded Hilkiah, and Ahikam the son of Shaphan, and Abdon the son of Micah, and Shaphan the scribe, and Asaiah a servant of the king's, saying, **Go, enquire** of the LORD **for me**, and **for them** that are left in Israel and in Judah, **concerning the words** of the book that is found: **for great is the wrath of the LORD that is poured out upon us**, because our fathers have not kept the word of the LORD, to do after all that is written in this book" (2 Chronicles 34:18-21).

Behold, Josiah "rent his clothes"! Why? "**Great** is **the wrath of the LORD** that is poured out upon us because our fathers have not kept the word of the LORD, to do after all that is written in this Book!" How do you look at *Church history*? Do you view the centuries of consistency in *extrabiblical Church history* as the measuring stick for truth? When Josiah looked at *Church history*, he recognized that his fathers had not kept the word of the Lord! He was terrified and tenderhearted! He did humble himself, rent his clothes, and wept after he heard the words of the Bible! Why? Because they condemned them and him! He found that men like him were consistently condemned throughout history, and that, consistently, all throughout Church history, the people of God often slipped into hell, and this time he was in desperate straits to be one of those few inconsistent persons who went through with God. In such a state of brokenness and horror, Josiah sent for a prophet, hoping to hear of God's mind toward Josiah and Israel right then, if haply, in that very moment in time, there could be a possibility for mercy and hope. As it is written, "Hate the evil, and love the good, and establish judgment in the gate: **IT MAY BE** that the LORD God of hosts will be gracious unto the remnant of Joseph" (Amos 5:15). And again, "Seek ye the LORD, all ye meek of the earth, which have wrought His judgment; seek righteousness, seek meekness: **IT MAY BE** ye shall be hid in the day of the LORD'S anger" (Zeph. 2:3). Huldah the prophetess sent back a word of a scarce salvation:

> "Thus saith the LORD, Behold, I will bring evil upon this place, and upon the inhabitants thereof, even all the curses that are written in the book which they have read before the king of Judah: Because they have forsaken Me, and have burned incense unto other gods, that they might provoke Me to anger with all the works of their hands; therefore my wrath shall be poured out upon this place, and shall not be quenched. And as for the king of Judah, who sent you to enquire of the LORD, so shall ye say unto him, Thus saith the LORD God of Israel concerning the words which thou hast heard; <u>Because</u> **thine heart was tender**, and **thou didst humble thyself before God**, **when thou heardest His words** against this place, and against the inhabitants thereof, and **humbledst thyself before Me**, and didst **rend thy clothes**, and **weep before Me**; **I have even heard thee also**, saith the LORD. Behold, I will gather thee to thy fathers, and thou shalt be gathered to thy grave in peace, neither shall thine eyes see all the evil that I will bring upon this place, and upon the inhabitants of the same. So they brought the king word again." (2 Chronicles 34:24-28)

Because Josiah was elect and loved with an everlasting love, is this why God saved him? Inevitably YES! But is that why God saved him in the circumstances under the counsel of *God in the ways of man*? In other words, what was God's revealed mind and counsel directly before this word, when Josiah first heard the words of the Law? Was it wrath or love, damnation or salvation? Was Josiah saved because he was assured of his election, and therefore he believed he could never be damned, he could never aggravate the anger of God, and never be condemned? NAY! Josiah was saved by plainly hearing the word of God which declared his own damnation, by hearing that God was intent to destroy him...BUT God changed His mind! Did you not read it? God said, "**<u>Because</u>** thine heart was tender... **when thou**

heardest His words against this place" – it was then, by soul-riveting humility – bone-breaking, soul-shaking, garment-rending, and desperate-weeping – THEN God turned away His wrath, but NOT BEFORE! Why? God says of Josiah, "Because **thine heart was tender**, and **thou didst humble thyself** before God, when thou heardest the words against this place, and against the inhabitants thereof, and **humblest thyself before Me**, and didst **rend thy clothes**, and **weep** before Me; I have even heard thee also, saith the LORD" (2 Chron. 34:27)! God heard Josiah because of these things, not separate from them! Therefore, just previous to hearing the words of the law, and just before God observed Josiah's faith, repentance, humility, and weeping, the wrath and destruction prophesied by scripture was still yet impending upon Josiah, even though he lived his life the way he did up to that day, even though he had done all the righteousness that he knew of by verbal tradition. In this way, Josiah made his **election sure**, as it is written – "make your calling and election sure" (2 Peter 1:10).

If Josiah would have believed that he was the elect, and that this made impossible the possibility of wrath or damnation, he would not have been saved. I repeat, though he followed God with all of his heart for ten years up to that day, though he followed the ways of God as much as he knew them by the traditions and truth which was available to him, when he heard the truth as it was written, his eyes were opened to the wrath and damnation which was yet kindled…and had a priest taught Josiah the contrabiblical tenets of Calvinism, and Josiah encountered such a time like this, Calvinism would have blinded his eyes from seeing God's wrath and damnation, leaving him hopelessly hard-hearted and slipping into rightful woes. This terrifies me! Will you now open your eyes to the unadulterated truth, my reader, and will you follow that which theological systems account as inconsistent and historically nonexistent, and yet, will you follow it because it is biblical? Will you judge your integrity and weigh all of your works, numbering them throughout all your years, and decide that, everything you have done up to this day is availing to nothing, if, and only if, there is just a word of holy scripture which assures that wrath is yet against you – no matter how high your ministerial position is, no matter how kingly you have become to your generation – and though these things (by appearance) cry out your justification before the Almighty, will you hear the written word of God against the famed system of Calvinism, against the *extrabiblical* cloud of witnesses which shout to hold its tenets firm?

Are you elect of God? Then show it by looking steadfastly on the kindled wrath of God over your sin – when it is indeed kindled – and so be violent, be moved to wrestle for mercy! But instead, you vainly imagine yourself to be one of the eternally elect persons of God, when no man can know such a thing (except by prophetic revelation or present progressive blamelessness), when the greatest evidence of election is obedience, and yet you rest in disobedience thinking that God (from eternity past) thinks solely in an unchanging, ever-present love towards you, and so, you are deluded from the strong crying that would be the evidence of your eternal election. The sovereignty of God was manifest by softening Hezekiah's heart, so that he would humble himself to tears at the report of the word of God. So the question remains: has a report of the wrath of God, the warning of God, or the word of God humbled you to tears? Has a revelation of a present-tense wrath because of the written word of God's blame terrified you to broken humility? Then this is the evidence of your election! Election is not made sure by a comprehension of an eternal, unconditional love, or by the joy and thankfulness that comes from realizing the absence all possibilities of damnation, but rather, it comes from the awareness of the anger of God toward you when the written warnings of God are binding them upon your life. It was not a comprehension of the eternal, unchanging, everlasting love that saved these men; it was an acknowledgement and belief of present-tense damning wrath. Calvinism is an amalgamation of truth with a deadly mixture of lies; it is the same deadly doctrinal snares of historical false prophets, because it secures the former mindset of inordinate peace and safety, as the only possible faith for a Christian, and it disannuls, makes void, and hinders the latter comprehension from even entering the mind, namely, that destruction is impending upon them. "For when they shall say, Peace and safety; then sudden destruction cometh upon them, as travail upon a woman with child; and they shall not escape" (1 Thess. 5:3). "My people are destroyed for lack of knowledge" (Hos. 4:6).

> **Point to conclude:** *If Jeremiah, Joshua, Jacob, and Josiah had believed they were elect (according to the simplistic misappropriations of sovereign election which are common today), they would have been damned in their most desperate hour. Because they did believe they were not of the elect (**God in the ways of man**), they were fervent in mind to make their election sure, especially by the message of God which assured the terror of possible and sure wrath, if indeed, they lived in transgression of biblical warnings. They were not saved by believing they were the elect, but when they believed that their election was in danger, that they were presently damned at various points in time, they were so moved to a saving degree of repentance and faith, and ironic as it may be, this became the manifest quality of their election (**God in the ways of God**).*

THE DECEPTION OF GOD
-FROWARD FOR FROWARD
CHAPTER 15

"Let their way be **dark** and **slippery**: and **let the angel of the LORD persecute them**" – Psalm 35:6
"**God shall send** them **strong delusion**, that they should believe a lie" – 2 Thessalonians 2:11

This chapter is **an exploration of *the frowardness* of God:** the deep mysteries of the Lord's righteous anger when it is in the form of God-sent delusions coming upon men, to the end that men would be prepared for the day of their destruction.

> Psalm 18:25-26
> "With the merciful Thou wilt shew Thyself merciful; with an upright man Thou wilt shew Thyself upright; With the pure Thou wilt shew Thyself pure; and **with the froward Thou wilt shew Thyself froward.**"

> 2 Samuel 22:26-27
> "With the merciful Thou wilt shew Thyself merciful, and with the upright man Thou wilt shew Thyself upright. With the pure Thou wilt shew Thyself pure; and **with the froward Thou wilt shew Thyself unsavoury.**"

The "*frowardness*" of God is a term coined in Psalm 18:26, the first verse transcribed above. Do you remember this verse? In case you have forgotten, dear reader, let me refresh your memory and briefly rehearse what we have covered in preparation for the study of this holy and terrible attribute in God.

Since the chapter titled, "The Righteous Judgment of God," we have looked at how God does "laugh" and "mock" at condemned sinners (Ps. 1:24-29, 37:13). We have seen how this is linked to what is said to be *the frowardness of God*. Froward means – "perverse, ungovernable, and not willing to yield or comply with what is required" (Webster's 1828). We also noted how God does *lead forth* sinners into iniquity (Ps. 125:5), being led, if you will, by the hand of a **deception**. Deception is experienced by those men who are worthy of it. God, Who is most holy, reveals Himself in frowardness to the faithless. This can be perplexing, because we know that God cannot actually be *froward* or *perverse*, but He can *show Himself* this way to someone because He is veiled behind the darkness of a deception...a deception, mind

336

you, that has been earned by the exceeding sinfulness of wicked men. Think of it! Men are habitations of deception *by nature*, and every piece of furniture therein is enchanted by the devil. God has the right to *give men up into sin and deception, to leave them alone*, and they, being sinners, are left alone in the violence of themselves. Sin is a murderer! It rises in the bodily members of fleshly men like the adrenaline of rage, mounting up for soul suicide. God promises – "be sure your sin will find you out" (Num. 32:23) – but lo, even the mystery of iniquity is a mapped out in God's predestination! The dark night of deception is daytime to God. Deceptions lead lost men – like persons they speak to them – and sinners lift up their eyes so as to look for God, and lo, they see distortions, blasphemies, and lying visions which are damning delusions. Who are the prisoners of this lawless and awful experience? It is the **scorner** that "seeketh wisdom and **findeth it not**" (Prov. 14:6), and thus we understand that, if God can hide wisdom from a man, then He can hide Himself – even behind a veil of deception, darkening and imprisoning men into further iniquity. "Verily Thou art a God **that hidest Thyself**, O God of Israel, the Savior" (Isa. 45:15), and if the Savior is hidden, so is salvation. Furthermore, we can understand, this deception is one that reacheth to the very spiritual capacities which enable a man to understand anything at all. They become prisoners in a prison they know nothing about. A man cannot know if or when he is deceived – that is the nature of deception. A man is deceived when he thinks that he is not deceived. Deception is an unconscious prison house where all men feel free, and they all go about as their nature leads them in a parade of rioting in the "The Carnival of Carnality". These men cannot "understand judgment" (Prov. 28:5). "The wisdom of the prudent is to understand his way: but the folly of fools is **deceit**" (Prov. 14:8).

Leading into further attributes and surrounding factors which pertain to biblical scenarios of deception, God says that He, at such a time, does *hide His face* (Deut. 32:20). His face is the shining of saving Light, and outside of it there is no light. At such a time of deception, it is then that the friendly and saving relationship one did have with God has turned, so that God is turning from men, becoming to them the opposite image of the saving promise – break for break (Ezek. 16:59, 17:18-19). *Hiding His face* is one way to express it: showing the feeling of hopelessness, darkness, and absence in this woeful experience, but another way God describes this experience of wrath is that He *casts men away* from His Presence. Do you remember the word "*castaway*"? God has and will cast men away (Rom. 11:15) from Himself, but note this carefully – this causes their "fall" from salvation (Rom. 11:11-12). God's own sovereign decree darkens the eyes of their understanding into "blindness" (Rom. 11:7), or in other words, God gives them a "spirit of slumber" (Rom. 11:8). So it is written: "eyes that they should not see, and ears that they should not hear" (Rom. 11:8). Jeremiah sought to wrestle against this wrath in a castaway generation, but intercession was impossible (Jer. 15:1), the Covenant was broken (Jer. 14:21), and the entire generation, as it were, held the hand of a deception, were in the bliss of ignorance, the happiness of oblivion, and they were led right into the slaughter. This deception is stupidity and brutishness; it is animal-like unconsciousness! Like "an ox goeth to the slaughter" or "as a bird hasteth to the snare, and knoweth not that it is for his life" (Prov. 7:22-23)! Did you know that men can become such fools? Are you one of them? If you are, you may never come to know it. An ox standeth in the slaughter line, and suddenly, he's dead! Of this Jeremiah cried – "Then said I, Ah, Lord GOD! Surely **Thou hast greatly deceived this people and Jerusalem**, saying, Ye shall have peace; whereas **the sword reacheth unto the soul**" (Jer. 4:10)! At another time than this, even Jeremiah had been carried away in deception. He was temporarily caught in it and then recovered, and at the time, Jeremiah lamented to his God that, to him, God seemed to be *a deceiver* (Jer. 15:18, 20:7), and thus we can see that even Jeremiah, along with all God's choice prophets, did temporarily experience the *unsavory* experience of condemning wrath when God *shows Himself as a liar*. All this is to prepare the way for a further examination of the experiences of deception – through the frowardness of God – in the various ways deceptions reveal Him, or, the various ways He shows Himself to men in *unsavory images*. If Christians can temporarily or permanently fall under this experience of deception, shouldn't we need know about it, if haply we may guard against its surprise upon our souls? Lest we end up in the darkness fast asleep, given over to the decree of God, called "the spirit of slumber" (Rom. 11:8), half-awake and hardly hearing the salvific call – "Awake thou that sleepest, and arise from the dead, and Christ shall give thee light" (Eph. 5:14) – and, lo…we are unable to wake up! It is imperative that we understand this deception, especially how, at sundry times, the saints did experience and recover from it. We need to learn what merited a deception to come upon them, and how, afterward, they were enabled to recovered from it. Also, we must learn from the course of those saints who fell into a deception without recovery from the fall, who ultimately, were damned with the world. Finally, we must understand deceptions, generally speaking, as they pertain to sinners who serve as examples to learn from. In general, we must know the course of the damned as it pertains to deception. My reader, let our study of *this course* begin with Eli.

Eli

> *"And ere the Lamp of God went out in the Temple of the LORD,*
> *where the ark of God was…"*

In the days of Eli, his unfaithfulness procured a breach of promise for his priesthood, for him and his household (as formerly addressed). Let us look and consider what it is meant for "**the Lamp of God**" to go out. It was written of this Lamp that, namely, it was "the Lamp of God". God commanded this Lamp to be burning, always lit, emanating a perpetual light in the holy place. This is emblematic of the light of God's shining face when it shines upon a blessed generation. It was written, "**cause the Lamp to burn always**" (Ex. 27:20), and if it would go out, what would become of *the Spiritual Light of God's presence*? Indicative of this, it is said of this woeful generation that God "forsook the Tabernacle of Shiloh, the tent which He placed among men" (Ps. 78:60), and this was the place, God says, "where I set my name at the first" (Jer. 7:12). It was because of the Tabernacle-forsaking, people-rejecting, wrath of God that then, lo, the Lamp of God went out. It is as if God was

338

exiting, and by this was exclaiming, "Oh that I had in the wilderness a lodging place of wayfaring men; that I might leave my people, and go from them! For they be all adulterers, an assembly of treacherous men" (Jer. 9:2). Shockingly, God did become as a wayfaring man. He left His people, *literally*, giving over the ark of God into the hands of the Philistines, so that they, as it were, carried Him away into a foreign land. Seated upon His throne, the ark, God was willingly carried away by unholy hands!

This is a woeful judgment! The same kind is later spoken of: "I will cast you out of My sight, as I have cast out all your brethren, even the whole seed of Ephraim. Therefore pray not thou for this people, neither lift up cry nor prayer for them, neither make intercession to me; for I will not hear thee" (Jer. 7:15-16). God's Tabernacle is the ground of all intercessions and prayers, as God said, "My house shall be called of all nations the House of prayer" (Mark 11:17), but now it is emptied of His Majesty. Israel is darkened at the absence of God, and behold, God walks over to a boy, Samuel by name, and abides with him in the time of wrath. Samuel is ordained to be a voice for God in the midst of a Godless nation, so that God can declare His doings whensoever He wills. The very moment the Lamp of God went out, it was then that God walked over to the sleeping boy, Samuel, and graciously called his name! Samuel became the only light of God left in Israel. Darkness was upon the Tabernacle of God, the high priest of God (Eli), the priests (Eli's sons), and all other ministrations which bore the saving authority of the God of Israel were cast away. The spiritual climate of this day was *dark* so that, "The Word of the LORD was **precious** in those days; there was **no open vision**" (1 Sam. 3:1). These marks are those which characterize "days and times" which are given over to deception – "The Deception of God" – thus Eli's life and generation serve as an introduction to what will be, hereafter, repeated for centuries.

That which happened to the High Priest, the priestly lineage, and the Tabernacle of God, is a direct indicator of the spiritual climate that shall cover the whole land. Think of it! Eli, the High Priest – that was given "the breastplate of judgment" in the House of God, even "the Urim and the Thummim" – even he cannot go before the LORD (Ex. 28:30)! Access to God's presence was a direct line of salvific grace for Israel, and all the people wept, for it was obsolete. From another angle, now let us consider Israel's King, King Saul by name. He was given over to the torments and deceptions of demons! And more! He was locked under the silence of God at the hour of his need! Israel too, in subjection to their forsaken leader, did all abide under the spiritual curse of old, "thy heaven that is over thy head shall be brass" (Deut. 28:23), and no prayer was breaking through for hope or salvation. Ordered armies did set their feet upon a charted course with their King, marching forward, but Saul was spiritually blind…he was being led a thick deception, until finally, he and those following him, in all the pomp of their sophisticated marching order – "both fall into the ditch" (Lk. 6:39). "And when Saul enquired of the LORD, the LORD answered him not, neither by dreams, nor by Urim, nor by prophets" (1 Sam. 28:6). The high priest Eli, dark and without God, was reduced to hear the Word of God from a child whom God found faithful – little Samuel – and lo, the boy opened his mouth to speak, but what could he say? "The LORD said to Samuel, Behold, I will do a thing in Israel, at which both the ears of every one that heareth it shall tingle. In that day I will perform against Eli all things which I have spoken concerning his house: when I begin, will also make an end" (1 Sam. 3:11-12).

Balaam

Eli was reduced to hear from a child, but Balaam was reduced to hear from a mute ass! The Lord did put Balaam in derision before the saving help of a donkey, and why? To show the shame of a man worthy of God-sent deceptions! To show that deceptions do render geniuses of intelligence decidedly, both deaf and blind, and that "The Deception of God" is a demonic dimension making men dumber than a donkey. How did Balaam merit for himself such a demoting deception?

The elders and rulers of Moab came before Balaam with the "rewards of divination" with them, requesting of him that he would curse the Israelites that were quickly approaching their land (Num. 22:7). Balaam sought the Lord for His word concerning their request, and God's answer was brisk, brief, and clear – "Thou shalt not go with them; thou shalt not curse the people: for they are blessed" (Num. 22:12). Balaam obeyed the word of the Lord and told the elders, "Get you into your land: for the LORD refuseth to give me leave to go with you" (Num. 22:13). The King of the Moabites, named Balak, sent mightier princes than those who were formerly sent and gave the pledge of whatever honour or riches Balaam desired, if only Balaam would curse Israel. Balaam answered, "I cannot go beyond the word of the LORD my God, to do less or more" (Num. 22:18). Balaam said this with his mouth, but his heart went after the reward of unrighteousness. He desired the greater rewards which were now laid before him. He should not have, but he received the men for the night. He should have turned them away, but he wanted to seek the Lord for **another word,** if haply the Lord would change His mind and allow Balaam to curse Israel. Balaam, knowing the will of God already, sought to hear **another word** from God, but it was so that he could fulfill his lusts, and because of this, unbeknownst to Balaam – God deceived him. Balaam fell under "The Deception of God", in that, his death sentence came through an answer to his prayer:

> "And God came to Balaam at night, and said unto him, If the men come to call thee, rise up, and go with them; but yet the word which I shall say unto thee, that shalt thou do" (Num. 22:20).

God answered Balaam's prayer! He gave Balaam a change from the former instruction which was "more" (Num. 22:19) than what was commanded as obedience at the first: "And Balaam rose up in the morning, and saddled his ass, and went with the princes of Moab. **And God's anger was kindled because he went**..." (Num. 22:21-22). Balaam did what was told him by the LORD! Is that wrong? The Lord answered Balaam's prayer request, but Balaam would learn to regret that he had made this request! His request was motivated by his own sinful lust for money. God, knowing the hearts of all men, gave Balaam the judgment he deserved according to his heart, and shockingly, answered his prayer by giving him another command. Balaam had the perception that he was still in the favor of God! God is a heart-searching, motive-discovering, discerner, alive today, and in the NT dispensation He also saith: "**I will kill** her children with death; and all the Churches shall know that **I am He which searcheth the reins and hearts: and I will give unto every one of you according to your works**" (Rev. 2:23). God sent the command to Balaam to *go*, and Balaam *went*, because God wanted Balaam to go forth on his course to walk into a God-ordained execution. What is terrifying about this is that Balaam was deceived by God! Men emboldened by their lusts, and persistent in flesh-born prayerful requests, deserve deceptions. Balaam thought that he was obeying the Lord, and Balaam was obeying the Lord (in one sense), but this obedience was to his death when he thought it was to the furtherance of his life. Read the entire passage carefully:

"God's anger was kindled because he went: and the angel of the LORD stood in the way for an adversary against him. Now he was riding upon his ass, and his two servants were with him. And the ass saw the angel of the LORD standing in the way, and his sword drawn in his hand: and the ass turned aside out of the way, and went into the field: and Balaam smote the ass, to turn her into the way. But the angel of the LORD stood in a path of the vineyards, a wall being on this side, and a wall on that side. And when the ass saw the angel of the LORD, she thrust herself unto the wall, and crushed Balaam's foot against the wall: and he smote her again. And the angel of the LORD went further, and stood in a narrow place, where was no way to turn either to the right hand or to the left. And when the ass saw the angel of the LORD, she fell down under Balaam: and Balaam's anger was kindled, and he smote the ass with a staff. And the LORD opened the mouth of the ass, and she said unto Balaam, What have I done unto thee, that thou hast smitten me these three times? And Balaam said unto the ass, Because thou hast mocked me: I would there were a sword in mine hand, for now would I kill thee. And the ass said unto Balaam, Am not I thine ass, upon which thou hast ridden ever since I was thine unto this day? was I ever wont to do so unto thee? And he said, Nay. Then the LORD opened the eyes of Balaam, and he saw the angel of the LORD standing in the way, and his sword drawn in his hand: and he bowed down his head, and fell flat on his face. And the angel of the LORD said unto him, Wherefore hast thou smitten thine ass these three times? behold, I went out to withstand thee, because thy way is perverse before me: And the ass saw me, and turned from me these three times: unless she had turned from me, surely now also

I had slain thee, and saved her alive. And Balaam said unto the angel of the LORD, I have sinned; for I knew not that thou stoodest in the way against me: now therefore, if it displease thee, I will get me back again" (Num. 22:22-34)

Balaam is a foundational example, serving well to warn all men of God's deceptive powers for judgment. Many shall become followers of Balaam. Many will become prophets who "find no vision from the LORD" (Lam. 2:6-9), and also, when any vision comes from the LORD, it is to their destruction. With such prophets as this who are under a delusion, likewise it is written of the King and Priest: the Lord "hath despised in the indignation of His anger the **King** and the **Priest**" (Lam. 2:6). These are days when "the law is no more" (Lam. 2:9), when "the Lord hath cast off His altar, He hath abhorred His sanctuary" (Lam. 2:7). God has been aggravated by the incessant insincerity of religious men, men that pray in unfounded, bold, and unholy liberties before a God. Whatever they are thinking, their thoughts are overflowing without caution in what they are speaking, and look, they go quickly to God and tell all their heart to Him, but God doth otherwise warn – "Keep thy foot when thou goest to the House of God, and be more ready to hear, than to give the sacrifice of fools: for they consider not that they do evil. Be not rash with thy mouth, and let not thine heart be hasty to utter any thing before God" (Eccl. 5:1-2). That which is before the House of God on earth, it is before the presence of the God, the God of all the earth, dwelling in the holiness of heaven, and this awful loft Balaam did not heed. Balaam and Israel, lo, they uttered their sinful requests before God, and behold, "their way [became] dark and slippery", for "the angel of the LORD [did] persecute them" (Ps. 35:6)!

Israel

"He gave them their own desire;
they were not estranged from their lust" – Psalm 78:29-30 & Numbers 11.

Israel came to learn this awful procurement in the wrath of God, by the multitudes, when God herein executed it upon them. He deceived them and killed them – and "there they buried the people that lusted" (Num. 11:34). What was their lust? They were utterly taken in their iniquity and, like Balaam, they hastily made their complaint a prayer request to God: "Give us flesh that we may eat" (Num. 11:13). "They tempted God in their heart by asking meat for their lust" (Ps. 78:18), and that which they requested to God, the Omni-righteous, He *did not withhold from them*. He answered their prayer so as to give them what they asked for, and He gave them over to their sins, and again - it was by the deception of answered prayers. They thought they were still in His favor because He had answered their prayer request, but lo, He answered it so that He could slay them in His wrath. They fell into "The Deception of God." Yea, "while their meat was yet in their mouths, the wrath of God came upon them, and slew the fattest of them, and smote down the chosen men of Israel" (Ps. 78:30-31). "He called the name of that place Kibroth-hattaavah", which

342

means **graves of lust** (Num. 11:34). Do you trust God to answer your prayers? What about when you pray for your evil lusts? The answered prayers appear to be the smile of God upon you, and behold, before you have time to repent, you suddenly fall down dead.

This Israelite casualty in the wilderness was repeated again. God desired that they would learn to fear Him, to obey Him, to avoid the deceptions of God, but sadly, the rebellion exhibited here will be held fast, stiffnecked, until God brings upon Israel the same judgment over again. So it is written <u>again</u>, He "**gave them up unto their own hearts' lust**" (Ps. 81:12), only this time it would be in the midst of Canaanite cities, nations, armies, and kings, when before it was in the desert's hot elements which melted their convictions into the madness of covetous rebellion. What is your *wilderness trial*? What is your *Canaanite battle* with *terrifying giants*? Below in Psalm 81:10-16, read how the humility which was learned in the wilderness should have been a guiding example for subsequent generations to take heed to, that they would trust only in the Lord and avoid the same error, but like unto those that perished in the hot and deserted wilderness, even so, Israel perished in the hot and breathtaking trials of the Promised Land – again, procuring "The Deception of God".

> "I am the LORD thy God, which brought thee out of the land of Egypt: open thy mouth wide, and I will fill it. But my people would not hearken to my voice; and Israel would none of Me. **So I gave them up unto their own hearts' lust**: and they walked in their own counsels. Oh that my people had hearkened unto Me, and Israel had walked in my ways! I should soon have subdued their enemies, and turned my hand against their adversaries. The haters of the LORD should have submitted themselves unto him: but their time should have endured for ever. He should have fed them also with the finest of the wheat: and with honey out of the rock should I have satisfied thee" (Psalm 81:10-16).

Micaiah & Later Generations

Scarcely are heavenly scenes unveiled for human creatures to behold. Rare are the instances in which God's higher-righteous decrees of heaven are revealed to men, as if, momentarily, they are bystanders in the Supreme Court of God in heaven. In the life and ministry of Micaiah, HE DID behold a *heavenly scene* of magnanimous proportion! At the sight of it, in consideration with the things subsequently unfolded on earth below, all men of sound reason will be forced to solemnly conclude, "With Him is strength and wisdom: *the deceived* and *the deceiver are His. He leadeth counsellors* away spoiled, and *maketh the judges fools*" (Job 12:16-17)! "Are we stronger than He" (1 Cor. 10:22)!?

343

"Go, and prosper: for the LORD shall deliver it into the hand of the king" – 1 Kings 22:15

Micaiah was a lonely prophet that "sat alone" (Jer. 15:17), as Israel was filled with lying soothsayers. Nevertheless, Micaiah was enquired by Ahab the King of Israel often enough so that he had a well-known reputation. Ahab said of him, "I hate him; for he doth not prophesy good concerning me, but evil" (1 Kings 22:8). Ahab expected Micaiah to prophesy of harm and evil when, this time, he is endeavoring a battle in league with Jehoshaphat, the King of Judah. Jehoshaphat was loyal to the true God, and thus he compelled Ahab to call forth Micaiah to prophesy. Micaiah was then called to the court to give a word. When Micaiah arrived, about 400 prophets had already prophesied to King Ahab, "Go up to Ramothgilead, and prosper: for the LORD shall deliver it into the king's hand" (1 Kings 22:12). While Micaiah was traveling to the court of the kings with the messenger that retrieved him, the messenger pled with him to prophesy like all other men, like the rest of the prophets who said *something good*.

> "And Micaiah said, As the LORD liveth, what the LORD saith unto me, that will I speak. So he came to the king. And the king said unto him, Micaiah, shall we go against Ramothgilead to battle, or shall we forbear? And he answered him, **Go, and prosper: for the LORD shall deliver it into the hand of the king**" (1 Kings 22:14-15).

How can this be? Did the LORD lie? My reader, the LORD "hath spoken evil" (1 Kings 22:23) concerning Ahab by sending him a deception! God sent Ahab a delusion through the instrumentality of lying spirits, as Micaiah later told Ahab saying: "behold, the LORD hath put a lying spirit in the mouth of all these thy prophets" (1 Kings 22:23). The Lord spoke evil concerning Ahab, but, this was spoken in heaven, and from the High Ground up there, God decreed that a lying spirit would be sent down here. This evil spirit was empowered by God's determining decree, empowered to deceive, and so he succeeded to bring about the God-ordained deception upon Ahab. This was to the end that Ahab would be *convinced he was in the will of God*, being deceived, to confidently go forth, with peace, with joy, riding into his death. God spoke evil concerning Ahab, but Ahab was held captive by a lying deception. It was God's will for Ahab to think he was in the favorable will of God. When Micaiah was asked what the word of God was to Ahab, shockingly, Micaiah spoke of the very same decree which he saw and heard in heaven – "Go and prosper" (1 Kings 22:15). It was God's will that Ahab would go and die, by decree, and this decree manifested in the powers of lying spirits, preaching deceptions through a hoard of false prophets, passionately deceived, and crying out – "Go, and prosper: for the LORD shall deliver it into the hand of the King" (1 Kings 22:12). Four hundred strong and shouting, deceptions like sulfur smoke were filling the court of the Kings. The blackness was whirling about with invisible demonic powers, so that, without hearing a whispering voice men believed Satan's speeches, making

344

perfectly sane men deluded by a spiritual blinding, and in this, all the deceived men were rejoicing in the emotional charisma of a victory at war, roaring with confidence that was utterly astounding! God Almighty – even the Lord – He did ordain this, and "His hand formed the crooked serpent" (Job 26:13)! Please carefully review the historical account as it was written:

> "So he came to the king. And the king said unto him, Micaiah, shall we go against Ramothgilead to battle, or shall we forbear? And he answered him, Go, and prosper: for the LORD shall deliver it into the hand of the king. And the king said unto him, How many times shall I adjure thee that thou tell me nothing but that which is true in the name of the LORD? And he said, I saw all Israel scattered upon the hills, as sheep that have not a shepherd: and the LORD said, These have no master: let them return every man to his house in peace. And the king of Israel said unto Jehoshaphat, Did I not tell thee that he would prophesy no good concerning me, but evil? And he said, Hear thou therefore the word of the LORD: I saw the LORD sitting on His throne, and all the host of heaven standing by Him on His right hand and on His left. And the LORD said, Who shall persuade Ahab, that he may go up and fall at Ramothgilead? And one said on this manner, and another said on that manner. And there came forth a spirit, and stood before the LORD, and said, I will persuade him. And the LORD said unto him, Wherewith? And he said, I will go forth, and I will be a lying spirit in the mouth of all his prophets. And He said, thou shalt persuade him, and prevail also: go forth, and do so. Now therefore, behold, the LORD hath put a lying spirit in the mouth of all these thy prophets, and the LORD hath spoken evil concerning thee." (1Ki 22:15-23)

As Balaam and Israel prayed to God, now again, this King Ahab prays enquiries, and justice reacts to their insolence with damning deceptions. Ahab enquired of God to know His mind, will, or word, but with a rebellious heart, and God says: "rebellion is as the sin of witchcraft, and stubbornness is as iniquity and idolatry" (1 Sam. 15:23). This rebellious King met the description written in Ezekiel 14:3 which explains "The Deception of God":

> "Son of man, these men have set up their idols in their heart, and put the stumblingblock of their iniquity before their face: **should I be enquired of at all by them**?" Well, should He? In this chapter, God threatens such men that come to a prophet for *enquiry*: "I the LORD will answer him that cometh **according to the multitude of his idols**" (Ezek. 14:4).

What does this mean for God to answer a man according to his idols? It

345

means – DECEPTION – God says, "That I may take the House of Israel **in their own heart**, because they are all estranged from Me through their idols" (Ezek. 14:5). By the power of deceptions and woeful judgments, God says that He will make such men "a sign and a proverb" by the manner in which He does cut them off from His people. Further, when deceptions go forth through the prophesying of the prophets which are enquired of – GOD TAKES OWNERSHIP FOR IT: "And if the prophet be **deceived** when he hath spoken a thing, **I the LORD have deceived that prophet**, and I will stretch out My hand upon him, and will destroy him from the midst of my people Israel" (Ezek. 14:9)!

God said...

> *To Ahab* – "Go, and prosper: for the LORD shall deliver it into the hand of the King" (1 Kings 22:15).
>
> *To Balaam* – "If the men come to call thee, rise up, and go with them" (Num. 22:20).

These are *the commandments of God*, by higher decree, but not those which are laced with truth and life! On the contrary, they are laced with wrath and death. Thus God declares: "Wherefore **I gave them also <u>statutes</u> that were not good**, and <u>**judgments**</u> **whereby they should not live**; And **I polluted them in their own gifts**, in that they caused to pass through the fire all that openeth the womb, **that I might make them desolate**, to the end that they might know that I am the LORD" (Ezek. 20:25-26). In the same manner that God related to Ahab and Balaam, specifically, how He spoke to them a deception, Ezekiel 20:39 is exactly parallel in command to Israel: "As for you, O house of Israel, thus saith the Lord GOD; **Go ye, serve ye every one his idols,** and hereafter also, if ye will not hearken unto Me: but pollute ye my holy name no more with your gifts, and with your idols" (Ezek. 20:39).

God said...

> *To Israel* – "Go ye, serve ye every one his idols" (Ezek. 20:39).

These commandments of God are sovereign decrees which result in the hardening of men's hearts. Men are irresistibly compelled by these commands under the deceptive power of God. This is like as it is written in the NT: "God shall send them strong delusion, that they should believe a lie" (2 Thess. 2:11). Had God never sent the delusion, then such persons would not have believed a lie. Why does the Lord give such commandments of strong delusion? The next verse declares its purpose: "That they all might be damned who believed not the truth, but had pleasure in unrighteousness" (2 Thess. 2:12). The Lord says the same thing in Ezekiel 20:25-26 as the purpose of the delusion, when He said, "that I might make them desolate." There are many decrees of deception on the high plains of sovereign loft, more than we know, which all the attendants of the court hear continually, like Micaiah saw and heard just once. As the Lord said to Ahab, "go," and to Balaam, "go," God also says *to Israel...*

> *To Israel* – "Come to Bethel, and transgress; at Gilgal multiply

transgression; and bring your sacrifices every morning, and your tithes after three years: And offer a sacrifice of thanksgiving with leaven, and proclaim and publish the free offerings: for this liketh you, O ye children of Israel, saith the Lord GOD" (Amos 4:4-5).

To rebellious young men – "Rejoice, O young man, in thy youth; and let thy heart cheer thee in the days of thy youth, and walk in the ways of thine heart, and in the sight of thine eyes: but know thou, that for all these things God will bring thee into judgment" (Eccl. 11:9).

God deceives them to bring them into His desired furnace of destruction. He prepares for, not a haven of rest, but a dungeon of derision. "I will **hide My face** from them, **I will see what their end shall be**" (Deut. 32:20). God will take them to the place where men will call upon Him, being in derision, and then God will leave them there, confounded, tormented by the silent absence of God. God will lead them forth to lie down in God's guillotine. Here He will debag their faces and cause them to look up at the blade, ready to fall, and then they will call upon all things, and even Him, and then God will deride them and shame them! He will call upon their false gods to upbraid the false confidence they have had. God will mock them there and be glorified over the images of His jealousy which stole the love of the people from God. Like a jealous husband, He will have the idols in derision, not that they could have emotion nor even speak, but by their silence they will be derided in the hearts of the people laid waste and ready to die, forsaken in the hour of their deepest need. "He that sitteth in the heavens **shall laugh**: the Lord shall have them **in derision**" (Ps. 2:4). "But Thou, O LORD, **shalt laugh at them**; Thou shalt have all the heathen **in derision**" (Ps. 59:8). "And He shall say, Where are their gods, their rock in whom they trusted, Which did eat the fat of their sacrifices, and drank the wine of their drink offerings? **Let them rise up and help you, and be your protection**" (Deut. 32:38)! "**Go and cry unto the gods which ye have chosen**; let them deliver you in the time of your tribulation" (Judges 10:14)! Thus God says to men as He says to the tribe of Ephraim, "Ephraim is joined to idols: **let him alone**" (Hos. 4:17)!

By life or death, God will have the glory! Oh dear reader, do you want God to *leave you alone?* Like as God said that He did to Israel when, "He gave them their own desire; they were not estranged from their lust" (Ps. 78:29-30). Oh the terror of it! That aside from the sovereign restraint of God men will be left to themselves, and if God will determine the destruction of a soul, it can be said, simply, that He restrained them no more, gave them up, and let them go. "But my people would not hearken to my voice; and Israel would none of Me. **So I gave them up unto their own hearts' lust: and they walked in their own counsels**" (Psalm 81:11-12). "Wherefore **God also gave them up** to uncleanness through the lusts of their own hearts, to dishonour their own bodies between themselves" (Rom 1:24).

Such men as these are human vessels purposefully created, and now existing, to display the glory of God's wrath. What glory? The glory of the magnitude, severity, and awfulness of the climax when they are destroyed – *when* it is done, *how* it is done, and *why* it is done! When they are destroyed, it is a surprise, surprising the deceived! How they are destroyed will be a sign and wonder to all those who live thereafter; feared and derided! Why they die is a case God makes clear. "The way of transgressors is hard" (Prov. 13:15). God gives men deceptions to make their sins increase, to reach the glory mark, until God is able to justly reward their behavior with a certain severity of awful destruction which shall stand forever – forever famous – steering all men away from sin into the fear of God. God waits to awake His judgments until the hour of His glory, till sin exponentially increases and mounts up, and God rises above it, with a Warrior leap, striking it down to the depths of hell! Even so, remember this, so it shall be in the End of Days:

> "And I heard another voice from heaven, saying, Come out of her, my people, that ye be not partakers of her sins, and that ye receive not of her plagues. For her sins have reached unto heaven, and God hath remembered her iniquities. Reward her even as she rewarded you, and double unto her double according to her works: in the cup which she hath filled fill to her double. How much she hath glorified herself, and lived deliciously, so much torment and sorrow give her: for she saith in her heart, I sit a queen, and am no widow, and shall see no sorrow. Therefore shall her plagues come in one day, death, and mourning, and famine; and she shall be utterly burned with fire: for strong is the Lord God Who judgeth her" (Rev. 18:4-8).

Into the hour of their derision, thereto the deception of God leadeth them, and then, God looks upon them with the very face they gave to Him! *Scorn*, *mockery*, and *frowardness*! Elijah did well represent this at that famed Mountain faceoff: "And it came to pass at noon, that Elijah **mocked** them, and said, Cry aloud: for he is a god; either he is talking, or he is pursuing, or he is in a journey, or peradventure he sleepeth, and must be awaked" (1Ki 18:27). Like Elijah, Elisha spoke to the King of Israel (who was utterly joined to idolatry and rebellion) in the hour of his deepest need: "What have I to do with thee? **Get thee to the prophets of thy father, and to the prophets of thy mother**. And the king of Israel said unto him, Nay: for the LORD hath called these three kings together, to deliver them into the hand of Moab" (2Ki 3:13). Thus also Christ derided His sleeping disciples who refused to hear His call for watchful prayer, and so, they were left to the delusions of their temptations, and in turn – every one of them forsook and denied Christ. "Then cometh [Jesus] to His disciples, and saith unto them, **Sleep on now**, and take your rest: behold, the hour is at hand, and the Son of Man is betrayed into the hands of sinners" (Matt. 26:45).

When God delivers His nation and people over to a delusion, He is leading them into crying agony, and at the hour of uplifted prayers God's face is still turned away. Remember this verse? "Therefore it is come to pass, that **as he cried, and they would not hear; so they cried, and I would not hear**, saith the LORD of hosts" (Zech. 7:13). God is justified, He reasons, to abide behind the clouds of delusion. "Then shall they cry unto the LORD, but He will not hear them: He will even **hide His face from them at that time, as they have behaved themselves** ill in their doings" (Mich. 3:4). "Therefore will I also deal in fury: Mine eye shall not spare, neither will I have pity: and though they cry in Mine ears with a loud voice, yet will I not hear them" (Ezek. 8:18). Men who say, "there is no God", God will be no God to them! "They cried, but there was none to save them: even unto the LORD, but He answered them not" (Psalm 18:41)! "Therefore thus saith the LORD, Behold, I will bring evil upon them, which they shall not be able to escape; and though they shall cry unto Me, I will not hearken unto them" (Jer. 11:11). They can cry, pray, fast, and mourn, but all such humiliation is in – an unacceptable time – a woeful hour when God cannot be found. What agony! God saith, "When they fast, I will not hear their cry; and when they offer burnt offering and an oblation, I will not accept them: but I will consume them by the sword, and by the famine, and by the pestilence" (Jer. 14:12). Generations of men have read about these horrifying deceptions decreed by God, and so, men fear to be made like a deceived animal, a dumb ox, unknowingly led to the slaughter. Be wise, my reader, and "feel after" God so as to find Him now, if haply now is an hour when He may be found of you (Acts 17:27)! "Seek ye the LORD **while He may be found**, call ye upon Him **while He is near**" (Isa. 55:6).

Maybe you will run into one of God's messengers of deception, the false prophets, who preach the good promises of God to unrepentant men. They do "seeing vanity, and divining lies", "saying, Thus saith the Lord GOD, when the LORD hath not spoken" (Ezek. 22:28). With the help of demonic powers, the common people turn away from hearing God's voice and law which calls them to repentance and obedience. They continue in disobedience, but still believe God, that, in the hour of trouble God will help and save them. What a tragedy; it is NOT SO! "He that turneth away his ear from hearing the law, even his prayer shall be abomination" (Pro 28:9)! God will judge even their prayer as a sin (Ps. 109:7), even as the psalmist said: "If I regard iniquity in my heart, the Lord will not hear me" (Ps. 66:18).

My dear reader, have you thought long and hard about a God Who will put men, even saved men, under the awful experience written in Lamentations 3:1-8?

> "I am the man that hath seen affliction by the rod of His wrath.
> He hath led me, and brought me into darkness, but not into light.
> Surely against me is He turned; He turneth His hand against me
> all the day. My flesh and my skin hath He made old; He hath
> broken my bones. He hath builded against me, and compassed me
> with gall and travail. He hath set me in dark places, as they that
> be dead of old. He hath hedged me about, that I cannot get out:
> He hath made my chain heavy. Also when I cry and shout, He
> shutteth out my prayer. Thou hast covered Thyself with a cloud,

that our prayer should not pass through" (Lam. 3:1-8, 44).

Dear pastor, church member, or ministerial staff, have you ever sought to examine the state of your heart and life next to the biblical fruits of true Christianity, if haply, perhaps, your expectations notwithstanding, all of your church assemblies, services, songs, prayers, and religious duties are antagonizing, wearying, and troubling to God? Even as He said of old:

> "When ye come to appear before Me, who hath required this at your hand, to tread My courts? Bring no more vain oblations; incense is an abomination unto Me; the new moons and sabbaths, the calling of assemblies, I cannot away with; it is iniquity, even the solemn meeting. Your new moons and your appointed feasts my soul hateth: they are a trouble unto Me; I am weary to bear them. And when ye spread forth your hands, I will hide Mine eyes from you: yea, when ye make many prayers, I will not hear: your hands are full of blood" (Isa 1:12-15).

Are you included in His case of justice? Maybe this describes you, then, when God said, "Thus saith the LORD unto this people, Thus have they loved to wander, they have not refrained their feet, therefore the LORD doth not accept them; He will now remember their iniquity, and visit their sins. Then said the LORD unto me, Pray not for this people for their good. When they fast, I will not hear their cry; and when they offer burnt offering and an oblation, I will not accept them: but I will consume them by the sword, and by the famine, and by the pestilence" (Jer. 14:10-12).

Saints Who Recover - The Temporary Experience of the Deception of God

Did you know that it is possible for a godly man to fall? Whether it be in the OT, NT, or now, godly men have fallen into a spiritual condition which merits God's wrath. As the OT declares it, they fall into a place where God has **hidden His face from them**. Being cast off, they have fallen…and at such a time, if repentance is not obtained, then God acts in His righteous judgment to reflect their behavior – *froward for froward*, *scorn for scorn*, and *lie for lie*.

When God is unrepentant, He is, as it were, sleeping at the cry of His people, thus God is not awaking for their help and salvation. Therefore the people of God express a terrifying feeling of abandonment (Ps. 7:6-7, Isa. 51:9).

> Arise, O LORD, in Thine anger, lift up Thyself because of the rage of mine enemies: and **awake** for me to the judgment **that Thou hast commanded**. So shall the congregation of the people

compass Thee about: for their sakes therefore return Thou on high" (Psalm 7:6-7).

"**Awake, awake**, put on strength, O arm of the LORD; **awake**, as in the ancient days, in the generations of old. Art Thou not it that hath cut Rahab, and wounded the dragon?" (Isa. 51:9)

This feeling is as though God is sleeping. It is a feeling that God cannot or will not hear their cry for help. Sleep is when the consciousness of a living man is not awake, whether to be alarmed to do right or wrong, or to arise and intervene against some impending harm, thus men feel that God has forgotten what is right, good, true, or even commanded.

"Arise, O LORD; O God, lift up Thine hand: **forget** not the humble" (Ps. 10:12).

"How long wilt Thou **forget** me, O LORD? for ever? How long wilt Thou hide Thy face from me?" (Ps. 13:1).

"O deliver not the soul of Thy turtledove unto the multitude *of the wicked:* **forget** not the congregation of Thy poor for ever" (Ps. 74:19).

"I am **forgotten** as a dead man out of mind: I am like a broken vessel" (Ps. 31:12).

"I will say unto God my rock, Why hast Thou **forgotten** me? why go I mourning because of the oppression of the enemy?" (Ps. 42:9)

"Hath God **forgotten** to be gracious? Hath He in anger shut up his tender mercies?" (Ps. 77:9).

This reality is a strange paradigm that saints relate to God in! Men seek to awake and remind God, as if He can forget. They are giving "Him no rest" until He does His own will, and, through these means, God will be sure to do it. This is written: "And give Him no rest, till He establish, and till He make Jerusalem a praise in the earth" (Isa. 62:7). Now what you need to understand, my reader, is that, at such a time of God's departure, like unto sleep or forgetfulness, this is a time when the promises are breached, favor and mercy for salvation is absent, and wrath is kindled (Ps. 77:7-9). This is the temporary experience of Christians while they are under the deception of God. Do you remember the terms of castaways, or when God does cast off, and how this is connected to reprobation, and do you remember how each of these terms were experienced by God hiding His face from His people? Even so God does with His saints; to some it is temporary, to others it is unto reprobation, but when it is upon the saint who then recovers from it, he recovers from it because he recognizes the signs of it, and thus he prays...

"When Thou saidst, Seek ye My face; my heart said unto Thee, Thy face, LORD, will I seek. **Hide not Thy face far from me; put not Thy servant away in anger: Thou hast been my help; leave me not, neither forsake me, O God of my salvation**" (Ps. 27:8-9).

"LORD, by Thy favour Thou hast made my mountain to stand strong: **Thou didst hide Thy face, and I was troubled**" (Ps. 30:7).

"**Hide Thy face from my sins**, and blot out all mine iniquities" (Ps. 51:9).

"And **hide not Thy face from Thy servant;** for I am in trouble: hear me speedily" (Ps. 69:17).

"**Hide not Thy face from me** in the day when I am in trouble; incline Thine ear unto me: in the day when I call answer me speedily" (Ps. 102:2)

"Hear me speedily, O LORD: my spirit faileth: **hide not Thy face from me**, lest I be like unto them that go down into the pit" (Ps. 143:7)

Read of the experiential anguish of saints under the wrath of God:

"For day and night Thy hand was heavy upon me: my moisture is turned into the drought of summer" (Psalm 32:4).

"Have mercy upon me, O LORD, for I am in trouble: mine eye is consumed with grief, yea, my soul and my belly. For my life is spent with grief, and my years with sighing: my strength faileth because of mine iniquity, and my bones are consumed... **Make Thy face to shine upon Thy servant**: save me for Thy mercies' sake" (Ps. 31:9-10, 16).

When saints are under this type of delusive wrath, they are humiliated before the sovereignty of God. They recognize they are locked under a delusion unless God delivers them out of it, and while under it, they are under the leadership of His angry will.

"I was dumb, I opened not my mouth; because Thou didst it." (Psalm 39:9)

"O LORD, why hast Thou made us to err from Thy ways, and hardened our heart from Thy fear? Return for Thy servants' sake, the tribes of Thine inheritance." (Isaiah 63:17)

"Who can understand his errors? cleanse Thou me from secret

faults. Keep back Thy servant also from presumptuous sins; let them not have dominion over me: then shall I be upright, and I shall be innocent from the great transgression." (Psalm 19:12-13)

If the saints recover again, it is because God is hearing their cry, choosing to no longer hide His face from them. They express this as the saving experience of recovery:

"God be merciful unto us, and bless us; and cause **His face to shine upon us**" (Ps. 67:1).

"Give ear, O Shepherd of Israel, Thou that leadest Joseph like a flock; Thou that dwellest between the cherubims, shine forth. Before Ephraim and Benjamin and Manasseh stir up Thy strength, and come and save us. Turn us again, **O God, and cause Thy face to shine; and we shall be saved**... Turn us again, O God of hosts, and **cause Thy face to shine; and we shall be saved**...Turn us again, O LORD God of hosts, **cause Thy face to shine; and we shall be saved**" (Ps. 80:1-3, 7, 19).

"**Make Thy face to shine** upon Thy servant; and teach me Thy statutes" (Ps. 119:135).

"The LORD **make His face shine** upon thee, and be gracious unto thee" (Num. 6:25).

"There be many that say, Who will shew us any good? LORD, **lift Thou up the light of Thy countenance upon us**" (Ps. 4:6).

"For the righteous LORD loveth righteousness; **His countenance doth behold the upright**" (Ps. 11:7).

"Why art thou cast down, O my soul? and why art thou disquieted in me? Hope thou in God: for I shall yet praise him for **the help of His countenance**" (Ps. 42:5).

"For they got not the land in possession by their own sword, neither did their own arm save them: but Thy right hand, and Thine arm, and **the light of Thy countenance**, because Thou hadst a favour unto them" (Ps. 44:3).

"Blessed is the people that know the joyful sound: they shall walk, O LORD, **in the light of Thy countenance**" (Ps. 89:15).

"**Neither will I hide my face any more from them:** for I have poured out my spirit upon the house of Israel, saith the Lord GOD" (Ezek. 39:29).

353

It is an absolute necessity to understand the personal experience of saints who underwent the deceptions of God, when, at sundry times, He did hide Himself from them, but did you know that God can give over entire generations, nations, and centuries into delusions? What we understand the Covenant to be will shape our view and judgment of how righteous or backslidden our generation is, but how few men seek for understanding like this "as for hid treasures" (Prov. 2:4)? How few are the men who do realize that it is a "secret" (Psa. 25:14)? We must be as those "men that had understanding of the times, to know what Israel ought to do" (1 Chron. 12:32), as one that has "understanding in the visions of God" (2 Chron. 26:4-5) – Lest it be said of us, "O ye hypocrites, ye can discern the face of the sky; but can ye not discern the signs of the times" (Matt. 16:3)?

> "And when He was come near, He beheld the city, and wept over it, Saying, **If thou hadst known**, even thou, at least in this thy day, the things *which belong* unto thy peace! but now they are **hid from thine eyes**" (Luke 19:41-42).

Dear reader, how might we judge this in our day? How might we judge whether or not if, today, as in this old time, Christ is weeping over our destruction which is nigh and at hand? How shall we take heed to what is written in Ecclesiastes, when the preacher said: "Whoso keepeth the commandment shall feel no evil thing: and a wise man's heart discerneth both **time** and **judgment**. Because to every purpose there is **time** and **judgment**, therefore the misery of man is great upon him" (Ecclesiastes 8:5-6)?

HAVE YOU DISCERNED YOUR "DAY" & "TIME"?
CHAPTER 16

"Ye hypocrites, ye can discern the face of the sky and of the earth; but how is it that ye do not discern this time?" – Luke 12:56

"Where is the LORD?"
– Jer. 2:6, 8

It was said of Saul that he "enquired of the LORD," but "the LORD answered him not" (1 Sam. 28:6), but it is all the more terrifying when whole generations and times are given over to such a state where "there is no answer of God" (Micah 3:5-7). The prophets cry "how long," but God hides himself by a cloud of darkness, because men transgress what He commands! Men cry out, "how long," and they receive no answer from God, because He is saying: "How long will it be ere they attain to innocency" (Hos. 8:5)? Thus the people and prophets wander in confusion for generations long…

"We have heard with our ears, O God, our fathers have told us, what work Thou didst in their days, in the times of old" (Psalm 44:1).

"I remember the days of old" – Psalm 143:5 "I remember Thy judgments of old" – Psalm 119:49-53

"Look Thou upon me, and be merciful unto me, as Thou usest to do unto those that love thy name" – Psalm 119:132

"**Turn** Thou us unto Thee, O LORD, and we shall be turned; **renew our days as of old**" (Lam 5:21).

"**Have respect unto the Covenant:** for the dark places of the earth are full of the habitations of cruelty" (Psalm 74:20).

"Turn Thyself again… heal the **breaches**" – Psalm 60

"**Will He reserve His anger for ever? Will He keep it to the end?**" (Jer. 3:4-5)

"Moreover the word of the LORD came to me, saying, Go and cry in the ears of Jerusalem, saying, Thus saith the LORD; I remember thee, the kindness of thy youth, the love of thine espousals, when thou wentest after Me in the wilderness, in a land that was not sown. Israel was holiness unto the LORD, and the firstfruits of His increase: all that devour him shall offend; evil shall come upon them, saith the LORD. Hear ye the word of the LORD, O house of Jacob, and all the families of the house of Israel: Thus saith the LORD, What iniquity have your fathers found in Me, that they are gone far from Me, and have walked after vanity, and are become vain? **Neither said they, Where is the LORD** that brought us up out of the land of Egypt, that led us through the wilderness, through a land of deserts and of pits, through a land of drought, and of the shadow of death, through a land that no man passed through, and where no man dwelt? And I brought you into a plentiful country, to eat the fruit thereof and the goodness thereof; but when ye entered, ye defiled My land, and made Mine heritage an abomination. **The priests said not, Where is the LORD?** and they that handle the law knew Me not: the pastors also transgressed against Me, and the prophets prophesied by Baal, and walked after things that do not profit. Wherefore I will yet plead with you, saith the LORD, and with your children's children will I plead" (Jer. 2:1-9).

My reader, henceforth let us search out the telling signs of God's Presence when it fulfills the Covenant agreement, and on the contrary, His absence, wrath, curses, and breaches which are also in Covenant agreement. To do such a study, we will have to understand the following terms bulleted below. We will examine these spiritual realities in their OT and NT context, in this chapter and into chapters to come. When we come to understand how to *discern* our "day" and "time", it is my hope, in earnest longing for myself and all other saints, that we would, as God says, "lay these things to thy heart...remember the latter end of it" (Isa. 47:7). If we are made a "spoil" for the devil, given over to heresies as strong as "robbers," is it not because of "the LORD, He against Whom we have sinned? ...Therefore He hath poured upon [us] the fury of His anger, and the strength of battle: and it hath set [us] on fire round about" (Isa. 42:24-25). In all this outpouring of God's displeasure, let us not be as Israel was, who, God said, "knew not; and it burned him, yet he laid it not to heart" (Isa. 42:25)! Let us not be as those damned men to whom God said, "thou hast lied, and hast not remembered Me, nor laid it to thy heart" (Isa. 57:11). Oh how terrible it is! "The righteous perisheth, and no man layeth it to heart" (Isa. 57:1)! Your accountability at the Final Judgment has everything do with the truth which we are about to search out and discover, but I pray and hope that it will not be said of us, now, as He said in the old time – "Many pastors have destroyed My vineyard, they have trodden My portion under foot, they have made My pleasant portion a desolate wilderness. They have made it desolate, and being desolate it mourneth unto Me; the whole land is made desolate Because No Man Layeth It To Heart" (Jer. 12:10-11).

- ❖ *Spiritual Darkness & Blindness*
- ❖ *Spiritual Famine of Starvation & Dehydration*
- ❖ *Spiritual Drunkenness*

❖ *Spiritual Infancy*

In the day of Eli's impeachment from the holy office of High Priest in Israel, thence the glory of Israel was taken away, the means of grace through the ministerial office of the priests was made void, and "the Lamp of God went out in the Temple of the LORD" (1 Sam. 3:3). The Lamp signifies the spiritual health & life of the people of God, and therefore at such a time as this it can also be said – "the word of the LORD was precious [rare] in those days; **there was no open vision**" (1 Sam. 3:1). Can you relate?

To ask → **"Where is the Lord?"**

Is the same thing to ask, in other words→**"Where are the Lord's right-hand men?"**

"And ye shall be unto Me a Kingdom of Priests" – Exodus 19:6

When the priests are forsaken by God, it is an evil "time," but what about when God forsakes Israel's King? A man in this office, King Saul by name, lived the subsequent generation after Eli's death, and he, like Eli, was stripped of salvation, power, unction, and life - "the Spirit of the LORD departed from Saul, and an evil spirit from the LORD troubled him" (1 Sam. 16:14). Darkness was in the Tabernacle where only light should have been, and likewise, the dark spirits of the devil seized the king of Israel. Night after night, Saul was forcefully taken into demon-inspired imaginations and nightmares, into a hell-valley of troubles. Saul could have described his experience in the age-old words: "He hath fenced up my way that I cannot pass, and He hath set darkness in my paths. He hath stripped me of my glory, and taken the crown from my head" (Job 19:8-9). God sent an evil spirit to Saul, and do you think it would only trouble him? Where evil spirits dwell, they inflict the disease of spiritual decay, making sinners strong and emboldened in high-handed rebellions against God. The man Saul, having become demon-possessed, was filled with the premeditated and preplanned schemes of hell, and thus, when Saul did but follow his heart, behold – "Nob, **the city of the priests**, smote he with the edge of the sword, both men and women, children and sucklings, and oxen, and asses, and sheep, with the edge of the sword" (1 Sam. 22:19). What if Satan entered into you? What would you be feeling and thinking, and what would you end up doing? Some treachery of Judas would be rising in your members, no matter how fervent your love for God was at a former time, a time when you dwelt under the shadow of the Almighty. It was once written: "Satan entered into him. Then said Jesus unto him, That thou doest, do quickly" (John 13:27). We must understand this awful curse, to have satanic demons hovering about the people of God! They are smart, systematic, and superior to humanity in all ways and powers, and in their intellectual capacity, they do plan the downfall of the world's only hope – the people of God. They are the inventors of your generation's grand scheme of deception and annihilation.

Should we suspect anything different from a man given over to a devil, than when, lo, Saul set his face in a determinate purpose, contorted with the devil's twisted wrath, to destroy all the hope and salvation left in Israel – *the city of the priests*? Saul was so fearless! At former times, Saul would have bowed down to such holy men, holding them in respect, honor, and esteem, and now he is turned backwards! Saul failed to execute justice toward the heaven-hated people, the Amalekites, when God commanded him to utterly destroy them (women, children, animals, and all); then later, after demon possession, he totally annihilates *the city of the priests*, the heaven-loved, executing upon them the judgment that should have been done to the Amalekites. He shrank back from justice and was courageous in crime. He pitied the wicked so as to hear their cries for mercy, but he brutally slaughtered the righteous that deserved compassion and a sparing eye. An evil spirit replaced the Holy Spirit that was once within Saul, thus, lo, the good commands of God's holy will were no longer his charges. They no longer graced the inward parts of his heart. Now the fierce wrath of the devil was there! The corrupt springs of hell flowed from the innermost parts of his belly, and from him came rivers of poison. In such a time (a time of spiritual darkness when the Lamp of God went out), demons replaced the presence of God, deceptions replaced truth, and there was a decay of physical and spiritual means of salvation – the people were left utterly without hope. Eli and Saul were two examples of men who stood to influence Israel from two different vocational grounds, grounds of potential for great good or otherwise for great evil. They were meant to be instruments in God's hands for spiritual and physical salvation, but what happened to them continues to happen for centuries to come, shockingly, in greater and greater degrees. Long after these two men flew into the depths of hellfire where they belong, during the days of Jeremiah it was written:

> "For this gird you with sackcloth, lament and howl: for the fierce anger of the LORD is not turned back from us. And it shall come to pass at that day, saith the LORD, that the heart of the **king** shall perish, and the heart of the **princes**; and the **priests** shall be astonished, and the **prophets** shall wonder. Then said I, Ah, Lord GOD! surely **Thou hast greatly deceived this people** and Jerusalem, saying, Ye shall have peace; whereas the sword reacheth unto the soul" (Jer. 4:8-10).

When this company of men – the *king*, *princes*, *priests*, and *prophets* – is delivered over to *the deception of God*, then the whole city is made ready for wrath. God's purpose to destroy Israel is so pointed, lo, it cannot be turned back. When such men fall, the means of grace are eradicated. They become deceived-stupid like as a courageous blind man, confident they can lead well, "and if the blind lead the blind, both shall fall into the ditch" (Matt. 15:14). For several generations and centuries, renowned and notorious sinners against high Heaven reached marks of great infamy, but it was because one or all of *these offices* were in desolation. The generations of "The Judges" are a good example of this. They were a kingless people, and therefore they did what was "right in their own eyes" (Judges 17:6, 21:25). Without God's right-hand men, the people turned back and rebelled, and there has never been a *biblical revival* which was not initiated and sustained through chosen men employed for God's holy use, chosen vessels, to take the preeminent place of authority under God. There is no such thing as a "nameless, faceless revival" (as some imagine and seek after today). "By a prophet the LORD brought Israel out of Egypt, and by a prophet was he preserved" (Hos. 12:13). While thinking upon the centrality of these offices and how they are used to begin and sustain a biblical revival, see as well how they can have the opposite effect upon God's people. They can become the instruments of woe and of pervading deception, when these offices are a planting that God "hath not planted" (Matt. 15:13). Now look carefully at the cries of intercessors through the centuries when they prayed. Look specifically how God inspired their prayers, and look at what they prayed for! They prayed for salvation, rescue, and hope *through* the restoration of these very offices. They recognize that, without them, the nation becomes drunken, wayward, and weary in God-ordained deceptions.

> "Then He remembered **the days of old**, Moses, and His people, saying, **Where is He** that brought them up out of the sea with the shepherd of His flock? **Where is He** that put His Holy Spirit within him? That led them by the right hand of Moses with His glorious arm, dividing the water before them, to make Himself an everlasting Name? That led them through the deep, as an horse in the wilderness, that they should not stumble? As a beast goeth down into the valley, the Spirit of the LORD caused him to rest: so didst Thou lead Thy people, to make Thyself a glorious Name" (Isaiah 63:11-14).

Notice in what manner they do call upon and remember God! They recognize that there was once *a man* with *the Holy Spirit within him,* and that God, through men, led Israel by the right hand. The people have learned the awful experience of "times" given over to deception, namely, when men with unholy spirits are in leadership. So the people cried out! They knew that, if such an office was revived, then the people would follow on to obey God! They cried, "Let Thy hand be upon **the man of Thy right hand**, upon **the son of man whom Thou madest strong** for Thyself. **So will not we go back from Thee**: quicken us, and we will call upon Thy name" (Psalm 80:17-18)! They knew the holy rite of such Divine orders and callings, and how far have we fallen from this today? Today the "spiritual leaders" of the "church" are subject to a congregational democracy. The congregation shepherds the shepherd. They hire and fire the pastor, and so, the choicest pick of the multitude is a congregational conformist whose priority is to keep his job, and so → Hell's hirelings are preaching God's holy word! They are pragmatic men, prepared by pampered professors of classroom politics, and so, like the heathen vocations, these men are educated into authority and classroom-cultivated. They are just worldly enough to tickle the taste buds of men who are hungry for religiously-intelligent sinning. They are whitewashed on the outside, and they are skilled to whitewash other men. By Divine constitution, isn't it written somewhere, maybe, that preachers must be set apart by the Holy Ghost? The office requires an empowering of God, a supernatural gifting, given to men only by God! We must, like past centuries, recognize the vitality and holy necessity in keeping these offices hallowed, keeping them untouched by carnal interference. "Blessed is the man whom Thou choosest, and causest to approach unto Thee, that he may dwell in Thy courts: we shall be satisfied with the goodness of Thy house, even of Thy holy temple" (Psalm 65:4). Blessed are the people who live in such a time, when God said – "And I will restore thy judges **as at the first**, and thy counsellors as at the beginning: afterward thou shalt be called, The city of righteousness, the faithful city" (Isaiah 1:26). If God restored the saints with God-ordained and God-empowered "judges" and "counsellors," then God's people would be beautified in salvation, and they would be "as in the days of old, and as in former years" (Mal. 3:4).

These biblical Christians knew that they needed not just any man, nor a very intelligent man, but they needed a holy man. They knew that carnal wisdom could not discover the undiscoverable pathways of salvation. It is beyond all comprehension, brilliantly miraculous; therefore they are hidden "in the great waters." "Thy way is in the sea, and Thy path in the great waters, and Thy footsteps are not known. **Thou leddest Thy people like a flock by the hand of Moses and Aaron**" (Psalm 77:19-20). Can a carnal man be educated enough to "make all men see what is the fellowship of the mystery, which from the beginning of the world hath been hid in God, Who created all things by Jesus Christ: To the intent that now unto the principalities and powers in heavenly places might be known by the Church the manifold wisdom of God" (Eph. 3:9-10)? We need men who preach "with the Holy Ghost" upon them, that He, the Holy Ghost, would do the preaching! Then, verily, these are "things the angels desire to look into" (1 Peter. 1:12). It is better to have a Legion of angels stricken with eye-gaping amaze and wonderment, when behold, true pastors preach heavenly-rich wisdom under the power of the Holy Ghost, and yet, there is hardly a building; it is some lowly, nameless, Church congregation scattered somewhere in a land of poverty. Yea, this is better! Better than today's "church-popular"! Stadiums of men sit amazed and entertained, and there, the drooling demons make the dead men sing praise. The electronic charisma, the graphic-based fantasies, the bass-stimulated powers, this is the feeling of "god's presence" which has replaced regenerating powers. These electronic "churches" are full of sinners, not saints, that are sons of the old time magicians who bewitched the masses with magic, and now, behold, the aura of a light-show "Christian" religion makes dead-religion fantastic. Do you get the picture? Preaching is a hallowed office! An office which is, today, desecrated by unholy men! Their preaching is self-planned and self-invented, and "Christianity" has become a manmade religion!

> "We see not our signs: there is no more any prophet: neither is there among us any that knoweth how long. O God, how long shall the adversary reproach? Shall the enemy blaspheme Thy name for ever?" (Psalm 74:9-10)

In Isaiah 63:11-14, the prophet cried, "**Where is He,**" and in Psalm 74, the prophet cried, "neither is there among us any that knoweth **how long,**" thus, with the absence of God there is confusion, astonishment, perpetual backslidings, and overwhelming damnation in this "day," "time," and generation – this is the deception of God. This deception is like the sun gone down, the land sitting in darkness, the people in blindness all staggering about; they grope for stability but they have no hope. This deception is like a cloudless sky for a long famine, until starvation sets in and the people faint and collapse. Nutrient-depleted, water-dried, and energy-drained, each man steadily withers away in a long, slow, and steady dying. They look up for rain, but lo, there is nothing, and if there be "clouds they are without water [and] carried about of winds" (Jude 12). What is even worse, men who are in one such spiritual "time" are so deceived, they don't even think to cry out, "**Where is the Lord,**" or, "**How long**," because they are not even aware that their "day" is a time of wrath and deception, a time marked by the absence of God and His right-hand men.

Asa was born into such a generation. It was written then: "Now for a long season Israel hath been without the true God, and without a teaching priest, and without law" (2 Chron. 15:3). King Josiah was born into such a dark time that he didn't even have a Bible. He sought God for many years with only the verbal or written, uninspired traditions which were passed down through the centuries. With such a dim lamp for such a dark night, a man can scarcely walk! Blessed be God that the man Josiah was destined to rise up to the shining stars (to be among those faithful few who were used on earth and honored in heaven), and so, God led him to find out where the Bible was hidden (2 Chron. 34:3)! Note: until such a time came, Josiah was still under the wrath of God. God's wrath was ready to destroy him, it was not turned back simply because he followed the verbal traditions of men who were venerated by the religious authorities of his day, or his father's day, no matter how ancient. Blessed are those who are born into a generation which is equipped with the means of salvation - made ready and at hand – but most men are born into "old waste places" (Isa. 58:12). Such men do await the arrival of God's helping hand to rest upon a man, or men, who are called and equipped by God to fulfill the title, "The restorer of paths to dwell in" (Isa. 58:12). Oh, those blessed generations who do "hear a word behind" them, saying, "This is the way, walk ye in it, when ye turn to the right hand, and when ye turn to the left" (Isa. 30:20-21)! Blessed are those to whom God says, "Thine eyes shall see thy teachers," that they are no longer "removed into a corner" of darkness and obscurity (Isa. 30:20-21)! Such a day and time is blessed, but most men that fear God are brought low by the overwhelming deception and oppression of their day, and so, they collapse into the ashes of Habakkuk and lift up a like cry:

> "O LORD, how long shall I cry, and Thou wilt not hear! even cry
> out unto Thee of violence, and Thou wilt not save! Why dost
> Thou shew me iniquity, and cause me to behold grievance? for
> spoiling and violence are before me: and there are that raise up
> strife and contention. Therefore the law is slacked, and judgment
> doth never go forth: for the wicked doth compass about the

361

righteous; therefore wrong judgment proceedeth" (Hab. 1:2-4).

Now perhaps you may understand the spiritual language of a generation-long, nationwide deception. Perhaps you may be enabled by the Spirit of God, to have ears to hear, to learn, and so, perhaps you will be able to discern your "day" and "time"! Those who are unable to understand these things will never cry out to God, "How long," because they don't even know that they are under the wrath of God. We must, as Psalm 77 carefully details, remember what biblical mercy and salvation are, so that we might tell when and if they are manifest or absent in our "day." We must recognize what marks characterize the generation of God's wrath. If God ever reveals these hidden things to us, these blessed secrets, and we do see it with open eyes, then we must "lay it to heart," remember it, and stay upon it (Isa. 47:7, 42:25, 57:1, 11, Jer. 12:11); otherwise our damnation is sure.

"Having done all to stand" – Eph. 6

If it was easy to "lay it to heart," to stay upon God in the midst of a spiritually violent, religious culture, with its pressures and amazing threats, and the overwhelming false confidences that "Christians" do angrily wave over our head…if it was easy, then all men would stand firm! These thronging, threatening, blasphemers are innumerable, and of their number are those intimate acquaintances of our old man – our *friends & family*. Like the nightfall hunt of a pack of African wild hyenas, Oh! How they hound and intimidate! They terrorize predators of incomparable strength – even a lion pride – and it is by their swarming, group-circling, relentless and persistent dodging and turning that they weary the lions and make them heartless to hold their ground, and shockingly, the lion pride often surrenders the prey they worked so hard to kill. The lions slowly leave, glancing back, again and again, with faces that look almost confused, aggravated, and spooked. It is as if they don't know what just happened, or how it happened, like they were outwitted and amazed at the whole experience. Oh, the annoyance of these horrid hyenas! Their laugh-squealing screeches that incessantly sound while they swarm all around the lion pride! Have you ever seen it? Then you would know what I say! Right behind you and beside you, and all around you, it seems that they are an undefeatable kamikaze force that will not back down.

Circling deceptions and swarming masses of intimidations, this catastrophe is your spiritual scenery; and of a TRUTH God forewarned us – hold on to the faith and "lay it to heart" (Isa. 47:7, 42:25, 57:1, 11, Jer. 12:11) – or else you will lose it, you will be wearied by the whirlwind of lies, and finally, you will "let it slip" (Heb. 2:1)! Will you stand through the stormy tempest of your day? Look around you, and behold, "the rain descended, and the floods came, and the winds blew, and beat upon that house; and it fell: and great was the fall of it" (Matt. 7:27)…and "the people were astonished at His doctrine" (Matt. 7:28). Have you found a man of God? Whither you go (into what "house" & "pew"), or what Christian thing you do…who is the man that you do hear and see, who are the men that are set in authority to preach to you? Christ Jesus said once, "What went ye out into the wilderness to see? **A reed shaken with the wind?** But what went ye out for to see" (Matt. 11:7-8)? This was said by King Jesus, He referred to a single-man minority who stood alone – the faithful and great prophet, John the Baptist. He was endowed with the spirit of Elijah, and therefore, look at him, how he followed in Elijah's burdens. Look how he was laden heavy with this single cause – *laying truth to his heart* – so that, again in his day, truth might oppose lies and stand fast, even if it was against 400-to-1 odds. Elijah's life depended on whether or not he successfully laid the truth to his heart. When he believed that he failed the mission for which he was sent to accomplish, namely – to be different than his hypocritical fathers – it was then that *he no longer desired to live*! In the hour of Elijah's sorrow when the prophet was never lower, read how he prayed to end his life. Consider this: If you can't pray such a prayer you will not live such a life. "We don't see revival because we are willing to live without it" (Leonard Ravenhill).

> "But he himself went a day's journey into the wilderness, and came and sat down under a juniper tree: and he requested for himself that he might die; and said, It is enough; now, O LORD, take away my life; for I am not better than my fathers" (1 Kings 19:4).

We need hearts like the true prophets; then we will follow in their pathway of glory (Luke 6:22-23, 26), though it be ever so lined with thorny tribulations. None can walk it, and go on unscathed. Momentary, light afflictions – a little sweat, a little blood – the wicked have their reward in this life, but ours is above. Is what Christ said, about Christians in the first century, untrue for Christians today? What about you? Are you the "blessed" people, or are you under Christ's woe? "Blessed are ye, when men shall hate you, and when they shall separate you from their company, and shall reproach you, and cast out your name as evil, for the Son of Man's sake…for in the like manner did their fathers unto the prophets…Woe unto you, when all men shall speak well of you! For so did their fathers to the false prophets" (Luke 6:22-23, 26).

Spiritual Darkness

"Wherefore hidest Thou Thy face, and holdest me for Thine enemy?" (Job 13:24)

```
-----------------------------------
|         RELATED SERMONS         |
|                                 |
| "Spiritual Darkness" – Sean Morris |
-----------------------------------
```

When "a generation," called "a day" and "time," is given over to deceptions and desolations, then God *looks for a man* to **intercede**, a *prophet* to **prophesy**, and a *righteous man* to do **judgment**. Oh, that all of America could wake up to her spiritual condition, how a spiritual darkness and famine is upon the land! When God says, "My face will I turn also from them," He determines to destroy those whom He is turning from, and when physical destruction has come upon such persons then God will have His glory over the persecutors, putting them in derision, when before they sought to put Him in derision. God's glory over them will climax in the hour of their need, and it is then that they will be buried under delusions and the silence of God – "Then shall they seek a <u>vision</u> of the **prophet**; but the <u>law</u> shall perish from the **priest**, and <u>counsel</u> from the **ancient**" (Ezek. 7:22, 26).

> "Woe unto you that desire the day of the LORD! to what end is it for you? the day of the LORD is **darkness**, and **not light**. As if a man did flee from a lion, and a bear met him; or went into the house, and leaned his hand on the wall, and a serpent bit him. Shall not the day of the LORD be **darkness**, and **not light**? even **very dark**, and **no brightness in it**?" (Amos 5:18-20)

In such a day of "The Deception of God", the Lord turns away His face, the light that shines from it is gone, and thus deceptions like a pursuing lion do soon pounce upon and surprise those who are deceived. A generation without light is a generation without the word of God, for it is written, "Thy word is a lamp unto my feet, and a light unto my path" (Ps. 119:105), but without the revelatory grace of God, the Holy Spirit, the people will never bask in the lamp of God's word. The prophets Amos and Isaiah further expounded the woeful time when God, in wrath, turned the lights out.

> "And it shall come to pass in that day, saith the Lord GOD, that I will cause **the sun to go down at noon,** and **I will darken the earth in the clear day**: And I will turn your feasts into mourning, and all your songs into lamentation; and I will bring up sackcloth upon all loins, and baldness upon every head; and I will make it as the mourning of an only son, and the end thereof as a bitter day. Behold, the days come, saith the Lord GOD, that **I will send a famine in the land,** not a famine of bread, nor a thirst for water, but **of hearing the words of the LORD**: And they shall **wander** from sea to sea, and from the north even to the east, they shall run **to and fro to seek** the word of the LORD, and **shall not find it**. In that day shall the fair virgins and young men **faint for thirst**" (Amos 8:9-13).

> "Then shall they cry unto the LORD, but He will not hear them: He will even **hide His face from them at that time,** as they have behaved themselves ill in their doings. Thus saith the LORD concerning the prophets that make My people err, that bite with their teeth, and cry, Peace; and he that putteth not into their mouths, they even prepare war against him. Therefore **night** shall be unto you, that ye shall **not have a vision**; and **it shall be dark unto you,** that **ye shall not divine**; and **the sun shall go down**

over the prophets, and **the day shall be dark over them**. Then shall **the seers be ashamed**, and the **diviners confounded**: yea, they shall all cover their lips; **for there is no answer of God**" (Micah 3:4-7).

God turns His face away, and like the sunset steadily turns around the edge of the globe, going down, the darkness increasingly shrouds the land, and, lo, at this time, by interpretation, the demonic spirits of "the darkness of this world" take control of the people. The people are bound like as in a horse's bit and bridle, and they are deranged and driven madly into a head-on collision with the wrath of God! These demons are "the rulers of the darkness of this world", and "spiritual wickedness in high places" (Eph. 6:12), therefore where darkness is, they hold a lawful rule and reign. Do you know, my reader, that you must wrestle against demons, if haply, you might be saved (Eph. 6:12)!? When men are blinded by the delusive darkness of demons, they are rendered incapable to obey God. Men are left alone by God, and lo, the demons arrive – then men become spiritual animals – nasty, mindless, tasteless, stiffnecked swine. They wallow in a life of filth that is alienated from the life of God, because upon them is the plague of spiritual "blindness," and they, "having the understanding darkened" (Eph. 4:18), are utterly lost. Such men become reprobate, unsavable men, God says - hence the command: "Let them alone" (Matt. 15:14), and, "Give not that which is holy unto the dogs, neither cast ye your pearls before swine, lest they trample them under their feet, and turn again and rend you" (Matt. 7:6). Demons and devils cry out to God, requesting to enter into human beings, to possess them, and that God would take away, if there are any, spiritual walls (or hedges) of protection which keep demons at bay (Job 1:10). When God puts "an hedge about" a man to protect him from devils, they contend with God that He would take it away. They fight against holy angels to withstand them, hindering them from their holy services to elect saints (Dan. 10:13, Heb. 1:14). They seek to advance the gates of hell and extend the boundaries of the devil's dominion, and if they find – YOU – and you are a swine, they will contend with God for their rightful ownership of your body, because you have sold yourself for sin. This was that ancient cry of devils that wander the earth – "suffer us to go away into **the herd of swine**!" And if YOU, my reader, are so vile a man that you are a spiritual swine in the sight of God, Christ will answer the devil's request! "And He said unto them, Go. And when they were come out, **they went into the herd of swine**: and, behold, the whole herd of swine ran violently down a steep place into the sea, and perished in the waters" (Matt. 8:31-32) – and so, devils will possess you and violently drive you into your destruction.

Men are lost in the godless pitch-blackness of "the vanity of their mind" (Eph. 4:17), and therefore they do commit the deeds of devils, even the "unfruitful works of darkness" (Eph. 5:11), because they walk hand-in-hand with "the prince of the power of the air, the spirit that now worketh in the children of disobedience" (Eph. 2:2). Sadly, such men are no longer the workmanship of God (Eph. 2:10) but the workmanship of the devil, "taken captive by him at his will" (2 Tim. 2:26). At such a time that God does choose their delusions (Isa. 66:4), He does raise up fallen angels to become powers and principalities in the place of His Kingship over men. These NT passages describe generations of men under "The Deception of God", locked up under the power of evil spirits, therefore the principle is clearly established – whithersoever the absence of God is, there is the presence of the devil, and with devil is the absence of righteousness, and the pandemic of rebellious, hard-hearted men! Woe to the persons, woe to the families, woe to the cities, woe to the nations, to whom belongeth the awful curse of God

> "The LORD hath **mingled a perverse spirit** in the midst thereof: and they have caused Egypt to err in every work thereof, **as a drunken man staggereth in his vomit**" (Isa. 19:14).

Demons are the messengers of God's deception, and all they that drink of the cup of damnation do commune with their spirits and messages. Paul said, "I would not that ye should have **fellowship with devils**. Ye cannot drink the cup of the Lord, and the cup of devils: ye cannot be partakers of the Lord's table, and of **the table of the devils**" (1 Cor. 10:20-21). Men do rebel because "**the spirit of whoredoms is in the midst of them**, and they have not known the LORD" (Hos. 5:4), and at such a time, men do "seek the LORD; but they shall not find Him; **He hath withdrawn Himself from them**" (Hos. 5:5-6). "Do we provoke the Lord to jealousy? Are we stronger than He" (1 Cor. 10:22)?

This question was asked by Paul on the back side of 1 Corinthians 10:1-12. He had just referenced four instances in biblical history when tens of thousands fell down dead when they struck up courage to disobey God, and so, they put God's strength to the test. Thus Paul asks, "Are we stronger than He" (1 Cor. 10:22)!? Did you know that you can provoke God to jealousy, and be so dull of hearing that you follow fallen men? We are a generation of "Christians" who think we can never fall, when instead, we should "take heed lest [we] fall" (1 Cor. 10:12). Preacher! When will you ever preach a sermon making plain this question – "Are we stronger than He?" Or does your heady theology forbid such a sermon from ever entering your heart? It's time to get on our knees, preacher! Then our learning can continue…but preacher! Is that where your knowledge of God first began, or do you have what the flesh can fabricate? Do you have a compelling personality, or do you have vital reality with God's Person? Are you like Matt Chandler, who confessed, "I went into hundreds of meetings over my first seven years as pastor of The Village without asking for direction and wisdom, without asking for power and clarity," and who rudely confessed again, "I suck at praying"? The man is a preacher of his personality. He preaches what a puffed up, proud, seminarian studies a lifetime to regurgitate – HEAD KNOWELDGE – and what a surprise – dead men love it! And they love Matt Chandler! Chandler reflects on his reputation with a woeful observation, confessing: "In some places being used powerfully by God can get you killed and here it makes you "famous". Hear me confess this. I like it." Chandler thinks that he is being used powerfully by God, when, staggeringly, the man doesn't even pray to God and ask

Him for His help! This is an amazing deception! In a world that killed Christ, that is killing Christians, and when biblical scripture fames the suffering saints as examples, as the true saints, and Chandler concludes, even still, he is a famous man of God?! Preachers! Get on your knees and read Proverbs 2:3-6. Pray the trembling prayer, "O forsake me not utterly" (Ps. 119:8)! Or does your theology forbid such a prayer? Now you can't think like the Bible, speak like the Bible, feel like the Bible, pray like the Bible, and you certainly can't preach like the Bible – at least to mean what you say (see 1 Cor. 9:27). It is one thing to be cast away from God, but it is a more horrid thing to be cast away from God into the hands of a legion of devils! These unhallowed angels of hell do stand ready and catch those cast away souls who are forcefully reprobated by God. God reprobates individual persons, and even communities, wide-reaching also unto generations and times, as it is written…

> "What then? Israel hath not obtained that which he seeketh for; but the election hath obtained it, and the rest were **blinded** (According as it is written, God hath given them **the spirit of slumber, eyes** that they should **not see**, and **ears** that they should **not hear**;) unto this day. And David saith, Let their table be made **a snare**, and **a trap**, and **a stumblingblock**, and a recompence unto them: Let their eyes be **darkened**, that they may not see, and bow down their back alway" (Rom 11:7-10).

Thus God, in this way, does hide His gospel from every generation which He chooses delusions for. "But if our gospel **be hid**, it is **hid** to them that are **lost**: In whom the god of this world [**the devil**] hath **blinded** the minds of them which believe not, lest the light of the glorious gospel of Christ, Who is the image of God, should shine unto them" (2 Cor. 4:3-4). Therefore salvation is rightly coined to be – "God, Who commanded the **Light** to shine out of **darkness**, hath shined in our hearts, to give **the Light** of the knowledge of the glory of God in the face of Jesus Christ" (2 Cor. 4:6). And again, in the OT, "Moreover the **light** of the **moon** shall be as the **light** of the **sun**, and the **light** of the **sun** shall be **sevenfold**, as the **light** of **seven** days, in the day that the LORD bindeth up the **breach** of His people, and healeth the stroke of their **wound** " (Isa. 30:26). When God chooses delusions, then He gives "commandments that are not good," but when He chooses salvation, He commands – "Hear, ye deaf, and look, ye blind, that ye may see", praise God, and again, "I will bring the blind by a way that they knew not; I will lead them in paths that they have not known: **I will make darkness light before them**" (Isa. 42:13-20).

Do you remember that God can give commandments that are not good? "And He said, Go, and tell this people, Hear ye indeed, **but understand not**; and see ye indeed, **but perceive not**. Make the heart of this people **fat**, and make their ears **heavy**, and **shut their eyes**; lest they see with their eyes, and hear with their ears, and understand with their heart, and convert, and be healed" (Isa 6:9-10). Thus they become "the blind that have eyes, and the deaf that have ears" (Isa. 43:8). Blindness and deafness is heartlessness and faithlessness, and this destroys the people of God from a good, saving relationship with the Lord. Though God speaks, though they hear Him with their ears, and though there are many signs and wonders which have performed salvation for them, even signs and wonders which they did behold with their own *eyes*, there is a breakdown in **understanding** the spiritual concepts which save. ***They are spiritually incapacitated from knowledge in God.*** "They have not known nor understood: for He hath shut their eyes, that they cannot see; and their hearts, that they cannot understand. And none considereth in his heart, neither is there knowledge nor understanding" (Isa. 44:18-19). God will strive with men from all angles, but woe to the people whom God says: "the LORD hath not given you an heart to perceive, and eyes to see, and ears to hear, unto this day" (Deut. 29:1-4). God says to such – "Ye have seen all that the LORD did before your eyes...the great temptations which thine eyes have seen, the signs, and those great miracles: Yet the LORD hath not given you... eyes to see" (Deut. 29:2-4). This is animal-like stupidity, and they do deserve to be numbered among the most shameful of them, because, "it is happened unto them according to the true proverb, the dog is turned to his own vomit again; and the sow that was washed to her wallowing in the mire" (2 Peter 2:22). A vomit-eating, mire-wallowing, menstrual cloth-collecting serpent is an understatement, when describing the spiritual disgust God feels toward a son of the devil.

Darkness makes men blind, and blind men (by eye impairment or by black darkness) do stagger like drunken men (Job. 12:25). They are incapable of a mature relationship with someone, or, to do something of responsibility by and by. "The blind gropeth in darkness," and so, when God makes the sun go down and covers the land in darkness, all the prophets, priests, and people do grope helplessly in damnation (Deut. 28:29). This is the meaning of the prophet's word when he said: "We grope for the wall like the blind, and we grope as if we had no eyes: we stumble at noonday as in the night; we are in desolate places as dead men" (Isa. 59:10). Likewise to the incapacitation of *darkness* and *blindness*, so also it is with *spiritual famines*, which cause widespread *starvation* and *dehydration*, until men <u>faint</u> and <u>stagger</u>, until they <u>collapse</u>, and again, this is also just like the mindlessness and incoherency of *drunken men*. This is why darkness is not the only metaphorical term for the experience of nationwide deception, but also "famine" (Amos 8:9-13), and drunkenness.

Spiritual Famine Or Spiritual Desertification

A famine touches the fairest apples among women, and the strongest branch of young men – "fair virgins and young men" – and with them, all other men, they do "faint for thirst" (Amos 8:9-13)! A spiritual famine is just as it is written, and men are incapacitated from a saving relationship with God even while, behold, they relentlessly search for the words of God, and, alas, they cannot be found! It is a *famine* of God's <u>Presence</u>, God's <u>preachers</u>, and God's <u>holy word</u>!

No Rain = Famine

368

The presence of God and His holy word, is, none other, but the "rain" (Isa. 5:6), "the former rain", and "the latter rain" (Joel 2:23), showering salvific life to all of creation that is in desperate need of it. If rain-laden clouds overshadow your land, then look up, for it is about to be fulfilled as God said, "I will pour out of My Spirit upon all flesh: and your sons and your daughters shall prophesy, and your young men shall see visions, and your old men shall dream dreams: And on My servants and on My handmaidens I will pour out in those days of My Spirit; and they shall prophesy" (Acts 2:17-18)! This is the spiritual "rain" (Heb. 6:7) of salvation, and by interpretation, it is said that it makes men "enlightened," tasting "the heavenly gift," being "made partakers of the Holy Ghost," tasting "the good word of God," and "the powers of the world to come" (Heb. 6:4-5). Do you see the connection, the parallels, how the prophetic language of *light and darkness* is just as the language of *rain and famine*? Therefore, devils are the desertification of a country and nation! They are, perfectly named, "serpents and scorpions" (Lk. 10:19)! They are the inhabitants of waste places and cursed regions, slithering about, living among cursed men who have become a part of the howling desert of sin. Rightly named, these cursed men are the "thorns and thistles" (Heb. 6:6) among which the devils do hide, finding rest, shade, safety, and camouflage. Woe to these men, that devils do find comfort to draw near and commune with them! How horrid it is when God forsakes men! They are covered with dragons, serpents, scorpions, and devils!

On the contrary, what is it for God to save and receive men? Even so, it is written, "When the poor and needy seek water, and there is none, and their tongue faileth for thirst, I the LORD will hear them, I the God of Israel will not forsake them. I will open rivers in high places, and fountains in the midst of the valleys: I will make the wilderness a pool of water, and the dry land springs of water" (Isa. 41:17-18). Amen! And again, "He that believeth on Me, as the scripture hath said, out of His belly shall flow rivers of living water" (John 7:38)! Are you beginning to understand the prophetic language and meaning in these scriptures, and the following?

> "Then shall the lame man leap as an hart, and the tongue of the dumb sing: for in the wilderness shall waters break out, and streams in the desert. And the parched ground shall become a pool, and the thirsty land springs of water: in the habitation of dragons, where each lay, shall be grass with reeds and rushes" (Isa. 35:6-7).

> "Behold, I will do a new thing; now it shall spring forth; shall ye not know it? I will even make a way in the wilderness, and rivers in the desert. The beast of the field shall honour Me, the dragons and the owls: because I give waters in the wilderness, and rivers in the desert, to give drink to my people, my chosen" (Isa. 43:19-20).

369

"For I will pour water upon him that is thirsty, and floods upon the dry ground: I will pour my spirit upon thy seed, and my blessing upon thine offspring" (Isa. 44:3).

"That thou mayest say to the prisoners, Go forth; to them that are in darkness, Shew yourselves. They shall feed in the ways, and their pastures shall be in all high places. They shall not hunger nor thirst; neither shall the heat nor sun smite them: for He that hath mercy on them shall lead them, even by the springs of water shall He guide them" (Isa. 49:9-10).

This is salvation! Praise God! Well-watered lands and sprouting prosperity of life, shaded resting places beside green pastures that are circled about by still waters, and, lo, all inhabitants are satisfied! Much opposed to those hungering and thirsting men of perdition, these men drink deeply of "A River," Whose "streams whereof shall make glad the city of God, the holy place of the Tabernacles of the most High" (Ps. 46:4)! But lost men, the castaways, are men that have become the devil's apartment – his dwelling place. They make for him a habitable hole. They are an inviting place of refuge for the heaven-hated, fallen angels. These humans are comfortable scenery for hell's worthies. These scaled beasts of the dust do nestle inside of men, like a den in the desert for poisonous and drooling dragons.

Lost men do thirst in the desert of this world, and they may wander for something to quench and satisfy...they may think they are seeking God, but listen, it is not so! "None seeketh after God" (Rom. 3), and what they seek after is not God. Such men are given over to the insatiable appetite of sin which resides in the flesh and blood, and through the flesh resides the rule of demonic powers. "Hell and destruction are never full; so the eyes of man are never satisfied" (Prov. 27:20), thus were Saul, Esau, and many others, filled with an insatiable hatred for righteousness and its followers. Saul and Esau had a violent hunger for the blood of the righteous (David and Jacob), and lo, apart from the hand of God, it was insatiable. So do men thirst after God, yea, rightly, but a deception is when men search after God but cannot find Him! A deception is the absence of God like water from the desert wastelands, and trapped therein are the fainting wanderers who search for god, but the god they thirst for and seek after is not the one true God. Like Saul and Esau, these lost and Godless men will "put you out of the synagogues: yea, the time cometh, and that whosoever killeth you will think that he doeth God service" (John 16:2). When these brothers of Cain do find their "god," it is not the true God! It is the devil, and they are his ministers! "Satan himself is transformed into an angel of light. Therefore it is no great thing if his ministers also be transformed as the ministers of righteousness; whose end shall be according to their works" (2 Cor. 11:14-15).

They are men and women who take the name of the true God on their lips, but they follow a false god – a god that is created in their own mind, who lives and moves, but lo, it is a masked devil in disguise. By lying words from false prophets, heresies, and the "doctrines of devils," they do relish in a vain show of religion. "Now the Spirit speaketh expressly, that in the latter times some shall depart from the faith, giving heed **to seducing spirits, and doctrines of devils**" (1 Tim. 4:1). Their mouth "devoureth iniquity" (Prov. 19:28), but they are in denial, bethinking themselves continually that they really hunger and thirst for God. "God knows my heart," they say; "God knows my heart." Therefore, in a desert wilderness that is without water, they seek after "god" and are filled with him! They are feasting and fat, and know it not, that, behold, they are in a cursed time and generation under a God-ordained famine. "Deceiving and being deceived" (2 Tim. 3:13), they are the "liberty" preachers who need to be freed (2 Pet. 2:19)! They are a famine-stricken man dwelling in a desert wasteland, proclaiming to hell's rats and lizards, "I am rich, and increased with goods, and have need of nothing" (Rev. 3:17)! They sit at the banquet table of "the lord," and eat! They digest deceptions while dying of starvation. Therefore did King Jesus say to them – "knowest not that thou art **wretched**, and **miserable**, and **poor**, and **blind**, and **naked**" (Rev. 3:17)!? "Woe unto you that are full! For ye shall hunger" (Luke 6:25)! They take their fill, verily, as roots of bitterness drink up poisonous waters; as dead men in dead waters, stinking, they hate living water preaching. Every man to his thorny cactus, they go, drinking "iniquity like water" (Job 15:16).

They are "lovers of pleasures more than lovers of God" (2 Tim. 3:4). They are "despisers of those that are good" (2 Tim. 3:3). They hunger and thirst, and they seek after god, then they are filled to fatness, and with what? Their "god is their belly, whose glory is in their shame, who mind earthly things" (Php. 3:19). They are lovers of their vile bodies (Php. 3:21), their god is the deceiver, "The Father of Lies," the Old Serpent of Eden. God's word of truth has "no place" in them (John 8:37). They cannot "understand" God's speech or "hear" God's word (John 8:43), because, "he that is of God heareth God's words," they are not of God therefore they "hear them not" (John 8:47). They are in a spiritual famine, and, lo, they do eat like kings! How can it be? In a habitation of no food they "eat of their dainties" (Ps. 141:4). In a desert that is absent of God, in a howling wilderness that is absent of rain, they are seated for a delectable banquet of the devil's "deceitful meat" (Prov. 23:3). "Be not desirous of his dainties: for they are deceitful meat" (Prov. 23:3). The wicked, in a spiritual famine of God's living meats and drinks, eat and drink, are merry, and "waxed fat" (Deut. 32:15), reigning as kings on the earth (1 Cor. 4:8). They are the rich that wear soft clothing. They are rebels and rejecters of the rough raiment of the righteous (Matt. 11:8). Instead of feasting on truth, they devour lies. They are laughing and full, and woe to them (Lk. 6:25)! Christ says, "Ye are of your father the devil, and the lusts of your father ye will do. He was a murderer from the beginning, and abode not in the truth, because there is no truth in him. When he speaketh a lie, he speaketh of his own: for he is a liar, and the father of it" (John 8:44). Are you thirsty? Are you filled? Are you fainting? Are you seeking? Are you laughing? Are you weeping? Are you running? Are you willing? Bend your clay vessel over and bow down before the God of all Might – the Sovereign – before He puts you into "the hamster wheel" of your deception from whence you will never escape (Masao

Gonthier). Bow down forward, lest He decidedly say, looking upon the multitudes, including you, "let their eyes be darkened, that they may not see, and bow down their back alway" (Rom. 11:10).

> "Blessed are they which do hunger and thirst after righteousness: for they shall be filled" (Matt. 5:6) → but it is not so with those under the reprobating deception of God – "In that day shall the fair virgins and young men **faint for thirst**" (Amos 9:13).

> "Blessed are ye that weep now: for ye shall laugh" (Lk. 6:21), and, "they that sow in tears shall reap in joy" (Ps. 126:5) → but it is not so with those under the reprobating deception of God – "when he would have inherited the blessing, he was rejected: for he found no place of repentance, though he sought it carefully with tears" (Heb. 12:17, Gen. 27:36), for, "Esau have I hated" (Rom. 9:13).

> In a race, "one receiveth the prize," therefore "so run that ye may obtain" (1 Cor. 9:24), and, "let us run with patience the race that is set before us" (Heb. 12:1) → but no speed, temperance, or striving can avail for those who are under the reprobating deception of God – "So then it is not of him that willeth, nor of him that runneth, but of God that sheweth mercy" (Rom. 9:16).

~ EXAMINE YOURSELF ~
My reader, can you relate to these individuals?

The Promise They "abhor judgment and pervert all equity", and they are utterly taken in covetousness, and the love of money, "yet will they lean upon the LORD, and say, Is not the LORD among us? None evil can come upon us" (Micah 3:9, 11).

The Bible → "Why then is this people of Jerusalem slidden back by a perpetual backsliding? they hold fast deceit, they refuse to return. I hearkened and heard, but they spake not aright: no man repented him of his wickedness, saying, What have I done? every one turned to his course, as the horse rusheth into the battle. Yea, the stork in the heaven knoweth her appointed times; and the turtle and the crane and the swallow observe the time of their coming; but My people know not the judgment of the LORD. How do ye say, We are wise, and the law of the LORD is with us? Lo, certainly in vain made he it; the pen of the scribes is in vain. The wise men are ashamed, they are dismayed and taken: lo, they have rejected the word of the LORD; and what wisdom is in

372

them?" (Jer. 8:5-9)

"

The Temple →

Thus saith the LORD of hosts, the God of Israel, Amend your ways and your doings, and I will cause you to dwell in this place. Trust ye not in lying words, saying, The temple of the LORD, The temple of the LORD, The temple of the LORD, are these. For if ye throughly amend your ways and your doings; if ye throughly execute judgment between a man and his neighbour; If ye oppress not the stranger, the fatherless, and the widow, and shed not innocent blood in this place, neither walk after other gods to your hurt: Then will I cause you to dwell in this place, in the land that I gave to your fathers, for ever and ever. Behold, ye trust in lying words, that cannot profit. Will ye steal, murder, and commit adultery, and swear falsely, and burn incense unto Baal, and walk after other gods whom ye know not; And come and stand before Me in this house, which is called by My name, and say, We are delivered to do all these abominations?" (Jer. 7:3-10)

The Sacrifices, Incense, Solemn Assemblies, Feast Days, Holy Days, Offerings, Fasting, and Prayers ... →

"To what purpose is the multitude of your sacrifices unto Me? saith the LORD: I am full of the burnt offerings of rams, and the fat of fed beasts; and I delight not in the blood of bullocks, or of lambs, or of he goats. When ye come to appear before Me, who hath required this at your hand, to tread My courts? Bring no more vain oblations; incense is an abomination unto Me; the new moons and sabbaths, the calling of assemblies, I cannot away with; it is iniquity, even the solemn meeting. Your new moons and your appointed feasts My soul hateth: they are a trouble unto Me; I am weary to bear them. And when ye spread forth your hands, I will hide Mine eyes from you: yea, when ye make many prayers, I will not hear: your hands are full of blood" (Isa 1:11-15).

When the Lord pronounces prophetic damnation, they cannot hear it →

"And it shall come to pass, when thou shalt shew this people all these words, and they shall say unto thee, Wherefore hath the LORD pronounced all this great evil against us? or what is our iniquity? or what is our sin that we have committed against the LORD our God?" (Jer. 16:10)

They have boldness to venture upon the miraculous provision of God →

"Enquire, I pray thee, of the LORD for us; for Nebuchadrezzar king of Babylon maketh war against us; if so be that the LORD will deal with us according

like as the true prophets did, but they are false prophets.	to all His wondrous works, that he may go up from us" (Jer. 21:2).
They truly believe they have not sinned. ➜	"Yet thou sayest, Because I am innocent, surely His anger shall turn from me. Behold, I will plead with thee, because thou sayest, I have not sinned" (Jer. 2:35).
The sincerity of their deception can be heard in their prayers ➜	"Israel shall cry unto Me, My God, we know Thee" (Hos. 8:2)
Therefore, they assure themselves that wrath will not come, and rather salvation, but they don't even detect that spiritual wrath in the form of God-sent deceptions are already in full swing, therefore they do agree with the false prophets of their day. ➜	"They have belied the LORD, and said, It is not He; neither shall evil come upon us; neither shall we see sword nor famine" (Jer. 5:12). "Behold, they say unto Me, Where is the word of the LORD? let it come now" (Jer. 17:15). "Then said I, Ah, Lord GOD! behold, the prophets say unto them, Ye shall not see the sword, neither shall ye have famine; but I will give you assured peace in this place" (Jer. 14:13)
Spiritual messages & visions are communicated to the people which declare to them the person and attributes of God, therefore, they are a people of high spiritual activity. ➜	"I have heard what the prophets said, that prophesy lies in My name, saying, I have dreamed, I have dreamed. How long shall this be in the heart of the prophets that prophesy lies? yea, they are prophets of the deceit of their own heart; Which think to cause My people to forget My name by their dreams which they tell every man to his neighbour, as their fathers have forgotten My name for Baal" (Jer. 23:25-27)
When God offers mercy to them, if ever they are conscious of it, they cannot lay hold upon it because they believe there is no hope. ➜	"There is no hope: But we will walk after our own devices, and we will every one do the imagination of his evil heart" (Jer. 18:12).

Deception and reprobation cannot be any more clearly stated than when God does treat a people as these passages of scripture describe. The people seek to enquire of, in a feigned way, presuming the privilege of God's friendship, and...

→ "Behold, I am against them that prophesy false dreams, saith the LORD, and do tell them, and cause My people to err by their lies, and by their lightness; yet I sent them not, nor commanded them: therefore they shall not profit this people at all, saith the LORD. And when this people, or the prophet, or a priest, shall ask thee, saying, What is the burden of the LORD? thou shalt then say unto them, What burden? I will even forsake you, saith the LORD... Therefore, behold, I, even I, will utterly forget you, and I will forsake you, and the city that I gave you and your fathers, and cast you out of My presence" (Jer. 23:32-33, 39).

Spiritual Drunkenness

By way of introduction, it is vital to understand the connection between *spiritual darkness* and *spiritual sleep* with *spiritual drunkenness*. God self-defines this language for us, saying, *such and such* men are "drunken, but not with wine; they stagger, but not with strong drink" (Isa. 29:9), which means that they are *spiritually drunk* rather than *physically drunk*, and this spiritual condition, according to Isaiah 29:9-10, is directly connected to spiritual sleep:

> "Stay yourselves, and wonder; **CRY** ye out, and **CRY**: **they are drunken, but not with wine; they stagger, but not with strong drink. For the LORD hath poured out upon you the spirit of deep sleep, and hath closed your eyes:** the prophets and your rulers, the seers hath he covered" (Isa. 29:9-10).

Is this not a woeful scene? Instead of pouring out upon these people God's Holy Spirit, like the gladsome word given through Joel when God said, "I will pour out of My Spirit upon all flesh" (Joel 2:28-32, Acts 2:16-21), but here – WOE to them! – God is pouring out *another spirit*! It is the spirit of devils! And God hath "poured out" this "spirit" upon them! Do you remember the commandments of God which decree sovereign deceptions, called, the "statutes" of God which are "not good" (Ezek. 20:25)? Like those which were referenced before, God gave this command in Isaiah 6:9-11:

> "And He said, Go, and tell this people, Hear ye indeed, but

understand not; and see ye indeed, but **perceive not. Make the heart of this people fat, and make their ears heavy, and shut their eyes; lest they see with their eyes, and hear with their ears, and understand with their heart, and convert, and be healed.** Then said I, Lord, how long? And He answered, Until the cities be wasted without inhabitant, and the houses without man, and the land be utterly desolate" (Isa. 6:9-11).

God blinds men so that they *stumble* at the truth (Isa. 8:14). God hardens their heart so that they are *offended* (Isa. 8:13). Therefore, they walk the course of the deception of God, which is to "stumble, and fall, and be broken, and be snared, and be taken" (Isa. 8:15). How and why? God did "bind up the testimony" and "seal the law among" His disciples, which is, to hide it from all others who are not His disciples (Isa. 8:16, Lk. 8:10). Hiding the truth from them is, as God has coined it many times, the very same thing when He "hideth His face" (Isa. 8:17), and the spiritual effect of this is as it was written:

+ **"behold trouble and darkness, dimness of anguish; and they shall be driven to darkness"** – Isaiah 8:22
+ **"that they might go, and fall backward, and be broken, and snared, and taken"** – Isaiah 28:13

The hiding of God's face brings darkness upon the individual hearts of men, rendering them blind, and worse, they become demonized preachers who herald eye-blinding heresies. You may understand the metaphor of darkness, by now, but Isaiah describes this very same deception in other terms. When it is being poured forth from false prophets, Isaiah describes it in terms such as "wine" and "strong drink" (Isa. 28:7)! False prophets preach until everyone hearing them is intoxicated into body-poisoning drunkenness – until – "they err in vision, they stumble in judgment," and **"all tables are full of vomit and filthiness"** (Isa. 28:7-8). It was the lying demon-spirit which deceived Ahab and his 400 prophets, "deceiving and being deceived," but look closely at the spiritual language in which God defines the devil's deceptive powers and their effects: **"The LORD hath mingled a perverse spirit in the midst thereof,"** to the end that "they have caused [Ahab] to err in every work thereof, **as a drunken man staggereth in his vomit"** (Isaiah 19:14). Do you hear the language of it? Ahab was a "drunken man" staggering, and it was through the perversity of the demon possessed false prophets! Chasing a lying mirage because your senses are numbed to near-hallucination, because *spiritual starvation* and *dehydration* are setting in, because you are burning and beaten down by the heat of a dragon-infested desert land, you are wandering in the cursed wasteland which is under a *God-sent famine*. Well...we can understand this. But even so, just as this man, so is the man who has *gouged-out eyes* in a *darkened*, sunless land – double dark – so that men are left staggering about in *spiritual darkness*. These are horrid spiritual conditions which exclaim *incoherence*, *incapacity*, and *deception*, but there is one more great term which prophetic language uses to describe "The Deception of

376

God," and it is *spiritual drunkenness*. Staggering men are blind men or dying men, and also, they move in the same ways as intoxicated and drunken men – "as a drunken man staggereth in his vomit" (Isa. 19:14).

God calls men "blind," "ignorant," "dumb," "sleeping," "loving to slumber," "greedy," "shepherds that cannot understand" – and what spiritual term can all of this be compared with? "Come ye, say they, I will fetch **wine**, and we will fill ourselves with **strong drink**; and to morrow shall be as this day, and much more abundant" (Isa. 56:9-12). And again

> "All ye beasts of the field, come to devour, yea, all ye beasts in the forest. His watchmen are **blind**: they are all **ignorant**, they are all **dumb** dogs, they cannot bark; **sleeping**, lying down, loving to **slumber**. Yea, they are greedy dogs which can never have enough, and they are shepherds that **cannot understand**: they all look to their own way, every one for his gain, from his quarter. Come ye, say they, I will fetch **wine**, and we will fill ourselves with **strong drink**; and to morrow shall be as this day, and much more abundant." (Isaiah 56:9-12)

These men are trained in a craft which makes men *drunk*, and the devil knows that "whoredom and **wine**, and **new wine** take away the heart" (Hos. 4:11). Cursed are the people who have such men as their prophets and pastors! God warns, "Arise ye, and depart; for this is not your rest: because it is polluted, it shall destroy you, even with a sore destruction. If a man walking in **the spirit and falsehood do lie**, saying, I will prophesy unto thee of **wine** and of **strong drink**; **he shall even be the prophet of this people**" (Micah 2:10-11). Do you see the direct connection? How the lying *spirits of falsehood* deceive men by spiritual powers, resulting in that these men became spiritually drunk? Can you judge your time? "For this time is evil," God says, and it is Him that does "devise an evil" (Micah 2:3)! Namely, it is His sovereign decree which has let loose a hoard of fallen angels and demons to establish their "spiritual wickedness in high places," and thus they have dominion over the will of men (Eph. 6:12). Do you walk "according to the course of this world, according to the prince of the power of the air, the spirit that now worketh in the children of disobedience" (Eph. 2:2)? It is no coincidence that alcoholic drinks are often referred to as "*spirits*" by the vendors that sell them!

These wicked generations! They make God's holy people spiritually drunk with deceptions, and all men that stand apart from them are *sober*! They are under the influence of the sober Ghost! And look – behold the great clash – as drunken sinners angrily command the sober saints to – "prophesy not" (Amos 2:12)!

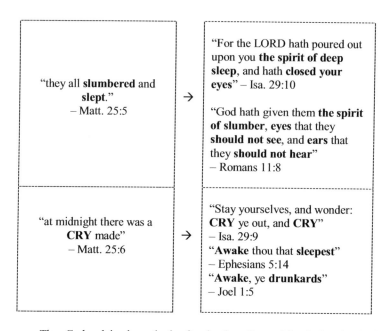

"they all **slumbered** and **slept**." – Matt. 25:5 →	"For the LORD hath poured out upon you **the spirit of deep sleep**, and hath **closed your eyes**" – Isa. 29:10 "God hath given them **the spirit of slumber, eyes** that they **should not see**, and **ears** that they **should not hear**" – Romans 11:8
"at midnight there was a **CRY** made" – Matt. 25:6 →	"Stay yourselves, and wonder: **CRY** ye out, and **CRY**" – Isa. 29:9 "**Awake** thou that **sleepest**" – Ephesians 5:14 "**Awake**, ye **drunkards**" – Joel 1:5

The God-ordained method of salvation for *spiritual drunkards* is – EXACTLY – just as the call for those who are *sleeping in the darkness* – "CRY OUT" (Isa. 29:9) and WAKE THEM UP! If you find yourself in the company of drunkards and sleepers, God commands, "STAY YOURSELVES", or, BE ASTONISHED and "WONDER" about it, and don't just wonder, but "**CRY** ye out, and **CRY**" the words – "**Awake** thou that sleepest" (Eph. 5:14), and again, "**Awake**, ye drunkards" (Joel 1:5)! This is God's trumpet-call for salvation to backslidden saints, and thus it is written – "at midnight there was a **CRY** made" (Matt. 25:6). Why was this cry made? Because the beloved virgins of God, the saints, "they all slumbered and slept" (Matt. 25:5), and God would have them "awake to righteousness" (1 Cor. 15:34). Woe to us! For we live in a generation which does not know what *spiritual drunkenness* is, and for that we should be **astonished** and **wondering**, being constrained forthwith, CRYING OUT.

My reader, has no one ever told you about spiritual drunkenness, and how in the *Last Days*, which are now, half of the saintly virgins will be caught lingering in a drunken slumber. They slumber and sleep too often, you see, until finally…when they wake up for preparations just as Judgment nigh approaches, look at them! They will go here…then they will go there…seeking to fear and trying to prepare, but behold – "THE DOOR WAS SHUT" (Matt. 25:10). My reader, you have not been told about spiritual drunkenness because, these days, the pastors give the strong drinks. This day is woefully like the old generation in which God said, "their fear toward me is taught by the precept of men" (Isa. 29:13). My reader, let God make his own case; let Him tell you about why there is a generation-wide oblivion and

378

ignorance that regenerate men can fall into damnable spiritual conditions, and how awful the warning! We are forewarned of a sweeping plague of slumber which apprehends and damns half of God's darling virgins! Does this make you wonder? Let God give an account of His own doings, for after all, it was and is He that "hath poured out upon you the spirit of deep sleep", and of drunkenness, "and hath closed your eyes" (Isa. 29:10), and for what?

> "Stay yourselves, and wonder; **CRY** ye out, and **CRY: they are drunken, but not with wine; they stagger, but not with strong drink. For the LORD hath poured out upon you the spirit of deep sleep, and hath closed your eyes:** the prophets and your rulers, the seers hath he covered. And the vision of all is become unto you as **the words of a book that is sealed**, which men deliver to one that is learned, saying, Read this, I pray thee: and he saith, I cannot; **for it is sealed**: And the book is delivered to him that is not learned, saying, Read this, I pray thee: and he saith, **I am not learned**. Wherefore the Lord said, Forasmuch as this people draw near me with their mouth, and with their lips do honour me, but have removed their heart far from me, and **their fear toward me is taught by the precept of men**: Therefore, behold, I will proceed to do a marvellous work among this people, even a marvellous work and a wonder: for the wisdom of their wise men shall **perish**, and the understanding of their prudent men shall be **hid**." (Isaiah 29:9-14)

The Spirit of God is a Holy Spirit, not an unholy one, and, it is likewise a sober Spirit instead of a drunken one. My reader, God would sober you up! He would wake you up! Therefore is it said, "And be not drunk with wine, wherein is excess" (Eph. 5:18). My reader, do the opposite! Rather "be filled with the Spirit" (Eph. 5:18)! Be filled with alcohol or the Spirit of God, for the two have the opposite effects. Do you think that Paul was meaning literal "wine" when he preached against drunkenness in Ephesians 5:18? Surely Paul knew of the prophetic language well already, the language which coined the spiritual typology of wine and drunkenness as a renowned symbol of carnality and darkness (Isaiah 19:14, 28:7-8, 29:9-10, 56:9-12, Hosea 4:11, Micah 2:10-11); thus Paul would so render it again here, in Ephesians 5, above other places. Why? For in this chapter, he did sorely rebuke "*fools*" who are in "*darkness*," commanding them to live righteously, henceforth, to dwell rather in the "*wisdom*" of spiritual "*Light*" (Eph. 5:6-17). Paul's very next charge is connected to the former charges by the word – "and" – and, look, is it of any significance to you that he immediately renders the same calling through different typology? → "And be not drunk with wine, wherein is excess; but be filled with the Spirit" (Eph. 5:18)! My reader, he knew that spiritual darkness, foolishness, blindness, and slumber, are all the same spiritual definitions as spiritual drunkenness...and there are still more evidences:

379

> "But ye, brethren, are **not in darkness**, that that Day should overtake you as a **thief**. Ye are all **the children of light**, and the **children of the day**: we are not **of the night**, nor **of darkness**. Therefore let us not **sleep**, as do others; but let us **watch** and be **sober**. For **they that sleep sleep in the night**; and **they that be drunken are drunken in the night**. But let us, who are **of the day**, be **sober**, putting on the breastplate of **faith** and **love**; and for an helmet, the **hope of salvation**. For God hath not appointed us to wrath, but to obtain salvation by our Lord Jesus Christ" (1 Thessalonians 5:4-9).

My dear reader, in the exact same context as Ephesians 5 is written in, now again in 1 Thessalonians 5, the correlating metaphors are in sync. Paul says again to the Church of Thessalonica, "For **they that sleep sleep in the night**; and **they that be drunken are drunken in the night**. But let us, who are **of the day**, be sober, putting on the breastplate of **faith** and **love**; and for an helmet, the **hope** of **salvation"** (1 Thess. 5:7-8). "Darkness" (1 Thess. 5:4) and "Light" (1 Thess. 5:5), "day" (1 Thess. 5:5) and "night" (1 Thess. 5:5), are categorically connected to spiritual "sleep" (1 Thess. 5:6) and standing awake, but to be awake is otherwise rendered as, to "watch" (1 Thess. 5:6). Finally, showing all metaphorical renderings from the OT to the NT in there perfect consistency, now again, to "sleep" and to be awake are directly parallel to the spiritual drunkenness and spiritual sobriety – therefore Paul declares, "and they that be **drunken** are **drunken in the night**…but let us, who are **of the Day**, be **sober**" (1 Thess. 5:7-8). Sobriety is "**faith** and **love**," and whosoever has these two fruits abounding in their life do also have a sound and sure "hope of salvation" (1 Thess. 5:8). "For in Jesus Christ neither circumcision availeth any thing, nor uncircumcision; but **faith which worketh by love**" (Gal. 5:6). The only way the Day of the Lord will take you as a thief in the night, is, if you are surprised by it, and you are found by the Lord in an unprepared condition. Only those in spiritual darkness, slumber, and drunkenness will be such persons; hence, Christians should be telling the *season* of the Lord's coming, how that "it is near, even at the doors" (Matt. 24:32-33), and therefore they should be awake and watching for the exact day and hour of His coming! Noah was preparing for 120 years, and then the floods came! So what about you? Will you hear the terrifying words of the Savior as He speaks today? Hear ye Him, when He said:

> "For the Son of Man is as a man taking a far journey, who left his house, and gave authority to his servants, and to every man his work, and commanded the porter to **watch**. **Watch ye therefore**: for ye know not when the master of the house cometh, at even, or at midnight, or at the cockcrowing, or in the morning: **Lest coming suddenly He find you sleeping. And what I say unto you I say unto all, Watch**" (Mark 13:34-37).

Do the awful words of the Savior grip your soul into attention, when He said: "Lest coming suddenly He find you **sleeping**" (Mk. 13:36)?! A man who is awake in the night, and watching, is not surprised by a thief; even so, let us not be suddenly surprised by the Lord! The Lord will be a thief on that Day, yea, but only to the damned. Let it not be so with you! Hear ye the Lord again, when He said:

> "Let your loins be girded about, and your **lights burning**; And ye yourselves like unto men that **wait for their lord**, when he will return from the wedding; that when he cometh and knocketh, they may **open unto him immediately**. <u>Blessed</u> are those servants, whom the lord when he cometh shall **find watching**: verily I say unto you, that he shall gird himself, and make them to sit down to meat, and will come forth and serve them. And if he shall come in the second watch, or come in the third watch, and **find them so**, <u>blessed</u> are those servants. <u>And this know</u>, **that if the goodman of the house had known what hour the thief would come, he would have watched, and not have suffered his house to be broken through. Be ye therefore ready also: for the Son of Man cometh at an hour when ye think not**" (Luke 12:35-40).

> **"If therefore thou shalt not watch, I will come on thee as a thief, and thou shalt not know what hour I will come upon thee**" (Rev. 3:3).

Preachers of God's damning deception do make men lighthearted and spiritually lewd. They are ungovernable, unruly fellows, characteristic of men who are physically intoxicated by drinking. Even so, "Wine is a **mocker**, strong drink is **raging**: and whosoever is **deceived** thereby is not **wise**" (Proverbs 20:1). Men who sit long under their pastoring do therefore "forget the law and pervert the judgment" (Prov. 31:4-5). My reader, look at it all! It is FORBIDDEN! It is written, "Neither shall any priest drink wine, when they enter into the inner court." (Ezekiel 44:21, Lev. 10:9). God forbids the drinking of wine in the "inner court," scripture declares, but now men administer strong drinks and intoxicating evil spirits from the inner court of God's NT House! I mean in our "churches!" There, even there, the pastors make men to be *mockers* who refuse to relate to God in obedient living. They refuse to acknowledge the necessity of obedience, they continually welcome lascivious living, and in it they feel no danger. They actually believe that their disobedience is disconnected and irrelevant to their eternal destiny. Mockers do, therefore, mock God, like drunkards they are, intoxicated and at odds with God's sober truth: →"Be not deceived; GOD IS NOT MOCKED: for whatsoever a man soweth, that shall he also reap. For he that soweth to his flesh shall of the flesh reap corruption; but he that soweth to the Spirit shall of the Spirit reap life everlasting" (Gal. 6:7-8).

Drunken men are not watching men, nor praying men (Lk. 21:34-36). According to the scripture they are sleeping men, rendered unready. UNREADY, I mean, for Christ's return! They make room for disobedience, plan provisions for the flesh, and they suppose, vainly, that they will have the time to repent later. They angrily reject accountability, reproof, and truth, like married men in Mexico – OH THE SHAME! They are living now, only for pleasure, caught up in a vacation island mirage where everyone rejoices in sin. These men meet the horrid description of damned men who Christ warned of, when He said:

> "if that servant say in his heart, My lord delayeth His coming;
> and shall begin to beat the menservants and maidens, and to **eat**
> and **drink**, and to be **drunken**; The lord of that servant will come
> in a day when he looketh not for him, and at an hour when he is
> not aware, and will cut him in sunder, and will appoint him his
> portion with the unbelievers" (Luke 12:45-46).

Spiritually speaking, will you be caught by Christ unready? Being made unready through prayerlessness is an unwatchful behavior in the night of this world. Take heed then, my reader, to one of the most terrifying passages in the Bible: →

> "And take heed to yourselves, lest at any time your hearts be
> overcharged with surfeiting, and **drunkenness**, and cares of this
> life, and so that day come upon you unawares. For as a snare
> shall it come on all them that dwell on the face of the whole
> earth. **Watch ye therefore, and pray always**, that ye may be
> accounted worthy to escape all these things that shall come to
> pass, and to stand before the Son of Man" (Luke 21:34-36).

Spiritual drunkards are the mockers and scoffers of the Last Days (Jude 18, 2 Peter 3:3). Even though they heard of it, that there should be a strong delusion in the last days which is God-sent, they think they can have a little space of time for unholy lusts of "pleasure in unrighteousness" (2 Thess. 2:12). Subtly therein, though they know it not, they are taken by **God's delusion**, and, lo, they bless themselves in their heart, even still (Deut. 29:19), that they, their friends, and most people they know, are not among the number of the "Great Falling Away." Men do not live like it is the Last Days; it is apparent. Most have fallen into the delusion of easy, unrepentant sensuality, or in other words, into BABY "Christianity," and they vainly trust that they have not become a part of that Great, prophetic, Last Days dilemma called the "Great Falling Away".

Spiritual Drunkenness → Spiritual Infancy

> "In that day shall the LORD of hosts be for a crown of glory, and
> for a diadem of beauty, unto the residue of His people, And for a
> spirit of judgment to him that sitteth in judgment, and **for**
> **strength to them that turn the battle to the gate.** But they also
> have **erred** through **wine**, and through **strong drink** are out of

382

the way; the **priest** and the **prophet** have **erred** through **strong drink**, they are swallowed up of wine, they are out of the way through **strong drink**; they err in vision, they **stumble in judgment**. For all tables **are full of vomit and filthiness**, so that there is no place clean. <u>Whom shall He teach knowledge? and whom shall He make to understand doctrine?</u> **Them that are weaned from the milk, and drawn from the breasts.** For precept must be upon precept, precept upon precept; line upon line, line upon line; here a little, and there a little: For with stammering lips and another tongue will he speak to this people. To whom he said, This is the rest wherewith ye may cause the weary to rest; and this is the refreshing: **yet they would not hear.** But the word of the LORD was unto them precept upon precept, precept upon precept; line upon line, line upon line; here a little, and there a little; **that they might go, and fall backward, and be broken, and snared, and taken.**" (Isaiah 28:5-13)

Do you remember the passages in Isaiah which did connect spiritual slumber with deception, darkness, and blindness, and how this same experience also was synonymous with spiritual drunkenness, and that all of this was through the instrumentality of false prophets? Just above is a key passage of this number, previously referenced, but here it is posted in its fullness. In this passage, there is a new term which prophetic language undertakes to depict the same spiritual condition as the other terms heretofore covered. Most recently we have studied how false prophets make men *spiritually drunk*, so that they cannot hear the word of God. Intoxicating them is the incapacitating deception which makes men spiritually irresponsive to the good commandments of God, and then, "the bad commandments" (Ezek. 20:25) of God lay hold upon the people so that they, "go, and fall backward, and [are] broken, and snared, and taken" (Isa. 28:13). Those who are under such a delusion are, rightly called, spiritually *drunken men*. Hence, the preaching of false prophets is rightly described as "strong drink." Now look closely in the passage above...do you see how these intoxicated men are described to be *baby children* (*infants* or *babes*)? Don't look for the exact name "*baby*" but look for the description matching the word. Infants are those who are not **weaned from the breasts**. They are **only able to drink milk**. "Who" and "whom," the prophet asks, shall be the able recipients of saving "knowledge" and "doctrine"? The prophet answers his own question, saying, "**Them that are weaned from the milk and drawn from the breasts**," the same persons who are not *spiritually drunken* by the "strong drink" of false prophets.

Does this make sense to you, how *spiritual infants* are likened as, and are equivalent to, *spiritually drunken* men? Does it make sense to you how both are descriptive synonyms for the same damning deception? Perhaps you would never think of a baby child's behavior as a comparable parallel to the spiritual synonyms which we have covered thus far. You may not call babies *fools* either. Fools, like drunkards, are also called *blind* men who are *in darkness*, biblically speaking. Oh reader, deny yourself and listen to God – "Out of His mouth cometh knowledge and understanding" (Prov. 2:6). If God said it, if you read it, then don't reject it! If this makes no sense to you, then you need to understand the depravity of *children*. Even the New Testament confirms these spiritual synonyms with explicit reference! See Romans 2:17-20:

> "Behold, thou… art confident that thou thyself art a guide of **the blind**; a light of **them which are in darkness**, an instructor of **the foolish**, a teacher of **babes**…" (Rom. 2:17-20)

Drunken men are certainly **foolish men**, but are not **children** like the **fools** and **drunkards**? Baby children, like drunken men, are forbidden to engage in issues of *responsibility*. Rightly so! Would you commit matters of responsibility and high cost into the hands of a child? Whatever the arena of the secular work force – labor laws, driving laws, athletic qualifications, and education laws – the bottom line is, children are irresponsible and untrustworthy. They cannot be trusted to respond in a manner to meet the task. A fool would trust a child to drive safely behind the wheel of an automobile. A fool would rest easy while a child runs around with a knife in his little hand, pointing up. A fool trusts in a fool, and there is so much of a fool in you, that, if you are a companion of fools you will become a fool. It is rightly said that, "a companion of fools shall be destroyed" (Prov. 13:20).

Drunken men are touchy and intemperate, huggy and hateful. They are unpredictable and entertained by the most simplistic or cruel things… and when grown men are drunk, they become like little children that are carried away in unrestrained foolishness to follow "the lord of the flies." Drunken men need a chaperone, a caring hand, a stable person, a watchful eye, a coherent thinker, a designated driver, or else they will fall in a ditch, crash a car, disrespect and rebel, transgress and deny, wander and get lost. They are robbed of wit and a mature mind! They do therefore need *a babysitter*! This reveals the shame of it all! They have altogether become like chaotic, unruly, ignorant, foolish *children*. They (both drunken men and baby children) cannot be trusted to care for themselves, to keep their possessions, or even their clothes – how shameful! They cannot cross the road without a guiding hand, nor can they cross the letter T so as to write, or make an organized and calculated plan. Drunkards are in the ungodly bliss of mindless pleasure in sin. It is the depraved lusts in grown men that they, in this way, become like children again, and so they loose themselves from the confinements of "real life." Sinners tarry long at the drink to loose themselves of the confinements of conscience! Certain sins which they would have otherwise been embarrassed to do, they are rather emboldened to do, for their raging depravity longs to be numb to the pricking of a guilty conscience. Have you ever seen a *shameless* child, a child who just doesn't know better? So are the shameless drunks! Drunkenness renders men shameless to commit shameful desires, and society excuses it as "ok", because the man is drunk. "He is just having a good time," saith the mockers. Drunken men are excused from their behavior, and at sundry times, they are applauded and held in honor on the morrow, so naturally, men would rather be drunk silly so they can be extremely sinful.

Drunken men, furthermore, are a druggie's friend; they both revel together and make themselves insane in sin. They are sin-brothers in shackles and bonds, addicted to the devil's board games where everyone who plays wins. My reader, can you look reality in the face?! Men long to eat the sprouting magic rising from a cow's dung! What a horror! Can you imagine it? Men have been reduced to such a darkened mind that they look after, meditate upon, and earnestly long for a cow to excrete his waste, making a "cow patty," and they, as it were, are huddling around it, gazing upon it, hoping, just for one rising mushroom, and, alas, they may fulfill their lusts! God created bacteria-infested, poisonous dung to stink for a reason, but these men have become animal-like hungry, heathen. While they digest these unhallowed "shrooms", they hallucinate, if haply that they might see devils, or at least the fantastic tales of devils. And oh, the horror! How men admire cow dung as precious, and the invaluable pearls of God's everlasting word as profane. They refuse the godly and sober meditation of God's word. They deny the hopeful wonder therein, that they might see God! This wicked and sinful depravity is a near kin to what is called "vile affections," "against nature," profaning "the natural" use of creation, and doing that which is "unseemly," and their God-hating love for the world has led them to this awful rejection point where "God also gave them up to uncleanness" and "dishonour" (Rom. 1:24-26). "Woe unto them that call evil good, and good evil; that put darkness for light, and light for darkness; that put bitter for sweet, and sweet for bitter" (Isa. 5:20)! Take heed that, you too, do not get to the Judgment seat having won for yourself the reputation of "dogs" and "swine!" These are hell's worthies! Thus God, not a man, calls them filthy animals, and He saith again, lo! "Give not that which is holy unto dogs, neither cast ye your pearls before swine" (Matt. 7:6)!

From another angle, drunken men seek another release – like from the anxiety and pressure of providing for their necessities, from incurred debt because of living in luxury, from melting emotions staggering with the swinging economy, and the frightening potential of life savings suddenly lost – and so, the sanity of the world stands or falls with these things. This is as God said, "all these things do the Gentiles seek" (Matt. 6:32), and when they ought to humble themselves and become children before God, the Father, the God of heaven and earth, they rather intoxicate themselves so as to act out their nature as children of the devil, caught up in the fairy tale of a drunken conscience. What they think, feel, say, and do, is not in memory or mind; they are blown with the wind of vanity and gladness without a conscience. They do not know the heavenly Father, so they would rather know nothing at all but the unhindered pleasures of sin – drunken-foolish like a shameless baby, they are utterly incapable of the ability to blush. Drunken men are numbed tasteless like swine, and they cannot even feel their face! Thus they can lie down and sleep in putrid messes of stinking filth, in life-threatening climates of the cold, and, when hungry, they can eat trash, rotten food, poison, and slime. Their faces are numb, their mind like a wild child made dumb, they riot in the dark and live for nightlife - they are the devil's harlot-lover and adulterous wife.

> "Woe unto them that rise up early in the morning, that they may **follow strong drink**; that continue **until night**, till wine inflame them! And the harp, and the viol, the tabret, and pipe, and wine, are in their feasts: but they regard not the work of the LORD, neither consider the operation of His hands...Therefore hell hath enlarged herself, opened her mouth without measure: and their glory, and their multitude, and their pomp, and he that rejoiceth, shall descend into it" (Isa. 5:11-12, 14).

> "For they that sleep sleep in the **night**; and they that be **drunken** are **drunken** in the **night**. But let us, who are **of the day**, be **sober**, putting on the breastplate of faith and love; and for an helmet, the hope of salvation" (1 Thess. 5:7-8).

> "And that, knowing the time, that now it is high time to awake out of **sleep**: for now is our salvation nearer than when we believed. The **night is far spent**, the day is at hand: let us therefore cast off the **works of darkness**, and let us put on the **armour of light**. Let us walk honestly, **as in the day**; not in rioting and **drunkenness**, not in chambering and wantonness, not in strife and envying" (Rom 13:11-13).

Children are not the innocent, adorable creatures men make-believe them to be. They are embodiments of Adamic rebellion that invent evil, live to lust, and foolishness is so bound up in their heart! Nevertheless, how sweet they are when foolishness is driven from them. They are so bound up in foolishness that there is but one hope for their eternal and temporary souls to be saved – their foolishness must be driven from them **by the rod**. "Foolishness is bound in the heart of a child; but the rod of correction shall drive it far from him" (Prov. 22:15). This is a matter of heaven or hell! "Withhold not correction from the child: for *if* **thou beatest him with the rod, he shall not die**. Thou shalt **beat him with the rod**, and shalt deliver his soul from **hell**" (Prov. 23:13-14).

The "I love you" of a child is often as insanely simplistic as drunken men, and they too do repeatedly say that phrase to their drunken comrades or their designated babysitters. They love in word, but their heart and deeds are far from reflecting their words. They are as those feigning Israelites in the wilderness, of whom it was said: "They did flatter Him with their mouth, and they lied unto Him with their tongues" (Ps. 78:36). Baby children will not love you, they will even hate you, unless the rod does drive from them the blinding, darkening, intoxicating foolishness they do love, or else they may literally forsake you when the time is opportune. They are unruly, relentless to disobey, grudgingly loving, loud and uncontrollable, whose luxury is chaos. The child cannot rest from sin...therefore if you don't correct him, then you will have no honor, obedience, or rest from him. Therefore it is written, "Correct thy son, and he shall give thee rest" (Prov. 29:17). If you let their sinful nature **go on unrestrained** from chastening, the nature will take its course in the most violent direction God's sovereignty will allow. Thus it is written, "Chasten thy son **while there is hope**, and let not thy soul spare for his crying" (Prov. 19:18). You don't spare for his crying, and, Lord willing, God will spare him when he cries out to Him. If you don't spare now, then God may spare his soul later – lest he end up in hell where sinners endlessly cry without the hope of God's pitiful eye. The nature of the child is enslaved to foolishness, and it is a faithful saying: fools perish in hell! "A child left to himself" will never have saving "wisdom" (Prov. 29:15). When an adult parent understands the eternal and temporary vitality in discipline, then he or she understands the course that depravity will take a child into; therefore the parent feels the responsibility to interrupt this course set on hell! Parents, I adjure thee! See that your children are on a runway of inevitable destruction, from birth, that you may be emboldened to ignore the child's tear-stained face that begs from you unrighteous pity. Crocodile tears will fool you, parents, as your children dramatize false pains and great fears. I say again, you will be able to endure the wearisome cries they howl, howling until their energy dies, if indeed, by grace, you remember – what is the trouble of 77 nights of wrestling against their Adamic nature, next to the eternal night of hell that awaits them? Will you trouble yourself, now, that you might keep their souls from trouble? It is HATE to allow a child to happily run the broad way to hell – you must make him cry! And spare not for his crying! Therefore it is written, "He that spareth his rod hateth his son: but he that loveth him chasteneth him betimes" (Prov. 13:24). Amen.

A BIBICAL STUDY OF
SPIRITUAL INFANCY
CHAPTER 17

The incapacitating effect of...

Blindness,

Darkness,

Starvation,

Dehydration,

and *Drunkenness* → is scripturally the same
condition as when a man is
a *Baby Child in grace.*

Newborn children, known as infants or babies, are what the scripture is referring to in the passages of scripture which we are studying. They are those children which are of such a young age that they cannot eat meat (or strong foods). At such an age, the children are utterly reliant upon the milk from their mother's breasts. They are such, which Isaiah 28:9 described them, children not "weaned from the milk and drawn from the breasts," or as the New Testament puts it, they are "babes in Christ" which are "fed" with "milk and not with meat: for hitherto [they are] not able to bear it" (1 Cor. 3:1-2). In the NT, furthermore, Hebrews 5:11-14 uses the same descriptive terms – they are such as "have need of milk and not strong meat," because they are as "a babe," and "strong meat belongeth to them that are of full age." In these two passages just referenced, 1 Corinthians 3:1-2 and Hebrews 5:11-14, it must be noted that the audience the writer is referring to are regenerate Christians (called "babes **in Christ**"), but they are incapacitated in such a way that they cannot "discern good and evil" (Heb. 5:14). In other words, these individuals have fallen from a state of Christian "**perfection**" (1 Cor. 2:6, Heb. 6:1). In Hebrews 6:1, the author states that their need is to "go on" (or grow up) into "perfection", which is a man who does not have to lay again the foundation of what is called, "the principles of the doctrine of Christ" (Heb. 6:1), or, "the first principles of the oracles of God" (Heb. 5:12), which are those things which maintain a saving relationship with the Lord in the life of a regenerate believer (otherwise known as a present progressive faith in the gospel). Two of six things mentioned which refer to the first, foundational, principles of faith in the gospel are: "**repentance** from dead works and of **faith** toward God." If a man falls away from believing and following these six things (the foundation and first principles), he will then become *carnal* instead of *spiritual*, as Paul says of the "babes in Christ" in 1 Corinthians 3 – "ye are yet carnal" (1 Cor. 3:1-3). Carnal men are fools, and fools are not wise, therefore these "babes in Christ," who can only drink milk, are as Isaiah says they are – those who are disqualified and unable to learn "**knowledge**," those who cannot "**understand doctrine**" (Isa. 28:9). To deny "**repentance**" and "**faith** toward God," my reader, is the same deed as denying the <u>gospel</u> itself. As a result, the individual is excluded from the gospel's *saving powers* which effectually work in them that believe, namely, the powers to "mortify the deeds of the body" instead of living "after the flesh" (Rom. 8:13); therefore these babes in Christ are called "**carnal**" men.

Spiritual infancy is not a condition which is of immediate onset after the *second birth*, like as it is in the *first birth*. It is not a condition which is inevitable, subjective to the slow process of growth through time until finally, the child reaches an adolescent's coherency. The physical and biological first birth, which is unquestionably in comparison, would suggest that the second birth has a gradual growth pattern of a similar timeline, that growth out of spiritual infancy should be the same as growth out of physical infancy, but the scriptures are careful to withhold and deny such an application.

The scriptures speak unitedly concerning the operation of God in **salvation begun**: there is a *sudden* and *instantaneous* formation of the image of Christ when a man is born again (Eph. 4:24, Col. 3:10, Gal. 4:19), and spiritual infancy is a spiritual condition wherein *this salvific image is lost*. Therefore, my reader, any regenerate man, at any degree of glory and growth, at once and suddenly, at the loss

> "For we ourselves also were sometimes foolish, disobedient, deceived, serving divers lusts and pleasures, living in malice and envy, hateful, and hating one another. But **after** that the kindness and love of God our Saviour toward man **appeared**, not by works of righteousness which we have done, but according to his mercy he saved us, by the washing of **regeneration**, and **renewing** of the Holy Ghost; Which he shed on us abundantly through Jesus Christ our Saviour; That being justified by his grace, we should be made heirs according to the hope of eternal life." (Titus 3:3-7)

of faith and repentance, will fall into such a state where the image of Christ is lost, and therein, until the man recovers faith and repentance again, is henceforth considered a *spiritual infant*. Spiritual infancy is not ruled or determined by carnal time, therefore, as is commonly the problem, regenerate men who have been saved for 10 years are still spiritual babies! We must understand that spiritual infancy is not exactly comparable to physical infancy, and therefore, we must strictly apply ONLY what the scriptures apply. At salvation begun the image of Christ is formed, but the brilliance of its shining strength is differing in each regenerate man henceforth according to the differing proportions of sovereign grace which God has distributed to every man. Meaning, not all have the same measure of faith as others (Rom. 12:3), and not all have the same fruitfulness as others do yield (1 Cor. 15:10), but "some thirty, and some sixty, and some an hundred" (Mark. 4:8). This image may have variations of glory and brilliance, but infancy is when the image which was formed is lost, the spiritual dominion of Christ is compromised, and there is a great war for the soul within and without the regenerate man!

With more doctrinal terms: the second birth, at the moment of regeneration, is so drastic that it can be called a **new** birth, and it is of such transforming power that, afterward, the man is declared to be a *new creation* that all the world can behold (2 Cor. 5:17; see also the conversion experience described in 1 Thess. 1:4-10). This conversion is of such power that the image of Christ is immediately formed, with overwhelming evidence, within the man's heart, words, and deeds. However, spiritual infancy is when the regenerate man is turned back from <u>NEW</u> to <u>OLD</u> again. All of the doctrinal terms which describe salvation unitedly speak the same. At salvation the image of Christ is immediately formed so that the individual is brought from *blindness* to *sight* (Acts 26:18), *darkness* to *light* (Acts 26:18), *death* to *life* (Eph. 2:1), *alienation* from God to *communion* with God (Col. 1:21-22, 1 Jn. 1:3, 1 Cor. 1:9), *enmity* of mind to Divine *friendship*, which is "in Spirit and in Truth" (Rom. 8:5-8, John 4:24), a *slave of sin* to a *bondman of grace* (Rom. 5:21), a *captive* now made *free* (John 8:34-36), and foremost of all terms, the man is brought from the *carnal man* into a *spiritual man*, or, the *carnal mind* into the *spiritual mind* (Rom. 8:5-8) – all of this, because the man is indwelt with the Holy Ghost. After this <u>instantaneous</u>, <u>sudden</u>, and <u>miraculous</u> change has taken place, then the experience of these salvific virtues of grace depends upon the **maintenance** of saving faith and repentance in the gospel message that, at the first, saved in this grand envelopment of glory, and as long as saving faith is presently and progressively held firm unto the end, so also, all the virtues of salvation will live in and through the man, welling up, as it were, carrying him into eternal life (Gal. 2:20, John 7:38). "The Spirit is life because of righteousness" (Rom. 8:10).

You see, beloved, God has given mankind salvation in Christ through the indwelling of the Holy Spirit, but men must *walk* in Him by the maintenance

> "As ye have therefore received Christ Jesus the Lord, so **walk** ye in Him." (Col. 2:6)
>
> "This I say then, **Walk** in the Spirit, and ye shall not fulfil the lust of the flesh." (Gal. 5:16)

of saving faith henceforth. If a man fails to maintain saving faith – he falls – from the glory of grace in which he formerly stood, from the virtues heretofore described, so that the image of Christ which was formed within him is now <u>marred</u> and <u>distorted</u> – being <u>conflicted</u> and <u>disrupted</u> – by all that Christ had before (suddenly, instantaneously, and miraculously) saved the man from: *blindness*, *darkness*, *death*, *carnality*, *alienation of mind*, the *absence of God*, thoughts of *enmity* against God, *malice* and *wickedness* (1 Cor. 5:8), and the *captivity* of *sin* through the *devil* (2 Tim. 2:25-26).

> "My little children, of whom I travail in birth
> again **until Christ be formed in you**" –
> Galatians 4:19

If the regenerate man fails to maintain saving faith and repentance, then consequentially, Christ is no longer *living* in the man (so as to *fill* him and *rule* him), thus when Christ is no longer living through the man, the man is, now, walking as a normal man. Is this not a great **FALL?**! This is exactly what Paul was describing the Corinthian babes to be, saying, "are ye not **carnal** and **walk as men**" (1 Cor. 3:3), and again, "**are ye not carnal**" (1 Cor. 3:4)? Is this not a great horror, a great distortion of what once was a shining salvation, so that, we can see how Christ needs to be "formed" in such men again (Note: Galatians 4:19, in context, is spoken to backslidden saints who are, at present, in a damnable spiritual condition, which means, this re-formation of Christ within them is the restoration of salvation)! Until then, when Christ is re-formed, what these men represent and express to this fallen world is an *infantile expression* of who Christ is, a *drunken distortion* of His character and Person, and oh, what a shame! When the world ought to see a clear image of Christ in Christians, look at them - it is but a *foolish* man when Christ is *wise*, a *drunken* man when Christ is *sober*, a *slothful, sleepy*, and *dark* picture when Christ is *diligent, watchful, awake*, and *full of Light*! A revival of saving faith and repentance would <u>suddenly</u> establish maturity, which is grace that establishes a saving and "full" formation of Christ within, and this brings the man into what Hebrews 5:14 calls, a "full age" (like that of a responsible youth in comparison to the immaturity of an infant). This "full age", in Hebrews 5:14, is the renewal of saving faith and repentance again (Heb. 6:1), the instantaneous ascent out of the drunken stupor of spiritual infancy, so that, again – Praise God! – the regenerate man is able to set his affection on things above (Col. 3:1-3)! This "full age" of Hebrews 5:14 does not mean to compare the age maturity of a "younger" man with an elder in the faith, for both of them do, already, savingly walk in Christ by the maintenance of faith and repentance. This revival from infancy is like when the man was first born again, how Christ was immediately formed within, for this re-formation of Christ is accomplished by the same old gospel-power and Godspeed! The man does not have to wait two or three years before this infantile, drunken display of carnality and death is removed. We must not look at this operation through the weakness of human flesh. Nay, we must not follow the ungodly suggestion that, **year after year**, at last, we can expect men to grow out of this woeful estate of infancy…but let us, rather, besiege these sick souls with gospel-healing – gospel preaching – "Jesus Christ and Him crucified" (1 Cor. 2:2) – with gospel praying and weeping (1 Thess. 3:10) – until, God willing…these souls might have a revival of life through the power of the Spirit of God. My reader, hear the glad tidings! This is an operation as <u>quick</u> and <u>powerful</u> as the first regeneration, and the last, for it is like "the twinkling of an eye" is fast (1 Cor. 15:52)!

My reader, these sick souls are on the brink of the second death, and like Spurgeon exclaimed, though they may not want a reviving, or seek it, "they need REVIVING, and they MUST HAVE IT"! Oh the painful astonishment of it all, that infantile, backslidden, and sickly regenerate men are spirit-dead (Rev. 3:1), so much so that they cannot understand saving grace! You can plead with so many forcible words, and, alas, they cannot see it! It takes nothing less than the reviving powers of the gospel-grace to awake and restore them to health! Of such, Spurgeon did lamentably write:

"There is, a condition of mind which is even more sad than either of the two above mentioned; it is a thorough, gradual, but certain decline of all the spiritual powers. Look at that consumptive man whose lungs are decaying, and in whom the vital energy is ebbing; it is painful to see the faintness which suffuses him after exertion, and the general languor which overspreads his weakened frame. Far more sad to the spiritual eye is the spectacle presented by spiritual consumptives who in some quarters meet us on all hands. The eye of faith is dim and overcast, and seldom flashes with holy joy; the spiritual countenance is hollow and sunken with doubts and fears; the tongue of praise is partially paralyzed, and has little

---

Contextual Verses Addressed Within the Quote

"Give not that which is holy unto the dogs, neither cast ye your pearls before swine, lest they trample them under their feet, and turn again and rend you" – Matthew 7:6

"Because thou sayest, I am rich, and increased with goods, and have need of nothing; and knowest not that thou art wretched, and miserable, and poor, and blind, and naked: I counsel thee to buy of Me gold tried in the fire, that thou mayest be rich; and white raiment, that thou mayest be clothed, and that the shame of thy nakedness do not appear; and anoint thine eyes with eyesalve, that thou mayest see" – Revelation 3:17-18

"Why should ye be stricken any more? Ye will revolt more and more: the whole head is sick, and the whole heart fain" – Isaiah 1:5

---

to say for Jesus; the spiritual frame is lethargic, and its movements are far from vigorous; the man is not anxious to be doing anything for Christ; a horrible numbness, a dreadful insensibility has come over him; he is in soul like a sluggard in the dog-days, who finds it hard labor to lie in bed and brush away the flies from his face. If these spiritual consumptives hate sin they do it so weakly that one might fear that they loved it still. If they love Jesus, it is so coldly that it is a point of question whether they love at all. If they sing Jehovah's praises it is very sadly, as if hallelujahs were dirges. If they mourn for sin it is only 'with half-broken hearts, and their grief is shallow and unpractical. If they hear the Word of God they are never stirred by it; enthusiasm is an unknown luxury. If they come across a precious truth they perceive nothing particular in it, any more than the cock in the fable, in the jewel which he found in the farmyard. They throw themselves back upon the enchanted couch of sloth, and while they are covered with rags they dream of riches and great increase of goods. It is a sad, sad thing when Christians fall into this state; then indeed they need reviving, and they must have it, for "the whole head is sick and the whole heart faint." Every lover of souls should intercede for declining professors that the visitations of God may restore them; that the Sun of righteousness may arise upon them with healing beneath his wings." – Spurgeon, "What Is A

392

Revival?"

Paul said to the Corinthians, "And I, brethren, could not speak unto you *as unto spiritual*, but *as unto carnal*" (1 Cor. 3:1) – this is the woeful incapacity of infants! These backslidden saints are now in bondage to a spiritual condition which is without saving repentance and faith (Heb. 6:1), and therefore, when it states that they cannot "discern both good and evil", it means that they are, as a heathen man, incoherently staggering in hypocrisy and rigidity, bent on rebellion to devour iniquitous-foolishness. Such men can't feel the sting of the conscience, the fear of God's rebukes, they can't find grace to hate sin or love God! A babe has left off the hallowedness of "repentance"! And worse, they are not ashamed about it! Open their ears to their God-given conscience which shouts – CONDEMNED – then they would be ashamed of their evil behavior...then they would bow down in heavy repentance...yea, they would mournfully return to God...but their mind is rendered drunken like a shameless child reveling in wild behavior without a consciousness! Staggeringly, they are without a saving degree of guilt! Do you see how they are as a drunken man in this pointed and doctrinally precise way, for neither a drunken man nor an infant child can "*discern* both good and evil" (Heb. 5:14). Spiritual infancy is a wicked and evil *incapacity* - woe to them! Their heart is imprisoned in the *foolishness* of no-repentance and faithlessness – to a damnable degree. When an evil is committed, alas, there is no *discernment* that it is sinful and wicked, and thus there is no repentance, because there is no *saving knowledge* of the goodness of God and the sinfulness of evil. Before a man is able to "*discern* good and evil", he will not choose the good for the love of it, or disdain the evil because he understands the sinfulness of it; thus, it is written: he is like an infant child who shamelessly wanders *without knowledge* of good or evil. Infancy is the time "before the child shall *know* to refuse the evil, and choose the good" (Isa. 7:15-16). Infant children are, biologically, rendered unable to *discern* the paths of righteousness and repentance in God, for they have "no *knowledge* between good and evil" (Deut. 1:39). Can you see it clearly now? This spiritual condition is as perverted and shameful as the unrepentant shamelessness of drunken men – cursed men – who are like a cursed field of thorns and briers, like heaping and entangling pricks with strangling arms, and they are choking out the holy seed of God at last. Under outpouring showers of promise and power for righteousness, lo, this ground is diseased-*dull* – unable to hear, fear, and obey (Heb. 5:11, 6:4-8).

When Paul said to the Corinthian babes, "And I, brethren, could not speak unto you *as unto spiritual*, but *as unto carnal*", it can very well be rephrased to, "I could not speak unto you as unto *the living*, but as unto *the dead*; as unto *the seeing*, but as unto *the blind*; as unto *God's friends*, but as unto *His enemies*; as unto *bondmen of grace*, but as unto *slaves of sin*, as unto *the free*, but as unto *Satan's captives* who need liberty; as unto *the wise*, but as unto *fools*; as unto *the watchful*, but as unto *the sleepers*; as unto *the sober*, but as unto *the drunkards*; as unto *the righteous*, but as unto *the wicked*; as unto *the perfect*, but as unto *the fallen*; as unto *the blameless*, but as unto *the blamable*; as unto *the delectable fields* of fruitful vineyards, but as unto *thorny fields* of *pricking sinners*; as unto *gold, silver,* and *precious stones*, but as unto *wood, earth, hay,* and *stubble*." These are the weak *cowards* who run from giants, who will not "be strong in the Lord" (Eph. 6:10). These are the Christian soldiers turned *deserters* because they are afraid of the devil, which run away as though weaponless, and against God's wishes and His cries, they will not be clad in the whole armour of God. These are *weary* of the narrow path, and sleeping, but they will awake to a nightmare at last. They are weary because they have forsaken the right: they have hated the Promised Land, the Promised Man, and the soul-rest of the weariless – the Savior's Breast. These are the *sleepers* who won't awake, who never prepare any oil to take, who cannot imagine standing before Judgment's gates.

"Knowledge" = "Understanding" = "Doctrine" (Isa. 28:9) = **Wisdom** (1 Cor. 2:6).

"We speak **wisdom** among them that are **perfect**"
(1 Cor. 2:6).

"The righteousness of the **perfect** shall direct his way: but the
wicked shall fall by his own wickedness." (Prov. 11:5)

Isaiah said that these babies can't understand saving truth; therefore they are like the *spiritual drunkards*, but they are drunk and intoxicated by *carnality* - therefore, here also, the apostle Paul agrees with Isaiah. Paul restates the spiritual principles of incapacity in 1 Corinthians with great detail, revealing exactly, just as Isaiah spoke, the very same spiritual characteristics as with spiritual drunkards. Look with me carefully at the doctrinal case which is made from chapter 2 onward, into chapter 3:1-3, wherein Paul approaches unto, reasons with, and seeks the recovery of the spiritual babes, certainly from a different angle than Hebrews, but it is with the same argument pattern and final conclusion.

Paul said that when he came to preach to the Corinthians, he came not with "enticing words of man's **wisdom**" (1 Cor. 2:4), but nevertheless, he did not deny that he did preach **wisdom** to certain persons who were of qualification. At Paul's first interaction with the Corinthians, meaning, when they were unconverted, probably the time of his first arrival in Corinth, Paul preached "Jesus Christ and Him crucified" alone, avoiding all deviations from this foundation. Paul knew that if he were to go on to other matters, he would be going away from "the first principles of the oracles of God," or, "the principles of the doctrine of Christ" (Heb. 5:12, 6:1). To go onward to more advanced things from this first foundation would then build upon this foundation – matters which were called "**wisdom**" by the apostle Paul – and if the foundation is not properly laid at the first, or, if it suffers some imperfection and breaks, that which is built aloft will suffer a great fall. At such a time when a

394

formerly sound foundation is moved, is made imperfect, or breaks, all building which is aloft would be urgently ceased until all imperfections are revived into fixed immovableness. Let it be clearly understood, my reader, that Paul did not deny that he spoke in wisdom, but he only spoke of the wisdom of God with those who are "able" to "hear" it (Heb. 5:11), "bear it" (1 Cor. 3:2), understand it, and receive it, or in other words, the ones who are able to chew it up and swallow it, to eat and then digest it. Paul said, "Howbeit we speak **wisdom** among them that are **perfect**: yet not the wisdom of this world, nor of the princes of this world, that come to nought" (1 Cor. 2:6). Paul called this "the **hidden wisdom**," because it is hidden from two kinds of people (1 Cor. 2:7): it is hidden from "**the natural man**" (1 Cor. 2:14) and the "**babe in Christ**," who also is called a "**carnal**" man (1 Cor. 3:1-4). Please read the following verses very carefully:

"But **the natural man** receiveth not the things of the Spirit of God: for they are foolishness unto him: neither can he know them, because they are **spiritually discerned**" (1 Corinthians 2:14).

"I, brethren, **could not speak** unto you as **unto spiritual**, but **as unto carnal**…for hitherto ye were not able to **bear it**, neither yet now are ye **able**" (1 Cor. 3:1-2).

> "Hidden Wisdom" = Hidden Christ
>
> "Verily Thou art a God that **hidest** Thyself, O God of Israel, **the Savior**" – Isaiah 45:15
>
> "Hidden Wisdom" = Hidden Face
>
> "And I will wait upon the LORD, that **hideth His face** from the house of Jacob, and I will look for Him" – Isaiah 8:17

"**Hidden wisdom**" is only given to and received by those who are called a "**spiritual**" man (1 Cor. 2:15), which, at that time, the Corinthians were not. Paul clearly declared that he *could not speak* to the Corinthian "babes in Christ" "as unto spiritual" men, but rather "as unto **carnal**" men (1 Cor. 3:1) – because they were given over to the delusions of uncontrollable, incapacitating **carnality**. Paul was naming their ungodly behavior by the rhetorical question – "**are ye not carnal**" (1 Cor. 3:4)? In 1 Corinthians 2:6-16, Paul spoke of the "**hidden wisdom**" of God which is "a mystery" to all natural men and carnal Christians, and he explained the conditions whereby this mystery is revealed to men. It is hidden from "the princes" who crucified Christ, men who are "**natural** men," simply because these things are not **naturally** understood. Paul explained that these things are **spiritual** in how they are "revealed" (1 Cor. 2:10). This means that it is not by the "eye" or the "ear", the memory, mind, or "heart of man" (1 Cor. 2:9), but God has to grant to men *spiritual* eyes, ears, and hearts. Paul argued that the Spirit that comes from God makes men to "know the things that are freely given to us of God" (1 Cor. 2:12), things which are otherwise hidden; therefore a man cannot understand the things of God without the aid of the Spirit that comes from God.

Just as a man cannot know the mind of a man, but only the spirit of a man that is in a man does know the mind of a man, so it is with the mind, knowledge, and heart of God – "even so the things of God knoweth no man, but the Spirit of God" (1 Cor. 2:11). However, if a natural man is given the Spirit of God, and he is therefore born of God after His Spirit, <u>AND</u> HE IS ABIDING IN THE SPIRIT, then the conditions are met which allows those things which are "spiritually discerned" (1 Cor. 2:14) to be revealed, things which "the Holy Ghost teacheth; comparing spiritual things with spiritual" (1 Cor. 2:13). Paul explained how these things are held by, acquired, and committed to "the spiritual man," when he said, "he that is spiritual judgeth all things" (1 Cor. 2:15). Why the *spiritual man*? That man has the Spirit of God, which knows the mind of God, so it is said – "For who hath known the mind of the Lord, that he may instruct Him? But we have the mind of Christ" (1 Cor. 2:16). These spiritual men do know the mind of God, because the Spirit of God is instructing them of the mind of God, therefore they are said to have the very mind of Christ, or as Romans 8:6 puts it, they are "spiritually minded." "For who hath known the mind of the Lord?" Indeed no one, except those who have the Spirit of God! And He, the Holy Ghost, reveals the mind of the Lord to the children of God who abide in Him. Therefore, "Whom shall He teach knowledge? And whom shall He make to understand doctrine?" – Isaiah asks! It is those that have the Spirit of God in a saving relationship, meaning that they are presently abiding in Him; therefore they are not **natural men** or **carnal Christians**. Both of these persons are ensnared by the natural, carnal, and fallen nature of man to a damnable degree – denying "repentance" & "faith" (Heb. 6:1) – which is what it means to fall from a **perfect** state while you are a regenerate Christian. Therefore these Christians need to learn **_again_** the saving gospel truths which they once knew, which is "**repentance** from dead works and **faith** towards God" (Heb. 6:1). Had they not left off from faith in these truths, then they would not have become carnal. They would still be abiding in the Spirit of God, and so, they would be enabled to eat the strong-meat wisdom in God. "For if ye live after the flesh, ye shall die: but if ye through the Spirit do mortify the deeds of the body, ye shall live" (Rom. 8:13).

"The Hidden Wisdom" (1 Cor. 2:7) → "But if our Gospel be HID" (2 Cor. 4:3)
"Blinded the minds" (2 Cor. 4:4)

God hides wisdom from regenerate men when they leave off faith in saving truths, which a man cannot leave off and still be in a saved spiritual condition – presently & progressively saved. "We are made partakers of Christ, if we hold the beginning of our confidence stedfast unto the end" (Heb. 3:14). In 2 Corinthians 3:6 - 4:6, we can see the language of the OT used again in the NT. Do you remember the saying of scripture of how God **hides His face**, and do you remember what the spiritual consequences are when this happens? Do you remember how often this spiritual reality was spoken about in the prayers, wrestlings, and strivings of all saints in the OT? Also, do you remember how they praised God, how they were exalted in glories, when, namely, He did not hide His face but reveal it – turning it upon them – and do you remember how they did exclaim that it SHINED with LIGHT?! Oh, how often did they cry out this same cry in so many different words: → "Cause Thy face to shine and we shall be saved" (Ps. 80:19)! And again, "Lift Thou up the light of

396

Thy countenance upon us" (Ps. 4:6)! They knew that this was the secret of how the living Lord would presently and progressively reveal the saving knowledge of God – even by the shining face of God, unhidden and beheld – thus the prayers went up: "Make Thy face to shine upon Thy servant; and teach me Thy statutes" (Ps. 119:135). Without it, they could not have **understanding, knowledge, doctrine,** or **wisdom.** These very terms in the same metaphorical language, are the very way 2 Corinthians 3:6 - 4:6 does describe what happens when Christ savingly reveals Himself to lost souls! Is Jesus Christ shining His face upon you, or is He hiding it from you?

When men were lost, NT or OT, it is when "their minds were blinded," and their minds were blinded because there was a veil over the heart,

> Psalm 34:12-16 & 1 Peter 3:10-12 are other references which cite "the face" of God which is a spiritual signal for you, or against you, which is parallel to it being hidden or shining.

which is also directly connected to the spiritual meaning behind why Moses had a veil over his face as the light from it was dimming (2 Cor. 3:13-14). Moses was a typological picture of God and Christ, in that his face did shine with a bright light…but now the NT states that when the Lord Jesus Christ is revealed to men, "the vail shall be taken away" (2 Cor. 3:16)! This unveiling is done by the "Spirit of the Lord" (2 Cor. 3:17), and so, "we all **with open face** beholding as in a glass **the glory of the Lord** are changed into the same image from glory to glory, even as by the Spirit of the Lord" (2 Cor. 3:18). We have an "open face" because there is no veil over the face of Christ, like as, the rather, how there was a veil over the face of Moses, and at present – Hallelujah – the face of Jesus Christ does shine upon us! The face of Christ ever shines in unfading brightness! It is ingratiated with glory, and when men are saved, it is because God does the very same thing that what was so earnestly and repeatedly prayed for in the OT – that "the light" from "the image of God" would "shine unto" men, even "the light of the knowledge of the glory of God **in the face of Jesus Christ**" (2 Cor. 4:6)! What is happening? God is lifting up **the light of His countenance** upon men by the unveiling of His face, which means that it is no longer hidden, and also, therefore, all the blindness of spiritual darkness is gone. What happened to men at the first – at regeneration and initial salvation – must be presently and progressively experienced, therefore the regenerate saints must abide in the shining face of Christ at all times.

"Blinded the minds of them which believe not" – 2 Cor. 4:4

If the light of God's face shines upon regenerate converts – they see – for darkness has fled away, but it is the contrary when regenerate converts do backslide from saving faith, repentance, and gospel-grace…then the saints are described in such ways as – the man is "**blind** and **cannot see** afar off" (2 Peter 1:9), is "in **darkness,**" "stumbling," "walketh in **darkness,**" "and knoweth not whither he goeth, because **darkness hath blinded his eyes**" (1 John 2:9-11). In such a spiritual condition as this where the shining face of God is evidently hidden from them, Christ is able to drop upon them the damnable charge – "knowest not thou art…**blind?**"

And, "I counsel thee to buy of Me," to "anoint thine eyes with eyesalve, that thou mayest **see**" (Rev. 3:17-18). My reader, just as those who are natural (unconverted or unregenerate) have their minds blinded (2 Cor. 4:4) because of the absence of Christ's shining face, even so, regenerate Christians can temporarily or forever be overcome into the woeful state of Christ turning away and hiding His face (like as the OT describes). Such a man as this is blinded in darkness just as the cited passages do declare! The man has thus become the fool who is unable to bear wisdom, and "the wisdom of the prudent is to understand his way: but the folly of fools is deceit" (Prov. 14:8). These men don't understand their way anymore, just as was cited: he "knoweth not whither he goeth." Likewise Christ rebuked him, "knowest not thou," and therefore, both of them, are utterly "stumbling." These men have become babies in need of constant attention! They have become as the *sleeping, foolish virgins* who need to WAKE UP, as Ephesians 5:7-17 delivers the striking charge – "**Awake** thou that **sleepest**, and arise from **the dead**, and Christ shall give thee **Light**" (Eph. 5:14)!

> "…the rest were **blinded** (According as it is written, God hath given them **the spirit of slumber**, eyes that they should **not see**, and ears that they should **not hear**;) unto this day" (Romans 11:7-8, Isa. 29:10)

Do you know the context of the passages written above? Men don't sleep while under the hot rays of the noonday sun, nor do any Christians sleep under the shining face of the Holy and True, Only Brilliant Messiah. Such sleeping Christians are like dead men, lost in the darkness of dead carnality, therefore they cannot be rightly called spiritual men. With no recovery, such men will not be called Christian men. They have "a name that [they] livest, and art **dead**" (Rev. 3:3). To be *dead* is obviously a damnable condition, is it not? You will either be judged "**quick**" (alive) or "**dead**" "at [Christ's] appearing and His Kingdom" (2 Tim. 4:1, 1 Pet. 4:5). Again it is written that these men need to arise from the dead, and it is because they have fallen from a "**perfect**" state (Rev. 3:2). If they don't repent then Christ will say, alas, they are not "worthy". This means, woe to them! He will blot out their names out of the book of life (Rev. 3:4-5)! "Ye are all the children of the Light, and the children of the day: we are not of night, nor of darkness. Therefore let us not **sleep**, as do others; but let us watch and be sober" (1 Thess. 5:5-6). Sleepers – "their eyes they have closed" (Matt. 13:15) – and therefore they need to hear the saying, "Awake thou that sleepest" (Eph. 5:14), but if they do not hear the "cry made" (Matt. 25:6) to wake them up, sleeping on and on in their horrid slothfulness, then lo, they will wake up to find no oil in their lamps, feeling sluggish and "foolish," wishing they would have woken up with the wise at the sundry times they did go "to them that sell" oil to buy it (Matt. 25:2). If you don't guard against the enchantments of the devil, then you too, as they did, will somehow fall asleep, here and there, "ten times" (Num. 14:22), and it is because you are not walking "circumspectly," guarding against surprise or danger. "See then that ye walk **circumspectly**, not as **fools** but as **wise**" (Eph. 5:15).

"For Thou art not a God that hath pleasure in wickedness: neither shall evil dwell with Thee. The **foolish** shall not stand in Thy sight: Thou hatest all workers of iniquity." (Ps. 5:4-5)

If a child's heart is bound up in foolishness, then *children are fools* (Prov. 22:15). If a man is a baby child in spiritual maturity, or a fool, can such a one go to heaven? Are not the fools those that did not go "in with Him" (the Bridegroom) "to the marriage" because "the door was shut" (Matt. 25:10)!? Did not those fools stand without, crying, "Lord, Lord, open to us" (Matt. 25:11)! When infant children grow up, then they are enabled to understand carnal responsibilities, consequences, and dangers, and then they responsibly meet the demands of life. The warning of God is, therefore, consistent and SURE. When a regenerate man turns back into this state of *foolishness*, *irresponsibility*, and **untrustworthiness** which constitutes him as obedient to God as a "babe" in Christ, it is just as a regenerate man can turn from *holiness* into **unholiness**, *spirituality* into *carnality*, *light* into *darkness*, *sight* into *blindness*, *righteousness* into *sin*, likewise therefore, they can turn from the spiritually *perfect* or *mature* man into *baby children* – from *wisdom* into *foolishness*. This putting off of the *new man* and putting on of the *old man* is a putting off of Christ, and "of Him are ye in Christ Jesus, Who of God is made unto us **wisdom**, and righteousness, and sanctification, and redemption" (1 Cor. 1:30). To put off *Christ* is to put off *wisdom*, and to put on the *old man* is to put on *foolishness*.

"…the rest were **blinded**…God hath given them **the spirit of slumber**, eyes that they should **not see**, and ears that they should **not hear**…" -Romans 11:7-8	→	"Stay yourselves, and wonder; **CRY** ye out, and **CRY**: they are **drunken**, but not with wine; they **stagger**, but not with strong drink. For the LORD hath poured out upon you **the spirit of deep sleep**, and hath **closed your eyes**: the prophets and your rulers, the seers hath he covered." -Isaiah 29:9-10
"For this people's heart is waxed gross, and *their* ears are **dull of hearing**, and their eyes they have closed; lest at any time they should see with *their* eyes, and hear with *their* ears, and should understand with *their* heart, and should be converted, and I should heal them" – Matthew 13:15	→	"Dull of Hearing" – Heb. 5:11

Are you beginning to see what the NT writers were referencing when they used such vocabulary as we have, heretofore, been biblically defining? Are you discovering how the Bible interprets itself? These baby children are incapacitated from a saving relationship with God. They are said to be overcome in the very same state that Christ said was a damnable, **blinding, darkness** upon the Jews – "their ears are **dull of hearing**" (Matt. 13:15) = "**dull of hearing**" (Heb. 5:11) – which is the same state which was just previously addressed, called *spiritual sleep*, or in Romans

11:7-8, "**the spirit of slumber**." How is it so? These regenerate Christians have become woeful babies – now they are blind, darkened, famished, starving, spiritually drunk, and utterly incapacitated under a delusion from God – where **saving wisdom** is utterly **hidden** from them! Are these understandable parallels to you, my reader? So also it is comparably parallel to see that spiritual infants are spiritually incapacitated like spiritual drunkards. Think about these two individuals still more: Children are utterly incapacitated, for, they have no able "senses", and why? Their mind is underdeveloped so that they cannot "discern both good and evil" (Heb. 5:11-14). They have underdeveloped organs and no teeth, which means, if they were served strong foods or meats then they would choke on it or vomit it up, as they would be unable to chew it or digest it. They are those who cannot bear to eat meat. They are cast upon the only hope of life, which is, the breasts of a woman for milk, and their minds and memories are underdeveloped so that they *easily forget* about things. This is as 2 Peter 1:9 states: "he hath **forgotten** that he was purged from his old sins," or as James 1:24 puts it, he "beholdeth" himself in a mirror and then "goeth his way, and straightway **forgetteth**" what he saw. Their eyes are underdeveloped, and literally, they "cannot see afar off" (2 Peter 1:9)! Babies can see things only if they are right in front of their face. They have as much capability to see as a full-grown man who has "pricks in [his] eyes," which, again, is an OT parallel to the NT spiritual experience of a blind babe (Num. 33:55). "But whoso looketh into the perfect law of liberty, and continueth therein, he being not **a forgetful hearer**, but a doer of the work, this man shall be blessed in his deed" (James 1:25). A man dull of hearing is a forgetful hearer, a "foolish man," and Jesus Christ said, "every one that heareth these sayings of Mine, and doeth them not, shall be likened unto **a foolish man**, which built his house upon sand: And the rain descended, and the floods came, and the winds blew, and beat upon that house; and it fell: and great was the fall of it" (Matt. 7:26-27).

What is the bottom line? Babies need milk so that they can *develop* and *grow*, and when they grow, then they are made more able to stand against all of the opposing forces which assail regenerate Christians, namely, "every wind of doctrine by the slight of men, and cunning craftiness, whereby they lie in wait to deceive" (Eph. 4:14). Those who fall away are rendered unstable by the winds of the devil's doctrines, and again it is clearly stated, these men are said to be "**the children**" who are "tossed to and fro and carried about with every wind," because they have fallen from the state of "**a perfect man**" (Eph. 4:13). They are in need of the ministrations of grace by preaching (like the giving of milk) which is to the "**perfecting of the saints**" (Eph. 4:12). Do you see the *perfect* parallels addressed thus far?

"Babes in Christ" → (1 Cor. 3:1-2)	Paul says, "I have fed you milk" → (1 Cor. 3:1-2)	That they might become "them that ar perfect" (1 Cor. 2:6)
"He is a Babe" → (Heb. 5:12-13)	Paul says, is in "need of milk" → (Heb. 5:12-13)	That they might "go on unto perfection" (Heb. 6:1)
"Children" → (Eph. 4:14)	Paul says, are in need of "perfecting" → (Eph. 4:12)	That they might become "a perfect man" (Eph. 4:13)

Just as it was written in the OT concerning the necessity of *knowledge*, *doctrine*, and *wisdom* for salvation, so it is with these baby children. Children are tossed to and fro by every wind, which is to say they are being deceived by men "because they have no knowledge" (Isa. 5:13). "Therefore my people are gone into captivity, because they have no **knowledge**: and their honourable men are famished, and their multitude dried up with thirst" (Isaiah 5:13), God says. The time, when there is "no truth, nor mercy, nor knowledge of God in the land" (Hos. 4:1), is a terrible woe! God says, "My people are destroyed for **lack of knowledge**: because thou hast **rejected knowledge**, I will also reject thee, that thou shalt be no priest to Me: seeing thou hast forgotten the law of thy God, I will also forget thy children" (Hos. 4:6). "The people that doth not **understand** shall fall" because they are those which "commit whoredom" (Hos. 4:14). In such a way, "Whoredom and wine and new wine take away the heart" (Hos. 4:11), and children are taken in spiritual adulteries against God – becoming *carnal, worldly, enemies* of God (James 4:4).

"A reed shaken by the wind" – Matthew 11:7
"Being rooted and grounded in love" – Eph. 3:17
"Rooted and built up in him" – Col. 2:7
"Grow up" – Eph. 4:15

Baby children are underdeveloped and easily moved like the planting of a very young and feeble reed, shaken by the wind. They have need of growth like as a reed is in need of growth; otherwise it is helplessly moved by the winds of deceit and false doctrine. A man will be saved only **if**, the Bible says, "If ye continue in the faith **grounded** and **settled**, and be **not moved away** from the hope of the gospel, which ye have heard, and which was preached to every creature which is under heaven; whereof I Paul am made a minister" (Col. 1:23). If a man becomes shallow-rooted (Mark. 4:6), or in other words, without the rooting and grounding necessary (Eph. 3:17, Col. 1:23, 2:6), then they will "endure but for a time" (Mark. 4:17) instead of **to the end**. But Christ declares: "he that **endureth to the end** shall be saved" (Matt. 10:22). As reeds without deep root do shake and turn with every wind, so do baby children, and as children are tossed to and fro, so are drunken men.

Ephesians 4:1-6 calls for worthiness of Christian vocation in being *perfect* in *God's unity* and *oneness*, which means that Christians should be unified and one with one another, as the Trinity is unified and one with One Another. These verses (4:1-6) press upon the reader the shamefulness of disunity, showing how it is the inevitable woe of infant delinquency. According to Ephesians 4:11-16, babies are incapacitated from saving oneness with God, and therefore, incapacitated from saving oneness with the brethren in God. This pattern of addressing perfect oneness (Eph. 4:1-6) was for the purpose of leading into a focused address of individual and corporate perfection (Eph. 4:12-13), making plain for the reader exactly what is gained by perfection and lost by infancy. All of this is meant to enforce the strength of rebuke upon spiritual infants (here called "children" in Eph. 4:14). This very same pattern can be seen in 1 Peter 1:13-17 and 1 Peter 1:18-25, both of which prepare the reader for the rebuke of spiritual infants (here called "newborn babes" in 1 Pet. 2:2).

1 Peter 1:13-2:11 is the last passage in the NT, which we have yet to address with closeness, of those passages which directly focus upon the spiritual condition of infancy by name. 1 Peter 1:13-17 calls for the worthiness of *perfection* in *God's holiness*, 1 Peter 1:18-25 calls for the worthiness of *perfection* in *God's eternality* (or unfailing power and love), and like as Ephesians 4, the "newborn babes" of 1 Peter 2:1-2 are utterly delinquent and wildly transgressing the graces of God for perfection. Even though perfection is not explicitly mentioned in 1 Peter 1:13-17 or 1 Peter 1:18-25, the principles of perfection are carefully taught and applied. Henceforth, the apostle Peter calls for a calling which was first preached by the prophet Isaiah. To understand this, it is best to read the passages side by side:

Isaiah 8:13-22

"Sanctify the LORD of hosts himself; and let him be your fear, and let him be your dread. And **He shall be for a Sanctuary; but for a Stone of stumbling and for a Rock of offence to both the houses of Israel**, for a gin and for a snare to the inhabitants of Jerusalem. And many among them shall stumble, and fall, and be broken, and be snared, and be taken. **Bind up the testimony, seal the law among my disciples.** And I will wait upon the LORD, that hideth His face from the house of Jacob, and I will look for him. Behold, I and the children whom the LORD hath given me are for signs and for wonders in Israel from the LORD of hosts, which dwelleth in mount Zion. And when they shall say unto you, Seek unto them that have familiar spirits, and unto wizards that peep, and that mutter: should not a people seek unto their God? for the living to the dead? To the law and to the testimony: if they speak not according to this word, it is because there is **no light in them**. And they shall pass through it, hardly bestead and hungry: and it shall come to pass, that when they shall be hungry, they shall fret themselves, and curse their king and their God, and look upward. And they shall look unto the earth; and behold trouble and darkness, dimness of anguish; and they shall be driven to darkness."

1 Peter 2:1-10

"Wherefore laying aside all malice, and all guile, and hypocrisies, and envies, and all evil speakings, As newborn babes, desire the sincere milk of the word, that ye may grow thereby: If so be ye have tasted that the Lord is gracious. To whom coming, as unto **a Living Stone, disallowed indeed of men**, but **chosen of God**, and precious, Ye also, **as lively stones**, are **built up a spiritual house, an holy priesthood, to offer up spiritual sacrifices, acceptable to God by Jesus Christ.** Wherefore also it is contained in the scripture, Behold, I lay in Sion a Chief Corner Stone, elect, precious: and he that believeth on Him shall not be confounded. Unto you therefore which believe He is precious: but unto them which be disobedient, the Stone which the builders disallowed, the same is made the Head of the Corner, And a Stone of stumbling, and a Rock of offence, even to them which stumble at the word, being disobedient: whereunto also they were appointed. But ye are a chosen generation, a royal priesthood, an holy nation, a peculiar people; **that ye should shew forth the praises of him who hath called you out of darkness into his marvellous light**: Which in time past were not a people, but are now the people of God: which had not obtained mercy, but now have obtained mercy."

What was prophesied in Isaiah 8:13-22 has come to pass, and it is recited by Peter as a calling of continual relevance for all regenerate Christians, and thus it is re-urged upon the disciples of Christ in this letter - disciples who, unlike the heathen, have been brought out of the darkness. This call out of darkness (Isa. 8:17, 20, 22) is a call, namely, that worthily joins the regenerate saints with Christ in His reproach, rejection, suffering, and humiliation, which simultaneously, joins them with His glory, grace, hallowedness, sanctity, Divine-acceptance, and Divine-Building – The Temple – being built together in saving connection with Him. A man must therefore "purge himself" from defilement and darkness (Eph. 5:7-11), including those who are in darkness (2 Cor. 6:14-7:1), and "he shall be a vessel unto honour, sanctified, and meet for the Master's use, and prepared unto every good work" (2 Tim. 2:20-21). As Christ was disallowed, we must become "as He is" (1 Jn. 4:17, 2:6), that we might be a "lively stone" as He was "a Living Stone" (perfection in His rejection). Our rejection by worldlings verifies the ceremonial right of our communion and connection with God's House, meaning that we are not in darkness but separate from it – Hallelujah! – and to all of such positional and spiritual grace God says, "I will receive you" (2 Cor. 6:17)! Therefore we are called out of darkness in how we are rejected by it, and likewise we don't have fellowship with it (Eph. 5:11); herein we stand as a holy priesthood in the praises of God's preciousness in light! This priesthood has been "called out of darkness into His marvellous light" (1 Pet. 2:9), and we can see this calling out of darkness expressly prophesied in Isaiah 8:13-22. Rejection is the priestly attire and robes of acceptance wherewith God calleth His children – "Come unto Me." Therefore "we have an altar, whereof they have no right to eat which serve **the Tabernacle**. For the bodies of those beasts, whose blood is brought into the sanctuary by the high priest for sin, are burned without the camp. Wherefore Jesus also, that He might sanctify the people with his own blood, suffered without the gate. **Let us go forth therefore unto Him without the camp, bearing His reproach.** For here have we no continuing city, but we seek one to come. **By Him therefore let us offer the sacrifice of praise to God continually**, that is, the fruit of our lips giving thanks to His Name" (Heb. 13:10-15).

Do you see the exact call of 1 Peter 2:1-10? It is a call for priestly veracity, for living stones for a living building in God's presence, beautified for a display of His praise, and those worthy of this are made worthy through saving faith and repentance – or perfection – which enables God to show the world His "praises" through you (1 Pet. 2:9), even "the stature of the fulness of Christ" (Eph. 4:13)! Only one thing remaineth, the conditions of perfection in the plethora of callings through gospel-grace, and thereby, God's people will be established in saving union with God. Then they, being built up in Him, will shine forth for Him in the zenith of His glory to a dying world! The call for perfection and suffering CLIMAXES with God's happy acceptance of us, and He – the Builder – will join us to His Name, stature, and praise, so that, worthily, we shall be the famed and world-renown House of God (John 17:20-26, Eph. 4:12-13, 1 Pet. 2:9).

Men heavenly-wise, God's robes despised, for rags-carnality

God's fools they were, clad in promises sure, they captives-were-made-free
But turned back again, against Christ's surety – sinned – and will not bow the knee
God's way is mocked, the apostles left shocked, and who can make babies see?
Wisdom is sealed, and understanding locked, they're unprepared for eternity
In a baby's crib, by false prophets rocked, they're thoughtlessly dreaming foolishly.
((1 Cor. 2:6, 3:1, 3:3-4) (1 Cor. 3:17-18) (1 Cor. 4:8) (1 Cor. 4:18-21, 2 Cor. 13:7)
(1 Cor. 2:6-3:3))

Are you the man, clothed in earth, His Temple to defile?
Then you, be sure, no change from this, you'll perish in the fire.
But others, who, in furnace go, will come out more entire,
Because, like gold, the flames perfect, more purity to admire,
And these, God chooses, to array – He found them not a liar.
((2 Tim. 2:20-21) (Jer. 6:28-30) (James 1:3-4) (1 Pet. 1:7) (Isa. 63:8))

Heaven's rain, upon cursed men, worsens the pain in the latter end,
Because they, a field, of open earth, drank heaven's rain of life-giving worth,
And to what end? Against His grace they sinned – walking unworthily.
Behold then – God – His frowning face, over a field that yielded thorns for grace
This, God watches, and He waits, His longstanding patience to tire,
For they aren't right, in Heaven's sight, they think of Him a liar,
Until, alas, their destined fate – a burning and unquenchable fire.
((2 Pet. 2:20) (Heb. 6:8) (Heb. 6:8) (2 Pet. 3:9, Jer. 15:6) (1 Jn. 5:10))

These, evil souls, to hell will go, and shall deeper torments know,
Because, they did, the Savior believe, and His graces happily receive,
But now, they hold, Him as a liar – they are destined for the fires,
God's sons, they were, but now 'tis sure, they are unsavable backsliders.
((Heb. 3:12)(1 Jn. 5:10))

The House of God is not built with stubble, hay, and earth,
But gold, silver, and precious worth.
The stones twinkle and glow, in a glory alien to earth,
Showing "forth the praises" of the second birth.
((1 Cor. 3:12-15)(1 Pet. 2:9, Eph. 4:13))

Out of darkness called, from sin cast away, such men are received by God,
Stones disallowed, by sinners make, the precious Temple of God.
Forsaken by, worldly-wise fools – the angels stand and applaud
You're fitly joined, to Christ Who is, the forsaken Wisdom of God.
((1 Pet. 2:9, 2 Thess. 1:4-5)(1 Pet. 2:4-8)(Lk. 10:21)(Isa. 8:14-16))

Are you the Lord's, recognizable son, because you are glorified in His Image?

Are you His choice stone, heaven-hallowed in light, set in His House for His Visage?
Are you His comfortable, garden increase, bearing gladsome fruits for His Vintage?
((Rom. 8:29, 36, Heb. 11:16, 13:10-16, 1 Pet. 2:21)(Rev. 21:9-22)(John 15:7-27))

Or are you strangling thorns which devour heavenly rain,
Unsalvageable metals which in the fires remain,
With the crackling thorns on cursed fields the same?
((Heb. 6:8)(Ezekiel 22:17-22)(Eccl. 7:6))

The Book of HEBREWS

Hebrews 5:11-14	→	**A Babe's Delinquency** A Historical Parallel to God's Divine curse is in reference: they are "dull of hearing" (Matt. 13:15, Rom. 11:7-8). They are described as those who are "dull of hearing", which is imprisonment in a heart without "repentance" and "faith" (Heb. 6:1); therefore they are unable to "discern both good and evil" in the sense of saving repentance and faith.
Hebrews 6:1	→	**Fallen from Perfection**
Hebrews 6:3-6	→	Recovery is unsure – damnation is the sure threat, and possibly, the inevitable end
Hebrews 6:7-8	→	**Typological Parallel** – an effort to show the shamefulness of the estate Babes are described to be as a field of unworthy yield given the most valuable and life-giving rain of salvation (a rain which is biblically famed as salvific: Acts 2:16-21, Joel 2:28-32). The charging demand and hopeful call of God is: a demand of "perfect" (Lk. 8:14) fruitfulness worthy of so great a rain-shower's wealth (Heb. 6:7-8). The THREAT – Babes, like the thorny field, are worthy to burn in fire.

The Book of 1st CORINTHAINS

1 Corinthians 2:1-3:3	→	**A Babe's Delinquency** Typological Parallel is used: the laws of *revelation* and *hiding*, which are like the laws of *light* and *darkness*, or *God's Face revealed* and *turned away*, therefore babes are lost because, for them, wisdom is "hidden," for they are

		yet "not able to bear it."
1 Corinthians 2:6	→	**Fallen from Perfection**
1 Corinthians 3:12-23	→	Typological Parallel – an effort to show the shamefulness of the estate The typology in view is in reference to **The Temple of God** : Babes are of such a condition that they are unworthy vessels, defiling and unholy vessels which defile the house of God (called wood, hay, stubble, and earth), and for God's House, God demands stones which do not defile, stones that are not worldly-wise, spiritual-fools. The THREAT – Babes, like the defiling vessels, are worthy to burn in fire ("him shall God destroy" - 3:17). Note: The value, preciousness, and acceptance of the stone is on this basis: is it worldly-wise or godly-wise?
1 Corinthians 3:15-18	→	Recovery is Unsure – damnation is the sure threat, and possibly, the inevitable end (not all are saved by the fires).
1 Corinthians 4:8-21	→	Threat to Chasten the Babes – because they are worldly-wise and rejecting the suffering of God's wisdom

The Book of EPHESIANS

Ephesians 4:1-6	→	Perfection in God's Unity – an effort to show the shamefulness of perfection lost
Ephesians 4:12-13	→	Perfection results in the zenith of God's glory – "the stature of the fulness of Christ"
Ephesians 4:14-15	→	A Babe's Delinquency – those who are fallen from perfection (vv. 12-13), who are not, therefore, unified with the brethren and built up to God's glory. They are rather, "tossed to and fro", which is a reference of a Typological Parallel (planting, grounding, and rooting unto a saving establishment in the gospel), and they are not grounded – meaning that they are deceived from "the truth" that is "in love".
Ephesians 4:16	→	Typological Parallel – we should be nourished through oneness, like as a body is joined together and thus flourishes. Note: The bodily connection of togetherness is a metaphorical parallel to **the building of the Temple**, which, as well, has been

		aforementioned in Ephesians 2:19-22.

The Book of 1st PETER

1 Peter 1:13-17	→	**Perfection in God's Holiness** – an effort to show the shamefulness of perfection lost
1 Peter 1:18-25	→	**Perfection in God's Eternality** – and effort to show the shamefulness of perfection lost
1 Peter 2:1-3	→	**A Babe's Delinquency** – those who are fallen from perfection Babes do therefore abide in a state of unholiness (1:13-17), being without steadfastness (1:18-25), and therefore they have such damnable fruits as described (1 Pet. 2:1), and being thus, they are accepted by the world and rejected by God – contrary to their calling (see 1 Peter 2:4-8) – when they should be rejected by the world and accepted by God, or, as another typological parallel so calls it, staying out of darkness and showing forth the praises of the Light (1 Pet. 2:9).
1 Peter 2:4-8	→	**Typological Parallel** – an effort to show the shamefulness of the estate The typology in view is in reference to **The Temple of God** : which demands elect, precious, and lively stones, and babes are of no such worthiness. Note: The value, preciousness, and acceptance of the stone is on this basis: is it like Christ and therefore disallowed of men, or in other words, is it worldly-wise or godly-wise? One cannot be savingly connected to Christ – the Living Stone – if he is not like Christ, who was and is disallowed and rejected of men. And if one cannot be savingly connected to Christ, the Chief Corner Stone, then he cannot be a stone for the Temple of God's glory. *A call to be acceptable stones of **the Temple**
1 Peter 2:9-10	→	**Typological Parallel** – we should be arrayed in glory and duty as God's priestly ministers of old *A call to be acceptable ministers of **the Temple** (in the light so as to show God's praise).
		Perfection results in the zenith of

407

| 1 Peter 2:9 | → | God's glory – "the praises of Him" are shown forth and revealed, exactly as Ephesians 4:13 describes "the stature of the fulness of Christ." |
| 1 Peter 2:4-9 | → | **Typological & Historical Parallel** established in Isaiah 8:13-22 – the calling from darkness to light, worldly-wise to God's wisdom, earthly acceptance to earthly rejection, unacceptable stones to acceptable stones, all of which are fit for **the Temple's building**. |

For those regenerate men who still need a restoration from infant delinquency, from a fallen condition of imperfection in grace, they must be striven with by those who are right with God! The call to CRY out against the babes, to be their holy conflict – this is THE ROD for the baby-fools – and by this redemptive plan we must engage them, if so be they may be saved. However, let us be prepared to suffer, for this conflict will result in what Paul and Peter described as spiritual honor by earthly rejection (1 Cor. 4:8-17, 2 Cor. 4:8-18, 6:3-10, 11:23-33, 1 Peter 2:1-25, 3:8-17, 4:1-19). Henceforth unto the end of this chapter, we must examine this biblical method of salvation for infants. This is a method which is rightly named – "At Midnight There Was A **Cry** Made" (Matt. 25:6, Isa. 29:9)! – a method Paul calls God's Rod upon the baby children.

The ROD

"A whip for the horse, a bridle for the ass, and a **rod** for the fool's back" (Prov. 26:3).

"As a dog returneth to his vomit, so a **fool** returneth to his folly" (Prov. 26:11).

"In the lips of him that hath understanding **wisdom** is found:
but a **rod** is for the back of him that is **void of understanding**" (Prov. 10:13).

"The **wisdom** of the **prudent** is to **understand his way**: but the folly of **fools** is **deceit**" (Prov. 14:8).

There is a time when a true pastor does approach the flock of God with an intimidating "heaviness" (2 Cor. 2:1). The heaviness comes from a God-placed burden, and the pastor continues, without relief, until those persons, for whom the burden is, are pressed down with the holy matter. What was Paul's burden in the aforementioned verse citation? He was burdened by the wicked backslidings of regenerate believers in Corinth. Paul was spiritually heavy because the people were carnally light. The spiritual condition of the people was a grave and eternally dangerous dilemma. Paul was heavy because if the Corinthians woke up to their spiritual condition, they – themselves – would suddenly "let [their] laughter be turned to mourning, and [their] joy to heaviness" (James 4:9)! Pastors ought to always come to the flock and find gladness and happiness by their presence, but not so if they are, at present, held in the gall of sin and the web of iniquity (2 Cor. 2:1-4). Though Paul would come in personal "heaviness" (2 Cor. 2:1), it was not unmixed with "anguish of heart", "many tears", and "much affliction" (2 Cor. 2:4). Though Paul threatens that his coming is with "heaviness", "power", "the ROD" (2 Cor. 4:18-21), and unsparing judgments (2 Cor. 13:1-5), before his arrival and upon it, and during the wielding of such a beating that the ROD of God would inflict, Paul said, "I shall bewail many which have sinned already, and have not repented..." (2 Cor. 12:21). Whether weeping, or a heavy countenance which delivered pride-breaking words like a rod to the back of fools, Paul was in the Spirit of true, holy, pure, and jealous love (2 Cor. 11:2-3). My reader, this message was of similar force – as a rod upon the foolish – but before the rod did lash, the Spirit of God did cause me to weep in anguish of heart...thus I entreat you now, do not murmur against the beating lest, if haply, you need it. The rod is not an instrument of meekness and gentleness, as Paul said, "What will ye? Shall I come unto you with a rod, or in love, and in the spirit of meekness" (1 Cor. 4:21). God's word, spoken by God's Spirit, can only be heard by God-given ears. "He that hath an ear, let him hear what the Spirit saith unto the Churches" (Rev. 3:22). Such a Spirit, heretofore described, did seize me with anguish of heart and weeping in the opening prayer of this message... and then, the same grace which seized me at the first, did cause me to stand up and deliver this beating by God's holy rod - see the following sermon.

RELATED SERMONS
"Opening Prayer"
"The Rod" – Sean Morris

When a Christian did backslide into a blamable state (fallen from **perfection**, **light**, **sobriety**, **seeing**, **hearing**, and **faith**), then the apostles did undertake the same redemptive action as actual parents would to a baby child bound on the broad way to hell – THE ROD. Children deny their parents as fools deny God (Ps. 14:1, 53:1). Children that are left unrestrained in their foolishness are a grief to their parents (Prov. 17:25, 19:13, 29:15); even so, adult men allow their infantile foolishness to rule their adult bodies unto the grief of the Arch-Adult, their Creator

(Prov. 17:25, 19:13, Eph. 4:30). Children hate knowledge and love foolishness. They are, therefore, **unteachable** and **unlearned**, until growth develops the capacities which enable one to **learn** matters of **grave responsibility**, weighty **knowledge**, or that which God calls saving **wisdom** & **doctrine**. They can no more learn *saving doctrine* and *wisdom* than **a baby child can eat meat**. They do therefore need the ROD.

> "Now some are puffed up, as though I would not come to you. But I will come to you shortly, if the Lord will, and will know, not the speech of them which are puffed up, but the power. For the kingdom of God is not in word, but in power. What will ye? Shall I come unto you with **a ROD**, <u>or</u> **in love**, and **in the spirit of meekness?**" (1Co 4:18-21)

Just as the scriptures do teach that children need a rod, so Paul said to the backslidden, baby Christians of Corinth – "shall I come unto you with **a ROD**, <u>or</u> **in love**, and **in the spirit of meekness**" (1 Cor. 4:21)? "The rod" is directly opposite to the expression of tender "love" and gentle "meekness"! Please understand this! This time which Paul was warning of, wherein he needed to use "a ROD" rather than a "spirit of meekness," IS NOT the same circumstance that calls for "all longsuffering and doctrine" (2 Tim. 4:2), "patient," an "apt to teach" mentality that is "gentle unto all men," or a "meekness instructing" mentality, as 2 Timothy 2:24-25 so clearly outlines. Please don't mistake me, 2 Tim. 2:24-25 is not to be nullified or made void…all longsuffering, patient, gentle, and meek teaching and instruction must be first accomplished, and then, if all of this does fail, or the severity of the sin at hand does demand otherwise, which is exactly the situation Paul was dealing with, then he speaks of the time of the ROD, declaring that, it is the opposite of what is understood to be meekness and gentleness. Saints will waver or totter from the way of holiness, but if they are seeking God with a broken heart and willing mind, so as to bear the first fruits of repentance, the circumstance would allow for meek instruction and gentle teaching. However, if a man is not repentant, is unwilling to follow God in some way, to the degree where they are falling into a damnable condition… my reader! This is a time, not of meekness or gentleness, but rather authoritative, judgmental (2 Cor. 13:1) preaching according to the power of God (2 Cor. 13:4), which is, namely, the power to excommunicate if repentance is not obtained (2 Cor. 13:2). This mind and heart of the apostle Paul, which was forewarned of in 1 Corinthians 4:18-21, did eventually come upon the Corinthians in 2 Corinthians 12:20-13:11:

> "<u>For I fear, lest, when I come, I shall not find you such as I would</u>, and **that I shall be found unto you such as ye would not**: lest there be debates, envyings, wraths, strifes, backbitings, whisperings, swellings, tumults: And lest, when I come again, my God will humble me among you, and **that I shall bewail many which have sinned already**, and have not repented of the

410

uncleanness and fornication and lasciviousness which they have committed. This is the third time I am coming to you. In the mouth of two or three witnesses shall every word be established. I told you before, and foretell you, as if I were present, the second time; and being absent now I write to them which heretofore have sinned, and to all other, that, if I come again, I will not spare: Since ye seek a proof of Christ speaking in me, which to you-ward is not weak, but is mighty in you. For though He was crucified through weakness, yet He liveth by the power of God. For we also are weak in Him, but we shall live with Him by the power of God toward you. **Examine yourselves, whether ye be in the faith; prove your own selves**. Know ye not your own selves, how that Jesus Christ is in you, **except ye be reprobates**? But I trust that ye shall know that we are not **reprobates**. Now I pray to God that ye do no evil; not that we should appear approved, but that ye should do that which is honest, though we be as reprobates. For we can do nothing against the truth, but for the truth. For we are glad, when we are weak, and ye are strong: and this also we wish, even your **perfection**. Therefore I write these things being absent, lest being present I should use sharpness, according to the power which the Lord hath given me to edification, and not to destruction. Finally, brethren, farewell. Be **perfect**, be of good comfort, be of one mind, live in peace; and the God of love and peace shall be with you" (2 Corinthians 12:20-13:11).

Paul was forewarning them that he was coming to them a third time, and Paul had heard that many had not repented of specific sins which he had dealt with already (see how Paul names them in 2 Cor. 12:20-21). As a parent does not want to beat his child with a rod, Paul acknowledged the likelihood of his arrival that, he said, "I shall not find you such as I would" (2 Cor. 12:20). As a child does not want to be beaten by a rod, as his little face is cast down at the sight of an approaching parent who knows of rebellion worthy of the rod, even so, Paul said that he was coming to Corinth, and that, "I shall be found unto you such as ye would not" (2 Cor. 12:10). The Corinthians had become foolishness-bound baby children, in need of the "rod of correction" (Prov. 22:15). By this point, their "foolishness" had become infamous, and with long instruction it had been denounced and rebuked, and, lo, it was still "bound in the heart of the child" (Prov. 22:15)! Paul painstakingly exposed the "foolishness" of the gospel-gate ("the strait gate") and the narrow way, or in other words, initial regeneration by a personal crucifixion, and the path of morality of the cross-bearing, self-denying disciples in Christ! The 1st and 2nd chapters of 1 Corinthians do deal directly with the Corinthian foolishness, and how they had been disqualified from the wisdom of God. Do you see how spiritual fools do need the ROD? Trace with me this thematic vein throughout the 1st and 2nd letters to the Corinthians, so that 2 Corinthians 12:20-13:11 is properly contextualized.

In 1 Corinthians chapters 1-2, Paul preached to them under a burden to make plain how the Corinthians had become spiritual fools. To become a spiritual fool is, in other words, to be worldly-wise, when the Corinthians should rather have been spiritually wise men who are worldly fools, because God's wisdom is at enmity to worldly wisdom. Paul continued with the same burden into 1 Corinthians chapter 3, emphatically declaring a reaching-out, rescue cry to the worldly-wise, sin-bound Corinthians – "Let no man deceive himself. If any among you seemeth to be wise in this world, let him become a fool, that he may be wise. For the wisdom of this world is foolishness with God. For it is written, He taketh the wise in their own craftiness. And again, The Lord knoweth the thoughts of the wise, that they are vain" (1 Cor. 3:18-20).

Paul continued with the same burden into 1 Corinthians chapter 4, and here he descriptively compared two courses of "Christian" morality – the worldly-wise interpretation of Christian morality in comparison with the worldly-foolish (God's wisdom) interpretation of Christian morality. Paul explained how circumstantial prosperity, peace, and honor is, in the heathen's eyes (worldly, carnal wisdom), the greatest indicator of favor from God, and the absence of these things is suggested as the consequences of rebellion, wickedness, and backsliding. Paul reproved his spiritual children in that they had forsaken the ways of their spiritual father, and those of Jesus Christ, and he said – "We are **fools** for Christ's sake, but ye are **wise** in Christ, we are **weak**, but ye are **strong**; ye are **honourable**, but we are **despised** … **buffeted** … **reviled** … **persecuted** … **defamed**…and…**made as filth**" (1 Cor. 4:10-13). Salvation for the Corinthians would be a turning around, turning their morality upside down, and a following after the ways of God exemplified in Paul (spiritual wisdom instead of worldly wisdom, making them spiritual men instead of carnal Christian men). Thus Paul commanded them, "be ye followers of me…of my ways which be in Christ, as I teach every where in every Church" (1 Cor. 4:16-17). Do you think that Paul was convinced that "foolishness was bound in the heart" of his spiritual children (Prov. 22:15)? Paul knew that false prophets had deceived the Corinthians to believe in and follow after a worldly-wise pseudo-Christian morality. In 2 Corinthians, he called them out on several fronts (2 Cor. 10:12, 11:3-33). How sad it is that Corinth did "suffer fools gladly" and forsake the wise way of salvation (2 Cor. 11:19), and that they were pushed to the verge of forsaking the apostle Paul altogether! Paul responded in heartfelt agony, saying, "Now I pray to God that ye do no evil; not that we should appear approved, but that ye should do that which is honest, though we be as reprobates" (2 Cor. 13:7). With all of this in mind, we are brought to the climactic passage of 2 Corinthians 12:20-13:11, referenced here again for your review:

> "For I fear, lest, when I come, I shall not find you such as I
> would, and **that I shall be found unto you such as ye would
> not**: lest there be debates, envyings, wraths, strifes, backbitings,
> whisperings, swellings, tumults: And lest, when I come again, my
> God will humble me among you, and **that I shall bewail many**

which have sinned already, and have not repented of the
uncleanness and fornication and lasciviousness which they have
committed. This is the third time I am coming to you. In the
mouth of two or three witnesses shall every word be established.
I told you before, and foretell you, as if I were present, the second
time; and being absent now I write to them which heretofore have
sinned, and to all other, that, if I come again, I will not spare:
Since ye seek a proof of Christ speaking in me, which to you-
ward is not weak, but is mighty in you. For though He was
crucified through weakness, yet He liveth by the power of God.
For we also are weak in Him, but we shall live with Him by the
power of God toward you. **Examine yourselves, whether ye be
in the faith; prove your own selves**. Know ye not your own
selves, how that Jesus Christ is in you, **except ye be reprobates**?
But I trust that ye shall know that we are not **reprobates**. Now I
pray to God that ye do no evil; not that we should appear
approved, but that ye should do that which is honest, though we
be as reprobates. For we can do nothing against the truth, but for
the truth. For we are glad, when we are weak, and ye are strong:
and this also we wish, even your **perfection**. Therefore I write
these things being absent, lest being present I should use
sharpness, according to the power which the Lord hath given me
to edification, and not to destruction. Finally, brethren, farewell.
Be **perfect**, be of good comfort, be of one mind, live in peace;
and the God of love and peace shall be with you" (2 Corinthians
12:20-13:11).

As a parent will not spare for the crying of his child who is being beaten
under the rod, even so, Paul would "not spare" (2 Cor. 13:2) the Corinthians. Paul
was coming to examine their faith! He forewarned them to examine their own faith
before his arrival (2 Cor. 13:5), to prepare them, if haply, they might be brought into
agreement with a potential conclusion that Paul would test and conclude upon them
all – that if they could not repent of the sins which were aforementioned, then, lo,
they would be "reprobates" who failed the test on whether, Paul said, "Jesus Christ is
in you." (2 Cor. 13:5). The greatest evidence that Jesus Christ is in a man is present
progressive repentance from sin (Matt. 18:15-17); hence, if a man can't repent, then
he is not presently considered as a saved man – one whom is lawfully and spiritually
possessed by the Spirit of Jesus Christ. Upon Paul's arrival, he was going to test and
find out all unrepentant men, that he might then put them under the rod of
excommunication. In this way, the whole Church (and especially Paul) was
"punishing" and "inflicting" the wayward children (2 Cor. 2:6) with the ROD.
Excommunication is called "punishment" and "infliction" in 2 Corinthians 2:6, which
is in reference to when they excommunicated the man spoken of in 1 Corinthians
chapter 5. Paul said that he "judged" this man with "the power of the Lord Jesus,"
and through excommunication, the man was delivered over to "Satan for the

destruction of the flesh, that the spirit may be saved in the day of the Lord Jesus" (1 Cor. 5:5). This is the hope that comes with using the beating ROD of rebuke and "sharpness" (2 Cor. 13:10), or the rod of excommunication, that it will save these wayward children and drive the damnable foolishness away from them. You see, my reader, the use of the rod that Paul was speaking of is the very same context as the use of the rod for the foolishness-bound, fallen, unregenerate children of literal, physical Israel. Both cases are a damnable condition, persons whose only hope is the rod, and so Paul used it and spared not, only hoping for their repentance and faith to be restored. Restoration into a saving relationship with the Lord was his only wish, as Paul said, "and this also we wish, even your **perfection**" (2 Cor. 13:9).

To the flesh and the world, or might I say to the worldly-wise, backslidden Christian – Mercy is **gentleness**, compassion is **acceptance** and **tolerance**, and humility is a teachable spirit *always* ready and willing to unlearn obedience and relearn **compromise**. There is a place for gentleness, but not for the wicked and foolish (Christian or non-Christian). There is a place for compassion to motivate acceptance and tolerance (Jude 22), but not for the backslidden, carnal, wicked men who are strictly forbidden by God to go on without judgment. For then, this would be the toleration of a manner of sin which God warns is intolerable to overlook. Rather, true compassion and love *in these circumstances* is **heaviness** (2 Cor. 2:1), **chastening** (Rev. 3:19), **the rod** instead of a **spirit of meekness** (1 Cor. 4:18-21), **sharpness** (2 Cor. 13:10, Gal. 4:20, Titus 1:13), **punishment** through **affliction** instead of holy kisses (2 Cor. 2:6-8), and **separation** without **sparing** (2 Cor. 12:19-13:11). Such a man of God does just this! He is under the burden of God that professors of Christianity must prove their faith (2 Cor. 1:23-24, 2:9-10, 3:1-3, 6:3-4, 7:2, 11, 15-16, 8:6-9, 24, 9:8-10, chapter 10, 12:11-12, 12:19-13:4) or be **excommunicated without sparing** (2 Cor. 13:2). This form of pastoring is true love (1 Cor. 13:6). Practicing this judgment is a Christian soldier's decoration, even the medals of honor borne by our Lord and Captain - persecution, accusation, slander, hatred, and seditions (John 15:20, 2 Cor. 13:7). The wisdom of God standeth sure: "Open rebuke is better than secret love. Faithful are the wounds of a friend; but the kisses of an enemy are deceitful" (Prov. 27:5-6). To the feelings of the flesh, TRUE LOVE is painful, even as a wound.

Charity does not seek laughter for the guilty (James 4:9). True pastors seek the **godly sorrow** of the guilty (2 Cor. 7:8-10), that they would "be afflicted, and mourn, and weep" (Jas. 4:9). What do you expect to see when you look upon a true pastor in the hour of carnality and foolishness? Even the disposition of the pastor seems to cry out, "let your laughter be turned to mourning, and your joy to heaviness" (Jas. 4:9), as he visits, preaches to, exhorts, and rebukes the wayward ones. When have you ever seen a gentle lamb cast off its meek and gentle demeanor, rise up, and "beat" (Prov. 23:14) a man with a ROD? NEVER! But parents do this to their children (Prov. 23:14) as shepherds do to wayward sheep, and even more, shepherds do smite the wolves until they leave with shattered jaws and broken teeth. The true pastors are therefore grave in their communications with such persons who

414

are in spiritually foolish conditions, while other "pastors," other mock-ministers and the like, are deluded to think that **kindness** is **lightheartedness**. "I want to make them to feel comfortable with me," they say. "Heaviness will make the people think I am unkind instead of nice," they fear. "They can repent just after we play volleyball," they hope. Preacher! Your vain thoughts, your methodology, is a poisonous medicine for an already poisoned soul. You say – "I need to show them I care by playing games and rolling dice" – but this is a serpent's bite! You are sinking spiritual fangs into their flesh and your carnality is the venom, and God will make you pay the price! Alas! You are caught up in the foolishness of a child's mentality! You have become a child and adopted their methodology! Do you think I am kidding!? I am shocked and appalled at how many "Christian" groups do "ice break," playing funny games of ridiculous, idle, and childish entertainment, of such immaturity it feels like a children's school recess! Bankrupt of spiritual joy and Christ-centered edification, these spiritual counterfeits entertain themselves with idleness, with personalities and ironies. They have turned from blatant sin into Christless communities of "love" and "care" that are centered on men. They have half-repented into a morality of imitating Christ's commandments, and, lo, they are without Christ! Any passer-by who is full of the Holy Ghost would quickly detect that such a people are all blind to the invisible realm of spirituality in Christ. As sober as a soldier, lo, the man of God would retire to his closet in agony…

> "No preacher is going to skip into the pulpit with the "good news" that the church won the top honors in the interchurch bowling league if he has come from the closet of prayer with eternity blazing in his eyes." - Leonard Ravenhill

> "No preacher leaves the closet with a sweat on his soul and offers a world of rebels the feeble utterance, 'God loves you,' without also stating, 'God is angry with the wicked every day (Ps. 7:11).'"
> - Leonard Ravenhill

Pull out the rod, and a child will lose the smiles **fast**! Oh! Put the childish games aside! At this time a pastor is NOT even to behave in "meekness" toward the baby-man. It is not the hour of entreaties, but of "charges" and commands (1 Thess. 5:27, 1 Tim. 1:3, 5:7, 21, 6:17, 13, 2 Tim. 4:1). Nay, a true pastor does not show the face of toleration and acceptance if indeed the person is not being accepted by God. They don't just carry the message in word only, but in heart, and in "Spirit" (1 Cor. 2:4), so that they are under the power of the message. Even so, the message is rightly called a BURDEN! And therefore, their body language does speak the weighty words: "let your laughter be turned to mourning and your joy to heaviness" (Jas. 4:9). It is a countenance-sobering demeanor, downcasting the countenance of sinning-saints who are intoxicated in a Godless happiness. How sobering, how agonizing? How heavy is the prayer that Charles Wesley prayed for the wayward and backslidden children of God?

"O wouldst Thou break the fatal snare
Of carnal self-security,
And let them feel the wrath they bear,
And let them groan their want of Thee,
Robb'd of their false pernicious peace,
Stripp'd of their fancied righteousness.

"Long as the guilt of sin shall last,
Them in its misery detain;
Hold their licentious spirits fast,
Bind them with their own nature's chain,
Nor ever let the wanderers rest,
Till lodged again in Jesus' breast." – Charles Wesley

At such times, true pastors are neither laughing nor in lightness, and rather, they are in mourning and heaviness. Therein they do *feelingly* speak saving messages to backslidden fools, if haply, by God's intervening grace, the hearers might *feel* what they preach! Spurgeon believed that if what he preaches does burn in his heart, it is sure to burn in the hearts of the congregation that hears him. True charity feels the spiritual conditions at hand, and he reflects them by his demeanor, as it was written – "Remember them that are in bonds, **as bound with them**; and them which suffer adversity, **as being yourselves also in the body**" (Heb. 13:3). If you knew the balm of Gilead for sick souls, that it is for them to *mourn* and *weep*, then you would *mourn* and *weep* over them to help them *mourn* and *weep* for themselves! "Be afflicted, and mourn, and weep," Pastor James pled (Jas. 4:9)! Is this not why God commanded and compelled Ezekiel to "Sigh therefore, thou son of man, with the breaking of thy loins; and with bitterness sigh before their eyes" (Ezek. 21:6), for Ezekiel bore a message from God which, when the people heard it, and when it came to pass, "every heart shall melt, and all hands shall be feeble, and every spirit shall faint, and all knees shall be weak as water" (Ezek. 21:7). Let weeping Whitefield speak to you on the matter, and judge ye, my readers, what interpretation he took on how the God-sent messenger should pastor baby-child, backslidden, fools:

"Tremble for fear God should remove His candlestick from you. Labourers are sick. Those who did once labour are almost worn out... There are few who like to go out into the fields. Broken heads and dead cats are no longer the ornaments of a Methodist. These honourable badges are now no more. Langour has gotten from the ministers to the people; and, if you don't take care, we shall all be dead together. The Lord Jesus rouse you! Ye Methodists of many years' standing, shew the young ones, who have not the cross to bear as we once had what ancient Methodism was.

Don't be angry with a poor minister for weeping over them who will not weep for themselves. If you laugh at me I know Jesus smiles. I am free from the blood of you all. If you are damned for want of conversion, remember you are not damned for want of warning. YOU ARE GOSPEL-PROOF; and, if there is one place in hell deeper than another, God will order a gospel-despising Methodist to be put there. God convert you from lying a-bed in the morning! God convert you from conformity to the world! God convert you from lukewarmness! Do not get into a cursed antinomian way of thinking, and say, "I thank God, I have the root of the matter in me! I thank God, I was converted twenty or thirty years ago; and, though I can go to the public-house, and play at cards, yet, I am converted; for once in Christ, always in Christ." Whether you were converted formerly or not, you are perverted now. Would you have Jesus catch you napping, with your lamps untrimmed? Suffer the word of exhortation. I preach feelingly. I could be glad to preach till I preached myself dead, if God would convert you. I seldom sleep after three in the morning; and I pray every morning, "Lord, convert me, and make me a new creature today!" -George Whitefield

Like George, Charles Spurgeon knew the heart of the matter, even if his doctrines and deeds were a looser hand than that which gripped his heart. With many colorful words, he too, made clear the woeful scene at hand – a pastor's heart at conflict with foolish backsliders – and when reading Spurgeon's words you can see the very picture heretofore examined, as it were, framed by a silver tongue of eloquence. Within the article titled, "What Is A Revival?", the unutterable emotions in God, the God of George Whitfield, are aflame in the same vehement message yet again, in Spurgeon, for another generation, time, and people to feel the heat. Spurgeon's words cry out with surging emotion – "Forsake the foolish and live" (Proverbs 9:6)!

"Workers in the Sunday-schools, tract distributors, and other laborers for Christ, what different people they become when grace is vigorous from what they are when their life flickers in the socket! Like sickly vegetation in a cellar, all blanched and unhealthy, are workers who have little grace; like willows by the water-courses, like grease with reeds and trashes in well-'watered valleys, are the servants of God who live in his presence. It is no wonder that our Lord said, "Because thou art neither cold nor hot, I will spue thee out of my mouth," for when the earnest Christian's heart is full of fire it is sickening to talk with lukewarm people. Have not warmhearted lovers of Jesus felt when they have been discouraged by doubtful sluggish people, who could see a lion in the way, as if they could put on express speed and run over them? Every earnest minister has known times when he has felt cold hearts to be as intolerable as the drones in the hive are to the working bees. Careless professors are as much out of place as snow in harvest among truly living Christians. As vinegar to the teeth and smoke to the eyes are these sluggards. As well be bound to a dead body as forced into union 'with lifeless professors; they are a burden, a plague, and an abomination. You turn to one of these cold brethren after a graciously earnest prayer-meeting, and say with holy joy, "What a delightful meeting we have had!" "Yes," he says carelessly and deliberately, as if it were an effort to say so much, "there was a good number of people." How his frostbitten words grate on one's ear! You ask yourself, 'Where has the man been? Is he not conscious that the Holy Ghost has been with us?'

Does not our Lord speak of these people as being cast out of his mouth, just because he himself is altogether in earnest, and consequently, when he meets with lukewarm people he will not endure them? He says, "I would thou wert cold or hot," either utterly averse to good or in earnest concerning it. It is easy to see his meaning. If you heard an ungodly man blaspheme after an earnest meeting, you would lament it, but you would feel that from such a man it was not a thing to make you vexed, for he has only spoken after his kind, but when you meet with a child of God who is lukewarm, how can you stand that? it is sickening, and makes the inmost spirit feel the horrors of mental nausea."

Paul approached the situation of baby Christians just as he approached the situation of *sleeping*, *darkened*, *blinded*, *foolish*, and *backslidden* Christians. It was a situation where he must not spare them, or else they would infect the rest of the body of Christ. Not only does the scripture say, "forsake the foolish and live" (Prov. 9:6), and most assuredly promise, the "companion of fools shall be destroyed" (Prov. 13:20), but this is stated because fools are said to be those who are like a "Body of Christ" infection that violently spreads, like a lump of dough is entirely overcome by a little "leaven" (1 Cor. 5:6). The infected ones who spread their leaven are the ones ill-behaving with "malice and wickedness" (1 Cor. 5:8). They are also called those who are in darkness, like the fool, and this is the same voice of the OT which saith – "the fool walketh in darkness" (Eccl. 2:14). Darkness is an unpardonable spiritual condition when it is without restoration. We "were sometimes darkness, but now are [we] light in the Lord," and we must therefore "walk as children of light" (Eph. 5:8), which is, having "no fellowship with the unfruitful works of darkness" (Eph. 5:11), nor, by necessity, them who are in darkness. How could we have fellowship with them that are in darkness!? It is not even possible, if indeed we are in the Light! The apostle John said, "This then is the message which we have heard of him, and declare unto you, that **God is Light**, and **in Him is no darkness at all**. If we say that we have fellowship with Him, and walk in darkness, we lie, and do not the truth: But if we walk in the Light, **as He is in the Light**, **we have fellowship one with another**, and the blood of Jesus Christ His Son cleanseth us from all sin" (1 Jn. 1:5-7). My reader, you must understand that backslidden Christians are not to be taken lightly! We are called to "come out from among them and be separate" (2 Cor. 6:17)! They are right now, at least temporarily, and hopefully not eternally, fallen from grace...which means that they have fallen into *unbelief*, *unrighteousness*, and *darkness*, and the scriptures declare what the bottom line is for such men – "Be ye not unequally yoked together with *unbelievers*: **for what fellowship hath**

418

righteousness with _unrighteousness_? **And what communion hath light with _darkness_**" (2 Cor. 6:14)? "Touch not the unclean thing" (2 Cor. 6:17) and "purge out therefore the old leaven that ye may be a new lump, as ye are unleavened" (1 Cor. 5:7), as ye are in the **light**, **believing**, and in **righteousness**. "Therefore put away from among yourselves that **wicked person**" (1 Cor. 5:13). These backslidden Christians who have come to hate "instruction," "knowledge," "understanding," do now mock God (Gal. 6:7) by mocking sin (Prov. 14:9), and they must be severely dealt with so that they might hear the signal and wake up, "that they may recover themselves out of the snare of the devil, who are taken captive by him at his will" (2 Tim. 2:26). Severe words will rightly represent the "severity" of God (Rom. 11:22). As fleeing from a contagious, incurable, airborne disease – as the black plague – God commands, "Go from the presence of a foolish man, when thou perceivest not in him the lips of knowledge" (Prov. 14:7), for we are "not to keep company" (1 Cor. 5:11) with such a one in the name of Christ.

Spiritual Incapacity _is when_ **_saving wisdom is hidden_**, _and this position of spiritual darkness is_ **_The Deception of God._**

Jesus Christ preached and proclaimed the verses which were descriptive of "The Deception of God" that the Lord sent upon the damned generation of the Babylonian Captivity, but He preached them as the prophetic description of the 1st century Jews. Those Jews of the 1st century, like unto the Jews of the Babylonian Captivity, were under a deception, and therefore they willingly crucified their Messiah. As God wanted Ahab to go up to Ramothgilead and die there, so also God wanted His Son to be rejected and crucified, praise God! But what were the definitive terms which described the deception of those Jews of the 1st century? They had an inability to "**hear**," "**see**," "**understand**," or "**perceive**" (Matt. 13:14). They were called "**dull of hearing**," men with "**eyes closed**," therefore they were doomed to be detained from grace to be "converted" or "healed" (Matt. 13:15). They were said to have "**blinded eyes**" and "**hardened hearts**" (John 12:40). Do these descriptions sound familiar? These terms are the very same spiritual delusions which are indicators of God casting away a generation of people, according to Romans chapter 11. In Romans 11:5-12, God makes the case that He did cast away the Israelites to save, receive, elect, or in other words, "graft in" the Gentiles instead (in one sense, temporarily). Before Romans chapter 11 ended, Paul described what the Lord had done to the Israelites and Gentiles through a helpful metaphor – a branch-laden olive tree (Rom. 11:16-23).

Romans 11 explains how the Israelites were under God's delusion, and were therefore, in the metaphor, **_the broken off branches_**, but the elect Gentiles were **_the grafted in branches_**. Nevertheless, **there is a warning given to the Gentile Church of the NT Dispensation**! The grafted in Gentile branch represents the dispensation of the New Covenant in Christ. The 1st century Israelites were "broken off" (Rom. 11:17), because God "spared not" (Rom. 11:21) from His castaway wrath, but, lo, the elect, saved, newly grafted in Gentiles in Christ must – "take heed, lest He

419

also **spare not thee**. Behold therefore the goodness and severity of God: on them which fell, severity; but toward thee, goodness, if thou continue in His goodness: otherwise thou also shalt be **cut off**" (Rom. 11:22). Therefore God is indicating that He can and will, in these very terms, *cast away*, *reprobate*, *blind*, *break off*, put to *sleep*, *incapacitate*, *harden hearts*, *close eyes*, bring *dullness of hearing* and an inability to *perceive* or *understand*, so the man can't repent or be *healed* – but LOOK – this is castaway, reprobating wrath to the REGENERATE Christian GENTILES, the very same experience that came upon the Jews of the 1st century. Therefore it should be highly significant to you and I, when and if we find written in the New Testament such spiritual conditions described as *darkness*, *blindness*, *spiritual deafness*, *dullness of hearing*, *slumber*, etc…for this language is the very same wording of the former, God-sent, damning delusion! My reader, such spiritual conditions in such words do indicate the NT damning delusion which was forewarned as a potential danger in Romans 11. The language of the NT is exactly parallel to these experiences described and coined in the OT, for they are the very same in the New Covenant arena. So also we must conclude that since all of these descriptive words are the characteristics of persons under the temporary or finally damning delusion of God in the OT & NT experience, and, seeing that they also describe, are interconnected to, and are synonymous with the NT experience of being a spiritual infant or a "babe in Christ", then to be a "babe in Christ" is to be under the damning delusion of God from which a man has a need to be savingly recovered from. Frankly, babes in Christ are going to hell if they don't repent!

"Be not highminded, but FEAR." – Romans 11:20

Perhaps you have been taught to never fear such an experience, but oh! Will you hear it? The same men who cast away their fears of God's wrath do often become castaways! Instead, we should cast away our high-mindedness and learn to FEAR, lest we become, like the others, a NT castaway (Deut. 17:18-19). You are highminded if you fancy yourself the peculiar, prized selection of God, forcefully concluding that, because you are prized by God then you deserve Him to respect your person in the case of you bring spiritually backslidden. Then you believe that, whether you are right with God or not, He will always savingly persevere you. God is no respecter of persons – not to the Abrahamic seed (physically or spiritually) – nor to you. The false prophets did always teach the people to trust that God will have a partial respect with them because of His promises, and with history in view, they vainly imagine that all of God's historically famous favor that He bestowed upon the seed of Abraham is now upon them – "We are Abraham's seed" (Lk. 3), they exclaim! – And so the Jews would solace themselves, but all the while, they were in bondage to impenitent sin. God showed us what He thinks about respecting their persons. God signals His message to them by turning His shining face away from them, and, lo, by turning it upon the Gentiles, raising them up – Hallelujah! – So that the Gentiles became "Abraham's seed" (Gal. 3:29)! Never assume a promise is yours while the holy justice of God is provoked by your unfaithful behavior…God can fulfill His promise without you, in some mysterious way we cannot comprehend.

Don't think so highly of yourself! That is what the text warns against. Rather, let us FEAR...let us be low-minded.

Appendix of Qualification: For an OT typological parallel, Leviticus 26:14-46 explains the different phases of chastisement in proportion to the measure of iniquities committed, and in this case it is five phases (1st (26:16-17), 2nd (26:18-20), 3rd (26:21-22), 4th (26:23-26), 5th (26:27-39)). There are, as it were (according to typological and Covenant parallels), five phases of increasingly intensifying chastisements wrought upon backsliders, and only the last phase inflicts with the power of excommunication from the Church (or ejection from the Promised Land for the OT, Lev. 26:27-39). Leading up to this final phase there is a partial and increasing measure of delivering over in which God delivers soul and body over to satanic powers, curse, and defeat – until finally the man is altogether fallen into the judgment: "deliver such an one unto Satan for the destruction of his flesh" (1 Cor. 5:5). Preceding and leading up to this final stage of chastisement, there are lesser phases of spiritual and physical affliction, none of which hold the power of excommunication. Like the physical alien armies which would invade, oppress, and take Israel captive during certain phases of chastisement, the invaders of the NT dispensation are satanic spirits, or, alien armies of temptation which lead into oppression or captivity of actual sin committed. These temptations or actual sins increasingly intensify, to the agony of soul and body, and devils are connected to this process of chastening as it intensifies more and more. This is how God uses devils as an instrument – a ROD – just like He used heathen armies for OT Israel. This ROD delivers NT Christians over into *drunkenness*, *darkness* & *the spirit of sleep*, *desertification*, and *adulterous rioting*. When graces for perseverance are taken away from the regenerate man, then suddenly, he is overtaken by the instruments of death and afflicted, and God willing, the man is brought to repentance quickly thereby long before he ever comes near to absolute captivity into sin and the final result – eventual excommunication. This means, when the light of God's face begins to dim, or when you get just a bit soul-sluggish and sleepy, or just a little desert-dry and weary, or just a little flirtatious with worldly lusts, then turn to God with haste – turn at His chastening – and by God's grace it will go no further. But if you persist without responding in repentance, then the lashes of the ROD just increase with strength, intensifying the pain of every blow, and the demon spirits are those forces which will inflict these horrid spiritual conditions: *drunkenness* (Isa. 19:14, Micah 2:10-11), *darkness* & *the spirit of sleep* (Isa. 29:9-10, Eph. 6:12, 2 Cor. 4:3-6), *desertification* (Luke 10:19), *adulteries* (Hos. 4:12, 5:4, 1 Tim. 4:1, James 4:7).

NT Darkness to Light: The Gospel of Regeneration

Initial Salvation – The Gospel of Promise

> "To open their eyes, and to turn them from **darkness** to **light**, and
> from the power of Satan unto God, that they may receive
> forgiveness of sins, and inheritance among them which are

sanctified by faith that is in me." Acts 26:18

If NT regenerate Christians can turn back to and experience spiritual darkness, popular religion would exclaim, "how can it be?" "Was it not the gospel promise that we would be turned from darkness to light?" Indeed it was, and is, thus we have been born again and made "meet to be partakers of the inheritance of the saints in light," because, God "hath delivered us from the power of darkness, and hath translated us into the Kingdom of His dear Son" (Col. 1:12-13). We have become the children of God, or children of Light, because "God is light, and in Him is no darkness at all" (1 John 1:5), and "in Him was life; and the life was the light of men" (John 1:4). Verily, in God's Kingdom "there shall be no night there," "for the glory of God [will] lighten it, and the Lamb is the light thereof," therefore all of those that "are saved shall walk in the light of it" (Rev. 21:23-25)! In this way we have become, by Spirit, nature, and law: "the children of Light" (John 12:36, 1 Thess. 5:5). In other words we are, "the children of the Day: we are not of the night, nor of darkness" (1 Thess. 5:5). This is *initial salvation*, as it is at the first experience, empowered by binding promises, but will you know that there is a *present progressive* necessity to keep your first faith in the gospel of grace, so that you do *presently* and *progressively* abide in the Light of God, otherwise you will return back into the darkness of carnality, the Godless world, and its ruling unholy angels will be the spirits of your communion?

Present Progressive Salvation – The Gospel by Command

Your regeneration was by the power of God when He did effectually call you with the gospel call, and the power of this PAST TENSE experience should be walked out at present, presently and progressively in your today. Thus, you "should shew forth the praises of Him Who hath called you **out of darkness into His marvelous Light**" (1 Peter 2:9). Henceforth you must "**continue in the faith** grounded and settled, and be not moved away from the hope of the gospel" (Col. 1:23), and therefore, "as ye have therefore received Christ Jesus the Lord, so **walk ye in Him**" (Col. 2:6) – and He is Light! "For we are made partakers of Christ, if we hold **the beginning of our confidence stedfast unto the end**" (Heb. 3:14). Now, if there were no possibility to fall from the gospel-empowering grace of God, then there would be no possibility to **fall into *darkness***, to *walk in darkness*, to dwell in another reality than what is purchased, performed, and promised in the gospel. The NT Churches were evidently in danger of falling into, and often in need of recovery from, darkness! *The gospel of promise*, which regenerated souls from darkness into light, is also presented *by a command* which I call – *The Gospel by Command*. Look at *the gospel by command* and reckon it into your theological persuasion. Look how the apostles acknowledged their regenerate brethren to be in damnable spiritual conditions, conditions which were upon them because of a slipping out of saving faith in the gospel promises. The apostles commanded the slipping saints to walk out in and lay hold upon the gospel promises:

422

"For ye were sometimes darkness, but now are ye light in the Lord: walk as children of light: (For the fruit of the Spirit is in all goodness and righteousness and truth;) Proving what is acceptable unto the Lord. And have no fellowship with the unfruitful works of darkness, but rather reprove them" (Eph. 5:8-11).

"Walk as men" – 1 Cor. 3:3)
"Walketh in Darkness" – 1 John 2:11
"Abideth in Death" – 1 John 3:14
"If ye live after the flesh ye shall die" – Rom. 8:13
"Arise from the dead" – Eph. 5:14
"Walk... not as fools, but as wise" – Eph. 5:15

According to Romans 13:11-14, if you do not "put on the armour of Light," which is to abide in the Light, then you are not putting on Jesus Christ Who is eternal life (1 John 2:11, 3:15, 5:11); you are in darkness instead of light, which is to say, in other terms, that you are sleeping. To put on Christ is to put on the armour of Light, which is Jesus Christ, and if this is not done, then you have not obeyed the gospel which is *by command* – "awake out of sleep!" Those that sleep do sleep in the night, and we are called to be awake! According to Ephesians 5:8-17, sleeping is to be dead, a fool, and in a damnable condition, which would be, like as Romans 13:11-14 would agree, a Christless condition. Therefore a sleeping Christian who is, by gospel promise and initial salvation – "now light in the Lord" – but at present walking in darkness, he is denying the gospel of God. What is the gospel by command? It is, "Walk as Children of Light" (Eph. 5:8). Those who do not are "dead" "fools" (Eph. 5:15-17). Need I remind you of the woeful cries which were shouted to the Savior – "Lord, Lord, open to us" (Matt. 25:1-13)? A Christian that walks in darkness "abideth in death" rather than the light, and thus Christ (1 John 5:11-12), the One and only Dwelling Place of "eternal life" (1 John 3:14-15), is not abiding in him. This spiritual condition is a walking in carnality, in foolishness, in darkness, in death, and in blindness...does all of this sound familiar? "He that loveth his brother abideth in the **light**, and there is none occasion of stumbling in him. But he that hateth his brother is in **darkness**, and walketh in **darkness**, and knoweth not whither he goeth, because that **darkness hath blinded his eyes**" (1 John 2:10-11).

By birth and gospel promise we are in the Light, but if we turn to darkness, we are in danger of eternal judgment and excommunication (2 Cor. 6:14, 1 John 1:5-7). We are therefore, as Philippians 2:15-16, under the damning "rebuke" of God because we are not "blameless," because we should rather "shine as lights in the world holding forth the word of life." If this is our condition, as Philippians 2:15-16 warns against, then on the final Day of Judgment we will NOT be reckoned as children of God, or otherwise put, "children of Light." Now can you tell the plain meaning of the following passages?

"But the day of the Lord will come as a thief in the night; in the which the heavens shall pass away with a great noise, and the elements shall melt with fervent heat, the earth also and the works that are therein shall be burned up. **Seeing then** that all these things shall be dissolved, **what manner of persons ought ye to be in all holy conversation and godliness, Looking for and hasting unto the coming of the day of God**, wherein the heavens being on fire shall be dissolved, and the elements shall melt with fervent heat? Nevertheless we, according to His promise, **look for** new heavens and a new earth, wherein dwelleth righteousness. **Wherefore, beloved, seeing that ye look for such things, be diligent that ye may be found of him in peace, without spot, and blameless.**" -2 Peter 3:10-14

"Then Jesus said unto them, Yet a little while is the light with you. Walk while ye have the light, lest darkness come upon you: for **he that walketh in darkness knoweth not whither he goeth**. While ye have light, believe in the light, **that ye may be the children of light.** These things spake Jesus, and departed, and did hide himself from them." -John 12:35-36

"But ye, brethren, are not in **darkness**, that that Day should overtake you as a thief. Ye are all **the children of light**, and **the children of the day**: we are not **of the night**, nor **of darkness**. Therefore let us not sleep, as do others; but let us **watch** and be **sober**. For **they that sleep sleep in the night**; and **they that be drunken are drunken in the night**. But let us, who are **of the day**, be sober, putting on the breastplate of **faith** and **love**; and for an helmet, the **hope** of **salvation,**" -1Th. 5:4-8

"For the Son of Man is as a man taking a far journey, who left his house, and gave authority to his servants, and to every man his work, and commanded the porter to **watch**. **Watch ye therefore**: for ye know not when the master of the house cometh, at even, or at midnight, or at the cockcrowing, or in the morning: **Lest coming suddenly He find you sleeping. And what I say unto you I say unto all, Watch.**" -Mark 13:34-37

"Let your loins be girded about, and your **lights burning**; And ye yourselves like unto men that **wait for their lord**, when He will return from the wedding; that when He cometh and knocketh, they may **open unto him immediately**. Blessed are those servants, whom the lord when He cometh shall **find watching**: verily I say unto you, that He shall gird himself, and make them to sit down to meat, and will come forth and serve them. And if He shall come in the second watch, or come in the third watch, and **find them so,** <u>blessed</u> are those servants. <u>And this know,</u> **that if the goodman of the house had known what hour the thief would come, he would have watched, and not have suffered his house to be broken through. Be ye therefore ready also: for the Son of Man cometh at an hour when ye think not."** -Luke 12:35-40

The Gospel By Promise	The Gospel By Command
(FINISHED IN THE PAST)	(AT PRESENT)
God tells you what He has done. How He walked.	God tells you what you must do, in Him & through Him. How you must walk, in Him & through Him.
~ Imputed Righteousness (Rom. 8:10, Eph. 2:8-9, 1 Cor. 6:11)~	*~Works Righteousness (1 Cor. 6:9-10, Eph. 2:10)~* Walk: Col. 2:6, Gal. 5:16, 25, Eph. 4:17, 5:8, 1 Cor. 3:3, 1 John 2:6

1) **Light**
  + Acts 26:18, Eph. 5:8, Col. 1:12-13
  + Rev. 21:23-25

1) **Light**
  + Php. 2:15-16, Eph. 5:8-11 – John 3:19-20, John 12:36, 46, 1 Thess. 5:5
  + 1 John 1:5-7, 2 Cor. 6:14
  + Rom. 2:19-20 – 1 Cor. 3:3, "walk as men", "walk in darkness", "walk in death", "walk in Him" "as He walked"
  + Final Salvation: Prov. 4:18, 1 Peter 1:19, Rev. 21:23-25

NT Foolishness to Wisdom: The Gospel of Regeneration

Initial Salvation – The Gospel by Promise

"But unto them which are called, both Jews and Greeks, Christ the power of God, and the **wisdom** of God."
-1 Cor. 1:24

"But of Him are ye in Christ Jesus, Who of God is made unto us **wisdom**, and righteousness, and sanctification, and redemption."
-1 Cor. 1:30

Present Progressive Salvation – The Gospel by Command

"Who is a **wise man** and endued with **knowledge** among you? let him shew out of a good conversation **his works** with meekness of **wisdom**. But if ye have bitter envying and strife in your hearts, glory not, and lie not against the truth. **This wisdom descendeth not from above**, but is **earthly, sensual, devilish**. For where envying and strife is, there is confusion and every evil work. But the **wisdom that is from above** is first pure, then peaceable, gentle, and easy to be intreated, full of mercy and good fruits, without partiality, and without hypocrisy. And the fruit of righteousness is sown in peace of them that make peace." -James 3:13-18

Need I say more about the eternal destiny of fools than what has already been referenced in Ephesians 5:15-17 and Matthew 25:1-13? But there is much, much more! Wisdom in those passages is expressively where the Divine Life of Christ abides, and therein is eternal life. This is confirmed again in James 3:13-18. According to this passage, if you are without heavenly wisdom, then you are without the "perfection of fruits" (Lk. 8:14) which the Father looks after with demand, for God has chosen you from this world to make you wise in Him (1 Cor. 1:27). The worldly-wise Corinthian is snared in what James calls "wisdom that descendeth not from above," wisdom that is rather "earthly, sensual," and even "devilish" (James 3:15)! Devilish wisdom exhibits the character of demons. Devilish wisdom exhibits the character of the devil's world (2 Cor. 4:4). If a man bears the evil fruits of foolishness, then the world will hear and understand him very well (1 John 4:5-6), even in popular esteem (Lk. 6:26), but if a man is in the wisdom of God, the world will hate him (1 John 3:13). The world is like an antichrist harlot who seduces the spiritual fools away from the wisdom of virginity (2 Cor. 11:2-4), purity (Matt. 5:8), and marital faithfulness (Jas. 4:4). She, the harlot of hypocritical religion, "subtil of heart" (Prov. 7:10), sets her seductive eyelids a-fluttering toward fools. She doeth it as a pursuer of them, as it were, just as it was written of old – "For at the window of my house I looked through my casement, and beheld among the simple ones, I discerned among the youths, a young man void of understanding, passing through the street near her corner; and he went the way to her house, in the twilight, in the evening, in the black and dark night: and, behold, there met him a woman with the attire of an harlot, and subtil of heart" (Prov. 7:6-10). Therefore, God saith, "without are…whoremongers" (Rev. 22:15).

"Ye adulterers and adulteresses, know ye not that friendship of the world is enmity with God? Whosoever therefore will be a friend of the world is the enemy of God." -James 4:4

"Mrs. Worldly-Wise Christianity" loves the fools, and she hunts them with her venomous lusts! Even by sexual lewdness they will know her – by adultery (James 4:4) – and that, against GOD! But the adultery will be subtle to the eye, you see, like a secret crime done for one dark night. It will be a covering up of carnality with religious shows of reputable religiosity, men glorying in men and lying against the truth (Jas. 3:14). Saints ought to live out their wise, pure, regenerate natures, walking in virginity, as a Bride that is "holy and without blemish" (Eph. 5:27), a

426

nature which the world does not know, a nature that the world utterly even hates (1 John 3:1, John 17:14-16)! "Let no man deceive himself. IF any man among you seemeth to be wise in this world, let him become a fool, that he may be wise" (1 Cor. 3:18). This is *the gospel by command*! Do you hear it? "Let him become a fool that he may be wise" (1 Cor. 3:18). But Oh! How often do saints turn back to baby, blamable, dark, drunken, foolish, adulterous "Christianity," a worldly, cool, civilized, acceptable "Christianity" that is not worthy to be called Christianity at all! They are therefore "carnal, and walk as men" (1 Cor. 3:3), rendered unable to receive the meats of saving *wisdom* (1 Cor. 2:6), and they are henceforth unable to go on with God, because they have left off saving *faith* and *repentance* (Heb. 6:1). Becoming carnal, now they abide in *death* (Rom. 8:6-7), fast asleep on Delilah's knees, arising again but at enmity with God and apostolic exemplification. Will you then understand the rebuke of Paul now, as he said it to the worldly-wise, baby-fools, and carnal-Corinthians?

> "Now ye are full, now ye are rich, ye have reigned as kings without us: and I would to God ye did reign, that we also might reign with you. For I think that God hath set forth us the apostles last, as it were appointed to death: for we are made a spectacle unto the world, and to angels, and to men. We are fools for Christ's sake, but ye are wise in Christ; we are weak, but ye are strong; ye are honourable, but we are despised. Even unto this present hour we both hunger, and thirst, and are naked, and are buffeted, and have no certain dwelling place; And labour, working with our own hands: being reviled, we bless; being persecuted, we suffer it: Being defamed, we intreat: we are made as the filth of the world, and are the offscouring of all things unto this day" (1Co 4:8-13).

> "…Wherefore I beseech you, be ye followers of me…my ways which be in Christ, as I teach every where in every Church" (1Co 4:16-17).

The Gospel By Promise	The Gospel By Command
(FINISHED IN THE PAST)	(AT PRESENT)
God tells you what He has done. How He walked.	God tells you what you must do, in Him & through Him. How you must walk, in Him & through Him.
~ Imputed Righteousness (Rom. 8:10, Eph. 2:8-9, 1 Cor. 6:11)~	*~Works Righteousness (1 Cor. 6:9-10, Eph. 2:10)~* Walk: Col. 2:6, Gal. 5:16, 25, Eph. 4:17, 5:8, 1 Cor. 3:3, 1 John 2:6
2) Wise ⟱1 Cor. 1:24, 30	**2) Wise** ⟱Matt. 25:1-13, Eph. 5:15-17, ⟱James 1:5, 3:13-18, 1 Cor.

427

1:27, 2:6, 13, 3:1, 18, 4:8-
10, 16 – Rom. 2:19-20

NT LOST TO SAVED
- THE GOSPEL OF REGENERATION
CHAPTER 18

The Gospel By Promise	The Gospel By Command
(FINISHED IN THE PAST)	(AT PRESENT)

The Gospel By Promise (FINISHED IN THE PAST)

God tells you what He has done. How He walked.

~ Imputed Righteousness (Rom. 8:10, Eph. 2:8-9, 1 Cor. 6:11) ~

1) **Dead (crucified & mortified)**
   - Rom. 6:2-3, Gal. 2:20, 5:24, Col. 3:3
   - Col. 2:20
   - "he that is dead is freed from sin" (Rom. 6:7)

2) **Resurrection (Risen)**
   - Eph. 2:5-6, Col. 3:3-4
   - Php. 3:18-20

3) **Baptized**
   - Rom. 6:3, 1 Cor. 12:13, Gal. 3:27
   - POWER - Lk. 24:49
   - FULLNESS - Eph. 1:23

The Gospel By Command (AT PRESENT)

God tells you what you must do, in Him & through Him.
How you must walk, in Him & through Him.

~Works Righteousness (1 Cor. 6:9-10, Eph. 2:10)~
Walk: Col. 2:6, Gal. 5:16, 25, Eph. 4:17, 5:8, 1 Cor. 3:3, 1 John 2:6

1) **Die (Crucify & Mortify)**
   - Col. 3:5, Rom. 8:13
   - 1 Cor. 15:31 – "I die daily"
   - 2 Cor. 4:10-12

2) **Resurrection**
   - Col. 3:1-2 "set your affections on things above"
   - Col. 2:20, Romans 6:10-12
   - Looking... (affections/treasure = eyes) Php. 3:20, 2 Peter 3:10-14, 2 Cor. 4:18, Matt. 6:21, Rev. 2:26-27, 3:21

3) **Baptized**
   - Gal. 4:19 "travail in birth... Christ be formed"
   - Eph. 3:17 "Christ may dwell in your hearts by faith"
   - FULLNESS - Eph. 3:19, 4:10, 13, 5:18

	♣ POWER - Col. 1:11, Eph. 1:19, 3:16, 20, 2 Thess. 1:11, Eph. 6:10
4) Put on & Put off ♣ Gal. 3:27, Col. 3:9-10	**4) Put on & Put off** ♣ Col. 3:12, 14 ♣ Rom. 13:12, 14 ♣ Eph. 6:11, 4:22, 24
5) Quickened (Alive, Living, & Revived) ♣ "And you hath He quickened who were dead" (Eph. 2:1). ♣ "when we were dead in sins, hath quickened" (Eph. 2:5).	**5) Quickened (Alive, Living, & Revived)** ♣ Rev. 3:1, Eph. 5:14, 1 John 3:14, James 5:19-20, 1 Jn. 5:16 ♣ 1 Peter 4:5, 2 Tim. 4:1

Dear reader, the entire work of Christ is separated all across the scriptures in the expressed categories above: "**The Gospel By Promise**" & "**The Gospel By Command**"

Crucified/Mortified/Buried – The Gospel of Regeneration

Initial Salvation

A Christian is "crucified with Christ" (Gal. 2:20). Personal crucifixion is, as you can see, a past tense experience. It was enabled by the gospel promise, thus the sinner is "baptized into His [Christ's] death", being "buried with Him by baptism into death" (Rom. 6:3-4). And again it is written, "ye are dead and your life is hid with Christ in God" (Col. 3:3). At this initial beginning, "they that are Christ's have crucified the flesh with its affections and lusts" (Gal. 5:24) by the blessed promise, "[Christ] died unto sin once: but the life that He liveth, He liveth unto God" (Rom. 6:10); even so, from that single death comes freedom to all that die in Him – "he that is dead is freed from sin" (Rom. 6:7).

As for a Christian who has been "crucified" to carnality and the flesh, is it theretofore impossible for him to walk in carnality again, as a natural man would (1 Cor. 3:3), so as to commit "the works of the flesh" (Gal. 5:19)? It is not impossible. The man can backslide from faith. Thus, when a man is faltering from faith in the gospel promise, the NT pastors briskly command – "The Gospel By Command."

> "For if ye live after the flesh, ye shall die: but if ye **through the Spirit do mortify the deeds of the body**, ye shall live." –Rom. 8:13

> "**Mortify therefore your members which are upon the earth**; fornication, uncleanness, inordinate affection, evil concupiscence, and covetousness, which is idolatry." –Col. 3:5

It is understood in the holy scriptures that, "there is therefore now no condemnation to them which are in Christ Jesus, **who walk not after the flesh**, but after the Spirit" (Rom. 8:1). Look closely at what the passage details! There IS condemnation for those that walk after the flesh! The gospel promise is that we are *dead*, and by faith we must daily appropriate the power of freedom in the purchase of the gospel. Then, "as [we] have therefore received Christ Jesus the Lord" into initial and instantaneous freedom, we will "walk" "in Him" Who is freedom (Col. 2:6, John 8:31-32). This is the walk of a **present progressive** believer in the gospel of grace. Such a one is therefore obeying the gospel by command. How do you *crucify* or *mortify* that which is already *dead*? It is done by faith in the promise that you are already dead, past tense; then your old man who exists in your body of death will be mortified *presently and progressively*. Now will you understand that you will go to hell if you walk in the works of the flesh instead of the works of the Spirit?

> "Now the works of the flesh are manifest, which are these; Adultery, fornication, uncleanness, lasciviousness, Idolatry, witchcraft, hatred, variance, emulations, wrath, strife, seditions, heresies, Envyings, murders, drunkenness, revellings, and such like: of the which I tell you before, as I have also told you in time past, that they which do such things shall not inherit the kingdom of God. But the fruit of the Spirit is love, joy, peace, longsuffering, gentleness, goodness, faith, meekness, temperance: against such there is no law. And they that are Christ's have crucified the flesh with the affections and lusts. If we live in the Spirit, let us also walk in the Spirit." -Gal 5:19-25

Present progressive mortification causes a man to avoid "the works of the flesh" that are described in Galatians 5:19-20, and so, these individuals will be finally recognized as Christ's people. Why? "They that are Christ's have crucified the flesh with the affections and lusts" (Gal. 5:24)! Will you be recognizable by God when He comes to the earth, even a God that judges according to works? Do you remember how that the word of God said, "by works a man is justified, and not by faith only" (James 2:24)? Even so, are you one of those that will be set aside on the right hand of Christ by recognition, one of those men of the company that "are Christ's" according to Galatians 5:24? In other words, are you one who has turned from "dead works"

(Heb. 6:1) to the Living God, into the grace of the new creation of God's "workmanship" (Eph. 2:10), the walk that Christ calls "My works" (Rev. 2:26), the wisdom that is recognizable by "works with meekness of wisdom" (James 3:13), enveloped in the Light which expels the "works of darkness" (Eph. 5:11, Rom. 13:12), even so, the life that is evidently crucified to "the works of the flesh" in their manifestations, because the very "affections and lusts" of your body are *presently and progressively* killed (Gal. 5:19, 24)!? Then you will be *finally saved*.

Resurrected & Ascended – The Gospel of Regeneration

Initial Salvation

> "Even when we were dead in sins, [He] hath quickened us together with Christ (by grace ye are saved;) And hath **raised us up** together, and made us to **sit together** in heavenly places in Christ Jesus." -Eph. 2:5-6

> "For ye are dead, and your life is hid with Christ in God. When Christ, Who is our life, shall appear, then shall ye also appear with Him in glory." -Col. 3:3-4

> "…enemies of the cross of Christ:…who mind earthly things.) For our conversation is in heaven; from whence also we look for the Saviour, the Lord Jesus Christ." -Php. 3:18-20

> "And if children, then heirs; heirs of God, and joint-heirs with Christ" (Rom. 8:17), and "all are yours." -1 Cor. 3:22

Spoken of as a **past tense** experience, God has "**raised us up** together and made us to **sit together**" (Eph. 2:5-6) with Christ Who is enthroned at the right hand of God. This was done by God through our co-participation and union in Christ's resurrection and ascension. We are "raised", made "to sit together" (Eph. 5:6), not with ourselves, but we are "hid with Christ in God" (Col. 3:3). Redeemed humanity is mysteriously one at the seat of God's Government! This positional redemption initially compels the earth-dwelling Christians into heavenly alignment. "For as many as are led by the Spirit of God, they are the sons of God" (Rom. 8:14). Seeing that this has been experienced, we are under a holy obligation to walk in Christ's rule by thought, word, and deed, like as if we are guided by a story-Book He is authoring. Then the world begins to see our lifestyle as a living revelation of Christ. Leaving many affected and some admiring, the Christians solemnly confess - "our conversation is in heaven" (Php. 3:20)! Who can tell of this Great Kingdom's story? Who can describe the many mansions, their sizable patterns, colors, and glory? None can! Notwithstanding the world does read it in our hearts, it is "known and read of all

432

men" (2 Cor. 3:2), "written not with ink, but with the Spirit of the living God; not in tables of stone, but in fleshly tables of the heart" (2 Cor. 3:3)! We have a childlike participation in a steep and honorable Kingdom, by unworthy right, standing as an inheriting child before his Father's boundless possessions. Amazingly, we are "joint-heirs with Christ" (Rom. 8:17)! For this cause, it was once said that to Christians, "all things are yours; whether Paul, or Apollos, or Cephas, or the world, or life, or death, or things present, or things to come; all are yours; And ye are Christ's; and Christ is God's" (1 Cor. 3:21-23).

Present Progressive Salvation

Affections → **"If ye be risen with Christ**, seek those things which are above, **where Christ sitteth at the right hand of God**. Set your affection on **things above**, not on things on earth." -Col. 3:1-2

Reigning Powers → "For in that He died, He died unto sin once: but in that He liveth, He liveth unto God. Likewise reckon ye also yourselves to be dead indeed unto sin, but alive unto God through Jesus Christ our Lord. **Let not sin therefore reign** in your mortal body, that ye should obey it in the lusts thereof" -Rom. 6:10-12

If our *initial salvation* has raised us co-enthroned, this position is of high ground of empowering grace in God. Being identified with and in Christ's ascension and throne-rule, so also we ought to **walk in** the Spirit's "rule" *presently and progressively* (Php. 3:16). Hence, we should not "**mind earthly things**" (Php. 3:19), but those things which are in and about Christ, where He is and what He is doing, because our co-participation in His resurrected life, that He lives *presently and progressively*, should be walked in right now. Therefore the scripture states, "If ye be risen…seek those things which are above where Christ sitteth at the right hand of God." It is commanded of us – IF YE BE RISEN – then <u>our personal affections</u> should be "mercies, kindness, humbleness of mind, meekness, longsuffering; forbearing one another, and forgiving one another" (Col. 3:12-13). IF we are NOT RISEN, then our personal affections would rather be, "fornication, uncleanness, inordinate affection, evil concupiscence, and covetousness, which is idolatry" (Col. 3:5). By position, we are different from all other men who are not risen and ascended in Christ, therefore by command we are to walk in gospel-liberties. All other men are compelled to "mind earthly things" (Php. 3:18-19), or as Colossians 3:2 states it, "things on the earth". They are in bondage to humanity's "vile body" (Php. 3:21), or as Colossians 3:5 describes it, "your members which are upon the earth" (Col. 3:5). Wherefore the rather, brethren, by the resurrection we are enabled to search out the depths of the members of God (1 Cor. 2:10).

Romans 6:10-12 clarifies **the gospel by command** in the terms of how the saint has a daily responsibility to "reckon" the resurrection truths, and if he successfully does this, then he will walk in the liberty and freedom which the gospel has purchased: letting "not sin therefore reign in" his "mortal body" that he "should obey it in the lusts thereof". Either Christ reigns or sin reigns. Christ's ascended spiritual condition of freedom and life becomes the positional point of our <u>reckoning</u>. This is *presently* and *progressively* redeeming their bodily members from their former king's reigning powers, from where "sin hath reigned" into where in Christ, "even so might grace reign through righteousness" (Rom. 5:21). The religious rule which Christians reckon is Christ's law of the Kingdom of heaven. The prayer He prayed, "Thy Kingdom come. Thy will be done in earth, as it is in heaven" (Matt. 6:10) – this is done inside of Christian men. Even so Christ said, "the Kingdom of God is within you" (Lk. 17:21). Daily reckoning religious laws which are existing with free course in the Kingdom of heaven is a daily longing after another world's King; therefore it is said, "unto them **that look for Him** shall He appear the second time without sin unto salvation" (Heb. 9:28). In this way, we can also see the spiritual meaning behind such words spoken by the Lord when He said, "For **where** your treasure is, there will your heart be also" (Matt. 6:21), meaning that we should be "rich toward God" (Lk. 12:21) with laid up "treasures in heaven" (Matt. 6:20). Where are your spiritual eyes? The suffering, lashed, scared, stoned, beaten, and poor man, the apostle Paul, he said that he did "faint not" even while his "outward man" did "perish" (2 Cor. 4:16). He said that while he thus suffered, "the inward man is renewed day by day", that it was all just a "light affliction", for behold, he saw in heaven an "exceeding and eternal weight of glory" (2 Cor. 3:16-17). Do you think his heart was in heaven? Hear Paul's secret in his own word – the rule of Christian faith – "While we look not at things which are seen, but at the things which are not seen: for the things which are seen are temporal; but the things which are not seen are eternal" (2 Cor. 4:18). Now can you understand the burden of God to maintain *present progressive* salvation, like as what is preached by the following passage? In the *present progressive,* or continual looking unto Christ for, daily power to walk in the resurrected life, I tell you, the desires are so strong that Christians would rather be entirely resurrected altogether to fly away from this sin-ridden earth. For this we are burdened like a man bowing down in soul-groaning, even like, as it were, the groans of all creation (Rom. 8:19-23) are joining hands with the Bride (Rev. 22:17), and the Bride cries out – oh, to be free from this earthly life (2 Cor. 5:1-4)! Such men are rightly called Christians, Christ-obsessed, groaning in desire to be where Christ is in bodily resurrection! These are the children that will be worthily called "the children of the resurrection" (Lk. 20:36), men and women that will be "accounted worthy to obtain that world, and the resurrection from the dead" (Lk. 20:35), and why? Their heart, affections, conversation, mind, will, and rule is in heaven! What a tragedy that with so many Christians it is not so!

God is LOVE – TRUE!
But a world that is wrong, MEN LOVE.

Flesh, Fashion, & Fame!
Men gather for the fights, footballs, foolishness, and games.
Shouts of lust, the whistles blow!

434

Men are entertained, amazed, eye-addicted to the show.
Men memorize rags, do all their numbers know!
For their winners' footsteps they do heave and blow.

For their winners they whine! They watch them all the time!
They think that they know God but to His footsteps they are blind.
Chapter and verse, oh right, they don't have the time!
Kneeling down in broken repentance, for what? Oh yeah, their sin is out of mind.
"I got saved when I was six, you see!?" And now for the world they run free.

Heaven would be a hell for unholy men.
They would loathe the Savior and long for sin,
Desiring a break from heaven for all the hobbies of natural men.

In bondage to praise for endless days Him Who is heaven-famous?!
These men would rather go back home to earth and watch the world-famous!

Doctrines → "Wherefore if ye be dead with Christ from the rudiments of the world, why, **as though living in the world**, are ye subject to ordinances…" -Col. 2:20

Christians are commanded to abide in heaven's principles and heavenly statutes instead of human principles and earthly statutes which make up doctrines or philosophies. There is an other-worldly law and alien power at the ascension of Christ. We are removed from all that is called "the rudiments of the world" (Col. 2:20). Therefore Paul makes the staggering admonishment, "**why as though living in the world** are ye subject to ordinances, (Touch not; taste not; handle not" (Col. 2:20-21)? Paul speaks of them as if they are not even living in the world anymore! And so, he refutes the heresies of philosophy and doctrine which are earthly-minded or humanly applicable.

Each of the verses above is a direct application of **the gospel by command**. A saint is obedient to these commands by believing in the gospel of grace which immediately empowers them in the realities of initial salvation, therefore presently and progressively they should continue in these salvific powers – by personal affection, reigning rule, and doctrine. Maybe you are trying to look to Christ by faith for present progressive obedience to the gospel commands of the resurrection and ascension, but are you OBEDIENT to them? Did you know that you can "look for such things" and be too slothful about it, to the end that you are found of Christ at His return in a condition which you would eternally regret: namely, not "in peace", with spots, and blamable?

"But the day of the Lord will come as a thief in the night; in the which the heavens shall pass away with a great noise, and the elements shall melt with fervent heat, the earth also and the works that are therein shall be burned up. Seeing then that all these things shall be dissolved, what manner of persons ought ye to be in all holy conversation and godliness, **Looking for** and hasting unto the coming of the day of God, wherein the heavens being on fire shall be dissolved, and the elements shall melt with fervent heat? Nevertheless we, according to His promise, **look for** new heavens and a new earth, wherein dwelleth righteousness. Wherefore, beloved, **seeing that ye look for such things**, be diligent that ye may be found of him **in peace, without spot**, and **blameless**" -2 Pet. 3:10-14

Did you know that Christ will judge your present progressive obedience to these gospel commands, and, if you are in a spiritual condition which is unworthy, earthly instead of heavenly, or overcome by the world instead overcoming the world, then Christ will say to you like He said to others, "I have a few things against thee" (Rev. 2:20), which means that He will dispel you from your resurrection, ascension, coheir qualification in Him. Lo, see how Christ said, "I will give unto every one of you according to your works", "And he that overcometh, and keepeth my works unto the end, to him will I give power over the nations: And he shall rule them with a rod of iron; as the vessels of a potter shall they be broken to shivers: even as I received of my Father" (Rev 2:26-27). Your coheir, co-enthronement, Kingdom inheritance is on the line! Present progressive obedience to the gospel call is present progressive salvation, and such will be rewarded with final salvation. Those that are presently and progressively walking in their co-enthronement with Christ to overcome the world, to live in holiness, will be finally seated upon His Throne in a consummating salvation to fulfill these words: "To him that overcometh will I grant to sit with Me in My Throne, even as I also overcame, and am set down with My Father in His Throne" (Rev 3:21).

Baptized – The Gospel of Regeneration

Initial Salvation

"Know ye not, that so many of us as were **baptized** into Jesus Christ were **baptized** into His death?" -Rom. 6:3

"For as many of you as have been **baptized** into Christ have put on Christ." -Gal 3:27

"Buried with Him in **baptism**, wherein also ye are risen with him through the faith of the operation of God, Who hath raised Him from the dead. And you, being dead in your sins and the uncircumcision of your flesh, hath He quickened together with Him, having forgiven you all trespasses." -Col. 2:12-13

436

"For by one Spirit are we all **baptized** into one body, whether we be Jews or Gentiles, whether we be bond or free; and have been all made to drink into one Spirit" -1 Co. 12:13

The baptism of the Spirit of God is not an after-salvation experience. It is said to be a past tense experience of a Christian when, as a lost man, he was united in the death of Jesus Christ. The baptism is not of water, it is when the individual is "baptized **into His death**" (Rom. 6:3), or into freedom, for "he that is dead is freed from sin" (Rom. 6:7). This baptism is the Spiritual "operation of God", wherein the lost individual dies with Christ in burial, and is raised up with Christ in resurrection (Col. 2:12-13), for, "as many of you as have been **baptized** into Christ have put on Christ" (Gal 3:27). Baptism unites all races into "one body" in Christ (1 Cor. 12:13). My reader, water baptism cannot do any of these operations, nor could this be referring to the "second blessing" interpretation of the baptism of the Spirit, because all of these operations refer to *initial salvation*.

Power → "And, behold, I send the promise of my Father upon you: but tarry ye in the city of Jerusalem, until ye be endued with power from on high." -Luke 24:49

When a man hears the phrase, "baptism of the Spirit", the outpouring at Pentecost is most often recalled to mind. It was then that the apostles were baptized in the Spirit of God. By operation, it was then that the New Covenant was initiated within them. Jesus called this baptism "the promise of the Father", which He spoke to them about. In John 14-16, Christ told them how He would have to go away so that He, the Holy Ghost, would come, and that it was better that Christ left so He would come (John 16:7). For this promise, they waited until it came, and suddenly they were "endued with power from on High" (Lk. 24:49). Can you see how the endowment of spiritual power and the Spirit's baptism are interconnected? This is vital to understand because there are many regenerate Christians that do not *presently and progressively* know the "exceeding greatness of His power to us-ward who believe" (Eph. 1:19). Nevertheless, at initial salvation, all men experience the "power of God" (Rom. 1:16)! By necessity, men are converted when the gospel reveals Christ, not "in word only, but also in power, and in the Holy Ghost, and in much assurance" (1 Thess. 1:5). To free an enchained bondman behind the gates of hell who is utterly surrounded by the fallen angelic host of Satan, by necessity, it takes *the power of God* to spoil principalities and powers, to triumph over them, to raise dead men to life and turn darkness to light, reconciling sinners to God and granting them eternal life.

Power = Fullness of the Spirit → "Wherefore I also, after I heard of your faith in the Lord Jesus, and love unto all the saints, Cease not to give thanks for you, making mention of you in my prayers; That the God of our Lord Jesus Christ, the Father of glory, may give unto you the spirit of wisdom and

437

revelation in the knowledge of Him: The eyes of your understanding being enlightened; that ye may know what is the hope of His calling, and what the riches of the glory of His inheritance in the saints, And what is the exceeding greatness of His power to us-ward who believe, according to the working of His mighty power, **Which He wrought in Christ, when He raised Him from the dead, and set Him at His own right hand in the heavenly places, Far above all principality, and power, and might, and dominion, and every name that is named, not only in this world, but also in that which is to come: And hath put all things under His feet, and gave Him to be the head over all things to the Church,** Which is His body, **the fulness of Him that filleth all in all.**"-Ephesians 1:15-23

In Ephesians 1:15-23, firstly, Paul revealed that he had an unceasing burden in prayer for the Ephesians (Eph. 1:16). Then Paul told us what he was asking for. There are three prayer requests made for the Ephesians which would all be answered through what Paul calls "the spirit of wisdom and revelation in the knowledge of Him", or in other words, "the eyes of your understanding being enlightened" (Eph. 1:17-18). If God answered Paul's request so that the Lord gave the Ephesians the spirit of revelation and enlightenment that he was asking for, then, as you can see, the Ephesians would have "wisdom" and "understanding in "the knowledge of Him." Then Paul got more specific about what wisdom, understanding, and knowledge of God he actually wanted the Ephesians to obtain. It is summarized in three requests: 1) "the hope of His calling, 2) "the riches of the glory of His inheritance in the saints", 3) the exceeding greatness of His power to us-ward who believe" (Eph. 1:18-19). Notice how one of Paul's requests was that the Ephesians would know "the exceeding greatness of His power to us-ward!" This is a very significant prayer in relation to the words of Jesus Christ concerning baptism, how He said: "tarry... until ye be endued with power from on high" (Luke 24:49). If Paul wanted the people of God to understand the power of God, notice how he did not communicate to them that they needed to be baptized with the Spirit of God, so as to, afterward, understand the power of God. He said nothing of the sort! Paul did not command them to pray, fast, and strive after "the second blessing" until God gave them the "Baptism of the Spirit" experience. In fact, Paul had stated that the Ephesians already had "all spiritual blessings in heavenly places in Christ" (Eph. 1:3)! If the saints of Ephesus had already received "all spiritual blessings", how then could they be in need to receive another one, one that they have not yet received? Paul, who evidently was not burdened for the baptism of the Spirit like as the second blessing doctrine teaches it, was, rather, burdened that the saints would have revelation and enlightenment of what had already been given to them at salvation, so that when they received revelation of it, then they would have the faith and understanding to appropriate it!

How could the Ephesians obtain a greater revelation of "the hope of His calling", "the riches of the glory of His inheritance in the saints", and "the exceeding greatness of His power to us-ward who believe?" Well, Paul told us: "according to the working of His mighty power" in the second blessing baptism of the Spirit? No! "Which He wrought in Christ, when He raised Him from the dead, and set Him at His own right hand in the heavenly places, far above all principality, and power, and might, and dominion, and every name that is named, not only in this world, but also in that which is to come: and hath put all things under His feet, and gave Him to be the head over all things to the Church, which is His body, the fulness of Him that filleth all in all" (Eph. 1:20-23). Paul said that there is hope, riches of glory in inheritance, and surpassing power available to Christians when we properly know what He did, in wisdom, knowledge, and revelation, what exactly God did in Christ when He "raised Him from the Dead" – THE RESURRECTION – "set Him at His own right hand in the heavenly places" – THE ASCENSION & GLORIFCATION – and what relation this is to "all principality, and power, and might, and dominion" in "this world".

If we properly understand the work of Christ at the cross – His Death, Burial, Resurrection, & Ascension – and how that relates to us who are regenerate in Him, then we will know the hope of our calling, the riches of the inheritance of the saints, and the surpassing power to us who believe. Behold, Paul preached the very revelation that he prayed for us to obtain! Why does Christ's resurrection mean power to us? Because, "you hath He quickened [or raised from the dead], who were dead in trespasses and sins" (Eph. 2:1)! Why does Christ's ascension and glorification at the throne mean power to us? Because God "hath raised us up together and made us sit together in heavenly places in Christ Jesus" (Eph. 2:6)! What does Christ's enthronement over powers and principalities of this world have to do with power being given to us? We are still in the world, which resides under the dominion of "the prince of the power of the air" (Eph. 2:2), who is Satan, and all those that rule with him in his antichrist revolt called, "principalities," "powers," "the rulers of the darkness of this world," and "spiritual wickedness in high places" (Eph. 6:12). If Christ's throne is above these worldly rulers, and yet, we too are with Christ where He is seated, in domain of rulership that is above earthly rule, then what is under Christ's feet is also under our feet! This means POWER! And we need it! For we do "wrestle against" these powers of darkness while we sojourn on earth, but lo! In Christ there is surpassing great power given to us already in that we are seated with Him at His throne, which means, "the power of His might" is already given to us, victory is already secured, therefore by faith we can "be strong in the Lord" (Eph. 6:10). This enthronement of Christ's glory is the most blessed estate of the visible and invisible creation of God! Christ's throne is the most highly favored seat in the whole of existence! And lo, there we are seated with Him! If we are with Christ at the Father's "own right hand in the **heavenly places**" (Eph. 1:20), then it is understandable why it was said that God has "blessed us with all spiritual blessings in **heavenly places** in Christ" (Eph. 1:3).

Now please, look with me at one final point of great significance! Christ's resurrection, ascension, and glorification is said to be with the Church, which is called: "the fullness of Him that filleth all in all" (Eph. 1:23). What does "the fulness of Him that filleth all in all" have to do with surpassing power available to us? Well, if we had wisdom, revelation, and enlightenment to understand "the love of Christ which passeth knowledge" (Eph. 3:19), namely in His resurrection, ascension, and glorification, then we would understand that we are filled with "the fulness of Him that filleth all in all" already! And if we understood this, by faith, then it would be a reality in our walk, and thus, presently and progressively, we would be "filled with the Spirit" (Eph. 5:18), or, "filled with all the fulness of God" (Eph. 3:19). By a lack of revelation knowledge in the gospel's work in relation to us now on earth, then we will not appropriate or experience what has already been accomplished and given at the day of our conversion.

Present Progressive Salvation

Faith expressed through power is a worthy demand of God for those who have been, verily, endued with power already (Eph. 1:19, Col. 1:10-11, 2 Thess. 1:11-12). It is going to take the strength and power of God Almighty to overcome all the ruling hosts and forces of wickedness in this world (Eph. 6:10-11). It is easy to understand that we need the baptism of the Spirit to be saved, that this is salvation; but as a saint goes from glory to glory, then he will continually be renewed in his mind of the greatness of God's power which is readily available to them in Christ, already and now, because of the past tense work of "The Baptism of the Spirit". However, if a saint falls from this enlightenment (Eph. 1:18) and so begins to be weak and cowardly (Rev. 21:8) against the enemies of sin, so as to be overcome therein (2 Pet. 2:20), then such a one needs to reckon the power of the gospel again which saved them once (Rom. 1:16), which overcomes death (Eph. 1:20, 1 John 5:4), and keep this faith unto the end: "For God hath not given us a Spirit of fear; but of power, and of love, and of a sound mind. Be not thou therefore ashamed of the testimony of our Lord..." (2 Tim. 1:7-8). The common man does understand that power was revealed at Pentecost, but this was only an example of what we should thereafter believe in God for! The gospel by promise is that we have been given **the fullness of the power of God** – "the strength of His might" (Eph. 6:10) – and so, how can we be given more power that we don't already have? Likewise, in Christ we have already been blessed with "all spiritual blessings in heavenly places in Christ" (Eph. 1:3), so how could we be blessed with another one?

> "And to know the love of Christ, which passeth knowledge, that ye might **be filled with all the fulness of God**." -Eph 3:19

"And be not drunk with wine, wherein is excess; but **be filled with the Spirit.**" -Eph 5:18

As a man can be initially crucified/dead/mortified by promise, and at present is commanded to reckon and appropriate the gospel truths to walk in their reality and power on earth today, which is to say he is mortifying again those already mortified members, therefore in such termed commands therein hinges salvific, holy, walking and living. Likewise it is with being filled with the Spirit of God! We are already filled with the fulness of Christ that filleth all in all, just as we are already resurrected with Christ, but all the power and potentials of this resurrection have not been accessed by faith and walked out in; so also, the present progressive command to maintain faith in the gospel is to be filled with the Spirit of God – the gospel by command. To be filled with the Spirit of God at a younger glory than an elder will have a different degree of sanctification in it, therefore a more mature image of Christ revealed to the world, but keeping the faith of the gospel is to, at your degree of sanctification, overcome the sin that God is making known to you (to the degree of what is known to be Christian perfection), and so, Christ is living and you are not. In other words, Christ is formed in you. Now, when you are backslidden in a damnable state like as the Galatians were when they did fall from grace, Paul said to them, "My little children, of whom I travail in birth again **until Christ be formed in you**" (Gal. 4:19). How could Paul travail in birth over those who were already born again? It is not that they could be born again, again, but that Paul was speaking of their restoration to a saving relationship in Christ, and this travailing, is a second travailing, a travailing again - because Paul already labored to see them come to the birth at one time. At the birth, they were born again into a saving faith in the gospel of grace so that Christ was savingly formed in them (i.e. they were walking after the Spirit and mortifying the flesh, thus He was living and they were dying), but now they did backslide from the gospel truths so that Christ was no longer living, they were no longer walking in the Spirit, and they were striving after God in the flesh, thus Paul said Christ needed to be formed in them again in a saving degree, which is also called "perfection" (Gal. 3:2-3).

> "He that descended is the same also that ascended up far above all heavens, **that He might fill all things**.) And He gave some, apostles; and some, prophets; and some, evangelists; and some, pastors and teachers; For the **perfecting** of the saints, for the work of the ministry, for the edifying of the body of Christ: Till we all come in the unity of the faith, and of the knowledge of the Son of God, unto **a perfect man**, unto the measure of the stature of **the fulness of Christ**…" -Eph 4:10-13

> "And to know the love of Christ, which passeth knowledge, that ye might **be filled with all the fulness of God.**" –Eph. 3:19

The very same principles are seen in Ephesians 4:10-13. The Church ministers, called apostles, prophets, evangelists, pastors, and teachers, do labor by

441

prayer and preaching just as Paul was to the Ephesians, to the end that they would have revelation and faith to walk in the gospel truths – gospel by promise and gospel by command – unto a saving spiritual condition, otherwise put, "the perfecting of the saints" (Eph. 4:12). Personal Christian perfection, or "the perfecting of the saints," leads to corporate perfection. Corporate perfection is when the entire Church is savingly walking in the Person and stature of Christ to a degree of "**fulness**" (Eph. 4:13). When each individual saint of the Church walks in "the fulness of Him that filleth all in all" (Eph. 1:23), then the entire Church will reveal "the fulness of Christ" (Eph. 4:13). Personal perfection in each saint will cause the whole Church to be "fitly joined together" (Eph. 4:16), so that everyone is one, "a perfect man" (Eph. 4:13). Christ's work, the cross, burial, resurrection, ascension, and glorification, is so "that He might fill all things" (Eph. 4:10), and foremost of all that He would be revealed in the world through the Church! Therefore, personal perfection is personal fullness, and corporate perfection is corporate fullness, and in the book of Ephesians, these terms serve as present progressive commands to experience and maintain saving faith in the gospel, from glory to glory, just as there is mortification from glory to glory. Paul's burden for personal fullness is written in Ephesians 3:19, and this experience, like the phraseology of Galatians 4:19, is said to be the establishment of the saving, gospel truth – "that Christ may dwell in your hearts by faith" (Eph. 3:17). Can you see the exact parallel that this phrase is to, "until Christ be formed in you" (Gal. 4:19)? The experience of a continual, present progressive faith in the gospel, causes the individual to walk in what was first purchased and wrought. Christ's purchase and working was to make the body of Christ, all of us, filled with "the fulness of Him that filleth all in all" (Eph. 1:23), therefore we must walk out in the gospel command to "be filled with the fulness of God" present-progressively! This *worthy walk* of gospel-enabling grace and faith is what the apostles continually strove after, and they did *scarcely* attain it in these NT Christians (1 Peter 4:18). Perhaps now you are beginning to understand the overwhelming burden which expands throughout the NT writings, which is, to work out your salvation (Php. 2:12). Perhaps then you will take notice of the exact parallels of perfect union in each gospel synonym of all other epistles and inspired writings, and thus understand the following burdens of prayer and preaching:

> "Cease not…making mention of you in my prayers…that you may know…what is the exceeding greatness of His power." -Eph. 1:16-19

> "For this cause I bow my knees…that He would grant you… to be strengthened with might." – Eph. 3:14-16

> "do not cease to pray for you… that ye might walk worthy … strengthened with all might according to His glorious power." -Col. 1:9-11

> "Wherefore also we pray always for you, that our God would count you worthy…fulfill…the work of faith with power." -2 Thess. 1:11

"Night and day praying exceedingly that we... might perfect that which is lacking in your faith." – 1 Thess. 3:10

"Whom we preach, warning every man, and teaching every man in all wisdom; that we may present every man **perfect** in Christ Jesus: Whereunto I also labour, striving according to His working, which worketh in me mightily." -Col 1:28-29.

```
┌─────────────────────────────────────────────┐
│            RELATED SERMONS                    │
│                                               │
│        "The Ark And Ephesians"                │
│           – Sean Morris                       │
└─────────────────────────────────────────────┘
```

Put on Christ – The Gospel of Regeneration

Initial Salvation

"For as many of you as have been baptized into Christ **have put on Christ.**" -Gal 3:27

"Lie not one to another, <u>seeing that</u> ye **have put off** the old man with his deeds; And **have put on** the new man, which is renewed in knowledge after the image of him that created him." -Col 3:9-10

The scriptures speak of the gospel experience of ***initial salvation*** as this: we "have put on Christ" (Gal. 3:27). All of a regenerate Christian's present experience of walking in Christ is by "<u>seeing that</u>" "(Col. 3:9) truth – the truth of freedom that Christ purchased by the gospel – namely that, we "have **put off** the old man with his deeds and have **put on** the new man" (Col. 3:9-10), already, and now we can walk in Christ freely! Therefore it is written, "As ye have therefore received Christ Jesus the Lord, so walk ye in Him" (Col. 2:6). Now, as a saint has already been mortified but is commanded to mortify himself daily, and as a man has already been risen with Christ but is commanded to live and access realities in and around Christ at His throne, and as a man has already been baptized/endured with power/filled with the fullness of the Spirit of Christ but is commanded to be filled with the fullness of the Spirit daily, so also a man has put on Christ but is commanded to put on Christ daily – this is the ***Gospel by Command***.

Present Progressive Salvation

"**Put on** therefore, as the elect of God, holy and beloved, **bowels of mercies**, kindness, humbleness of mind, meekness,

443

longsuffering; Forbearing one another, and forgiving one another, if any man have a quarrel against any: even as Christ forgave you, so also do ye. And above all these things **put on charity**, which is the bond of perfectness." -Col 3:12-14

"That ye **put off** concerning the former conversation **the old man**, which is corrupt according to the deceitful lusts; And be renewed in the spirit of your mind; And that ye **put on the new man**, which after God is created in righteousness and true holiness." -Eph 4:22-24

Colossians 3:12-14 commands the putting on of "bowels of mercies" which is from "the new man" (Col. 3:10), Who is Christ that lives in them, and in this way they are to do EVERTHING, "in word or deed, do all in the name of the Lord Jesus" (Col. 3:17). The new man is the Spirit of the Living God, Who is our "newness of life" (Rom. 6:4). This putting on is an abiding in, a walking in the Person and inner workings of Christ, called here the "bowels" (Col. 3:12) of the new man, or "the bowels of Jesus" (Php. 1:8), which are "holy and beloved" springs of all the fruits you see listed in those scriptures. Thus, to put on Christ it is also to "put on charity", establishing perfect unity in all of the body of Christ (Col. 3:14).

"The night is far spent, the day is at hand: let us therefore cast off the works of darkness, and let us **put on the armour of light**. Let us walk honestly, as in the day; not in rioting and drunkenness, not in chambering and wantonness, not in strife and envying. But **put ye on the Lord Jesus Christ**, and make not provision for the flesh, to fulfil the lusts thereof." -Rom 13:12-14

Romans 13:12-14 commands the putting on of "the armour of Light" which also is Christ; therefore there is a direct reference to this gospel by command saying, "put ye on the Lord Jesus Christ". All of this is the same burden of God in each epistle, but this specific phraseology of the gospel is most common in these three books of Paul (Col. 3, Rom. 13, Eph. 4). Ephesians 4:22-24 speaks of the old man as the former conversation which a Christian man must, by faith, put off today, and then "put on the new man" which is the creation of God in their souls – "created in righteousness and true holiness". Now again, to maintain saving faith in the gospel of grace, a man will then maintain obedience to these gospel presentations given by command rather than promise, but if you study these passages carefully, you will find the same need for ever-present and increasing revelation to be given as the saint has a greater view of his own sins next to the righteousness of God, and so the saint will go from glory to glory by keeping faith in the gospel. Perhaps now you will understand that revelation and faith are the two objects of grace which do increase as a saint goes from glory to glory, and then you will understand the burden of these passages below:

"seeing that ye" (Col. 3:9)
"seeing that ye" (1 Peter 1:22)

"**renewing of your mind**"(Rom. 12:2)
"**renewed in knowledge**"(Col. 3:10)
"**renewed in the spirit of your mind**"(Eph. 4:23)

"**But now... put off all these**" (Col. 3:8)
"**Wherefore putting away**" (Eph. 4:25)
"**Wherefore laying aside**" (1 Peter 2:1)

"all things that pertain" (2 Peter 1:3-4)
"all spiritual blessings in heavenly places" (Eph. 1:3).

"**wisdom** and **revelation** in the **knowledge** of Him" (Eph. 1:19)
"filled with the **knowledge** of His will... all **wisdom** and **spiritual understanding** ...increasing in the **knowledge** of God" (Col. 1:9-10).
"grow in grace and in the **knowledge** of our Lord" (2 Peter 3:18)
"I pray... love may abound yet more and more in **knowledge** and in all **judgment**" (Php. 1:9-11).

"**If so be that ye** have heard Him, and have been taught by Him" (Eph. 4:20-21).
"**If so be that ye** have tasted that the Lord is gracious" (1 Peter 2:3).
"the excellency of the knowledge of Christ Jesus my Lord" (Php. 3:8).

When a man holds fast to the liberty given by the gospel purchase ***presently and progressively***, the man is "seeing that" (Col. 3:9, 1 Pet. 1:22) he has "put off" the old man and "put on" the new man already, and so by faith's reckoning, he is "renewed" in the "mind" (Col. 3:10, Eph. 4:23, Rom. 12:2) unto an empowering walk of "putting away" (Eph. 4:25, Col. 3:8) and "laying aside" (1 Pet. 2:1) the evil deeds listed in Col. 3:5, Ephesians 4:25-32, and 1 Peter 2:1: "fornication, uncleanness, inordinate affection, evil concupiscence, and covetousness, which is idolatry," "lying, angry wrath, stealing, corrupt communication, bitterness, wrath, anger, clamour, evil speaking, malice," "malice, guile, hypocrisies, envies, and all evil speaking." Such a man that walks this way is having the "wisdom, revelation, knowledge, and spiritual understanding" that the apostles are praying for (Eph. 1:19, Col. 1:9-10, 2 Peter 3:18, 1 Php. 1:9-11), and as it increases in measure, so the glories brighten into greater expressions of Christ!

Quickened (Alive, Living, & Revived) – The Gospel of Regeneration

Initial Salvation

"And you hath He quickened who were dead" (Eph. 2:1).

"when we were dead in sins, hath quickened" (Eph. 2:5).

Salvation is described in a past tense experience termed in this way: when you were dead you were then quickened. This simply means, brought from **death** to

life in Christ, which is, **carnality** to **Spirituality**, because "to be **carnally** minded is **death**; but to be **spiritually** minded is **life** and peace" (Rom. 8:6). Now what happens when a Christian, who has passed from death to life, is no longer walking in the Spirit, but rather the flesh which is death?

Present Progressive Salvation

> "And unto the angel of the Church in Sardis write; These things saith He that hath the seven Spirits of God, and the seven stars; I know thy works, **that thou hast a name that thou livest, and art dead.**" -Rev 3:1

> "Wherefore He saith, Awake thou that sleepest, and **arise from the dead**, and Christ shall give thee light." -Eph 5:14

> "We know that we have **passed from death unto life**, because we love the brethren. He that loveth not his brother **abideth in death.**" -1 Jn. 3:14

To a regenerate Church of God, Christ said, "thou hast a name that thou **livest**, and art **dead**" (Rev. 3:1), yet they were at one time living rightly with God. A regenerate man will be judged at present, at death, or at the Judgment as dead, if he has left off saving faith in the gospel which results in the *quickening power* of *life over death* & sin. Christ is reproving the Church in Revelation 3:1 with loss of salvation as the consequence in view. This should be understood by the plain terms Jesus used when He said, "thou...art dead" (Rev. 3:1), but later Christ ends this reproof of the Church of Sardis with unarguable clarity, saying, "He that overcometh, the same shall be clothed in white raiment; and I will not blot out his name out of the book of life, but I will confess his name before My Father, and before His angels" (Rev. 3:5). Now look closely at Ephesians 5:14. Do you see how the apostle appeals to the regenerate Ephesians that they "were sometimes darkness" but now were "light in the Lord" (Eph. 5:8) because of their initial salvation, and yet, do you see how this means that they were sometimes dead but now they were alive in the Lord? You see, they were made light and alive at initial salvation, but they were not walking in the light or life of Christ! Paul judges that, at this point, they were considered spiritually dead in the sight of God. The appeal for repentance is clear: "Arise from the dead and Christ shall give thee light" (Eph. 5:14). All the saints of the past understood that they could fall into a damnable condition of spirituality even though they were already alive by regeneration, therefore they prayed:

"Thou, which hast shewed me great and sore troubles, shalt **quicken** me again, and shalt bring me up again from the depths of the earth." -Ps. 71:20
"So will not we go back from Thee: **quicken** us, and we will call upon Thy name." -Ps. 80:18
"My soul cleaveth unto the dust: **quicken** Thou me according to Thy word." -Ps. 119:25
"Turn away mine eyes from beholding vanity; and **quicken** Thou me in Thy way." -Ps. 119:37
"Behold, I have longed after Thy precepts: **quicken** me in Thy righteousness." -Ps. 119:40

"**Quicken** me after Thy lovingkindness; so shall I keep the testimony of Thy mouth." -Ps. 119:88

"I am afflicted very much: **quicken** me, O LORD, according unto Thy word." -Ps. 119:107

"Hear my voice according unto Thy lovingkindness: O LORD, **quicken** me according to Thy judgment." -Ps. 119:149

"Plead my cause, and deliver me: **quicken** me according to Thy word." -Ps. 119:154

"Great are Thy tender mercies, O LORD: **quicken** me according to Thy judgments." -Ps. 119:156

"Consider how I love Thy precepts: **quicken** me, O LORD, according to Thy lovingkindness." -Ps. 119:159

"**Quicken** me, O LORD, for Thy name's sake: for Thy righteousness' sake bring my soul out of trouble" -Ps. 143:11

"When lust is conceived it bringeth forth sin: and sin, when it is finished bringeth forth **death**" (James 1:14), so that when a regenerate Christian backslides into a blamable state of **darkness** and **death**, firstly, they are spiritually dead (which is a recoverable condition, hence the appeal to repent), and if they tarry long in this dead rebellion then there remains only one conclusion: at the time limit of God's choosing, they will be reprobated into an unrecoverable condition of spiritual death, doomed for the second death, and since they were once dead, then alive, and now irrevocably dead in their sins again, they are said to be "twice dead" (Jude 12). James 5:19-20 speaks directly on this grave matter. All Christians are exhorted to help recover their brethren from spiritual death before it reaches the threshold of judgment when it becomes an irrevocable reprobation into second death! "**Brethren, if any of you** do err from the truth, and one convert him; Let him know, that he which converteth the sinner from the error of his way shall **save a soul from death, and shall hide a multitude of sins**". A reprobate man is a man who cannot repent, who cannot be interceded for with Christian intercessory prayer, as it is written: "If any man see **his brother** sin a sin which is not **unto death**, he shall ask, and He shall give him **life** for them that **sin not unto death**. There is **a sin unto death**: I do not say that he shall pray for it" (1 Jn. 5:16). Why does John say, "I do not say that he shall pray for it?" Because the NT threshold of reprobation is in view; therefore that which is said in the Old Testament is echoed in the New: "Therefore pray not thou for this people, neither lift up cry nor prayer for them, neither make intercession to Me: for I will not hear thee" (Jer. 7:16). "Then said the LORD unto me, Pray not for this people for good..." (Jer. 15:11).

A regenerate man must obey the gospel by command, which is to "arise from the dead", even though he is already alive and risen, and so he must lay hold upon the powers of life that are in Christ to walk in Him, lest they be found to be as those which do abide in death, as 1 John 3:14 warns. Perhaps now you may understand the warnings of Christ, The Judge of Christians, when He said – "he that overcometh shall not be hurt of the second death" (Rev. 2:11). Dear reader, reckon this fact! Christ will judge regenerate Christians as He judges the regenerate Churches in Revelations 2-3, as the apostles are burdened for and seek the salvific perfection of saving faith with continuance in all regenerate Churches that were committed to their care (as seen by all the gospel language covered thus far); therefore it is imperative that we understand that we are alive by initial salvation, we must presently and progressively be alive in Christ, so as to walk in His life (Gal. 5:25), to the end that we are judged worthy of salvation by keeping the faith unto the end. Christ returning to judge between *the quick* and *the dead* means the same to say, Christ will judge between *the revived* and *the dead*, and yet, today men have made revival out to be an eternally insignificant experience in regenerate Christians. Will you understand the burden of the New Testament and look at these passages straight on, and present-progressively walk in the revived life of a Christian, even so to be judged quick on that last day? Perhaps you will understand this burden now:

> "Who shall give account to him that is **ready to judge the quick and the dead...**" -1 Pet. 4:5

> "I charge thee therefore before God, and the Lord Jesus Christ, **Who shall judge the quick and the dead** at His appearing and His kingdom..." -2 Tim. 4:1

When true pastors are moved by saving graces to reach this hallowed and salvific goal, a present progressive revival shines and arouses the ever-lingering saints. They rise up and join those who are ever-abounding, and the Church meetings are like as Martin-Lloyd Jones did so precisely describe:

> "That is what happens in revival and thus you get this curious, strange mixture, as it were, of great conviction of sin and great joy, a great sense of the terror of the Lord, and great thanksgiving and praise. Always in a revival there is what somebody once called a divine disorder. Some are groaning and agonizing under conviction, others praising God for the great salvation. And all this leads to crowded and prolonged meetings. Time seems to be forgotten. People seem to have entered into eternity." – "What is Revival"

This is the normal Christian life of a healthy and persevering biblical Church, according to the New Testament standard. Are you prepared for the Judgment? Namely, of them who are "the quick and the dead"?

THE PARTIAL COMPLETION OF THE GOSPEL
-PRESENT PROGRESSIVE SALVATION EXPLAINED
CHAPTER 19

"Mark **the perfect man**, and behold the upright: for the end of that man is peace."
– Psalm 37:37

Regenerate Christians were *initially* saved, must *presently* and *progressively* be saved, and will be *finally* saved when the gospel consummates at Christ's coming. Therefore we wait, and do not now have the full salvation which is to come – the "salvation to be revealed" (1 Peter 1:5). In the previous study leading up to this section, the Gospel was amplified by *promise* and *command* in five separate and definitive terms – *crucified*, *resurrected*, *baptized*, *put on*, and *quickened*. When this is understood, we can see that *the call of the Gospel* was not merely a single-sensed calling, or a single-sensed salvation, but it *initially* began, then it *presently* and *progressively* continues in the personal walk of a true believer. Lastly, when these two senses of the Gospel call are savingly kept, then the believer is led into the Gospel's fulfillment and *final* consummation for which it was set forth – the call's conclusion – the third sense of salvation – the final resurrection – "the high *calling* of God in Christ Jesus" (Php. 3:14).

There are various other terms descriptive of the salvific work of Christ accomplished in the true believer, and by them we can also see an exhaustive explanation of what we now have in the *partial completion* of the gospel experience here on earth, and that which will *be finally consummated* in the end – the final resurrection. When these are cited and paralleled next to each other, like the notations below, it is easier to understand the holistic mindset of the inspired writers in their terminology, phraseology, teaching, rhetoric, and theology.

- Adopted now (Rom. 8:15) – Consummating Adoption to come   (Rom. 8:23)
- Redeemed now (1 Cor. 1:30) – Consummating Redemption to come (Php. 3:14, Rom. 8:23).
- Regeneration now (Titus 3:5) – Consummating Regeneration to come(Rom. 8:18-21, Php. 3:12-14)
- Kingdom within you now (Lk. 17:21, Col. 1:13, Eph. 2:6)–Consummating Kingdom to come (2 Tim. 4:1, Rev. 3:21)
- On Mount Zion now (Heb. 12:22)–Consummating ascent upon Mount Zion to come (Rev. 14:1-5)
- Resurrection now (Rom. 6:4) – Consummating Resurrection to come (1 Cor. 15:50)
- Eternal Life now (1 John 3:15, 5:12-13) – Consummating Eternal Life to come (2 Cor. 5:1-4, 1 Tim. 6:12)
- Overcoming power now (Eph. 2:5, 1 John 5:4) – Consummating Overcoming power to come (1 Cor. 15:54-57)
- Defeat of Death now(Rom. 8:2, 6, Eph. 2:5)–Consummating Defeat of Death to come (1 Cor. 15:54-57)

✦ In the Light now(Eph. 5:8)– Consummating, Eternal Day of Light to come(Prov. 4:18, 2 Peter 1:19, Rev. 21:23-25)
✦ Seeing God now(2 Cor. 3:17-18, 1 Cor. 13:12, Heb. 11:27)–Consummating revelatory sight to come (1 John 3:2)
✦ Perfect Now (Heb. 10:14) – Consummating Perfection to come (Php. 3:12, 1 Cor. 13:10, Prov. 4:18)
✦ "As He is" now (1 John 4:17) – Consummating conformity, "as He is" in glory, to come (1 John 3:2, Rev. 2:27)
✦ Knowing Him now (1 John 2:4, John 17:3) – Consummating knowing, "even as also I am known" to come (1 Cor. 13:12)
✦ Elect now (2 Jn. 1:1, 13, 1 Pet. 1:2) – Consummating Election to come (2 Peter 1:10)
✦ Called now (1 Cor. 1:26) – Consummating Calling to come (Php. 3:14)
✦ Chosen now (1 Peter 2:9) – Consummating Choice to come (Matt. 22:14, Rev. 17:14)

The above notations can be briefly explained like this: We have been partakers of Christ's death; however, the consummating victory over death will not be actualized until after the fullness of the gospel of Christ's Kingdom is consummated. We have been *resurrected* (Rom. 6:4), *regenerated* (Tit. 3:5), we have overcome *death* (Eph. 2:5), and *inherited* the Kingdom of God (Lk. 17:21), but we await a final consummating *resurrection* (1 Cor. 15:42-50), *regeneration* (Rom. 8:18-21, Php. 3:12-14), defeat of *death* (1 Cor. 15:54-57), and *inheritance* of the Kingdom of God (1 Cor. 15:50). In this manner we await a "salvation to be revealed" (1 Pet. 1:5), which is not yet full, and we strive for the calling of this final freedom (Php. 3:14).

At the final consummation of the gospel, which is our salvation, then "that which is perfect is come", which means our salvation experience, which is presently "in part", is done away with, and our reconciliation, which was "in part", is done away with; therefore, then it will be the final resurrection wherein begins the face-to-face encounter of saints with God, to ever be with God in eternal, <u>sinless</u> **perfection** (1 Cor. 13:9-10). There are two verses in NT scripture which preach the consummation of salvation as *perfection* (1 Cor. 13:10, Php. 3:12, Prov. 4:18). This is understandable, because we are to strive to "be accepted of Him" (2 Cor. 5:9-10) on that final Day, and our acceptance rewards to us an eternity of sinlessly dwelling with God in His <u>sinless *perfection*</u>. Here, the end of the gospel call is spoken of in the term "**perfection**". If the Gospel call's consummation is spoken of in this term – "perfection" – could there be other senses of this very same word which define the *initial* or *present progressive* forms of the gospel? For example, the word "resurrection" describes the consummating end of the gospel call (1 Cor. 15:50), but it also describes the *initial* and *present progressive* experience of a believer (Rom. 6:4). In the very same way, the word "perfection" is used. I have cited two verses which use the word "perfection" as the consummating end of the gospel (1 Cor. 10:13, Php. 3:12), but I will soon cover at least 20 other uses of the word "perfect", "perfected", or "perfection", which all refer to the *initial* and *present progressive* experience of the gospel call. There would be a drastic change in our prayers and preaching if we understood the meaning behind these words. Where the gospel is preached (*initially*, *present-progressively*, or *finally*), eternity hangs in the balance! Does a man desire to obtain *final perfection*, which is the *final resurrection*? Let him obtain the two senses of perfection which are attainable now in Christ: *initial* and *present progressive* perfection.

The entire goal of the NT pastors was to cause the Church to be an acceptable *presentation* to Christ at His coming, meaning, they are in a perfect, complete, saving relationship in the NT Covenant sense. If a man is perfectly fulfilling all five senses of the *initial* and *present progressive* experience of the gospel call – crucified, resurrected, baptized, put on, quickened – then such a one is "**perfect**", in its *initial* and *present progressive* sense, and for a man to be perfect, then he is also, biblically speaking – *blameless* (*unblameable*, *without blame* & *offence*, *unreprovable* & *without rebuke*, *faultless*, and *sincere*), *holy* (*sanctified*), and *without blemish* and *spot*. These new terms that I have listed are separated into four other categories which make up, as you will see, more gospel synonyms which define God's approval and acceptance of a NT Christian *initially*, *present-progressively*, and *finally*, and if the NT believer is not acceptable to God in any of these three senses of the gospel call, then God uses one of the four categories of terms to express and define His disapproval and rejection of them. Therefore, all of these terms hold the utmost weight because they are descriptive of a person's saving faith in the gospel experience, *initially*, *present-progressively*, and *finally*, and so also these terms are used in the very same three contextual scenarios or senses in NT scripture. In these terms, we can see the burden of salvation expanded beyond the five terms of the gospel and salvation which we have already discussed. These four terms which make up four categories of study are charted below, and following this chart, they are divided and expounded in their sense and meaning.

The Gospel By Promise	**The Gospel By Command**
(FINISHED IN THE PAST)	(AT PRESENT)
God tells you what He has done. How He walked.	God tells you what you must do, in Him & through Him. How you must walk, in Him & through Him.
~ Imputed Righteousness (Rom. 8:10, Eph. 2:8-9, 1 Cor. 6:11)~	*~Works Righteousness (1 Cor. 6:9-10, Eph. 2:10)~* Walk: Col. 2:6, Gal. 5:16, 25, Eph. 4:17, 5:8, 1 Cor. 3:3, 1 John 2:6
1) **Perfect & Complete**	1) **Perfect & Complete**
♦ "ye are complete in Him" (Col. 2:10)	♦ Perfect as a Christian (Lk. 6:40, Col. 1:28-29, 4:12, Eph. 4:12, 1 Cor. 2:6, 2 Cor. 13:9, 11, Php. 3:15, 2 Tim. 3:17, Heb. 6:1, 13:21, James 3:2)
♦ "For by one offering He hath perfected for ever them that are sanctified" (Heb. 10:14)	♦ Perfect faith (James 2:21-22, 1 Thess. 3:10)
	♦ Perfect love (1 John 2:5, 4:12, 17)
	♦ Perfect holiness (2 Cor. 7:1)
	♦ Perfect works (Rev. 3:2, Heb. 13:21, 2 Thess. 2:16-17)

451

2) Blameless (unblameable, without blame & offence, unreprovable & without rebuke, faultless, sincere)

+ "chosen us in Him before the foundation of the world, that we should be holy and without blame before Him in love" (Eph. 1:4)
+ "to present you holy and unblameable and unreproveable in His sight" (Col. 1:22)
+ PROMISE: 1 Cor. 1:8-9

3) Holy & Sanctified

+ "chosen us in Him before the foundation of the world, that we should be holy and without blame before Him in love" (Eph. 1:4)
+ Col. 1:22, Heb. 10:10, 1 Peter 1:2, 1 Cor. 6:11

4) Without Blemish & Spot

+ Gal. 2:20
+ Christ: Exodus 12:5, Num. 19:2, Lev. 22:19-22, 1 Cor. 5:7, John 1:29, 1 Pet. 1:19

2) Blamelessness (unblameable, without blame, unreprovable)

+ "clearing of yourselves" – 2 Cor. 7:11
+ "obtained good report" - Heb. 11:2, 39
+ Revelation 2:4, 14, 20, 23, 3:2
+ Fault: 1 Cor. 6:6, Gal. 6:1, Jude 24, Rev. 14:5
+ Blame: Gal. 2:11 (14, 17-18), Php. 2:15, 1 Thess. 3:13, 5:23-24, 1 Tim. 5:7, 2 Peter 3:14
+ Offence: Php. 1:10
+ Sincere: Php. 1:10
+ Without rebuke: Php. 2:15, 1 Tim. 6:14, Rev. 3:19, Hos. 5:9, Isa. 51:20, Psalm 80:16

3) Holy & Sanctified

+ Heb. 12:14, 1 Thess. 3:13, 4:3, 7, 5:23-24, 2 Tim. 2:21, 1 Peter 1:14-17, 2 Peter 3:11, Rev. 21:27, 22:11
+ 1 Tim. 2:15, 1 Peter 3:11

4) Without Blemish & Spot

+ Rom. 12:1-2
+ James 1:26-27, 3:2-6, 2 Peter 3:14,1 Tim. 6:14
+ Corporate: Rom. 15:16-19, Ephesians 5:25-27, 2 Peter 2:13, Jude 12)

The Church, upon regeneration, is initially saved, and to be initially saved, then you have undergone the gospel experience called "imputed righteousness". If you have imputed righteousness, then, lawfully speaking, you have the righteousness of Christ covering you. Therefore at this point, you are savingly in perfection/completion; you are savingly, perfectly, and completely joined to Christ! If a man has *imputed righteousness*, but then fails to maintain his saving faith, this is a failure to maintain unity with the life of the righteous Christ which indwells him; therefore he will not produce Christ's *works righteousness* (called "My works" [Rev. 2:26]). If a man does not have works righteousness, then he has *dead faith*, and if it is not *revived* or made *alive* again, then he too will be judged *dead*, without God, Christ, and imputed righteousness – thus he has fallen from *perfection* into *blame*. If a man falls from a saving relationship with Christ, which is by saving faith apart from works, and then those inward, immediate, and empowering qualities of the gospel are not walked out, which means that the powers of *initial* salvation are not *presently* and *progressively* experienced by the individual, then there is no present progressive works righteousness. If a man falls from works righteousness and yet pleads for salvation because he once had imputed righteousness, he is arguing for mercy because he once believed the gospel which he no longer believes at present. Scripture overwhelmingly declares that such a man will not be saved except by the restoration of faith and repentance.

When a man is in *perfection*, he is in blamelessness (unblameable, without blame and offence, unreprovable and without rebuke, faultless, and sincere), because he is in the first and active virtues of salvation which clothe a man in the lawful righteousness of Christ's sinless perfection; but they (those Christians who are perfect initially or present-progressively) are NOT sinlessly perfect by deed until they are finally resurrected at the gospel's consummation. Therefore also, as a man will be called perfect and blameless, so also he is called holy and sanctified for the same reasons which stem from his *saving connection to Christ*. He has inward and immediate holiness and sanctification (by nature, Spirit, and law), and is also, therefore, without blemish and spot in the eyes of God. All of this is because he has been baptized with salvation in the Spirit of God, Whose work is to make you *crucified*, *dead*, *buried*, *resurrected*, and *ascended* with Christ. Therefore he has put on Christ, and seeing that He is the man's righteousness, nature, life, and new man, he is all of these characteristics charted above at *initial* salvation – but will you know that to maintain those characteristics in *present progressive* salvation is the main burden of the NT writers? As exhaustively as we have covered the other five biblical terms which encapsulate the Gospel by Promise paralleled with the Gospel by Command, the four terms recently charted above are even more exhaustive! When a man comes to understand these terms and their relationship to the purpose of salvation (initially, present-progressively, and finally), it becomes evident that – SALVATION – is the central focus of scriptural preaching and the whole work of the ministry for NT elders, and it required all the talents of the 5 Holy Ghost-empowered offices to even maintain SALVATION! NOT to maintain abundant rewards in heaven, NOT to bring an eternally insignificant work of revival into your church, but to establish YOUR eternal life in the gospel call of *present progressive* salvation! The question then remains, are you REVIVED!? You may have initially been in revival at your *initial* salvation, but are you *presently* and *progressively* being revived; walking in a continual state of revival? The biblical picture of the final commitment of the Church-Bride to God is called "The Presentation". Christian or pastor, do you have this burden? Do you even understand it?

*** The Presentation ***

"Whom we preach, warning every man, and teaching every man in all wisdom; that we may **present** every man perfect in Christ Jesus: Whereunto I also labour, striving according to His working, which worketh in me mightily" (Col. 1:28-29)

"To **present** you holy and unblameable and unreproveable in His sight" (Col. 1:22)

"That He might sanctify and cleanse it with the washing of water by the word, that He might **present** it to Himself a glorious Church, not having spot, or wrinkle, or any such thing; but that it should be holy and without blemish" (Eph. 5:26-27).

"Now unto Him that is able to keep you from falling, and to **present** you faultless before the presence of His glory with exceeding joy, to the only Wise God our Saviour, be glory and majesty, dominion and power, both now and ever. Amen" (Jude 24-25).

"For I am jealous over you with godly jealousy: for I have espoused you to one Husband, that I may **present** you as a chaste virgin to Christ" (2 Cor. 11:2).

WORTHY →	"pray always" (2 Thess. 1:11) "do not cease to pray" (Col. 1:9-10) "exhorted, comforted, & charged" (1 Thess. 2:11-12)
PERFECTION →	"Night & Day praying exceedingly" (1 Thess. 3:10) "preaching, warning, teaching, all wisdom, labour, striving, His working, mightily" (Col. 1:28-29)
ABOUNDING/ WITHOUT OFFENCE →	"I pray" (Php. 1:9-10) "put you always in remembrance" (2 Pet. 1:12) "stir you up by putting you in remembrance" (2 Pet. 1:13) "always in remembrance" (2 Pet. 1:15)

RELATED SERMONS

"The Presentation" – Sean Morris

"Worthiness" – Sean Morris

"Christian Perfection" – Sean Morris

Perfection – The Gospel of Regeneration

The Gospel By Promise	The Gospel By Command
(FINISHED IN THE PAST)	(AT PRESENT)
God tells you what He has done. How He walked.	God tells you what you must do, in Him & through Him. How you must walk, in Him & through Him.
~ *Imputed Righteousness (Rom. 8:10, Eph. 2:8-9, 1 Cor. 6:11)*~	~*Works Righteousness (1 Cor. 6:9-10, Eph. 2:10)*~
	Walk: Col. 2:6, Gal. 5:16, 25, Eph. 4:17, 5:8, 1 Cor. 3:3, 1 John 2:6

The Gospel By Promise

1) **Perfect & Complete**
   - "ye are complete in Him" (Col. 2:10)
   - "For by one offering He hath perfected for ever them that are sanctified" (Heb. 10:14)

The Gospel By Command

1) **Perfect & Complete**
   - Perfect as a Christian (Lk. 6:40, Col. 1:28-29, 4:12, Eph. 4:12, 1 Cor. 2:6, 2 Cor. 13:9, 11, Php. 3:15, 2 Tim. 3:17, Heb. 6:1, 13:21, James 3:2)
   - Perfect faith (James 2:21-22, 1 Thess. 3:10)
   - Perfect love (1 John 2:5, 4:12, 17)
   - Perfect holiness (2 Cor. 7:1)
   - Perfect works (Rev. 3:2, Heb. 13:21, 2 Thess. 2:16-17)

How relevant is *The Doctrine of Perfection*?

Please hear me, and let us understand this vital doctrine, even if the language of it is foreign or distasteful to your Christian vocabulary! Don't let those heretics who preach sinless perfection cause you to reject anyone who renders a correct teaching on the matter. I beg you, please!

A correct view of biblical history would prove to us its utter necessity! Biblical history describes the lives, generations, and centuries of God's work of salvation in terms of personal and corporate *perfection*. Oh, will you hear it!? Depending on whether or not they obtained biblical "perfection", this determined

455

their destiny of heaven or hell! The scripture explicitly states that Job (Job 1:1, 8, 2:3, 8:20), Noah (Gen. 6:9), Abraham (Gen. 17:1-2), Joshua (Deut. 18:13), David (Psalm 101), Solomon (1 Kings 11:4, with his repentance, which is in Ecclesiastes), and Hezekiah (1 Kings 20:3) went to heaven because they were *perfect*. As for all other heaven-bound men, even though it was not explicitly mentioned that they were "*perfect*", they nevertheless followed the ways of them who were called "*perfect*". The scripture, likewise, does explicitly state that Abijam (1 Kings 15:3), Asa (In light of 2 Chron. 15:17, comparatively to 2 Chron. 16:7-13), and Amaziah (2 Chron. 25:2) went to hell because of a single indictment – that they were NOT *perfect*. Furthermore, every major vocation is taught the saving expression of their office and duties by the term *perfection*. Kings (Psalm 101), Priests (Lev. 22:21), Judges (2 Chron. 19:9), Warriors (Ps. 18:32), and all, were taught what it is to be *perfect* in the execution of their office, and depending on whether or not they were perfect, they went to heaven or hell. All other men and women of every generation were taught perfection in the principle of its meaning, even though the very word is not explicitly used. Let it therefore alarm us, if, haply, we don't understand what biblical perfection is!

Initial Perfection

A Christian is *initially perfect* because of the crucifixion, death, burial, resurrection, and ascension of Jesus Christ. In other words, the Christian's personal experience of these five senses of the gospel (as formerly and exhaustively addressed) makes him: "complete in Him" (Col. 2:10). Christ's work is sinlessly perfect; so is His gospel call, and as far as we are partial participants of these five senses of the gospel now on earth, we will be full participants of them in the time to come, but as for our initial salvation, it can only be called a perfecting NOW unto FOREVER: "For by one offering He hath perfected for ever them that are sanctified" (Heb. 10:14). This perfecting is a work performed at present, right now, and it is a promise of God unto forever, just like perseverance is promised. Abiding in this invaluable gift of eternal blessedness, one must be careful to abide in the gospel truths the scriptures do outline as a practical walk of saving faith, without which no man will continue to be perfectly sanctified by the blood of Christ, by law, spirit, or conscience. Two passages of gospel-walk-commands which hold in jeopardy the precious, cleansing, eternally powerful blood, now and in times to come, are Hebrews 10:19-31 & 1 John 1:5-7. Both passages describe a warning of disqualifications for the eternally perfecting attributes of the gospel, and in these two passages specifically, the present continuous perfecting power of the blood is addressed. In Hebrews 10:26-29, we read of a man's disqualification from the atoning power of the Lamb's sacrifice, even though he was already "sanctified" by "the blood" of the NT "Covenant" (Heb. 10:29). 1 John 5:7 holds in eternal jeopardy the very same quality, which is the present continuous cleansing power of the blood of Christ which "cleanseth us from all sin" (1 John 5:7). In this address, I have only focused on the perfection of the gospel as it has related to the blood, but I have already covered the other five senses of the gospel experience (crucifixion, death, burial, resurrection, and ascension) with their *present progressive* necessity as it pertains to perfection, and also how this is for the victory finish of *final perfection* for eternity.

Present Progressive Perfection

Seeing this, we ourselves can understand why Christ would send people to hell because they are not "perfect". Perfection is the fruitfulness demanded of all Christians, and it is obtained by all Christians who hold to saving faith presently, progressively, and continuously. At initial salvation a man is therefore perfect, as a Christian, and the perfecting powers of the gospel do make possible a man's present progressive perfection as a Christian. *Perfect faith* in the individual, as he responds to the gospel (initially and present progressively), will make the man walk in *perfect love* (true faith leads to charity), *perfect holiness* (true faith unites the Christian to the **Holy** Ghost causing immediate and instantaneous holiness, and a walking in His holiness henceforth), and *perfect works* (true faith is revealed through works of righteousness). Above, in the column of present continuous perfection, you can see these various forms of perfection cited in the scripture.

> "Whom we preach, warning every man, and teaching every man in all wisdom; that we may present every man **perfect** in Christ Jesus: Whereunto I also labour, striving according to His working, which worketh in me mightily" (Col 1:28-29).

> "Night and day praying exceedingly that we might see your face, and might **perfect** that which is lacking in your faith..." (1Th 3:10)

When we finally understand the eternal significance of perfection, the NT scriptures come alive in a new way. However gripping they were formerly to us when we read them, now they are terrifyingly hallowed in their address of a Christians' eternal hope of heaven and the woeful fate of hell, presently and progressively. Perhaps now we can understand why Paul did pray "night and day" "exceedingly" to "perfect" the faith of the saints in the NT times (1 Thess. 3:10). Some people have never prayed night and day exceedingly for anything! And lo, Paul is thus burdened for perfection in the regenerate Church! Perhaps now we can understand: all of our ingratiation to "preach", to "warn every man", and our "teaching", in every capacity of "all wisdom" that we are enabled to speak, or, with all the stamina, "labour", and "striving" we are enabled to continue to speak with, is all for the final, climactic, END of the Christian's destiny where he will be judged (at his death or Christ's return) on whether he is *perfect* or not. Paul's sole pursuit as an apostle, pastor, teacher, and preacher is to present the Bride of Christ *perfect* to Christ (Eph. 4:12-13) – at "The Presentation" – and shockingly, this task is scarcely accomplished (1 Peter 4:18)! Is this why you exist in your ministerial office, preacher, "to present every man **perfect** in Christ Jesus" (Col. 1:28)!?

> "To **present** you holy and unblameable and unreproveable in His sight" (Col. 1:22)

"That He might <u>sanctify</u> and <u>cleanse</u> it with the washing of water by the word, that He might **present** it to Himself a glorious Church, not having <u>spot</u>, or wrinkle, or any such thing; but that it should be <u>holy</u> and <u>without blemish</u>" (Eph. 5:26-27).

When a Christian is presented *perfect* in Christ, then he is also presented "**<u>holy</u>**", "**<u>unblameable</u>**", and "**<u>unreproveable</u>**" in God's sight (Col. 1:22). When a man is "holy", "unblameable", and "unreproveable" in God's sight, he is also <u>sanctified</u> and <u>cleansed</u> without <u>spot</u> or <u>wrinkle</u>, both holy and without <u>blemish</u>, as the Bride must be. The only way the Bride (the Church & individual Christians) will make it to heaven, is if they are *presented* to God in this condition. These terms do not describe some special END TIME *"revival people"*! These terms describe those who are initially, present-progressively, and finally saved – in any and every generation, all throughout time. All of the Church that will be *finally saved* did abide in the present continuous gospel power which makes a man meet these descriptive terms of *an acceptable presentation*, which is Christian *perfection*, so that the perfection he has now will open the door of everlasting, sinless perfection in heaven – Praise God! All preaching and pastoring is to the end that saints may continue in perfection and finally be saved – walking in revival so that they might be judged as the revived (the quick), that they will be recognized and accepted by God as the Bride. God will "present it to Himself a glorious Church" in this very way! Some await a revival in the end times because they recognize that "the church" today does not meet the standard described in Ephesians 5:26-27, but let us understand the terms! If you don't meet these terms which describe the acceptable presentation of the Bride to God, then you will not be reckoned as a part of the Bride by God, which is salvation! Rather, as Christ said, you will be cast forth from the Vine of salvation, though you were savingly engrafted into Christ, and in the END the Husbandman will have a Vine with no withering, fruitless, or diseased branches on it! So also you, regenerate Christian – if God finds you (at your death or at His return) as an unholy spot, blemish, or mark upon His corporate Bride (the Church), He will remove you from Himself as one that does not have the right garment for the occasion. "And He saith unto him, Friend, how camest thou in hither not having a wedding garment? And he was speechless. Then said the King to the servants, Bind him hand and foot, and take him away, and cast him into outer darkness; there shall be weeping and gnashing of teeth. **For many are called, but few are chosen.**" (Matthew 22:12-14). In preparation for the presentation of your soul to God to "be accepted of Him" (2 Cor. 5:9-10), you must be kept "from falling" and "faultless before the presence of His glory" (Jude 24), "as a chaste virgin to Christ" (2 Cor. 11:2), for no "adulterer" will be accepted as a part of the Bride (James 4:4).

*********************←Point to Prove→***********************

The false prophets or heretical messages of our day preach that ***Revival*** *is eternally insignificant and inconsequential, and therefore, an option to obtain or refuse by each individual's* *choice of pursuit. So likewise therefore, **all of its synonyms** are also preached as an option without any eternal consequence. As a result, to the loss of many souls into a Godless eternity, the people are blinded by preachers of peace who keep asleep revival-less persons, when, lo, God would have them wake up from their carnal peace and look straight on at their trouble.*

****

"O LORD, **revive** Thy work in the midst of the years,
in the midst of the years make known; **in wrath remember mercy**"
(Habakkuk 3:2).

Revival cannot be eternally insignificant, for, it is directly related to the **WRATH** of God. I say again in another way, it has everything to do with the **MERCY** of God unto salvation. When you pray for revival, do you pray – "**in wrath remember mercy**" (Hab. 3:2)? The synonyms of *revival* are formerly listed in the four categories we are mapped to examine, including the five senses of the gospel we have already examined, and more specifically this category called "**perfection**" we are addressing now → falling from personal revival is also a falling from *perfection as a Christian* (Col. 1:28-29, Eph. 4:12, 2 Cor. 13:9, 11), which is falling from *perfecting works* in Christ (Rev. 3:2, Heb. 13:21, 2 Thess. 2:16-17), *perfected holiness* (2 Cor. 7:1), *perfected faith* (James 2:21-22, 1 Thess. 3:10), and as John addresses it, *perfected love* (1 John 2:5, 4:12, 17). Likewise as falling from personal or corporate revival, to fall from perfection is to, at present, incur the just penalties of reprobating and casting-away wrath (2 Cor. 13:5), though God will give a space of time for repentance that you may potentially but not certainly escape it.

"Though I walk in the midst of trouble, Thou wilt **revive** me:
Thou shalt stretch forth Thine hand against the wrath of mine
enemies, and Thy right hand shall **save me**. The LORD will
perfect that which concerneth me: Thy **mercy**, O LORD,
endureth for ever: **forsake not** the works of Thine own hands"
(Ps. 138:7-8).

Revival is the reestablishing of **perfection** when, at the present time, the saint has sinfully fallen from it. Being found in the midst of the troublous conflict of im**perfection**, it is then that David cries out for *revival*, saying, "Thou wilt **revive** me", and by this he pointedly means, "Thy right hand shall **save** me". *Salvation* and *revival* are biblical synonymous! David clearly has his eyes of hope upon saving "**mercy**" and therefore prays for it, saying, "**forsake not** the works of Thine own hands". By this he means himself. The supplication to God could be otherwise rendered, "O forsake me not utterly" (Ps. 119:8). This scenario of high crime, desperate need, present trouble, and eternal consequence is, let the reader understand, the hour of need for *REVIVAL*! Every biblical saint that ever strove for revival did so under the same emotional press and salvific aim. Revival is a reestablishment of salvation and mercy in the midst of salvation-interrupting wrath, a wrath which is, potentially, able to be infuriated until the man of God is forsaken; otherwise the wrath is pacified because salvific revival interrupts the conflict of wrath in however it was manifesting and pursuing the individual or corporate body. This wrath-interrupting, saving work of God is altogether understood as God perfecting the saints, or as David said, "The LORD will **perfect** that which concerneth me" (Ps. 138:7-8).

If you are a babe in Christ, it is because you have fallen from **perfection** (1 Cor. 2:6, Heb. 6:1, Eph. 4:13-14). This is when growth is stunted into a standstill, that is, until the gospel truths are reestablished in the heart of the believer. While a believer maintains saving faith in the gospel, he is growing as a young Christian into older age, but as a youth, the perfected saint is not understood to be a babe, therefore he is able to eat the meat of wisdom. To be of "full age" is a spiritual stature in a saint enabling him to eat God's manifold meats of wisdom. Such a one has grown to the spiritual-biological faculties which can digest meat, as seen in those that are of a young or youthful age (1 Pet. 5:5) beyond the years of a baby child (Heb. 5:12-14). With wisdom and understanding being increased in his life, then he is becoming more aware of his own sinfulness, inwardly and outwardly, in heart and practice, which simultaneously makes him become more aware of the nature, Person, holiness, faith, love, and judgment of God. In this course there are, therefore, greater works of repentance being wrought in his life, with greater works of faith, but as he is increasing from one glory to the next, each greater glory gained is the natural work of sanctification (*present progressive salvation*) which God accomplishes as a response to the saint's continuance of saving faith in the gospel. When a saint falls from saving faith in the gospel, he also falls from the blessed operations of God which will perform in the man "the increase" (1 Cor. 3:7), to "grow in grace" (2 Pet. 3:18) and "abound" (2 Pet. 1:8) in the perseverance of continual "increasing" (Col. 1:10), which *sanctification* and *present progressive salvation* describe.

From one glory to the next, there is a new and greater revelation of sin (in heart and practice) which enlightens the saint, and thus the saint is convicted by God to repent of these formerly unknown sins, then to believe in Christ (by the gospel) to overcome this formerly unknown evil behavior. When the saint is so ingratiated into this overcoming experience, it is by his *present progressive* steadfastness of faith in the gospel, granting power over death. In other words, the saint is empowered by the gospel-promised faithfulness of God Who did *initially* conquer, but also promised to *presently* and *progressively* conquer and keep, unto the very end. Present progressive faith in God's faithfulness manifests the inner workings of perseverance in personal **revival**. In this way, we can see the specific place *present progressive* faith has in the work of sanctification, and how that sanctification – a life of increasing, abounding, and growing – is a mark that one is keeping saving faith in the gospel; therefore if a man loses this growth, then he is not having saving faith in the gospel, which is a falling from perfection into blame and all the various other terms of God's disapproval and rebuke.

460

Do you see it? There is a ***present progressive*** perfection which is spoken of as a process of continual achievement, which is a greater degree of perfection in Christ than what was formerly had, but in all stages, one must be perfect to be saved even though those who are older in Christ will look different than those who are younger in Christ, as they maintain their own stage of perfection, but when either one of them fall, the fruits of carnality which do arise are immediately the same, but when repentance is had again, the recovered state is vastly different as the age chasm of glories was formerly different. Each individual is recovered back into the stage of glory which they had before they fell, or near it (generally speaking), depending, of course, on how long one remains fallen and how severe the sins were which were committed. Verses which speak clearly in the language of this present progressive attainment of perfection are in James 1:4, 1 Peter 5:10, Galatians 3:3, and Hebrews 13:21, but all four of these books are dealing with the rebuke and denouncing of the behavior of saints who are falling from perfection into the various terms which describe a fallen saint from perfection: ***blamed***, ***blemished*** & ***spotted***, ***unholy*** & ***unsanctified***, etc..

"Now the God of peace, that brought again from the dead our Lord Jesus, that great Shepherd of the sheep, through the blood of the everlasting covenant, **Make you perfect in every good work to do His will, working in you** that which is wellpleasing in His sight, through Jesus Christ; to Whom be glory for ever and ever. Amen" (Heb. 13:20-21).

"For this cause we also, since the day we heard it, do not cease to pray for you, and to desire that ye might be **filled with the knowledge of His will in all wisdom and spiritual understanding**; That ye might **walk worthy** of the Lord unto all pleasing, **being fruitful in every good work, and increasing in the knowledge of God**; Strengthened with all might, according to His glorious power, unto all **patience** and **longsuffering** with **joyfulness**" (Col 1:9-11).

"And beside this, giving all **diligence**, add to your faith **virtue**; and to virtue **knowledge**; And to knowledge **temperance**; and to temperance **patience**; and to patience **godliness**; And to godliness **brotherly kindness**; and to brotherly kindness **charity**. **For if these things be in you**, and **abound**, they make you that ye shall neither be **barren** nor **unfruitful** in the **knowledge** of our Lord Jesus Christ. But he that lacketh these things is blind, and cannot see afar off, and hath forgotten that he was purged from his old sins. Wherefore the rather, brethren, give **diligence** to make your **calling** and **election** sure: for if ye do these things, ye shall never **fall**: For so **an entrance shall be ministered** unto you abundantly into the everlasting kingdom of our Lord and

Saviour Jesus Christ" (2Pe 1:5-11).

Do you see? Each glory is another trial, another trying of the faith with another form of the gospel presentation put to the believer who has a greater revelation of sin and righteousness being revealed to him as he grows, and, if the believer maintains that faith which he had from the beginning, then he will maintain perfection from glory to glory. In each glory plane of higher ground, it can be said also that he is being made perfect because he is reaching another greater form of perfection in his practical conformity to Christ - inwardly and outwardly. Thus, to fall from the *increasing* (Col. 1:9-11, 1 Thess. 3:12-4:1, 4:10) and *abounding* (1 Thess. 3:12-4:1, 2 Peter 1:5-11, 2 Cor. 8:7-9) raceway, this is *the spirit of err* (2 Pet. 3:17-18) and damnation. Hebrews 13:21 is a good example of what it would look like to walk this road of increasing good works (Titus 3:8, 14, 2 Thess. 2:16-17) for each stage of perfection in Christ, stating that this road is God "working in you" "every good work" according to your stage of sanctification, which we can see is vital for salvation, so much so that it can be rightly said that we are *working out our sanctification*, but not this merely, but we are commanded to "work out [our] salvation **with fear and trembling**" (Php. 2:12). Sanctification is present progressive salvation! Therefore we can see that Christian perfection by saving faith does make a man abide in this "stedfastness" of a man who is enabled to "grow in grace". Thus the book of 2 Peter was closed, "Ye therefore, beloved, seeing ye know these things before, beware lest ye also, being led away with **the error** of **the wicked**, **fall from your own stedfastness**. But **grow in grace**, and in the **knowledge** of our Lord and Saviour Jesus Christ. To him be glory both now and for ever. Amen" (2 Pet. 3:17-18).

Blamelessness – The Gospel of Regeneration

The Gospel By Promise (FINISHED IN THE PAST)	**The Gospel By Command** (AT PRESENT)
God tells you what He has done. How He walked.	God tells you what you must do, in Him & through Him. How you must walk, in Him & through Him.
~ Imputed Righteousness (Rom. 8:10, Eph. 2:8-9, 1 Cor. 6:11)~	*~Works Righteousness (1 Cor. 6:9-10, Eph. 2:10)~* Walk: Col. 2:6, Gal. 5:16, 25, Eph. 4:17, 5:8, 1 Cor. 3:3, 1 John 2:6
1) **Blameless (unblameable, without blame & offence, unprovable & without rebuke, faultless, sincere)**	1) **Blameless (unblameable, without blame & offense, unreproveable & without rebuke, faultless, sincere)** ꙮ "clearing of yourselves" – 2 Cor. 7:11

462

- "chosen us in Him before the foundation of the world, that we should be holy and without blame before Him in love" (Eph. 1:4)
- "to present you holy and unblameable and unreproveable in His sight" (Col. 1:22)
- PROMISE: 1 Cor. 1:8-9

- "obtained good report" - Heb. 11:2, 39
- Revelation 2:4, 14, 20, 23, 3:2
- Fault: 1 Cor. 6:6, Gal. 6:1, Jude 24, Rev. 14:5
- Blame: Gal. 2:11 (14, 17-18), Php. 2:15, 1 Thess. 3:13, 5:23-24, 1 Tim. 5:7, 2 Peter 3:14
- Offence: Php. 1:10
- Sincere: Php. 1:10
- Without rebuke: Php. 2:15, 1 Tim. 6:14, Rev. 3:19, Hos. 5:9, Isa. 51:20, Psalm 80:16

Initial Blamelessness

"Blessed be the God and Father of our Lord Jesus Christ, Who hath blessed us with all spiritual blessings in heavenly places in Christ: According as He hath chosen us in Him before the foundation of the world, that we should be **holy** and **without blame** before him in love" (Eph. 1:3-4).

"Who shall also **confirm you unto the end, that ye may be blameless in the Day of our Lord Jesus Christ**. God is faithful, by Whom ye were called unto the fellowship of His Son Jesus Christ our Lord" (1 Co. 1:8-9).

According to the purpose of God in salvation, and according to predestination in God's absolute sovereignty, God has chosen those who will be saved, and lo, they will be presented "holy and **without blame** before Him." These are descriptive terms of those who will be presented and accepted before the Judgment Seat. If a studious disciple of the Lord searched the NT scriptures for an understanding about biblical *blamelessness*, the discoveries would be startling! "The Day of our Lord Jesus Christ", as 1 Corinthians 1:8-9 holds it in view, is the constant burden which energizes the preaching, praying, and pursuit of every saint for *personal* and *corporate blamelessness*. The sheer number of times that the biblical pastors of inspired scripture are mindfully dominated about preparing for Judgment Day is shocking! We must understand that God's eternal purpose for the elect is to present them "**holy** and **without blame**" before God (Eph. 1:3-4), that the promises of God do pointedly deliver from *blamableness* before God (1 Cor. 1:8-9); nevertheless, it is the responsibility of each saint to have faith, lay hold upon, and walk out in *blamelessness* before God. *Initial blamelessness* is instantaneous and immediate, but *present progressive blamelessness* is commanded; therefore God's confirming grace makes a man blameless "UNTO THE END" when he appears before the Judgment at "the Day of our Lord Jesus Christ" (1 Cor. 1:8-9).

> "And you, that were sometime alienated and enemies in your mind by wicked works, yet now hath He **reconciled in the body of His flesh through death**, <u>to present you</u> **holy** and **unblameable** and **unreproveable** in His sight: **If** ye continue in the faith grounded and settled, and be not moved away from the hope of the gospel, which ye have heard, and which was preached to every creature which is under heaven; whereof I Paul am made a minister" (Colossians 1:21-23).

> "I have somewhat against thee" – Rev. 2:4
> "I have a few things against thee" – Rev. 2:14
> "I have a few things against thee" – Rev. 2:20
> "I will give unto every one of you according to your works" – Rev. 2:23
> "I have not found thy works **perfect** before God" – Rev. 3:2

We are *initially blameless* in Christ because of the imputed righteousness therein, but *present progressive blamelessness* is obtained by walking in the faith, to keep it, to be a man that does "continue in the faith grounded and settled", and is "not moved away from the hope of the gospel" (Col. 1:21-23). Christ Jesus saves sinners "in the body of His flesh through death", for what? "To present you **holy** and **unblameable** and **unreproveable** in His sight" (Col. 1:21-23). However, notice the **IF**! "If ye continue in the faith", Paul says! The NT writers continually press upon the memory of the saints the dangers of those who "draw back" (Heb. 10:38-39) from faith in the gospel. They are pressed to keep the faith steadfastly until "He that shall come will come" (Heb. 10:37), that is, Jesus Christ the Lord. If the saint maintains saving faith *presently* and *progressively*, then they will, as "the elders" of Hebrews 11 did, "obtain a good report" (Heb. 11:2, 39)…but what is a bad report? What does it mean for a man to be found *in blame* before God on that final Day? This is what is meant in the verses above cited from Revelation 2:4, 14, 20, 23, 3:2. At this time, Jesus Christ has something **against you**, some point to **blame you** on, proving by it that you have fallen from saving faith in the gospel of Christ. Each of these regenerate Churches who were found blamed were charged to repent or perish.

Faith is judged by indicating evidences, a man's fruits, and if they be "in" them and "abounding" (as 2 Peter 1:5-14 taught), there is *no blame* before God. If a saint falls, he must get back up again and be revived, which is to believe in the gospel again, and with the reviving of their faith they are enabled to have a blameless repentance from however they fell into the damnable spiritual condition. Of course, this *blameless* repentance is judged by its fruits (2 Cor. 7:10-11). When such fruits are in the heart and deed of the man unto *perfection* (Lk. 8:14, Rev. 3:2), then salvation is maintained because they did, in this way, obtain a "clearing of themselves" (2 Cor. 7:11) from the manner in which they were blamed by God.

464

"Now unto him that is able to keep you from **falling**, and to present you **faultless** before the presence of His glory with exceeding joy..." (Jude 1:24)

"Brethren, if a man be overtaken in a **fault**, ye which are spiritual, restore such an one in the spirit of meekness; considering thyself, lest thou also be tempted." (Gal. 6:1)

What does it mean to be found at fault before God, rather than "faultless before the Presence of His glory" (Jude 1:24)? In Jude 1:24, faults are equated with the spiritual condition of one who has *fallen*. Is there a NT burden about saints "falling?" For a saint to *fall*, it is a falling from saving faith into a damnable condition (1 Cor. 10:12, 2 Peter 1:10-11, 3:17, Rom. 11:11-12, 1 Tim. 3:6, 6:9, James 5:12, 2 Thess. 2:3, Heb. 4:11). To be "overtaken in a fault", or fallen, is a blind condition in danger of Judgment (Matt. 7:1-5), and at such a time a man needs to be recovered, but, lo, the man cannot see that he may, by his own graces, recover himself. Therefore he needs a "spiritual" man (Gal. 6:1) to help recover him, a man that can "see clearly" (Matt. 7:5) how to "restore" (Gal. 6:1) from the overtaking blindness. Paul rebuked the Corinthian Church, saying, "there is utterly a **fault** among you" (1 Cor. 6:6), and it was because there were no spiritual men (those who fit the description, "a wise man" [1 Cor. 6:5] or "ye which are spiritual" [Gal. 6:1]), who were rising to the task of judgment and reconciliation between the brethren as Galatians 6:1 and Matthew 7:1-5 reference, and as you know, dear reader, neither foolish men nor carnal men are heaven-bound. We must be *wise* and *spiritual* to be saved, for this is the gospel purchase! A very similar passage in James 5:19-20 gives the same charge for NT Christians to restore their brethren from fallen and damnable conditions, otherwise called *faults* or *blame*. Both prayer and preaching are the means of restoration for these *fallen* saints (James 5:16-20). The danger to be fought against is clear: "Brethren, if any of you do err from the truth, and one convert him; Let him know, that he which converteth the sinner from the error of his way shall save a soul from death, and shall hide a multitude of sins." Do you think the biblical pastors and apostles did exhibit a different burden than this? Read of their burdens and see what ailed their souls, see what drove them to prayer and preaching!

Apostolic & Pastoral Burden

"And this I pray, that your love may **abound** yet more and more in **knowledge** and in all **judgment**; That ye may approve things that are excellent; that ye may be **sincere** and **without offence** till the Day of Christ" (Php. 1:9-10).

"Wherefore, my beloved, as ye have always **obeyed**, not as in my presence only, but now much more in my absence, work out your own **salvation** with **fear** and **trembling**. For it is God which worketh in you both to will and to do of His good pleasure. Do all things without murmurings and disputings: That ye may be **blameless** and **harmless**, the sons of God, **without rebuke**, in the midst of a crooked and perverse nation, among whom ye shine as lights in the world; Holding forth the word of life; that I may rejoice in the Day of Christ, that I have not run in vain, neither laboured in vain" (Php. 2:12-16).

"Night and day praying exceedingly that we might see your face, and might **perfect** that which is **lacking in your faith**? Now God Himself and our Father, and our Lord Jesus Christ, direct our way unto you. And the Lord make you to increase and abound in love one toward another, and toward all men, even as we do toward you: To the end He may stablish your hearts **unblameable** in **holiness** before God, even our Father, at the coming of our Lord Jesus Christ with all His saints. Furthermore then we beseech you, brethren, and exhort you by the Lord Jesus, that as ye have received of us how ye ought to walk and to please God, so ye would abound more and more" (1Thess 3:10-4:1).

Comparing Scripture

"That thou keep this commandment **without spot, unrebukeable**, until the appearing of our Lord Jesus Christ" (1 Tim. 6:14).

"Ephraim shall be desolate in the day of **rebuke**" (Hosea 5:9).

"**Rebuke** me not in Thy wrath" (Psalm 38:1).

"Thy sons have fainted, they lie at the head of all the streets, as a wild bull in a net: they are full of the fury of the LORD, the **rebuke** of thy God" (Isaiah 51:20).

"The LORD shall send upon thee cursing, vexation, and **rebuke**, in all that thou settest thine hand unto for to do, until thou be destroyed, and until thou perish quickly; because of the wickedness of thy doings, whereby thou hast forsaken me" (Deuteronomy 28:20).

"It is burned with fire, it is cut down: they perish at the **rebuke** of Thy countenance" (Psalm 80:16).

"Neither murmur ye, as some of them also murmured, and were destroyed of the destroyer" (1 Cor. 10:10).

Saints who are under the wrath of God have become His enemies (James 4:4) or adversaries (Heb. 10:27), as was formerly addressed in detail. Such a state is a *rebukable* state (1 Tim. 6:14), which God seeks to prevent us from, that we might rather be the "sons of God **without rebuke**" (Php. 2:15). If God's sons will be "**without rebuke** in the midst of a crooked and perverse nation", it will be that they are uncorrupted by the crookedness and perversion around them; but if they are corrupted, God saith: "They have corrupted themselves, their spot is not the spot of His children: they are a perverse and crooked generation" (Deut. 32:5). The *rebuke* of God is a mark indicating damnation (Hos. 5:9, Isa. 51:20, Psalm 80:16), of curse and destruction (Deut. 28:20); thus it is feared by the righteous who are cast off and backslidden (Psalms 38:1, 6:1). To be without rebuke is also to be "**blameless** and **harmless**" (Php. 2:15). My reader, renew your mind and understand, tremble and imagine the possibility, if haply, you stand before the Lord your Master suddenly to discover – not the joy of God, but His **rebuke**! And lo! It proceedeth out of His mouth with damnable force like as it was written of old, "they perish at the **rebuke** of Thy countenance" (Ps. 80:16)! My reader, you will be like all things which perished at the rebuke of God's countenance in time past: "burned with fire" and "cut down" (Ps. 80:16).

As you can see, *faults*, *blame*, *offense*, *rebukable*, and *insincerity* are all damnable characteristics of those who fall from **perfection**. In Galatians 2:11-18, the word **blame** describes a damnable state of a regenerate man (the apostle Peter), and the apostle Paul was the spiritual man who interceded with judgment to stay the plague of carnality that was striking Peter and all those who followed him. 1 Thess. 3:10-4:1 & Philippians 1:9-19 do show the apostolic burden for blamelessness to be great – so great that there is ceaseless prayer for its maintenance, and how scarcely it is obtained?! The infamous sin of "murmurings and disputings" became infamous because it was one way men were reprobated from salvation in centuries past – the same men whose reprobation stands for our example that we should not follow them in it (1 Cor. 10:10-12). Therefore this sin is warned against as a matter of *fear and trembling* over our *present progressive* salvation and *blamelessness*, lest we are under the NT *rebuke* of God warned of in Php. 2:12-16! Are you a complainer?

> "Fight the good fight of faith, **lay hold on eternal life**, whereunto thou art also **called**, and hast professed a good profession before many witnesses. I give thee charge in the sight of God, Who quickeneth all things, and before Christ Jesus, Who before Pontius Pilate witnessed a good confession; That thou keep this commandment **without spot, unrebukeable, until the appearing of our Lord Jesus Christ:** (1 Tim. 6:12-14)

> "As many as I love, I **rebuke** and chasten: be zealous therefore, and repent." (Rev. 3:19)

Even Timothy needed the fierce warnings of God to continue on, to lay hold upon eternal life! 1 Thessalonians 5:23-24 and 1 Corinthians 1:8-9 show how the promises and calling of God for *blamelessness* is a gift of God, but like as eternal life, must be as 1 Timothy 6:12 states, *laid hold upon*, so also our *blamelessness* and *unrebukableness* must be *laid hold upon* (1 Tim. 6:14, Peter 3:14). Those who are in a *rebukable* and *blamable* state are confronted with the *rebukes* of Christ to repent or perish, and if a man understood the good mind of the Lord behind it, and that it was given in love to save their souls, then they would respond to the "rebuke" so as to

467

clear themselves (2 Cor. 7:11) from it, being recovered into salvation's final presentation – "**unrebukeable** until the appearing of our Lord Jesus Christ" (1 Tim. 6:14).

> "Who shall ascend into **the hill of the LORD**? or who shall stand in His holy place? He that hath clean hands, and a pure heart; who hath not lifted up his soul unto vanity, nor sworn deceitfully. He shall receive the blessing from the LORD, and righteousness from the God of his salvation. This is the generation of them that seek Him, that seek Thy face, O Jacob. Selah" (Psalm 24:3-6).

> "And I looked, and, lo, a Lamb stood **on the Mount Sion**, and with him an hundred forty and four thousand, having His Father's name written in their foreheads. And I heard a voice from heaven, as the voice of many waters, and as the voice of a great thunder: and I heard the voice of harpers harping with their harps: And they sung as it were a new song before the throne, and before the four beasts, and the elders: and no man could learn that song but the hundred and forty and four thousand, which were redeemed from the earth. These are they which were not **defiled** with women; for they are **virgins**. These are they which follow the Lamb whithersoever He goeth. These were redeemed from among men, being the firstfruits unto God and to the Lamb. And in their mouth was found no guile: for they are **without fault** before the Throne of God" (Rev. 14:1-5).

Duncan Campbell reported the wondrous Revival of the Isle of Lewis to the world via the internet. Today, these recordings are listened to across the world! Duncan argued that the work of *reviving grace* was an outpouring in fulfillment to one primary text's conditions. He affirms that a similar revival can be experienced if indeed we meet these very same conditions outlined by his primary text. Namely, one must meet the conditions of Psalm 24:3-6. What I desire for my reader to see is: Though other fulfillments of this promise can be shadowed in time, the apex of this passage is finally fulfilled at the *final salvation* of God's people, and, what is terrifying is that Duncan preached this as conditions for Revival, but he left the people unaware that these conditions are, biblically and contextually speaking, conditions for *final salvation*, so the people imagine a revival experience that is eternally insignificant for their own souls, and that it is only for the salvation of lost souls, but God is signifying that these conditions are for the *final salvation* of regenerate souls! And if the saints will obtain this final standing before God, it is because they have been *initially* and *present-progressively* standing with God on the holy mount of Zion (Heb. 12:22-23). How does one know if they are *presently* and *progressively* standing on Mount Zion? According to Psalm 24:3-6 & Revelation 14:1-5, you must have – "clean hands," "a pure heart," a denial of "vanity" and false swearing, "not defiled with women," as "virgins," as one that does "follow the Lamb withersoever He goeth," having no "guile" in the mouth and "without fault" before the Throne. Are you one of those "who shall ascend the Hill of the LORD" so as to be *finally saved*? Then *presently* and *progressively* abide in such a character of blamelessness – personally for sure, and God willing, corporately!

Holiness & Sanctification – The Gospel of Regeneration

The Gospel By Promise (FINISHED IN THE PAST)	**The Gospel By Command** (AT PRESENT)
God tells you what He has done. How He walked.	God tells you what you must do, in Him & through Him. How you must walk, in Him & through Him.
~Imputed Righteousness (Rom. 8:10, Eph. 2:8-9, 1 Cor. 6:11)~	*~Works Righteousness (1 Cor. 6:9-10, Eph. 2:10)~* Walk: Col. 2:6, Gal. 5:16, 25, Eph. 4:17, 5:8, 1 Cor. 3:3, 1 John 2:6
1) **Holy & Sanctified**	1) **Holy & Sanctified**
⁜ "chosen us in Him before the foundation of the world, that we should be <u>holy</u> and without <u>blame</u> before Him in love" (Eph. 1:4) ⁜ Col. 1:22, Heb. 10:10, 1 Peter 1:2, 1 Cor. 1:30, 6:11	⁜ Heb. 12:14, 1 Thess. 3:13, 4:3, 7, 5:23-24, 2 Tim. 2:21, 1 Peter 1:14-17, 2 Peter 3:11, Rev. 21:27, 22:11 ⁜ Women: 1 Tim. 2:15, 1 Peter 3:5

Initial Holiness & Sanctification

"According as He hath chosen us in Him before the foundation of the world, that we should be **holy** and without blame before him in love." (Eph. 1:4)

"But of him are ye <u>in Christ Jesus</u>, Who of God is made unto us **wisdom**, and **righteousness**, and **sanctification**, and **redemption**." (1 Co. 1:30)

"And such were some of you: but ye are **washed**, but ye are **sanctified**, but ye are **justified** in the name of the Lord Jesus, and by the Spirit of our God." (1 Co. 6:11)

> "And you, that were sometime alienated and enemies in your
> mind by wicked works, yet now hath He <u>reconciled</u> In the body
> of His flesh through death, <u>to present</u> you **holy** and **unblameable**
> and **unreproveable** in His sight: **If ye continue in the faith**
> grounded and settled, and be not moved away from the hope of
> the gospel, which ye have heard, and which was preached to
> every creature which is under heaven; whereof I Paul am made a
> minister." (Col. 1:21-23)

As referenced before, Ephesians 1:4 states that Christians are not only chosen to be "without blame" but also "**holy**". *Initially*, Christians are holy because "in Christ Jesus" we become what Christ was made for us to become: "wisdom, and righteousness, and **sanctification**, and redemption (1 Cor. 1:30). So from our *initial* salvation onward, it can be said of us in the past tense that we "were" lost but now "are washed", "**sanctified**", and "justified" (1 Cor. 6:11). This entire work was done by the work of the gospel! This could not be stated any clearer than it is in Colossians 1:21-23, and keep in mind that Paul emphasized that this is the work of the gospel *initially*, BUT we must keep the faith that we had *initially*, with *present continuance*, "not moved away" from it, and if we are moved away then we will be *unholy*, blamable, and reprovable in God's sight.

Present Progressive Holiness & Sanctification

> "For this is the will of God, even your **sanctification**, that ye
> should abstain from fornication: That every one of you should
> know how to possess his vessel in **sanctification** and honour; Not
> in the lust of concupiscence, even as the Gentiles which know not
> God: That no man go beyond and defraud his brother in any
> matter: because that the Lord is the avenger of all such, as we
> also have forewarned you and testified. For God hath not **called**
> us unto uncleanness, but unto **holiness**" (1Thess. 4:3-7).

> "And the very God of peace **sanctify** you <u>wholly</u>; and I pray God
> your <u>whole</u> <u>spirit</u> and soul and <u>body</u> be preserved **blameless** unto
> <u>the coming of our Lord Jesus Christ</u>. Faithful is He that **calleth**
> you, Who also will do it" (1Thess. 5:23-24).

Holiness is certainly an initial possession at *initial salvation*, and it is promised to us by the blessed promises of God (1 Thess. 5:23-24), but is it violently prayed for and sought after in your life personally, for your own sake, and is it violently sought after in your prayers for your regenerate brothers' and sisters' sakes? This is the very picture we see in 1 Thess. 3:10, 12-13, and we can see the preachers preaching it in 1 Thess. 4:3-7. In bodily deeds, they are seeking the *present continuous* holiness and sanctification of the people of God, so that they would walk out the performance of the blessed promise of God written in 1 Thess. 5:23-24. Have

470

you ever asked yourself the question, "what manner of persons ought ye to be in **all holy conversation** and godliness", so that, haply, you are "found of Him in peace, without spot, and blameless" (2 Peter. 3:11, 14)? In other words, do you have *holiness* in your life to a measure and degree of *blameless perfection*? So many people quote Hebrews 12:14, "**without holiness** no man shall see the Lord", but do they really know that they must *presently and continuously* lay hold upon holiness of spirit and body (1 Thess. 5:23, 2 Cor. 7:1)? It is needful that we have that "DAY" (2 Pet. 3:11-14) in mind as the scriptures continually inculcate, for Christ's consummated Kingdom will not have one unholy person in it (Rev. 21:27, 22:11)! We, with our sisters in the Lord, will be saved as long as we keep the "IF" – if we "continue in faith and charity and **holiness** with sobriety" (1 Tim. 2:15).

> "Wherefore gird up the loins of your mind, be sober, and hope to the end for the grace that is to be brought unto you at the revelation of Jesus Christ; **As obedient children**, not fashioning yourselves according to the former lusts in your ignorance: But **as He which hath called you is holy, so be ye holy in all manner of conversation**; Because it is written, **Be ye holy; for I am holy**. And if ye call on the Father, Who without respect of persons judgeth according to every man's work, pass the time of your sojourning here in fear"
> (1 Pet. 1:13-17).

At your death, or the revelation of Jesus Christ, you will have to face the Judgments of God, and if you are not "as obedient children" but rather disobedient children, if you are unholy instead of "as He which hath called you is holy", then you are falling short of the gospel experience God has "called you" into. If you do not fulfill this call so as to be holy, then don't expect to escape the wrath and rebukes of God at Judgment. You suppose that He will respect your person, perhaps, because He knows that you are His son. But reader, He will not breach judgment because you call Him Father, and He will not respect your person even if you respect your person. Let this sink down into your ears: "And if ye call on the Father, Who without respect of persons judgeth according to every man's work, pass the time of your sojourning here in fear" (1 Pet. 1:17).

Without Spot & Blemish – The Gospel of Regeneration

The Gospel By Promise	**The Gospel By Command**
(FINISHED IN THE PAST)	(AT PRESENT)

God tells you what	God tells you what you must do,
He has done.	in Him & through Him.
How He walked.	How you must walk, in Him
	& through Him.

~ Imputed Righteousness (Rom.	*~Works Righteousness (1 Cor. 6:9-10,*
8:10, Eph. 2:8-9, 1 Cor. 6:11)~	*Eph. 2:10)~*
	Walk: Col. 2:6, Gal. 5:16, 25, Eph. 4:17,
	5:8, 1 Cor. 3:3, 1 John 2:6

1)   Without Blemish & Spot

✦   Gal. 2:20

✦   Christ: Exodus 12:5, Num. 19:2, Lev. 22:19-22, 1 Cor. 5:7, John 1:29, 1 Pet. 1:19

1)   Without Blemish & Spot

✦ Rom. 12:1-2

✦ James 1:26-27, 3:2-6, 2 Peter 3:14,1 Tim. 6:14

✦ Corporate: Rom. 15:16-19, Ephesians 5:25-27, 2 Peter 2:13, Jude 12

Initially Without Spot & Blemish

> "I am crucified with Christ: nevertheless I live; yet not I, but Christ liveth in me: and the life which I now live in the flesh I live by the faith of the Son of God, Who loved me, and gave Himself for me." (Gal. 2:20)

"Without spot" and "blemish" are descriptive terms for sacrifices, and if you are called to meet such a description, then it will be by a personal offering to God *as a sacrifice*. These terms are sacrificial terms for acceptable or unacceptable sacrifices and offerings (Numbers 19:2), and regenerate Christians are described to be, already, in past tense terms, "crucified with Christ" (Gal. 2:20). The cross is the NT altar for sacrifice! The Roman crucifix was the altar of the Lamb of God Who was, "a Lamb **without blemish** and **without spot**" (1 Peter 1:19), and on what He was offered upon, we are called to die with Him there, *initially* and *present-progressively*, so that we may be accepted *finally* (Rom. 15:16-19). If we will present ourselves to God that we might be *presently* and *progressively* a "living sacrifice" (Rom. 12:1-2), we must therefore be "without blemish" and "without spot" like our Lord, in our Lord, and through our Lord. Nothing else is acceptable.

Present Progressively Without Spot & Blemish

Present Command

"I beseech you therefore, brethren, by the mercies of God, that ye present your bodies **a living sacrifice, holy, acceptable** unto God, which is your **reasonable service**. And be not conformed to this world: but be ye transformed by the renewing of your mind, that ye may prove what is that good, and acceptable, and **perfect**, will of God" (Rom 12:1-2).

Comparing Scriptures

"The next day John seeth Jesus coming unto him, and saith, Behold the **Lamb of God**, which taketh away the sin of the world" (John 1:29).

"Christ our Passover is sacrificed for us" (1 Corinthians 5:7).

"Your lamb shall be **without blemish**" (Exodus 12:5).

"Ye shall offer at your own will a male **without blemish**, of the beeves, of the sheep, or of the goats. But whatsoever hath a blemish, that shall ye not offer: for **it shall not be acceptable for you**. And whosoever offereth a sacrifice of peace offerings unto the LORD to accomplish his vow, or a freewill offering in beeves or sheep, **it shall be perfect to be accepted**; there shall be **no blemish** therein. Blind, or broken, or maimed, or having a wen, or scurvy, or scabbed, ye shall not offer these unto the LORD, nor make an offering by fire of them upon the altar unto the LORD" (Leviticus 22:19-22)

Here is the *present progressive* command given to regenerate Christians, that they would become acceptable offerings, all on the altar, living sacrifices. What are the terms of acceptance? **Holy** offerings are the only **acceptable** offerings! My reader, you must understand the language and terminology used for sacrifices. Jesus Christ was "our Passover" Lamb that was "sacrificed for us" (1 Cor. 5:7), a "Lamb of God" (John 1:29) that was, as the law required, "**without blemish**" (Exodus 12:5). Offerings to the Lord must be of a certain holiness, which is also called without spot, without blemish, or "perfect," for nothing else will be "acceptable" by God for an offering (Lev. 22:19-22). Notice how "**perfect**" (Lev. 22:21) and "acceptable" (Rom. 12:1) Christians, offered to God as "**perfect**" sacrifices, are enabled to know and prove what is the "**perfect** will of God" (Rom. 12:2).

If a man is not perfect as a sacrifice, he will not prove what is the perfect will of God. Falling from perfection is falling from God's perfect will being proven, and the phrase, "**to prove**", is in repetitive reference in the letters to the Corinthians as a salvific requirement. Paul is under the burden of God, that the regenerate Christians at Corinth do *prove their faith* (2 Cor. 1:23-24, 2:9-10, 3:1-3, 6:3-4, 7:2,

11, 15-16, 8:6-9, 24, 9:8-10, chapter 10, 12:11-12, 12:19-13:4), or be excommunicated without sparing (2 Cor. 13:2). Therefore, it is likewise said in Romans 12:1-2 that a saint must **prove the will of God.** Like as babes in Christ cannot receive wisdom so that they are handicapped from going on with God in His will, here we see a parallel reality that those who fail to be acceptable sacrifices experience the delusion that they cannot know or prove what God's perfect will is.

> "If any man among you seem to be religious, and bridleth not his tongue, but deceiveth his own heart, this man's religion is vain. **Pure** religion and **undefiled** before God and the Father is this, To visit the fatherless and widows in their affliction, and **to keep himself unspotted from the world**" (Jas. 1:26-27).

> "Wherefore, beloved, seeing that ye look for such things, be diligent that ye may be found of him in peace, **without spot**, and blameless" (2 Pet. 3:14).

> "That thou keep this commandment **without spot**, unrebukeable, until the appearing of our Lord Jesus Christ" (1 Tim. 6:14).

In James 1:26-27, the apostle James gives a focused address on exactly how a person is "to keep himself unspotted from the world". He boldly divides the saved from the lost by whether or not the man can bridle the tongue – otherwise his religion and confession of faith is "vain". He who is not "swift to hear, slow to speak, slow to wrath" (Jas. 1:19), in other words, is the man that "bridleth not his tongue". James calls this overflowing of evil from the nature through the tongue "filthiness and superfluity of naughtiness" (Jas. 1:21). Note how he believes it is filthy or defiling, making a man impure rather than pure, thus James moves directly to defend that "**pure** religion and **undefiled**" has everything to do with the tongue. If the tongue is overflowing with "filthiness" then the world's defiling evils are controlling it, springing up from the inward nature of the old man. Jesus Christ preached the very same principles of saving religion by purity, defilement, and filthiness:

> "And He said, That which cometh out of the man, that **defileth** the man. For from within, **out of the heart** of men, proceed evil thoughts, adulteries, fornications, murders, Thefts, covetousness, wickedness, deceit, lasciviousness, an evil eye, blasphemy, pride, foolishness: All these evil things come **from within**, and **defile** the man" (Mark 7:20-23).

> "A good man out of the good treasure **of the heart** bringeth forth good things: and an evil man out of the evil treasure bringeth forth evil things. But I say unto you, That every **idle word** that men shall speak, they shall give account thereof in the Day of Judgment. For **by thy words** thou shalt be **justified**, and **by thy**

474

words thou shalt be **condemned**" (Matthew 12:35-37)

Therefore James makes it clear and plain that "the perfect man" is able to bridle both the tongue and body (Jas. 3:2), and whosoever is not able to bridle the tongue is therefore defiled by its excretion of filthiness "that it defileth the whole body and setteth on fire the course of nature" (Jas. 3:6). This defiling of the body is otherwise termed by James as being spotted by the world (James 1:27). We should rather, as Peter says, be careful to maintain such a "holy conversation of godliness" (2 Peter 3:11), that we might be found by Christ to be "without spot" on the Day of Judgment (2 Peter 3:14). So, the gospel confession, initially and present-progressively, is the commandment given to all regenerate Christians that we must "keep" the commandments, and ourselves, "without spot, unrebukeable, until the appearing of our Lord Jesus Christ" (1 Tim. 6:14).

> "Husbands, love your wives, even as Christ also loved the
> Church, and gave himself for it; That He might **sanctify** and
> **cleanse it** with the **washing** of water by the word, That He might
> present it to himself a glorious Church, **not having spot**, or
> **wrinkle**, or **any such thing**; but that it should be **holy** and
> **without blemish**" (Ephesians 5:25-27).

> "That I should be the minister of Jesus Christ to the Gentiles,
> ministering the gospel of God, that the offering up of the Gentiles
> might be **acceptable**, being **sanctified by the Holy Ghost**. I have
> therefore whereof I may glory through Jesus Christ in those
> things which pertain to God. For I will not dare to speak of any of
> those things which Christ hath not wrought by me, to make the
> Gentiles **obedient**, **by word and deed**, Through mighty signs
> and wonders, by the power of the Spirit of God; so that from
> Jerusalem, and round about unto Illyricum, I have fully preached
> the gospel of Christ" (Romans 15:16-19).

Will we ever learn how to *presently and progressively* keep ourselves "unspotted by the world" as James 1:27 says, and "without spot" as 2 Peter 3:14 and 1 Tim. 6:14 command, so that we might be a part of the *final salvation* of the saints which is called – The Presentation of the Bride to Christ – or – The Offering Up of the Gentiles – made up of those saints which are rightly called "**holy** and **without blemish**" (Eph. 5:27) in "**word and deed**" (Rom. 15:18)?!

THE GOSPEL CALLING
CHAPTER 20

"In flaming fire taking vengeance on them that know not God,
and that **obey not the gospel** of our Lord Jesus Christ" (2 Thess. 1:8)

The Gospel was first preached to Abraham. In the following verses we can see that by faith he **obeyed** it. This Gospel was preached in this very specific way - God "**CALLED**" (Heb. 11:8-10).

> "By faith Abraham, when he was **called** to go out into a place which he should after receive for an inheritance, **obeyed**; and **he went out**, not knowing whither he went. By faith he sojourned in the land of promise, as in a strange country, dwelling in tabernacles with Isaac and Jacob, the heirs with him of the same promise: For he looked for a city which hath foundations, whose Builder and Maker is God" (Heb. 11:8-10).

> "Look unto Abraham your father, and unto Sarah that bare you: for I **called** him alone, and blessed him, and increased him" (Isa. 51:2).

> "Who didst **choose** Abram, and **broughtest him forth** out of the Ur of the Chaldees, and gavest him the name Abraham" (Neh. 9:7).

This gospel **call** to Abraham was historically recorded in Genesis 12:1-3, and Hebrews 11 cites it to be Abraham's first *saving* response to the gospel call. After this time, through many trials for many years, Abraham maintained saving faith, and so he became a biblical beacon of salvation – an example for NT Christians to follow. God's gospel call to Abraham was a call to "go out" (Heb. 11:8). God preached the OT type of the gospel in these very words: "**Get thee out** of thy country, and from thy kindred, and from thy father's house, unto a land that I will shew thee" (Gen. 12:1). Abraham responded to *the gospel call,* and so, he was separated from country and kindred, both *inwardly* and *outwardly*, even as it is now for Christians in the NT. We too are separated from the devil's country (*this world*). We too are born again into another family or kindred (*God's*).

This call severed Abraham from his former kin, so that from him a chosen lineage could be established as a generational line of salvation. Abraham separated from the house of his father, Terah, and with Abraham was the company of God's called out ones (The Church). To mark this separation, God instituted an *outward sign* to be put upon all the males of His newly born Church:

> "And God said unto Abraham, Thou shalt keep **My covenant** therefore, thou, and thy seed after thee in their generations. This is My covenant, which ye shall keep, between Me and you and thy seed after thee; Every man child among you shall be **circumcised**. And ye shall **circumcise** the flesh of your foreskin; and it shall be **a token of the covenant betwixt Me and you**...And the **uncircumcised** man child whose flesh of his foreskin is not circumcised, **that soul shall be cut off from his people; he hath broken My covenant.**" (Genesis 17:9-11, 14)

Let my reader understand: outward circumcision was of such importance to God that, without it, "that soul shall be cut off from his people"! Circumcision was the very "token of the Covenant" of salvation that God was working in the midst of this called out company. However, it was not the *physical circumcision* that saved these men, was it?

Was the OT law a salvation which was wrought through the means of "earthly things" (John 3:12), to be understood by us as a Covenant of mere "carnal commandment" (Heb. 7:16) and "carnal ordinances" (Heb. 9:10) which are strictly physical, and that alone? Then one would conclude, wrongly, that a Jew is a true Jew who is one "outwardly", and all the practices of the *gospel figures* and *lawful shadows* which <u>reveal Christ</u> were strictly "outward in the flesh", meaning that, nothing ever touched the man in "the heart", and nothing ever saved the man "in the Spirit", "inwardly" and "by nature", rather than "outwardly" (Rom. 2:25-29). If we were to conclude to this interpretation and faith, we too, like the unsaved Jews of the 1st century who were dead men's bones, would have "a zeal for God, but not according to knowledge", and we would be "going about to establish [our] own righteousness" because we are "ignorant of God's righteousness" (Rom. 10:1-3). The OT law is more than physical ordinances! Behind the physical ordinances are messages – messages which contain gospel powers, messages which hinge upon saving faith, and each one, according to God's will, is "a figure" of Christ's gospel message which was to come, so that, heretofore unto the New Covenant dispensation, all men were saved by grace through faith, apart from works, by a revelation of the gospel of Christ by shadow.

Of the Carnality (or Physically), Outwardly	Of the Spirit (or Nature), Inwardly
"The law of a **carnal** commandment" – Heb. 7:16 "**A figure** for the time then present" – Heb. 9:9 "**Carnal** ordinances" – Heb. 9:10	"For circumcision verily profiteth, if thou keep the law: but if thou be a breaker of the law, **thy circumcision is made uncircumcision. Therefore if the uncircumcision keep the righteousness of the law, shall not his uncircumcision be counted for circumcision?** And shall not uncircumcision which is **by nature**, if it fulfill the law, judge thee, who by the letter and circumcision dost transgress the law? For he is not a Jew, which is one **outwardly**; neither is that circumcision, which is **outward in the flesh**: But he is a Jew, which is one **inwardly**; and circumcision is that of **the heart**, in **the Spirit**, and not in the letter; whose praise is not of men, but of God." – Rom. 2:25-29

My reader, we have already looked at, with great detail, how the Israelites who were called out of Egypt in the Exodus generation were spiritually saved by a vital union to the pre-Incarnate Christ. Remember how the Passover sacrifice was not a dead ordinance, but it was a message of saving faith (Heb. 11:28)? Do you remember how the waters of the Red Sea were not mere ocean waters but a spiritual baptism (1 Cor. 10:1-2, Heb. 11:29), how the Manna was not a mere piece of bread but "spiritual meat" (1 Cor. 10:3), how the water from the Rock was not a mere river of waters but a "spiritual drink" (1 Cor. 10:4), how the Rock was not a mere piece of stone but a "spiritual Rock" – and "that Rock was Christ" (1 Cor. 10:4)? Even so it is here, in Genesis 17, with the physical circumcision. It is not a mere physical circumcision that is "outward in the flesh", but this is also a message of saving faith, resulting in a spiritual circumcision of the heart, in the Spirit, creating communion with the pre-Incarnate Christ! It has always been true, all throughout the OT generations, that a Jew "is not a Jew, which is one outwardly; neither is that circumcision, which is outward in the flesh: But he is a Jew, which is one inwardly; and circumcision is that of the heart, in the Spirit, and not in the letter; whose praise is not of men, but of God" (Rom. 2:25-29). The Lord preached that it was a *spiritual circumcision* that saved men all throughout the OT scriptures:

> "And the LORD thy God will **circumcise thine heart**, and the heart of thy seed, to love the LORD thy God with all thine heart, and with all thy soul, that thou mayest live." (Deuteronomy 30:6)

> "**Circumcise** therefore the foreskin **of your heart**, and be no more stiffnecked." (Deuteronomy 10:16)

> "Circumcise yourselves to the LORD, and take away **the**

foreskins of your heart, ye men of Judah and inhabitants of Jerusalem: lest my fury come forth like fire, and burn that none can quench it, because of the evil of your doings." (Jeremiah 4:4)

Abraham, and all saved men in the OT, were of such that had their hearts circumcised, that had the Spirit of God within them, so that the chief token of the OT Covenant was a spiritually circumcised seed of Abraham that did "love the LORD [their] God with all [their] heart, and with all [their] soul" (Deut. 30:6). Therefore these men, who had circumcised hearts, did "keep the righteousness of the law", which means they loved God so as to "fulfil the law" (Rom. 2:26-27), for if they had not kept the righteousness of the law, then their "circumcision is made uncircumcision" (Rom. 2:25)! The spiritual work of the law, *spiritual circumcision*, is what saves a man, and not the outward, physical circumcision – so much so that if a man is spiritually circumcised, then God will judge him to be as the physically circumcised, and vice versa: if a man is physically circumcised and not spiritually circumcised, then his physical circumcision will be counted as uncircumcision! Herein is the bottom-line principle validating the outward, carnal, physical precepts of the law which are kept – a spiritual salvation!

This very reality can be seen in the subsequent generations after the physical ordinance was instituted in Genesis 17. Abraham's seed did abound, and although all of them were physically circumcised, not all were spiritually circumcised – therefore there was enmity, division, and separation continuously – and Isaac separated from Ishmael, Jacob from Esau, Joseph from his brothers, all the way until the Exodus generation. Not all of the men who were the children of Abraham did inherit the promises of salvation (called the promises to Abraham and his seed), but only those who were the *spiritual seed* of Abraham…but this *spiritual seed* was mingled in the vast lineage of Abraham's *physical seed*. The physical circumcision was the physical "token" (Gen. 17:11) upon all the "covenant" (Gen. 17:9) inheritors after Abraham; however, vast numbers of Abraham's sons who were physically circumcised became disqualified from their inheritance in Abraham. This is because they were denounced from the family of Abraham altogether, as a father would renounce the existence of a son. Even so, these literal, physical children of Abraham came to have no spiritual inheritance in Abraham.

I repeat, it must be understood that even in the midst of Abraham's seed which became this chosen lineage, again and again the gospel call went forth, being preached over and over, to the end that *Abraham's seed was severed from Abraham's seed, Jew from Jew, kin from kin*; Isaac *from* Ishmael, Jacob *from* Esau, Joseph *from* his brethren. This continued in all the generations from Joseph to Jesus Christ. The chief example of all *salvific divisions* in the midst of Abraham's seed is Jesus Christ, how He was severed from the Jews in the flesh. This "*Jew severing from Jew*" gospel call is of great significance in the New Testament.

Study the centuries of history to trace the lines that came forth from

Abraham's flesh, and you will find that salvation is *of the Lord* and not of the flesh, and of the vast amount of carnal seed which came from Abraham, you will find that "the purpose of God according to election" did stand to **call forth the seed**, "not of works, but of Him that **calleth**" (Rom. 9:11). Therefore God chose Isaac rather than Ishmael, and said, "In Isaac shall thy seed be **called**" (Rom. 9:7), and by the power of the gospel experience, Isaac was Abraham's *spiritually circumcised*, and worthy, seed. "What then? Israel hath not obtained that which he seeketh for; but the election hath obtained it, and the rest were blinded" (Rom. 11:7). As you may know, after Isaac was **called** and Ishmael was rejected, so also Jacob was called and Esau was rejected. God says of Jacob, "I have **called** him" (Isa. 48:15). And again:

> "Hearken unto Me, O Jacob and Israel, my **called**; I am He; I am the first, I also am the last." (Isa. 48:12)

Several centuries after Abraham's death, it came to pass that his seed was bound in Egyptian slavery, and from there God saved Abraham's seed, both *physically and spiritually*. I repeat, God saved them *spiritually* and *not just physically* (as we have studied), and for this reason their Exodus from Egypt is exactly synonymous to the gospel experience heretofore described, when God said:

> "When Israel was a child, then I loved him, and **called** My son out of Egypt." (Hos. 11:1)

God called this special and elect seed of Abraham into a spiritual salvation, so that God might be with them, dwell among them, and be in them. God spoke of His communing Presence as the very purposeful reason He saved Israel (the Exodus generation). God had a divine objective for the gospel **call** of salvation, and it was thus:

> "I will take you to Me **for a people**, and I will **be to you a God**: and ye shall know that I am the LORD **your God**, which bringeth you out from under the burdens of the Egyptians." (Ex. 6:7)

To be taken by God *as a people*, for Him to be *their God*, is a very fearful and difficult thing! It is not easy for a sinful people to survive when an infinitely Holy God does come near to them, to be in their very midst. When the Israelites came to the desert of Sinai and "camped before the Mount" (Ex. 19:2), God gave them conditions for survival in His Presence:

> "Ye have seen what I did unto the Egyptians, and how I bare you on eagles' wings, and **brought you unto Myself**. Now therefore, **if** ye will **obey My voice** indeed, and keep my Covenant, then ye shall be a peculiar treasure unto Me above all people: for all the earth is Mine: And ye shall be unto Me a **Kingdom of priests**, and an **holy nation**." (Ex. 19:4-6)

480

God did walk with Adam and Eve in the Garden of Eden in a perpetual friendship, because of their sinless innocence. Adam and Eve knew the Presence of God well (Gen. 3:8). Yet for God to be Israel's God, to dwell in the midst of a fallen, sinful, and guilty people, this was an astonishing and terrifying endeavor, and yet this was, and is, God's very express purpose in salvation – "**that I may dwell among them: I am the LORD their God**" (Ex. 29:46). This great Covenant was initiated at Sinai, and here at the beginning, remember how the people scarcely survived the terrifying experience? How much more difficult will it be, and with how much more scarcity will Israel continue to dwell with God? My reader, you must see this purpose of God repeated over and over, emphasized and reemphasized by God, so that when you think of salvation, what it is and what it accomplishes, you will immediately think wondrously about a people in the midst of the Presence of God.

> "And **I will dwell among** the children of Israel, and **will be their God**. And they shall know that **I am the LORD their God**, that brought them forth out of the land of Egypt, **that I may dwell among them: I am the LORD their God.**" (Exodus 29:45-46)

> "And I will set My Tabernacle **among you**: and my soul shall not abhor you. And **I will walk among you**, and **will be your God**, and **ye shall be My people.**" (Lev. 26:11-12)

Now, in a very real way, a true Jew is one that is *with God*, and therefore the Jews do keep the law by *nature* and *Spirit*. Also, a Jew is one who is with God so as to be in *continuing fellowship with Him*, one who is not separate from Him. A true Jew is a member of the "Church in the wilderness" (Acts 7:38), and all of them partook of the spiritual salvation of God (1 Cor. 10:1-4), and therefore, like *circumcision*, they were empowered "inwardly", "by nature", "of the heart", and "in the Spirit" to keep the righteousness of the law (Rom. 2:24-29)! With the Mosaic Law, God made sure the holy seed's separation from all once-born imposters. To keep the whole Church pure, holy, and clean, God instituted strict laws of execution for any Israelite who forsook the spiritual salvation of God, evidenced by keeping the righteousness of the law, by turning to a mere carnal expression of the carnal commandments, or a form of godliness, denying the power of God to keep the righteousness of the law. Therefore, anyone who sinned "presumptuously", or willfully, would be "cut off from among his people" (Numbers 15:30-31), just like Ishmael was cut off from Isaac, and Esau from Jacob, which are examples of this in the generations before the Mosaic Law was instituted. After the Mosaic Law was instituted, the laws of execution ensured that all who were forsaking a vitally real and *spiritual salvation*, which is evidenced by men turning from heartfelt obedience to willful sinning, which is a failure to keep the righteousness of the law, were cut off from the congregation. Even so, the men would be separated from the rest of the seed of Abraham who were the spiritual seed of Abraham indeed, not merely the once-born physical seed of Abraham.

In this way we can see that to be in the Presence of God is salvation gained. To be cast away from God's presence is salvation lost. The Gospel for the OT saints was to bring them to God, and so in a very *typological* way, like as from a shadow pointing to a reality, we are with God now by the work of Christ accomplished on the cross! So it is in the NT, "For Christ also hath once suffered for sins, the just for the unjust, **that He might bring us to God**, being put to death in the flesh, but quickened by the Spirit" (1 Peter 3:18). God saves us by a gospel calling which calls us "out from among them" into separation (2 Cor. 6:17), for the express purpose to be of the number that dwells in God's presence, and the NT inspired authors quote this OT salvific purpose as God's stated purpose in NT salvation. The NT authors cite the OT gospel call: → "I will **dwell in them**, and **walk in them**; and **I will be their God**, and they shall **be My people**. WHEREFORE **come out from among them**, and be ye separate" (2 Cor. 6:16-17). Praise God! It is today in NT reality, as it was said in OT typology:

> "But I have said unto you, Ye shall inherit their land, and I will give it unto you to possess it, a land that floweth with milk and honey: I am the LORD your God, **which have separated you from other people**. Ye shall therefore **put difference between clean** beasts **and unclean**, and **between unclean** fowls and clean: and ye shall not make your souls abominable by beast, or by fowl, or by any manner of living thing that creepeth on the ground, **which I have separated from you as unclean**. And **ye shall be holy unto Me: for I the LORD am holy, and have severed you from other people, that ye should be Mine**."
> (Leviticus 20:24-26)

The NT gospel calling is for sinners who were once "without Christ", "having no hope and without God in the world" (Eph. 2:12), but the Jews who were merely Jews *by flesh* and not *by the Spirit*, they too were lost and without God. They too had their "understanding darkened, being alienated from the life of God through the ignorance that is in them, because of the blindness of their heart" (Eph. 4:18), and why? "God hath given them the spirit of slumber, eyes that they should not see, and ears that they should not hear... their eyes [were]

"...For they are not all Israel, which are of Israel: Neither, because they are the seed of Abraham, are they all children: but, In Isaac shall thy seed be **called**." – Rom. 9:6-7

"Now we, brethren, **as Isaac was**, are **the children of promise**. But as then **he that was born after the flesh persecuted him that was born after the Spirit**, even so it is now. Nevertheless what saith the scripture? Cast out the bondwoman and her son: for the son of the bondwoman shall not be heir with the son of the freewoman. So then, brethren, we are not children of the bondwoman, but of the free." (Galatians 4:28-31)

"Born After Spirit" – Gal. 4:29
"Children of the Bondwoman" – Gal. 4:31
"Children of the Free" – Gal. 4:31
"Children of Promise" – Gal. 4:28

482

darkened, that they may not see, and bow down their back alway" (Rom. 11:8-10). Even so it was for Ishmael and Esau, and all those like them…they were enemies of the gospel calling. They were born unto Abraham after the flesh, yet never born into him, or God, after the Spirit. Paul cites the perpetuity of the second birth gospel as an OT and NT reality in Galatians 4:28-30. Paul emphasizes that the seed of Abraham was at enmity one with another in two representative spiritual families, and he states that as it was then, even so it is now in the NT dispensation – "But as then he that was **born after the flesh** persecuted him that was **born after the Spirit**, <ins>even so it is now</ins>" (Gal. 4:29). The two different origins of birth represent two different, irreconcilable families, families that are without friendship, so that, for the sake of salvation for the second-born family of God, there is a necessity of separation. Thus it was said: "**Cast out** the bondwoman and her son" (Gal. 4:30). Did you know that the spiritual reality of being "born again" is here affirmed to be an OT and NT means of salvation (here in Galatians 4:28-30)? Jesus Christ shamed Nicodemus for his ignorance of the second birth gospel call of salvation! Christ Jesus understood this to reveal just how fallen and degenerate Israel was, that their pastoral rulers like Nicodemus knew nothing of the second birth. Jesus said – "Art thou a master of Israel, and knowest not these things" (John 3:10)? The *second birth* is the *second circumcision*, it is the *spiritual seed* which claims the *spiritual inheritance* in Abraham, and to be ignorant of this is to be ignorant of salvation altogether.

This is how it has always been in the OT law, not for the law of *circumcision* only, but for all practices of the law. Take, for example, the law of *sacrifices*. It is not the *physical sacrifices* that save, is it? For, then, *physical circumcision* would also have the power to save a man, wouldn't it? If a man has no spiritual reality with God, and he brings a sacrifice for atonement without any true repentance from sin, it is unacceptable to God (keep in mind that repentance is a spiritual gift given by God, granted as a fruit of saving faith). A man cannot repent unless, *inwardly*, the Spirit of God is working, therefore God disqualifies all carnal, outward, physical sacrifices which are without this spiritual work within the heart:

> "The sacrifice of the wicked is an abomination to the LORD: but the prayer of the upright is His delight." (Proverbs 15:8)

> "The sacrifice of the wicked is abomination: how much more, when he bringeth it with a wicked mind?" (Proverbs 21:27)

My reader, when a man is keeping the law *physically*, and not *spiritually*, then God will say, "<ins>To what purpose</ins> is the multitude of your sacrifices unto Me? saith the LORD: I am full of the burnt offerings of rams, and the fat of fed beasts; and I delight not in the blood of bullocks, or of lambs, or of he goats. When ye come to appear before Me, who hath required this at your hand, to tread my courts? Bring no more vain oblations; incense is an abomination unto Me; the new moons and sabbaths, the calling of assemblies, I cannot away with; it is iniquity, even the solemn meeting. Your new moons and your appointed feasts my soul hateth: they are a trouble unto Me; I am weary to bear them. And when ye spread forth your hands, I will hide Mine eyes from you: yea, when ye make many prayers, I will not hear: your hands are full of blood" (Isa. 1:11-15). Why are the physical sacrifices such an abomination to God? It is because there is no *spiritual sacrifice* being made by the people! Without a *second circumcision*, there is no salvation; even so, here, in the law of sacrifices – without a *second sacrifice* there is no salvation! What is the *second sacrifice*? David explains it exactly in Psalm 51:16-19.

> "For Thou desirest not sacrifice; else would I give it: Thou delightest not in burnt offering. **The sacrifices of God are a broken spirit: a broken and a contrite heart, O God, Thou wilt not despise.** Do good in Thy good pleasure unto Zion: build Thou the walls of Jerusalem. **Then shalt Thou be pleased with the sacrifices of righteousness, with burnt offering and whole burnt offering: then shall they offer bullocks upon Thine altar**." (Psalm 51:16-19)

Before David endeavored to bring *physical sacrifices*, he brought before God the *spiritual sacrifices* of heartfelt repentance with a "broken spirit: a broken and a contrite heart", for he knew that, without this, God would despise the *physical sacrifice*. This heartfelt repentance, otherwise known as full surrender – offering your body as a living sacrifice (Rom. 12:1-2) – is a *spiritual sacrifice* which is acceptable to God, and saving, without which, all *physical, outward, carnal* fulfillments of the law become vain and unacceptable! Hosea calls repentant words and prayers, "so will we render **the calves** of our lips" (Hos. 14:2), for verily, to God, these are the spiritual sacrifices of "calves" which do save a soul in truth! Therefore God said to apostate Israel, unless they "put away the evil of [their] doings", "cease to do evil", "learn to do well", "seek judgment", "relieve the oppressed", "judge the fatherless", and "plead for the widow" (Isa. 1:16-17), then he would hate, reject,

> "...if thou be a breaker of the law, thy circumcision is made uncircumcision" – Rom. 2:25
>
> If thou be a breaker of the law, thy sacrifices are made to be no sacrifices.
>
> "...if the uncircumcision keep the righteousness of the law, shall not his uncircumcision be counted for circumcision?" – Rom. 2:26
>
> If those who do not make physical sacrifices do keep the righteousness of the law, shall not his no sacrifices be counted as sacrifices?
>
> If a wicked man gets circumcised, my reader, the man must be circumcised again! If a wicked man makes a sacrifice, the man must make a sacrifice again!
> There is a second circumcision and sacrifice, spiritual in nature, which does save a man, and all physical institutions do show figures of these spiritual realities!

and be troubled by *physical sacrifices*. Whether in the OT or NT, it was a spiritually real and vital reality with the very Spirit of God – a *walk* with God – that saved a man! Could the prophet Micah make it any more clear for us that this was the understanding of all those who were "children of promise" and "born after the Spirit" in the OT (Gal. 4:28-29)?

> "Wherewith shall I come before the LORD, and bow myself before the high God? shall I come before him with burnt offerings, with calves of a year old? Will the LORD be pleased with thousands of rams, or with ten thousands of rivers of oil? shall I give my firstborn for my transgression, the fruit of my body for the sin of my soul? He hath shewed thee, O man, what is good; and what doth the LORD require of thee, but to do justly, and to love mercy, and **to walk humbly with thy God**?" (Micah 6:6-8)

If a man is not spiritually saved, evidenced by keeping the righteousness of the law, then the physical circumcision becomes uncircumcision to God. Even so, without a spiritual salvation evidenced by keeping the righteousness of the law, the physical sacrifices become no sacrifice at all in the sight of God.

Take, for another example, the law of *washings*. Wicked Israelites can wash themselves with waters, they can sprinkle themselves with lawful sprinklings, but if they have not been *washed again*, *spiritually* speaking, then the *physical washing* is vain. God will still say, again, "wash you, make you clean" (Isa. 1:16). It is not *physical washings* but the *spiritual washing* that reaches *to the heart* in the *inner man* that saves! Thus God said – "O Jerusalem, **wash thine heart** from wickedness, that thou mayest be saved. How long shall thy vain thoughts lodge within thee?" (Jeremiah 4:14)

Take, for another example, the law of *cleanness*. One can make himself *physically* and *lawfully clean* according to the *outward* man, but God will say to him, "make you clean" **again** (Isa. 1:16)! How? Uncleanness is not merely a ceremonial transgression, but it is a matter of moral law as well! All manner of immorality, or the transgression of the righteousness of the law, is considered as uncleanness, whether it be in the OT or NT (Job 33:9, 15:14). Men are <u>born</u> unclean, therefore Eliphaz says, "what is man, that he should be clean? And he which is <u>born</u> of a woman, that he should be righteous" (Job 15:14)? David confirms this again, declaring, "Behold, I was <u>shapen</u> in iniquity, and in sin did my mother <u>conceive me</u>" (Ps. 51:5). David cried out for the spiritual washings and cleansings which were of God by the Spirit of God, when, lo, he was in desperate need of it. He cried – "**Wash me** throughly from mine iniquity, and **cleanse me** from my sin...Behold, Thou desirest **truth in the inward parts**: and in **the hidden part** Thou shalt make me to know wisdom. **Purge me** with hyssop, and I shall be **clean**: **wash me**, and I shall be whiter than snow" (Ps. 51:2, 6-7). David knew that he could not wash himself, cleanse himself, or make himself clean by the mere outward ordinances of keeping the letter of the law, but he cried out to God that He would wash him, *spiritually speaking*, "by the **washing** of regeneration and **renewing** of the Holy Ghost" (Titus 3:5). David knew that his heart was unclean, and that God was going to condemn him if he didn't have truth in the "**inward parts**", not merely the **outward parts** (Ps. 51:6). David specifically cried

485

out for this need, saying – "**Create** in me **a clean heart**, O God; and **renew a right spirit within me**. Cast me not away from **Thy presence**; and take not **Thy Holy Spirit** from me" (Ps. 51:10-11)! Cleanness must first be spiritual, "by nature", "inwardly", "of the heart", and "in the Spirit" (Rom. 2:25-29)! Indeed, "who can say, I have made my heart clean, I am pure from my sin" (Prov. 20:9)? NOT ONE! But if God cleans a man, then it can be done! And God will save all those that "are of **a clean heart**" (Ps. 73:1), which is inward, and He will cast away all the rest into damnation, whether they are outwardly clean or not!

A man may lift up his hands and spread them forth in prayer, according to the law, but God will say: "...when ye spread forth your hands, I will hide Mine eyes from you" (Isa. 1:15). In other words, you must lift up your hands *again*, *spiritually speaking*, and the salvific work must reach *to the heart*, even that, in other words – "Let us **lift up our heart with our hands unto** God in the heavens" (Lamentations 3:41)!

A man may rend his garments so as to seek the attention of God's salvific help, but God will say that you must rend your garments **again**! "And **rend your heart**, and not your garments, and turn unto the LORD your God: for He is gracious and merciful, slow to anger, and of great kindness, and repenteth him of the evil." (Joel 2:13) A man my likewise fast, but if it is not a turning of *the heart* to God, *spiritually speaking*, then God will say that the man must fast *again*, or in other words, He denounces the legitimacy of the first fast, saying – "did ye at all fast unto Me, even to Me" (Zech. 7:5)? If a man fasts *outwardly* without the Spirit of God, then the people will quickly find out that God rejected it. They will then say as they once said – "Wherefore have we fasted, say they, and **Thou seest not**? Wherefore have we afflicted our soul, and **Thou takest no knowledge**" (Isa. 58:3)? They must fast *again*!

A man may begin to cry aloud to God, and pray, but God will say, "they have not cried unto Me **with their heart**" (Hos. 7:14), if indeed the deed is not done with the Spirit of God. God does most fearfully declare, "He that turneth away his ear from hearing the law, **even his prayer shall be abomination**" (Prov. 28:9). All the men of God in the OT knew this truth, that "if [they] regard iniquity in [their] **heart**, the Lord will not hear [them]" (Ps. 66:18). Oh, how woeful is the condition, as the lamentation cried aloud – "Also when I cry and shout, He shutteth out my prayer...Thou hast covered Thyself with a cloud, that our prayer should not pass through" (Lam 3:8, 44)! In such a case, the man must pray *again*!

If a man has *one* pair of eyes and *one* pair of ears, and he tarries all day long before Nehemiah, before Ezra, before the teaching priest and the Levite, is it of any good at all if it be merely *outward attendance*? God will say, you need to hear *again*, you need to see *again*, and you need a *second* pair of eyes and a *second* pair of ears! A man can "have eyes, and see not", and "have ears, and hear not" (Jer. 5:21). The Lord has to give them spiritual eyes, ears, and hearts, as it is written: "Yet the LORD hath not given you an heart to perceive, and eyes to see, and ears to hear, unto this day" (Deuteronomy 29:4). See also Isaiah 6:9-10, Ezekiel 12:2, Matthew 13:13-17, Revelation 2:7, 11, 17, 29, 3:6, 13, 22, 13:9.

In the light of eternity, *one* pair of eyes does not matter, does it? Likewise, *one* pair of ears does not matter, does it? There is a spiritual biology behind salvation; even so, there is *spiritual circumcision* (a *second* circumcision), *spiritual sacrifices* (a *second* sacrifice), *spiritual cleanness* (a *second* cleansing), a *spiritual Manna* (a *second* Manna), a *spiritual water* (a *second* water), a *spiritual Rock* (a *second* Rock), a *spiritual eyesight* (a *second* pair of eyes), a *spiritual hearing* (a *second* pair of ears), besides all the *physical* manifestations of these things! Even so, is it of any wonder then that a man must be *spiritually born* (a *second* birth) into *the family of Abraham*, made into the *spiritual seed of Abraham*, a *spiritual heir*, inheriting a *spiritual inheritance*, following after *spiritual deeds of righteousness*, after the image of God the Father? Is it of any wonder that "they are not all Israel, which are of Israel: Neither, because they are the seed of Abraham, are they all children: but, In Isaac shall thy seed be **called**" (Rom. 9:6-7)? Is it of any wonder that, by the spiritual salvation of God, manifest in the spiritual realities of the law and figures of gospel shadows, God *separated* the saved from the unsaved, the righteous from the unrighteous, the spiritual from the carnal, the second-born from the once-born, and so, Abraham from Terah, Isaac from Ishmael, Jacob from Esau, Joseph from his brothers, righteous Israelites from unrighteous Israelites (under the Mosaic Law), and finally, foremost of all, Jesus Christ from the once-born Jews of the 1st century?

All throughout the centuries, there was a *spiritual seed* and *family* in the midst of the literal, physical seed of Abraham, and they held sole rights to the *spiritual inheritance* of *heaven*. To denounce and be in oblivion to the *second family* of Abraham (the *spiritual* family), the *second seed* of Abraham (the *spiritual* seed), the *second inheritance* of Abraham (the *spiritual* inheritance), is to denounce and be ignorant of the *second circumcision* of Abraham (the *spiritual* circumcision). This *second-born family*, *seed*, company of *heirs*, who were second-time circumcised, *spiritually speaking*, was at enmity with the *once-born family*, *once-born seed*, *once-born* company of *heirs*, who were *one-time circumcised*, and they both were the Jews of Abraham's literal physical seed. To believe and preach that literal, physical circumcision is what saves a man, instead of the second circumcision, which was spiritual and of the heart (Deut. 30:6), is the same message as preaching that all once-born, literal, physical children of Abraham are saved, irrelevant of whether or not they are spiritually born unto Abraham at all ("born again"). This is why Jesus Christ was astonished that Nicodemus didn't understand the doctrine of being born again (John 3)! Jesus said to Nicodemus, "Art thou a master of Israel, and knowest not these things…If I have told you **earthly things**, and ye believe not, how shall ye believe if I tell you of **heavenly things**" (John 3:10, 12)? Nicodemus was under the age-old, ancient deception that salvation was attained by making "clean the outside of the cup and platter", even though the "inward part is full of ravening and wickedness" (Luke 11:39). Jesus Christ, alongside all the OT prophets, did rebuke the once-born Jews, saying, "Ye fools, did not He that made that which is **without**

487

make that which is **within** also" (Luke 11:39-40)? But it was inevitable that the once-born men fall into heretical, damnable deception, because they are once-born, which means that they are a plant which the Father "hath not planted", which means that they only have one pair of eyes – making them *spiritually blind*! Jesus Christ sought to expose the heretical teaching that they created about the law of cleanness and washings, and stated that the origin of this heresy is because they are not born of God into a second pair of spiritual eyes:

> "But in vain they do worship Me, teaching for doctrines the commandments of men. And He called the multitude, and said unto them, Hear, and understand: Not that which **goeth into** the mouth defileth a man; but that which cometh out of the mouth, this defileth a man. Then came His disciples, and said unto him, Knowest Thou that the Pharisees were offended, after they heard this saying? But He answered and said, **Every plant**, which **My heavenly Father hath not planted**, shall be rooted up. Let them alone: they be **blind leaders** of the **blind**. And if the **blind** lead the **blind**, both shall fall into the ditch. Then answered Peter and said unto him, Declare unto us this parable. And Jesus said, Are ye also yet without understanding? Do not ye yet understand, that whatsoever entereth in at the mouth goeth into the belly, and is cast out into the draught? But those things which proceed out of the mouth come forth from the heart; and they defile the man. For out of **the heart** proceed evil thoughts, murders, adulteries, fornications, thefts, false witness, blasphemies: These are the things which defile a man: but to eat with unwashen hands defileth not a man." (Matthew 15:9-20)

Therefore, as Jesus said to the once-born Pharisees, who were at enmity with Him, "let them alone"; even so, Ishmael was at enmity to Isaac, Esau was at enmity to Jacob, Joseph's brothers were at enmity to Joseph. Every time, in every generation, the same age-old method of salvific holiness was preached – "Cast out" the once-born, God says; thus we must cast out the castaways from the holy grounds of the Church! Have you heard the NT call?

"Get thee out" – Gen. 12:1

"Come out" – 2 Cor. 6:17

"purge out" – 1 Cor. 5:7

"put away" – 1 Cor. 5:13

"Cast out" – Gal. 4:30

"from among yourselves" – 1 Cor. 5:13

"out from us" – 1 John 2:18-19

"taketh away" & "cast forth" – John 15:1, 6
"take him away, and cast *him* into outer

"So shalt thou put the evil away from the midst of thee" – Deut. 13:5

"So thou shalt put the evil away from among you" – Deut. 17:7

"…thou shalt put away the evil from Israel" – Deut. 17:12

"…so shalt thou put the evil away from among you" – Deut. 19:19

"…so thou shalt put evil away from

darkness" – Matt.22:13
"castaway" – 1 Cor. 9:27
"reprobate" – 2 Cor. 13:5

among you" – Deut. 20:21

"Every plant, which My heavenly Father hath not planted, shall be rooted up. **Let them alone**: they be blind leaders of the blind. And if the blind lead the blind, both shall fall into the ditch." (Matt. 15:13-14)

"among you" – Deut. 13:11
"among you" – Deut. 13:14
"among you" – Deut. 18:10
"among you" – Deut. 19:20
"among you" – Deut. 21:21, 24
"among them" – Lev. 15:31
"among the children of Israel" – Lev. 22:32

Jesus Christ preached this with authority, persistence, and great opposition! In the 1st century, the land of Israel was crawling with Israelites who were children of Abraham by flesh and the devil by spirit, and Christ utterly shocked them with His fierce denouncement of their privileges, salvation, and inheritance as children of the Abrahamic lineage! Jesus addressed some of these very persons in John 8:31-47. NOTE: they were Jews which were called "believers". Beginning in verse 31, He addressed those of the Jews that *"believed on Him"*, which is Christ. Since it says they "believed on Him," what do you think Jesus did say? Will Jesus commend their faith? Many today profess to believe in Jesus Christ and God. Many do commend any individual who professes faith, but read what Jesus said to these men that *believed*:

"As He spake these words, **many believed. on Him**. Then said Jesus to those Jews **which believed on Him**, If ye continue in My word, then are ye My disciples indeed; And ye shall know the **truth**, and the truth shall make you **free**. They answered Him, **We be Abraham's seed**, and were never in bondage to any man: how sayest Thou, Ye shall be made free? Jesus answered them, Verily, verily, I say unto you, Whosoever committeth sin is the servant of sin. And the servant abideth not in the house for ever: but the Son abideth ever. If the Son therefore shall make you free, ye shall be free indeed. I know that ye are Abraham's seed; but ye seek to kill Me, because my word hath no place in you. I speak that which I have seen with My Father: and ye do that which ye have seen with your father. They answered and said unto Him, **Abraham is our father**. Jesus saith unto them, If ye were Abraham's children, ye would do the works of Abraham. But now ye seek to kill Me, a man that hath told you the truth, which I have heard of God: this did not Abraham. **Ye do the deeds of your father.** Then said they to him, We be not born of fornication; we have one Father, even God. Jesus said unto them, If God were your Father, ye would love Me: for I proceeded forth and came from God; neither came I of Myself, but He sent Me.

Why do ye not understand my speech? even because ye cannot hear my word. **Ye are of your father the devil, and the lusts of your father ye will do.** He was a murderer from the beginning, and abode not in the truth, because there is no truth in him. When he speaketh a lie, he speaketh of his own: for he is a liar, and the father of it. And because I tell you the truth, ye believe Me not. Which of you convinceth Me of sin? And if I say the truth, why do ye not believe Me? He that is of God heareth God's words: ye therefore hear them not, because ye are not of God." (John 8:30-47)

These Jews believed on him (v. 30) and yet were not free from the bondage of sin (vv. 31-32); therefore they did not savingly believe on Him, meaning therefore that they were once-born men. They were utterly unable to understand Jesus, because they had not the help of the Spirit of God (v. 33). They had an outward form of the gospel for the Jews, but it was this alone that they clave to for salvation. Their gospel was that salvation would come through *the seed of Abraham*, and thus they professed, **"we be Abraham's seed"** (v. 33), thinking that this justified them. The scripture says, "Now to Abraham and his seed were the promises made" (Gal 3:16). Jesus knew the Pharisees were Abraham's seed according to the flesh (*outwardly*), but He showed them how they were not the *spiritual children* of Abraham (*inwardly*), and that they were rather the *spiritual children* of Satan (vv. 36-47).

Jesus said that the truth makes men free (John 8:32), and the Pharisees were truthless and carnal. They could not receive the words of Jesus Christ. Jesus said, **"the words** that I speak unto you, they are **spirit**, and they are **life**" (John 6:63). Without the aid of the Spirit of God, you cannot receive Jesus' spiritual words. "The natural man receiveth not the things of the Spirit of God: for they are foolishness unto him: neither can he know them, because they are spiritually discerned" (1 Cor. 2:14). The Pharisees professed to be the children of Abraham and God (John 8:33, 41), but Jesus Christ rebuked them and said, "If God were your Father, ye would love Me" (John 8:42). And again, "Why do ye not understand My speech? Even because ye cannot hear My word. **Ye are of your father the devil**, and the lusts of your father ye will do" (John 8:43-44). Jesus shows us a spiritual pattern that we can judge all men by – their deeds. A person's deeds are a true indicator of what *spiritual offspring* they are of. Jesus said, **"ye do the deeds of your father"** (John 8:41). Deeds reveal the *spiritual fatherhood* and *motherhood*. Regenerate women must therefore be – **"as daughters of Sarah"** (1 Peter 3:6) – and they will be saved as long as they "do well", as Sarah did. A spiritual son of Abraham is a son of God, and a spiritual daughter of Sarah is a daughter of God. Jesus Christ said: "If ye were Abraham's children, ye would do the works of Abraham" (John 8:39), and so likewise, if ye were Sarah's children, ye would do the works of Sarah.

Today, many claim to be the children of God, yet they live nothing like Him! As for the term "Abraham's seed", a true Christian has become Abraham's seed according to Galatians 3:29: "and if ye *be* Christ's, then are ye **Abraham's seed**, and heirs according to the promise". The question is not what you profess, nor whom you confess, but, what are the **deeds** that you do? Do you confess or deny Him by your deeds (Titus 1:16)? Multitudes of Jews that were Abraham's seed after the flesh did worship God with lip service and confessions, but in their heart they hated Him and loved the devil! God said, "This people draweth nigh unto Me with their mouth, and honoureth Me with their lips; but their heart is far from Me" (Matt. 15:8). Do you do the works of Abraham and the works of God, or the works of men and the devil? That question is the bottom line! The deeds you do will determine your father, your birth, and the validity of your salvation, even as the modern proverb goes, "many talk the talk, but do they walk the walk"? And if you don't walk the walk, you will be damned! You will go to hell! Even as it is written, "*there is* therefore now no condemnation to them which are in Christ Jesus, **who walk not after the flesh, but after the Spirit**" (Romans 8:1).

> "*[14]* Be ye not unequally <u>**yoked together**</u> with unbelievers: for **what fellowship** hath righteousness with unrighteousness? and **what communion** hath light with darkness? *[15]* And **what concord** hath Christ with Belial? or **what part** hath he that believeth with an infidel? *[16]* And **what agreement** hath the temple of God with idols? for ye are the temple of the living God; as God hath said, *I will dwell in them, and walk in them; and I will be their God, and they shall be my people.* *[17]* Wherefore come out from among them, and be ye separate, saith the Lord, and <u>touch not the unclean thing;</u> and I will receive you, *[18]* And will be a Father unto you, and ye shall be my sons and daughters, saith the Lord Almighty.* *[1]* Having therefore these promises, dearly beloved, let us cleanse ourselves from all filthiness of the flesh and spirit, perfecting holiness in the fear of God.*"
> (2 Corinthians 6:14-7:1)

The gospel call to **holiness** is a conditional <u>command</u> bound with **promises**. The call is a break of **yoke**! Why? The power of the gospel establishes this purpose of God through regeneration, which is a supernatural severing from unbelievers. The break of yoke is a break of **fellowship**, **communion**, **concord**, and **agreement**, and this can be understood when a man understands the work of salvation as a transformation and separation from the world. A "divine nature" segregates **fellowship**, voids **commonality**, and establishes spiritual enmity with all unbelievers and this world (2 Peter 1:4). Reception of this gospel is a reception of "**come out from among them**," and so we become children of Abraham who did obey his gospel, "get thee out" (Gen. 12:1, Heb. 11:8). If you receive this gospel, a gospel that is, in this way, a gospel of holiness, you are received by God and He becomes your new spiritual Father, being born again His son or daughter (2 Cor. 6:18). This is the unavoidable purpose of God in the gospel, past, present, and forever. Such an *imputation* of holiness by the indwelling of the regenerating Holy Ghost begets holy living in *deed* as the manifest qualities of Abraham's seed.

Now we must understand that the gospel is called "**A Calling**", and this gospel is a saving union with Christ – "**at-one-ment**" – where man is placed *in Christ*. Thus we are separated from the earth and are born into a life and conversation from heaven (Php. 3:20). We have a new Family and Father, and we do become "strangers and pilgrims in this world", because we crucify our flesh (1 Peter 2:11, Col. 3:5). Therefore the gospel call is a call to be Abraham's spiritual seed, which is also Christ's seed, and therefore we are called to be the sons of God – spiritually circumcised – "For we are the circumcision, which worship God in the spirit, and rejoice in Christ Jesus, and have no confidence in the flesh" (Phil. 3:3).

Those that are savingly "called" (Rom. 9:24) by the gospel calling are then called, God says, "My people" (Rom. 9:25) and "children of the Living God" (Rom. 9:26). If you are a child of God, then you are like God's child – Jesus Christ – Who was called the "firstborn among many brethren". If you will be called God's child, you will be a man who is "conformed to the Image of [God's] Son" (Rom. 8:29). Jesus Christ repeatedly explained the various ways in which Christians are made savingly one with God. He prayed for Christians and said, "As Thou Father, art in Me, and I in Thee, **that they may be one in Us**" (John 17:21). We are one in Him and Them! This oneness with God is spoken of as the glory of God (John 17:22), the love of God (John 17:23, 15:9-10), the saving knowledge, or intimate knowing, of God (John 10:14-15, 17:3, 1 John 2:4), and it is a life that lives by God (John 6:56-57). Read how Jesus Christ explained NT salvation:

GLORY →   "And the **glory** which Thou gavest Me I have given them; that they may be one, even as We are One." (John 17:22)

LOVE →   "I in them, and Thou in Me, that they may be made perfect in one; and that the world may know that Thou hast sent Me, and hast **loved** them, as Thou hast **loved** Me." (John 17:23) "As the Father hath **loved** Me, so have I **loved** you: continue ye in My **love**. If ye keep my commandments, ye shall abide in My **love**; even as I have kept My Father's commandments, and abide in His **love**." (John 15:9-10)

KNOW →   "I am the good Shepherd, and **know** My sheep, and am **known** of Mine. As the Father **knoweth** Me, even so **know** I the Father: and I lay down My life for the sheep." (John 10:14-15)

ALIVE →   "He that eateth My flesh, and drinketh My blood, dwelleth in Me, and I in Him. As the **living** Father hath sent Me, and I **live** by the Father: so he that eateth Me, even he shall **live** by Me." (John

6:57)

Can you see the pattern?

ALIVE → "as We are One"
LOVE → "as Thou hast loved Me"
"as the Father hath loved Me, so I have loved you…
"as I have kept My Father's commandments" "abide in My love"
KNOW → "I…know My sheep, and am known of Mine"
"As the Father knoweth Me, even so know I the Father"
GLORY →"As… I live by the Father: so…live by Me"

So also it is written: "as the Father hath **sent** Me, even so **send** I you."
(John 20:21)
"He that **heareth** you **heareth** Me; and he that **despiseth** you
despiseth Me; and he that **despiseth** Me **despiseth** Him that
sent Me." (Luke 10:16)
"He that **receiveth** you **receiveth** Me, and he that **receiveth**
Me **receiveth** Him that **sent** Me." (Mat 10:40)
"He that **receiveth** whomsoever I send **receiveth** Me; and he
that **receiveth** Me **receiveth** Him that **sent** Me." (John 13:20)

There is a sense in which all of these verses are true. The gospel call is a man's saving connection and **union** to Christ. This "calling" of God still goes forth into the world that is crawling with professing Jews, now called "Christians", and like as the 1st century, most of these professing believers ARE NOT THE SPIRITUAL SEED OF GOD! People do not understand it! What happened to the Jews in the 1st century is prophesied to happen to the regenerate Church after the 1st century, which is NOW, and it is called a God-sent delusion for the preparation of "The Great Falling Away"! The spiritual climate of the 1st century Jewish people is like the spiritual climate of the Church in the last days, and not just upon those professing believers of religion, but by a Great Falling Away from those regenerate believers who were the true Church indeed!

THE GREAT FALLING AWAY
CHAPTER 21

"And ere the Lamp of God went out in the Temple of the LORD,
where the ark of God was…" (1 Sam. 3:3)

*"Remember therefore from whence thou art **fallen**, and repent,*
and do the first works; or else I will come unto thee quickly, and
will remove thy candlestick out of his place, except thou repent."
(Rev. 2:5)

Give Christ the glory, for He is the Resurrected Judge, "Who walketh in the midst of the **seven golden candlesticks**" (Rev. 2:1), even as He said, "I will dwell in them, and walk in them; and I will be their God, and they shall be My people" (2 Cor. 6:16). So John does testify of Christ and say: "I turned to see the voice that spake with me. And being turned, I saw **seven golden candlesticks**; And **in the midst** of the **seven candlesticks** One like unto the Son of Man, clothed with a garment down to the foot, and girt about the paps with a golden girdle" (Rev. 1:12-13). As it was in Eli's day when "ere **the Lamp of God** went out in the Temple of the LORD", so also we see **the NT Lamps** of God now called Christ's candlesticks, and the Lord does solemnly warn the NT Israelites that five out of the seven Churches which are addressed presently stand in a damnable condition. If they fail to obtain the repentance that Christ demands, then God will <u>remove the spiritual Candlestick</u>, and thus, for them: "the lights go out on the road to hell" (Rolfe Barnard). The threat which was spoken to Ephesus, "**I…will remove thy candlestick**", is the same castaway, reprobating, deluding, and damning power that was decreed and unleashed upon the OT saints during the days of Eli & Saul, and in subsequent centuries as formerly and exhaustively detailed in our study. When God departed from Israel in the days of Eli, and subsequent generations, it was because His people were falling from saving grace, thus they were denounced to be His people by the enacting sign of God's absence. Without God's presence, they were not His people, and if they were not holy and out from among the lost, but rather they were falling away from Him into the lost estate of those who were once-born, then God would leave them and become "as a wayfaring man" (Jer. 14:8). This was therefore, as is quoted in reference, describing a great falling away in the OT times: virginity and purity to adultery, faithfulness to treachery, and so men fell away from God, He Who they were formerly with (Jer. 9:2).

"A Great Falling Away" – 2 Thess. 2:3

"I. A general apostasy, *there would come a falling away first,* <u>2Th 2:3</u>. By this apostasy we are not to understand a defection in the state, or

494

from civil government, but in spiritual or religious matters, from sound doctrine, instituted worship and church government, and a holy life. The apostle speaks of some very great apostasy, not only of **some converted Jews or Gentiles**, but such as should be very general, though gradual, and should give occasion to the revelation of rise of *antichrist, that man of sin.* This, he says (2Th 2:5), he had told them of when he was with them, with design, no doubt, that they should not take offence nor be stumbled at it. And let us observe that no sooner was Christianity planted and rooted in the world than there began to be a defection in the Christian church. It was so in the Old Testament church; presently after any considerable advance made in religion there followed a defection: soon after the promise there was revolting; for example, soon after men began to call upon the name of the Lord all flesh corrupted their way, - soon after the covenant with Noah the Babel-builders bade defiance to heaven, - soon after the covenant with Abraham his seed degenerated in Egypt, - soon after the Israelites were planted in Canaan, when the first generation was worn off, they forsook God and served Baal, - soon after God's covenant with David his seed revolted, and served other gods, - soon after the return out of captivity there was a general decay of piety, as appears by the story of Ezra and Nehemiah; and therefore it was no strange thing that after the planting of Christianity there should come **a falling away**." - Matthew Henry

There must be "**A GREAT FALLING AWAY** first, and that man of sin be revealed" (2 Thess. 2:3), and then the end shall come, and even Matthew Henry recognizes the historical consistency of this falling away to be upon those who are within the Church! As he said above, "some converted Jews or Gentiles", but God does not say some but MANY! Do you remember how we have carefully noted the deception of God, its working and names, and now, like those OT saints, and even back in the 1st century, we do see Christians born again into light, made blameless, faultless, holy, sanctified, without blemish and spot, wise, quickened, and revived, and they were being turned back to darkness, blame, fault, unholy and unsanctified behavior, making themselves blemished and spotted by the world, found unwise fools, and finally, they are altogether spiritually dead and in need of *revival*. As of now, the truth of the matter lieth hard upon us, and we are pressed, yea, we hang down under the pressure of its misery. A long time has passed since the 1st century Church and we have been darkened from the light that shined in virgin purity, but let us note the first beginnings of "the falling away" that lieth hard upon us now, and let us see that it began back then. Pointing to this, Paul said, "the mystery of iniquity **doth already** work" (2 Thess. 2:7), which means that it was at work already in his day. This is as it is said again by the apostle John in 1 John 4:1, "many false prophets are gone out into the world" (1 John 4:1), and, the "spirit of antichrist whereof ye have heard that it should come; and **even now already is it in the world**" (1 John 4:3). The one man, the anti-Christ, he will come, but before he comes there are *many antichrists* which will come, as John affirms in 1 John 2:18-19. In comparison to those passages just referenced in the 2nd chapter of 1 John, 1 John 4:4-6 reveals the same context of these assaulting antichrist spirits at work, specifically that their effect shall be upon the **saints** (the regenerate) resulting in a GREAT FALLING into deception, scattering, and reprobation. Notice the two emboldened parts of the cited verses below. The context clearly shows this falling away happening among those regenerate persons within the Church.

> "Love not the world, neither the things that are in the world. If any man love the world, the love of the Father is not in him. For all that is in the world, the lust of the flesh, and the lust of the eyes, and the pride of life, is not of the Father, but is of the world. And the world passeth away, and the lust thereof: but he that doeth the will of God abideth for ever. Little children, it is the last time: and as ye have heard that antichrist shall come, even now are there many antichrists; whereby we know that it is the last time. They went out from us, but they were not of us; for if they had been of us, they would no doubt have continued with us: but they went out, that they might be made manifest that they were not all of us." (1 Jn. 2:15-19)

> "Beloved, believe not every spirit, but try the spirits whether they are of God: because many false prophets are gone out into the world. Hereby know ye the Spirit of God: Every spirit that confesseth that Jesus Christ is come in the flesh is of God: And every spirit that confesseth not that Jesus Christ is come in the flesh is not of God: and this is that spirit of antichrist, whereof ye have heard that it should come; and **even now already is it in the world**. Ye are of God, little children, and have overcome them: because greater is He that is in you, than He that is in the world. They are of the world: therefore speak they of the world, and the world heareth them. We are of God: he that knoweth God heareth us; he that is not of God heareth not us. Hereby know we the spirit of truth, and the spirit of error." (1 Jn. 4:1-6)

Those that go "**out from us**" (1 John 2:18-19) – the regenerate Church – are those castaways of God which we must cast out through Church judgment (1 Cor. 5:13). For those who are unrepentant of their sin, they are presently in a condition that is "no more worthy to be called [God's] son" (Lk. 15:19), nor should the man be "called a brother" (1 Cor. 5:11). He should rather be called a "heathen" man or a "publican" (Matt. 18:17), because he is doing the deeds of the heathen instead of the deeds of God. Salvation begun was a saving union to God's Presence; thus men are "called the children of the Living God" (Rom. 9:26), but salvation lost is being cast away from God's presence, which then results in an excommunication which casts them away from the local Church ("taken away" [1 Cor. 5:2], "purge out" [1 Cor. 5:7], "put away" [1 Cor. 5:13]) – because God will no longer be their "Father", nor they His "sons" and "daughters" (2 Cor. 6:18). So also, since they have turned to the

496

flesh and therein become entangled and overcome, they are now judged to be "of the world" and the devil, instead of God, and they can no longer hear, understand, respond to, and obey the saving truth of God (1 John 4:5-6, Matt. 13:15). Take some time with me to look closely at the evidences behind why this is the correct interpretation of 1 John 2:15-19 and 1 John 4:1-6. If we desire to understand the language in 1 John, then we must understand the language of the apostle John's other book, the Gospel of John, and so we will find the true interpretation by "comparing spiritual things with spiritual" (1 Cor. 2:13).

> "I am the true vine, and my Father is the husbandman. Every branch **in Me** that beareth not fruit **He taketh away**: and every branch that beareth fruit, He purgeth it, that it may bring forth more fruit. Now ye are clean through the word which I have spoken unto you. **Abide** in Me, and I in you. As the branch cannot bear fruit of itself, except it **abide** in the vine; no more can ye, except ye **abide** in Me. I am the Vine, ye are the branches: He that **abideth** in Me, and I in him, the same bringeth forth much fruit: for without Me ye can do nothing. If a man **abide** not in Me, he is **cast forth** as a branch, and is withered; and men gather them, and **cast them into the fire**, and they are burned." (John 15:1-6)

The NT doctrine of reprobation is detailed in John 15 by the Testator of the Covenant Himself: Jesus Christ. In verses 1-8, Christ describes the relationship of "the Husbandman" with two different branches which are both *in Jesus* - as Jesus said - "every branch **in Me**" (John 15:1). Jesus Christ is, as declared in another place, "The Root and Fatness" which is "Holy" (Rom. 11:16-17). Firstly in John 15, it must be recognized that both branches are *in Jesus* (the Vine); thus Jesus says, "Every branch **in Me** that beareth not fruit He taketh away: and every branch that beareth fruit, He purgeth it, that it may bring forth more fruit" (John 15:1), and you can't be *in Jesus* while at the same time you are unregenerate. In this parable, Jesus describes the process of how God "taketh away" the fruitless branches and "purgeth" the fruitful branches, and those two branches are two different regenerate Christians who are in Jesus. Desiring that all saints would be a fruitful Christian, Jesus teaches how to be fruitful branches (in Him) instead of the fruitless ones. Reprobation is when the Husbandman "**taketh away**" your connection to Christ, and thus you are "**cast forth as a branch, and is withered; and men gather them, and cast them into the fire, and they are burned**" (John 15:2, 6). Notice in verse 6 it says that they are "cast forth," which again references a casting away from Christ when previously they were savingly "engrafted" into Christ (John 15:6, Rom. 11:17, Jas. 1:21). If a man who was in Jesus could not be cast forth from Him, would a doctrinally sound man ever say, like Paul, who, when he was fighting to subdue his flesh at "any means" in which it would arouse itself to snare him, that he fights this exhaustive battle to avoid the danger – "lest... I myself should be a **castaway**" (1 Cor. 9:27). If a man is **cast away**, what is he cast away from if he was never with Christ, grafted into Him, under

497

the influences and graces of the Spirit's indwelling power?

The disciples heard this teaching in John 15 with fearful wondering – wondering how they might be the fruitful branch instead of the reprobate branch. By this teaching, Jesus meant for us to understand the secret to bearing fruit in Him. The Lord teaches the secret of fruitfulness in this very parable so that men might escape being "cast forth" or a "castaway" (John 15:6, 1 Cor. 9:27), and Jesus says, "abide in Me, and I in you. As the branch cannot bear fruit of itself, except it abide in the Vine; no more can ye, except ye abide in Me. I am the Vine, ye are the branches: he that abideth in Me, and I in him, the same bringeth forth much fruit: for without Me ye can do nothing" (John 15:4-5). What must we do to be fruitful (having already been engrafted as a branch in Jesus)? We must *abide in Jesus Christ*.

Notice that being <u>engrafted</u> into the Vine is *different* than <u>abiding</u> in the Vine. The single difference between both branches that are **in Jesus** is that one did *abide* in Jesus and the other didn't, but both were engrafted into the Vine already. The engraftment is regeneration, imputed righteousness, and immediate justification (lawfully and spiritually), but abiding in Jesus Christ is maintaining the saving faith that you had from the beginning, enabling the man to be filled with the graces and powers of regeneration for present progressive victory over the world's damnable forces of sin. When men maintain saving faith in the gospel (that which "ye have heard from the beginning"), they will *continue in the Son* as an engrafted branch, avoiding the fate of those that *discontinue* to be **in the Son**. The discontinuance of being in the Son of God, the Vine, is not only preached in John 15, but with further reference it is preached in 1 John directly after 1 John 2:15-19. Here in 1 John, the apostle warned of the same principle written in John 15 – castaway branches which discontinue to be in the Vine – a principle echoed again in Romans 11:22, rephrasing it to be, "otherwise thou also shalt be cut off" (Rom. 11:22).

> "...**continued with us**..." – 1 John 2:19
> "...**continue in the Son**...' – 1 John 2:24

1 John is a doctrinally focused commentary about the practice of "**abiding**"; a term first introduced in John 15. It is written, "If that which ye have heard from the beginning shall remain in you, ye also shall **continue in the Son**, and in the Father" (1 John 2:24, see also John 15:7). The word *continue* does show the possibility of *discontinuing*, and the secret of continuing in the Son of God is repeated in the same terms as John 15 – "Let that therefore **abide** in you" (1 John 2:24). **Abiding** is an equivalent to the biblical word **walk**, and he that does not (through faith) **walk** out the faith of the gospel, which is in the newness of the Spirit, the new man, or the new creation, then he will be reprobated, discontinued, and cast forth from the Son. Those who undergo reprobation will be made manifest when they go "out from us" (that is, the Church assembly), for as long as they had "continued in the Son" and been "of us", then doubtlessly, the writer proves, "they would no doubt have continued with us," but if they did not "continue in the Son", how will they continue in the assembly (1 John 2:19, 24)? Many people presume that this passage

(1 John 2:19) means that such individuals at reference were, they say, "NEVER of us," but this is out of context from the following verse and charges that the apostle does give to the remaining Christians who have not yet left the Church's companionship. John pled with them to continue to be "of us," which is, a continuing "in the Son" (1 John 2:24). This is taught in the fifth verse down from verse 19, therefore it must be rightly understood to mean that – a discontinuing with the assembly of the saints (the body of Christ on earth) does happen by a discontinuing with the Son of God in personal salvation, but it cannot mean that these individuals were *never of us,* which the text does not say, nor could it say this, lest the gospel of John's secret of abiding is in different principles and consequences than how it is taught the book of 1 John. Surely, when John used the word "abide" in 1 John 2:24, he had in mind what he wrote in John 15, which is the foremost teaching on "abiding" in the whole of the New Testament.

Abiding is the secret of bearing fruit. Being fruitful is a manifestation of saving faith. No matter what the descriptive terms or metaphors, the NT scriptures continually present the same picture from different angles. Fruitfulness is the primary burden of the NT pastors, and to open it up before the people of God, they use a plethora of metaphors. One that is helpful to parallel the teaching, "abiding in the Vine", is the metaphor using light and darkness, rendering the same burden in different terms – only we must "abide in the light". Spiritually and lawfully, Christians have been made into light from the darkness (2 Cor. 4:4-6), as formerly addressed, but are they "*walking*" or *abiding* in this reality, truth, and spiritual empowerment? Paul writes in Ephesians 5:8, "For ye were sometimes darkness, but now are ye light in the Lord: **walk as** children of light." If they do walk as children of light (*walk* = *abide*), then they will, according to Ephesians 5:9-17, bear the "fruit of the Spirit" that is "in all goodness and righteousness and truth", which is manifest in the holy living men who do not have "fellowship with the unfruitful works of darkness," or that is to say, men who are *continuing in the Light*. In 1 John, the apostle John thoroughly examines the profession of "he that saith he is in the Light" and explains that he is not in the light if he does not walk in the Light; thus the apostle is teaching the means to *continue in the Light* (1 John 2:9), just as John's burden was to "**continue in the Son**" (1 Jn. 2:24). As a second witness, John emphasizes to the reader – to be outside of the Light is to be outside of the umbrella of Christ's salvific blood. "If we say that we have fellowship with Him, and walk in darkness, we lie, and do not the truth: But if we walk in the light, as He is in the light, we have fellowship one with another, and <u>the blood of Jesus Christ His Son cleanseth us from all sin</u>" (1 John 1:6-7). Do you see the scriptural consistencies building this interpretation? Our confessions of faith must be tried and found pure according to the fruits of our faith. Thus it was written in 1 John, "Beloved, believe not every spirit, but try the spirits whether they are of God: because many false prophets are gone out into the world" (1 John 4:1).

1 John is a trying of spirits and confessions, as formerly noted. Two other confessions are addressed in chapter two: "he that saith, I know Him" and "he that

saith he **abideth** in Him" (1 John 2:4, 6). Those who say they abide must then walk according to the nature, empowerment, and Spirit of their salvation – thus, "He that saith he **abideth** in Him ought himself also so to walk, even as He walked" (1 John 2:6, Luke 6:40). This **walk** (Gal. 5:16) is a keeping of the commandments of God by faith, therefore, "He that saith, I know Him, and keepeth not His commandments, is a liar, and the truth is not in him" (1 John 2:4). John says this is *perfected love,* and "hereby know we that we are in Him" (1 John 2:5). On the final day of Judgment, God will not judge an un-perfected Christian as being "in Him", though at present (if they are not reprobate) they are still spiritually "in Him", or lawfully able to be revived again in Him through faith and repentance. Yet if you die having fallen from a state of "perfection" (Heb. 6:1, 1 Cor. 2:6), you will be damned. That is falling from *perfection as a Christian* (Col. 1:28-29, Eph. 4:12, 2 Cor. 13:9, 11), which is, falling from *perfecting works* in Christ (Rev. 3:2, Heb. 13:21, 2 Thess. 2:16-17), *perfected holiness* (2 Cor. 7:1), *perfected faith* (James 2:21-22, 1 Thess. 3:10), and as John addresses it, a *perfected love* (1 John 2:5, 4:12, 17). And reader, this must be understood: to fall from perfection is to, at present, incur the just penalties of reprobating and casting-away wrath (2 Cor. 13:5, 9, 11), though God will give a space of time for repentance that you may escape it (Rev. 2:21).

> "But whoso keepeth His word, in him verily is the love of God perfected: hereby know we that we are in Him. He that saith he **abideth** in Him ought himself also so to walk, even as He walked." (1 John 2:5-6)

> "God is love; and he that dwelleth in love dwelleth in God, and God in him. Herein is our love made perfect, that we may have boldness in the day of Judgment: because as He is, so are we in this world." (1 John 4:16-17)

Are you burdened to, by faith, "continue in the Son, and in the Father," knowing exactly the grounds, laws, effects, and tests to know if "truly our fellowship is with the Father, and with His Son Jesus Christ" (1 John 1:3, 7)? "If we" know these truths, the question remains, are we "walking" in these truths – for many are they which "saith I know him" (1 John 2:4), "saith he abideth in him" (1 John 2:6), and "saith he is in the light," (1 John 2:9) and yet walk **contrary to these professions**. "It is the last time" (1 John 2:18), "and the world passeth away, and the lust thereof: but he that doeth the will of God abideth for ever" (1 John 2:17); but do you "**abide** in Him; that when He shall appear, we may have confidence, and not be ashamed before Him at His coming" (1 John 2:28)? Are we worthy to "be called the sons of God" (1 John 3:1) and therefore walking "**as** He is in the Light" (1 John 1:7), in "the truth" or "of the truth" **as** He is the Truth (1 John 2:4, 3:19, John 14:6), in "His Word" **as** He is the Word (1 John 1:10, 2:4, 24, 28, John 1:1), in righteousness "even **as** He is righteous" (1 John 3:7), in love **as** "God is love; and he that dwelleth in love dwelleth in God, and God in him" (1 John 4:16), to "lay down our lives for the brethren" even **as** "He laid down His life for us" (1 John 3:16)? If so, then "the world knoweth us not" **as** "it knew Him not" (1 John 3:1) and we have a holy "hope" that we may be purified "even **as** He is pure" (1 John 3:3). We need this "understanding, that we may know Him that is true" (1 John 5:20). We must be sure we are walking in Him in all these specified ways, for "herein is our love made perfect, that we may have boldness in the Day of Judgment: because **as He is**, so are we in this world. There is no fear in love; but **perfect love** casteth out fear: because fear hath torment. He that feareth is not made perfect in love" (1 John 4:17-18).

Abiding in Christ maintains spiritual fruitfulness, and therefore maintains a saving connection to Christ, which therefore maintains a saving communion in the corporate body of Christ, the Church. If a man discontinues to abide in Christ, then he discontinues being fruitful, and if he discontinues fruitfulness then he will, like as the man's excommunication in 1 Corinthians chapter 5, discontinue fellowship in the assembly of the saints. However, if the man repents from his sins unto fruitfulness again, a saving (perfection) fruitfulness as described in 2 Corinthians 7:10-11, then the man will be allowed to continue in the midst of the assembly of the saints because, evidently by the fruits, he is back in the presence of the Son of God!

It is time that men see and understand God's burden, that Christians prove their faith (1 Cor. 1:23-24, 2:9-10, 3:1-3, 6:3-4, 7:2, 11, 15-16, 8:6-9, 24, 9:8-10, chapter 10, 12:11-12, 12:19-13:4). It is time that regenerate Christians pray for and attain mercies for present-tense abiding in Christ, lest they too are cast away (1 Cor. 9:27) from the Vine of Christ. Such a call for examination was done by Paul when he commanded the Corinthians with the utmost authority, "Examine yourselves, whether ye be in the faith; prove your own selves. Know ye not your own selves, how that Jesus Christ is in you, except ye be **reprobates**" (2 Cor. 13:5). Such men and women that are addressed here by Paul would, by this time, likely be castaways, because when they were fallen, they sinned away their space to repent, and Paul laments the fact that they possibly "have not repented" (2 Cor. 12:21) because they cannot repent (2 Tim. 2:25-26). A man cannot repent if he does lack the virtue of the Vine by a holy, reprobating, severing from Christ when He said, "He taketh away" (John 15:1). Though eternal life was a present possession to them (as seen in 1 John 3:15), it is because Jesus Christ the Vine is that eternal life (1 John 5:11-12), and if a man can discontinue from Jesus Christ, then a man can and does discontinue from eternal life. Eternal life is only in Jesus Christ, and it is your present possession if you are judged by God to be in Him.

Such a man who has sinned himself into reprobation has fallen into a state of death (Rev. 3:1), being unable to recover himself again from it. Thus the man has sinned a sin, but not just any sin. He has sinned a sin which is unto death, meaning, he is outside of the possibilities of intercession (by Christ or Christians in Christ). There are many sins which are not unto death, which, if a man sins, a Christian "shall ask, and [God] shall give him life for them that sin not unto death. There is a sin unto death: I do not say that he shall pray for it" (1 John 5:16). Did you know that, like as God's people can become His enemies (James 4:4, Heb. 10:27), they can also become sinners when they were formerly saints, and that a man can be temporarily dead (Rev. 3:1), or in darkness (1 John 2:11), but then recovered from it? God says of saints who have fallen into sin: "***Brethren***, if any of you do err from the truth, and one convert him; let him know, that he which converteth the sinner from the error of his way shall save a soul from death, and shall hide a multitude of sins" (James 5:19-20). Do you want to continue to be alive? Then abide in and walk in the Spirit (Gal. 5:24-25, Rom. 8:13).

We have seen the ascended Christ warn His beloved Churches of reprobation, but during His earthly ministry He did exclaim so many warnings to the regenerate Church it is utterly shocking! The parables of Christ in the gospel accounts, which we shall soon cover in detail, reveal what will happen to the company of "the called out ones" (the Christians) when the Lord returns to judge their faith. He will prove them and see if they have enduring faith or not. Why would they need enduring faith? Christ said these fearful words of His returning Judgment – "shall He find faith on the earth" (Lk. 18:7-8)? He was speaking this question in direct reference to the enduring faith and prayers of "His own elect"! Why would Christ ask this soul-searching and terrifying question if He could never lose His elect? Why would He say this if their names could never be blotted out of the Book of Life (Rev. 3:5)?

The scriptures prophesy and forewarn that "in latter times some shall depart from the faith" (1 Tim. 4:1), and you cannot depart from the faith if you have never been in the faith, like as how you cannot depart from God if you have never been with God (Heb. 3:12-13), or like as you cannot fall if you have never risen into standing graces (1 Thess. 3:8). If a man falls away, what does he fall away from, if indeed the man was never saved? Indeed, "perilous times shall come", which now are, but marvel at this: that this fight that is called "perilous times" had already begun in the NT times! Take note that the perilous times are afflictions from those who are still professors of godliness in Christ, only now they don't have the gospel Spirit of power in their life, thus they gather for themselves teachers that preach unsound doctrine from the spirit of the world:

> "…In the **last days perilous times** shall come… having a form of godliness, but denying the power thereof: **from such turn away**…the **time will come** when they will not endure sound doctrine…" (2 Tim. 3:1, 5, 4:3)

> "They are of the world: therefore speak they of the world, and the world heareth them." 1 John 4:5

So also consider Christ's description of the great falling away:

> "Then shall they deliver **you** up to be afflicted, and shall kill **you**: and **ye** shall be hated of all nations for My Name's sake. And then shall **many** be offended, and shall **betray one another**, and

502

shall **hate one another**. And many false prophets shall rise, and shall **deceive many**. And because iniquity shall abound, **the love of many shall wax cold. But he that shall endure unto the end, the same shall be saved.**" Matt. 24:9-13

Let me put this solemn question to you in another way! How can a man's love for God wax cold if he never had hot love in the Spirit of God? In this very same context Jesus declares that the love, which does "endure to the end", endures all the persecutions during the great falling away. Endurance is a keeping of love to God in the midst of these times, the great falling away, when circumstances seek to suffocate faith. In these last days, we will be so hard-pressed with persecution and betrayal, namely and the foremost hurtful of all is, the betrayal from regenerate Christians when they do betray other regenerate Christians! This antichrist revolution shall begin *within* the regenerate Churches, and it also will assail it *without*! Look carefully at Jesus' description of the falling away in Matthew 24 cited above. "Then shall **many** be offended", Christ says, and He speaks that their offense will cause what? A betrayal of Christian bonds one to another. Among those that once loved one another, even they will then "betray one another and shall hate one another", so that their love is turning into hatred. The "**many**" offended are also the same group of persons in description when Christ says the false prophets are arising to "deceive **many**", and further, Christ directly references this same company, called the "**many**", describing that THEIR LOVE has WAXED COLD, which proves that they once HAD LOVE and then lost it – which means that their love DID NOT ENDURE the FALLING AWAY delusion which assailed those within the Church.

As a further confirmation of these truths, the books of Jude and 2 Peter chapter 2 depict this same fight for the faith against the falling away, describing again that it had *already begun* at that time, and in addition to this, Acts chapter 20 names these "grievous wolves" (false prophets) to be persons who were saved and then turned away, like as 2 Peter 2:1-3 speaks of "false prophets" "**among you**" (meaning a part of the regenerate Church), and so again these passages declare that men will arise and "**many**" of the regenerate Church will be deceived by them! Acts 20 is a farewell sermon from the apostle Paul to the elders of Ephesus. Elders were not merely regenerate Christians but Elders, and therefore we can be doubly sure they were regenerate! And yet Paul said of them, "of your own selves shall men arise" (Acts 20:30)!

"Take heed therefore unto yourselves, and to all the flock, over the which the Holy Ghost hath made you overseers, to feed the Church of God, which He hath purchased with His own blood. For I know this, that after my departing shall grievous **wolves enter in among you**, not sparing the flock. Also **of your own selves shall men arise**, speaking perverse things, to **draw away disciples after them**. Therefore watch, and remember, that by the space of three years I ceased not to warn every one night and day with tears." (Acts 20:28-31)

Paul was weeping day and night over a falling away which was to come shortly after his departure from Ephesus, and today men can't even believe saints can fall away, let alone weep over it! The battle was already violently upon the NT saints, and they were, back then, already recognizing the characteristics of the Last Days delusion coming upon them (Jude 17-21). They were urged and charged to be saints that "earnestly contend for the faith which was once delivered unto the saints", but it was because the deluded offenders who were "ordained to this condemnation", who were chosen as instruments of delusion to bring about the falling away – even these men were at work in subverting-heresies inside of the Church; Jude was stating that they had – "crept in unawares" – attacking the doctrines of the grace of God (Jude 3-4) which they did, at one time, savingly interpret, apply, walk out in, and believe (Jude 5-8)! These men are New Testament examples of those who were "saved", but after salvation they fell away and then were doomed to be "destroyed", like as their OT fathers who were "saved" but "afterward destroyed" (Jude 5).

"let it not be once named **among you**" (Eph. 5:3)
"taken away from **among you**" (1 Cor. 5:2)
"Put away from **among yourselves**" (1 Cor. 5:13)
"**among you** that believe" (1Thess. 2:10)
"come out from **among them**" (2 Cor. 6:17)

Peter is battling against "damnable heresies" from "false teachers **among you**", which is the regenerate Church, and they are "privily" brought in (2 Peter 2:1). These false teachers were so effective that "**many** shall follow their pernicious ways" (2 Peter 2:2), like as Christ said in Matthew 24:9-13, "false prophets… shall deceive **many**"! It is stated further of these false teachers and their followers, "they speak great swelling words of vanity" and "they allure through the lusts of the flesh, through much wantonness, those that were clean escaped from them who live in error" (2 Peter 2:18). Now please, let me address the controversies surrounding this passage and make plain the true meaning, by God's able grace. First, let us read the entire passage which is at hand:

> "For when they speak great swelling words of vanity, they allure through the lusts of the flesh, through much wantonness, those that were **clean escaped from them who live in error**. While they promise them liberty, they themselves are the servants of corruption: for of whom a man is overcome, of the same is he brought in bondage. For if **after they have escaped the pollutions of the world** through the knowledge of the Lord and Saviour Jesus Christ, they are **again entangled therein, and overcome**, the latter end is worse with them than the beginning. For it had been better for them not to have known the way of righteousness, than, **after they have known it, to turn from the holy commandment** delivered unto them. But it is happened

unto them according to the true proverb, The dog is **turned** to his own vomit again; and the sow that was **washed** to her wallowing in the mire." (2 Pet. 2:18-22)

A key to understanding this passage is noting the language of the entire book of 2 Peter. If 2 Peter 2:18-22 is speaking of falling away from salvific grace, then how does 2 Peter term salvation when it is first begun?

"According as His divine power hath given unto us all things that pertain unto life and godliness, through the knowledge of him that hath called us to glory and virtue: Whereby are given unto us exceeding great and precious promises: that by these ye might be partakers of the divine nature, **having escaped the corruption that is in the world through lust**." (2 Pet. 1:3-4).

My point to prove here is that, in verse 4 of chapter 1 the gospel promises did regenerate the lost man by "the divine nature", which in turn did effectually cause the man to be in a condition which was said to be "**having escaped the corruption that is in the world through lust**" (2 Peter 1:4). Compare the two passages below and see if you can tell anything in common:

"having **escaped the corruption that is in the world through lust**" – 2 Pet. 1:4
"after they have **escaped the pollutions of the world**…they are again entangled therein, and overcome" – 2 Pet. 2:20

In 2 Peter 1:4, those who are partakers of the divine nature have escaped the *corruptions* of this world through lust, while in 2 Peter 2:20, the individuals that are again entangled in and overcome by sin were once "clean escaped" from (2 Peter 2:18) this error which they are now entangled in, error which is called the *pollutions* of the world. It is absurd to conclude that those who have "escaped the corruption that is in the world" (2 Pet. 1:4) are a different company of persons from those who have "escaped the pollutions of the world" (2 Pet. 2:20)! The divine nature that caused lost men to escape "the corruption that is in the world" is the same divine nature that caused men to escape "the pollutions of the world". Corruption and pollution are descriptive of the very same spiritual reality: → SIN.

Now you may say, "But these people are called a pig and a dog in 2 Peter 2:22!" And since these terms, a pig and a dog, are commonly used to describe lost people, men argue that those persons described in 2 Peter 2:18-22 must have been once-born and lost the entire time. If these men in 2 Peter 2:18-22 are unregenerate, lost, unbelievers, and the intent of the author in calling them a dog and a sow is to reveal this very thing, then ANSWER ME THIS QUESTION: → How does a dog *vomit* and a sow get *washed*? How can a lost, unregenerate, unbeliever ever *vomit* and be *washed*? Look closely at the direct context of what these verbs are describing in the passage…

"But it is happened unto them according to the true proverb, The dog is turned to his own **vomit** again; and the sow that was **washed** to her wallowing in the mire."
(2 Peter 2:22)

To "vomit" is to repent of sin, and to be "washed" is to be "clean escaped" from the filthiness of sin (2 Peter 2:18, 22)! The man did savingly repent so that he was removed from his sin, like vomit is removed from the body, and the man was savingly washed from the mire of sin until he was "clean" (2 Pet. 2:18) – but how could an unregenerate man ever experience this? How could an unregenerate man *vomit* and be *washed*? But if the dog and the sow do describe a regenerate believer who has fallen away from saving grace, then it makes perfect sense why he vomited (savingly repented) and was washed (forgiven clean), and seeing that the man fell away from grace and is lost again, the author points out the brutish stupidity of such a thing, calling the man as dumb as a dog who eats his own vomit that he once threw up and turned away from, and again, the man is as confused as a sow who values the mire above the "washing of regeneration" (Titus 3:5). The horror of the crime which is committed is well displayed by these two animals! It would be a very strange thing to describe an unregenerate man, a lost man, as one who was "clean escaped from them who live in error" (2 Peter 2:18), one who previously "escaped the pollutions of the world", and then is "AGAIN entangled therein and overcome" (2 Peter 2:20), or a man who had a former state of salvific freedom and then fell into a "latter end" which is worse for him, now, specifically because he had "known the way of righteousness" and then did "turn from the holy commandment" (2 Peter 2:21). All of those things are impossible for unregenerate believers!

Therefore 2 Peter 2:18-22, like the other passages, does reveal the ongoing battle against a falling away that was already in progress before Peter's death. Christ preached FIVE PARABLES of the same burden! It was prophesied at the conception of the Old Covenant that there would be **a great falling away** (Lev. 26:44), and so Christ prophesied of this horrifying fall and delusion which He shall send upon the earth, like things to what had been done by the God of deceptions in the OT (Jer. 4:10), yet this time unto worldwide unity amongst unholy, darkened, godless, men. Sinners are made ready for the coming of the antichrist while Christians are made ready for the coming of Christ. The prince of darkness is coming for his "children of the night" (1 Thess. 5), the "sons of Belial" (2 Cor. 6), the "workers of iniquity" (Matt. 7:22), for they all do the deeds of their father, the devil, but Christ is coming for His "children of the day" (1 Thess. 5), the "sons of God" (Php. 2:15, 2 Cor. 6:18), and those who work righteousness as a fulfillment of their gospel call, who therefore "have no fellowship with the unfruitful works of darkness" (Eph. 5:11).

Oh! How "**many**" Christians are being turned to darkness, carnality, and blame, living unworthy of their calling! Even all the same characteristics of the OT deception of God are working in the NT time period, and how much more now?! Christians who are born again into light, made blameless, faultless, holy, sanctified, without blemish and spot, wise, quickened, and revived, even they are FALLING AWAY, being turned back to darkness, blame, fault, unholy and unsanctified behavior, making themselves blemished and spotted by the world, made into unwise fools, and finally, into dead men in need of revival! They are spiritual babies! Spiritual drunkards! But will you understand that when a person does this, then their childhood under God does discontinue? God will no longer call them His sons or daughters, because they do not behave like His sons or daughters.

Could it be that, as Moses prophesied of apostasy to OT regenerate Israelites, so Christ prophesied of apostasy to NT regenerate Israelites? How many centuries did pass by that were filled with apostasy and chaos, and how increasingly did the apostasy grow, until finally, that great END came in the Israelite captivity and dispersion? Likewise, how many centuries of like chaos and apostasy can we see in extrabiblical Church history since the purity of the 1st century Church? How rarely have we seen faithful men arise, moved by the Holy Ghost, ushering in moves of God that lastingly revived souls? And consider this, that these were not mere *revivals*, merely moving of God, but moves of saving grace, and however many fell back asleep into an un-revived, un-quickened spiritual condition – all of these men were eternally lost. Now can we conclude that today, as we dwell in the dark eve of the Antichrist, that we are further along in "the last days" than when the 1st century began the dispensation which was called "the last days"? Therefore we can suspect that *these days* are like "the Days of Noah", days when 8 souls were saved in a world full of people, so we should not be counting the thousands but rather that which can be numbered with our two hands – quite possibly, thus are the days in which we approach! When Jesus Christ comes, "shall He find faith on the earth" (Lk. 18:8)? Don't answer God with words, dear reader! Rend your heart and get on your face! Read this verse and do likewise – "He putteth his mouth in the dust: if so be there may be hope" (Lam. 3:29).

THE NT GOSPEL CALL TO WORTHINESS
CHAPTER 22

Will you be called God's Son on Judgment Day?
Do your deeds reflect that?

Do you remember how Jesus Christ declared that you are Abraham's seed if you **do the deeds of Abraham**? Do you remember how this same spiritual principle is applied to being called **a child of God**? If God is your Father, then you will do the deeds of God - this is the essence of ***worthiness***. We live in a day when men believe that their adoption as God's son or daughter does disannul the dangers of Judgment Day, but it is not so! If you call on God as your Father, then you will be judged by God concerning the legitimacy of that claim, and if you are found worthy to bear the name of God, then you are living worthy of the gospel calling of God. This is as it is written:

> "And if ye call on the Father, Who without respect of persons judgeth according to every man's work, pass the time of your sojourning here in fear." (1 Pet. 1:17)

You see dear reader, you must live in such a way that you are blamelessly keeping "the gospel call", present-progressively without rebuke, and if you fail to do this, then you will not be, what Paul called, "sons of God without **rebuke**" (Php. 2:15), which is to say that God will find you in such a state which deserves His ***rebukes*** (Rev. 3:19) at Judgment Day! "One shall say, I am the LORD'S; and another shall call himself by the name of Jacob; and another shall subscribe with his hand unto the LORD, and surname himself by the name of Israel" (Isa. 44:5), and so it is today, but are you worthy to bear the Name of God? Many will say to God in that day, "Lord, Lord"... we have done this, and this, and this other thing "in Thy name" (Matt. 7:22), "Nevertheless the foundation of God standeth sure, having this seal, **The Lord knoweth them that are His. And, let every one that nameth the name of the Christ depart from iniquity**" (2 Tim. 2:19). Are you a son of God without rebuke? Do you live worthy of your **calling**? Do you know what your calling is?

> "As ye know how we exhorted and comforted and charged every one of you, as a father doth his children, that ye would **walk worthy** of God, Who hath **called** you unto His kingdom and glory." (1 Thess. 2:11-12)

"**Called** unto the fellowship of His Son Jesus Christ our Lord" – 1 Cor. 1:9
"Hereunto were ye **called**: because Christ also suffered for us… ye should follow in His steps" – 1 Peter 2:21
"Walk worthy of the vocation wherewith ye are **called**" – Eph. 4:1, "called in one body" – Col. 3:15
"**Called** you out of darkness in His marvellous light" – 1 Peter 2:9
"**Called** us to glory and virtue" – 2 Peter 1:3
"God hath not **called** us unto uncleanness, but unto holiness" –1 Thess. 4:7
"Lay hold on eternal life, whereunto thou art **called**" – 1 Tim. 6:12
"When he was **called** to go out… he sojourned in the land of promise" (Heb. 11:8-9), and we are thus "as strangers and pilgrims" because we have obeyed our calling to "come out from" (2 Cor. 6:17) among the world to "abstain from fleshly lusts, which war against the soul" (1 Pet. 2:11).
"Holy brethren, partakers of the heavenly **calling**" – Heb. 3:1

We have been called out of the world and into the Presence of God, through Christ; therefore we are the Church of God. The word "Church" describes a local congregation or assembly, and also, it is a universal people around the globe who obeyed the gospel of God, who came out of the world to be born of another. Spiritually they have become the "**called out ones**". This is the work of **the cross**! As Paul did affectionately declare, "God forbid that I should glory, save in the cross of our Lord Jesus Christ, by Whom the world is crucified unto me, and I unto the world" (Gal. 6:14). The word "Church" in the scripture, which is ekklesia in the Greek, literally means "**called out ones**", and that calling is the gospel of Christ. One must become the Church by nature and then live as the Church by deed, and they will live worthy of their calling.

> "Be ye not unequally **yoked** together with **unbelievers**: for what **fellowship** hath **righteousness** with **unrighteousness**? and what **communion** hath **light** with **darkness**? And what **concord** hath **Christ** with **Belial**? or what **part** hath he that **believeth** with an **infidel**? And what **agreement** hath **the temple of God** with **idols**? for ye are the temple of the living God; as God hath said, **I will dwell in them, and walk in them; and I will be their God, and they shall be my people.** <u>Wherefore</u> **come out from among them**, and **BE YE SEPARATE**, saith the Lord, and **touch not the unclean thing**; and **I will receive you, And will be a Father unto you, and ye shall be my sons and daughters**, saith the Lord Almighty. Having therefore <u>these promises</u>, dearly beloved, let us cleanse ourselves from all filthiness of the flesh and spirit, perfecting **holiness** in the fear of God." (2 Corinthians 6:14-7:1)

If you are not living worthy of your calling, it is because you have turned back into *unrighteousness*, you have fallen away, and therefore you are in *darkness*, *carnality*, *blame*, etc., and God, at this point and in result of this, will no longer dwell

509

with you nor call you His son or daughter. He will no longer be your Father! You are no longer worthy to dwell with Him! The promises of 2 Corinthians 7:1, which the Christians are exhorted to lay hold upon, enable a man to savingly be in God's Presence. As God said, "I will dwell in them and walk in them". In this way, a people does become God's people and He is their God, or in other terms, they are God's sons and daughters and He is their Father, as He said, "I will receive you... be a Father... and ye shall be my sons and daughters" (2 Cor. 6:18). Christians have already become believers, and therefore the spiritual **yoke** to unbelievers is broken *by nature*. They have already become the righteousness of God (2 Cor. 5:21), therefore they have no spiritual **fellowship** with unrighteousness in carnal men *by nature*. They have already become the **light** of the world, therefore they have no **communion** with unbelievers who are still yet in **darkness**. They do abide in Christ, keep His word (1 John 2:4) and His law (John 13:34, Gal. 6:4, Rom. 8:4), therefore henceforth, they have no **concord** with lawless children of **Belial**. They are saved believers, therefore they have no religious **part** with unbelieving infidels because there is no **agreement** between the two. This enmity, or non-agreement, is as sharp as the OT conflict between the Temple of God and idols, and why is this? Christians have become the Temple of God and the world is polluted with devilish sin-worship through anti-God idolatry. Seeing then that God says of Christians, "I will dwell in them, and walk in them; and I will be their God, and they shall be my people", henceforth we ought to live worthy of such an indwelling, and so personally and corporately walk according to the spiritual laws, realities, and holy ways that the salvation and indwelling of a thrice-Holy God would demand. Now consider again those tenets above which are the calling of God. Each one of them is because the individual saint is called out of the world and into the Presence of God, and because they are in the Presence of God, then they must live out and walk in the DEEDS that such a divine nature is worthy of! They must walk out their nature, or in other words, walk in their God's Presence. This calling is carefully and exhaustively broken down for us all throughout the NT books! We must look at what God's Presence is, and from there we can understand our calling.

"As He is, so are we in this world." (1 John 4:17)

"**Called** unto the <u>fellowship</u> of His Son Jesus Christ our Lord" – 1 Cor. 1:9

We are called to live in and walk in the Presence of God, to be conformed to what God is BY DEED. We are called unto the <u>fellowship</u> of God's Son in this saving union of oneness, and when that fellowship or communion with Him is broken in our personal relationship to God's Presence that dwells in us, then the following experiences of the gospel, also described as our calling, are not experienced, hence we are to be blamed instead of being judged "blameless in the day of our Lord Jesus Christ" (1 Cor. 1:8), and we will **not** be recognized by God as His sons (2 Cor. 6:18-7:1). What we are by nature, we must become by DEED, and this is *worthiness*. This is Paul's continual burden for the Church of God. Paul can summarize all of his preaching in the forms of exhortation, comforting words, and charges, but all of these communicative expressions have the same final burden: Paul says, "That ye would **walk worthy** of God, Who hath called you unto His Kingdom and glory" (1 Thess. 2:12). Your eternity will be decided upon in the language, "if you will 'be accounted **worthy**'" (Lk. 20:35, 21:36). All those who enter Paradise will enter because their life relationship to the gospel call was one that makes them of the number that God says, "they are **worthy**" (Rev. 3:4).

If we do walk in Christ (our nature), then we will become like as He was in deed, and therefore, the world will respond to us in the same way the world responded to Christ. According to 1 Peter 2:21, this is a fulfillment of our calling, for, "Hereunto were ye **called**: because Christ also suffered for us... **ye should follow in His steps**" (1 Peter 2:21). Worthiness of the gospel calling is perfection, and therefore we will be "**as He is in this world**" (1 John 4:17). We must live worthy of our profession, which is, "he that saith he abideth in Him ought himself also so to **walk, even as He walked**" (1 John 2:6). Worthiness is the response of saving faith, and since faith must be kept initially, presently and progressively, and finally, so also worthiness is spoken of as an attribute of initial salvation (Matt. 10:37-39, 22:8), present progressive salvation (1 Thess. 2:11-12, Eph. 4:1), and final salvation (2 Thess. 1:5, 11, Rev. 3:4, Luke 20:35-36, 21:36). Will you be "counted worthy of the Kingdom of God"? Then you must walk worthy of your calling to suffer as 1 Peter 2:21 said. Paul encourages and comforts the Thessalonican Church, that they are worthy for the Kingdom of God BECAUSE they are suffering. Read it carefully:

> "So that we ourselves glory in you in the Churches of God for
> your patience and faith in all your persecutions and tribulations
> which ye endure: Which is a manifest token of the righteous
> judgment of God, **that ye may be counted worthy of the
> kingdom of God**, for which ye also suffer: Seeing it is a
> righteous thing with God to recompense tribulation to them that
> trouble you; And to you who are troubled rest with us, when the
> Lord Jesus shall be revealed from heaven with His mighty angels,
> In flaming fire taking vengeance on them that know not God, and
> that **obey not the gospel** of our Lord Jesus Christ." (2 Th. 1:4-8)

The Church was going through "persecutions and tribulations" because they were called to "suffer" for the Kingdom of God, and this suffering was the manifest **token** that God would count them **worthy** of the Kingdom of God. In this way, they had obeyed the gospel calling, and as for the others, they would suffer the vengeance of God. You see, we are called by and into the Name of God, into His Presence, and thus we must not "blaspheme the **worthy** name by the which [we] are called" (James 2:7). We are now "called the sons of God: therefore the world knoweth us not, because it knew Him not" (1 John 3:1), and when we walk out our nature, then the world will hate us as it hated Him. In His nature, we are in His Name (Col. 3:17), worthily walking in Him, therefore the world beholds Christ like they did in Paul's life, who said, "for me to live is Christ" (Php. 1:21). In His nature, we are truly confessing Christ by word and deed (Titus 1:17), "wherefore God is not ashamed to be called [our] God", when otherwise He would be ashamed (Mk. 8:38). We must persevere in the deeds of our salvific gospel calling, and thus, like Abraham, be "called the friend of God" (James 2:23). Suffering, as we have just reviewed, with many other attributes of God which demand the overflow of Christ's DEEDS, must be kept to live **worthy** of the gospel, **worthy** to be called the sons of God, but all of these deeds have the same common root of origin - they overflow the characteristics of the Presence of God that indwell the believer, or, they are an overflow of the divine NATURE.

Behavior "as dear children" (Eph. 5:1) of God, is, behavior "as obedient children" (1 Pet. 1:14), and at Judgment Day they will be the "sons of God without rebuke" (Php. 2:17). Living otherwise, men will be called "the children of disobedience" (Eph. 2:1). Their eternal fate resides like the solemn warning – "Let no man deceive you with vain words: for because of these things cometh the wrath of God upon **the children of disobedience** (Eph. 5:6, Col. 3:6). Such persons are living in a manner which does not represent the calling to be holy, or as Paul said, "called to be saints" (1 Cor. 1:2, Rom. 1:7), therefore they are living in a way which does not "becometh saints" (Eph. 5:3), and that is to say that they are not living in a way which is worthy of the name saint (which means holy one), and likewise they are not living in a way "as becometh the gospel" call (Php. 1:27). *Becometh* is a synonym to *worthiness*. These verses I have cited are in various places throughout scripture, and they address different nature-to-deed calls of worthiness, but what you need to see is that God must "account" you "worthy" to be called "the children of God", and when you see this, then you will understand all the argumentation which we shall soon cite and examine.

> "The children of this world marry, and are given in marriage: But they which shall be **accounted worthy** to obtain that world, and the resurrection of the dead, neither marry, nor are given in marriage: Neither can they die any more: for they are equal unto angels; and are **the children of God**, being **the children of the resurrection**." (Luke 20:34-36)

Those that obtain the resurrection were "**accounted worthy**", or judged worthy. Are you prepared? Do you know that you will be reckoned with by God? This is a verb which described God's Final Judgment upon God's talent-gifted Christians! It is written, "After a long time the Lord of those servants cometh, and **reckoneth with them**" (Matt. 25:19), and your worthiness of the gospel-talent of the Holy Ghost will be reckoned with by God. God questions you – what have you done by DEED with what you have been given in salvation by NATURE? If you do not live worthy of your calling, "some thirtyfold, some sixty, and some an hundred" (Mark. 4:20), or in other words, again, some 10 talents, 4 talents, and 2 talents, each one showing forth works of righteousness to their proper perfect multiplication which is evidence that imputed righteousness is within them (Matt. 25:14-30), then you will

512

be, like the unfruitful branches (John 15:6), "cast" "into outer darkness: there shall be weeping and gnashing of teeth" (Matt. 25:30). And again, if you do not bring forth the fruits of "herbs meet" to God's requirements of you, accounting that you are a field which is planted by the choicest seed, watered by so great an outpouring of the Holy Ghost, namely, the rains of being enlightened, tasting of the heavenly gift and the good word of God, and experiencing the powers of the world to come (Heb. 6:4-5), and still, even when these Holy Spirit rain showers are continually coming upon you so that you do drink them up "oft", you will not bring forth a worthy and meet measure of fruits! And rather, you bring forth "thorns and briers"! Then man, you are unworthy of Paradise. I am sorry for you, for you are "nigh unto cursing, whose end is to be burned" (Heb. 6:7-8).

We are called out of the world for another name – to be called "children of the Living God" (Rom. 9:26) – thus Luke 20:36 states the name of our reward in these terms: we shall be called "the children of God" and "the children of the resurrection". So also we must achieve the final reward of our calling, or as Paul phrases it, "press toward the mark for **the prize of the high calling** of God" (Php. 3:14), which is to be worthily judged and called "the children of Light" (John 12:36, 1 Thess. 5:5) and "the children of the Day" (1 Thess. 5:5), worthy to obtain the resurrection of God's eternal Day, which is, "the Perfect Day" (Prov. 4:18, 1 Peter 1:19, Rev. 21:23-25). Walk in the spirit of Christ's resurrection now (Rom. 6:4), and you will be worthy to be called one of the children of resurrection then (Lk. 20:36), and likewise, walk in the light of Christ now (Eph. 5:8), and you will be worthy to enter God's eternal Day of Light which shall never diminish in heaven (Rev. 21:23-25). Worthy, meet (Heb. 6:7-8, Matt. 3:8), and becometh (Php. 1:27, Eph. 5:2, 1 Tim. 2:10, Titus 2:1, 3) are all synonymously used to bring into reference the DEMAND of fruits, works, and deeds for professing believers to inherit heaven – and heaven is only reserved as an inheritance for the heirs, the sons of God, and none other; thus if God does not call you His son, then you do not have the inheritance of heaven (Gal. 4:1, 6-7, Rom. 8:17). Matthew 5:43-48 does match this DEMAND perfectly:

"GOD, HIS WAY IS PERFECT" – Psalm 18:30

"…keep the commandments of the LORD thy God, to **walk in His ways**, and to fear Him" (Deut. 8:6).
"Blessed is every one that feareth the LORD; that **walketh in His ways**." (Ps. 128:1)

"Ye have heard that it hath been said, Thou shalt love thy neighbour, and hate thine enemy. But I say unto you, **Love your enemies**, **bless** them that curse you, **do good** to them that hate you, and pray for them which despitefully use you, and persecute you; **That ye may be the children of your Father** which is in heaven: for He maketh His sun to rise on the evil and on the good, and sendeth rain on the just and on the unjust. For if ye love them which love you, what reward have ye? do not even the publicans the same? And if ye salute your brethren only, what do ye more than others? do not even the publicans so? Be ye therefore **perfect, even as your Father which is in heaven is perfect.**" (Mat 5:43-48)

"But love ye your enemies, and do good, and lend, hoping for nothing again; and your reward shall be great, and ye shall be the children of the Highest: for He is kind unto the unthankful and to the evil. Be ye therefore merciful, **as your Father also is merciful.**" (Luke 6:35-36).

Christian, you are called to live worthy of the gospel. Therefore you are called to be "as your Father" is (Lk. 6:36), which means that you walk in Him, and when you walk in Him, you do His deeds. God does love His enemies. He does good to them and blesses them, and how? By shining the sun and raining rain upon them. So also, if you are "perfect" you will be "as your Father" (Matt. 5:48), which means that you do what He does by walking in

---

> ### "Be Perfect" – Matt. 5:48
> ---
> "Be ye therefore perfect, even as your Father which is in heaven is perfect." (Matt. 5:48)
> "Be ye therefore merciful, as your Father also is merciful." (Lk. 6:36)
>
> "…every one that is **perfect** shall be **as his Master.**" (Luke 6:40)
> "Be ye therefore perfect, **even as your Father** which is in Heaven is **perfect.**" (Matt. 6:48)

Him. "He that saith he abideth in Him ought himself also, so to **walk, even as He walked**" (John 2:6). In this way must be "as He is" (1 John 4:17) in walk. Can you see how Christian perfection is to be "as He is" (1 John 4:17)? In Matthew 5:43-48 & Luke 6:35-36, the attribute of God's merciful love is in direct view, thus we can see that Christian perfection is to be "as your Father" (Matt. 6:48), and from henceforth as we examine "perfection", whatever attribute is in view about Who God is, or, what are the manner of His ways, to be perfect in "Christian perfection" is to be "as He is". God's way is perfect; therefore we must be perfect by walking in His ways. "Ye do the deeds of your father" (John 8:41).

"that ye may be the children of Light" (John 12:36)
"that ye may be the children of your Father" (Matt. 6:45)

John 12:36 says, "walk… that ye may be the children of Light", and now, here in Matthew 5:43, it states that we should love as God loves, which is being as He is, which is also being perfect as He is perfect (Matt. 5:48), and all of this is to the end "that ye may be the children of your Father" (Matt. 5:45), God says! For, if you do not do these things and are not "as He is in this world" (1 John 4:17), then you will not be called a child or son of God on the Last Day of Judgment! Christian perfection (Php. 3:15), which is saving faith, does lay hold upon the gospel calling

(Php. 3:14) in a worthy "walk" (Eph. 4:1) right NOW, presently and progressively, so that in the Final Judgment you will obtain final, sinless perfection (Php. 3:12) in the gospel consummation. To be perfect like as Matthew 5:48 states is a present progressive COMMAND which is obtainable, at present, and thus the NT writers labor for Christian perfection with all their might, bearing in mind that it is an eternally significant cause (Col. 1:28-29)! "The disciple is not above his Master: but every one that is **perfect** shall be **as his Master**" (Luke 6:40). Can you now understand and see the meaning behind these verses? We'd better understand what Christian perfection is! There is no other reason for the gifts of the Spirit to empower Church ministers except that they would, by grace, cause the people to be established in and maintain perfection (Eph. 4:12-13). Hear of Paul's exhausting devotions to this supreme goal: "Whom we preach, warning every man, and teaching every man in all wisdom; that we may present every man **perfect** in Christ Jesus: Whereunto I also labour, striving according to His working, which worketh in me mightily" (Col. 1:28-29). Perfection was heard about, it was evidently a supreme topic in his preaching, warning, and teaching, and, in this cause he was laboring, striving, and working according to the mighty power of God – yet is Christian perfection so alien to you that you don't even know what it is? Has your congregation ever heard you speak of it, and is it in your prayers that you pray to God? Paul's heart was utterly rent over the spiritual necessity of each individual's perfection in Christ – so much so, he did so earnestly pray – "NIGHT AND DAY praying EXCEEDINGLY that we might see your face, and might **perfect** that which is lacking in your faith" (1 Thess. 3:10)! A matter so grave, so heavy, Paul was continually cast upon his knees, prostrated on his face, standing in the nights with hands lifted up, praying and praying, exceedingly, and lo, WOE TO US – we don't even understand what it is! Christian perfection is a matter of eternity, and do you think that you are a biblical pastor or elder, and yet you don't know what this subject pertains to? May the Lord have mercy! Then preacher, know this, you are not the man of God for the hour! Let this agonizing lamentation of God sink down into your ears – "Oh that My people had hearkened unto Me, and Israel had **walked in My ways**" (Ps. 81:13)!

"GOD IS LOVE" – 1 John 4:16

"But whoso keepeth His word, in him verily is the love of God perfected: hereby know we that we are in Him. He that saith he **abideth** in Him ought himself also so to walk, even as He walked." (1 John 2:5-6)

> **"Perfect Love"** – (1 John 2:5, 4:12, 17-18)
> ---
> "GOD IS LOVE; and he that dwelleth in love dwelleth in God, and God in him." (1 John 4:16)

"God is love; and he that dwelleth in love dwelleth in God, and God in him. Herein is our love made perfect, that we may have boldness in the day of Judgment: because as He is, so are we in this world." (1 John 4:16-17)

515

Are you burdened to, by faith, "continue in the Son, and in the Father", knowing exactly the grounds, laws, effects, and tests to know if "truly [your] fellowship is with the Father, and with His Son Jesus Christ" (1 John 1:3, 7)? "If

RELATED SERMONS

"Perfect Love, Do You Have It?"
– Sean Morris
"The Secret of Boldness"
– Sean Morris

we" know these truths, the question remains: are we "walking" in these truths? For, many are they which "saith I know Him" (1 John 2:4), "saith he abideth in Him" (1 John 2:6), and "saith he is in the Light," (1 John 2:9) and yet, they walk **contrary to these professions**. "It is the last time" (1 John 2:18), "and the world passeth away, and the lust thereof: but he that doeth the will of God abideth for ever" (1 John 2:17), but do you "**abide** in Him; that when He shall appear, we may have confidence, and not be ashamed before Him at His coming" (1 John 2:28)? Are we worthy to "be called the sons of God" (1 John 3:1) and therefore walking "**as** He is in the Light" (1 John 1:7), in "the truth" or "of the truth" **as** He is the Truth (1 John 2:4, 3:19, John 14:6), in "His Word" **as** He is the Word (1 John 1:10, 14, 2:24, 28, John 1:1), in righteousness "even **as** He is righteous" (1 John 3:7), in love **as** "God is love; and he that dwelleth in love dwelleth in God, and God in him" (1 John 4:16), to "lay down our lives for the brethren" even **as** "He laid down His life for us" (1 John 3:16)? If so, then "the world knoweth us not" **as** "it knew Him not" (1 John 3:1) and we have a holy "hope" that we may be purified "even **as** He is pure" (1 John 3:3). We need this "understanding, that we may know Him that is true" (1 John 5:20). We must be sure we are walking in Him in all these specified ways, for, "herein is our love made **perfect**, that we may have boldness in the Day of Judgment: because **as He is**, so are we in this world. There is no fear in love; but **perfect love** casteth out fear: because fear hath torment. He that feareth is not made **perfect** in love" (1 John 4:17-18).

"in him verily is the love of God **perfected**" (1 John 2:5)
"**the love of the Father** is not **in him**" (1 John 2:15)

Perfect love is not describing how God perfectly loves you, but it is how you are perfectly abiding in the love of God which is in you, which must be perfectly formed in you, so then you are loving God and loving the brethren with a "perfect" degree of His love, and thus it can be said that your love is "as He is". This perfect love does not describe God's love toward you but your love, in Christ, toward God, and when a man is perfected so that he, in this way, does keep God's commandments (1 John 2:3-6), the Christian man is living worthy of his profession (1 John 2:3-6), so to "walk even as He walked" (1 John 2:6), thence it will be said at Judgment Day, "as [Christ] is so [was] [he] in this world" (1 John 4:17). Here in 1 John 4:17, again, there is an exact comparison to 1 John 2:5-6 – perfection is declared as an eternal necessity, and without it one will not continue in the Son of God, wherein is eternal life, but will rather be cast forth into the torments of fire. 1 John 2:5-6 is John's first introduction of the phrase, "perfect love", and from here in chapter 2, and onward, the burden of perfect love and its need to be formed within the Christian is explained and applied. The apostle John expounds the very attributes of this love in its relationship to "the world", self-sacrifice for the brethren regarding money and goods, and generally speaking, keeping the words of God with obedience. In 1 John 2:15-17, the world is the topic at hand, but not the world only, but, John explains, if a man loves the world then perfect love is not in him, or as John phrases it here, "the love of the Father is not in him" (1 John 2:15). In the book of 1 John, this means GOD IS NOT IN YOU (1 John 2:5-6). In other words, you will be condemned in this judgment on the Final Day if you do not repent and change your ways! Do you see the burden? Is "the love of the Father" in you? This is the burden of perfect love.

> "Hereby perceive we **the love of God**…" (1 John 3:16)
> "…how dwelleth **the love of God** in him?" (1 John 3:17)

In 1 John 3:16-17, the apostle John performs a more specified examination of perfect love. To discern the love of God in the Christian, he focuses on certain charitable deeds toward the brethren, but the same question is at hand – does the love of God dwell in you? If the author is explaining to the reader that "hereby perceive we the love of God" (1 John 3:16), and not in some other way, but "hereby", then we ought to listen up and pay attention, because, in 1 John, the apostle is showing that if you don't have the love of God in you, then you don't have God or eternal life! John declares how the love of God is perceived, and it is within a man when he is laying down his life for the brethren like as Christ loved the Church and laid down His life for them (1 John 3:16, John 13:34, 15:12-14, Eph. 5:1-2). Then John applies an exact scenario at hand, of practical deeds relevant to us all, and by such deeds being present or absent, even so the love of God is present or absent from the soul of the man – "But whoso hath this world's good, and seeth his brother have need, and shutteth up his bowels of compassion from him, how dwelleth the love of God in him" (John 3:17)? This question, "how dwelleth the love of God in him?", is to say, if a man does not give to the necessities of the brethren when he has goods to give, then the love of God is not in this man, which means that he is not "perfect in love", and thus, he has no reason to be assured of salvation at the Judgment because God will judge him to be without God. Why?

"GOD IS LOVE" – 1 John 4:16

> "If we love one another, God dwelleth in us, and His love is **perfected** in us." (1 John 4:12)
> "**God is love**; and he that dwelleth in love dwelleth in God, and God in him. Herein is our love made **perfect**, that we may have boldness in the Day of Judgment: because **as He is, so are we in this world**."
> (1 John 4:16-17)

Why will a man be judged to be without God if he is without love? GOD IS LOVE! And if we are "as He is" in love, then we have perfected love. To be "as He is" is the foundational essence of what Christian perfection is. Whatever attribute of God is in focus, if we are "as He is" in that attribute, then, concerning that attribute in God we are savingly perfected in it, and thus, this is one of the evidences of our saving faith. Most people interpret 1 John 4:17 entirely out of context from 1 John 2:5-6, 15-17, 3:16-17, 4:12, & 16! Even so, people believe that God is teaching that Christians are never to fear the possibility of going to hell. Reader, if you don't have "perfect love", then you should not have "boldness", which means fearlessness, to face the Judgment of God, because then you will surely be given over to eternal torments (1 John 4:18). However, if you do have perfect love, then you can have boldness and fearlessness that you are not going to perish. Nevertheless, you should still fear Him, namely God, because He is able to make you perish, even though you are not perishing (Lk. 12:5). This is as Christ said, "But I will forewarn you Whom ye shall fear: Fear Him, which after He hath killed hath power to cast into hell; yea, I say unto you, fear Him" (Lk. 12:5)! Therefore let us conclude this final statement – we are always to fear God, that He is **_able_** to cast us into hell, but we are only to fear that He **_will_** cast us into hell if we are not "perfect" in Him. So, how about you? Are you perfected in Christ? "Perfect Love – Do You Have It?"

We have seen Christian perfection with the attribute of God's LOVE, but the doctrine of perfection is used to focus on many multifaceted attributes in God – like His ONENESS, HOLINESS, STRANGENESS, ILLUMINATING LIGHT, GLORY AND VIRTUE, ETERNALITY, and HEAVENLINESS. For now, let us move on to the next attribute at hand which would greatly help understand the doctrine of perfection.

"GOD IS ONE" – Mk. 12:29

"Walk worthy of the vocation wherewith ye are **called**" – Eph. 4:1
"**called** in one hope of your calling" – Eph. 4:4
"**called** in one body" – Col. 3:15

    "**GOD IS ONE**" (Mk. 12:29), even though He is three Persons, and each of Them dwell in perfect Oneness and Unity. So also, it is expected and demanded that those that are in God ought to be one (John 17:21-23), for they are, as Christ said to the Father, "one in US". Our calling is in the unity of ourselves with God, and thus this results in the unity of one another. We must therefore keep "**the unity of the Spirit in the bond of peace**" (Eph. 4:3). "One Lord, one faith, one baptism, One God and

> **"Perfect in one"** – John 17:23
> **"A Perfect Man"** – Eph. 4:13
> **"Perfectly Joined Together"** – 1 Cor. 1:10
> **"The Bond of Perfectness"** – Col. 3:14
> --
> God is One; and he that dwelleth in oneness dwelleth in God, and God in him. God is unified; and he that dwelleth in unity dwelleth in God, and God in him.

518

Father of all, Who is above all, and through all, and in you all" (Eph. 4:5-6), does empower us to be "a perfect man", all of us together, in the unity of our nature and indwelling Person, Jesus Christ – "**perfect** in one" (John 17:23). This unity is attained by each individual Christian's "perfection", Eph. 4:12 declares, and when individual Christians maintain perfection, then they will come to corporate "perfection" which is called "the unity of the faith" (Eph. 4:13). This doctrine of unity called "perfection" in Ephesians 4:12 and 4:13 came from the doctrine of Christ in John 17:23, coining the phrase – "perfect in one". All the "**perfect**" (Eph. 4:12-16) Christians are unified because they are dwelling in unity with the Spirit of God, and all those who are walking after the flesh are creating the divisions in the body of Christ (1 Cor. 3:1-3). You are "as He is" (1 John 4:17) or "as men" (1 Cor. 3:3) in your walk, and thus your conversation creates unity as He is, or it creates divisions (1 Cor. 1:10, 3:3). Walking worthy of "the vocational calling", as it is termed in Eph. 4:1, is rephrased in Php. 1:27 as, "Let your conversation be as it **becometh** the gospel of Christ", which Paul says is UNITY, in "one spirit, with one mind striving together for the faith of the gospel" (Php. 1:27). To be perfect is to be, therefore, individually (Eph. 4:12) and corporately (Eph. 4:13) with "no divisions", that we "speak the same thing", "**perfectly joined together** in the same mind and in the same judgment" (1 Cor. 1:10), but it is all because we are perfect with our God's Spirit Who is the nature, empowerment, and substance of our oneness.

GOD "IS HOLY" – 1 Peter 1:16

"God hath not **called** us unto uncleanness, but unto holiness" – 1 Thess. 4:7

"as He which hath called you is holy" – 1 Peter 1:14-17

"**called** to be saints" – 1 Cor. 1:2, Rom. 1:7

"**Perfecting Holiness**" – 2 Cor. 7:1

God is holy; and he that dwelleth in holiness dwelleth in God, and God in him.

"Whose Name is Holy" – Isa. 57:15
"holy and reverend is His Name" – Ps. 111:9

GOD IS HOLY –

"Be ye holy **FOR I AM HOLY**" (1 Peter 1:16). The question of perfecting holiness brings to the forefront the question: are you "as your Father is", Who is holy, so that you will be found truthful of your claim that you are a child of God? If we are God's "children" (1 Pet. 1:14), let us therefore recognize our calling which He has called us into by the gospel, namely, to be HOLY, and let us further recognize that, just because we are the children of God by nature and we call God Father by confession, this does not exclude the dangers of Judgment if we are not **perfect in holiness,** as 2 Corinthians 7:1 warns, or, **holy as He is holy**, as 1 Pet. 1:16 commands. Do you understand this Judgment BAR!? Peter WARNS all those persons who call God "Father" – to FEAR – as the faith-filled and reasonable response to the fact that God calls you to be holy! "If ye call on the Father, Who without respect of persons judgeth according to every man's work, pass the time of your sojourning hear in fear" (1 Pet. 1:17). Read the passage in its entirety before we continue:

> "As obedient children, not fashioning yourselves according to the former lusts in your ignorance: But as He which hath **called** you is holy, so be ye holy in all manner of conversation; Because it is written, Be ye holy; for I am holy. And if ye call on the Father, Who without respect of persons judgeth according to every man's work, pass the time of your sojourning here in fear..." (1 Pet. 1:14-17)

Peter is expounding all the principles of "perfect" holiness, but he does it without the word "perfect" being used. As the apostle John brought the people to consider "perfect love" in the light of Judgment Day, so now Peter is preaching on perfect holiness on God's Judgment Day. The doctrine of perfection was understood by all the apostles and pastors of the 1st century Church. The apostle Paul preaches the same principles of **perfect holiness** in 2 Corinthians 6:14-7:1, and I hope that I would not have to exposit the entire passage in detail, because I have already addressed it several times. But look with me at a few points of emphasis. What is the burden of Paul? It is "perfecting holiness" (2 Cor. 7:1), and why? It is because God's presence is in their midst (2 Cor. 6:16), and He will not continue in their midst, nor will He call them His sons or daughters, if they are not maintaining a holiness, otherwise known as a separateness, which is accomplished by coming out from among unholy things. The Judgment of the saints on Judgment Day is of primary view in the passage, how that God will judge the legitimacy of their claim to be God's "sons and daughters". Direct instructions are given so that Christians will, as Peter preaches it, be holy as God is holy, only now it is Paul speaking to the Corinthians. Hanging in jeopardy is the blessed promise: "I will be a Father unto you, and ye shall be My sons and daughters, saith the Lord Almighty" (2 Cor. 6:18). If you want to lay hold of these blessed promises for your Judgment Day experience, Paul says that you better perfect holiness in the fear of God, which is, a separation from "unbelievers", "unrighteousness", "darkness", "Belial", "infidels", and "idols", in context of what the passage is meaning, and rather abide in God's presence which is "righteousness", "light", "Christ", and "the Temple of the Living God" (2 Cor. 6:14-16).

"Without holiness no man shall see the Lord" (Heb. 12:14).

God is "holy, holy, holy" (Rev. 4:8), His Spirit is a "Holy Spirit" (1 Thess. 4:8), and those that walk in Him are "holy" (Heb. 12:48), therefore they are not strangers but citizens and friends of "the holy city" (Rev. 21:2). No one who is not holy "may enter in through the gates into the city" (Rev. 22:14), "and there shall in no wise enter into it any thing that defileth" (Rev. 21:27). God's "name is Holy" (Isa. 57:15), and if you seek to lay claim that you are of His name, you must, THEREFORE, be holy.

GOD IS A STRANGER

***Strangeness** in the world is a synonymous doctrine to **holiness**…*

We are "**called**" "as Strangers and Pilgrims in this world" (Heb. 11:8, 1 Peter 2:11).

"By faith, Abraham, when he was **called** to go out into a place which he should after receive for an inheritance, obeyed; and he went out, not knowing wither he went. By faith he sojourned in a land of promise, as in a strange country, dwelling in tabernacles with Isaac and Jacob, the heirs with him of the same promise: For he **looked for a city** which hath foundations, whose Builder and Maker is God… These all died in faith, not having received the promises, but having seen them afar off, and were persuaded of them, and embraced them, and confessed that they were strangers and pilgrims on the earth. For they that say such tings declare plainly that they seek a country. And truly, if they had been mindful of that country from whence they came out, they might have had opportunity to have returned. But now they desire a better country, that is, an heavenly: Wherefore God is not ashamed to be called their God: for He hath prepared for them a city." (Heb. 11:8-11, 13-16)

"Dearly beloved, I beseech you, **as strangers and pilgrims**, abstain from fleshly lusts, which war against the soul." (1 Peter 2:11)

"Remember Lot's wife" (Luke

A Perfect Stranger
Perfect Strangeness

God is a Stranger; and he that dwelleth in strangeness dwelleth in God, and God in him.

"walk before Me and be thou **perfect**"(Gen. 17:1-2). Abraham is the fulfillment of perfection by strangeness.

"Thou shalt be **perfect** with the LORD thy God" (Deut. 18:13).
Those that followed in Abraham's ways were also perfect with God in the strangeness of their calling, therefore, after Abraham's strangeness, there came the commandment for Israelite strangeness in the conquest of Canaan. The Israelites had to keep holy strangeness from the native Canaanites among whom they were going to dwell.

"A **perfect** heart" and "a **perfect** way" is described in Psalm 101:1-8.
David, arisen after Joshua's land-conquering generation, still exemplifies the doctrine of strangeness in perfection with God, here now, as before, but in the paradigm of the established Kingdom in David's rule.

"**perfecting** holiness" (2 Cor. 7:1).
Holiness is strangeness and it must be perfected, thus also the OT showed the necessity of perfection in the P. land or the House of God.

THE LAND - "For the upright shall dwell in the land, and the **perfect** shall remain in it" (Prov. 2:21).

THE HOUSE OF GOD - "**Holiness** becometh thine house, O LORD, for ever" (Ps. 93:5), and, "so the workmen wrought, and the work was

521

17:32) while "looking for new heavens and a new earth, wherein dwelleth righteousness" (2 Peter 3:13).

perfected by them, and they set the house of God in his state, and strengthened it" (2 Chron. 24:13).

Furthermore: "be **watchful**" (Rev. 3:1-3) – "denying ungodliness and worldly lusts…godly in this present world; **Looking for**" (Titus. 2:11-14) – "…all holy conversation and godliness…**looking for** and hasting" (2 Peter 3:11-12) – "**watch and be sober**" (1 Thess. 5:6) – "having a desire to depart" (Php. 1:23) – Groaning, earnestly desiring, and burdened "that mortality might be swallowed up of life" (2 Cor. 5:1-4). "And when these things begin to come to pass, then look up, and lift up your heads; for your redemption draweth nigh." (Lk. 21:28)

GOD IS A STRANGER – He is an enemy and alien to this world, and when we walk in Him we will be "as He is". God is otherworldly because He is not of this world. Why? It is written, "The whole world lieth in wickedness" (1 John 5:19). Contradicting this world are those twice-born Christians who were born of another world. Therefore they are not "of the world" (1 John 2:16, 4:5). They are free from the "pollutions of the world" (2 Peter 2:20), and this is because they are "of God" (1 John 5:19), or, "of the Father" (1 John 2:16). To be a stranger is to be born from another origin than that of this world's natives who are countrymen of carnality. They are natural men, born "of blood", and they need to be born into a family of lineage that is "of God" (1 John 1:13), thus it is written that we are hated, otherworldly strangers, suffering in this world but ruling in "the world to come" (Mark. 10:30, Lk. 18:30, Heb. 2:5, 6:5). To be a stranger is to be a man in a foreign land, far away from what is called home. A traveler is not a treasurer. They are far away from what they call "treasure" (Matt. 6:21). All their time here on earth is but "sojourning" (1 Pet. 1:17) – "this world is not my home, I'm just a-passing through, my treasures are laid up somewhere beyond the blue" ("This World is Not My Home", Jim Reeves).

If you are rejected by this world, then you are worthy to be received by God (2 Thess. 1:4-5). If you can be "heard" by this world, and you "hear" them, then you cannot "hear" God or His people, comparatively as if you and they speak a different language or a foreign tongue, and everything is rendered strange. If you are ashamed of God, then He will be ashamed of you, but if you confess, live in, and preach God, then this world will be ashamed of you. Christians "desire a better country" than this world and do therefore confess the Lord, "wherefore God is not ashamed to be called their God" (Matt. 10:32-40, Heb. 11:16). To be "godly in this present world" (Titus 2:11-14) is to be anti-god against "the god of this world" (2 Cor. 4:4) – "as lights in the world" (Php 2:15) against the "rulers of the darkness of this world" (Eph. 6:12).

For this reason, if we walk in the flesh by denying the gospel call (Gal. 5:24-25, 6:14), then we become friends with the world, and also, enemies and adulterers to God (James 4:4). We must not be friends with the devil, who is "the god of this world" (2 Cor. 4:4), who also is called the "prince of the power of the air" (Eph. 2:2). If we make friends with him, then the devil's spirit will work in us. Then, we are not "obedient children" of 1 Peter 1:14, but rather, we are the "disobedient children" of Ephesians 2:2. If we are friends with God, we are enemies of the devil, and if the devil's spirit rules in this world, therefore is the world full of the chaos of carnality, while we, the anarchists against the devil's tyranny, are those holy ones who are not "taken captive by him at his will" (2 Tim. 2:26). As for the devil's sinful world, love it not, or else it is adultery to God (Jas. 4:4)! A stranger does therefore know no man, as chaste "virgins" (2 Cor. 11:2-4, Rev. 14:4), for we are preserved for heaven's Bridegroom. All those that indulge in carnality rather than spirituality will die (Rom. 8:13). Strangers are those that do not –this is our "**strangeness**" (1 Pet. 4:1-4) – that we "abstain from fleshly lusts", because "God is Spirit" (John 4:24) and not flesh! "No flesh should glory in His presence" (1 Cor. 1:29). "We are the circumcision which worship God in the Spirit, and rejoice in Christ Jesus, and have no confidence in the flesh" (Php. 3:3), the "true worshippers" of God (John 5:23).

New creatures (2 Cor. 5:21) walk in the "new man" (Col. 3:10), which is "newness of life" (Rom. 6:4) in Jesus' living Person and "name" (Col. 3:17), therefore all such persons are strangers in a world of fallen men. New men belong to a new world, the "new Jerusalem" (Rev. 21:2), the "new heaven and a new earth" (Rev. 21:1), where dwelleth Him Who said, "Behold, I make all things new" (Rev. 21:5). God is "holy, holy, holy" (Rev. 4:8), His Spirit is a "Holy Spirit" (1 Thess. 4:8), and those that walk in Him are "holy" (Heb. 12:48), therefore they are not strangers, but citizens and friends of "the holy city" (Rev. 21:2), for none other "may enter in through the gates into the city" (Rev. 22:14). "There shall in no wise enter into it any thing that defileth" (Rev. 21:27). God is a Holy Spirit, The Stranger of this unholy world, and so are all those that live and move in Him. Therefore the world does "think it **strange** that" we "run not with them to the same excess of riot, speaking evil" (1 Peter 4:4), but this is no surprise! We should "think it not **strange**" (1 Peter 4:12) that they are offended at our **strangeness**. Christian, the world is "where thou dwellest, even where Satan's seat is" (Rev. 2:13), but you are "made" to "sit together" with Christ (Eph. 2:6) "far above all principality and power" (Eph. 1:21), therefore you must walk according to another King's Reigning Rule – "that as sin hath reigned unto death, even so might grace reign through righteousness unto eternal life by Jesus Christ our Lord" (Rom. 5:21). If we "walk as men" (1 Cor. 3:3), then we do walk in sin, but if we "walk in Him" (Col. 2:6), then we will walk contrary to every earthly rule (Php. 3:16-21). Therefore a Christian has "a desire to depart" rather than stay on earth (Php. 1:23), because, to look to God is to look away from this world, and again, to look for the world to come "wherein dwelleth righteousness" is to look away from this world wherein dwelleth sin (2 Peter 3:13).

God is a stranger, so that the world knows Him not (1 John 3:1). If you are saved, it is because you have come to know Him Who the world does not know (1 John 2:4), and how many will come before the gates of God's eternal Kingdom and boldly declare, "open up the doors of entrance for me", and why? The Kingdom of God is what they sang about, stood praying unto heretofore, and then at last, they arise to claim their eternal crown that is their own, and, lo, alas! He that sitteth upon the Throne of Grace, He that unctionizes every man unto a bold approach into heaven's holy ground, even He saith unto them – "I know you not" – "and ye begin to stand without, and to knock at the door, saying, Lord, Lord, open unto us; and He shall answer and say unto you, I know you not whence are" (Lk. 13:25).

GOD IS HEAVEN

A synonym to holiness and strangeness is heavenliness…

"Holy brethren, partakers of the **heavenly calling**" – Heb. 3:1
"For our conversation is in **heaven**" – Php. 3:20
We are NOT "living in this world" – Col. 2:20
"But Jerusalem which is **above** is free, which is the mother of us all" - Gal. 4:26

> ## Perfectly Heavenly
> --
> God is heaven; and he that dwelleth in heaven dwelleth in God, and God in him.
>
> "just men made **perfect**" – Heb. 12:23

"Now therefore ye are …fellowcitizens with the saints, and of the household of God" (Eph. 2:19), and "ye are come unto mount Sion, and unto the city of the living God, the **heavenly** Jerusalem, and to an innumerable company of angels, To the general assembly and Church of the firstborn, which are **written in heaven**, and to God the Judge of all, and to the spirits of just men made **perfect**" (Heb. 12:22-23).

"Who shall **ascend** into the hill of the LORD? or who shall stand in his holy place? He that hath clean hands, and a pure heart; who hath not lifted up his soul unto vanity, nor sworn deceitfully. He shall receive the blessing from the LORD, and righteousness from the God of his salvation. This is the generation of them that seek him, that seek thy face, O Jacob. Selah." (Psalm 24:3-6)

"And I looked, and, lo, a Lamb stood on the mount Sion, and with him an hundred forty and four thousand, having His Father's name written in their foreheads. And I heard a voice from heaven, as the voice of many waters, and as the voice of a great thunder: and I heard the voice of harpers harping with their harps: And they sung as it were a new song before the throne, and before the four beasts, and the elders: and no man could learn that song but the hundred and forty and four thousand, which were redeemed from the earth. These are they which were not defiled with women; for they are virgins. These are they which **follow the Lamb whithersoever He goeth**. These were redeemed from among men, being the firstfruits unto God and to the Lamb. And in their mouth was found no guile: for they are without fault before the

524

throne of God." (Rev. 14:1-5)

GOD IS HEAVEN, it can be said, for He is what is heavenly about heaven. God is heavenly and His Spirit is called "the **heavenly** gift" (Heb. 6:4), and if we walk in Him, then we are walking worthy of our "**heavenly** calling" (Heb. 3:1). This heavenly calling lives in the setting of our "affections" (Col. 3:1-3) and "conversation" (Php. 3:20) on heaven, from whence is our salvation in the very "**heavenly** things" (Heb. 8:5), where Christ is standing in His virtuous salvation (Heb. 9:23-24), and if we thus walk worthily we will be unashamedly called God's worthy inheritors of His "**heavenly**" country (Heb. 11:16), "the **heavenly** Jerusalem" (Heb. 12:22). Therefore also, your name has then abided past the dangers of being blotted out from the heavenly BOOK, which is to say that your name is still written there – "written in **heaven**" (Heb. 12:23). In fact, it can be said that "our conversation is in **heaven**" (Php. 3:20) in such a real, spiritual, and lawful way, so much so that we are not "living in this world" anymore (Col. 2:20). In this way we are already come unto the "Mount Sion" of heaven (Heb. 12:22), even now, but we await a consummating ascension unto the physical "Mount Sion" (Rev. 14:1-5) which is to come. Those that stand with the "Lamb" (Rev. 14:1) on that final day, all of them will be arrayed in holiness on the Mountain of God! These are there with the Lamb in the end, because they did follow the Lamb of heaven while on earth. They were in Him by nature and deed! Jesus said, "If any man serve Me, let him follow Me; and where I am, there shall also My servant be: if any man serve Me, him will My Father honour" (John 12:26). Those that were with Him on earth are worthy for heaven! "These are they which follow the Lamb withersoever He goeth" (Rev. 14:4)! "Let us go forth therefore unto Him without the camp, bearing His reproach. For here have we no continuing city, but we seek one to come" (Heb. 13:13-14).

God is the builder of heaven, and, "we have a building of God, an house not made with hands, eternal in the heavens" in Christ (2 Cor. 5:1), "Whose house are we if we hold fast the confidence and the rejoicing of the hope firm unto the end" (Heb. 3:6, 14). God's face is the light of heaven (Rev. 21:23-25), and those that "are saved shall walk in the light of it", not only then but NOW (2 Cor. 3:17-18, 4:3-6)! God's nature is the purity of heaven, and, "it doth not yet appear what we shall be: but we know that, when He shall appear, we shall be like Him; for we shall see Him as He is" (1 John 3:2). In a sinlessly perfect way, God does consummate the gospel (1 Cor. 13:10, Php. 3:12), culminating in our regeneration into His sinless perfection for all eternity! Jesus Christ is "on High" (Heb. 1:3)! Amen! Therefore we are called by what is said to be, "the high calling of God in Christ Jesus" (Php. 3:14). In a gospel sense, it is as if God has said to us – "come up hither" (Rev. 11:12).

"GOD IS LIGHT" – *1 John 1:5*

"**Called** you out of darkness into His marvellous light" – 1 Peter 2:9

"GOD IS LIGHT".
Being made one with God, you are in the Light, for God is Light (1 John 1:5-7). "Our fellowship is with the Father, and with His Son Jesus Christ" (1 John 1:3), and, "GOD IS

> **Perfect Light**
> ---
> God is light; and he that dwelleth in light dwelleth in God, and God in him.
> "Walk in the Light, **as He is in the Light**" (1 John 5:7), and this is Christian perfection in the attribute of God that He is light.

LIGHT, and in Him is no darkness at all" (1 John 1:5), of necessity therefore, "If we say that we have fellowship with Him, and walk in darkness, we lie, and do not the truth: But if we **walk in the Light, as He is in the Light**, we have fellowship one with another, and the blood of Jesus Christ His Son cleanseth us from all sin" (1 John 1:5-7). "I am the light of the world" (John 9:5), Jesus said, but also He furthermore said, "ye are the light of the world" (Matt. 5:14). Though this section is short, let it be sufficient for you, my reader, because I have already addressed the spiritual biology of light and darkness in great detail.

GOD IS GLORY & VIRTUE

"**Called** us to glory and virtue" – 2 Peter 1:3
"…that our God would count you **worthy** of this **calling**… That the Name of our Lord Jesus Christ may be **glorified** in you and ye in Him…" – 2 Thess. 1:11-12

GOD IS GLORY AND VIRTUE – "In God is my salvation and My glory" (Ps. 62:7). We are called to show forth the glory of God to the world (1 Pet. 2:9), and, God's glory is His Person (John 15:1, 5) which we have been connected to. He is the virtue from His glory we are nourished up in, and thus, His Name is also His person (Col. 3:17).

> **Perfect Glory & Virtue**
> ---
> God is glory; and he that dwelleth in glory dwelleth in God, and God in him. We must be as He is in this way NOW (Jn. 17:22), and in the time to come we shall also be enveloped by His glory in a consummating finality!

A Christian going deeper into His person is therefore described as an "image" transformation "from glory to glory" (2 Cor. 3:18). His Image is His glory, and this Image is our predestinated end (Rom. 8:29). To be an extension from God, we are therefore, filled with the glory of His personal deeds of glory, called His own works (Eph. 2:10), and in another placed called "the fruits of the Spirit" (Gal. 5:21). Let it be understood then: God's glory is His Person, goodness, and name, and so again, God's glory is His face (Ex. 33:18-20)!

"I beseech Thee, **shew me Thy glory**… I will make **My**

goodness pass before thee... I will proclaim the **Name of the LORD** before thee... thou canst not see **My face**: for there shall no man see Me, and live." (Exodus 33:18-20)

"I kept them in Thy Name" (John 17:12)", Jesus said, and those who are kept in His Name will also have, as Jesus said, the "**glory**... I have given them; that they may be **one, even as We are One**" (John 17:22). Did you understand that?! The glory of God is our oneness in Him! Therefore let us be channels only for the Master's Holy Spirit. Jesus Christ said of the Holy Ghost, "He shall **glorify** Me: for He shall receive of Mine, and shall shew it unto you" (John 16:14). If we walk in Him, then we will be "**a glorious Church**" (Eph. 5:26-27) – arrayed worthy to be in marital union with the Living King of heaven! Glory marries Glory! God's glory is the chief end of our lives as Christians. All efforts that are properly aimed do point to the glory of God. God is glory, to walk in God is to walk in glory, and therefore, perfection in glory is to glorify God! Paul taught that a man must walk in "the work of faith with power", so that, "the name of our Lord Jesus Christ" would be "**glorified**", and, this is so that "our God would count [us] **worthy** of this **calling**". Consider the entire passage:

> "Wherefore also we pray always for you, that our God would count you **worthy of this calling**, and fulfill all the good pleasure of His goodness, and the work of faith with power: That the Name of our Lord Jesus Christ may be **glorified** in you and ye in Him, according to the grace of our God and the Lord Jesus Christ." (2 Thess. 1:11-12)

Is this the aim of all your prayers? Is this your understanding of *worthiness* and *perfection*? The purchase of the gospel is for this end – to "**glorify** God in your body, and in your spirit, which are God's" (1 Cor. 6:20) – and there is no excuse if you are rendered impotent and without grace for glory.

Now we see God's glory in part because we have been saved, but there is a consummation of His glory to come! Jesus said, "Father, I will that they also, whom Thou hast given Me, be with Me where I am; that they may behold **My glory**, which Thou hast given Me: for Thou lovest Me before the foundation of the world" (John 17:24). "**Glory** shall be revealed in us" (Rom. 8:18) at "the manifestation of **the sons of God**" (Rom. 8:19), and then all of creation will follow into "the **glorious** liberty of **the children of God**" (Rom. 8:21)! This is when "He shall come to be **glorified** in His saints, and to be admired in all them that believe... in that Day" (2 Thess. 1:10). We shall see Him then in His glory, "**face to face**" (1 Cor. 13:12), being "glorified together" (Rom. 8:17) with Him!

GOD IS ETERNAL LIFE

"Lay hold on eternal life, whereunto thou art **called**..." – 1 Tim. 6:12

GOD IS ETERNAL LIFE – "And this is the record, that God hath given to us eternal life, and this life is in His Son. He that hath the Son hath life; and he that hath not the Son of God hath not life" (1 John 4:11-12). If we

> **Perfected in His Eternality**
> --
> God is eternal; he that dwelleth in perpetuity of character dwelleth in God and God in him.

"walk" (1 John 2:6) in the Son of God, or abide in Him, we will "continue in the Son" (1 John 2:24), and so we shall be worthily "as He is", as rightful inheritors of eternal life (1 John 4:17). Let us learn **how He is,** so that we might become "as He is". He is perpetually consistent, steadfast, unchanging in righteousness, and enduring in charity. The eternality of God in which we must be perfected in right NOW, in this life, refers to those powers available in Him which perpetuate His character in us.

> "Seeing ye have purified your souls in obeying the truth through the Spirit unto unfeigned love of the brethren, see that ye love one another with a pure heart fervently: **Being born again, not of corruptible seed, but of incorruptible,** by **the word of God, which liveth and abideth for ever**. For all flesh is as grass, and all the glory of man as the flower of grass. The grass withereth, and the flower thereof falleth away: But the word of the Lord endureth for ever. And this is the word which by the gospel is preached unto you." (1 Pet. 1:22-25)

We have been born again by an eternally enduring word of God, thus our love, which was borne, and is now sustained by, the power of God's word, should also be eternally enduring. This is the "as He is" logic of worthiness taught in 1 Peter 1:22-25. God, Who is eternal life, Whose attributes are eternally enduring, Who is the Word of God and the seed of our birth, is the reason that our attributes in Him should be enduring throughout the time of our sojourning here on earth. The birth seed is "incorruptible", the word of God "liveth and abideth for ever", therefore we should love one another with an incorruptible, ever living and abiding love. This is the due expectation of the enduring powers, therefore we should endure in His character by His enduring nature. If we were called to love after the flesh, live in the flesh, or rely upon the flesh, then, understandably, it would be justifiable that our love is withering and falling like a fading grass flower. "Charity" in God "never faileth", nor ceaseth to be (1 Cor. 13:8), though prophesies, tongues, and knowledge does. Charity in God "beareth all things...endureth all things", and, it shall not ever "vanish away" (1 Cor. 13:7-8), and having been given His Spirit, we are responsible to persevere in His ways. We have not been given a spirit that fades and vanishes, but of eternality and perpetuity, thus let us persevere unto the end, into eternity, by and through the unfailing Spirit.

"Thy Name, O LORD, endureth for ever; and Thy memorial, O LORD, throughout all generations." (Ps. 135:13)

We should endure, for He endured all things (Heb. 2:17-18, 4:15), and He is with us now as He promised, "Lo, I am with you always, even unto the end of the world" (Matt. 28:20). He is with us now on earth, lifting our heads up to look, and lo, there again, He standeth in heaven for us as a "lively hope" (1 Peter 1:3). Yea, there He is! And He "maketh intercession for us" (Rom. 8:34)! This is not temporary! God is able to save everlastingly, forever, and all throughout your sojourning in time! Why? Let the scripture declare the answer: "Wherefore He is able also to save them to the uttermost that come unto God by Him, seeing **He ever liveth** to make intercession for them" (Heb. 7:25)! He is our "living way" (Heb. 10:20), and in Him we should "know the way" (John 14:4), because He is "the way" (John 14:6). He is the "author" of our faith, the writer of our salvation story, and lo, He is the "finisher" of faith, of every true story, writing them all up for eternal glory (Heb. 12:1-2). We should be "confident of this very thing, that He which hath **begun** a good work in you will **perform it until the Day** of Jesus Christ" (Php. 1:6). He is the living waters from the living fountain that faileth not! He is, as He declared from enthroned glory – "I am Alpha and Omega, the beginning and the end. I will give unto him that is athirst of the fountain of the water of life freely" (Rev. 21:6). Jesus said, "I am the resurrection, and the life: he that believeth in Me, though he were dead, yet shall he live: And whosoever liveth and believeth in Me shall never die" (John 11:25-26).

The life of God is not some neutral cloud of gas. The life of God is righteousness and not neutrality, and we have His life in us if we have His Spirit. Are you alive? "The Spirit is life **because of righteousness**" (Rom. 8:10). Are you righteous? Our righteousness should be enduring in the eternality of His life, because, He can never die. "To be carnally minded is death" (Rom. 8:6). Do not "walk as men" (1 Cor. 3:3) in the passions and lusts of men, for all of this is passing away. Don't be of the flesh, don't abide in the flesh, or in anything of this world! "The world **passeth away**, and the lust thereof: but he that doeth the will of God **abideth for ever**" (1 John 2:17). His life is forever, and so is His will! Live in Him, "for what is your life? It is even a vapour, that appeareth for a little time, and then vanisheth away" (James 4:14). We should overcome the world because He has overcome the world, and therefore, "He that is born of God overcometh the world" (1 John 5:4). Therefore Jesus said that, "in Me ye might have peace. In the world ye shall have tribulation: but be of good cheer, **I have overcome the world**" (John 16:33, Rev. 3:21). Do you have "eternal life abiding" in you (1 John 3:15)? So walk in it; as He is eternal in existence, as He is perpetually steadfast in righteousness and purity, so be it with you – Amen.

GOD is PERFECT, LOVE, ONE, HOLY, A STRANGER, HEAVEN, LIGHT, GLORY & VIRTUE, & ETERNAL LIFE.

Do you see how GOD IS, what GOD IS, and how that, even so we MUST BE, and that this is *Christian perfection*? Do you believe the gospel? It does savingly unite us to God so that we can walk in Him, Whom the world hates! Will you walk in Christ so that your living "is Christ" (Php. 1), and so, you will be "as He is" (1 John 4:17) – or rather, will you walk in yourself like the rest of humanity that do "walk as men" (1 Cor. 3:3)? Are you seeing these principles clearly? Written again just below is the template verse which I was able to frame all other attributes of perfection in. With this same vein of logic as seen in this template verse, please read and study the following points after this verse. These points cover more attributes than the eight which I have just written about. Each one is an explicit reference which is pointed to something of how God is, and how we must be "as He is" in perfection, that is, if we wish to be finally saved. These things are "the Image of His Son" (Rom. 8:28-29).

~~~~~~~~~

*"Herein is our love made perfect, that we may have boldness in the Day of Judgment: because **as He is, so are we in this world**. There is no fear in love; but perfect love casteth out fear: because fear hath torment. He that feareth is not made **perfect** in love." (1 Jn. 4:17-18)*

*"every one that is **perfect** shall be **as his Master**." (Lk. 6:40)*

*"**Called** according to His purpose… to be conformed to **the Image of His Son**." (Rom. 8:28-29)*

~~~~~~~~~

We have been called by the Gospel which has made us one with Him (John 17), which has placed us in Him (Rom. 8:1)…therefore we must be like Him (inwardly) because we have been made like Him by **NATURE**:

- ❖ "as We are One" (John 17:22)
- ❖ "as Thou hast loved Me" (John 17:23)
- ❖ "as the Father hath loved Me" (John 15:9)
- ❖ "as the Father hath sent Me" (John 20:21-23)
- ❖ "as the Father knoweth Me" (John 10:14-15)
- ❖ "as the Living Father hath sent Me and I live by the Father" (John 6:56-57)
- ❖ "as I am not of this world" (John 17:14, 16, 1 John 3:1, 2:15-17)
- ❖ "as Christ was raised up" (Rom. 6:4)
- ❖ "as those…alive from the dead" (Rom. 6:13)
- ❖ as the eternally enduring word of God from which we were born (1 Peter 1:22-25)
- ❖ "as lively stones" (1 Peter 2:4-8)

Perfect Faith - (James 2:21-22, 1 Thess. 3:10)

Perfect Christian – (Matt. 6:43-48, Lk. 6:35-36, 40, Col. 1:28-29, 4:12, Eph. 4:12, 1 Cor. 2:6, 2 Cor. 13:9, 11, Php. 3:15, 2 Tim. 3:17, Heb. 6:1, 13:21, James 3:2)

These bullet points outline God's NATURE and salvific works. When a man sees and understands these principles of the faith, which can be summarized as The Person & Work of Christ, and when he is properly

- ❖ "as strangers and pilgrims" (1 Peter 2:11)
- ❖ "as obedient children" (1 Peter 1:14-16)
- ❖ "as He is holy" (1 Peter 1:14-16)
- ❖ "as He is in the Light" (1 John 1:5-7)
- ❖ "as He walked" (1 John 2:6)
- ❖ "as He is pure" (1 John 3:7)
- ❖ "as He is righteous" (1 John 3:7)
- ❖ "as He is so are we in this world" (1 John 4:17)
- ❖ "as the elect of God, holy and beloved" (Col. 3:12, 13)

related to them by faith, believing on Jesus Christ's Person and salvific works, then the Christians will be conformed to Christ's nature so as to be empowered to live by, and walk in, Him. The tie that binds a man to the Person and Work of Christ is "perfect faith" in these principles, so the apostles seek to perfect the faith, and when this is perfected, so is the Christian, thus they do the DEEDS of their Father, because they are conformed to the Nature, Image, & Person of the Son.

We must also, therefore, walk in our **NATURE** which was a free gift given to us once, and thereto promised to abide forever, and so outwardly our life will follow that which is alive inwardly; thus we must be "as He is" by **DEED**:

- ❖ "as I have **done**" (John 13:15) → (Eph. 5:25, Php. 2:5, Col. 1:24, Php. 3:10-11)
- ❖ "even as your Father which is in heaven is perfect"(Mt.6:48).
- ❖ "as your Father also is merciful" (Lk. 6:36)
- ❖ "as his Master" (Lk. 6:40)
- ❖ "as I had pity" (Matt. 18:33)
- ❖ "as I have loved you"(John 13:34, 15:12, Eph. 5:2, 1 John 3:16)
- ❖ "as I have kept My Father's commandments" (John 15:10)
- ❖ "as God for Christ's sake hath forgiven you" (Eph. 4:32)
- ❖ Rest, "as God did from His" works (Heb. 4:10)
- ❖ "as Christ received us" (Rom. 15:7)
- ❖ "as Christ also hath loved us" (Eph. 5:2)
- ❖ Husbands: "as Christ also loved the Church" (Eph. 5:25)
- ❖ Wives: "as daughters of Sarah" (1 Peter 3:6)
  - o "If ye were Abraham's children, ye would do the works of Abraham" (John 8:39), and so likewise, if ye were Sarah's children, ye would do the works of Sarah.
- ❖ "as Christ forgave you" (Col. 3:13)

"as Christ hath suffered for us" (1 Peter 4:1, see 1 Peter 2:21-23)

- ❖ "as He walked" (1 John 2:6)
- ❖ as He laid His down life (1 John 3:16)
- ❖ as Paul (1 Cor. 11:1)

Perfect Works – (Rev. 2:26, 3:2, Heb. 13:21, 2 Thess. 2:16-17)

Jesus says that salvation is granted to him that "keepeth My works unto the end" (Rev. 2:26). When a man sees the Person and salvific work of Christ and believes on Him with perfect faith, then such a one will have perfect works. Being unified with the Nature and Person of Christ within is accomplished by seeing the entirety of His historical and living works of salvation today, and then you are enabled to walk in Him Who is in you, and not merely imitate Him; thus, you are by DEEDS conformed to "the image of His Son" (Rom. 8:28), which is living worthy of your calling.

- ❖ "as in the Day" (Rom. 13:13), see also the contrast: "as in the night" (1 Thess. 5:6)
- ❖ "as I also overcame" (Rev. 3:21)

❖ as the truth (Eph. 4:21, Titus 1:1, 2 John 1-4, 9, 3 John 3-4)
  ○ Jesus Christ is "The Truth" (John 14:6), and the Holy Spirit is "The Spirit of Truth" (John 16:13), thus we must be "walking in the truth" (2 Jn. 4), "for the Truth's sake, which dwelleth in us, and shall be with us for ever" (2 Jn. 2). Therefore, when we speak as proper channels only, we do speak as the "oracles of God" (1 Peter 4:11), and on this wise, Christ said: "He that heareth you heareth Me; and he that despiseth you despiseth Me; and he that despiseth Me despiseth Him that sent Me" (Lk. 10:16, John 13:20, Matt. 10:40).

Now do you understand the charges of God to lay hold upon, live worthy of, and make sure your calling? Do you understand the charge: "Wherefore the rather, brethren, give diligence to make **your calling** and election **sure**: for **if** ye **DO THESE THINGS**, ye shall never **fall**" (2 Peter 1:10)? Is your **calling sure**?

> **Eternal Life Sure:** We must lay hold upon the consummating eternal life which is to come (1 Tim. 6:12).

> **Election Sure:** We must lay hold upon election, even though we are elect now (2 Peter 1:10). As the elect, we are regenerate, thus our nature is the nature of the elect; so is our charge then – we must "put on therefore, as the elect of God, holy and beloved, bowels of mercies, kindness, humbleness of mind, meekness, longsuffering; forbearing one another, and forgiving one another, if any man have a quarrel against any: even as Christ forgave you, so also do ye" (Col. 3:12). How do you know if your election is sure? Ask yourself this question according to the tests of scripture: are you fulfilling the purpose of God for which He has elected you, which purpose is "to be conformed to the Image of His Son" (Rom. 8:29), or in other words, are you in the Image of God's Son Jesus Christ – in NATURE and in DEED? Or in other words, are you perfect? Will you be of those, God says, "upon whom My Name is called" (Acts 15:17), not only now, but in the END?

> **Perfection Sure:** In this very same sense, we must lay hold upon the consummating perfection to come, even though we are perfect now. This is done by walking in the attainable perfection presently and progressively, unto the end.

WORTHY →   "pray always" (2 Thess. 1:11)

"do not cease to pray" (Col. 1:9-10)

"exhorted, comforted, & charged" (1 Thess. 2:11-12)

PERFECTION → "Night & Day praying exceedingly" (1 Thess. 3:10)

"preaching, warning, teaching, all wisdom, labour, striving, His working, mightily" (Col. 1:28-29)

ABOUNDING/
WITHOUT OFFENCE → "I pray" (Php. 1:9-10)

"put you always in remembrance" (2 Pet. 1:12)

"stir you up by putting you in remembrance" (2 Pet. 1:13)

"always in remembrance" (2 Pet. 1:15)

THE CONDESCENSION
WITHDRAWN
CHAPTER 23

❖ *Thematic Point of Reference: The Pattern of the Promises*

There is a **pattern the promises and Covenants** are given in, making them appear to be irrelevant of, and impossible to have any binding conditions which subject the promises to, the responsibility of man. Thus, when the promises are read, it appears that there is no possible way there could be conditions, in that they appear to be without possible breach by the nature of **God's faithful word,** and completely reliant upon **the sovereign work of God alone.**

Of many matters I would like to make a sum: There is a way of *God in the ways of man* which is emotionally <u>responsive</u> to man, whether in love or in hatred, and this is God's relationship to us by *condescension.* By <u>responsive</u> I mean, He loves and hates in response to what men DO, for He does not negate the fact that what a man does by deed is a manifestation of what a man believes in heart. Such an existence of God in this way of *condescension* affects His will, counsel, mind, word, Covenant, and promise, and these affect eternal salvation and damnation. Studying the biblical and historical accounts of the *many called,* and of this many how many did eventually fall, or how few eventually persevered, it becomes evident that these persons received and related to the promises of God in a consistent *pattern.* I call it "The Pattern of the Promises." When this is understood and the disciple of Christ is familiarized with these *scriptural consistencies*, then the hard persuasion behind one of the most popular Calvinistic arguments is easily discovered as folly.

PATTERN #1: Our Only Hope – God's Faithfulness

It is said, as I have, and do wholly agree, *the word of God **promises** eternal security.* It is true! I never disaffirmed this. Again, let me repeat, the word of God does emphatically **promise** eternal security. However, is it biblically accurate to assume that none can come short of these **promises**, slip away from their performance, and substantiate the anger of God's holy *breach* which is made possible through a change of mind, which, if it is held fast in God it leads to an eventual

534

reprobation? Need I give the answer? There are, without a doubt, *conditions* to these blessed promises! The NT promises parallel the pattern of the promises, Covenants, and experiences which the saints of the OT underwent throughout history, and these saints with their promises and Covenants I have thoroughly addressed already, and will again remind the reader of their significance.

As for the New Testament, the promises of "Eternal Security" are clearly declared:

> "Being confident of this very thing, that **HE which hath begun** a good work in you **will perform** it until the day of Jesus Christ." (Philippians 1:6)

> "**Faithful** is **HE** that calleth you, Who also will do it." (1 Thessalonians 5:24)

> "**Who** shall also confirm you unto the end, that ye may be blameless in the day of our Lord Jesus Christ. God is **faithful**, by Whom ye were called unto the fellowship of His Son Jesus Christ our Lord." (1 Corinthians 1:8-9)

> "There hath no temptation taken you but such as is common to man: but God is **faithful**, **Who** will not suffer you to be tempted above that ye are able; but will with the temptation also make a way to escape, that ye may be able to bear it." (1 Corinthians 10:13)

These promises are given by God, performed by God, and are as sure as **the faithfulness of God**, *but what if you doubt that God is faithful?* What if you are unbelieving of these promises and so, you believe God is lying, or as 1 John 5:10 terms this sin, you are thus making "Him a liar" by your unbelief (1 Jn. 5:10)? Long ago, I read a systematic theology by a renowned "conservative" scholar, whose name I will forbear to mention. He concluded that these passages which clearly affirm "eternal security" are easy to be understood, clear, or simple. Conversely, the scholar argued that the opposing passages used by the Armenian camp which taught that you could lose your salvation were difficult to understand, complex, and unclear. He thought that "we" should never call into question those things which the scriptures teach that are clear, repetitive, and consistent, because of that which is difficult to understand, complex, and unclear. This sounded like good *logic* at the time. From this point onward, I unconsciously blinded myself to the warnings written within the NT which clearly taught that you could lose your salvation. I did not know I was doing this. When I read or studied one of the passages which warned of falling from grace, I would harden my heart against this teaching, believing it to be an impossibility. I was sure the scriptures promised eternal security, and therefore I assumed there could be *no conditions* to those promises. I thought that if the word of God said that you could lose your salvation, then the Bible contradicted itself. I had no conception of any reasonable or biblical alternative. With a desire to defend the infallibility of the word of God, I hardened my heart against the clear teachings of falling from grace, and these passages I then excused as complex. I was sincere! Truly, I did not see any refutation to the arguments I had against falling from grace. To further my confidence, when I did meditate and trust that I was eternally secure, divine manifestations of the Spirit of God for practical grace were deployed to my soul. Because of this, I thought all the more that eternal security was the complete truth. God did meet with me, ingratiate me, and fill me betimes because, I affirm again, eternal security IS a doctrine FOR the believing saints and *NONE can be saved by ANY OTHER MEANS but THIS foundation rock of the faithfulness of God.* A man is saved by believing that he is eternally secure under the faithfulness of God! Praise the Lord!

To further my assurance that eternal security was irrefutably sound, and the lone conclusion able to be drawn from the scripture, I saw some promises which were **bound with** and *inseparable from the sovereignty of God*, and I knew that the scriptures taught that God was sovereign. My experience, and more importantly, scripture, both affirmed this wonderful truth, and how I loved the sweet humility of a saint under the Sovereign Wing of God the Father. Look at the inseparable nature of the following promises which are much like the former ones:

> "My sheep hear My voice, and I know them, and they follow Me:
> And I give unto them eternal life; and **they shall never perish,
> neither shall any man pluck them out of My hand**. My Father,
> which gave them Me, is greater than all; and **no man is able to
> pluck them out of my Father's hand**. I and My Father are
> One." (John 10:27-30)

> "And Jesus said unto them, I am the bread of life: he that cometh
> to Me shall never hunger; and he that believeth on Me shall never
> thirst. But I said unto you, That ye also have seen Me, and
> believe not. **All that the Father giveth Me shall come to Me;
> and him that cometh to Me I will in no wise cast out.** For I
> came down from heaven, not to do Mine own will, but the will of
> Him that sent Me. And this is the Father's will which hath sent
> Me, that **of all which He hath <u>given</u> Me I should <u>lose</u> nothing**,
> but should raise it up again at the last day. And this is the will of
> Him that sent Me, that every one which seeth the Son, and
> believeth on Him, may have everlasting life: and I will raise him
> up at the last day." (John 6:35-40)

You see, I knew that initial salvation (justification by faith & regeneration) was begun by God (Php. 1:6), and if it was begun by Him, how could anyone stop Him from finishing His desire, or as John 6 and 10 affirm, how could anyone "pluck them out of" God's hand? How could God lose something that He states is dependent upon His own sovereign gifts? How can God say, "all which" the Father "hath given" Christ, concerning all of them, that it is the determination of God that He "should lose nothing"? It is clear logic – "they shall never perish," as much as God shall never be defeated in greatness, for He "is greater than all!" These are precious promises! They are meant to be preached in this very way! It is an exaltation of the sovereignty of God, the faithfulness of God, the eternal fulfillment of all His eternal counsels, covenants, and promises!

However, to say that it is impossible for any to fall away or be lost is a misappropriation, a complete oblivion that the promises hinge upon *conditions*. Thus, there is also oblivion to the condescension of God in the ways of man, and the biblical, historical pattern of the sovereignty of God's counsels, promises, and eternal purposes which were established through the many breaches, changes, and fallings of saints in time past.

For example, a Calvinist would state the "*nevers*" with absolute confidence that, because the scripture says *never*, then all conditions are impossible and nonexistent. BUT: is this the sole possibility with all the ways of God in view? Has God ever said "*never*" before in a promise, and that promise was justifiably *breached*, or fallen short of, though all similar characteristics of God's faithfulness, sovereignty, and greatness appear to make impossible its failure?

In the NT, for example, Jesus said in John 6:35-40, "of all which He hath given Me I should lose nothing," for these are they which GOD has GIVEN. Then how is it said of Judas in John 17:11-12, in Jesus' prayer to the Father: "those that THOU GAVEST Me [Jesus] I have kept, and none of them is lost, **but** the son of perdition; that the scripture might be fulfilled"? Judas and the rest were given, and yet he wasn't kept, so he was lost. This is the clear terminology and phraseology used in John 6, repeated in John 17. An additional NOTE: Judas was elsewhere affirmed by Christ to be His friend (Ps. 41:9, John 13:18, Matt. 26:50), which is a term for saved individuals (Jas. 2:23), and in the citation of Christ wherein Jesus references the prophecy of His betrayal, there Judas is said to be one "whom I trusted" (Ps. 41:9), speaking of Christ's trust in Judas, and this term of trustworthiness, again, is only an attribute of saved individuals (1 Cor. 4:2, 7:25, Matt. 25:21, Lk. 12:42). In regards to the former point made about Judas, carefully read John 6:35-40 & John 17:11-12 and see for yourself:

> "And Jesus said unto them, I am the bread of life: he that cometh to Me shall never hunger; and he that believeth on Me shall never thirst. But I said unto you, That ye also have seen Me, and believe not. **All that the Father giveth Me shall come to Me; and him that cometh to Me I will in no wise cast out.** For I came down from heaven, not to do Mine own will, but the will of him that sent Me. And this is the Father's will which hath sent Me, that **of all which He hath <u>given</u> Me I should <u>lose</u> nothing**, but should raise it up again at the last day. And this is the will of him that sent Me, that every one which seeth the Son, and believeth on him, may have everlasting life: and I will raise him

up at the last day." (John 6:35-40)

"And now I am no more in the world, but these are in the world, and I come to Thee. Holy Father, keep through Thine own name those whom Thou hast given Me, that they may be one, as We are. While I was with them in the world, I kept them in Thy name: those that Thou gavest Me I have kept, and **none of them is lost**, but the son of perdition; that the scripture might be fulfilled." (John 17:11-12)

Like as this clear instance, however hard it may be for you to swallow, I plead with you to remember all that we have covered thus far. Of all that we have covered, let's look at the sum. If we use the reasoning of popular Calvinists, we do therefore, and we must, negate the priestly covenant of Eli, the kingly covenant of Saul, the Abrahamic Covenant to the exodus generation, the Davidic Covenant to David, the Mosaic promise to Joshua, the prophetic covenant to Jeremiah, and the difficulty in attaining promises before a Holy God as seen in the lives of Jacob and Josiah, to name a few. The words "perpetual," "everlasting," and "for ever" were spoken to Eli (Exodus 29:9, 40:15, 1 Sam. 2:35). The word "for ever" was spoken to Saul (1 Sam. 15:35). The Abrahamic Covenant is called an "immutable counsel" (Heb. 6:17-18), which is fixed, until the *literal and physical exodus generation* is saved, safe-dwelling, and land-inhabiting. The Davidic Covenant was of unfailing faithfulness (Psalm 89:33), unbreakable words (Psalm 89:34), and immutable changelessness (Psalm 89:35), with the word "for ever" promised to the throne of David in Solomon's *literal physical lineage* (2 Sam. 7:12-16, 1 Chron. 17:10-14). God said to Joshua that He would never leave him or fail him (Joshua 1:5), as the promises of Matt. 28:20 and Heb. 13:5 are for us in the NT, yet in Joshua 7:12, God threatens to leave Joshua. Does it mean anything to you that God said to the generation after Joshua, "I said I will *never* break My Covenant with you" (Judges 2:1), but they rebelled and God invoked the condition to the promises of *forever* and *never*, saying, "Wherefore I also said, I will not drive them out from before you" (Judges 2:3), and this led to their eventual corruption unto damnation. Remember again how the greatness of God is committed to Jeremiah, as God said, "I am with thee to deliver thee" (Jer. 1:8). Who is greater than God? He is as a "Defenced city," an "Iron pillar," a "Brasen wall" for Jeremiah, against all that fight against him. The devil and a world of iniquity, all of these fight against Christians, and to us it is said like as Jeremiah, "they shall fight against thee; but they shall not prevail against thee; for I am with thee, saith the LORD, to deliver thee" (Jer. 1:17-19). Nevertheless, God pronounces the prophetic woe to Jeremiah, in Jeremiah 15:14, that the Babylonians (God's destroying wrath) will prevail against him.

As for the Abrahamic Covenant, the prophets complained, "Doth *His promise* fail for evermore" (Psalm 77:8)? As for the Davidic Covenant, the prophets were baffled and questioning God – why had He "*made void* the Covenant" (Psalm 89:39) which He swore to perform (Psalm 89:49), which He said He would not "lie" about nor "fail" to perform because of His "faithfulness" (Psalm 89:33, 35)? Yet how can it be? Likewise, Jeremiah's complaint echoed with the same words when he questioned God, "Wilt Thou be altogether unto me *as a liar*, and as waters that *fail*" (Jer. 15:18)? This is as the question in Psalm 89:49: "Lord, where are Thy former lovingkindness, *which Thou swarest* unto David in Thy truth?"

My readers, all promises and counsels which are "immutable," eternal, and forever, which have failed, been breached, or changed, were indeed changed, nevertheless, they will be mysteriously fulfilled in Christ or otherwise forgotten under the mystery of God's higher righteousness and impossible law-breaking powers. The "*forevers*" will be fulfilled even as God said to Jesus, "The LORD hath sword, and will not repent, Thou art a priest **for ever** after the order of Melchizedek" (Psalm 110:4). As God stated of the priesthood of Christ, *so are all the prophetic attributes of Christ*, but not all were stated in such a manner as Psalm 110:4. Rather, they were mysteriously **hidden** in *unfulfilled promises in previous Covenants*, covenants given to other individuals who *fell* short of those promises in their day, so that *through their failure and fall Christ may arise*. Yet, will you understand that their failure and fall was a genuine failure of promise and fall from salvation?

"Through their fall salvation is come." (Rom. 11:11)

Jesus Christ is the mystery of prophecy, promise, salvation, and Covenant. The purpose of God for Christ to descend into incarnation, ascend back up, and then come again – this purpose was eternal – and in Jesus Christ, all things draw their significance. Nevertheless, besides this eternal purpose there were temporary purposes in God by way of condescension. God was intent on other salvations, promises, and Covenants (willful of them in the counsel "**God in the ways of man**"), but because of the sins of the persons to whom these salvific promises were given, they never came to pass. It was therefore – "**through their fall**" – that God changed His mind from the performance of the promises given to them, thus in another plan arising in a later time, but bounding thereto from eternity past, lo, "salvation is come" to us in Christ (Rom. 11:11)! They all fell from the good will of God in their lives (God in the ways of man), but it was for a mysterious, predestinated, and eternal purpose of Jesus Christ to become manifest in the sovereign will of God (God in the ways of God). Men fell from the will of **God in the ways of man** because of the determination of the will of **God in the ways of God.**

Through the fall of the Exodus generation, the Abrahamic Covenant is pending until the work of Christ consummates and entirely fulfills it. *Through the fall* of Solomon, the Davidic Covenant is pending till the work of Christ consummates and entirely fulfills it. *Through the fall* of the literal, physical Judaistic nation and people of God in the first century (at the first coming of Christ), the consummated promises of God for the full salvation of literal, physical Israel are pending until the work of Christ consummates and entirely fulfills it; temporarily *through this fall*, the predestinated purpose to reconcile the whole (Gentile) world to Himself is manifest till the fulfillment of the Abrahamic and Davidic Covenants are accomplished, wherein, conclusively, all of physical Israel will be saved, but this is at the end of time after the fullness of the Gentiles comes in. This is the binding and loosing, the blinding and choosing of God!

You see, the salvation of physical Israel is an eternal, predestinated, immutable, unchanging counsel (of God in the ways of God); nevertheless, how it will be finally attained and what hindered it throughout time must be considered by those who are saved today, because we are saved by fulfilling mysterious extensions of the same Covenants and promises which they fell short of. What hindered the promised salvation from coming in a consummation? It was the people, when and how they did fall, and it was in the times after their fall that God did repent with repentances that changed former details of the previous Covenant, and when all circumstances, salvations, and condemnations were and are completed throughout time, the Covenant will be completed by the unrepentant, immutable purpose of God – unchanging from and unto eternity. It is the unrepentant purpose of God that governs all the repentances. As for Israel, they are elect through an unrepentant election (Rom. 11:28), "For the gifts and calling of God" toward them "all" (Rom. 11:26) "are without repentance" (Rom. 11:29), though throughout time the literal, physical, and spiritual Israelites, both individuals and generations, were damned through God's repentances, until the persons of His unrepentant love are all saved and the generation of His unrepentant calling doth arise in the end of time. Yet, in the past and now, every breach and pending work done until the salvation of all of Israel is completed, all of this is a part of the sovereign purposes of God, and shockingly, God has now "concluded" both Gentiles and Jews "in unbelief that He might have mercy upon all" (Rom. 11:32)! That is to say, He has concluded them both to fall because sovereignty did cast them away, but it was that He might have mercy upon all (the remnant elect) when He does save them throughout time and in the end. Of this sovereign and mysterious wonder, the Spirit exclaims, "O the depth of the riches both of the wisdom and knowledge of God! How unsearchable are His judgments, and His ways past finding out! For who hath known the mind of the Lord? Or who hath been His counsellor? Or who hath first given to Him, and it shall be recompensed unto him again? For of Him, and through Him, and to Him, are all things: to Whom be glory for ever. Amen" (Rom. 11:33-36). Let the reader that hath ears to hear, say, Amen! "The Lord be magnified" (Ps. 40:16)!

Now listen: many do claim that since the NT Christ arose in the place of these fallen men, the Covenant given to Him is without repentances and therefore un-breach-able; it is eternal in nature and originating from His perfection in the unavoidable performance of all the tenets of the NT. This sounds very viable, but one who asserts this is discounting the entire reason God does change His mind, repents of promises, and allows men to fall away from salvation after they have been saved. God's repentances are caused by the corrupt sinfulness of men which provokes God - Who relates to men in condescension (God in the ways of man). For repentances to cease, the sinfulness of man must cease. If the sinfulness of man ceased, then there would be no more condescension to men, and men would no more be humans which

540

dwell in a body of death. Some may argue that the sinfulness of man has been dealt with by NT regeneration, and so the liability which comes from the uprising sinfulness of saved men is no longer there – but this cannot be true. If the sinfulness of saved men ceased to be a problem in the NT, then there would be no possibility for a saint to ever provoke God like as those men and women of the OT did provoke Him – leading them into the eventual breach of their promises and salvation – but the NT affirms this as a possibility by using these very instances of these men and women in OT as examples of viable realities in the NT experience (see 1 Cor. 10, Heb. 3-4, etc.). The problem of original sin is **partially** subdued in a **partial** deliverance of God (in an **incomplete** state), yet God's people remain in a body of death, and wait, until the final consummation of the gospel is completed at the END. Therefore, since we are partial participants in the gospel gifts, we are still under the possibility of falling away into sinful, wrath-provoking behavior before a Holy God. Yet, in the END, when sin is removed in full, then shall the saints be bound in the eternality of Christ's purchased Covenant - then all the "forevers" will be fulfilled in those who persevered to the END.

- Adopted now (Rom. 8:15) – Consummating Adoption to come (Rom. 8:23)
- Redeemed now (1 Cor. 1:30) – Consummating Redemption to come (Php. 3:14, Rom. 8:23).
- Regeneration now (Titus 3:5) – Consummating Regeneration to come(Rom. 8:18-21, Php. 3:12-14)
- Kingdom within you now (Lk. 17:21, Col. 1:13, Eph. 2:6)–Consummating Kingdom to come (2 Tim. 4:1, Rev. 3:21)
- On Mount Zion now (Heb. 12:22)–Consummating ascent upon Mount Zion to come (Rev. 14:1-5)
- Resurrection now (Rom. 6:4) – Consummating Resurrection to come (1 Cor. 15:50)
- Eternal Life now (1 John 3:15, 5:12-13) – Consummating Eternal Life to come (2 Cor. 5:1-4, 1 Tim. 6:12)
- Overcoming power now (Eph. 2:5, 1 John 5:4) – Consummating Overcoming power to come (1 Cor. 15:54-57)
- Defeat of Death now(Rom. 8:2, 6, Eph. 2:5)–Consummating Defeat of Death to come (1 Cor. 15:54-57)
- In the Light now(Eph. 5:8)– Consummating, Eternal Day of Light to come(Prov. 4:18, 2 Peter 1:19, Rev. 21:23-25)
- Seeing God now(2 Cor. 3:17-18, 1 Cor. 13:12, Heb. 11:27)–Consummating revelatory sight to come (1 John 3:2)
- Perfect Now (Heb. 10:14) – Consummating Perfection to come (Php. 3:12, 1 Cor. 13:10, Prov. 4:18)
- "As He is" now (1 John 4:17) – Consummating conformity, "as He is" in glory, to come (1 John 3:2, Rev. 2:27)
- Knowing Him now (1 John 2:4, John 17:3) – Consummating knowing, "even as also I am known" to come (1 Cor. 13:12)
- Elect now (2 Jn. 1:1, 13, 1 Pet. 1:2) – Consummating Election to come (2 Peter 1:10)
- Called now (1 Cor. 1:26) – Consummating Calling to come (Php. 3:14)
- Chosen now (1 Peter 2:9) – Consummating Choice to come (Matt. 22:14, Rev. 17:14)

Do you remember all the ways in which the NT does describe our salvation to be only partially completed? Therefore, as long as we await the fulfillment of our gospel-Covenant in Christ, then, on this matter, we are as our brethren in the Church of the OT. We, like them, do await the fulfillment of our promises. Above is a doctrinal overview of what exactly is spoken of to be partial and incomplete in our Covenant, and what will be consummated at the fulfillment of our promises in Christ. We still await our consummating salvation from the problem of sin, which is, the full and complete fulfillment of our promises in Christ, and at that fullness, then there is an initiation of all the forevers and nevers of the Covenants of God, for then, God saith of Himself: → "repentance shall be hid from Mine eyes".

"I will ransom them from the power of the grave; I will redeem them from death: O death, I will be thy plagues; O grave, I will be thy destruction: **repentance shall be hid from Mine eyes**."
(Hosea 13:14)

"Thy people also **shall be all righteous**…" – Isaiah 60:21

In the end, "repentance shall be hid from [His] eyes", but that does not negate all those generations and persons who perished because God did repent of His purpose to save them in their salvific promises because of their SIN. Repentance will cease when the problem of sin does cease. Of what nature is the **END**? It is the resurrection, the condescension withdrawn, inaugurating the full reign of the Messianic King Jesus, Who will fully recreate the laws of all creation and remove the curses of sin, and fully reconcile, resurrect, redeem, and save His partially recreated Christians, and for this they did faithfully wait. But Oh! How the devil and false prophets do craft doctrinal nets of persuasion - of false confidences in error! Error I say! Some men suppose that they are the "elect" persons, possessors of inalienable rights - that God must save them no matter what they do or believe at present. Such men are high-minded (Rom. 11:20), *higher* than His high ways, they suppose; therefore they do continuously think that they know *the way He will take* to fulfill His own promises, fancying themselves to be an object of God's final choice. In this way, men and women have been beguiled by heresy through the misappropriation of the promises of God, emboldened to disobedient behavior, and oblivious to the severity of God's wrathful repentances. He can repent over you as a physical or spiritual Israelite, then replace you, and His word will be accounted of to be true, though it seemed impossible to you – "How unsearchable are His judgments, and His ways past finding out!" These proud men suppose that there are no other ways His promise can be fulfilled but by the salvation of their own souls – but God, not winking at the continuous rebellion of saved men, did, through the centuries, make the performance of the promises of salvation a mystery, an unsearchable wonder that can't be found out. Do you suppose that you are bound to His salvation because of an immutable word of His righteousness? God can repent of His choice of you and choose a stone to replace you, yea, and this stone could become you! I repeat, it can be you, and then God will still be as He always will be, as He will finally reckoned by all to be – perfectly true: "For I say unto you, that God is able of these stones to raise up children unto Abraham" (Luke 3:8). God failed you? No, God reprobated you. He cast you away, and then He replaced you, and then that stone became you. He would more quickly redeem a lying, Canaanite, already-condemned harlot whose heart is full of faithful obedience than you, you proud Christian Pharisee, supposing that you are preferred because you are God's chosen people, and thus, you embolden yourself in fearless rebellion. You may fancy yourself that you are the elect, but God hath forewarned – "make your calling and election sure" (2 Pet. 1:10).

Do you see what I am saying? Some argue, "All the former covenants and promises could be breached, but not Christ's." This is true when the Covenant, gospel, and call is consummated, and *until then*, the problem of sin before a Holy God can still provoke the Lord to repentance. As in all the former Covenants wherein a breach was possible, our Covenant is **partial**, **incomplete**, and **unfulfilled**. We have been partakers of Christ's death; however, the consummating victory over death will not be actualized until after the fullness of the gospel of His Kingdom is consummated. We have been *resurrected* (Rom. 6:4), *regenerated* (Tit. 3:5), we have overcome *death* (Eph. 2:5), *inherited* the Kingdom (Lk. 17:21), but we await a final consummating *resurrection* (1 Cor. 15:42-50), *regeneration* (Rom. 8:18-21, Php. 3:12-14), defeat of *death* (1 Cor. 15:54-57), and an *inheritance* of the Kingdom of God (1 Cor. 15:50). In this manner we await a "salvation to be revealed" (1 Pet. 1:5), which is not yet revealed in full, and we strive for the calling of this final freedom (Php. 3:14) – therefore we have a necessity to obey this charge – "make your calling and election sure!" His Kingdom and rule, those things purchased by His priestly atonement, have not been completely fulfilled, and with the fulfillment of this work, there will be the final fulfillment of the Abrahamic and Davidic Covenants, with all other remaining promises, covenants, prophecies, or mysteries that revealed Christ and His work. Christ's work in the New Covenant has not been completely fulfilled, nor have all the other promises and Covenants been fulfilled in Him yet. Why can the Covenants fail for individuals, or be changed for peoples and generations? SIN! Why is it possible for God to repent of a good will, of love, or of salvific purposes? SIN! Why must it ever continue to be? SIN! Why will the promises no longer change after Christ's Messianic consummation? There will be no more SIN! Why would God never repent again? SIN is what makes God change His mind, and with its final eradication, there will be no potential for wrath or destruction. How did He change throughout these generations and times, when we know that God cannot change? **The Condescension of God!** Why will He no longer change at the consummation? **The condescension is removed and "the ways of man" become a nonexistent relational capacity used by God henceforth!**

Your Ascent or God's Descent – *The Condescension Withdrawn*

> ### *Condescension Withdrawn* → Final Resurrection → Sinless Perfection → An Eradication of Human Ways and Capacities Active in All Humans → Therefore A Final Removal of God in the Ways of Man → *Condescension Withdrawn*

The eternal purpose of God is that, through the fall of man, through the open display of the insufficiency of men, upon the devastating consequences of their

543

fall, the depth of their disobedience is bitterly made evident, and a platform and stage is formed for Christ to appear and fulfill, save, and become the mystery by which the Word of God and Covenants of Salvation are forever, eternally, and finally fulfilled.

> "But unto you that fear My Name shall **the Sun of Righteousness** arise with healing in His wings…" – Malachi 4:2

Behold Christ's sufficiency! For now it hath broken the bitter night by the break of dawn so that the *early morning* is upon us, and lo, He ariseth as the sun riseth up – strength to strength – "as the shining Light, that shineth more and more unto the Perfect Day" (Prov. 4:18), but tarry a while now and understand, the Perfect Day is not yet upon us, for then the noon day strength of the Son of God's Kingdom would have chased away all darkness and night. Verily, there are yet enemies of Jesus Christ and His seed lurking as shadows and following men about, who must soon be frightfully subdued. He reigns now, therefore the early morning is upon us, but "He must reign, till He hath put all enemies under His feet" (1 Cor. 15:25). Let us therefore rejoice in the morning and eagerly watch after the Son of God's rising; I say, let us patiently wait for His Highness to reach His heights, and then, let us rejoice in the light of the Perfect Day. "When that which is perfect is come", namely, "the Perfect Day" (Prov. 4:18), "then that which is in part shall be done away" (1 Cor. 13:10). God has promised a worldwide rule to the Davidic King Jesus, as He said in Psalm 37:6, "And He shall bring forth Thy righteousness as the Light, and Thy judgment as the noonday" (Ps. 37:6). Christ's sufficiency is brilliantly made manifest after the bitter fall of men is deeply understood, that from the bitter darkness the triumph of Christ is appreciated in the sweet brilliance of the unfailing, faithfulness of God in Christ, Who could not and will not fall or fail. Yet for this blissful eternity to be inaugurated with a power of changeless glory, Christ must fill all, be in all, and take paramount supremacy over all, ridding His Kingdom of man-like iniquity and the whole body of death - thus at the resurrection men shall be as the angels (Mark 12:25).

> "Do ye not therefore err, because ye know not the scriptures,
> neither the power of God? For when they shall rise from the
> dead, they neither marry, nor are given in marriage; but are as the
> angels which are in heaven." (Mark. 12:24-25)

At this point when flesh is removed, the glory of Christ fills all, and the mark of the prize is won, for there is a complete conformity of man to Christ. This is the condescension underlined! It is His resurrection, and in it men will have their ascension, then His immutable ways and promises will be our comprehension – "then shall I know even as I am known" (1 Cor. 13:12). Brethren, this is why we were "apprehended" (Php. 3:12)! Now we are in the dispensation of **partial salvation** because we are in the relational capacities of the condescension. "Now I know in **part**" (1 Cor. 13:12), the scripture plainly declares, and as it were, the morning light has just begun the glorious illumination of the world. It is still yet only partly day; for its perfection let us wait for His rising to power and preeminence. When the

544

condescension is removed, then "that which is in **part** shall be done away with" (1 Cor. 13:10), my calling (Php. 3:14) will be complete (Php. 3:12), and "that which is perfect is come" (1 Cor. 13:10). This perfect is salvation, complete, consummated, and come, and those who are "perfect" *now* (Php. 3:15) in this NT dispensation before the resurrection, which is an attainable *perfection* for the now, do strive for an unattainable "perfection" (Php. 3:12) that will be accomplished at the resurrection, which is sinless perfection – the purpose and end of our gospel call. When the perfect is come, Christ has come, and when He is here, there will be no more falling, failure, mutability, repentances, nor any condescension. The men are removed from their limitations and glorified into the eternality of Christ's life, coexisting in His glorified spiritual sensations – "then shall I know even as also I am known" (1 Cor. 13:12).

How does God know a man? We do not know! God's knowledge is without boundary and limit, the depths of His searching out are infinite; how can a man know how much, or to what magnitude, God knows a man?! We know this much, "The spirit of man is the candle of the LORD, searching all the inward parts of the belly" (Prov. 20:27). Metaphors can only partially reveal God's majesties, for we cannot understand the unexplainable except by those things of our physical world which do hold a partial similitude. God knows a man like as a man knows his own home, and in such, the man searches every corner as with the light of a candle until no part is left unknown. So God knows a man, and infinitely more so and beyond! But can it be said then, as God knows a man, even so, men will know God?! That "then shall I know even as also I am known" (1 Cor. 13:12)!? This is a glorification! Think of it! No candle could search out the unsearchable Mansion that God is!

No amount of men in cooperation for any great length of time, no collective powers of human thought and mind, could search out the inner Person of God if He were a Castle-like Mansion of luxurious rooms. The search would be endless for an infinite number of candle-bearing men who searched relentlessly, if they sought to know and discover the treasures of Who God is – if they could, as it were, go into God as God goes into man to search him out, and finally, to leave nothing uncovered and unknown! Psalms of holy wonder were penned by astonished prophets as they considered how infinitely deep, how immeasurably surmountingly God does know a man, but how then should we react to man knowing God as God knows a man!?

> "Thou knowest my downsitting and mine uprising, Thou
> understandest my thought afar off. Thou compassest my path and
> my lying down, and art acquainted with all my ways. For there is
> not a word in my tongue, but, lo, O LORD, Thou knowest it
> altogether. Thou hast beset me behind and before, and laid Thine
> hand upon me. Such knowledge is too wonderful for me; it is
> high, I cannot attain unto it. Whither shall I go from Thy Spirit?
> or whither shall I flee from Thy Presence? How precious also are
> Thy thoughts unto me, O God! how great is the sum of them! If I
> should count them, they are more in number than the sand: when

I awake, I am still with thee." (Psalm 139:2-7, 17-18)

God KNOWS YOU! He knows you with innumerable thoughts like as and beyond the very sands of the sea, but to be swallowed up with another glory comparable to this story, only that in it, then, you KNOW GOD! I cannot suggest all the boundaries of what this experience may be, or, if we will or will not have an omniscience of God like as He has an omniscience of us. A fool would conclude this matter with certainty, but I believe that the scriptures teach us to conclude it with a holy uncertainty coupled with worship and awe. Even though we do not know "what we shall be", nevertheless we do know a little of something – "we shall be like Him" (1 John 3:2).

We will NOT *know God* through the capacities available in a human's comprehension, or any man-like limitations, therefore there will be no hindrance from a FULL revelation of God to man instead of the limited revelations done on the earth below. The feeble weakness and sinfulness of our human frame will be gone and we will be able to SEE GOD – when otherwise we would be consumed by the Face of God – all these limitations were the capacities limited in the ways of men. We will know God even as we are fully known by God! God does not know men after the comprehension of human beings; God knows men through the spiritual senses in an other-worldly comprehension, so that there is nothing in us that can be hidden from Him. By parabolic expression, it is to say: "The spirit of man is the candle of the LORD, searching all the inward parts of the belly" (Prov. 20:27). God knows our thoughts, heart, intentions, and ways. "Man's goings are of the LORD," and He knows our deeds (Prov. 20:24). On earth, we know God in **part**.

Partly, the scripture says, as a visual reflection through a piece of glass, instead of face-to-face communion. This reflection is dim, dark, and unclear. *Partly*, as the firstfruits are but a part of the harvest, a small incomparable part to the reaping of the whole harvest, as a drop of pleasure is to an ocean of heavenly bliss stretching with an immeasurable border. These things speak of our limited and hindered communion with God because of our sinful, fallen, and fleshly stature. Yet, what we know of now is *a part* of what is to come, a taste – though it is dark in comparison like a dim reflection. There is an unsearchable wisdom, unknowable ways, and "ocean-deep", mind-shattering attributes of God to be revealed when the condescension is removed. "Eye hath not seen, nor ear heard, neither have entered into the heart of man" the things of ascended, glorified unity and intimacy with the Triune King. It will be an intimacy, Jesus says, "as I received of My Father" (Rev. 2:27). It will be an unknowable revelation, the dark glass will be shattered, and we will look full and straight-eyed into the face of God, even He that has an unknowable name! We will see Him! "Beloved, now are we the sons of God, and it doth not yet appear *what we shall be*: but we know that, when He shall appear, **we shall be like Him; for we shall see Him as He is**" (1 John 3:2). Now we see Him, but not as He is, only through the condescension of a reflected, dark, dim glass. So powerful is this Person that His reflected image saved the un-savable sinners of earth! Sinners are saved, conformed to His image, having become image bearers themselves of this Image of Christ – and the burning flash and seething brand was but a reflection of God. At them – these image-bearing sinners – the world does wonder or rage, and it is shaken because familial posterity is fractured, and its bonds torn asunder. These sinners who caught a ray of the reflection of God do now reflect Him to others, though God does dwell behind the veil of their flesh. Men do therefore respond to Christians in love and praise to God or hatred and violent rage. None can see Him and not be saved. Those who continue to see Him do walk in His way. None can see God, Who is love, and not love. It is a killing (Gal. 2:20), saving (Eph. 2:8), and constraining (2 Cor. 5) love. These are the spiritual rays of the Image of Jesus Christ which have reflected off of a dark, diminished, unclear glass - salvation in the condescension.

As our salvation is partial now, so we have a partial salvation from sin; yet if our vision of His image was no longer in part and we saw face to face this Person of God, then our salvation from sin would not be partial, and our fleshly body of death, which contained the remnant of devilish enmity, would be burned up at His presence. Therefore, the condescension of God through a reflective glass is the spiritual revelation of the Person of God our fleshly faculties can endure and still live with. What is to come cannot be endured by flesh; it is an unveiling of the Face of God without limitations and condescension. "No man hath seen God at any time; the only begotten Son, which is in the bosom of the Father, He hath declared Him," but the Son will take us to be where He was before His incarnation. Where? To behold the glory He had with the Father, and this glory will be in and upon us (in some sense) because He is one and with us, therefore we will be as "a white stone," and "in the stone a new name written which no man knoweth save He that receiveth it" (Rev. 2:17). Jesus said, "I will write upon him the name of My God," "and I will write upon him My New Name" (Rev. 3:12). It is not that we become God, or become parallel to God, but are completely dominated by God, in perfect union with God, so that in and through God are all things for God, and we, forever, do unworthily participate and experience, through the charity of God's undying energy, the ceaseless praise and worship of God! "We shall be like Him; for we shall see Him as He is" (1 John 3:2). No man "knoweth" what will be known with this white stone, or the name that God will give - this is the name that Jesus says is "My New Name." There is an unknowable knowing which will be known, which will be hereafter revealed, infinitely beyond that which we know now.

> "All things are delivered unto Me of my Father: and no
> man knoweth the Son, but the Father; neither knoweth
> any man the Father, save the Son, and *he* to
> whomsoever the Son will reveal *him.*" (Matt. 11:27)

This is the climax, the consummation, the final and perfect resurrection! This is heaven, perfect unity with the Godhead, basking in His eternal Life. "And this is life eternal, that they might know Thee the only true God, and Jesus Christ, Whom

Thou hast sent" (John 17:3). All things are "that I may know Him" (Php. 3:10). But in contrast to *now*, in what we experience *here* in this body of death, still yet hindered from His glory, there is yet a knowing Him that unspeakably exceeds what we know now. "Then shall I know even as also I am known" (1 Cor. 13:12). This glory to come is the reward of Christ's sufferings and the fulfillment of His priestly prayer:

> "And the glory which Thou gavest Me I have given them; that
> they may be one, even as We are One: I in them, and Thou in Me,
> that they may be perfect in one; and that the world may know that
> Thou hast sent Me, and hast loved them, as Thou hast loved Me.
> Father, I will that they also, whom Thou hast given Me, be with
> Me where I am; that they may behold My glory, which Thou hast
> given Me: for Thou lovedst Me before the foundation of the
> world. O righteous Father, the world hath not known Thee: but I
> have known Thee, and these have known that Thou hast sent Me.
> And I have declared unto them Thy name, and will declare it: that
> the love wherewith Thou hast loved Me may be in them, and I in
> them" (John 17:22-26)!

God shall transform this vile body into a glorious body, into a frame which can bear the deadly explosions of ecstasy which emanate from His unlimited Person. God shall take you up, as it were, into the bosom of the Father where ne'er a man hath been! That which has been declared shall be unveiled! Faith shall pass away, with prophecy, into endless and blinding, brilliantly shining, Face-to-face mesmerizing experiences of all-consuming charity. This is that which, in God, "abideth for ever" (1 John 2:17), and "God is love" – thence you are no longer a mere man but are as angels, for "no **man** hath seen God at any time." "God is love" (1 John 4:16), and when He comes, "prophecies shall fail," "tongues shall cease," and "whether there be knowledge, it shall vanish away". The knowing of this God will be in an unknowable way, the dark glass of human limitations and sensations will be shattered by a personal, resurrected revelation of God's face, unto endless expressions of Charity which can never pass away. "For now we see through a glass, darkly; but then **face to face**: now I know in *part*; but then shall I know **even as I am known**" (1 Cor. 13:12).

Consider the wonder of the dark glass! I, as a regenerate man, have experienced measures of joy. The Kingdom of God is righteousness, peace, and joy, and it has come into my heart. I have tasted the firstfruits of the Kingdom of God, and therefore have a partial understanding of what joy is like, experientially, like as it is in heaven, because I taste heaven's fruit of joy on earth in Christ's heavenly Person Who dwells within me. Yet, there is a full harvest to come which is incomparable to the first fruits now. There is a glorious liberty and full revelation, a removal of the condescension and shattering of the partial. I worship God "in Spirit and in truth" because I have beheld a reflection of the face of God ricocheted off of a dark glass. Now, "where the Spirit of the Lord is there is liberty," but there is another glorious liberty to come (Rom. 8:21). "We all with open face beholding in a **glass** the glory of the Lord, are changed into the same image from glory to glory, even as by the Spirit of the Lord," but there is another glory to come (1 Cor. 15:35-57). That which I see now which is so bright that it enlivens such a pile of dust as me, changing me into His image and causing the world to rage and wonder – this brightness is darkness comparatively to what is to come.

****

A beaming ray from His eternal, shining FACE (2 Cor. 3:18),
Ricocheted from a dark glass and gave me saving GRACE (Titus 3:4),
That in this place which I do live, I might shew forth His marvelous praise (1 Peter 2:9).

My pile of dust was enlivened by a light-empowered, wind-like gust,
From the ricocheted ray of Light there was a mighty and saving thrust.
To spread a gospel of a twice-born seed and race,
Which were born from another created law and place.

*A ricocheted ray of Light struck a pile of dust, and at it does the world wonder, but what will the world think when this Light shines without a ricochet, without a reflection or a darkening change of direction, diminishing the power, efficacy, and clarity times seven? Then this Light straightway rises upon the saints through a transfiguring resurrection, elevating the world and all creation into a corporate participation of our recreation, because **God is descending without condescension**!*

The ecstasy of prophecy, visions of glory, and praises of doxology – these are the "glory to glory" experiences of the New Testament story, yet all these are childish things compared to the glory of the coming King. Prophecies shall fail, tongues shall cease, and knowledge vanisheth away when God, like the sun, ariseth in revelatory strength like as the noonday. All these former things were in part, yea, the vision they revealed was comparatively stark, and they are immature expressions like a child's foolish art. Childish things will be put away when our comprehension of God is an impossible apprehension. These mediums of glory will be a thing of the past, they will shatter like glass as the blink of an eye is fast, they will be expressions of God like dark shadows at last, and when they were the means of grace, they were likened to the unclear pigment of bronze-like reflective glass. God's curtain, the heavens, will unveil God very soon, and the angels will announce it with a trumpet-like boom. The eternal beauty of godly sincerity existing within the Persons of the Trinity, as they, for Each Other, have perfect and unending, mutual charity, then, coexisting within the Trinity the saints will have unimagined unity with God as co-participants of their everlasting charity, thus at the descent of God, the New Jerusalem will have its rose-like bloom, petals of unfading glory filling the world with its heavenly perfume.
****

"For we know **in part**, and we prophesy **in part**. But when that which is **perfect** is come, then that which is **in part** shall be done away. When **I was** a child, **I spake** as a child, **I understood** as a child, **I thought** as a child: but when I became a man, I put away **childish things**. For now we see through a **glass**, **darkly**; but then face to face: now **I know in part**; but then shall **I know** even **as also I am known**. And now abideth faith, hope, charity, these three; but the greatest of these is charity." (1 Corinthians 13:9-13)

I speak, understand, and think what I am, as a child comparatively to what we shall be in the end, for then we shall be "as He is" (1 John 3:2). To be "as He is" changes our relationship with Him as much as it changes what we are, therefore we, with Him, shall know an unknowable experience and nearness in speaking, understanding, and thinking. Everything I know, am, speak, think, and understand, are all childish things compared to the maturity of these experiences, intelligent understandings, clear speaking, and unimaginable thinkings which are to come in what we shall be. To us now, in this way, "it doth not yet appear what we shall be" (1 John 3:2).

What has been revealed now is "unknowably" infantile compared to what is to come, and this childlike expression of grace is but a ricochet from His shining face, sending the world into hatred or praise! This is the power of God! While it is a reflection, a glass-like vision dark in expression, I do remain a creation of grace which is underneath the resurrected, consummated prize, and all of my present understanding of grace and righteousness according to the Spirit of Christ's resurrection is like a child's explanation of what he saw at the zoo, his coloring and drawing of what he imagines in his mind, and, lo, I am bound to think like a child, but when Christ returns I will become a man of grace! In this, prophecies and knowledge will pass away, charity and perfect conformity will arrive, and I will be swallowed up in God's unknowable ways. This is "the glory which shall be revealed in us" (Rom. 8:18)! We shall be "glorified together" with Christ in throne-like majesty and crown-casting wonder. We will be "joint-heirs with Christ" (Rom. 8:17)! We are "the firstfruits of the Spirit," a bounty infantile compared to the collection to come, and "we ourselves groan within ourselves, waiting for the adoption, to wit, the redemption of our body" (Rom. 8:23). Also, "the creature itself also shall be delivered from bondage into the glorious liberty of the children of God" (Rom. 8:21). "When He shall come to be glorified in His saints, and to be admired in all them that believe", we shall be "caught up together with them in the clouds, **to meet the Lord in the air**: and so shall we ever be with the Lord" (2 Thess. 1:10, 1 Thess. 4:17).

We shall be transformed and "raised a spiritual body", because the former body cannot endure the glory of God. We shall be brought so nigh to God that we must be given new bodies, lest, by the sheer glory of joy we would but die with its pains. It is a happiness so strong it is otherworldly, unearthly, heavenly in glory, and to the earthly it is deadly; a happiness that hurts – "a love strong as death" (Song of Songs). The expressions of His love cannot be endured. Until we are glorified, we cannot endure His glory. I have tasted of His fruit, but a man cannot digest a harvest.

550

This is what is spoken of in 1 Corinthians 15. The earthly body will break, the Spirit of God, which is the seed of Christ, will come forth from this vile body, and what was hidden within it will burst forth and fill the world, recreating it and hiding all things in God (1 Cor. 15:37-38).

> "But some man will say, How are the dead raised up? and with what body do they come? Thou fool, that which thou sowest is not quickened, except it die: And that which thou sowest, thou sowest not that body that shall be, but bare grain, it may chance of wheat, or of some other grain: But God giveth it a body as it hath pleased him, and to every seed his own body." (1 Corinthians 15:35-38)

> *When this earthen pitcher is finally broken,*
> *the Lord will fulfill all that was spoken. As*
> *there are different glories of different earthly*
> *bodies, a celestial body we need, and we*
> *shall be overcome and hidden in Christ's*
> *increase, name, and seed (1 Cor. 15:40).*

> "All flesh is not the same flesh: but there is one kind of flesh of men, another flesh of beasts, another of fishes, and another of birds. There are also celestial bodies, and bodies terrestrial: but the glory of the celestial is one, and the glory of the terrestrial is another." (1 Corinthians 15:39-40)

> *We were saved and were made to shine and*
> *therefore we were called the light of the world, but*
> *this light which did shine upon us was reflected by*
> *a dark glass, and our brightness, it was like the*
> *moon whose rays emanate from the sun at last,*
> *and we shined in the night piercing darkness with*
> *the right, until the end of our earthly plight.*

> "There is one glory of the sun, and another glory of the moon, and another glory of the stars: for one star differeth from another star in glory." (1 Corinthians 15:41)

Yet there is coming a day, a "Perfect Day" (Prov. 4:18), a day of incorruption, incomparable shining, where all other glory is but "weakness" and "dishonour" compared to the glory and power to come. God is inexpressible, and yet He was expressed through a "natural body," and there comes a "spiritual body" which will bear the fullness of His name and fame. The seed of Christ was sown into individual persons with bodies of flesh. These bodies, as the body of the seed, are carriers of the life of Christ. This is the *resurrection* sown *now* – the life of Christ experienced within every believer by the power of His resurrection, which they presently and inwardly participate in. Yet, this resurrection will eventually be completed, the body of death will be shed, and the glory of the *resurrection now* is comparable to the *resurrection to come*, as the glory of the moon to the sun, as reflective rays in darkness to the shining Sun at noonday. The "quickening spirit" of the second Adam shall rule at last, filling all things with Himself. Lo, "All things are for Him through Him and to Him" (Rom. 11). We shall "bear the image of the heavenly," namely, the "Second Man" Who "is the Lord from heaven" (1 Cor. 15:47, 49). The saints will perfectly and completely glory in God. God shall fill all things with His presence and glory through the final removal of flesh. As God hath said, "No flesh should glory in His presence" (1 Cor. 1:29), and again, all the world will be filled with His glory (Hab. 2:14)!

> "Now this I say, brethren, that flesh and blood cannot inherit the kingdom of God; neither doth corruption inherit incorruption. Behold, I shew you a mystery; We shall not all sleep, but we shall all be changed, In a moment, in the twinkling of an eye, at the last trump: for the trumpet shall sound, and the dead shall be raised incorruptible, and we shall be changed. For this corruptible must put on incorruption, and this mortal must put on immortality. So when this corruptible shall have put on incorruption, and this mortal shall have put on immortality, then shall be brought to pass the saying that is written, Death is swallowed up in victory. O death, where is thy sting? O grave, where is thy victory? The sting of death is sin; and the strength of sin is the law. But thanks be to God, which giveth us the victory through our Lord Jesus Christ." (1 Corinthians 15:50-57)

Condescension withdrawn is a straightway descent of God, an unhindered expression of God; even as it was when those holy men experienced God by an ascent into heaven, so likewise, there is coming a day when heaven comes down, and God, without condescension, will, with His holy heaven, DESCEND. The powers of God created heaven, and God is heaven, and if He descends without condescension, He will transform the earth into heaven – and all men will behold the new heaven and the new earth! As His will was done above, so it will be done below. At this time, the Covenant of Christ will be fulfilled. At this time, there will be no more condescension, no more will, word, or relationship in the ways of man. Men will be glorified and dwell in His everlasting glory foretold by the promises, Covenants, and exultant praises throughout time. The promises and praises of this exalted God were patterned to foretell this triumphant END. As the saints waited for this END throughout history, they were bewildered by breaches, broken under God's heavy hand of wrath, and terrified by His repentances. Why? God found out their SIN. False prophets would not have it so; they claim the guilty to be possessors of glory. They fancy themselves to be "the saved", that they are, irrevocably, "the elect", and thus, they unconsciously open their minds to the seduction of sin. They believe they are the elect and they are sure, but they fail to make their calling and election sure (2 Peter

1:10). This is their horrid woe: their unrighteous assurance that they will be, finally, the elect, causes them to fail to make their election sure. Their banner is eternal security, and the armory of graces have they left behind, not knowing that there is a warfare that must be won if a man of sin is to win the prize.

PATTERN #2: *God's Eternality, Sovereignty, & Higher Righteousness Exalted*

It is essential that you understand that the Covenant of Christ is not yet fulfilled. The problem of sin is with us today as it was with those of former Covenants. The promises take the same patterns as the former ones, and as always, the conditions are clear and equally binding. The promises are presented with convincing power, because they are pointedly reliant on God's work of faithfulness, until the reader, being exercised by reason and righteousness, will feel disarmed from gainsaying against them, and resign at last to surrender to the safety of faith. This is one of the reasons why an intermittent glorification of the sovereignty of God with the eternal perfectness of all the promises has become a pattern of preaching in the scripture. When one ventures to study all the promises of God throughout the centuries, he will quickly see that this is no strange occurrence. However, the burden I have been compelled to make plain to the reader is that God's eternal perfectness, sovereignty, and higher righteousness does not negate the possibility of breaches, failures, fallings, and repentances – for these are enabled by the condescension of God. These exultations are the glory of God's "eternal purpose" which He will fulfill, in its time – but which is not fulfilled yet. Therefore, while we are yet unglorified, therefore we are *partially* saved, seeing, resurrected, living, light-inhabited, kingdom dwellers. When we will be glorified, we will be *fully* saved, face-to-face seeing, finally resurrected, fully living, without the presence of the body of death, and dwelling in the unapproachable light and Kingdom which has come. While yet in relation to God, by His condescension, there can be a falling away from grace, but the glory of God is always capitalized in the praises of eternal security so that men will, by faith, be persuaded that they are eternally secure, and those that have fallen are accounted with the wicked, which are forgotten.

~~~~~~~~~~~~~~~~~~~~~~~~

Impossibilities

In this section I will address things I have already addressed heretofore, but it is to put you in mind and memory of what was already covered, to the end that I may successfully establish the point at hand now, and remember, because of the exhaustiveness of this study and how unfamiliar you may be with its subjects, I have taken leave to be repetitive.

~~~~~~~~~~~~~~~~~~~~~~~~~

*God is not a man and therefore does not repent (God in the
ways of God), but He has repented (God in the ways of man),
and yet still never repented (God in the ways of God).*

When Saul was rejected as King, God repented of His mind to save Saul, which salvation, God said, was formerly intended to be forever; nevertheless in the very passage where God "**repented** that He had made Saul king over Israel", it is written for the glory of God - "The strength of Israel will not **lie** nor **repent**: for **He is not a man**, that HE should **repent**" (1 Sam. 15:35, 29). In the end, when men fall, it cannot taint the glory of God: His word, will, and promises are still immutable, everlasting, and sure – and all that we see otherwise in biblical history are darkened happenings within the tent of time and condescension. If men fall, it will be because of an unrepentant purpose decreed in heaven by the King Who reigns above the orchestra of events and time. If they fall, it is "whereunto also they were appointed" (1 Pet. 2:8), and this appointment was never repented of, though He repented within time of a genuine purpose by condescension.

*God casts His people away (God in the ways of man), but He
cannot make them castaways (God in the ways of God);
He forsakes them (God in the ways of man), but He cannot
forsake them (God in the ways of God).*

Though these realities are real, experiential, warned of, feared by the godly, interceded against by the prophets, and are forever the doom of the reprobate – there are promises which declare that it is an *impossibility* for God to **cast off, cast away**, and **forsake** His people ((Jer. 31:37, 33:24, Psalm 94:14) → [casting off] (Psalm 94:14, 1 Sam. 12:22, 1 Kings 6:13, Neh. 9:31) → [forsaking]), but these scriptures refer to the *final* and *entire* annihilation of Israel, not the annihilation of *nearly all* except a *remnant,* and it in no way negates biblical history when the many promise-bound saints rebelled through the centuries and so lost their salvation. Parallel to this are the instances of God's *repentances*, but God promises with *an unrepentant purpose* that He will never *fully* and *entirely* annihilate His people (Rom. 11:29).

*God changes (alters) His word (God in the ways of man), but
He cannot alter it, change it, or lie (God in the ways of God);
He changes (God in the ways of man), but He cannot change,
and never changed (God in the ways of God).*

They wronged His righteous faithfulness which was toward them, like as is represented in Isaiah 63:8, and God did plead with them according to their wrong that they did toward His righteous goodness, saying – "**I said, I will never break My Covenant with you**" (Judges 2:1) – and this promise of God they despised by disobeying His commanding voice (Judges 2:2). On this the promises hinged, and God dealt with them – *break for break* – thus He said: "**Wherefore I also said**, I will

554

not drive them out from before you; but they shall be as thorns in your sides, and their gods shall be a snare unto you" (Judges 2:3). Hovering high above, and transcending over, the events of time as they unfolded throughout history, there is an **unbreakable eternality in God's promise**, though throughout time there were so many who perished in the justice of *break for break*. This is the mystery of damnation which God executed upon His backsliding children through the centuries. It was not that men understood it entirely, so as to understand all the ways it was entirely just, but rather, they were *bewildered* and *confounded* about it. Thus they were led to pray to God – "Thou hast made **void** the Covenant of Thy servant" (Ps. 89:39). Their complaint was that it was **VOID**. It is not surprising that they were confused, because God said: "So shall My Word be that goeth forth out of My mouth: it shall not return unto Me **void**, but it shall accomplish that which I please, and it shall prosper in the thing whereto I sent it" (Isaiah 55:11). They knew the promise and oath of God: "My Covenant will I not **break**, nor **alter** the thing that is gone out of My lips. Once have I sworn by My holiness that I will not **lie** unto David" (Ps. 89:34-35). God's justice was termed ***break for break*** in Ezekiel 16 & 17, as formerly addressed; thus in Psalm 89, the bewildered prophet feels as though God is being *froward* and *deceptive*. The prophet feels as though he is beholding a froward face upon God, and in the representative stead of all the Israelites, the prophet cries: "How long, LORD? Wilt Thou **hide** Thyself for ever? Shall Thy **wrath** burn like fire?...Lord, where are Thy former **lovingkindnesses**, which Thou **swarest** unto David in Thy **truth**" (Ps. 89:46, 49)? This prophet feels deceived because he remembered that God said, "I will not lie unto David" (Ps. 89:35).

Jeremiah knew the feeling of shame and adverse darkness under the shadow of the froward face of God. He cried, "O LORD, Thou hast **deceived** me, and I was **deceived**: Thou art stronger than I, and hast prevailed" (Jer. 20:7). And again, "Why is my pain perpetual, and my wound incurable, which refuseth to be healed? Wilt Thou be altogether unto Me as a **liar**, and as waters that fail" (Jer. 15:18) – and Jeremiah knew that God had said of Himself that He would not – "suffer My faithfulness to **fail**" (Ps. 89:33). These cries of Jeremiah were all in the dilemma when his personal, prophetic covenant that he had with God (Jeremiah 1) was breached, without Jeremiah knowing it; therefore he was deceived, he felt deceived, thus he speaks of deception in his personal ministry and relationship with God (Jer. 15:18 & 20:7), as was formerly addressed. Jeremiah was the intercessor for the generation of the captivities who also, like unto Jeremiah's personal experience, underwent the woeful darkness of the froward face of God, when God turned their light into darkness, but unlike Jeremiah's quick restoration back into the favor of his covenant with God, this generation was never able to recover themselves. For them, just retributions of deception fell upon them unto their reprobation. My reader, let these words of inspired scripture cry aloud in your conscience as if you were beholding Jeremiah himself when he was gasping, confounded, and crying loud and long – AHHHH! "Then said I, Ah, Lord GOD! Surely Thou hast **greatly deceived** this people and Jerusalem, saying, Ye shall have peace; whereas the sword reacheth unto the soul" (Jer. 4:10)! The form of this deception is *break for break*; thus

Jeremiah cries on behalf of the generation: "Do not abhor us, for Thy name's sake, do not disgrace the throne of Thy glory: remember, **break not Thy Covenant** with us" (Jer. 14:21), but for them there was no hope (save a small remnant). Intercession was impossible… "Then the LORD said unto me, Though Moses and Samuel stood before Me, yet My mind could not be toward this people: cast them out of My sight, and let them go forth" (Jer. 15:1). Though it is impossible that God would eternally and everlastingly break His Covenant (Jer. 33:20), God is able to reprobate generations and persons from the company of those bound in this saving Covenant for the glory of His wrath against lying children. "Children that will not lie" (Isa. 63:8) are the ones to whom God will NOT _show_ Himself as a liar, and so He will save them by the keeping performance of His promises and oaths. It is impossible for God to be evil, impure, and froward; likewise it is "impossible for God to lie" (Heb. 6:8), but in retributive _deceptions,_ God brings upon man a just penalty of his action done vertically toward Him, and thus He can _show_ Himself to be _froward_ to them. By _show_ Himself, I mean that He appears to be this way in the God-ordained deception upon their own mind – _froward for froward, impure for impure, break for break_, and _lie for lie_ – nevertheless, in God's higher righteousness it cannot be so. "Wilt Thou be altogether unto Me **as a liar**" (Jer. 15:18), Jeremiah asked of God, though he knew that it was written of God that He "will not lie" (Ps. 89:35).

As many as will fall must fall. Before reprobation, when a Christian is in a damnable state, it is against God they do

> ### RELATED SERMONS
>
> "God's Eternal Love Seen from Gethsemane"
>
> - Jake Gardner

wrestle, against His will to damn them, and if haply they prevail, "it may be" that they will find personal or corporate mercy in their day, but if they for salvation do not prevail – _God is not in need of them to fulfill His promises_. God can "of these stones" "raise up children unto Abraham" (Lk. 3:8). The false prophets presume upon the promises of God, supposing that they are unable to fall from them, and that God is indebted to perform salvation with them, and it is not so. He does not respect their person, because God can make a stone into their person. The great struggle through the centuries has been the difficulty and scarcity with which Israel attained or maintained salvation, but the bottom line made sure by these struggles is – if you are in defiance of the warnings of God, even as the chosen, elect, called, and covenanted people, _God will do the impossible to fulfill His word, with or without you_. God does not need you, _even if all reason, logic, and possibilities demand it, though all promise and purpose prophesy it – a stone can replace you as God justly reprobates you, and still all His words will be true_. IF you are elect, called, and regenerate now, and yet fallen, "it may be," "haply," "peradventure" God will grant you repentance; it does not say there is no alternative but God granting the fallen regenerate man repentance, BECAUSE God does not _need you_ to fulfill the integrity of His word! Is that not what is written? They that are fallen from grace are "those that oppose themselves," and they will find salvation "if God **peradventure** will give them repentance to the acknowledging of the truth; and that they may recover themselves out of the snare of the devil, who are taken captive by him at his will" (2 Tim. 2:25-26). Peradventure He may decide to restore you, and peradventure He may decide otherwise. He is impossibly, unimaginably perfect in His ways – look up and blush, and whisper: "Amen".

"Abba, Father, *all things are possible unto Thee*…"
(Mark 14:36)

Do you know that Christ means what He said when He prayed, "Abba, Father, all things are possible unto Thee" (Mark 14:36)? This was the agonized cry of the Savior of the world as He prayed in Gethsemane. It was the predestinated plan of God from eternity past to slay the Lamb of God for the sin of the world. The whole host of elect and precious persons were everlastingly in the mind of God before He ever created their soul or knit them together wonderfully in their mother's womb. Before ever the earth was, He did have His elect souls, their faces, their names, and all the numerous hairs on their body, every one of them foreordained for glory! Foreordained I say, "according as He hath chosen us in Him before

If God does rewrite the elect's names which were evidently written before the foundation of the world, what can we say about this? God can rewrite eternity's plan! Yet you may complain and say – "then His 'promises' 'fail', His 'Covenant' is 'void', His word is 'altered', and He is 'a liar' – but who are you to question Him? He says He knows not these persons! Such were the complaints of the saints in time past in their exact words. God did such things then, and can He not do them now?

the foundation of the world, that we should be holy and without blame before Him in love: Having predestinated us unto the adoption of children by Jesus Christ to Himself, according to the good pleasure of His will… in Whom also we have obtained an inheritance, being predestinated according to the purpose of Him Who worketh all things after the counsel of His own will" (Eph. 1:4-5, 11). Before the foundation of the world, the chosen were chosen, and elect, and predestinated; therefore the names of the Book of Life were written and set, as much as His unchanging choice predestinates and determines all things by His sovereign power. Again it is written to the Christians that "God hath from the beginning chosen you to salvation" (2 Thess. 2:13), and, they are "elect according to the foreknowledge of God the Father" (1 Peter 1:2); but how, my dear reader, can the following scripture be answered? "He that overcometh, the same shall be clothed in white raiment; and I will not blot out his name out of the Book of Life, but I will confess his name before My Father, and before His angels" (Rev. 3:5). This Book is not any other book, but the book of the elect, and any careful and honest study of this Book will reveal this. Those that perish do perish because their names are not written in the book, and the names were written before time began, before Christ spoke this in Revelation 3:5. Those names are said to be unmovable names, inerasable names, unchangeably there – the very time they were written, the power of predestination, and the changeless glory of His love toward the elect do all exclaim this truth! Even the scriptures say that the men that are lost are lost because their "names were not written in the Book of Life from the foundation of the world" (Rev. 17:8), and, "whosoever was not found written in the Book of Life was cast into the Lake of fire" (Rev. 20:15). What truth is being communicated, but that those who are regenerate are therefore written in the Book, and those in the Book were there before the foundation of the world, thus their salvation was predestinated; but somehow Jesus Christ the Lord is able to change this book within time!? This should baffle us all! Creating shock, wonder, praise, humiliation, fear, and honor in our hearts toward God. How can it be? All things are possible with God!

The fact that all things are possible with God has never more powerfully been communicated but in the time when Christ acknowledges before the Father that He can, as a wise preacher once said as a paraphrase of what Christ is acknowledging, "Thou [Father] art able to rewrite eternity's plan" (J.M. Gardner). How? The Lamb of God was slain, Revelation 13:8 states, "from the foundation of the world", and this is clearly seen in Revelation 5:6 when Christ appears from eternity past after the throne is set in heaven (Rev. 4:2-3) and before all things were created on earth (Rev. 4:11); so also then, the Lamb of God appeared long before the first century, and Christ is described to be in this place of timeless eternity – "A Lamb as it had been slain" (Rev. 5:6), meaning already crucified. His sacrifice and the plan of it were both timeless and eternal, thus He was the Lamb of God "slain from the foundation of the world" (Rev. 13:8); and yet, Christ knew and understood when He approached the agony of the cross where He would become sin under the wrath of God's intense hatred for sin – and the love He had known uninterrupted, unblemished, and perfectly outpoured upon Him from eternity past would then be turned into wrath – being in an agony because of this, He was pressed in a righteous desire not to undergo such a thing, out of love for the Father in His heart…with the reality in mind that He was able to pray to the Father another plan than what has already been predestinated from eternity, and God would do it – because He could rewrite eternity's plan and do the impossible! Revealing this truth, He boldly declared to the disciples, "Thinkest thou that I cannot now pray to My Father, and He shall presently give Me more than twelve legions of angels" (Matt. 26:53)? It is not that it cannot be; it can be – though the scriptures, the Book of Life, and eternity's realities are against it, it can be! Though His sacrifice was "foreordained before the foundation of the world", it still can be (1 Pet. 1:20)! This is the very thing that Christ was acknowledging when He said, "Abba, Father, all things are possible unto Thee; take away this cup from Me: Nevertheless not what I will, but what Thou wilt" (Mark 14:36). Will you disagree with the acknowledgement of Christ and say that such a thing is not possible? Christ prayed this prayer out of the agony that He would, for the first time ever, and for the only time ever, experience the castaway wrath of God to forsake Him on the cross – He thus prayed what He prayed – but beforehand, He set His will to the utter subjection that sinless righteousness was in its glory, for He was a servant to the Father, preferring the Father, and loving to the Father unto the END – thus was His prayer, "Father, glorify Thy Name", and the Father answered back from Heaven, one of three times in biblical history He did ever do this in the life of His dear Son: "Then came there a voice from heaven, saying, I have both glorified it, and will glorify it again" (John 12:28)! Hallelujah! Look closely at the Master and His mind toward suffering, our great "Captain" of salvation (Heb. 2:10): "Now is my soul troubled, and what shall I say? Father, save Me from this hour: but for this cause came I unto this hour. Father, glorify Thy Name. Then came there a voice from heaven, saying, I have both glorified it, and will glorify it again" (John 12:27-28)!

"Known unto God are all His works from the beginning of the world." (Acts 15:18)

God can make a stone become a child of Abraham. We don't need to understand how that is or could be. With God, it is, if He wants it to be. Though all possibilities and laws of creation join hand in hand with what you think is logical, and though men riot against it, with God it is possible, perfect, and logical. With God, all His works have been "finished from the foundation of the world" (Heb. 4:3). Though He worked for six days to create the earth, He did not work, and His works were ever finished beforehand. Though God repented of making Saul King, He did not repent, and His repentances have ever ceased since the foundation of the world. Though Christ was incarnate and crucified within time, He was slain before time, even "slain from the foundation of the world" (Rev. 13:8). The impossible is possible, but will you acknowledge it? *God does repent, but He cannot repent. God casts His people away (castaways), but He cannot make them castaways; He forsakes them, but He cannot forsake them. God changes His word (alters it), but He cannot alter it, change it, or lie. He changes, but He cannot change.*

These attributes and sayings impossibly exist in God, but these are not to be understood by us. The height of this matter is well expressed by Adam Clarke. Though I disagree with the final conclusions he draws about the *omniscience* of God (written in other portions of his writings but not here), I do confess to and agree with him in: the unlimited transcendence of God beyond all of our understandings, and therefore the infinite condescension He has undergone to stoop into the grounds of our limited understanding; thus we are left with wondrous statements like Revelation 13:8, and infinitely lofty thoughts like the expressions well written and accounted of by Clarke: "The foreknowledge of God is never spoken of in reference to Himself, but in reference to us: in Him properly there is neither foreknowledge nor afterknowledge. Omniscience, or the power to know all things, is an attribute of God, and exists in Him as omnipotence, or the power to do all things. He can do whatsoever He will; and He does whatsoever is fit or proper to be done. God cannot have foreknowledge, strictly speaking, because this would suppose that there was something coming, in what we call futurity, which had not yet arrived at the presence of the Deity. Neither can He have any afterknowledge, strictly speaking, for this would suppose that something that had taken place, in what we call preterity, or past time, had now got beyond the presence of the Deity. As God exists in all that can be called eternity, so He is equally everywhere: nothing can be future to Him, because He lives in all futurity; nothing can be past to Him, because He equally exists in all past time; futurity and pretereity are relative terms to us; but they can have no

559

relation to that God Who dwells in every point of eternity; with whom all that is past, and all that is present, and all that is future to man, exists in one infinite, indivisible, and eternal Now."

When God speaks, He "calleth those things which be not as though they were" (Rom. 4:17), and we must, through faith, lay hold upon these realities and promises so as to become them (Rom. 4:18), but your eternal election will finally determine if you will fulfill the word of God for salvation or reprobation. All reprobations that will happen until the consummation of the gospel, covenants, and salvation, will be forgotten, ruled out of mind (Heb. 10:17, Ezek. 3:7, 18:24), and God's perfect fulfillment of salvation and promise will be His glory now and then! Psalm 105 glorifies the Abrahamic Covenant as perfectly fulfilled, as if there was never any breach to it. Why? NO breach can taint the glory of His immutable faithfulness, and no fall of men will "be mentioned" (Ezek. 18:24) or "remembered" (Ezek. 3:7) as a scratch to the untouchable gold of God's goodness - nor could "The Golden Chain" be marred or rusted! Tremble at the saying and give God the glory: "Behold, I, even I, will utterly forget you" (Jer. 23:39). God cannot lie, thus it is said, "He remembered His holy promise and Abraham His servant" (Psalm 105:42), and all "breaches" are forgotten (Numbers 14:30-34). To them that will be saved, it will be under the banner and name of God "Who keepest Covenant and mercy", though to diverse persons, He breached it for justice as He forewarned He would do (Neh. 9:31-33). So it is in Romans 8:28-30. This is "The Golden Chain" of God's eternal glory!

> "And we know that all things work together for good to them that love God, to them who are the called according to His purpose. For whom He did foreknow, He also did predestinate to be conformed to the image of His Son, that He might be the firstborn among many brethren. Moreover whom He did predestinate, them He also called: and whom He called, them He also justified: and whom He justified, them He also glorified." (Romans 8:28-30)

It cannot be broken, though it has been broken through history; such links are unmentionable, nonexistent, and forgotten, while the glory of salvation and His faithfulness is the praise of His saints now, and in the END! No good thing can come to man without due thanks to His sovereign hand, and no bad thing can come except in God it was preplanned. God is the sole possessor of all His rights, and in them are included all things in His powers. It is in HIS power to break off links to this chain as others were "broken off" from the tree of salvation (Rom. 11:17), but whatever has temporarily befallen this golden chain, and all the removed names in the Book of Life is of no effect on the eternality of God's name, election, love, and salvation!

*The names written before the foundation of the world will be there **forever**,*
*And what happens within the hours, days, and centuries of time cannot **ever**,*
*The glories of God's timeless, eternal purposes **sever**!*

God is the possessor of these rules and powers *within* and *outside* of time, working all things to the glory of Himself – showing the world wrath and mercy (Rom. 9:22-23). Hear ye His powers:

> "See now that **I**, *even* **I**, *am* **He**, and *there is* no god with Me: **I** kill, and **I** make alive; **I** wound, and **I** heal: neither *is there any* that can deliver out of **My hand**." (Deut. 32:39)

> "That they may know from the rising of the sun, and from the west, that there is none beside Me. I am the LORD, and there is none else. I form the light, and create darkness: I make peace, and create evil: I the LORD do all these things. Drop down, ye heavens, from above, and let the skies pour down righteousness: let the earth open, and let them bring forth salvation, and let righteousness spring up together; I the LORD have created it. **Woe unto him that striveth with his Maker! Let the potsherd strive with the potsherds of the earth. Shall the clay say to Him that fashioneth it, What makest Thou?** Or thy work, He hath no hands? Woe unto him that saith unto his father, What begettest thou? Or to the woman, What hast thou brought forth?" (Isaiah 45:6-10)

As He forms light, so He creates darkness, and because light can turn to darkness, will you now strive with your Maker? Shall "the clay say" anything to God, dishonoring Him, as a reviler to a father, "what begettest Thou? Or to the woman, what hast thou brought forth?" Many would accuse the doctrine of losing salvation that it is based upon a misunderstanding of grace, reliance upon works, and a negating of faith. Ye hypocrites! If we believe we have received salvation, not apart from but through saving faith, how then is the loss of saving faith a salvation based upon works? If faith gained was no work, then faith lost is also no work. The sovereignty of God is evidenced by a man's inability to come to Christ, because the man has an inability to believe – meaning faith "is the gift of God" (Eph. 2) "according as God hath dealt to every man" (Rom. 12:3). But what if God, in His sovereignty, does shew forth those who are elect as "vessels of wrath fitted to destruction" by their eventual discontinuance of faith and repentance, while formerly, they were able to obtain salvation through faith and repentance, and conclusively, He glorifies His own eternal integrity before, during, and after their fall, as an exultation of judgment outside the realm of our logical comprehension and understanding?! Thus, it is a glorification of God's sovereignty. Of this glory, it is written, "no flesh can glory in His presence", therefore these attributes of judgment are to be wondered at from below, a looking up at the loft of infinite purity in sovereign, just pleasure.

What is the glorification? It is consistently declared as the capstone and governor of all events and circumstances, judgments and condemnations, perseverances and salvations. God would have it that His people, throughout all the events which are on the relational plane of God in the ways of man, throughout all the uncertainty and difficulty to keep the narrow way, beholding others fall away and all the venomous damages Satan succeeds upon God's people – God would have it that His people never come to think that God has slipped off of His throne! He would have us understand that He has infinitely condescended, and whatsoever they see now is infinitely below Him, under Him, and securely ruled by Him Who sits as the immovable Determinate and completely sovereign King – The Only Wise Potentate.

If God desires (in the ways of God) to shower upon your life as a converted man "the riches of His glory", He will show you the glory of His sovereign "mercy" (Rom. 9:23). He will therefore continue to work in you the perseverance of all those who are elect after His eternal counsel. He will "**incline our hearts** unto Him, to walk in His ways, and to keep His commandments, and His statutes, and His judgments, which He commanded our fathers" (1 Kings 8:58). If you "run the way of His commandments", and finish your course through keeping the faith (1 Tim. 6:7), it is because God did ever "enlarge" your "heart" (Ps. 119:32). If you have put on the helmet of hope, and escaped damnable shame, it is because God "caused" you "to hope" (Ps. 119:49). If you fall, and God grants you repentance, if you are wounded by Him, and from Him you seek healing - you must seek it now like as all the brethren sought, saying: "Heal me, O LORD, and I shall be healed; save me, and I shall be saved: for Thou art my praise" (Jer. 17:14). During this raging "war against your soul" (1 Pet. 2:11) all throughout your days, in this present progressive struggle against the lethal end of sin (Jas. 1:15), if ever or always you desire freedom, your request is subject the dispensation of His sovereign will, and you cannot turn yourself. Knowing this – that if you cannot be turned from evil to God, then your course is set on damnation – therefore our brethren of old did pray this prayer, with hands lifted up: "turn Thou me, and I shall be turned; for Thou art the LORD my God" (Jer. 31:18). You may be of *eternal value* to God, that in you, this express purpose would be fulfilled, to shew forth the power of His wrath (Rom. 9:22). Under this fear the faithful groan, "**incline not my heart** to any evil thing" (Ps. 141:4). God is hope (Ps. 39:7), God is holding stability (Ps. 71:6), God is the continual source and praise of initial and present progressive salvation, and at all times the godly are made to understand, "my praise shall be continually of Thee" (Ps. 71:6). If you are silenced into hellfire, behold, "Thou didst it," said the psalmist to God (Ps. 39:9). If you never turn back from God, behold, it is of God - "So will not we go back from Thee: quicken us, and we will call upon Thy name. Turn us again, O LORD God of hosts, cause Thy face to shine; and we shall be saved" (Ps. 80:18-19). My fellow brethren in truth, I pray that your ministers who are as a flame of fire (Heb. 1:14, Rev. 2:1, 8, 12) do say to your soul, "And the Lord **direct your hearts** into the love of God, and into the patient waiting for Christ" (2 Thess. 3:5). Faith's beginning, perseverance, and end, is God's glory, so all the saints like stars emanate God's good praises, shining light in the darkness of night, giving heaven its sparkling diamonds and due honor. When I see many fall away, and in their reprobation they introduce damnable heresies with a wolverine viciousness, still then I will know that these are men "of old ordained to this condemnation" (Jude 4), doing that "whereunto also they were appointed" by predestination, that by Potter-like ordination they have become "them which stumble at the word" (1 Peter 2:8). The darkness of night is not ruled without Light (Gen. 1:14-19). God hath therefore forbidden the quarrel, "Why hast Thou made me thus" (Rom. 9:20). If some of these stars lose their place, what can be said? They are "wandering stars, to whom is reserved the blackness of darkness for ever" (Jude 13).

In the end, God's glory takes preeminence! As it was written in Romans 8, those that are called will be glorified. This is true to them who are predestinated to be glorified. Those who are called, and yet not glorified, were predestinated to be damned. In the showcase of God's glory, there are precious stones laden on all fixtures of gold. One is the glory of God to save and the other the glory of God to damn. In these two works, throughout the sojourning of time, God seeks to get Himself a Name. Eternally, it is not possible for the elect to be deceived, but within the temporary dispensation of God's condescension, the temporary elect can be deceived, but all those that were deceived and fell can ne'er blemish the eternal glory of the saying, "if it were possible" in Matthew 24:24 and Mark 13:22.

Jesus said "the gates of hell will not prevail against my Church," but this does not mean that they never have in OT Church history, nor never will in NT Church history since the day Christ spoke that word, but in the END, the gates of hell will not prevail. All of God's enemies are not yet under Christ's feet, and all of God's friends do not always gather with Him at present that He might daily put under their foes (Eph. 6:11-18). Unfortunately, because of Matthew 16:18, men understood Christ to mean that the gates of hell shall never prevail against the Church. Those poor souls on whom the gates of hell do prevail against, even they "shall not be remembered" (Ezek. 3:20, 18:24) as the Church. God's credit goes on undaunted and unmarred by these. In this instance, Christ did not say or mean never, and even if He did, those who fall He will forget and sever (John 15:6), and God will fulfill every promise of never and forever, but now hell rages to catch holy men through our fleshly body (Jas. 3:6), the world (2 Cor. 4:4, Eph. 2:2-3, Matt. 23:15), and the reigning principalities (Eph. 6:12). Now, in our day, men seek to gain confidence through the study of *extra-biblical* Church history, supposing that therein lies the consistent witness of the faithful Church throughout time, and anything that they find new or inconsistent from the pages of *extra-biblical* Church history spanning since the first century, this doctrine or deed is dismissed and named heretical, because it is a "new thing" from the witness, they suppose, of what God has kept from the gates of hell throughout time. On this one promise, men seek to follow the mass witness through the centuries, when a true study of *biblical* Church history would reveal the truth of the saying, "many are called and few are chosen." Which will you follow, the many or the few?

The NT Visitation of God – *Final Judgment & Final Salvation*

The Mysterious Development of Salvific Promises → Abrahamic – Priestly Mosaic Ceremonial – Kingly Davidic – New Testament – End of Days Salvation

The Mysterious Development of Damning Woes → Assyrian & Babylonian Captivities – 70 AD – End of Days Woe & Condemnation

> "…upon this Rock I will build My Church; and the gates of hell shall not prevail against it" – Matt. 16:18

How fared "the Church in the wilderness" (Acts 7:38) against the gates of hell? How many raced and won the prize they raced for, of all the children of the OT Church which were "born after the Spirit" (Gal. 4:29)? Since the days of Moses, the prophetic foretelling of the Israelite nation's falling away, eventual destruction, and final dispersion was ever looming over their heads. Centuries passed, one after another, and there were generations of much mercy wherein God did pour out His Spirit but a little, granting that He would raise up some men of His right hand for the lightening of the load. Even when all deserved to die, some Spirit-empowered leaders were enabled to preserve some small remnant alive in God. Oh! How hard these years, decades, and centuries were, and how awfully did iniquity increase at each generation unto the next. Even after the brief lives of those faithful few, some of which who were enabled to cause their generation to stand up for Jesus, these generations of Israel did quickly return back to the former crest of rebellion the previous generations left off at, and then from thence, they rose beyond it for greater heights for hell. Overlooking the entire span of these centuries of Israelite Church history, one would be a fool to conclude that "the gates of hell" did never prevail against the Church of God. This is to assert that the Church and Covenant of God was *always* fulfilled, standing fixed because of the people's obedience, thus standing successfully as a defense against hell's advances to breach its walls, so that God did not lose one, some, or any of His children to whom He was savingly related. What unlearned man would make such a claim!? Furthermore, what characteristic marked those rising lone-leaders who are chronicled as heroes of biblical history, upon whom was the Spirit of Revival? They did not follow their fathers, they did not follow the anti-God, anti-remnant majority of people who ruled the contemporary religion that civilized men held in honor, and they were appalled at the pervading conclusions of unbiblical traditions that bowed to the ancients with an unrighteous respect, ancient men who were stiffnecked to disobey the Bible. These Spirit-empowered leaders refused to yield to all these men, and they contended against all the exasperating pressures to bend the straight way crooked. They trusted in God by casting the hope of their entire life upon the infallible Writ of God's Book – the Bible. They were a Book-keeping, Bible-reading, scripture-memorizing, truth-copywriting, testimony-singing, and truth-preaching people! Praise God!

Yea, the Church found in *biblical* history, called the "Church in the wilderness" (Acts 7:38), is our example Church, and not another! *Biblical* history gives us the surety that these were true Churches, whose events of history were recorded and protected by the inspiration and providence of God, recordings which can be trusted as accurate, with God-verified salvations in true works of saving graces, all of which should be trusted as genuine. This is biblical history – history which should be trusted and quoted, but *extra-biblical* history has been the primary study of "Christianity" today, and why!? Because men believe that they can never come short of the promises of

> *The books of **extra-biblical Church history** are covered with the finger prints of fallibility, for, it is the work of humanity, but the Church history of God is God-chronicled and God-protected, therefore it is called God's word – God breathed – though it is on a piece of meager paper, a tangible page, able to be handled and held, able to deteriorate and age. It is infallibility borne in the most unexpected place from the most unexpected persons. It is, as it were, infallibility borne in a manger.*

God, and so, when they look at the centuries which have passed since the conception of the NT Church in the 1st century, they do conclude that there has been a thriving, persevering work of God throughout the centuries, and because it has thrived, it does therefore hold for us the honor of antiquity, or, truth that lasts the test of time, and thus, any confession which does not match with what can be traced throughout the centuries, they conclude, is not a part of the Church which Jesus promised to keep, and is therefore a modern and alien invention of man – it is "a new thing" which cannot be trusted. While I believe that a remnant was kept in saving graces, I do not believe the Covenant was maintained in its fullness, which means, not all those whom God intended to save were saved, not all of the glory that God intended to have was had, and not all the truth which does keep the saved saints persevering was being taught and held fast to. What I am pressing upon my reader is the sober question, could God raise up a Josiah generation on the eve of woes, just before the revelation of the antichrist? If we would be a Josiah generation, then we would be "a new thing," which really is a reviving of the old thing formerly written, the Covenant of God, but if this is so, then we would have to be different from the majority of centuries of Church history. Are we prepared for that? To be like Josiah who denied the majority witness of "church" history and confession, for he held to the infallibility of the written word of God alone?

Men trust in *extra-biblical* history as if it is accurate, preserved, and infallible. They know so little of *biblical* Christianity, and what they did ever know about it, they forget, because they are so busy remembering what *extra-biblical* history says. Let me be as clear as I can! Men look at the centuries of *extra-biblical* "church" history and conclude, if it cannot be found and traced throughout the centuries as the common confession of all the remnant, then we should never believe it, accept it, and adhere to it, and why? Jesus said, "…upon this Rock I will build My Church and the gates of hell shall not prevail against it" (Matt. 16:18), and they conclude that this meant that *extra-biblical* history will show the infallible witness of true confessions of theology and doctrine, when not even biblical history demonstrated such preservation, consistency, and generation-to-generation Covenantal, doctrinal, and theological perfection. Men should be looking at *extra-biblical history* and conclude what Peter concluded when he studied *biblical Church history's* chief lesson – and what was it!? "The righteous" were "scarcely saved" (1 Peter 4:18), or as Jesus Christ said it, "many are called and few are chosen" (Matt. 22:14)!

Looking at *biblical history*, after carefully noting all of which we have studied thus far, there is no mystery behind the words of Christ, "Many are **called** and few are **chosen**" (Matthew 22:14). Many were saved, or, were of the companies which were saved, and of these two types, few persevered to be found of God as "**the chosen**." Without these terms definitively referenced, this is what we have been tracing throughout *biblical history*. With the entire history of God's people in mind, Peter observed this sweeping conclusion throughout the centuries: many righteous men are called, and of the called, few and scarce are those who are finally chosen. In his own words he put it, "If the righteous scarcely be saved, where shall the ungodly and the sinner appear" (1 Peter 4:18)? Was this not the burden of the Lord Jesus for His Church of the "last days"?

Satan's craft to beguile the holy was, and is, to preach *promises* without the coexistence of *conditions*. Satan preached to Jesus the *promise* of Psalm 91:11-12 in Matthew 4:6, but Jesus answered him again with the *condition* to that promise's performance in Matthew 4:7. As Satan preached, so his son-servants spew out the same lies (John 8:44), yet Calvinism is an organized web which preys upon God's people, catching them in false confidences in true promises, persuading men that conditions are nonexistent, inapplicable, and irrelevant. Satan cloaked his lure by the promises of God, and "no marvel," this was his appearance of righteousness (2 Cor. 10:14), but he has crafted a theological system of corruption, namely Calvinism, which hath in it great and wonderful truths, and through them he doth employ the ignorant to his ruinous causes which deceive the righteous. As Satan was to Jesus, so "they" become. By doctrine or deed, they preach and praise the promises of God, and yet they are in complete denial and oblivion to the conditions. Jesus' defense against Satan was a burden consistent with the truth and warning found throughout *biblical Church history* – beware of the CONDITIONS!

Thus far, we have studied how God renounced the generations of the Exodus and the Babylonian Captivity, both serving as typified relationships God has with saved persons. Now consider this: What God did to the generation of Jesus Christ was parallel to what was done to the generation of the Babylonian Captivity.

The dispersion (known as The Assyrian and Babylonian Captivities) was spoken of by God as His "visitation" (Jer. 10:15). When God visited His people, He was executing upon them the justice of the Covenant agreement according as it was written, every man according to their works (Prov. 24:12). When He visited, He judged them as He found them, which means that, before His visitation comes, during this undetermined amount of time, the people have a space to find mercy and repentance. God's visitation was the hour of judgment, an hour too late for repentance, and so also, Jesus Christ spoke of His return and His Judgment of the Church! He speaks of it in the strict terms of Judgment *according to works*. It is a day to fear, a day to prepare for, so that we are told that all former days before this final Day are given for the purpose that men would find grace for repentance through saving faith, that they might be thus prepared. For this reason I have titled this section, "The Visitation and Final Judgment", for, the NT visitation of Christ is like the OT visitation of God as seen in the dispersion, so that Christ's return will be unto a people who are staggeringly unprepared for Him. When Christ returns, large portions of His people will be damned by Him, as it was already written that many were first called unto salvation, but in the end few were chosen unto its everlasting enjoyments. This is a pattern which is consistent and repeated all throughout the centuries of biblical Church history, but now, much more, it shall be in the Last Days just before His return.

Thus, as we have thoroughly addressed repeatedly, Romans 11:13-23 prophesied the very same conditions of a falling away happening to the NT Church, and also this was the very burden of Christ during the latter end of His earthly ministry. As for what happened to the 1st century, do I need to remind you again? God gave them a "spirit of slumber," eyes that see not and ears that hear not. The sovereignty of God was at work to blind them into damnation, and though they were, in type, saved persons, covenanted peoples, called sons and daughters, God's wife, etc., and as the generation of the Babylonian Captivity was made ready for the curses of God's wrath through the casting-away deception of God, likewise Jesus' generation was prepared for wrath in 70 AD (another type of God's visitation), but this 70 AD experience was only a partial fulfillment, and parallel to those prophecies of Christ. Will we understand our day in the light of those unfulfilled prophecies!? Will we understand that what happened in 70 AD was only a partial fulfillment of the wrath which was prophesied in those prophetic woes? Therefore, there is yet a generation that must be prepared to drink in the vials of God's holy anger! As the generation of the Babylonian Captivity was prepared to drink in the wrath of God – being led thereto by the Deception of God – so also the 1st century generation of Jesus Christ was prepared, even so we must expect to fulfill the unfulfilled prophecies of the Babylonian Captivity by the OT prophets, and to fulfill the unfilled prophecies of Jesus Christ after 70 AD; even so, a generation must be prepared by a strong, delusive, deception of God – a "strong delusion" – so that the generations preceding the last prepare the stage for the coming of the Anti-Christ. In the generation of the antichrist's arrival, with him is the woeful generation who will fulfill all the words of this Book which did prophesy a curse. We therefore should expect, EVEN NOW, a great "**FALLIING AWAY**" (2 Thess. 2:3-12)!

567

This very curse was called being a "castaway", among other terms, which all define reprobation. This very terror is prophesied to happen within the dispensation of the New Covenant. Again I say, Jesus Christ warned of this repeatedly; He preached on it as the weighty theme of His latter ministry to His disciples! Paul dealt with this theological wonder in Romans chapter 11:13-25. In summary, Paul proved that if God cast away Israel, He could cast away His saved Church in like manner. "Some of the branches" were "broken off" (Rom. 11:17), and then the Church was grafted in, but as God broke the former branches off, so also, He can break the NT Church off, "casting away" (Rom. 11:15) saints who were made "holy" (Rom. 11:16) by "the root and fatness of the olive tree" (Rom. 11:17). Therefore LOOK, CHURCH – look at the many called and how few were chosen in the biblical ages already passed. Look at *Biblical Church history,* and understand just how few there are that were saved, and later were finally saved. Therefore FEAR – "Be not highminded, but fear: For if God spared not the natural branches, take heed, lest He also spare not thee. Behold therefore the goodness and severity of God: on them which fell, severity; but toward thee, goodness, if thou continue in His goodness: otherwise thou also shalt be cut off" (Rom. 11:20-22).

Let me close this chapter with two points.

1) **WRATH**: That great and terrible Judgment Day of God, which was prophesied in the major and minor prophets, was partially, but not perfectly, fulfilled in the Babylonian Captivity, then again in the 1st century doom of 70 AD, and we await a final and more perfect fulfillment of all those prophetic woes – but that is not all we are waiting for, praise God!

     i. **NOTE**: These prophetic woes were in response to God's people who were in rejection and rebellion. They provoked this wrath from God to come, and preceding the actual woes of annihilation, God gave them over to spiritual plagues of castaway wrath…and all of these terms which were applied to those individuals in the Babylonian Captivity are applied to the 1st century Jews, and again, are applied to the NT Church dispensation, and they were already the raging conflict still in the 1st century – and it was prophesied, from there, to get worse and worse unto a great "falling away!"

2) **SALVATION**: So also, along with the prophetic woes, even so we await the Covenant and prophetic promises of salvation! We await still the final fulfillment of the Abrahamic and Davidic Covenants, and also the prophetic promises of the major and Minor Prophets which expounded all the ways in which these two major Covenants will be mysteriously and eternally fulfilled. So we wait, because each one of these promises and

Covenants were partially, but not perfectly, fulfilled, just like the prophetic woes.

As a result of understanding this…we should be conscious that we are as the Israelites, who lived in those wayward generations which led up to the Babylonian Captivity, and we should learn from the valiant footsteps of those who lived in seasons of revival (Jehoshaphat, Hezekiah, and Josiah), therefore we should strive to be different from those rebellious persons who walked out the course of deception, which in turn, hastened the day of wrath. We should pray to the Lord the same old prayer of Habakkuk: "O LORD, **revive** Thy work in the midst of the years, in the midst of the years make known; in **wrath** remember **mercy**" (Habakkuk 3:2). Each backslidden generation brought the day of God's visitation just a little nearer. They did not know the day or hour in which it would arrive, and neither do we. You can see how Hezekiah recognized that he was born into a generation in which the wrath of God was upon Israel (2 Chron. 29:10). Therefore, with desperation he sought to be different – DIFFERENT FROM BIBLICAL CHURCH HISTORY – for he recognized that he lived in a day which was prophesied to be a backsliding catastrophe! So also, we can see this exact same heart in the NT Christians as they meditated upon, and as they prepared for, the Final Judgment and/or Christ's return (the NT visitation). Men should be making their "election sure" instead of fancying themselves that they are the elect, by a presumptuous, unfounded, untried, and unwise assurance.

Though many have and will come short of the promises of salvation, it must be that the promises of salvation come to their consummating fulfillment, as will the prophetic promises of wrath. Below are some of these unchangeable *forevers…*

WRATH

Amos 8:7
The LORD hath sworn by the excellency of Jacob, Surely **I will never forget** any of their works.

Ezekiel 24:14
I the LORD have spoken it: it shall

"I will never forget" – Amos 8:7
"I will not go back…neither will I repent" – Ezek. 24:14
"I have purposed it and will not repent, neither will I turn back from it" – Jer. 4:28
"I thought to punish you… and I repented not" – Zech. 8:14
"…I will not turn away the punishment thereof…" – Amos 2:4
"…I will not turn away the punishment thereof…" – Amos 2:6
"it shall not return any more" – Ezek. 21:5
"is not turned back from us" – Jer. 4:8
"shall not return" – Jer. 30:24

come to pass, and I will do it; **I will not go back**, neither will I spare, **neither will I repent**; according to thy ways, and according to thy doings, shall they judge thee, saith the Lord GOD.

Jeremiah 4:28

For this shall the earth mourn, and the heavens above be black: because I have spoken it, **I have purposed it, and will not repent, neither will I turn back from it**.

Zechariah 8:14

For thus saith the LORD of hosts; **As I thought** to punish you, when your fathers provoked Me to wrath, saith the LORD of hosts, and **I repented not**

Amos 2:4

Thus saith the LORD; For three transgressions of Judah, and for four, **I will not turn away** the punishment thereof; because they have despised the law of the LORD, and have not kept His commandments, and their lies caused them to err, after the which their fathers have walked:

Amos 2:6

Thus saith the LORD; For three transgressions of Israel, and for four, **I will not turn away** the punishment thereof; because they sold the righteous for silver, and the poor for a pair of shoes;

Ezekiel 21:5

That all flesh may know that I the LORD have drawn forth my sword out of his sheath: **it shall not return** any more.

Jeremiah 4:8

For this gird you with sackcloth, lament and howl: for the fierce anger of the LORD **is not turned back** from us.

Jeremiah 30:23-24

Behold, the whirlwind of the LORD goeth forth with fury, a continuing whirlwind: it shall fall with pain upon the head of the wicked.
The fierce anger of the LORD **shall not return**, until He have done it, and until He have performed the intents of His heart: in the latter days ye shall consider it.

Isaiah 24:19-25:1

The earth is utterly broken down, the earth is clean dissolved, the earth is moved exceedingly.
The earth shall reel to and fro like a drunkard, and shall be removed like a cottage; and the transgression thereof shall be heavy upon it; and it shall fall, and not rise again.
And it shall come to pass in that day, that the LORD shall punish the host of the high ones that are on high, and the kings of the earth upon the earth.
And they shall be gathered together, as prisoners are gathered in the pit, and shall be shut up in the prison, and after many days shall they be visited.
Then the moon shall be confounded, and the sun ashamed, when the LORD of hosts shall reign in mount Zion, and in Jerusalem, and before His ancients gloriously.
O LORD, Thou art My God; I will exalt Thee, I will praise Thy Name; for Thou hast

done wonderful things; Thy counsels of old are faithfulness and truth.

Isaiah 14:24-26 (*The judgment of Assyria, the Devil, and Babylon, and the salvation of God's people*)
The LORD of hosts hath sworn, saying, Surely as **I have thought, so shall it come to pass**; and as **I have purposed, so shall it stand**:
That I will break the Assyrian in my land, and upon my mountains tread him under foot: then shall his yoke depart from off them, and his burden depart from off their shoulders.
This is **the purpose** that is purposed upon the whole earth: and this is the hand that is stretched out upon all the nations.

Yes, my dear reader, galloping from eternity past is this great occasion of wrath that God is seeking to bring upon the earth, and it is for His own eternal glory (Rom. 9:22)! We can see many of these prophetic woes, which He has eternally determined, by how God speaks in the explicit wording which affirms that He will not "*repent*" from, "*return*" or "*turn*" from, nor "*forget*" these purposes. Do you remember how God warned men to repent of their sins, lest He become so aggravated at evil that He is moved into an unrepentant, unrelenting mind of wrath? In such cases, He uses the same affirmations like the wording of the verses above, commanding repentance – "lest My fury go out like **fire, and burn that none can quench it**, because of the evil of your doings" (Jer. 21:12) – and He does mean it as He says it, even an *unquenchable fire* – and He will fulfill it! The fire of God's fury, even this *unquenchable fire-like wrath*, has been rushing from eternity past to consume "vessels of wrath" in an unquenchable Lake of Fire – and therein, in the Lake of Fire, the prophetically declared *forevers* of wrath shall be fulfilled! These slaves of sin, these once-born men, with all the twice-dead saints who turned sinners again, they, along with the devils that ruled over them, shall be judged by the Ruler of heaven and hell – Jesus Christ – and He will take them against their own will, and "cast [them] into the Lake of Fire and brimstone…and [they] shall be tormented day and night for ever and ever" (Rev. 20:10)!

SALVATION

Psalm 110:4
The LORD hath sworn, and **will not repent**, Thou art a priest **for ever** after the order of Melchizedek.

Psalm 132:11
The LORD hath sworn in truth unto David; He **will not turn from it**; Of the fruit of thy body will I set upon thy throne.

"will not repent… forever" – Ps. 110:4
"will not turn from it" – Ps. 132:11
"suffer My faithfulness to fail…
My Covenant will I not break
nor alter the thing that is gone out of My lips…
…I will not lie…" – Ps. 89:33-35
"shall not return" – Isa. 45:23
"it shall not return unto Me void" – Isa. 55:11
"repentance shall be hid from Mine eyes" – Hos. 13:14

Psalm 89:33-35

Nevertheless my lovingkindness will I not utterly take from him, nor **suffer my faithfulness to fail**.
My covenant will I not break, nor **alter the thing that is gone out of my lips**. Once have I sworn by my holiness that **I will not lie** unto David.

Isaiah 45:23

I have sworn by Myself, the word is gone out of my mouth in righteousness, and **shall not return**, That unto Me every knee shall bow, every tongue shall swear.

Isaiah 55:11-12

So shall my word be that goeth forth out of my mouth: **it shall not return unto Me void**, but it shall accomplish that which I please, and it shall prosper in the thing whereto I sent it.
For ye shall go out with joy, and be led forth with peace: the mountains and the hills shall break forth before you into singing, and all the trees of the field shall clap their hands.

Hosea 13:14

I will ransom them from the power of the grave; I will redeem them from death: O death, I will be thy plagues; O grave, I will be thy destruction: **repentance shall be hid from Mine eyes**.

You see, the word of the Lord was spoken, and then it was not brought to pass because it was "**prolonged**" from being performed, but there is a day and generation in which "it shall be no more **prolonged**" (Ezek. 12:25). There is a "day" in which, God says, "There shall none of My words be **prolonged** any more, but the word which I have spoken shall be done" (Ezek. 12:28). Do you know what "day" this is? There is a "time" in which God has chosen, God says, "that I will perform that good thing **which I have promised**" (Jer. 33:14), even though it was stalled, repented of, and prolonged for so many generations! Do you know this "time"? My reader, don't despise how God stalls the Day of His coming! He does this for us, because we have not come to repentance, and He does not want to bring the Final Judgment of His return prematurely, while there are certain elect saints still in unrepentance, while there is a Bride yet blemished and wrinkled. "The Lord is not slack concerning His promise, as some men count slackness; but is longsuffering to us-ward, not willing that any should perish, but that all should come to repentance" (2 Peter 3:9)! Nevertheless, there is a day in which ALL of that which was promised shall come to pass.

God wants men to know the surety of His Covenant, meaning that it is "everlasting," "ordered," "and sure" (2 Sam. 23:5), which is to signify that it is set in order to be fulfilled in its ordained "day" and "time". This "everlasting," "ordered," and "sure" purpose of God is also called the "sure mercies of David" (Isa. 55:3). In manifold ways which God argues, proves, and exclaims, these promised mercies are and shall be "SURE"! God wants men to know that there are certain things in which

He speaks, as "the LORD," and not in the ways of man (Mal. 3:6), things which are irrevocably spoken from the loft of His absolute sovereignty over all things. Likewise, when God speaks of something in the loft of His Person, outside of the capabilities within God's condescension, He links these words with a certain righteousness, that, if these words were not fulfilled, then there would be unrighteousness in God, for it is righteous for God to fulfill the word when it is connected to eternal purposes of "love" or "hate" (Rom. 9:13). With this in mind, it is understandable why the saints were and are utterly perplexed when God does not fulfill a word which He has spoken, and by compulsion they thence resolve that there must be some high *mystery* hidden in the heavens, which is veiled in a most holy, higher righteousness. This *mystery* is progressively and increasingly explained throughout the centuries, thanks to God, Who allowed that the prophets would be employed in the task of seeking out, standing attentive to, and watching after explanations of any further revelation, and they spent their whole life purpose inquiring of such **mysteries** (1 Peter 1:10). At "sundry times" in "diverse manners" (Heb. 1:1) they did see, understand, and from thence declared mysteries "hid in God" since "the beginning of the world" (Eph. 3:9). These eternal, unchanging, and timeless purposes of God are spoken on earth by His Spirit through prophets, and thus, it is only right that God would fulfill these words by His determinate powers, which we know do transcend creation and time. Therefore, because it is only right that these eternal purposes come to pass, or because it is righteous that nothing in creation and time can disrupt the good desires of God, we can understand that God wants to show men the certainty of what He says, and so, when He speaks a word that is, God says, "gone out of My mouth in righteousness" (Isa. 45:23), we will know that it is God's righteousness which will fulfill that word! Have you ever meekly pled with the Lord that He would hear your prayers and save you, pleading that, an answer to your prayers for this cause would be a deed done, as David said to God, "in Thy righteousness" (Ps. 143:1)? It is important then to understand what this means! The question this verse should arouse in us is, what is righteous about a word that goes forth, God says, "in righteousness"? As in this word which is encased in God's claimed and stated "righteousness," which is cited in Isaiah 45:23 and Psalm 143:1, so also God wants to show what is *faithful about His faithfulness* (Ps. 89:33), and what is *the truthfulness of truth* and *the uprightness of upright* when deeds are "done in truth and uprightness" (Ps. 111:8). You see, when God speaks a word in His ways, which are, "in righteousness" (Isa. 45:23), "by My holiness" (Ps. 89:35), and "done in truth and uprightness" (Ps. 111:8), or any other like attribute that is connected to the words and deeds of God, we must come to understand exactly what eternal purposes God is pointing toward, to know, what exactly what God's attributes will eventually accomplish, and, what exactly God is assuring us of.

> "They **stand fast for ever** and **ever**, and are done in truth and uprightness." – Ps. 11:8

First let me address this…all of these attributes are spoken of as eternal realities in the Person of God, realities which shall be proven as everlasting throughout all the happenings of time; they shall be known by all men, especially redeemed men, and they will magnify Him in these titles with everlasting praises, and that means that these words are directly in reference to the FOREVER purposes of God which He will perform on the earth! Read the following verses and remember, no word in scripture is without immeasurable depths, deeper-than-the-oceans unsearchable depths, and no word is without invaluable richness, even riches which are hidden from angels' eyes in heaven. Therefore, when the forevers of God are stated, bound with everlasting attributes, these are not idle words of empty detail about vague, unspecific, and unidentifiable attributes in God's words and deeds! Heaven's most dignified and godly angels do long to look upon such mysterious riches, and, lo, these mysteries are not explained in heaven! Nay, they are found on earth, in the hearts of the prophets and saints, on the tongues of holy men, even the things which the breath of God called – "the unsearchable riches of Christ" and "the manifold wisdom of God" (Eph. 3:9-10), "which things the angels desire to look into" (1 Peter 1:12)! Men of such caliber were: the prophets of old and new, and the 1st century Church which was beautified into a "glorious Church" (Eph. 5:27), which is to say that they were the envy of the Jews, a bright beacon of hope for the entire Gentile world, which was turning the devil's world upside down – making men who had formerly fled from God to flee from sin. Now listen, my reader, if these men understood something **exactly specific** when they worshipped God for His "righteousness", "holiness", "truth", and "uprightness", or at other times, His "faithfulness", "mercy", "covenant", "wonder", and "praise", it remains therefore that we need to study, identify, and discover what they understood about these attributes, with exactitude, so that we, like them, might worship God "with the understanding also" (1 Cor. 14:15).

> "Thy **faithfulness** is unto all generations" – Ps. 119:90
> "His work is honourable and glorious: His righteousness endureth for ever" – Ps. 111:3
> "the truth of the LORD endureth for ever" – Ps. 117:2

The Holy Ghost renders each of these attributes as the chief praises of God, and foremost of all, the inspired psalmist repeated – "He is good...His mercy endureth for ever." Therefore, it remains as a vital priority for us, who are the children of untimely birth into an adulterous generation, that we must understand, more than all other attributes hailed in God – the MERCY of God – and exactly, what is so "plenteous" (Ps. 103:8), "rich" (Rom. 9:23) in it, and what is surely meant by how it endures forever.

> "Mercy shall be built up for ever" – Ps. 89:2

The mercy of God is the motivator for salvation, as we have exhaustively addressed in the chapter, "Mercy On Whom I Will Have Mercy," and thus for it to be "built up for ever," it must be that His Covenant, or the agreement of salvation, must also be forever. Therefore is it written: "He commanded His Covenant for ever" (Ps. 111:9).

"The works of His hands are verity and judgement; all His commandments are **sure**. They **stand fast for ever** and **ever**, and are done in truth and uprightness. He sent redemption unto His people: **He commanded His covenant for ever**: Holy and Reverend is His Name. The fear of the LORD is the beginning of wisdom: a good understanding have all they that do His commandments: **His praise endureth for ever**" – Ps. 111:7-10

The Lord's mercy endures forever to establish His Covenant of salvation in its final consummation, and therefore, men praise God that His mercy and faithfulness endure forever EVEN if and though, at present, mercy is not establishing the Covenant of salvation for regenerate individuals who are born into a backslidden generation. Do you believe that? Ezekiel 20 is like no other chapter in the whole of scripture, but by theme and purpose there are many other chapters which are devoted to communicate the exact same theme at hand! Such chapters are Nehemiah 9, Deuteronomy 7, Psalm 89, and Psalm 106. By now you know the content of these chapters, but look with me at the very shocking attributes of God in view, attributes which I did forbear to highlight heretofore!

Remember that Deuteronomy 7 addresses the Abrahamic Covenant promises, Psalm 89 the Davidic Covenant promises, and Nehemiah 9 and Psalm 106 the Abrahamic and Davidic promises – each chapter is devoted to communicate how the promises have been *breached* in the former generation or generations (Deut. 7, Neh. 9, Psalm 106), and/or, the promises have been, and are being, *breached* at the present generation (Psalm 89, Psalm 106). Furthermore, Psalm 89 and Psalm 106 are entirely devoted to the acknowledgment of the promises of God in the Covenants, so also the psalmists do rehearse what God said and did, but most importantly, these psalms are an intercessory lamentation for the Covenants that were presently breached, broken, cast off, and destroyed in their day; thus they cried out for salvation – but what is so amazing about the psalms is that they still praise the Lord for His faithfulness and mercy, in that it is *FOREVER ENDURING* while they are in the midst of a breach of promise, wrath is breaking forth, and they are bewildered, astonished, and full of perplexity!

PSALM 89 - THE DAVIDIC COVENANT -
"I will sing of the mercies of the LORD for ever: with my mouth will I make known Thy faithfulness to all generations. For I have said, Mercy shall be built up for ever: Thy faithfulness shalt Thou establish in the heavens." (Psalm 89:1-2)
"And the heavens shall praise Thy wonders, O LORD: Thy faithfulness also in the congregation of the saints." (Psalm 89:5)

"O LORD God of hosts, who is strong LORD like unto Thee? Or to Thy faithfulness round about Thee?" (Psalm 89:8)

"But My **faithfulness** and My **mercy** shall be with Him: and in My Name shall his horn be exalted." (Psalm 89:24)

Amazing! Is it not? They were singing of the mercy and faithfulness of God, but they had no idea where it was, and were in the utter agony of oblivion in why it was gone, failed, and fallen, from the previous generations longstanding, unto theirs. Nevertheless, they knew it would rise again! But would it rise again with them *in particular*, even their generation of all the generations of men past and future? This they knew not. This is just like the praises of God which Habakkuk uttered in chapter 3, and how he pled, "in wrath remember **mercy**", for he desired mercy for himself so that he would be hid in the day of wrath, but even if he was not, nor all of Israel, he did still sing and praise the Lord for salvation!

> Habakkuk 3:16-19
>
> "When I heard, my belly trembled; my lips quivered at the voice: rottenness entered into my bones, and I trembled in myself, that I might rest in the day of trouble: when he cometh up unto the people, he will invade them with his troops. Although the fig tree shall not blossom, neither shall fruit be in the vines; the labour of the olive shall fail, and the fields shall yield no meat; the flock shall be cut off from the fold, and there shall be no herd in the stalls: Yet I will rejoice in the LORD, I will joy in the God of my salvation. The LORD God is my strength, and He will make my feet like hinds' feet, and He will make me to walk upon mine high places. To the chief singer on my stringed instruments."

This is amazing to me! "Seek ye the LORD, all ye meek of the earth, which have wrought His judgment; seek righteousness, seek meekness: **it may be** ye shall be hid in the day of the LORD'S anger" (Zeph. 2:3). When you enter your church assembly and "sing of the mercies of the LORD for ever", what is so *forever* and *faithful* about the mercy of God that you are singing about? To the psalmists, it is not that those of the regenerate multitude can never fall away from, or fail to obtain, the promise of salvation, but it is that God will **eventually** and **finally**, in a great consummation, fulfill the promises in the **resurrection, and thence, changelessly forevermore.**

PSALM 106 - THE ABRAHAMIC & DAVIDIC COVENANTS-
"Praise ye the LORD. O give thanks unto the LORD; for He is good: for His **mercy endureth for ever.**" (Ps. 106:1)

This psalm is like as Psalm 89. Read Psalm 106:4-5, 47-48 – it is the psalmist's fervent appeal to be saved, for he is presently under the wrath of God. He prays for salvation, hoping that God may repent and remember the Covenant for him. The last verses of the psalm are prayers for saving grace, and unlike other psalms, there is no confident reckoning or triumphant proclamation that God has heard or will hear his prayer unto salvation. The psalm ends without any evidence that the man is confident that he is, or will be, saved, therefore, while presently under the wrath of God, here again, to my amazement, the psalmist's opening line is the same praise of God in Psalm 89 – "His mercy endureth for ever"! The psalmist desires for God to remember His Covenant (Lev. 26:42), which also is to remember him for personal salvation therein. The psalmist rehearses how great God's mercies have been in the past toward His wayward, backsliding people (like as the law commands that a man should do, see Psalm 78:5-7)...but specifically, the psalmist rehearses the **multitude of mercies** that are in God; the psalmist said, "we have sinned with our fathers, we have committed iniquity, we have done wickedly" (Ps. 106:6), in the beginning of salvation in the Abrahamic Covenant, and after salvation in the Abrahamic Covenant was already begun and established, they "tempted God" to their great destruction thenceforth, so much so that God "should destroy them," and He did destroy many of them (Ps. 106:23), and yet, by the riches of His glorious mercy, the multitude of His mercies, God "saved" (Ps. 106:8) them in the beginning, and still, He continued to save a remnant thenceforth because Moses "stood before Him in the breach to turn away His wrath" (Ps. 106:23). After Moses' death (Ps. 106:33), it appears that the psalmist traces the future generations, beginning with Joshua, through the Judges, up into and through the Davidic Covenant until the final dispersion (I conjecture), and all the while, the psalmist points out and recognizes how many times Israel rebelled and deserved total annihilation (Ps. 106:34-43)...but God did not totally annihilate them, and did rather hear and save them when they were laden with "affliction," and thence when they lifted up an intercessory "cry" for salvation (Ps. 106:44). The psalmist recognizes that this cry and answer of salvation was the praise of God's glory, that He "remembered for them His Covenant, and repented according to **the multitude of His mercies**" (Ps. 106:45). For this reason, being instructed by the **near annihilation** and **scarce salvation** of God's people throughout the centuries, the psalmist praises God's mercy, that it is a great "multitude" of mercies that "endureth for ever" (Ps. 106:45, 1)! Therefore, because of this, the psalmist has hope, even though he is not presently saved, for he knows that God can, but is not obliged to, repent from destroying wrath and save him, when and if he calls upon Him. Having all of this in mind, it is then that the psalmist ends the song with this hopeful cry – "Save us, O LORD our God, and gather us from among the heathen, to give thanks unto Thy Holy Name, and triumph in Thy praise. Blessed be the LORD God of Israel **from everlasting to everlasting**: and let all the people say, Amen. Praise ye the LORD" (Ps. 106:47-48). What is **so good** about God, what is so **thankworthy** and **praiseworthy**, insomuch that it can be said, "His mercy endureth for ever" (Ps. 106:1)? It is that NOT ALL of the regenerate people God were castaways! Nay, shockingly, a small remnant is spared for present and/or eventual, consummating salvation, and "they shall inherit the land for ever..." (Isa. 60:21)! Is that what is amazing about the grace of God to you?

Deuteronomy 7 -THE ABRAHAMIC COVENANT-
"because the LORD loved you..." – Deut. 7:8

"because He would keep the oath which He had sworn unto your fathers..." – Deut. 7:8
"He is God, the faithful God" – Deut. 7:9
"which keepeth Covenant and mercy" – Deut. 7:9

This faithfulness of God is mentioned in reference to the following: the parents of the audience that God is herein speaking to did fall away from their salvation and were lost, and God's mercy, and His promised oath - and covenant - keeping faithfulness, are magnified in this very specific way, that the generation now in Covenant with God is raised up for salvation in the stead of their parents! This is undeserved! The children of the castaway parents deserved total annihilation. God desired and spoke to accomplish (see Numbers 14:11-12) a total annihilation of them, but He did not do this because He is an oath- and Covenant-keeping God in mercy and faithfulness! Now, what is so loving, merciful, faithful, and keeping about God? It is that some, even that anyone, even a small remnant at all, or any at all of the whole multitude of regenerate persons, are saved, in your generation and/or in the end of time, and it is not that none can be lost or fall away who were formerly saved, otherwise the parents of this generation would have been preserved! Furthermore, God forewarned this generation that if they did not maintain His command to them, which required holiness from the Canaanites (see Deut. 7:11-12, 1-5, 25-26), then God warns them, even this remnant, that He will destroy them "suddenly" (Deut. 7:4), for God had made a name for Himself in the castaway wrath He showed to former generations when He: "repayeth them that hate Him to their face, to destroy them: He will not be slack to him that hateth Him, He will repay him to his face" (Deut. 7:10) – He is willing to keep that reputation. The language here, in Deuteronomy 7, which very specifically speaks that God keeps His Covenant and oath to the magnification of His mercy and faithfulness...became a foundational understanding of what the mercy and faithfulness of God was; therefore, henceforth the people of God do echo these attributes of God in prayers, praises, and prophetic books, with the exact same meaning as Deuteronomy 7. All events of history, including Deuteronomy 7, sung the same sounds in the same songs, resounding the everlasting understanding – the Lord is "the Great, the Mighty, and the Terrible God, Who keepest Covenant and mercy" (Neh. 9:32). This is written, as you can see, in Nehemiah 9:32, and it is a comprehensive summary of the biblical history of God's people. Nehemiah built the same historical and contextual foreground of God's words and deeds, tracing it through history, event to event, until finally, Nehemiah lifted up the praise of what is so merciful about the Covenant-keeping virtues of God. Oh! It is the multitude of God's Covenant-keeping mercies that salvific mercy is available at all for latter generations, when, behold, He did reprobate the former...thus God is "terrible" and merciful, and, behold, He has "goodness and severity" (Rom. 11:22)! "Behold therefore the goodness and severity of God: on them which fell, severity; but toward thee, goodness, if thou continue in His goodness: otherwise thou also shalt be cut off" (Rom. 11:22).

Amazingly, to the staggering of my soul into worship, the ever-enduring mercy of God is praised in backslidden generations, even while no mercy is presently given and the promises remain breached! Why? Oh, how happy I am to declare it to my reader! The brethren knew that, *one day*, though it may not be *their day*, the promises will be fulfilled, or in other words, though wrath is burning now in *their day*, it will not burn forever! Wrath seems like it burns forever, but Oh! God's mercy endures forever! Yea, there is a greater and longer lasting energy than wrath, at least for God's chosen people, and that is, "His mercy endureth for ever!"

> "And He shall send Jesus Christ, which before was preached unto
> you: Whom the heaven must receive until the times of **restitution
> of all things**, which God hath spoken by the mouth of all His
> holy prophets since the world began." (Acts 3:20-21)

The Covenants are clear to declare a forever salvation which is with a forever enduring mercy (with all other attributes included in their eternal titles), and these things will be fulfilled in the **consummation** or **restitution of all things**. The prophets who communicated these Covenants spoke, as a whole, not just of the second advent of Christ (which initiates the resurrection or the condescension withdrawn), because if anyone will be saved in any generation before the resurrection, it is because mercy endured beyond the near-annihilating wrath of God in their personal and corporate lives, but saved individuals or generations will, at the resurrection, rise again to inherit any promises which were left unfulfilled in their day, and they were saved in a salvific work which was experiential in enough of the promises, so as to be finally saved when they stand before the Judgment Seat. When these persons stand before the Judgment or at the millennial reign of Christ, and afterwards, they will obtain all the promises in their forevers, forevermore!

> "...the times of **restitution of all things**..." (Acts 3:20-21)

> "then shall ye know that I the LORD **have spoken it, and performed it**, saith the
> LORD." (Ezek. 37:14)

At THIS TIME – the resurrection – men will know that God's word is performed, and therefore God says – "then shall ye know that I the LORD have spoken it, and **performed it**, saith the LORD" (Ezek. 37:14). How do I know what time this is, and what is the time that the Abrahamic Covenant shall be finally fulfilled forevermore? Look carefully at this time, saints, so that heretofore you may look forward to it, praising God, for the eventual deeds which God's everlasting mercies shall perform. Look now at the context in which Ezekiel 37:14 was written in:

> Ezekiel 37:12-14 **- THE ABRAHAMIC COVENANT FULFILLED-**
> Therefore prophesy and say unto them, Thus saith the Lord GOD; Behold,
> O my people, I will open your graves, and cause you to come up out of
> your graves, and bring you into the land of Israel. And ye shall know
> that I am the LORD, when I have opened your graves, O my people, and

brought you up out of your graves, And shall put my spirit in you, and ye shall live, and I shall place you in your own land: **then shall ye know that I the LORD have spoken it, and performed it, saith the LORD.**

"Thy people also shall be all righteous... they shall inherit the land for ever... (Isa. 60:21)

This time is "The Condescension Withdrawn," which happens at the resurrection. At this time, God will fulfill everything promised and covenanted, and as the Lord said – "then" – but not another time, "then shall ye know that I the LORD **have spoken it, and performed it**, saith the LORD" (Ezek. 37:14). When God says that He speaks something "in righteousness" (Isa. 45:23), "by My holiness" (Ps. 89:35), "done in truth and uprightness" (Ps. 111:8), it is meant to make clear that He will not fail to fulfill what He is speaking of at that very moment, so that the promise will not "**fail**", "**break**", "**alter**", or "**lie**", or, that His word "**shall not return**" (Isa. 45:23), and again, "**shall not return unto Me void**" (Isa. 55:11), because at the time of the resurrection, God said, "**repentance shall be hid from Mine eyes**" (Hos. 13:14). Why and how is it possible that repentance shall then, at this time, be hid from God's eyes? IT IS BECAUSE of the resurrection, or "The Condescension Withdrawn." Review the verses from which these quotations are made, and you can evidently see that the consummating time in which God will bring to pass these changeless words is after the resurrection, and, if ever you were saved by the promises or Covenants of God in any single generation, your salvation was but a partial expression of a greater fulfillment to come!

> Isaiah 45:23
> I have sworn by Myself, the word is gone out of My mouth in righteousness, and **shall not return**, That unto Me every knee shall bow, every tongue shall swear.
>
> Isaiah 55:11-12
> So shall My word be that goeth forth out of My mouth: **it shall not return unto Me void,** but it shall accomplish that which I please, and it shall prosper in the thing whereto I sent it.
> For ye shall go out with joy, and be led forth with peace: the mountains and the hills shall break forth before you into singing, and all the trees of the field shall clap their hands.
>
> Hosea 13:14
> I will ransom them from the power of the grave; I will redeem them from death: O death, I will be thy plagues; O grave, I will be thy destruction: **repentance shall be hid from Mine eyes.**

Think of it! Think of such a time when God will never repent from the purpose of love and mercy! So that, everlastingly, God will fulfill such words which He spoke when He said:

- "neither will I hide My face **any more** from them: for I have poured out My Spirit upon the house of Israel" – Ezek. 39:29
- "with **everlasting kindness** will I have mercy on thee" – Isa. 54:8
- "so **have I sworn** that I would not be wroth with thee, nor rebuke thee" – Isa. 54:9
- "my **kindness shall not depart** from thee, neither shall the Covenant of peace be **removed**, saith the LORD that hath mercy on thee" – Isa. 54:10
- "I will not **turn away** from them… they **shall not depart** from Me" - Jer. 32:37-44

These words of promise make up "an everlasting Covenant" which is called "the sure mercies of David" (Isa. 55:3). These promises, and others like them, shall have their fulfillment in the resurrection, but, these promises are also ***double sensed***. They do begin and establish the New Covenant of Christ, partially and present-progressively, but they will have their final consummating fulfillment in the resurrection. Other 1st and 2nd Advent promises that are double sensed in this way are: Jeremiah 31:31-40, Jeremiah 32:37-44, Isaiah 54-55, Hosea 2:18-23, and Isaiah 49. The Lord will initiate and partially fulfill the promises of God in the 1st Advent because of His faithfulness, like as His faithfulness continued and did not totally annihilate God's saved people in generations past, generations before the New Covenant, and when the problem of sin is no more during the time of the resurrection, or the 2nd Advent of Christ, it is then that God will finally fulfill the Covenants in Christ – "Because of the LORD that is faithful" (Isa. 49:7). The power of these promises is progressively being fulfilled in dispensations, and during times of wrath they are kept alive, and enduring, notwithstanding those who are reprobated, and so, the New Covenant dispensation which is before the resurrection is powered by the very same promises which shall eventually and finally save literal, physical Israel, and in turn, empower the millennial reign after the 1st resurrection, and then, also, empower the full manifestation of the New Heaven and New Earth reality after the 2nd resurrection. The stress of this Covenant is a looking forward to the consummation – for in its consummation, all of these forever glories shall be changelessly established! Read how the prophets continually referenced this "time" of forever glories to be a time of the resurrection, which is also the same time when, simultaneously, God will establish the Kingdom of God to cover the whole world, and like the saints, the world – itself – will be regenerated and made new.

> "And in that day will I make a covenant for them with the beasts of the field, and with the fowls of heaven, and with the creeping things of the ground: and I will break the bow and the sword and the battle out of the earth, and will make them to lie down safely. And I will betroth thee unto Me for ever; yea, I will betroth thee unto Me in righteousness, and in judgment, and in lovingkindness, and in mercies. I will even betroth thee unto Me in faithfulness: and thou shalt know the LORD. And it shall come to pass in that day, I will hear, saith the LORD, I will hear the

heavens, and they shall hear the earth; And the earth shall hear the corn, and the wine, and the oil; and they shall hear Jezreel. And I will sow her unto Me in the earth; and I will have mercy upon her that had not obtained mercy; and I will say to them which were not My people, Thou art My people; and they shall say, Thou art my God." (Hosea 2:18-23)

"The voice of joy, and the voice of gladness, the voice of the bridegroom, and the voice of the bride, the voice of them that shall say, Praise the LORD of hosts: **for the LORD is good; for His mercy endureth for ever**: and of them that shall bring the sacrifice of praise into the house of the LORD. For I will cause to return the captivity of the land, as at the first, saith the LORD." (Jeremiah 33:11)

Here again, at this time we can see the age-old, long-lasting praise of God exclaimed – "For the LORD is good; for His mercy endureth for ever"! This is like a capstone, a pillar's crown, which magnifies to me that then, at this time, mercy has endured throughout all the evil days! This hallowed time is what the saints of every age waited for, and for them, at this time, forever has become "the now." Forevermore the Davidic Throne will be lifted high, and down the steep, hallowed, white-transparent steps which lead thereto flows a waterfall of righteousness, faithfulness, and mercy, and time has ceased to exist!

I have seen an amazing thing in the scriptures! Firstly, it is God's mercy that He keeps any men alive at all, for He would be just if He decided upon the kindled repentings which raged in His holy heart, and again be sorry that He made man upon the earth (Neh. 6:5-7) until He destroys them all. Still today, everyone, from their birth – "every imagination of the thoughts of his heart" is "only evil continually" – nevertheless, God set a bow in the heavens that He will never destroy the world again like at Noah's day, which means, namely, that God will not destroy the world again by water. Now the Noahic rainbow does declare for us this unchanging purpose in God, and the love of God is magnified over His enemies, in that, "He maketh His sun to rise on the evil and on the good, and sendeth rain on the just and on the unjust" (Matt. 6:45). Thus it is God's mercy and love that anyone, any man at all, is kept alive! I believe that this is one of the main things which is meant by the sayings:

"Thy mercy, O LORD, is in the heavens; and Thy faithfulness reacheth unto the clouds" (Psalm 36:5).
"For Thy mercy is great above the heavens: and Thy truth reacheth unto the clouds" (Psalm 108:4).
"Thy faithfulness is unto all generations: Thou hast established the earth, and it abideth" (Psalm 119:90).

Secondarily, it is the mercy of God that He is "longsuffering" toward His

582

people, because they provoke Him, over and over, to desire a full destruction of them by a total annihilation (2 Peter 3:9). It is the mercy of God that any of the regenerate multitudes are alive at all! And, there are certain other verses which are connected with the faithfulness of God "in the heavens," like Psalm 36:5, and these verses refer to the ever-enduring mercy of God to accomplish the final and eventual salvation of Israel...

> "For this is as the waters of Noah unto Me: for as I have sworn that the waters of Noah should no more go over the earth; so have I sworn that I would not be wroth with thee, nor rebuke thee." (Isa. 54:9)

At the return of Christ, which is also the resurrection, this verse will be accomplished, as formerly noted, but what is astonishing to me is how God affirmed His ever-enduring faithfulness when He connected it with the fixed positions of creation. In this, He showed the verity of His word which fixed them in their places when they were created at the beginning of the world, and also, we can see the verity of His word of mercy which was spoken in the days of Noah. All of this is to say, as God keeps all these things in their places, fixed, firm, enduring, and sure, so God will keep the purpose of Israel's final salvation. God is powering this eternal purpose for Israel like the undying energies of these created beacons of love, health, and life. BUT, God also says that they are emblems which reveal another unchanging, eternal, unrepentant purpose in God – which is to save His people in all the forevers – and so God says:

> "His seed shall endure for ever, and his throne **as the sun** before Me. It shall be established for ever **as the moon**, and as a faithful witness in the heaven. Selah." (Psalm 89:36-37)

Read carefully of those prophecies which connect these two things:

THE ABRAHAMIC AND DAVIDIC COVENANTS FULFILLED

> "The voice of joy, and the voice of gladness, the voice of the Bridegroom, and the voice of the Bride, the voice of them that shall say, Praise the LORD of hosts: **for the LORD is good; for His mercy endureth for ever**...For I will cause to return the captivity of the land, as at the first, saith the LORD... I will perform that good thing which I have promised...For thus saith the LORD; David shall never want a man to sit upon the throne of the house of Israel...Thus saith the LORD; **If ye can break My Covenant of the day, and My Covenant of the night, and that there should not be day and night in their season; Then may also My Covenant be broken with David My servant, that he should not have a son to reign upon his throne; and with the Levites the priests, My ministers.** As the host of heaven cannot be numbered, neither the sand of the sea measured: so will I multiply the seed of David My servant, and the Levites that minister unto Me...Thus saith the LORD; If My Covenant

be not with day and night, and if I have not appointed the ordinances of heaven and earth; Then will I cast away the seed of Jacob, and **David My servant**, so that I will not take any of his seed to be rulers over **the seed of Abraham**, Isaac, and Jacob: for I will cause their captivity to return, and have mercy on them." (Jer. 33:11, 14, 17, 20-22, 25-26)

Do you see how God specifically referenced "David" and "the seed of Abraham"? Do you see how He referenced the stars and sand as a witness of what God will surely do on earth, without repentance, in direct reference to the words of the Abrahamic Covenant? So also, God referenced His Covenant with the day and night, which also is with the sun and moon…now look carefully, and see how much God repeatedly emphasizes this peculiar witness to affirm what will become of the King Messiah Who will be upon the Davidic throne: →

"They shall fear Thee **as long as the sun and moon endure**, throughout all generations. He shall come down like rain upon the mown grass: as showers that water the earth. In His days shall the righteous flourish; and abundance of peace **so long as the moon endureth**. He shall have dominion also from sea to sea, and from the river unto the ends of the earth. They that dwell in the wilderness shall bow before Him; and his enemies shall lick the dust. The kings of Tarshish and of the isles shall bring presents: the kings of Sheba and Seba shall offer gifts. Yea, all kings shall fall down before him: all nations shall serve Him." (Psalm 72:5-11)

"His name shall **endure for ever**: His name shall be **continued as long as the sun**: and men shall be blessed in Him: all nations shall call Him blessed. Blessed be the LORD God, the God of Israel, Who only doeth wondrous things. And blessed be his glorious name **for ever**: and let **the whole earth** be filled with his glory; Amen, and Amen." (Psalm 72:17-19)

"All the ends of the world shall remember and turn unto the LORD: and all the kindreds of the nations shall worship before Thee. For the kingdom is the LORD'S: and He is the governor among the nations. All they that be fat upon earth shall eat and worship: all they that go down to the dust shall bow before Him: and none can keep alive his own soul. A seed shall serve Him; it shall be accounted to the Lord for a generation. They shall come, and shall declare His righteousness unto a people that shall be born, that He hath done this."
(Psalm 22:27-31)

As the scriptures state, this Davidic throne shall rule the whole world, and this is in fulfillment of the word spoken in Numbers 14:21, a word which was

584

rewarded to Moses through his intercessory prayers against a total annihilating wrath - "But as truly as I live, **all the earth** shall be filled with the glory of the LORD" (Numbers 14:21).

"And the LORD shall be King over **all the earth**: in that day shall there be one LORD, and His Name One." (Zechariah 14:9)

"**All nations** whom Thou hast made shall come and worship before Thee, O Lord; and shall glorify Thy Name." (Psalm 86:9)

"For **the earth shall be filled with the knowledge of the glory of the LORD**, as the waters cover the sea." (Habakkuk 2:14)

"**The Kingdoms of this world** are become the kingdoms of our Lord, and of His Christ; and He shall reign **for ever and ever**." (Rev. 11:15)

Now remember, God said to David - personally - "But My faithfulness and My Mercy shall be with him: and in My Name shall his horn be exalted" (Psalm 89:24). And God said of David's seed – exactly his seed, which was Solomon – that his throne would last forever, but shockingly, God shows His higher-righteous and irresistible powers when He calls Jesus Christ by the Name – David – making Christ fulfill this word about David, and, that Christ's Kingdom shall be forever just as the Davidic Covenant states:

Jeremiah 30:9
But they shall serve the LORD their God, and **David** their king, whom I will raise up unto them.

Ezekiel 34:23-24
And I will set up one shepherd over them, and he shall feed them, even my servant **David**; he shall feed them, and he shall be their shepherd. And I the LORD will be their God, and my servant **David** a prince among them; I the LORD have spoken it.

Ezekiel 37:24-25
And **David** my servant shall be king over them; and they all shall have one shepherd: they shall also walk in my judgments, and observe my statutes, and do them. And they shall dwell in the land that I have given unto Jacob my servant, wherein your fathers have dwelt; and they shall dwell therein, even they, and their children, and their children's children for ever: and my servant **David** shall be their prince **for ever**.

Hosea 3:5

Afterward shall the children of Israel return, and seek the LORD their God, and **David** their king; and shall fear the LORD and His goodness in the latter days.

Psalm 145:13
Thy Kingdom is an **everlasting** Kingdom, and Thy dominion endureth throughout **all generations**.

Daniel 2:44
And in the days of these kings shall the God of heaven set up a kingdom, which shall **never be destroyed**: and the kingdom shall not be left to other people, but it shall break in pieces and consume all these kingdoms, and it shall stand **for ever**.

This is the mysterious fulfillment of the Davidic Covenant in Christ! Does that amaze you? It should! Most well-studied Christians do know this, but there is something else that is astounding which we must understand so that we can praise God for what He is, according to the scriptures, most praiseworthy for! How is God made great? Read carefully:

Psalm 98:1-9
A Psalm. O sing unto the LORD a new song; for He hath done marvellous things: His right hand, and His holy arm, hath gotten Him the victory.
The LORD hath made known His **salvation**: His **righteousness** hath He openly shewed in the sight of the heathen.
He hath remembered His **mercy** and His **truth** toward the house of Israel: **all the ends of the earth have seen the salvation of our God.**
Make a joyful noise unto the LORD, all the earth: make a loud noise, and rejoice, and sing praise.
Sing unto the LORD with the harp; with the harp, and the voice of a psalm.
With trumpets and sound of cornet make a joyful noise before the LORD, the King.
Let **the sea** roar, and the fulness thereof; **the world**, and they that dwell therein.
Let **the floods** clap their hands: let **the hills** be joyful together
Before the LORD; for He cometh to judge the earth: with righteousness shall He judge the world, and the people with equity.

Do you see how the psalmist, under the inspiration of God, is speaking to "the sea", "the world", "the floods", and "the hills", but why? Have you ever understood it? We can well remember how Psalm 19:1-3 describes creation in a personified way, making it to have a voice of communication, for, its existence and purposes do communicate that which every language can understand, but there is *something different* than personification spoken HERE in the Davidic Kingdom's worldwide fulfillment. This is the time when worldwide salvation is revealed, the time when God comes to establish His Kingdom and judgment, a time which is simultaneously the resurrection, and – with climatic GLORY – this is the time when the world – the plants, animals, soils, seas, the sun, stars, and universal laws in created order – everything – shall be regenerated! What I mean is that at this time, the earth will go from what it is now, namely, how it "groaneth and travaileth in pain" (Rom. 8:22), for now it is subject to the curse of sin which is called "the bondage of corruption" (Rom. 8:21). At Christ's return - then - the whole world and all that is in it will be gloriously translated from **groaning** and **travail** into **singing**, like as a standing ovation of **applause**, even all the trees of the field **clapping their hands**, and how?! Why? Why will "the sea" and "the world" "roar", and why will "the floods clap their hands," and why will "the hills be joyful together" (Ps. 98:7-8)!? For such a long-lasting amount of time, the promises of God have been stalled, or prolonged, and for so long a time God has long-suffered His sinning saints (2 Peter 3:9), but at this time that the created world itself praises God, it is because God brought His Davidic Kingdom upon the earth with His appearing, and with this: the sudden, immediate, and glorious "manifestation of the sons of God" (Rom. 8:19)! Yea, just as the sunrise is like a bridegroom coming out of his chamber (Ps. 19:5), then God, even Christ, will be The "Bridegroom coming out of His chamber" to rescue His Bride, and He "rejoiceth as a strong man to run a race" (Ps. 19:5) – "And the city had no need of the sun, neither of the moon, to shine in it: for the glory of God did lighten it, and the Lamb is the light thereof. And the nations of them which are saved shall walk in the light of it: and the kings of the earth do bring their glory and honour into it" (Rev. 21:23-24)!

"For the LORD will have mercy on Jacob, and will yet choose Israel, and set them in their own land: and the strangers shall be joined with them, and they shall cleave to the house of Jacob...The LORD hath broken the staff of the wicked, and the scepter of the rulers. He who smote the people in wrath with a continual stroke, he that ruled the nations in anger, is persecuted, and none hindereth. The whole earth is at rest, and is quiet: they break forth into singing. Yea, the fir trees rejoice at thee, and the cedars of Lebanon, saying, Since thou art laid down, no feller is come up against us." (Isa. 14:1, 5-8)

"Sing, O ye heavens; for the LORD hath done it: shout, ye lower parts of the earth: break forth into singing, ye mountains, O forest, and every tree therein: for the LORD hath redeemed Jacob, and glorified himself in Israel." (Isa. 44:23)

"Behold, these shall come from far: and, lo, these from the north and from the west; and these from the land of Sinim. Sing, O heavens; and be joyful, O earth; and break forth into singing, O mountains: for the LORD hath comforted His people, and will have mercy upon His afflicted...Thus saith the Lord GOD, Behold, I will lift up Mine hand to the Gentiles, and set up My

587

standard to the people: and they shall bring their sons in their arms, and thy daughters shall be carried upon their shoulders. And kings shall be thy nursing fathers, and their queens thy nursing mothers: they shall bow down to thee with their face toward the earth, and lick up the dust of thy feet; and thou shalt know that I am the LORD: for they shall not be ashamed that wait for Me…all flesh shall know that I the LORD am thy Saviour and thy Redeemer, the Mighty One of Jacob." (Isa. 49:12-13, 22-23, 26)

"For ye shall go out with joy, and be led forth with peace: the mountains and the hills shall break forth before you into singing, and all the trees of the field shall clap their hands" (Isa. 55:12).

"Let the heavens be glad, and let **the earth** rejoice: and let men say among the nations, The LORD reigneth. Let **the sea** roar, and the fulness thereof: let **the fields** rejoice, and all that is therein. Then shall **the trees** of **the wood** sing out at the presence of the LORD, because He cometh to judge the earth." (1 Chron. 16:31-33)

What a glory! The resurrection! And the whole world will follow the children of God in their final regeneration, called – "the redemption of our body" (Rom. 8:23). So it is written, my reader, and furthermore – I repeat – this is the exclamation of God's "righteousness", "faithfulness", and "truth"! Verily, from the beginning of salvation and to this final end, God is praised for His faithfulness, primarily that it will work this final and glorious END, and thanks be to God for every partial manifestation theretofore!

Romans 8:18-23
For I reckon that the sufferings of this present time are not worthy to be compared with the glory which shall be revealed in us. For the earnest expectation of the creature waiteth for the manifestation of the sons of God. For the creature was made subject to vanity, not willingly, but by reason of Him Who hath subjected the same in hope, Because the creature itself also shall be delivered from the bondage of corruption into the glorious liberty of the children of God. For we know that the whole creation groaneth and travaileth in pain together until now. And not only they, but ourselves also, which have the firstfruits of the Spirit, even we ourselves groan within ourselves, waiting for the adoption, to wit, the redemption of our body.

2 Corinthians 5:1-4
For we know that if our earthly house of this tabernacle were dissolved, we have a building of God, an house not made with

hands, eternal in the heavens. For in this we groan, earnestly desiring to be clothed upon with our house which is from heaven: If so be that being clothed we shall not be found naked. For we that are in this tabernacle do groan, being burdened: not for that we would be unclothed, but clothed upon, that mortality might be swallowed up of life.

Revelation 22:16-17
"I Jesus have sent Mine angel to testify unto you these things in the Churches. I am the root and the offspring of David, and the bright and morning star. And the Spirit and the Bride say, Come…"

"And righteousness shall be the girdle of his loins, and faithfulness the girdle of his reins." (Isaiah 11:5) → "The wolf also shall dwell with the lamb, and the leopard shall lie down with the kid; and the calf and the young lion and the fatling together; and a little child shall lead them." (Isaiah 11:6)

"O LORD, Thou *art* my God; I will exalt Thee, I will praise thy name; for Thou hast done wonderful *things; thy* **counsels of old** *are* faithfulness *and* **truth**." (Isaiah 25:1) → "He will swallow up death in victory; and the LORD GOD will wipe away tears from off all faces; and the rebuke of His people shall He take away from off all the earth: for the LORD hath spoken it." (Isa. 26:8)

"And He that sat upon the throne said, Behold, I make all things new. And He said unto me, Write: for these words are true and faithful." Revelation 21:5 → "And I saw a new heaven and a new earth: for the first heaven and the first earth were passed away; and there was no more sea." (Rev. 21:1)

"…an everlasting sign that shall not be cut off" (Isa. 55:13)!
"…everlasting joy shall be unto them" (Isa. 61:7)!

The Bride groans and mourns until the consummating forever comes – and the whole earth with her – they both are awaiting their own final and redemptive regeneration! O let us praise Him with understanding, then, when we sing of His faithfulness and mercy! Though we, like David, be near death by His wrath and judgments (Psalm 143:2-4, 7-9), and though we are scarcely escaping the annihilation that takes out so many saints throughout the generations, let us appeal rightly, before our God, on the basis of the righteousness of His faithfulness to save His Name (Ps. 143:11-12), and that we would be a part of this Name which He determined to preserve and glorify forever! Thus we can pray with understanding, and say - "Hear my prayer, O LORD, give ear to my supplications: in Thy faithfulness answer me, and in Thy righteousness" (Psalm 143:1).

Let the scriptures, and not a man's false imaginations, "shew forth" the "lovingkindness" and "faithfulness" of God (Ps. 92:2), in what it is exactly. According to the word of God in Psalm 92, and for a conclusion to this chapter...even though the wicked do flourish now (92:7), they will not flourish forever. They have risen up and *flourished,* but it is so that they might be destroyed forever (92:7), and even their destruction is not now so that the righteous do flourish instead, the psalmist explains, it shall eventually come to pass that the righteous will be saved and *flourishing* instead of the wicked (92:14). If this exaltation of the righteous did not eventually and forever happen, then it could be said that God is unrighteous, but God will do this very thing because He is righteous, to show forth His righteousness, as it was said in the last line of the psalm – "To shew that the LORD is upright: He is my rock, and there is no unrighteousness in Him" (92:15). When the psalmist undertakes the holy burden to "shew forth" the "lovingkindness" and "faithfulness" of the LORD, it is to show forth this very thing, that eventually and forever, the righteous shall be saved and flourishing forever in the Covenants of God, even though it is not so now!!

> "For I am the LORD, I change not; therefore ye sons of Jacob are not consumed." (Mal. 3:6)

"I AM THE LORD" means that God is not a man, and therefore, because "God is not a man" (Num. 23:19), and again, because "He is not a man" (1 Sam. 15:29), He will not change His mind or word from the eventual, final, and forever salvation of Israel, even though He has changed His mind and word of salvation over so many generations and persons. As it was then, in the lives of those generations and persons when His word changed, it will not be in the END, because *God in the ways of man* will cease to exist when God establishes His word toward Israel. Then, it will be the resurrection, "The Condescension Withdrawn". His word will be performed toward Israel, and why? "For I am God and not a man" (Hos. 11:9), God said, which means that this purpose and word which was spoken in His ways, His sovereignty, and according to His predestination, will come to pass, and understandably so, for everything that is spoken in His ways, instead of our ways, does not "change" (Mal. 3:6), is "immutable" (Heb. 6:17), has "no variableness" or "turning" (Jas. 1:17), and is "for ever" (Eccl. 3:14), because God "cannot lie" (Titus 1:2) and "will not lie nor repent" (1 Sam. 15:29, Num. 23:19); even so, it is "impossible for God to lie" (Heb. 6:18). This "gift" and "calling" of God is "without repentance" (Rom. 11:29), for THE FINAL generation of Israel which shall be saved in the END, who shall be saved condescension-removing resurrection power, and as for all the former Israelites which underwent a breach of promise or word, which is a repentance of God unto their damnation, even though they were formerly saved, and EVEN IF YOU DON'T UNDERSTAND HOW IT CAN BE SO, understand this – God can condescend to man in man's ways of purpose and word, and thus He can change, but eternity does always remain the same – and if you have a problem with that, then remember this one truth about God – how Job said, "He is not a man, as I am, that I should answer Him, and we should come together in judgment" (Job. 9:32).

590

"THE GOODNESS OF GOD LEADETH THEE TO REPENTANCE"
-ROMANS 2:4
CHAPTER 24

How is repentance wrought in the regenerate children of God?

"Their fear toward Me is taught by the precept of men." (Isa. 29:13)

I am continually amazed at how "the law is slacked", how "judgment doth never go forth", how "wrong judgment proceedeth" (Hab. 1:4)! A corrupted law and wrong judgments sent forth through unending media streams, echoed back again by the church on every corner – it is all like a house of mirrors built up around each human soul, making them lost in a warped reality. God says, "Blessed are the poor in spirit: for theirs is the Kingdom of heaven" (Matt. 5:3), but depravity makes men rich in self-righteousness, a pseudo-religious sincerity, and they are honest people who are honestly deceived. They are sincere and religious but Godless…and therefore the mass of men who live in a certain generation become the final authority of faith and practice. They all join hand in hand as one voice to collectively decide on matters of conscience and religion, self-inventing the moral compass of righteousness and unrighteousness, self-identifying the feeling and communications of God's love and wrath, and self-verifying the persons who will make up the populations of heaven and hell – and they do it all without God. The "thing" is right or wrong as the mass of people do decide it to be. Then, to help this cause, hell spawns for them such colorful preachers, a people's preacher instead of God's preacher, and they become, therefore, preacher parrots, pet preachers, repeating and resounding what tickles the clubhouse-congregation to passion and humor. Their sermons have just enough religious symbolism and biblical phraseology to suffocate the guilty conscience. The audience leaves built up in bondages, but feeling well, feeling like they are doing something right for "Jesus" in their life. The devil sought out for himself pastors that are, behold, "men after man's own heart". Willful sin is like an addictive hobby, and what is the matter with it, right!? Every "Christian" has his hobbies…and so, time passes, degeneration takes its awful course, and this collective conscience of once-born men unites in a terrifying direction – they become impassioned to destroy the true work of the living Spirit of Jesus Christ. "When He is come, He will reprove the world of sin, and of righteousness, and of judgment" (John 16:8), and when He moves in the midst of these religious circles, so that a person comes to be convicted of sin, then the people will call the conviction – itself – a sin, that the man is doubting God's love, but this is because their faith <u>is</u> a "peacefulness of conscience" on the broad way, a "solid faith" without sincere conviction, an unashamed boldness, without fear, while reveling in personal hypocrisies. Real sin is treated like pets to tame – "pet sins". The people learn to cage their pet sins just at the right times, some just for a little while, and the animals learn to behave themselves, you see, at least for the hour of religion, but these pet sins are coddled and cherished, the people are encouraged to "live abundantly" in a life which is condemned, and it is because their pet sins have become culturally acceptable pleasures. Behold the conclusion of the whole matter – God says, "Their fear toward Me is taught by the precept of men" (Isa. 29:13). Reader, do you think what people say about "the fear of God" is directly connected to a person's repentance?

> You may think that the unregenerate multitudes which meet the former description do need to hear about the condemning fear of God, but is there any way Satan has deceived us, even the regenerate multitudes, so that we have heresies which corrupt and suppress the messages of the Holy Spirit which provoke "godly fear" (Heb. 12:28) and "terror" (2 Cor. 5:11)?

Let us examine this through this question: → how is repentance wrought in the regenerate children of God? In answer to this question, many Calvinists would think of God's chastening, but I suppose that the most learned Calvinists would think that the man needs *a greater revelation of the love of God*. That can be rephrased to, "*a greater revelation of the goodness of God which leads to repentance*". Calvinists view God in His sovereign, eternal, changeless aspects of existence, and relate to God in this view alone, therefore they believe that God can **never be angry with a Christian again**. Therefore wrath will never be preached to the regenerate multitude to motivate repentance. Essentially, Calvinists believe that they do love God "<u>enough</u>" so that they will always repent. The Bible would call this *high-mindedness*, but nevertheless, this whole understanding permeates the very interpretive lens of a Calvinist as he or she studies the word of God. Everything is viewed through this foundational perspective, and therefore men become blind to what the scriptures actually teach.

> "Or despisest thou the riches of His **goodness** and **forbearance** and **longsuffering**; not knowing that **the goodness of God leadeth thee to repentance**? But after thy hardness and impenitent heart treasurest up unto thyself wrath against the day of wrath and revelation of the righteous judgment of God; Who will render to every man according to his deeds." (Rom. 2:4-6)

Might I ask the relevant question? What is a scripturally backed definition of God's "**goodness**", "**forbearance**", and "**longsuffering**"? We can interpret these attributes of God how we *feel* that they mean, or how these attributes exist in our ordinary human lives. Or, we can look up a modern or historical dictionary and

592

choose one of all the definitions therein rendered, or its synonyms therein listed, and now in a matter of seconds the word is exhaustively amplified. We can look up the words in a Greek lexicon, or in Hebrew, and see the various definitions of the root word used elsewhere in scripture. We can look up the secular history of each of the words, or the etymology of the words…After all of this, we can think we are getting somewhere in our journey to interpret the word of God, but let me plead with you all! Let us first look up the roots of the word in biblical instruction, in biblical history, within the safeguard of absolute inerrancy, and then let us look up every other instance it is used. Let us look, firstly, at each word in chronology from Genesis to Revelation, in each context, until finally we can grasp exactly what the biblical definition of the word is, and then let us conclude our searching and resolve, "this is the meaning indeed". Yea, let us not wander into further inquiries so as to bring this definition into doubt. If we venture elsewhere into the aforementioned grounds (Greek, Hebrew, history, systematized theology, dictionary, or etymology), let it be to enlarge upon the meaning already established by the infallibly-holy and definitively-peculiar exactitude of inspired scripture.

We must not err, my beloved brethren, by seeking God's definitions amongst godless men, wresting God's writing because of the uninspired pens of fallible men who claim "such and such" from history, who imagine "such and such" because of what is discoverable through original language proficiency, who affirm "such and such" as a legitimate and definitive trespass against the Book's defining Author – God Almighty – I speak so as to defend Him, for the Lord's sake: such men are puffed up in the hot air of scholarship, whose idolatry is intelligence, and they, hating humility and hallowing human education, do bow down to the hierarchy of a self-invented, unbiblical, para-Church authority. We are rejecting biblical verity for extra-biblical ideologies – pearls for pride – we are rejecting *sola scriptura* for the vulnerable and sabotaged manuscripts of human-documented, human-collected, God-rejected "church" history. The childlikeness of Peter the fisherman - he is chided, the God-ordination of the uneducated man is denounced as laughable, and with the eyes of faith effectually gouged out, men follow a system of God-unprotected philosophies and ideologies which are venerated because they are antique. Let us not seek the Living among the dead! Be astonished at this – these pastors preach without broken hearts! They are arrayed in graduation robes with hands blood red! With honorable letters by their name, look at them; they are prayerless preachers without any shame! Fattened for hibernation and prepared, and for what? For nothing but a long sleep…every one of them can be found deep within the dark cave of their three-thousand-book personal library – this is the bane of their existence. Nevertheless, let us have the holy resolve found in the Holy Ghost – in the purity of true meekness and void of pride – and let us assuredly exclaim: I am "wiser", "I have more understanding than all my teachers," "I understand more than the ancients, because I keep Thy precepts" (Psalm 119:97-100). The inspired psalmist was not proud when he said that.

Please, let me bring my question before you again. What is a scripturally backed definition of God's "**goodness**", "**forbearance**", and "**longsuffering,**" so that we might preach on these magnificent attributes of God when the Lord's people are in need of repentance?

Just as people quote that "God is faithful," or, "His mercy endureth forever," and these truths are abused to mean the near opposite of what they actually do mean, so also, many quote the saying that it is "the riches of His goodness and forbearance and longsuffering" which leads a man to repentance. They interpret this to mean that men need to see the goodness of God, and not the fear of God, when they are in need of repentance. Such persons understand that the goodness of God is something entirely disconnected from the wrath of God, or the fear of God, but again, it is the contrary!

Forbearance

I suppose, when men think of the forbearance that God has over His children, they think that God is not as a man, and they understand this to mean that, what makes men terribly angry, and also, how quickly men are angered, comes to be incomparable to how God would behave in these scenarios, and that God, Who is infinitely more loving than men, would in these situations be much more "slow to anger" (Ps. 103). For example, when a man would get terribly and uncontrollably angry over his children, it is then that God would be just "a little displeased" (Zech. 1:15). So also, when a man might be harsh, or even harmful, when he corrects his child in such scenarios, God would use perfect wisdom and gentleness to His children, which means that He would "correct thee in measure," a measurement much less than man (Jer. 30:11). I know that this may sound right and pleasing to you, my reader, but is that a correct comparison? Are the three passages which I quoted from in their correct contexts and application? Sadly, analogies from the life experiences of humanity are the definitive paradigm which interprets the Bible these days, and this leads into heresy! I beg you, again, for we are confronted with the same dilemma! What is a scripturally backed definition of God's slowness to anger (Ps. 103)? What does it means for God to have a little displeasure (Zech. 1:15), or a calculated correction in a measure (Jer. 30:11)!? If you would read those passages, you would understand that God's slowness to anger, little displeasure, and correction in measure magnifies the wonder that God left any of His people alive – and only nearly annihilated them – for they deserved a total annihilation! Now, if the near annihilation of God's people was a primary aspect in view when speaking the former three phrases, what do you think God has in mind about *forbearance*?

> "Yet many years didst Thou **forbear** them, and testifiedst against them by Thy Spirit in Thy prophets: yet would they not give ear: therefore gavest Thou them into the hand of the people of the lands. Nevertheless for Thy great mercies' sake Thou didst not utterly consume them, nor forsake them; for Thou art a gracious and merciful God." (Nehemiah 9:30-31)

594

This verse serves as a correct interpretative lens for the word "forbearance". Do I need to comment on it? You remember the context of Nehemiah chapter 9, don't you? I hope this astonishes you into the holy wonder of how backslidden our generation is, and oh, how wrong we have got it!

Goodness

"…the goodness of God leadeth thee to repentance" – Rom. 2:4
"For He is GOOD" – Psalms 106:1, 107:1, 118:1, 29

"Praise the LORD for His goodness" – Psalm 107:8, 15, 21, 31

Likewise to the other words, *the goodness* of God is used exactly like *the enduring mercy* of God. "The goodness of God endureth continually" (Ps. 52:1), the scripture exclaims! It is not that the goodness of God makes people repent by focusing on some attribute which is disconnected from God's wrath, but the goodness of God is good because when men are unrepentant and then they look upon the wrath of God hovering overhead, understanding that it is breaking forth to a possible near annihilation, and then, when they are distressed over it so as to call upon the Lord in tearful, repentant fear – the goodness of God is that He will hear and save such a man! Tragically, men believe that it is the goodness of God which makes impossible fear, and men are to believe that because God is good, then there is no wrath, but it is the contrary! When men behold the wrath of God, it is then that men are enabled to obtain the saving goodness of God (Ps. 106:1, 107:1, 8, 15, 21, 31)!

Longsuffering

"The Lord is not slack concerning His promise, as some men count slackness; but **is longsuffering to us-ward**, not willing that any should perish, but that all should come to **repentance**." (2 Peter 3:9)

"And account that **the longsuffering of our Lord is salvation**; even as our beloved brother Paul also according to the wisdom given unto him hath written unto you." (2 Peter 3:15)

Please my reader, listen closely. The two verses above perfectly place the biblical use of the word "longsuffering." These two verses are from the same chapter, and they are only five verses apart from one another. If we want to know what is so saving and repentance-working about a biblical understanding of God's *longsuffering*, then we ought to be pointed to look upon the emotional expression upon God's face which is impressed upon the reader in this chapter. In other words, what is the author pointing the reader to at this time, in the surrounding context of these two passages!? What impression do you get? Is longsuffering an attribute of God which is altogether disconnected from God's wrath or fear, or the potential of damnation? Let us read these verses from 2 Peter in their surrounding context, starting from verse 7 instead of verse 9:

> "But the heavens and the earth, which are now, by the same word are kept in store, reserved unto fire against the Day of Judgment and **perdition** of **ungodly** men. But, beloved, be not ignorant of this one thing, that one day is with the Lord as a thousand years, and a thousand years as one day. The Lord is not slack concerning His promise, as some men count slackness; but **is longsuffering to us-ward**, not willing that any should perish, but that all should come to **repentance**. But the day of the Lord will come as a thief in the night; in the which the heavens shall pass away with a great noise, and the elements shall melt with fervent heat, the earth also and the works that are therein shall be burned up. <u>**Seeing then**</u> that all these things shall be dissolved, what manner of persons ought ye to be **in all holy conversation and godliness**, Looking for and hasting unto the coming of the day of God, wherein the heavens being on fire shall be dissolved, and the elements shall melt with fervent heat? Nevertheless we, according to His promise, look for new heavens and a new earth, wherein dwelleth righteousness. Wherefore, beloved, seeing that ye look for such things, be diligent that ye may be found of Him **in peace**, **without spot**, and **blameless**. And account that **the longsuffering of our Lord is salvation**; even as our beloved brother Paul also according to the wisdom given unto him hath written unto you…" (2 Peter 3:7-15)

When you read this passage, recognize that the author is pointing toward the judgment of God against the ungodly at the END of the world, and the ability for a regenerate Christian to spend away, abuse, be hardened against, and despise the longsuffering of God, by refusing to repent, spurning and disregarding how that the longsuffering of God stalls final judgment because the regenerate man is not repenting. Seeking to get the attention of the unrepentant regenerate persons still lingering in the world, Peter warns them to SEE something, or, to LOOK upon something! What is it? Is it the feelings of *no fear* or *no wrath*!? No! Peter points them to look and see how the "earth," "the works" therein, and the "ungodly men" are doomed for "perdition," so that when they are "seeing then" all of this (2 Peter 3:11), they should be careful to repent and keep repentance, so that they would be found "in all holy conversation and godliness" (2 Pet. 3:11), "in peace, without spot, and blameless" (2 Peter 3:14) at Christ's coming. If they do not repent, let my reader take note, that they will not be in peace, without spot, and blameless at Christ's coming, because he is not in all the holiness of godliness that God would require.

Tender Mercies

"tender mercies" – Psalm 103:4
"very pitiful and of tender mercy" – James 5:11

The "tender mercies" and "gentleness" (Ps. 18) of God, also, just as the former attributes, are contrary to the common understanding. I remember the heresies of one man who I knew in the past – he constantly speaks of the tenderness of God in an unbiblical sense, and, such a one also falsely understands that mercy is the central theme of the whole Bible. This is not so! God is the central theme of the whole Bible, and in God, two colors of His glory are displayed, and they are – Saving Mercy & Condemning Wrath – FOR HIS GLORY. God's glory is the central theme of the Bible, in these two colors.

Let me attempt to establish this very clearly, as with all the aforementioned biblical attributes in God. The tender mercies of God, for Job, did not make impossible the experience of the wrath of God! As the verse above states, God was "very pitiful and of tender mercy" to Job (Jas. 5:11), but do you know what Job went through?! Have you any biblical recollection? Let Job's own words cry out the experience of WOE that was upon him, that you may know now that God's tender mercy does not negate the experience, or danger, of WRATH upon a saved, just, upright, perfect man who falls into sin. Tender mercies and pity come to lift a soul like Job's out of bitter agony and lamentation, BUT IT WAS THE WRATH of God which bound him and beat him into bitter agony and lamentation!

"Wherefore hidest Thou Thy face" – Job 13:24
"Wherefore…holdest me for Thine enemy" – Job 13:24
"He teareth me in His wrath, Who hateth me" – Job 16:9
"His archers compass me round about, He cleaveth my reins asunder" – Job 16:13
"Behold, I cry out of wrong, but I am not heard: I cry aloud, but there is no judgment. He hath fenced up my way that I cannot pass, and He hath set darkness in my paths"
– Job 19:7-8
"He hath destroyed me" – Job 19:10
"kindled His wrath against me…counteth me unto Him as one of His enemies" – Job 19:11

The pity and tender mercy of God is that God saved Job from His wrath, but this merciful salvation was NOT without the outpouring of God's wrath upon Job at the first! A man in bitter agony and lamentation does not reach forth for wrath and condemnation, but being mindful of the mercy, pity, longsuffering, forbearance, and goodness in God, he reaches forth for salvation through repentance. Exactly as this experience was for Job, even so, again and again, the psalmists underwent the same things. They spoke of them in the exact same ways and words, bitterness and breaking. When the psalmist prayed, "Have mercy upon me, O God, according to Thy lovingkindness: according to the multitude of Thy tender mercies blot out my transgressions" (Ps. 51:1), it did not mean that the man was in no danger of wrath, that he was not being exercised by the threatening of wrath, or was not under the very bitter crushing of wrath at that very moment –they were in the midst of a soul-threatening and fiercely destroying wrath, and thus, they did cry out in repentance and hope for "tender mercies" to undeservedly save them! You know the context of Psalm 51, don't you!? David knew God would cast him away even as He did King Saul, and so he cried out for mercy: "Cast me not away from Thy Presence; and take not Thy Holy Spirit from me" (Ps. 51:11). All of these verses below are prayerful cries from the very straits of wrath:

"Remember, O LORD, thy tender mercies and thy lovingkindnesses; for they *have been* ever of old." (Ps. 25:6)	→	"Look upon mine affliction and my pain; and forgive all my sins." (Ps. 25:18)
"Hear me, O LORD; for thy lovingkindness *is* good: turn unto me according to the multitude of thy tender mercies." (Ps. 69:16)	→	"Hide not Thy face from Thy servant; for I am in trouble." (Ps. 69:17)

When such men were under the wrath of God, and then they called upon the tender mercies of God, this did not mean that they were absolutely sure they would be forgiven and delivered. Need I comment on the context of Psalms 77, 103, and 79?

"Hath God forgotten to be gracious? hath He in anger shut up His tender mercies?" (Ps. 77:9)

"Who redeemeth thy life from destruction; Who crowneth thee with lovingkindness and tender mercies."
(Ps. 103:4)

"O remember not against us former iniquities: let Thy tender mercies speedily prevent us: for we are brought very low." (Ps. 79:8)

Chastening & The ROD

"I will be his Father, and he shall be My son. If he commit iniquity, I will chasten him with the **ROD** of men, and with the **stripes** of the children of men"
– 2 Samuel 7:14

"…I will visit their transgression with the **ROD**, and

598

their iniquity with **stripes**" – Psalm 89:32

Few words so pointedly direct our thoughts to God's Fatherly compassion and paternal love, besides the words "Chastening" and "the ROD". How many times have you heard a man gladly, and loudly, with the sharp tones of carnal pride, declare – "I am a child of God!" – and you know the man is set on devouring iniquity? As devastating as this is, it has a root. Men and women, of the regenerate houschold of God and the once-born mass of Americanized "Christianity", do believe that because they are a child of God, therefore God will not "hide" Himself, not for a little while or "forever", and His "wrath" will never "burn like fire" (Psalm 89:46). "Look", they say, "God hath spoken", and what are they pointing at? They point to God's Fatherly "ROD" and Paternal "stripes", how that, by promise, the intent behind it is for the oath – "Nevertheless My lovingkindness will I not utterly take from him, nor suffer My faithfulness to fail" (Psalm 89:33). Now PLEASE, my reader, look closer, and at ALL of the scripture, and we can quickly see how the psalmist of Psalm 89 did plainly disagree (Ps. 89:38-53).

Most people are not ignorant, at least, that "the ROD" is the biblical instrument used by the parents to chasten a stubborn and disobedient child, but they suppose that when they are that disobedient child of God, that they, always, without fail, will be turned to repentance and faith again, that it is an absolute impossibility that they could be lost in such a state unto eternal damnation. The foremost NT scriptures which are *commonly* used to define and interpret what God's chastening is are the following verses:

> "And ye have forgotten the exhortation which speaketh unto you as unto children, My son, despise not thou the chastening of the Lord, nor faint when thou art rebuked of Him: For whom the Lord loveth He chasteneth, and scourgeth every son whom He receiveth." (Hebrews 12:5-6)

> "As many as I love, I rebuke and chasten: be zealous therefore, and repent." (Rev. 3:19)

Do you think that you have the correct interpretation on what biblical chastening is, and more specifically, the emotional mind of God behind the beating of the ROD? Could God ever be angry when He beats with the rod? What about the purposes and potentials of being beaten by the rod, is it dangerous and can it be damnable? When common people read these two verses above, they would not think so, despite the staggering clarity in the wider context of Rev. 3:19. What many do not know is that the verses quoted in Hebrews 12:5-6, which was written before John wrote the book of Revelation, originate from the OT:

> "My son, despise not the chastening of the LORD; neither be weary of His correction: For whom the LORD loveth He

correcteth; even as a Father the son in whom He delighteth.
Happy is the man that findeth wisdom..."
(Proverbs 3:11-13)

"Behold, happy is the man whom God correcteth: therefore
despise not thou the chastening of the Almighty. For He maketh
sore, and bindeth up: He woundeth, and His hands make whole."
(Job 5:17-18)

When encountering the exact same sentences or phrases in two different
books, like the two verses above, we can understand that the later book is quoting the
earlier book, and seeing that the book of Proverbs was written after the book of Job
(probably dated pre-flood), then we can understand that Solomon (the author of
Proverbs) had Job's interpretation and experience of chastening in his mind as he
quoted it in Proverbs 3:11-13. Therefore it is necessary for us to study the book of
Job that we might understand what biblical chastening is, according to Job, and not
according to our own human philosophies, or, how we chasten our children at "such
and such" a time, with "such and such" a purpose and potential. In Job 5:17-18,
God's correction and chastening was describing what Job was going through at that
time, and though Eliphaz was not perfectly correct in his assessment of why Job was
being chastened, Job did not disagree that he was being chastened. Fatherly
chastening is by the ROD, as formerly mentioned; therefore Job speaks of his
experiences as a product of God's beating ROD upon him:

"Let Him take His **rod** away from me, and let not His fear terrify
me..." (Job 9:34)
"Their houses are safe from fear, neither is the **rod** of God upon
them." (Job 21:9)

In Job 9:34, Job speaks of the rod of God as something that is terrifying
him. In Job 21:9, Job acknowledges the rod to be used upon a choice people, the
godly and regenerate children of God, which means that it is not used upon the once-
born wicked of the earth, and again, here, like as before, this chastening rod has the
power of destruction which seizes men with fear. Do you understand the significance
of this reference in Job? Job considers his experiences of suffering as the work of
God's Fatherly, compassionate ROD! Consequentially, therefore, all of these
experiences listed below are categorically defined as chastening. What Job underwent
was, therefore, an inerrant and biblical demonstration of what it is, definitively, for a
choice servant of God to go under the Paternal ROD:

"Wherefore hidest Thou Thy face" – Job 13:24
"Wherefore...holdest me for Thine enemy" – Job 13:24
"He teareth me in His wrath, Who hateth me" – Job 16:9
"His archers compass me round about, He cleaveth my reins
asunder" – Job 16:13

600

"Behold, I cry out of wrong, but I am not heard: I cry aloud, but there is no judgment. He hath fenced up my way that I cannot pass, and He hath set darkness in my paths"
– Job 19:7-8
"He hath destroyed me" – Job 19:10
"kindled His wrath against me…counteth me unto Him as one of His enemies"
– Job 19:11

Is this how you understand chastening, and the ROD? You may vainly assert that I have taken an enormous and unverified leap, that I am, in some way, forcing this experience to define God's Paternal chastening. My reader, let us look further, for yet another book (written after Job) speaks of chastening and the rod in the same exact context of definition and description, exactly parallel with Job's experience and affirmation. In fact, Job's exact experience of chastening under the rod, as he described it above, namely that it was an affliction of *the wrath of God*, is the exact same description of God's chastening and the rod in biblical inspiration henceforth. If the experience of chastening by God's rod is not "endured" so that the person is brought under "subjection" to God by it, which means they are brought to repentance through it, then they will not be saved, but destroyed (Heb. 12:7, 9). We must come under subjection to our Father, for there, and only there, is the place that we might continue to "live" (Heb. 12:9). Therefore did the godly saints learn to pray:

"O LORD, rebuke me not in Thine anger, neither chasten me in Thy hot displeasure. Have mercy upon me, O LORD; for **I am weak**: O LORD, heal me; for **my bones are vexed**." (Ps. 6:1-2)
"O LORD, rebuke me not in Thy wrath: neither chasten me in Thy hot displeasure. For **Thine <u>arrows</u> stick fast in me**, and Thy hand **presseth me sore**." (Ps. 38:1)
"O LORD, correct me, but with judgment; <u>not in Thine anger</u>, **lest Thou bring me to nothing**." (Jer. 10:24)
"Let Thy tender mercies come unto me, **that I may live**: for Thy law *is* my delight." (Ps. 119:77)

Do you think these inspired writers had something in their mind, by definition, which is fundamentally different and thus contradicting your understanding of what God's chastening is? Would you ever, naturally, pray the prayers that these men prayed, fearing with the fear that they are affrighted with? My reader, it is the *human philosophies* which have led you astray! You are thinking that God is, naturally, like your nature, and now you cringe in distaste, and at what? Do you think God is a "monster" of a Person now, and you are, rather, a good parent? God gives better *gifts* than you – more valuable, meritorious, and merciful – and God gets angrier than you, He *chastens* better than you, delivering chastisement-blows of harder, more precise, life-threatening power, which then, as you can see, became terrifyingly famous throughout history. As for God the Father, whether it be the

601

goodness of His blessing, or, the severity of His wrath, whether it be the compassion of His condescension and humility, or, the overpowering fierceness of His punishment; my reader, "if ye then, being evil," knoweth how to "give good gifts" to your children, and also, "if ye then, being evil," knoweth how to demand "reverence" from your children by the severity of chastisement and "correction" you deliver, "**how much more**" mature, superior, infinitely perfect, and trustworthy is God's Parenting in both veins, and, "**shall we not much rather** be in subjection to the Father of spirits" (see Matt. 7:11 & Heb. 12:9)? When God said of us that we are parents – comparatively "evil" – when in the light of God's Parenting, He means to explain that our *parenting philosophies* are stinking with depravity, are twisted with corruption, that they are inferior in <u>fatherly</u> compassion and <u>fatherly</u> chastening. He means to show us that we would never "love mercy" or "do justly" like as He does, and therefore we need to learn of Him, His ways, and "walk humbly with [our] God" (Micah 6:8).

Do you want to understand this kind of chastening which is according to scripture – biblical *chastening*? The most significant passage, which frames all definitive verses thereafter, is found in Leviticus 26:28, where God says – "I, even I, will **chastise** you seven times for your sins." This is spoken in the 5th of 5 phases of chastening which God afflicts Israel with, in the case that they are in rebellion and disobedience ((1st) 26:16-17, (2nd) 26:18-20, (3rd) 26:21-22, (4th) 26:23-26, and (5th) 26:27-39). Read the wider context of the 5th phase of chastening, and see just what emotions and determinations God had in his heart when He was chastising them!

> "And if ye will not for all this hearken unto Me, but walk
> contrary unto Me; Then I will walk contrary unto you also **in
> fury**; and I, even I, will **chastise** you seven times for your sins.
> And ye shall eat the flesh of your sons, and the flesh of your
> daughters shall ye eat. And **I will destroy** your high places, and
> cut down your images, and **cast your carcases** upon the carcases
> of your idols, and **my soul shall abhor you**. And I will make
> your cities **waste**, and bring your sanctuaries unto **desolation**,
> and I will not smell the savour of your sweet odours. And I will
> bring the land into **desolation**: and your enemies which dwell
> therein shall be astonished at it. And **I will scatter you among
> the heathen**, and will draw out a sword after you: and your land
> shall be **desolate**, and your cities **waste**. Then shall the land
> enjoy her sabbaths, as long as it lieth desolate, and ye be in your
> enemies' land; even then shall the land rest, and enjoy her
> sabbaths. As long as it lieth desolate it shall rest; because it did
> not rest in your sabbaths, when ye dwelt upon it. And upon them
> that are left alive of you I will send a faintness into their hearts in
> the lands of their enemies; and the sound of a shaken leaf shall
> chase them; and they shall flee, as fleeing from a sword; and they
> shall fall when none pursueth. And they shall fall one upon

another, as it were before a sword, when none pursueth: and ye shall have no power to stand before your enemies. And ye shall **perish** among the heathen, and the land of your enemies shall **eat you up**. And they that are left of you shall **pine away** in their iniquity in your enemies' lands; and also in the iniquities of their fathers shall they **pine away** with them." (Leviticus 26:27-39)

This is the wrath of God in the great dispersion, otherwise called the captivities, the OT near-annihilation which should have been a total annihilation and reprobation! My reader, the Assyrians and Babylonians are, God says, "**the ROD** of Mine anger" (Isa. 10:5, 15, 24, Micah 6:9)! God brought them upon Israel and Judah, and God beat them down! Jeremiah laments this chastening in the stead of all Israel, and said – "I am the man that hath seen affliction by **the ROD** of His wrath" (Lamentations 3:1). This amazes and astounds me! The biblical consistency and clarity which comes by a proper, balanced, unadulterated study of God's word! My reader, in the book of Lamentations, Jeremiah describes the experience of God's near-annihilating wrath to be exactly the same as what Job experienced:

Job	Lamentations
"Wherefore hidest Thou Thy face" – Job 13:24 "Wherefore…holdest me for Thine enemy" – Job 13:24 "He teareth me in His wrath, Who hateth me" – Job 16:9 "Behold, I cry out of wrong, but I am not heard: I cry aloud, but there is no judgment. He hath fenced up my way that I cannot pass…	"against me is He turned" – Lam. 3:3 "The Lord was an enemy: He hath swallowed up Israel" – Lam 2:5 "He hath… pulled me in pieces: He hath made me desolate" – Lam. 3:11 "when I cry and shout, He shutteth out my prayer" – Lam. 3:8 "He hath hedged me about, that I cannot get out…He hath inclosed my ways with hewn stone" – Lam. 3:7,9
…and He hath set darkness in my paths" – Job 19:7-8 "He hath destroyed me" – Job 19:10 "kindled His wrath against me…counteth me unto Him as one of His enemies" – Job 19:11 "His archers compass me round about, He cleaveth my reins asunder" – Job 16:13	"brought me into darkness, but not into light" – Lam. 3:2 "He was unto me as a bear lying in wait, and as a lion in secret places" – Lam. 3:10 "Thou hast not pardoned" – Lam. 3:42 "Thou hast not pitied" – Lam. 3:43 "desolation and destruction" – Lam. 3:47 "bent His bow" & "caused the arrow" – Lam. 3:12-13, 2:4

Jeremiah, the writer of Lamentations, the prophet of the Captivities, addresses this event of chastening in Jeremiah 30:11-14 with the very same witness:

> "For I am with thee, saith the LORD, to save thee: though I make
> a full end of all nations whither I have scattered thee, **yet will I
> not make a full end of thee**: but I will correct thee in measure,
> and will not leave thee altogether unpunished. For thus saith the
> LORD, Thy bruise is incurable, and thy wound is grievous. There
> is none to plead thy cause, that thou mayest be bound up: thou
> hast no healing medicines. All thy lovers have forgotten thee;
> they seek thee not; for I have wounded thee with the wound of an
> enemy, with the **chastisement** of a cruel one, for the multitude of
> thine iniquity; because thy sins were increased." (Jeremiah 30:11-14)

As we have, in former chapters, exhaustively addressed the near annihilation of God's people in the Captivities, we can understand that, this chastisement was one of condemnation and salvation, hatred and merciful redemption, but *only those who survived it were redeemed by it*. Not all chastening is a condemning stroke from God's ROD. Remember how there were four phases of wrath which went before this fifth phase, all of which were not of the intensity of the fifth phase. When the first four phases of wrath were not responded to, and sin remained yet un-surrendered, the flames of wrath which burned against sin did turn upon the people who held it dear. The five phases increasingly intensified until when, God said, "I will chastise you seven times for your sins" (Lev. 26:28). Job underwent the severity of such definitively parallel chastening as the generation of the Captivities because he thought evil of God, accusing Him, to the point that he desired to argue for God's apparent injustice against himself, and thus left off the integrity of faith and patience which he held to in the beginning of his trial.

Job's experience of chastening and the ROD was not peculiar. Just as you have seen above, David also, and the other psalmists, with others, describe temporary or permanent experiences of wrath with the same vocabulary and phraseology, only it is in their personal lives. The whole of scripture could be exhausted to echo these realities, but let these clear and explicitly categorized verses conclude the biblical meanings of God's Chastening and ROD for now.

The rod is for someone who is in a damnable condition, which is:

> "him that is void of understanding" – Prov. 10:13
> "for the fool's back" – Prov. 26:3, 17:10
> "evil" – Prov. 20:30

In the case of physical children:

> "He that spareth his **rod** hateth his son: but he that loveth him
> **chasteneth** him betimes." (Prov. 13:24)
> "**Foolishness** is bound in the heart of a child; but the **rod** of

correction shall drive it far from him." (Prov. 22:15)

"Withhold not correction from the child: for if thou beatest him with the **rod**, he shall not <u>die</u>. Thou shalt beat him with the **rod**, and shalt deliver his soul from <u>hell</u>."
(Prov. 23:13-14)

"The **rod** and reproof give **wisdom**: but a child left to himself bringeth his mother to shame." (Prov. 29:15)

The rod is used for physical children who are in a condition which is damnable. To confirm this, the scriptures affirm that chastening with the rod is a saving experience from death and hell, and from foolishness. It is a means of grace, a holy instrument, by which God will interrupt and suppress the course and chaos of depravity, making room for heartfelt conviction and eventual salvation.

Chastening & The ROD = Judgment Beginning at the House of God

"**For the LORD shall judge His people**, and repent Himself for His servants, <u>when</u> He seeth that **their power is gone**, and **there is none shut up, or left**." (Deut. 32:36)

"For the time is come that **judgment must begin at the house of God**: and if it <u>first</u> begin at us, what shall <u>the end</u> be of them that obey not the gospel of God? And **if the righteous scarcely be saved**, where shall the ungodly and the sinner appear?" (1 Peter 4:17-18)

Judgment must begin at the House of God. People acknowledge this with their mouth – but what does it mean? How do we interpret and understand what is meant for God to *judge the House of God*? The meaning is exactly in context with the passage above, in Deuteronomy 32:36. This verse is the closest verse of the exact expression of what is in reference in 1 Peter 4:17-18, "**Judgment must begin at the House of God**... and if the righteous scarcely be saved, where shall the ungodly and the sinner appear?" What is so *scarce* about the *salvation* of the people of God, specifically speaking, after Fatherly *chastening* & *judgment*!? It is that "there is none shut up or left" (Deut. 32:36)! It is that God has nearly annihilated them in His *judgment* and *chastening* (Deut. 32:26-27)!

"**The LORD shall judge His people**" – Deut. 32:36

"For we know Him that hath said, **Vengeance** belongeth unto Me, I will recompense, saith the Lord. And again, **The Lord shall judge His people**. It is a fearful thing to fall into the hands of the living God." (Hebrews 10:30-31)

"For the Day of **vengeance** is in Mine heart...therefore He was turned to be their enemy, and He fought against them." (Isa. 63:4, 10)

Both Deut. 32 & Isa. 63 reference God as their Father, and Deut. 32:36 references wrath and annihilation as "judgment", which is also called the vengeance of God in Isa. 63, meaning exactly that. It is the vengeance of God toward God's people! This is the exact rendering of the words used in Hebrews 10:30-31, speaking again, but now in the NT, to the children of God that lost their salvation (Heb. 10:26-29). "Judgments are prepared for scorners," and God's people can become scorners (Prov. 19:29). "Stripes [are] for the back of fools", and God's people can become fools (Prov. 19:29). "Vengeance" comes upon the "adversaries" (Heb. 10:27) and "enemies" of God (Jas. 4:4), and God's people can become such men (Isa. 63:10). In biblical history, how exactly did Judgment **BEGIN** at the house of God, so that, **secondarily**, it did **afterward**, fall upon the heathen? This is the very heart of 1 Peter 4:17-18! The apostle understands this to be a reality alive, or still applicable, in the New Covenant dispensation. As in the case of the captivities, which were the greatest judgment of God upon His people in the Old Covenant, it was perfectly exemplified that Israel and Judah, firstly, were judged by the wrath of God, and this was the beginning of God's judgments, but then, secondarily, God turned to the heathen with the rest of His judgments.

> "And I am **very sore displeased** with the heathen that are at ease: for I was but **a little displeased**, and they helped forward the affliction. Therefore thus saith the LORD; I am returned to Jerusalem with mercies: my house shall be built in it, saith the LORD of hosts, and a line shall be stretched forth upon Jerusalem." (Zechariah 1:15-16)

> "Behold, I will send and take all the families of the north, saith the LORD, and Nebuchadrezzar the king of Babylon, my servant, and will bring them against this land, and against the inhabitants thereof, and against all these nations round about, and will utterly destroy them, and make them an astonishment, and an hissing, and **perpetual desolations**. Moreover I will take from them the voice of mirth, and the voice of gladness, the voice of the bridegroom, and the voice of the bride, the sound of the millstones, and the light of the candle. And this whole land shall be a desolation, and an astonishment; and these nations shall serve the king of Babylon seventy years. And it shall come to pass, when **seventy years** are accomplished, that I will punish the king of Babylon, and that nation, saith the LORD, for their iniquity, and the land of the Chaldeans, and will make it **perpetual desolations**." (Jeremiah 25:9-12)

> "For I am with thee, saith the LORD, to save thee: **though I**

make a full end of all nations whither I have scattered thee, yet **will I not make a full end of thee**: but I will **correct thee in measure**, and will not leave thee altogether unpunished." (Jeremiah 30:11)

"Fear thou not, O Jacob my servant, saith the LORD: for I am with thee; for **I will make a full end of all the nations whither I have driven thee**: but **I will not make a full end of thee**, but **correct thee in measure**; yet will I not leave thee wholly unpunished." (Jeremiah 46:28)

"Begin at the House of God" → Near Annihilation (scarcely saved)
"Where Shall the Ungodly and Sinner Appear?" → Total Annihilation

Israel 1ˢᵗ → "Slay utterly old and young, both maids, and little children, and women: but come not near any man upon whom is the mark; and **begin at my sanctuary**. Then they began at the ancient men which were **before the House**." (Ezekiel 9:6)

"In **a little wrath** I hid my face from thee **for a moment**; but with everlasting kindness will I have mercy on thee, saith the LORD thy Redeemer." (Isaiah 54:8)

"For thus hath the LORD said, The whole land shall be desolate; **yet will I not make a full end**."
(Jeremiah 4:27)

"Go ye up upon her walls, and destroy; **but make not a full end**: take away her battlements; for they are not the LORD'S."
(Jeremiah 5:10)

"Nevertheless in those days, saith the LORD, **I will not make a full end with you**." (Jeremiah 5:18)

"Behold, the eyes of the Lord GOD are upon the sinful kingdom, and I will destroy it from off the face of the earth; saving that **I will not utterly destroy the house of Jacob**, saith the LORD. For, lo, I will command, and I will sift the house of Israel among all nations, like as corn is sifted in a sieve, yet shall not the least grain fall upon the earth." (Amos 9:8-9)

The Heathen (Assyria & Babylon) 2ⁿᵈ → "And I will render unto Babylon and to all the inhabitants of Chaldea all their evil that they have done in Zion in your sight, saith the LORD." (Jeremiah 51:24)

"Nebuchadrezzar the king of Babylon hath devoured me, he hath crushed me, he hath made me an empty vessel, he hath swallowed me up like a dragon, he hath filled his belly with my delicates, he hath cast me out. The violence done to me and to my flesh be upon Babylon, shall the inhabitant of Zion say; and **my blood upon the inhabitants of Chaldea, shall Jerusalem say**." (Jeremiah 51:34-35)

"Therefore, ye mountains of Israel, hear the word of the Lord GOD; Thus saith the Lord GOD to the mountains, and to the hills, to the rivers, and to the valleys, to the desolate wastes, and to the cities that are forsaken, which became a prey and derision to the residue of the heathen that are round about; Therefore thus saith the Lord GOD; Surely in the fire of my jealousy have I spoken against the residue of the heathen, and against all Idumea, which have appointed my land into their possession with the joy of all their heart, with despiteful minds, to cast it out for a prey." (Ezekiel 36:4-5)

"For the day of the LORD is near upon all the heathen: as thou hast done, it shall be done unto thee: thy reward shall return upon thine own head. For as ye have drunk upon my holy mountain, so shall all the heathen drink continually, yea, they shall drink, and they shall swallow down, and they shall be as though they had not been." (Obadiah 1:15-16)

Don't you remember how many of the prophets did present their holy complaints to the Lord, being in an agony, because the heathen were "at ease" (Zech. 1:15) in "prosperity" (Ps. 73:3) while Israel was "plagued" (Ps. 73), judged, and brought low? Habakkuk does encapsulate the same complaint very well, when he said: "Thou art of purer eyes than to behold evil, and canst not look on iniquity: wherefore lookest Thou upon them that deal treacherously, and holdest Thy tongue when the wicked devoureth the man that is more righteous than he" (Hab. 1:13)?

Again, Jeremiah says, "Wherefore doth the way of the wicked prosper? Wherefore are all they happy that deal very treacherously? Thou hast planted them, yea, they have taken root: they grow, yea, they bring forth fruit: Thou art near in their mouth, and far from their reins" (Jer. 12:1-2). God's answer is: Chastening is meant for the salvation of a remnant that was to be "plucked out of the fire" (Zech. 3:2). In the midst of the fires of annihilation, it is there that God is burning, smelting, and refining, making ready a people that would go through with Him unto the end, thus He says in Isaiah 48:10: "Behold, I have refined thee, but not with silver; I have chosen thee in the furnace of affliction" (Isa. 48:10). Do you see how all of these judgments are meant for the salvation of a select and chosen remnant? Just as the NT affirms: "But when we are judged, we are chastened of the Lord, that we should not be condemned with the world" (1 Cor. 11:32).

"…we went through the fire…" – Psalm 66:12
 "…save with fear, pulling them out of the fire" – Jude 1:23
"…the furnace for gold" – Proverbs 17:3
"…gold tried in the fire" – Revelation 3:18
"…he himself shall be saved; yet so as by fire" – 1 Corinthians 3:15

The intention of God to save through *judgment* (1 Cor. 11:32, see also "The Purpose & Intent for Salvation") is exactly parallel to the metaphorical rendering of the same experience, wherein, *chastening* and *judgment* upon God's people is called *the furnace of fire* (for salvific-smelting and damnable-annihilation, and universally, for the trying of the faith). This beating of God's ROD of anger is exactly parallel to when God burns Israel to save her. The fires of God are simultaneously *intended to save* and *intended to annihilate*, but not all will savingly respond to the fires (Amos 4:11, Jer. 6:28-30), whose heat increases by phases of intensity, until a near annihilation transpires with a remnant plucked out (Isa. 48:9).

Psalm 66:8-15
Proverbs 17:3, 25:4
Isaiah 1:25, 48:8-12
Jeremiah 6:28-30
Ezekiel 22:17-22
Daniel 12:10
Malachi 3:1-3

"Yea, thou heardest not; yea, thou knewest not; yea, from that time that thine ear was not opened: for I knew that thou wouldest deal very treacherously, and wast called a transgressor from the womb. For my name's sake will I defer mine anger, and for my praise will I refrain for thee, that I cut thee not off. Behold, I have refined thee, but not with silver; I have chosen thee in the furnace of affliction. For mine own sake, even for mine own sake, will I do it: for how should my name be polluted? and I will not give my glory unto another. Hearken unto me, O Jacob and Israel, my called; I am he; I am the first, I also am the last" (Isaiah 48:8-12).

He took the whole nation of Israel and cast her into the flames of His fierce and destroying wrath, until, nearly all were burned up – AND THEN – God reached into the furnace of wrath and pulled out a small remnant, smelted and soft, a brand from the burning, ready now, after suffering the heat of the most vehement flames – God's chastening – they are molded into "a vessel for the Finer" (Prov. 25:4). Ezekiel 6:8-10 accurately declares how this people, finally, after being fire-burned and ROD-broken will mourn their sinful deeds at last:

> "Yet will I leave a remnant, that ye may have some that shall escape the sword among the nations, when ye shall be scattered through the countries. And they that escape of you shall remember me among the nations whither they shall be carried captives, because I am broken with their whorish heart, which hath departed from me, and with their eyes, which go a whoring after their idols: and they shall lothe themselves for the evils which they have committed in all their abominations. And they shall know that I am the LORD, and that I have not said in vain that I would do this evil unto them" (Ezekiel 6:8-10).

Being saved by *fire* is – EXACTLY AS – being saved by the *chastening ROD* & *House-judgments*. God chastened Israel as a whole nation like as a parent would judge a single child, but God, in high, holy, and terrifying severity, beat with the ROD in wrath, hot displeasure, and fierce anger, until finally, the whole body of the single child nearly died (the Israelite nation), but scarcely though, life was spared...the child is now wounded, bleeding, and bruised, suffering a loss of limbs, and the ability to walk, but God does heal the child with miraculous powers so that the bruises heal the heart, the wounds heal without scars, the limbs and legs grow back to walk and keep the strait and narrow path, so that in the END, though the child was near death, you would not know it at last.

"But ye that did cleave unto the LORD your God are alive every one of you this day"
– Deut. 4:4

The chastening of the Captivities is a more intensified expression of what formerly happened to the Exodus generation, when nearly all of that generation died in reprobating wrath. In the Exodus generation *and* the Captivities, generally speaking, all that "did cleave unto the LORD" were enabled to remain alive (Deut. 4:4). Those that did remain alive were, primarily, the children of the Exodus generation, and they were instructed as to what their eyes have seen, that it was, namely, "the **chastisement** of the LORD your God". They saw, Moses said, "the **chastisement** of the LORD your God, His greatness, His mighty hand, and His stretched out arm...and what He did unto you in the wilderness, until ye came into this place; and what He did unto Dathan and Abiram, the sons of Eliab, and the son of Reuben: how the earth opened her mouth, and swallowed them up, and their households, and their tents, and all the substance that was in their possessions, in the midst of all Israel:...your eyes have seen all the great acts of the LORD which He did" (Deut. 11:1-7), and this example is pointedly applied to the NT children of God with a fearful warning – "Now all these things happened unto them **for ensamples**: that are written **for our admonition**, upon whom the ends of the world are come. **Wherefore** let him that thinketh he standeth **take heed lest he fall**" (1 Cor. 10:11-12). With this in mind, do you think Paul was defining biblical chastening, as mentioned in 1 Corinthians 11:31-32, with a different understanding than the previous chapter's awful annals (recounted in 1 Corinthians 10:1-12, stemming from what Deut. 11:2 called "chastisement"). It is understandable, then, why Paul declared chastening to be a means for redemption, and it is – just that – for those who survive it, but it is condemnation for those who die in it (with few exceptions). While watching men die, be chastened therewith, let us avoid dying like unto their example! While watching men fall, be chastened therewith, let us take heed lest we fall, and so become like unto them.

God is intent on salvation, even if, like as the generation of the Captivities, he must nearly annihilate an entire generation, and thus he did to the Exodus generation by breach of promise, by plagues of power, until the exercise of chastening motivated their children to learn and behave differently. Again, those that live through the chastening of God, they are the ones who are redeemed by it, but in the process of it – **so many will perish in it**.

According to God's argument of what resulted from the judgments and chastening in the Captivities, salvation arose from the most unlikely of places which self-righteous, religious backsliders would wonder to learn. We need to learn this lesson today, like as the children of the Exodus generation learned their lessons, and henceforth persevered. As a result of God judging the children of God **first**, in the Captivities, since God judged Israel through the heathen's instrumentality (coupled with other means), the heathen were aroused to blaspheme and speak proudly against God and His people. The heathen were estranged from what actually happened, and how God gave Israel into their hand, thus they were compelled thence to speak "strangely". This is what they said...

> "Our hand is high, and the LORD hath not done all this"
> – Deut. 32:27

> "Because thou saidst, 'Aha', against My sanctuary, when it was profaned; and against the land of Israel, when it was desolate; and against the house of Judah, when they went into captivity;"
> – Ezek. 25:3

> "Because thou hast clapped thine hands, and stamped with the feet, and rejoiced in heart with all thy despite against the land of Israel...therefore...I will cause thee to perish out of the countries: I will destroy thee..." – Ezek. 25:6-7

"Because that Moab and Seir do say, Behold, the house of Judah is like unto all the heathen; therefore, behold…I will execute judgments upon Moab" – Ezek. 25:8-11

"Because that Tyrus hath said against Jerusalem, Aha, she is broken that was the gates of the people: she is turned unto me: I shall be replenished, now she is laid waste… Behold, I am against thee, O Tyrus, and will cause many nations to come up against thee, as the sea causeth his waves to come up" – Ezek. 26:3

Do you see how this blasphemy of the heathen does move the heart of God with such force, pressing Him into the desire to save His people from total annihilation (Deut. 32:26-27, Isa. 48:9-12)? It is because the Lord's own Name is connected with His people, and blasphemed, resulting in the greatest evil to the Most Good – God's Name. It is in this way that *the righteous are scarcely saved* from **the judgment of God** which *began* with them, and woefully, thence, turned upon the heathen men! It amazes me that God saves His people in this way, repenting from a present-tense annihilation – God, feelingly desiring a total annihilation of them, changes both mind and emotion, and moves into love and salvation, because – lo, the heathen blasphemed the Church who was being smitten down by God, saying, "This is Zion, whom no man seeketh after" (Jer. 30:17), accusing them that it was not God who smote them, that their God is no God, and these things happened by their own hand. When God was judging His people, they came to such a low estate, and deplorable, because of the strokes of the ROD in wrath, the flames of the furnace in licking destruction, the world of heathen men spoke strangely about it, and against God's people. Then God, suddenly, responding to this accusatory speech of ill-fame, decidedly turned to save Israel and destroy the heathen! Oh that God would speak of such loving redemption to His people, saying, "For I will restore health unto thee, and I will heal thee of thy wounds, saith the LORD;" and it is because the heathen blasphemed! Namely, God says, "because they called thee [God's people] an Outcast, saying, This is Zion, whom no man seeketh after" (Jer. 30:17). To read that this is the very signal for God's salvation is amazing, but to be such a people (a NT biblical Church) chastened by God, then likewise, buried under strange blasphemies and sharp denouncement as in a grave of ignominy…and from thence, recognizing, as from the valley of humiliation, that this condemning, double-tongued, slander of the devil is the very signal of salvation which God is hearing, responding to, and arising against – putting it to shame and contradicting it – with trumpet-loud MERCY for the world to marvel at glory endowed! For such, this is an unforgettable wonder! "And as he passed over Penuel the sun rose upon him, and he halted upon his thigh" (Genesis 32:31). Praise God!

"Groanings Which Cannot Be Uttered" – Romans 8:26
Examining King David in the Psalms

There are nearly 74 Psalms which are explicitly titled or credited to King David. By vocabulary and phraseology, it is apparent that David is deeply convicted over his sins, often in straits of wrath compelling him into astounding intercessory experiences, and yet, the horrifying reality is that these very same NT terms, experiences, and intercessions are spurned by the church. These terms are explicit identifiers of God's plaguing wrath; whence it is falling, saints sought to be recovered therefrom, but if they fail to be recovered from the temporary experience therein, then, at last, the signaling strokes of these experiences which were meant for redemptive chastening turn into eternal dooms. All of these experiences – like the Rod, the furnace of fire, and House-judgments – are meant for redemption if the people of God survive them. Survival is, namely, by responding to it in the same manner that *David exemplifies*. He is, for us, a patterned saint, and we need to learn to behave like he did, for we too, like him, will be in such straits henceforth categorized and addressed.

ARROWS

Secondary Witness	King David
"He hath bent His bow, and set me as a mark for the arrow. He hath caused the arrows of His quiver to enter into my reins." (Lamentations 3:12-13)	"For thine arrows stick fast in me, and Thy hand presseth me sore. There is no soundness in my flesh because of thine anger; neither is there any rest in my bones because of my sin. For mine iniquities are gone over mine head: as an heavy burden they are too heavy for me. My wounds stink and are corrupt because of my foolishness." (Psalm 38:2-5) *(Contextually, arrows are representative of wrath aimed at wicked men – Ps. 7:12-13, 18:14, 21:12, 64:7, 144:6)*

SPIRITUAL DESERTIFICATION

Secondary Witness	King David
"And the LORD shall guide thee continually, and satisfy thy soul in drought, and make fat thy bones: and thou shalt be like a watered garden, and like a	"When I kept silence, my bones waxed old through my roaring all the day long. For day and night Thy hand was heavy upon me: my moisture is turned into the drought of summer.

spring of water, whose waters fail not." (Isaiah 58:11) "Therefore they shall come and sing in the height of Zion, and shall flow together to the goodness of the LORD, for wheat, and for wine, and for oil, and for the young of the flock and of the herd: and their soul shall be as a watered garden; and they shall not sorrow any more at all." (Jeremiah 31:12) "He that believeth on Me, as the scripture hath said, out of his belly shall flow rivers of living water." (John 7:38)	Selah. I acknowledged my sin unto thee, and mine iniquity have I not hid. I said, I will confess my transgressions unto the LORD; and Thou forgavest the iniquity of my sin. Selah." (Psalm 32:3-5) "A Psalm of David, when he was in the wilderness of Judah. O God, Thou art my God; early will I seek thee: my soul thirsteth for thee, my flesh longeth for thee in a dry and thirsty land, where no water is..." (Psalm 63:1) "To the chief Musician, Maschil, for the sons of Korah. As the hart panteth after the water brooks, so panteth my soul after thee, O God. My soul thirsteth for God, for the living God: when shall I come and appear before God? My tears have been my meat day and night, while they continually say unto me, Where is thy God?" (Psalms 42:1-3)

DROWNING IN FLOODS OF WATERS

Secondary Witness	King David
"Waters flowed over mine head; then I said, I am cut off." (Lamentations 3:54) "For Thou hadst cast me into the deep, in the midst of the seas; and the floods compassed me about: all Thy billows and Thy waves passed over me. Then I said, I am cast out of Thy sight..." (Jonah 2:3-4).	"To the chief Musician upon Shoshannim, A Psalm of David. Save me, O God; for the waters are come in unto my soul. I sink in deep mire, where there is no standing: I am come into deep waters, where the floods overflow me." (Psalm 69:1-2) "Then the waters had overwhelmed us, the stream had

	gone over our soul: Then the proud waters had gone over our soul." (Psalm 124:4-5)

"Thy wrath lieth hard upon me, and Thou hast afflicted me with all Thy waves. Selah." (Psalm 88:7)

"Deep calleth unto deep at the noise of Thy waterspouts: all Thy waves and Thy billows are gone over me." (Psalm 42:7) |

SPIRITUAL DARKNESS

Secondary Witness	King David
"He hath led me, and brought me into darkness, but not into light." (Lamentations 3:2)

"When His candle shined upon my head, and when by His light I walked through darkness..." (Job 29:3)

"Arise, shine; for thy light is come, and the glory of the LORD is risen upon thee. For, behold, the darkness shall cover the earth, and gross darkness the people: but the LORD shall arise upon thee, and His glory shall be seen upon thee. And the Gentiles shall come to thy light, and kings to the brightness of thy rising." (Isaiah 60:1-3)

"Therefore I will look unto the LORD; I will wait for the God of my salvation: my God will hear me. Rejoice not against me, O mine enemy: when I fall, I shall arise; when I sit in darkness, the | "For Thou wilt light my candle: the LORD my God will enlighten my darkness." (Psalm 18:28)

"A Psalm of David. The LORD is my light and my salvation; whom shall I fear? the LORD is the strength of my life; of whom shall I be afraid? Hide not Thy face far from me; put not Thy servant away in anger: Thou hast been my help; leave me not, neither forsake me, O God of my salvation." (Psalm 27:1, 9)

"For they got not the land in possession by their own sword, neither did their own arm save them: but Thy right hand, and Thine arm, and the light of Thy countenance, because Thou hadst a favour unto them." (Psalm 44:3)

"For the enemy hath persecuted my soul; he hath smitten my life down to the ground; he hath made me to dwell in darkness, as those |

LORD shall be a light unto me." (Micah 7:7-8)	that have been long dead...Hear me speedily, O LORD: my spirit faileth: hide not Thy face from me, lest I be like unto them that go down into the pit." (Psalm 143:3, 7) "O send out Thy light and Thy truth: let them lead me; let them bring me unto Thy holy hill, and to Thy tabernacles." (Psalm 43:3) "Blessed is the people that know the joyful sound: they shall walk, O LORD, in the light of Thy countenance." (Psalm 89:15)

The *arrows* of God – likewise the spiritual *desertification, drowning floods*, and *plaguing darkness* – they are meant for the world, namely to condemn them, but if we are in unrepentant sin, we will be thus judged. We are chastened by these plagues that we might repent and recover our saintly standing in grace, unto obedience, thus we are chastened by them "that we should not be condemned with the world" (1 Cor. 11:32), but if we fall into these plagues without recovering from them, expressly because we are not being exercised unto fruits of repentance and holiness through them (Heb. 12:11), then our judgment will not be in this life only, but in the life to come, and we will perish with the heathen world of iniquitous sinners. We have become, as it is written, them that are "turned out of the way" (Heb. 12:13), them that "fail of the grace of God" (Heb. 12:15), them that become the "root of bitterness springing up" in the garden of God (Heb. 12:15, Deut. 29:18). Henceforth, let us look at how David was not condemned by these chastening plagues of judgment and wrath, but rather, exercised unto repentance and restoration, meekly responded to the goodness of God so that, for him, it became a redemptive process as it was meant by God to be. If haply we understand biblical chastening that we might identify the experience of it, and of necessity, by God's grace, we are exercised by it, then we will come to know the hope and happiness of the word spoken to the saints of old – "I will also leave in the midst of thee an afflicted and poor people, and they shall trust in the Name of the LORD" (Zeph. 3:12).

PSALM 25
"Remember not the sins of my youth, nor my transgressions...pardon mine iniquity; for it is great...forgive all my sins." (Ps. 25:7, 11, 18)

"The secret of the LORD is with them that fear Him; and He will shew them His covenant. Mine eyes are ever toward the LORD; for He shall pluck my feet out of the net. Turn Thee unto me, and have mercy upon me; for I am desolate and afflicted. The troubles of my heart are enlarged: O bring Thou me out of my distresses. Look upon mine affliction and my pain; and forgive all my sins." (Psalm 25:14-18)

Psalm 25 is thematic, for it represents the whole of David's pursuit – the Covenant's fulfillment – and his greatest burden of mind which interrupted the Covenant's fulfillment – his sins. David knew that his sin could, and did, provoke God to wrath, endangering David that, haply, God would be willing to "enter into judgment" (Ps. 143:2) with him. Therefore, see how David was ever praying for the Lord to forgive his sins (Ps. 25:7, 11, 18). What is the spiritual experience of wrath which David underwent if the Covenant was not being fulfilled in his life? David speaks of it like as the verses above: God's arrows of wrath aimed at and firing upon him until they were sticking fast into his soul, making grievous wounds, God's plague of wrath which brought a desertification of the soul, God's tempestuous wrath which brought drowning floods of water upon the soul, and God's plague of wrath in spiritual darkness because God turned away the saving light of His face. We can determine therefore, clearly, that David wrestled against the wrath of God in his lifetime, and it was for the *present progressive* confirmation of the Covenant promises!

Who in this entire world of men does experience the soul-crushing, body-depleting, and near-death pressures of wrestling against God's wrath for personal and corporate salvation, as seen in the life of the beloved of God, King David? The famed missionary to the Native Americans, David Brainerd by name, was one man of such experience, but tragically, he is written off to be a man of melancholy, of mental and clinical sickness, but his rapturous experiences of nearness to God's presence, the length and depth of his prayer life, and the revival powers that followed, all of these things are the envy of the children of God. It is with brokenness and astonishment that I have come to conclude, that Brainerd was in a right-standing relationship with God, and thereby, he was sensitive to, and responsive to, his own sinfulness, being aware of God's reactive and changing wrath; all the while he was in pursuit of the promises of God to be performed, but how terrible it is that his life of lowly repentance and mourning is the hiss of God's people, as they just brush it off?! They are of a stronger constitution, you see…but Brainerd's power is their praise and they go on powerless all their days! Why!? Apparently they have sin that they don't know about! But Brainerd knew it – oh, how he knew his wrath-aggravating sin! The secret of Brainerd's success in the Spirit of God was this very breaking experience which "Americanized Christianity" spurns as a psychological instability, when, in truth, these experiences were death to the flesh so that Brainerd might live to God. This was not merely Brainerd's melancholy, but godly sorrow. It was his deep wrestling against wrath, followed by rising successes of mercies won! Thus power endued and rested upon this humble man! Brainerd was an example, like King David, whose experiences of personal soul-travail against God's wrath men do likewise spurn, so that men are nearly unaware of God's wrath altogether, and it is because they refuse to suffer it. Leonard Ravenhill rightly said, "I get calls from all over the world, everyone wants my anointing and mantle…but nobody wants my sackcloth and ashes".

A Present Progressive Assurance of Salvation – Obtained by Intercession

Oh! How many do reckon and boast in the "sure mercies of David", and yet, they are completely oblivious to how David, for himself, made mercy sure! Might I suggest that we learn how David responded and related to the wrath of God, so that we can be like him?

Oh, that we would see the wrath of God, if indeed it is upon us! And then, that we would intercede in desperation, so as to say, "Hide not Thy face far from me; put not Thy servant away in anger: Thou hast been my help; leave me not, neither forsake me, O God of my salvation" (Ps. 27:9)! Will we ever be like David, that we might have Davidic mercies? Then let us, when necessary, be broken and pressed down under Davidic experiences of wrath, God's wrath, which was so often upon him. Let us burn in hatred and anger against our sin, so that, God would never burn us with wicked men. Let us undergo the process of present progressive

Thematic Template of the Psalms

We must seek God in intercession against wrath so that we can obtain *a present progressive, supernatural assurance that God will save.* This becomes the standing platform of our praise, for, grace has enabled a holy *reckoning of the promises of God*, so that, hour by hour, by and by, saving power clothes our conversation. Also, by the victories of intercession, certain revelations are cast beyond the present time into the future, by *a prophetic word or vision*, and by this we can declare future deeds of God's glory in our personal perseverance in salvation, even though the circumstantial foes presently in opposition do appear insurmountable. But Oh! What is missing today is that the people of God are not *wrestling against the wrath of God*, so that their praises, reckoning of the promises, or prophetic declarations of future perseverance are all without the performance of what is praised, reckoned, or prophesied!

salvation with the same language of David's intercessions, so that we can speak to God in the same coherent wording as biblical saints, but to do this we must first – stop – and look this ancient, biblical reality in the face. No shrinking back! No shrugging it off! Let us walk through the emotional traumas to a biblical proportion – as David and as Jacob – like when they did wrestle with their God. After intercession, we can, like them, arise again to praise God for His goodness and mercy, but let it be praised after we did have such a hard wrestle of intercession that we were brought to the point of fainting, and even death. With a clear conscience and of honest report, David did say – "**I had fainted**, unless I had believed to see the goodness of the LORD in the land of the living. Wait on the LORD: be of good courage, and He shall strengthen thine heart: wait, I say, on the LORD" (Psalm 27:13-14).

Have you ever been near **fainting** in a spiritual wrestle against wrath? This is why David wrote, "**I had fainted.**" This is no exaggeration! David is not a lying enthusiast who seeks to make your emotions tingle by poetic fantasies. Reader, HE WAS IN AN AGONY! Have you ever been taken to a spiritual cliff and pressed right to the edge, and from thence you looked down upon the blood-red rocks of wrath, upon which, at sundry times, God drove men into, because they would not repent at last? God terrorizes a good man's mind so that he will repent in time, and how? What can it be compared to? It is as when men who fear heights are brought up high, oh the feeling of it!

> *It is like a thousand fire alarms vibrating your emotions into sirens;*
> *Like a swarm of killer bees circling around your mental equilibrium;*
> *You are trying to gather your thoughts, but in the midst of bees you are lost.*
> *As it were, every swarming thought has a poisonous sting, and, lo,*
> *You are persecuted, swelling, stung-red, and burning-hot.*
> *You are relentlessly swinging but you cannot do a thing!*
> *You are in a craze and spinning around, you are made unsound in every sensibility,*
> *For because, with your senses stung, you cannot see – your thoughts are stinging bees!*
> *They climb into your eyes, ears, nose, and mouth, stinging relentlessly,*
> *And so much the more – you feel – there is no direction to flee!*

Behold the man, he is terrified into dizziness and is ready to **faint**...My reader, I find that David had similar experiences of inexpressible fears, so that, time and time again, David was tottering around the edges of bodily collapse, emotionally amazed with weeping and holy-gasp, crying aloud for *nights* and *days*, enduring long, bone-exposing fasts, and thus, he was near **fainting** betimes.

> *He was hallowed for heaven, yes, but he obtained saving graces by*
> *wrestling against wrath 70 x 7 times – for this reason repentance was his*
> *continual state of mind.*
> *David's exasperation and desperation, his soul-travailing, wrestling, and*
> *wailing, these must become our template of example, or else, what religious*
> *mountain are you climbing?!*
> *You claim everything else of David's, BUT WITHOUT THIS, it is a false*
> *reality, and so, men do presumptuously claim David's triumphant*
> *declarations without having them in actuality.*
> *A bunch of vain men, they are, reckoning promises without David's pain,*
> *laying claim to David's holiness without his chastening and shame.*
> *They are trampling underfoot the tear-stained cheeks, wrinkled old eyes,*
> *and callused knees of the poor man, David, whose life of wrestling with God*
> *was in perseverant entreaties!*
> *They will follow after only half of David's spiritual experiences and name,*

unwilling to mourn in David's sackcloth and ashes, so that, with him, they
might rise up beautified – the same.

Men do search the psalms to claim David's assurance of salvation for themselves, his eloquent and picture-perfect promises which he reckoned, and those prophetic visions he did write about and tell, which cause every generation to marvel how God did love David – and yet – to my utter astonishment – men are blind to David's wrestling against wrath – as if there were never any steep cliffs and narrow paths which did lead up to the peak of David's triumph at last. From its height of heaven's glory – from there David did say – "Surely goodness and mercy shall follow me all the day of my life: and I will dwell in the house of the LORD for ever" (Psalm 23:6), but men do mindlessly repeat the words while they are utterly falling away!

> *"...**groanings** which cannot be uttered..." – Romans 8:26*

> "I am weary with **my groaning**; all the night make I my bed to swim; I water my couch with my tears. Mine eye is consumed because of grief; it waxeth old because of all mine enemies." (Ps. 6:6-7)

"I am weak...my bones are vexed...my soul is also sore vexed: but Thou, O LORD, how long?" (Ps. 6:2-4), saith King David. At this point, David was under the "anger" and "hot displeasure" of God, so that God did cast him off and leave him (Ps. 6:4) into the hands of his "enemies" (Ps. 6:10). The wrath of God did put him in this place for a long period of time, so that, David reverently cried to God, "How long", and it was continuing for such a long period of time that David was feeling like he was going to die under its long-lasting severity. Thus he pled for God to "return" to him, for one express purpose – "For in death there is no remembrance of Thee: in the grave who shall give Thee thanks" (Ps. 6:5)? In this experience of wrath, herein described, you may think that David was praying for salvation, but how hard? You may think that you are an intercessor, but what is your experiential standard by which you measure yourself? Are your friends and companions, who are ever on the brink of lukewarmness, your measuring standards, "measuring [yourselves] by [yourselves], and comparing [yourselves] among [yourselves]," so that you think so highly of yourself (2 Cor. 10:12)? David should be the standard for what intercession looks like for the NT experience of intercession! Yes, I mean the NT experience of intercession AGAINST the wrath of God! David prayed hard and long, even so much that he said: "I am weary with **my groaning**; all the night make I my bed to swim; I water my couch with my tears. Mine eye is consumed because of grief; it waxeth old because of all mine enemies" (Ps. 6:6-7). My reader, he was weeping profusely all night long, and for many nights, until he said that his eye was waxing old. Those of you who have been through similar intercession, you know what he is saying. David said that his **groanings** were because of, and in intercession against, wrath, and he was groaning because he could no longer utter words to express the feelings of the soul that were upon him, by the heavy hand of the Holy Ghost.

"the Spirit itself maketh intercession for us with **groanings** which cannot be uttered"
– Romans 8:26

"I am weary with my **groaning**; all the night make I my bed to swim" – Ps. 6:6
"I have **roared** by reason of the disquietness of my heart...my **groaning** is not hid"
– Ps. 38:8-9
"...I forget to eat my bread. By reason of the voice of my **groaning** my bones cleave to my skin" –Ps. 102:4-5
"the LORD did behold the earth to hear the **groaning** of the prisoner; to loose..." – Ps. 102:19-20

"...the words of my **roaring**" – Ps. 22:1
"When I kept silence, my bones waxed old through my **roaring** all the day long" – Ps. 32:3
"My **sighing** cometh before I eat, and my **roarings** are poured out like waters" – Job 3:24

> Have you ever seen the connection between the NT description of "groanings" with the biblical example of King David and others, groaning because of the wrath of God? We must trace the word to its root!
> In plain clarity, we can now see, exactly what kind of groaning is in reference in the NT passage (Rom. 8:26-27), because the groanings are called *intercessory groanings*, which are groans because of, and against, the wrath of God, as seen in the psalms.

"the **sighing** of the needy" – Ps. 12:5
"my life is spent with grief, and my years with **sighing**" – Ps. 31:10
"Let the **sighing** of the prisoner come before Thee" – Ps. 79:11

> **"maketh intercession** for us"
> – Rom. 8:26
> **"maketh intercession** for the saints"
> – Rom 8:27

"the men that **sigh** and that cry" – Ezek. 9:4
"**Sigh** therefore, thou son of man, with the breaking of thy loins; and with bitterness **sigh** before their eyes" – Ezek. 21:6

> "Likewise the Spirit also helpeth our infirmities: for we know not what we should pray for as we ought: but the Spirit itself **maketh intercession** for us with **groanings** which cannot be uttered. And He that searcheth the hearts knoweth what is the mind of the Spirit, because He **maketh intercession** for the saints according to the will of God." (Romans 8:26-27)

David's intercessory *groaning*, *roaring*, and *sighing* interprets Romans 8:26-27 when it describes intercessory groaning in the New Testament dispensation – groaning which cannot be uttered with words. Groanings are exactly like roarings and sighings. How many vocal chords the groan engages, and to what force of amplification it does reach, this matters not. Roarings would be the loudest and most forceful engagement of the voice, while sighing is more disengaged and voiceless, silent but just as sore. Roaring and sighing can express the same inward turmoil that is within the man; they are just two forms of expression in the loudest and lowest forms of groaning.

David indicates that groaning is intercessory, even though it is an unutterable agony. He said in Psalm 38:9, "Lord, all my desire is before Thee; and my groaning is not hid from Thee." The groanings do communicate "the mind" and "will of God" (Rom. 8:26-27), which also is, as David says, "my desire" (Ps. 38:9), for the two have become one communication to God by the Holy Ghost, and though it is not an understandable communication to man, to God it is an unhidden meaning, clearly understood, fully expressing intercessory desires which otherwise could not "be uttered." David was saying that all of his desire was before God in the intercessory groanings of the Holy Ghost, so that the meaning of those groanings God understands! This is exactly what is referenced in Romans 8:26, when it is said that "the Spirit itself maketh intercession for us with groanings which cannot be uttered."

> "When **I kept silence**, my bones waxed old through my roaring all the day long. For day and night Thy hand was heavy upon me: my moisture is turned into the drought of summer. Selah. I acknowledged my sin unto Thee, and mine iniquity have I not hid. I said, I will confess my transgressions unto the LORD; and Thou forgavest the iniquity of my sin. Selah. For this shall every one that is godly pray unto Thee in a time when Thou mayest be found: surely **in the floods of great waters** they shall not come nigh unto him." (Psalm 32:3-6)

In all the former citations which used *groaning*, *roaring*, and *sighing*, each is a mark of salvation being wrought in the person who was in the midst of an outpouring of wrath, and, by those very means, they were interceding against the wrath of God. Now let us clearly note: we understand that these were intercessory *groanings*, *roarings*, and *sighings*, and therefore, they were wrought within the soul because of the kindled wrath of God, and the groanings, roarings, and sighings were manifesting to stand against it so as to pacify it; thus, when wrath is pacified then men do cease to *groan*, *roar*, and *sigh*. This is plainly evident in Psalm 32:3-6, cited just above. David was, at first, "silent" about his sins, which means that he was hiding and unrepentant over them, and therefore God poured out wrath to utterly chasten David's soul. This happened "all the day" and every day, until David did repent of his sin-hiding silence and unrepentant rebellion. David confessed this when he said, "I acknowledged my sin unto Thee, and mine iniquity have I not hid. I said, I will confess my transgressions unto the LORD; and Thou forgavest." At the moment that David ceased to be in rebellion, at the moment he repented of his silence and made known his sin by a humble confession to God, he was delivered from the afflicting wrath of God which pressed him into *groanings*, *roarings*, and *sighings*.

Oh! How eternity will prove that those men who "groaned" and "roared" on earth will not be those who groan and roar in hell! Those that hated their sins on earth will forget about them in heaven, while those that loved their sins on earth will regretfully remorse over them in hell! May I put to you a solemn question? Do you *groan* over your sins? If not, maybe it is because you do not believe in the wrath of God. Maybe it is because you do not see your sins which do provoke God's wrath, and perhaps your doctrine does not permit you to groan because you are taught by it that God cannot ever be angry with you again, now that you are regenerated. Just a little distance from God's presence, and behold, you are dazzled by eternally insignificant hobbies and entertainment, and you will not groan because you believe God would never change His compassionate face into an angry frown, or a gentle tone into a sharp, fiery rebuke!

> When I read the psalms I find that King David *groaned* and
> *roared* over his sin!
> I am so shocked and amazed how blinded "Christianity" is today!

Please, I beg you to reevaluate what you think intercessory prayer is, what a godly degree of conviction of sin is, what you see when you look up at the face of God, whether wrath or love, what spiritual condition you are presently in, how long and trying wrath's exercise was for David and the psalmists, and therefore how long you can expect it to be for you in similar circumstances! Have you ever experienced these things? If not, that should trouble you! That should confuse you! And you deserve confusion of face because of your sins and those of your fathers'! Confess to God, "O Lord, righteousness belongeth unto Thee, and unto us confusion of faces...O Lord, to us belongeth confusion of face...because we have sinned against Thee" (Dan. 9:7-8)! Yea, and then in your confusion, if God gives you mercy, why don't you *groan*, *roar*, and *sigh* over it! Then do that for many *days* and *nights*, even weeping, and God might have mercy upon you. Don't start making up reasons why this can't be the case for you now. Don't excuse yourself by taking sides with your deceitful heart, as it tells you all its reasons why you are more holy than King David, and therefore rightfully excluded from David's exercises of wrath. Why don't you try to seek God? Then you might understand what circumstances this experience of near annihilating wrath is a possible for NT Christians, like as it was for King David in the OT! Lest God says to you the fearful words of dissatisfaction and rejection, even the words of Jeremiah 6:10, and God passes you by. What a fate – that God does not enlighten your understanding to open up the truth before you, so as to take away the confusion you are in, and why? God says: "To whom shall I speak, and give warning, that they may hear? Behold, their ear is uncircumcised, and they cannot hearken: behold, the word of the LORD is unto them a reproach; they have no delight in it" (Jer. 6:10). Reader, you just don't care, so therefore you don't *groan*, *roar*, and *sigh*! Therefore you don't pray, you don't make many effectual prayers "with all perseverance" (Eph. 6:18), and so it is so – "yet made [you] not [your] prayer before the LORD [your] God, that [you] might turn from [your] iniquities and understand [God's] truth" (Dan. 9:13).

> "Mighty intercessors" of modern "Christianity," I adjure thee! I beg of
> thee! Does your intercession look like and feel like, is it long lasting like,
> and does it make you act like the following experiences written as the

inspired example of what intercession looks like?

"A Psalm of David, to bring to remembrance. O LORD, **rebuke** me not in Thy **wrath**: neither **chasten** me in Thy **hot displeasure**. For **Thine arrows** stick fast in me, and Thy hand presseth me sore. There is no soundness in my flesh because of Thine anger; neither is there any rest in my bones because of my sin. For mine iniquities are gone over mine head: as an heavy burden they are too heavy for me. My wounds stink and are corrupt because of my foolishness. I am troubled; I am bowed down greatly; I go mourning all the day long. For my loins are filled with a loathsome disease: and there is no soundness in my flesh. I am feeble and sore broken: I have **roared** by reason of the disquietness of my heart. Lord, all my desire is before Thee; and my **groaning** is not hid from Thee. My heart panteth, my strength faileth me: as for the light of mine eyes, it also is gone from me." (Psalm 38:1-10)

"A Prayer of the afflicted, when he is overwhelmed, and poureth out his complaint before the LORD. Hear my prayer, O LORD, and let my cry come unto Thee. **Hide not Thy face from me** in the day when I am in trouble; incline Thine ear unto me: in the day when I call answer me speedily. For my days are consumed like smoke, and my bones are burned as an hearth. My heart is smitten, and withered like grass; so that I forget to eat my bread. By reason of the voice of my **groaning** my bones cleave to my skin. I am like a pelican of the wilderness: I am like an owl of the desert. I watch, and am as a sparrow alone upon the house top. Mine enemies reproach me all the day; and they that are mad against me are sworn against me. For I have eaten ashes like bread, and mingled my drink with weeping, Because of Thine indignation and Thy wrath: for Thou hast lifted me up, and cast me down. My days are like a shadow that declineth; and I am withered like grass. But Thou, O LORD, shalt endure for ever; and Thy remembrance unto all generations. Thou shalt arise, and have mercy upon Zion: for the time to favour her, yea, the set time, is come. For Thy servants take pleasure in her stones, and favour the dust thereof. So the heathen shall fear the name of the LORD, and all the kings of the earth Thy glory. When the LORD shall build up Zion, He shall appear in His glory. He will regard the prayer of the destitute, and not despise their prayer. This shall be written for the generation to come: and the people which shall be created shall praise the LORD. For He hath looked down from the height of His sanctuary; from heaven did the LORD behold the earth; To hear the **groaning** of the prisoner; to loose those that are appointed to death; To declare the name of the LORD in Zion, and His praise in Jerusalem…" (Psalm 102:1-21)

"In Thee, O LORD, do I put my trust; let me never be ashamed: deliver me in Thy righteousness…I will be glad and rejoice in Thy mercy: for Thou hast considered my trouble; Thou hast known **my soul in adversities**; And hast not shut me up into the hand of the enemy: Thou hast set my feet in a large room. Have mercy upon me, O LORD, **for I am in trouble: mine eye is consumed with grief, yea, my soul and my belly. For my life is spent with grief, and my years with sighing: my strength faileth because of mine iniquity, and my bones are consumed.** I was a reproach among all mine enemies, but especially among my neighbours, and a fear to mine acquaintance: they that did see me without fled from me. I am forgotten as a dead man out of mind: I am like a broken vessel. For I have heard the slander of many: fear was on every side: while they took counsel together against me, they devised to take away my life. But I trusted in Thee, O LORD: I said, Thou art my God. My times are in Thy hand: deliver me from the hand of mine enemies, and from them that persecute me. **Make Thy face to shine upon Thy servant**: save me for Thy mercies' sake. Let me not be ashamed, O LORD; for I have called upon Thee: let the wicked be ashamed, and let them be silent in the grave. Let the lying lips be put to silence; which speak grievous things proudly and contemptuously against the righteous…For I said in my haste, **I am cut off from before Thine eyes**: nevertheless Thou heardest the voice of my supplications when I cried unto thee. O love the LORD, all ye His saints: for the LORD preserveth the faithful, and plentifully rewardeth the proud doer. Be of good courage, and He shall strengthen your heart, all ye that hope in the LORD." (Psalm 31:1, 7-18, 22-24)

"I said, I will take heed to my ways, that I sin not with my tongue: I will keep my mouth with a bridle, while the wicked is before me. I was dumb with silence, I held my peace, even from good; and my sorrow was stirred. My heart was hot within me, while I was musing the fire burned: then spake I with my tongue, LORD, **make me to know mine end, and the measure of my days, what it is; that I may know how frail I am. Behold, Thou hast made my days as an handbreadth; and mine age is as nothing before Thee: verily every man at his best state is altogether vanity.** Selah. Surely every man walketh in a vain shew: surely they are disquieted in vain: he heapeth up riches, and knoweth not who shall gather them. And now, Lord, what wait I for? my hope is in Thee. Deliver me from all my transgressions: make me not the reproach of the foolish. I was dumb, I opened not my mouth; because Thou didst it. **Remove Thy stroke away from me: I am consumed by the blow of Thine hand. When Thou with rebukes dost correct man for iniquity, Thou makest his beauty to consume away like a moth: surely every man is vanity.** Selah. Hear my prayer, O LORD, and give ear unto my cry; hold not Thy peace at **my tears**: for I am a stranger with Thee, and a sojourner, as all my fathers were. O spare me, that I may recover strength, **before I go hence, and be no more.**" (Psalm 39:1-13)

Wrath & Intercessions so Long →   "I cry unto Thee DAILY"
– Ps. 86:3-5
"MY DAYS are consumed…my days are like a shadow that declineth…"
(Ps. 102)
"For MY LIFE is spent with grief, and MY YEARS with sighing: my strength faileth because of mine iniquity, and my bones are consumed." (Psalm 31)

NOTE: In the midst of wrath and intercessions, it is not uncommon for the individual to lose the sense of assurance in their personal salvation.

Wrath so Severe it is Nearly Deadly → "Unto Thee will I cry, O LORD my rock; be not silent to me: lest, if Thou be silent to me, I become like them that go down into the pit." (Psalm 28:1)

"make me to know mine end, and the measure of my days, what it is; that I may know how frail I am. Behold, Thou hast made my days as an handbreadth; and mine age is as nothing before Thee: verily every man at his best state is altogether vanity… Remove Thy stroke away from me: I am consumed by the blow of Thine hand. When Thou with rebukes dost correct man for iniquity, Thou makest his beauty to consume away like a moth: surely every man is vanity… O spare me, that I may recover strength, before I go hence, and be no more." (Psalm 39) "my soul in adversities… for I am in trouble: mine eye is consumed with grief, yea, my soul and my belly… For I said in my haste, I am cut off from before Thine eyes…" (Psalm 31)

"Be merciful unto me, O Lord: FOR I CRY UNTO THEE DAILY. Rejoice the soul of Thy servant: For unto Thee, O Lord, do I lift up my soul. For Thou, Lord, art good, and ready to forgive; and plenteous in mercy UNTO ALL THEM THAT CALL UPON THEE." (Psalm 86:3-5)

David's prayers and intercessions were "fervent" (James 5). They were not mere whispers or silent monologues; they were with a lifted up voice and loud cries. Do you pray this way? Maybe it is because you are not as urgent as he was, because you don't see your sin or God's wrath like he saw it to be.

"For innumerable evils have compassed me about: mine iniquities have taken hold upon me, so that I am not able to look up; they are more than the hairs of mine head: therefore **my heart faileth me**." (Psalm 40:12)

"I had fainted, unless I had believed" – Psalm 27:13

Maybe if you were so convicted, or if your salvation was on the line, then you would fear so much so that your heart fails and your consciousness is near fainting because your inner turmoil and travail is so great. Then, like the following verses, you might bestir yourself to seek God like you never have before, except when you first sought after salvation in Christ.

"I cry unto Thee: make haste unto me; give ear unto my voice, when **I cry** unto Thee. Let my prayer be set forth before Thee as incense; and **the lifting up of my hands** as the evening sacrifice. Set a watch, O LORD, before my mouth; keep the door of my lips. Incline not my heart to any evil thing, to practise wicked works with men that work iniquity: and let me not eat of their dainties."
(Psalm 141:1-4)

"My knees are weak through fasting; my flesh faileth of fatness." (Ps. 109:24)

"no soundness in my flesh…no rest in my bones…an heavy burden…too heavy for me…my wounds stink…I am troubled...bowed down greatly...mourning all the day...feeble and sore broken...my heart panteth, my strength faileth" (Ps. 38:1-10)

"my bones cleave to my skin...weeping...the groaning of the prisoner" (Ps. 102)

Do you see how aware David was of his sins, thus he sought repentance of these sins so that he would not be a castaway?! If ever he did persevere, by God's grace, which he did, thence his spiritual walk is our example, and we should credit God's salvation to be great in the midst of these unavoidable experiences of sins uprising. This Psalm was written after the Covenant was established with David, and he was ruling as King at the time that his own house was being dedicated:

> "A Psalm and Song at the dedication of the house of David. I will extol Thee, O LORD; for Thou hast lifted me up, and hast not made my foes to rejoice over me. O LORD my God, I cried unto Thee, and Thou hast healed me. O LORD, Thou hast brought up my soul from the grave: Thou hast kept me alive, that I should not go down to the pit. Sing unto the LORD, O ye saints of His, and give thanks at the remembrance of His holiness. For His anger endureth but a moment; in His favour is life: weeping may endure for a night, but joy cometh in the morning. And in my prosperity I said, I shall never be moved. LORD, by Thy favour Thou hast made my mountain to stand strong: Thou didst hide Thy face, and I was troubled. I cried to Thee, O LORD; and unto the LORD I made supplication. What profit is there in my blood, when I go down to the pit? Shall the dust praise Thee? shall it declare Thy truth? Hear, O LORD, and have mercy upon me: LORD, be Thou my helper. Thou hast turned for me my mourning into dancing: Thou hast put off my sackcloth, and girded me with gladness; To the end that my glory may sing praise to Thee, and not be silent. O LORD my God, I will give thanks unto Thee for ever." (Psalm 30:1-12)

All the times of defeat and tarrying, previous to the point of the establishment of the Kingdom under David, were understood by him to be manifestations of wrath because of sin. Also, all future inability to continually secure the Kingdom of God under David was also credited as a manifestation of wrath because of sin. Psalm 60 is a perfect example of this, and with this psalm I will conclude this chapter:

> "To the chief Musician upon Shushaneduth, Michtam of David, to teach; when he strove with Aramnaharaim and with Aramzobah, when Joab returned, and smote of Edom in the valley of salt twelve thousand. **O God, Thou hast cast us off,**

Thou hast scattered us, Thou hast been displeased; O turn Thyself to us again. Thou hast made the earth to tremble; Thou hast broken it: heal the breaches thereof; for it shaketh. Thou hast shewed Thy people hard things: Thou hast made us to drink the wine of astonishment. Thou hast given a banner to them that fear Thee, that it may be displayed because of the truth. Selah. That Thy beloved may be delivered; save with Thy right hand, and hear me. God hath spoken in His holiness; I will rejoice, I will divide Shechem, and mete out the valley of Succoth. Gilead is mine, and Manasseh is mine; Ephraim also is the strength of mine head; Judah is my lawgiver; Moab is my washpot; over Edom will I cast out my shoe: Philistia, triumph thou because of me. Who will bring me into the strong city? Who will lead me into Edom? **Wilt not Thou, O God, which hadst cast us off? and Thou, O God, which didst not go out with our armies?** Give us help from trouble: for vain is the help of man. Through God we shall do valiantly: for He it is that shall tread down our enemies." (Psalm 60:1-12)

"MANY ARE CALLED BUT FEW ARE CHOSEN"
CHAPTER 25

"Turn, O **backsliding children**, saith the
LORD; for I am married unto you: and I will
take you **one of a city,** and **two of a family**,
and I will bring you to Zion."
(Jeremiah 3:14)

****

Answering "The Golden Chain"

The Sovereign Exaltation ➔ "Moreover whom He
did **predestinate**, them
He also **called**: and
whom He **called**, them
He also **justified**: and
whom He **justified**,
them He also **glorified**."
(Romans 8:30)

*God is not a man that He
should fail to glorify those
whom He has called, but some
have fallen from His promise
and intent by resisting Him as
He condescended to them in
their ways; nevertheless those
who cannot fall will not fall
because God's immutable will
predestinated them with
irresistible grace.*

The Scarce Salvation ➔ "For many are **called**,
but few are **chosen**."
(Matthew 22:14)

The Pastoral Burden ➔ "Make your **calling** and **election** sure." (2 Peter 1)

****

Studying history, we can see that there were many golden chains of the
promises of God, but was there ever an exception, a breach, a break of those golden
chains? That is the question. If there was never any break of the golden chains
throughout history, then we can expect there will be no breaks in the NT golden
chain, and if there are no breaks, then many are called and many are chosen, but
Christ says many are called and few are chosen. There can be exceptions WITHIN
TIME, but in eternity, in the arena upward in heaven where God dwells in His
Sovereign loft, the decrees of His golden chains never break, even if God has to do
the impossible and illogical outside of the realm of our understanding.

Many Golden Chains: *The Golden Chains Throughout History*

In Genesis 15:13-16, God swore the Canaanite land (Gen. 15:18-21) unto the fourth generation after Abraham (Gen. 15:13-16), called the Exodus generation, and this generation fulfilled the number which God promised them to be (Gen. 15:5); they were as the stars of heaven (Deut. 10:22, Neh. 9:23). This generation came "short" (Heb. 4:1) of their gospel promise and were cast away, forsaken, and rejected by God (Num. 14:34) through a holy ***breach*** of the Covenant promise; a holy ***broken*** promise. Now, this was to no fault or error in the integrity and faithfulness of God to perform His word. Intercessors, recognizing that the promises had been broken, cried out for their fulfillment (Ps. 77). All of the thousands of years leading up to the day of Christ, men were still pleading for and looking after the fulfillment of those promises (Luke 1:54-55, 72-73), and we, like them, are also waiting for those promises to consummate in Christ's rulership of the Land. We await their final, mysterious fulfillment, but there is no fault upon God because His former word was breached. The Abrahamic Covenant was a "golden chain" which cannot be broken, and though those persons who were called in its promise fell short of it, and though many generations in its call also fell short of it, it was the mercy of God that He did not entirely and utterly consume the whole seed of Abraham so as to make void the Covenant's final fulfillment altogether (Neh. 9:17, 19, 27, 31). It was God's mercy that He did not throw out the golden chain altogether but rather disintegrated some links to the chain, and with no flaw in the promise, for somehow the higher righteousness of God is able to take a just and righteous occasion to damn saved men because of their sin (Neh. 9:33). Rising up to vindicate God's faultlessness, God's people, the holy angels, and God's scripture still affirm that God kept His word perfectly, faithfully, and righteously (Neh. 9:7-8, 15, 23-25, 32, Psalm 105:8-11, 42), but the breach of promise upon those saved men/generations is never disannulled, disaffirmed, or denied **at the same time**. I say again, they recognized that God's faithfulness to perform the Covenant was magnified in that He kept the Covenant alive at all. They understood that God desired, thought to, and moved to destroy it altogether, many times, and therefore, to think that God would keep it alive for any further, partial, or a final mysterious fulfillment in Christ for all eternity – this is God's great faithfulness (Num. 9:31-32, Lam. 3:21). Had it not been for intercessors in every age standing against the wrathful mind of God to destroy the Covenant and His people, then it, and they, would not be alive today (Exodus 32:13). God hears their prayers and still affirms, the New Covenant is arisen to fulfill the age-old, first Covenant to the fathers' – or Abraham as the first father (Deut. 9:5, 26-29, 10:15-16, Micah 7:20, Lk. 1:54-55, 72-73, Rom. 11:28-29, Jer. 33:22-26).

Many persons and generations were participants in the promises of these Covenants, but they were damned, fell short of their calling, were not finally chosen, and how? God repented of His purpose to save them (as we have addressed with so great an exhaustiveness thus far unto this chapter), and when it says that "the gifts and calling of God are without repentance", it is meant to say that just as Nehemiah articulates Church history (Nehemiah 9) – though many perished and fell from the Covenant through God's holy repentances – nevertheless, it is alive and will finally be fulfilled with a single generation in the END, and that for all time, because this purpose is established without repentance, and all those who died having not seen the final fulfillment of it, but did look for and wait for it until death, will be resurrected to its fulfillment in the END of time. They were saved by these very promises in their life and in the life to come. In the end it shall be said – "this is My Covenant unto them, **when I shall take away their sins**" (Rom. 11:27). In the END **"repentance shall be hid from [His] eyes"** (Hos. 13:14), but that does not negate all those generations and persons who perished because God did repent.

In the very same manner as the Abrahamic Covenant, the Davidic Covenant is eternally fulfilled in Christ. Like the Abrahamic Covenant, it was, in its time and still today, a golden chain, though many generations and persons came short of the Covenant promises when they were participants in them as saved men. The Davidic Covenant's golden chain is altogether like unto Romans 8:28-32, but as was thoroughly addressed already, Solomon fell short of the final promise of that chain, and in subsequent generations God sought to fulfill the Covenant so as to give David's seed an eternal throne...nevertheless, David's throne was utterly cast down to the ground. For this reason the intercessors did arise and cry (Psalms 89, 132), and God did respond and speak to show the eternality of the Davidic Covenant's final fulfillment (Psalm 110:1), but this does not negate the holy breaches of the Covenant in the former, present, and future generations to come. The time of its fulfillment has partially begun with the ascension of Christ to the throne of David in heaven (Lk. 1:31-33, Acts 2:25-36), and yet remember, it is not fulfilled finally, eternally, without breachability until God makes all of Christ's enemies His footstool (Acts 2:35, 1 Cor. 15:24-28, 54-57). This is the end of our gospel-Covenant as well, because we are now links in the chain of the golden promises of the Davidic Covenant, and for its fulfillment in Christ do we wait, but God can break us off and raise up others to be saved by these promises, just like He did with those of times past (Rom. 11:18-22). They fell short of their calling, which, in Christ, is also our calling.

What is golden about the golden chain of Romans 8:28-32, what is faithful about the faithfulness of God, and what is merciful about the ever-enduring mercies of God to keep His Covenant? These acclamations do not mean that no one ever came short of and perished under a holy breach of those words of promise, but it is that *all did not*, *are not*, and *will not* come short of them, even though God desired, desires, and will desire to destroy all of His people in His holy, righteous anger against the sinfulness of the saints. Faithfulness and mercy do exclaim the wonder that a small amount, even that some of the people, are saved which are altogether just a FEW of the MANY that were called. That is a biblical explanation of the faithfulness and mercy of God! But oh! How many people just abuse the words of God!

632

What will you so fervently plead? That God says that He will "never leave thee nor forsake thee" (Heb. 13:5, Deut. 31:6), and therefore HE CANNOT ever leave you or forsake you and that is FINAL? Then why did God say, "I will never break My Covenant" (Judges 2:2), and yet He breached the promises for the rebellious generations? Will you plead that Christ said, "Lo, I am with you alway, even unto the end of the world" (Matt. 28:20), and therefore He means to say that it is impossible for Him to leave you, or ever forsake you, but to ALWAYS be with you? Will you just stand so fervently upon that word ALWAYS, as if there is no answer to you? Then why did God say to Joshua, "I will be with thee: I will not fail thee, nor forsake thee" (Josh. 1:6), and then later, "neither will I be with you any more" (Josh. 7:12)? Why did God say to Jacob, "I will not leave thee" (Gen. 28:15), and at the dark night of Jacob's soul God sought to leave him to destruction, and He said to Jacob, "let Me go" (Gen. 32:26)? Yea verily, at this time Jacob made his election sure instead of vainly trusting in election – he wrestled, clave, and cried, "I will not let Thee go", to God (Gen. 32:26)!

What else will you say? God says that He will, in the New Covenant, "put My fear in their hearts, that they shall not depart from Me" (Jer. 32:40), and therefore that means that NT Christians cannot depart from God? Then why does Hebrews 3:12 use the very same word and language to declare that a man can depart from God, and that we should fear and take heed to this, saying, "Take heed, brethren, lest there be in any of you an evil heart of unbelief, in departing from the Living God" (Heb. 3:12)? Or will you say that God cannot remember our sins anymore because He says, "their sins and iniquities I will remember no more" (Heb. 10:17), but then why does God say later in that chapter that He will remember men's sins if they begin to willfully sin against Him (Heb. 10:26-29)? Did not God say "their sins and iniquities I will remember no more" in Hebrews 10:17, which is in the same context as when He said, "all his righteousness shall not be remembered" (Ezek. 33:13)? And again, if the wicked turns from his wickedness then "none of his sins that he hath committed shall be mentioned unto him" (Ezek. 33:16). Do you see? The sin and righteousness which was not remembered in the OT was able to be remembered again, and the promise quoted in Hebrews 10:17 is also quoted from the OT in Jeremiah 31:34, thus would not Jeremiah's preaching be parallel to Ezekiel's? In the NT and OT there is a fear of falling short of the promises of God, because men understand that they can fall short of them!

In the midst of biblical chapters where the scripture is establishing a godly fear that men are able to fall away from grace, the promises of God's faithfulness and keeping power are inserted, because this leads the people to pray for their performance, seek after their verification and confirmation, and lay hold upon them, for truly, God's faithfulness is our only hope – but this does not make void and deny that men can come short of them! Such verses like 1 Corinthians 3:15, 10:13, Hebrews 6:9-10, Heb. 10:32-36 do not negate the truth of the surrounding warnings of falling into condemnation. These asserting words of hope are held right there in a good place, as the only beacon of hope for salvation, giving direction for the godly fear of a saint who is taking heed to himself, lest he falls.

The PURPOSE & INTENT for Salvation

> "when we are judged, we are chastened of the Lord, that we
> should not be condemned with the world."
> (1 Cor. 11:32)

> "that the spirit may be saved in the day of the Lord Jesus." (1
> Cor. 5:5)

You may argue that God does all of His "rebukes" (Heb. 12:5-6, Rev. 3:19) for the intention and purpose of salvation and not condemnation, in love and not in wrath, but that is to say that God has no will, desire, purpose, counsel, mind, emotion, and heart which can be fallen short of and resisted, as if there is no condescension of God in the ways of man, and as if there is no simultaneous will in God working within time which genuinely desires salvation but does not always obtain it. The scriptures are very clear – saved, righteous men are judged in this life for the specific purpose that they are saved in the life to come. Therefore for this intent and purpose are the righteous plagued, chastened, and troubled by God's wrath. As it is written, "when we are judged, we are chastened of the Lord, that we should not be condemned with the world" (1 Cor. 11:32). Will you stand on this, that it does exactly mean therefore that no man can be lost, condemned, and under eternal wrath at the final Judgment, only because this is *God's intent* or *purpose* for all these things? Then you are claiming that God can never come short of His salvific *intents* or *purposes*, and that there is no condescension of God which makes plain that salvific *intent* can be resisted by men and changed in God.

PURPOSE & INTENTION #1

> "O that there were such an heart in them, that they would fear
> Me, and keep all My commandments always, that it might be
> well with them, and with their children for ever" (Deut. 5:29)?!

Did not God desire the salvation of Israel so as to seek it through mighty revelations of His fear, as Moses explained the purpose for these things, "that His fear may be before your faces, that ye sin not" (Ex. 20:20)? And did not God so earnestly desire the salvation of this generation that He exclaimed the lamentation, "O that there were such an heart in them, that they would fear Me, and keep all My commandments always, that it might be well with them, and with their children for ever" (Deut. 5:29)?!

PURPOSE & INTENTION #2

> "O that thou hadst hearkened to My commandments! Then had

thy peace been as a river, and thy righteousness as the waves of the sea" (Isa. 48:18)!

Did not God do all that He did to Israel so that they would be saved (Isaiah 5:1-5), that that very purpose of salvation was HIS DESIRE behind all that He did? And it was resisted! And so, like God lamented over Israel in Deuteronomy 5:29, He also says of the dispersed generation, "O that thou hadst hearkened to My commandments! Then had thy peace been as a river, and thy righteousness as the waves of the sea" (Isa. 48:18)!

PURPOSE & INTENTION #3

"Oh that My people had hearkened unto Me, and Israel had walked in My ways" (Ps. 81:13)!

Again, to the generation which was commissioned to take the Promised Land to rule it forever, God lamented, "Oh that My people had hearkened unto Me, and Israel had walked in My ways" (Ps. 81:13)! And again, when He destroyed His House, He cried, "How is the gold become dim! How is the most fine gold changed! The stones of the sanctuary are poured out in the top of every street" (Lam. 4:1)!

PURPOSE & INTENTION #4 & #5

"How long will it be ere they attain to innocency (Hos. 8:5)!?

God desired for His people to be righteous and cried again on this matter, "How long will it be ere they attain to innocency (Hos. 8:5)!? Likewise also God lamented over the first century Jews, even weeping (Lk. 19:42), and He clearly declares that He desired to save them but they "would not" (Luke 13:34-35)!

Reader, God desired to save all of these generations and peoples, and I could cite more. God desired to save them and He used *judgment*, *fire*, *rebukes*, and *affliction* with the *intent* that the people He is lamenting over would have been so exercised – "that the spirit may be saved in the day of the Lord Jesus" (1 Cor. 5:5) – but just because this was God's purpose and intent, nevertheless it was resisted! Thus did God lament as He did. Therefore, when we see the salvific intent of God in the New Testament scriptures, as in 1 Corinthians 11:32 & 1 Corinthians 5:5, these verses do not mean that men cannot come short of that intention, purpose, desire, and pursuit of God! Now please, let me reason in another direction.

1) Your heresy is coming from the fact that you view God only in His sovereign ways – that He cannot change His mind, purpose, will, and desire when conditions are transgressed, resulting in a breach His word of promise. In other words, you are negating the condescension of God, God in the ways of man.

635

2) Furthermore, you are doing the work of a false prophet when you give unrepentant saints false peace, because, if the saved men in biblical history did not see that they were under the damning wrath of God at certain times in their lives, when indeed they were, they would not have been moved to repent.

You say that men cannot come short of this salvific intent and purpose, and therefore, God always fulfills His intentions, and I ask you this: why did God desire to give King Saul an eternal Kingdom (1 Sam. 13:13-14), and yet, he came short of that salvific desire in God? I could cite many more, but the bottom-ling two points are these: 1) Your heresy is coming from the fact that you view God only in His sovereign ways – that He cannot change His mind, purpose, will, and desire when conditions are transgressed, resulting in a breach His word of promise. In other words, you are negating the condescension of God, God in the ways of man. 2) Furthermore, you are doing the work of a false prophet when you give unrepentant saints false peace, because, if the saved men in biblical history did not see that they were under the damning wrath of God at certain times in their lives, when indeed they were, they would not have been moved to repent.

It is proven throughout biblical history that a fear of falling short of salvific promises, which is also an awareness of damning wrath alive in God when one is presently fallen short of the salvific promises of God, enabled saints to persevere and repent! God always was intent on Jeremiah's eternal salvation (Jer. 31:3), but within time God was angry with him so as to damn him. Jeremiah did not always abide in His delivering favour, though God said that He was with him "to deliver him", and that men "shall not prevail against" him (Jer. 1:19). In Jeremiah 15, God was intent on leaving Jeremiah in the hands of wicked men to be destroyed under God's wrath, along with the condemned people. We can see by his life and many others which we have covered, that, if the higher, hidden, and sovereign ways of God had been Jeremiah's sole meditation, had he believed that there could be no danger, damnation, or anger of God because of an everlasting love in God, it is then that he would have perished in his own self-justifying, unrepentant deceit. Likewise with Jeremiah, Hezekiah and Josiah believed the report of their condemnation and thus arose as the elect by that means of grace – grace to fear (Heb. 12:28-29)! "See that ye refuse not Him that speaketh" (Heb. 12:25), dear reader.

No, reader, you do not love God enough so that you will follow Him and be faithful just because you love Him. That is not true! You need to look up and meditate upon God's condescension, not only His eternality, sovereignty, and changeless glory. You need to recognize it when you look up, if haply, at a specific time in your life the wrath of God is kindled against you, even to damn you, because God has changed His mind toward you. At such a time, there can be simultaneous desires in God wrestling with one another! God no longer desiring to save you, and still yet desiring to save you! At such a time when God repents of desiring to save you, if then you repent and/or intercede against God's wrath, God can repent of the

636

desire to destroy you – thus your salvation will be persevered. But you will say, perhaps, that there is no possibility of God's repentance in the NT, affirming this by claiming there is no evidence of its existence, that the NT is clearly absent from and unlike the numerous accounts of God's repentances as seen in the OT. Not so, reader!

NT Intercessions & NT Repentances

POINTS TO PROVE

1) Christians can fall into damnable spiritual conditions.
2) The OT phrases like, "it may be", were used to acknowledge that God can repent of a damning purpose of wrath into a saving purpose of mercy, or vice versa, but at present the people don't know what God will do, and there are NT phrases of the exact same meaning use.
3) If there are no NT repentances in God, then there will not be any reference of NT intercessions in the present progressive salvation of saints, because intercession is a standing against wrath which is alive in the heart of God, until it is pacified. If it can be proven that there are NT intercessions, it is therefore proven that there are NT repentances.
4) Not only does Christ intercede in heaven, but, Christ, in Christian men, does intercede on earth. This further verifies that wrath is alive in God over NT, regenerate saints, and they have a need to recognize it when it is kindled.

1) Christians can fall into damnable spiritual conditions.

Christ's salvific work which was prophesied to come was declared in the terms that He would bring - light to darkness, water to desolate regions of desert, sight to the blind, and understanding to the foolish. If this is salvation at the first, and thus this is the experience when a man is saved, so also when a man falls from salvation then he falls from these experiences into the former spiritual state of their condemnation, which is a fallen state from salvific love to wrath, and thus it is into: → darkness, waterlessness, blindness, and foolishness. A denial of light, water, sight, and understanding, in NT and OT doctrine, is a denial of Christ. Oh, how we need to understand this! These are NT realities!

Damnable spiritual conditions mean spiritual deafness and blindness. Jesus Christ spoke the fearful words – "he that hath an ear, let him hear what the Spirit saith unto the Churches" (Rev. 3:13) – which grounds to the foundation a single question which does discern if your faith saves – do you hear His voice today? I am not asking you if you heard His voice yesterday. I am not asking you if you have ever heard His voice, or if you did hear His voice for a certain amount of time in the past right after you were saved. This question is the remaining truth which judges the reality you have with God – and your worthiness to bear the name Christian – do you hear Christ speak to you? For Christ to say this to the seven Churches in the province of Asia, it is to question the genuineness of their Christianity by these terms. The reader should walk away with question in their heart, "do I hear?" Or, "how would I know if I cannot hear?" But how many people today believe that they **always hear**, that they are never in danger of <u>not hearing</u>, and that hearing is an eternally insignificant concern for a regenerate Christian? We can so easily worship the victories experienced with God in time past, and so like Gideon, you worship a golden ephod which was made by the spoil of salvific victories wrought in the Lord. Do you know that you can go "blind" (Rev. 3:17)? You acknowledge that Jesus used the terrifying word, "Who hath ears to hear, let him hear" (Matt. 13:9), when He spoke to the multitudes of Israel which were mingling of two kinds of people - many reprobated and a few elect persons. Those that were reprobated had "eyes that they should not see, and ears that they should not hear" (Rom. 11:8), but it was said of the elect, "blessed are your eyes, for they see: and your ears, for they hear" (Matt. 13:16). Many amongst these multitudes sought after Christ, salvation, and obedience, but they could not understand the words of Christ, so that, "Israel hath not obtained that which he seeketh for; but the election hath obtained it, and the rest were **blinded**" (Rom. 11:7). Therefore we must understand, there would be no reason to speak the word, "he that hath an ear, let him hear" (Rev. 3:13), unless there are persons, still now, yet in the multitudes of the audience of regenerate persons of the Church who were once regenerate themselves, and who have fallen into blindness of eyes (Eph. 4:18) and dullness of hearing (Heb. 5:11), so that now they cannot hear or see, and thus, what happened to the Jews in the 1st century was a type of what is happening to the regenerate Church in the last days (Rom. 11:18-23).

2) **The OT phrases like, "it may be", were used to acknowledge that God can repent of a damning purpose of wrath into a saving purpose of mercy, or vice versa, but at present the people don't know what God will do. The NT parallel to these OT phrases are: →**

> "if God peradventure" (2 Tim. 2:25)
> "if God permit" (Heb. 6:3)
> "prove your own selves…except ye be reprobates"
> (2 Cor. 13:5)

When a man no longer has eyes to see and ears to hear, he has lost saving faith which grants such things; therefore the man cannot find repentance, because God is not giving it to him (2 Tim. 2:25, Heb. 6:6, 12:17). In all the preaching of the NT pastors, there was a believing and hoping of all things (1 Cor. 13:7), that the flock would be saved to the uttermost, that they would persevere to the end, but this never took away from their acknowledgement that this hope was underneath the Sovereign Judgment of a Holy God Who has the capability to cut men off from Christ – thus they would say things like, "if God peradventure" (2 Tim. 2:25), "if God permit" (Heb. 6:3), and "prove your own selves...except ye be reprobates" (2 Cor. 13:5).

"Brethren, if any of you do err from the truth, and one convert him; Let him know, that he which converteth **the sinner** from the error of his way shall **save a soul from death**, and shall **hide a multitude of sins**." (James 5:19-20)

"If any man see his brother sin a sin which is not unto death, he shall ask, and he shall give him life for them that sin not unto death. There is a sin unto death: I do not say that he shall pray for it." (1 John 5:16)

"pray not thou for this people, neither lift up cry nor prayer for them, neither make intercession to Me: for I will not hear thee." (Jer. 7:16, 14:11, 15:1)

"There is a sin unto death: I do not say that he shall pray for it" (1 John 5:16). Likewise, when a regenerate man who is backslidden is saved from the damnable condition they were backslidden into, they do not say that the man was not in eternal danger, but rather, "let him know" that he was "converted" and "saved" "from death" and "a multitude of sins" (James 5:19-20). They had a continual hope for their salvation (Heb. 6:9-10, 10:33-36, 1 Cor. 10:13) right beside and around legitimate conditions to the promises of God, which were acknowledgements that they can be lost. There was a time when a man could not repent anymore (Heb. 4:1, 6:6, 12:17), and when a man cannot repent anymore then God will not answer intercessions for that person anymore. What NT scripture better reinstates what God said to Jeremiah when He said, "pray not thou for this people, neither lift up cry nor prayer for them, neither make intercession to Me: for I will not hear thee" (Jer. 7:16, 14:11, 15:1), than when the apostle John said, "I do not say that he shall pray for it" (1 John 5:16)? There is a time where there is no more atoning forgiveness left (Heb. 10:26-29) in the NT, even though this sacrifice was of the eternally sanctifying kind (Heb. 10:14). As I have proven already, the forevers, nevers, eternals, and everlastings do not change the castaway capabilities in the holy righteousness of God's justice.

Men today don't even believe that God's wrath can be kindled over a saint, but all these spiritual experiences I have cited above are experiences which are ordained upon men because of the kindled wrath of God over their sin – blindness, deafness, desertification, darkness. If our prayers were of no significant intercession against the wrath of God then neither would our deeds be, yet scripture claims both to be changing eternity for souls. If there was no such thing as NT intercession, then, whether we preach or not, our words would not "save a soul from death" (Jas. 5:20), and certainly, the blood of such a one who is not saved – the same one that we should have preached to, but didn't – his blood would never be required at our hand because we had no real responsibility in the slaughtering of his eternal soul (Ezek. 3:18, 20). Is there no NT blood-guiltiness for silent preachers? Paul said to some unconverted men who refused the gospel when it was preached to them, "your blood be upon your own heads; I am clean" (Acts 18:6), so obviously Paul understood that he would have been a red-handed, guilty murderer in the sight of God if he failed to preach to them, but what about when regenerate Christians are not preached to in their hour of need; the hour they need salvation from the ever-present danger of backsliding into a damnable state?

"Again, When a righteous man doth turn from his righteousness, and commit iniquity, and I lay a stumblingblock before him, he shall die: **because thou hast not given him warning**, he shall die in his sin, and his righteousness which he hath done shall not be remembered; **but his blood will I require at thine hand**. Nevertheless **if thou warn** the righteous man, that the righteous sin not, and he doth not sin, he shall surely live, because he is warned; **also thou hast delivered thy soul**." (Ezekiel 3:20-21)

"And now, behold, I know that ye all, among whom I have gone preaching the kingdom of God, shall see my face no more. Wherefore I take you to record this day, **that I am pure from the blood of all men**. For **I have not shunned to declare unto you all the counsel of God**. Take heed therefore unto yourselves, and to all the flock, over the which the Holy Ghost hath made you overseers, to feed the Church of God, which He hath purchased with His own blood. For I know this, that after my departing shall grievous wolves enter in among you, not sparing the flock. Also **of your own selves** shall men arise, speaking perverse things, to draw away disciples after them. Therefore watch, and remember, that by the space of three years **I ceased not to warn every one night and day with tears**." (Acts 20:25-31)

What was said to Ezekiel, "thou hast delivered thy soul" (Ezek. 3:19), was a NT reality for Paul, and he preached this to the *regenerate elders* of the Church at Ephesus, because he knew that some of them would fall away and perish in their sins (Acts 20:29-31). Paul preached burdens, just like his Master Jesus did, in the light of a "Great Falling Away" which would come. If saved men could never be eternally lost, then Paul would never seek to be "pure from the blood of all men" (Acts 20:26), and he was specifically referencing **regenerate men's blood** in the chapter, and therefore, in the fear that blood would be accounted to his charge, he gave the complete and full message of salvation, which was all that they needed to hear to be present-progressively saved (Acts 20:27). But people today believe that what we do has nothing to do with the eternal destiny of regenerate persons. Therefore, what the preachers preach to regenerate persons will never "hide a multitude of sins" (James

5:20), but God would have men "**know**" the opposite message – "Let him **know**, that he which converteth the sinner from the error of his way shall save a soul from death, and shall hide a multitude of sins" (James 5:20).

3) **If there are no NT repentances in God, then there will not be any reference of NT intercessions in the present progressive salvation of saints, because intercession is a standing against wrath which is alive in the heart of God, until it is pacified. If it can be proven that there are NT intercessions, it is therefore proven that there are NT repentances.**

Christ in Heaven →   "**maketh intercession** for us" – Rom. 8:34
Christ in Christians → "**maketh intercession** for us" – Rom. 8:26
                           "**maketh intercession** for the saints" – Rom 8:27

Intercession is against the wrath of God, and
if it avails, it is against the wrath of God until
He repents of His purpose which was in His
heart.

As it is with preaching, so it is with prayer: there is intercessory prayer (Rom. 8:26-27) like as there is intercessory preaching, which saves a sinning saint from death, but if there was no wrath in God over sinning saints, then what would we be interceding against? There is only one kind of intercession that exists in the Bible, and it is when a man stands in between a threatened soul and an Angry God, and the intercessor stands against the wrath of God to try to turn it away! When God is minded to destroy a soul, then the NT intercessors do cry out... then God gives the saints "life for them that sin not unto death" (1 John 5:16). God was minded to destroy unto the second death, imprisoning the saint in spiritual death, but God changed His mind from that and gave life to the sinning saint, so that the man was, genuinely, a saved "soul from death" by a deliverance from "a multitude of sins" God was imputing into the man (James 5:19-20). This is the repentance of God at work! The regenerate man was sinless in the righteousness of Christ, so that God remembered his sin no more (Heb. 10:17), and then, God was imputing a "multitude of sins" upon the man, being angry with him, and he was then under the spiritual plague of darkness (1 Jn. 1:6) until, peradventure, repentance would be granted to the man. This spiritual darkness is a place which is not covered by "the blood of Jesus Christ" (1 Jn. 1:7), therefore God is seeing the sin, angry in destroying wrath, and only minded to save again by a holy repentance! Thus it is written that there is such a thing as NT "intercession" (Rom. 8:26-27)! Now remember, intercession did prevail to change the mind of God, because God was minded also, simultaneously, to save the man through the spiritual chastening of darkness, and God was minded to save the man the whole time – at the same time He was minded to destroy him – and these two desires in God wrestled with each other, like two Persons of the Trinity wrestling one another, and saints were included in the wrestle as workers together with God in mystical union, and behold, the sovereign, eternal, predestinated, changeless will in

God prevailed in the end over the condescended will of God! The theology of Calvinism asserts that, after a man is regenerated, then God can never be angry with that saint again! It is no wonder that Calvinistic circles are so confused about prayer! I knew one brother who, when he was a Calvinist, he chose to pray only for the lost. Why? He said that he would rather pray for sinners who are under the wrath of God rather than spending his time praying for saints who can never be under the wrath of God. He thought it strange to occupy his time to pray for the greater and lesser rewards of saints, and neglect praying for sinners bound for hell.

4) **Not only does Christ intercede in heaven, but, Christ in Christian men does intercede on earth. This further verifies that wrath is alive in God over NT, regenerate saints, and they have a need to recognize it when it is kindled.**

NT intercession is done by Christ in heaven (Heb. 7:25, Rom. 8:34), by Himself alone, for He is able to turn back the wrath of God on account of His own divine powers. What is done in heaven will likely be copied on earth by the mystical body and life of Christ in the Church, and so it is so; the Church does intercede by the Holy Ghost (Rom. 8:26-27). The Church's participation in Christ's intercessions does not take away from the sufficiency of Christ, nor does it add any merits to humanity. It is Christ in the Christians that empowers the intercessory prayers or preaching. You must understand the mystical union of the Church on earth with Christ in heaven, and through this lens look at the vitality of NT intercession as an eternally consequential operation. The co-responsibility of saints to obey God by intercessory prayer and preaching cannot be diminished, though we know that God is absolutely sovereign, for, "how shall they hear without a preacher" (Rom. 10:14)? Therefore I repeat, it is for this reason Paul feared blood-guiltiness when preaching was neglected.

MYSTICAL AMBASSADORIAL UNION

What is desired by God in heaven is put in the hearts of saints on earth, so that, being constrained by the love of God, they do pray the will of God back to Him in heaven, thus it is understood that when God moves His people move with Him. Pray, and God gives a man life for his sins (1 John 5:16), but it is Christ Who prays to forgive him, through men. He moves His people to pray for the man to have life, like as He is praying in heaven for the very same man. Christ is "the Head, from which all the body by joints and bands having nourishments ministered, and knit together, increaseth with the increase of God" (Col. 2:19). In this way of prayer, we can see an ambassadorial calling in our mystical union with Christ, so that when we pray a man is given life, but it is not that we are praying so much, but it is Christ praying through us – "praying in the Holy Ghost" (Jude 20). So whether we beseech a lost soul to repent, it is "in Christ's stead" "as though God did beseech" the man "by us" (2 Cor. 5:20). We don't merely represent Christ on earth in form, but in the very Spirit of Who God is. Thus it is said that He is alive and we are dead (Gal. 2:20). Therefore we have His mind, "the mind of Christ" (1 Cor. 2:16). When we have peace and joy, Jesus Christ says – "My peace" and "My joy" (John 14:27, 15:11). When we suffer, He is suffering, and when men persecute us, Christ says, "why persecutest thou Me" (Acts 9:4, 22:7, 26:14)? When sins are committed against us, it is not against us only but Him, and when we hunger, He hungers (Matt. 25:31-46), when we are lonely, He is lonely (Matt. 25:31-46), when we are forsaken, He is forsaken (Matt. 25:31-46). When we are sick, He is sick (Matt. 25:31-46), when we are preaching, He is preaching (1 Cor. 1:21), and when men hear us, they hear Him (Lk. 10:16). Therefore it is said, "If any man speak, let him speak **as the oracles of God**; if any man minister let him do it as of **the ability which God giveth**: that God in all things may be glorified **through Jesus Christ**" (1 Peter 4:11). "He that heareth you heareth Me; and he that despiseth you despiseth Me; and he that despiseth Me despiseth Him that sent Me" (Lk. 10:16). "He that receiveth you receiveth Me, and he that receiveth Me receiveth Him that sent Me" (Matt. 10:40). And again, "He that believeth on Me, believeth not on Me, but on Him that sent Me" (John 12:44), and thus He also said, "If they have persecuted Me, they will also persecute you; if they have kept My saying, they will keep yours also" (John 15:20). Like as God said to Samuel, "they have not rejected thee, but they have rejected Me, that I should not reign over them" (1 Sam. 8:7), so it is with the ambassadorial presence of God's people on earth, in Christ. So also God said of Ezekiel, "Israel will not hearken unto thee; for they will not hearken unto Me" (Ezek. 3:7).

SUFFERING

Paul, walking out the course of his life's calling, did suffer, but he said that his suffering was not for himself but for the elect saints that would be saved through his ministry in Christ. "I suffer trouble... Therefore I endure all things for the elect's sakes, that they may also obtain the salvation which is in Christ Jesus with eternal glory" (2 Tim. 2:9-10). He described this way of suffering as an intercessory work when he said, "death worketh in us, but life in you" (2 Cor. 4:12), so that he said again in the same passage, "all things are for your sakes" (2 Cor. 4:15). Paul called these sufferings Christ's sufferings, and that he was fellowshipping (Php. 3:10) with Christ in His sufferings, even that he was filling up in his (Paul's) body and life that which was lacking in what was to be suffered by Christ's life on earth, because Christ is still alive. Paul said his sufferings were for the Church when he said, "my sufferings for you", in Colossians 1:24, but these sufferings were Christ's in Paul's body. Thus he said, "my sufferings for you, and fill up that which is behind of **the afflictions of Christ** in my flesh **for His body's sake, which is the Church**" (Col. 1:24). In a shocking way, we can see that, for Paul, "to live is Christ" (Php. 1:21). He said again, "Yea, and if I be offered upon **the sacrifice and service of your faith**, I joy, and rejoice with you all. For the same cause also do ye joy, and rejoice with me" (Php. 2:17). Paul's work, prayers, preaching, ministry, life, and therefore also sufferings, were all a manifestation of the life of Christ saving the Church on earth, and it was through men (in the means of grace). Though a man can ever say that flesh and blood are their glory (1 Cor. 1:29), in a non-idolatrous way, Paul said that he and the apostles were the glory of the Church, and they are the Church's rejoicing in the

Day of Judgment – "my tribulations for you, **which is your glory**" (Eph. 3:13), and again, "**we are your rejoicing**...in the day of the Lord Jesus" (2 Cor. 1:14). They are not rejoicing in Paul but in Christ, for, "who then is Paul, and who is Apollos" (1 Cor. 3:5)? "So then neither is he that planteth any thing, neither he that watereth; but **God** that giveth the increase" (1 Cor. 3:7).

Who is Paul? The Church in the NT did not recognize and relate to men after their fleshly persons and names. They did not know Paul after the flesh anymore. They understood that Christ was living through Paul. This ambassadorial mentality is explained in 2 Corinthians 5:16-20, and more specifically in these words – "wherefore henceforth know we no man after the flesh: yea, though we have known Christ after the flesh, yet now henceforth know we Him no more" (2 Cor. 5:16). Paul's office and ministry to the Church is such a vital means of grace for the present progressive salvation of the elect that Paul says, whether he is afflicted or comforted, "**it is for your consolation and salvation**" (2 Cor. 1:6).

CHURCH JUDGMENTS

The intercessory, ambassadorial relationship of Christians is at work in the evidences – suffering, preaching, comfort, and praying – even so, it is with *Church judgments*. The Church is a living representation of the Kingdom of God in heaven, so that, whatever is happening in the Kingdom of God *in heaven* should be executed *on earth,* in the Church, which is the Kingdom of God on earth. Therefore, if God is angry with a saint so as to damn him, and He is holding sin against him, then he is to be excommunicated from the Church. The evidence that God is holding sin against the man is in the fact that God is withholding grace to repent of sin. Such men are to be thrust out of the Church (the Kingdom of God on earth) because they are thrust out of their citizenship in heaven (the Kingdom of God in heaven). The Church is a representation of God's ruling grounds! If you are not forgiven by God Who dwells in heaven, at this time, the Church authority in the apostles will be ambassadors of this heavenly edict, and, they would not forgive your sins on earth, but they do this "in the Person of Christ" (2 Cor. 2:10). So, Christ did not forgive them in heaven, and His Person which dwelt in the apostles on earth, He also did not forgive them, but as individual Christians the apostles did not have a grudge against any man. The anger and unforgiveness is God's! Therefore they thrust the man out of the Church fellowship (God's grounds). This is called "judging" in 1 Corinthians chapter 5. The apostles would, in this way, judge in the Person of Jesus Christ for excommunication, which is, holding the person's sins against the person to deliver them over to Satan (1 Cor. 5:3-6). Paul did this, he said, "in the name of our Lord Jesus Christ...with the power of our Lord Jesus Christ" (1 Cor. 5:4). Also the opposite work is done upon a soul when he is received back into the Church. Paul calls it forgiveness, which means that the person who was previously excommunicated because Christ did not forgive him is now received again because Christ has forgiven him. Again Paul acts as an ambassador of Christ when he said, "forgave I it in the Person of Christ" (2 Cor. 2:10), and so the man who was excommunicated in 1 Corinthians chapter 5 is received again at the later time (2 Corinthians 2:6-11). Note: the evidence that Christ forgave the backslidden, formerly damned, and excommunicated man was that God gave the man repentance evidenced by the proper fruits (2 Cor. 7:10-11), therefore such a one passed the test that Christ is still in him and he is not reprobated (2 Cor. 13:5). If God never gave the man repentance again unto life, it is by this men can see that God has reprobated him (2 Tim. 2:25-26), therefore he would never be received back in the Church. The Church ministers are to walk in Christ to do His will on earth, "as it is in heaven" (Matt. 6:10). These awfully fearful, ambassadorial powers were called keys to the Kingdom of God, and were shown to be, primarily, the sole ambassadorial honor to the apostolic ministers, and during times of excommunication the powers are exercised by them (or the elders presiding over the Churches). Verses which show this peculiar power which I speak of are as follows:

> "And I will give unto thee the keys of the kingdom of heaven: and whatsoever thou shalt bind on earth shall be bound in heaven: and whatsoever thou shalt loose on earth shall be loosed in heaven." (Matt. 16:19)

> "Verily I say unto you, Whatsoever ye shall bind on earth shall be bound in heaven: and whatsoever ye shall loose on earth shall be loosed in heaven. Again I say unto you, That if two of you shall agree on earth as touching any thing that they shall ask, it shall be done for them of my Father which is in heaven. For where two or three are gathered together in my name, there am I in the midst of them." (Matt. 18:18-20)

> "Whosoever sins ye remit, they are remitted unto them; *and* whosoever *sins* ye retain, they are retained." (John 20:23)

NT intercession exists in individuals of the Church upon the same principles as *these ambassadorial powers*. I find that all of these biblical principles of intercessory labors through NT Christians do all resemble the very same intercessory powers of the OT prophets who did, in like manner to the spiritual saints in the NT, stand before an angry, destroying God to plead for the salvation of God's people – though salvation is always, and will always be the work of God, and Him alone! I account of all these things to doctrinally justify the necessity of NT intercessory prayer for saints under the wrath of God and the existence of NT repentance in God's condescension. When God is desirous to destroy and damn saints by holding their sins against them, a saint must intercede against the wrath of God just as the OT saints did! God is, as He was in Ezekiel's day, saying again: "I sought for a man among them, that should make up the hedge, and stand in the gap before Me for the land, that I should not destroy it: but I found none. Therefore have I poured out Mine indignation upon them; I have consumed them with the fire of My wrath: their own way have I recompensed upon their heads, saith the Lord GOD" (Ezek. 22:30-31). Even as Elijah prayed until salvation came to Israel, so we are to pray for salvific rain to fall (Heb. 6:7), and like as Elijah, whose like spirit we now have in Christ, we are to intercede for our brethren who are overtaken in error, who are under the wrathful penalty of a multitude of sins. This is the shocking and compelling context of James 5:14-20! Read it carefully please.

> "Is any sick among you? let him call for the elders of the Church; and let them pray over him, anointing him with oil in the name of the Lord: And the prayer of faith shall save the sick, and the Lord shall raise him up; and if he have committed sins, they shall be forgiven him. Confess your faults one to another, and **pray one for another, that ye may be healed. The effectual fervent prayer of a righteous man availeth much.** Elias was a man subject to like passions as we are, and **he prayed earnestly that it might not rain: and it rained not on the earth by the space of three years and six months. And he prayed again,** and the heaven gave rain, and the earth brought forth her fruit. Brethren, if any of you do err from the truth, and one convert him; Let him know, that he which converteth the sinner from the error of his way shall save a soul from death, and shall hide a multitude of sins." (Jas 5:14-20)

Who more than the lonely man Elijah did bring a damned nation to its knees again? It was him, and him alone, in God's Spirit, who stood against the 400 prophets of Baal, and so, by the intercession of judgment he did do again what he had done for 3 years up to that day. He prayed intercessory prayers, that God would end the famine, with fervency and 7-time persistence just as he prayed for three years that God would bring the famine. The same fervency and persistence seen that day was done every day, to bring and take away the famine. Do you think God is trying to speak to us something of our responsibility to intercede, seeing that we have the same spirit as Elijah? When God's NT Israelites are under a spiritual famine, when the desertification of the soul and fruitlessness are laying waste regenerate men on every side – what will you do? Nothing, because God is sovereign and you can't do anything? Pray for rain, NT Elijah, God says to all NT Christians! And God will bring forth the RAINS to end the spiritual desertification of souls, causing fruit to spring up within them, ending the famine, the dehydration, reviving life in them that were sitting in death! A dry season is a sin season, a cursed condition, thus let the spiritual saints pray for the rain of God's salvation to return, and so, God's damning powers of wrath will be turned away. The multitude of sins which He is holding against them can be forgiven!

The Covenant is in desolation, the earth in spiritual devastation.
False prophets are intoxicated by the promises of God while a godly man can scarcely be found.
The multitudes are in fetters – in false confidences they are bound,
And they are emboldened to un-repentance by indoctrinations unsound.
Oh, that one man would remember God and in faith look around,
By a truth laden heart may the breach be found.

It is the Last Days and God has hidden His old ways,
Yet men do stand in the gap and for the Covenant they do pray,
To finish the chapter of time by resurrecting Josiah's days.

Surely Revival God would send if faith did impart a river parting wind.
Elisha bids his master bye with a hopeful, loud, uplifted cry.
Eyes raised up, he looks up high, watching chariots of fire making Elijah fly.
Scene is over; Elisha's heart in unrest, his prayer was answered – double portion is blessed.
Elisha surpasses Elijah's spiritual crest, he lays hold on Elijah's mantel and approaches the test.
His mind memorable of Elijah's God, Elisha's memory is with preparation shod.
Elisha's hand does grip the mantle tight while the river approaches and is nigh in sight.
Mantle going forth, no doubt of any sort, the call to God is lifted up as the prophet's first and continual resort.

"Where is the LORD God of Elijah", was Elisha's cry,
And echoing in my heart is a perpetual like sigh.
As the moving life and a rushing river in my veins
My eyes ever behold the Bride of Christ in her stains,

That throughout all the personal suffering I undergo now, and in every change, my eyes widen in a stedfast looking for the subsequent revelatory glory to brighten the dark glass, and in part or whole, make this grief assuage:

That with a more open face I may behold His shining face,
Comprehending the labor-sufficient, gloriously powerful, resurrection grace,
And so find the knowledge of God empowers in His perfecting, cleansing, Bride-baptizing praise.
Thus I would be: Tried in His holy fire, clothed in His precious, majestic, warlike attire,
Seated in the heavenlies I would be sufficient and entire,
 To wash the Bride under the perfect influence of His governing Empire.

And thus, bear the mark of His perfect signature ensuring a daily Son-rise to brighten the world with the fullness of the stature of Christ. Thus is the Covenant, to outshine the physical world declaring the reality and "at hand" illumination of the Kingdom of Heaven for the world to understand. That, in likeness to the sun, its rays to shed abroad to the whole world the touch of His life-giving power, that to the ends of the world none have been exempt from the merciful nearness of the gospel of God interrupting some facet of the dark and hopeless society and time, by the momentary passing of The Presence, work, and Person of eternal life. Namely, Jesus Christ the Lord – Amen and let it be Lord.

A Liar in the Church

"Because with **lies** ye have… strengthened the hands of the
wicked, that he should not return from his wicked way, by
promising him life: therefore ye shall see no more vanity, nor
divine divinations: for I will deliver **My people** out of your hand:
and ye shall know that I am the LORD."

647

(Ezek. 13:22-23)

Because of eternal security preachers, men believe that there is no simultaneous will of God working contrary to the sovereign will, emotions, and promises of God, therefore there is no conception that God seeks to know a man by *the trial of his faith* to see if the man will fear God, and furthermore, find him out in trials, fires, visitations, or finally, at Christ's appearing. Men do therefore conclude, there is nothing that Abraham, David, nor any saved man could commit as a sin, so that God would turn upon them to "make void the Covenant" (Ps. 89:39) rather than "make it" (Gen. 17:1-2). They are persuaded that because God "said...forever", that always, inevitably, and without exception this means forever (1 Sam. 2:30), "perpetual", and "everlasting" (Ex. 29:9, 40:15), for every saved individual. Today it is tragic! Men don't even know what *biblical perfection* is! And no wonder – they are lulled to sleep by false doctrines. God's beloved saints are turned into "sinners" "at ease in Zion" (James 5:20, Amos 6:1)! Even in this state, men don't fear damnation. Men cannot tell when or if they are in a damnable condition! David, Hezekiah (Jer. 26:16-19), Jonah, Josiah, Jeremiah, and Jacob were saved by seeing this – that when they were under the wrath of God as regenerate men, they saw it, they recognized it, and so they "cried" (Jonah 2:9), and God heard the voice of their "weeping" (Ps. 6:8) when they "wept" (Hos. 12:4). Remember how God said to Hezekiah, "I have seen thy tears" (Isa. 38:5), and again to Josiah, "because thine heart was tender, and thou didst...weep before Me; I have even heard thee also, saith the LORD" (2 Chron. 34:27). We have fat, faithless, fearless, and tearless Christians today, and let the blame be put upon eternal security! Again, God said to David, "the LORD hath heard the voice of my weeping" (Ps. 6:8), but you are too spiritual to weep for fear of damnation? You just love God so much that you don't need to fear? Maybe your false "god" that you have made up in your own mind will name himself after your name, but the God of the Bible named Himself after David's name – and he wept in fear for damnation as a regenerate man many times! Moses, Jonah, David, Lot, Hezekiah, Joshua, Jeremiah, Jacob, Josiah, even all of them returned to God because they knew that God was promising them condemnation – this truth made them free at a time when the promise of life would have damned them forever! Oh my reader, I beg you to hear and understand it!

Called – Elect – Chosen – Foreknown

This section is intended to be a brief, outlined overview of the terms titled above to prepare the reader for the next section. If "The Golden Chain" of Romans 8:28-30 can be dissolved, and yet, in a higher, mysterious righteousness of God, He declares it, even still, infallible in its links, untouched by the happenings of condescension and time, then the terminology which identifies *predestination* and *election* – "**called**", "**elect**", "**chosen**", and "**foreknown**" – should also represent this mysterious contradiction. Therefore, there is a kind of collision in terms, between the eternality of what is forever and outside of time with what is mutable and

648

experienced inside of time. Sovereignty in God's eternality, here again, like as all other places formerly addressed, is still exulted right beside the condescension of God's will, word, and works.

Called → Elect → Chosen → Foreknown → ✹ ← Foreknown ← Chosen ← Elect ← Called

If God's condescension is contradicting sovereign, eternal, unchanging glories in this chain, then these very terms – "called", "elect", "chosen", and "foreknown" – will all have a real and genuine meaning, use, and experience, according to how God speaks it and performs it inside of time, and this contradicts the real and genuine meaning, use, and experience outside of time. This is just as we have studied and noted thus far, how there is a will and word of God (*God in the ways of man*) which is contradictory to the will and word of God (*God in the ways of God*), but they both exist simultaneously in God. We should not be surprised to find these four terms – "called", "elect", "chosen", and "foreknown" – to indicate realities in both spectrums of God's relationship to man (*God in the ways of man* & *God in the ways of God*). Should we be at all surprised that we could add the four bullet points below to the previous list of terms which was used as *initial* and *present progressive* salvation, and also that which is *finally* to be consummated?

- **Elect now** (2 Jn. 1:1, 13, 1 Pet. 1:2) – **Consummating Election to come** (2 Peter 1:10)
- **Called now** (1 Cor. 1:26) – **Consummating Calling to come** (Php. 3:14)
- **Chosen now** (1 Peter 2:9) – **Consummating Choice to come** (Matt. 22:14, Rev. 17:14)
- **Know Him now** (1 John 2:4, John 17:3) – **Consummating knowing, "even as also I am known" to come** (1 Cor. 13:12)

CALLED

1) Initial & Present Progressive Salvation of Calling:

We have studied "The Gospel Calling" of NT Christianity in great detail, and I hope it is now needless to say, yet again, that the "calling" of a man means initial salvation, and as we have studied all the terms of the calling experientially described (light, holiness, etc.), when a man comes short of this experience, he is falling short of the experiential terms of what his salvific calling is (falling from light to darkness, holiness to unholiness, etc.), thus in this way we can see that this calling refers to *initial* and *present progressive* salvation.

Matt. 22:14, Jude 1, Rom. 1:7, 9:7, 1 Cor. 1:2, 1 Peter 2:9, 1 Cor. 1:26, Heb. 9:15, Gal. 1:15-16, 1 Thess. 2:11-12, Eph. 1:18, 4:4

2) Final Salvation (on Judgment Day) of Calling:

We must make our "calling" "sure" if we want to be saved (2 Peter 1:10). This corresponds with the burden

Rev. 17:14, Php. 3:14, 2 Thess. 1:11, 2 Peter 1:10, 1 Tim 6:12, Eph. 1:18, 4:4 2 Cor. 6:17-18 (called sons of God).

of Paul, which was to "walk worthy of God" (1 Thess. 1:12), for, if a man walks in those adverse sins which are at enmity with God, it is then that God will no longer acknowledge such a one as His son or daughter. We must make our calling as "sons" and "daughters" sure by walking in God, and not in the flesh (2 Cor. 6:18).

3)   Predestination of Calling:

If a man is initially called, and then walks worthy of
1 Cor. 7:20 (sovereign ordination of birth, race, family, habitation, carnal vocation, & events), Rom. 11:29, Rom. 9:7, 11, 24-26, 2 Tim. 1:9 (sovereign election for salvation)

that calling so as to presently and progressively abide in that calling, then the calling is "sure," and if a man successfully walks in these three senses of calling which describe salvation (*initial*, *present progressive*, and *final*), we can be assured that he has done it by **eternal election**. The calling of God *outside of time* did irresistibly lay hold upon the man, and so, salvation was begun and finished.

CHOSEN or ELECT

1)   Initial & Present Progressive Salvation of Chosen:

John 15:16-19, 1 Peter 1:2,
Romans 16:13, Neh. 9:7
(same as called, Heb. 11:18)

2)   Final Salvation (on Judgment Day) of Chosen:

Matt. 22:14, Mark. 13:20,
Rev. 17:14, 2 Peter 1:10

We must lay hold upon election, even though we are elect now (2 Peter 1:10). As the elect, we are regenerate, thus our nature is the nature of the elect, and so we are charged thereto, that we must "put on therefore, **as the elect of God**, holy and beloved, bowels of mercies, kindness, humbleness of mind, meekness, longsuffering; forbearing one another, and forgiving one another, if any man have a quarrel against any: even as Christ forgave you, so also do ye" (Col. 3:12). Like the preciousness of the precious "Living Stone," which was "chosen of God" and "elect" (1 Peter 2:4, 6), we are supposed to abide in Him in spiritual union and become "lively stones" ourselves, which means that we are abiding in His nature and deed, and thus, we too walk out the preciousness of our choosing and election, being built together as a House that is a dwelling place for Him. How do you know if your election is sure? Ask yourself this question according to the tests of scripture. Are you fulfilling the purpose of God for which He has elected you for, which purpose is, "**to be conformed to the Image of His Son**" (Rom. 8:29), or in other words, are you in the Image of God's Son Jesus Christ – in **NATURE** and in **DEED**? In other words, are you *perfect*? Will you be one of those to whom God says, "upon whom My Name is called" (Acts 15:17), not only now but in the END?

3) <u>**Predestination** of Chosen:</u> Eph. 1:4-5, John 15:16-19,
2 Thess. 2:13, Ps. 78:67-68, Mark
13:20

If a man walks out in the three experiences of salvation termed in the word chosen (***initial, present progressive***, and ***final*** salvation), it is certain that it is because of the irresistible and eternal choosing of God.

<u>KNOWN or FOREKNOWN</u>

1) <u>**Initial & Present Progressive**</u>
<u>**Salvation of Knowing:**</u> Gal. 4:9, 1 Cor. 8:3, 2 Tim.
2:19, 1 John 2:4, John 10:14-
15, 27, 17:3, Jer. 31:34, Ps. 1:6,
Nah. 1:5-7, Amos 3:1-2

2) <u>**Final**</u> **Salvation (on Judgment Day) of Knowing:**
Matt. 7:23, Lk. 13:25-27, Rev. 3:5,
13:8, 17:8, 2 Tim. 2:19, Amos 3:1-2

3) <u>**Predestination** of Knowing:</u> Rom. 8:28, Jer. 1:5, Rom. 11:2, 1
Peter 1:2

The same definitive principles in the words "knowing" or "foreknown" are perfectly aligned with the other three terms – "called", "chosen", and "elect" – but before I address this term in great detail, I would like to show you the colliding, side by side, scriptural examples of these terms, so that, when it is all understood side by side, then we can accept it as the same mystery patterned all throughout the scripture. In this way, we can avoid the heresy of "eternal security" and receive the clear burden of God that He desires us to have. To exposit the term "known" or "foreknown", ***foreknowledge, election***, and ***the Book of Life*** must be addressed as well, and unto this I will arrive before long.

"Many Are Called But Few Are Chosen" – Matt. 22:14

"Behold, I, even I, will **utterly** "his righteousness which he hath done shall not
forget you" (Jer. 23:39)→ be remembered"-Ezek. 3:20
"shall not be mentioned" – Ezek. 18:22
"shall not be mentioned" – Ezek. 18:24

What is the burden of God that I am trying to finally release to the reader, unhindered by heresies and doctrines of man? It is that "many are called but few are chosen" – THE VERY SAME BURDEN as Jesus Christ the Savior, the Caller, & the Chooser! The scripture solemnly sounds the alarm: → "**Many**" – "**many**" – "**many**" (Matt. 24:9-13) – "**many**" (2 Peter 2:2) – "**Many** are called, but few are chosen" (Matt. 22:14). Oh, how we need to hear it!

The word *calling* refers to the eternal, determinate election of God (*God in the ways of God*) in Romans 9:7-8. It is stated that "In Isaac shall thy seed be **called**." This was quoted by Paul from Genesis 21:12, "In Isaac shall thy seed be **called**". Those that are called, in this sense, are called by an irresistible grace, and therefore they all are perseverant to the end. If this was the only meaning of the word "**called**," there would be an irreconcilable conflict with what Jesus meant in Matthew 22:14, "For many are **called**, but few are chosen".

Likewise to the word called, the word *chosen* is used by Christ in this verse, saying – "few are **chosen**." If this was the only meaning of the word chosen, there would be similar irreconcilable conflicts. Those that are called after the meaning of the word calling in Romans 9:7-8 can never fall or fail to inherit salvation, *initial* or *final*. Those that are called in the sense that Jesus spoke in Matthew 22:14 did fail to inherit salvation. Likewise, speaking in terms of the exodus generation who were bound under the prophetic oaths of the Abrahamic Covenant, they were saved by God (as documented formerly), and therefore they were "called" of God. God affirms this by the prophet Hosea in chapter 11:1, "When Israel was a child, then I loved him, and **called** my son out of Egypt." This generation was called in the sense that they were *initially* saved, but as we studied, we found that they were not *finally* saved. Their calling was by promises and oaths, and yet there were "few" of the "many" called that obtained the *final* salvation which they were called to. *Initially* called is *initial* salvation. To fall from the *final* salvation is to fall from the calling in every sense, which results in a disannulment of the original Covenant-choice of God. This is the exact meaning of the word "chosen" in Matthew 22:14. Chosen is used in Matthew 22:14 in distinction from the sense of the word "calling" that Christ used as a final attainment of salvation; therefore it is an irreversible choice of God **at the END**. Yet, in other parts of scripture, "chosen" is used exactly as the meaning of the word "calling" in Matthew 22:14, which means that chosen is used as *initial* salvation rather than *final* salvation. This *initial* salvation definition can be seen in Deuteronomy 10:15 – "Only the LORD had a delight in thy fathers to love them, and He **chose** their seed after them, even you above all people, as it is this day," and again, "And because He **loved** thy fathers, therefore He **chose** their seed after them, and brought thee out in His sight with His mighty power out of Egypt." Further references can be found, but these suffice the matter for now (Deut. 7:7-8).

It is not strange that the word "chosen" refers to *initial* salvation instead of *final* salvation, like as the word "calling" refers to *initial* salvation in Matthew 22:14. Other like uses of the word "calling" in the NT show the NT parallel to the meaning and use of the word "chosen" in Deut. 10:15 & 7:7-8. Read carefully the following verses in context and compare them to the former verses:

"For the promise is unto you, and to your children, and to all that are afar off, even as many as the Lord our God shall **call**." (Acts 2:39)

"Among whom are ye also **the called** of Jesus Christ: To all that be in Rome, beloved of God, called to be saints: Grace to you and peace from God our Father, and the Lord Jesus Christ." (Romans 1:6-7)

"For ye see your **calling**, brethren, how that not many wise men after the flesh, not many mighty, not many noble, are **called**: But God hath **chosen** the foolish things of the world to confound the wise; and God hath **chosen** the weak things of the world to confound the things which are mighty; And base things of the world, and things which are despised, hath God **chosen**, yea, and things which are not, to bring to nought things that are: That no flesh should glory in His presence." (1 Corinthians 1:26-29)

As you can see in 1 Cor. 1:26-29, like as the word "calling" refers to *initial* salvation, so also is the word "chosen" used as *initial* salvation *in the NT*. In 1 Peter 2:9, it is said to the New Testament Church – "Ye are a **chosen** generation, a royal priesthood, an holy nation, a peculiar people; that ye should shew forth the praises of Him Who hath **called** you out of darkness into His marvellous light" (1 Peter 2:29). Here we have the synonymous use of the words *"called"* and *"chosen"* as *initial* salvation, yet this verse in 1 Peter 2:29 is but a NT quotation from what happened in the OT with the Exodus generation. Why? These very same words and phrases were used to describe the calling of God to them. 1 Peter 2:9 is a quotation of Exodus 19:4-7. Look at them side by side:

"Ye have seen what I did unto the Egyptians, and how I bare you on eagles' wings, and brought you unto Myself. Now therefore, if ye will obey My voice indeed, and keep My covenant, then ye shall be a **peculiar** treasure unto Me above all people: for all the earth is Mine: And ye shall be unto Me a kingdom of **priests, and an holy nation**. These are the words which thou shalt speak unto the children of Israel. And Moses came and called for the elders of the people, and laid before their faces all these words which the LORD commanded him." (Exodus 19:4-7)

"But ye are a chosen generation, a royal **priesthood, an holy nation**, a **peculiar** people; that ye should shew forth the praises of Him Who hath called you out of darkness into His marvellous light." (1 Peter 2:9)

As a further confirmation of this biblical parallel, a later prophet who understood this same concept wrote in Psalm 135:4, using the word "chosen" synonymously with the effect of a people or person becoming God's treasure:

> "For the LORD hath **chosen** Jacob unto himself, and Israel for
> His **peculiar treasure**." (Ps. 135:4)

> "Blessed is the nation whose God is the LORD; and the people
> whom He hath **chosen** for His own **inheritance**." (Ps. 33:12)

Heretofore, what can altogether be understood is that God saves in *initial* salvation by the word "chosen", having the same effect as the word "calling" used in Matthew 22:14 and elsewhere (NT & OT), and this word is used to describe a saving work of God upon a man whereby he becomes a treasure and inheritance unto God, yet these well-saved and chosen (*initial* salvation) saints which are in view in these scripture references, namely the Exodus generation, were not finally chosen (*final* salvation) by God, in the sense of the word used in Matthew 22:14.

If men were chosen in final salvation after the meaning of Christ's words in Matthew 22:14, this could, and would only, be done because they were chosen by God in the sense of eternal predestination; this "chosen" being synonymous with eternal election and thus bearing the inevitable fruit of perseverance. Consider the comments of the renowned Richard Baxter, known by his book "The Reformed Pastor." He was writing on the mystery of *falling from grace*, even though the fallen man was soundly *called* by God unto regeneration, experienced a degree of sanctification, and then he did yet fail to persevere to the final END.

> "Consider, that the doctrine of perseverance hath nothing in it to encourage security. The very controversies about it, may cause you to conclude, that a certain sin is not to be built upon a controverted doctrine. Till Augustine's time, it is hard to find any ancient writers, that clearly asserted the certain perseverance of any at all. Augustine and Prosper maintain the certain perseverance of **all the elect**, but deny the certain perseverance of all that are regenerated, justified, or sanctified; for they thought that more were regenerate and justified than were elect, of whom some stood (even all the elect) and the rest fell away: so that I confess, I never read one ancient father, or Christian writer, that ever maintained the certainty of the perseverance of all the justified, of many hundred, if not a thousand years after Christ." (Richard Baxter, "The Reformed Pastor")

If "chosen" and "calling" are both used to mean *initial* salvation, are they both used as *final* salvation? We know that Matthew 22:14 uses "chosen" to mean *final* salvation, but can the word "calling" be so expanded, like as the word "chosen" was? Yea, it can. *Final* salvation referred to by the word "chosen" is also referred to by the word "election", hence the saying, "make your calling and election sure" (2 Peter 1:10). Election, performed by the predestinating powers of God, is motivated by *an unchanging and everlasting love* in God which is peculiar to His chosen human vessels. This peculiar love is so profound that it makes men, who are mere vessels of clay, the Almighty's "peculiar treasure!" This love can be seen in the life of Jacob...

Jacob is the chief example of eternal, predestinating election, and God says of him that he was chosen in "the purpose of God according to **election**" (Rom. 9:11). Why was Jacob chosen? It is because God said, "Jacob have I loved" (Rom. 9:13, Mal. 1:2-3). Jacob is called of God, "Mine elect," in Isaiah 45:4, and this is one of the few uses of this exact expression in all of scripture. Predestination is often expressed in the word "**chosen**", like as in Isaiah 44:1-2 states – "Yet now hear, O Jacob my servant; and Israel, whom I have **chosen**: Thus saith the LORD that made thee, and formed thee from the womb, which will help thee; Fear not, O Jacob, my servant; and thou, Jesurun, whom I have **chosen**." Furthermore, in both Testaments, they are declared to be synonymous, as the following two verses reveal:

> "And except that the Lord had shortened those days, no flesh should be saved: but for the **elect's** sake, whom He hath **chosen**, He hath shortened the days." (Mark 13:20)

> "Ye have not **chosen** Me, but I have **chosen** you, and ordained you, that ye should go and bring forth fruit, and that your fruit should remain: that whatsoever ye shall ask of the Father in My name, He may give it you. These things I command you, that ye love one another. If the world hate you, ye know that it hated Me before it hated you. If ye were of the world, the world would love his own: but because ye are not of the world, but I have chosen you out of the world, therefore the world hateth you." (John 15:16-19)

Do you remember that the words "calling" (Rom. 9:11), "election" (Rom. 9:11, 11:5, 7), "love" (Rom. 9:13), and "foreknown" (Rom. 11:2) are all used in the acropolis-argument of the apostle Paul in Romans, chapters 9-11, where Paul addresses sovereignty, salvation, and damnation in the light of "**many**" falling into damnation (Rom. 11:11-12, 17, 20-21) through blindness (Rom. 11:7-10, 25) and reprobation (cast away, Rom. 11:1-2, 15)? So also, Jesus preaches this burden of God in Matthew 22:14: "For **many** are called but few are chosen." Even still, the word of God verifies and lifts up the sovereign expressions of God's workings, as always, in the verses so famously coined as "The Golden Chain," and there these words (foreknown, called, elect) are used again. Election is mentioned in the same line of reasoning in Romans 8:33, after the Golden Chain is preached in Romans 8:28-30:

> "The Golden Chain"
> "And we know that all things work together for good to them that love God, to them who are the called according to His purpose. For whom He did **foreknow**, He also did predestinate to be conformed to the image of His Son, that He might be the firstborn among many brethren. Moreover whom He did

predestinate, them He also called: and whom He **called**, them He also justified: and whom He justified, them He also glorified." (Romans 8:28-30)

Like as the words "called" and "chosen" (meaning elect or loved) are divided into their different uses in Matthew 22:14, in parallel ways the word "foreknown" (known, knew, known) is used in the same way. In 'The Golden Chain", there is another word which is yet to be introduced to my reader, and this word also serves as biblical language for election. The word is – *foreknow*. Those whom God did *foreknow*, they are the *called* by predestination (rather than merely initial salvation), and thus they do abide in the unbreakable chain of promises that do follow – the *called*, *justified*, and *glorified*. Yet Jesus is preaching another very different burden! He preaches how such a one that is *called* is not always *glorified*. For this to be possible, it would mean that, as Richard Baxter did soundly address, there is a certain perseverance of all the eternally *elect*, but not a certain perseverance of all that are *regenerate*, *justified*, or *sanctified*. It would mean that there are more persons that are regenerate and justified than are eternally elect. It would mean that all who are regenerate, who are not elect, will inevitably fall away. The elect do, on the contrary, endure the tempest and stand the test of God's holy proving, called "The Trial of Your Faith" (1 Peter 1:7). Concerning the *foreknowledge* of God, or God's *foreknowing*, there are four uses of this word, just as there are three uses of the words "called" and "chosen". The four senses of its use throughout scripture are, as formerly stated, *initial* salvation, *present progressive* salvation, and *final* salvation, and those that persevere to final salvation are *predestinated* to that end by an eternal, unchanging election ("chosen" or "loved").

By "*foreknowledge*", I mean the definition from that phrase in Romans 8:28-29, where God said, "for whom He did **foreknow** He did also predestinate." Concerning its meaning, John Gill's commentary precisely states it –

"The **foreknowledge** of God here, does **not** intend His prescience of all things future; by which He foreknows and foretells things to come, and which distinguishes Him from all other gods; and is so called, not with respect to Himself, with whom all things are present, but with respect to us, and which is eternal, universal, certain, and infallible; for in this sense He foreknows all men, and if this was the meaning here, then all men would be predestinated, conformed to the image of Christ, called by grace, justified and glorified; whereas they are a special people, whom God has foreknown: nor is this foreknowledge to be understood of any provision or foresight of the good works, holiness, faith, and perseverance of men therein, upon which God predestinates them to happiness; since this would make something out of God, and not His good pleasure, the cause of predestination; which was done before, and without any consideration of good or evil, and is entirely owing to the free grace of God, and is the ground and foundation of good works, faith, holiness, and perseverance in

656

them: but this regards the everlasting love of God to His own people, His delight in them, and approbation of them; in this sense He knew them, He foreknew them from everlasting, affectionately loved them, and took infinite delight and pleasure in them; and this is the foundation of their predestination and election, of their conformity to Christ, of their calling, justification, and glorification."

Therefore, as many Calvinists correctly argue, this *foreknowing* is not a matter of the omniscience or prescience of God, but of the predestination of God, the determination of God, the fore-election or fore-loving of God, or a knowing before, which has been consistently referential to the elective love of God toward choice vessels. "*Foreknowledge*" is a *fore-knowing* of a specially chosen and loved person, like as God said to Jeremiah – "Before I formed thee in the belly **I knew thee**" (Jer. 1:5). This knowing is a fore-loving, which is the origin of God's fore-election, as God said to Jeremiah in another place – "The LORD hath appeared of old unto me, saying, Yea, I have loved thee with an **everlasting love**: therefore with lovingkindness have I drawn thee" (Jer. 31:3). In this very same way, God foreknew others. The emphasis behind God's foreknowing of an individual is, they were cherished in love and mercy "being not yet born, neither having done any good or evil" (Rom. 9:11), and in the purpose of mercy for God's glory, they were thereto created and formed. In this way they were "**afore** prepared unto glory" (Rom. 9:23).

This foreknowledge is not merely an attribute of those that are called to a special office, as Jeremiah was called to the office of a prophet (Jer. 1:5), or as Paul was called to the office of an apostle. If the words, "separated me from my mother's womb" were only used for the foreknowledge and fore-choosing of special office holders, then this principle would only be spoken to those special persons. This phrase is expressly given to Paul's call in Galatians 1:15-16. In full, it says, "But when it pleased God, **Who separated me from my mother's womb,** and **called** me by His grace, To reveal His Son in me, that I might preach Him among the heathen; immediately I conferred not with flesh and blood..." (Galatians 1:15-16). You can see a reference to his salvation therein, but also it is used for the special calling of office which he had, like as it was said in Acts 22:14 where the word "chosen" is used – "And he said, The God of our fathers hath **chosen** thee, that thou shouldest know His will, and see that Just One, and shouldest hear the voice of His mouth" (Acts 22:14). This "chosen" is certainly referencing the special office of an apostle, one of the credentials being a personal sight of the risen Lord (1 Cor. 9:1, 15:5-8). The word "chosen" is used in the OT in similar fashions (Ps. 78:70, 2 Chron. 6:6). Yet, as the word "chosen" is not only used in reference to special office bearers, but in all the senses as formerly detailed, so "foreknowledge" works the same way.

It is written of Moses that God knew him in a special way. Twice did Moses plead for the special graces which originate from the choice title: "God knew him", Moses saying back to God what God said of him – "I know thee by name" (Ex. 33:12, 17). Some may infer this to be referring to his special office as a prophet, but I cannot help but recognize other special graces throughout the scriptures which come from God knowing, remembering, keeping near, and looking after the account of all *the names* of His well-beloved. As God said of His people in Isaiah 49:15-16, "Can a woman forget her sucking child, that she should not have compassion on the son of her womb? Yea, they may forget, yet will I not forget thee. Behold, **I have graven thee upon the palms of my hands**; thy walls are continually before Me." Verily, God knoweth all of them "*by name*" that are graven upon His own hands! That is, even more intimately than a mother knows her own suckling child! God is preaching the *impossibility* of forgetfulness, which is the ever-presence of His helping graces, or the perseverance of His salvific mercies, which motivate the lavished outpouring of the intense devotion God has toward certain choice individuals – thus God argues that He will *never forsake* them (see Isa. 49:14). Aren't these the graces of those who are elect?

God is a keeper of these names, the names of the saved, as Jesus said – "your **names are written** in heaven" (Luke 10:20). These that had names written in heaven were co-participants and co-inheritors of what Christ suffered for and purchased by the riches of His own life. Therefore, Jesus, becoming a saved man's Advocate and Mediator, says of those individuals who He saves, "I will confess **his name** before My Father which is in heaven" (Rev. 3:5). Following the principle of *foreknowledge*, all these names are likewise known, written, and chosen before their birth, which also is the principle behind predestination in eternal election. If you perish, it is because you are of those "whose **names** were not written in the book of life **from the foundation of the world**" (Rev. 17:8). If you are not finally saved, at the Judgment Seat, then you are of those persons' names which were "not found written in the book of life" (Rev. 20:15). In this sense, it is as if God does not know your name, like as the sense when God said to others, "I know you not whence ye are" (Lk. 13:27). It is to be understood by these passages that those who are found written in the Book of Life – they do partake of graces which make impossible their failure, fall, or rebellion, and these graces make sure their perseverance through horrific sufferings and trials. It is obvious that these are the promise-bound saints, saved by His supernatural graces, who can know in their lifetime that they are of those "names" "in the Book of Life" (Php. 4:3).

The foreknowing of individuals is the special and everlasting love God has for individuals outside of time, and to be created by these everlasting affections of God, then your course will be ordained for salvation, nearness to God, and His glory. So also, the very experiences of grace which draw and empower a man to salvation are also spoken of in terms of **pre**determination, **pre**destination, **fore**ordination, and like phrases which emphasize God's plan **beforehand**. These are terms of eternal election which do emphasize the **FOREVER** of God's good will, love, and promise to a soul. The very reason that it was **pre**planned by God is because of election, as the verse immediately below in Romans 9:11 states the point of planning for election to be when the humans are – "being not yet born." It is at this time that election and elective graces are ordained, given, determined, and predestinated to be showered

upon the human being which is yet to be physically created. **Predestinated means –**
PRE- or BEFOREHAND – destinated, and thus are all the experiences of salvation:

Calling →   **"being not yet born**...the purpose of God according to
                election... of Him that **calleth"** – Rom. 9:11
                "which was **given** us in Christ Jesus **before the world began"** –
                2 Tim. 1:9

Chosen →   "God hath **from the beginning chosen** you to salvation"
                – 2 Thess. 2:13
                "chosen us in Him before the foundation of the world"
                – Eph. 1:4-5

Election →   "**Elect** according to the **foreknowledge** of God the Father"
                – 1 Peter 1:2
                "**afore prepared** unto glory" – Rom. 9:23

Wisdom →   "which God **ordained before the world** unto our glory"
                – 1 Cor. 2:7

Righteousness → "God hath **before ordained** that we should walk in them" – Eph.
                2:10

The Book of Life →"whose names were not written in The Book of Life **from the**
                foundation of the world" – Rev. 17:8

The astonishing, everlasting love of God is at work in salvation, and all of
these citations do exclaim this clear message. Nevertheless, in perfect consistency to
all other words, phrases, doctrines, and patterns, God reserves the right to do the
humanly illogical and impossible – because that which is earthily incomprehensible
is heavenly comprehensible. Therefore God can forget, has forgotten, and threatens to
forget your name, *erase* your name, and *know you no more*. In Revelation 3:5, God
speaks of sin as obstacles which are dangerous affronts to perseverance, and Christ
gives present-tense threats that these sins must be overcome for the sake of their
continued salvation. God saith:

> "He that overcometh, the same shall be clothed in white raiment;
> and I will not blot out **his name** out of the book of life, but I will
> confess **his name** before my Father, and before His angels."
> (Rev. 3:5)

> "God shall **take away his part out of the book of life**, and out
> of the holy city, and from the things which are written in this
> book." (Rev. 22:19)

659

"Behold, I, even I, will **utterly forget** you" (Jer. 23:39)→

"his righteousness which he hath done shall not
be remembered"-Ezek. 3:20
"shall not be mentioned" – Ezek. 18:22
"shall not be mentioned" – Ezek. 18:24

What God has said and promised – made known as the laws of His relationship, mind, and heart to man – if they in any wise repay Him evil for good, God will do likewise to them! Just as God said to Eli – "**I said indeed** that thy house, and the house of thy father, should walk before Me **for ever**: but now the LORD saith, Be it far from Me; for them that honour Me I will honour, and they that despise Me shall be lightly esteemed" (1 Sam. 2:30). This is like as God said in Psalm 18:25-26, "With the merciful Thou wilt shew Thyself merciful; with an upright man Thou wilt shew Thyself upright; With the pure Thou wilt shew Thyself pure; and **with the froward Thou wilt shew Thyself froward.**" Woe to the man who is rewarded according to his works, who deserves as recompense the reflection of God, when He reflects back to you what you have done toward Him: *scorning* for *scorning, hatred* for *hatred, lying* for *lying,* and *froward* for *froward.* As it is written of God, "Surely He scorneth the scorners: but He giveth grace unto the lowly" (Prov. 3:34). Astonishingly, here too, like as all other places previously cited, the **forevers** and **nevers** of God are not beyond breach, mutability, and holy alteration by God in condescension, and it is for holy justice that this impossibility is done, while the eternality of God's heaven-high, sovereign counsel is still untouched, golden, perfectly infallible, and immutably accomplished.

"Here is the patience of the saints: here are they that keep the
commandments of God, and the faith of Jesus."
– Rev. 14:12

It can be said: keep your name in the Book of Life – keep your clothing white – "keep the faith" (Rev. 14:12) – "keep yourselves in the love of God" (Jude 21) – and "make your calling and election sure" (2 Pet. 2:10)! You see, these senses are different than the sovereign elective forms formerly noted. As it is with God's use of the words "calling" and "chosen", so it is with God's "foreknowing", diversely applied in different senses, yet patterned, parallel, and consistent with each other. All of this is very telling to the context of the saying of Christ, "**Many are called but few are chosen**" (Matthew 22:14).

We love God because He first loved us, and we know God because He first knew us, or likewise, because He does known us now. As it is written, "But now, after that **ye have known God**, or rather are **known of God**, how turn ye again to the weak and beggarly elements, whereunto ye desire again to be in bondage" (Galatians 4:9)? This knowing of God, again, is similar to the foreknowledge of God in predestination (specifically that it is love), but this is love is a present-tense experience in present progressive salvation. We love because His love is reciprocated in us, by Him, through us, back to Him (1 John 4-5). Yet this is likewise what is experientially meant by the present-tense knowing of God; it is a knowing of God by Him knowing us, and this knowing of Him is by an indwelling possession which causes regeneration. As it is written…

> "If any man love God, the same is **known of Him**." (1 Cor. 8:3)

This "knowing" is in the sense of His presence being salvificly near, causing us to experience His salvific purposes at present. The Shepherd, therefore, shepherds His sheep, and none other:

> "I am The Good Shepherd, and **know My sheep, and am known of Mine**." (John 10:14)

This is affirmed in the NT and OT, as God says of the righteous – "the LORD **knoweth the way of the righteous**" (Ps. 1:6) and "hath respect unto the lowly: but the proud **He knoweth afar off**" (Ps. 138:6). In this sense, God is near to the lowly and afar off from the proud, therefore the lowly know Him in this salvific sense because they are no more aliens to Him. This experience of God's near, salvific presence is well-stated by the psalmist in Psalm 17:3, "Thou hast proved mine heart; Thou hast **visited me** in the night; Thou hast tried me, and shalt find nothing; I am purposed that my mouth shall not transgress" (Ps. 17:3). So David says, "O LORD, Thou hast searched me, and **known me**," and with this is the assurance and good hope: "Search me, O God, and **know my heart**: try me, and **know my thoughts**: and see if there be any wicked way in me, and lead me in the way everlasting" (Ps. 139:23-24). If you are His, therefore, you are dwelling in the power of His near presence in regeneration, *presently* and *progressively*, which makes you righteous - this is what it means to *presently* know Him and be known by Him in a saving sense. "The foundation of God standeth sure, having this seal, **The Lord knoweth them that are His**. And, let every one that nameth the name of Christ depart from iniquity" (2 Tim. 2:19). God hath forbidden and made impossible any other way, "and they **that are Christ's**" have crucified the flesh with the affections and lusts" (Gal. 5:24). The knowing of God is, in one sense, *predestination*; in another sense, it is begun at the regeneration of *initial* salvation and is vitally experiential and conditional in *present progressive* salvation, lest *finally*, in the end, when God looks upon you, He will not know you because you left off knowing Him. You see? Your turning to sin is a "departing from the living God" (Heb. 3:12). One ought not to do this, lest He cease to call you His son, or Christ's, because you left off *presently* and *progressively* crucifying the flesh with its affections and lusts (Gal. 5:24, Rom. 8:13, Col. 3:5). The Knowing of God is therefore understood in *predestination*, *initial*, *present progressive*, and *final* salvation.

"Behold, I, even I, will **utterly forget** you" (Jer. 23:39)→

"his righteousness which he hath done shall not be remembered"-Ezek. 3:20
"shall not be mentioned" – Ezek. 18:22
"shall not be mentioned" – Ezek. 18:24

Is this not the burden of Jesus Christ? That He would know you *when He finds you*, that when He sees you, He would call you His own? Oh reader, maybe you have forgotten the burden of Jesus Christ! This burden was preached and repeated, and with its repetition you see its urgency, gravity, and necessity to be understood! There are four parables in a row in Matthew 24-25 (Faithful and Evil Servants, Wise and Foolish Virgins, Talent-Laden Servants, and the Goats and the Sheep); each of these sirens the same eternal consequence of the terrifying and final end of those saints who were not ready for His coming. In the parable of the Master's House (Lk. 13:23-30), the Wise and Foolish Virgins (Matt. 25:1-13), and in the warning of Matthew 7:21-23, each given in context surrounding similar parabolic teachings, JESUS CHRIST SAID – "I **know you not whence ye are**," and, "He shall say, I tell you, **I know you not whence ye are**; depart from Me, all ye workers of iniquity" (Lk. 13:25, 27), and again, "**I know you not**" (Matt. 25:12), and again, "then will I profess unto them, **I never knew you**: depart from Me, ye that work iniquity" (Matt. 7:23)! In these sayings, is there not an alarm to professing and true Christians to be ready for Him at His coming? Have you ever considered that, though He knew you once, that He can "utterly forget you" (Jer. 23:39), and all the righteousness that you have done can be no longer "remembered" (Ezek. 3:20)? That when you appear before Him on the Last Day, you could be nothing but an alien to Him, a worldling, "as an heathen man and a publican" (Matt. 18:17)? This is as Jesus saying, "I called you; you fell away into sin", and finally, He does not know you, choose you, and has rejected you, therefore He blotted out your name from the Book of Life. The presence of this name in the Book of Life, which was eventually blotted out, affirms that this individual was regenerated and therefore chosen/elect, known, and called; however; God breached those promises and oaths to cast him away in wrath. By these parabolic expressions, we can see the burden of Jesus Christ, and when this burden is received by faith, then an individual will be pressed in a sense of urgency of soul, a feeling of frightful necessity to prepare for His sudden appearance. Who are these individuals? They are a company that is called into His service, who will be judged in the condition in which they are found in, and responded to according to how their works determine. An emotional surge should electrify your soul into zeal to be ready, because, imagine it! Imagine yourself pounding on the shut and bolted door of the Kingdom of God, and lo, you find yourself irreversibly thrust out and forgotten by God. Note: If you do not forget God and thrust Him out of your life, He will not thrust you out of His Kingdom nor ever forget you. Yet, so many rule out themselves because they understand that they are known by God, and they assume that they could never cease to be known by Him. They are called by God, and wrongly believe that they could never cease to be called His. They are chosen by Him, and they believe that they could never cease to be chosen by Him. With these understandings, they have become oblivious to the burden of Jesus Christ, and they do not understand the scarcity of those who are *finally chosen* in comparison to those who were *initially chosen*, or as Jesus stated it, those who are *finally chosen* in comparison to those "*many*" who were *called*. This is the burden of Jesus Christ – The difficulty and scarcity of salvation!

Do you remember when one asked Jesus Christ, "Lord, are there few that be saved" (Lk. 13:23)? Do you remember what He said? "And He said unto them – "Strive to enter in at the strait gate: for **many**, I say unto you, will seek to enter in, and shall not be able."

*What does it mean for Christ to **know you not**?*
*What does it mean for the Bride to **make herself ready**?*

If the living Lord has any burden for His Churches TODAY…would it be any different than these parables? Would it not be a burden of where they stand *at present*, in comparison to where they MUST be at His coming or their death (Rev. 2:4-5, 14, 20, 3:2, 15-17), under the strict observance (Rev. 2:1, 23) of how God does *know them now* (Rev. 2:2, 13, 19, 3:1, 8, 15), their souls hanging in jeopardy as to whether or not God will *confess* and *know them then* (Rev. 3:1, 5), with the necessity of their END determining where they will eternally stand (Rev. 2:26, 2:7, 10-11, 17, 3:11-12, 20-22)?

It is undeniable that these parables in the gospels are in reference to saved, regenerate individuals. Jesus Christ is burdened for those who are a part of the regenerate Church and how they still stand in jeopardy of losing or discontinuing their salvation. As Revelation chapters 2-3 depicted those regenerate persons in danger, so also the four parables in Matthew 24-25 do likewise. The Parable of the Servants (Matt. 24:42-51) is made up of those who are **called** His "**servant**" (Matt. 24:46), which no heathen is called, and the burden of Christ is that they would be **called faithful**, **wise**, and therefore saved, by making themselves "**ready**" (Matt. 24:44-45). The Parable of the Wise and Foolish Virgins (Matt. 25:1-13) is made up of those who are **called virgins**, which no heathen is called (2 Cor. 11:2), which the betrothed yet unmarried bride is to remain until the day of her marital union. And again, "they that were **ready**" were "**wise**," therefore **saved** (Matt. 25:9-10). The Parable of the Talents (Matt. 25:14-30) is made up of those who are **called servants**, which no heathen is called (1 Cor. 7:22), nor could the heathen have a spiritual and supernatural talent which he must be faithful with. Like the **foolish virgins** "slumbered and slept" and so were found **un-prepared**, so also the "wicked and slothful servant" was found to deserve "outer darkness" and "weeping and gnashing of teeth" (Matt. 25:30), proving himself to be, finally, no servant of God. The Parable of the Sheep and the Goats (Matt. 25:31-46) is made up of those who were likewise professors of the Lord, held accountable to Christians' acts of service and laws of love (Gal. 6:2, John 13:34, John 15:12-14), and He separates and calls one from the other to finally be His or not by the works they did to Him, through each one, unto each other as Christians. Are there few that be saved?

Different parables accent different angles of this woeful or blessed appearance of Christ. The first parable had no reference of numbers. As for the virgins, *half were lost*. As for the talent-committed servants, *one of three were lost*. As for the sheep and the goats, the two companies of **many persons** were divided and each one sounded with the voice of multitudes, likewise is the picture of Matthew 7:21-23 – "**Many** will say to Me in that day, "Lord, Lord, have we not prophesied in Thy Name? And in Thy Name have cast out devils? And in Thy Name done many wonderful works?" Again I question, "Are there few that be saved" (Lk. 13:23)?

According to the burden of Christ in Revelation, if He had returned to the seven Churches in the province of Asia, which were made up of many house Churches within the single name "Church" of each domain (and sometimes, each Church would include thousands of converts, of all of these multitudes of people) – *five out of seven* would have been cast into hell, and at that point in time, they were found to be in a damnable condition! If Christ returned at that very moment in time, He would have damned five out of seven Churches, or in other approximate terms, *5,000 out of 7,000 persons damned* who were initially saved and regenerated! Imagine it in more personal terms – name 7 persons you know to be genuine converts, and then write their names down on a piece of paper. Then, let the reader understand…the way is so narrow and strait that it is likely that 5 out of those seven persons you named are in a damnable condition right now, and only two of those persons would, right now, be welcomed into everlasting life! Cross off five out of the seven names, and consider: if you all died now, then only few of the many that are called would be saved! As for Revelation, these are not persons, but whole Churches, or even the generation of men saved in that time and province, therefore these numbers refer to five out of seven of the representative multitudes! These numbers are just like the twelve spies that spied out the Promised Land, because they represented the multitudes which eventually followed their evil report unto damnation. Of the twelve spies, *two out of twelve were saved.* Paralleled by multitudes, 2 out of 12 spies were saved, and likewise, 11 out of 12 tribes were entirely annihilated (20 year old males and upward)! Only the tribe of the Levi was saved from the reprobation, because they did not go out to war, and therefore they were not a part of that last quarrel with God that resulted in their reprobation. 2 out of 12 spies being saved is just alike to how 1 out of 12 tribes were saved! The ten spies were snared in unbelief, and then 600,000 men of war followed them in their damnation. Only the untold number of wives and children that these 600,000 men, including the tribe of the Levites, still had the possibility to persevere in salvation, and this is not counting all the thousands that died up to that day, or those who died after that day through other similar provocations (especially those of the tribe of Levi, because they would shortly have their own great falling away within their tribe; see Numbers 16-17). "Are there few that be saved?" Surely this is the understanding of Jesus in the saying – "Many are called but few are chosen"! Surely this is what is concluded by a true study of *biblical Church history*, and yet this is the very antithesis of modern "wisdom"; thus it is no wonder we look nothing like the scriptural expression of what biblical Christianity is, when we cannot even follow the promises and warnings of the Bible. Or will you now tell me that this is not what Christ is saying in Matthew 22:14?

The Marriage & The Called, Chosen, and Faithful

"Thou hast a **few** names even in Sardis which have not defiled **their garments**..." (Rev. 3:4)

"Behold, I come as a thief. Blessed is he that watcheth, and keepeth his garments, lest he walk naked, and they see his shame." (Rev. 16:15)

"Turn, O backsliding children, saith the LORD; for I am married unto you: and I will take you **one of a city**, and **two of a family**, and I will bring you to Zion." (Jeremiah 3:14)

Few are chosen, and of the many in the Church of Sardis, few were said to be worthy to escape the threatening blotting-out powers of God, but this context is directly in reference to salvation in terms of "garments", which I will now turn to examine. When the marriage of the Lamb is come, and this being the contextual situation for those called and chosen individuals in Matthew 22:1-14, the company at jeopardy are those who are on trial to determine whether or not their garments are *worthy* for so honorable a procession. This is in clear connection with the NT necessities and prerequisites laid upon the Bride for marriage (Eph. 5:26-27); thus, in the parable, the guests do hold the same parabolic connections with those that are blessedly regenerate and still on trial to be proven **ready** (see Luke 14 alongside Matthew 22). When "the marriage of the Lamb is come," it is because the Bride "hath made herself **ready**" (Rev. 19:7), and note – READINESS and WORTHINESS are the same burden which motivated the terrifying parabolic sermons of Christ incarnate (the Bridegroom) at the latter end of His ministry and life. He wanted His people to remember something. These parables were His dying burden, that they might eternally live by His death – and be READY. He knows what is fitting for the marriage He has chosen. A Bride termed *ready* meets the expressed image - "**sanctify**," "**cleanse**," "a **glorious** Church, not having **spot**, or **wrinkle**, or **any such thing**; but that it should be **holy** and **without blemish**" (Eph. 5:26-27). As she is to be honorable by apparel, by color and needlework, in perfect holiness arrayed, so the Bride makes ready her reception by "fine linen, clean and white" (Rev. 19:7-9), as is the burden of Christ for individuals in His presence - "the same shall be clothed in white raiment" (Rev. 3:5) – and so it is with the Bride's garments, "the fine linen [which] is **the righteousness of the saints**" (Rev. 19:7-9). Look at the passage closely:

"Let us be glad and rejoice, and give honour to Him: for the marriage of the Lamb is come, and His wife hath **made herself ready**. And to her was granted that she should be **arrayed** in **fine**

linen, clean and white: for the fine linen is the **righteousness of saints**. And he saith unto me, Write, **Blessed** are they which are **called** unto **the marriage supper** of the Lamb. And he saith unto me, These are the true sayings of God." (Revelation 19:7-9)

None outside of this dress code, calling, or stature shall *finally* be recognized as the Bride, for, "they that are with Him [the Bridegroom] are **called**, and **chosen**, and **faithful**" (Rev. 17:14). What is Jesus Christ's burden in the five parables formerly addressed? Be ready, for final judgment is surprisingly imminent, and it exacts eternal costs upon souls! And, lo, of the many chosen, few are chosen - of the many known, few are known - of the many called, few are called – or, of the many called, few are chosen. Nevertheless, "**Blessed** are they which are **called** unto the marriage supper of the Lamb." As it was in those parables, it is no different in Matthew 22:1-14 (and likewise to this, other parables like John 15:1-7). Look closely at the parable of the Marriage Dinner:

Matthew 22:1-14

Gen. 12:1
2 Cor. 6:17
1 Cor. 5:7
1 Cor. 5:13
Gal. 4:30
1 Cor. 5:13
1 John 2:18-19
John 15:1, 6
Matt. 22:13
1 Cor. 9:27
2 Cor. 13:5
Matt 15:13-14

[1] And Jesus answered and spake unto them again by parables, and said, [2] The kingdom of heaven is like unto a certain king, which made **a marriage** for his son, [3] And sent forth his servants to **call** them that were **bidden** to the wedding: and they would not come. [4] Again, he sent forth other servants, saying, Tell them which are **bidden**, Behold, I have prepared **my dinner**: my oxen and *my* fatlings *are* killed, and all things *are* ready: come unto the marriage. [5] But they made light of *it*, and went their ways, one to his farm, another to his merchandise: [6] And the remnant took his servants, and entreated *them* spitefully, and slew *them*. [7] But when the king heard *thereof*, he was wroth: and he sent forth his armies, and destroyed those murderers, and burned up their city. [8] Then saith he to his servants, The wedding is ready, but they which were **bidden** were not **worthy**. [9] Go ye therefore into the highways, and as many as ye shall find, **bid** to the marriage. [10] So those servants went out into the highways, and gathered together all as many as they found, both bad and good: and the wedding was furnished with **guests**. [11] And **when the king came** in to see the guests, he saw there a man which had not on **a wedding garment**: [12] And he saith unto him, **Friend**, how camest thou in hither not having a wedding garment? And he was speechless. [13] Then said the king to the servants, **Bind him hand and foot, and take him away, and cast *him* into outer darkness; there shall be weeping and gnashing of teeth.** [14] For many are **called**, but few *are* **chosen**.

Revelation 17:14 says that those that stay with Christ (the Bridegroom) for eternity are those who are "**called**, and **chosen**, and **faithful**." This is the burden of

666

Christ. *Initial* salvation is one thing, but Christ's burden is *final* salvation. Therefore, we must not only be of the many **called** to the Marriage Supper of the Lamb, merely, but we must persevere to the final END to be the **called**, **chosen**, and **faithful** - for many are **called** but few are **chosen**. Revelation 19:7-9 portrays a parallel picture to compare Matthew 22:1-14. With both of these in view, there are those who are of the blessed company that are called to the marriage supper of the Lamb, and yet, while abiding at the dinner and waiting for the meal, before the supper of the final marriage, Christ goeth about the company and finds one unworthy. It is a man attending this marriage dinner (which can only be attended by the *initial calling*) who does not have white raiment. The burden of Christ is that they would be in white raiment WHEN HE COMES to investigate and look upon His guests – so that the guests (those initially called) would not be fools but wise, not slothful but faithful, not unprofitable and wicked but obedient, in no need of expulsion at the END when Christ separates one from the other, and they all react with utter shock that He does not know multitudes of them anymore. In this case, the man is shocked speechless – "And He saith unto him, Friend, how camest thou in hither not having **a wedding garment**? And **he was speechless**" (Matt. 22:12).

Let the reader understand that those who attended the wedding dinner are the called (v. 3) or "bidden." In context, those that refused to come and attend are the Jews, whom, at this time in the 1st century, God was casting away from Himself, so God sought out others (the Gentiles), but of these others *not all that are called are chosen*. Look at the NT use of the word called, and recognize, at this time the regenerated Christian has entered into the Church, which is, the spiritual arena of the Marriage Dinner where they sup with Christ until His consummated return and final marriage dinner. There is a calling in which we partake of the spiritual reality that makes us a "friend" of God. There is a stature of holiness and obedience which makes us meet to abide in this place of holy communion with the Living God, and that stature of holiness which we had must not be forfeited along the passing of time. We, being those holy persons called into the presence of God, must be worthy of this calling, lest when He comes we will be expelled from His presence, forfeiting our rights in His presence because of the insulting, unacceptable, perverse, un-holiness we are now walking in – profaning our holy calling. Those who are initially called by regeneration must live worthy of their calling, which is to "make sure" your gospel calling *presently* and *progressively*, until you are *finally* found by Christ to be the called and chosen because you are worthy of salvation.

The calling of *initial* salvation is as exhaustive as the calling of *present progressive* salvation. By initial salvation, it is meant, not called out from our homes into an assembly…it is another calling out! Today men add to the church them that are unsaved, but in the New Testament, "the Lord added to the Church daily such as should be saved" (Acts 2:47). According to the word of God, only the Lord can add to or build a Church. It is written, "except the LORD build the house, they labour in vain that build it" (Ps 127:1). Is there any question as to Who should build the Church, or what persons are chosen by God to be added to the Church? We have been saved by Him "Who hath **called** you out of darkness into His marvelous light" (1 Peter 2:9). He "hath **called** us to glory and virtue" (2 Peter 1:3). "God hath not **called** us unto uncleanness, but unto holiness" (1 Thess. 4:7). Holiness, glory, virtue, and light are in Christ, and herein is our unity and calling. We are "**called** in one body" (Col. 3:15), "**called** in one hope of your calling" (Eph. 4:4), and supremely, "in this He has **called** us unto eternal life (1 Tim. 6:12), a "high **calling**" of the redemption of our body in an eternal resurrection (Phil. 3:14). We are called out of the world by being born of heaven. We have been "**called** unto the fellowship of His Son Jesus Christ our Lord" (1 Cor. 1:9). We are born of another place, but we still abide in this world. Here we walk out our calling, and we await the inheritance of the world to come (1 Cor. 3:22). Therefore, the Christian is "**called** to go out into a place which he should after receive for an inheritance," and for us, that place is the world (Hebrews 11:8). That is to say, rephrased, we are called out of the world, but we are left waiting in the world for the world to be given to us – but it is not presently ours, nor Christ's, in this sense, even though in a higher sense "all things are yours" in Him (1 Cor. 3).

The constitution of the Church assembly is inherently defined in the meaning of the very word "Church". God's calling re-creates, and this does enable us to have a worthy fellowship in a congregation of "the called out ones," in whose midst is the chief centerpiece of affection in a Person, the Caller and Elector Himself. As our calling is, so we must be in assembly, holy unto the Lord. "As obedient children, not fashioning yourselves according to the former lusts in your ignorance: but **as He which hath called you is holy, so be ye holy** in all manner of conversation; because it is written, BE YE HOLY; FOR I AM HOLY" (1 Peter 1:14-16). Today men add to the church, but only God can add to the Church, and that is by an effectual, irresistible calling of salvation. The calling is the work of the Lord, the "assembling of ourselves" is the teaching of scripture, and in physically assembling we become a local Church (Hebrews 10:25). Let us limit the **local Church** to them that **are the Church**; let men call to assemble only those certain ones that have already been called of God. God has called for a congregation because of the new creation.

As for the ***present progressive*** necessity to be worthy of this calling, as Christ ***presently*** and ***progressively*** walks about, judges, and has a reactionary relationship to His people in Revelation 2-3, Christ said to the Church of Sardis – "Thou hast a **few** names even in Sardis which have not defiled their garments; and they shall **walk with Me in white**: for they are **worthy**. He that overcometh, the same shall be **clothed in white raiment**; and I will not **blot out his name out of the book of life**, but I will confess his name before My Father, and before His angels" (Rev. 3:4-5). Those that "sup" with Christ ***presently*** and ***progressively*** (Rev. 3:20-22), will sup with Him ***finally*** (Matt. 8:11, Lk. 12:37, 13:29), if He finds us well-abiding in His presence in power. Likewise, those that ***presently*** keep their garments, they keep the faith, and ever receive of Christ the "white raiment" that they "mayest be clothed, and that the shame of [their] nakedness do not appear" (Rev. 3:18). Do you remember the hope of Paul when he said that God "would count [you] worthy of this calling" (2 Thess. 1:11)? These are those who will be called "His saints" (2 Thess. 1:10), those that have rightly been unregretful and perseverant in faithfulness, and in this way they have desired God's "heavenly" banquet – "wherefore God is not ashamed to be called their God: for He hath prepared for them" such a supper (Heb. 11:16).

> "I speak not of you all: I know whom I have **chosen**: but that the
> scripture may be fulfilled, **He that eateth bread with Me hath
> lifted up his heel against Me.**" (John 13:18)
> "Yea, Mine own familiar **friend**, in whom **I trusted**, which **did
> eat of My bread, hath lifted up his heel against Me**" (Ps. 41:9)

There is a perseverant end whereby we must obtain the confirmation of God's oaths (Heb. 6:15-16), by avoiding the conditional threat of breaches (Heb. 4:1), and thus our friendship with God (Jas. 2:23) is not discontinued. As a saint must keep His garments "white", "worthy", and wedding-honorable, so a saint must keep "the righteousness of the saints" – as holy ones (Rev. 19:8). If you do not, your life and works misrepresent your name, and God, Who is infinitely holy, will not accept your person, nor justify your nakedness, just as God, of necessity, required Abraham to justify His friendship through "works" (James 2:21-26). All this, likewise, can be understood through when the King Christ did cast away His onetime "friend" (Matt. 22:12), Judas. Do you see how the scripture is explicitly stating that he was a friend of Christ? Even so, we can become a typological-traitor like Jesus' "friend" Judas (Psalm 41:9, John 13:18, Matt. 26:50, John 6:36-40, 7:16-17, 17:11-12). Likewise as with these angles in which salvation is explained, it is just a different picture of the same object. Salvation is explained in different metaphors with the same rules. There is a plethora of parabolic expressions of the *initial*, *present progressive*, and *final* salvation at hand for Christians, which follows the same thrust of rhetoric and burden – God being called your God (Heb. 11:16), and you, being called His sons and daughters (1 John 3:1, Heb. 11:24, 2 Cor. 6:17-7:1), "walking worthy of the vocation wherewith ye are called" (Eph. 4:1, Lk. 19:13, Matt. 25:14), following in the Spirit and deeds of Christ's Person as a fulfillment of your calling (1 Peter 2:21, 1:15, 3:9, 2 Pet. 1:3, 1 Thess. 4:7), representing deeds worthy of the regenerating and unifying powers of His corporate Person (Col. 3:15, Eph. 4:1-4), abiding in the principles where Christ will not leave you but stay with you in Presence. These citations represent but a few of which we have already covered. In this way, Christians have been "called unto the fellowship of His Son", Jesus Christ our Lord (1 Cor. 1:9, 1 John 1:5-11, 2:1-7, Eph. 5:1-15). Verily, the entirety of the NT echoes the same burden as the parables of Jesus Christ.

The Epistles: *A Commentary, Echo, and Practical Application of the Parables of Jesus Christ – How Do You Preach to & Pray for Christians to Prepare Them for the Day of Christ?*

> "And that, knowing the time, that now it is high time to awake out of sleep: for now is our salvation nearer than when we believed. The night is far spent, the day is at hand: let us therefore cast off the works of darkness, and let us put on the armour of light." (Rom. 13:12)

"The day is at hand," the apostle Paul proclaims (Rom. 13:12). "Knowing the time, that now it is high time" that "the night is far spent, the day is at hand" he says, in light of this, "let us therefore cast off the works of darkness, and let us put on the armour of light" (Rom. 13:11-12). What is this day? Urgency exudes from the words "let us therefore," but what is this day? Reader, there is a salvation which you must prepare for, a "salvation ready to be revealed in the last time" (1 Peter 1:5).

> "Be not deceived; God is not mocked: for whatsoever a man soweth, that shall he also reap. For he that soweth to his flesh shall of the flesh reap corruption; but he that soweth to the Spirit shall of the Spirit reap life everlasting. And let us not be weary in well doing: for in due season we shall reap, if we faint not." (Gal. 6:7-9)

> "And this I pray, that your love may abound yet more and more in knowledge and in all judgment; That ye may approve things that are excellent; that ye may be sincere and without offence till the day of Christ." (Php. 1:9-10)

"In due season we shall reap" Paul writes to the Galatians (6:9), but if a man reaps, then he must have sown. Reader, do you know where you must sow, that you may reap "everlasting life" (Gal. 6:7-9)? To the Philippians, Paul is burdened of things they must do, and he, teaching them to do these things, says to the Philippians that these things done well are for the purpose "that ye may be sincere and without offence till the day of Christ" (Php. 1:10). Many preach some other thing, or perhaps all the things *you don't have to do*, but Paul preached what men must do! Depending on what we do, and God's judgment of these deeds, we will be sincere or insincere, under offense or without offense, and all this is during the time of trial which is "till the day of Christ." "Till the day of Christ," he says, but what is the day of Christ? Truly, saints, we have "turned to God" from sin, and we are commanded "to wait for His Son from heaven", but is there any chance we can be found by Him in a manner which we desire not - namely, insincere and under offence (1 Thess. 1:9-10, Php. 1:10)?

"As ye know how we exhorted and comforted and charged every

670

one of you, as a father doth his children, That ye would walk worthy of God, Who hath called you unto His kingdom and glory." (1Thess. 2:11-12)

"Night and day praying exceedingly that we might see your face, and might perfect that which is lacking in your faith..." (1Thess. 3:10)

"And the Lord make you to increase and abound in love one toward another, and toward all men, even as we do toward you: To the end He may stablish your hearts unblameable in holiness before God, even our Father, at the coming of our Lord Jesus Christ with all His saints." (1Thess. 3:12-13)

"Wherefore also we pray always for you, that our God would count you worthy of this calling, and fulfil all the good pleasure of His goodness, and the work of faith with power." (2 Thess. 1:11)

If we are waiting for the Son of God to appear, what should we expect of that day? Reader, the Lord Jesus Christ "shall judge the quick and the dead at His appearing and His Kingdom" (2 Tim. 4:1). Saints, "God hath called you unto His kingdom and glory", but do you "walk worthy of God" and this calling (1 Thess. 2:12)? Will you be "counted worthy of the Kingdom of God" (2 Thess. 1:5)? Brethren, you should know "the times and the seasons", that "ye have no need that I write unto you" – this is a healthy focus of soul (1 Thess. 5:1). You must "know perfectly" how "the Day of the Lord so cometh" and how "at the coming of our Lord Jesus Christ", your hearts would be found "unblameable in holiness before God" (1 Thess. 5:2, 3:13). You must trust and obey God "to the end He may stablish your hearts unblameable in holiness before God, even our Father, **at the coming of our Lord Jesus Christ** with all His saints" (1 Thess. 3:13). Would you even perceive if there was something "lacking in your faith" that would be of such a vital alarm that would cause you and your pastor to begin, "night and day," "praying exceedingly" until your faith is perfected (1 Thess. 3:10)? Grasping the true message of the New Testament, you would righteously tremble at the perpetual need to be perfect, and seeing this need, you and your pastor would "pray always for you, that our God would count you worthy of this calling" (2 Thess. 1:11). O Christian, you do have a calling, and it is contained in commandments - and if you understood the New Testament, you would take heed to yourself, "that thou keep this commandment without spot, unrebukeable, until the appearing of our Lord Jesus Christ" (1 Tim. 6:14). What must you, not another, be prepared for "against that day", to "find mercy of the Lord in that day" (1 Tim. 2:12, 18)? Search these scriptures with that question!

Can you say, "there is laid up for me a crown of righteousness, which the Lord, the righteous judge, shall give me at that day" (2 Tim. 4:8)? Do you know with certainty that God will "preserve [you] unto His heavenly Kingdom" (2 Tim. 4:18)?

In this manner, with understanding, are you "looking for that blessed hope, and the glorious appearing of the great God and our Savior Jesus Christ" (Titus 2:13)? Do you know your calling, namely **the gospel**, and are you careful to obey it? For "the Lord Jesus shall be revealed from heaven with His mighty angels, in flaming fire, taking vengeance on them that know not God, and that obey not the gospel of our Lord Jesus Christ: who shall be punished with everlasting destruction from the presence of the Lord, and from the glory of His power..." (2 Thess. 1:7-9)

> "Blessed is the man that endureth temptation: for when he is tried, he shall receive the crown of life, which the Lord hath promised to them that love Him." (James 1:12)

> "We are confident, I say, and willing rather to be absent from the body, and to be present with the Lord. Wherefore we labour, that, whether present or absent, we may be accepted of Him. For we must all appear before the judgment seat of Christ; that every one may receive the things done in his body, according to that he hath done, whether it be good or bad. Knowing therefore the terror of the Lord, we persuade men; but we are made manifest unto God; and I trust also are made manifest in your consciences." (2 Cor. 5:8-11)

O, may the Church recognize the blessedness of a man, after "when he is tried," then "he shall receive the crown of life, which the Lord hath promised to them that love Him" (James 1:12). "The righteous Judge" shall give to those that are worthy "a crown of righteousness" "at that day," but does that day terrorize you (2 Tim. 4:8)? "Knowing therefore the terror of the Lord" by a stedfast looking at THIS DAY when "we must all appear before the Judgment seat of Christ; that every one may receive the things done in his body, according to that he hath done, whether it be good or bad;" being "confident" you will stand before the presence of the Lord – have you therefore been pressed to "labour" that you "may be accepted of Him" (2 Cor. 5:8-11)?

> "Know ye not that they which run in a race run all, but one receiveth the prize? So run, that ye may obtain. And every man that striveth for the mastery is temperate in all things. Now they do it to obtain a corruptible crown; but we an incorruptible. I therefore so run, not as uncertainly; so fight I, not as one that beateth the air: But I keep under my body, and bring it into subjection: lest that by any means, when I have preached to others, I myself should be a castaway." (1 Cor. 9:24-27)

> "Wherefore let him that thinketh he standeth take heed lest he fall." (1 Co 10:12)

> "Wherefore the rather, brethren, give diligence to make your

calling and election sure: for if ye do these things, ye shall never fall." (2 Pet. 1:10)

Have you even recognized how you may "run" this Christian "race" wherein you "may be accepted of Him" when you "appear before" Him (1 Cor. 9:24-27)? The Bible commands to "so run, that ye may obtain" this "incorruptible" "crown", but it is obtained because you are - so running - so are you? Paul was not running or fighting "as uncertainly", but he took heed to "any means" by which he could "fall" lest he be one that "thinketh he standeth" and yet is falling – yea, he made his "calling and election sure" (1 Cor. 9:24-27, 10:12, 2 Peter 1:10). Such a "meekness" must abide in the heart of a "diligent", certain runner, so that he is not subtly overtaken by "forgetfulness"; rather he is a blessed "hearer" and "doer" of the word of God "which is able to save your souls" (2 Peter 1:9-10, James 1:21-25). Is your faith that you will obtain your crown "dead" or alive, can your "faith save" you, or are you a "vain man" with no understanding of how your "faith" is "made perfect" (James 2:14, 20, 22)? Are you "wanting" something, or are you a "wise man" – examine yourself – "glory not, and lie not against the truth" (James 1:4-5, 3:13-18). Has your wisdom borne fruits of friendship with the world, or are you foolish and forsaken by the world, they being invigorated to hate you because of "the fruit of righteousness" in your life (James 3:13-14, 4:4, 1 Jn. 3:1)? The "friends" and "enemies" of God are separated by "works," "wisdom," "knowledge," and "faith" (James 2:23, 4:4, 3:13), but have you even looked into your heart in obedience to the commandment given, "stablish your hearts: for the coming of the Lord draweth nigh," a looking to recognize damnable sins and "saving foundations" (1 Tim. 6:19), the "conversation" (James 3:13) of "acceptable sanctification" (Rom. 15:16, 18, 2 Cor. 5:9) and the "castaways" "reprobation" (1 Cor. 9:27, 2 Cor. 13:5) – "lest ye be condemned: Behold, the Judge standeth before the door" (James 5:7-9)?

"At the appearing of Jesus Christ", will you have "praise and honour and glory?" How will you "be found" (1 Peter1:7)? If you understood this life as "the trial of your faith", you would surely "pass the time of your sojourning here in fear" (1 Peter 1:7, 17)! "Though it be tried with fire", it is that it might "be found" as pure gold and worthy of eternal life, however, God judges the faith "without respect of persons" and "judgeth according to every man's work" (1 Peter 1:7, 17). Are you holy in conversation and deed, "as Christ", "because it is written, be ye holy for I Am holy" (1 Peter 1:16, 4:1)? If you are "following" in "His steps" (1 Peter 2:21), then you are "as obedient children" (1 Peter 1:14), "as newborn babes" (1 Peter 2:1), "as lively stones" (1 Peter 2:5), "as strangers and pilgrims" (1 Peter 2:11), and finally, you even have the "same mind" as Christ (1 Peter 4:1). O, that the Church would bear the burden of the "sober" "watch" for "the end of all things at hand" (1 Peter 4:7), called "the day of visitation" (1 Peter 2:12) "at the appearing" and "revelation of Jesus Christ" (1 Peter 1:7, 13)! "When His glory shall be revealed", will you be "a partaker of the glory that shall be revealed" (1 Peter 4:13, 5:1)? "When the Chief Shepherd shall appear", will you be accounted of God a sheep that is "astray," or rather, against that day will God have prepared you so as to "make you perfect, stablish, strengthen, settle you" (1 Peter 5:4, 2:25, 5:10)? All of us, saved and unsaved, are they "who shall give account to Him that is ready to judge the quick and the dead" (1 Peter 4:5); yea, and do you even know your "today" by the litmus test of scripture, if Christ will say, "I have not found thy works perfect before God" (Rev. 3:2), and, "I know thy works, that thou hast a name that thou livest, and art dead" (Rev. 3:1)? Do you have such a perception of the holiness of God and the terribleness of this day that you say, "Amen", that "the righteous scarcely be saved" (1 Peter 4:18)? O, "make your calling and election sure", that you may not "fall" from "an entrance" "into the everlasting kingdom of our Lord and Savior Jesus Christ" (2 Peter 1:10-11).

The word of God exclaims the manner and preparations we must undergo to be ready at the "coming of our Lord Jesus" (2 Peter 1:16). We are taught and reminded over and over of the past-time judgments of God to prepare us for the Judgment of God that is as "the day dawn" ahead (2 Peter 1:19). What judgment? That "God spared not the angels that sinned" "and spared not the old world", but now ungodly men with the heavens and earth are "reserved unto fire against the day of Judgment and perdition of ungodly men" (2 Peter 2:4-5, 3:7). God has shown "the vengeance of eternal fire" to Sodom (Jude 7), the "everlasting chains under darkness unto the Judgment of the Great Day" to the angels that sinned (Jude 6), but God will "execute Judgment" again (Jude 15) – "Behold, the Lord cometh with ten thousand saints, to execute judgment upon all, and to convince all that are ungodly among them of all their ungodly deeds which they have ungodly committed, and of their hard speeches which ungodly sinners have spoken against Him" (Jude 14-15). "But the day of the Lord will come as a thief in the night; in the which the heavens shall pass away with a great noise, and the elements shall melt with fervent heat, the earth also and the works that are therein shall be burned up. Seeing then that all these things shall be dissolved, what manner of persons ought ye to be in all holy conversation and godliness, looking for and hasting unto the coming of the day of God, wherein the heavens being on fire shall be dissolved, and the elements shall melt with fervent heat? Nevertheless we, according to His promise, look for new heavens and a new earth, wherein dwelleth righteousness. Wherefore, beloved, seeing that ye look for such things, be diligent that ye may be found of Him in peace, without spot, and blameless" (2 Peter 3:10-14). Behold the "Judgment now of a long time lingereth not", and of the wicked God says, "their damnation slumbereth not" (2 Peter 2:3); we should not think it lingereth, but rather, because of the narrow, holy Judgment of our Lord in the scarcity of the salvation, we should "account that the longsuffering of our Lord is salvation", for He is "longsuffering to us-ward, not willing that any should perish, but that all should come to repentance" (2 Peter 3:9, 15). The longsuffering of the Lord is our salvation, for, when He forbears to judge now, it is so that we may be perfected and established at the Judgment, so as to be saved.

Are you burdened to, by faith, "continue in the Son, and in the Father," knowing exactly the grounds, laws, effects, and tests to know if "truly our fellowship is with the Father, and with His Son Jesus Christ" (1 John 1:3, 7)? "If we" know these truths, the question remains, are we "walking" in these truths – for many are they which "saith I know Him" (1 John 2:4), "saith he abideth in Him" (1 John 2:6), and "saith he is in the light" (1 John 2:9), yet walk **contrary to these professions**. "It is the last time" (1 John 2:18), "and the world passeth away, and the lust thereof: but he that doeth the will of God abideth for ever" (1 John 2:17), but do you "abide in Him; that when He shall appear, we may have confidence, and not be ashamed before Him at His coming" (1 John 2:28)? Are we worthy to "be called the sons of God" (1 John 3:1) and therefore walking "**as** He is in the Light" (1 John 1:7), in "the truth" or "of the truth" **as** He is the Truth (1 John 2:4, 3:19, John 14:6), in "His Word" **as** He is the Word (1 John 1:10, 14, 2:24, 28, John 1:1), in righteousness "even **as** He is righteous" (1 John 3:7), in love **as** "God is love; and he that dwelleth in love dwelleth in God, and God in him" (1 John 4:16), to "lay down our lives for the brethren" even **as** "He laid down His life for us" (1 John 3:16)? If so, then "the world knoweth us not" **as** "it knew Him not" (1 John 3:1), and we have a holy "hope" that we may be purified "even **as** He is pure" (1 John 3:3). We need this "understanding, that we may know Him that is true" (1 John 5:20). We must be sure that we are walking in Him in all these specified ways, for "herein is our love made perfect, that we may have boldness in the Day of Judgment: because **as He is**, so are we in this world. There is no fear in love; but perfect love casteth out fear: because fear hath torment. He that feareth is not made perfect in love" (1 John 4:17-18). All of this is "the truth" (2 John 1); you must be found "walking in truth" (2 John 2:4), and these means of understanding make up "the doctrine of Christ" (2 John 9). "He that abideth in the doctrine of Christ, he hath both the Father and the Son. If there come any unto you, and bring not this doctrine, receive him not into your house, neither bid him God speed" (2 John 9-10). Being "led away with the error of the wicked", as to subtly compromise the doctrine of Christ, will cause you to "fall from your own stedfastness", and this can happen by hypocritical deeds **with truthful confessions**, therefore "beware lest ye also" follow the backslidings of those who are backslidden in the New Testament (2 Peter 3:17).

Many may say that saints cannot be in danger of perishing, but Christ, in forbearance to return, appeals to five of seven Churches in Revelation 2-3 to repent – for if He had returned right then, only two would have been scarcely saved out of seven. Henceforth Jesus exercised their minds to urgency by repeatedly preaching about the fearful, sudden, irreversible consequences of being found unworthy at His return (Matt. 24-25) – as He saith, "And all the Churches shall know that I am He which searcheth the reins and hearts: and I will give unto every one of you according to your works" (Rev. 2:23). "Or else," He threatens – "Repent; or else I will come unto thee quickly, and will fight against them with the sword of my mouth" (Rev. 2:16). "Repent, and do the first works; or else I will come unto thee quickly, and will remove thy candlestick out of his place, except thou repent" (Rev. 2:5). "But that which ye have already hold fast till I come" (Rev. 2:25), "Behold, I come quickly: hold that fast which thou hast, that no man take thy crown" (Rev. 3:11). According to the promises of God, true Christians are "rich, and increased with goods, and have need of nothing" (Rev. 3:17)…and this, perhaps "thou sayest" (Rev. 3:17), but Jesus saith again, "I know thy works" (Rev. 3:15). Do you know if you have "gold tried in the fire, that thou mayest be rich" (Rev, 3:18), or "knowest not that thou art wretched, and miserable, and poor, and blind, and naked" (Rev. 3:17)?

The Sovereign Exaltation ➔ "Moreover whom He did **predestinate**, them He
also **called**:
and whom He **called**, them He also **justified**:
and whom He **justified**, them He also **glorified**."
(Romans 8:30)

The Scarce Salvation ➔ "For many are **called**, but few are **chosen**." (Matthew 22:14)

The Pastoral Burden ➔ "Make your **calling** and **election** sure…"
(2 Peter 1:10)

In this burden, we can see the principles of OT "visitation" as the primary angle from which "Final Judgment" is preached in the NT, and the imminency of sudden death or Christ's surprising thief-like return upon the unprepared propounds these principles in the minds of the people to be ready & prepared.

A Pastor's Sermons to Make Sure Biblical Mercy
–Leave Them Terrified By Final Judgment

"PEPARE TO MEET THY GOD" – Amos 4:12
"The Great and Terrible Day of the LORD" – Joel 2:31
"KNOWING THEREFORE THE TERROR OF THE LORD"
– 2 Cor. 5:11
"our God, The Great, The Mighty, and The Terrible God" – Neh. 9:32
"The Day of the LORD is Great and very Terrible; and who can abide it?" –
Joel 2:11

Final judgment should be prepared for! Its sudden arrival is just like the visitations of God's judgment in former generations in the OT. We, in the NT, walk in a Covenant of partially fulfilled promises, like as former Covenants, and side by side, the promises are also the forewarning that the partially fulfilled prophetic woes of the OT are still to come in a consummation in the end of the world. These woes will be experienced then, and they are preached to God's NT people just like their former, partially fulfilled, types were preached in the OT. Thus in the NT, the Christian people are called to prepare to meet their God, and not just any meeting, but to be judged by God according to how He finds them on the day of this meeting, which is the same context of relationship of OT "visitations" (God in the ways of man). But sadly, men do not prepare for this Day, because they fancy themselves possessors of the promises under the lens of **God in the ways of God** – but God explicitly says He will judge men according to the realm of human comprehension and understanding – God in the ways of man – ACCORDING TO THEIR WORKS.

Men DO NOT get to the Judgment Seat and hear that they are denied heaven because of election without reference to anything that is on our own comprehensible plane of understanding of the righteous justice executed in God's judgment. It is written, they are "judged out of those things which were written in the books, **according to their works**" (Rev. 19:12). Again it is said, "they were judged every man **according to their works**" (Rev. 19:13).

God is, dear reader, even to His dearest, a Judge according to a man's works. This attribute of FEAR is taught to the NT Christians as something to be ever-remembered about God. "And if ye call on the Father, Who without respect of persons **judgeth according to every man's work**, pass the time of your sojourning here in **fear**" (1 Peter 1:17). Again it is written that God is no respecter of persons. Even elect persons who didn't make their *election sure* by *deed* and *fruit* (2 Peter 1:4-15). Even promise-laden persons who are under the "forevers" and "nevers" of God's own oath and word. In this aspect and spectrum of God's Judgment, God is making the point to men that **their deeds must line up with their faith** - and in this way, they will be declared righteous inheritors of that which they were born again for. This is as Abraham was "**justified by works** when he had offered Isaac his son upon the altar" (Jas. 2:21). By this instance, he passed **the trial of his faith** (Heb. 11:17-19), and God, Who examined him as if He didn't know his heart (Gen. 22:1), then rested assured that Abraham was worthy of the Covenant of salvation (Gen. 22:12, 16-18), and likewise, Abraham became assured of his inheritance of it (Heb. 6:13-20). What is God pointing to in all of this? OBEDIENCE and WORKS are important to Him!

> "Was not Abraham our father justified by works, when he had offered Isaac his son upon the altar? Seest thou how faith wrought with his works, and by works was faith made perfect? And **the scripture was fulfilled** which saith, Abraham believed God, and it was imputed unto him for righteousness: and he was called the Friend of God. Ye see then how that **by works a man is justified**, and not by faith only. Likewise also was not Rahab the harlot justified by works, when she had received the messengers, and had sent them out another way? For as the body without the spirit is dead, so faith without works is dead also."
> (James 2:21-26)

"The scripture was fulfilled" (Jas. 2:23). Note: there is a distinction between deeds of the law, which subvert and nullify faith (dead works; see Rom. 3:20), and those deeds of the Spirit & faith in obedience to the voice of God (living works; see Rev. 3:26), the latter perfects faith rather than destroys it, saves a man rather than damns him, establishes grace and righteousness by deed rather than standing in opposition to saving grace.

In the end, the Book of Life's account of election will not be mentioned alone, nor other means of salvation which are *apart from works*; God will be focused upon *the works* of <u>sinners</u> and <u>saints</u>! By **this standard alone** God will separate them (Matt. 25:31-46, Matt. 7:24-27). This was the **terror** of Paul. He knew that his works were evidences of the genuineness of his faith. Therefore Paul resolved, "wherefore we labour!" "WHEREFORE WE LABOUR," Paul says, for what? "That whether present or absent, we may **be accepted of Him**", and that is, before the Judgment Seat of Christ Who judgeth according to the labour of every man's deeds. Consider carefully the whole passage:

> We are confident, I say, and willing rather to be absent from the body, and to be present with the Lord. **WHEREFORE WE LABOUR**, that, whether present or absent, **we may be accepted of Him**. For we must all appear before the Judgment Seat of Christ; that every one may receive the things done in his body, according to that he hath done, whether it be good or bad. Knowing therefore **THE TERROR OF THE LORD**, we persuade men..." (2 Cor. 5:8-11)

Do you know this terror of Judgment Day which energized Paul? Even the apostle Paul, a far more holy and beloved of a man than we! This judgment of God is biblical, historical, and richly stated - (Ps. 62:12, Isa. 3:10-11, Jer. 17:10, 32:19, Ezek. 18:30). God wants men to know that He will not be mocked, as if He would allow men and women to go to heaven by some other means than that which *vindicates His righteousness* in choosing them, and so, *by their works*, walk, deeds, and conversation, they are rewarded an entrance in heaven. God would have men know that He purposes, for His glory, that He would be worshipped according to an *understandable righteousness*…in other words, that we would worship God "with the understanding also", so that in the case that we are saved or condemned, we are facing a judgment which is an evident representation of our works (1 Cor. 14:14-15). "For the Son of Man shall come in the glory of His Father with His angels; and then He shall reward **every man according to His works**" (Matt. 16:27). Men of God need to be conscious of the reality that Christ DOES, right now, presently, stand in the midst of a regenerate congregation of saints to judge and respond to **men's works**, and as the judgment is on earth which goes before Final Judgment, so is Final Judgment. Christ Jesus wants "all the Churches" to know this for sure, forgetting it not: "And I will kill her children with death; and all the Churches **shall know** that **I am He which searcheth the reins and hearts: and I will give unto every one of you according to your works**" (Rev. 2:23).

If we disbelieve this, we are mocking God. This is what the unbiblical misappropriation of Calvinistic election has done to men when they remove themselves from the consequences of **their works**, when they relate to God without respect to their works! This is a deception that the Lord repeatedly warns against, saying, "Be not deceived; God is not mocked: for whatsoever a man soweth, that shall he also reap. For he that soweth to his flesh shall of the flesh reap corruption;

but he that soweth to the Spirit shall of the Spirit reap life everlasting" (Gal. 6:7-8). Thus, rightly minded before the comprehensible righteousness of God, Who will judge man according to His works, men do understand their condemnation and salvation, and therefore they must set themselves in earnest to *prepare* themselves to be *ready*, though they are presently regenerated – making their calling and election sure, even though they are the elect. "And, BEHOLD, I come quickly; and my reward is with Me, **to give every man according as his work shall be.**" (Rev. 22:12)

Did you hear that? What you sow, that you shall reap! God wants us to understand this, and anything else is utter mockery (Gal. 6:7-8, Hos. 10:12, 8:7). "The wicked worketh a deceitful work: but to him that soweth righteousness shall be a sure reward" (Proverbs 11:18). Concerning what you DO, God will love or hate you (Prov. 6:17-19). God will be famous to repay and perfectly remember all sinners' sins, whatsoever they are (Psalm 137:7, 2 Thess. 1:6). Sinners will therefore confess, "as I have done, so God hath requited me" (Judges 1:7). "For the day of the LORD is near upon all the heathen: **as thou hast done, it shall be done unto thee:** thy reward shall return upon thine own head" (Obadiah 15). This judgment of God according to works "is a righteous thing" (2 Thess. 1:6); therefore judgment according to works is called "The Righteous Judgment of God" (Rom. 2:5). This is altogether for the heathen and the righteous (2 Cor. 5:8-11). Those who have come speaking another thing are the "mockers" who have come "in the last time," which is now (Jude 18). Don't let anything, not even your understanding of sovereign, elective, irresistible grace, cause you to take your mind off of your deeds, for concerning these God will judge your faith at Final Judgment. Is Calvinism your deceiver by taking your mind off of a biblical understanding of works righteousness, so leaving you unprepared for the Final Judgment?

"Let no man **deceive** you with vain words" (Eph. 5:6).
"Be not **deceived**" (1 Cor. 6:9-10).
"Let no man **deceive** you" (1 John 3:7).
"**deceiveth** his own heart" (Jas. 1:26, Matt. 12:36-37).
"Be not **deceived**" (1 Cor. 15:33).

THE ASSURANCE OF ETERNAL ELECTION
CHAPTER 26

❖ <u>**NOTE**</u>: *I have already shown how the Covenant of Abraham was still able to be breached in Abraham's personal life and walk (see "Abrahamic Exemplification").*

The NT Christians had an assurance of present-tense election which was communicated as interconnected to eternal election in the Book of Life written before the world began. God desires for men to have an assurance of their eternal election, and this is why He speaks the forevers and nevers, with all election language such as:

Calling →   "**being not yet born**…the purpose of God according to **election**… of Him that **calleth**" – Rom. 9:11
       "which was **given** us in Christ Jesus **before the world began**" – 2 Tim. 1:9

Chosen →   "God hath **from the beginning chosen** you to salvation" – 2 Thess. 2:13
       "chosen us in Him before the foundation of the world" – Eph. 1:4-5

Election →   "**Elect** according to the **foreknowledge** of God the Father" – 1 Peter 1:2
       "**afore prepared** unto glory" – Rom. 9:23

Wisdom →   "which God **ordained before the world** unto our glory" – 1 Cor. 2:7

Righteousness →   "God hath **before ordained** that we should walk in them" – Eph. 2:10

The Book of Life → "whose names were not written in The Book of Life **from the foundation of the world**" – Rev. 17:8

We know that Jeremiah had an assurance of his eternal election (Jer. 31:3). So also in the NT, eternal security is preached, and God wants His beloved Christians to know the forever eternality of His saving love, even by their eternal election being assured to their hearts, but how? Abraham is our chief example for this doctrine – the assurance of eternal election – or – the assurance of salvation.

Believe His Word! – NT _Covenanted Love_ is the Same

Message of Promise as _Eternal Election_

"And we desire that every one of you do shew the same **diligence** to the **full assurance** of <u>hope unto the end</u>: That ye be not **slothful**, but followers of them who through **faith** and **patience** <u>inherit the promises</u>." (Hebrews 6:11-12)

Just after the writer of Hebrews warned the NT regenerate Christians he was writing to of reprobation, he then affirms to them that his hope and desire in preaching this message is that they would have a biblically founded "full assurance of

"**diligently** seek Him" – Heb. 11:6
"Looking unto Jesus" – "**diligently**" - Heb. 12:2, 15
"giving all **diligence**" – 2 Pet. 1:5
"give **diligence**" – 2 Peter 1:10

"**diligently** hearken to the voice of the LORD" - Ex. 15:26
"keep thy soul **diligently**" – Deut. 4:9
"teach them **diligently**" – Deut. 6:7
"Ye shall **diligently** keep the commandments" – Deut. 6:17
"if ye shall hearken **diligently** unto My commandments" – Deut. 11:13
"**diligently** learn" – Jer. 12:16

"Thou wicked and **slothful** servant" – Matt. 25:26

hope unto the end" (Heb. 6:11), or in other words, a biblically founded assurance of salvation, which is attained by, and not apart from, the "diligence" of faith, not "slothfulness", of those who were perseverant unto the end in their own lives. The use of the words "diligent" and "slothful", across Testaments New & Old, are used as terms for the saved or damned (see citations), and this strengthens the evidence that the writer is burdened that they would obtain a biblical assurance of salvation by diligence, rather than the self-deception that one is assured of their salvation while still abiding in slothfulness. Without "faith", "patience" (which means stedfastness), and "diligence", a man should not have "assurance" and "hope" he will be saved, for without these a man will not "inherit the promises" of eternal life – this is the bottom-line burden of this passage. Secondarily, the writer pointed the Hebrew Christians to "them", desiring that they, that is, those faithful men of former generations, would serve as examples of a walk of faith that is worthy of biblical assurance by which he will obtain what he is assured for and "inherit the promises". In pointing the reader to examples of faith by saying, "followers of them", the writer immediately turns to the foremost example of biblical "assurance" to learn from, namely Abraham, for the remainder of the chapter.

"For when God made promise to Abraham, because He could swear by no greater, He sware by Himself, Saying, Surely blessing I will bless thee, and multiplying I will multiply thee. And so, **after he had patiently endured**, he **obtained the promise**. For men verily swear by the greater: and an oath for **confirmation** is to them an end of all strife. Wherein God, willing more abundantly to shew unto the heirs of promise the immutability of His counsel, **confirmed** it by an oath: That by two immutable things, in which it was impossible for God to lie, we might have a **strong consolation**, who have fled for refuge to lay hold upon the hope set before us: Which hope we have as an anchor of the soul, both sure and stedfast, and which entereth into that within the veil; Whither the forerunner is for us entered, even Jesus, made an high priest for ever after the order of Melchisedec." (Hebrews 6:13-20)

Reader, the secret of Abraham's sure inheritance is that he obtained it "after he had patiently endured"; it was then that "he obtained the promise". "After", the writer says, referencing that a certain amount of time passed wherein Abraham was tried by God, and then after this it was granted to him that he might have a "strong consolation", or in other words, "a full assurance of hope unto the end", or, an assurance of eternal election. The day of this great assurance of salvation which Abraham obtained was the day in which he completed the trial of his faith, whereby God said, "now I know that thou fearest Me", when Abraham offered up his son Isaac as a sacrifice to God. This instance was called, "when he was tried" (Heb. 11:17-19), "he" meaning Abraham, so this instance is exemplary and typological of the completion of the "trial of" Abraham's faith (1 Pet. 1:7). So also, we should not have assurance and hope of eternal life if, when we are tried, or after we are tried, we did fail the trial. This experience of trial for Abraham was toward the latter end of his life, a life in which he endured continual trials of God for decades, that is until, the writer of Hebrews says he "obtained the promise" by passing this final trial. So he becomes an example of a man who obtains the promise by passing the trials. What was the significant thing that God did to make it sure to Abraham, or assure him, that he would be saved? What gave him his strong consolation?

At this time, after he was tried with offering up Isaac, God knew him and found him faithful according to his deeds, and thus, God vindicated His own righteousness for choosing Abraham for the Covenant, and at this time, after he was found faithful by deeds, then the Covenant was sworn to be given to Abraham. It was already promised, but now it was sworn in. This swearing of God had never happened before, nor had God ever said to Abraham, "now I know"; thus what is in view for the reader to understand is that we must be faithful in our trials by the same diligence, patience, and faith, as Abraham, and we will thus have a biblical hope, assurance, and consolation given to us by the witness of the Spirit of God. This biblical assurance of salvation and immutable, eternal election is not separate from God's condescension by which He comes to try you to see and know you after your deeds, nor is it separate from God's context of Judgment whereby He seeks to finally Judge you according to the comprehensibility of works righteousness (God in the ways of man). The writer of Hebrews, as I have already cited, affirms this experience to be the time when Abraham "obtained a good report" (Heb. 11:2) by perseverance, and we also must be perseverant like him (Heb. 11:13-19). Abraham kept faith to the end (Heb. 11:17-19), as did Isaac (Heb. 11:20), Jacob (Heb. 11:21), and Joseph (Heb. 11:22), unto their dying day! And if a man does not do this, then God will disown him, be ashamed of him (Heb. 11:16), and reject him. Why? James explains the point of the matter – God will be vindicated and justified in choosing who from among His people are His final chosen in the END, and it is by their faithfulness in deed, through trial, found ready today!

> "But wilt thou know, O vain man, that faith without works is dead? Was not Abraham our father justified by works, when he had offered Isaac his son upon the altar? Seest thou how faith wrought with his works, and by works was faith made perfect? And the scripture was fulfilled which saith, Abraham believed God, and it was imputed unto him for righteousness: and he was called the Friend of God. Ye see then how that by works a man is justified, and not by faith only. Likewise also was not Rahab the harlot justified by works, when she had received the messengers, and had sent them out another way? For as the body without the spirit is dead, so faith without works is dead also" (James 2:20-26).

What is the burden of this section in James? "What doth it profit, my brethren, though a man say he hath faith, and have not works? Can faith **save** him" (James 2:14)? The burden is, are you now (present-progressively), and will you be finally, **saved**? How do you have the assurance of salvation now? James declares in verses 20-26 that it is not apart from "works" (James 2:24)! As it was said in Hebrews 6:13-20 that Abraham, at this time of offering Isaac, obtained the promises, so here in James 2:23, it states that **the scripture was fulfilled** when it said that Abraham's faith rewarded to him imputed righteousness (salvation apart from works), or in other words, the righteousness in God choosing and saving Abraham is that righteousness was imputed to him by faith apart from works, and then he did continue in saving faith by walking in works righteousness, and thus, God is not ashamed, regretful, or repentant that He has made a Covenant with Abraham, and rather, is assuring him or any man like him that he is assured everlasting life in the everlasting potency of the promises and oaths of God! All your experience is supposed to build in you "hope, and hope maketh not ashamed" for such a man as this, for God will not take away the Holy Ghost from him (Rom. 5). If Abraham did not walk "perfect" before God (Gen. 15:1-2), which is diligent faith and patience, then God would not have given him the assurance of eternal election and salvation, nay, but rather, He would have reprobated him, been ashamed of him, repented that He had saved him, and vindicated His own righteousness for rejecting Abraham because he was not walking in works that verified his faith!

The Covenant was on the line for Abraham, to be fulfilled and performed or breached and lost, and so Abraham walked perfect and obtained the promises, fulfilled the scriptures, and so also God preaches to you promises, oaths, and scriptures in the NT which, in the same way, you are to strive after and obtain them. God will seek to persuade you of the "immutability of His counsel" and all "immutable things" in His changeless faithfulness, both in "promise" and "oath", and the utter impossibility it is for God to lie, all for the purpose that you would trust God's faithfulness, truthfulness, and changelessness, that you would be assured of your changeless, eternal election, but it is not apart from justifying Him for choosing you by making sure your final choosing or election, assuring yourself in this means of sureness, and laying hold upon the promises! Otherwise, you also will be cut off because you believed God was a liar, unfaithful, evil, and froward, and you rewarded for yourself reprobating wrath.

Preach the forevers, nevers, and God's immutable, without repentance, changeless faithfulness and salvation – so as to persuade the believer to believe…but if the believer is deceived to be unbelieving, which is manifest by the deeds of darkness and sin, and he goes on unrecovered from this state, then God will be just to breach His forevers and nevers; He will not show the froward man His immutability but His mutability, repentance, and changes on His word of salvation for them by way of condescension. How the changeless perfectness of God in heaven (outside of time) can be reconciled with the changing, reactionary will and word by way of condescension (within time), no man can know, but at least we can understand the scriptural consistency behind how and why He does what He does when He does it.

God desires to show men His love through preaching His faithfulness, eternality, and immutability, exclaiming that falling from perseverance is an impossibility, but to believe that God is a liar so as to judge Him unfaithful, rather than to judge Him faithful (Heb. 11:11), this is an awful evil! Especially in regard to all that God has promised! God seeks to make men afraid so that they will not forget about and fail to perform the conditions to the promise, and God seeks to make men assured of His love. Consider the contrasting words:

FEAR→ "**Ye cannot** serve the LORD:" He is "holy" and "jealous", thus He will not pardon – Josh. 24:19

LOVE → "**We are well able** to overcome it" – Num. 13:30

LOVE → (Num. 14) "The Lord delight in us," "He will bring us"…neither fear the people; "the Lord is with us" (13:30) "stilled the people," "let us go up at once"

FEAR → "Be careful to maintain good works" – Titus 3:8

LOVE → "Be careful for nothing" – Php. 4:6

FEAR → "wherefore we labour, **that** whether present or absent, **we may be accepted of Him**" – 2 Cor. 5:9

LOVE → "To the praise of the glory of His grace, wherein **He hath made us accepted in the beloved**" – Eph. 1:6

FEAR → GOD commands – "Let Me go!"…*that I might leave you Jacob –*

684

	Gen. 32:26
LOVE →	God promises – "I will not leave thee" – Gen. 28:15
FEAR →	"neither will I be with you any more, except…" – Josh. 7:12
LOVE →	"I will not fail thee, nor forsake thee" – Josh. 1:5

We could go on, couldn't we? Do you remember all that we have covered thus far? Therefore dear reader: Believe God to be immutable, forever, never, and therefore faithful & truthful, while keeping the conditions, and you will experience the performance of the promise presently and progressively, and thus, the Holy Ghost can give you the assurance of your salvation and eternal election. To end this writing, I must close with a section in which I preach this great LOVE which is in the NT – exactly "what manner of love" God has for us, just as it should be preached, believed, and applied, with the fearful conditions in mind of which I have spent this entire book until this point seeking to prove, justify, and make plain to the reader. The purpose of this book was not to show the love of God, but the fear of God, so that a man would rightly interpret and apply the love of God. But oh! I cannot end this book without a section on the love of God, lest my readers misplace themselves in a worldly fear (instead of a godly fear), which leads them to disbelieve God rather than believe His promises, faithfulness, and mercy.

"What Manner of Love" – 1 John 3:1

The chief expression of faith is irresistible grace! When trusting in the fullness of His love through the written word, I do reckon, believe, and exalt the

RELATED SERMONS

"Why Weepest Thou?" – Sean Morris
"Looking Unto Jesus" – Sean Morris
"Pursued, Overtaken, & Blessed" – Sean Morris
"Good Hope Through Grace" – Sean Morris

grace of God in its irresistible virtues to have saved me, to presently save me, and finish my salvation to the end. *"Behold, **what manner of love** the Father hath bestowed upon us, that we should be called the sons of God: therefore the world knoweth us not, because it knew Him not." (1 John 3:1)* Behold the scripture commands! Look at, consider, understand, perceive, digest, comprehend, and know exactly, specifically, practically, relevantly **what manner of love** God has toward you. Behold in this study, Lord willing, what manner of love.

"Have mercy upon me, O LORD, for I am in trouble:
mine eye is consumed with grief, yea, my soul and my
belly. For my life is spent with grief, and my years with
sighing: my strength faileth because of mine iniquity,

and my bones are consumed... Blessed be the LORD:
for He hath shewed me His marvellous kindness in a
strong city. For I said in my haste, I am cut off from
before Thine eyes: nevertheless Thou heardest the
voice of my supplications when I cried unto Thee. O
love the LORD, all ye His saints: for the LORD
preserveth the faithful, and plentifully rewardeth the
proud doer. Be of good courage, and He shall
strengthen your heart, all ye that hope in the LORD."
– Ps. 31:9-10, 21-24

There are many times when a saint will feel the groaning of Psalm 31:9-10: *"Have mercy upon me, O LORD, for I am in trouble: mine eye is consumed with grief, yea, my soul and my belly. For my life is spent with grief, and my years with sighing: my strength faileth because of mine iniquity, and my bones are consumed."* There will be many times where we will think or say things hastily that are fueled by a sore chastening of God justly exercised upon us because of our sin. At such times our hasty, unspiritual thoughts will be hopeless or depressive, like the psalmist wrote, *"For I said in my haste, I am cut off from before Thine eyes."* However, by the blessed faithfulness of God, by His great mercies, He will magnify His love to where we confess and learn what the psalmist learned: *Blessed be the LORD: for He hath shewed me His marvellous kindness in a strong city. Nevertheless Thou heardest the voice of my supplications when I cried unto Thee. O love the LORD, all ye His saints: for the LORD preserveth the faithful, and plentifully rewardeth the proud doer. Be of good courage, and He shall strengthen your heart, all ye that hope in the LORD.* The road is rough, and faith is a fight, but God will draw us to Himself by a willing choice or bit and bridle, the easy way or the hard way.

The simple truths in the glad gospel of God do provide a
certain entrance behind the holy veil.
They should convince saints to flee to His embrace having
confidence they will not see a dispelling angry face.
Cease from striving in an endless chase to find this
heavenly and holy embrace!
God's own vows bear upon His mind as He looks after your
sojourning throughout time.
If you stop your ears or close your eyes, or do all you can
to embrace more lies,
Throughout all your groaning, in every weary sigh, the
whispers of His love are still so nigh.
The chastening of God like a loving breeze does draw your
soul back to its knees.

The experience of the psalmist in Psalm 31 is a biblical and perfect

686

reflection of what I often suffer on account of my sin. Describing such a time, I wrote the following poem to represent this trial and seeming hopelessness, then my deliverance and praise of His name. The following content of the whole document is an exposition of what was revealed to me in that delivering love of God.

Irresistible Grace ** Irresistible Love

My musings of God in the knowledge of the Holy did persuade me
*of the experiential possibility of **resistible grace**.*
This caused me to think that there is no assurance of delivering
grace if ever I did, at present, sinfully provoke God to the face,
Even while feeling that I didn't want to sin, striving and yet
unable to escape the devil's chase.
Drawn to salvation I was, drawn through perseverance I must be, but if presently
under His angry blame, by sin overcome, handicapped, and lame: how will I ever
escape the judgment of sinners and inevitably, eternally be the same?
My musings became a maze and I was lost for many days, terrifically terrorized by
the annals of history, His wrath my heart did amaze – will I be of the few that are
scarce to be saved in the "unsearchable" holiness of God's ways?
If His present will could think to kill, God pursuing man though in dusty frame they
lay still - if I think this is His will, that this is my case at present and now, to whence
can I flee to make my heart still?
Gasping for air, dizzy in strength, fainthearted in fearfulness, He grabbed my hand,
He lifted me up upon the sea to stand, then guided me back from sea to land.
He simplified the maze, showed me a refuge in His ways, He comforted my heart that
was fretting in craze.
Resistible grace, there is no greater calamity, sinners reliant upon themselves is a
present-tense insanity, but in the refuge of His ark, the Sabbath of His loving heart,
He directs man to see that His love is the same as at the salvific start.
By the promises of God He told me the way, that resistible grace is for those who fall
away, but unto me He did solemnly and soundly say that irresistible grace is the
faithful, salvific, and only way. It is the message of His divine love covenanted from
*above shining a perpetual emblem of first and finishing, **irresistible love**.*

The love of God is the only escape, our only salvation, and there is no other way but to trust in the faithfulness of God that is active and living through **unmerited favor** (the favor God gives irrelevant of works, the favor God gives to the most unworthy and unlovely, the most vile and wicked, the favor that is not contingent, dependent, or conditional to any merit that you could have) – and there is a sure way to be beset (or eventually damned), when one trusts in his own faithfulness and loses sight of God's. The love of God must **first be received**, then the obedience to God that you seek can be accomplished – but only in this order and never reversed. Oh, but how subtly our flesh or the devil reverses the order! We must first be engrafted

687

into the Vine, and when in the Vine, we must have the life of the Vine nourish, quicken, and animate the engrafted branch – then the branch can/will bear fruit.

> "I am the Vine, ye are the branches: He that abideth in Me, and I in Him, the same bringeth forth much fruit: for without Me ye can do nothing." (John 15:5)

We have been connected to a "holy root" (Rom. 11:16), from which comes all the holiness that is in the Person of Christ. We have been made to partake "of the root and fatness of The Olive Tree" which is Christ Jesus, the root and fatness of The Vine of Christ, but how often do we try to obey the commandments of God without the nourishment of The Root? If you try to obey God and feel ill-nourished, powerless, impotent, or dry for the task, it is because you are trying to bear fruit without being filled with the virtue-life of The Vine, the nourishing power of the root which is the fatness for flowering fruitfulness. Somehow the devil has deceived you to "boast" in some other wellspring, trust some other sustenance than that of Christ "the Root," "But if thou boast, thou bearest not the Root, but the Root thee" (Rom. 11:18). You cannot bear fruit except by the Vine, except being borne and nourished by the root; thus, cease striving to obey the commandments of God without first looking to the love of God wherein is virtue to obey. Branch of the Vineyard, dost thou see that the Father God Himself does look upon you for fruit? First look at the free lovingkindness, nourishment, life, and godliness of the Person of Christ (the love of God), then by that love and life-giving feed from the Vine, bring forth fruit unto the Fatherly Husbandman. First, receive His love, then by that love, obey. Relate to the Vine and be ever quickened to gladsome obedience unto a satisfied Fatherly Judge. Jesus says unto you, Christian, make "my joy" "remain in you" (John 15:11). It is the joy of the Son, Jesus Christ, to bring forth fruit to the Father; therefore let Christ have His own way within you, let Him bring forth fruit to the Father in and through you. Let Christ have His joy, be a channel only, that the Father may rejoice in Jesus Christ "formed in you" (Gal. 4:19)! Abounding fruitfulness (2 Peter 1) God does command, abounding fatness Christ does supply, to satisfy the Father throughout every season – "His leaf also shall not wither, and whatsoever He doeth shall prosper" (Ps. 1:3). Many men try to please the Father, but rather cease ye from man (and *yourself), walk as Christ, and the Father will be well-pleased.*

> "He spake also this parable; A certain man had a fig tree planted in his vineyard; and he came and sought fruit thereon, and found none. Then said he unto the dresser of his vineyard, Behold, these three years I come seeking fruit on this fig tree, and find none: cut it down; why cumbereth it the ground? And he answering said unto him, Lord, let it alone this year also, till I shall dig about it, and dung it…" (Luke 13:6-8)

> "For the vineyard of the LORD of hosts is the house of Israel, and the men of Judah His pleasant plant: and He looked for judgment, but behold oppression; for righteousness, but behold a

cry." (Isaiah 5:7)

The Father is only pleased with a certain amount of fruit yielded by the branch. It is easy for us to be motivated by the waiting and expectant eyes of the Father that will judge our fruit without compromise. It is easy to remember that our Father is He "Who without respect of persons judgeth according to every man's work" (1 Peter 1:17), and therefore it is easy to be gripped with a consciousness of an expectant, judging, righteous Husbandman. Nevertheless, all our strivings to bring forth the right measure of fruit to the Father will be to no avail if we don't first look to The Vine. Jesus said, "without Me ye can do nothing." The Father is only pleased with a certain amount of fruit, but the Son (The Vine) is pleased to accept us how we are in unmerited favor, fill us with His own life and power, empowering us to meet the required yield of fruit the Father demands. The Son (The Vine) is pleased to accept us because we have been engrafted into Him already. He is pleased to accept us freely and in unmerited favor. He knows our powerless estate to bring forth fruit. He knows we are dead and cursed. Jesus said, "Without Me ye can do nothing", and herein is His matchless love – saying to us, without Me, DO NOTHING.

> "Just as I am, though tossed about with many a conflict, many a doubt,
> Fightings and fears within, without, O Lamb of God, I come, I come.
> Just as I am, poor, wretched, blind: Sight, riches, healing of the mind,
> Yea, all I need, in Thee to find, O Lamb of God, I come, I come."
> ("Just As I Am, Without One Plea", Charlotte Elliott)

We must relate to God in a dual manner, being filled with the Son of God's unmerited favor and fruitfulness, then "in Him" looking unto the Father, expecting loving satisfaction in His eyes. You have become the abode of the Father and the Son, the place of joy wherein they have come to celebrate their love one toward another. You are the vessel and channel wherein the Son desires to cause the Father's heart to rejoice. You are the storehouse wherein the Son has chosen to bring forth and store up much fruit to the Father's delight. You are the cup of pleasure to the Father, of which He is blessed to drink from, for now thou dost overflow with Living Waters. The full expression of faith and revelation through this work of God in man results in a hiddenness of self within the transcendence of the Father's glorious relationship to the Son of God and the Holy Ghost. It is a losing of yourself, becoming lost in the Trinity, till Their love One for Another does simultaneously make you aware of your absence and unworthiness yet present-tense participation and actual experience of this wondrous relationship - being dead, nevertheless living, yet not you but Christ (Gal. 2:20).

> "Herein is my Father glorified, that ye <u>bear much fruit</u>; so shall
> ye be my disciples. **As the Father hath loved Me, so have I
> loved you: continue ye in my love**. If ye keep my
> commandments, ye shall **abide in my love**; even as I have kept
> my Father's commandments, and abide in His love. These things
> have I spoken unto you, that my joy might remain in you, and

that your **joy might be full**." (John 15:8-11)

First, you must receive the love of God, and then by that love which you have received - obey. You must become "rooted and grounded in love" to "know the love of Christ," that "Christ may dwell in your hearts" being "filled with all the fullness of God" (Eph. 3:16-21). To "know the love of Christ," as it is stated in Eph. 3, is not some understanding that is carnally in your mind. This spiritual understanding is like the first salvific "illumination" (Heb. 10:32), but it is a present-tense "enlightening" (Eph. 1:18) which comes by a personal revelation given by God to you. Therefore, this revelation does result in the experiential reality of Christ dwelling in your heart (the faculty and seat of your being, emotions, and will). In a spiritual sense, you must be rooted and grounded in love! The roots of the Tree do extend deep into the soil to give the tree strength to be immovable against the winds and weights that do shake it and to draw from the soil into the tree the nourishment of water necessary for growth. If the roots are deeply grounded and far-reaching to the watery regions of the underground soil, then the tree will be healthy and unshakable. The source of our health and unshakableness in Christ is by depth and nourishment in the love of God. Know the love of God; then you will know the fullness of the possessing, empowering, living Christ – being "filled with the fullness of God." Cease from striving to be filled with the Spirit, and feast upon the full written and living revelation of the love of God in Christ; then, as you behold the love of God, you will be filled with the Spirit. It is easy to be "carried about with every wind of doctrine" (Eph. 4:14) when you are weak and shallow-rooted like "a reed shaken with the wind" (Matt. 11:7). "But we are not of them who draw back unto perdition; but of them that believe to the saving of the soul" (Heb. 10:39).

> **"Exceeding greatness of His power to us-ward who believe**,
> according to the working of His mighty power, which He
> wrought in Christ..." (Eph. 1:19-20)

"That your joy might be full." (John 15:11)

The Lord wants you to have a revelation of His love; the love of God that convinces you of the **surpassing great power** of God working in you that dwarfs all enemies of sin or wrestlings of hell, resulting in an inevitable victory and rejoicing. The revelation of God shows you the greatness of God's power, yea, but that power must be appropriated to your daily life (words, thoughts, and deeds) to give you the means by which all your desires could be fulfilled, to be as holy as you thirst for "that your joy might be full" (John 15:11). Think of the words of Christ: "for Thine is the Kingdom, and the power, and the glory, for ever. Amen." (Matt. 6:13) All saints can say this when worshipping God, because of the measure of grace and glory they have already tasted and experienced at their salvation. Praising the Father, they can say, "Thine is the Kingdom, and the power, and the glory!" But, dearly beloved, have you recognized that God has chosen you as His vessel by which He wants to shew forth His Kingdom, power, and glory throughout all the earth? God has not called you to glorify Him in your name but, Jesus said, "Whatsoever ye shall ask in My Name, that will I do, that the Father may be glorified in the Son. If ye shall ask any thing in My Name, I will do it" (John 14:13-14). God will and desires to "lead you not into temptation" but deliver you from evil in the fullness of His Kingdom power and glory, to the end that you might have the appropriation of the fullness of His power wherein you might be conformed to the fullness of His Person – "till all shall see Christ only, always, living in me" ("Have Thine Own Way", Adelaide A. Pollard). That is God's own way!

Many say "Thine is the Kingdom," but God would have you learn to live worthy of the calling He has given you in this great Kingdom! Give God the glory that He has the Kingdom, power, and glory to fulfill the chief purpose of delivering YOU from sinful temptations (Matt. 6:13). We know that God has surpassing great power, but what we don't understand is that this power is "to us-ward" (Eph. 1:19). Think of all the Kingdom and power of God, and then attribute it to this single purpose: to deliver you from temptation. "And lead us not into temptation, but deliver us from evil: For Thine is the kingdom, and the power, and the glory, for ever. Amen" (Matthew 6:13). Pray for yourself as the apostles prayed for the Churches – "Wherefore also we pray always for you, that our God would count you worthy of this calling, and fulfill all the good pleasure of His goodness, and the work of faith with power: That the name of our Lord Jesus Christ may be glorified in you and ye in Him, according to the grace of our God and the Lord Jesus Christ" (2 Thess. 1:11-12).

> "And Elisha prayed, and said, LORD, I pray Thee, **open his eyes**, that he may **see**. And the LORD opened the eyes of the young man; and he saw: and, behold, the mountain was full of horses and chariots of fire round about Elisha."
> (2 Kings 6:17)
>
> "Are they not all ministering spirits, sent forth to minister for them who shall be heirs of salvation?" (Hebrews 1:14)

The Kingdom of God is glorious – full of power and virtue! God hath set the eyes of the hosts of heaven – even the "ministers" that are a flame of fire – God hath set their eyes upon you. You are the apple of His eye (He and all His hosts), the vineyard of His pleasure, the object of His complete investment unto all the powers of His immeasurable Kingdom in heaven. Can you consider all the "Kingdom, power, and glory" that is God's and then imagine the faultless, inerrant, perfection with which God would perform His own fervent purpose to "lead you into no temptation but deliver you from evil"? This is why you don't need to pray this prayer in "meaningless repetitions", but simply ask once (Matt. 6:8). God wants you to understand that He is mindful of your needs, that He is a Father Who "knoweth what things ye have need of, before ye ask Him" (Matt. 6:8), and is fully intending, commanding, and overshadowing you to accomplish your needs before you even spoke. God is He "Who maketh His angels spirits, and His ministers a flame of fire" (Heb. 1:7) in the glory of His own Kingdom, that they might be "set forth to minister for them who shall be heirs of salvation" (Heb. 1:14). Can you end the Lord's Prayer to God with all of your heart, with the fullness of its meaning in your mind: "And lead us not into temptation, but deliver us from evil: For Thine is the Kingdom, and the power, and the glory, for ever. Amen" (Matt. 6:13)?! Pray that God would open your eyes even as He did to the servant of Elisha – "I pray Thee, open his eyes, that he may see" (2 Kings 6:17). "The angel of the LORD encampeth round about them that fear Him, and delivereth them" (Ps. 34:7).

> "Thine is the Kingdom, and the power, and the glory, for ever."
> (Matt. 6:13)

The glory of an angel is one magnitude, but the glory of the Son is another. If the fierce eyes of flaming angels do set their mind to the task of deliverance, what of the exalted Son Himself Who has purposeful "eyes" "as a flame of fire" (Rev. 1:14)? If you caught a glimpse of His eyes, you would fall "at His feet as dead", thus you would be ever delivered and free, for what can be compared with the power of the Son Who hath determined to destroy all your sin and every residue of the devil? Pray that God would open your eyes till you fall "at His feet as dead," till you "yourself" see Christ only always living in you – "For He that is dead is freed from sin" (Rom. 6:7). Give glory to God and fall at His feet. Pray that God would open your eyes to see the Son of God Who died to set you free (John 8:32-33), Who came to the earth to "destroy the works of the devil" (1 John 3:8). He hath made your sin His enemy, your sanctification His warfare, yet can you imagine that HE will lose this fight and war that He has undertaken to accomplish in your soul? God has pledged Himself to you with His own word! If you are yet unbelieving – EVEN STILL – then you are "he that believed not God" and you have "made Him a liar" (1 John 5:10).

> "Death is swallowed up in victory." (1 Cor. 15:54)

> "But I see another law in my members, warring against the law of
> my mind, and bringing me into captivity to the law of sin which
> is in my members. O wretched man that I am! who shall deliver
> me from **the body of this death**?"
> (Romans 7:23-24)

> "For the law of the Spirit of life in Christ Jesus **hath made me
> free** from the law of sin and death." (Romans 8:2)

Will you believe that the **Throne of the Lamb** is impotent against all the works of the devil, winds of temptation, or any residue of death that would grievously defile your mind and heart? Will you believe that the "sceptre of righteousness", which "is the sceptre of" Christ's Kingdom, can be compared to the sceptre of iniquity (Heb. 1:8)? There is no wrestling, "nor wisdom nor understanding nor counsel against the LORD" (Prov. 21:30). "There are many devices in a man's heart," devices against the saints, and even devices of death in the body;

"nevertheless the counsel of the LORD, that shall stand" (Prov. 19:21). Will you exclaim to God the glories of His Kingdom and so bid them to come into your heart, upon earth, as it is in heaven – exclaim and say – "Death is swallowed up in victory. O death, where is thy sting? O grave, where is thy victory" (1 Cor. 15:54-55)? Christ came to defeat death and hath risen to reign in a life that rules in righteousness, "that as sin hath reigned unto death, even so might **grace reign through righteousness** unto eternal life by Jesus Christ our Lord" (Rom. 5:21). Do you see a "warring" against your mind (Rom. 7:23), even "fleshly lusts which war against the soul" (1 Peter 2:11)? Are you aware of the "law of sin which is" in your members (Rom. 7:23-24)? Are you able to loudly lament, "O wretched man that I am" (Rom. 7:24)? Now look to His Kingdom and all the heavenly host exclaiming, "Death is swallowed up in victory!" "Seek those things which are above, where Christ sitteth on the right hand of God" (Col. 3:1). Shout the same Hallelujah that is resounding up there, and bid the Kingdom come into your heart, bid His will be done on earth, as it is in heaven, in your "earthen vessel." Afterward, you will see that "the law of the Spirit of life in Christ Jesus hath made" you "free from the law of sin and death" (Rom. 8:2), that death, wretchedness, and the warring of sin is defeated. With the fullness of faith and revelation, acknowledging all of these things, is it possible for you to continue in sin (Rom. 6:1)? If God does open "the eyes of your understanding" (Eph. 1:18), you will exclaim the verdict of the Kingdom, the heavenly praise of the "victory," namely, that God has forbidden a continuance of sin. Therefore, "How shall we, that are dead to sin, live any longer therein" (Rom. 6:2)? Possessed, empowered, resurrected, and relating to God in His Kingdom, the Lord Christ has given you a commandment – "Let not sin therefore reign in your mortal body, that ye should obey it in the lusts thereof" (Rom. 6:12).

> "And hath raised us up together, and made us sit together in
> heavenly places in Christ Jesus..." (Ephesians 2:6)

Do you live as though God hath not already said to Jesus Christ, "Sit on my right hand, until I make Thine enemies Thy footstool" (Heb. 1:13)? God hath made your sin Christ's enemy, hath enthroned Him as the active impending force against all your foes, "that we may boldly say, the Lord is my helper, and I will not fear" (Heb. 13:6): therefore "there shall no evil befall thee," "neither shall any plague" of sin "come nigh thy dwelling" (Ps. 91:10) – thou art risen "up together" and seated "together in heavenly places in Christ Jesus" (Eph. 2:6), and He, even He, has become "thy habitation" (Ps. 90:9). Glory, glory, glory "in the cross of our Lord Jesus Christ, by Whom the world is crucified" unto you, and you "unto the world" (Gal. 6:14). God is putting all of Christ's enemies under His feet – this is the channel of the glorious Kingdom power! Now you, right now, put all of your enemies under Christ's feet, "that the name of our Lord Jesus Christ may be glorified in you and ye in Him, according to the grace of our God and the Lord Jesus Christ" (2 Thess. 1:12). Christ drank the cup of God's wrath, and there is not a drop left for you; now raise up your sins before the fierce face of God. Put them before His face, that He may be satisfied when He consumes them like the fat of lambs that became sin (Ps. 37:20).

Put them before His face, that He may burn them away with His anger. Put every one of your sins with all the enemies of the Lord, "and <u>hang them up</u> before the LORD against the sun, that the fierce anger of the LORD" may be satisfied" (Num. 25:4).

> "To whom God would make known what is the **riches of the glory** of this mystery among the Gentiles; which is **Christ in you, the hope of glory…**" (Colossians 1:27)

> "It came even to pass, as the trumpeters and singers were as one, to make one sound to be heard in praising and thanking the LORD; and when they lifted up their voice with the trumpets and cymbals and instruments of musick, and praised the LORD, saying, For He is good; for His mercy endureth for ever: **that then the house was filled with a cloud, even the house of the LORD;** So that the priests could not stand to minister by reason of the cloud: for the glory of the LORD had filled the house of God." (2 Chronicles 5:13-14)

Give glory to God – "the LORD reigneth; let the people tremble: He sitteth between the cherubims; let the earth be moved" (Ps. 99:1)! Give glory to God, give glory to Christ, even "Christ in you the hope of glory" (Col. 1:27). Glory in Christ Who reigneth in heaven, be moved with the earth and resolve with trembling that Christ reigneth in you – henceforth, let it be known unto you, and let it be beheld by all, that "sin shall not have dominion over you" (Rom. 6:14). Heart, mind, soul, strength subdued in glory, under a sceptre sublime. The Temple is filled with Shekinah glory "so that" the "royal priesthood" of the whole body of Christ cannot "stand to minister by reason of the cloud: for the glory of the LORD" has "filled the house of God" (2 Chron. 5:14). Give glory to God, and then obey God by walking in His glory, that these words will not be your end: "This evil people, which refuse to hear words, which walk in the imagination of their heart, and walk after other gods, to serve them, and to worship them, shall even be as this girdle, which is good for nothing. For as the girdle cleaveth to the loins of a man, so have I caused to cleave unto Me the whole house of Israel and the whole house of Judah, saith the LORD; that they might be unto Me for a people, and for a name, and for a praise, and for a glory: but they would not hear" (Jer. 13:10-11). Avoid such a fate, and be thou diligent therein to avoid it, thus say to God and confess the great remedy – "We have thought of Thy lovingkindness, O God, in the midst of Thy Temple" (Ps. 48:9). Be as those priests and holy people in the days of Solomon (2 Chronicles 5:13-4). Praise Him, sing to Him, play instruments to Him, and say to Him that "He is good; for His mercy endureth for ever" – then your house will be filled with the glorious mind of Christ, with all of your emotions captivated in the cloud of His presence.

> "The God of peace, that brought again from the dead our Lord Jesus, that Great Shepherd of the sheep, through the blood of the everlasting covenant…" (Heb. 13:20)

The love of God must be appropriated in the wake of the unfathomable accomplishments and immeasurable expressions of His commended manners of love: → To one, ever-present, irresistible purpose of God that none can stand against – to *"make you perfect in every good work to do His will, working in you that which is wellpleasing in His sight through Jesus Christ; to Whom be glory for ever and ever. Amen"* (Heb. 13:21). Jesus Christ died to make God "the God of peace" to you. Jesus Christ was "brought again from the dead", that He might become the "Great Shepherd of the sheep." Jesus Christ shed His blood to give you everlasting vows and timeless promises for you to trust in, even an incorruptible blood to seal them in before the favor of the Almighty. "Through the blood of the everlasting Covenant", God does strive to teach you His love, unveil all its mysteries, until you become "perfect in every good work to do His will," until He is "working in you that which is wellpleasing in His sight through Jesus Christ." *"The God of peace, that brought again from the dead our Lord Jesus, that Great Shepherd of the sheep, through the blood of the everlasting covenant make you perfect in every good work to do His will, working in you that which is wellpleasing in His sight through Jesus Christ; to Whom be glory for ever and ever. Amen"* (Heb. 13:20-21).

> "Now our Lord Jesus Christ **Himself**, and God, **even our Father**, which hath loved us, and hath given us everlasting consolation and good hope through grace, **Comfort your hearts, and stablish you in every good word and work.**" (2 Thessalonians 2:16-17)

Who can resist the person of Jesus Christ when He, "**Himself**", does take upon Himself this supreme purpose? Who cannot believe when it is God, "**our Father**," that hath already "loved us" and "given us" this manner of love "through grace?" What purpose? He is purposeful, and fiercely devoted, to work in us "every good word and work!" This is the "comforting" and "stablishing" of our hearts. Is not our sin the source of all discomfort? Is it not the Father's natural affection to comfort His children? Your Creator God has made Himself your spiritual Father, hath taken upon Himself the form of a servant, hath so loved you that He follows you everywhere you go, will be with you all throughout time, thinks upon you every waking moment, watching beside you, guarding and protecting you, teaching and serving you – and with all this wondrous and lofty lovingkindness, it is His desire that we are *comforted* in our hearts! He desires that we would recognize that it is His duty to work in us "every good word and work," and seeing He is faithful and full of everlasting love and grace, we have no reason to faint in this fearful, impossible calling. The love of God is that, though you are presently beset by sin, He does look upon you to conquer your sin with the fierceness of His hatred of it, the fervency of His love to you, with a replacement of that sin with "every good word and work", wherein there can be nothing encircling your soul but the comfort of your establishment. Believe His word, trust His grace, and God will spiritually reveal to you the great revelation of His sustaining, persevering love! Till you can say with the Spirit-inspired psalmist: "Thou art my hiding place; Thou shalt preserve me from trouble; Thou shalt compass me about with songs of deliverance. Selah" (Psalm 32:7). "Now we have received, not the spirit of the world, but the spirit which is of God; that we might know the things that are freely given to us of God" (1 Cor. 2:12). God wants to comfort you, all ye that are lost through Satan's beguiling, your emotions in a graveyard of self-pity – look away from yourself - "not a striving to have faith...but a looking off to the Faithful One" (Hudson Taylor). Let God "comfort your hearts" by the wondrous truth that your perseverance is dependent upon His faithfulness and not your own. You may feel defenseless and insecure, but He is your defender and security; look unto Him and be ye enamored by His comfort and grace.

> "But God **commendeth His love** toward us, in that **while we were yet sinners**, Christ died for us." (Rom. 5:8)

My meditation concerning this verse is a very specific aspect of the love of God – that He loved us "while we were yet sinners" (Rom. 5:8). This certain aspect of His love is called the commendation of His love: that in this state and with this deed there can be no greater love (Rom. 8:32). "If God be for us, who can be against us? He that spared not His own Son, but delivered Him up for us all, how shall He not with Him also freely give us all things" (Rom. 8:31-32)? God says "freely"! What stops me from freely receiving God's love all the time? It is when I am convinced that God is not for me in some way, or perhaps presently angry with me. I do not have trouble trusting in God's love when I know that I have put on Christ, **but this love that I speak of now put Christ on me**. If this love had its free course, then God would put Christ on me every day, remortify me, reactivate all the virtues that overcame me **at the first**. If we know that He first loved us while we were yet sinners, we can then understand that He will love us while we are sinning saints! If He loved us while we were sinners and put Christ on us, who can stop Him from loving us while we are sinning saints till He puts Christ on us evermore (in appropriation and spiritual renewal)?

> "For by grace are ye saved through faith; and that not of yourselves: it is the gift of God: not of works, lest any man should boast." (Eph. 2:8-9)

> "Being confident of this very thing, that He which hath begun a good work in you will perform it until the day of Jesus Christ..." (Philippians 1:6)

Salvific Love is "not of yourselves" (Eph. 2:8). The love of God by grace did work saving faith into your heart at the beginning; if from the beginning it was "not of yourselves," how then can His "workmanship" "unto good works" not continue upon us? If God began the work, how then will He not continue it? When God saved you, He saved you by His own power and glory, stripping you of all self-righteousness and dead works, leaving you in a state of heart wherein you wholly magnified His name for His complete performance of regeneration – God made you a man that could not boast! God did astound you with the beginning of His works and did cause your soul to make its boast in God, but with the continuance of that performing work, God will finish you as "His workmanship" in "every good work" "until the day of Jesus Christ!" As you were astounded at the first, be ye astounded now. Look unto your heavenly Father with holy honor in your eyes and speak ye to Him with this in mind! As He began it, HE SAYS, He will be faithful to perform it to the end! Whatsoever He ever calls you to do, think upon every word or work of obedience you can imagine...now resign these things wholly to be God's business and work and not your own, for "faithful is He that calleth you, Who also will do it" (1 Thess. 5:24). Look upon what HE will do - A course of consecutive, consistent, constant comforts as He divinely works every word and work convenient to the calling.

What particularly is consoling my mind is *the expectation* that ought to be held fast in a saint who has experienced this love already. If the love originated from the free will of God, then I can be assured that it will continue in the free will of God! There was a love of God that did pursue me, "draw me," reveal to me, and unblind me to the blessed appearance of "the kindness and love of God" (Tit. 3:4). If God did appear in "kindness and love", I need to look steadfastly to the end on this "kindness and love!" This love is the product of an electing love, and if I could trust that this election is not temporary, then I could rejoice truly in a persevering love that ever grants faith to experience the Covenanted and vowed love of God.

> "So then it is not of him that willeth, nor of him that runneth, but of God that sheweth mercy." (Rom. 9:16)

Think of this expectation that can come from the persuasion that you are eternally elect of God. You can know, irrelevant of your works, no matter what you will or how you run, that God will show mercy to you which grants a perpetual manifestation of saving faith in your heart until you perpetually surrender to the saving love of God all your days. A sweet consolation this would be! But, except by prophetic revelation, we cannot know if we are the eternally elect who will never be blotted out of the book of life (Rev. 3). Thus, what manner of love is the resting of a saint on earth, still sojourning through time and trial? What can we trust in, what manner of love is to console us? Can we then turn to our *willing* and *running* as a means to obtain mercy? Nay, oh man, this is sure disaster! *Resistible grace, there is no greater calamity, sinners reliant upon themselves is a present-tense insanity!* Then what can we rest in – what is the Covenanted message of love toward us now?

> "My little children, these things write I unto you, that ye sin not. And if any man sin, we have **an advocate** with the Father, Jesus Christ the righteous: And He is **the propitiation for our sins**: and not for ours only, but also for the sins of the whole world." (1 John 2:1-2)

2 Thess. 3:3, 5; Jer. 31:18; Ps. 141:4, 119:32, 36

God vows a love that encapsulates the same comforts, experience, promise, and perseverance that was appropriated by Romans 9:16. Rest saints, in the love of God that is covenanted to you by voice and promise – the love of God that delivers me from my sin and performs the good mind, will, and works of Christ within me. Being in Christ now, at present, is all the hope and glory that you will ever need! He is the "Secret Place" and safe "Shadow of the Almighty" (Psalm 91:1). Brethren, we know it is possible to fall away, but it is only possible if you call God a liar by unbelief! Though we do not believe in the manmade doctrine of "eternal security", we must believe, trust, and adore the promises of God which do promise us eternal security! There is security, brethren, there is nothing to fear; God will perform every work and wipe away every tear!

I had deceived myself to think that this love was not a certain shadow, because I thought this was the love of eternal election alone. I was wrong; this love is the very message of commitment to us as His children – that His love is a commitment and covenant wherein He takes upon Himself the duty of our full salvation/sanctification. It is a defense against temptation with a manifestation of obedience, and therefore is a deliverance from unbelief with a manifestation of faith unto the keeping power of God. God promises to defeat any unbelief, reservation, or resistance against His lovingkindness, and to grant you perpetual manifestations of faith, enabling a full surrender into the love of God, which is a resolve with the feeling of dissolving into the love of God that salvificly drowns you in His will. Do you find yourself defensive or resistant against the love of God? This is rebellion, and God will defeat it. When this is my trust (feeling wholly delivered from temptation, see Matt. 6), I do feel as though I am dead, that there is nothing left living of myself, and that I cannot do anything but obey. At this time, I am able to say with a clear conscience, "How shall we, that are dead to sin, live any longer therein" (Rom. 6:2)? Seeing that God has taken upon Himself to personally defeat all uprisings of myself – any resistance I may stubbornly fall into – seeing that God defeats all of this, it is as if there is nothing left but Christ. And if Christ defeats me and lives, I cannot do anything but believe, because I am dead. How can a dead man resist God – or how can I not obey every word of God when I am fully possessed by God? When there is nothing left of me to hinder the work and will of God, there is nothing left but a ceaseless fountain of the working, willing, delivering, and empowering Person of God within. God defeated the evil hindrance and hallowed this house to be full of His hallowed incense – He is manifesting fruits of heaven in the heathen as a thick cloud of Shekinah pleasure. "Not a striving to have faith…but a looking off to the Faithful One" (Hudson Taylor). Cease from striving to believe (a manifestation of obedience), cease from striving against unbelief (a manifestation of sin), cease from even trying to look to Christ (present tense - mortify, put on, be filled with the Spirit); recognize first that God has already killed you and there is nothing left of you, thus how can you not look to Him, for He looketh in you. The manifestation of obedience overcoming all manifestations of conscious sin is the vowed love of God by promise, spiritually and lawfully a finished accomplishment, and presently an experience when fully trusted. How to get faith? Cease striving for it, because you are already fortified in it, even every spiritual blessing and all things that pertain unto life and godliness in Christ Jesus (Eph. 1:6, 2 Pet. 1:4).

God is devoted to me even while I am yet in sin, even after its ugly fingers have gripped or defiled my heart in some manner – the love of God has not ceased. The delight of God may have – yet not the love – for He ever waits for one look of faith for God to deliver from this encroaching enemy. Somehow I have been easily deceived that this is not the love of God. I think perhaps it is because of the perception that He is angered against sin, even to hellfire, when a saint is to be blamed. Yet there is an ever-present escape vowed to us that we might escape this anger, and it is the promised love of God unto vital, empowering obedience. In situations like this, I will feel stuck underneath His fierce countenance, because I will feel as though my only escape is the sovereign will of God manifesting saving faith in my heart...but my flesh deceives me from setting my mind on this, for, what does the experience of sovereign, elective love do? It manifests saving faith in the heart without the willing, running, or consciousness of the individual. Thus, I should not wait to see if God loves me (in the ways of God), nor feel handicapped as if He does not presently love me (in the ways of God of sovereign, eternal, elective love), but LOOK, the vows of His ever-present love are upon me (God in the ways of man/His covenanted voice), and He is angry until I trust in this delivering, unfathomable, empowering love that grants the faith/obedience that I need. Indeed, we have reason to be in terror, for "To day if ye will hear His voice, harden not your hearts" (Heb. 4:7). Only let the end of this fear drive you to the Covenanted salvation of God. Let this fear drive away hopelessness, any idea of mercilessness, any imagination that you are now helpless if God is presently angry with your behavior. By this fear look to the way of escape: "Seeing then that we have a great High priest, that is passed into the heavens, Jesus the Son of God, let us hold fast our profession. For we have not an high priest which cannot be touched by the feeling of our infirmities; but was in all points tempted like as we are yet without sin. Let us therefore come boldly unto the Throne of Grace, that we may obtain mercy, and find grace to help in time of need" (Heb. 4:14-16). Your fear of God should drive you to a fearless and bold approaching to the grace, mercy, and help of God, softening any hardness of heart you presently have against obedience, so as to make the yoke of His service easy and free. God knows all the points of your temptation, and He says to come to the Throne of His power which is friendly to you because of the grace of the Great High Priest. Do you believe He can help you, in times of hopelessness? Then believe that He will help you now – fearfully flee to a fearless appropriation of mercy, grace, and obedience. Amen.

This love is the love He loved me with while I was yet a sinner, for He was angry enough to kill and send me to hell, loved me enough to die and plead His delivering, free love to me in the gospel, and desires that I do resign myself fully to this love. Thus He loved me while I was yet a sinner and is willing/waiting to give me all things while I am a sinning saint, thus the overcoming, conquering love that saved me at first is the persevering love that will save me to the end. He that delivered you from Egypt by His mighty power promises to deliver the Promised Land to you by the same power. He came down to deliver you then, and He will come down to fight for you now – believe His word and trust His grace.

When the chief experience of being dead has permeated my heart, I have a perception that Christ lives: He motivates, leads, thinks, and puts on my heart, so that if temptation is present it cannot find me, because I am dead and He liveth. When I am able to obtain this experience of trust and expectation, it comes by trusting the particular scriptures of His delivering mind and lovingkindness to me as a sinner. "Lead us not into temptation, but deliver us from evil" embodies the "delivering" love of God…that, when temptation comes or sin is conceived, God still loves me and is desirous to deliver me. When I am protected in a fortress of care, active protection, and mindful defense wherein God defeats all my temptations that arise by His own understanding (not mine), it is then that I experience the reality of being dead. Truly, at this place of spiritual experience, I feel as though "my will is a gladsome bird imprisoned in a cage of grace", for I find myself lost, hidden, and overcome by the active, working will/life/purpose of God. God is the fighter and fortitude against my temptation and members, encircling me as an able deliverer. "God is our refuge and strength, a very present help in trouble" (Ps. 46:1). "I will love Thee, O LORD, my strength. The LORD is my rock, and my fortress, and my Deliverer; my God, my strength, in Whom I will trust; my buckler, and the horn of my salvation, and my high tower" (Ps. 18:1-2).

"Thou sweet, beloved will of God, My anchor ground, my fortress hill,
My spirit's silent, fair abode, In Thee I hide me and am still.

O Thou, that willest good alone, Lead Thou the way – Thou guidest best;
A little child, I follow on, And trusting, leaning upon Thy breast.

Thy beautiful, sweet will, my God, Holds fast in its sublime embrace
My captive will, a gladsome bird, Prisoned in such a realm of grace.

Within this place of certain good, Love evermore expands her wings,
Or nestling in Thy perfect choice, Abides content with what it brings.

Oh, lightest burden, sweetest yoke, It lifts, it bears my happy soul,
It giveth wings to this poor heart; My freedom is Thy grand control.

Thy wonderful, grand will, my God, With triumph now I make it mine;
And faith shall cry a joyous Yes! To every dear command of Thine."
(Andrew Murray)

How do I balance the near-annihilating wrath of God with the tender mercies of the LORD? The near-annihilating wrath of God should reveal to us the

700

sinfulness of sin, specifically and especially the sin of **unbelief** in God's awesome, praiseworthy, thankworthy, overwhelming, faithful love, and so, we should be pressed by this godly fear, and with it pushing behind us, we are forced into the direction of God's "Throne of Grace", from which He calleth us to boldly approach unto, with fearlessness, "in full assurance" (Heb. 10:22), that there we "obtain the mercy, and find grace to help in time of need" (Heb. 4:16). Run nowhere else but into the loving, keeping, preserving, persevering arms of a Great Savior, and the doctrine of the fear of God is working in you what it should. The *fear* of God enables one to *fearlessly* approach the Throne!

Concluding Statement

"Many of them also which used curious arts brought their books together, and burned them before all men: and they counted the price of them, and found it fifty thousand pieces of silver." – Acts 19:19

"For Thy sake we are killed all the day long; we are accounted as sheep for the slaughter." – Romans 8:36

Men of more sound understanding lived in generations different than now, a time when ordinary and meek men were so used to turn lost men to God! Sinners were saved! Men who would have burned in the Presence of God for all eternity, they rather broke their idols and burned their books of witchcraft. The city backlashed the bold repentance and faith of countrymen crucified with Christ, and this clash created the predestinated witness that God sought after at last (Rom. 8:36) – "we are accounted as sheep for the slaughter". This climactic Image of Christ living in the Church on earth was sealed by this God-ordained, yet mysterious clash, man to man, when holy men and unholy men, with God, met face to face. These 1st century Christians "endured such a contradiction of sinners" in their "striving against sin" (Heb. 12:3-4), which meant that they rejected their popular cliques, did upset their family unity, and became the troublesome aggravation of society's honorable elite who domineered in idolatrous fraternities! The self-obsessed "nobility" of the city was the power class of the heathen – emboldened in sin – and they, even they, FEARED that their life of sin was in danger! Can you imagine it!? The highest class of wealth and power which fared sumptuously in sin and debauchery, even they were melting with fear that their livelihood of sin was in danger of extinction! The idolatry-fueled economy was crashing into a depression with no economist making the claim, but streetside bonfires hailing Jesus' Name! Men were in fear, fear for the safety of their world of lies and sin, that this Christ in men would utterly end it at last! Therefore did the servants of the devil bestir themselves to violently oppose it with boundless immorality. Blaming God and beautifying the devil, they shed the blood of their converted family, friends, and fellow countrymen. Do you see the point? These Christians had POWER; therefore sinners feared to let them have a fair-standing freedom to preach in the public eye. Doomed to do the devil's will, the heathen murdered the righteous children of Christ, and no wonder; it is just like they did to Christ. It was because Christ in their countrymen was destroying sin (1 Jn. 3:8)! This Christ in the 1st century Christian men – He did "fill Jerusalem" (Acts 5:28), and then "every where" (Acts 21:28, 28:22) else in "the world" (Acts 24:5), with sin-destroying, sinner-saving Truth! "I am the Truth" – saith Christ! Oh! Will we ever recover that wondrous secret of abiding in the Lord?

Oh! Let God reason with us again, reasons why we should walk worthy!

While dwelling in the world…I must not, I cannot be of the world!

"Behold, I give unto you power to tread on serpents and scorpions,
and over all the power of the enemy: and nothing shall by any means hurt you."
(Luke 10:19)

This world, a snake-infested path filled with Satan's wrath,
Yet I know my enemies shall be heeled-down at last (Gen. 3:15).
I will not dwell on my unregenerate past,
My Father in heaven did against the devil laugh.

"And the Dragon was wroth with the woman, and went to make war with the remnant of her seed, which keep the commandments of God, and have the testimony of Jesus Christ." (Rev. 12:17)

When walking near the devil and I hear his loud Texas rattle,
I will not be powerless like the herding animals, the goat or cattle.
I will not retreat while having sufficient armor for this Battle.

"Put on the whole armour of God, that ye may be able to stand against the wiles of the devil. For we wrestle not against flesh and blood, but against principalities, against powers, against the rulers of the darkness of this world, against spiritual wickedness in high places. Wherefore take unto you the whole armour of God, that ye may be able to withstand in the evil day, and having done all, to stand. Stand therefore…" (Eph. 6:11-14)

Should I cry wolf while dwelling safe behind the Shepherd's staff? (Matt. 7:15, 10:16)
Should I gasp while at heaven's height, while I am utterly out of the enemy's sight?
(Prov. 18:10)
Then I am afraid of black when I am dressed in white! (Rev. 3:5)
Can I believe the devil's threats while I yet hear My Father's laugh?
Which sound should I trust while on this grueling, narrow path?

"But the word is very nigh unto thee, in thy mouth, and in thy heart, that thou mayest do it." (Deut. 30:14, Rom. 10:8)
"Set me as a seal upon Thine heart, as a seal upon Thine arm: for love is strong as

702

death; jealousy is cruel as the grave: the coals thereof are coals of fire, which hath a most vehement flame." (Song. 8:6)

I will not be weak when in a body of strength, (Heb. 11:34, Eph. 6:10)
When I know my Author has finished my race at length. (Rom. 9:16)
I will not be dead while abiding in Life,
For love stronger than death made me the Savior's wife.
I will not be a hopeless human while abiding with Hosanna.
I will not go hungry in the desert while surrounded by Manna. (John 6:58)
There is a Rock that follows me, in Whose cleft I can continually resort for free, so how could I remain thirsty? (1 Cor. 10:4)
Dehydration or starvation, is there need for migration? From Christ there is no depravation or separation, shadow of turning, or segregation!

"All that the Father giveth Me shall come to ME, and him that cometh to Me I will in no wise cast out." (John 6:37)

Could it be that a Christian could not see? (John 14:4)
Barren when grafted into a fat and fruitful Vine? (John 15:5, Rom. 11:17)
Forgetful while having a Holy Ghost memory and mind? (John 14:26, 1 Cor. 2:16)
Confounded while Spirit-led, unforgiven while under the crimson red? (Rom. 8:14)
Undiscerning after all that the Book has said,
Wandering in the dark with a light over my head? (Ps. 18:28, Job 29:3-4, Ps. 119:105)
Murmuring when rewarded by the Judge's weights weighed? (Rom. 8:33-34)
Unhealed from my wounds after I am cut by His blade? (Jer. 8:22, Heb. 4:12)
At the giants dismayed, when at the feet of the Almighty we prayed? (Deut. 7:17-21)
Looking for carnal help when Christ in me already obeyed? (Col. 2:6, Col. 2:10)

Can I be poor while in a Treasure House of gold? (Col. 1:27)
Foolish when with the Ancient Creator of old? (Prov. 8:22-31)
A coward when He is bold, I am burning in a Consuming Fire and yet still cold?
(Prov. 28:1, Heb. 12:29)

Grace, Grace, an ocean of grace with its billows o'er me rolled!
Can I calculate salvation, number the waves, or grab a hold?

"Thou knowest my downsitting and mine uprising, Thou understandest my thought afar off. Thou compassest my path and my lying down, and art acquainted with all my ways. For there is not a word in my tongue, but, lo, O LORD, Thou knowest it altogether. Thou hast beset me behind and before, and laid Thine hand upon me. Such knowledge is too wonderful for me; it is high, I cannot attain unto it. Whither shall I go from Thy spirit? or whither shall I flee from Thy presence? How precious also are Thy thoughts unto me, O God! how great is the sum of them! If I should count them, they are more in number than the sand: when I awake, I am still with Thee." (Psalm 139:2-7, 17-18)

703

Should I be doubting a story already told?
In the timelessness of His charity can I break my predestinated mold? (Jer. 31:3, Rom. 9:13)
Earthly-minded while in His resurrection,
Can I then be found without lasting affection? (1 Peter 1:22-23)
I cannot believe the devil's threats,
The Father in heaven laughs at his fish-empty nets. (Lk. 5:10)
I will not be dismembered from those with whom I am one!
For this reason He did come! (Col. 2:19, John 17:21-23)
I cannot sleep or slumber while under the noonday sun!
I cannot lose a race in which He doth in me run! (Rev. 1:16, 2 Cor. 3:18)

RELATED SERMONS

"Patient in Tribulation - The Conflict Against Faith"
– Sean Morris

Printed in Great Britain
by Amazon.co.uk, Ltd.,
Marston Gate.